EGON RONAY'S Lucas GUIDE 1983

to Hotels, Restaurants, Inns
in Great Britain and Ireland

including

> ## Economy Evening Meals,
>
> ## Economy Hotels,
>
> ## Bargain Weekends in the British Isles
>
> ## & Survey of Theatre Catering

First published by Egon Ronay Organisation Ltd 1982
Greencoat House, Francis Street, London SW1P 1DH
First published in the United States in 1983 by
Holt, Rinehart and Winston, 383 Madison Avenue,
New York, New York 10017
Published simultaneously in Canada by Holt, Rinehart
and Winston of Canada, Limited
Copyright © 1982 Egon Ronay
All rights reserved, including the right to reproduce
this book or portions thereof in any form
ISBN 0–03–063331–1
Library of Congress Catalog Card Number 74–644890
First American Edition
Printed in Great Britain by Jarrold and Sons Ltd, Norwich
Cartography by David L Fryer & Co, Henley-on-Thames
Maps based on Ordnance Survey Material reproduced
with the permission of the Controller HMSO
Produced by Egon Ronay Organisation Ltd

Layout and typography by Barbara Ronay

CONTENTS

Lucas engineering for world transport pages 65–67, 158–159, 228–229, 286–287, 350–351, 450–451, 488–489, 642–643, 714–715, 734–735, 836–837

Lucas service agents 664

Town maps including sights and establishments

EXPLANATION OF SYMBOLS

	Restaurants	Restaurants	Restaurants
★	Cooking much above average	Cuisine bien au-dessus de la moyenne	Küche sehr über dem Durchschnitt
★★	Outstanding cooking	Cuisine remarquable	Hervorragende Küche
★★★	Best cooking in the British Isles	La meilleure cuisine des Iles Britanniques	Beste Küche der britischen Inseln
Ⓢ	Friendly service	Personnel aimable	Freundliche Bedienung
♨	Cooking by proprietor or his family	Le patron ou sa famille fait la cuisine	Der Inhaber oder seine Familie kocht selber
🍷	Wine list classification (details on page 25)	Classification de la carte des vins (précisions page 25)	Weinkarte-Klassifizierung (für ausführliche Information siehe Seite 25)
About £ . . . for two	The approximate cost (except on pages 195–210) of a three-course meal including wine, coffee, service and VAT. This is based on a choice from among average-priced items on the menu and includes one of the least expensive bottles of wine. If there is a set menu, this will usually come to less.	Prix approximatif (pages 195–210 exceptées) d'un repas complet pour deux personnes, vin, café, taxe et service compris, basé sur un choix de plats et d'un vin à prix modéré. Lorsqu'il y a un menu à prix fixe, le prix du repas est en général moins élevé.	Der ungefähre Preis einer Mahlzeit mit drei Gängen (jedoch nicht auf Seiten 195–210) einschließlich Wein, Kaffee, Bedienung und MWSt für zwei Personen. Berechnet auf einer Auswahl einiger Gerichte in mittlerer Preislage, zusammen mit einer billigen Flasche Wein. Menüs, soweit vorhanden, sind in der Regel billiger.
● Set L	Price of a set lunch	Déjeuner à prix fixe	Tagesmenüpreis, Mittags
● Set D	Price of a set dinner	Dîner à prix fixe	Tagesmenüpreis, Abends

	Hotel accommodation	Hôtel (cuisine non incluse)	Hotelunterkunft
85–100% De Luxe	De Luxe	De Luxe	Luxushotel
70–84% Grade 1		Première Classe	Klasse 1
50–69% Grade 2		Deuxième Classe	Klasse 2
HOTEL ...	Ungraded because of rebuilding or similar circumstances	Non classé à cause de travaux ou de circonstances semblables	Unklassifiziert wegen Umbau oder ähnliche Umstände
Ⓜ	Owner-managed inn or hotel or tenanted inn	Auberge ou hôtel géré par le propriétaire ou auberge confiée à un gérant	Gasthof oder Hotel unter der Leitung des Besitzers oder Gasthof mit einem Pächter
E	Executive hotel, explained on page 21	Hôtel pour cadres supérieurs (voir page 21)	Manager Hotels (Details siehe Seite 21)
£A–£F	Hotel price categories. See page 7 for explanation.	Catégories des prix des hôtels. Voir page 7.	Hotel Preiskategorien: Erklärung siehe auf Seite 7.
♔♔♔♔♔♔	Degree of luxury	Degré de luxe de l'établissement	Luxusgrad
♿	Establishment considered by the management as suitable for wheelchairs.	Selon la direction, l'établissement peut accueillir les voitures des invalides.	Geeignet für Rollstühle, laut der Direktion.
Credit	Credit cards accepted by the establishment	Cartes de crédit acceptées par l'établissement	Kreditkarten werden angenommen
Banquets .../...	The maximum/minimum numbers for a meal in a separate room.	Maximum/minimum de couverts dans une salle particulière.	Maximum/minimum Anzahl von Gästen in einem separaten Raum.
	We print the name of the proprietor, manager or tenant who has been in charge for at least five years.	Nous publions le nom du propriétaire ou du gérant quand celui-ci est en place depuis au moins cinq ans.	Wir veröffentlichen die Namen jener Eigentümer und Geschäftsführer, die diese Position mindestens seit fünf Jahren bekleidet haben.

BASIS OF OUR GRADING SYSTEM

Hotels and Inns

In our unique grading system the percentage shown on each hotel entry, except for 'Economy Hotels', is an individual rating arrived at after careful testing, inspection and calculation. According to their percentage rating, hotels are further classified in three categories as de luxe, grade 1 and grade 2. ('Economy Hotels' are explained below.)

We assess hotels on 22 factors, many relating to the quality of service. Some refer to public rooms—their cleanliness, comfort, state of repair and general impression. Bedrooms are looked at for size, comfort, cleanliness and decor. The exterior of the building, private and public bathrooms, efficiency of reception, conduct and appearance of the staff and the room service are among other factors. The percentage is arrived at by comparing the marks given for each of the 22 factors with the maximum the hotel could have achieved.

The size of the hotel and the prices charged are not considered in the grading, *nor are their restaurants*.

If we recommend meals in a hotel or inn, a separate entry is made for its dining room.

There are often thin dividing lines between hotels and inns. We distinguish an inn from an hotel by its more modest accommodation, usually in the public rooms. For our purposes an inn is either a pub with superior, hotel-like accommodation or a small hotel with a bar and the atmosphere of a pub. Inns are not graded.

Country House Hotels Explanation on page 22.

London Economy Hotels

'Economy Hotels' is a category for modest hotels with limited facilities and with accommodation of a reasonable standard. They are below our usual limit of a 50% grading.

Restaurants

We only include restaurants where the cooking comes up to our minimum standards, however attractive the place may be in other respects. We take into account how well the restaurant achieves what it sets out to do, as reflected in the menu, decor, prices, publicity, atmosphere, clientele aimed at, etc., factors that add up to some sort of expectation. A modest eating place may have a number of stars, and a luxurious restaurant may be awarded no stars, as the *star* symbol indicates excellence of cooking, not of decor. The degree of luxury is indicated by the *crown* symbol.

In awarding the symbol ⑤ for *service,* we do not count formalities, but the essence of good service: friendliness, the capacity to put customers at ease on arrival and to make them feel at home while they are there, as well as sorry to leave.

Economy Evening Meals in London

'Economy Evening Meals in London' cover inexpensive dinners of reasonable quality, but not always up to our usual standards.

We have raised our minimum standards and therefore establishments previously included and not now in the Guide or appearing with different gradings have not necessarily lowered their standards.

HOTEL PRICE CATEGORIES

Continuous rises in hotel charges, which are inevitable in view of inflation in the whole economy, mean that even prices obtained just before going to press become out of date soon after publication. As prices quoted in an annual Guide must inevitably be comparative, we print categories from A to F rather than actual prices.

The categories are based on the price, Summer 1982, of a *double room for two occupants with bath, including English breakfast, 10% service & VAT:*

£A–over £85
£B–£65 to £85
£C–£50 to £65
£D–£37 to £50
£E–£27 to £37
£F–under £27

Prices quoted for Eire are in Irish punts.

We took the price of double rooms: there are far fewer single rooms and, therefore, their prices are less representative. Our basis is the *lowest* double-room price because this usually applies to the majority of rooms.

Where our calculations show the price to be just above or below the borderline between two categories, we symbolise the price as, for example, **£C/D**.

SUMMARY OF COVERAGE

This Guide includes the following number of establishments:

Hotels	1380	Restaurants	953
Inns	85	Economy restaurants	92
Economy hotels	60		
		Total	2570

THE EGON RONAY ORGANISATION

Although best known for this annual Guide, first published in 1957, our researches and publications have included the whole field of catering, and, apart from occasional publications, we produce three other annuals —*Just a Bite, Egon Ronay's Lucas Guide for Gourmets on a Family Budget*, and *Egon Ronay's Bulmer Pub Guide* which assesses bar food and accommodation at pubs and inns, the next editions of which will be brought out in March and February 1983 respectively; and *Egon Ronay's TWA Guide to Good Restaurants in Europe's Business Cities*, publication: January 1983.

Our researches are carried out by full-time professional inspectors with catering backgrounds. After testing their good taste and knowledge of international cooking thoroughly, we train them for many weeks in the Organisation to achieve common standards of judgement with as much objectivity as this field allows. Their professional identities are not disclosed until they seek information from the management after paying their bills.

Our Guide to eating in Europe's business cities is based on the researches and assessments of a multi-national group of eight respected gastronomes and connoisseurs.

To find establishments for forthcoming Guides, we normally rely on re-inspection of current listings; a research programme drawn up from readers' recommendations; and requests for visits from proprietors of establishments (these latter two categories being subject to careful vetting).

We are completely independent in editorial selections and judgement and do not accept advertising, payment or hospitality from establishments we cover.

Celebrations tend to be spontaneous. So it's good to know that with the American Express Card you can set the style. With consummate ease. The Card is warmly welcomed at good restaurants, hotels, stores and car-hire and airline offices in Britain and around the world.

SET THE STYLE

So whether you're celebrating success or merely making overtures, do it on the American Express Card.

If you're not yet enjoying the benefits of Cardmembership, pick up an application form from any branch of Lloyds Bank or telephone Brighton (0273) 696933, for an application form.

Don't leave home without it.

GOLD PLATE AWARDS

Our annual awards for the Hotel and Restaurant of the Year are Gold Plates engraved with the winners' names and retained until the next year's awards. *They do not necessarily denote the best establishments*, but are awarded to a hotel and a restaurant whose consistent excellence or enterprise we find outstanding.

The Winners for 1982

**HOTEL OF THE YEAR
Ston Easton Park
Ston Easton, Somerset**
Enterprising spirit and outstanding management have quickly lifted this new country house hotel above others. Lovely setting, friendly atmosphere and incomparable decor are its hallmarks.

**RESTAURANT OF THE YEAR
La Tante Claire
London SW3**
This small restaurant is the culinary home of a true artist, Pierre Koffmann, whose originality, perfectionism and finesse are without parallel in London.

Previous Years

Hotel of the Year

1969
Lygon Arms, Broadway (Hereford & Worcester)
1970
Inn on the Park, London W1
1971
Inverlochy Castle, Fort William (Highland)
1972
Berkeley Hotel, London SW1
1973
Gleneagles Hotel, Auchterarder (Tayside)
1974
Sharrow Bay Country House Hotel, Ullswater (Cumbria)
1975
Ashford Castle, Cong (Co. Mayo), Eire
1976
Chewton Glen Hotel, New Milton (Hampshire)
1977
Gravetye Manor, East Grinstead (West Sussex)
1978
The Ritz, London W1
1979
Connaught Hotel, London W1
1980
Royal Crescent Hotel, Bath (Avon)
1981
Plough & Harrow, Birmingham (West Midlands)

Restaurant of the Year

1969
Thornbury Castle, Thornbury (Avon)
1970
Le Poulbot, London EC2
1971
Box Tree Cottage, Ilkley (West Yorkshire)
1972
Le Gavroche, London SW1
1973
Kildwick Hall, Kildwick (West Yorkshire)
1974
Shezan, London SW7
1975
Wilton's, London SW1
1976
Horn of Plenty, Gulworthy (Devon)
1977
Carrier's, London N1
1978
McCoy's, Staddle Bridge (North Yorkshire)
1979
Les Quat' Saisons, Oxford (Oxfordshire)
1980
Sharrow Bay Country House Hotel, Ullswater (Cumbria)
1981
The Waterside Inn, Bray (Berkshire)

Photo: BTA Ston Easton Park, Ston Easton, Somerset

Pierre Koffmann
La Tante Claire, London

STARRED RESTAURANTS

Three Star Restaurants 

London
La Tante Claire

England
Bray-on-Thames, Berkshire, Water-
side Inn
Gulworthy, Devon, Horn of Plenty

Two Star Restaurants 

London
Le Gavroche
Hyatt Carlton Tower, Chelsea Room
Interlude de Tabaillau
Ma Cuisine
Mirabelle

England
East Grinstead, West Sussex,
   Gravetye Manor Restaurant
Hintlesham, Suffolk, Hintlesham Hall
Ilkley, West Yorkshire, Box Tree
   Restaurant
New Milton, Hampshire, Chewton
   Glen Hotel, Marryat Room
Oxford, Oxfordshire, Les Quat'
   Saisons
Ullswater, Cumbria, Sharrow Bay
   Hotel Restaurant

One Star Restaurants ★

London
L'Arlequin
Bagatelle
Berkeley Restaurant
Boulestin
Brasserie St Quentin
Carrier's
Chez Nico
Connaught Hotel
   Restaurant
Daphne's
Dorchester,
   The Terrace
Gay Hussar
Inter-Continental
   Hotel, Le Soufflé
Ken Lo's Memories
   of China
Mijanou
Odette's
Odin's
Le Poulbot
Shezan
Le Suquet

England
Abberley, Hereford &
   Worcester — Elms Hotel, Brooke Room Restaurant
Ashford, Kent — Eastwell Manor Restaurant
Bath, Avon — Priory Hotel Restaurant
Battle, East Sussex — Netherfield Place Restaurant
Birmingham, West Midlands — Plough & Harrow Hotel Restaurant
Birmingham, West Midlands — Rajdoot
Brighton, East Sussex — Le Français
Brockdish, Norfolk — Sheriff House
Chagford, Devon — Gidleigh Park Hotel Restaurant
Corse Lawn, Gloucestershire — Corse Lawn House
Dartmouth, Devon — Carved Angel
Dedham, Essex — Le Talbooth
Freshford, Avon — Homewood Park Restaurant
Fressingfield, Suffolk — Fox & Goose
Grasmere, Cumbria — Michael's Nook Restaurant
Haslemere, Surrey — Lythe Hill Hotel, Auberge de France
Haslemere, Surrey — Morels
Helford, Cornwall — Riverside
Herstmonceux, East Sussex — Sundial

Leamington Spa, Warwickshire	Mallory Court Restaurant
Limpsfield, Surrey	Old Lodge
Louth, Lincolnshire	Forbidden Fruits
Malvern, Hereford & Worcester	Croque-en-Bouche
Nantwich, Cheshire	Rookery Hall Restaurant
Northleach, Gloucestershire	Old Woolhouse
Pool-in-Wharfedale, West Yorkshire	Pool Court
Shipdham, Norfolk	Shipdham Place Restaurant
Staddle Bridge, North Yorkshire	McCoy's Restaurant
Stockbridge, Hampshire	Sheriff House
Ston Easton, Somerset	Ston Easton Park
Storrington, West Sussex	Manley's
Taunton, Somerset	Castle Hotel Restaurant
Underbarrow, Cumbria	Tullythwaite House

Scotland

Crinan, Strathclyde	Crinan Hotel, Lock 16 Seafood Restaurant
Fort William, Highland	Inverlochy Castle Restaurant
Gullane, Lothian	Greywalls Hotel Restaurant
Inverness, Highland	Station Hotel Restaurant
Kinlochbervie, Highland	Kinlochbervie Hotel Restaurant
Knipoch, Strathclyde	Knipoch Hotel Restaurant
Ledaig, Strathclyde	Isle of Eriska Hotel Restaurant
Peat Inn, Fife	The Peat Inn
Tarbert, Strathclyde	Stonefield Castle Hotel Restaurant

Wales

Llandewi Skirrid, Gwent	Walnut Tree Inn
Newport, Dyfed	Pantry

Channel Islands

St Saviour, Jersey	Longueville Manor Restaurant
Sark, Sark	Aval du Creux Hotel Restaurant

Northern Ireland

Saintfield, Co. Down	Barn

Eire

Cork, Co. Cork	Arbutus Lodge Hotel Restaurant
Dublin, Co. Dublin	Patrick Guilbaud
Dunderry, Co. Meath	Dunderry Lodge Restaurant
Kenmare, Co. Kerry	Park Hotel Restaurant
Shanagarry, Co. Cork	Ballymaloe House Restaurant

A map of starred restaurants appears on the following page.

Starred Restaurants around Britain and Ireland

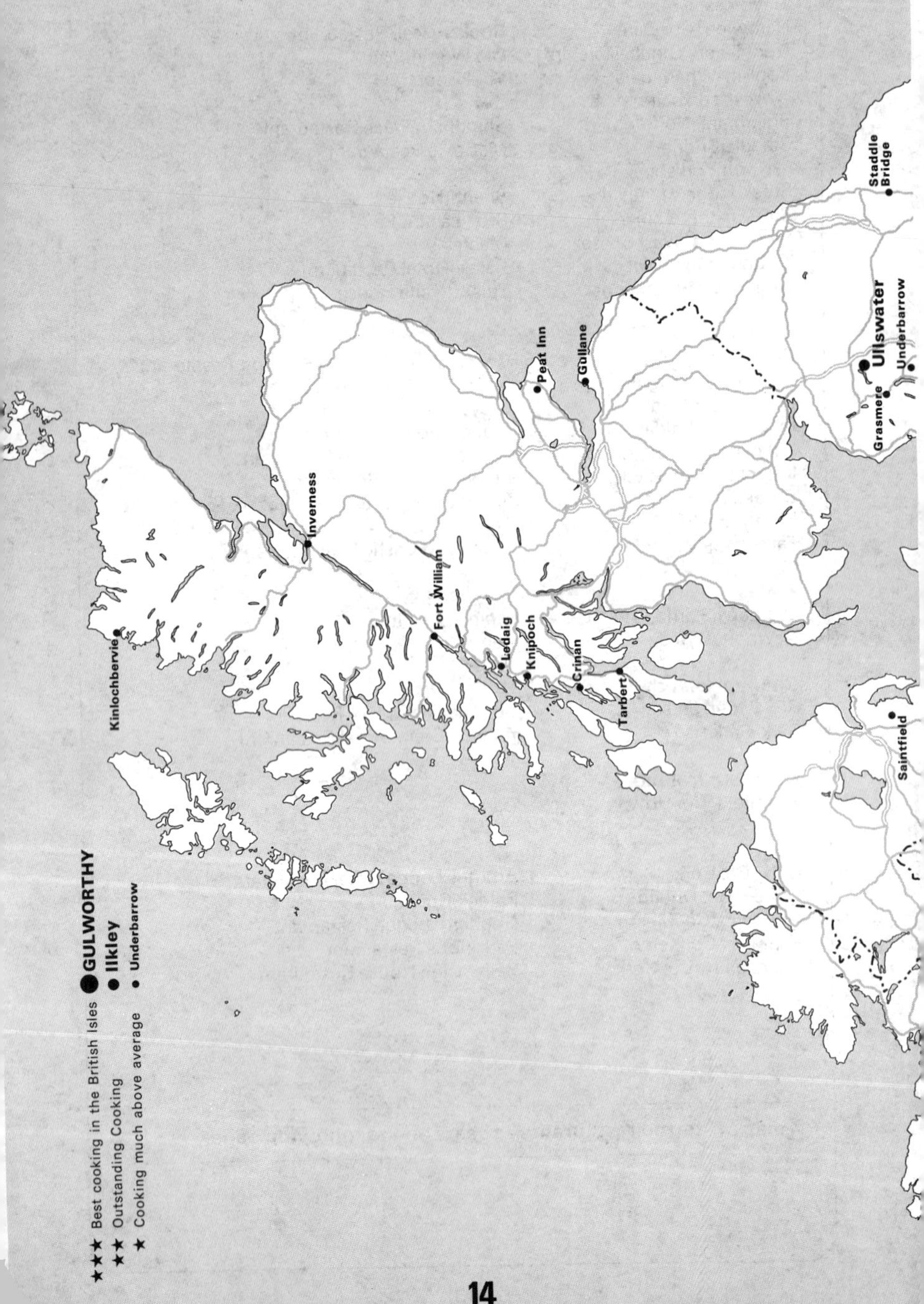

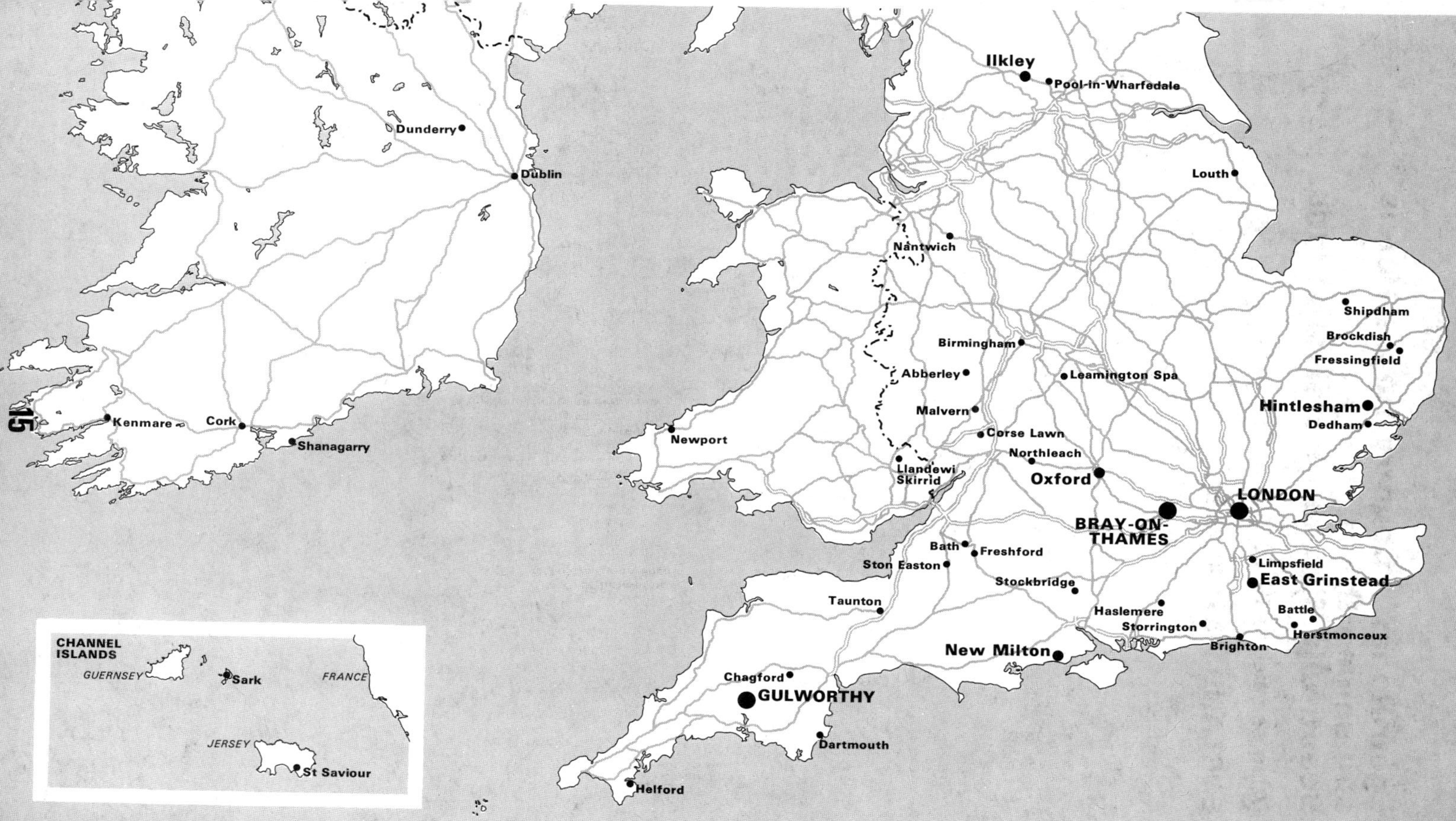

Shipdham
Brockdish
Fressingfield
Hintlesham
Dedham
Louth
Limpsfield
East Grinstead
Battle
Herstmonceux
LONDON
Brighton
Pool-in-Wharfedale
Leamington Spa
Storrington
BRAY-ON-THAMES
Haslemere
Ilkley
Oxford
Corse Lawn
Northleach
Stockbridge
New Milton
Birmingham
Freshford
Abberley
Malvern
Bath
Nantwich
Llandewi Skirrid
Ston Easton
Taunton
GULWORTHY
Chagford
Dartmouth
Newport
Helford
Dublin
Dunderry
Shanagarry
Cork
Kenmare

CHANNEL ISLANDS
GUERNSEY
Sark
FRANCE
JERSEY
St Saviour

15

Egon Ronay's Country House Hotels and some other Beautifully Situated Hotels and Inns

(Also see pages 18-20 and 22)

ENGLAND AND WALES

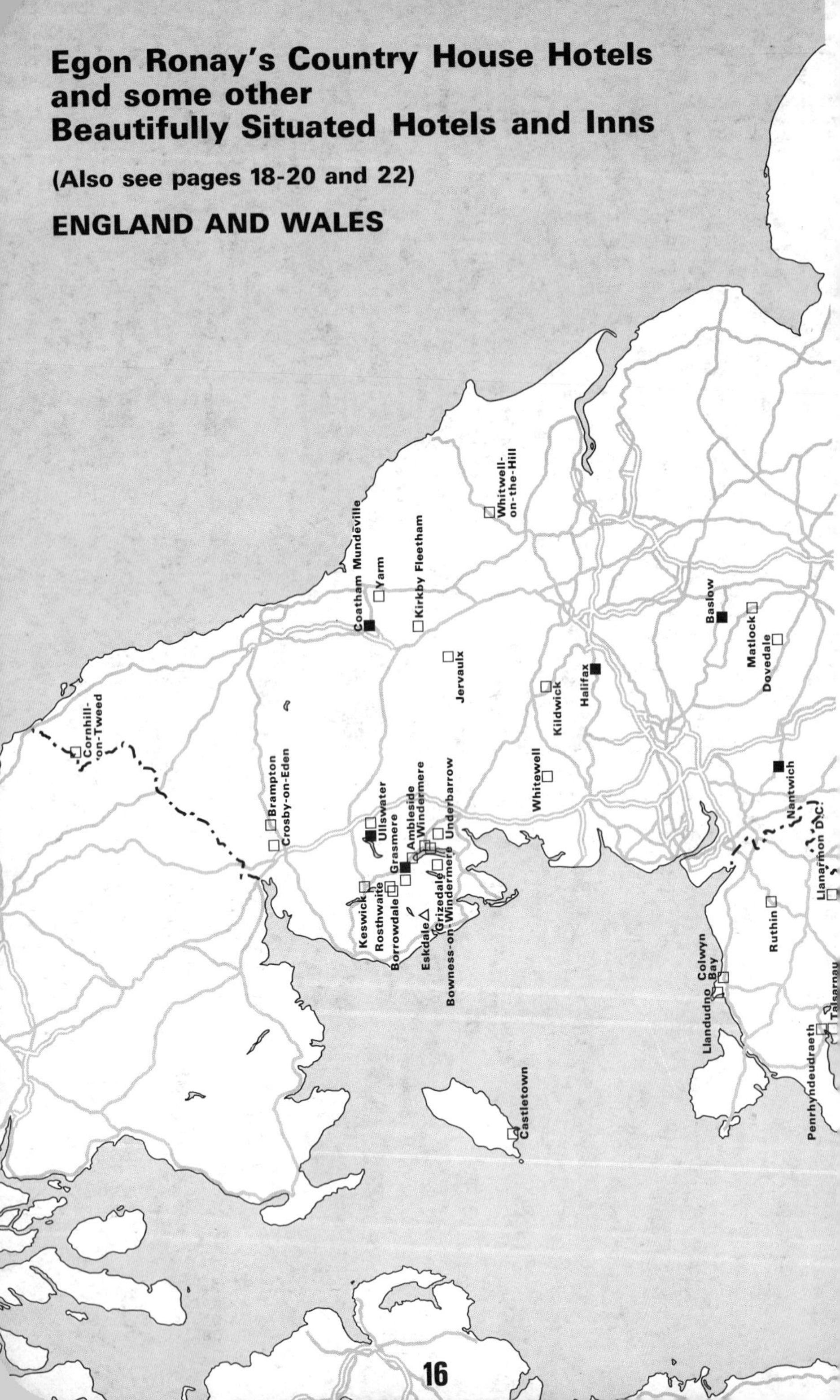

Bontddu
Penmaenpool
Tal-y-Llyn
Eglwysfach
Aberystwyth
Pant Mawr
Abergwesyn
St David's
Lake Vyrnwy
Abberley
Shrawley
Malvern
Ledbury
Ross-on-Wye
Tintern Parva
Thornbury
Rothley
Oakham
Shipdham
Leamington Spa
Stratford-upon-Avon
Walton
Six Mile Bottom
Dedham
Cheltenham
Shurdington
Bibury
Amberley
Malmesbury
Streatley-on-Thames
Castle Combe
Beanacre
Freshford
Hunstrete
Ston Easton
Warminster
Horton-cum-Studley
Newgate Street Village
Hadley Wood
Harrow Weald
Marlow
Egham
Bagshot
Winchester
Haslemere
Storrington
Walberton
East Grinstead
Ashford
Battle
Rushlake Green
Climping
Woody Bay
Heddon's Mouth
Saunton
Simonsbath
Chittlehamholt
Sturminster Newton
Burley
Lymington
Bransgore
New Milton
Freshwater
Studland Bay
Bonchurch

ISLES OF SCILLY
Tresco

Whimple
Gittisham
Chedington
Branscombe
Chagford
Moretonhampstead
Ashburton
Torquay
Padstow
Hellandbridge
Newquay
Golant
Carlyon Bay
St Ives
Portloe
Veryan
Hope Cove
Kingsbridge
Salcombe
St Mawes
Budock Vean
Praa Sands
Lamorna Cove

Country House Hotel
Beautifully Situated Hotel
Beautifully Situated Inn

© 1982 Egon Ronay's Guides
Crown Copyright Reserved

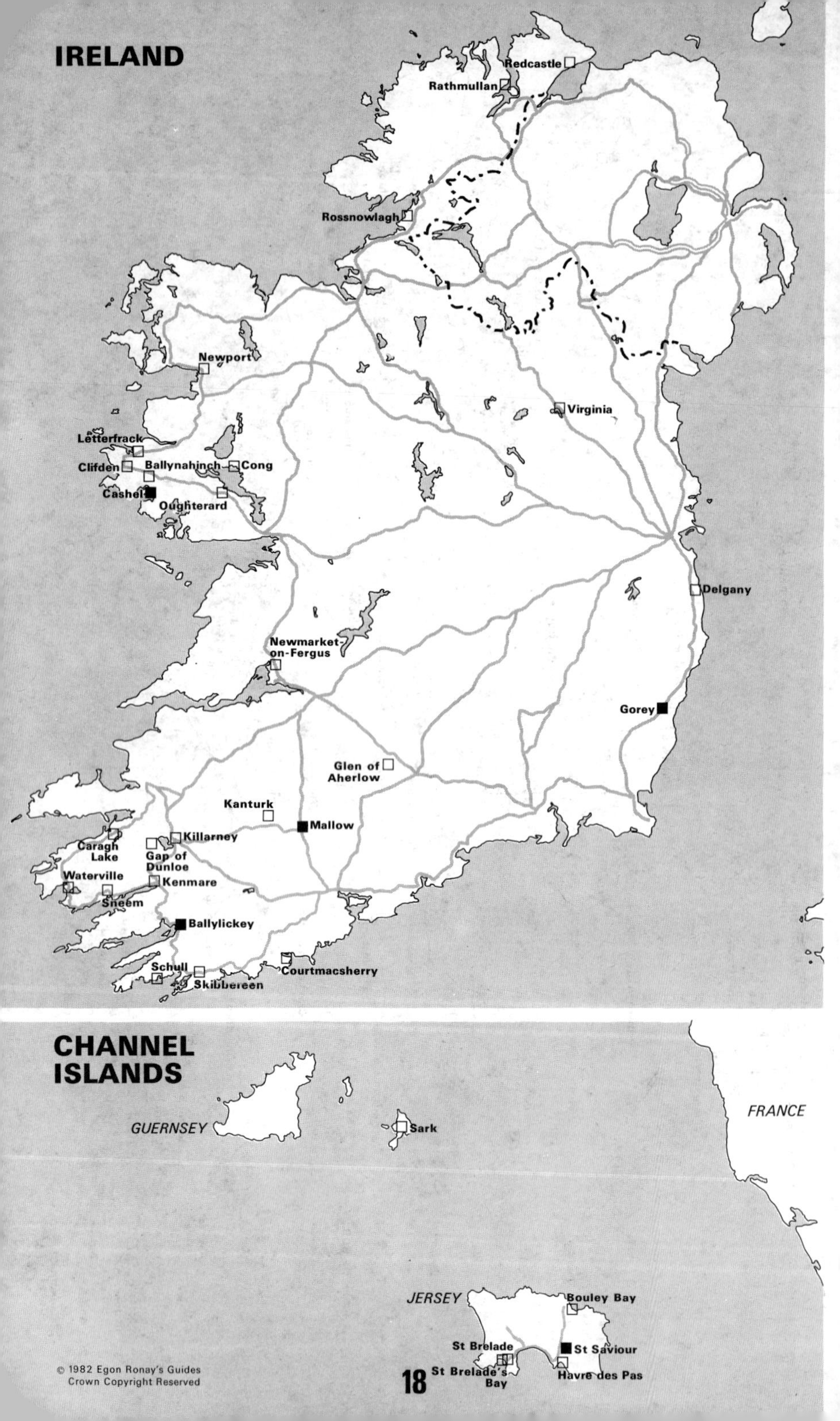

IRELAND
Redcastle
Rathmullan
Rossnowlagh
Newport
Virginia
Letterfrack
Clifden
Ballynahinch
Cong
Cashel
Oughterard
Delgany
Newmarket-on-Fergus
Gorey
Glen of Aherlow
Kanturk
Mallow
Killarney
Caragh Lake
Gap of Dunloe
Waterville
Kenmare
Sneem
Ballylickey
Schull
Courtmacsherry
Skibbereen
CHANNEL ISLANDS
GUERNSEY
Sark
FRANCE
JERSEY
Bouley Bay
St Brelade
St Saviour
St Brelade's Bay
Havre des Pas

18

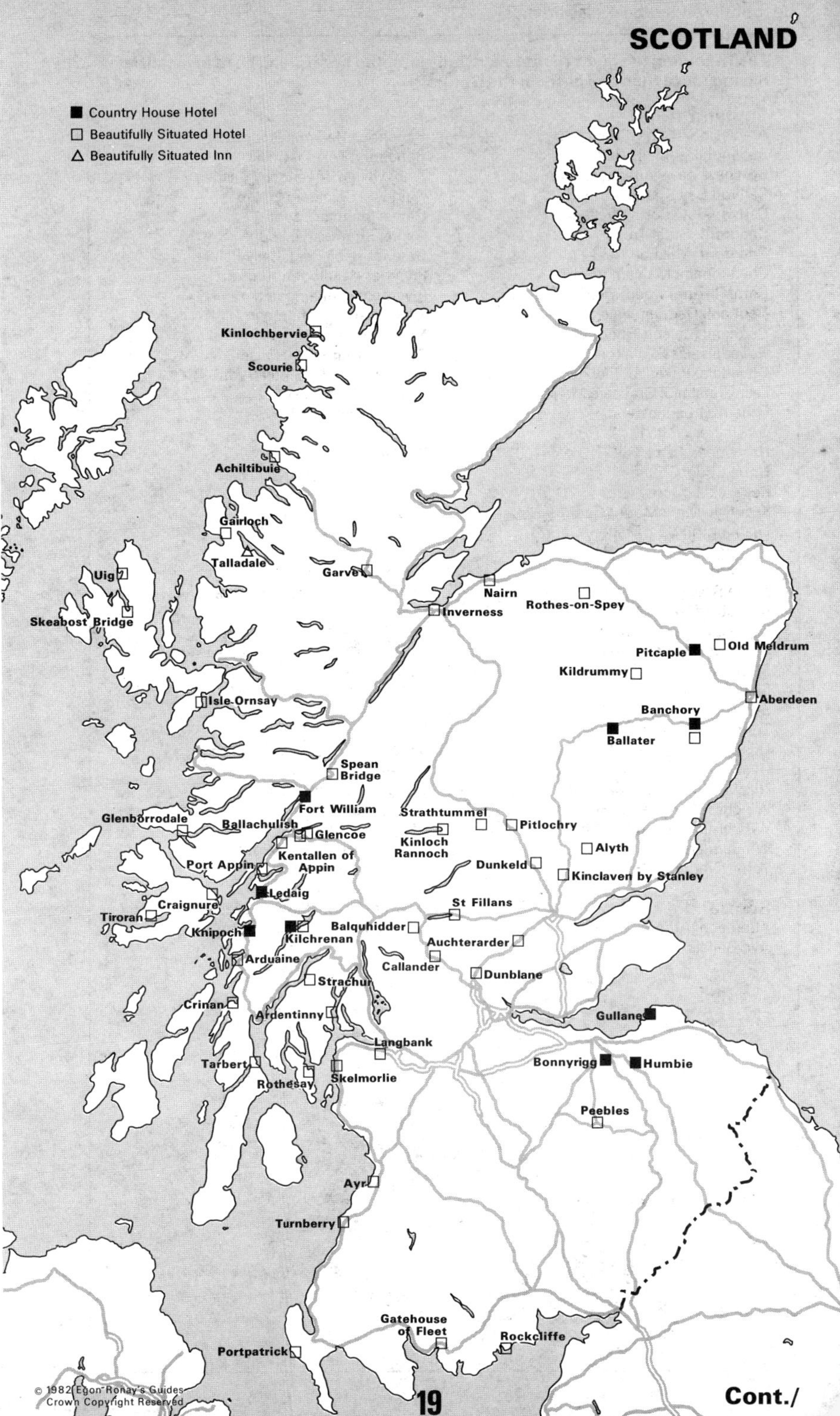

SCOTLAND

Country House Hotel
Beautifully Situated Hotel
Beautifully Situated Inn

Kinlochbervie
Scourie
Achiltibuie
Gairloch
Talladale
Uig
Garve
Skeabost Bridge
Nairn
Inverness
Rothes-on-Spey
Pitcaple
Old Meldrum
Kildrummy
Isle Ornsay
Banchory
Aberdeen
Ballater
Spean Bridge
Fort William
Glenborrodale
Ballachulish
Strathtummel
Pitlochry
Glencoe
Kinloch Rannoch
Alyth
Port Appin
Kentallen of Appin
Dunkeld
Kinclaven by Stanley
Ledaig
Craignure
St Fillans
Tiroran
Balquhidder
Knipoch
Kilchrenan
Auchterarder
Arduaine
Callander
Strachur
Dunblane
Crinan
Ardentinny
Gullane
Langbank
Tarbert
Bonnyrigg
Humbie
Rothesay
Skelmorlie
Peebles
Ayr
Turnberry
Gatehouse of Fleet
Rockcliffe
Portpatrick

19

Cont./

The following list gives those beautifully situated hotels which are in localities having more than one entry in the Guide:

England

Ambleside: Rothay Manor
Bagshot: Pennyhill Park
Bowness on Windermere: Burnside
Carlyon Bay: Carlyon Bay
Carlyon Bay: Porth Avallen
Chagford: Great Tree
Chagford: Mill End
Cheltenham: Malvern View
Cornhill-on-Tweed: Tillmouth Park
Dedham: Dedham Vale
Dedham: Maison Talbooth
Dovedale: Izaak Walton
Dovedale: Peveril of the Peak
East Grinstead: Gravetye Manor
Egham: Great Fosters
Grasmere: White Moss House
Haslemere: Lythe Hill
Hope Cove: Cottage
Keswick: Lodore Swiss
Keswick: Mary Mount Country House
Leamington Spa: Mallory Court
Lymington: Passford House
Malvern: Cottage in the Wood
Matlock: Riber Hall
Newquay: Headland
St Ives: Tregenna Castle
St Mawes: Hotel Tresanton
Salcombe: South Sands
Salcombe: Tides Reach
Stratford-upon-Avon: Welcombe
Torquay: Osborne
Ullswater: Leeming on Ullswater
Ullswater: Old Church
Ullswater: Sharrow Bay Country House
Winchester: Lainston House
Windermere: Langdale Chase
Windermere: Miller Howe
Yarm: Crathorne Hall

Scotland

Aberdeen: Ardoe House
Ayr: Belleisle
Banchory: Raemoir House
Banchory: Tor-na-Coille
Fort William: Inverlochy Castle
Gairloch: Shieldaig Lodge
Garve: Inchbae Lodge
Garve: Strathgarve Lodge
Gatehouse of Fleet: Cally Palace
Inverness: Culloden House
Inverness: Dunain Park
Kilchrenan: Taychreggan
Nairn: Newton
Peebles: Cringletie House
Peebles: Peebles Hotel Hydro
Pitlochry: Green Park
Scourie: Eddrachilles

Wales

Llandudno: Bodysgallen Hall
Ruthin: Ruthin Castle
St David's: Warpool Court
Tintern Parva: Wye Valley

Channel Islands

Havre des Pas: Hotel de la Plage
St Brelade: Atlantic
St Brelade's Bay: Hotel l'Horizon
St Brelade's Bay: St Brelade's Bay
Sark: Aval du Creux
Sark: Hotel Petit Champ

Eire

Ballylickey: Ballylickey House
Caragh Lake: Ard-na-Sidhe
Caragh Lake: Caragh Lodge
Clifden: Abbeyglen
Kenmare: Park
Killarney: Aghadoe Heights
Killarney: Castlerosse
Killarney: Hotel Europe
Newmarket-on-Fergus: Dromoland Castle
Oughterard: Currarevagh House

EXECUTIVE HOTELS
'E'

Our unique Executive Hotel category applies to those establishments that meet the needs of executives who require efficiently provided facilities, coupled with luxurious comfort, as the tools of their trade while on official business.

This category is based on certain minimum requirements as follows:

1. Our de luxe or grade 1 classification.
2. Telex.
3. Direct dial telephones with message warning lights.
4. Room service of snacks and beverages until midnight.
5. TV and radio in all rooms.
6. Early morning service of breakfast from 5am.
7. Early morning check out facility from 5am.
8. Constantly manned porters' desk.
9. Adequate writing surfaces and supply of stationery in all rooms.
10. The hotel should be able to provide a snack even if it is only a sandwich and drink throughout the day and evening.
11. 24-hour laundry service.

The only exceptions made have been where not more than *one* of the least important criteria was not met.

LONDON
Athenaeum
Hotel Bristol
Britannia
Capital
Churchill
Dorchester
Drury Lane
Europa
Gloucester
Grosvenor House
Hilton International
  London
Holiday Inn (Chelsea)
Holiday Inn (Marble Arch)
Holiday Inn
  (Swiss Cottage)
Howard
Hyatt Carlton Tower
Hyde Park
Inn on the Park
Inter-Continental
John Howard
May Fair
Montcalm
Portman Inter-Continental
Ritz
Royal Garden
Royal Lancaster
Savoy
Selfridge
Sheraton Park Tower
Tower
Waldorf

LONDON AIRPORTS
Gatwick
Copthorne
Gatwick Hilton
  International
Gatwick Penta
Heathrow
Heathrow Penta
Holiday Inn
Sheraton-Heathrow
Sheraton Skyline

ENGLAND
Bagshot: Pennyhill Park
Birmingham: Albany
Birmingham: Holiday Inn
Birmingham: Metropole & Warwick
Birmingham: Plough & Harrow
Bristol: Holiday Inn
Bristol: Ladbroke Dragonara
Chester: Grosvenor
Dover: Holiday Inn
Droitwich: Château Impney
Haslemere: Lythe Hill
Leeds: Ladbroke Dragonara
Leicester: Holiday Inn
Liverpool: Atlantic Tower
Liverpool: Holiday Inn
Longhorsley: Linden Hall
Manchester: Hotel Piccadilly
Middlesbrough: Ladbroke Dragonara
Newcastle upon Tyne: Gosforth Park
Newcastle upon Tyne: Holiday Inn
Nottingham: Albany
Plymouth: Holiday Inn
Poole: Quay
Portsmouth: Holiday Inn
Slough: Holiday Inn
South Normanton: Swallow
Stratford-upon-Avon: Hilton International
Torquay: Imperial
York: Viking

SCOTLAND
Aberdeen: Holiday Inn
Aberdeen Airport: Holiday Inn
Edinburgh: George
Edinburgh: Ladbroke Dragonara
Glasgow: Albany
Glasgow: Grosvenor
Glasgow: Holiday Inn

CHANNEL ISLANDS
St Brelade's Bay: Hotel l'Horizon

NORTHERN IRELAND
Belfast: Belfast Europa

EIRE
Cork: Jurys
Dublin: Berkeley Court
Dublin: Blooms
Dublin: Burlington
Dublin: Jurys

EGON RONAY'S COUNTRY HOUSE HOTELS

Our quest in the last four years has detected and established a new, elite category of small hotels, in many respects the cream of British hostelries and certainly unsurpassed in other countries. Usually they are imposing country mansions, transformed by dedicated owners, often husband-and-wife teams, with unerring taste for attractive interiors and a true understanding of the essence of service. They have turned—some are in the course of turning—fine, attractively set buildings into civilised and polished hostelries with all-round excellence and good food often of star standard. They are created by—and for—sophisticated individualists.

England

Ashford: Eastwell Manor
Baslow: Cavendish Hotel
Battle: Netherfield Place
Beanacre: Beechfield House
Bonchurch: Winterbourne Hotel
Chagford: Gidleigh Park
Chedington: Chedington Court
Climping: Bailiffscourt Hotel
Coatham Mundeville: Hall Garth
Dedham: Maison Talbooth
East Grinstead: Gravetye Manor
Freshford: Homewood Park Hotel
Gittisham: Combe House Hotel
Grasmere: Michael's Nook
Halifax: Holdsworth House
Hunstrete: Hunstrete House
Leamington Spa: Mallory Court

Malmesbury: Whatley Manor
Nantwich: Rookery Hall
New Milton: Chewton Glen Hotel
Oakham: Hambleton Hall
Rushlake Green: Priory Hotel
Shipdham: Shipdham Place
Shurdington: Greenway Hotel
Ston Easton: Ston Easton Park
Storrington: Little Thakeham
Sturminster Newton: Plumber Manor
Thornbury: Thornbury Castle Hotel
Ullswater: Leeming on Ullswater
Ullswater: Sharrow Bay Country House Hotel
Warminster: Bishopstrow House
Whimple: Woodhayes
Winchester: Lainston House

Scotland

Ballater: Tullich Lodge
Banchory: Raemoir House Hotel
Bonnyrigg: Dalhousie Castle
Fort William: Inverlochy Castle
Gullane: Greywalls Hotel
Humbie: Johnstounburn House
Kilchrenan: Ardanaiseig Hotel
Knipoch: Knipoch Hotel
Ledaig: Isle of Eriska
Pitcaple: Pittodrie House Hotel

Channel Islands

St Saviour: Longueville Manor

Eire

Ballylickey: Ballylickey House Hotel
Cashel: Cashel House Hotel
Gorey: Marlfield House Hotel
Mallow: Longueville House

Husbands have been caught trying to play records on it.

It's a hob that's as unique as System One's built-in oven and grill.

An oven and grill that doesn't just look the best built-in cooker money can buy.

It performs like it.

Its Sola®Grill cooks evenly right along its length and breadth.

So there are no burnt erings from the middle, and nothing half-cooked from the ends.

It also gives you seven shelf positions instead of the usual six, can cook 40 buns on two trays, gobble up a 31 lb turkey and even clean itself.

It only takes one look to realise System One is quite an amazing cooker.

One that couldn't be mistaken for anything but the best.

TI NEW WORLD LIMITED, FREEPOST, WARRINGTON WA4 1BR.

Little wonder.

System One's hob is like no other hob anyone's seen before.

For a start, even a man will notice it's got a lid. But not just any lid.

A lid that's heat-resistant and as tough as the average work top.

It's also totally safe, being counter balanced and having a valve that automatically cuts off the gas the moment you start to close it.

When it's open it acts as a splash back that cleans with a wipe.

What it so elegantly covers are four burners that can give you the gentlest of simmers or the most furious of boils.

And if your milk should happen to spill over, there's no crying over it. Its burners are sealed to the hotplate, so you simply sponge up any mess.

THE PERFECT WINE LIST

The perfect wine list may not exist, but we look for something near it in those we grade 'outstanding'. These are some points of style and content which we consider.

Since non-*a.c.* wines from *appellation contrôlée* regions in France no longer exist, it is unnecessary to indicate that any wine from such a region is *a.c.* VDQS and *Vins de Table* should, however, be shown as such. We strongly support observance of the EEC law which forbids any suggestion, by place in the list or by description, that a *Vin de Table* has any connection with an *a.c.* region.

The listing of 'follow-on' vintages, e.g. '1979/80', should be restricted to lesser wines, and only when the vintages are of comparable quality and price. While a disclaimer may protect the restaurateur from the Trades Descriptions Act should he accidentally serve a bottle different from that listed, the customer should know that although an alternative may be offered, he is not compelled to accept it. Of course, if lists are kept up to date, such situations should not arise.

A common fault is omission of bottling details. Now that most clarets are château-bottled, a note at the head of the page reading 'Château-bottled unless otherwise indicated' may be better than a repetition of 'ch.b.' on many lines. Bordeaux, French or English bottling should be distinguished.

In Burgundy, Rhône and the Loire, English, French or domaine bottlings should be distinguished, and the name of the shipper or grower is essential, even if there is a vineyard name too.

A serious list must have a balance of good and lesser vintages. Long lists of great names, all either from 'off-vintages' or far too young to drink, are not impressive.

Some otherwise good lists are marred by being put together haphazardly. Long sections such as claret can be subdivided by vintage, by smaller geographical units and, of course, by price. But a long list where the only order is that of bin-number helps nobody.

GRADING OF WINE LISTS

Wine Lists are appraised and graded in three categories:

Above Average
Superior
Outstanding

The criteria of assessment include the choice of vintages; a balanced representation of areas within one or two countries, or internationally; appropriate nomenclature and designation; indication of reliable sources of supply; enterprise in specialisation or unusual though valid features.

It may count against a cellar if the wine list is not constantly updated, including the one sent to us. We consider the reliance on a general warning regarding the substitution of unavailable vintages inadequate.

It will be vital for wine lists to indicate whether wines are château- or estate-bottled.

We consider that the restaurants below have **outstanding** wine lists this year.

London
A l'Ecu de France
Au Jardin des Gourmets
Berkeley Restaurant & Le Perroquet
Café Royal
Capital Hotel Restaurant
Claridge's Causerie & Restaurant
L'Escargot
Le Gavroche
Inn on the Park, Four Seasons
    Restaurant & Lanes Restaurant
Inter-Continental Hotel, Le Soufflé
Mijanou
Mirabelle
Montcalm Hotel, La Varenne
Pomegranates
Ritz Hotel, Louis XVI Restaurant
Savoy Hotel Grill Room &
    River Room
Scott's
La Tante Claire
Walton's

England
Aston Clinton, Buckinghamshire:
    Bell Inn
Battle, East Sussex: Netherfield Place
Beanacre, Wiltshire: Beechfield
    House
Bourton-on-the-Water,
    Gloucestershire: Rose Tree
Bowness on Windermere, Cumbria:
    Porthole Eating House

Bray-on-Thames, Berkshire:
    Waterside Inn
Bristol, Avon: Harveys
Chagford, Devon: Gidleigh Park
Chedington, Dorset: Chedington
    Court
Chiddingfold, Surrey: Crown Inn
    Restaurant
Chilgrove, West Sussex: White Horse
    Inn
Coggeshall, Essex: White Hart
Dartmouth, Devon: Carved Angel
Dedham, Essex: Le Talbooth
East Grinstead, West Sussex:
    Gravetye Manor

Continued

Fressingfield, Suffolk: Fox & Goose
Harrogate, North Yorkshire: Number
  Six
Hintlesham, Suffolk: Hintlesham Hall
Ilkley, West Yorkshire: Box Tree
  Restaurant
Lymington, Hampshire: Stanwell
  House Hotel, Railings Restaurant
Malvern, Hereford & Worcester:
  Croque-en-Bouche
New Milton, Hampshire: Chewton
  Glen Hotel, Marryat Room
Oakham, Leicestershire: Hambleton
  Hall
Oxford, Oxfordshire: Restaurant
  Elizabeth
Oxford, Oxfordshire: Les Quat'
  Saisons
Pool-in-Wharfedale, West Yorkshire:
  Pool Court
Rushlake Green, East Sussex:
  Priory Hotel
Shepton Mallet, Somerset: Bowlish
  House
Speldhurst, Kent: George & Dragon,
  Oak Room
Swallowfield, Berkshire: Mill House
Taunton, Somerset: Castle Hotel
Thornbury, Avon: Thornbury Castle
Ullswater, Cumbria: Leeming on
  Ullswater

Ullswater, Cumbria: Sharrow Bay
  Country House Hotel
Uppingham, Leicestershire:
  Lake Isle
Walshford, North Yorkshire: Bridge
  Inn, Byron Room
Wentbridge, West Yorkshire:
  Wentbridge House Hotel

Scotland
Fort William, Highland: Inverlochy
  Castle
Gullane, Lothian: La Potinière
Peat Inn, Fife: The Peat Inn
Port Appin, Strathclyde:
  Airds Hotel
Uphall, Lothian: Houston House

Wales
Llandewi Skirrid, Gwent: Walnut
  Tree Inn

Eire
Cork, Co. Cork: Arbutus
  Lodge Hotel
Dublin, Co. Dublin:
  Le Coq Hardi
Dunderry, Co. Meath: Dunderry
  Lodge
Shanagarry, Co. Cork: Ballymaloe
  House

CELLAR OF THE YEAR 1982
EGON RONAY/ARMAGNAC AWARD

This year the panel of three, under *Egon Ronay's* chairmanship, to choose the winner of the trophy consisted of:

Patrick Grubb M.W., Director and Head of the Wine Department at Sotheby's.

Paul Henderson, owner of Gidleigh Park Hotel, Chagford, Devon, and last year's winner.

The panel was advised by *David Wolfe*, wine consultant to the Egon Ronay Organisation.

Skilled selection of vintages, shippers and growers was a prime consideration. Balance, and the absence of poor vintages, counted for more than comprehensiveness. Yet the winner is the most comprehensive cellar in the country:

WHITE HORSE INN, CHILGROVE

not so much for its encyclopaedic French and German sections, as for its choice of the best wines from these and other countries.

The panel in session (left to right) David Wolfe, Patrick Grubb, Egon Ronay, Paul Henderson and Trevor Barker of 'Food and Wine from France'.

LONDON HOTELS

in order of rating

De luxe

92%	Berkeley	88%	Hyatt Carlton Tower
92%	Claridge's	88%	Ritz Hotel
92%	Connaught Hotel	87%	Savoy Hotel
92%	Dorchester Hotel	86%	Sheraton Park Tower
90%	Inn on the Park	85%	Inter-Continental Hotel
88%	Grosvenor House		

Grade 1

83% Athenaeum Hotel
82% Hyde Park Hotel
81% Hotel Bristol
81% Hilton International London
81% Howard Hotel
81% Selfridge Hotel
80% Churchill Hotel
79% Holiday Inn (Chelsea)
79% Lowndes Hotel
79% May Fair Hotel
79% Portman Inter-Continental Hotel
78% John Howard Hotel
78% Royal Garden Hotel
78% Royal Lancaster Hotel
78% Stafford Hotel
77% Britannia Hotel
77% Gloucester Hotel
77% Montcalm Hotel
77% Waldorf Hotel
76% Capital Hotel
76% Holiday Inn (Swiss Cottage)
76% Tower Hotel
75% Ladbroke Westmoreland Hotel
75% Westbury Hotel
74% Brown's Hotel
74% Dukes Hotel
74% Park Lane Hotel
73% Europa Hotel
73% Goring Hotel
72% Holiday Inn (Marble Arch)
71% Drury Lane Hotel
71% The White House
70% Chesterfield Hotel
70% Royal Trafalgar Hotel

Grade 2

69%	Basil Street Hotel	62%	Coburg Hotel
69%	Blakes Hotel	62%	Strand Palace Hotel
69%	Cumberland Hotel	62%	Washington Hotel
69%	Hilton International, Kensington	61%	Great Eastern Hotel
		61%	Royal National Hotel
69%	Royal Westminster Hotel	60%	Bloomsbury Crest Hotel
69%	St George's Hotel	60%	London Penta Hotel
68%	Cavendish Hotel	60%	Londoner Hotel
68%	Curzon Hotel	60%	Mount Royal Hotel
68%	Kensington Palace Hotel	60%	Portobello Hotel
68%	New Berners Hotel	60%	Rembrandt Hotel
67%	London Belgravia	59%	Royal Angus Hotel
67%	London Tara Hotel	58%	Barkston Hotel
67%	Hotel Russell	58%	Embassy House Hotel
66%	Cadogan Hotel	58%	Hogarth Hotel
66%	Cunard International Hotel	58%	Royal Scot Hotel
66%	Ladbroke Clive Hotel	57%	Bonnington Hotel
66%	London Embassy Hotel	57%	Clarendon Court Hotel
66%	London International Hotel	57%	Grosvenor Hotel
66%	London Metropole	57%	Imperial Hotel
66%	New Mandeville Hotel	57%	Kingsley Hotel
66%	Piccadilly Hotel	57%	Post House Hotel (Bayswater)
66%	St Ermin's Hotel	57%	White's Hotel
65%	Elizabetta Hotel	56%	Central Park Hotel
65%	Hendon Hall Hotel	56%	Cora Hotel
65%	Kennedy Hotel	56%	Pastoria Hotel
65%	Kensington Close Hotel	55%	Carnarvon Hotel
65%	Royal Horseguards Hotel	55%	Post House Hotel (Hampstead)
64%	Clifton-Ford Hotel		
64%	Great Western Royal Hotel	55%	Wilbraham Hotel
64%	Regent Crest Hotel	54%	Stratford Court Hotel
64%	Swiss Cottage Hotel	53%	Gore Hotel
63%	Charing Cross Hotel	53%	Harewood Hotel
63%	Durrants Hotel	52%	West Centre Hotel
63%	Great Northern Hotel	50%	Ebury Court Hotel

not graded Londonderry Hotel *(Under renovation)*

Airport Hotels
Grade 1

77%	Sheraton Skyline	62%	Berkeley Arms Hotel
76%	Gatwick Hilton International	62%	Post House Hotel (Horley)
73%	Gatwick Penta Hotel		
72%	Sheraton-Heathrow Hotel	62%	Skyway Hotel
71%	Copthorne Hotel	59%	Chequers Hotel
70%	Heathrow Penta Hotel	58%	Ariel Hotel
70%	Holiday Inn	58%	Gatwick Moat House
		58%	Post House Hotel (West Drayton)

Grade 2

67%	Saxon Inn	56%	Crest Hotel, Gatwick
66%	Excelsior Hotel	55%	Master Robert Motel

Continued

Economy Hotels in Alphabetical Order

Alexander Hotel
Alison House Hotel
Apollo Hotel, W2
Apollo Hotel, W8
Aster House
Atlas Hotel
Bardon Lodge
Campden Court Hotel
Century Hotel
Chesham House Hotel
Colin House Hotel
Colonnade Hotel
Columbia Hotel
Concord Hotel
Cranley Gardens Hotel
Craven Gardens Hotel
Culford House
Eden House Hotel
Eden Park Hotel
Eden Plaza Hotel
Elizabeth Hotel
Executive Hotel
Frognal Lodge Hotel
George Hotel
Grosvenor Court Hotel
Henry VIII Hotel
Jenkin's Hotel
Knightsbridge Green Hotel
Ladbroke Kensington Court Hotel
Lancaster Court Hotel
Leicester Court Hotel

Leinster Towers Hotel
Hotel Lexham
Hotel Lily
London Park Hotel
Lonsdale Hotel
Manor Court Hotel
Merryfield House
Milford House
Montague Hotel
Mornington Lancaster Hotel
Hotel Oliver
Hotel One Two Eight
Onslow Court Hotel
Park House
Park Plaza Hotel
Parkwood Hotel
Pembridge Court Hotel
Philbeach Hotel
President Hotel
Prince Hotel
Royal Park Hotel
Ruskin Hotel
Stanhope Court Hotel
Sumner Hotel
Surtees Hotel
Tavistock Hotel
Terstan Hotel
Tudor Court Hotel
Willett House Hotel
Worcester House

ENGLAND

Home Counties
88%	New Milton, Hampshire	Chewton Glen
86%	Ashford, Kent	Eastwell Manor
85%	Winchester, Hampshire	Lainston House
80%	East Grinstead, West Sussex	Gravetye Manor
80%	Eastbourne, East Sussex	Grand
79%	Battle, East Sussex	Netherfield Place
78%	Portsmouth, Hampshire	Holiday Inn
77%	Bagshot, Surrey	Pennyhill Park
77%	Brighton, East Sussex	Grand
77%	Harpenden, Hertfordshire	Moat House
76%	Climping, West Sussex	Bailiffscourt
76%	Eastbourne, East Sussex	Cavendish
76%	Storrington, West Sussex	Little Thakeham
75%	Haslemere, Surrey	Lythe Hill
73%	Rushlake Green, East Sussex	Priory
72%	Dover, Kent	Holiday Inn
72%	Egham, Surrey	Great Fosters
71%	Brighton, East Sussex	Brighton Metropole
71%	Eastbourne, East Sussex	Queen's
70%	Dorking, Surrey	Burford Bridge
70%	Rusper, West Sussex	Ghyll Manor

Isle of Wight
70%	Bonchurch	Winterbourne

Thames Valley & Chilterns
82%	Windsor, Berkshire	Oakley Court
78%	Marlow, Buckinghamshire	Compleat Angler
77%	North Stoke, Oxfordshire	Springs
75%	Woodstock, Oxfordshire	Bear
73%	Aston Clinton, Buckinghamshire	Bell Inn
71%	Slough, Berkshire	Holiday Inn

East Anglia
79%	Dedham, Essex	Maison Talbooth
76%	Six Mile Bottom, Cambridgeshire	Swynford Paddocks
71%	Woodbridge, Suffolk	Seckford Hall
70%	Shipdham, Norfolk	Shipdham Place

East Midlands
82%	Oakham, Leicestershire	Hambleton Hall
76%	Leicester, Leicestershire	Holiday Inn
73%	Baslow, Derbyshire	Cavendish
72%	South Normanton, Derbyshire	Swallow
70%	Nottingham, Nottinghamshire	Albany

West Midlands
81%	Birmingham, West Midlands	Metropole & Warwick
80%	Birmingham, West Midlands	Plough & Harrow
80%	Leamington Spa, Warwickshire	Mallory Court
77%	Broadway, Hereford & Worcester	Lygon Arms
76%	Abberley, Hereford & Worcester	Elms
76%	Droitwich, Hereford & Worcester	Château Impney

Continued

75%	Shifnal, Shropshire	Park House
75%	Stratford-upon-Avon, Warwickshire	Hilton International
74%	Coventry, West Midlands	De Vere
73%	Stratford-upon-Avon, Warwickshire	Billesley Manor
73%	Stratford-upon-Avon, Warwickshire	Welcombe
73%	Wishaw, Warwickshire	Belfry
72%	Birmingham, West Midlands	Holiday Inn
71%	Birmingham, West Midlands	Albany
70%	Ludlow, Shropshire	Feathers
70%	Warwick, Warwickshire	Ladbroke Mercury

North East

81%	Longhorsley, Northumberland	Linden Hall
79%	Yarm, Cleveland	Crathorne Hall
78%	Bolton Abbey, North Yorkshire	Devonshire Arms
78%	Kirkby Fleetham, North Yorkshire	Kirkby Fleetham Hall
77%	Kildwick, West Yorkshire	Kildwick Hall
76%	Newcastle upon Tyne, Tyne & Wear	Gosforth Park
75%	Rotherham, North Yorkshire	Carlton Park
75%	Scarborough, North Yorkshire	Royal
74%	Newcastle upon Tyne, Tyne & Wear	Holiday Inn
72%	Boroughbridge, North Yorkshire	Crown
72%	Middlesbrough, Cleveland	Ladbroke Dragonara
71%	Coatham Mundeville, Co. Durham	Hall Garth
71%	Halifax, West Yorkshire	Holdsworth House
71%	Jervaulx, North Yorkshire	Jervaulx Hall Country House
70%	Harrogate, North Yorkshire	Hotel Majestic
70%	Leeds, West Yorkshire	Ladbroke Dragonara
70%	Stockton-on-Tees, Cleveland	Swallow
70%	York, North Yorkshire	Viking

North West & Lake District

84%	Nantwich, Cheshire	Rookery Hall
80%	Chester, Cheshire	Chester Grosvenor
78%	Ullswater, Cumbria	Sharrow Bay Country House
77%	Manchester, Greater Manchester	Hotel Piccadilly
76%	Grasmere, Cumbria	Wordsworth
76%	Keswick, Cumbria	Lodore Swiss
75%	Ullswater, Cumbria	Leeming on Ullswater
74%	Grasmere, Cumbria	Michael's Nook
73%	Liverpool, Merseyside	Holiday Inn
72%	Windermere, Cumbria	Miller Howe
71%	Birkenhead, Merseyside	Bowler Hat
71%	Liverpool, Merseyside	Atlantic Tower
70%	Ambleside, Cumbria	Rothay Manor
70%	Handforth, Cheshire	Belfry

West Country

89%	Ston Easton, Somerset	Ston Easton Park
88%	Bath, Avon	Royal Crescent
82%	Torquay, Devon	Imperial
82%	Warminster, Wiltshire	Bishopstrow House
81%	Hunstrete, Avon	Hunstrete House
80%	Thornbury, Avon	Thornbury Castle
79%	Bournemouth, Dorset	Royal Bath
79%	St Mawes, Cornwall	Hotel Tresanton
78%	Bath, Avon	Priory
78%	Taunton, Somerset	Castle
77%	Bournemouth, Dorset	Carlton
77%	Chagford, Devon	Gidleigh Park
77%	Freshford, Avon	Homewood Park
75%	Beanacre, Wiltshire	Beechfield House
75%	Malmesbury, Wiltshire	Whatley Manor
75%	Plymouth, Devon	Holiday Inn
75%	Salcombe, Devon	Marine

74%	Bristol, Avon	Ladbroke Dragonara
74%	Gittisham, Devon	Combe House
74%	Moretonhampstead, Devon	Manor House
74%	Poole, Dorset	Quay
74%	St Ives, Cornwall	Tregenna Castle

74%	Whimple, Devon	Woodhayes
72%	Bristol, Avon	Holiday Inn
72%	Budock Vean, Cornwall	Budock Vean
72%	Shurdington, Gloucestershire	Greenway
72%	Wareham, Dorset	Priory
71%	Castle Combe, Wiltshire	Manor House
71%	Salcombe, Devon	Tides Reach
71%	Tetbury, Gloucestershire	Close at Tetbury
70%	Bristol, Avon	Grand
70%	Chedington, Dorset	Chedington Court
70%	Hatch Beauchamp, Somerset	Farthings Country House
70%	Sturminster Newton, Dorset	Plumber Manor

SCOTLAND

92%	Fort William, Highland	Inverlochy Castle
88%	Auchterarder, Tayside	Gleneagles
87%	Dunblane, Central	Cromlix House
80%	Glasgow, Strathclyde	Holiday Inn
78%	Bonnyrigg, Lothian	Dalhousie Castle
77%	Aberdeen Airport, Grampian	Holiday Inn

Continued

77%	Inverness, Highland	Culloden House
77%	Turnberry, Strathclyde	Turnberry
76%	Aberdeen, Grampian	Huntly
76%	Edinburgh, Lothian	George
75%	Aberdeen, Grampian	Holiday Inn
75%	Edinburgh, Lothian	Ladbroke Dragonara
75%	Glasgow, Strathclyde	Grosvenor
75%	Knipoch, Strathclyde	Knipoch Hotel
74%	Kilchrenan, Strathclyde	Ardanaiseig
73%	Ledaig, Strathclyde	Isle of Eriska
72%	Glasgow, Strathclyde	Albany
72%	Gullane, Lothian	Greywalls
72%	Langbank, Strathclyde	Gleddoch House
71%	Ballater, Grampian	Tullich Lodge
70%	Banchory, Grampian	Raemoir House
70%	Callander, Central	Roman Camp
70%	Humbie, Lothian	Johnstounburn House
70%	Kinclaven by Stanley, Tayside	Ballathie House
70%	Nairn, Highland	Clifton
70%	Nairn, Highland	Newton
70%	Peebles, Borders	Peebles Hotel Hydro
70%	Pitcaple, Grampian	Pittodrie House

WALES

79%	Newport, Gwent	Celtic Manor
74%	Llandudno, Gwynedd	Bodysgallen Hall
70%	Cardiff, South Glamorgan	Park

CHANNEL ISLANDS

79%	St Saviour, Jersey	Longueville Manor
75%	St Brelade's Bay, Jersey	Hotel l'Horizon
74%	Bouley Bay, Jersey	Water's Edge
72%	St Brelade, Jersey	Atlantic
70%	St Helier, Jersey	Grand
70%	St Peter Port, Guernsey	Old Government House

NORTHERN IRELAND

77%	Holywood, Co. Down	Culloden
71%	Belfast, Co. Antrim	Belfast Europa
70%	Dunmurry, Co. Antrim	Conway

EIRE

90%	Cong, Co. Mayo	Ashford Castle
88%	Kenmare, Co. Kerry	Park
85%	Dublin, Co. Dublin	Berkeley Court
83%	Newmarket-on-Fergus, Co. Clare	Dromoland Castle
82%	Gap of Dunloe, Co. Kerry	Dunloe Castle
77%	Sneem, Co. Kerry	Parknasilla
76%	Dublin, Co. Dublin	Blooms
76%	Newmarket-on-Fergus, Co. Clare	Clare Inn
74%	Dublin, Co. Dublin	Jurys
74%	Gorey, Co. Wexford	Marlfield House
74%	Mallow, Co. Cork	Longueville House
73%	Killarney, Co. Kerry	Hotel Europe
71%	Ballylickey, Co. Cork	Ballylickey House
71%	Cork, Co. Cork	Imperial
71%	Dublin, Co. Dublin	Burlington
71%	Killiney, Co. Dublin	Fitzpatrick Castle
70%	Caragh Lake, Co. Kerry	Ard-na-Sidhe
70%	Cashel, Co. Galway	Cashel House
70%	Cork, Co. Cork	Jurys

RESTAURANT FRANÇAIS
IMPERIAL HOTEL
2113
Wherever you are...
BARCLAYCARD
VISA
4929 123 456 789
For full details
about Barclaycard and an
application form, pick up a booklet at
any branch of Barclays Bank, or write to
Department M.A., Barclaycard, Northampton, NN1 1SG.

HAMMERSMITH
Cunard International

EARL'S COURT
Barkston
Concord (B)
Elizabetta
Hogarth
Ladbroke Kensington
Court (B)
Manor Court (B)
Oliver (B)
Philbeach (B)
Terstan (B)

GLOUCESTER ROAD
Eden Plaza (B)
Gloucester
Leicester Court (B)
London International
Penta
Stanhope Court (B)
Tudor Court (B)

KNIGHTSBRIDGE

HYDE PARK CORNER

SOUTH KENSINGTON
Alexander (B)
Aster House (B)
Onslow Court (B)
Park House (B)
Prince (B)
Rembrandt
Sumner (B)

KNIGHTSBRIDGE
Basil Street
Campden Court (B)
Capital
Executive (B)
Holiday Inn (Chelsea)
Hyde Park
Lowndes
Sheraton Park Tower

HYDE PARK CORNER
Berkeley
Hilton
Inn on the Park
Inter-Continental
Londonderry

KING'S CROSS
Great Northern
Royal Scot

RUSSELL SQUARE
Bloomsbury Crest
Bonnington
Cora
George (B)
Imperial
Jenkin's (B)
Lonsdale (B)
Montague (B)
President (B)
Royal National
Ruskin (B)
Russell
Tavistock (B)

HOLBORN
Kingsley

COVENT GARDEN
Drury Lane

GREEN PARK
Bristol
Brown's
Cavendish
Chesterfield
Dukes
May Fair
Park Lane
Ritz
Stafford

PICCADILLY CIRCUS
Piccadilly
Royal Angus
Royal Trafalgar

LEICESTER SQUARE
Pastoria

(B) Budget/Economy Hotel

LONDON RESTAURANTS WITH DISTINCTLY NATIONAL COOKING

Brazilian
Paulos'

Caribbean
Le Caraïbe

Chinese
Chinatown
Crystal Palace
Diamond
Gallant
Golden Duck
Good Earth, NW7
Good Earth, SW3
Good Friends
Green Cottage
Happy Garden
Hongs
Hunan
Hung Toa
Ken Lo's Memories of China
Kites
Kuo Yuan
Ley-On's
Loon Fung
Mandarin Kitchen
Pangs
Paper Tiger
Poons
Poons & Co
Poons of Covent Garden
Shu Shan
Shu Shan II
Tai-Pan
Tiger Lee
Yangtze

English
Baron of Beef
Dorchester Grill Room
English Garden
English House
Finches
Hungry Horse
Simpson's-in-the-Strand
Wilton's

French
Ark
L'Artiste Affamé
L'Aubergade

Bagatelle
Berkeley Restaurant
Boulestin
Brasserie St Quentin
Hotel Bristol, Louis D'Or Restaurant
Bubb's
Bunny's
Café Jardin
Capital Hotel Restaurant
Cassis
Le Chef
Chez Gerard
Chez Nico
Chez Solange
Connaught Hotel Restaurant
Daphne's
Dorchester, The Terrace
Four Seasons
Le Gamin
Le Gavroche
Gavvers
Grosvenor House, Ninety Park Lane
Les Halles
Hyatt Carlton Tower, Chelsea Room
Inter-Continental Hotel, Le Soufflé
Interlude de Tabaillau
Keats
Ma Cuisine
Ménage à Trois
Mes Amis
Mijanou
Mirabelle
Monsieur Thompsons
No Name Place
Peachey's
Le Poulbot
Pyramid
Relais des Amis
La Tante Claire
The White House Restaurant

Greek & Greek Cypriot
Bitter Lemons Taverna
White Tower

Hungarian
Gay Hussar

Indian & Pakistani
Gaylord
Great Mughal

Holy Cow
Kundan
Last Days of the Raj
Marzi's
Salloos
Shezan
Shireen
Standard
Tagore
Tandoori of Chelsea
Viceroy of India
Vijay

Italian
Apicella 81
Barbarella
La Barca, SW6
La Barca, SE1
Cecconi's
Como Lario
Eleven Park Walk
Estoril da Luigi e Roberto
La Famiglia
Gondolière
Gran Paradiso
Meridiana
Mimmo d'Ischia
Montpeliano
La Pavona
Rose
Rossetti
San Carlo
San Lorenzo Fuoriporta
San Ruffillo
Tiberio
Topo d'Oro
Vasco & Piero's Pavilion
Villa dei Fiori

Japanese
Ajimura
Asuka
Fuji
Ginnan
Hilton International Kensington,
    Hiroko Restaurant
Ikeda
Masako
Nanten Yakitori
Shogun
Suntory
Yamaju

Jewish
Bloom's, Golders Green
Bloom's, Whitechapel

Korean
Arirang Korean Restaurant
La Corée
Kaya

Portuguese
Os Arcos

South-east Asian
Equatorial
Melati, Great Windmill Street
Melati, Peter Street
New Rasa Sayang

Thai
Busabong
Chaopraya
Siam

Tunisian
Sidi Bou Said

OPEN AIR EATING IN LONDON

L'Artiste Assoiffé, W11
Bagatelle, SW10
Brinkley's, SW10
Café Jardin, W1
Chanterelle, SW7
La Croisette, SW10
Dan's, SW3
Del Monico's, W1
La Famiglia, SW10
Four Seasons, N1
Frederick's, N1
Gran Paradiso, SW1
Great Mughal, W2
Hungry Horse, SW10

Legends, W1
Meridiana, SW3
Mijanou, SW1
Mirabelle, W1
Odette's, NW1
Paulos', WC2
Peachey's, NW3
Pollyanna's, SW11
San Carlo, N6
San Lorenzo Fuoriporta, SW19
Sheekeys, WC2

Economy Restaurants

Anemos, W1
L'Artiste Musclé, W1
Brasserie des Amis, SW3
Fingal's, SW6
Il Fornello, WC1
Grumbles, SW1
Hard Rock Café, W1
Kalamaras, W2
Ormes, SW4
Pontevecchio, SW5
Romano's, W9
Le Routier, NW1
Scats, SW1

SUNDAY EATING IN LONDON

CENTRAL LONDON

Chelsea & South Kensington
Bitter Lemons Taverna (D)
Busabong
Chanterelle
La Croisette
Crystal Palace
Drakes
English Garden
La Famiglia
Golden Duck
Good Earth
Hungry Horse
Marzi's
Meridiana
Paper Tiger
Le Quai St Pierre
September
Shu Shan II
Standard
Le Suquet
Tai-Pan
Tandoori of Chelsea
Tiger Lee (D)
Walton's

City
Tower Hotel, Princes Room

**Covent Garden, Strand &
  Bloomsbury**
Drury Lane Hotel, Maudie's
  Restaurant
Howard Hotel, Quai d'Or
  Restaurant
Interlude de Tabaillou (L)
Kites
Last Days of the Raj (D)
Savoy Hotel, River Room
Tagore (D)
Waldorf Hotel, Wellington
  Restaurant

Islington
Grapes

**Kensington, Bayswater &
  Paddington**
Ark (D)
Great Mughal
Holy Cow (D)
Leith's (D)
Mandarin Kitchen
Siam

Topo d'Oro
Yangtze

Knightsbridge
Berkeley Restaurant
Brasserie St Quentin
Capital Hotel Restaurant
Hyatt Carlton Tower, Chelsea Room
Hyatt Carlton Tower, Rib Room
Hyde Park Hotel, Grill Room
Mes Amis
Sheraton Park Tower, The Trianon

Mayfair & Park Lane
Athenaeum Hotel Restaurant
Hotel Bristol, Louis D'Or Restaurant
Brown's Hotel, L'Apéritif
  Restaurant
Claridge's Causerie
Claridge's Restaurant
Connaught Hotel Restaurant
Dorchester Grill Room
Europa Hotel, Diplomat Restaurant
Grosvenor House, Ninety Park Lane
Ikeda (D)
Inn on the Park, Four Seasons
  Restaurant
Inn on the Park, Lanes Restaurant
  (L)
Inter-Continental Hotel, Le Soufflé
Relais des Amis
Scott's (D)
Shogun (D)
Trader Vic's

Oxford Street & Marble Arch
Churchill Hotel, No. 10 Restaurant
Gaylord
Montcalm Hotel, La Varenne (D)

Piccadilly & St James's
A l'Ecu de France (D)
Café Royal, Grill Room & Le Relais
Dukes Hotel, St James's Room
  Restaurant
Estoril da Luigi e Roberto
Legends (L)
Ritz Hotel, Louis XVI Restaurant

Soho & Leicester Square
Diamond
Equatorial
Fuji (D)
Gallant
Happy Garden

Continued

Ley-On's
Loon Fung
Manzi's (D)
New Rasa Sayang
Shu Shan
Swiss Centre, Chesa

Tottenham Court Road
Chez Gerard

Victoria
Goring Hotel Restaurant

EAST END
Bloom's, Whitechapel
Chinatown
Good Friends

NORTH WEST
Bloom's, Golders Green
Bunny's
Capability Brown (L)
Good Earth
Green Cottage
Hongs
Kuo Yuan
Peter's (L)
Rossetti

San Carlo
Viceroy of India
Vijay
Villa dei Fiori
Walker's (L)

SOUTH EAST
Casa Cominetti (L)
Spread Eagle (L)

SOUTH WEST
No Name Place (L)
Pollyanna's
Rose (L)
San Lorenzo Fuoriporta

WEST
Hilton International Kensington,
   Hiroko Restaurant
Monsieur Thompsons
Pangs

HOTELS WITH SWIMMING POOLS

INDOOR

LONDON
Berkeley
Grosvenor House
Holiday Inn (Chelsea)
Holiday Inn (Marble Arch)
Holiday Inn (Swiss Cottage)
Kensington Close

LONDON AIRPORTS
Gatwick
Gatwick Hilton International
Heathrow
Heathrow Penta
Holiday Inn
Sheraton-Heathrow
Sheraton Skyline

HOME COUNTIES
Dover, Kent: Holiday Inn
East Grinstead, West Sussex: Ye Olde
   Felbridge
Hollingbourne, Kent: Great Danes
Hythe, Kent: Hotel Imperial
Portsmouth, Hampshire: Holiday Inn
Shedfield, Hampshire: Meon Valley Hotel,
   Golf & Country Club

THAMES VALLEY & CHILTERNS
Slough, Berkshire: Holiday Inn

EAST ANGLIA
Blakeney, Norfolk: Blakeney
Cambridge, Cambridgeshire: Cunard
   Cambridgeshire
Hethersett, Norfolk: Park Farm

EAST MIDLANDS
Leicester, Leicestershire: Holiday Inn
Matlock Bath, Derbyshire: New Bath

WEST MIDLANDS
Birmingham, West Midlands: Albany
Birmingham, West Midlands: Holiday Inn
Warwick, Warwickshire: Ladbroke
   Mercury

NORTH EAST
Bradford, West Yorkshire: Baron
Hackness, North Yorkshire: Hackness
   Grange Country
Harrogate, North Yorkshire: Hotel Majestic
Newcastle upon Tyne, Tyne & Wear:
   Gosforth Park
Newcastle upon Tyne, Tyne & Wear:
   Holiday Inn
Scarborough, North Yorkshire: Palm Court
South Milford, North Yorkshire: Selby
   Fork

NORTH WEST & LAKE DISTRICT
Bowness on Windermere, Cumbria:
   Belsfield
Grasmere, Cumbria: Wordsworth
Handforth, Cheshire: Pinewood
Keswick, Cumbria: Lodore Swiss
Liverpool, Merseyside: Adelphi
Liverpool, Merseyside: Holiday Inn
Manchester, Greater Manchester:
   Britannia

Continued

WEST COUNTRY
Barnstaple, Devon: Barnstaple Motel
Bristol, Avon: Holiday Inn
Budock Vean, Cornwall: Budock Vean
Chittlehamholt, Devon: Highbullen
Failand, Avon: Redwood Lodge
Golant, Cornwall: Cormorant
Hope Cove, Devon: Lantern Lodge
Lower Slaughter, Gloucestershire:
   Manor
Milton Damerel, Devon: Woodford Bridge
Newquay, Cornwall: Atlantic
Newquay, Cornwall: Hotel Bristol
Newquay, Cornwall: Headland
Ottery St Mary, Devon: Salston
Padstow, Cornwall: Treglos
Plymouth, Devon: Holiday Inn
Salcombe, Devon: Marine
Salcombe, Devon: Tides Reach
Saunton, Devon: Saunton Sands
Sidmouth, Devon: Victoria
Tewkesbury, Gloucestershire: Tewkesbury
   Park
Thurlestone, Devon: Thurlestone
Torquay, Devon: Imperial
Torquay, Devon: Kistor
Torquay, Devon: Palace
Torquay, Devon: Rainbow House
Woolacombe, Devon: Woolacombe Bay

SCOTLAND
Aberdeen, Grampian: Holiday Inn
Aberdeen Airport, Grampian: Holiday Inn
Auchterarder, Tayside: Gleneagles
Aviemore, Highland: Coylumbridge
Glasgow, Strathclyde: Holiday Inn
Kinloch Rannoch, Tayside:
   Loch Rannoch
Langbank, Strathclyde: Gleddoch House
Peebles, Borders: Peebles Hotel Hydro
Stranraer, Dumfries & Galloway:
   North West Castle
Turnberry, Strathclyde: Turnberry

WALES
Aberdyfi, Gwynedd: Trefeddian
Aberystwyth, Dyfed: Conrah Country
Chepstow, Gwent: St Pierre Golf &
   Country Club
Llandudno, Gwynedd: Empire
St David's, Dyfed: Warpool Court
St Mellons, South Glamorgan:
   St Mellons

CHANNEL ISLANDS
St Brelade's Bay, Jersey: Hotel l'Horizon
St Helier, Jersey: Grand

NORTHERN IRELAND
Londonderry, Co. Londonderry:
   Everglades

EIRE
Ballina, Co. Mayo: Downhill
Bunratty, Co. Clare: Fitzpatrick's Shannon
   Shamrock
Carrickmacross, Co. Monaghan:
   Nuremore
Cork, Co. Cork: Jurys
Dublin, Co. Dublin: Berkeley Court
Dublin, Co. Dublin: Burlington
Dublin, Co. Dublin: Jurys
Dundalk, Co. Louth, Ballymascanlon
Galway, Co. Galway: Corrib Great
   Southern
Galway, Co. Galway: Great Southern
Gap of Dunloe, Co. Kerry: Dunloe Castle
Killarney, Co. Kerry: Hotel Europe
Killarney, Co. Kerry: Great Southern
Killarney, Co. Kerry: Torc Great Southern
Killiney, Co. Dublin: Fitzpatrick Castle
Rosslare, Co. Wexford: Kelly's Strand
Sneem, Co. Kerry: Parknasilla Hotel
Waterville, Co. Kerry: Waterville Lake
Wexford, Co. Wexford: Talbot

OUTDOOR

LONDON
Holiday Inn (Chelsea)

LONDON AIRPORTS
Gatwick
Chequers
Post House
Heathrow
Excelsior
Skyway

HOME COUNTIES
Bagshot, Surrey: Pennyhill Park
Bognor Regis, West Sussex: Royal Norfolk
Borehamwood, Hertfordshire: Elstree
   Moat House
Brockenhurst, Hampshire: Ladbroke
   Balmer Lawn
Burley, Hampshire: Burley Manor
Climping, West Sussex: Bailiffscourt
Cobham, Surrey: Ladbroke Seven Hills
Cooden, East Sussex: Cooden Beach
Dorking, Surrey: Burford Bridge
Dorking, Surrey: White Horse
East Grinstead, West Sussex: Ye Olde
   Felbridge
Eastbourne, East Sussex: Grand
Egham, Surrey: Great Fosters
Havant, Hampshire: Post House
High Halden, Kent: Hookstead House
Lymington, Hampshire:
   Passford House
Lyndhurst, Hampshire: Lyndhurst Park
Lyndhurst, Hampshire: Parkhill
New Milton, Hampshire: Chewton Glen

Newgate Street Village, Hertfordshire:
  Ponsbourne
Redbourn, Hertfordshire: Aubrey Park
Rusper, East Sussex: Ghyll Manor
Sanderstead, Surrey: Selsdon Park
Sedlescombe, East Sussex: Brickwall
Silchester, Hampshire: Romans
Southampton, Hampshire: Post House
Steyning, West Sussex: Springwells
Storrington, West Sussex: Little Thakeham
Stubbington, Hampshire: Crofton Manor
Walberton, West Sussex: Avisford Park
Weybridge, Surrey: Oatlands Park

ISLE OF WIGHT
Bembridge: Highbury
Bonchurch: Winterbourne
Freshwater: Farringford
Sandown: Melville Hall
Shanklin: Cliff Tops
Ventnor: Royal

THAMES VALLEY & CHILTERNS
Ascot, Berkshire: Berystede
North Stoke, Oxfordshire: Springs
Oxford, Oxfordshire: TraveLodge
Reading, Berkshire: Post House
Stoke Mandeville, Buckinghamshire:
  Belmore
Wallingford, Oxfordshire: Shillingford
  Bridge

EAST ANGLIA
Barnham Broom, Norfolk: Barnham
  Broom
Brentwood, Essex: Post House
Ipswich, Suffolk: Post House
Lowestoft, Suffolk: Victoria
Norwich, Norfolk: Post House
South Walsham, Norfolk: South Walsham
  Hall

EAST MIDLANDS
Matlock Bath, Derbyshire: New Bath
Nottingham, Nottinghamshire: Novotel

WEST MIDLANDS
Birmingham, West Midlands: Post House
Bodymoor Heath, Warwickshire: Marston
  Farm
Broadway, Hereford & Worcester: Collin
  House
Church Stretton, Shropshire:
  Stretton Hall
Coventry, West Midlands: Novotel
Leamington Spa, Warwickshire: Mallory
  Court
Meriden, West Midlands: Manor
Ross-on-Wye, Hereford & Worcester:
  Pengethley
Shifnal, Shropshire: Park House
Shrawley, Hereford & Worcester:
  Lenchford
Stratford-upon-Avon, Warwickshire:
  Billesley Manor

NORTH EAST
Bradford, West Yorkshire: Novotel
Chester-le-Street, Co. Durham: Lumley
  Castle
York, North Yorkshire: Mount Royale

NORTH WEST & LAKE DISTRICT
Blackburn, Lancashire: Saxon Inn
Bowness on Windermere, Cumbria:
  Belsfield
Bowness on Windermere, Cumbria:
  Old England
Faugh, Cumbria: String of Horses
Keswick, Cumbria: Lodore Swiss
Manchester Airport, Greater Manchester:
  Excelsior
St Michael's on Wyre, Lancashire:
  Rivermede Country House

WEST COUNTRY
Alveston, Avon: Post House
Bath, Avon: Priory
Belstone, Devon: Skaigh House
Bideford, Devon: Durrant House
Bournemouth, Dorset: Carlton
Bournemouth, Dorset: Durley Hall
Bournemouth, Dorset: East Cliff Court
Bournemouth, Dorset: Highcliff
Bournemouth, Dorset: Ladbroke Savoy
Bournemouth, Dorset: Hotel Normandie
Bournemouth, Dorset: Royal Bath
Carlyon Bay, Cornwall: Carlyon Bay
Castle Combe, Wiltshire: Manor House
Cheltenham, Gloucestershire: Hotel de la
  Bere
Chittlehamholt, Devon: Highbullen
Dulverton, Somerset: Carnarvon Arms

Continued

Dursley, Gloucestershire: Stinchcombe
  Manor
Exmouth, Devon: Devoncourt
Failand, Avon: Redwood Lodge
Fairy Cross, Devon: Portledge
Falmouth, Cornwall: Falmouth
Ferndown, Dorset: Dormy
Gloucester, Gloucestershire: Tara
Golant, Cornwall: Cormorant
Hatherleigh, Devon: George
Helland Bridge, Cornwall: Tredethy
Horn's Cross, Devon: Foxdown Manor
Hunstrete, Avon: Hunstrete House
Lamorna Cove, Cornwall: Lamorna Cove
Limpley Stoke, Wiltshire: Cliffe
Looe, Cornwall: Talland Bay
Lynmouth, Devon: Tors
Malmesbury, Wiltshire: Whatley Manor
Mortehoe, Devon: Rockham Bay
Mudeford, Dorset: Avonmouth
Mullion, Cornwall: Polurrian
Newquay, Cornwall: Atlantic
Newquay, Cornwall: Headland
Newquay, Cornwall: Hotel Riviera
Paignton, Devon: Palace
Paignton, Devon: Redcliffe
Plymouth, Devon: Mayflower Post House
Plymouth, Devon: Novotel Plymouth
St Ives, Cornwall: Tregenna Castle
Salcombe, Devon: Marine
Sidmouth, Devon: Victoria
Stoborough, Dorset: Springfield Country
Studland Bay, Dorset: Knoll House
Swindon, Wiltshire: Post House
Thurlestone, Devon: Thurlestone
Torquay, Devon: Gleneagles
Torquay, Devon: Grand
Torquay, Devon: Imperial
Torquay, Devon: Livermead Cliff
Torquay, Devon: Livermead House
Torquay, Devon: Osborne
Torquay, Devon: Palace
Torquay, Devon: Rainbow House
Torquay, Devon: Toorak
Veryan, Cornwall: Nare
Weston-super-Mare, Avon: Grand Atlantic
Wincanton, Somerset: Holbrook House
Woolacombe, Devon: Woolacombe Bay
Yelverton, Devon: Moorland Links

ISLES OF SCILLY
Tresco: Island

SCOTLAND
Aberdeen Airport, Grampian: Aberdeen
  Airport
Auchterhouse, Tayside: Old Mansion
  House
Gatehouse of Fleet, Dumfries & Galloway:
  Cally Palace
Moniaive, Dumfries & Galloway: Woodlea
Nairn, Highland: Golf View
North Berwick, Lothian: Marine

Pitlochry, Tayside: Atholl Palace
Selkirk, Borders: Philipburn House
Tarbert, Strathclyde: Stonefield Castle

WALES
Abersoch, Gwynedd: Porth Tocyn
Caernarfon, Gwynedd: Stables
Coychurch, Mid Glamorgan: Coed-y-
  Mwstwr
Fishguard, Dyfed: Fishguard Bay
Gwbert-on-Sea, Dyfed: Cliff
Penrhyndeudraeth, Gwynedd: Hotel
  Portmeirion
Robeston Wathen, Dyfed: Robeston
  House

CHANNEL ISLANDS
St Martin's, Guernsey: St Margaret's
  Lodge
St Peter Port, Guernsey: Duke of
  Richmond
St Peter Port, Guernsey: Old Government
  House
Bouley Bay, Jersey: Water's Edge
Gorey, Jersey: Old Court House
Portelet Bay, Jersey: Portelet
St Brelade, Jersey: Atlantic
St Brelade, Jersey: La Place
St Brelade's Bay, Jersey: Hotel Château
  Valeuse
St Brelade's Bay, Jersey:
  St Brelade's Bay
St Clement's Bay, Jersey: Hotel
  Ambassadeur
St Peter, Jersey: Mermaid
St Saviour, Jersey: Longueville Manor
Sark, Sark: Hotel Petit Champ

ISLE OF MAN
Castletown: Castletown Golf Links
Douglas: Palace

NORTHERN IRELAND
Dunadry, Co. Antrim: Dunadry Inn
Dunmurry, Co. Antrim: Conway

EIRE
Ballylickey, Co. Cork: Ballylickey House
Castledermot, Co. Kildare: Kilkea Castle
Clifden, Co. Galway: Abbeyglen
Cork, Co. Cork: Jurys
Dingle, Co. Kerry: Sceilig
Dublin, Co. Dublin: Jurys
Glounthaune, Co. Cork: Ashbourne House
Killarney, Co. Kerry: Castlerosse
Kinsale, Co. Cork: Actons
Oughterard, Co. Galway: Connemara
  Gateway
Rosslare, Co. Wexford: Kelly's Strand
Shanagarry, Co. Cork: Ballymaloe House

HOTELS WITH FISHING, GOLF, RIDING, SQUASH, AND TENNIS

FISHING

ENGLAND

Coarse

Bagshot, Surrey: Pennyhill Park
Basildon, Essex: Crest
Beanacre, Wiltshire: Beechfield House
Beccles, Suffolk: Waveney House
Bodymoor Heath, Warwickshire:
   Marston Farm
Bredwardine, Hereford & Worcester:
   Red Lion
Burbage, Wiltshire: Savernake Forest
Cambridge, Cambridgeshire:
   Garden House
Chollerford, Northumberland: George
Churt, Surrey: Frensham Pond
Cornhill-on-Tweed, Northumberland:
   Tillmouth Park
Darlington, Co. Durham: Blackwell
   Grange Moat House
Droitwich, Hereford & Worcester:
   Château Impney
Dunchurch, Warwickshire: Dun Cow
Egham, Surrey: Runnymede
Grasmere, Cumbria: Wordsworth
Greta Bridge, Co. Durham: Morritt Arms
Haslemere, Surrey: Lythe Hill
Hollingbourne, Kent: Great Danes
Horning, Norfolk: Petersfield House
Hoveton, Norfolk: Hotel Wroxham

Huntingdon, Cambridgeshire: Old Bridge
Hythe, Kent: Hotel Imperial
Lyndhurst, Hampshire: Parkhill
Marlow, Buckinghamshire:
   Compleat Angler
Mottram St Andrew, Cheshire:
   Mottram Hall
Nantwich, Cheshire: Rookery Hall
Needingworth, Cambridgeshire:
   Pike & Eel
Newby Bridge, Cumbria: Swan
Norwich, Norfolk: Hotel Nelson
Otterburn, Northumberland: Percy Arms
St Michael's on Wyre, Lancashire:
   Rivermede Country House
Shorne, Kent: Inn on the Lake
Shrawley, Hereford & Worcester:
   Lenchford
South Walsham, Norfolk: South Walsham
   Hall
Streatley-on-Thames, Berkshire: Swan
Sudbury, Suffolk: Mill
Sutton Coldfield, West Midlands:
   Penns Hall
Ullswater, Cumbria: Leeming on Ullswater
Ullswater, Cumbria: Old Church
Wallingford, Oxfordshire: Shillingford
   Bridge
Walton, Warwickshire: Walton Hall
Wansford, Cambridgeshire: Haycock Hotel

Continued

Wareham, Dorset: Priory
Windermere, Cumbria: Langdale Chase
Windsor, Berkshire: Oakley Court
Windsor, Berkshire: Old House
Winsford, Somerset: Royal Oak Inn
Woodbridge, Suffolk: Seckford Hall

Game
Ashburton, Devon: Holne Chase
Ashford, Kent: Eastwell Manor
Barnham Broom, Norfolk: Barnham
   Broom
Baslow, Derbyshire: Cavendish
Bibury, Gloucestershire: Swan
Bilbrook, Somerset: Dragon House
Bredwardine, Hereford & Worcester:
   Red Lion
Castle Combe, Wiltshire: Manor House
Chagford, Devon: Gidleigh Park
Chagford, Devon: Mill End
Chittlehamholt, Devon: Highbullen
Chollerford, Northumberland: George
Cooden, East Sussex: Cooden Beach
Cornhill-on-Tweed, Northumberland:
   Tillmouth Park
Crooklands, Cumbria: Crooklands
Croxdale, Co. Durham: Crest
Dulverton, Somerset: Carnarvon Arms
East Grinstead, West Sussex:
   Gravetye Manor
Fairford, Gloucestershire: Bull
Frenchbeer, Devon: Teignworthy
Gittisham, Devon: Combe House
Greta Bridge, Co. Durham: Morritt Arms
Hackness, North Yorkshire: Hackness
   Grange
Hawkchurch, Devon, Fairwater Head
Heddon's Mouth, Devon: Hunter's Inn
Horton, Dorset: Horton Inn
Kingham, Oxfordshire: Mill

Lifton, Devon: Arundell Arms
Lower Slaughter, Gloucestershire:
   Manor
Malmesbury, Wiltshire: Whatley Manor
Milton Damerel, Devon: Woodford Bridge
Moretonhampstead, Devon: Manor House
Much Birch, Hereford & Worcester:
   Pilgrim
Otterburn, Northumberland: Percy Arms
Ottery St Mary, Devon: Salston
Rosthwaite, Cumbria: Scafell
Rowsley, Derbyshire: Peacock
Rushlake Green, East Sussex: Priory
Samlesbury, Lancashire: Tickled Trout
Ston Easton, Somerset: Ston Easton Park
Sturminster Newton, Dorset:
   Plumber Manor
Ullswater, Cumbria: Leeming on Ullswater
Ullswater, Cumbria: Old Church
Upper Slaughter, Gloucestershire:
   Lords of the Manor
Warminster, Wiltshire: Bishopstrow
   House
Whitewell, Lancashire: Whitewell
Yarm, Cleveland: Tall Trees

Sea
Aldeburgh, Suffolk: Brudenell
Branscombe, Devon: Masons Arms
Brixham, Devon: Quayside
Budock Vean, Cornwall: Budock Vean
Fairy Cross, Devon: Portledge
Falmouth, Cornwall: Greenbank
Fowey, Cornwall: Riverside
Hythe, Kent: Hotel Imperial
Mawnan Smith, Cornwall: Meudon
Mousehole, Cornwall: Lobster Pot
Mudeford, Dorset: Avonmouth
Newquay, Cornwall: Atlantic
Newquay, Cornwall: Hotel Riviera

Praa Sands, Cornwall: Lesceave Cliff
Salcombe, Devon: Marine
Salcombe, Devon: South Sands
Salcombe, Devon: Tides Reach
Sunderland, Tyne & Wear: Seaburn
Thornton-le-Fylde, Lancashire:
    River House
Torquay, Devon: Livermead Cliff
Torquay, Devon: Livermead House
Torquay, Devon: Palace
Tresco, Isles of Scilly: Island
Veryan, Cornwall: Nare
Worthing, West Sussex: Eardley

SCOTLAND

Coarse
Auchterarder, Tayside: Gleneagles
Banchory, Grampian: Tor-na-Coille
Bonnyrigg, Lothian: Dalhousie Castle
Humbie, Lothian: Johnstounburn House
Kilchrenan, Strathclyde: Taychreggan
Kinclaven by Stanley, Tayside: Ballathie
    House
Kinloch Rannoch, Tayside: Loch
    Rannoch
Lochgair, Strathclyde: Lochgair
Pitlochry, Tayside: Green Park
Strathtummel, Tayside: Port-an-Eilean

Game
Aberdeen, Grampian: Ardoe House
Achiltibuie, Highland: Summer Isles
Ardvasar, Highland: Ardvasar
Auchterarder, Tayside: Gleneagles
Balquhidder, Central: Ledcreich
Banchory, Grampian: Raemoir House
Banchory, Grampian: Tor-na-Coille
Beattock, Dumfries & Galloway:
    Auchen Castle
Callander, Central: Roman Camp
Connel, Strathclyde: Ossian's
Contin, Highland: Craigdarroch Lodge
Dornoch, Highland: Burghfield House
Dryburgh, Borders: Dryburgh Abbey
Dunblane, Central: Cromlix House
Dunkeld, Tayside: Dunkeld House
East Linton, Lothian: Harvester's
Fort William, Highland: Inverlochy Castle
Gairloch, Highland: Gairloch
Gairloch, Highland: Shieldaig Lodge
Garve, Highland: Inchbae Lodge
Garve, Highland: Strathgarve Lodge
Gatehouse of Fleet, Dumfries & Galloway:
    Cally Palace
Gatehouse of Fleet, Dumfries & Galloway:
    Murray Arms
Glencoe, Highland: King's House
Glenlivet, Grampian: Blairfindy Lodge
Hollybush, Strathclyde: Hollybush House
Invershin, Highland: Invershin
Isle Ornsay, Highland: Kinloch Lodge
Kenmore, Tayside: Kenmore
Kilchrenan, Strathclyde: Ardanaiseig
Kilchrenan, Strathclyde: Taychreggan

Kildrummy, Grampian: Kildrummy Castle
Kinclaven by Stanley, Tayside:
    Ballathie House
Kinloch Rannoch, Tayside: Loch
    Rannoch
Lanark, Strathclyde: Cartland Bridge
Langbank, Strathclyde: Gleddoch House
Lochgair, Strathclyde: Lochgair
Pitlochry, Tayside: Green Park
Port William, Dumfries & Galloway:
    Corsemalzie House
Scourie, Highland: Eddrachilles
Scourie, Highland: Scourie
Skeabost Bridge, Highland: Skeabost
    House
Spean Bridge, Highland: Letterfinlay
    Lodge
Strathtummel, Tayside: Port-an-Eilean
Talladale, Highland: Loch Maree
Ullapool, Highland: Royal

Sea
Achiltibuie, Highland: Summer Isles
Ardentinny, Strathclyde: Ardentinny
Connel, Strathclyde: Ossian's
Gairloch, Highland: Gairloch
Gatehouse of Fleet, Dumfries & Galloway:
    Murray Arms
Glenborrodale, Highland: Glenborrodale
    Castle
Kyle of Lochalsh, Highland: Lochalsh
Ledaig, Strathclyde: Isle of Eriska
Portpatrick, Dumfries & Galloway:
    Knockinaam Lodge
Portree, Highland: Rosedale
Scourie, Highland: Eddrachilles
Skeabost Bridge, Highland: Skeabost
    House
Strachur, Strathclyde: Creggans Inn
Tarbert, Strathclyde: Stonefield Castle
Ullapool, Highland: Royal

WALES

Coarse
Beddgelert, Gwynedd: Royal Goat
Betws-y-Coed, Gwynedd: Gwydyr
Chepstow, Gwent: St Pierre Golf &
    Country Club
Dolgellau, Gwynedd: Gwernan Lake
Glyn Ceiriog, Clwyd: Golden Pheasant
Ruthin, Clwyd: Ruthin Castle

Game
Betws-y-Coed, Gwynedd: Gwydyr
Brechfa, Dyfed: Tŷ Mawr Country House
Dolgellau, Gwynedd: Gwernan Lake
Glyn Ceiriog, Clwyd: Golden Pheasant
Lake Vyrnwy, Powys: Lake Vyrnwy
Llangollen, Clwyd: Hand
Pant Mawr, Powys: Glansevern Arms
Robeston Wathen, Dyfed: Robeston
    House
Talsarnau, Gwynedd: Maes-y-Neuadd
Tal-y-Llyn, Gwynedd: Tyn-y-Cornel

Continued

Sea
Gwbert-on-Sea, Dyfed: Cliff
Penmaenpool, Gwynedd: George III
Penrhyndeudraeth, Gwynedd:
   Hotel Portmeirion
St David's, Dyfed: Warpool Court

CHANNEL ISLANDS

Sea
Gorey, Jersey: Moorings
St Clement's Bay, Jersey:
   Hotel Ambassadeur

ISLE OF MAN

Sea
Castletown: Castletown Golf Links

NORTHERN IRELAND

Game
Dunadry, Co. Antrim: Dunadry

Sea
Portaferry, Co. Down: Portaferry

EIRE

Coarse
Ballina, Co. Mayo: Downhill
Blessington, Co. Wicklow: Downshire
   House
Carrickmacross, Co. Monaghan:
   Nuremore
Glen of Aherlow, Co. Tipperary:
   Aherlow House
Kanturk, Co. Cork: Assolas Country House
Killarney, Co. Kerry: Aghadoe Heights
Mallow, Co. Cork: Longueville House
Newmarket-on-Fergus, Co. Clare:
   Dromoland Castle
Virginia, Co. Cavan: Park

Game
Ballina, Co. Mayo: Downhill
Ballinahinch, Co. Galway: Ballinahinch
   Castle
Ballylickey, Co. Cork: Ballylickey House
Blessington, Co. Wicklow: Downshire
   House
Cahir, Co. Tipperary: Kilcoran Lodge
Caragh Lake, Co. Kerry: Ard-na-Sidhe
Caragh Lake, Co. Kerry: Caragh Lodge
Carrickmacross, Co. Monaghan:
   Nuremore
Cashel, Co. Tipperary: Cashel Palace
Castledermot, Co. Kildare: Kilkea Castle
Cong, Co. Mayo: Ashford Castle
Gap of Dunloe, Co. Kerry: Dunloe Castle
Kanturk, Co. Cork: Assolas Country House
Killarney, Co. Kerry: Aghadoe Heights
Killarney, Co. Kerry: Cahernane
Killarney, Co. Kerry: Hotel Europe
Mallow, Co. Cork: Longueville House

Moyard, Co. Galway: Crocnaraw
Newmarket-on-Fergus, Co. Clare:
   Dromoland Castle
Newport, Co. Mayo: Newport House
Oughterard, Co. Galway: Currarevagh
   House
Rathmullan, Co. Donegal: Rathmullan
   House
Redcastle, Co. Donegal: Red Castle
Renvyle, Co. Galway: Renvyle House
Skibbereen, Co. Cork: Liss Ard House
Virginia, Co. Cavan: Park
Waterville, Co. Kerry: Waterville Lake

Sea
Courtmacsherry, Co. Cork:
   Courtmacsherry
Dingle: Co. Kerry: Sceilig
Newport, Co. Mayo: Newport House
Rathmullan, Co. Donegal: Rathmullan
   House
Redcastle, Co. Donegal: Red Castle
Renvyle, Co. Galway: Renvyle House
Rossnowlagh, Co. Donegal: Sand House
Waterville, Co. Kerry: Waterville Lake

GOLF

LONDON AIRPORTS
Heathrow, Holiday Inn

ENGLAND
Bagshot, Surrey: Pennyhill Park
Barnham Broom, Norfolk: Barnham
   Broom

Budock Vean, Cornwall: Budock Vean
Cambridge, Cambridgeshire: Cunard
    Cambridgeshire
Carlyon Bay, Cornwall: Carlyon Bay
Chittlehamholt, Devon: Highbullen
Freshwater, Isle of Wight: Farringford
Hythe, Kent: Hotel Imperial
Moretonhampstead, Devon: Manor House
Newquay, Cornwall: Headland
St Ives, Cornwall: Tregenna Castle
Sanderstead, Surrey: Selsdon Park
Shedfield, Hampshire: Meon Valley Hotel,
    Golf & Country Club
Stratford-upon-Avon, Warwickshire:
    Welcombe
Studland Bay, Dorset: Knoll House
Tewkesbury, Gloucestershire: Tewkesbury
    Park
Thurlestone, Devon: Thurlestone
Torquay, Devon: Palace
Washington, Tyne & Wear: George
    Washington
West Runton, Norfolk: Links Country Park
Weybridge, Surrey: Oatlands Park
Wishaw, Warwickshire: Belfry

SCOTLAND
Auchterarder, Tayside: Gleneagles
Gatehouse of Fleet, Dumfries & Galloway:
    Murray Arms

Kenmore, Tayside: Kenmore
Langbank, Strathclyde: Gleddoch House
Pitlochry, Tayside: Pitlochry Hydro
Turnberry, Strathclyde: Turnberry

WALES
Chepstow, Gwent: St Pierre Golf &
    Country Club
Gwbert-on-Sea, Dyfed: Cliff

ISLE OF MAN
Castletown, Isle of Man: Castletown Golf
    Links

EIRE
Carrickmacross, Co. Monaghan:
    Nuremore
Cong, Co. Mayo: Ashford Castle
Newmarket-on-Fergus, Co. Clare:
    Clare Inn
Newmarket-on-Fergus, Co. Clare:
    Dromoland Castle
Newport, Co. Mayo: Newport House
Redcastle, Co. Donegal: Red Castle
Renvyle, Co. Galway: Renvyle House
Rossnowlagh, Co. Donegal: Sand House
Shanagarry, Co. Cork: Ballymaloe House
Sneem, Co. Kerry: Parknasilla
Virginia, Co. Cavan: Park
Waterville, Co. Kerry: Waterville Lake

Continued

RIDING

ENGLAND
Bagshot, Surrey: Pennyhill Park
Bilbrook, Somerset: Dragon House
Burley, Hampshire: Burley Manor
Cheltenham, Gloucestershire: Hotel de la
   Bere
Exford, Somerset: Crown
Freshford, Avon: Homewood Park
Hythe, Kent: Hotel Imperial
Nottingham, Nottinghamshire:
   Post House
Rusper, West Sussex: Ghyll Manor
St Ives, Cornwall: Tregenna Castle
Sanderstead, Surrey: Selsdon Park
Stoborough, Dorset: Springfield Country
Thornton-le-Dale, North Yorkshire: Hall

SCOTLAND
Langbank, Strathclyde: Gleddoch House
Ledaig, Strathclyde: Isle of Eriska
Peebles, Borders: Peebles Hotel Hydro

WALES
Glyn Ceiriog, Clwyd: Golden Pheasant

CHANNEL ISLANDS
St Saviour, Jersey: Longueville Manor

EIRE
Courtmacsherry, Co. Cork:
   Courtmacsherry
Dingle, Co. Kerry: Sceilig
Gap of Dunloe, Co. Kerry: Dunloe Castle
Killarney, Co. Kerry: Hotel Europe
Moyard, Co. Galway: Crocnaraw
Newport, Co. Mayo: Newport House
Renvyle, Co. Galway: Renvyle House
Rossnowlagh, Co. Donegal: Sand House
Shanagarry, Co. Cork: Ballymaloe House
Skibbereen, Co. Cork: Liss Ard House
Sneem, Co. Kerry: Parknasilla

SQUASH

LONDON
Kensington Close

LONDON AIRPORTS
Gatwick, Copthorne

ENGLAND
Barnham Broom, Norfolk: Barnham
   Broom
Birmingham, West Midlands: Albany
Birmingham, West Midlands: Metropole &
   Warwick
Bramley, Surrey: Bramley Grange
Brandon, Warwickshire: Brandon Hall
Brockenhurst, Hampshire: Ladbroke
   Balmer Lawn
Burnham, Buckinghamshire: Burnham
   Beeches
Cambridge, Cambridgeshire: Cunard
   Cambridgeshire
Cheltenham, Gloucestershire: Hotel de la
   Bere
Chittlehamholt, Devon: Highbullen
Clayton-le-Woods, Lancashire: Pines
Cobham, Surrey: Ladbroke Seven Hills
Coventry, West Midlands: Novotel
Failand, Avon: Redwood Lodge
Great Driffield, Humberside: Bell
Harrogate, North Yorkshire: Hotel Majestic
Haslemere, Surrey: Georgian

Hythe, Kent: Hotel Imperial
Keswick, Cumbria: Lodore Swiss
Leamington Spa, Warwickshire: Mallory
  Court
Liverpool, Merseyside: Adelphi
Milford, Surrey: Milford House
Milton Damerel, Devon: Woodford Bridge
Moretonhampstead, Devon: Manor House
Mullion, Cornwall: Polurrian
Neasham, Co. Durham: Newbus Grange
Newcastle upon Tyne, Tyne & Wear:
  Gosforth Park
Newquay, Cornwall: Atlantic
Newquay, Cornwall: Hotel Riviera
Ottery St Mary, Devon: Salston
Portsmouth, Hampshire: Holiday Inn
St Ives, Cornwall: Tregenna Castle
Salcombe, Devon: Tides Reach
Saunton, Devon: Saunton Sands
Shedfield, Hampshire: Meon Valley Hotel,
  Golf & Country Club
Simonsbath, Somerset: Simonsbath
  House
South Walsham, Norfolk: South Walsham
  Hall
Tewkesbury, Gloucestershire: Tewkesbury
  Park
Thornton-le-Dale, North Yorkshire: Hall
Thurlestone, Devon: Thurlestone
Torquay, Devon: Imperial
Torquay, Devon: Livermead House
Torquay, Devon: Palace
Torquay, Devon: Rainbow House
Walberton, West Sussex: Avisford Park
Wallingford, Oxfordshire: Shillingford
  Bridge
Washington, Tyne & Wear: George
  Washington
Weston-under-Penyard, Hereford &
  Worcester: Wye
Westonbirt, Gloucestershire: Hare &
  Hounds
Weybridge, Surrey: Oatlands Park
Wincanton, Somerset: Holbrook House
Woolacombe, Devon: Woolacombe Bay
Yarm, Cleveland: Tall Trees

SCOTLAND
Aberdeen Airport, Grampian: Skean Dhu
Auchterarder, Tayside: Gleneagles
Auchterhouse, Tayside: Old Mansion
  House
Banchory, Grampian: Tor-na-Coille
Glasgow, Strathclyde: Holiday Inn
Inverness, Highland: Kingsmills
Langbank, Strathclyde: Gleddoch House
North Berwick, Lothian: Marine
Peebles, Borders: Peebles Hotel Hydro
Pitcaple, Grampian: Pittodrie House
Troon, Strathclyde: Sun Court

WALES
Chepstow, Gwent: St Pierre Golf &
  Country Club
Gwbert-on-Sea, Dyfed: Cliff

St Mellons, South Glamorgan: St Mellons
Wolf's Castle, Dyfed: Wolfscastle Country

NORTHERN IRELAND
Dunmurry, Co. Antrim: Conway
Holywood, Co. Down: Culloden

EIRE
Ballina, Co. Mayo: Downhill
Carrickmacross, Co. Monaghan: Nuremore
Cork, Co. Cork: Jurys
Dundalk, Co. Louth: Ballymascanlon
Killiney, Co. Dublin: Court
Killiney, Co. Dublin: Fitzpatrick Castle
Redcastle, Co. Donegal: Red Castle
Rosslare, Co. Wexford: Kelly's Strand
Wexford, Co. Wexford: Talbot

TENNIS

LONDON AIRPORTS
Heathrow, Holiday Inn

ENGLAND
Abberley, Hereford & Worcester: Elms
Ashford, Kent: Eastwell Manor
Bagshot, Surrey: Pennyhill Park
Barnham Broom, Norfolk: Barnham
  Broom

Continued

Beanacre, Wiltshire; Beechfield House
Bodymoor Heath, Warwickshire: Marston Farm
Bognor Regis, West Sussex: Royal Norfolk
Bournemouth, Dorset: Highcliff
Bramley, Surrey: Bramley Grange
Broadway, Hereford & Worcester: Lygon Arms
Brockenhurst, Hampshire: Ladbroke Balmer Lawn
Budock Vean, Cornwall: Budock Vean
Burnham, Buckinghamshire: Burnham Beeches
Cambridge, Cambridgeshire: Cunard Cambridgeshire
Carlyon Bay, Cornwall: Carlyon Bay
Castle Combe, Wiltshire: Manor House
Chagford, Devon: Gidleigh Park
Cheltenham, Gloucestershire: Hotel de la Bere
Chittlehamholt, Devon: Highbullen
Climping, West Sussex: Bailiffscourt
Cobham, Surrey: Ladbroke Seven Hills
Darlington, Co. Durham: Blackwell Grange Moat House
Dedham, Essex: Maison Talbooth
Dovedale, Derbyshire: Peveril of the Peak
Droitwich, Hereford & Worcester: Château Impney
Dursley, Gloucestershire: Stinchcombe Manor
Egham, Surrey: Great Fosters
Evershot, Dorset: Summer Lodge
Exmouth, Devon: Devoncourt
Failand, Avon: Redwood Lodge
Fairy Cross, Devon: Portledge
Ferndown, Dorset: Dormy
Frenchbeer, Devon: Teignworthy
Freshford, Avon: Homewood Park
Freshwater, Isle of Wight: Farringford
Hackness, North Yorkshire: Hackness Grange Country
Harrogate, North Yorkshire: Cairn
Harrogate, North Yorkshire: Hotel Majestic
Harrogate, North Yorkshire: Old Swan
Haslemere, Surrey: Lythe Hill
Helmsley, North Yorkshire: Feversham Arms
Hethersett, Norfolk: Park Farm
Horn's Cross, Devon: Foxdown Manor
Horton-cum-Studley, Oxfordshire: Studley Priory
Hunstrete, Avon: Hunstrete House
Hythe, Kent: Hotel Imperial
Ilkley, West Yorkshire: Craiglands
Keswick, Cumbria: Lodore Swiss
Longhorsley, Northumberland: Linden Hall
Lower Slaughter, Gloucestershire: Manor
Lymington, Hampshire: Passford House
Lyndhurst, Hampshire: Lyndhurst Park
Marlow, Buckinghamshire: Compleat Angler

Matlock Bath, Derbyshire: New Bath
Milton Damerel, Devon: Woodford Bridge
Moretonhampstead, Devon: Manor House
Mullion, Cornwall: Polurrian
Nantwich, Cheshire: Rookery Hall
New Milton, Hampshire: Chewton Glen
Newbury, Berkshire: Elcot Park
Newgate Street Village, Hertfordshire: Ponsbourne
Newquay, Cornwall: Headland
North Stifford, Essex: Stifford Moat House
North Stoke, Oxfordshire: Springs
Oakham, Leicestershire: Hambleton Hall
Paignton, Devon: Palace
Paignton, Devon: Redcliffe
Redbourn, Hertfordshire: Aubrey Park
Rusper, West Sussex: Ghyll Manor
St Ives, Cornwall: Tregenna Castle
Sanderstead, Surrey: Selsdon Park
Saunton, Devon: Saunton Sands
Shedfield, Hampshire: Meon Valley Hotel, Golf & Country Club
Sidmouth, Devon: Victoria
Silchester, Hampshire: Romans
Six Mile Bottom, Cambridgeshire: Swynford Paddocks
Slough, Berkshire: Holiday Inn
South Milford, North Yorkshire: Selby Fork
South Walsham, Norfolk: South Walsham Hall
Stoborough, Dorset: Springfield Country
Storrington, West Sussex: Little Thakeham
Stratford-upon-Avon, Warwickshire: Billesley Manor
Studland Bay, Dorset: Knoll House
Sturminster Newton, Dorset: Plumber Manor
Thurlestone, Devon: Thurlestone
Torquay, Devon: Grand
Torquay, Devon: Imperial
Torquay, Devon: Livermead House
Torquay, Devon: Osborne
Torquay, Devon: Palace
Torquay, Devon: Toorak
Veryan, Cornwall: Nare
Walberton, West Sussex: Avisford Park
Walsall, West Midlands: Crest
Walton, Warwickshire: Walton Hall
Warminster, Wiltshire: Bishopstrow House
Weston-super-Mare, Avon: Grand Atlantic
Westonbirt, Gloucestershire: Hare & Hounds
Weybridge, Surrey: Oatlands Park
Whitwell-on-the-Hill, North Yorkshire: Whitwell Hall Country House
Wincanton, Somerset: Holbrook House
Windermere, Cumbria: Langdale Chase
Woolacombe, Devon: Woolacombe Bay
Yelverton, Devon: Moorland Links

SCOTLAND
Airth, Central: Airth Castle
Auchterarder, Tayside: Gleneagles
Auchterhouse, Tayside: Old Mansion
    House
Borgue, Dumfries & Galloway: Senwick
    House
Contin, Highland: Craigdarroch Lodge
Dunblane, Central: Cromlix House
Dunkeld, Tayside: Dunkeld House
Fort William, Highland: Inverlochy Castle
Gairloch, Highland: Gairloch
Gairloch, Highland: Shieldaig Lodge
Gatehouse of Fleet, Dumfries & Galloway:
    Cally Palace
Gatehouse of Fleet, Dumfries & Galloway:
    Murray Arms
Gullane, Lothian: Greywalls
Inverness, Highland: Culloden House
Kelso, Borders: House O'Hill
Kentallen of Appin, Highland: Ardsheal
    House
Kilchrenan, Strathclyde: Ardanaiseig
Kinclaven by Stanley, Tayside: Ballathie
    House
Ledaig, Strathclyde: Isle of Eriska
Lewiston, Highland: Lewiston Arms
Moniaive, Dumfries & Galloway: Woodlea
Nairn, Highland: Golf View
Nairn, Highland: Newton
North Berwick, Lothian: Marine
Peebles, Borders: Cringletie House
Peebles, Borders: Peebles Hotel Hydro
Pitcaple, Grampian: Pittodrie House
Pitlochry, Tayside, Atholl Palace
Pitlochry, Tayside: Pitlochry Hydro
Rothesay, Strathclyde: Glenburn
Tarbert, Strathclyde: Stonefield Castle
Troon, Strathclyde: Sun Court
Turnberry, Strathclyde: Turnberry

WALES
Aberdyfi, Gwynedd: Trefeddian
Abersoch, Gwynedd: Porth Tocyn
Chepstow, Gwent: St Pierre Golf &
    Country Club
Coychurch, Mid Glamorgan: Coed-y-
    Mwstwr
Lake Vyrnwy, Powys: Lake Vyrnwy
Llandudno, Gwynedd: Bodysgallen Hall
Penrhyndeudraeth, Gwynedd: Hotel
    Portmeirion
St Mellons, South Glamorgan: St Mellons
Wolf's Castle, Dyfed: Wolfscastle Country

CHANNEL ISLANDS
Portelet Bay, Jersey: Portelet
St Brelade, Jersey: Atlantic
St Brelade's Bay, Jersey: St Brelade's Bay

ISLE OF MAN
Castletown, Isle of Man: Castletown Golf
    Links

NORTHERN IRELAND
Holywood, Co. Down: Culloden

EIRE
Ballina, Co. Mayo: Downhill
Ballinahinch, Co. Galway: Ballinahinch
    Castle
Blessington, Co. Wicklow: Downshire
    House
Caragh Lake, Co. Kerry: Caragh Lodge
Cashel, Co. Galway: Cashel House
Castledermot, Co. Kildare: Kilkea Castle
Clifden, Co. Galway: Abbeyglen
Cong, Co. Mayo: Ashford Castle
Dingle, Co. Kerry: Sceilig
Dundalk, Co. Louth: Ballymascanlon
Gap of Dunloe, Co. Kerry: Dunloe Castle
Glounthaune, Co. Cork: Ashbourne House
Gorey, Co. Wexford: Marlfield House
Kanturk, Co. Cork: Assolas Country House
Kenmare, Co. Kerry: Park
Kilkenny, Co. Kilkenny: Newpark
Killarney, Co. Kerry: Aghadoe Heights
Killarney, Co. Kerry: Cahernane
Killarney, Co. Kerry: Castlerosse
Killarney, Co. Kerry: Great Southern
Killarney, Co. Kerry: Torc Great
    Southern
Killiney, Co. Dublin: Fitzpatrick Castle
Limerick, Co. Limerick: Limerick Inn
Newmarket-on-Fergus, Co. Clare:
    Dromoland Castle
Oughterard, Co. Galway: Connemara
    Gateway
Rathmullan, Co. Donegal: Rathmullan
Redcastle, Co. Donegal: Red Castle
Renvyle, Co. Galway: Renvyle House
Rosslare, Co. Wexford: Kelly's Strand
Rossnowlagh, Co. Donegal: Sand House
Shanagarry, Co. Cork: Ballymaloe House
Skibbereen, Co. Cork: Liss Ard House
Sneem, Co. Kerry: Parknasilla
Virginia, Co. Cavan: Park
Waterford, Co. Waterford: Ardree
Waterville, Co. Kerry: Waterville Lake

CREDIT, TRAVEL & ENTERTAINMENT CARDS

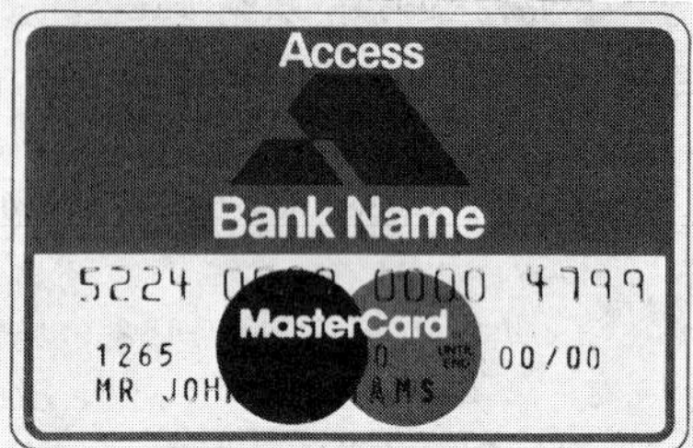

ACCESS

Headquarters Address:
Access
Joint Credit Card Co. Ltd
Southend on Sea, Essex SS2 6QQ
Tel: Southend (0702) 352211
Apply for an Access card free of charge at any bank displaying the Access sign or at the above address. MasterCard and Eurocard are accepted at all Access retail and service establishments.

AMERICAN EXPRESS

Membership Application
American Express Company
Amex House, P.O. Box 63
Edward Street, Brighton
Sussex BN2 1YL
Personal membership: £17·50 enrolment fee and £17·50 annual subscription; £10 for each additional family member on the same account. For details regarding applications for American Express Cards please phone Brighton (0273) 696933

BARCLAYCARD

Headquarters Address:
Barclaycard
Northampton NN1 1SG
Tel: Northampton (0604) 21100
Holders of all VISA cards are welcome wherever they see the familiar blue, white and gold badge. Most of the best-known hotels and restaurants in the United Kingdom welcome Barclaycard.

DINERS CLUB INTERNATIONAL

Membership Information:
Diners Club House, Kingsmead
Farnborough, Hampshire
Tel: (0252) 516261
Personal membership: £17·50 per annum; £10 entrance fee; £10 for each additional family card on the same account. Company membership: £17·50 first member; £10 entrance fee; £10 each additional member. Unlimited bulk membership on one centralised account: £120 per annum; £10 entrance fee. *Signature* magazine sent free to members.

AN OFFER FOR ANSWERS— A DISCOUNT ON THE NEXT GUIDE

Readers' answers to questionnaires included in the Guide prove invaluable to us in planning future editions, either through their reactions to the contents of the current Guide, or through the tastes and inclinations indicated. Please send this tear-out page to us *after you have used the Guide for some time*, addressing the envelope to:

Egon Ronay Organisation, Greencoat House, Francis Street, London SW1P 1DH.

As a token of thanks for your help, we will enable respondents (in the British Isles only) to obtain the 1984 Guide post free from us at one third discount off the retail price. We will send you an order form shortly before publication, so that answering the questionnaire imposes no obligation to purchase.

This offer closes 30 September 1983.
All answers will be treated in confidence.

Please tick

1. Are you

		Under 21?	☐
		21–30?	☐
		31–45?	☐
male?	☐	46–65?	☐
female?	☐	over 65?	☐

2. Your occupation ....

3. Do you possess any previous editions of this Guide?   1978 ☐
    1979 ☐   1980 ☐   1981 ☐   1982 ☐

4. Do you refer to this Guide

four times a week?	☐	once a week?	☐
three times a week?	☐	once a fortnight?	☐
twice a week?	☐	once a month?	☐

5. How many other people, apart from yourself, refer to this Guide (including those in your home and place of work)? ....

6. Do you choose your eating place from our bargain section in London?

		3 out of 4 times	☐
always	☐	2 out of 4 times	☐
never	☐	1 out of 4 times	☐

Continued

7. Do you choose your London accommodation at 'Economy Hotels' (from the bargain section)? | Yes | No |

8. Do you use the 'Bargain Winter Weekend' section? | Yes | No |

9. Do you have our 'Just A Bite' Guide?

1979	
1980	
1981	
1982	
1983	

10. Do you have our Pub Guide?

1980	
1981	
1982	
1983	

11. What subject(s) would you like us to survey or what improvements do you suggest?

....

....

....

12. Do you occupy more than one home? | Yes | No |

Do you own the house you live in? | Yes | No |

13. Your car

Make........................... cc................................... year.......................

Please *print* your name and address here if you would like us to send you an order form for the 1984 Guide.

Name...

Address...

....

....

YOU'RE WELCOME

You're welcome at over 470 Tourist Information Centres in England where you'll receive friendly help with accommodation and holiday ideas.

Many of them can even book a room for you. You can spot these Centres by the Accommodation Service Signs:

Those who offer our Holiday Information Service can give you information about the whole country. If there's one in your town you can go there for help in planning your trip:

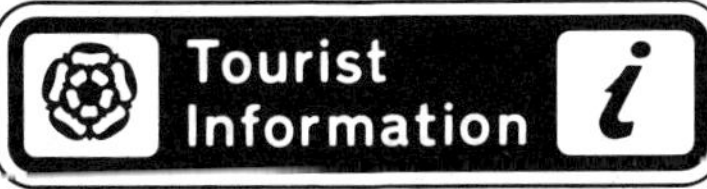

A free Directory of Tourist Information Centres is available from your nearest TIC or direct from the English Tourist Board at 4 Grosvenor Gardens, London SW1W 0DU.

RSJ
13a Coin Street, SE1
✆ *Tube Waterloo*
Open Lunch 12–2.30 Dinner 6–11.30
Closed L Sat, all Sun & Bank Holidays
About £18·50 for two
Delightful monkfish terrine and lamb cutlets roasted with honey and rosemary are typical of the varied dishes available in this informal, simply furnished restaurant. Home-made sweets, mostly based on fruit. Booking advisable.

Tel: 01–928 4554

(see also p. 207)

SAVOY HOTEL, THAMES FOYER
Strand, WC2
✆ *Tube Temple*
Open 4–7.30
Set afternoon tea £3·75 Shrimp & smoked salmon salad £3·20
Afternoon tea is served promptly at 4pm in the sedate and tranquil surroundings of this opulent hotel lounge. From 5.30 onwards there are pre-theatre snacks of salads and savoury bites. The Savoy's own blend of tea is deliciously refreshing.
Credit Access, Amex, Barclaycard

Tel: 01–836 4343

(see *Just a Bite* guide)

SWISS CENTRE, CHESA
2 New Coventry Street, W1
✆ *Tube Piccadilly Circus*
Open Lunch 12–2.30 Dinner 6–12
Closed Christmas Day
About £29 for two
Pick a light Swiss starter like air-dried beef, then go on to something like succulent lamb cutlets with mange-tout and finish with an exquisite mousse. Enjoy it all with a bottle from the superior wine list.
Credit Access, Amex, Barclaycard, Diners

Tel: 01–734 1291

(see also p. 305)

TRATTORIA IMPERIA
19 Charing Cross Road, WC2
✆ *Tube Leicester Square*
Open Lunch 12–2.45 Dinner 6–11.25
Closed Sun & Bank Holidays
About £18·50 for two
A really lively atmosphere and enjoyable Italian food make this a very popular little trattoria—especially at lunch time. Dishes range from favourites like minestrone and cannelloni to the unusual duck with peach sauce. *Credit* Access, Amex, Barclaycard, Diners

Tel: 01–930 8364

(see also p. 209)

YOUNG VIC THEATRE BAR
66 The Cut, SE1
✆ *Tube Waterloo*
Open 10.30 till 30 minutes after evening performance ends; lunch only when no performance
Closed Sun & Bank Holidays
Chinese vegetables 95p Pork & bean casserole £1·10
Morning coffee, light lunches, afternoon teas and theatre suppers all play their part in the life of this popular refectory-style restaurant. The attractive counter display ranges from quiches and salads to hot dishes. Ring to check opening times.

Tel: 01–633 0133

(see *Just a Bite* guide)

This is the age of the train ⇌

Continued

Paddington & Marylebone

CARAVAN SERAI
50 Paddington Street, W1   *Tel:* 01–935 1208
☻ *Tube Baker Street*
Open Lunch 12–2.45 Dinner 6–10.45, Sun 6–11.30
About £18·50 for two
Juicy marinated prawns cooked in a clay oven are one of the highlights in this friendly restaurant specialising in authentic Afghan cuisine. Yoghurt and spices are also used to telling effect with lamb and chicken. *Credit* Access, Amex, Barclaycard, Diners   (see also p. 198)

LE CHEF
41 Connaught Street, W2   *Tel:* 01–262 5945
☻ *Buses 6, 7, 8, 12, 15, 16, 36B, 88*
Open Lunch 12,30–2.30 Dinner 7–11.30, Sat 7–11
Closed L Sat, all Sun, Mon, Bank Holidays & 2 weeks August
About £26 for two
Enjoy a taste of French country cooking in the informal atmosphere of this popular bistro. Robust regional dishes like fish soup, sautéed veal provençale and poussin lyonnaise are prepared in forthright fashion. Booking advisable. *Credit* Access   (see also p. 242)

LE DODO GOURMAND
30 Connaught Street, W2   *Tel:* 01–258 3947
☻ *Buses 6, 7, 8, 12, 15, 16, 36B, 88*
Open Lunch 12.30–2.30 Dinner 7–10.30
Closed Sun, Christmas Day & 1 January
About £29 for two
Uncomplicated French dishes like lamb brochettes and colourful Mauritian-Creole specialities such as cod marinated in saffron, coriander and mustard are popular in this little restaurant. Bernard de Rosnay is a charming and urbane host.
Credit Access, Amex, Barclaycard, Diners   (see also p. 249)

GREAT MUGHAL
2 Hyde Park Square, W2   *Tel:* 01–258 3507
☻ *Buses 12, 88*
Open Lunch 12–3 Dinner 6.30–11.30
Closed Christmas & Boxing Day
About £30 for two   ♿
It pays to be adventurous in this luxurious North Indian restaurant, so follow the advice of the courteous waiters if you want to sample some of the more unusual dishes on the varied menu. Meticulous, authentic cooking. *Credit* Access, Amex, Barclaycard, Diners   (see also p. 262)

GYNGLEBOY
27 Spring Street, W2   *Tel:* 01–723 3351
☻ *Tube Paddington*
Open 11–3 & 5.30–9
Closed Sat, Sun & Bank Holidays
Game pie £2·30 Ham off the bone £2·15
A Victorian atmosphere pervades this dark, sawdust-strewn wine bar, where the bill of fare includes smoked fish, savoury pies and cold meats with gargantuan salads. Finish with fresh fruit or Stilton.
Credit Access, Amex, Barclaycard, Diners   (see *Just a Bite* guide)

This is the age of the train ⇒

LA LUPA
23 Connaught Street, W2   *Tel:* 01–723 0540
⊖ *Buses 6, 7, 8, 12, 15, 16, 36B, 88*
Open Lunch 12–2.45 Dinner 6.30–11.30
Closed Sun, L Bank Holidays & 3–4 days Christmas
About £18 for two
Classical Roman decor sets the tone for this attractive basement restaurant. Seasonal specialities and regional dishes supplement the varied menu of well-prepared Italian favourites like fettuccine and saltimbocca alla romana. *Credit* Access, Amex, Barclaycard, Diners   (see also p. 204)

MAISON SAGNE
105 Marylebone High Street, W1   *Tel:* 01–935 6240
⊖ *Tube Baker Street*
Open 9–5 (Sat till 12.30)
Closed Sun & Bank Holidays
Chicken & mushroom vol-au-vent £1·50 Florentine 55p
Tempting cakes and pastries catch your eye in the window of this smart little pâtisserie, where the choice ranges from marzipan rolls and florentines to lovely croissants and brioches. Lunchtime savouries too. Unlicensed.   (see *Just a Bite* guide)

LE P'TIT MONTMARTRE
15 Marylebone Lane, W1   *Tel:* 01–935 9226
⊖ *Tube Bond Street*
Open Lunch 12–2.30 Dinner 6–11
Closed L Sat, all Sun & Bank Holidays
About £31 for two
Food comes first in this reliable, simply furnished restaurant, where the menu features mainly classic French-style dishes like eggs Benedict and veal dijonnaise served with nicely cooked fresh vegetables. *Credit* Access, Amex, Barclaycard, Diners   (see also p. 291)

RAW DEAL
65 York Street, W1   *Tel:* 01–262 4841
⊖ *Tube Baker Street*
Open 10am–10pm
Closed Sun & Bank Holidays
Salad platter £1·95 Hot savoury £1·10
A splendid array of imaginative salads plus daily hot dishes like braised parsnips or brussels sprouts with chestnuts draw the crowds to this simple little vegetarian restaurant. Very busy at lunch time. Unlicensed. *Credit* Access, Amex, Barclaycard, Diners   (see *Just a Bite* guide)

SIDI BOU SAID
9 Seymour Place, W1   *Tel:* 01–402 9930
⊖ *Tube Marble Arch*
Open Lunch 12–3 Dinner 6–11.30
Closed Sun & Bank Holidays
About £22 for two
Two brothers run this coolly decorated little restaurant where the emphasis is on traditional Tunisian cooking. Choose from various types of couscous and tajine, piquant salads and pastries, with scented coffee to finish. *Credit* Access, Amex, Barclaycard, Diners   (see also p. 303)

This is the age of the train ⇒

Engineering For World Transport

Engineering for World Transport

The A300 Airbus relies on actuation systems supplied by Lucas Aerospace in conjunction with LAT, for the precise operation of the aircraft's wing flaps and slats. During take-off and landing, these secondary flight controls become primary in importance and their reliable actuation is vital.

Lucas Aerospace also supplies the tailplane trim actuator, which governs the pitch attitude of the A300 and helps the pilot to balance the arcraft aerodynamically to counteract load variations.

SUMMING UP

Twenty-five Years

CONTENTS

Section layout by Humphrey Stone

FRANKLY SPEAKING

I wish I could say that it has all been tremendous fun, that I have enjoyed every minute of it, that I would do it all over again.

But it wasn't at all like that.

My distilled memories are those of constant struggle, above all to make ends meet; a seemingly unwinnable obstacle race against time and printing deadlines, twisting a thousand arms to get things done, constant anxiety that hundreds of tasks beyond my overstretched timetable would not be done well enough by others. Not to mention the paranoid notion that I should have visited every restaurant and hotel myself and the never-ending, but unjustified, worry about even the best inspector's assessments.

So, you might well ask, what has made Egon run?

Perhaps the force that has driven me—and still does, undiminished—was the obsession with excellence and talent, with improving things and being mercilessly scathing about mediocrity and sloppiness. It's an obsession that made me dangerously oblivious of financial and manpower problems, even of my own physical strength, and many

By courtesy of South Wales Echo

'Now you know why we insist you pay for it before you eat it!'

a time brought me and my enterprise to the brink of disaster. It is clearly naive and unwise, but I treat obstacles as largely imaginary things which tend to disappear if ignored or, by hook or by crook, can be overcome.

It isn't a tendency with which one is born. My parental home and restaurants, and strict school in Budapest, developed my second nature. In my mid teens, I often accompanied my father on his regular nightly visit to the kitchens of one of his restaurants before the start of dinner service. He entered the chef's domain with a fistful of long spoons to taste every soup, sauce and dish down to the potatoes, with the chef de cuisine in his wake, like a consultant surgeon followed by the senior registrar, criticising, praising, condemning, to the surrounding staff in white. Could that have been the seed from which this Guide grew?

And could its philosophy have been developed at the numerous meetings to which my father started to take me when I was 18 to listen, as a mute observer, to discussions about the problems of my family's five restaurants, leaders in their field? Not a single instance do I recall when profits, and how to achieve and increase them, were discussed. Talk always centred on how to improve things even further, in cooking, service, decor, staff, etc. It was taken for granted that profit would follow – and it did: my father became the capital's fifth biggest taxpayer.

His was a methodical progress I could not afford to emulate. For business strategy, when the aims are high, you need capital, which I did not have as I had to leave everything behind when I left Hungary in 1946. Not for me the five-year, let alone twenty-five-year, plan. I lurched from milestone to milestone, every time amazed that I got there. I must have been crazy to have had confidence in winning through, and, although in the most dire need for a few hundred pounds, to have driven my inspectors to spend thousands, without ever limiting their expenditure on test meals or hotel rooms. Nor did financial considerations ever stop me from having a new establishment visited irrespective of distance or prices – seemingly a prescription for financial disaster.

It certainly was a rum set-up at the start – if you can call an office of very nearly wardrobe size, with me and my part-time secretary and a part-time salesman, a set-up. In the first year I researched, wrote, proofread and oversaw the setting and printing of the Guide (having insisted on being my own publisher) and I had to sell it, too. My salvation was my part-time salesman, the son of a big ex-landowner with a historic name from Hungary, whose only connection with my subject was a stint as commis waiter (he was penniless) and whose knowledge of bookselling was as sub-elementary as mine. Haphazard selling would be an understatement: we drove or walked along London's main streets and made a sales pitch at every bookshop we found. The sale of six books was most satisfactory, twenty-four being a cause for jubilation.

'He doesn't normally stay in for lunch. Perhaps it's Egon Ronay's head.'

But the man without whose imagination I would be nowhere was the advertising manager of the Ford Motor Company, Bob Adams, who took three advertising pages in the 96-page first edition and a large number of books, thus making the printing of the first issue possible.

The next year or two were salad days. In an old friend, Geza Luby, an ex-diplomat who was working for the BBC foreign service, I found a man of impeccable taste, knowledge and judgement (he is still with me) with whom I kept scouring the country, oblivious of fatigue or of my family. We had four meals every day: three—or four—dishes for me, one for him for lunch; then speeding to the next restaurant, sometimes 15 to 20 miles away, before it closed, where it was one course for me and three or four for him for the second lunch; da capo sin al fine for dinner and the same next day, and the day after that—ad infinitum, it seemed. And between breakfast and lunch I wrote up the previous day's four restaurants in descriptions much longer than in today's Guide.

In the fourth year I had three inspectors and, in addition to inspecting, I wrote 1,000 long entries, the whole book—an experience nothing could induce me to repeat. We now have two resident and four part-time copy writers. I only have time to write 40 to 50 stories a year, but I do prepare all the editorial introductions and, of course, inspect whenever I can.

I never had any doubt about my own views of restaurants and hotels or any hesitation about expressing them firmly, having been a professional restaurateur and hotelier for 25 years before I began to write. So when I started my weekly dining-out column in 1953 (it ran for six years, in the *Daily Telegraph* and later in the *Sunday Telegraph*), it was easy to compete authoritatively with my opposite numbers, none of whom had been professional restaurateurs. For the same reason, caterers largely respected my views, even if they didn't always like what they read.

I made my first attacks on British Rail food (far worse than today) and motorway catering in the '50s in the *Daily Telegraph*, well before the Guide started, and I have never ceased to campaign against bad catering in monopolistic situations. Yet some people think I only started our campaigns to increase Guide sales. I have always felt upset and angry when food, particularly simple food, was incompetently prepared, and that's why my colleagues and I have made such surveys, not because we thought it was a good sales gimmick to do so. Those under attack didn't–and don't–accept these as my motives. (Just think: our 1980 survey of airlines cost some £16,000–impossible to recoup from sales.)

With the exception of some 60 to 80 restaurants where they know me well, I am not recognised. A certain columnist made a crack about this: 'Egon Ronay need not worry about being recognised', he wrote. 'He has the most forgettable face I know.' The simple reason is that my face is not generally known, so eating out anonymously presents no problems. This was confirmed to my great embarrassment when I took two important business friends to a West End hotel restaurant, having

booked under another name. The head waiter, who had been wine butler in a restaurant I managed some 20 years before, recognised me, rushed to my table and said: 'Mr Ronay–it's so good to see you! Tell me, where are you working now?'

Now that the Guide's name has become so widely known, I am increasingly deprived of something I greatly enjoy–good conversation. Try as hard as I will, people insist on changing the subject to food and wine. Cocktail parties and similar gatherings are absolutely taboo: there is always someone who collars me in the first five minutes and asks: 'I wonder when you visited the Red Lion in Backwoods last? Do you realise that they don't serve lentil soup any more . . .?!' Perhaps I should carry a printed sheet on me for such occasions, explaining that, between our four Guides, we publish nearly 5,000 entries annually, work with 12 professional inspectors, etc., etc., and that, please God, may we talk about the theatre, politics, education or religion–in fact, *anything* but restaurants?

Another unfulfilled wish of mine is not to have to fast all day when I am invited to dinner at a private house. God forbid I should not be able to finish *all* the food my hostess invariably insists on heaping on to my plate irrespective of my craving for a small helping of simple cooking after all the restaurant meals of the week. Invariably I end up with a large portion of a complicated concoction, by no means always good. And I must think of a different excuse when taken out to business luncheons, a time of the day when I try not to eat or drink very much: the 'medical check up this afternoon' ploy is wearing thin.

But the one thing I never tire of, to my surprise, is visiting a restaurant I haven't been to before. My anticipation and excitement are invariably that of an opera enthusiast before a new production: so many facets to enjoy, so many factors to click for a successful evening. Food, like singing in an opera, is, of course, the paramount aspect, just as the art of an opera star is as ephemeral as the art of a great chef, except that the latter cannot even be taped. One feels–or should feel–privileged and humble when the perfect feat happens: it's unique, it's for the night and it's for me. This is what makes the experience so exciting.

On almost every occasion I get nostalgic about my days as a restaurateur. Once you have been in the business, the urge to return never leaves you, just as in the theatre, and, having seen so much I imagine that I would be better than most–a fantasy I would never dare to put to the test. I wouldn't have to provide cutlery: all those I have criticised over many years would bring their own sharpened knives.

THOSE WERE THE DAYS

A lot of things have changed since Egon Ronay conceived the idea of his first Guide. Just cast your mind back—if you're old enough, of course—to that autumn of 1957.

Harold Macmillan, you will remember, was Prime Minister then, having come through the Suez crisis the year before, and was already beginning to tell the nation it had 'never had it so good'. And indeed, rationing was a fast-fading memory, unemployment was under half a million, and the buses ran on time.

The bank rate, however, was raised to 7 per cent and inflation was beginning to cause slight worries, as was an epidemic of influenza—a particularly sinister variety dubbed Asian—which was killing the elderly and keeping one child in four away from school. But it did not prevent Prince Charles from starting his first term as a boarder at Cheam School in Hampshire.

At about the same time, Malcolm Muggeridge caused a stir by asking in the *Saturday Evening Post*, 'Does England Really Need a Queen?' It was a mild, reasoned piece which was as polite as polite could be towards the person of Her Majesty, but Muggeridge was roundly rebuked on all sides for raising such an issue just as the Queen and Prince Philip were about to embark on a tour of Canada and the United States, and the BBC withdrew an invitation to explain his views on *Panorama* after calls from outraged viewers.

Yes, *Panorama* existed then, although it probably didn't enjoy as wide a following as the weekly saga of that sterling British Bobby, *Dixon of Dock Green*. BBC television was already 21 years old, but believe it or not, a lot of people lived without a set in their homes. They had to struggle through the day by listening to the Home, Light or Third on their radios, starting perhaps with *Mrs Dale's Diary*, or *Music While You Work*, in the morning. At lunchtime there was the *Billy Cotton Band Show* (Wakey, wakey! anyone who can't remember that), and sometimes *Hancock's Half Hour*, and in the evening, of course, there were the *Archers* (some things never change).

Life was altogether more innocent then. An article in *The Times* headed 'Gay Day in London' referred to the Lord Mayor's Show, there was no such thing as the pill and sex shops were undreamt of. But the Wolfenden Report upset a bishop or two by recommending that homosexual acts between consenting adults not be a criminal offence.

Nor did women then question their role as selfless wives, mothers and secretaries. 'If a woman loses her reputation as a good cook, what has she left?' wondered one woman's page columnist, and countless advertisements showed beaming family groups, not a hair out of place and thrilled to bits with the dazzling evidence of cleanliness all around.

You could, of course, escape a housebound destiny by being a film star. This was the age of the bosom, and Jayne Mansfield (41 – meaning inches) carried all before her on a much-publicised visit to London. But Gina Lollobrigida, Marilyn Monroe, Sophia Loren, Diana Dors and their respective measurements were never out of the limelight for very long.

Not for them the sack, the straight-up-and-down fashion phenomenon that swept the land like wildfire that autumn. Everyone said how frightful it had looked in the '20s, and then went out and bought one. Alternatively, the young could also wear the 'jive' look – T-shirt, three-quarter length jeans, flat pumps and lipstick – and be indistinguishable from many of their daughters today.

However attired, the young spent many fruitless hours loafing around in coffee bars, listening to skiffle and buying 'pop' records – 750,000 copies of Paul Anka's 'Diana' in two months and 500,000 copies of Elvis Presley singing 'Gotta Lotta Lovin' to Do'. The record boom was hailed as a revival of home entertainment such as the Victorians had enjoyed, but it did not meet with everyone's approval. Frank Sinatra, for one, thought that rock and roll was 'sung, played and written for the most part by cretinous goons'.

Young and old alike flocked to the cinema to see *Bridge on the River Kwai*, while those with more esoteric tastes could watch Brigitte Bardot bathing in asses' milk while wondering what Gloria Swanson as her wicked mother-in-law Agrippina would get up to next in a film called *Nero*. *Lucky Jim* (the movie) was enjoying some success, and *Band of Angels*, in which Yvonne de Carlo was sold to Clark Gable as a slave, very little.

Meanwhile, out in the real world Khrushchev and Mao Tse-tung were meeting in Moscow, and President Eisenhower was threatening to send state troops in to Little Rock, Arkansas, if Governor Faubus continued to bar black children from white schools. The Russians sent a dog called Laika forever into space, and also perfected a TV screen capable of receiving coloured pictures.

At home, the Labour Party Conference rejected a left-wing motion to renounce the H-bomb. Dr Julian Huxley and Desmond Morris unveiled an exhibition of paintings by two chimpanzees, and the Duke of Bedford, invited to hear groups like the Skiffle Cats from Pinner at the Café de Paris, complained that there were 'so few places left to go to in London these days'. But he obviously hadn't seen Egon Ronay's Restaurant Guide, which even told you where to get a three-course meal for 7s 6d. Those were the days!

THE EGON RONAY
ORGANISATION AT WORK

Scene—any Monday morning in our Victoria office

Monday morning—first thing—Roger Mordan (*right*), Guides Director, and Hilary Wharton (*left*), Research Director, meet to discuss the week's research programme.

A fortnightly inspectors' meeting to exchange experiences and to maintain a unified approach.

Inspectors map out the next fortnight's research task, book accommodation, reserve tables and catch up on outstanding reports.

Egon Ronay (*centre*) and Geza Luby—in charge of inspections—finalise star ratings and hotel gradings. Gerry Osipczak, Egon Ronay's PA, takes notes.

The new batch of reports brought in by the inspectors is logged into enormous ledgers by Coreen Williams. She is our 'continuity girl', who keeps track of every report. Behind her Sharon Smith (*left*) and Jocelyn Stoddard (*right*) are typing the manuscripts for the printers.

This is probably the most detailed information file on catering establishments in Britain. Wendy Daniel (*right back*), Production Director, controls the system. Roseleen Colgan (*left*) files and prepares file cards for each new Guide recommendation.

These files are just some of the thousands containing correspondence with praise of, or complaints about, hotels and restaurants. Roseleen and Rosa Ludwick (*right*) keep them up to date.

In another part of the office Jenny Lefley (*centre*), Marketing Director, and David Hunt (*left*), Sales Director, discuss new sales ideas.

Barbara Ronay designs layout and typography of the Guides.

Donald Gray, Senior Director with advertising assistant Lynn Sanders.

Ruth Stanton, Press & Promotions Director, follows up the results of her dealings with the media.

The wordsmiths—*(left to right)* Jo Perry subedits and proofreads; Julanne Arnold is Editorial Director; Peter Long and David Mabey are resident copywriters.

Vivienne Alexander, Office Manager; Dee Horn *(back)* is receptionist and telephonist.

Ken Bullen passes on the latest figures to his assistant, Betty Pottersman *(right)*. She scrutinises the inspectors' daily expense claims.

INSPECTING THE INSPECTORS

Inspectors come in all shapes and sizes: serious or witty, bohemians with an artistic eye or Germanically thorough, introvert bachelors or fugitives from wilting marriages, shrewd apprentices preparing for their own futures as restaurateurs, or simply those in a rut searching for any fresh role in life. They have one thing in common: they all love food, or–if such passionate feelings about food are beyond some English people–at least they have a deep interest in it.

Basically, of course, they seek a job to earn a living–except in the case of one applicant who turned out to be a Lloyd's underwriter bent upon turning his great hobby, eating, into a way of life. He seemed to be a most practised eater-out so we employed him. A letter came, instead of him, on the appointed day, asking for one week's grace as his butler had just run off with his housemaid. But he did eventually come and proved to be a man of taste. He drove around in a Bentley and his wife had to meet him periodically at an appointed spot–with his shirts: it would have been unthinkable not to have them handwashed. He was critical of the food but never of the service, which he found, without a single exception, to be most attentive and deferent even in the unlikeliest places. Our puzzlement ended when it was discovered that, even in the simplest godforsaken pub or café, he never failed to dine in a dinner jacket, a lifelong routine we eventually persuaded him to change.

Not all our problems have had their bright side. An early-middle-aged inspector was sought by the police, having run off with a vicar's underage daughter. The police obligingly saved us from colossal embarrassment by withholding the name of his employers from the press, as it wasn't eating but a different kind of gluttony he was guilty of.

Passion of sorts played its part in the perennial indecision of a young barrister who had been wanting to leave every three months to start his career in law but stayed on for three years, incapable of tearing himself away from food, his consuming interest.

A young Chinese lady whom we had trained for visiting Oriental restaurants was subjected to one of our periodical checks by a senior inspector. He was impressed by the judgement and general approach of his young companion. But while he was paying the bill, he noticed that she slipped something into her bag. He was startled by the freely given information that she was merely pinching an ashtray: 'But I do it in every restaurant. Since I started with you, I have collected a suitcaseful.' We denied her further opportunities.

In times when we couldn't find enough suitable applicants in England, we searched overseas. A young Scandinavian aristocrat, claiming to be an accomplished gourmet, served but a week of his training period before it was discovered that his idea of a dainty, appetite-whetting aperitif was filling himself with a whole pint of Guinness before every lunch as well as dinner.

From Paris came a dashing and sophisticated Russian prince with a legendary name well known from Tolstoy's *War and Peace*. During his weeks of training he proved himself a true connoisseur of good food and, alas, of much else besides. The senior inspector with whom he had to serve his apprenticeship became more and more desperate: our Russian friend, mostly late for the morning start, had to be hauled out of bed, more often than not, from the side of an attractive female companion, once or twice identified as the hotel receptionist. He lost our trust, if not our admiration.

At a much riper age such pastimes don't occupy the imagination quite as much. An elderly, very reliable inspector sent a reasonably good report about a certain hotel and so it carried our recommendation in the following year's Guide, except that we printed his only reservation: 'noticeable plumbing noise at night'. A considerably younger inspector, visiting the same place the following year, horrified us by reporting that we had been recommending a popular house of assignation.

But how do we choose inspectors?

Most of the numerous letters we receive answering our three or four annual small ads in *The Times* personal column are blatantly useless. Five or six interviews are set up every time. It doesn't take more than ten minutes to see whether the applicant has good taste and common sense—the two salient attributes. Part of our informal chat, once the candidate is at ease, may run like this.

ER: 'What's your favourite dish?'
Good Candidate: 'I love game, particularly saddle of hare or roast larded venison.'
Hopeless Candidate: 'I like everything.'

ER: 'What is the best dish you have ever had in your life?'
Good Candidate (after long thought): 'About six months ago, in St Malo, a plate of moules marinière with beautifully fresh bread and a chunk of butter.'
Hopeless Candidate (replies instantly): 'Coq au vin.' ER: 'When was that?' *HC:* 'Three days ago.'

ER: 'When did you eat out last and where?'

Good Candidate: 'I can't afford to eat out much . . . it must be all of three weeks–in an attractive little pub in the Thames Valley.'

Hopeless Candidate: 'We eat out frequently near our home in Pinner, where we know quite a few excellent little restaurants. The last time was three days ago.'

ER: 'Can you recall what you had to eat?'

Good Candidate: 'A lentil soup, then a very tender piece of roast rib of beef with spring greens and jacket potatoes.' ER: 'Dessert?' *GC:* 'I'm afraid not–I couldn't resist the Stilton.' ER: 'Coffee?' *GC:* 'Yes. As a matter of fact, it was rather weak.'

Hopeless Candidate: 'It's a little difficult to remember . . . ah, yes, it was the coq au vin I mentioned before.' ER: 'Anything before that?' *HC:* 'Some fruit juice or other . . . no, sorry, it must have been potted shrimps.' ER: 'Desserts?' *HC:* 'Ice cream.'

ER: 'What in particular did you like about your main course?'

Good Candidate: 'The meat was very succulent and tender and they must have used some salt and pepper on it. Also, the spring greens were still a little on the crisp side, not limp.'

Hopeless Candidate: 'Oh, I just like chicken cooked the French way.'

ER: 'Do you do any cooking at home?'

Good Candidate: 'I am not a cook but sometimes I make omelettes (and am supposed to be reasonably good at that) and occasionally the Sunday joint, but my wife is Italian and such a good cook that there is no need for me to cook much.'

Hopeless Candidate: 'Oh, yes, I do . . . simple things, like grills. I do steaks or grilled sole or I roast a chicken–as I said, I like chicken . . .'

ER: 'What did you drink?'

Good Candidate: 'We didn't have wine with our meal because I know their draught beer, which is very good. But we did have a glass of Sylvaner before lunch.'

Hopeless Candidate: 'Actually I prefer white wine with most dishes.' ER: 'What kind?' *HC:* 'Medium.'

In the 'Hopeless Candidate' it was impossible to discover any indication of genuine interest in food or the slightest attraction to the pleasures it gives. The 'Good Candidate' gave several clues to his love of good eating and his surprisingly good taste, and he showed a lack of pretence. He may well have been cunning and given the answers he thought his interviewer wanted to hear. Even then, he knew how good taste manifests itself, something people without it have no way of knowing.

Strangely, the general belief is that expert knowledge of technical details is of paramount importance. Not so. We are never impressed by people who instantly recognise a particular herb or spice in a sauce or who can pinpoint vineyards, let alone vintages. That only proves a retentive memory and very extensive practice. It certainly does not, in itself, make a good judge of food and wine. It is infinitely more important to know, unmistakably, that a particular sole véronique is an excellent dish, with the fish's texture well preserved, the sauce light and striking the right balance between sweet and dry, than to discern that a Sauternes was used in the sauce.

Nor is a gastronome overawed by the ridiculous concentration, the intense sniffing, swirling and similar liturgy, in which most professional wine tasters indulge. They are obviously treating it as a science. Precious few among them get real enjoyment and pleasure out of actually drinking good wines as opposed to discussing them as if they were abstract.

But it isn't enough to have gathered a group of good inspectors. After training them to get on to the same wavelength comes managing them, which is as much of a skill as inspecting itself. The psychological key lies in knowing whom to send where, what weight to attribute to the opinion of one as opposed to the other, to surmise from between the lines of a report that it is safer to double-check through an additional visit by someone else.

'What a marvellous job', it is often said. 'You can't have much difficulty in finding the right people.'

It takes about a hundred applicants to find two inspectors for training, one of whom is likely to prove useless. . . .

'Excuse me Professor, there's a Mr Egon Ronay to see you.'

THE SURVIVORS

Seven restaurants which were recommended in
the first edition of the Guide are still run by the
same people (or members of their family) as then and
are still worthy entries in our current edition.

The photograph shows (*standing, left*)
Chef Jean Drees, Mirabelle: the only 'grand
restaurant' chef still in the same post after all this time.
(*right*) **Mr Anthony Manzi** of **Manzi's,** formerly the
House of Hamburger: the latest of four generations
to run Soho's most consistently good
fish restaurant.

(*centre*) **Mr Victor Sassie,** proprietor of the
Hungarian restaurant the **Gay Hussar:**
rumours of his retirement have proved premature.
Victor Sonvico (Mr Victor), manager, **Mirabelle:**
25 years ago he was head waiter.
Mrs Eileen Stais, White Tower: she and Mr J. P. Stais
have been running this Greek restaurant
since 1938. **Mr Luigi Contini** has been their chef
for over 25 years.

(*front*) **Mrs Lucille Marks, Wilton's,** has
continued to maintain the high standards of
this traditional English restaurant which she
helped her husband to run until his death.
Mr Egon Ronay. Mr David Cominetti, Casa Cominetti,
Catford: the 25 guide entries only record a fraction of
the 66 years of this Italian restaurant's success.

(*not shown*) **Mr Alistair Greig,** proprietor, the
Guinea Grill.

THE THINGS WE HAVE DONE...!

We have never had complexes about being critical and out-spoken: 'Scandalously inferior,' the first Guide rounded on public school feeding. 'Gastronomic rape, except that they don't even derive pleasure from it,' we said later about food in Wales. 'Embezzlement!' we accused restaurants pocketing some of the service charge. 'Worst advertisement for British womanhood' is how we characterised 'frosty, unconcerned receptionists'. 'Appalling and filthy' (motorway cafés), 'harassing harridans' (chambermaids), 'fraudulent and impertinent' (serving frozen vegetables as fresh), 'hotel guests dripping at breakfast' (the result of the size of bath towels), 'cesspool' (in which pub glasses are washed up), 'drainworthy' (the cooking of vegetables), 'Mediterranean stable boys without even pidgin English' (the measure of waiting skill) . . .

Random pickings from hundreds of similar remarks which were not coined to impress. They were tools, born from anger, used in campaigns we have waged over the years to bring about improvements.

Campaigns—like motorways . . . fresh vegetables . . . licensing laws . . . battery chickens . . . coffee . . . hospital food . . . government loans for hotels . . . etc, etc.

In our annual 'Summing up' chapter we pleaded, prodded, suggested and fulminated. And our annual surveys of public fields of catering, mostly in monopolistic situations allowing no choice, were the result of painstaking and costly research.

A stocktaking of battles which proved to be unwinnable and those which had noticeably improved matters is revealing. We ourselves are surprised to find how early we had started to stir up some causes that have later become subjects of public opinion pressure or ended up as music hall jokes. And naturally we are pleased that we can claim some results.

★ ★ ★

Way back in 1963 we started to advocate **shorter menus** as easier to live up to. The language of menus, too, was too flamboyant in the days of 'farm-gathered peas' and ducklings invariably 'Aylesbury' and beef 'Aberdeen'. But in vain did we suggest a test case for the application of the Trades Descriptions Act to PR menuese. Food snobs and business hosts felt that bed-sheet-sized menus were more important than the cooking which so few could appreciate in those days.

1963 'If menus were limited to dishes cooks *can* cook . . .'
1964 'Menus unnecessarily ambitious.'
1966 'Preoccupation with culinary encyclopaedia.'

Eventually the effect started to be felt.

1968 'The shrinking of menus has a lot to do with general improvements.'
1969 'Menus are at last shorter.'
1971 'The length of menus – with exceptions – is in reverse ratio to the standard of cooking.'

★ ★ ★

It is a paradox that receptionists, overwhelmingly women, should display so little femininity. **Friendly reception** is something that neither we nor the press which took up our cause could bring about. Yet how we tried!

1966 'Reception desks a veritable barrier. Receptionists seldom display a warm smile.'
1968 'Receptionists are forbidding figures. A manager said: "I don't encourage friendliness in receptionists – otherwise customers will ask them too many questions."'
1979 'Our inspectors are received more like squatters than hotel guests. How about a smile . . . making us feel welcome, let alone wanted.'
1981 'Reception has been dehumanised in chain hotels.'

Even greater efforts went into our castigation of the **early morning harassment by chambermaids**. Nothing, it seems, will change that breed.

1964 'Chambermaid left no doubt how unwelcome we were after 9.30am.'
1966 'They ride their broomsticks . . . prematurely hounding you out of your room . . . barging in without knocking . . . strict, sadistic . . . immune to "don't disturb" notices.'

1970   'Chambermaids are the worst harassers.'

1972   'To keep possession of your room after 8.30 becomes a trial of strength. The phalanx of bonneted viragos gather in the scullery ready for the fray at 8am.'

Perhaps we can derive consolation from the even worse routine of chambermaids in Russia. A report in *The Times* said:

1982   'At the crack of dawn a cleaning woman came in with a bucket, took one look and said "Carry on. You're not in my way."'

★ ★ ★

Searching for **fresh vegetables** in a restaurant was a hopeless quest until the late sixties. Prodding was our method to such an extent that in 1966 we announced the publication of a list in the following year's Guide reflecting all restaurants whose menu, under a separate heading, listed fresh vegetables. In 1967 this list contained 19 restaurants out of 1,005 – a small but worthwhile start.

1965   'Fraudulent and impertinent use of frozen vegetables . . . it reflects the chef's laziness, the management's indifference and the customers' gullibility.'

1966   'As to fresh vegetables, we shall fight on even if it may be a losing battle. There *are* fresh vegetables besides cauliflower in the solar system.'

1967   'The service of fresh vegetables for which we have been pleading for years seems to show a tiny improvement . . . a Scottish landlady told us she served fresh vegetables in order to give her customers a change from their home cooking!'

1969   'Now that we have started to use fresh vegetables, it is time we learnt how to cook them . . . drainworthy – though fresh – vegetables swimming in water, colourless and expensive.'

1972   'It is now normal to be told by the head waiter which vegetables are fresh.'

★ ★ ★

The absence of **fresh fruit** in eating places was just as inexplicable as the reluctance to serve fresh vegetables, even in the heart of the best vegetable and fruit growing regions.

1965   'The restaurateur is his own enemy by refusing to keep a fresh fruit basket.'

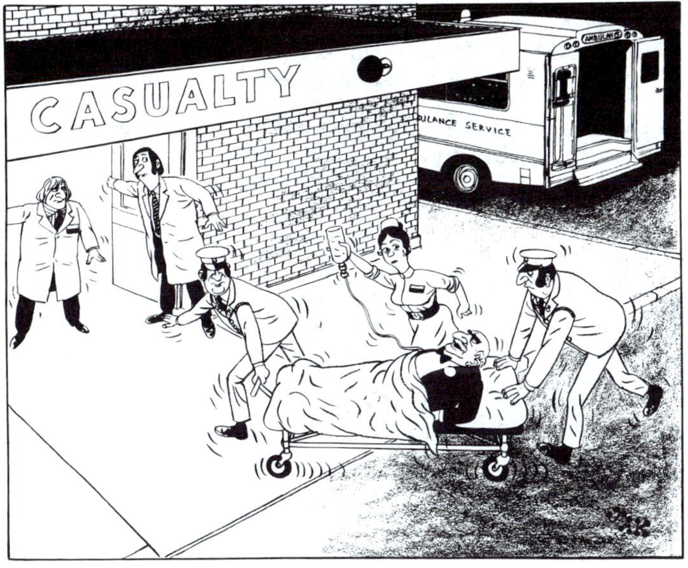

'Are you sure it's got the Egon Ronay seal of approval?'

★ ★ ★

In 1973 we decided to grasp a particularly difficult nettle and researched **food in hospitals**. We had to enlist the help of what was then called The Junior Hospital Doctors Association whose interest to help us lay in their own suffering from the same cooking. They facilitated our anonymous visits as their guests. Six years later we reverted to the subject and produced a second survey which diagnosed no improvements. However, it showed that there *were* one or two hospitals able to produce excellent fare on the standard budget. It is a sad reflection that even though the media concentrated its attention on this nationally important matter about which there was a widespread outcry and although the media backed our efforts, in the end hospital food stayed just as abominable, and patients still have nothing pleasant to look forward to, that will break the disheartening hospital routine.

★ ★ ★

1973   'Bad purchase ... unseasoned, overcooked, mushy vegetables ... poor, fatty, overcooked or dried out meat ... inedible and indigestible liver ... puddings worst of all ... food of nauseating appearance ... insensitivity towards the psychological aspect so important for the sick ... the Ministry has a duty to half a million patients a day.'

1979   'General improvements can be made without substantial increases in expenditure.'

We were very annoyed about comparisons that could be made between bath towels (if they could be called that) in this country and on the Continent: British **hotel towels** used to be just a laugh.

1966   'If hotel management realised the amount of bad blood created by tatty and tiny bath towels, they wouldn't squeeze the last thread out of their linen.'

1967   'Bath towels are notoriously small and leave one shivering as well as wet.'

1980   'Could raging inflation (talking of cost cutting) lead to hotel guests dripping at brakfast?'

★ ★ ★

The inbred reluctance of restaurateurs to abandon traditional routine, however useless, is amazing–nowhere more apparent than in the absurd **pricing of wines**. The whole force of public opinion is by now against the suicidal habit of adding a minimum of 100 per cent irrespective of the purchase price. Wine turnover in restaurants could easily double if a more intelligent pricing policy were adopted and customers were not discouraged from drinking better wines.

1963   'Restaurants are the worst enemies of their own wine turnover ... nonsensical pricing policy ... the price of British Transport Hotel wines is a national scandal.'

1964   'There is no logical reason why restaurateurs should expect 30 shillings profit on a bottle bought for 30 shillings when they are satisfied with 10 shillings profit on those bought for 10 shillings and just as costly to handle and store.'

1972   'Carafe wines have been devalued in quality, revalued in price and are unrewarding to order.'

It only needed one year's highlighting of some uncomfortable, sagging, narrow **hotel beds** to draw the press's attention to this problem. Articles and cartoons abounded and improvements soon became evident.

1965   'Too many hotel beds are out of date and sub-standard.'

★ ★ ★

The traditional reputation of **hotel breakfasts** many years ago turned into traditional disrepute: alas, it has become worse and worse. The only catering place where you can get a really good old English breakfast and consume it in comfort is at a pub.

1964   'The general state of breakfast at hotels is deplorable . . . poorly laid, cheap trays, disgusting and undrinkable coffee, cold and leathery toast.'

1966   'The high quality of the English hotel breakfast is a myth. It is abysmally bad, with bad coffee, low quality marmalade or jam, half the essentials left off the tray.'

1970   'Hotel breakfast is one of the heavier crosses we have to bear on our inspections.'

1982   'Even machines should be fed with decent tea . . . help-yourself breakfast is a sadly spreading practice.'

★ ★ ★

A relatively less important part of breakfast, however, has improved over the years. You can now obtain **fresh orange juice** for breakfast.

1964   'Tinned and nasty fruit juices.'

1966   'Always tinned fruit juice . . . there is no excuse for not serving *fresh* orange juice or grapefruit juice in a hotel.'

★ ★ ★

It has been a constant source of annoyance that one cannot make oneself understood in one's own country as far as restaurant waiters are concerned. In spite of the high unemployment figures, it is still **difficult to recruit British staff.** While the British have now started to change their minds about being employed in the catering industry, this is limited to an interest in the higher echelons: if a British person seeks employment in the catering industry, he wants to be a manager.

1966   'Even though there is an acute staff shortage, one wonders about the wisdom of employing staff without the slightest knowledge of even pidgin English.'

1969   'The Ministry of Labour insists that no waiter can be employed without four years' experience abroad but it would also be helpful to subject the applicant to a two-minute language test at British Consulates.'

1970   'Foreign waiters are loud, undisciplined and ignorant of the simple courtesies partly because of their scant knowledge of English . . . wine waiting is a shambles, with Italian sommeliers at the bottom of the heap.'

1973   'Employers have to fall back on the untrained dregs of society.'

1977   'School leavers cannot get jobs yet caterers have to make do with Mediterranean stable boys stuck into striped T-shirts and called waiters. Thanks to catering colleges and universities we have plenty of conductors but members of their orchestras can only whistle.'

1981   'Waiting skills on the level of farm hands with no English.'

★ ★ ★

One of the earliest objections we had was to **table-lamps** and **cooking at the table**. Nowadays the situation is reversed and it has become an excellent habit to dish out the food in the kitchen and, according to the tenets of nouvelle cuisine, to present a pretty plate of food.

1962   'It is heartbreaking how head waiters prostitute crêpes Suzette and sadistically burn them at the stakes of abominable table-lamps.'

1963   'Many a gastronomic highlight must have burnt out on abominable table-lamps . . . the mesmerised public lets itself be impressed by purposeless jiggery-pokery . . . head waiters run amok and flame everything they can lay their hands on . . . if chefs saw waiters and apprentices tamper with the result of skill and art, the relationship between kitchen and waiting staff would be even worse than it traditionally is.'

★ ★ ★

It is difficult to recall that years ago it was practically impossible to get a decent cup of **coffee** after a meal but even today the widespread espresso coffee is as unpalatably bitter as it is strong—not a patch on its Italian counterpart.

1966   'It is absurd that the two simple rules of using enough coffee and making it frequently during mealtimes are ignored by nine out of ten caterers.'

1972   'The main problem is stewing: it is not freshly made.'

★ ★ ★

The controversial question of obligatory **service charges** has become something of a hobby-horse of the annual 'Summing up' chapters. Very early on we thought it an anomaly that one should find a service charge on one's bill even when service was bad or non-existent. Tipping according to the level of service received seemed then – and still does to us – a much better method but the public, too lazy to work out how much to tip, prefers the obligatory system which is now irreversible.

There is still a problem, however: some of the items under 'service charge' are simply pocketed by the management.

1965 'Obligatory service charge is an abomination. The public must refuse to be dictated to and refuse to pay unless it is justified by the service.'

1969 'Abolishing tipping is tantamount to increasing prices by the tips that will be left just the same.'

1973 'Service charges are conducive to staff complacency . . . charges are often embezzled by those managements which don't distribute them fully.'

We were never able to accept the harmful reputation lent to this country's catering by the abysmal food served at **tourist centres**. When we researched them thoroughly, particularly in London, the shameful discoveries made front page headlines and the abhorrence was widespread.

1976 'The Department of the Environment did not exercise effective supervision and control of the standards of food and service though they have the right to do so stipulated in the catering contracts. The Department said "it doesn't come into it because the conditions are in the Lease and we are dealing with organisations experienced in this field".'

1978 'Crowds eat with apparent satisfaction and with no complaints . . . the public gets the catering it is prepared to accept.'

With no other campaign have we achieved results comparable with the one waged over **motorway cafés**. By no means all places have improved but many of them have out of all recognition and to the satisfaction of millions of motorists. The public interest was so great that it led to the setting up of the Prior Commission of Inquiry.

1964 'Ministry of Transport policy goes by bank balances instead of proven catering standards when tenders are sifted.'

1967 'Big chains with gold-mining concessions must really be pulled up by the Ministry of Transport who should exercise their right and duty in supervision . . . filthy state of some motorway restaurants.'

'Have you made a reservation?'

1972 'They are the nadir of British catering–not one of them would merit inclusion as a restaurant in the Guide.'

1975 'No systematic improvements in motorway catering until the Department of the Environment concerns itself seriously with the standard of food.'

1978 'Most of the food is dreadful.'

All these years some horrifying details were realistically reflected in the write-up of individual motorway service areas.

Worldwide interest of unexpected proportions was aroused by our survey of **airline food**. We flew each transatlantic airline between this country and North America three times. A league table of airlines was the result and we took them vividly to task for the horrors they served up. Great improvements took place thanks to the media interest focused on the problems and sustained for months.

1980 The lot of air passengers is a dismal one. Why don't airlines limit themselves to a few carefully thought out dishes that will stand the inevitable culinary punishment?'

Our advocacy, for three consecutive years, of **government loans** for the building and improving of hotels was the forerunner of the government loan scheme for which the White Paper was published in 1968.

1965　'Prohibitively expensive money for development is to blame for high hotel prices ... short-sightedness of present and past governments.'

1966　'Once again we plead emphatically for government action. If the Government will not arrange cheaper money, long-term, interest free loans, or create tax and other incentives, our exports will suffer gravely. The Irish Republic has achieved excellent results with the policy we advocate.'

We criticised the government White Paper published in 1968 in the following year:

1969　'The loan schemes are not sweeping enough and are mingy: only immovable fixtures–bricks and mortar–must be built from loans and grants, no improvements are allowed for decor and other creature comforts. We hope restaurants will be included in this new scheme.'

★ ★ ★

On the other hand we seemed to remain helpless concerning **hotel prices**.

1965　'London is the world's most expensive hotel capital if you compare value for value.'

1978　'Unrealistic increase of prices (for the Jubilee) to capitalise on conditions ... the UK will earn the reputation for being overpriced and no longer affordable by tourists.'

1981　'Who will be the Laker of the hotel industry and take the lead in reducing London's hotel prices?'

★ ★ ★

Perhaps our inability to stem the deterioration in **room service** in hotels is not surprising as it is a worldwide trend caused by rocketing overheads.

1976　'A hotel manager when asked whether room service was provided said "You had better say it isn't in case it is expected."'

1978　'The depersonalisation of hotel service: kettles instead of early morning tea service ... we seem to accept this meekly.'

1982　'We are reluctant to rate hotels with no porterage as Grade One ...'

★ ★ ★

We can still not put up with the decline of **sweets**. Contrary to belief, it is not calorie consciousness that causes it but false economies in reducing overheads.

1966   'The almost total absence of sweets, substituted by a
       miserable list of ice-cream concoctions.'
1972   'What has become of puddings? Ice-cream is the ubiquitous
       and often only theme for variations.'
1980   'The abundance of sweet trolleys is in inverse proportion to
       the quality of desserts. It reflects the British customer as a
       gastronomic voyeur rather than a discerning eater . . . we
       wish also that more hot sweets were available.'
1982   'Conspicuous lack of imagination on sweet trolleys, many of
       which have disappeared altogether and have been replaced
       by gastronomically invalid and not home-made ice-cream
       combinations.'

★ ★ ★

Our plea to introduce **table d'hôte** meals more widely was taken up
by the trade press and bore good results in 1982, so much so that it
almost amounted to a general reduction in restaurant prices.

1981   'The feeling of security imparted by an all-inclusive price
       works wonders. The new pricing policy in some restaurants
       (examples were quoted) led to a full house daily. Table
       d'hôte prices can be a magnet. This year we give prominence
       to set meal prices in entries.'

★ ★ ★

We have always felt strongly about monopolistic catering situations,
so we could not have left out **food at airports**. Surprisingly, it proved to
be a more difficult nut to crack than motorways.

1975   'The British Airports Authority, just as its opposite number
       in respect of motorways, does not exercise effective
       supervision and control of food and service, though it has
       the duty to do so according to caterers' contracts.'
1982   In a comparative survey of European airports–'Almost
       every airport is let to a single catering company which is as
       outdated as it would be to have a single caterer for all cafés,
       restaurants, pubs and bars in–say–Gravesend.'

★ ★ ★

Another monopolistic situation exists, of course, on Channel **ferries**
once you are on the boat. On the other hand the standard of food is as
good a reason as any to choose a particular line where there is a
selection.

1981   'Ferries resemble water borne bus stations . . . the standard
       of food so awful that it constitutes by far the worst aspect
       for a trip by ferry . . . anything will do for the captive
       customer . . . take our advice: take your own.'

Sad to report, our attack on **battery chicken**, sustained over the years, was perhaps a lost cause from the start. Big business and the public's complacency are to blame, although, to mention two examples, Sainsbury's and Marks & Spencer can still supply chickens for which they prescribe sanity in feeding as well as rearing conditions.

1962   'For years we have not come across a single dish of decent roast chicken—to the glory, no doubt, of chicken manufacturing batteries.'

1964   'Oh, for the days of natural chicken ... we invite restaurants to come forward and state if they use free-range birds.'
1966   'The tasteless, soft, wet wood-shavings that stick to something resembling chicken bones.'
1968   'Chicken is a forgotten taste ... turned out of eerie batteries, tasting of wet cottonwool.'

★ ★ ★

There were numerous other causes for which we fought, even if not in what can be called a full-blown campaign. We tried to persuade **hotels** that it is not absolutely essential to **run their own restaurants** or even to *have* a traditional restaurant if they cannot ensure high standards. We pinpointed one of the many reasons for the **low quality of food at hotels** as opposed to independent restaurants. We decried the absence of **room-charge displays**, before these became obligatory. But in vain did we object to the now widespread rule in so many hotels of having to **pay in advance**.

We drew attention to the cross that businessmen **leaving hotels early in the morning** have to bear. 'Is it beyond the capability of hotels to organise two, three or more cashier points to avoid nerve-racking queues?', and as recently as 1982 we complained about hotels advertising a **reduction** for customers who are employees of **corporations and companies**. This is tantamount to punishing individual hotel guests.

In 1971 we urged the radical relaxation of **licensing laws**, and the general interest in **real ale** came many years after we had started to be active in this field. The disgusting and dangerous way in which **glasses** are **washed up** in pubs has *always* revolted us.

★ ★ ★

But with all our criticism and castigation there was never any doubt left that we are trying to help restaurateurs by being **constructive**. Our criticism has never been generalised and has always tried to pinpoint where the fault lay. From the beginning we said:

1963 'Generalisations about low standards of British catering are irresponsible, misinformed and unjust. Those who make the accusations are guilty of indifference about where they eat and what they order.'

★ ★ ★

After a quarter of a century of scourging mediocrity and incompetence, it is satisfying to record that about half of our campaigns were successful. Our consolation for the efforts spent on battles we have lost is that perhaps some have lit a long fuse.

"Watch it — someone else with a touch of the old Egon Ronays .."

A DAY IN THE LIFE OF AN INSPECTOR

Hello. My name's Tim Broadbent, and I've got the best job in the world—well, so everyone tells me. 'You do *what?*' I hear them cry, incredulous. '*Eat?*—for a *living?* Gerraway.'

This particular morning, though, I'd be hard put to agree with their appraisal of life as one of Egon Ronay's full-time hotel and restaurant inspectors. A dismal Tuesday in February is not the ideal time to wake up in a North Wales holiday resort, and having arrived here last night after driving up from one of the regular inspectors' meetings (held at the London office to discuss current trends, new 'finds', successes and disappointments), I'm afraid I must disagree with the readers who recommended this establishment. *They* may have had 'the time of their lives' among 'friendly staff' and 'lived it up' on 'super food that was very reasonably priced', but I hardly think the majority of our readers would have been happy with 'French Onion Soup' (fresh from the packet), 'Chef's Pâté' (which Barbara Woodhouse's canine pupils would have shunned) and 'Beuof Stroggernorf' (*sic*) accompanied by yesterday's frozen vegetables—which had since been simmering quietly on the corner of a stove! You really do wonder sometimes if you're in the right place.

As for the 'friendly staff', they've made me feel a perfect nuisance ever since I got here: I've only just elicited enough information from the 'receptionist' to find my room, I've been turfed out of the dining room ''cos when it's quiet I likes to get orf early' and I've prevented persistently knocking chamberpersons from carrying out their duties this morning by staying in bed 'til nearly half past 8, silly me! And the carpets have had an argument with the skirting boards; and the furniture hasn't been replaced since the coupons ran out in 1948; and there's no hot water with which to fill the cracked washbasin; and no, I don't want someone else's soap; and yes, it was cold when the heating went off between 10 and 7. And worst of all, the telly wasn't working so I missed *Fawlty Towers*—obligatory viewing for everyone in the catering trade.

Ah well, you can't win 'em all, and on this occasion, I'll just pay up and be off, but all new recommendations are welcomed and followed through, forming an integral part of our programme of visits in addition to checking last year's entries.

Lunch is an hour's drive away–another new recommendation I see. I stop in a quiet lay-by to write a brief account of last night's experiences leading to the hotel's non-recommendation, as well as to fill out the all-important tally of expenses incurred (failure to do this has been known to result in terms of up to three months of surveying motorway service stations!). Paperwork complete, I'm soon tucking into minestrone (home-made and very good), spaghetti carbonara (the pasta nicely al dente and the sauce rich and creamy) and veal escalopes in a

"I THOUGHT YOU'D LIKE TO KNOW THAT EGON RONAY AND A FRIEND, DRESSED AS TRAMPS, INTEND VISITING YOUR CAFE SHORTLY!"

well-flavoured Marsala sauce, served with crisp, fresh vegetables and rounded off by a tangy lemon mousse–not at all outstanding, but a thoroughly worthy new entry. After settling the bill I introduce myself to the delighted Italian chef-patron. He'd written to us on opening the restaurant and asked for an anonymous visit (this is another way of finding possible new entries), and I collect details of opening times, etc., to send on to London with my report, menus and a wine list (for separate perusal by an expert in the field).

While on the road, we keep an eye out for possible 'chance' visits, not only for the *Hotel and Restaurant Guide*, but also for *Just a Bite* and the *Pub Guide*, and between lunch and checking into the hotel that I have booked tonight, it's worth stopping in a couple of towns en route to see what's about.

Bingo! Old Mrs Jones makes all her own featherlight cakes and crams freshly baked ham into home-made bread for a sandwich that's a meal in itself, washed down with generous pots of fresh tea and coffee. She's 'sort of heard of *Just a Bite*' but is amazed to think that we might be interested in her homely efforts, and although any comment on our part is strictly taboo, it's hard to hide a smile of approval of éclairs, florentines, fruit cake and cream sponges, all beautifully made.

So, after a poor start, the day is looking up. And tonight looks promising—an elegant country house hotel, currently highly rated and the restaurant starred last year; definitely an evening to look forward to. Thankfully I'm not disappointed as I sit alone, conspicuously perhaps, among the couples and parties in a sumptuous, panelled dining room, enjoying (oh yes, I still enjoy good food!) the four or five courses that usually make up a test meal. 'Aren't you ever recognised?' friends ask. Well, I probably was when on a particularly snowy Monday night I booked a table for one and then let it slip that I was driving 70 miles to sit at it. But the ability to cook won't suddenly manifest itself in people who can't cook, and if there is any doubt, a revisit can always be arranged.

Back upstairs, it's not quite time to relax—tomorrow's visits have to be planned. There's no lunch within striking distance, but a couple of pubs are on my list to be looked at, and I'll be drinking orange juice at them because there's a 100-odd-mile drive to tomorrow night's hotel and the end of another day. Typical? Well, there's not really any such thing, especially considering the more bizarre missions such as flying to Miami for one night as part of the transatlantic airline survey, or eating two curries a day for three weeks while compiling a list of ethnic entries. Today has been, shall we say, representative.

And now I think I've earned a nightcap, so I'll fall into one of those vast armchairs by the open fire, clutching a glass of something good, and maybe swop occupations with my fellow guests.

'Me? Oh, I've got the best job in the world.'

LAUNCHING LUNCHES

Never do things simply if you can complicate them.

This strikes me, in retrospect, as an appropriate motto for almost a quarter of a century of annual lunches to mark our publication days.

Not for us the straightforward banquet, the dull four courses, predictably bland at best. So, over the years, we have injected plenty of drama into the proceedings and so much excitement for ourselves that the annual panic stations before the event made us doubt, every year, whether we were quite sane to go through this trauma year after year – except that we love it.

One of the guests, making the trip annually from Paris, found the key at last year's event. He scrutinised the immensely complicated menu (see illustration), munched his successive courses and when I thought the oracle was about to make an enlightening gastronomic comment, he remarked: 'You like to live dangerously.'

In the faraway simple(?) days, all we did was to invite five chefs, each of whom was to prepare one of the five courses. Supervising their invasion of the host chef's domain now seems a relatively small difficulty. Even so, it needed an accomplished diplomat's skill to persuade one chef to do nothing but the soup and dissuade four from doing the main course.

As in gambling, we needed greater risks and bigger stakes every year.

Once we had five kitchens constructed overnight and the chefs performed under our very nose, with Wynford Vaughan Thomas giving a running commentary, skilfully reflecting the drama of cooking as things kept coming literally to the boil.

On one of these occasions we gathered our guests in five separate groups of tables adjoining each of the special kitchens. We made them get up after every course and move to tables near the next kitchen, so they could taste the cooking of each. Clement Freud startled one of the guests by asking, 'Haven't I met you in Glasgow?' It was a moment before she realised that the previous kitchen had been manned by a Glaswegian team.

But we had to edge still nearer the brink. Five chefs came with their teams from five European Common Market countries (France, Belgium, Italy, Germany, Denmark) to Gleneagles, where we trebled the traumas and turned the event into a thriller. Would all the chefs arrive in time? Would the ingredients, some of which they brought with them, be admitted by the customs? Would chef Deligne of the Taillevent in Paris meet with disaster? The 400 crayfish he had brought with him were obviously at the point of death when they arrived the day before the lunch. Their life was only prolonged by a brainwave: they were rushed to the nearby loch, plunged into it and kept there until next morning to die at the moment in accordance with predestination and gastronomy. It was an October day and the fog came down in London, preventing 100 guests from taking off on schedule. A miraculous break in the weather saved us from serving the fruits of immense labour to empty seats.

By this time the annual banquet had become completely divorced from the publicity angle, as it was held two or three days following the publication date, after the media showed its interest in the Guide's contents. The lunch became an obsessive act of gastronomic brinkmanship, but also a fixture in the London calendar impossible to abandon.

We wanted still more excitement and bravura, so we took over Maxim's beautiful public dining room in Paris and decided to take five British chefs right into the lion's den. We went over with the five teams for a rehearsal, and they were dismayed at the tiny size of Maxim's legendary kitchens. 'How can your 26 cooks work in such absurdly confined space?' I dejectedly asked Louis Vaudable, the proprietor. He explained: 'They are not chefs, they are acrobats.' We flew all 120 guests from London to Paris, and it proved to be our most successful lunch yet, though many a French eyebrow was raised by the presence of a woman chef (from Devon) as well as the resounding Scottish bagpipes piping the company into the dining room, not to mention the superbly good cooking.

As if this hadn't been enough, we have since added a further multiple twist to the formula. For the last two years we have constructed four different menus, which would have been simple enough, except that each of the four teams prepared a complete four-course meal and the guests, divided into four groups, were served the first course from one team, the second course from another—and so on. Sixteen dishes not only had to be the teams' specialities, but had to fit, like a jigsaw puzzle, into four menus to make gastronomic sense. And just to add a little further embellishment, we chose 12 wines at several wine tastings so that each of the four menus could be accompanied by three different wines, plus the champagne aperitif and the Armagnac. (See the menu for our 1981 launching on pages 104–5.)

The thing has grown into a monster and it is fascinating, not to say frightening, how it has acquired its own momentum, like a computer run berserk.

Now just to develop the thing further, we thought that next year we might....

KEY

Chef/patron Jean-Louis Taillebaud
Interlude de Tabaillau, London

Chef Christian Delteil
Chewton Glen Hotel, New Milton, Hampshire

Chef/patronne Sonia Stevenson
The Horn of Plenty, Gulworthy, Devon

Chefs/patrons Malcolm Reid & Colin Long
Box Tree, Ilkley, West Yorkshire

WINES

Mumm Crémant de Cramant, Blanc de Blancs

Chardonnay 1977, *Estate bottled, Alexander Valley Vineyards*

Corton Clos de la Vigne au Saint 1972 *(Prosper Maufoux)*

Forster Ungeheuer Riesling Beerenauslese 1976
Erzeugerabfüllung Gutsverwaltung Deinhard

Grande Fine Armagnac, *Janneau*, 1939

Bolivar Havana Cigars

CO-ORDINATED BY

Chef de Cuisine: Bernard Gaume

Maître d'Hôtel: Jean Quéro

Menu I

Consommé de pigeon sauvage forestière

Médaillons de sole à la mousse de cresson

L'agneau en tranches à la Mauleon

Timbale de fraises Box Tree

Menu II

Potage de laitue au lard

Dariole de homard cardinal

Magret de canard au vinaigre de framboise

Parfait glacé Louise Bavouzet

Menu III

Dodine de poulet de Bresse pistachée

Bar de Cornouaille, sauce moutarde

Pigeonneau de Bresse au ragoût d'escargots

Marquise au chocolat sauce café

Menu IV

Salade de chasse vigneronne

Gâteau de cuisses de grenouilles à l'estragon

Noisette d'agneau Edouard VII

Crème brûlée aux pommes

Table Manners

The distinguished historian, the late James Laver, who linked fashions with the social and economic events of the times, duly noting such facts as the effects of war and the temporary dominance of one sex or the other, might well have found a similar relationship concerning food in this country—especially as regards the changes in restaurants.

Since the Second World War, and at an increased pace over the past 25 years, a transformation has taken place almost unawares, so that we are surprised to find just how much change we have accepted; and this pattern has exactly followed social and economic changes and certainly recognises a growing part played by women, who now own and run a growing number of restaurants at many levels.

It was, of course, the war which shook us up—not surprisingly. With its ending, there was a longing for gaiety and colour after the blackout, the rationing, the ubiquitous rubble and the stress of determined cheerfulness. Above all, we wanted relaxation. And where does one relax more completely than over a good meal? Especially, I may add, as a woman, without the cooking and the washing-up!

The first impact (which eventually affected the restaurant world profoundly) was *colour*. Visiting Norway immediately after hostilities ceased, I found them painting everything in pale, sky colours. 'Space, freedom, peacefulness,' one of the paint manufacturers explained. The British, who had not been occupied, were more stimulating in their tastes. Out went the faded red plush of many an establishment that had maintained the same decor since Edwardian days: in came almost anything cheerful, not always tasteful, to say the least.

The Festival of Britain had many results, with a lot of new ideas emerging. Out, for instance, went the standard thick white dinner plate.

Grander establishments had always known how to use delicate design and colour in their tableware; and Wedgwood, doyen of the direction of good taste to its rightful place, already supplied, for example, the Berkeley and the Savoy, including the River Room, and some of the grand old shipping lines such as the Orient, often with exclusive designs. (Also many humbler establishments, some of which could be found in the first Egon Ronay guide.) But there was not, in the first few years, a rush towards good taste—rather a gradual, often timid experimentation.

Then things moved. The public began to go abroad; and a much wider section of the nation got new ideas. Wine began to be enjoyed to a much greater extent, and many a home sported a Mateus rosé bottle lamp on the table. The restaurants sprouted colour in tableware, cloths and napkins (and also began to use PAPER!).

But the important factor in the change was the explosive growth of a new public which wanted to eat out.

With recovery, there also began to be much more money about. Women were increasingly earners in their own right, and the idea of a 'meal out' was no longer an 'occasion' but was becoming a pleasant habit cutting right through class. Travel certainly taught us. Slackish member of the EEC we may be; but we have taken to our bosoms (or, more accurately, our stomachs) habits, customs and food from the dreaded foreigner, to our benefit . Not so much to our benefit perhaps, though convenient at times, has been increasing informality in the dress of the diners. Jeans go to strange places nowadays.

Until this new way of eating out began, the restaurant world was dominated by the French, with quarters like Soho supplying the other culinary varieties. To a large extent, this is still true today; the French way with food is classic and conservative,

Continued

The 'Sultan' design in Wedgwood bone china hotelware highlights the fine cuisine and atmosphere in the restaurant of the Plough & Harrow Hotel, Birmingham. The hotel received the 1981 Hotel of the Year Award presented by Egon Ronay's Lucas Guide.

In the picture, from left, are Oscar Bassam, Restaurant Manager, John Sweeney, Chef de Cuisine, and Mario de Freitas, Sommelier.

no matter that the 'nouvelle cuisine' has its adherents; and the owner, not his customers, decides on the surroundings and appurtenances. 'Plus ça change' remains the motto.

The first major postwar invaders in ethnic cuisine were the Italians–their arrival did not only affect food. First came the dark *trattoria*, plus fishing nets, the inevitable Chianti flask (which did that wine's image no good), dark beams and a general cosiness that made for an ideal family outing. No sooner had we got used to that than Apicella brought in cool white walls and trailing plants. One of the pleasures of Italian food presentation is the beautiful way they have with vegetable arrangements–and I often wonder to what extent these displays have influenced a growing demand for well-designed, fine quality tableware for home use.

Here we come to the most dramatic alteration in the restaurant world– service, its character and its personnel. Who remembers, with perhaps more affection nostalgically than at the time, the pre-war waiter? Permanently bent in service, dinner jacket somewhat splashed except in the grander establishments, rather cravenly anxious to please and, round the corner often, alas, given to careless hygiene–why did we love him so? He did try and he was an oppressed race, dependent on our largesse, in the days when 'Service' on the bill did not represent a compulsory Danegeld.

The transition has been complete. Largely due to those first Italian invaders, dressed in anything from white shirts and black bow-ties above elegantly tight trousers, to fishermen, gondoliers and bandits, costume for waiters has been transformed, at least in anywhere that can be called informal. On the whole, it is good, because it is friendly, merry and pretty efficient, as becomes a race who like their food and regard the ideal restaurant as an extension of the home; and there still remain those muchloved figures of old Soho, where the foreign waiter has always set the pattern. Observe that the English waiter has almost disappeared in for-

mal surroundings. He survives in majesty where majesty is still apparent. Sometimes the extrovert is rather too prominent. What would the serious Edwardian diner have done about the 'singing waiter' or the often abominable Muzak? I hate to think–or to listen.

The mass opening of restaurants with distinctly national cooking, from about 25 years ago, is something we have taken in our stride. The remarkable thing about some of them is the rise in status. What was once a place or cuisine generally associated with students is now likely to be highly regarded and patronised by those with conservative tastes and no need to find bargains. Many of these restaurants, which include those with Greek, Indian and Pakistani, Chinese and South-east Asian cuisine, have created charming and imaginative surroundings and adopted good table furnishings. Many, including excellent French and Italian speciality groups, use–yes, Wedgwood.

Incidentally, a brief look overseas reveals that more and more hotels and restaurants–from Canada and Switzerland to Japan and Australia– are using this 225-year-old English company's tableware. Over 60 per cent of production at the Staffordshire factory is exported, and Wedgwood is increasingly popular with airlines concerned with improving in-flight passenger comfort.

Returning to Britain–so far, I have been thinking mostly of 'feet under the table' places. Changing times bring changing manners; so do changing pockets. Recession following on affluence has affected life styles sharply; so, while good restaurants survive, the wine bar, which has arrived and flourished during the past ten years, has widened the choice for sociable souls with limited means. A choice of wine by the glass or the bottle, and something to go with it, has proved a pretty good formula and a bit of Laver-like evidence.

Having evolved into something entirely British, not quite the Austrian heuriger, not the pavement café and quite different from the hamburger bar

Continued

Wedgwood bone china tableware is to be found in many of the hotels and restaurants featured in the 1983 Egon Ronay's Lucas Guide. Most of these establishments use the company's specially created hotelware, but some have chosen designs from the collection of slightly finer bone china which is available to the general consumer in retail outlets. For example, 'Bianca', top left' is used at the Maison Talbooth, Dedham, and the Oliver Restaurant, Harrogate; 'Westbury', bottom right, is in the Four Seasons Restaurant at London's Inn on the Park, and 'Hathaway Rose', top right, enhances afternoon tea at Brown's Hotel, also in London.

Distinctive 'Insignia' fluted shapes were introduced for hotel and restaurant use in 1980. So many people wanted to buy this tableware for use at home that four patterns, including 'Gardenian Insignia', bottom left, are now available from Wedgwood Rooms in department stores.

or the international pizzeria, the wine bar is a very civilised place. It varies from the near-pub to the elegant, and while the psychologist might find something interesting in varying decors, the criminologist could have only one idea as to why the plain white dinner plate is back (albeit, perhaps, bearing a famous name), where the lighting is often low and service often 'self'.

Not that the customer always lacks enterprise, as a true happening in one of London's most prestigious hotels demonstrates. This hotel has rather lovely silver serving plates (the sort that are removed when the first course arrives). One day, the hall porter noticed that a departing guest looked a little stout around the chest. There was a clatter as he reached the revolving door and out fell two of these decorative objects. 'Sir,' cried the porter, rushing forward, 'I can't possibly allow you to take these away not properly wrapped.' He propelled the guest to his desk, carefully tied up the plates—and presented the bill.

One of the best buys I ever made was at a sale—a complete dinner set of Mason's Ironstone for exactly £3. (It was a long time ago!) A lot still survives and—impressed by its magnificent strength—I made enquiries, to discover the pattern is still available and that the company is now in the Wedgwood Group. I had already discovered that a high proportion of the bone china used in restaurants, of all levels, bore 'Wedgwood' on the base; and I make no secret of the fact that I defy manners and turn plates up, since they are very relevant now that we cannot buy fine dinner services for £3—even in a sale!

The ubiquity of Wedgwood bone china commercially is almost certainly because of its superb property for wear. Bone china, correctly made, is the strongest of all ceramic bodies—and one of the oldest firms in the business has, since 1759, acquired a great deal of know-how.

Today, technology has enabled the manufacture of bone china hotelware, which is slightly thicker than the normal product. Its strength would endear it to anyone in the catering business, where, perhaps, beautiful design alone might not; but the company, which has always been motivated by what one can only call enlightened self-interest, has had the brilliant idea of offering exclusive designs to its patrons. (Look under your plate next time a design pleases you in a restaurant.)

Wedgwood started, like all the best enterprises, as a family business and the old traditions persist. It is not sentimentality but good business that the company cares for the customer's satisfaction, that it pioneers design and technically inclined achievements, and is always on the lookout for possible improvement—all practices initiated by the founder, Josiah Wedgwood I, the 'father of English potters'. I am personally much interested in the encouragement of good design allied to practical purposes. 'Top Fifty' inscribed china plaques, awarded to just 50 caterers worldwide in alternate years, are one of the company's interests. They are given to those customers who provide outstanding gastronomic excellence, at acceptable prices, with consistently high standards of presentation and service in pleasant surroundings. I am happy to report that my own consistent favourite got one, confirming my high view of Wedgwood's good judgement and good taste! So, although my brief was *not* to write a 'plug' for this famous house, I cannot refrain from putting in three cheers for the Potteries in general, since that is near where I was born—and for Wedgwood in particular—and may enlightened self-interest never wane.

Peta Fordham

(*on behalf of Josiah Wedgwood & Sons Limited*)

The Basil Street Hotel in London has an old-world charm. Ted Kowalski, foreground, has been Maître d'Hôtel since 1945 in the restaurant overlooking the Brompton Road and in which the 'Tresco' pattern in Wedgwood bone china hotelware is used.

SURVEY OF THEATRE BUFFETS & RESTAURANTS

SUMMARY

Theatre managers have a captive audience and they are taking advantage of them.

In this country we are lucky enough to have some of the finest and most civilised theatres in the world—yet the standards of theatre catering are deplorable. Overseas visitors, who think so highly of our artistic enterprise, are apt to reach the wrong conclusion in general about this country's catering.

Glyndebourne is a case in point: with guests paying something like £25 per head for a meal with wine in the blatantly ostentatious restaurant, it isn't surprising that many choose to take with them their picnic baskets and eat the traditional alfresco meal.

Some new municipal theatres, like Plymouth, are at least making an effort, but it's by no means completely successful; too often, though, catering comes bottom of their list—a dismal afterthought hardly worth considering.

The symptoms of this national malaise are chronic in every sense of the word: there's far too much reliance on inferior products (bought-in pâtés, quiches and, above all, sweets are the main culprits, although the Royal Shakespeare Theatre at Stratford does have the distinction of providing home-made puddings); vegetables are almost always dreadful in every way and service is perfunctory. There must be scores of small caterers who could do the job more successfully, and it's a telling irony that the only two theatres rated 'Good' in our survey—the Greenwich and the Lyric—did their own catering.

Speed and efficiency are the prime considerations, the theory being that people who eat in theatre restaurants have no time for a leisurely meal. So a minimum effort is expended on preparation, dishes are reheated and rehashed to save time and costs, and there's definitely no place for cooking to order.

But even when the food is modest—just a few sandwiches or quiches—it has no right to be awful. We don't expect haute cuisine or imagine that every theatre chef should aspire to artistry, but it is not much to ask for fresh, well-prepared food, even if it is intended for a quick bite between acts. We hope that this survey will give theatre catering managers pause for thought; perhaps they will realise that it isn't good enough to offer their patrons indifferent or inedible food, and that eating at the theatre should be a satisfying, enjoyable experience.

OUR RESEARCH METHOD

Two members of our regular team of professional inspectors researched the catering facilities in theatres in London and the provinces for four weeks during June and July.

In London we inspected those theatres offering anything from just a piece of quiche to those that served full meals. In the provinces we concentrated only on those theatres that provide a full restaurant service.

Having tested a total of 295 items of food, we have classified establishments as 'Good' (2); 'Acceptable' (13); 'Poor' (15); 'Appalling' (7). The two theatres whose catering qualified as 'Good' were both informal buffets. None of the theatre restaurants would qualify for recommendation in this Guide.

London Theatres

Appalling

Aldwych Theatre Aldwych, WC2
Rock-bottom in more ways than one, this grubby little basement bar shows scant regard for personal comfort and no interest in providing pleasant or wholesome food. As the cheesecake and quiche on the menu hadn't arrived, we were left with only a choice of tasteless pre-wrapped sandwiches.

Poor

Barbican Bistro Barbican Centre, EC2
Integrated with the Waterside Café, this is a completely characterless room, and the food on display is really not to be recommended. The pâté was not only greasy and unpleasant, but horrendously overpriced at £1·25 for half a slice; the cold chicken was bland, the ham dry, the quiche heavy. At least the salads looked colourful, but sadly lacked any flavour or individuality.

Acceptable

Barbican, Cut-Above Restaurant Barbican Centre, EC2
Don't take the name too seriously, even though this striking, colourfully designed restaurant is the gastronomic jewel of the Barbican; the food is uneven, with modest peaks but also with much that is badly prepared or disappointing. We found the minestrone harshly flavoured, vegetables handled without care and the cold table a very tired display of what looked like yesterday's meats, and dull salads, not to mention a sweet trolley that was really dreadful. But there were favourable points, like the creamy smoked salmon mousse and the succulent roasts from the carvery. So, enjoy the view, choose carefully, but don't expect too much in the way of culinary expertise.

Poor

Barbican, Waterside Café Barbican Centre, EC2
If it wasn't for the impressive terracing, fountains and ponds outside, you might be deceived into thinking that you were in a motorway café, with its lurid plastic-laminate decor, inept service and anonymous atmosphere. The food is dismal, too, and we had to endure tasteless Southern-fried chicken, watery plaice and gritty, unappetising chilli con carne. Only enormous wholemeal baps packed with salad saved the day, and from our experience it's best to finish with fresh fruit salad rather than risk the perils of leaden cheesecake or rough ginger sponge. The Barbican really should be able to do better than this.

Good

Greenwich Theatre, Crowder's Buffet Crooms Hill, SE10
Bare boards, Victorian lampshades and colourful prints give this buffet the informal atmosphere of a wine bar, with food to match. Forget the commercial pâté, sausage rolls and pasties and settle for a home-made hot dish like mildly spiced pork curry, delicious cheese and onion quiche or excellent pink roast beef with fresh, colourful salads. A hunk of well-kept

Continued

Stilton is also infinitely preferable to tasteless bought-in gâteaux. Only offhand service mars the pleasure of eating here.

Poor

Hampstead Theatre Club Swiss Cottage Centre, NW3
The activity in the tiny bar suggests that this is a lively, well-supported theatrical concern. Pre-show drinks obviously come first, but there are various sandwiches with fillings like cream cheese and green pepper or salmon and cucumber. Useful only if you are desperately hungry.

Poor

King's Head Theatre Club 115 Upper Street, N1
Arrive by seven if you want a meal before the show at this intimate theatre behind a lively old pub. The menu offers a dish of the day plus a few starters and sweets, and the food does have its good points: our tender chicken was served with a very pleasant creamy mushroom sauce and the vegetable quiche had a reasonable flavour, although it suffered from being kept warm for too long. But vegetables were dreadfully overcooked and the fresh fruit salad was a very basic affair, showing its age and with a dreadful topping.

Good

Lyric Theatre Buffet King Street, W6
On summer evenings you can unwind on the terrace, away from the buzz of activity inside this pleasant, contemporary-style buffet. The quality of the food is generally good, although the undoubted stars of the show are the freshly prepared, imaginative salads like refreshing mint and cucumber or delightful watercress with sultanas and strawberries. We also enjoyed robust pea and ham soup, creamy spinach quiche and a plentiful helping of tasty cannelloni, as well as rich chocolate gâteau. In all, a very useful place for hungry theatregoers.

Poor

National Theatre, Box Office Buffet SE1
Lack of seating space in the entrance hall of the National Theatre complex means that you will probably be forced to eat standing up. The food is an uninspired selection of basic rolls and sandwiches, so-called Danish pastries (a world away from the real thing) and cheesecake, plus watery tea and stale coffee.

Poor

National Theatre, Cottesloe Buffet SE1
No more than a little snack counter tucked in one corner of the entrance to the Cottesloe, this buffet offers a very limited selection of dull sandwiches, fresh fruit and confectionery. As dismal coffee and cold milk are the only drinks available, it's not surprising that the bar is a much more popular venue.

Acceptable

National Theatre, Lyttleton Buffet SE1
Savoury pies and pâtés on the colourful display of cold dishes here look more interesting than they taste, but salads are generally crisp and reasonably seasoned, and cakes are acceptable providing they're fresh. Coffee is a better bet than tea.

Acceptable

National Theatre, Olivier Buffet SE1
A view of the Thames provides distraction here, and there's a good choice of food available. Run-of-the-mill sandwiches, nondescript quiche and bland chicken pie were hardly memorable, but the apple pie was pleasant, with a nice filling and crisp firm pastry. The tea was like awful murky water and bore no resemblance to the national beverage.

Acceptable

National Theatre Restaurant SE1
Masses of grey concrete and plate glass plus surly staff combine to make this a cold, unwelcoming restaurant where the food, though grandly styled, is no more than acceptable. Good-quality meats like veal steak, rack of lamb and

duck are well cooked but their natural flavour is overwhelmed by anonymous brown saucing, and other dishes like seafood chowder and trout stuffed with fish mousse are rather bland. Vegetables are awful in every respect.

Appalling

New London Theatre Bar Drury Lane, WC2

A theatre that can bask in the glory of productions like *Cats* really ought to offer its patrons something better than soggy mass-produced quiche—the *only* sustenance available in the stylish first-floor bar. Treat yourself to a box of chocolates instead.

Acceptable

Riverside Studios Restaurant Crisp Road, W6

Riverside Studios is a hive of artistic activity, but the quality of food available in the ground-floor restaurant seems to have slipped. It's all very rustic and down-to-earth, with dishes like spicy vegetable curry and well-dressed salads outshining underseasoned turnip and potato soup, bland spinach quiche and cloying cheesecake. And a smile from the surly waitresses would work wonders.

Poor

Round House Chalk Farm Road, NW1

Renowned as a bastion of the avant-garde and a centre for new trends, the Round House is disappointing and predictable when it comes to food. The choice is pedestrian to say the least, and although much is freshly bought-in, the overall quality is poor: bland chicken and ham pie with leaden pastry, tasteless asparagus quiche, watery rice salad and dull, unseasoned cottage pie.

Appalling

Royal Court Theatre Circle Bar Sloane Square, SW1

The more controversial productions at the Royal Court may make the headlines, but there's nothing memorable or noteworthy about the abysmal offerings available in the drab, dirty Circle Bar. All we found were a few slices of heavy, indigestible cheesecake and miserably brewed tea. Dramatic doings clearly get top priority here.

Acceptable

Royal Opera House Crush Bar Betterton Street, WC2

Founded on the belief that great art should be performed in graceful and elegant surroundings, Covent Garden is a paragon of civilised virtues. So it's surprising that the Crush Bar should serve a basically mundane selection of cold food: crisp salads with plump king prawns, rare roast beef and rather dry smoked trout, nice sandwiches and reasonable sweets. Service is helpful and efficient.

Acceptable

Sadlers Wells Buffet 369 St John's Street, EC1

In contrast to the sophisticated dance productions at Sadlers Wells, the food served in the buffet could not be simpler or more down-to-earth. There's a reasonable choice of sandwiches with tasty fillings ranging from cheese and tomato to prawn and egg, but the quality of the bread should be improved. Cakes can vary: our cheesecake was poor, while the chocolate gâteau had a deliciously light home-made flavour. Hot strong coffee is the only drink available, but the bar is close at hand.

Poor

Westminster Theatre, Foyer Restaurant Palace Street, SW1

In the same room as the snack bar, this restaurant has nothing to recommend it: white tablecloths do little to improve the drab decor, the service is uncaring and slovenly, and the cooking lacks any kind of expertise. Only home-made split pea soup was remotely acceptable, the rest of our meal being dreadful: the pâté was bitter, chicken with macaroni was a ghastly overcooked mess, vegetables were, without exception, badly prepared, and the chocolate and orange mousse had almost turned to liquid.

Continued

Poor

Westminster Theatre Snack Bar Palace Street, SW1
There's an all-pervading grubbiness about this snack bar, reinforced by the awful food available at the self-service counter. Our visit was a chapter of disasters: greasy sausage rolls; desperately overcooked and shrivelled lamb chops with a revolting tomato sauce; a bland casserole tasting of reheated leftovers and stale Danish pastries with a taste of revival by microwave. A thoroughly unenjoyable experience.

Acceptable

Young Vic Theatre Bar 66 The Cut, SE1
'Excellent value for money' might be the motto of this pleasant, simple restaurant manned by helpful counter assistants. Best bets are the home-made hot dishes like vegetarian chilli or tasty double lamb chop in a light mint-flavoured gravy. Salads are fresh and varied, and even bought-in items are reasonably good and well presented.

Provincial Theatres

Poor

Coventry: Belgrade Theatre, Stagebite Restaurant
This attractive Victorian-style restaurant with its brass fittings, old advertisements and carved mirrors promises a great deal, but the all-American food is far from inspiring. The menu—a news sheet full of puns and joky dish names—may raise a smile, and the hamburgers which top the bill are certainly meaty and well cooked. Unfortunately, boring salads, unpleasantly flavoured chicken soup and lemon meringue pie with dreadful topping let the side down. Young waitresses work hard at their task, but it's all much ado about nothing.

Acceptable

Croydon: Ashcroft Theatre, Fairfield Restaurant
A twisting, hospital-style corridor leads to this anonymous restaurant overlooking a modern office block. It's hardly an endearing setting, but the service is pleasant and the food mostly acceptable. Meat is carefully chosen and simply cooked and vegetables are reasonably well handled, but there's also a plethora of convenience soups (at least the chef knows how to follow directions on a packet!), and sweets such as sickly black cherries in tough puff pastry leave a lot to be desired. So choose carefully if you want a good meal.

Appalling

Crewe: Lyceum Theatre Restaurant

Visitors to this dismal restaurant may well call to mind those immortal words of Tony Hancock, 'I thought my mother's cooking was bad, but . . .'; to say that the food here is disgusting is perhaps being a little generous. We were confronted by vile quiche (seemingly just melted cheese and tinned tomatoes on a leaden pastry case, and served with brown gravy!), stringy chicken pieces, overcooked sprouts that were the consistency of papier-mâché and—the final horror—thick, stodgy apple pie swamped with custard. Unbelievably, the place seems to do a roaring trade.

Acceptable

Derby: Playhouse Restaurant

Theatregoers could do worse than make a beeline for this pleasant, informal bistro-cum-wine bar. There are some quite enterprising dishes on the short menu, like freshly prepared stuffed peppers, fried frogs' legs and halibut steak, as well as perennial favourites such as pâté (home-made but without much flavour), sirloin steak (well cooked but somewhat dry) and burgers. Although there's a certain lack of finesse and some dishes can be rather bland, the food is acceptable, and service is very friendly.

Poor

Glynde: Glyndebourne Festival Opera Restaurant

The familiar image of Glyndebourne is one of elegantly dressed couples reclining by the lake with champagne and picnic hampers. There's also a smart modern restaurant for interval meals, but despite white-gloved waitresses and a somewhat ostentatious, horrendously overpriced menu, the food consists of bland, unexciting dishes like our thin vichyssoise, tasteless lobster cocktail and overcooked duck with bitter orange sauce. Such a beautiful place really deserves finer food than this.

Acceptable

Guildford: Yvonne Arnaud Theatre Restaurant

Overlooking a wooded garden and a stream, this smart restaurant seems far removed from the confines of the theatre, and it offers very acceptable food. The menus provide a vast selection, the table d'hôte being the most interesting, and there are unqualified successes like our eye-catching vegetable terrine and home-made chicken liver pâté. Roast duck with a nicely flavoured honey sauce was also enjoyable, but sweets were indifferent in choice as well as quality.

Appalling

Hereford: Nell Gwynne Theatre Restaurant

Despite paintings on the walls and modern pine tables, theatre-goers venture into this restaurant at their peril: it's quite simply a gastronomic disaster area. There is too much reliance on commercial products of very poor quality, and some things such as our inedible bitter cheesecake seem to be kept well beyond their normal shelf life. Other atrocities we noted included soggy garlic bread, tasteless braised beef in a foul glutinous gravy, dried-up peas and stewed sprouts.

Appalling

Liverpool: Playhouse Restaurant

There's an uneasy blend of ultra-modern and ornate Victorian decor in this circular restaurant, where the food shows the worst kind of pretentiousness used to disguise blatantly ill-treated raw materials. From our first mouthful of greasy pâté to the cloying, inedible sauce of stringy fillet steak chasseur and soggy lemon meringue pie to finish, the impression was one of unrelenting horror and dismay.

Poor

Mold: Clwyd Theatre, Harlequin Restaurant

Although this theatre is the new home of the prestigious Welsh National Opera, the food in the austere, windowless restaurant is nothing to sing about. Its main function may be to provide convenient sustenance during

Continued

Wagnerian marathons and the like, but there's no excuse for thin, sharply flavoured soup, carelessly cooked meat, awful vegetables kept in hot water for ages, and fruit pies with a paltry amount of glutinous filling.

Poor

Norwich: Theatre Royal Restaurant

There are shades of the staff canteen in this dingy, narrow restaurant, despite the colour photos of the stars on the walls. The food is a sad spectacle: our prawn cocktail was watery, so-called coq au vin tasted of neither wine nor chicken, and chocolate gâteau was dull and heavy. In fact, the only redeeming feature was a meaty home-made pâté—which suggests that with a little more effort and enterprise, standards could be greatly improved.

Poor

Nottingham: Theatre Royal Restaurant

Even though this theatre has benefited greatly from recent modernisation, catering still comes bottom of the list, and this restaurant—elegant though it is—offers a disappointing choice of food. The simple menu seems to be based on convenience foods or poor-quality fresh ingredients: prawn cocktail consisted of watery defrosted prawns in a mixture of bottled mayonnaise and tomato ketchup, soup was tasteless minestrone, gammon was tough and Black Forest gâteau was powdery.

Poor

Pitlochry: Festival Theatre, Brown Trout Restaurant

Space, comfort and fine views are plus marks in this modern restaurant but, despite some thoughtful planning, the set menu is a real disappointment. To be fair, we did enjoy a creamy smoked mackerel pâté and light strawberry gâteau, but the rest was dire: French onion soup had the colour of black treacle, the chef's speciality was a sorry concoction of anaemic pork in a nondescript sweetish sauce, and the wafer-thin venison in red wine sauce was a travesty, resembling a packaged TV dinner more than a restaurant dish.

Acceptable

Plymouth: Theatre Royal Restaurant

A brand new theatre deserves a full-scale, properly run restaurant, and Plymouth should be saluted for recognising this need. The setting is clean and smart and the menu shows plenty of imaginative touches. Seafood holds the limelight (our mussels in rich cream sauce were highly enjoyable) and other unusual offerings include duck with Marsala and clotted cream and veal escalope stuffed with Brie and salmon. A pity that vegetables and sweets are rather disappointing.

Acceptable

Stratford-upon-Avon: Royal Shakespeare Theatre, Box Tree Restaurant

Visitors who come to celebrate the Bard may be filled with anticipation when perusing the short, varied menu in this smart restaurant. But blandness and lack of finesse tend to dull enterprising dishes like ballotine of duck and Stilton steak (although this was juicy and cooked to order). Vegetables tell the same sad tale, but there's an unexpected flourish at the end of the meal with splendid home-made sweets like rich crème brûlée and chocolate mousse.

Appalling

Worthing: Connaught Theatre Restaurant

Inferior convenience foods in this dreary first-floor restaurant are treated without one iota of skill or care, and so-called fresh ingredients are dreadfully abused: our pâté was greasy and tasteless, the overcooked steak was rancid and the gammon turned out to be a tough, rubbery lump of processed shoulder. Add to this grubby tablecloths and poorly cleaned cutlery, and the result is the worst kind of charade. The one positive note is affable service.

Egon Ronay's
Cocktail Bar
Guide
MARTINI
MARTINI
THE BIANCO
MARTINI
ROSSO
MARTINI
VERMOUTH
BIANCO
MARTINI
REGISTERED TRADE MARK
VERMOUTH
ROSSO

Birmingham · *Holiday Inn, West End & Poolside Bars*

Central Square, Holliday Street · *West Midlands*
021–643 2766
Open West End 7–10.30 Pool 5.30–10.30
Screwdriver £1·50 Harvey Wallbanger £1·65
P ample: ATV Centre multi-storey

Choose between the leafy airiness of the Poolside Bar and the rich comfort of the Edwardian-style West End Bar. Both offer a good range of drinks, including some of Henry Henriques' cocktail creations. Live music after 9 in West End Bar.

Birmingham · *Midland Hotel, Castillane Bar & Peel's Bar*

New Street · *West Midlands*
021–643 2601
Open 10.30–2.30 & 5.30–10.30
Whisky Sour £1·80 Speciality cocktails £2
P ample: NCP behind hotel

Gabriel Quinn–finalist in the UK Bartenders' Guild Cocktail Barman Competition–has a repertoire of some 200 original creations. Enjoy your choice in the dignified panelled bar, hung with fine old oil paintings. Pianist most evenings.

Birmingham · *Plough & Harrow Hotel*

Hagley Road, Edgbaston · *West Midlands*
021–454 4111
Open 10.30–2.30 & 6–12, Sun 12–2 & 7–10.30
Pina Colada £2·25 Rob Roy £1·50
P ample: own car park

Peter Lawler and his assistant keep the customers happy with a wide range of expertly prepared cocktails in this elegant bar. Juices are freshly squeezed, and drinks are served with particularly tasty nibbles. Pianist.

Brighton · *Fagan's*

77 East Street · *East Sussex*
Brighton (0273) 27433
Open 12–2.30 & 6–11, Sun 12–2 & 7–10.30
Singapore Sling £1·85 Damson Queen £2·25
P difficult: meter parking

Young waitresses take your orders as you sit among the palms and ferns at this fashionable bar near the seafront. There's a list of more than 70 up-market cocktails (some non-alcoholic), as well as down-to-earth pints of beer.

Brighton · *Hacienda Heights*

135 Western Road · *East Sussex*
Brighton (0273) 21868
Open 11.30–2 & 6–11, Sun 7–10.30 **Closed** L Sun
Bev's Kiss £1·65 Mai Tai £3·25
P ample: Churchill Square car parks

White-painted tables, wicker chairs and potted plants give an alfresco air to this popular little bar. The cocktail list is long and includes one or two non-alcoholic mixtures. Happy hour 6 to 7.30, Sunday 7 to 7.30.

Brighton · *Old Ship Hotel, Tetts Bar*

King's Road · *East Sussex*
Brighton (0273) 29001
Open 11–2.30 & 6–11, Sun 12–2 & 7–10.30
Moscow Mule £1·50 Tetts Surprise £1·60
P difficult: meter parking

Shields and trophies from the UK Bartenders' Guild are testimony to the skills of Albert, head barman at this grand old seafront hotel. A pianist completes the classic picture in the warm panelled room. Happy hour (half price) 6 to 7 Saturday.

ATLANTIC BREEZE
½ measure of Vodka
⅕ measure of Martini Extra Dry
⅙ measure of Blue Curaçao
⅙ measure of Galliano

Shake, strain into an ice-filled glass. Decorate with orange, etc.

MANHATTAN
½ measure of Scotch Whisky
¼ measure of Martini Extra Dry
¼ measure of Martini Rosso
Dash of Angostura Bitters

Stir, strain into a glass and serve with a cherry.

Cover photograph taken from the world famous Martini Terrace, London.

Martini is…perfect cocktails.

Bristol
Central Park

37 College Green · *Avon*
Bristol (0272) 276426
Open 10.30–2.30 & 5.30–10.30 (Fri & Sat till 11,
Sun 7–10.30)
Tequila Sunrise 95p Harvey Wallbanger £1·40
P ample: multi-storey in Trenchard Street

Brash, colourful and noisy, this roomy bar with New York decor offers a good selection of cocktails (they'll mix ones not on the list), along with real ale and wines. Taped music, and singing waiters! Happy hour (25 per cent off) 5.30 to 7, Sun 7 to 8.

Bristol
Grand Hotel, Brass Nails Cocktail Bar

Broad Street · *Avon*
Bristol (0272) 291645
Open 12–2.30 & 5.30–11 (Sun 7–10.30)
Pina Colada £2·25 Pussy Foot £1·50
P limited: hotel car park in Rupert Street

A strikingly contemporary bar, with smart leather-backed chairs and a mirrored ceiling. Specialities include champagne with various fresh fruit purées. Live music at night. Half-price cocktails and free mixers with spirits during happy hour (6 to 7 Monday to Saturday).

Bristol
Holiday Inn, Panache Bar

Lower Castle Street · *Avon*
Bristol (0272) 294281
Open 11.30–3 & 5.30–11, Sun 12–2 & 7–10
Singapore Sling £2·30 Harvey Wallbanger £2·30
P ample: multi-storey next door

A veritable jungle of greenery gives a garden-café atmosphere to this roomy modern bar. The list of cocktails, which changes each month, includes the popular Mixed Doubles for two. A pianist plays six nights a week.

Edinburgh
George Hotel, Gathering of the Clans Bar

George Street · *Lothian*
031–225 1251
Open 11–11, Sun 11–2.30 & 6.30–11
Daiquiri £2·25 White Heather £2·50
P limited: meter parking

As its name suggests, there's a strong Scottish theme in this elegant, club-like bar, where display cases of clan shields line the walls. The cocktail list includes old favourites and house specials like Kidnapped and Rob Roy.

Edinburgh
Roxburghe Hotel Cocktail Bar

38 Charlotte Square · *Lothian*
031–225 3921
Open 11.30–2.30 & 5.30–11 **Closed** L Sun
Pimm's No. 1 £1 Rusty Nail £1·40
P limited: meter parking

The Roxburghe is conveniently situated in Edinburgh's business centre, and its cocktail bar with its own entrance in George Street is just the place for a quiet drink. The room is quite elegant, with pillar-box red walls, olive green banquette seating and Victorian-style glass lamps.

Glasgow
Albany Hotel

Bothwell Street · *Strathclyde*
041–248 2656
Open 12.30–2.30 & 6.30–10.30 **Closed** L Sat & all Sun
Brandy Alexander £1·75 Bucks Fizz £2·25
P ample: own car park

Local business people favour this smart, modern bar with its wood-lined ceiling and comfortable burgundy-coloured armchairs. Besides the usual spirited concoctions, the Albany offers a few non-alcoholic cocktails like Pussyfoot and Coconut Derby.

MILLION DOLLAR
1 measure of Martini Extra Dry
1 measure of Pineapple Juice
6 measures of Gin
2–3 dashes Grenadine
½ egg to each drink

Stir with cracked ice and add a spoonful of orange water on top.

BAMBOO
¼ measure of Martini Extra Dry
¼ measure of Martini Rosso
½ measure of Dry Sherry

Stir well and strain into a glass.

Martini is…perfect cocktails.

Glasgow — *Charlie Parker's*

Royal Exchange Square · *Strathclyde*
041–221 0798
Open 11–11, Sun 7–11
Manhattan £1·75 Caribbean Cooler £1·95
P difficult: meters

Right in the heart of Glasgow's bustling commercial centre, Charlie Parker's is snazzily decked out in mid-Manhattan style, with glossy wallpaper, high-backed winged sofas and a white grand piano. Casually smart young staff mix cocktails with style and a smile.

Glasgow — *Holiday Inn*

Argyle Street · *Strathclyde*
041–226 5577
Open 11–2.30 & 5–11, Sun 12.30–2.30 & 6–11
Planters Punch £2·30 Mixed Doubles £3·80
P ample: own car park

Forget the cold outside and relax over a drink in this warmly decorated bar. The list of cocktails changes monthly with the signs of the Zodiac, and a popular choice for couples is the speciality Mixed Doubles. A pianist plays every night except Sunday.

Leeds — *Ladbroke Dragonara Hotel, Rosewood Bar*

Neville Street · *West Yorkshire*
Leeds (0532) 442000
Open 11–3 & 5.30–10.30, Sun 12–2 & 7–10.30
Blue Horizon £1·20 Don's Irish Cream £1·50
P limited: hotel car park

'You name it, I'll mix it' could be the motto of cheerful Don Brewer, for many years head barman at this smart modern place. Tweedy brown armchairs are comfortable and relaxing, and there's a piano/double bass duo every weekday evening.

Leeds — *Queen's Hotel Cocktail Bar*

City Square · *West Yorkshire*
Leeds (0532) 31323
Open 10.30–3 & 5.30–10.30, Sun 12–2 & 7–10.30
Bucks Fizz £1·60 Diana's Delight £2·25
P ample: station car park

The atmosphere of the '30s survives in this smartly fitted bar, where head barman Les Minton and his assistant offer a wide selection of cocktails—and if you want something not on the list, they'll mix that, too.

Liverpool — *Adelphi Hotel, American Bar*

Ranelagh Place · *Merseyside*
051–709 7200
Open 11.30–2.30 & 6–10.30 **Closed** Sat & Sun
Daiquiri £1·40 Adelphi £1·60
P ample: own car park

In comfortably elegant surroundings, affable Brian Heaton, drawing on 17 year's experience, will mix you anything from a simple fizz to his special Adelphi, made with Amaretto, Kahlua, orange Curaçao, grenadine, fresh cream and nutmeg!

Liverpool — *Atlantic Tower Hotel, Stateroom Cocktail Bar*

Chapel Street · *Merseyside*
051–227 4444
Open 12–2.30 & 6.30–10.30 **Closed** Sun
Strawberry Blonde £2·50 Stateroom Cocktail £3
P ample: own car park

Enjoy a hint of liner luxury in this comfortable modern bar, where Stephen Hannaway produces popular cocktails as well as some seductively named specials of his own. A resident pianist heightens the sophisticated nightclub atmosphere.

Liverpool

Holiday Inn, Spyglass Bar

Paradise Street · *Merseyside*
051–709 0181
Open 12–3 & 5–10.30 **Closed** Sun
Gin Fizz £1·60 Charlie's Angel £2·20
P ample: multi-storey in Hanover Street

Brass lanterns, ships' compasses and captains' chairs lend a seafaring atmosphere to this pleasant, welcoming bar. John Kinsella keeps things swimming along with a selection of well-made cocktails, including a special double of the month.

London

Cadogan Hotel, Langtry Bar

75 Sloane Street SW1
01–235 7141
Open 11–3 & 5.30–11, Sun 12–2 & 7–10.30
Cadogan Classic £2 Jersey Lily £2
P ample: car park in Cadogan Place Gardens
⊖ Tube Sloane Square

Mementoes of Lillie Langtry and her friends provide an interesting talking point in this intimate bar, which was once the lovely lady's drawing room. Cocktails are served in delicate lily-shaped glasses to the strains of a soothing piano in the lounge next door.

London

Café Royal, Nicol's Bar

68 Regent Street W1
01–437 9090
Open 11–3 & 5.30–11, Sun 12–2 & 7–10.30
Americano £1·50 Champagne cocktail £2·25
P limited: meters in side streets
⊖ Tube Piccadilly Circus

Drink in style in this classic cocktail bar, with its elaborately moulded ceiling, marble-topped tables and red plush and gilt chairs. It's an ideal place for relaxing with friends, and there are at least 60 cocktails to choose from, served by Bruce and his charming waitresses.

London

Coconut Grove, Polo Bar

3 Barrett Street W1
01–486 5269
Open 12–3 & 5.30–11, Sun 7–10.30 **Closed** L Sun
Coco Loco £2·50 Brooklyn Bomber £3·10
P difficult: meters
⊖ Tube Bond Street

If you like music with your cocktails, join the young and trendy in this lively, well-run and very popular bar, whose '30s decor features potted plants and pictures of flappers. Alternatively, sip outside at one of the white-painted tables and watch the world go by.

London

Dorchester Hotel Bar

Park Lane W1
01–629 8888
Open 11–3 & 5.30–12, Sun 12–2 & 7–10.30
Bloody Mary £3·40 Grasshopper £3
P ample: hotel car park
⊖ Buses 2, 2B, 16, 30, 36B, 73, 74, 137

Resplendent in its tasteful blue and cream decor, this impeccably beautiful bar is an elegant, inviting place. Head barman Giuliano and his team are courteous and efficient, and their cocktails (ingredients are helpfully listed for each) are served with superb canapés. There's a pianist every evening except Sunday.

London

Hilton Hotel, Trader Vic's Tiki Bar

22 Park Lane W1
01–493 7586
Open 12–3 & 5.30–11, Sun 12–2 & 7–10.30
Barbados Punch £2·50 Tokyo Sour £3·20
P ample: NCP under hotel
⊖ Tube Hyde Park Corner

Polynesia in Park Lane, this renowned bar combines marvellous atmosphere with delightful presentation of exotic drinks, many of them rum-based. Under a woven grass roof hung with native lanterns, foursomes can enjoy their festive cocktails from a ceremonial communal bowl!

MARTINI CONTINENTAL
¼ measure of Gin
⅛ measure of Martini Extra Dry
⅛ measure of Martini Bianco
1 dash of Benedictine
1 dash of Lemon Peel Juice
1 Cherry
½ tumblerful of broken ice

Half fill the tumbler with broken ice and add the Gin. Add the Martini Bianco and Extra Dry and the Benedictine. Stir well and pass through a strainer into a cocktail glass. Serve with a cherry and a dash of lemon peel juice.

VODKATINI
⅔ measure of Martini Extra Dry
⅓ measure of Vodka

Stir and serve with a twist of lemon peel.

Martini is … perfect cocktails.

London — *Holiday Inn (Chelsea), Bohemian Bar*

Sloane Street SW1
01–235 4377
Open 11–3 & 5.50–11, Sun 12–2 & 7–10.30
Cool of the Day £2·75 Bermuda Rose £3
P limited: meter parking
⊖ Tube Knightsbridge

Wander out to a table by the swimming pool beneath its sliding sun roof, and Efisio's exotic drinks will conjure up visions of a tropical island. If you like your surroundings more traditional and more English, the drinks taste just as good in the comfort of the club-like bar. Pianist in the evening.

London — *Hyatt Carlton Tower, Chelsea & Rib Room Bars*

Cadogan Place SW1
01–235 5411
Open 11–3 & 5.30–11, Sun 12–2 & 7–10.30
Rachel £2·70 Alexander £2·40
P ample: car park under hotel
⊖ Buses 19, 22, 137

The cheerful, informal Chelsea Bar is a popular spot for enjoying anything from a fresh orange juice or a silver tankard of champagne to one of the cocktail creations of head barman Kemal. Downstairs in the Rib Room Bar there's a half-price happy hour from 5.30 to 7 Monday to Friday.

London — *Hyde Park Hotel, Cavalry Bar*

Knightsbridge SW1
01–235 2000
Open 11–3 & 5.30–11, Sun 12–2 & 7–10.30
Old Fashioned £2·60 French 75 £3·50
P difficult: meter parking
⊖ Tube Knightsbridge

Nobody enters this smart, sophisticated little bar without a cheery greeting from barman Charles Street, whose domain it has been for the past 20 years. All drinks—the list includes two-dozen cocktails and 33 whiskies—are served in fine crystal glasses and come with particularly tasty nibbles.

London — *Lafayette Cocktail Bar*

32 King Street SW1
01–930 1131
Open 5.30–11.30 **Closed** Sat & Sun
Lafayette Tropical £2·70 Scorpion £2·90
P limited: meter parking
⊖ Tube Green Park

The atmosphere is intimate, the clientele young and the greeting friendly in this smart, comfortable bar, where the cheerful Errol beavers away producing a wide range of tempting, generously served concoctions, including many of his own creations. All cocktails are £1 less during happy hour, which stretches from 5.30 to 9.30.

London — *Master's Cocktail Bar*

190 Queen's Gate SW7
01–581 5666
Open 12–3 & 5.30–11, Sun 12–2
Blue Movie £2·50 Pink Lady £2·50
P ample: meter parking
⊖ Buses 9, 52, 73

Oak panels and oil paintings grace the softly lit bar of this popular place, where the emphasis is very much on comfort and old-fashioned elegance. Well-garnished cocktails are presented in enormous tulip-shaped glasses, and there are bar nibbles. Drinks are half price in the happy hour, which runs from 5.30 to 8.

London — *Park Lane Hotel, Harry's Bar*

Piccadilly W1
01–499 6321
Open 11–3 & 5–11, Sun 12–2 & 7–10.30
Dry Martini £1·80 Champagne Cocktail £3
P limited: hotel garage
⊖ Tube Green Park

With a piano tinkling quietly in the background, you'll feel far removed from the hustle and bustle of Piccadilly as you relax with a drink in this luxurious bar. The cocktail list is conventional, but head barman David, successor to the legendary Harry Harris, is always happy to mix special requests.

AMERICANO
⅔ measure of Martini Rosso
⅓ measure of Campari
Ice

Pour over ice in large wine glass. Fill with soda, stir, and add a twist of lemon peel, and a dash of Angostura Bitters.

DRY MARTINI
½ measure of Martini Extra Dry
½ measure of Dry Gin

Stir well with ice. Strain and serve with twist of lemon peel or an olive.

Martini is…perfect cocktails.

London
Savoy Hotel, American Bar

Strand WC2
01–836 4343
Open 11–3 & 5.30–11, Sun 12–2 & 7–10.30
Manhattan £2·10 Royal Silver £3·65
P ample: own car park
⊖ Tube Temple

In contrast to the old-world elegance of the rest of the hotel, the American Bar is bright and ultra-modern. The atmosphere is relaxing, service under head barman Victor is unobtrusive and highly professional, and drinks are served with some delicious nibbles and hot bites.

Manchester
Midland Hotel Cocktail Bar

Peter Street · *Greater Manchester*
061–236 3333
Open 11.30–2 (Fri 12–2) & 5.30–10.30 **Closed** L Sat & all Sun
White Lady £1·70 Stinger £1·70
P ample: NCP at rear

A comfortable American-style bar, where genial head barman Claude Peglion will be pleased to mix the cocktail of your choice, even if it's not on his list. Small tables dotted around the room create a cosy and intimate atmosphere. Happy hour 5.30 to 7.

Manchester
Piccadilly Hotel, Vintage Bar

Piccadilly Plaza · *Greater Manchester*
061–236 8414
Open 12.30–2.30 & 6.30–10.30 (Fri & Sat till 11)
Bucks Fizz £3·50 Tom Collins £1·20
P ample: own car park

Marjorie Harper always has a warm welcome for visitors to this smart, stylish bar, which enjoys fine views over the city. Champagne is the speciality, served either in crystal glasses or tankards. A very popular place for business people to unwind.

Newcastle upon Tyne
Gosforth Park Hotel, Silver Ring Bar

High Gosforth Park · *Tyne & Wear*
Wideopen (089 426) 4111
Open 10.30–2.30 & 6.30–10.30, Sun 12–2 & 7–10.30
Gin Fizz £1·75 Fallen Angel £2
P ample: own car park

Pictures of famous racehorses line the walls of this relaxing bar. The printed list of cocktails is short, but barman Michael Macriss has a great many more at his fingertips. There's also a poolside bar. Dance band Tuesday to Saturday evenings.

Newcastle upon Tyne
Ricks

44 Cloth Market · *Tyne & Wear*
(0632) 323159
Open 11–3 & 5.30–10.30, Sun 7–10.30 **Closed** L Sun
Gin Fizz £1·50 Blood & Sand £2
P limited: street parking

Every one of the staff can mix 100 cocktails from memory in this informal, many-mirrored bar which also offers 19 imported beers. Happy hour (spirits half price, all cocktails £1·50) every lunch time and 5.30 to 6.30 Monday to Saturday.

Newcastle upon Tyne
Swallow Hotel Cocktail Bar

Newgate Arcade · *Tyne & Wear*
(0632) 325025
Open 11–3 & 5.30–10.30, Sun 12–2 & 7–10.30
Moomba Cocktail £1·60 Copacabana £1·40
P ample: car park in Clayton Street

A spacious rooftop bar, with deep modern armchairs and splendid views across the city. Head barman Tony Diaz has over 100 concoctions in his repertoire, and he also declares, 'Name a base, state dry, medium or sweet, and I'll invent something you'll like!'

MAKING WAVES

Put in a medium size wine glass 1 lump of sugar, 2 dashes of Angostura Bitters poured on to the sugar, 1 lump of ice, 1 measure of Martini Rosso.

Fill with iced Martini Asti Spumante, add a twist of lemon peel and stir slightly.

SNAKE IN THE GLASS

1 measure of Benedictine
2 teaspoonfuls Lemon juice
8 measures of Martini Asti Spumante (chilled)
1 long narrow strip of cucumber peel

Pour the Benedictine and lemon juice over the peel. Add the Asti Spumante and stir. Let the cocktail stand for a few minutes.

Martini is…perfect cocktails.

Martini is...
perfect cocktails
MARTINI
ROSÉ
MARTINI
THE BIANCO
MARTINI
ROSSO
MARTINI
EXTRA DRY
MARTINI
MARTINI
MARTINI
MARTINI

1,001 BARGAINS

BED & BREAKFAST UNDER £27 FOR TWO

ENGLAND
Home Counties
Bishop's Stortford, Hertfordshire:
    Dane House
Canterbury, Kent: Ebury
Godalming, Surrey: Lake
Goudhurst, Kent: Star & Eagle
Lewes, East Sussex: White Hart
Little Wymondley, Hertfordshire:
    Redcoats Farmhouse
Pulborough, West Sussex: Chequers
Woking, Surrey: Wheatsheaf

East Anglia
Hethersett, Norfolk: Park Farm

East Midlands
Derby, Derbyshire: Gables
Lincoln, Lincolnshire: Moor Lodge
Marston Trussell, Northamptonshire:
    Sun Inn

West Midlands
Birmingham, West Midlands:
    Berrow Court
Burton upon Trent, Staffordshire:
    Riverside Inn
Burton upon Trent, Staffordshire:
    Stanhope Arms
Church Stretton, Shropshire:
    Stretton Hall
Stourbridge, West Midlands: Talbot
Tern Hill, Shropshire: Tern Hill Hall

North East
Berwick-upon-Tweed,
    Northumberland: Castle
Great Driffield, Humberside: Bell
Hexham, Northumberland:
    Beaumont
Middleton in Teesdale, Co. Durham:
    Teesdale
Piercebridge, Co. Durham: George
Romaldkirk, Co. Durham:
    Rose & Crown

Rosedale Abbey, North Yorkshire:
    Milburn Arms
Yarm, Cleveland: Tall Trees

North West & Lake District
Charnock Richard, Lancashire:
    TraveLodge
Chester, Cheshire: Ye Olde King's
    Head
Eskdale, Cumbria: Bower House
Grasmere, Cumbria: Rothay Bank
Heversham, Cumbria: Blue Bell
Knutsford, Cheshire: La Belle Epoque
Meal Bank, Cumbria:
    High Laverock House
St Annes-on-Sea, Lancashire:
    Chadwick
Sandbach Heath, Cheshire:
    Chimney House
Whitehaven, Cumbria:
    Roseneath Country House
Whitewell, Lancashire: Whitewell

West Country
Chideock, Dorset: Chideock House
Dulverton, Somerset: Carnarvon
    Arms
East Stoke, Dorset:
    Kemps Country House
Heddon's Mouth, Devon:
    Hunter's Inn
Hellandbridge, Cornwall:
    Tredethy Country
Lynton, Devon: Lynton Cottage
Mortehoe, Devon: Rockham Bay
St Austell, Cornwall: White Hart
Whimple, Devon: Woodhayes

SCOTLAND
Ardvasar, Highland: Ardvasar
Banchory, Grampian: Tor-na-Coille
Barrhead, Strathclyde: Dalmeny Park
Biggar, Borders: Hartree Country
    House

Dulnain Bridge, Highland:
  Muckrach Lodge
Dulnain Bridge, Highland: Skye of
  Curr
Garve, Highland: Inchbae Lodge
Invershin, Highland: Invershin
Kelso, Borders: House O' Hill
Lewiston, Highland: Lewiston Arms
Lockerbie, Dumfries & Galloway:
  Dryfesdale
Moffat, Dumfries & Galloway:
  Annadale
Muir of Ord, Highland: Ord Arms
Pitcaple, Grampian: Pittodrie House
Strathblane, Strathclyde: Kirkhouse
  Inn
Strathtummel, Tayside: Port-an-
  Eilean

WALES
Beaumaris, Gwynedd:
  Ye Olde Bull's Head
Betws-y-Coed, Gwynedd: Gwydyr
Caernarfon, Gwynedd: Stables
Crickhowell, Powys: Bear
Dolgellau, Gwynedd: Gwernan Lake
Newton, Powys: Bear
Pant Mawr, Powys: Glansevern Arms
St David's, Dyfed: St Non's
Swansea, South Glamorgan: Dolphin
Three Cocks, Powys: Three Cocks
Tintern Parva, Gwent: Wye Valley
Wolf's Castle, Dyfed:
  Wolfscastle Country

CHANNEL ISLANDS
St Martin's, Guernsey:
  St Margaret's Lodge
St Brelade's Bay, Jersey:
  Hotel Château Valeuse

NORTHERN IRELAND
Portaferry, Co. Down: Portaferry

EIRE
Ballinahinch, Co. Galway:
  Ballinahinch Castle
Ballylickey, Co. Cork:
  Sea View
Clifden, Co. Galway:
  Abbeyglen
Clifden, Co. Galway:
  Hotel Alcock & Brown

BARGAIN WEEKENDS

All hotels listed are also included in the main sections of the Guide, where individual entries can be consulted.

When are these bargains available?

Dates published are those within which bargain weekend schemes operate in 1982–83. Most hotels do not include Bank Holidays, particularly Christmas and Easter. Many hotels also offer package terms for other times of year and for longer periods.

How many nights are included?

Quotations are for two or three weekend nights. Where we state 'Any two nights' any two consecutive nights in the week can be chosen. Most hotels will offer a third night at similar rates.

How much does it cost?

Prices are for one person for two or three nights, on the basis of two people sharing a double room. There may well be a supplementary charge for single occupancy. Many hotels offer special rates for children.

We have quoted for a room with private bathroom unless stated otherwise. It may be possible to pay slightly less for a room without bath.

What do you get?

Bargain-break holidaymakers are entitled to all the hotel's facilities—see entries in the main part of the Guide for details. Meals quoted apply to every day of the stay unless stated otherwise. A full English breakfast is served unless a continental breakfast is indicated.

We would advise you to check before booking that the price quoted is for a bargain weekend.

Hotels are listed by regions on the following pages:

London

Athenaeum Hotel	November–30 April **2 nights £60** Breakfast (book 01–937 0088)
Barkston Hotel	November–February **2 nights £34** Breakfast
Bloomsbury Crest Hotel	November–April **2 nights £32** Breakfast
Cadogan Hotel	1 October–4 May **2 nights £37·90 (£33·90 13 Dec–14 Feb)** Breakfast
Cavendish Hotel	November–February **2 nights £57** Breakfast
Charing Cross Hotel	27 October–5 April **2 nights £32·60** Breakfast
Clarendon Court Hotel	1 September–30 April **Any 2 nights £19** Continental breakfast
Coburg Hotel	All year **2 nights from £44** Breakfast, £6 per meal towards lunch or dinner
Cumberland Hotel	November–February **2 nights £48** Breakfast
Ebury Court	November–end March **2 nights £35·50** Breakfast
Gloucester Hotel	November–30 April **2 nights £41** Breakfast (book 01–937 0088)
Gore Hotel	All year **2 nights £30 (£33 after 31 March)** Breakfast
Great Eastern Hotel	14 October–25 April **2 nights £32·60** Breakfast

Great Northern Hotel	14 October–25 April **2 nights £32·60** Breakfast
Great Western Hotel	14 October–25 April **2 nights £32·60** Breakfast
Grosvenor Hotel	14 October–25 April **2 nights £29·60** Continental breakfast
Hendon Hall Hotel	All year **2 nights £42 (£46 after 1 April)** Breakfast, dinner
Hogarth Hotel	1 September–30 April **2 nights £19** Continental breakfast
Inn on the Park	November–March **Any 2 nights £135** Breakfast, dinner
Kensington Close Hotel	November–February **2 nights £39** Breakfast
Kensington Palace Hotel	1 October–4 May **2 nights £37·90 (£33·90 13 Dec–14 Feb)** Breakfast
Kingsley Hotel	November–February **2 nights £34** Breakfast
Leicester Court Hotel (see p. 217)	1 November–31 March **Any 2 nights £31** Breakfast, dinner
London Embassy Hotel	8 October–14 April **2 nights £38** Breakfast
London Metropole Hotel	1 October–31 March **2 nights £34·50** Breakfast
London Tara Hotel	All year **2 nights £35** Breakfast
Lowndes Hotel	1 October–4 May **2 nights £37·90 (£33·90 13 Dec–14 Feb)** Breakfast

Onslow Court Hotel (see p. 220)	1 November–31 March **2 nights £25·50** Breakfast
Post House Hotel (Bayswater)	November–February **2 nights £39** Breakfast
Post House Hotel (Hampstead)	November–February **2 nights £39** Breakfast
Regent Crest Hotel	November–30 April **2 nights £32** Breakfast
Royal Angus Hotel	1 October–4 May **2 nights £37·90 (£33·90 13 Dec–14 Feb)** Breakfast
Royal Garden Hotel	November–30 April **2 nights £41** Breakfast (book 01–937 0088)
Royal Horseguards Hotel	1 October–4 May **2 nights £37·90 (£33·90 13 Dec–14 Feb)** Breakfast
Royal Lancaster Hotel	November–30 April **2 nights £41** Breakfast (book 01–937 0088)
Royal Scot Hotel	1 October–4 May **2 nights £37·90 (£33·90 13 Dec–14 Feb)** Continental breakfast
Royal Trafalgar Hotel	1 October–4 May **2 nights £37·90 (£33·90 13 Dec–14 Feb)** Breakfast
Royal Westminster Hotel	1 October–4 May **2 nights £37·90 (£33·90 13 Dec–14 Feb)** Breakfast
Hotel Russell	November–February **2 nights £48** Breakfast
St George's Hotel	November–February **2 nights £48** Breakfast
Selfridge Hotel	1 October–4 May **2 nights £37·90 (£33·90 13 Dec–14 Feb)** Breakfast

Strand Palace Hotel	November–February **2 nights £39** Breakfast
Swiss Cottage Hotel	1 October–31 March **2 nights £35** Breakfast, £2·50 per meal towards dinner
Tower Hotel	1 October–4 May **2 nights £37·90 (£33·90 13 Dec–14 Feb)** Breakfast
Waldorf Hotel	November–February **2 nights £48** Breakfast
West Centre Hotel	November–30 April **2 nights £26** Breakfast
Westbury Hotel	November–February **2 nights £62** Breakfast
The White House	November–30 April **2 nights £35** Breakfast (book 01–937 0088)
White's Hotel	November–February **2 nights £39** Breakfast

London Airports

Berkeley Arms Hotel (Heathrow)	8 October–14 April **2 nights £36** Breakfast, dinner
Chequers Hotel (Surrey)	1 October–4 May **2 nights £39·90 (£35·90 14 Dec–13 Feb)** Breakfast, dinner
Post House Hotel (Heathrow)	November–February' **2 nights £39** Breakfast

Home Counties

Alton Hampshire **Grange Hotel**	All year **2 nights £44** Breakfast , dinner & 1 lunch

Alton Hampshire **Swan Hotel**	November–March **2 nights £39** Breakfast, dinner & Sunday lunch
Arundel West Sussex **Norfolk Arms Hotel**	1 November–Easter **Any 2 nights from £44** Breakfast, dinner
Ashford Kent **Eastwell Manor**	November–March **Any 2 nights £70 (excl. Fri & Sat)** Breakfast, £10 per meal towards dinner
Bagshot Surrey **Pennyhill Park Hotel**	November–March **2 nights £59·50** Breakfast, dinner
Basingstoke Hampshire **Red Lion Hotel**	November–March **2 nights £39** Breakfast, lunch & Sunday dinner
Beaulieu Hampshire **Montagu Arms Hotel**	1 November–31 March **Any 2 nights from £49·50** Breakfast, dinner
Bembridge Isle of Wight **Highbury Hotel**	1 November–1 June **2 nights £27·50** Breakfast
Berkhamsted Hertfordshire **Swan Hotel**	All year **2 nights £40** Breakfast, dinner
Bishop's Stortford Hertfordshire **Dane House Hotel**	All year **2 nights £40** Breakfast, dinner & Sunday lunch
Bognor Regis West Sussex **Royal Norfolk Hotel**	All year **Any 2 nights from £40·50** Breakfast, lunch or dinner
Bonchurch Isle of Wight **Winterbourne Hotel**	28 January–mid May **Any 2 nights £44** Breakfast, dinner
Bosham West Sussex **Millstream Hotel**	November–May **Any 2 nights £43** Breakfast, £7 per meal towards lunch or dinner
Brighton East Sussex **Bedford Hotel**	1 October–31 March **2 nights £38·55** Breakfast
Brighton East Sussex **Brighton Metropole Hotel**	1 October–4 May **2 nights £43·90 (£39·90 13 Dec–14 Feb)** Breakfast, dinner

Brighton East Sussex **Courtlands Hotel**	All year **2 nights £50** Breakfast, lunch or dinner
Brighton (Hove) East Sussex **Dudley Hotel**	November–February **2 nights £55** Breakfast, dinner
Brighton East Sussex **Grand Hotel**	1 November–31 March **2 nights £48·50** Breakfast, lunch or dinner
Brighton East Sussex **Old Ship Hotel**	All year **2 nights from £45** Breakfast, lunch or dinner
Brighton East Sussex **Royal Albion Hotel**	1 October–4 May **2 nights £43·90 (£39·90 13 Dec–14 Feb)** Breakfast, dinner
Brighton East Sussex **Royal Crescent Hotel**	1 October–1 March **2 nights £44** Breakfast, lunch or dinner
Brighton East Sussex **Sackville Hotel**	All year **2 nights £39 (£44 after 1 April)** Breakfast, lunch or dinner
Brockenhurst Hampshire **Carey's Manor Hotel**	23 October–30 June **Any 2 nights £43·70 (£49·70 after 31 March)** Breakfast, dinner
Bromley Kent **Bromley Court Hotel**	November–August **2 nights £39·75** Breakfast, Saturday dinner
Burley Hampshire **Burley Manor Hotel**	1 November–Easter **Any 2 nights from £44** Breakfast, dinner
Camberley Surrey **Frimley Hall Hotel**	November–February **2 nights £45** Breakfast, dinner
Canterbury Kent **Chaucer Hotel**	November–February **2 nights £46** Breakfast, dinner
Canterbury Kent **County Hotel**	All year **2 nights £37·50** Breakfast, lunch or dinner
Canterbury Kent **Ebury Hotel**	All year **2 nights £32·50 (£36·50 after March)** Breakfast, dinner

Chichester West Sussex **Chichester Lodge**	August–April **Any 2 nights £45** Breakfast, dinner
Chichester West Sussex **Dolphin & Anchor Hotel**	November–February **2 nights £52** Breakfast, dinner
Chiddingfold Surrey **Crown Inn**	30 September–31 March **Any 2 nights £49·50** Breakfast, dinner
Churt Surrey **Frensham Pond Hotel**	All year **2 nights £46** Breakfast, dinner
Churt Surrey **Pride of the Valley Inn**	November–February **2 nights £43** Breakfast, dinner
Climping West Sussex **Bailiffscourt Hotel**	1 October–31 March **2 nights £33·75 (Sun–Thurs)** Breakfast
Cooden East Sussex **Cooden Beach Hotel**	1 November–31 March **Any 2 nights £60** All meals
Crawley West Sussex **George Hotel**	November–February **2 nights £40** Breakfast, dinner
Dorking Surrey **Burford Bridge Hotel**	November–February **2 nights £55** Breakfast, dinner
Dorking Surrey **Punch Bowl Hotel**	November–March **2 nights £39** Breakfast, dinner & Sunday lunch
Dorking Surrey **White Horse Hotel**	November–February **2 nights £45** Breakfast, dinner
Dover Kent **White Cliffs Hotel**	October–May **2 nights £32** Breakfast, dinner & 1 lunch
Eastbourne East Sussex **Burlington Hotel**	All year **Any 2 nights from £76** Breakfast, dinner
Eastbourne East Sussex **Cavendish Hotel**	1 November–31 March **2 nights £53** Breakfast, lunch or dinner

Eastbourne East Sussex **Chatsworth Hotel**	October–April **Any 2 nights £40** Breakfast, dinner
Eastbourne East Sussex **Grand Hotel**	1 November–31 March **2 nights £70** Breakfast, lunch or dinner
Eastbourne East Sussex **Mansion Hotel**	1 October–1 April **2 nights £30** Breakfast, dinner
Eastbourne East Sussex **Queen's Hotel**	1 November–31 March **2 nights £48** Breakfast, lunch or dinner
Eastbourne East Sussex **Wish Tower Hotel**	November–February **2 nights £42** Breakfast, dinner
Egham Surrey **Runnymede Hotel**	1 October–4 May **2 nights £52·90 (£48·90 13 Dec–14 Feb)** Breakfast, dinner
Farnham Surrey **Bush Hotel**	November–March **2 nights £45** Breakfast, dinner & Sunday lunch
Fleet Hampshire **Lismoyne Hotel**	All year **2 nights £45·25** Breakfast, dinner & Sunday lunch
Goodwood West Sussex **Richmond Arms Hotel**	All year **2 nights £52 (£56 after 1 April)** Breakfast, dinner
Guildford Surrey **Angel Hotel**	November–February **2 nights £45** Breakfast, dinner
Hadley Wood Hertfordshire **West Lodge Park**	1 September–25 April **2 nights £45** Breakfast, £9 towards lunch or dinner
Haslemere Surrey **Georgian Hotel**	October–May **2 nights £38·50** Breakfast, dinner
Haslemere Surrey **Lythe Hill Hotel**	All year **Any 2 nights £58·50 (£63.50 after 8 April)** All meals
Hatfield Hertfordshire **Comet Hotel**	8 October–14 April **2 nights £34** Breakfast, dinner

Havant Hampshire **Post House Hotel**	November–February **2 nights £46** Breakfast, dinner
Hemel Hempstead Hertfordshire **Post House Hotel**	November–February **2 nights £41** Breakfast, dinner
Herstmonceux East Sussex **White Friars Hotel**	All year **Any 2 nights from £42** Breakfast, lunch or dinner
Hertingfordbury Hertfordshire **White Horse Inn**	November–February **2 nights £41** Breakfast, dinner
High Halden Kent **Hookstead House**	October–April **Any 2 nights from £37·50** Breakfast, dinner
Hollingbourne Kent **Great Danes Hotel**	November–30 April **2 nights £39·50** Breakfast, lunch or dinner (book 01–937 0088)
Hythe Kent **Hotel Imperial**	All year **Any 2 nights from £45** Breakfast, £8 towards lunch or dinner
Hythe Kent **Stade Court Hotel**	All year **Any 2 nights from £35** Breakfast, lunch or dinner
Lewes East Sussex **Shelleys Hotel**	All year **2 nights £42 (£52 after 1 May)** Breakfast, dinner
Lewes East Sussex **White Hart Hotel**	All year **Any 2 nights from £39** Breakfast, lunch or dinner
Little Wymondley Hertfordshire **Redcoats Farmhouse Hotel**	1 October–31 March **2 nights £39** Breakfast, dinner
Lymington Hampshire **Passford House Hotel**	1 November–31 May **Any 2 nights from £48** Breakfast, dinner
Lymington Hampshire **Stanwell House Hotel**	1 October–31 March **Any 2 nights from £44** Breakfast, dinner
Lyndhurst Hampshire **Crown Hotel**	November–March **2 nights £40** Breakfast, dinner & Sunday lunch

Lyndhurst Hampshire **Lyndhurst Park Hotel**	1 November–Easter **Any 2 nights from £44** Breakfast, dinner	
Lyndhurst Hampshire **Parkhill Hotel**	1 October–31 March **Any 2 nights from £51** Breakfast, dinner	
Maidstone Kent **Larkfield Hotel**	November–March **2 nights £39** Breakfast, dinner & Sunday lunch	
Middle Wallop Hampshire **Fifehead Manor**	1 November–31 March **2 nights £45** Breakfast, dinner	
Midhurst West Sussex **Spread Eagle Hotel**	29 October–26 May **Any 2 nights £37·50 (£45 Fri & Sat)** Breakfast, dinner	
New Milton Hampshire **Chewton Glen Hotel**	1 November–30 March **Any 2 nights from £88** Breakfast, dinner	
Northiam East Sussex **Hayes Arms**	27 September–27 April **Any 2 nights £50** Breakfast, dinner	
Petersfield Hampshire **Langrish House**	All year **Any 2 nights £34 (except Sun)** Breakfast, £5 per meal towards dinner	
Pulborough West Sussex **Chequers Hotel**	All year **Any 2 nights £36** Breakfast, dinner	
Redbourn Hertfordshire **Aubrey Park Hotel**	All year **2 nights from £41** Breakfast, lunch or dinner	
Romsey Hampshire **White Horse Hotel**	November–February **2 nights £52** Breakfast, dinner	
Rye East Sussex **Mermaid Inn**	1 October–30 April **Any 2 nights from £50** Breakfast, dinner	
St Albans Hertfordshire **Noke Hotel**	1 October–4 May **2 nights £37·90 (£34·90 13 Dec–14 Feb)** Breakfast, dinner	
Sanderstead Surrey **Selsdon Park Hotel**	November–April **2 nights from £59** Breakfast, dinner	

Sedlescombe East Sussex **Brickwall Hotel**	8 October–31 May **Any 2 nights from £37** Breakfast, dinner	
Shedfield Hampshire **Meon Valley Hotel Golf & C.C.**	All year **Any 2 nights £47 (£52 after 10 March)** Breakfast, lunch or dinner	
Shepperton Middlesex **Warren Lodge**	All year **Any 2 nights £30·36** Breakfast	
Southampton Hampshire **Dolphin Hotel**	5 November–February **2 nights £40** Breakfast, dinner	
Southampton Hampshire **Polygon Hotel**	November–February **2 nights from £46** Breakfast, dinner	
Southampton Hampshire **Post House Hotel**	November–February **2 nights £41** Breakfast, dinner	
Southampton Hampshire **Southampton Park Hotel**	1 November–Easter **2 nights £36** Breakfast, dinner	
Southsea Hampshire **Pendragon Hotel**	November–February **2 nights £46** Breakfast, dinner	
Southsea Hampshire **Royal Beach Hotel**	1 October–30 April **2 nights £39** Breakfast, dinner	
Stevenage Hertfordshire **Roebuck Inn**	November–February **2 nights £41** Breakfast, dinner	
Storrington West Sussex **Little Thakeham**	November–April **2 nights £40 (Mon–Fri)** Breakfast	
Stubbington Hampshire **Crofton Manor Hotel**	1 October–29 April **2 nights £70** All meals	
Sway Hampshire **Pine Trees Hotel**	1 November–31 March **2 nights from £48** Continental breakfast, dinner	
Tonbridge Kent **Rose & Crown Hotel**	November–February **2 nights £45** Breakfast, dinner	

Tunbridge Wells Kent **Spa Hotel**	All year **2 nights £40** Breakfast, lunch or dinner	
Ventnor Isle of Wight **Royal Hotel**	November–February **2 nights from £38** Breakfast, dinner	
Walberton West Sussex **Avisford Park Hotel**	All year **2 nights from £42·50** Breakfast, dinner	
Welwyn Hertfordshire **Heath Lodge Hotel**	All year **2 nights £20** Breakfast	
West Chiltington West Sussex **Roundabout Hotel**	29 October–30 June **Any 2 nights from £38** Breakfast, dinner	
Weybridge Surrey **Oatlands Park Hotel**	1 November–31 March **2 nights £38** Breakfast, lunch or dinner	
Weybridge Surrey **Ship Hotel**	1 October–4 May **2 nights £39·90 (£35·90 13 Dec–14 Feb)** Breakfast, dinner	
Winchester Hampshire **Wessex Hotel**	November–February **2 nights £55** Breakfast, dinner	
Worthing West Sussex **Beach Hotel**	1 October–30 April **2 nights £41·40** Breakfast, dinner	
Worthing West Sussex **Chatsworth Hotel**	1 September–30 April **2 nights £35·90** Breakfast, dinner	
Worthing West Sussex **Eardley Hotel**	All year **2 nights £36** Breakfast, dinner	

Thames Valley

Ascot Berkshire **Berystede Hotel**	November–February **2 nights £50** Breakfast, dinner	
Aylesbury Buckinghamshire **Bell Hotel**	November–February **2 nights £45** Breakfast, dinner	

Banbury	November–February
Oxfordshire	**2 nights £43**
Whately Hall Hotel	Breakfast, dinner

Beaconsfield	1 November–3 March
Buckinghamshire	**2 nights £44**
Bellhouse Hotel	Breakfast, lunch or dinner

Burford	All year
Oxfordshire	**Any 2 nights from £45**
Golden Pheasant Hotel	Breakfast, £7·50 per meal towards dinner

Burford	1 October–30 April
Oxfordshire	**Any 2 nights £38**
Inn for all Seasons	Breakfast, dinner

Burford	30 October–14 March
Oxfordshire	**Any 2 nights £40**
Lamb Inn	All meals

Burnham	All year
Buckinghamshire	**2 nights £39·50**
Burnham Beeches Hotel	Breakfast, £9·50 towards dinner

Chenies	1 October–4 May
Buckinghamshire	**2 nights £49·90 (£45·90 13 Dec–14 Feb)**
Bedford Arms Hotel	Breakfast, dinner

Gerrards Cross	1 November–31 March
Buckinghamshire	**2 nights £45**
Bull Hotel	Breakfast, lunch or dinner

Henley-on-Thames	1 November–28 February
Oxfordshire	**2 nights £40**
Red Lion Hotel	Breakfast, £7·50 per meal towards dinner

Horton-cum-Studley	1 October–1 May
Oxfordshire	**Any 2 nights from £57·60 (£59·60 after 28 February)**
Studley Priory Hotel	Breakfast, dinner

Hungerford	All year
Berkshire	**2 nights £39·50 (£41·50 after 1 April)**
Bear at Hungerford	Breakfast, lunch or dinner

Kingham	3 October–1 April
Oxfordshire	**Any 2 nights £39·50**
Mill Hotel	Breakfast, dinner

Middleton Stoney	All year
Oxfordshire	**Any 2 nights £35**
Jersey Arms	Breakfast, lunch or dinner

Newbury	November–February
Berkshire	**2 nights from £40**
Chequers Hotel	Breakfast, dinner

Newbury Berkshire **Elcot Park Hotel**	All year **Any 2 nights from £39·50** Breakfast, lunch or dinner
Newport Pagnell Buckinghamshire **TraveLodge**	November–February **2 nights £24** Continental breakfast
Oxford Oxfordshire **Randolph Hotel**	November–February **2 nights £57** Breakfast, dinner
Oxford Oxfordshire **TraveLodge**	November–February **2 nights £24** Continental breakfast
Pangbourne Berkshire **Copper Inn**	All year **2 nights £39·50 (£41 after 31 March)** Breakfast, £9·50 per meal towards dinner
Reading Berkshire **Post House Hotel**	November–February **2 nights £41** Breakfast, dinner
Shipton-under-Wychwood Oxfordshire **Lamb Inn**	1 November–31 March **2 nights £30** Breakfast, dinner
Shipton-under Wychwood Oxfordshire **Shaven Crown Hotel**	1 November–12 April **Any 2 nights £40** Breakfast, dinner
Stoke Mandeville Buckinghamshire **Belmore Hotel**	All year **2 nights £24·60** Continental breakfast, dinner
Streatley-on-Thames Berkshire **Swan Hotel**	All year **2 nights £40** Breakfast, lunch or dinner
Thame Oxfordshire **Spread Eagle Hotel**	All year **2 nights from £40** Breakfast, £5·75 per meal towards dinner
Wallingford Oxfordshire **George Hotel**	All year **2 nights £52 (£56 after 1 April)** Breakfast, dinner
Wantage Oxfordshire **Bear Hotel**	All year **2 nights £40** Breakfast, £10 per meal towards dinner
Windsor Berkshire **Castle Hotel**	November–February **2 nights from £51** Breakfast, dinner

Windsor Berkshire **Oakley Court Hotel**	All year **2 nights £58** Breakfast, dinner
Windsor Berkshire **Old House Hotel**	1 October–30 April **2 nights £60** Breakfast, dinner
Woodstock Oxfordshire **Bear Hotel**	November–March **Any 2 nights £59** Breakfast, dinner
Yattendon Berkshire **Royal Oak Hotel**	1 October–27 March **2 nights £39·75** Breakfast, £10 per meal towards dinner

East Anglia

Aldeburgh Suffolk **Brudenell Hotel**	November–February **2 nights £44** Breakfast, dinner
Aldeburgh Suffolk **Wentworth Hotel**	10 October–31 April **Any 2 nights £40** Breakfast, dinner
Barnham Broom Norfolk **Barnham Broom Hotel**	All year **Any 2 nights from £44** Breakfast, dinner
Beccles Suffolk **Waveney House Hotel**	16 October–25 April **Any 2 nights £42** Breakfast, dinner
Blakeney Norfolk **Blakeney Hotel**	All year **Any 2 nights from £40** Breakfast, dinner
Blakeney Norfolk **Manor Hotel**	15 November–11 May **Any 2 nights from £29·50 (£35 after 12 February)** Breakfast, dinner & 1 lunch
Braintree Essex **White Hart Hotel**	November–February **2 nights £38** Breakfast, dinner
Brentwood Essex **Post House Hotel**	November–February **2 nights £44** Breakfast, dinner
Bury St Edmunds Suffolk **Angel Hotel**	November–May **2 nights £48** Breakfast, £10 per meal towards dinner

Bury St Edmunds Suffolk **Suffolk Hotel**	November–February **2 nights £44** Breakfast, dinner	
Cambridge Cambridgeshire **Arundel House Hotel**	All year **2 nights £39 (£42·30 after 31 March)** Breakfast, dinner	
Cambridge Cambridgeshire **Cunard Cambridgeshire Hotel**	All year **2 nights £53 (£59·50 after 11 March)** Breakfast, lunch or dinner	
Cambridge Cambridgeshire **Garden House Hotel**	November–March **Any 2 nights £52** Breakfast, £8 per meal towards dinner	
Cambridge Cambridgeshire **Gonville Hotel**	October–April **2 nights £41 (£44 after 1 March)** Breakfast, £5·50 per meal towards lunch or dinner	
Cambridge Cambridgeshire **University Arms Hotel**	1 October–31 May **2 nights £41 (£44 after 31 March)** Breakfast, dinner	
Carlton Colville Suffolk **Hedley House Park Hotel**	All year **2 nights £28** Breakfast, £3 per meal towards dinner	
Coggeshall Essex **White Hart Hotel**	All year (except August) **2 nights £50** Breakfast, dinner & Sunday lunch	
Colchester Essex **Rose & Crown Hotel**	All year **2 nights £21·50** Breakfast	
East Dereham Norfolk **Phoenix Hotel**	November–February **2 nights £45** Breakfast, dinner	
Epping Essex **Post House Hotel**	November–February **2 nights £42** Breakfast, dinner	
Framlingham Suffolk **Crown Hotel**	November–February **2 nights £45** Breakfast, dinner	
Frinton-on-Sea Essex **Frinton Lodge Hotel**	29 October–26 May **Any 2 nights £37·50** Breakfast, £7 per meal towards lunch or dinner	
Great Dunmow Essex **Saracen's Head Hotel**	November–February **2 nights £43** Breakfast, dinner	

Great Yarmouth Norfolk **Carlton Hotel**	1 September–30 April **Any 2 nights £39·90** Breakfast, dinner
Horning Norfolk **Petersfield House Hotel**	All year **Any 2 nights £36·50** Breakfast, dinner
Huntingdon Cambridgeshire **Old Bridge Hotel**	1 October–31 March **2 nights from £31** Breakfast
Ipswich Suffolk **Belstead Brook Hotel**	All year **2 nights £35·95** Breakfast, lunch or dinner
Ipswich Suffolk **Great White Horse Hotel**	November–February **2 nights £41** Breakfast, dinner
Ipswich Suffolk **Marlborough Hotel**	All year **2 nights £48** Breakfast, £10 per meal towards dinner
Ipswich Suffolk **Post House Hotel**	November–February **2 nights £42** Breakfast, dinner
King's Lynn Norfolk **Duke's Head Hotel**	November–February **2 nights £45** Breakfast, dinner
Lavenham Suffolk **Swan Hotel**	November–February **2 nights £55** Breakfast, dinner
Long Melford Suffolk **Bull Hotel**	November–February **2 nights £52** Breakfast, dinner
Lowestoft Suffolk **Victoria Hotel**	All year **2 nights from £36** Breakfast, dinner
Maldon Essex **Blue Boar Hotel**	November–February **2 nights £41** Breakfast, dinner
Newmarket Suffolk **White Hart Hotel**	November–February **2 nights £41** Breakfast, dinner
Norwich Norfolk **Castle Hotel**	1 November–31 March **2 nights £36** Breakfast, lunch or dinner

Norwich Norfolk **Lansdowne Hotel**	8 October–14 April **2 nights £35** Breakfast, dinner	
Norwich Norfolk **Maid's Head Hotel**	All year **2 nights from £38** Breakfast, dinner	
Norwich Norfolk **Hotel Nelson**	All year **Any 2 nights from £43** Breakfast, lunch or dinner	
Norwich Norfolk **Hotel Norwich**	29 October–10 March, 27 May–27 October **Any 2 nights from £41** Breakfast, lunch or dinner	
Norwich Norfolk **Post House Hotel**	November–February **2 nights £46** Breakfast, dinner	
Ormesby St Margaret Norfolk **Ormesby Lodge**	All year **2 nights £46** Breakfast, dinner	
Needingworth Cambridgeshire **Pike & Eel**	1 October–31 March **Any 2 nights £35** Breakfast, lunch or dinner	
Peterborough Cambridgeshire **Great Northern Hotel**	14 October–5 April **2 nights £32·60** Breakfast	
Peterborough Cambridgeshire **Saxon Inn**	All year **2 nights £35** Breakfast, dinner	
St Ives Cambridgeshire **Slepe Hall Hotel**	All year **Any 2 nights from £39·50** Breakfast, dinner	
Six Mile Bottom Cambridgeshire **Swynford Paddocks**	1 January–30 April **2 nights £59** Breakfast, dinner	
Sudbury Suffolk **Mill Hotel**	1 October–31 March **Any 2 nights £42** Breakfast, dinner	
Thetford Norfolk **Bell Hotel**	November–February **2 nights £52** Breakfast, dinner	
Wansford Cambridgeshire **Haycock Inn**	1 October–31 March **2 nights from £31** Breakfast	

West Runton Norfolk **Links Country Park Hotel**	All year **Any 2 nights from £37·50** Breakfast, lunch or dinner
Weybourne Norfolk **Maltings Hotel**	November–May **Any 2 nights £52** All meals
Woodbridge Suffolk **Seckford Hall Hotel**	8 October–24 April **2 nights £59·50** Breakfast, dinner & Sunday lunch

East Midlands

Bakewell Derbyshire **Rutland Arms**	8 October–14 April **2 nights £38** Breakfast, dinner
Barnby Moor Nottinghamshire **Ye Olde Bell Hotel**	November–February **2 nights £43** Breakfast, dinner
Baslow Derbyshire **Cavendish Hotel**	1 November–28 February **2 nights £27·50** Breakfast
Bedford Bedfordshire **Woodlands Manor**	All year **2 nights £36** Breakfast, dinner
Crick Northamptonshire **Post House Hotel**	November–February **2 nights £43** Breakfast, dinner
Derby Derbyshire **Midland Hotel**	14 October–25 April **2 nights £47·60** Breakfast, dinner
Dovedale Derbyshire **Izaak Walton Hotel**	29 October–10 March **Any 2 nights £40** Breakfast, lunch or dinner
Dovedale Derbyshire **Peveril of the Peak Hotel**	November–February **2 nights £52** Breakfast, dinner
Dunstable Bedfordshire **Old Palace Lodge Hotel**	All year **2 nights £24** Breakfast
Grantham Lincolnshire **George Hotel**	All year **2 nights £33 (£35 after 26 May)** Breakfast, £6·50 towards lunch or dinner

Bargain weekends

Grimsthorpe Lincolnshire **Black Horse Inn**	4 October–2 April **2 nights £39·50** (without bath) Breakfast, dinner	
Hope Derbyshire **House of Anton**	All year **Any 2 nights £45** Breakfast, dinner	
Leicester Leicestershire **Grand Hotel**	8 October–14 April **2 nights £38** Breakfast, dinner	
Leicester Leicestershire **Post House Hotel**	November–February **2 nights £42** Breakfast, dinner	
Lincoln Lincolnshire **Eastgate Post House Hotel**	November–February **2 nights £49** Breakfast, dinner	
Lincoln Lincolnshire **Moor Lodge Hotel**	All year **2 nights £30** Breakfast	
Lincoln Lincolnshire **White Hart Hotel**	November–February **2 nights £48** Breakfast, dinner	
Loughborough Leicestershire **King's Head**	8 October–14 April **2 nights £34** Breakfast, dinner	
Luton Bedfordshire **Strathmore Hotel**	1 October–4 May **2 nights £39·90** (£35·90 13 Dec–14 Feb) Breakfast, dinner	
Matlock Derbyshire **Riber Hall**	15 October–15 April **Any 2 nights £62** Breakfast, £10 per meal towards dinner	
Matlock Bath Derbyshire **New Bath Hotel**	November–February **2 nights £49** Breakfast, dinner	
Northampton Northamptonshire **Saxon Inn**	All year **2 nights £43** All meals	
Nottingham Nottinghamshire **Albany Hotel**	November–February **2 nights £45** Breakfast, dinner	
Nottingham Nottinghamshire **Post House Hotel**	November–February **2 nights £45** Breakfast, dinner	

Nottingham
Nottinghamshire
Strathdon Hotel

1 October–4 May
2 nights £37·90 (£33·90 13 Dec–14 Feb)
Breakfast, dinner

Oundle
Northamptonshire
Talbot Hotel

November–March
2 nights £42
Breakfast, dinner & Sunday lunch

Rothley
Leicestershire
Rothley Court

All year
2 nights £19·50
Breakfast

Rowsley
Derbyshire
Peacock Hotel

8 October–14 April
2 nights £60
All meals

South Normanton
Derbyshire
Swallow Hotel

November–March
2 nights £38
Breakfast, dinner & Sunday lunch

Southwell
Nottinghamshire
Saracen's Head

November–March
2 nights £44
Breakfast, dinner & Sunday lunch

Stamford
Lincolnshire
George of Stamford

1 October–31 March
2 nights £31
Breakfast

Uppingham
Leicestershire
Falcon Hotel

All year
2 nights £29
Breakfast, dinner

Woburn
Bedfordshire
Bedford Arms

All year
2 nights £52 (£56 after 1 April)
Breakfast, dinner

Woodhall Spa
Lincolnshire
Dower House Hotel

October–April
Any 2 nights £39
Breakfast, dinner

Woodhall Spa
Lincolnshire
Golf Hotel

All year
Any 2 nights £40 (£44 after 26 May)
Breakfast, lunch or dinner

West Midlands

Abberley
Hereford & Worcester
Elms Hotel

November–March
Any 2 nights £75
Breakfast, dinner

Alcester
Warwickshire
Cherrytrees Hotel

October–March
2 nights £32·50
Breakfast, dinner

Birmingham West Midlands **Albany Hotel**	November–February **2 nights £45** Breakfast, dinner	
Birmingham West Midlands **Metropole & Warwick**	1 October–31 March **2 nights £32·60** Breakfast	
Birmingham West Midlands **Midland Hotel**	All year **Any 2 nights from £40** Breakfast, £7·20 per meal towards dinner	
Birmingham West Midlands **Post House Hotel**	November–February **2 nights £39** Breakfast, dinner	
Birmingham West Midlands **Royal Angus Hotel**	1 October–4 May **2 nights £37·90 (£33·90 13 Dec–14 Feb)** Breakfast, dinner	
Birmingham West Midlands **Strathallan Hotel**	1 October–4 May **2 nights £37·90 (£33·90 13 Dec–14 Feb)** Breakfast, dinner	
Birmingham Airport West Midlands **Excelsior Hotel**	November–February **2 nights £44** Breakfast, dinner	
Brandon Warwickshire **Brandon Hall Hotel**	November–February **2 nights £40** Breakfast, dinner	
Broadway Hereford & Worcester **Broadway Hotel**	All year **Any 2 nights £54** Breakfast, £7·95 per meal towards dinner	
Broadway Hereford & Worcester **Collin House Hotel**	1 November–31 March **Any 2 nights £45** Breakfast, dinner	
Broadway Hereford & Worcester **Dormy House**	All year **2 nights £68** Breakfast, £9 per meal towards dinner	
Broadway Hereford & Worcerster **Lygon Arms**	November–March **Any 2 nights £78** Continental breakfast, £12 per meal towards dinner	
Church Stretton Shropshire **Stretton Hall Hotel**	All year **2 nights £30·50** Breakfast, dinner & Sunday lunch	
Coventry West Midlands **De Vere Hotel**	1 November–31 March **2 nights £40** Breakfast	

Coventry West Midlands **Hotel Leofric**	8 October–14 April **2 nights £38** Breakfast, dinner	
Coventry West Midlands **Post House Hotel**	November–February **2 nights £42** Breakfast, dinner	
Droitwich Hereford & Worcester **Château Impney Hotel**	All year **2 nights £45·90** Breakfast	
Droitwich Hereford & Worcester **Raven Hotel**	All year **2 nights £36·90** Breakfast	
Dunchurch Warwickshire **Dun Cow Hotel**	All year **2 nights £55** All meals	
Evesham Hereford & Worcester **Evesham Hotel**	21 October–25 April **2 nights £45 (£37·50 1 Dec–16 Feb)** Breakfast, dinner & 1 lunch	
Hereford Hereford & Worcester **Green Dragon Hotel**	November–February **2 nights £45** Breakfast, dinner	
Kenilworth Warwickshire **Clarendon House Hotel**	All year **2 nights £35** Breakfast, dinner	
Kenilworth Warwickshire **De Montfort Hotel**	1 November–31 March **2 nights £32** Breakfast	
Leamington Spa Warwickshire **Regent Hotel**	All year **Any 2 nights from £36·50** Breakfast, lunch or dinner	
Ledbury Hereford & Worcester **Hope End Country House Hotel**	March–November **Any 2 nights £55** Breakfast, dinner	
Ludlow Shropshire **Feathers Hotel**	1 November–31 March **Any 2 nights £54** Breakfast, dinner	
Malvern Hereford & Worcester **Abbey Hotel**	1 November–31 March **2 nights £49** Breakfast, lunch or dinner	
Malvern Hereford & Worcester **Cottage in the Wood Hotel**	1 October–30 April **Any 2 nights from £59·50** Continental breakfast, dinner	

Malvern Hereford & Worcester **Foley Arms Hotel**	All year **Any 2 nights £44** Breakfast, £5 per meal towards lunch or dinner	
Meriden West Midlands **Manor Hotel**	1 November–31 March **2 nights £33** Breakfast	
Newcastle-under-Lyme Staffordshire **Clayton Lodge Hotel**	8 October–14 April **2 nights £34** Breakfast, dinner	
Newcastle-under-Lyme Staffordshire **Post House Hotel**	November–February **2 nights £42** Breakfast, dinner	
Newton Solney Staffordshire **Newton Park Hotel**	8 October–14 April **2 nights £35** Breakfast, dinner	
Oswestry Shropshire **Wynnstay Hotel**	November–February **2 nights £41** Breakfast, dinner	
Ross-on-Wye Hereford & Worcester **Pengethley Hotel**	All year **Any 2 nights £32** Breakfast, dinner	
Rugby Warwickshire **Three Horseshoes Hotel**	27 May–27 October **2 nights £42** Breakfast, lunch or dinner	
Shifnal Shropshire **Park House Hotel**	All year **2 nights £45** All meals (bar lunch Saturday)	
Shrawley Hereford & Worcester **Lenchford Hotel**	All year **Any 2 nights £44** Breakfast, £7 towards dinner	
Shrewsbury Shropshire **Lion Hotel**	November–February **2 nights £45** Breakfast, dinner	
Solihull West Midlands **George Hotel**	8 October–14 April **2 nights £35** Breakfast, dinner	
Solihull West Midlands **St John's Hotel**	1 September–30 April **Any 2 nights from £35·90** Breakfast, dinner	
Stafford Staffordshire **Tillington Hall Hotel**	November–March **2 nights £36·50** Breakfast, dinner & Sunday lunch	

Stoke-on-Trent Staffordshire **North Stafford Hotel**	November–February **2 nights £39** Breakfast, dinner	
Stone Staffordshire **Crown Hotel**	All year **2 nights £24** Breakfast	
Stratford-upon-Avon Warwickshire **Alveston Manor Hotel**	November–February **2 nights £53** Breakfast, dinner	
Stratford-upon-Avon Warwickshire **Billesley Manor Hotel**	October–March **Any 2 nights £54** Breakfast, dinner	
Stratford-upon-Avon Warwickshire **Shakespeare Hotel**	November–February **2 nights £55** Breakfast, dinner	
Stratford-upon-Avon Warwickshire **Stratford House Hotel**	1 November–31 March **Any 2 nights £30** Breakfast	
Stratford-upon-Avon Warwickshire **Welcombe Hotel**	14 October–25 April **2 nights £48·60** Breakfast, dinner	
Sutton Coldfield West Midlands **Moor Hall Hotel**	All year **2 nights £34 (£35 after 10 March)** Breakfast, lunch or dinner	
Sutton Coldfield West Midlands **Penns Hall Hotel**	8 October–14 April **2 nights £36** Breakfast, dinner	
Tern Hill Shropshire **Tern Hill Hall Hotel**	November–April **2 nights £40** Breakfast, dinner	
Uttoxeter Staffordshire **White Hart Hotel**	All year **2 nights £13·50** Breakfast	
Walsall West Midlands **Baron's Court Hotel**	All year **2 nights £29** Breakfast, 1 dinner	
Walton Warwickshire **Walton Hall Hotel**	All year **2 nights from £44** Breakfast, £7 per meal towards dinner	
Weston under Penyard Hereford & Worcester **Wye Hotel**	All year **2 nights £40** Breakfast, dinner	

Westland
British airways
G-BBDG
IIAF
N64
FAA
G-BBVM
EDGHILL

Engineering for World Transport

Over a hundred distinct types of civil and military aircraft and helicopters rely on the expertise of Lucas Aerospace. All are in international service, involving some 300 operators in over 100 countries.

Dedicated to the design, development and production of advanced control, actuation and generating systems and equipment, Lucas Aerospace can quite literally be described as a High Technology company, operating at the limit of known engineering techniques, often with new and sophisticated materials.

Wishaw West Midlands **Belfry Hotel**	November–March **2 nights from £41·50** Breakfast, dinner & Sunday lunch	
Wolverhampton West Midlands **Mount Hotel**	8 October–14 April **2 nights £36** Breakfast, dinner	
Wolverhampton West Midlands **Park Hall Hotel**	8 October–14 April **2 nights £34** Breakfast, dinner	
Worcester Hereford & Worcester **Giffard Hotel**	November–February **2 nights £50** Breakfast, dinner	

North East

Alnwick Northumberland **White Swan Hotel**	November–March **Any 2 nights £36** Breakfast, dinner & Sunday lunch	
Bamburgh Northumberland **Lord Crewe Arms Hotel**	October & 31 March–27 May **Any 2 nights £40** Breakfast, dinner	
Barnsley South Yorkshire **Ardsley House Hotel**	All year **2 nights from £41·50** Breakfast, £5 per meal towards dinner	
Bawtry South Yorkshire **Crown Hotel**	November–February **2 nights £42** Breakfast, dinner & Sunday lunch	
Belford Northumberland **Blue Bell Hotel**	November–March **Any 2 nights £36** (without bath) Breakfast, dinner & Sunday lunch	
Berwick upon Tweed Northumberland **Castle Hotel**	18 October–30 May **Any 2 nights £38** Breakfast, dinner	
Berwick upon Tweed Northumberland **King's Arms Hotel**	All year **Any 2 nights £38** Breakfast, dinner	
Beverley Humberside **Beverley Arms Hotel**	November–February **2 nights from £43** Breakfast, dinner	
Billingham Cleveland **Billingham Arms Hotel**	1 October–4 May **2 nights £37·90 (£34·90 13 Dec–14 Feb)** Breakfast, dinner	

Bingley West Yorkshire **Bankfield Hotel**	8 October–14 April **2 nights £36** Breakfast, dinner	
Boroughbridge North Yorkshire **Crown Hotel**	All year **2 nights £35** Breakfast, £5·75 towards 1 lunch, £6·50 per meal towards 2 dinners	
Boroughbridge North Yorkshire **Three Arrows Hotel**	8 October–14 April **2 nights from £32** Breakfast, dinner	
Blanchland Co. Durham **Lord Crewe Arms Hotel**	9 October–25 May **2 nights £40 (£45 after 14 March)** Breakfast, dinner & Sunday lunch	
Bradford West Yorkshire **Victoria Hotel**	November–February **2 nights from £35** Breakfast, dinner	
Bramhope West Yorkshire **Parkway Hotel**	8 October–14 April **2 nights £33** (without bath) Breakfast, dinner	
Bramhope West Yorkshire **Post House Hotel**	November–February **2 nights £45** Breakfast, dinner	
Chester-le-Street Co. Durham **Lumley Castle Hotel**	October–April **2 nights £39·75** Breakfast, dinner	
Chollerford Northumberland **George Hotel**	November–March **Any 2 nights £42** Breakfast, dinner & Sunday lunch	
Cleethorpes Humberside **Kingsway Hotel**	All year **2 nights £36** Breakfast, dinner	
Coatham Mundeville Co. Durham **Hall Garth**	All year **2 nights £40** Breakfast, £5 per meal towards lunch or dinner	
Cornhill-on-Tweed Northumberland **Collingwood Arms Hotel**	All year **Any 2 nights £35** Breakfast, dinner	
Darlington Co. Durham **King's Head Hotel**	November–March **2 nights £34** Breakfast, dinner & Sunday lunch	
Darrington West Yorkshire **Darrington Hotel**	All year **2 nights £39·50** Breakfast, dinner	

Doncaster South Yorkshire **Earl of Doncaster**	November–March **2 nights £37** Breakfast, dinner & Sunday lunch
Doncaster South Yorkshire **Punch's Hotel**	8 October–14 April **2 nights £33** (without bath) Breakfast, dinner
Durham Co. Durham **Royal County Hotel**	November–March **2 nights £42** Breakfast, dinner & Sunday lunch
Gateshead Tyne & Wear **Five Bridges Hotel**	November–March **2 nights £32** Breakfast, dinner & Sunday lunch
Grassington North Yorkshire **Wilson Arms Hotel**	1 November–27 March **Any 2 nights £40** Breakfast, dinner
Greta Bridge Co. Durham **Morritt Arms Hotel**	October–April **Any 2 nights £34** Breakfast, dinner
Hackness North Yorkshire **Hackness Grange Country Hotel**	1 November–31 March **Any 2 nights from £44·50** Breakfast, dinner
Halifax West Yorkshire **Holdsworth House**	All year **2 nights £40** Breakfast, dinner
Harrogate North Yorkshire **Cairn Hotel**	1 October–4 May **2 nights £47·90** (£43·90 13 Dec–14 Feb) Breakfast, dinner
Harrogate North Yorkshire **Crown Hotel**	November–February **2 nights £46** Breakfast, dinner
Harrogate North Yorkshire **Granby Hotel**	October–April **Any 2 nights £39·50** Breakfast, dinner
Harrogate North Yorkshire **Hotel Majestic**	November–February **2 nights £46** Breakfast, dinner
Harrogate North Yorkshire **Russell Hotel**	14 October–31 March **2 nights £36·75** Breakfast, dinner
Harrogate North Yorkshire **Hotel St George**	November–March **2 nights £42** Breakfast, dinner & Sunday lunch

Harrogate North Yorkshire **Studley Hotel**	1 October–31 March **2 nights £46** Breakfast, £9 per meal towards dinner	
Hartlepool Cleveland **Grand Hotel**	14 October–5 April **2 nights £32·60** Breakfast	
Helmsley North Yorkshire **Black Swan Hotel**	November–February **2 nights £59** Breakfast, dinner	
Helmsley North Yorkshire **Feversham Arms Hotel**	All year **Any 2 nights from £34** Breakfast, dinner	
Hexham Northumberland **Beaumont Hotel**	29 October–4 April **2 nights £32** Breakfast, £6 per meal towards dinner & Sunday lunch	
Holywell Green West Yorkshire **Rock Inn**	All year **2 nights £40** Breakfast, dinner	
Hovingham North Yorkshire **Worsley Arms Hotel**	1 November–31 March **Any 2 nights £39 (£42 after 1 Jan)** Breakfast, dinner	
Howden Humberside **Bowmans Hotel**	All year **2 nights £40** Breakfast, 2 dinners & 1 lunch	
Huddersfield West Yorkshire **George Hotel**	November–February **2 nights £40** Breakfast, dinner	
Hull Humberside **Royal Station Hotel**	14 October–5 April **2 nights £32·60** Breakfast	
Ilkley West Yorkshire **Craiglands Hotel**	November–February **2 nights from £43** Breakfast, dinner	
Jervaulx North Yorkshire **Jervaulx Hall Country House Hotel**	4 October–Easter **Any 2 nights £44** Breakfast, dinner	
Kirkby Fleetham North Yorkshire **Kirkby Fleetham Hall**	All year **Any 2 nights from £50** Breakfast, dinner	
Kirkbymoorside North Yorkshire **George & Dragon Hotel**	November–Maundy Thursday **Any 2 nights from £12** Breakfast (dinner must be taken at hotel)	

Knaresborough North Yorkshire **Dower House Hotel**	29 October–31 March **2 nights £45** Breakfast, dinner
Leeds West Yorkshire **Merrion Hotel**	All year **2 nights £42 (£46 after 1 April)** Breakfast, dinner
Leeds West Yorkshire **Hotel Metropole**	November–February **2 nights from £40** Breakfast, dinner
Leeds West Yorkshire **Queen's Hotel**	14 October–5 April **2 nights £32·60** Breakfast
Middleton-in-Teesdale Co. Durham **Teesdale Hotel**	1 November–30 April **Any 2 nights £61** All meals
Monk Fryston West Yorkshire **Monk Fryston Hall Hotel**	All year **2 nights from £42** Breakfast, dinner
Neasham Co. Durham **Newbus Grange Hotel**	All year **2 nights £40·50** Breakfast, Sunday lunch & 1 dinner
Newcastle upon Tyne Tyne & Wear **County Hotel**	1 October–4 May **2 nights £39·90 (£35·90 14 Dec–13 Feb)** Breakfast, dinner
Newcastle upon Tyne Tyne & Wear **Gosforth Park Hotel**	1 October–4 May **2 nights £49·90 (£45·90 14 Dec–13 Feb)** Breakfast, dinner
Newcastle upon Tyne Tyne & Wear **Royal Station Hotel**	14 October–5 April **2 nights £32·60** Breakfast
Newcastle upon Tyne Tyne & Wear **Royal Turks Head Hotel**	1 October–4 May **2 nights £39·90 (£35·90 14 Dec–13 Feb)** Breakfast, dinner
Newcastle upon Tyne Tyne & Wear **Swallow Hotel**	November–March **2 nights £34** Breakfast, dinner & Sunday lunch
Otterburn Northumberland **Percy Arms Hotel**	November–March **Any 2 nights £36** Breakfast, dinner & Sunday lunch
Pickering North Yorkshire **Forest & Vale Hotel**	1 October–30 April **Any 2 nights £40** Breakfast, dinner

Pocklington Humberside **Feathers Hotel**	October–March **2 nights £32·50** Breakfast, dinner	
Ripon North Yorkshire **Ripon Spa Hotel**	All year **Any 2 nights from £38** Breakfast, £7·50 per meal towards dinner	
Romaldkirk Co. Durham **Rose & Crown Hotel**	November–February **Any 2 nights £37** Breakfast, dinner	
Scarborough North Yorkshire **Holbeck Hall Hotel**	All year **Any 2 nights £52** Breakfast, dinner	
Scarborough North Yorkshire **Palm Court Hotel**	1 October–31 May **2 nights from £43·70** Breakfast, dinner	
Scarborough North Yorkshire **Royal Hotel**	October–April **2 nights from £40** Breakfast, dinner & Sunday lunch	
Scarborough North Yorkshire **Hotel St Nicholas**	All year **Any 2 nights from £49** Breakfast, dinner	
Sheffield South Yorkshire **Grosvenor House Hotel**	November–February **2 nights £50** Breakfast, dinner	
Sheffield South Yorkshire **Hallam Tower Hotel**	November–February **2 nights £45** Breakfast, dinner	
South Milford South Yorkshire **Selby Fork Hotel**	November–March **2 nights £40** Breakfast, dinner & Sunday lunch	
Stockton-on-Tees Cleveland **Swallow Hotel**	November–March **2 nights £38** Breakfast, lunch or dinner	
Sunderland Tyne & Wear **Mowbray Park Hotel**	1 October–4 May **2 nights £37·90 (£34·90 13 Dec–14 Feb)** Breakfast, dinner	
Sunderland Tyne & Wear **Seaburn Hotel**	November–March **2 nights £36** Breakfast, dinner & Sunday lunch	
Thornaby-on-Tees Cleveland **Golden Eagle Hotel**	1 October–4 May **2 nights £37·90 (£34·90 13 Dec–14 Feb)** Breakfast, dinner	

Thornaby-on-Tees Cleveland **Post House Hotel**	November–February **2 nights £39** Breakfast, dinner	
Wakefield West Yorkshire **Post House Hotel**	November–February **2 nights £39** Breakfast, dinner	
Wakefield West Yorkshire **Swallow Hotel**	November–March **2 nights £36** Breakfast, dinner & Sunday lunch	
Washington Tyne & Wear **George Washington Hotel**	All year **Any 2 nights £45** Breakfast, £5·50 towards lunch or dinner	
Washington Tyne & Wear **Post House Hotel**	November–February **2 nights £41** Breakfast, dinner	
Wentbridge West Yorkshire **Wentbridge House Hotel**	All year **2 nights £28·70** Continental breakfast	
Whitwell-on-the-Hill North Yorkshire **Whitwell Hall Country House Hotel**	1 October–30 April **Any 2 nights £40 (£49 after 31 March)** Breakfast, dinner	
Willerby Humberside **Willerby Manor Hotel**	All year **2 nights £33** Breakfast, dinner	
Wooler Northumberland **Tankerville Arms**	September–June **Any 2 nights £32** Breakfast, dinner	
York North Yorkshire **Abbots Mews Hotel**	1 November–31 May **Any 2 nights £30** Breakfast, dinner	
York North Yorkshire **Chase Hotel**	All year **2 nights £45·90** Breakfast, lunch or dinner	
York North Yorkshire **Dean Court Hotel**	30 October–30 July **Any 2 nights £52** Breakfast, dinner	
York North Yorkshire **Judges Lodging**	1 October–3 May **Any 2 nights £49** Continental breakfast, dinner	
York North Yorkshire **Mount Royale Hotel**	All year **Any 2 nights £50 (except Sunday)** Breakfast, dinner	

York North Yorkshire **Post House Hotel**	November–February **2 nights £49** Breakfast, dinner
York North Yorkshire **Royal Station Hotel**	14 October–5 April **2 nights £48·60** Breakfast, dinner

North West

Alderley Edge Cheshire **Edge Hotel**	All year **2 nights £40** Breakfast
Alston Cumbria **Lowbyer Manor**	1 May–31 July **Any 2 nights £45** Breakfast, dinner
Altrincham Cheshire **Bowdon Hotel**	All year **2 nights £42** Breakfast, dinner
Altrincham Cheshire **Cresta Court Hotel**	All year **2 nights £38** Breakfast, £6 per meal towards dinner
Altrincham Cheshire **George & Dragon Hotel**	November–March **2 nights £35** Breakfast, dinner & Sunday lunch
Ambleside Cumbria **Rothay Manor**	1 November–30 Dec, 3 January–31 March **Any 2 nights from £71 (from £78 after 3 Jan)** Breakfast, dinner
Bassenthwaite Lake Cumbria **Pheasant Inn**	8 November–13 March **Any 2 nights £44** All meals
Beeston Cheshire **Wild Boar Motor Lodge Inn**	8 October–14 April **2 nights £40** Breakfast, dinner
Blackpool Lancashire **Imperial Hotel**	1 October–4 May **2 nights £43·90 (£39·90 13 Dec–14 Feb)** Breakfast, dinner
Blackpool Lancashire **Savoy Hotel**	12 November–22 May **2 nights £36** All meals
Bolton Lancashire **Pack Horse Hotel**	November–March **2 nights £35** Breakfast, dinner & Sunday lunch

Bowness on Windermere Cumbria **Belsfield Hotel**	November–February **2 nights £45** Breakfast, dinner	
Bowness on Windermere Cumbria **Burnside Hotel**	November–February **2 nights £43** Breakfast, dinner	
Bowness on Windermere Cumbria **Old England Hotel**	November–February **2 nights from £52** Breakfast, dinner	
Braithwaite Cumbria **Ivy House Hotel**	March–November **2 nights £35** Breakfast, dinner	
Brampton Cumbria **Farlam Hall Hotel**	17 November–17 April (except February) **Any 2 nights £48 (except Tues)** Breakfast, dinner	
Bucklow Hill Cheshire **Swan Hotel**	November–March **2 nights £40** Breakfast, dinner, Sunday lunch	
Carlisle Cumbria **Hilltop Hotel**	November–March **2 nights £34** Breakfast, dinner & Sunday lunch	
Charnock Richard Lancashire **TraveLodge**	November–February **2 nights £24** Continental breakfast	
Chester Cheshire **Abbots Well Motor Lodge**	8 October–14 April **2 nights £38** Breakfast, dinner	
Chester Cheshire **Blossoms Hotel**	1 October–4 May **2 nights £52·90 (£48·90 13 Dec–14 Feb)** Breakfast, dinner	
Chester Cheshire **Grosvenor Hotel**	November–March **Any 2 nights £62** Breakfast, £10 per meal towards dinner	
Chester Cheshire **Mollington Banastre Hotel**	All year **Any 2 nights from £39** Breakfast, lunch or dinner	
Chester Cheshire **Post House Hotel**	November–February **2 nights £46** Breakfast, dinner	
Chester Cheshire **Ye Olde King's Head Hotel**	November–March **Any 2 nights £34** (without bath) Breakfast, dinner & 1 lunch	

Crooklands Cumbria **Crooklands Hotel**	All year **Any 2 nights from £39** Breakfast, lunch or dinner	
Crosby-on-Eden Cumbria **Crosby Lodge Hotel**	1 October–30 April **2 nights £50** Breakfast, dinner	
Eskdale Cumbria **Bower House Inn**	1 November–3 April **Any 2 nights £26** Breakfast, dinner	
Faugh Cumbria **String of Horses**	October–April **Any 2 nights £32·50** Breakfast	
Grasmere Cumbria **Michael's Nook**	1 November–31 March **2 nights £64** Breakfast, dinner	
Grasmere Cumbria **Swan Hotel**	November–February **2 nights £52** Breakfast, dinner	
Grasmere Cumbria **White Moss House**	Mid March–1 May & 1 July–20 August **2 nights £60 (£64 after 31 Dec) (Mon–Thurs)** Breakfast, dinner	
Grasmere Cumbria **Wordsworth Hotel**	November–March **Any 2 nights £58** Breakfast, dinner	
Handforth Cheshire **Belfry Hotel**	All year **2 nights £75** Breakfast, dinner	
Haydock Merseyside **Post House Hotel**	November–February **2 nights £43** Breakfast, dinner	
Heversham Cumbria **Blue Bell**	1 October–27 June **2 nights £39** Breakfast, dinner	
Kendal Cumbria **County Hotel**	1 October–4 May **2 nights £43·90 (£39·90 13 Dec–14 Feb)** Breakfast, dinner	
Kendal Cumbria **Woolpack Hotel**	November–March **Any 2 nights £40** All meals	
Keswick Cumbria **Keswick Hotel**	November–February **2 nights £46** Breakfast, dinner	

Keswick Cumbria **Mary Mount Country House Hotel**	January–March **Any 2 nights £48 (except Sat & Sun)** All meals
Leigh Greater Manchester **Greyhound Motor Hotel**	8 October–14 April **2 nights £33** Breakfast, dinner
Liverpool Merseyside **Atlantic Tower Hotel**	1 October–4 May **2 nights £39·90 (£35·90 13 Dec–14 Feb)** Breakfast, dinner
Liverpool Merseyside **St George's Hotel**	November–February **2 nights £44** Breakfast, dinner
Lytham St Anne's Lancashire **Clifton Arms Hotel**	29 October–26 May **2 nights £41** Breakfast, £7 per meal towards lunch or dinner
Manchester Greater Manchester **Grand Hotel**	November–February **2 nights £48** Breakfast, dinner
Manchester Greater Manchester **Midland Hotel**	14 October–25 April **2 nights £32·60** Breakfast
Manchester Greater Manchester **Hotel Piccadilly**	8 October–14 April **2 nights £38** Breakfast
Manchester Greater Manchester **Portland Hotel**	1 October–4 May **2 nights £42·90 (£39·90 13 Dec–14 Feb)** Breakfast, dinner
Manchester Greater Manchester **Post House Hotel**	November–February **2 nights £45** Breakfast, dinner
Manchester Airport Greater Manchester **Excelsior Hotel**	November–February **2 nights £44** Breakfast, dinner
Mealbank Cumbria **High Laverock House Hotel**	1 October–30 June **Any 2 nights £34** Breakfast, dinner
Morecambe Lancashire **Midland Hotel**	All year **2 nights £40** Breakfast, dinner
Mottram St Andrews Cheshire **Mottram Hall Hotel**	November–March **2 nights £42** Breakfast, dinner & Sunday lunch

Nantwich Cheshire **Rookery Hall**	All year **2 nights £75 (£85 after 4 April)** Breakfast, dinner	
Newby Bridge Cumbria **Swan Hotel**	1 September–30 April **Any 2 nights £45** Breakfast, dinner	
St Annes-on-Sea Lancashire **Chadwick Hotel**	1 November–31 March **Any 2 nights £32·80** All meals	
St Michael's on Wyre Lancashire **Rivermede Country House Hotel**	31 October–23 December & February **2 nights £22** Breakfast, £2·30 per meal towards dinner	
Southport Merseyside **Bold Hotel**	All year **2 nights £18** Breakfast	
Southport Merseyside **Prince of Wales Hotel**	All year **2 nights £46·50** Breakfast, dinner	
Stockport Greater Manchester **Alma Lodge Hotel**	8 October–14 April **2 nights £34** Breakfast, dinner	
Thornton-le-Fylde Lancashire **River House**	All year **2 nights £40** Breakfast, dinner & Sunday lunch	
Ullswater Cumbria **Leeming on Ullswater**	1 November–20 March **Any 2 nights £64** Breakfast, dinner	
Underbarrow Cumbria **Greenriggs Country House Hotel**	5 November–20 May **2 nights £44** Breakfast, dinner & Sunday lunch	
Warrington Cheshire **Lord Daresbury Hotel**	All year **2 nights £36·50** Breakfast, £6·50 towards lunch & dinner	
Whitehaven Cumbria **Roseneath Country House Hotel**	All year **2 nights £42** Breakfast, dinner	
Windermere Cumbria **Langdale Chase Hotel**	5 November–30 April **Any 2 nights from £44** Breakfast, dinner	

West Country

Alveston Avon **Alveston Post House**	November–February **2 nights £46** Breakfast, dinner
Amberley Gloucestershire **Amberley Inn**	All year **Any 2 nights from £37** Breakfast, lunch or dinner
Ashburton Devon **Holne Chase Hotel**	1 October–31 March **Any 2 nights £42 (£37 16 Nov–11 Feb)** Breakfast, dinner
Barnstaple Devon **Imperial Hotel**	November–February **2 nights from £42** Breakfast, dinner
Bath Avon **Lansdown Grove Hotel**	All year **Any 2 nights from £46** Breakfast, £7·75 per meal towards lunch or dinner
Bath Avon **Pratt's Hotel**	1 November–Easter **Any 2 nights from £44** Breakfast, dinner
Bath Avon **Priory Hotel**	1 November–28 April **Any 2 nights from £69·10** Continental breakfast, dinner
Bath Avon **Royal Crescent Hotel**	November–March **Any 2 nights £85** Breakfast, dinner
Bath Avon **Royal York Hotel**	October–April **Any 2 nights £43·65** Breakfast, dinner
Beanacre Wiltshire **Beechfield House Hotel**	30 October–1 April **Any 2 nights £55** Breakfast, dinner
Bibury Gloucestershire **Swan Hotel**	1 November–14 April **Any 2 nights £52·50** Breakfast, dinner & 1 lunch
Bideford Devon **Yeoldon House**	1 October–26 May **Any 2 nights from £39·50** Breakfast, dinner
Bilbrook Somerset **Dragon House Hotel**	1 October–30 June **2 nights £32·50** Breakfast, dinner

Bournemouth Dorset **Carlton Hotel**	1 October–31 March **Any 2 nights £75** Breakfast, lunch or dinner
Bournemouth Dorset **Durley Hall Hotel**	1 November–30 April **Any 2 nights £38** Breakfast, dinner
Bournemouth Dorset **East Cliff Court Hotel**	22 October–June **2 nights from £38** Breakfast, dinner
Bournemouth Dorset **Highcliff Hotel**	All year **Any 2 nights from £44** Breakfast, lunch or dinner
Bournemouth Dorset **Hotel Normandie**	October–May **Any 2 nights £39·50** Breakfast, dinner
Bournemouth Dorset **Palace Court Hotel**	All year **2 nights £54·50** Breakfast, dinner
Bournemouth Dorset **Queen's Hotel**	27 October–9 May **Any 2 nights £35 (£36 after 10 May)** Breakfast, dinner
Bournemouth Dorset **Royal Bath Hotel**	1 November–31 March **2 nights £69** Breakfast, lunch or dinner
Branscombe Devon **Masons Arms**	1 November–31 March **Any 2 nights £44** Breakfast, dinner
Bristol Avon **Grand Hotel**	All year **2 nights £40 (£44 after 27 May)** Breakfast, lunch or dinner
Bristol Avon **Unicorn Hotel**	November–30 April **2 nights £39·50** Breakfast, meal voucher for lunch or dinner (book 01–937 0088)
Brixham Devon **Quayside Hotel**	1 October–31 May **Any 2 nights from £41 (£43 after 31 March)** Breakfast, dinner
Bude Cornwall **Strand Hotel**	November–February **2 nights from £38** Breakfast, dinner
Budock Vean Cornwall **Budock Vean Hotel**	All year **Any 2 nights £37** Breakfast, dinner

Burbage Wiltshire **Savernake Forest Hotel**	All year **Any 2 nights from £40** Breakfast, dinner	
Carlyon Bay Cornwall **Porth Avallen Hotel**	1 October–30 April **Any 2 nights £40** Breakfast, dinner	
Castle Combe Wiltshire **Manor House Hotel**	1 November–31 March **Any 2 nights £70 (except Fri & Sat)** Breakfast, dinner	
Chagford Devon **Easton Court Hotel**	1 November–31 March **Any 2 nights £39** Breakfast, dinner	
Chagford Devon **Mill End Hotel**	22 October–31 March **Any 2 nights £39** Breakfast, dinner	
Chalford Gloucestershire **Springfield House Hotel**	September–May **Any 2 nights £40** Breakfast, dinner	
Chedington Dorset **Chedington Court**	1 October–30 June **Any 2 nights from £48 (from £52 after 31 March)** Breakfast, dinner	
Cheltenham Gloucestershire **Hotel de la Bere**	November–30 April **Any 2 nights £52** Breakfast, £9 per meal towards dinner	
Cheltenham Gloucestershire **Carlton Hotel**	All year **2 nights £40** Breakfast, dinner	
Cheltenham Gloucestershire **Golden Valley Hotel**	1 October–4 May **2 nights £45·90 (£41·90 13 Dec–14 Feb)** Breakfast, dinner	
Cheltenham Gloucestershire **Lilleybrook Hotel**	All year **2 nights £39·50** Breakfast, lunch or dinner	
Cheltenham Gloucestershire **Malvern View Hotel**	1 November–31 March **Any 2 nights £48** Breakfast, dinner	
Cheltenham Gloucestershire **Queen's Hotel**	November–February **2 nights £57** Breakfast, dinner	
Chipping Campden Gloucestershire **Kings Arms Hotel**	November–March **2 nights £40** Breakfast, dinner	

Chipping Campden Gloucestershire **Noel Arms Hotel**	1 November–1 May **Any 2 nights from £42** Breakfast, dinner
Christchurch Gloucestershire **King's Head Hotel**	29 October–26 May **2 nights £43 (£47 from 10 March)** Breakfast, dinner
Cirencester Gloucestershire **Stratton House Hotel**	1 November–18 May **2 nights £48** Breakfast, dinner
Coleford Gloucestershire **Speech House Hotel**	November–February **2 nights £49** Breakfast, dinner
Dartmouth Devon **Royal Castle Hotel**	November–March **Any 2 nights £40** Breakfast, dinner & 1 lunch
Dulverton Somerset **Carnarvon Arms Hotel**	18 October–30 April **Any 2 nights £38·75** Breakfast, dinner
Dunkirk Avon **Petty France Hotel**	November–30 April **Any 2 nights from £46·80** Breakfast, £9 per meal towards dinner
Dunster Somerset **Luttrell Arms Hotel**	November–February **2 nights £52** Breakfast, dinner
Dursley Gloucestershire **Stinchcombe Manor**	September–30 April **Any 2 nights £48** Breakfast, dinner
Evershot Dorset **Summer Lodge Hotel**	1 October–31 May **Any 2 nights £48** Breakfast, dinner
Ewen Gloucestershire **Wild Duck Inn**	1 November–31 March **2 nights £45** Continental breakfast, lunch & dinner
Exeter Devon **White Hart Hotel**	All year **2 nights £24** Breakfast
Exford Somerset **Crown Hotel**	1 September–30 April **Any 2 nights £39·90** Breakfast, dinner
Exmouth Devon **Devoncourt Hotel**	22 October–17 April **2 nights £35·65** All meals

Failand Avon **Redwood Lodge Hotel**	All year **2 nights £45** Breakfast, dinner & Sunday lunch	
Fairy Cross Devon **Portledge Hotel**	21 September–20 December **Any 2 nights £45** Breakfast, dinner	
Falmouth Cornwall **Falmouth Hotel**	1 October–16 May **Any 2 nights £39** Breakfast, dinner	
Falmouth Cornwall **Greenbank Hotel**	17 September–2 May **2 nights £42·50** Breakfast, dinner	
Ferndown Dorset **Dormy Hotel**	1 November–31 March **2 nights £50** Breakfast, lunch or dinner	
Frenchbeer Devon **Teignworthy**	1 November–23 December, 27 January–31 March **Any 2 nights £59** Breakfast, dinner	
Freshford Avon **Homewood Park Hotel**	November–March **2 nights £62 (Sun to Thurs)** Breakfast, dinner	
Frome Somerset **Mendip Lodge Hotel**	1 October–20 May **2 nights £40** Breakfast, dinner	
Glastonbury Somerset **George & Pilgrims Hotel**	1 October–30 April **Any 2 nights from £40** Breakfast, lunch or dinner	
Gloucester Gloucestershire **Tara Hotel**	All year **2 nights £33** Breakfast	
Golant Cornwall **Cormorant Hotel**	1 November–30 April **Any 2 nights £20** Breakfast	
Hatch Beauchamp Somerset **Farthings Country House Hotel**	1 October–31 March **2 nights from £55** Breakfast, dinner	
Hawkchurch Devon **Fairwater Head Hotel**	October, March–mid May **Any 2 nights £43** Breakfast, dinner & 1 lunch	
Heddon's Mouth Devon **Hunter's Inn**	October–May **Any 2 nights £35** Breakfast	

Bargains

Hellandbridge Cornwall **Tredethy Country Hotel**	5 November–3 April **2 nights £30** Breakfast, dinner
Hope Cove Devon **Cottage Hotel**	1 November–31 March **Any 2 nights £29·65** Breakfast, dinner
Hope Cove Devon **Lantern Lodge Hotel**	1 November–31 May **Any 2 nights from £40** Breakfast, dinner
Kingsbridge Devon **Buckland-Tout-Saints Hotel**	All year **Any 2 nights from £44 (from £48 after 27 May)** Breakfast, lunch or dinner
Lacock Wiltshire **Sign of the Angel**	1 November–31 March **Any 2 nights £45** Breakfast, dinner
Lamorna Cove Cornwall **Lamorna Cove Hotel**	20 November–30 April **Any 2 nights £37** Breakfast, dinner
Lifton Devon **Arundell Arms Hotel**	15 October–8 May **Any 2 nights £40 (£46·50 after 31 March)** Breakfast, dinner
Limpley Stoke Wiltshire **Cliffe Hotel**	All year **Any 2 nights from £35** Breakfast, dinner
Looe Cornwall **Talland Bay Hotel**	1 November–18 December & 11 February–30 April **Any 2 nights £38·30 (£41·50 after 1 March)** Breakfast, dinner
Lostwithiel Cornwall **Carotel Motel**	30 September–1 June **Any 2 nights £32** Breakfast, dinner
Lower Slaughter Gloucestershire **Manor Hotel**	1 October–31 May **Any 2 nights £58** Breakfast, dinner
Lower Swell Gloucestershire **Old Farmhouse Hotel**	3 October–28 April **Any 2 nights £22** Breakfast
Lynmouth Devon **Tors Hotel**	19 March–31 May **Any 2 nights £37** Breakfast, dinner
Lynton Devon **Lynton Cottage Hotel**	26 March–28 May, 4 June–3 July **Any 2 nights £42·20** Breakfast, dinner

Malmesbury Wiltshire **Whatley Manor Hotel**	All year **Any 2 nights from £62** Breakfast, dinner	
Mawnan Smith Cornwall **Meudon Hotel**	20 October–1 May **Any 2 nights £44** Breakfast, dinner	
Mere Wiltshire **Old Ship Hotel**	Mid October–end May **Any 2 nights from £36** Breakfast, dinner	
Mickleton Gloucestershire **Three Ways Hotel**	1 October–11 March **Any 2 nights £38·96** Breakfast, lunch or dinner	
Milton Damerel Devon **Woodford Bridge Hotel**	All year **Any 2 nights £50** Breakfast, dinner	
Moreton-in-Marsh Gloucestershire **Manor House Hotel**	1 November–30 April **Any 2 nights £54·50** Breakfast, dinner	
Moreton-in-Marsh Gloucestershire **Redesdale Arms**	October–March **Any 2 nights £42** Breakfast, dinner	
Moretonhampstead Devon **Manor House Hotel**	14 October–25 April **2 nights £52·60** Breakfast, dinner	
Mudeford Dorset **Avonmouth Hotel**	November–February **2 nights £49·50** Breakfast, dinner	
Mullion Cornwall **Polurrian Hotel**	April–July **Any 2 nights £41** Breakfast, dinner	
Newquay Cornwall **Hotel Bristol**	25 September–21 May **2 nights £42** Breakfast, dinner	
Newquay Cornwall **Headland Hotel**	March–May **Any 2 nights £23** Breakfast	
Newquay Cornwall **Hotel Riviera**	All year **2 nights from £35** Continental breakfast, dinner	
North Petherton Somerset **Walnut Tree Inn**	All year **2 nights £30** Breakfast, dinner	

Ottery St Mary Devon **Salston Hotel**	1 November–16 September **Any 2 nights from £35** Breakfast, £5 per meal towards lunch or dinner	
Paignton Devon **Palace Hotel**	November–February **2 nights from £44** Breakfast, dinner	
Paignton Devon **Redcliffe Hotel**	1 November–31 March **Any 2 nights £32** Breakfast, dinner	
Painswick Gloucestershire **Painswick Hotel**	All year **2 nights £46** Breakfast, dinner	
Plymouth Devon **Astor Hotel**	All year **2 nights £36** Breakfast, dinner	
Plymouth Devon **Duke of Cornwall Hotel**	29 October–26 May **2 nights £36 (£40 after 10 March)** Breakfast, lunch or dinner	
Plymouth Devon **Mayflower Post House Hotel**	November–February **2 nights £53** Breakfast, dinner	
Portloe Cornwall **Lugger Hotel**	1 September–30 April **2 nights £39·90** Breakfast, dinner	
Praa Sands Cornwall **Lesceave Cliff Hotel**	1 September–27 June **Any 2 nights £36** Breakfast, dinner	
St Ives Cornwall **Garrack Hotel**	5 April–25 June **Any 2 nights £32** Breakfast, dinner	
St Ives Cornwall **Trecarrell Hotel**	1 November–28 March **Any 2 nights £34·50** Breakfast, dinner	
St Ives Cornwall **Tregenna Castle Hotel**	14 October–25 April **2 nights £52·60** Breakfast, dinner	
Salcombe Devon **Marine Hotel**	27 September–30 April **Any 2 nights from £68** Breakfast, dinner	
Salcombe Devon **St Elmo Hotel**	May–October **Any 2 nights from £33** Breakfast, dinner	

Salcombe Devon **Tides Reach Hotel**	30 September–30 November, 1 March–1 May **Any 2 nights £38** Breakfast, £3 per meal towards dinner
Salisbury Wiltshire **White Hart Hotel**	November–February **2 nights £49** Breakfast, dinner
Saunton Devon **Saunton Sands Hotel**	November–May **Any 2 nights from £45** Continental breakfast, lunch & dinner
Seavington St Mary Somerset **Pheasant Hotel**	September–March **2 nights £35** Breakfast, dinner
Sennen Cornwall **Tregiffian Hotel**	1 March–30 June, 11 September–31 October **Any 2 nights £36** Breakfast, dinner
Shaftesbury Dorset **Grosvenor Hotel**	November–February **2 nights £45** Breakfast, dinner
Shaftesbury Dorset **Royal Chase Hotel**	All year **Any 2 nights from £39** Breakfast, £7 per meal towards lunch or dinner
Sherborne Dorset **Post House Hotel**	November–February **2 nights £48** Breakfast, dinner
Shipton Gloucestershire **Frogmill Inn**	October–March **2 nights £31** Breakfast, dinner
Sidmouth Devon **Belmont Hotel**	All year **2 nights from £40** All meals
Sidmouth Devon **Fortfield Hotel**	1 October–19 May **Any 2 nights £40 (£42 after 17 March)** Breakfast, dinner
Sidmouth Devon **Victoria Hotel**	1 October–27 May **Any 2 nights from £53** Breakfast, dinner
Somerton Somerset **Red Lion Hotel**	October–March **2 nights £40** Breakfast, dinner
Stow-on-the-Wold Gloucestershire **Fosse Manor Hotel**	November–May **Any 2 nights £43 (£38 midweek)** Breakfast, dinner

Stow-on-the-Wold
Gloucestershire
Royalist Hotel

8 November–1 April
Any 2 nights £37·50
Breakfast, dinner

Street
Somerset
Wessex Hotel

All year
2 nights £29
Breakfast, dinner

Stroud
Gloucestershire
Bear of Rodborough

November–March
2 nights £46
Breakfast, dinner & Sunday lunch

Swindon
Wiltshire
Blunsdon House Hotel

All year
2 nights £39·50 (£43·50 after 9 March)
Breakfast, dinner

Swindon
Wiltshire
Post House Hotel

November–February
2 nights £41
Breakfast, dinner

Swindon
Wiltshire
Wiltshire Hotel

All year
2 nights £42 (£46 after 1 April)
Breakfast, dinner

Taunton
Somerset
Castle Hotel

1 October–30 April
2 nights £64 (£59 January–February)
Breakfast, £11·90 per meal towards dinner

Taunton
Somerset
County Hotel

November–February
2 nights from £40
Breakfast, dinner

Teignmouth
Devon
Venn Farm Country House Hotel

1 November–30 May
Any 2 nights from £40
Breakfast, dinner

Tetbury
Gloucestershire
Close at Tetbury

All year
Any 2 nights from £52
Breakfast, dinner

Tetbury
Gloucestershire
White Hart Hotel

All year
Any 2 nights from £39·50
Breakfast, £8·50 per meal towards dinner

Tewkesbury
Gloucestershire
Tewkesbury Park Hotel

1 September–30 April
2 nights £39·90
Breakfast, dinner

Thurlestone
Devon
Thurlestone Hotel

24 September–26 May
Any 2 nights from £49
Breakfast, dinner

Torquay
Devon
Gleneagles Hotel

April–mid June & September–October
Any 2 nights £37
Breakfast, dinner

Torquay Devon **Grand Hotel**	4 October–24 April **Any 2 nights from £52 (£46 November–March)** Breakfast, dinner
Torquay Devon **Imperial Hotel**	November–February **2 nights £77** Breakfast, dinner
Torquay Devon **Kistor Hotel**	25 September–27 May **Any 2 nights £39 (£44 after 26 March)** All meals
Torquay Devon **Livermead Cliff Hotel**	All year **Any 2 nights £36·25 (£42 after 10 March)** Breakfast, lunch or dinner
Torquay Devon **Livermead House Hotel**	October–May **Any 2 nights £36·25 (£42 after 10 March)** Breakfast, lunch or dinner
Torquay Devon **Osborne Hotel**	1 October–31 March **Any 2 nights £36** Continental breakfast, dinner
Torquay Devon **Palace Hotel**	All year **Any 2 nights £46** Breakfast, dinner
Torquay Devon **Rainbow House Hotel**	September–May **2 nights £42** Breakfast, dinner
Torquay Devon **Toorak Hotel**	31 October–27 March **Any 2 nights £41·50** Breakfast, dinner
Upper Slaughter Gloucestershire **Lords of the Manor Hotel**	1 November–31 March **Any 2 nights from £48** Continental breakfast, £9 per meal towards dinner
Weston-super-Mare Avon **Grand Atlantic Hotel**	November–February **2 nights from £45·50** Breakfast, dinner
Westonbirt Gloucestershire **Hare & Hounds Hotel**	29 October–25 August **Any 2 nights from £39** Breakfast, lunch or dinner
Wimborne Minster Dorset **King's Head Hotel**	November–February **2 nights £45** Breakfast, dinner
Wincanton Somerset **Holbrook House Hotel**	All year **Any 2 nights from £39** Breakfast, lunch or dinner

Woody Bay Devon **Woody Bay Hotel**	1 September–30 June **Any 2 nights £39 (£43 after 31 March)** Breakfast, dinner
Yelverton Devon **Moorland Links Hotel**	All year **2 nights £40 (£45 after 26 May)** Breakfast, £7 per meal towards lunch or dinner
Yeovil Somerset **Little Barwick House**	October–April **Any 2 nights £12·50** Breakfast (dinner must be taken at hotel)

Scotland

Aberdeen Grampian **Caledonian Hotel**	1 October–4 May **2 nights £43·90 (£39·90 13 Dec–14 Feb)** Breakfast, dinner
Aberdeen Grampian **Station Hotel**	14 October–5 April **2 nights £32·60** Breakfast
Anstruther Fife **Craw's Nest Hotel**	October–July **Any 2 nights £48** All meals
Ardentinny Strathclyde **Ardentinny Hotel**	1 April–7 November **Any 2 nights £39 (£43 June–August)** Breakfast, dinner
Auchterarder Tayside **Gleneagles Hotel**	November–March **Any 2 nights £75** Breakfast, dinner
Aviemore Highland **Badenoch Hotel**	November–February **Any 2 nights £34** Breakfast, dinner
Aviemore Highland **Post House Hotel**	November–February **2 nights £44** Breakfast, dinner
Aviemore Highland **Strathspey Hotel**	1 October–4 May **Any 2 nights £45·90** Breakfast, dinner
Ayr Strathclyde **Pickwick Hotel**	1 October–31 March **Any 2 nights £30** Breakfast, dinner
Ballachulish Highland **Ballachulish Hotel**	All year **Any 2 nights £36** Breakfast, dinner

Ballachulish Strathclyde **Stewart Hotel**	April–May & September–October **Any 2 nights £44·50 (£46·75 from September)** Breakfast, dinner
Banchory Grampian **Raemoir House Hotel**	1 October–1 March **Any 2 nights £40** All meals
Banchory Grampian **Tor-na-Coille Hotel**	October–March **2 nights £40** All meals
Banff Grampian **County Hotel**	All year **Any 2 nights from £37** Breakfast, dinner
Barrhead Strathclyde **Dalmeny Park Hotel**	All year **2 nights £32** Breakfast, dinner
Beattock Dumfries & Galloway **Auchen Castle Hotel**	1 September–30 April **Any 2 nights £39·90** Breakfast, dinner
Biggar Borders **Hartree Country House Hotel**	October–July **Any 2 nights £26** Breakfast, 1 bar lunch
Bonnyrigg Lothian **Dalhousie Castle**	November–March **Any 2 nights £55** Breakfast, lunch or dinner
Borgue Dumfries & Galloway **Senwick House Hotel**	October–February **Any 2 nights £28·50** Breakfast, dinner
Bridge of Allan Central **Royal Hotel**	All year **Any 2 nights from £34** Breakfast, lunch or dinner
Callander Central **Roman Camp Hotel**	1 November–31 March **Any 2 nights £44** Breakfast, dinner
Coatbridge Strathclyde **Coatbridge Hotel**	All year **2 nights £33·90** Breakfast, dinner
Crinan Strathclyde **Crinan Hotel**	Mid March–end June **Any 2 nights £31** Continental breakfast
Dirleton Lothian **Open Arms Hotel**	1 November–15 May **Any 2 nights £34** Breakfast, lunch or dinner

Dryburgh Borders **Dryburgh Abbey Hotel**	All year **Any 2 nights from £52·50** Breakfast, dinner & 1 lunch	
Drymen Central **Buchanan Arms**	1 November–31 March **Any 2 nights from £34** Breakfast, dinner	
Dundee Tayside **Angus Hotel**	1 October–4 May **2 nights £37·90 (£33·90 13 Dec–14 Feb)** Breakfast, dinner	
Dunfermline Fife **King Malcolm Hotel**	1 October–4 May **2 nights £37·90 (£33·90 13 Dec–14 Feb)** Breakfast, dinner	
East Kilbride Strathclyde **Bruce Hotel**	November–March **2 nights £34** Breakfast, dinner & Sunday lunch	
East Kilbride Strathclyde **Stuart Hotel**	1 October–4 May **2 nights £37·90 (£33·90 13 Dec–14 Feb)** Breakfast, dinner	
Edinburgh Lothian **Barnton Hotel**	1 October–4 May **2 nights £39·90 (£35·90 13 Dec–14 Feb)** Breakfast, dinner	
Edinburgh Lothian **Braid Hills Hotel**	1 October–1 May **2 nights £51** All meals	
Edinburgh Lothian **Caledonian Hotel**	14 October–5 April **2 nights £54·40** Breakfast, dinner	
Edinburgh Lothian **Ellersley House Hotel**	October–April **2 nights £23** Breakfast	
Edinburgh Lothian **Howard Hotel**	15 October–15 May **2 nights £42** Breakfast, dinner	
Edinburgh Lothian **King James Hotel**	1 October–4 May **2 nights £45·90 (£41·90 13 Dec–14 Feb)** Breakfast, dinner	
Edinburgh Lothian **North British Hotel**	14 October–5 April **2 nights £50** Breakfast, dinner	
Edinburgh Lothian **Post House Hotel**	November–February **2 nights £46** Breakfast, dinner	

Edinburgh Lothian **Roxburghe Hotel**	All year **2 nights £39·50 (£52·50 from 1 May)** Breakfast, lunch or dinner	
Edinburgh Lothian **Royal Scot Hotel**	November–March **2 nights £39** Breakfast, dinner & Sunday lunch	
Fochabers Grampian **Gordon Arms Hotel**	1 October–June **2 nights £40** Breakfast, dinner	
Garve Highland **Inchbae Lodge Hotel**	4 September–1 April **Any 2 nights £30** Breakfast, dinner	
Gatehouse of Fleet Dumfries & Galloway **Murray Arms Hotel**	All year **Any 2 nights from £36** Breakfast, dinner	
Glasgow Strathclyde **Albany Hotel**	November–February **2 nights £43** Breakfast, dinner	
Glasgow Strathclyde **Central Hotel**	14 October–5 April **2 nights £32·60** Breakfast	
Glasgow Strathclyde **Lorne Hotel**	All year **2 nights £38 (£42 after 1 Jan)** Breakfast, £4·50 per meal towards lunch & £6·50 per meal towards dinner	
Glasgow Strathclyde **North British Hotel**	14 October–5 April **2 nights £32·60** Breakfast	
Glasgow Airport Strathclyde **Excelsior Hotel**	November–February **2 nights £44** Breakfast, dinner	
Glenborrodale Highland **Glenborrodale Castle Hotel**	November–February **2 nights £52** Breakfast, dinner	
Glencoe Highland **King's House Hotel**	1 April–31 October **Any 2 nights £42** Breakfast, dinner	
Glenrothes Fife **Balgeddie House Hotel**	All year **2 nights £23** Breakfast	
Hawick Borders **Kirklands Hotel**	September–June **2 nights £32** Breakfast, dinner	

Humbie Lothian **Johnstounburn House**	1 October–30 June **Any 2 nights £46 (£50 after 30 April)** Breakfast, dinner
Invergarry Highland **Inn on the Garry**	April–October **Any 2 nights £53** All meals (incl. wine)
Inverness Highland **Kingsmills Hotel**	31 October–28 May **2 nights £44 (£49 after 5 March)** Breakfast, £7 per meal towards dinner
Inverness Highland **Station Hotel**	14 October–5 April **2 nights £47·60** Breakfast, dinner
Isle of Gigha Strathclyde **Gigha Hotel**	1 October–31 March **Any 2 nights £37·50** Breakfast, dinner
Kelso Borders **House O'Hill**	1 November–31 March **2 nights from £42** (without bath) All meals
Kenmore Tayside **Kenmore Hotel**	March–August **2 nights £48 (Mon–Fri)** Breakfast, dinner
Kildrummy Grampian **Kildrummy Castle Hotel**	5 March–30 April **Any 2 nights £40** Breakfast, dinner
Kinclaven by Stanley Tayside **Ballathie House Hotel**	15 October–2 April **2 nights £40** Breakfast, dinner
Kinloch Rannoch Tayside **Loch Rannoch Hotel**	1 November–31 March **Any 2 nights from £42** Breakfast, dinner
Kyle of Lochalsh Highland **Kyle of Lochalsh Hotel**	14 October–5 April **2 nights £47·60** Breakfast, dinner
Langbank Strathclyde **Gleddoch House**	All year **2 nights £38** Breakfast
Largs Strathclyde **Marine & Curlinghall Hotel**	1 September–30 April **Any 2 nights £39·90** Breakfast, dinner
Lewiston Highland **Lewiston Arms Inn**	October–March **2 nights £26** Breakfast, dinner

Lockerbie Dumfries & Galloway **Dryfesdale Hotel**	1 October–30 March **Any 2 nights £36** Breakfast, £5 per meal towards dinner	
Milngavie Dumfries & Galloway **Black Bull Hotel**	1 October–4 May **2 nights £37·90 (£33·90 13 Dec–14 Feb)** Breakfast, dinner	
Moffat Dumfries & Galloway **Annandale Hotel**	March–May & September–November **Any 2 nights £25** Breakfast, dinner	
Moffat Dumfries & Galloway **Beechwood Country House Hotel**	1 October–31 March **Any 2 nights £45** Breakfast, dinner	
Muir of Ord Highland **Ord Arms**	September–April **2 nights £40** Breakfast, dinner	
Newton Stewart Dumfries & Galloway **Bruce Hotel**	1 October–31 May **Any 2 nights £52 (excl. Sun)** Breakfast, dinner	
North Berwick Lothian **Marine Hotel**	November–February **2 nights from £47·50** Breakfast, dinner	
Peebles Borders **Cringletie House Hotel**	24 October–22 December, 4 March–19 May **Any 2 nights £49·50 (£54·90 after 31 March)** Breakfast, dinner	
Peebles Borders **Park Hotel**	November–March **2 nights £39** Breakfast, dinner & Sunday lunch	
Peebles Borders **Peebles Hotel Hydro**	October–April **Any 2 nights from £39** Breakfast, dinner	
Peebles Borders **Tontine Hotel**	November–February **2 nights £41** Breakfast, dinner	
Perth Tayside **Royal George Hotel**	November–February **2 nights £45** Breakfast, dinner	
Perth Tayside **Station Hotel**	14 October–5 April **2 nights £47·60** Breakfast, dinner	
Pitlochry Tayside **Atholl Palace Hotel**	November–February **2 nights from £44** Breakfast, dinner	

Pitlochry Tayside **Green Park Hotel**	24 March–10 May **Any 2 nights £45** All meals
Portpatrick Dumfries & Galloway **Knockinaam Lodge Hotel**	October–22 December & March–May **Any 2 nights £45** Breakfast, dinner
Rothesay Strathclyde **Glenburn Hotel**	27 September–31 March **Any 2 nights £33** Breakfast, dinner
Rothes-on-Spey Grampian **Rothes Glen Hotel**	March–May & October–mid November **2 nights £57·20** Breakfast, dinner
St Andrews Fife **Old Course Hotel**	14 October–5 April **2 nights £47·60** Breakfast, dinner
St Andrews Fife **Rufflets Hotel**	1 November–30 April **Any 2 nights £38** Breakfast, dinner
Selkirk Borders **Philipburn House Hotel**	September–May **2 nights from £40** All meals
Skelmorlie Strathclyde **Manor Park Hotel**	October–Easter **2 nights £39·50** Breakfast, dinner
Stranraer Dumfries & Galloway **North West Castle Hotel**	1 October–30 June **2 nights from £38** All meals
Troon Strathclyde **Marine Hotel**	1 November–31 March **Any 2 nights from £42** Breakfast, dinner
Troon Strathclyde **Sun Court Hotel**	1 October–30 April **2 nights £47** All meals
Turnberry Strathclyde **Turnberry Hotel**	14 October–5 April **2 nights £59·50** Breakfast, dinner

Wales

Barry South Glamorgan **Mount Sorrel Hotel**	1 October–31 May **2 nights £30** Breakfast, dinner

Beaumaris Gwynedd **Bulkeley Arms**	September–June **2 nights £35** All meals
Bontddu Gwynedd **Bontddu Hall Hotel**	27 September–23 December **Any 2 nights £38·90** Continental breakfast, lunch & dinner
Brechfa Dyfed **Tŷ Mawr Country House Hotel**	All year **Any 2 nights £44** Breakfast, dinner
Caernarfon Gwynedd **Stables Hotel**	1 September–30 June **2 nights £42** Breakfast, dinner & Sunday lunch
Cardiff South Glamorgan **Angel Hotel**	October–April **Any 2 nights £39·95** Breakfast, dinner
Cardiff South Glamorgan **Inn on the Avenue**	All year **2 nights £45** Breakfast, dinner
Cardiff South Glamorgan **Park Hotel**	All year **2 nights £42 (£45 after 6 May)** Breakfast, £6 per meal towards lunch or dinner
Cardiff South Glamorgan **Post House Hotel**	November–February **2 nights £40** Breakfast, dinner
Carmarthen Dyfed **Ivy Bush Royal Hotel**	November–February **2 nights £43** Breakfast, dinner
Colwyn Bay Clwyd **Hotel Seventy Degrees**	All year **2 nights £49·50 (£57·50 1 July–31 August)** Breakfast, dinner & 1 lunch
Coychurch Mid Glamorgan **Coed-y-Mwstwr Hotel**	1 February–30 November **2 nights £70** Breakfast, dinner & Sunday lunch
Deganwy Gwynedd **Deganwy Castle Hotel**	1 October–31 March **Any 2 nights £40** Breakfast, dinner
Eglwysfach Powys **Ynyshir Hall Country House Hotel**	1 November–31 March **Any 2 nights £56** Breakfast, dinner
Fishguard Dyfed **Fishguard Bay Hotel**	1 October–30 April **Any 2 nights £38** Breakfast, dinner

Glyn Ceiriog Clwyd **Golden Pheasant Hotel**	1 September–30 April **Any 2 nights from £39·90** Breakfast, dinner	
Gwbert-on-Sea Dyfed **Cliff Hotel**	All year **Any 2 nights from £40** Breakfast, £6 per meal towards lunch or dinner	
Lake Vyrnwy Powys **Lake Vyrnwy Hotel**	1 March–30 April **Any 2 nights £55** All meals	
Llandudno Gwynedd **Empire Hotel**	All year **Any 2 nights from £40** Breakfast, dinner	
Llandudno Gwynedd **St George's Hotel**	All year **Any 2 nights from £37** Breakfast, lunch or dinner	
Llanelli Dyfed **Stradey Park Hotel**	November–February **2 nights £41** Breakfast, dinner	
Llangollen Clwyd **Hand Hotel**	All year **Any 2 nights from £30** Breakfast, £6 towards lunch or dinner	
Llangollen Clwyd **Royal Hotel**	November–February **2 nights £45** Breakfast, dinner	
Machynlleth Powys **Wynnstay Hotel**	November–February **2 nights £41** Breakfast, dinner	
Merthyr Tydfil Mid Glamorgan **Baverstock's Hotel**	All year **2 nights £45** All meals	
Mold Clwyd **Chequers Hotel**	1 October–4 May **2 nights £39·90 (£35·90 13 Dec–14 Feb)** Breakfast, dinner	
Monmouth Gwent **King's Head Hotel**	All year **Any 2 nights £45** Breakfast, dinner	
Northophall Clwyd **Chequers Hotel**	All year **2 nights from £30** Breakfast, dinner & 1 lunch	
Pant Mawr Powys **Glansevern Arms**	1 November–31 March **Any 2 nights £31** Breakfast, dinner	

Pembroke Dyfed **Wheeler's Old King's Arms Hotel**	All year **2 nights from £20** Breakfast	
Presteigne Powys **Radnorshire Arms Hotel**	November–February **2 nights £47** Breakfast, dinner	
Robeston Wathen Dyfed **Robeston House**	October–March **Any 2 nights £44** Breakfast, dinner	
Ruthin Clwyd **Castle Hotel**	All year **2 nights £27** Breakfast, dinner	
Ruthin Clwyd **Ruthin Castle**	All year **Any 2 nights £42·50 (£45·50 after 6 May)** Breakfast, lunch or dinner	
St David's Dyfed **St Non's Hotel**	1 October–31 March **Any 2 nights from £33** Breakfast, dinner	
St David's Dyfed **Warpool Court Hotel**	19 September–20 May **2 nights £42·50** Breakfast, dinner & 1 lunch	
St Mellon's South Glamorgan **St Mellon's Hotel**	All year **2 nights £45** Breakfast, £4 per meal towards lunch, £5 per meal towards dinner	
Swansea West Glamorgan **Dragon Hotel**	November–February **2 nights from £46** Breakfast, dinner	
Talsarnau Gwynedd **Maes-y-Neuadd Hotel**	1 October–30 April **Any 2 nights £39·50** Breakfast, dinner	
Three Cocks Powys **Three Cocks Hotel**	1 October–30 June **Any 2 nights from £40** (without bath) Breakfast, dinner	
Tintern Parva Gwent **Beaufort Hotel**	8 October–14 April **2 nights £36** Breakfast, dinner	
Tintern Parva Gwent **Royal George Hotel**	November–February **2 nights £43** Breakfast, dinner	
Tintern Parva Gwent **Wye Valley Hotel**	All year **Any 2 nights £37·50** Breakfast, £2·50 per meal towards lunch, £7·50 per meal towards dinner	

Channel Islands

Sark	May–September
Sark	**2 nights £36 (Mon–Fri)**
Aval du Creux	All meals

Northern Ireland

Dunadry	All year
Co. Antrim	**2 nights £38**
Dunadry Inn	Breakfast, 1 lunch & 1 dinner

Dunmurry	November–February
Co. Antrim	**2 nights £53**
Conway Hotel	Breakfast, dinner

Eire

Ballina	October–April
Co. Mayo	**2 nights £46**
Downhill Hotel	Breakfast, dinner

Caragh Lake	1 April–1 September
Co. Kerry	**Any 2 nights £28**
Caragh Lodge	Breakfast

Cashel	October–1 May
Co. Tipperary	**2 nights £60**
Cashel Palace Hotel	Breakfast, dinner

Castlebar	November–March
Co. Mayo	**2 nights £21**
Breaffy House Hotel	Breakfast

Castledermot	November–March
Co. Kildare	**2 nights £21**
Kilkea Castle	Breakfast

Clifden	1 March–31 May
Co. Galway	**Any 2 nights £36**
Abbeyglen Hotel	Breakfast, 1 dinner

Dundalk	September–June
Co. Louth	**Any 2 nights £43**
Ballymascanlon Hotel	Breakfast, 1 dinner

Ennis	November–March
Co. Clare	**2 nights £21**
West County Inn	Breakfast

Glounthaune Co. Cork **Ashbourne House Hotel**	All year **2 nights from £27·50** Breakfast, 1 dinner	
Kanturk Co. Cork **Assolas Country House**	1 May–30 September **2 nights £63·20** Breakfast, dinner	
Killarney Co. Kerry **Aghadoe Heights Hotel**	1 September–30 April **Any 2 nights £35·90** Breakfast, dinner	
Killarney Co. Kerry **Castlerosse Hotel**	November–March **2 nights £21** Breakfast	
Killiney Co. Dublin **Court Hotel**	All year **2 nights £30** Continental breakfast	
Killiney Co. Dublin **Fitzpatrick Castle Hotel**	October–30 April **2 nights £42** Breakfast, dinner	
Letterfrack Co. Galway **Rosleague Manor Hotel**	1 April–30 June & 1 September–1 November **Any 2 nights £46** Continental breakfast, dinner	
Moyard Co. Galway **Crocnaraw**	September–July **2 nights £45** Breakfast, dinner	
Rosslare Co. Wexford **Casey's Cedars Hotel**	1 September–30 April **Any 2 nights £35·90** Breakfast, dinner	
Shanagarry Co. Cork **Ballymaloe House**	1 November–1 March **2 nights £80** Breakfast, dinner	
Virginia Co. Cavan **Park Hotel**	November–March **2 nights £21** Breakfast	
Waterford Co. Waterford **Ardree Hotel**	October–March **2 nights £32** Breakfast, 1 dinner	
Waterford Co. Waterford **Granville Hotel**	July–December **2 nights £30·50** Breakfast, 1 dinner	
Wexford Co. Wexford **White's Hotel**	November–March **2 nights £21** Breakfast	

ECONOMY EVENING MEALS IN LONDON

Reasonable quality of food although not always up to our usual restaurant standards

UP TO APPR. £18.50 FOR TWO

Two courses, half carafe of wine, coffee, service, VAT—at the time of going to press

Economy evening meals can be had at the following restaurants, which are listed in the main London section of the Guide. (Note that prices in the main section include three courses and a full bottle of wine.)

Ajimura	Last Days of the Raj
Ark	Ley-On's
Bitter Lemons Taverna	Mandarin Kitchen
Bloom's, Golder's Green	Manzi's
Bloom's, Whitechapel	Melati, Great Windmill Street
Chinatown	Melati, Peter Street
Como Lario	New Rasa Sayang
La Corée	Newports
Crystal Palace	Paper Tiger
Diamond	Poons
Equatorial	Poons & Co.
Ginnan	Shu Shan
Good Friends	Shu Shan II
Green Cottage	Sidi Bou Said
Happy Garden	Standard
Hongs	Tagore
Hung Toa	Vijay
Jack's Place	Wat's House
Kuo Yuan	Yangtze
Langan's Bistro	

Map 23 A5
01–373 3502
About £16 for two
Closed 25 December
♨ Tube Earl's Court

Adam's Rib House 239 Old Brompton Road *SW5 0EA*

A must for lovers of succulent barbecued ribs and chicken with tangy sauces, this pleasant restaurant also offers soup, hot garlic bread, salads and tasty sweets. *Credit* Access, Amex, Barclaycard

Lunch Sun only noon–6.30pm *Dinner* 6.30pm–1am

Map 24 B2
01–580 5907
About £12·50 for two
Closed Bank Hols
♨ Tube Goodge Street

Anemos 32 Charlotte Street *W1R 1HJ*

Charcoal-grilled kebabs and garlic sausages with hot pitta bread are among the Greek favourites available at this popular taverna. Taramasalata, moussaka and baklavas are authentic, too. *Credit* Access, Amex, Diners

Lunch 12–3 *Dinner* 6–12, Sun 6–11

Map 25 A4
01–493 6150
About £12·50 for two
Closed L Sun, Bank Hols
♨ Buses 9, 14, 19, 22, 25, 38

L'Artiste Musclé 1 Shepherd Market *W1Y 7HS*

A blackboard menu announces the day's fare in this busy, friendly wine bar: robust country pâté, tasty quiche and various salads, plus a hot special. Cheesecake and gâteaux to finish.

Lunch 12–3 *Dinner* 5.30–12, Sun 7–11

Map 21 D6
01–274 9163
About £18 for two
Closed most Bank Hols
♨ Buses 2, 3, 37, 40, 68, 172, 196

Au Provençal 295 Railton Road, Herne Hill *SE24 0JP*

Tasty French provincial dishes ranging from soupe de poissons to daube de bœuf with lovely vegetables make up the menus in this agreeable restaurant. Budgeters should choose with care.

Lunch Sun only 12.30–2 *Dinner* 7–10.30

Map 22 A1
01–221 7502
About £7 for two
Closed Mon & Christmas
♨ Buses 7, 15, 23, 27, 28, 31

Baba Bhelpoori House 118 Westbourne Grove *W11 2RR*

Variety's the spice of life in this simple Indian vegetarian restaurant, where savoury snacks like samosas, pooris and dosas are satisfying and well prepared. Unlicensed, so drink refreshing yoghurt-based lassi.

Lunch 12–3, Sat & Sun noon–10pm *Dinner* 6–10.30, Sat & Sun 6–10

Map 21 B5
01–736 7110
About £16 for two
Closed Bank Hols & 10 days Christmas
♨ Tube Fulham Broadway

Bagley's 7 Broxholme House, New King's Road *SW6 4SA*

In the relaxed surroundings of this cosy little restaurant, capable cooking by Nick Wain produces English dishes notable for their fine fresh flavours and tasty sauces. *Credit* Access, Amex, Barclaycard

Lunch Sun only 12.45–2.30 *Dinner* 7.30–11.30   ♿

Map 24 B2
01–636 4174
About £16 for two
Closed Sun, Bank Hols & 3 weeks August
♨ Tube Goodge Street

Bertorelli Bros 19 Charlotte Street *W1P 1HB*

Flavours are foremost in this traditional family-run restaurant, whose vast menu ranges from Breton pâté and taramasalata to Hungarian goulash and baked jam roll. Book for lunch. *Credit* Access, Barclaycard

Lunch 12–2.30 *Dinner* 6–10   ♿

Map 20 B1
01–349 4386
About £11 for two
Closed Sun & Bank Hols
♨ Buses 104, 143, 263

Blue Angel 3 Long Lane *N3 2PR*

A varied selection of English and Central European dishes is available all day long–from robust red bean soup and Black Forest ham to omelettes and superb sautéed chicken. *Credit* Access

Meals 10am–11pm

Map 23 C4
01–584 9012
About £17 for two
Closed 25 December
✆ Tube Knightsbridge

Brasserie des Amis 27 Basil Street *SW3 1BB*

Bright, smart and friendly, this popular brasserie offers a good choice of tasty dishes like garlic mushrooms, pissaladière, gigot de chevreuil and speciality brochettes. *Credit* Access, Amex, Barclaycard, Diners

Lunch 11.30–3 *Dinner* 6.30–11, Sun 6.30–10.30

Map 23 A4
01–603 4422
About £16 for two
Closed 25 & 26 Dec
✆ Tube High St Kensington

Byblos 262 Kensington High Street *W8 6ND*

Feast on authentic Lebanese fare in this friendly little restaurant designed like a tent. Varied hors d'œuvre, kebabs and specials like couscous or stuffed lamb. *Credit* Access, Amex, Barclaycard, Diners

Meals noon–midnight

Map 24 B3
01–437 9090
About £13 for two
Closed Sat, Sun & Bank Hols
✆ Tube Piccadilly Circus

Café Royal Bar 68 Regent Street *W1R 6EL*

Lunches and early suppers offer a good choice of cold meats and salads, along with hot specials such as goulash, roast beef and excellent chicken pie. *Credit* Access, Amex, Barclaycard, Diners

Lunch 12–3 *Dinner* 5.30–8

Map 22 D1
01–935 1208
About £18·50 for two
✆ Tube Baker Street

Caravan Serai 50 Paddington Street *W1 3RQ*

Specialities from the clay oven like our marinated king prawns are an excellent choice here, and there's a good range of spicy Afghan dishes. Budget-eaters should choose carefully. *Credit* Access, Amex, Barclaycard, Diners

Lunch 12–2.45 *Dinner* 6–10.45, Sun 6–11.30

Map 20 B3
01–286 3741
About £18 for two
Closed Sun & 3 days Christmas
✆ Tube Westbourne Park

Caribbean Sunkissed Rest. 49 Chippenham Rd *W9 2AH*

Enjoy a feast of authentic West Indian fare in this cheerful restaurant: spicy pepperpot soup, curried goat, chicken in rum sauce, with rice and vegetables like okra and breadfruit. *Credit* Access, Barclaycard

Lunch 12–3 *Dinner* 6–10.45

Any person using our name to obtain free hospitality is a fraud. Proprietors, please inform the police and us.

Map 20 B3
01–722 5959
About £17 for two
Closed Sun, Bank Hols & August
✆ Tube St John's Wood

La Casalinga 64 St John's Wood High Street *NW8 7SH*

Friendly young waiters serve in this simple trattoria, where reliably cooked Italian dishes like chicken cacciatore are supplemented by daily specials such as halibut with butter sauce. Attractive sweets.

Lunch 12–3 *Dinner* 6–11.15

Map 23 B4
01–937 6912
About £17·50 for two
Closed Sun, Bank Hols & 3 wks Aug/Sept
✆ Buses 9, 33, 49, 52, 73

Casa Porrelli 1a Launceston Place *W8 5RL*

Enjoyable Italian cooking in a cheerful setting. Minestrone and pasta are particularly good, and other favourites include scampi fritti, veal escalope and grilled spring chicken. *Credit* Access, Amex, Barclaycard, Diners

Lunch 12–2.30 *Dinner* 6–10.30 &

Map 20 C3
01–722 1956
About £18 for two
Closed L Sat, all Sun &
Mon & Bank Hols
Tube Chalk Farm

Chalcot's 49 Chalcot Road *NW1 8LS*

From pâté de lapin to salmon with sorrel and lemon cheescake, everything's carefully prepared and attractively presented in this pleasant little restaurant. Particularly good service. *Credit* Access, Barclaycard, Diners

Lunch 12.30–3 *Dinner* 7–11

Map 20 C3
01–267 9820
About £15 for two
Closed D Sun, Mon, Bank
Hs, 2 wks Sept, 1 wk Xmas
Tube Camden Town

Chalk & Cheese 14 Chalk Farm Road *NW1 8AA*

A friendly little bistro, where Ray Curran's seasonally changing menus offer dishes like home-made soup, grilled trout, rack of lamb and puddings such as brown bread ice cream. *Credit* Access, Amex, Barclaycard

Lunch Sun only 12–3 *Dinner* 7–11

Map 25 C4
01–839 7282
About £15 for two
Closed 25 & 26 Dec
Tube Charing Cross

Charing Cross Hotel, Betjeman Carving Restaurant Strand *WC2N 5HX*

An attractive display of hot and cold joints, vegetables and salads dominates this lofty, pillared room, where the set lunches offer excellent value for money. *Credit* Access, Amex, Barclaycard, Diners

Meals noon–10.30pm

Map 24 A3
01–629 2669
About £15 for two
Closed Sun & L Bank
Holiday Mon
Tube Bond Street

Chicago Pizza Pie Factory 17 Hanover Square *W1R 9AJ*

Friendly, fashionable and very American, this buzzing basement restaurant is constantly crowded with devotees of spicy stuffed mushrooms, delicious deep-dish pizzas and rich cheesecake. Service is suitably slick and efficient.

Meals 11.45am–11.30pm

Map 25 B4
01–930 8279
About £15·50 for two
Closed Sun & Bank Hols
Tube Piccadilly Circus

Colombina 4 Duke of York Street *SW1Y 6JP*

A pleasantly relaxed restaurant, whose extensive menu includes most of the usual Italian favourites. Cooking is capable, and service friendly and smart. *Credit* Access, Amex, Barclaycard, Diners

Lunch 12–3 *Dinner* 6–11

Map 22 A3
01–229 3794
About £12 for two
Closed Sun & Bank Hols
Tube Notting Hill Gate

Costas Grill 12 Hillgate Street *W8 7SR*

Food gets top priority in this popular, unassuming restaurant dominated by lamb turning on the spit. Appetising Greek favourites like sheftalia and moussaka are freshly cooked and informally served.

Meals noon–10.30pm

Map 24 B2
01–636 1057
About £13 for two
Closed L Sat, all Sun, Bank
Hols & 3 wks summer
Tube Goodge Street

Cypriana Kebab House 11 Rathbone Street *W1P 1AF*

Attractive plants deck the entrance to this simple taverna, where Mrs Soteriou prepares tasty Greek and Cypriot specialities from houmus and avgolemono to afelia, kebabs and kleftiko. *Credit* Barclaycard, Diners

Lunch 12–2.30 *Dinner* 6–11.30

Map 23 C4
01–589 6117
About £13 for two
Closed 25 & 26 Dec
Tube South Kensington

Daquise 20 Thurloe Street *SW7 2LT*

For 25 years this simple café-restaurant has offered authentic Polish and Russian specialities, from hearty soups and spicy sausages to stuffed cabbage and meatballs, plus excellent pâtisserie.

Meals noon–midnight.

Map 21 A5
01–748 9393
About £18 for two
Closed 25 & 26 Dec
⊖ Tube Hammersmith

Da Gianbruno 6 Hammersmith Broadway *W6 7AL*

Run with friendly Italian charm, this informal trattoria has a varied menu of reliably prepared dishes ranging from spaghetti alle vongole to tender veal chop with sage. *Credit* Access, Amex, Barclaycard, Diners

Lunch 12–3 *Dinner* 6–11.30

Map 20 C3
01–387 5556
About £7 for two
Closed Mon & 25 Dec
⊖ Tube Euston

Diwana Bhel-Poori House 121 Drummond Street *NW1 2HL*

There's always a crowd at Mr Patel's splendid little restaurant, where the formula for success is tasty, well-prepared Indian vegetarian dishes at very reasonable prices. Unlicensed. *Credit* Access, Barclaycard

Meals noon–10.45pm

Map 22 A1
01–221 0721
About £10 for two
Closed Mon & 25 December
⊖ Buses 7, 15, 23, 27

Diwana Bhel-Poori House 50 Westbourne Grove *W2 5SH*

Indian vegetarian dishes offer great value for money at this friendly, informal restaurant. Try tasty pooris and dosas, or sample several different dishes on the set lunch. Unlicensed. *Credit* Access, Barclaycard

Lunch 12–3 *Dinner* 6–10.45

Map 25 A6
01–730 8147
About £16·50 for two
⊖ Tube Victoria

Ebury Court Hotel Restaurant 26 Ebury Street *SW1V 0LU*

An elegant pink dining room, where simple dishes like eggs florentine, salmon mayonnaise, boiled silverside and grilled rumpsteak are prepared with a skilled experienced hand. *Credit* Access, Barclaycard

Lunch 12–2, Sat 12–1.30 *Dinner* 7–9

Map 23 D4
01–730 5447
About £16 for two
Closed 4 days Christmas
⊖ Buses 11, 39

Ebury Wine Bar 139 Ebury Street *SW1W 9QU*

Booking is essential at this popular wine bar, where the choice of simple, well-prepared food ranges from eggs Madras and cannelloni to grills and salads. *Credit* Access, Amex, Barclaycard, Diners

Lunch 11–3, Sun 12–2.30 *Dinner* 5.30–11, Sun 7–10.30

Map 24 B2
01–636 1953
About £15 for two
Closed Sun & Bank Hols
⊖ Tube Great Portland St

Efes Kebab House 80 Great Titchfield Street *W1P 7AF*

Perfectly cooked kebabs and other charcoal-grilled specialities are the main attraction at this admirable Turkish restaurant. Varied starters like stuffed aubergine. Book. *Credit* Access Amex, Barclaycard

Meals noon–11.30pm

Map 23 B5
01–589 2401
About £16·50 for two
Closed 25 & 26 Dec
⊖ Tube South Kensington

Il Falconiere 84 Old Brompton Road *SW7 3LQ*

A cheerful, popular trattoria featuring tasty dishes ranging from minestrone and pasta to veal escalope and grilled sole with prawn and caper sauce. Nice sweets, too. *Credit* Access, Amex, Barclaycard, Diners

Lunch 12–2.45 *Dinner* 6–11.45

Map 21 B6
01–736 2418
About £15 for two
Closed Sun & Bank Hols
⊖ Buses 28, 91, 295

Filling Station Bistro 144 Wandsworth Bridge Road *SW6 2UH*

The welcome is friendly and the cooking excellent at this charming bistro. Choices range from Camembert croquettes to grilled poussin with mango and darkly tempting chocolate mousse. *Credit* Access, Barclaycard

Dinner only 7.30–12

When certain members of our staff retire, we find them a nice place in the country.

Whitbread's magnificent Shire Horses are not employed purely for show. They all work for their living.

By delivering beer within the City of London and its immediate surroundings, these beautiful animals serve a practical purpose as well as continuing a well loved tradition. When they're not making deliveries, Whitbread's Shires may well be involved in an important ceremonial occasion. Which, as descendants of the chargers at Agincourt, seems only fitting.

They can often be seen drawing the coach of the Lord Mayor or the Speaker of the House of Commons.

For most of the year, the Shires are housed in stables at our Chiswell Street Brewery. But for their summer holidays they can relax and gambol freely in the beautiful surroundings of our hop farm at Beltring, near Paddock Wood, Kent.

And when the time comes, it's the perfect place for the Shires to enjoy a well-earned retirement.

Map 21 B5
01–736 1195
About £18 for two
Closed L Sat, all Sun,
Easter & 1 wk Xmas
☻ Tube Parsons Green

Fingal's 690 Fulham Road *SW6 5SA*

A homely, rustic restaurant where varied dishes like gazpacho and rack of lamb with rosemary are carefully prepared and informally served. Choose carefully to stay within budget. *Credit* Access, Barclaycard

Lunch 12.30–2.30 *Dinner* 8–11.30

Our inspectors are our full-time employees; they are professionally trained by us.

Map 20 B2
01–435 1541
About £17 for two
Closed Sun & Bank Hols
☻ Tube Belsize Park

La Fondue at Bunny's 7 Pond Street *NW3 2PN*

At this charming little place, part of Bunny's Restaurant, the three-course set menu for two centres round a delicious fondue–cheese, meat or vegetable. For single diners there's a steak.

Dinner only 6.30–11, Sat 6.30–11.30

Map 24 C1
01–837 4584
About £16 for two
Closed Sun & some Bank Hols
☻ Tube Russell Square

Il Fornello 150 Southampton Row *WC1B 5AL*

A friendly, family-run trattoria, whose long menu offers pasta, veal specialities, fish dishes, omelettes, salads and grills, all well cooked and attractively presented. *Credit* Access, Amex, Barclaycard, Diners

Meals 11.30am–11pm   ♿

Map 23 C6
01–352 7179
About £16·50 for two
Closed some Bank Hols & 9 days Christmas
☻ Bus 39

Foxtrot Oscar 79 Royal Hospital Road *SW3 4HN*

From delicious moussaka to eggs Benedict, from timbale of scallops to sausage and mash, there's an international flavour to the menu in this stylish, welcoming restaurant. *Credit* Access, Amex, Barclaycard, Diners

Lunch 12.30–2.30, Sun 12.30–2.45 *Dinner* 7.30–12.45

Map 23 B6
01–352 8692
About £18 for two
Closed 25 December
☻ Buses 14,31

Foxtrot Tango 14 Hollywood Road *SW10 9HY*

Choose anything from a simple hamburger or salad to an unusual speciality like veal chop with avocado sauce in this smart modern restaurant (formerly Jake's). *Credit* Access, Amex, Barclaycard, Diners

Lunch 12.30–2.30 *Dinner* 7.30–11.45

Map 20 C3
01–278 1938
About £15 for two
Closed Sun & Bank Hols
☻ Tube King's Cross

Ganpath 372 Gray's Inn Road *WC1X 8BB*

Helpful, enthusiastic staff will guide you through the menu at this simply decorated restaurant, which specialises in authentically prepared, subtly spiced South Indian vegetarian dishes. *Credit* Access

Lunch 12–3 *Dinner* 7–11   ♿

Map 21 B6
01–731 6381
About £17 for two
Closed L Sat, all Sun & most Bank Hols
☻ Tube Parsons Green

Gastronome One 313 New King's Road *SW6 4RF*

A smart, friendly restaurant where the new French chef prepares tasty dishes like cheese soufflé, lotte au poivre vert and daube de bœuf. Nice vegetables. *Credit* Access, Barclaycard

Lunch 12–2.30 *Dinner* 7–11   ♿

Map 21 A6
01–785 9151
About £14 for two
Closed D Sun & Bank Hols
⊖ Buses 14, 22, 30, 39, 74, 85, 93, 220, 264

Gavin's Bistro 5 Lacy Road, Putney *SW15 1HN*

Splendid down-to-earth home cooking is the hallmark of this cosy little restaurant: delicious soups, main dishes like baked ham or roast lamb, tasty fresh vegetables and marvellous sweets.

Lunch 12–2.30 *Dinner* 7–11, Sat 7–11.30

Map 22 A2
01–727 7969
About £11 for two
⊖ Tube Notting Hill Gate

Geales Fish Restaurant 2 Farmer Street *W8 7SN*

The place for outstanding fish and chips–from cod to conger eel and shark, cooked to order in lovely crisp batter. *Credit* Access **Closed** Sun, Mon, Bank Hols & day after, 3 weeks July/August & 2 weeks Christmas

Lunch 12–3 *Dinner* 6–12, Sat 6–11

Map 7 A4
01–567 5237
About £15·50 for two
Closed 2 days Easter & 3 days Christmas
⊖ Tube Ealing Broadway

Gino's 70 The Mall, Ealing *W5 5LS*

Classic Italian favourites like osso bucho, spaghetti alla vongole and various pizzas tempt passers-by into this lively restaurant, where the cooking is thoroughly enjoyable and the service unhurried.

Lunch 12–3 *Dinner* 6.30–11.30, Fri & Sat 6.30–12

Map 21 C5
01–834 0149
About £15 for two
Closed L Sat, D Sun & Bank Hols
⊖ Tube Victoria

Grumbles 35 Churton Street *SW1V 2LT*

Informal and unpretentious, this popular bistro offers a good range of robust, tasty dishes, from haddock smokies and onion soup to chicken chasseur and fillet steak. *Credit* Access, Amex, Barclaycard, Diners

Lunch 12.30–3, Sun 1–3 *Dinner* 6–11.55

Map 24 B1
01–388 1640
About £14 for two
⊖ Tube Warren Street

Gurkha Tandoori 23 Warren Street *W1P 5DE*

Tandoori specialities–mainly chicken and lamb–are among the attractions of this tiny restaurant. Others include excellent bhajias, biryanis and Nepalese dishes. *Credit* Access, Amex, Barclaycard, Diners

Lunch 12–2.45 *Dinner* 6–11.45

Map 22 D3
01–629 0382
About £14 for two
Closed 25 December
⊖ Tube Hyde Park Corner

Hard Rock Café 150 Old Park Lane *W1Y 3LN*

The crowds still flock to this friendly, noisy restaurant to enjoy some of the best American-style food in town: charbroiled steaks, burgers, salads, sandwiches, milkshakes and daunting ice cream sundaes.

Meals noon–12.15am, Sun noon–midnight

Map 20 B3
01–722 1869
About £13 for two
Closed D Fri, all Mon, Jan, Xmas & Jewish Hols
⊖ Tube St John's Wood

Harry Morgan's 31 St John's Wood High Street *NW8 7NH*

Jewish favourites dominate the menu at this friendly, unassuming restaurant: the salt beef is excellent, and other popular choices include gefilte fish, latkes and chicken liver risotto. Grills and roasts, too.

Lunch 12–3, Sun noon–10pm *Dinner* 6–10

Map 23 B6
01–352 6797
About £17·50 for two
Closed 25 & 26 Dec
⊖ Buses 11, 19, 22, 31, 45, 49

Ho Lee Fook 368 King's Road *SW3 5UZ*

A large, friendly Chinese restaurant, where you'll find a good choice of well-prepared Cantonese dishes ranging from sesame prawns and steamed sea bass to crispy roast duck. *Credit* Access, Amex, Barclaycard, Diners

Meals noon–11.30pm ♿

Map 22 C3
01–235 2000
About £18·50 for two
Tube Knightsbridge

Hyde Park Hotel, Park Room Knightsbridge *SW1Y 7LA*

A harpist plays in the opulent surroundings of this grand dining room, where the best bets for budget-eaters are simple items like burgers, salads and omelettes. *Credit* Access, Amex, Barclaycard, Diners

Meals 12.30pm–11pm

Map 22 D3
01–409 3131
About £18·50 for two
Tube Hyde Park Corner

Inter-Continental Hotel Coffee House
1 Hamilton Place *W1V 0QY*
Sandwiches, salads, hamburgers and delicious hot dishes offer ample choice, but budget-eaters must choose carefully at this smart coffee shop. Excellent pâtisserie, too. *Credit* Access, Amex, Barclaycard, Diners

Meals 7am–midnight, Sat & Sun 7.30am–2am

Map 21 B4
01–221 6090
About £18 for two
Closed Mon, Easter &
24–26 December
Tube Holland Park

La Jardinière 148 Holland Park Avenue *W11 4UE*

A fresh, airy restaurant whose interesting French menu offers nicely prepared dishes such as crab croquettes, entrecôte au Roquefort and excellent duck in pastry. Friendly service. *Credit* Access, Amex

Lunch Sun only 12.30–2.30 *Dinner* 6.30–11.45

Map 24 D3
01–836 0651
About £16 for two
Closed 25 December
Tube Covent Garden

Joe Allen 13 Exeter Street *WC2E 7DT*

Popular with homesick New Yorkers and lovers of all things American, this lively basement restaurant does a roaring trade with exciting salads, spareribs, black bean soup and pecan pie.

Meals noon–1am, Sun noon–midnight

Map 22 B2
01–727 5082
About £16 for two
Closed Sun & Bank Hols
Tube Bayswater

Kalamaras 66 Inverness Mews *W2 3JQ*

Authentic Greek dishes are capably prepared in this friendly little taverna. The choice includes dolmades, Smyrna sausages, lamb and moussaka. Unlicensed. *Credit* Access, Amex, Barclaycard, Diners

Dinner only 7–11.30

Map 25 D6
01–379 7722
About £13·50 for two
Closed Sun & Bank Hols
Buses 1, 6, 9, 11, 13, 15, 23, 77

L. S. Grunts 12 Maiden Lane *WC2E 7NA*

Chicago-style deep-dish pizzas are the main attraction at this popular restaurant in a converted power station. Also salads, stuffed mushrooms, cheesecake and ice creams. *Credit* Access, Barclaycard

Meals noon–11.30pm

Map 23 C4
01–589 2950
About £14 for two
Closed Sun, Bank Hols &
last 3 weeks August
Buses 14, 30, 74

Luba's Bistro 6 Yeoman's Row *SW3 2AH*

Enjoyable Russian specialities attract a loyal following at this friendly bistro, along with grills, curries, spaghetti and lots more. Unlicensed, so bring your own. *Credit* Access, Amex, Barclaycard

Lunch 12–3 *Dinner* 6–11.30

Map 22 C2
01–723 0540
About £18 for two
Buses 6, 7, 8, 15, 16, 16A, 23, 36B

La Lupa 23 Connaught Street *W2 2AY*

Amidst classical Roman decor, enjoy Italian favourites, along with some less usual items like our fettuccine al Gorgonzola. *Credit* Access, Amex, Barclaycard, Diners **Closed** Sun, L Bank Hols & 4 days Christmas

Lunch 12–2.45 *Dinner* 6.30–11.30

Map 24 B1
01–580 5607
About £12 for two
Closed L Sun
⊖ Tube Goodge Street

Mahagopal 160 New Cavendish Street *W1M 7FJ*

Formerly the Uema, this unpretentious restaurant offers a wide choice of familiar Indian dishes, from tandoori chicken to spicy curries like mutton dhansak. Reliable cooking. *Credit* Access, Amex, Barclaycard, Diners

Lunch 12–3 *Dinner* 6–11.30, Sun 7–11.30

Map 20 B3
01–794 9981
About £13 for two
Closed 4 days Christmas
⊖ Tube Finchley Road

Mediterranean Kebab House 265 Finchley Road *NW3 6LU*

There's a good choice of kebabs at this friendly, modern restaurant, along with mezes, salads, chicken dishes and moussaka. Enjoyable sweets include kateif and baklava. *Credit* Access, Amex, Barclaycard, Diners

Lunch 12–2.30 *Dinner* 6–12

Map 22 A3
01–727 5452
About £15·50 for two
Closed L Sat, all Sun & Bank Hols
⊖ Tube Notting Hill Gate

Mildred's 135 Kensington Church Street *W8 7LP*

A friendly, informal atmosphere prevails at this bistro-style restaurant, where simple dishes like cream of broccoli soup, pork chop with apple sauce and roast chicken with lemon and herbs are prepared with skill.

Lunch 12–3 *Dinner* 7–10.30

Map 7 A5
01–948 2787
About £10 for two
Closed D Mon & Tues & 4 days Christmas
⊖ Buses 27, 37, 65, 71

Mrs Beeton 58 Hill Rise, Richmond *TW10 6UB*

Enthusiastically run by local housewives, this friendly little place offers tasty, value-for-money dishes like pâtés, vegetable soups and meaty casseroles. Nice puddings, too. Unlicensed, so bring your own.

Lunch 10–3.30 *Dinner* 6.30–10.30

Map 7 A4
01–567 2343
About £18·50 for two
Closed L Sun & 25 & 26 December
⊖ Tube Ealing Broadway

New Leaf 35 Bond Street, Ealing *W5 5AS*

Superb Peking and Szechuan-style cooking combines with friendly service to make this family-run restaurant a real winner. First-class raw materials, and neat modern decor. *Credit* Access, Amex, Barclaycard

Lunch 12–2.15 *Dinner* 6–11.45

Map 23 C4
01–589 4971
About £14·50 for two
Closed L Sat & 4 days Xmas & Easter
⊖ Tube South Kensington

Nineteen 19 Mossop Street *SW3 2LY*

Careful cooking attracts a strong following to this friendly little bistro. Tasty choices range from iced cucumber soup and crab mousse to calf's liver with a rich wine sauce and delicious puds like treacle tart.

Lunch 12–2.45 *Dinner* 7–11.45

Map 20 C3
01–387 4579
About £10·50 for two
Closed Sun & Bank Hols
⊖ Tube Camden Town

Nontas 16 Camden High Street *NW1 0JH*

Authentic Greek dishes are capably prepared in this congenial restaurant. The choice includes baked stuffed marrow, charcoal grills and mezes, as well as daily specials like afelia or kleftikou. *Credit* Access, Diners

Lunch 12–2.45 *Dinner* 6–11.30

Map 21 C6
01–673 2568
About £15 for two
Closed L Sun (summer) D Sun & 25 & 26 Dec
⊖ Buses 35, 37, 88, 137

Ormes 67 Abbeville Road *SW4 9JW*

There's something for everyone at this Victorian-style restaurant, where enjoyable dishes range from delicious vegetable and cheese chowder to steaks, beef olives and some scrumptious sweets. *Credit* Access, Barclaycard

Lunch 12–3 *Dinner* 7–10.45

Map 21 C6
01–228 9824
About £18 for two
Closed L Sat, all Sun &
25–30 December
☻ Buses 45, 77, 77A

Ormes at Lavender Hill 245 Lavender Hill *SW11 1JW*

A pleasant seafood restaurant, whose monthly-changing menu offers delights like Hungarian fish soup, baked trout and cod and chips. Also chicken and steak, plus a few super desserts. *Credit* Access, Barclaycard

Lunch 12–2.30 *Dinner* 7–11

Map 22 A3
01–229 4332
About £17 for two
Closed Sun & some Bank
Hols
☻ Tube Notting Hill Gate

La Paesana 30 Uxbridge Street *W8 7TA*

A popular restaurant, where enjoyable Italian favourites include home-made pasta, liver veneziana and tender scaloppina alla zingara. There's also a good choice of hors d'œuvre and sweets. *Credit* Amex, Barclaycard, Diners

Lunch 12–3 *Dinner* 6.30–12

Map 23 B6
01–352 0651
About £15 for two
Closed D 24 & 31 & all 25
& 26 December
☻ Buses 14, 45

Parsons 311 Fulham Road *SW10 9QH*

Slow-moving fans and luxuriant greenery set the scene in this very popular restaurant where the choice ranges from burgers to creamy onion soup, spaghetti and fried chicken, all generously served.

Meals 12.30pm–12.30am

Map 23 A4
01–937 0120
About £17 for two
Closed 24 December
☻ Tube Earl's Court

Phoenicia 11 Abingdon Road *W8 6AH*

Set menus offer a good introduction to Lebanese cuisine at this smart restaurant. The extensive à la carte includes hot and cold mezes and charcoal-grilled main courses. *Credit* Access, Amex, Barclaycard, Diners

Meals noon–11.45pm

Map 23 D5
01–730 5323
About £16·50 for two
Closed Mon & Bank Hols
☻ Tube Sloane Square

Pimlico Ristorante Italiano 89 Pimlico Road *SW1W 8PH*

Good ingredients and careful cooking make for enjoyable meals in this pleasant Italian restaurant, whose menu is supplemented by daily specials like osso bucho or sautéed rabbit with fresh herbs. *Credit* Access, Diners

Lunch 12–2.30 *Dinner* 7–11.30

Map 23 A5
01–373 9082
About £18·50 for two
Closed Bank Hols
☻ Tube Earl's Court

Pontevecchio 256 Old Brompton Road *SW5 9HR*

A lively trattoria full of style, where Italian specialities like saltimbocca are ably prepared and served with delicious vegetables. Budget-eaters should choose carefully. *Credit* Access, Amex, Barclaycard, Diners

Lunch 12.30–3 *Dinner* 7–12

Map 25 D6
01–836 6466
About £15 for two
Closed 25 & 26 Dec
☻ Buses 1, 6, 9, 11, 13, 15,
23, 77, 77A, 170, 172, 176

Porters 17 Henrietta Street *WC2E 8QH*

Splendid savoury pies, ranging from lamb and apricot to game, top the bill in this bustling, down-to-earth restaurant, while traditional puds include plum duff and treacle tart. *Credit* Access, Barclaycard

Lunch 12–3, Sat noon–11.30pm, Sun noon–10.30pm *Dinner* 5.30–11.30

We welcome complaints and bona fide recommendations on the tear-out pages for readers' comments. They are followed up by our professional team. Please also complain to the management instantly.

Map 7 B4
01–858 9222
About £15 for two
Closed L Sat, D Sun, 1 Jan
& 25 & 26 Dec
Buses 108b, 177, 180, 188

Le Premier Cru 328 Creek Road, Greenwich *SE10 9SW*

A pleasant restaurant near the *Cutty Sark*, where you can get anything from a lunchtime sandwich or two-course meal to an evening choice of sauced dishes, grills and excellent sweets. *Credit* Access, Amex, Diners
Lunch 12–3 *Dinner* 7–11

Map 7 A5
01–940 6777
About £12 for two
Closed Sun, Mon & 10
Aug–10 Sept
Tube Kew Gardens

Le Provence 14 Station Parade, Kew *TW9 3PZ*

English and French blend happily in this welcoming, informal restaurant, with tasty dishes ranging from roast chicken and liver and bacon to plaice meunière and loin of pork with rosemary. Unlicensed.

Lunch Sat only 12–2.30 *Dinner* 6–9.15

Map 23 B5
01–589 0529
About £17 for two
Closed L Sat, all Sun &
Bank Hols
Tube South Kensington

Pulcinella 30 Old Brompton Road *SW7 3DL*

A colourful basement restaurant offering a wide choice of Italian dishes ranging from minestrone with tripe to brains in a tasty sauce. Nicely cooked pasta, too. *Credit* Access, Amex, Barclaycard, Diners

Lunch 12–3 *Dinner* 6–12

Map 20 B3
01–328 9070
About £15 for two
Closed 25 & 26 Dec
Tube Kilburn

Raffles 391 Kilburn High Road *NW6 7QE*

Spicy North and South Indian specialities, including some vegetarian dishes, dominate the menu in this attractive restaurant. Steaks, omelettes and various sweets, too. *Credit* Access, Amex, Barclaycard, Diners

Lunch 12–3 *Dinner* 6–11.30

Map 23 C4
01–589 5970
About £17 for two
Closed D Sun & 4 days
Christmas
Tube Knightsbridge

Rascals 6 Beauchamp Place *SW3 1NG*

Variety's the key to this friendly restaurant: frankfurters and sauerkraut, poached egg in curry sauce, roasts and dishes like beef carbonnade are all well prepared. *Credit* Access, Amex, Barclaycard, Diners

Lunch 12–2.45, Sun 12–3 *Dinner* 6–12.45am

Map 20 B3
01–286 2266
About £15·50 for two
Closed L Mon, all Sun,
Bank Hols & 3 wks Aug
Tube Warwick Avenue

Romano's 30 Clifton Road *W9 1ST*

A friendly little trattoria offering enjoyable Italian dishes such as al dente tortellini and scallopine alla romana, plus grills and salads. Well-prepared vegetables, too. *Credit* Access, Amex, Barclaycard, Diners

Lunch 12–3 *Dinner* 6–11.30

Map 20 C3
01–485 0360
About £18 for two
Closed Bank Holidays
Tube Camden Town

Le Routier 13 Commercial Place, Chalk Farm Road *NW1 8AF*

This converted warehouse has the atmosphere of an informal French café, with cooking to match. The menu shows plenty of skill and imagination, but budget-eaters should choose carefully. *Credit* Access, Amex

Lunch 12.30–2.30, Sun 12.30–2.45 *Dinner* 7–10.45

Map 26 A3
01–928 4554
About £18·50 for two
Closed L Sat, all Sun &
Bank Hols
Tube Waterloo

RSJ 13a Coin Street *SE1 8YQ*

It's best to book at this lively restaurant, whose varied menu includes tasty French-style dishes like monkfish terrine and lamb with honey and rosemary. Excellent desserts, too. Budgeters choose carefully.

Lunch 12–2.30 *Dinner* 6–11.30

Map 22 C1
01–402 7722
About £15 for two
Closed Bank Hols
⊖ Tube Edgware Road

Salino 25 Sale Place *W2 1PU*

Sicilian specialities like veal with aubergines and mozzarella are highlights of the menu in this attractive trattoria, where simple Italian fare is the order of the day. *Credit* Access, Amex, Barclaycard, Diners

Lunch 12–3 *Dinner* 6–11.30

Map 23 D4
01–235 1668
About £16·50 for two
Closed D Sun & 3 days Xmas
⊖ Tube Knightsbridge

Scats 27 Motcomb Street *SW1X 8JU*

Varied, unpretentious food is offered in this informal brasserie, where the choice ranges from crisp smoked haddock fish cakes and tasty moules marinière to roast rack of lamb. *Credit* Access, Amex, Barclaycard, Diners

Lunch 12.30–2.45 *Dinner* 6.30–10.30

Map 21 B5
01–731 4248
About £11 for two
Closed L Mon & 1 week Christmas
⊖ Tube Fulham Broadway

Staveley's 642 King's Road *SW6 4DU*

Fish and chips are the speciality of this friendly, comfortable restaurant, where tasty fried cod, plaice, haddock and rockfish are served with lovely crisp chips. Steak and kidney pie for meat-lovers.

Lunch 12–3, Sat & Sun noon–midnight *Dinner* 6–12

Map 25 C6
01–734 1291
About £14 for two
Closed 25 December
⊖ Tube Piccadilly Circus

Swiss Centre, Rendezvous 2 New Coventry Street *W1V 7FJ*

Swiss-German specialities feature in this restaurant styled like a coffee shop. Interesting salads, veal sausages and burgers are offered, along with luscious gâteaux. *Credit* Access, Amex, Barclaycard, Diners

Meals 11.30am–midnight

Map 25 C6
01–437 2354
About £15 for two
Closed 25 December
⊖ Tube Leicester Square

Tai Ka Lok 18 Gerrard Street *W1V 7LA*

A varied menu of delicious Cantonese dishes brings crowds of Chinatown locals flocking to this simple, bustling little restaurant. Very generous portions of wholesome, authentic fare.

Meals noon–midnight

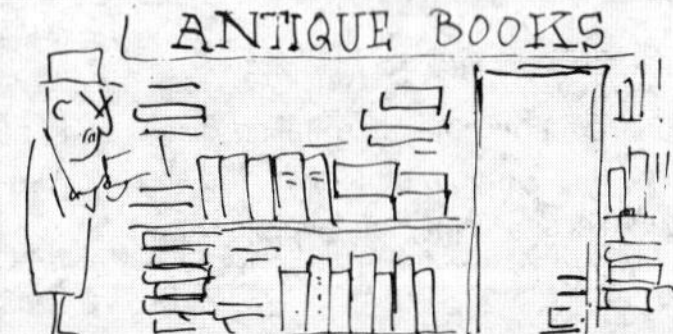

We publish annually, so make sure you use the current edition. It's worth it!

Map 22 A2
01–727 2980
About £16 for two
Closed Sun & 25 & 26 December
⊖ Tube Bayswater

Texas Lone Star West 117 Queensway *W2 4SJ*

As the menu suggests, you'll find Western saloon decor and a menu to please hungry cowboys, ranging from smoky spareribs and tasty tacos to meaty burgers and chilli as hot as you can take it.

Lunch 12–3 *Dinner* 6.30–1

Map 24 B3
01–734 5931
About £15 for two
⊖ Tube Piccadilly Circus

Topo Gigio 46 Brewer Street *W1R 3HN*

A smart modern basement restaurant decorated in true Italian style. The menu offers an extensive range of carefully prepared dishes such as saltimbocca alla romana. *Credit* Access, Amex, Barclaycard, Diners

Meals noon–11.30pm

Map 25 C6
01–930 8364
About £18·50 for two
Closed Sun & Bank Hols
Tube Leicester Square

Trattoria Imperia 19 Charing Cross Road *WC2H 0ES*

Reliable cooking is the hallmark of this busy little Italian restaurant, where the menu ranges from tagliatelle to veal alla milanese. Budget-eaters should choose carefully. *Credit* Access, Amex, Barclaycard, Diners

Lunch 12–2.35 *Dinner* 6–11.25

Our inspectors never book in the name of the Egon Ronay Organisation; they disclose their identity only after paying their bills.

Map 22 D3
01–235 8444
About £17 for two
Closed 25 & 26 Dec
Tube Knightsbridge

Upper Crust in Belgravia 9 William Street *SW1X 9HL*

Traditional pies with splendid puffed-up tops are featured in this simple panelled restaurant along with other English favourites like roasts, steaks and plum pudding. *Credit* Access, Amex, Barclaycard, Diners

Lunch 11.30–3 *Dinner* 6–11.15, Sun 6–11

Map 23 C4
01–584 1107
About £16·50 for two
Closed Sun, Good Fri & 25 & 26 Dec
Tube Knightsbridge

Verbanella 30 Beauchamp Place *SW3 1NJ*

Still as popular as ever, this trattoria offers well-prepared and nicely presented Italian favourites ranging from prosciutto and minestrone to marinated lamb with rosemary. *Credit* Access, Amex, Barclaycard, Diners

Lunch 12–3 *Dinner* 6–11.45

Map 22 D1
01–935 2174
About £16 for two
Closed Sun & Bank Hols
Buses 1, 2, 13, 30, 74, 113, 159

Verbanella 35 Blandford Street *W1H 3AE*

Very popular at lunch time, especially with Italians, this rustic trattoria offers enjoyable dishes ranging from spaghetti vongole to veal with ham and cheese. *Credit* Access, Amex, Barclaycard, Diners

Lunch 12–3 *Dinner* 6–11.30

Map 22 A2
01–229 9882
About £16 for two
Closed Sun, Easter & Christmas
Tube Notting Hill Gate

Verbanella 145 Notting Hill Gate *W11 3LB*

Colourful antipasti are a must in this ever-popular trattoria, and there are also tasty pasta dishes and favourites like pollo sorpressa. Excellent espresso to finish. *Credit* Access, Amex, Barclaycard, Diners

Lunch 12–3 *Dinner* 6–11.30

Map 23 C4
01–589 8444
About £14 for two
Closed 25 & 26 Dec
Tube Knightsbridge

Wolfe's 25 Basil Street *SW3 1BB*

A smart, well-run restaurant, where meaty six- or eight-ounce hamburgers are served with an imaginative variety of sauces and toppings. Also salads, omelettes, steaks and lots more. *Credit* Access, Amex, Barclaycard, Diners

Meals 11.30am–midnight 

Map 22 D1
01–487 4009
About £14 for two
Closed 25 December
Tube Bond Street

Woodlands 77 Marylebone Lane *W1M 5GA*

Order a thali (set meal) and explore the whole range of delights on offer at this stylish South Indian vegetarian restaurant. Dosas are a speciality. *Credit* Access, Amex, Barclaycard, Diners

Lunch 12–3, Sat & Sun noon–11pm *Dinner* 6–10.30

Map 25 B6
01–834 5413
About £16 for two
Closed L Sun, Good Fri &
3 days Christmas
✪ Tube Victoria

Yasmine 278 Vauxhall Bridge Road *SW1V 1BB*

A comfortable and smart little restaurant offering spicy tandoori dishes and a range of popular curries with tasty rice and nan bread. Helpful service. *Credit* Access, Amex, Barclaycard, Diners

Lunch 12–3 *Dinner* 6–12

ECONOMY HOTELS IN LONDON

'Economy Hotels' is a category comprising modest hotels with limited facilities. The accommodation is of a reasonable standard, but below our usual limit of 50% grading and with prices almost always much cheaper. Some call themselves 'private hotels' or 'unlicensed hotels'.

Hotels in the main London section of the Guide where prices are comparable to those in this section:

Central Park Hotel, W2

Clarendon Court Hotel, W9

Elizabetta Hotel, SW5

Embassy House Hotel, SW7

Hogarth Hotel, SW5

Imperial Hotel, WC1

Portobello Hotel, W11

Royal National Hotel, WC1

Alexander Hotel Ⓜ £ D/E

Map 23 B5
9 Sumner Place *SW7 3EE*
01–581 1591
Telex 917133
Rooms 36   *with TV* 36
with bath/shower 32
with telephone 36

⊖ Tube South Kensington

There's an air of gracious living about this elegant hotel, tastefully converted from three mid-Victorian houses. Housekeeping is impeccable, and the public areas are beautifully decorated and carpeted. The pine-furnished breakfast room has French windows opening on to a peaceful paved garden. Bright, comfortable bedrooms range from small with shower only to family size. No dogs. *Amenities* garden, 24-hour porterage.
Credit Access, Amex, Barclaycard, Diners

Alison House Hotel Ⓜ £ E

Map 23 D4
82 Ebury Street *SW1W 9QD*
01–730 9529
Proprietors Mr & Mrs F. A. Haggis
Rooms 11   *with TV* 11
with bath/shower 2
with telephone None
Closed December/January
⊖ Tube Victoria

Visitors can expect the friendliest of welcomes from Mr and Mrs Haggis on arrival at this neat, spotlessly clean hotel, and thoughtful extras like a glass of sherry, information sheets and plenty of reading matter add to the pleasure of a short stay. Compact bedrooms are cheerfully decorated and modestly furnished, and hearty breakfasts are served in a cosy basement room. Unlicensed. No dogs.
Amenities porterage.

Apollo Hotel £ E/F

Map 23 A4
18 Lexham Gardens *W8 5JE*
01–373 3236
Telex 264189
Manager Mr M. J. Monina
Rooms 60   *with TV* None
with bath/shower 38
with telephone 60
⊖ Bus 74

Friendly staff make guests feel very much at home at this white painted hotel, which stands in a Victorian terrace. Its public rooms include a spacious reception-foyer, a TV lounge, a pleasant bar and an airy dining room. Well-lit bedrooms have practical modern furnishings and very comfortable beds; bathrooms are nicely fitted. There are several family rooms. *Amenities* 24-hour porterage, lift. *Credit* Access, Amex, Barclaycard, Diners

Apollo Hotel Ⓜ £ F

Map 22 B2
64 Queensborough Terrace *W2 3SN*
01–229 6251
Proprietor Mr A. V. Avedissian
Rooms 18   *with TV* 18
with bath/shower 18
with telephone 18

⊖ Tube Queensway

Guests returning year after year testify to the popularity of this comfortable little hotel, run for the last 18 years by the welcoming Mr Avedissian. Cheerful public areas include reception, a lounge and a basement breakfast room. Good-sized bedrooms have attractive floral-design curtains and bedcovers, smart practical furnishings and well-maintained, up-to-date bathrooms.
Credit Access, Amex, Barclaycard

Our inspectors are our full-time employees; they are professionally trained by us.

Aster House Ⓜ £ F

Map 23 B5
3 Sumner Place *SW7 3EE*
01–581 5888

Rooms 12   *with TV* 12
with bath/shower 5
with telephone 12

⊖ Tube South Kensington

Standing at the end of a row of terraced houses just off Fulham Road, this family-run hotel offers friendly service and very clean, comfortable accommodation. Simply decorated, brown-carpeted bedrooms have large windows, adequate storage and writing space, TVs and telephones. Bright, well-kept bathrooms. Continental breakfast is served in the bedrooms. No dogs.
Amenities porterage.
Credit Access, Amex, Barclaycard

Atlas Hotel Ⓜ £ E/F

Map 23 A4
24 Lexham Gardens *W8 5JE*
01–373 7873
Telex 264189
Manager Mr M. J. Monina
Rooms 70   *with TV* None
with bath/shower 38
with telephone 70
⊖ Bus 74

Under the same management as its neighbour and sister hotel, the Apollo, this well-run establishment offers similar hospitality and equally comfortable, unpretentious accommodation in neatly fitted, prettily decorated bedrooms. It has a smart reception area, a little TV lounge and a cosy cocktail bar, and there's an attractive panelled breakfast room. Mr Monina has run both hotels for 22 years.
Amenities porterage, lift. *Credit* Access, Amex, Barclaycard, Diners

Bardon Lodge

£ F

Map 7 B5
15 Stratheden Road
Blackheath *SE3 7TH*
01–853 4051
Rooms 15 *with TV* 4
with bath/shower None
with telephone None
Closed Christmas
☎ Buses 53, 54, 75, 89, 108, 192

The Notts have turned this detached Victorian house into a pleasant, well-run hotel. Original ceilings and carved wooden fireplaces are features of the spacious ground-floor sitting room (with TV) and the breakfast room. Bedrooms (including five with tiled shower cubicles) are centrally heated and equipped with duvets; two family bedrooms have bunks. There are three carpeted public bathrooms. Unlicensed.
Amenities garden.

Campden Court Hotel

£ E

Map 23 C4
28 Basil Street *SW3 1AT*
01–589 6286

Rooms 18 *with TV* 18
with bath/shower 8
with telephone 18

☎ Tube Knightsbridge

Italian-style furnishings are gradually replacing the more basic fitted units in the bedrooms of this four-storey red-brick hotel. Rooms vary from compact singles to family size, and bathrooms are functional. The public areas are limited to a welcoming reception hall with a small lounge area. Continental breakfast is served in the bedrooms. Guide dogs only.
Amenities Lift.
Credit Amex, Barclaycard

We welcome complaints and bona fide recommendations on the tear-out pages for readers' comments. They are followed up by our professional team. Please also complain to the management instantly.

Century Hotel

£ E/F

Map 22 B2
18 Craven Hill Gardens *W2 3EE*
01–262 6644

Rooms 56 *with TV* 56
with bath/shower 56
with telephone 56

☎ Tube Lancaster Gate

Modest overnight comforts are provided at this five-storey hotel conveniently located for Paddington Station. Bedrooms, uniformly decorated in pleasing blues and mauves, have neat white fitted furniture and adequately equipped bathrooms. There's no separate lounge, but guests can relax in the little bar just off the reception area. The breakfast room in the basement is spacious and pleasant. *Amenities* 24-hour porterage, lift.
Credit Access, Amex, Diners

Chesham House Hotel 

£ F

Map 23 D4
64 Ebury Street *SW1W 9QD*
01–730 8513
Telex 912881
Proprietor Mr Eric Fletcher
Rooms 34 *with TV* 6
with bath/shower None
with telephone None
☎ Tube Victoria

Cheerful simplicity is the hallmark of this small hotel not far from Victoria Station. Bedrooms are functional and modern in style, and public bathrooms are adequate. There are 11 bedrooms in an annexe round the corner in Elizabeth Street, where accommodation is similar but only continental breakfast is available. Unlicensed. No dogs.
Amenities porterage, tea/coffee-making facilities in annexe.
Credit Amex, Barclaycard, Diners

Colin House Hotel Ⓜ

£ F

Map 23 D4
104 Ebury Street *SW1W 9QD*
01–730 8031

Rooms 11 *with TV* None
with bath/shower 1
with telephone None

☎ Buses 11, 39

The pleasant, newly carpeted breakfast room has a homely air in this Victorian terraced hotel, where energetic new owners generate a welcoming family atmosphere. Modestly equipped bedrooms of various sizes have pretty patchwork-design duvets to brighten their generally simple decor. Compact, modernised bathrooms are adequately fitted. Unlicensed. No dogs.

Colonnade Hotel Ⓜ

£ E

Map 20 B3
2 Warrington Crescent *W9 1ER*
01–286 2167   Telex 298930
Proprietors R. H. K. &
A. R. Richards
Rooms 52 *with TV* 52
with bath/shower 40
with telephone 52
☎ Tube Warwick Avenue

This charming Victorian hotel offers variety, individuality and high standards of comfort. Each bedroom is in a different style—traditional, modern, French, floral, etc. All have trouser presses, hairdryers and comfortable seating, and bathrooms are also very well equipped. Public areas include a welcoming reception-lounge, a Japanese-style bar and a tented dining room overlooking the attractive garden.
Amenities garden, 24-hour porterage, lift. *Credit* Access, Amex

We do not necessarily recommend the cooking at hotels whose restaurants are not separately listed.

Columbia Hotel  £E

Map 22 B2
95 Lancaster Gate *W2 3NS*
01–402 0021
Proprietor Mr M. Rose

Rooms 99   *with TV* 99
with bath/shower 77
with telephone 99
Tube Lancaster Gate

Just off the busy Bayswater Road, this large Victorian hotel, with its freshly painted facade and elegant pillared entrance, is smart and welcoming. Public rooms with ornate moulded ceilings include a lounge filled with deep old-fashioned armchairs and a pleasant bar. A sweeping staircase leads to the roomy, traditionally furnished bedrooms. Bathrooms are well equipped. *Amenities* 24-hour porterage, lift.
Credit Amex, Barclaycard

Concord Hotel £F

Map 23 A4
157 Cromwell Road *SW5 0TQ*
01–370 4151
Proprietor Mrs E. Hryniewicz
Rooms 40   *with TV* None
with bath/shower 15
with telephone 40

Tube Earl's Court

Two large Victorian terraced houses were converted into this warm, welcoming hotel. A chandelier lights the elegant foyer, and the roomy TV lounge, with comfortable modern chairs and large mirrors, is equally bright and appealing. Good-sized bedrooms, all with central heating, have simple decor and furnishings. Spruce bathrooms are adequately fitted, and housekeeping is excellent throughout the hotel. *Amenities* garden, 24-hour porterage.
Credit Amex

Cranley Gardens Hotel £E

Map 23 B5
8 Cranley Gardens *SW7 3DA*
01–373 3232
Telex 291855
Manager Ms Avril Mills
Rooms 85   *with TV* 85
with bath/shower 85
with telephone 85
Buses 14, 30, 45

Converted from four 19th-century terraced houses, this hotel is popular with tourists and visitors from overseas. Stylish, fully modernised public rooms include a busy foyer-lounge with an attractive bar as well as a basement breakfast room. Bedrooms are simply furnished in modern style and have compact, up-to-date bathrooms.
Amenities porterage, lift.
Credit Access, Amex, Barclaycard, Diners

Craven Gardens Hotel £E

Map 22 B2
16 Leinster Terrace *W2 3ES*
01–262 3167
Telex 8955622
Rooms 45   *with TV* 45
with bath/shower 41
with telephone 45

Tube Queensway

The facade of this friendly Bayswater hotel is in smart Georgian style, while the interior is much more modern and functional. The reception area and two lounges (one with a bar) are on the ground floor, and there's a large, bright breakfast room in the basement. Neatly fitted bedrooms include singles, doubles and family size. Tiled bathrooms are well equipped. No dogs.
Amenities lift.
Credit Access, Amex, Barclaycard, Diners

Culford House Hotel  £F

Map 23 D5
9 Culford Gardens *SW3 2TA*
01–581 3255

Rooms 21   *with TV* 21
with bath/shower 12
with telephone 21

Tube Sloane Square

This converted Victorian house just off King's Road boasts a very smart modern interior. Spacious bedrooms are fully carpeted and fitted with functional built-in units, and bathrooms are extremely well maintained. There are no public rooms apart from reception, but continental breakfast is served in your bedroom.
Amenities garden, tea/coffee-making facilities.
Credit Access, Amex, Baclaycard, Diners

Eden House Hotel £E

Map 23 B5
111 Old Church Street *SW3 6DX*
01–352 3403
Proprietors Mr & Mrs P. Johnson
Rooms 13   *with TV* 13
with bath/shower 8
with telephone None

Buses 11, 19, 22, 49

For 25 years the Johnsons have been welcoming visitors to their charming, well-kept hotel just off King's Road. Several of the spotless, simply furnished bedrooms have extra beds for children, and services like baby sitting and children's meals make it a useful place for young families. Breakfast is served in the bedrooms, and room service of beverages and snacks is available until 10.30pm. Unlicensed. *Amenities* garden.
Credit Access, Amex, Barclaycard, Diners

Eden Park Hotel   £ E

Map 22 B2
Inverness Terrace *W2 3JS*
01–229 1453

Rooms 138   *with TV* 138
with bath/shower 138
with telephone 138

⊖ Tube Bayswater

In a tree-lined terrace close to Hyde Park, this comfortable hotel has a Victorian facade and a thoroughly modern interior. Public areas include a reception with an adjoining TV lounge, and a pleasant bar with a striking mirrored ceiling. Centrally heated bedrooms (those in the annexe are quite small) have simple decor and neat fitted furniture; bathrooms are adequate. *Amenities* 24-hour porterage, lift.
Credit Access, Amex, Barclaycard, Diners

Eden Plaza Hotel   £ E

Map 23 B4
68 Queen's Gate *SW7 5JT*
01–370 6111
Telex 916228
Rooms 62   *with TV* 62
with bath/shower 62
with telephone 62

⊖ Tube Gloucester Road

Handily placed for the Kensington museums, this well-run hotel is very popular with overseas visitors. Open-plan public areas, which are stylishly modern and cheerfully furnished, include a comfortable lounge and bar. Double-glazed bedrooms, identically furnished with modern fitted units, have TVs, radios, telephones and information folders, and smartly tiled bathrooms are equipped with hairdryers. *Amenities* 24-hour porterage, lift, sauna.
Credit Access, Amex, Barclaycard, Diners

Elizabeth Hotel Ⓜ   £ E

Map 21 C5
37 Eccleston Square *SW1V 1PB*
01–828 6812

Rooms 25   *with TV* 5
with bath/shower 3
with telephone None

⊖ Tube Victoria

The impressive terraced house overlooking verdant gardens is kept in very good order and is conveniently situated not far from Victoria Station. Public rooms, including a lofty lounge and a neat basement breakfast room, are spotlessly clean. Comfortable bedrooms, which range from compact singles to spacious family rooms, are furnished and decorated in a variety of styles. No dogs. Unlicensed.
Amenities garden.

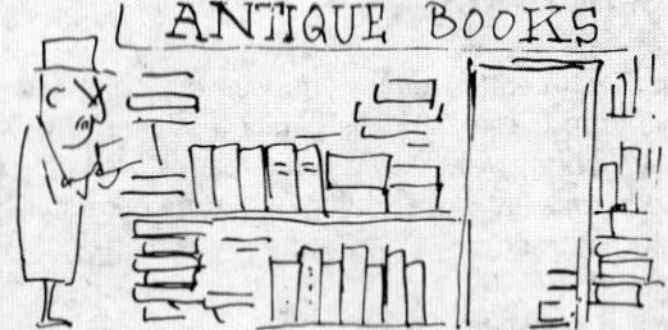

We publish annually, so make sure you use the current edition. It's worth it!

Executive Hotel Ⓜ   £ E

Map 23 C4
57 Pont Street *SW1X 0BD*
01–581 2424
Telex 263250
Rooms 29   *with TV* 29
with bath/shower 27
with telephone 29

⊖ Tube Knightsbridge

A grand little entrance hall, with plasterwork medallions and elaborate cornices, recalls a bygone era at this handsome red-brick hotel near the Knightsbridge shops. Other public areas like the breakfast room and tiny bar are cheerfully contemporary, and compact bedrooms, uniformly decorated in browns and beiges, have functional modern fittings. Adequate bathrooms. No dogs. *Amenities* porterage, tea/coffee-making facilities, lift, small car park.
Credit Access, Amex, Diners

Frognal Lodge Hotel   £ E

Map 20 B2
14 Frognal Gardens *NW3 6UX*
01–435 8238
Telex 8812714
Rooms 17   *with TV* 7
with bath/shower 7
with telephone 17

⊖ Tube Hampstead

Tucked away in a quiet spot near Hampstead High Street, this well-maintained five-storey hotel has pleasant modern accommodation. There's a functional bar-lounge with colour TV as well as a spacious breakfast room. Cheerfully decorated bedrooms (including several family rooms) are simply furnished and have plenty of wardrobe space. Bathrooms are adequately fitted.
Amenities garden, porterage, lift, snack bar (noon–9pm).
Credit Access, Amex, Barclaycard, Diners   ♿

George Hotel Ⓜ   £ F

Map 20 C3
58 Cartwright Gardens *WC1H 9EL*
01–387 1528

Rooms 43   *with TV* None
with bath/shower 3
with telephone None

⊖ Tube Russell Square

Part of a Georgian crescent near the railway stations for the north, this hotel is conscientiously run by the Barranco family. Simple, contemporary decor is a feature of the TV lounge and the terrazzo-floored breakfast room, as well as the neat staircase and landings. Bedrooms of various sizes have freestanding furniture and bold colour schemes. Fully tiled bath/shower rooms. No dogs.
Credit Access, Amex, Diners

Map 22 B1
144 Praed Street *W2 1HU*
01–262 3464
Telex 266217
Rooms 93 *with TV* 93
with bath/shower 93
with telephone 93

⊖ Tube Paddington

Grosvenor Court Hotel £ D/E

Travel-weary businessmen and tourists appreciate this smartly modernised hotel just a few steps from Paddington Station. Identical bedrooms, pleasantly fitted out in browns and creams, have built-in furniture, tea-makers, radios and neat little bathrooms. There's a drink-vending machine on the first floor, and the hotel has its own pub right next door.
Amenities tea/coffee-making facilities, lift, in-house movies.
Credit Access, Amex, Barclaycard, Diners

Our inspectors never book in the name of the Egon Ronay Organisation; they disclose their identity only after paying their bills.

Map 22 B2
19 Leinster Gardens *W2 3AN*
01–262 0117

Rooms 107 *with TV* 107
with bath/shower 107
with telephone 107

⊖ Tube Lancaster Gate

Henry VIII Hotel £ D/E

Smartly modernised behind its elegant Victorian facade, this pleasant hotel just off the Bayswater Road offers comfortable accommodation and plenty of amenities. The foyer has a relaxing lounge area featuring a plaster motif of Henry VIII, and there's an appealing bar as well as several function rooms. Well-fitted bedrooms all have their own neat little bathrooms. *Amenities* 24-hour porterage, tea/coffee-making facilities, lift, indoor swimming pool.
Credit Access, Amex, Barclaycard, Diners

Map 20 C3
45 Cartwright Gardens *WC1H 9EH*
01–387 2067
Proprietors Mr & Mrs Williams
Rooms 12 *with TV* None
with bath/shower None
with telephone None
Closed 1 week Christmas
⊖ Tube Russell Square

Jenkin's Hotel Ⓜ £ F

On the corner of a terraced crescent near Russell Square, this hotel has a pleasant homely atmosphere. The spacious TV lounge is comfortable and warmly decorated, and there's an attractive little breakfast room downstairs. Bedrooms have simple fitted or freestanding furniture, pretty patterned wallpapers and matching curtains. There are six spotlessly clean public bath or shower rooms. Unlicensed. No dogs.
Amenities garden.

Map 23 A5
33 Nevern Place *SW5 9NP*
01–370 5151

Rooms 35 *with TV* 35
with bath/shower 35
with telephone 35
Closed 2 weeks Christmas
⊖ Tube Earl's Court

Ladbroke Kensington Court Hotel £ D/E

A modern purpose-built hotel, handily placed for the Earl's Court Exhibition Centre, and with the added bonus of its own car park. Public rooms consist of a freshly decorated lounge-bar and a cheerful basement breakfast room. Uniformly styled bedrooms have attractive fitted units, ample seating and plenty of shelf and writing space. All have compact tiled bathrooms with showers. *Amenities* tea/coffee-making facilities, lift, car park.
Credit Access, Amex, Barclaycard, Diners

Map 22 B2
202 Sussex Gardens *W2 3UA*
01–402 8438

Rooms 42 *with TV* 42
with bath/shower 14
with telephone None
Closed 3 days Christmas
⊖ Tube Paddington

Lancaster Court Hotel £ F

Noted for its unfussy, spotlessly clean accommodation, this terraced hotel is convenient for travellers using nearby Paddington Station. Bedrooms are plainly decorated in functional modern style, and half are arranged as family units with one double and one single bed. Some have simple private bathrooms, others shower cubicles only. Breakfast is served in the cosy basement room. Unlicensed. No dogs. *Amenities* 24-hour porterage, in-house movies. *Credit* Access, Amex, Barclaycard, Diners

Map 23 B4
41 Queen's Gate Gardens *SW7 5NB*
01–584 0512
Telex 262180
Rooms 67 *with TV* None
with bath/shower 8
with telephone 67

⊖ Tube Gloucester Road

Leicester Court Hotel £ E

This handsome five-storey house makes a comfortable hotel offering pleasant accommodation. There's a nicely furnished TV lounge with views of the gardens, and a second lounge with glass panels and chintzy curtains. Large bedrooms have simple fitted units or fine old mahogany furniture as well as print curtains and wallpapers. Unlicensed.
Amenities 24-hour porterage, lift.
Credit Access, Amex, Barclaycard, Diners

Leinster Towers Hotel   £ D/E

Map 22 B2
Leinster Gardens *W2 3AU*
01–262 4591

Rooms 170   *with TV* 170
with bath/shower 170
with telephone 170

✆ Tube Queensway

Bright, modern public rooms at this well-maintained six-storey hotel include a cheerful, open-plan reception-lounge area, a little cocktail bar with attractive beige decor, and two conference rooms. Well-equipped bedrooms, with orange or deep red carpets and curtains, have practical fitted furniture and compact tiled bathrooms. All rooms have colour TVs and radio-alarms. No dogs. *Amenities* 24-hour porterage, tea/coffee-making facilities, lift.
Credit Access, Amex, Barclaycard, Diners

Hotel Lexham    £ E/F

Map 23 A4
32 Lexham Gardens *W8 5JU*
01–373 6471
Proprietor Mr L. Wilson
Rooms 63   *with TV* None
with bath/shower 15
with telephone 63

✆ Bus 74

This large four-storey hotel conveniently situated just off the busy Cromwell Road makes a useful base for visitors to the metropolis. There are two comfortable lounges (one with TV) and a spacious restaurant. Carpeted corridors lead to the bedrooms, which are comfortably furnished in a wide range of styles. Bathrooms are compact and spotlessly clean. Unlicensed. No dogs. *Amenities* 24-hour porterage, lift.
Credit Barclaycard

Hotel Lily    £ E/F

Map 23 A6
23 Lillie Road *SW6 1UG*
01–381 1881
Telex 918922
Proprietor Mr Allibhai
Rooms 100   *with TV* 100
with bath/shower 100
with telephone 100
✆ Tube West Brompton

Standing very close to Earl's Court Exhibition Centre, this friendly modern hotel has its own purpose-built conference suite, as well as basement car-parking facilities. There's no lounge, but chairs in the panelled reception area and a comfortable bar provide ample space for relaxation. Compact bedrooms are well equipped, and all have neat tiled bathrooms. No dogs. *Amenities* porterage, tea/coffee-making facilities, lift, sauna, in-house movies.
Credit Access, Amex, Barclaycard, Diners

London Park Hotel   £ F

Map 21 D5
Brook Drive
Elephant & Castle *SE11 4QU*
01–735 9191
Telex 919161
Rooms 388   *with TV* 388
with bath/shower 250
with telephone 388
✆ Tube Elephant & Castle

A tall, red-brick Victorian building, completely modernised inside, this large hotel is popular with tourists. One of the two bars adjoins the main foyer, while the other leads to the residents' lounge-cum-writing room. There's also a coffee shop. Good-sized bedrooms have contemporary fitted furniture and very comfortable beds. Compact, well-equipped bathrooms.
Amenities garden, 24-hour porterage, lift, coffee shop (10am–midnight).
Credit Access, Amex, Barclaycard, Diners   ♿

Lonsdale Hotel   £ E

Map 24 C1
9 Bedford Place *WC1B 5JA*
01–636 1812
Proprietor Peter Soutzos
Rooms 35   *with TV* None
with bath/shower 2
with telephone None

✆ Tube Russell Square

Two attractive Georgian houses make up this pleasant hotel, which stands near the British Museum between Russell Square and Bloomsbury Square. There's a comfortable TV lounge with deep armchairs and sofas, and a bright breakfast room. Good-sized, fully carpeted bedrooms, which can be adapted to family rooms, are tastefully furnished in a variety of styles. No dogs. Unlicensed.
Credit Access, Amex, Barclaycard, Diners

Manor Court Hotel    £ E

Map 23 B5
35 Courtfield Gardens *SW5 0PJ*
01–373 8585
Proprietor Mrs Panjwani
Rooms 88   *with TV* 88
with bath/shower 50
with telephone 88

✆ Tube Earl's Court

Behind its attractive white facade and red awnings, this quiet terraced hotel has spacious, comfortable public rooms: the reception-lounge has relaxing sofas and armchairs and glass-topped tables, and there's an open-plan bar in similar style and a separate TV lounge. Smartly furnished bedrooms have pleasant patterned bedspreads and matching curtains. Bathrooms are well equipped.
Amenities garden, porterage, lift, restaurant (7am–11pm).
Credit Access, Amex, Barclaycard, Diners   ♿

Changes in data may occur in establishments after the Guide goes to press. Prices should be taken as indications rather than firm quotes.

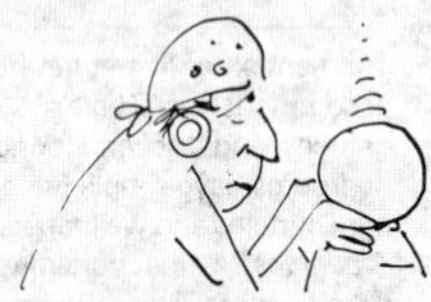

Merryfield House   £ F

Map 22 C1
42 York Street *W1H 1FN*
01–935 8326
Manager Mrs Bridget O'Brien
Rooms 8   *with TV* None
with bath/shower 8
with telephone None

Tube Baker Street

Book well in advance, as this neat little terraced hotel is immensely popular, thanks to the care with which Bridget O'Brien treats her guests. Cosy, traditionally furnished bedrooms have really pretty colour schemes and bright, boldly patterned wallpapers, plus spotless little bathrooms. TV is available on request. Breakfast is served in your bedroom, and there's also a tea/coffee dispenser. Unlicensed.

Milford House   £ F

Map 22 C1
31 York Street *W1H 1PX*
01–935 1935
Manger Miss V. Amor
Rooms 6   *with TV* None
with bath/shower 1
with telephone None

Tube Baker Street

Admirable Miss Amor keeps this attractive Georgian terrace house in really immaculate condition. Bedrooms vary in size, but all have modern fitted units, plenty of writing space and comfortable beds with duvets; bathrooms are compact and well fitted, with showers over the baths. There's no lounge, but a TV is installed in the breakfast room. Unlicensed. No dogs.
Amenities tea/coffee-making facilities.

Any person using our name to obtain free hospitality is a fraud. Proprietors, please inform the police and us.

Montague Hotel    £ D/E

Map 24 C1
Montague Street *WC1B 5BJ*
01–637 1001

Rooms 125   *with TV* None
with bath/shower 28
with telephone 125

Tube Russell Square

New owners have recently taken over this comfortable hotel converted from a row of Georgian town houses. A modern reception hall leads to the open-plan lounge-bar, and there's also a basement breakfast room. Good-sized bedrooms have unit furniture and attractively coordinated soft furnishings. Private bathrooms are compact and fully carpeted, while public ones are more basic. *Amenities* garden, lift.
Credit Access, Amex, Barclaycard, Diners

Mornington Lancaster Hotel   £ E

Map 22 B2
12 Lancaster Gate *W2 3LG*
01–262 7361
Telex 24281
Rooms 66   *with TV* 66
with bath/shower 66
with telephone 66
Closed 2 weeks Christmas
Tube Lancaster Gate

This fine Victorian mansion with lofty pillared porch is smart and impeccably maintained. Handsome mahogany panelling and green leather armchairs give the reception-lounge the atmosphere of a club, and there's a library-bar as well as a basement breakfast room with trellis wallpaper and potted plants. Compact, thoughtfully furnished bedrooms have superb beds (complete with duvets) and fully tiled bathrooms. *Amenities* lift, sauna.
Credit Access, Amex, Barclaycard, Diners

Hotel Oliver    £ F

Map 23 A4
198 Cromwell Road *SW5 0SN*
01–370 6881
Manager Mr S. Alibhai
Rooms 48   *with TV* 48
with bath/shower 48
with telephone 48

Tube Earl's Court

An attractive stairway with a brass balustrade leads up to this comfortably modernised hotel, whose public rooms include a little bar and a pleasant TV lounge with large arched windows. Bedrooms (singles, doubles, family) are uniformly fitted out with white unit furniture and colourful soft furnishings. All have TVs, telephones and adequate bathrooms. No dogs.
Amenities 24-hour porterage, lift, restaurant (7am–10pm).
Credit Access, Amex, Barclaycard, Diners

Hotel One Two Eight    £ F

Map 21 A4
128 Holland Road *W14 8BD*
01–602 3395
Props Mr & Mrs D. Novakovic
Rooms 30   *with TV* None
with bath/shower 16
with telephone 30
Closed 24 December–2 January
Tube Shepherd's Bush

You're certain of a warm welcome at this smart terraced hotel, kept by its owners in absolutely tip-top condition. Two lounges with cane furniture and potted plants are delightfully fresh and bright (one has TV), and there's a large basement breakfast room. Cosy, cheerful bedrooms have traditional furnishings including useful writing tables. Most have neat modern shower rooms or cubicles. Unlicensed.
Amenities garden, 24-hour porterage, tea/coffee-making facilities, lift.

Onslow Court Hotel   £ E

Map 23 B5
109 Queen's Gate *SW7 5LR*
01–589 6300

Rooms 133   *with TV* 133
with bath/shower 112
with telephone 133

● Tube South Kensington

This impressive period building, with elegant pillars and balconies, stands at the Old Brompton Road end of Queen's Gate. The open-plan reception-lounge is roomy and comfortable, and guests can also relax in the '30s-style coffee shop or the smart little bar. Bedrooms are large, airy and neatly furnished; bathrooms are well equipped. Helpful, friendly staff.
Amenities 24-hour porterage, lift, in-house movies.
Credit Access, Amex, Barclaycard, Diners

Park House    £ E

Map 23 C4
47 Egerton Gardens *SW3 2DD*
01–589 0715

Rooms 16   *with TV* 10
with bath/shower 10
with telephone 16

● Tube South Kensington

Close to the Knightsbridge shops and handy for South Kensington's museums, this smart red-brick hotel is run with loving care by Deborah Williams. Spacious, fully carpeted bedrooms (all are double-glazed) have elegant built-in units and chintzy fabrics, and compact bathrooms are well equipped. There's a bright, airy breakfast room in the basement. Unlicensed. No dogs. *Amenities* lift.
Credit Amex

Park Plaza Hotel    £ D/E

Map 22 B2
Lancaster Gate *W2 3NA*
01–262 5022
Telex 8954372
Rooms 360   *with TV* 360
with bath/shower 360
with telephone 360

● Tube Lancaster Gate

This large, handsome hotel, smartly modernised behind its impressive Edwardian facade, is a popular base for tour groups. Its public rooms include a spacious pillared reception hall, an open-plan lounge and two bars, one with a sedate club-like feel. Fair-sized bedrooms have practical fitted furniture and well-equipped, up-to-date bathrooms. Guide dogs only.
Amenities 24-hour porterage, lift, coffee shop (10.30am–10.30pm).
Credit Access, Amex, Barclaycard, Diners

Parkwood Hotel   £ E

Map 22 C2
4 Stanhope Place *W2 2HB*
01–402 2241
Telex 8812714
Rooms 18   *with TV* 18
with bath/shower 12
with telephone 18

● Tube Marble Arch

Handily placed for the Oxford Street shops and right opposite Hyde Park, this Victorian house with a pillared entrance has a lofty hallway, an attractive lounge area with TV, and a bright, modern breakfast room. Well-carpeted bedrooms, many with high ceilings and intricate plasterwork, have cheerful floral wallpaper and pleasing furnishings. Neat bathrooms are fully tiled. No dogs.
Credit Access, Amex, Barclaycard, Diners

Our inspectors are our full-time employees; they are professionally trained by us.

Pembridge Court Hotel    £ E

Map 22 A2
34 Pembridge Gardens *W2 4DX*
01–229 9977
Telex 298363
Proprietors Capra family
Rooms 35   *with TV* 35
with bath/shower 35
with telephone 35
● Tube Notting Hill Gate

The Capras have lavished more than 20 years of loving care on modernising this handsome Victorian house in a tree-lined road near Portobello market. Bright bedrooms (all with bath or shower) are compact and well fitted, with comfortable furnishings, TV and radio. A few in an extension are in simpler style. Attractive public rooms include a brick-walled reception area, a relaxing lounge and a cosy cocktail bar. *Amenities* 24-hour porterage.
Credit Access, Amex, Barclaycard, Diners

Philbeach Hotel    £ E/F

Map 23 A5
30 Philbeach Gardens *SW5 9EB*
01–373 1244

Rooms 41   *with TV* None
with bath/shower 13
with telephone None

● Tube Earl's Court

Situated in a quiet, tree-lined crescent, this hotel offers modest accommodation. There's a small reception and a basement bar with a cosy TV lounge, plus a restaurant overlooking the garden. Bedrooms are individually decorated and fitted with a mixture of traditional and modern furniture. Compact bathrooms are adequate. No children under 16.
Amenities garden, discothèque.
Credit Access, Amex, Barclaycard, Diners

President Hotel £E

Map 24 C1
Russell Square *WC1N 1DB*
01–837 8844
Telex 21822
Manager Stephen Walduck
Rooms 447 *with TV* 447
with bath/shower 447
with telephone 447
⊖ Tube Russell Square

Popular with parties of tourists, this is a well-run, purpose-built hotel with good modern facilities. A contemporary reception area leads to the large TV lounge and there's also a smart, streamlined bar. Nicely proportioned bedrooms have fitted furniture and floral patterned wallpaper, plus compact tiled bathrooms.
Amenities 24-hour porterage, lift, hairdressing, coffee shop (10am–2am).
Credit Access, Amex, Barclaycard, Diners

Prince Hotel Ⓜ £F

Map 23 B5
6 Sumner Place *SW7 3AB*
01–589 6488

Rooms 20 *with TV* 20
with bath/shower None
with telephone None

⊖ Tube South Kensington

Standing unostentatiously in a row of terraced town houses, this friendly hotel has a white-painted facade, a pillared entrance and attractive window boxes. Nicely carpeted public areas include a TV lounge with rich green curtains and deep, relaxing armchairs, and there's a bright, cheerful breakfast room. Pleasant bedrooms, with smart white freestanding furniture, come in single, double and family sizes; 14 have shower cubicles. Unlicensed. No dogs.
Amenities garden, porterage. *Credit* Access, Barclaycard

We welcome complaints and bona fide recommendations on the tear-out pages for readers' comments. They are followed up by our professional team. Please also complain to the management instantly.

Royal Park Hotel £F

Map 22 B2
5 Westbourne Terrace *W2 3UL*
01–402 6187
Manager Mr Cartwright
Rooms 60 *with TV* 40
with bath/shower 48
with telephone 60
Closed 24–26 December
⊖ Tube Paddington

Situated near Paddington Station and with easy access to all parts of the capital, this imposing hotel (originally a row of Victorian terraced houses) is convenient for short stays. The Hunt Bar is a popular venue and there's also a comfortable TV lounge with an impressive fireplace. Cheerful bedrooms have fitted units and prettily coordinated fabrics. All baths have shower attachments. No dogs. *Amenities* lift, snack bar (3pm–11pm).
Credit Amex, Diners

Ruskin Hotel Ⓜ £E/F

Map 24 C2
23 Montague Street *WC1B 5BN*
01–636 7388

Rooms 35 *with TV* None
with bath/shower 3
with telephone None

⊖ Tube Russell Square

This pleasant, well-kept little hotel in a terraced street just by the British Museum is a comfortable and convenient base for exploring the capital. There's a smart, stone-floored reception area, an elegant, relaxing lounge with TV, and a spacious breakfast room. Tastefully furnished bedrooms (many with attractive views of the square at the back) have washbasins and comfortable beds. No dogs. *Amenities* lift.
Credit Access, Amex, Barclaycard, Diners

Stanhope Court Hotel £E

Map 23 B4
46 Stanhope Gardens *SW7 5RT*
01–370 2161

Rooms 124 *with TV* 124
with bath/shower 54
with telephone 124

⊖ Tube Gloucester Road

A large Victorian mansion manned by smart, efficient staff. Public rooms, including a reception-lounge and an attractive reading room, retain their spacious proportions, and there's also a new cocktail bar. Large bedrooms are individually decorated and sensibly furnished. Bathrooms are well equipped.
Amenities garden, 24-hour porterage, tea/coffee-making facilities, in-house movies, ladies' hairdressing.
Credit Access, Amex, Barclaycard, Diners

Sumner Hotel £E

Map 23 B5
11 Sumner Place *SW7 3EE*
01–589 9854

Rooms 10 *with TV* None
with bath/shower 6
with telephone None

⊖ Tube South Kensington

Look for the number as there's no nameplate outside this attractive, friendly hotel. Inside, spacious bedrooms have attractive wicker furniture, check bedspreads and large windows. Six have their own spotlessly clean bath or shower rooms. There's also a cosy TV room with prints and potted plants, but no restaurant (continental breakfast is served in your room). Unlicensed.
Amenities porterage.

Surtees Hotel £ F

Map 21 C5
94 Warwick Way *SW1V 1SB*
01–834 7163

Rooms 10   *with TV* None
with bath/shower 1
with telephone None

⊖ Tube Victoria

Cheerful modern decor gives this small terraced hotel a most pleasing atmosphere, which is further enhanced by the efforts of charming manageress Miss Chatman. Hessian-covered walls and hanging baskets lend character to the basement breakfast room, which doubles as a TV lounge. Modernised bedrooms have attractive wall fabrics, pretty bedspreads and built-in furniture. Bathrooms are adequate.

Tavistock Hotel £ E/F

Map 24 C1
Tavistock Square *WC1H 9EU*
01–636 8383
Telex 263951
Manager Stephen Walduck
Rooms 301   *with TV* 301
with bath/shower 301
with telephone 301
⊖ Tube Russell Square

This large purpose-built hotel, which occupies almost one side of attractive Tavistock Square, is a popular place with tourists. It has a welcoming modern reception hall, and refreshments can be taken either in the residents' lounge or in the smartly contemporary wine bar. There's plenty of storage and writing space in the bedrooms, which have plain whitewood fitted units and neat, compact bathrooms. *Amenities* lift, 24-hour porterage, garage.
Credit Access, Amex, Barclaycard, Diners

Terstan Hotel Ⓜ £ F

Map 23 A5
29 Nevern Square *SW5 9PE*
01–373 5368
Proprietors Mr & Mrs S. Tabaka
Rooms 54   *with TV* 24
with bath/shower 24
with telephone 54

⊖ Tube Earl's Court

Popular with business and holiday visitors alike, this friendly family-owned hotel stands in a quiet residential square near Earl's Court Exhibition Centre. Lightwood panelling is a feature of the public areas, which include a lounge and separate TV room, both with low modern seating, and a little bar. Bedrooms are well lit and neatly furnished; those with private bathrooms also have TVs, and all have radios. *Amenities* lift.
Credit Access, Barclaycard

Tudor Court Hotel £ E

Map 23 B4
58 Cromwell Road *SW7 5BY*
01–584 8273
Manager Mrs K. Fairbrother
Rooms 89   *with TV* 89
with bath/shower 42
with telephone 89

⊖ Tube Gloucester Road

The promise of its fresh Victorian facade is amply fulfilled by the interior of this friendly, well-run hotel. Lofty bedrooms are particularly smart, with pretty floral wallpapers, good carpets, light oak furniture and useful luggage racks. Public areas include several comfortable lounges (one with TV) and a bright breakfast room. The hotel is now licensed.
Amenities porterage, lift.
Credit Access, Amex, Barclaycard, Diners

Willett House Hotel Ⓜ £ F

Map 23 D5
32 Sloane Gardens *SW1W 8DJ*
01–730 0634

Rooms 17   *with TV* 17
with bath/shower 14
with telephone None

⊖ Tube Sloane Square

Visitors appreciate the helpful friendliness of Mr and Mrs Nuñez, hosts at this impressive Victorian hotel. There's a pleasant reception area with comfortable easy chairs and a smart breakfast room in the basement. Pleasant bedrooms are traditionally furnished and provided with radios and good reading lights. Most have very small bathrooms (some with showers only). No dogs.
Amenities tea/coffee-making facilities.

We do not necessarily recommend the cooking at hotels whose restaurants are not separately listed.

Worcester House Ⓜ £ E

Map 7 A5
38 Alwyne Road
Wimbledon *SW19 7AE*
01–946 1300
Props Mr & Mrs John Dudley
Rooms 9   *with TV* 9
with bath/shower 8
with telephone None
⊖ Tube Wimbledon

Handily placed for tennis enthusiasts, this suburban red-brick house has been transformed into a comfortable hotel by Mr and Mrs Dudley. Compact, cheerfully decorated bedrooms have well-coordinated soft furnishings, and shower rooms are equipped with luxurious, ultra-modern fittings. As there are no public rooms, your hearty cooked breakfast is brought up to your bedroom. No dogs.
Amenities tea/coffee-making facilities, 24-hour porterage.

HOTELS, RESTAURANTS AND INNS

London	225
London Airports	313
England	323
Scotland	670
Wales	755
Channel Islands	775
Isle of Man	785
Ireland	787

LONDON

PUERILITY THEATRE
REVUSIJAZZAGANZOMEDY
PISH-TUSH
Jenkyn
WON'T WASH CLOTHES
MEET ME AT SALVAGE'S
READ THE Daily Error
CHARING
Get it at TO-DAY
23

A l'Ecu de France ♕♕ Ⓢ

Map 25 B4
111 Jermyn Street *SW1Y 6HB*
01–930 2837
Manager Mr N. Peduzzi

● **Set L** £10·50 **Set D** £14·50
incl. service
About £48 for two
Banquets 34/5
☻ Tube Piccadilly Circus

An elegantly formal restaurant, with sober brown decor and immaculate table settings. The extensive French-based menu ranges from artichoke hearts stuffed with crabmeat to calf's sweetbreads in white wine or tournedos in Madeira sauce. There's an attractive sweet trolley and an assortment of British and Continental cheeses. Service is both professional and friendly.
♟ *OUTSTANDING. Credit* Access, Amex, Barclaycard, Diners   ♿

Lunch 12.30–2.30 *Dinner* 6.30–11.30, Sun 7–10.30
Closed L Sat & Sun, Good Friday & 25 December

Ajimura Ⓢ

Map 25 D5
51 Shelton Street *WC2H 9HE*
01–240 0178
Proprietor Mr Susumu Okada
Japanese cooking
About £19 for two
☻ Tube Covent Garden

Friendly staff will help you with the long menu in this Japanese restaurant, where superbly fresh ingredients, careful preparation and colourful presentation are noteworthy. Good choice of set meals. *Credit* Access, Amex, Barclaycard, Diners *Lunch* 12–3 *Dinner* 6–11 **Closed** L Sat, all Sun & Bank Holidays *Banquets* 25/10 ● **Set L** from £4·50 **Set D** from £5·50   ♿

Alonso's ♟ ♕ 

Map 21 C6
32 Queenstown Road *SW8 3RX*
01–720 5986

Proprietor
Mr Alonso Galvez

● **Set L** £7·50
Set D from £11·25
About £30 for two
☻ Buses 45, 77, 77A, 137

The set menus in Alonso Galvez's pleasant flowery restaurant really do cater for all tastes. After a seafood pancake or cream of lobster soup, you could go on to grilled tandoori chicken, noisettes of pork in an orange sauce, or the formidable Indonesian beef and lamb casserole. Capable, imaginative cooking is enhanced by friendly, attentive service.
Credit Amex, Diners

Lunch 12.30–2.30 *Dinner* 7.30–11.30
Closed L Sat, all Sun & Bank Holidays

Anna's Place Ⓢ

Map 20 D2
90 Mildmay Park *N1 4PR*
01–249 9379

About £32 for two
☻ Buses 38, 73, 141, 171, 236, 277

Anna Hegarty is the most welcoming of restaurateurs, and you eat in the homely front room of her terraced house. The cooking is traditional, but full of imaginative touches: a tempting choice includes subtle aubergine soufflé with a hint of tarragon, pork fillet with ginger and delicious mange-tout, and moist chicken breast wrapped in a vivid green jacket of spinach. Informal service matches the amiable atmosphere. Book.

Dinner only 7.15–10.15
Closed Sun, Mon, 3 weeks Easter, August & 3 weeks Christmas

Apicella 81 

Map 24 B3
4 Mill Street *W1R 9TE*
01–499 1308

Italian cooking

About £37 for two
Banquets 20/–
☻ Buses 3, 6, 12, 13, 15, 23, 53, 88, 159

Apicella himself designed this attractive modern restaurant with its snow-white tablecloths and colourful plants and prints. The Italian menu is sensibly short, and cooking is consistently sound, from al dente pasta– delicious with seafood –to tender veal milanese and fresh, tasty vegetables. Superb pastries round off a most enjoyable meal. Attentive waiters serve.
Credit Access, Amex, Barclaycard, Diners

Lunch 12.30–3 *Dinner* 7–12
Closed L Sat, all Sun & Bank Holidays

Arirang Korean Restaurant 

Map 24 B2
31 Poland Street *W1V 3DB*
01–437 6633

Proprietors Mr & Mrs E. Wee
Korean cooking

● **Set L** £6·75 **Set D** £8·50
About £27 for two
☻ Tube Oxford Circus

Helpful, colourfully dressed waitresses will guide you through a pleasantly unusual meal at this unpretentious Korean restaurant. Use rice as the centrepiece for a feast of authentically spiced and strongly flavoured dishes like pickled cabbage, thinly sliced beef marinated in a sweet sauce and fragrant pokum woo-dong–fried noodles with meat, fish balls and vegetables. *Credit* Access, Amex, Barclaycard, Diners

Lunch 12–3 *Dinner* 6–11
Closed Sun & 25 & 26 December

Ark

Map 22 A3
35 Kensington High Street
W8 5BA
01–937 4294
Proprietor Mr Witt
French cooking

Excellent French bourgeois cuisine draws a large clientele to this well-established restaurant, so it's advisable to book. The short menu offers tasty, generously served dishes ranging from pied de porc ravigote and smoked haddock quiche to foie de veau provençale, ballotine de volaille and gigot d'agneau aux flageolets. Vegetables are fresh and crisp, and there are a few delicious sweets. *Credit* Access, Barclaycard, Diners

About £23 for two
⊖ Tube High Street Kensington

Lunch 12–3 *Dinner* 7–11.30
Closed L Sun, 4 days Easter & 4 days Christmas

L'Arlequin ★   

Map 21 C6
123 Queenstown Road *SW8 3RH*
01–622 0555

Christian Delteil has transferred his considerable talents from Chewton Glen to this simply appointed little restaurant, where his charming wife Genevieve leads the friendly, polished service. His brilliance and flair are very evident in outstanding mousses and sauces, and presentation of all dishes is outstanding. Vegetables are handled with great care, and memorable desserts include bavarois aux poires and the sensational vacherin 'L'Arlequin'–the thinnest layer of meringue encasing deliciously fruity blackcurrant ice cream.
Specialities sauté de ris de veau au vinaigre, ravioli de saumon frais au fenouil, fricassée de sole 'Petit Paul', gratin de pommes.
Credit Access, Barclaycard

● **Set L** £8·50
About £32 for two

⊖ Bus 137

Lunch 12–2 *Dinner* 7–10.30
Closed L Sat, all Sun, Mon, 25 & 26 December & 3 weeks August

Any person using our name to obtain free hospitality is a fraud. Proprietors, please inform the police and us.

L'Artiste Affamé   

Map 23 A5
243 Old Brompton Road *SW5 9HP*
01–373 1659

French cooking

A relaxed, appealing French restaurant, featuring eye-catching artefacts like a wine press, magic lanterns and an old kitchen range. There's a good choice of hors d'œuvre, including snails, ratatouille and poached egg Argenteuil, and we much enjoyed a tender chicken escalope with artichoke hearts and a well-made sauce béarnaise. Capable cooking is matched by obliging service. *Credit* Access, Amex, Barclaycard, Diners

About £25 for two
Banquets 20/–
⊖ Tube Earl's Court

Lunch 12.30–2.15 *Dinner* 6.30–11.15
Closed L Sat, all Sun, Bank Holidays & 24 December

L'Artiste Assoiffé

Map 21 B4
122 Kensington Park Road
W11 2EP
01–727 4714
Proprietor Mr Eric Armitage
About £27 for two
⊖ Tube Notting Hill Gate

Three attractive dining rooms in a Victorian town house make up this popular restaurant, where a good range of French-style dishes like duck with green peppercorn sauce is acceptably prepared. *Credit* Access, Amex, Barclaycard, Diners *Lunch* Sat only 12–2.45 *Dinner* 6.30–11, Sat 7–11
Closed Sun & Bank Holidays ● **Set L** £6·75 *Banquets* 30/10

Ashley's

Map 26 C1
10 Copthall Avenue *EC2R 7DJ*
01–638 9363

The menu is brief at this smart, welcoming basement restaurant in the heart of the City. The Spanish chef uses excellent materials for dishes like lamb cutlets with asparagus tips or veal kidneys berrichone, and his sauces show an expert touch. There's a choice of daily specials to tempt the regulars and home-made sweets include a delicious chocolate gâteau.
Credit Access, Amex, Barclaycard, Diners

About £40 for two
Banquets 60/25
⊖ Tube Bank

Lunch only 12–3
Closed Sat, Sun, Bank Holidays & 1 week Christmas

525
SUPER II
MF

Engineering for World Transport

Agricultural vehicles are built for the tough life. Most are powered by rugged diesel engines which in turn rely on a high precision fuel injection system to provide unfailing performance, whatever the job or terrain.

Lucas CAV is a world leader in the design and manufacture of diesel fuel injection pumps, injectors and filters. Made to incredibly fine precision standards, CAV equipment is built to endure, however arduous the operating conditions.

Map 21 C4

Berkeley Arcade
209a Baker Street *NW1 6AB*
01–486 5026

Japanese cooking

● **Set L** from £4 incl. service
Set D from £12
About £40 for two
⊖ Tube Baker Street

Asuka

White walls and sleek black furniture create an atmosphere of serene simplicity in this elegant Japanese restaurant. The menu covers the full range of familiar specialities like crisp tempura and beautifully arranged sashimi, some forming the basis of set meals. There are also seasonal specialities such as grilled asparagus with mustard and soya sauce or an ice-cold seafood salad. *Credit* Access, Amex, Barclaycard, Diners

Lunch 12–2.30 *Dinner* 6–10.30
Closed L Sat, all Sun & Bank Holidays

Map 25 A4

116 Piccadilly *W1V 0BJ*
01–499 3464
Telex 261589

Manager Mr R. F. Jones
Rooms 112
with bath/shower 112
Room phone Yes
Room TV Yes
Confirm by 6
Last dinner 10.30
Parking Ample
Banquets 50/2

Credit Access, Amex,
Barclaycard, Diners
⊖ Buses 9, 14, 19, 22, 25, 38, 55

Athenaeum Hotel   83%   *E*   £A

The dedicated manager and his friendly staff ensure that standards remain very high at this striking modern hotel overlooking Green Park. There's a fresh, outdoor feel about the comfortable pale-green lounge, with its potted plants and attractive statues, while in the bar plush seating and rich mahogany panelling evoke the atmosphere of an exclusive club. Most of the stylish bedrooms, which feature military-style yew furniture with tooled leather, have been redecorated in spring, summer or autumn themes, with appropriate colour schemes and cheerful zigzag patterned wallpaper. Fully tiled bathrooms are supplied with lots of little extras. *Amenities* lounge bar (24 hours), hairdressing, valeting, in-house movies.

Map 25 A4

116 Piccadilly *W1V 0BJ*
01–499 3464

● **Set L** £11·50 & £13·50
incl. wine & service
About £38 for two
⊖ Buses 9, 14, 19, 22, 25, 38, 55

Athenaeum Hotel Restaurant

Comfortable, elegant surroundings and friendly service are features of this relaxing restaurant, which offers capably cooked and attractively presented dishes. The choice ranges from bisque de homard and duck terrine to quenelles de sole Véronique and grills. Vegetables are handled with care, and to finish, choose from the cheeseboard or eye-catching sweet trolley. *Credit* Access, Amex, Barclaycard, Diners

Lunch 12.30–3, Sun 12.30–2.30 *Dinner* 6.30–10.30, Sun 6.30–10

Map 25 C5

5 Greek Street *W1V 5LA*
01–437 1816

● **Set L & Set D** £8·50
About £38 for two
⊖ Tube Tottenham Court Road

Au Jardin des Gourmets

Booking is essential at this elegant restaurant with its striking frontage and Art Nouveau decor. The menu features a good choice of generally well-prepared dishes like delicious fish terrine with sauce verte and juicy chicken baked in puff pastry with mushrooms. There are grills, too, and seasonal specialities such as moules marinière. ♟ *OUTSTANDING.*
Credit Access, Amex, Barclaycard, Diners

Lunch 12.15–3 *Dinner* 6.30–11.30, Sat 6–12
Closed L Sat, all Sun & L Bank Holidays

Map 20 B1

816 Finchley Road *NW11 6YL*
01–455 8853

French cooking
About £29 for two
⊖ Buses 13, 26, 102, 260

L'Aubergade

A friendly little bistro, where Monsieur Cattiaux prepares a selection of tasty French provincial dishes ranging from soufflé d'épinards to ballotine de volaille bourguignonne and tarte maison. *Credit* Amex, Barclaycard *Lunch* 12–2.30 *Dinner* 7–11 **Closed** L Sat, all Sun, 1 week Easter & 3 weeks Christmas *Banquets* 28/20

Bagatelle ★ Ⓢ

Map 23 B6
5 Langton Street *SW10 0JL*
01–351 4185
Proprietor Mr D. Marrocco

French cooking

● **Set L £8**
About £38 for two

You can eat in the cosy, elegantly appointed dining room of this restaurant or, on warm summer evenings, choose the garden at the rear, where the scent of honeysuckle mingles with the aroma of chef Ono's cooking. The short, well-balanced menu shows real flair and a lightness of touch in dishes like the eye-catching hot vegetable terrine served with delicate tomato sauce and thinly sliced pink breast of duck with a rich green peppercorn sauce. A friendly team of young waiters provides service with a smile.
Specialities concombre en surprise, panaché de poissons, carré d'agneau à la moutarde, crêpe Bagatelle.
Credit Access, Amex, Barclaycard, Diners

✆ Buses, 11, 22, 31

Lunch 12–2 *Dinner* 7–11
Closed Sun & Bank Holidays

Barbarella Ⓢ

Map 23 A6
428 Fulham Road *SW6 1DU*
01–385 9434
Proprietor Sandro Morelli
Italian cooking
About £32 for two
✆ Tube Fulham Broadway

There's an enjoyable selection of ably prepared Italian dishes at this smart restaurant and disco. Try baby octopus followed by the chef's agnolotti filled with cheese and spinach. Good sweets too.
Credit Access, Amex, Barclaycard, Diners *Dinner only* 8–1, Sat 8–2
Closed Sun & Bank Holidays *Banquets* 100/50

La Barca 🍷 Ⓢ

Map 21 B5
571a King's Road *SW6 2EB*
01–731 0039

Italian cooking

About £25 for two
Banquets 40/–
✆ Buses 11, 22

Choose with confidence from the long menu at this smart modern Italian restaurant. Cooking by the chef-patron and his Tuscan assistant is consistently capable and we much enjoyed our flavoursome stracciatella, al dente spaghetti with a tasty tomato and seafood sauce and a deliciously light dish of calf's brains with brown butter and capers. Friendly, obliging staff.
Credit Access, Amex, Barclaycard, Diners

Lunch 12–2.30 *Dinner* 7–11.30
Closed Sun & Bank Holidays

La Barca 🍷 Ⓢ

Map 21 D5
80 Lower Marsh *SE1 7AB*
01–928 2226
Italian cooking

About £25 for two
Banquets 40/6
✆ Tube Waterloo

Friendly Italian waiters serve in this smart restaurant, which is especially busy at lunchtime. There's an appetising hors d'œuvre trolley, and the long menu lives up to its promise, from excellent stracciatella and delicious pasta (try fusilli with cream and smoked salmon) to main courses like veal milanese. Vegetables are carefully handled and there are tempting sweets.
Credit Access, Amex, Barclaycard, Diners ♿

Lunch 12–2.30 *Dinner* 7–11.30
Closed L Sat, all Sun & Bank Holidays

Barkston Hotel 58% £D

Map 23 A5
Barkston Gardens *SW5 0ER*
01–373 7851
Telex 8953154
Manager Mr J. MacDonald
Credit Access, Amex, Barclaycard, Diners
✆ Tube Earl's Court

A friendly, modest hotel just off the Earl's Court Road. The open-plan foyer leads to a colourfully decorated lounge, and there's also a pleasantly club-like bar which serves as a convivial meeting place. Bedrooms vary in size from compact singles to vast twins, but all have coordinated colour schemes and practical modern furniture. Bathrooms are adequately equipped.

Rooms 74	*Room phone* Yes	*Confirm by* 6	*Parking* Difficult
with bath/shower 74	*Room TV* Yes	*Last dinner* 9.30	*Banquets* 60/–

Baron of Beef 👑 Ⓢ

Map 26 B1
Gutter Lane, Gresham St. *EC2V 6BR*
01–606 6961
Manager Peter Fletcher
English cooking
About £35 for two
✆ Tube St Paul's

Traditional English cooking in a handsome panelled restaurant, very popular at lunchtime. Roasts are the centrepiece of the menu, but there are also grills, fish dishes, cold appetisers and fruit-based desserts.
Credit Access, Amex, Barclaycard, Diners *Lunch* 12–3 *Dinner* 5.30–9.30
Closed Sat, Sun & Bank Holidays ● **Set L & Set D** £9 *Banquets* 80/40

Map 22 C3

8 Basil Street *SW3 1AH*
01–581 3311
Telex 28379
Manager Mr S. Korany
Credit Access, Amex,
Barclaycard, Diners
☻ Tube Knightsbridge

Rooms 109
with bath/shower 68

Basil Street Hotel 69% Ⓜ £ B

The long-serving manager's personal approach to the needs and comfort of his guests is one of the attractions of this charming hotel near Harrods. Spacious public rooms like the entrance hall and sitting rooms have a traditional style and elegance, and individually decorated bedrooms are bright, comfortable and spotlessly clean. Bathrooms, too, are well maintained. *Amenities* coffee shop (10am–3pm).

Room phone Yes	*Confirm by* 6	*Parking* Ample
Room TV Yes	*Last dinner* 9.45	*Banquets* 50/2

Map 25 B4

11 Swallow St, Piccadilly *W1R 7HD*
01–734 4756
Proprietor Mr Peter Bentley
Seafood
About £30 for two
☻ Tube Piccadilly Circus

Bentley's Oyster Bar & Restaurant Ⓢ

Delicious fresh seafood–from turbot, trout and sole to crab and lobsters–is served in the smart upstairs restaurant. At the ground-floor bar you can enjoy superb oysters straight from Colchester. *Credit* Access, Amex, Barclaycard, Diners *Lunch* 12–2.45 *Dinner* 6–10.30, Sat 6–10
Closed Sun & Bank Holidays *Banquets* 25/8

Map 22 D3

Wilton Place *SW1X 7RL*
01–235 6000
Telex 919252

Rooms 152
with bath/shower 152
Room phone Yes
Room TV Yes
Confirm by By arrang.
Last dinner 11
Parking Ample
Banquets 180/12

Credit Access, Barclaycard

☻ Tube Hyde Park Corner

Berkeley 92% £ A

This fine hotel is one of a rare breed, offering standards of service and housekeeping associated with an age more gracious than our own. As soon as you pass through the open-plan, marble-floored foyer you are transported to another world where courtesy reigns supreme. There are two sumptuous sitting rooms with panelling and crystal chandeliers, as well as a striking contemporary bar on two levels. Bedrooms are individually designed in modern or traditional style, with tastefully chosen furniture and fabrics. Bathrooms are luxuriously appointed with tiled or marble surfaces. No dogs. *Amenities* sauna, indoor swimming pool, discothèque (Mon–Sat), cinema, valeting, hairdressing.

Map 22 D3

Wilton Place *SW1X 7RL*
01–235 6000
Manager Mr Carlo Tanzi

French cooking

About £60 for two

☻ Tube Hyde Park Corner

Berkeley Restaurant ★ ♕♕♕ Ⓢ

With so many restaurants going down the path of informality it is a relief to find one where the style and atmosphere are of the more rigid old world. It is good to see, for a change, picture hats and morning coats (at Ascot or Royal garden party time), women dressed to the pin, Savile Row suits and not a tie-less collar in sight. The food, which rarely rises to any pinnacles, is reliable and the service in keeping with the style of bygone days. An elegant and pretty room.
Specialities quenelles de sole au champagne, piccata de veau Josephine, mignons de bœuf Clementine.  *OUTSTANDING.*
Credit Access, Barclaycard

Lunch 12.30–3 *Dinner* 6.45–11, Sun 6–10
Closed Sat

Map 22 D3

Wilton Place *SW1X 7RL*
01–235 6000

● **Set L** £4·75
About £45 for two
☻ Tube Hyde Park Corner

Berkeley Hotel, Le Perroquet ♕ Ⓢ

Lively music draws the young at heart to this superbly stylish restaurant with chrome and smoked-glass mirrors. Dinner features familiar items like oysters, snails, simple grills and more elaborate dishes like sweetbreads in a rich cream sauce, prepared from good raw materials and formally served. There's a buffet at lunch time, and the supper menu is available after 11.30pm.
 OUTSTANDING. Credit Access, Barclaycard

Lunch 12.30–3 *Dinner* 6.30–2am
Closed Sun & some Bank Holidays

Bill Bentley's   Ⓢ

Map 26 D1
Swedeland Court
202 Bishopsgate *EC2M 4NR*
01–283 1664
Proprietor Bill Bentley

A popular lunchtime rendezvous, where the simple decor and businesslike service match the honest, unfussy cooking. Seafood is the mainstay, ranging from oysters and moules marinière to langoustines provençale, sole in various guises and nicely sauced salmon with a garnish of tomatoes, mushrooms and shrimps. There are also grills, roasts and other meat dishes. 🍷*ABOVE AVERAGE. Credit* Access, Amex, Barclaycard, Diners

About £36 for two
❷ Tube Liverpool Street

Lunch only 12–3
Closed Sat, Sun & Bank Holidays

Bitter Lemons Taverna   🍸 Ⓢ

Map 21 B5
98 Lillie Road *SW6 7SR*
01–381 1069
Greek Cypriot cooking

Cheerful waiters help to bring this informal little Greek Cypriot restaurant to life. Authentic mezes (houmus, spicy sausages, stuffed vine leaves, etc.) offer a comprehensive selection from the simple menu. Book.
Credit Access, Barclaycard *Lunch* 12–2.45 *Dinner* 6–11.45, Sun 6–11.30

About £15 for two
❷ Tube West Brompton

Closed 4 days Christmas ● **Set L & Set D** £6·50 *Banquets* 40/30

Blakes Hotel   69%   £ A

Map 23 B5
33 Roland Gardens *SW7 3PF*
01–370 6701
Telex 8813500

There's something truly individual about the style and decor of this converted Victorian house. Wicker chairs fill the cosy foyer-lounge, while an enormous parasol marks the entrance to the dazzling basement bar. Pleasing bedrooms and luxurious suites (including several in a house across the road) have pretty drapes and superb fittings. Tiled bathrooms are very well equipped. No dogs. *Amenities* sauna.

Credit Access, Amex,
Barclaycard, Diners
❷ Buses 14, 30, 45

Rooms 50
with bath/shower 50

Room phone Yes	*Confirm by* 6	*Parking* Difficult
Room TV Yes	*Last dinner* 11.30	

Bloom's   Ⓢ

Map 20 B1
130 Golders Green Rd *NW11 8HB*
01–455 3033
Manager Mr M. Goldberg
Jewish cooking
About £17 for two
❷ Tube Golders Green

Splendid hot salt beef, gefilte fish and lockshen pudding are among the Jewish specialities served generously in this long-established, strictly kosher restaurant. Unlicensed. *Credit* Access, Barclaycard
Meals noon–9.30pm
Closed Fri, Sat & Jewish holidays

Bloom's

Map 21 D4
90 Whitechapel High St *E1 7RA*
01–247 6001
Manager Mrs Sadie Berman
Jewish cooking
About £18 for two
❷ Tube Aldgate East

Authentic Jewish specialities like tasty meat blintz, excellent salt beef and hearty lockshen pudding are generously served in this long-established, strictly kosher restaurant. Simple decor and efficient service.
Meals 11.15am–9.30pm, Fri 11.15am–2.15pm
Closed Sat, 25 December & Jewish holidays

Our inspectors are our full-time employees; they are professionally trained by us.

Bloomsbury Crest Hotel   60%   £ C/D

Map 24 C1
Coram Street
Russell Square *WC1N 1HT*
01–837 1200
Telex 22113
Credit Access, Amex,
Barclaycard, Diners
❷ Tube Russell Square

This busy hotel (formerly the Bloomsbury Centre) stands close to the British Museum. Completely refurbished bedrooms have smart new carpets and pretty bedspreads and curtains; all have neatly tiled bathrooms. Besides two bars–one with a Dickensian theme–there's an attractive coffee shop in 1930s style. Extensive conference facilities.
Amenities in-house movies, coffee shop (7.15am–11pm).   ♿

Rooms 250
with bath/shower 250

Room phone Yes	*Confirm by* 6	*Parking* Ample
Room TV Yes	*Last dinner* 11	*Banquets* 1,000/10

Bonnington Hotel 57% £D

Map 24 C1
92 Southampton Row *WC1B 4BH*
01–242 2828
Telex 261591
Manager Mr Alan Bostock
Credit Access, Amex,
Barclaycard, Diners
⊖ Tube Russell Square

Standards of housekeeping are high at this carefully modernised hotel situated on the fringes of the West End. The spacious foyer leads into a charming lounge which is overlooked by two balconies that serve as writing areas; there's also a smart cocktail bar with cosy alcove seating. Attractively decorated bedrooms have fitted units, colourful soft furnishings and radios. Bathrooms are fully tiled. &

Rooms 261
with bath/shower 102

| *Room phone* Yes | *Confirm by* 6 | *Parking* Difficult |
| *Room TV* Yes | *Last dinner* 9 | *Banquets* 120/80 |

Boulestin ★ ♔♔ Ⓢ

Map 25 D6
25 Southampton Street *WC2E 7JA*
01–836 7061

French cooking

About £50 for two

⊖ Tube Covent Garden

Sir Maxwell Joseph's flagship and personal pride, this is a most attractive, well-run place in which chef-manager Kennedy is given a free rein. One of the new generation of successful British chefs, he offers creations, often original, that never disappoint. If you feel fairly formal, it's a splendid choice for after the theatre; it's also well situated for lunch for the western part of the City.
Specialities fricassée de chanterelles aux œufs de canettes, escalope de saumon sauvage aux morilles, selle d'agneau farcie au crabe garnie aux petits légumes, magret de canard au chou-vert au vinaigre de Xérès.
♟ *SUPERIOR. Credit* Access, Amex, Barclaycard, Diners

Lunch 12.30–2.30 *Dinner* 7–11.15
Closed L Sat, all Sun, Bank Holidays & last 3 weeks August

Brasserie du Coin

Map 24 D1
54 Lamb's Conduit Street
WC1N 3LW
01–405 1717

About £24 for two
⊖ Buses 5, 19, 38, 55, 172

A bustling brasserie, where good fresh ingredients and capable cooking produce enjoyable French favourites such as moules marinière, coq au vin and bœuf bourguignonne. Simple sweets please, too. Polite, efficient service. *Credit* Access, Amex, Diners *Lunch* 12–3 *Dinner* 6–10.30
Closed Sat & Sun *Banquets* 50/12

Brasserie St Quentin ★ Ⓢ

Map 23 C4
243 Brompton Road *SW3 2EP*
01–589 8005

French cooking

● **Set L** £7·50
About £37 for two
Banquets 25/- (lunch only)

⊖ Tube South Kensington

This informal brasserie buzzes with life, and the atmosphere is matched by skilfully prepared, highly enjoyable food. The cooking is unmistakably French in style, ingredients are first class and sauces are made with real finesse. Soft quail's eggs on a bed of spinach between layers of light puff pastry makes an eye-catching starter; salads are well dressed, and perfectly cooked veal kidneys come with a characterful mustard sauce. Sweets such as tangy lemon tartlet provide an excellent finish.
Specialities feuilleté d'escargots à la crème d'ail, terrine de légumes et son coulis de tomates, caneton au citron vert, saumon sauce Nantua.
Credit Access, Amex, Barclaycard, Diners &

Lunch 12–3 *Dinner* 7–12, Sun 7–11.30
Closed Good Friday

Brinkley's ♧ Ⓢ

Map 23 B6
47 Hollywood Road *SW10 9HX*
01–351 1683

About £34 for two
Banquets 30/10
⊖ Buses 14, 31

Skill, enthusiasm and first-class materials are the secrets of success at this delightful restaurant. The menu's full of good things, from Caesar salad, hot cheese parcels and smoked salmon mousse as starters to main courses like pink-roasted rack of Welsh lamb and duck à l'orange served with perfectly timed vegetables. Delicious puddings, too. ♟ *ABOVE AVERAGE.*
Credit Access, Amex, Barclaycard, Diners

Dinner only 7.30–11.30
Closed Sun, Bank Holidays & 25 December–1 January

Map 25 B4

Berkeley Street *W1X 6NE*
01–493 8282
Telex 24561

Rooms 197
with bath/shower 197
Room phone Yes
Room TV Yes
Confirm by 6
Last dinner 8.30
Parking Ample
Banquets 50/4

Credit Access, Amex,
Barclaycard, Diners
⊖ Tube Green Park

Hotel Bristol   81%   *E*   **£ A**

An air of unobtrusive elegance is immediately apparent in the striking marble-floored foyer of this smart modern hotel. Public rooms, like the stylish cocktail bar and the impressive lounge, are attractively fitted out in distinctive Louis XV style. Double-glazed, air-conditioned bedrooms are spacious, with soft colours and fabrics helping to create a soothing atmosphere, and fully tiled bathrooms are well equipped. An interesting innovation is the allocation of an entire floor to bedrooms designed specifically for the businesswoman, with the emphasis firmly on feminine luxury. Staff are courteous and helpful. No dogs.
Amenities in-house movies, valeting, Ceefax.   &

Map 25 B4

Berkeley Street *W1X 6NE*
01–493 8282
French cooking

About £39 for two
⊖ Tube Green Park

Hotel Bristol, Louis d'Or Restaurant   

An elegant dining room in ornate Louis XV style forms a splendid setting for a menu of grills and classical French dishes. Service is formal, and cooking reaches consistent standards. *Credit* Access, Amex, Barclaycard, Diners
Lunch 12.30–2.30 *Dinner* 6–11, Sun 7–10
● **Set L** £10 incl. service **Set D** £12 incl. service

Map 22 D2

Grosvenor Square *W1A 3AN*
01–629 9400
Telex 23941

Rooms 434
with bath/shower 434
Room phone Yes
Room TV Yes
Confirm by 6
Last dinner 10
Parking Limited
Banquets 90/2

Credit Access, Amex,
Barclaycard, Diners
⊖ Tube Bond Street

Britannia Hotel   77%   *E*   **£ B**

Built in mock-Georgian style to blend in with the architecture of Grosvenor Square, this imposing seven-storey hotel re-creates the splendour and elegance of a bygone age. Corinthian columns dominate the facade, while inside there's a gracious entrance hall with a moulded ceiling, fine chandeliers and leather armchairs. The panelled Pine Bar has a marvellous relaxed atmosphere, while the Waterloo Despatch Bar is a reproduction of the pub on this spot where the news of Wellington's victory was first delivered to the Cabinet. Bedrooms are thoughtfully designed in Regency style, with mahogany furniture and well-equipped bathrooms. *Amenities* shopping arcade, hairdressing, coffee shop (8am–10.30am & noon–11pm).

Map 25 A4

Dover Street *W1A 4SW*
01–493 6020
Telex 28686
Manager Mr Bruce Banister

Rooms 129
with bath/shower 129
Room phone Yes
Room TV Yes
Confirm by 6
Last dinner 9.30
Parking Difficult
Banquets 90/2

Credit Access, Amex,
Barclaycard, Diners
⊖ Tube Green Park

Brown's Hotel   74%   **£ A**

High standards of old-world courtesy and polite, efficient service are maintained at this elegant, terraced Mayfair hotel, opened in 1837 by a former butler to Lord Byron. From the moment visitors register on arrival, sitting at a leather-topped desk, there's a feeling of traditional comfort and gracious living. The oak-panelled public rooms, with moulded ceilings, deep armchairs and open fires, include a peaceful writing room and a club-like cocktail bar. Bedrooms vary in size and style: most rooms have bold wallpaper and a combination of antique and reproduction furniture, while the newest are smartly up to date. All have well-equipped, spacious bathrooms.
Amenities men's hairdressing.

THE PURE DROP

In Praise of Water

In 1603, two English doctors imported 200 bottles of natural spring water from Spa in Belgium, and began a trend for enjoying its health-giving properties that has been popular ever since.

During the 17th and 18th centuries, English towns that were lucky enough to possess springs started to call themselves 'spas' and became fashionable retreats for wealthy people who hoped for speedy relief from ailments like gout and ulcers and who needed to cleanse their systems after eating and drinking to excess. Hordes of overweight, unhealthy citizens descended on Cheltenham, Leamington, Harrogate and, above all, Bath itself, which had long been famous for its baths and mineral water. (In 1750, the Royal Mineral Water Hospital was founded by one Dr William Oliver, a man who gained immortality by inventing those celebrated biscuits, Bath Olivers.)

The fashion for 'taking the waters' passed, but bottled mineral water was already waiting in the wings, and even in 1907 the Army & Navy Stores in London stocked 200 different varieties. Since then the market has been dominated by the French, but the British are now fighting back, and water from springs in the Peak District, the Malvern Hills, Perthshire and Shropshire is successfully bottled and sold to increasing numbers of people.

Everyone needs water—we are largely composed of it and would soon die without it. Tap water, of course, serves its purpose, but it is basically dull and is no match for natural spring water when it comes to flavour. The purest drop of all (100% H_2O) is distilled water, which is absolutely tasteless; the special character of spring water comes from the trace elements and minerals it contains—calcium, potassium, magnesium, lithium, sulphur and many others that are essential for the body's well-being. Each type of water has a different composition, and there's a subtle range of flavours to be appreciated by connoisseurs of the subject.

The attractions of bottled natural water—especially when it is slightly effervescent—are obvious. It's a deliciously refreshing, calorie-free alternative to alcohol, ideal for drivers, slimmers and those with a thirst; it can be drunk on its own with ice and lemon, or mixed with fruit juices and spirits. Because bottled water is rich in minerals it is also the most pleasant and palatable of medicines, helping to aid digestion, settle the stomach and aid recovery after sickness. At a time when the trend is towards more sensible, healthy eating and drinking, it has its natural place alongside wholemeal bread, free-range eggs and honey.

Fortunately we no longer need to rely on supplies of bottled water imported from abroad, as abundant springs in our own country can now provide us with the most perfect and simple drink in the world.

Brown's Hotel, L'Aperitif Restaurant ♛ Ⓢ

Map 25 A4
Dover Street *W1A 4SW*
01–499 6122

Manager Mr Barrie Larvin

● **Set L** £13·50
Set D £16 incl. service
About £46 for two
⊖ Tube Green Park

A relaxing panelled restaurant, with comfortable armchairs and elegant table settings. The menus offer a varied, interesting choice ranging from oysters in champagne sauce to steak Diane, fillet of veal in port sauce with black-berries, and sweets from an impressive trolley. Cooking and presentation are very capable, and service is smooth and friendly. 🍷 *ABOVE AVERAGE.*
Credit Access, Amex, Barclaycard, Diners

Lunch 12.15–2.30 *Dinner* 6–10, Sun 6.30–9.30

Bubb's Ⓢ

Map 26 A1
329 Central Markets *EC1A 9BN*
01–236 2435
Proprietors
Catherine & Peter Bubb
French cooking

About £28 for two
⊖ Tube Farringdon

Very popular with City lunchers, this simple bistro-style restaurant is noted for its authentic French cooking. The short menu features enjoyable dishes like calf's liver provençale, duck breast with limes and guinea fowl flambéed with Pernod, all accompanied by skilfully prepared fresh vegetables. There's also a small selection of sweets such as Grand Marnier soufflé. Book well in advance.

Lunch only 12.15–2
Closed Sat, Sun, Bank Holidays & August

Bunny's Ⓢ

Map 20 B2
7 Pond Street *NW3 2PN*
01–435 1541

French cooking

● **Set L** £5·75
About £31 for two
⊖ Tube Belsize Park

The atmosphere is friendly and informal at the Winstons' popular Victorian-style restaurant, and Keith Shudall's cooking is capable and imaginative. The interesting menu offers starters like caviare d'aubergine and deep-fried gruyère to precede roast duck (with a choice of sauces), sole meunière and carré d'agneau among the classic main courses. Sweets from the trolley are delicious, too. *Credit* Amex, Barclaycard

Lunch Sun only 12–3 *Dinner* 7–11
Closed Mon, D Easter Sun, all Good Fri, Aug Bank Holiday & 25 & 26 Dec

Busabong Ⓢ

Map 23 B6
329 Fulham Road *SW10 9QL*
01–352 4742
Proprietor Mrs Sue Kanasuta
Thai cooking
About £26 for two
⊖ Buses 14, 45

Authentic Thai specialities are served in the three dining rooms of this colourful restaurant. The choice is vast, and cooking is enjoyable, with a subtle blending of contrasting flavours typical of many dishes. *Credit* Access, Amex, Barclaycard, Diners *Lunch* 12.30–2.30 *Dinner* 6.30–11.30, Sun 6.30–10.30 **Closed** Christmas ● **Set D** £12 *Banquets* 80/–

Cadogan Hotel 66% £B/C

Map 23 D4
75 Sloane Street *SW1X 9SG*
01–235 7141
Telex 267893

Credit Access, Amex,
Barclaycard, Diners
⊖ Buses 19, 22, 137

Associations with Lillie Langtry and Oscar Wilde are part of the romantic attraction of this turreted, red-brick building, conveniently placed between the shopping centres of Knightsbridge and Chelsea. There's a pleasantly old-fashioned air about panelled public rooms like the lobby, lounge and bar, and individually decorated bedrooms are also comfortably traditional, with handsome furnishings and attractively tiled bathrooms. Friendly staff.

Rooms 66
with bath/shower 66

| *Room phone* Yes | *Confirm by* 6 | *Parking* Ample |
| *Room TV* Yes | *Last dinner* 10 | *Banquets* 35/4 |

Café Jardin ♛ Ⓢ

Map 24 A3
10 Lancashire Court
New Bond Street *W1Y 9AD*
01–493 2896

French cooking

● **Set L & Set D** from £5·95
About £42 for two
Banquets 25/10
⊖ Tube Bond Street

Alan Bird (formerly of Thomas de Quincey's) is chef at this attractive new restaurant, where he offers a sensibly short menu of intriguing French dishes ranging from light mousseline of sole with lobster sauce to grills and items like sautéed veal with noodles, which show a simpler touch. Cooking is based on excellent raw materials and generally reaches a high standard.
Credit Access, Amex, Barclaycard, Diners

Lunch 12–2.30 *Dinner* 7–11.30
Closed L Sat, all Sun, 1 January & 25 December

Map 24 B3
68 Regent Street *W1R 6EL*
01–437 9090
Manager Mr Peter Andresman

About £45 for two
⊖ Tube Piccadilly Circus

Café Royal, Grill Room & Le Relais ♔ ♔ ♔ ⑤

Both the opulent Grill Room and the more spacious but equally sumptuous Le Relais offer a good choice of grills and classically based entrées, cooked to a most acceptable standard. Enjoyable sweets. ♛ *OUTSTANDING*. *Credit* Access, Amex, Barclaycard, Diners *Lunch* 12.30–3, Sun 12.30–2.30 *Dinner* 6–11, Sunday 7–10.30 ● **Set L** from £9

Map 20 B2
351 West End Lane *NW6 1LT*
01–794 3234

● **Set L** £7·45
Set D Mon £6·95, Tues £9·45
About £38 for two
Banquets 24/8
⊖ Tube West Hampstead

Capability Brown ♟ ⑤

A new team has taken over at this pleasant restaurant, and cooking shows much flair and imagination. Our smoked salmon mousse was dressed with a sour cream and fennel sauce, while a refreshing tangerine sorbet preceded roast duck with a sauce containing whole raspberries. Vegetables are young and tender, and there's an attractive sweet trolley. Simpler lunch menu. *Credit* Access, Amex, Barclaycard, Diners

Lunch 12–2 *Dinner* 7–11.30
Closed L Sat, D Sun & all Bank Holidays

Map 23 C4
22 Basil Street *SW3 1AT*
01–589 5171
Telex 919042
Manager Mr K. Williams

Rooms 60
with bath/shower 60
Room phone Yes
Room TV Yes
Confirm by By arrang.
Last dinner 10.30
Parking Limited
Banquets 22/4

Credit Access, Amex,
Barclaycard, Diners
⊖ Tube Knightsbridge

Capital Hotel 76% *E* £ A/B

Just around the corner from Harrods in a quiet Knightsbridge street, this plush hotel is maintained with impeccable taste and thoughtful attention to detail. Ultra-modern silvery-grey decor gives the foyer a sophisticated atmosphere, and there are also two elegant, interconnecting function rooms. Stylish bedrooms are exceptionally well appointed with purpose-built fittings, bedside controls, push-button telephones and fridges blending perfectly with traditional carved pine furniture and rich leather bedheads. Marble-floored bathrooms are equally impressive and superbly equipped. There are several traditionally decorated suites in the older section of the hotel. ♿

Map 23 C4
22 Basil Street *SW3 1AT*
01–589 5171
Manager Mr Dieter Schuldt

French cooking

About £48 for two
⊖ Tube Knightsbridge

Capital Hotel Restaurant ♔ ⑤

Soft lights and stylish decor give this restaurant an elegant atmosphere well suited to the refined and skilful cooking of Brian Turner. His menu features delightfully presented French dishes ranging from fish soup and game terrine with watercress sauce to sautéed chicken with morels and various grills. Sauces and vegetables are excellent, and there are some gorgeous sweets. ♛ *OUTSTANDING*. *Credit* Access, Amex, Barclaycard, Diners ♿

Lunch 12.30–2.15, Sun 12.30–1.45 *Dinner* 6.30–10.30, Sun 7–9.45

Map 21 B6
182 Wandsworth Bridge Road
SW6 2UP
01–731 0732

Caribbean cooking

About £28 for two
⊖ Buses 28, 91, 295

Le Caraïbe ⑤

This informal little restaurant offers a menu of authentic Caribbean and Creole favourites, with almost every dish enlivened by West Indian herbs and spices. Stuffed crab with peppers makes a very tasty starter, and main courses include flavoursome sancoche (chicken, salt cod and coconut cream), curried goat and even flying fish. Leafy decor and Caribbean music provide a pleasant setting. *Credit* Access, Amex, Barclaycard, Diners

Dinner only 7.30–11.30
Closed Sun & 25 December

Map 21 B6
855 Fulham Road *SW6 5HJ*
01–736 4507

● **Set L** £3·95
About £26 for two
Banquets 16/8
⊖ Tube Parsons Green

Carlo's Place

An enormous old cast-iron stove sprouts pipes up to the ceiling of this busy bistro, while numbers of cuckoo clocks hang on the walls. A short seasonally changing menu offers enjoyable, freshly prepared dishes like flavoursome terrine maison, duck with ginger or simple grilled sole. There are always several daily specials, described enthusiastically by efficient, helpful and very friendly staff.

Lunch 12–3 *Dinner* 7–11.30
Closed L Sat, all Sun, Easter Mon & 24–30 December

We welcome complaints and bona fide recommendations on the tear-out pages for readers' comments. They are followed up by our professional team. Please also complain to the management instantly.

Map 7 A4
2 Hanger Lane
Ealing Common *W5 3HN*
01–992 5399 Telex 935114
Manager Mr G. Penturo
Credit Access, Amex,
Barclaycard, Diners
⊖ Tube Ealing Common

Carnarvon Hotel   55%   £D

This efficiently run businessman's hotel is a streamlined, modern brick building overlooking Ealing Common, conveniently placed for the M4 and Heathrow Airport. Attractive plants are a feature of the comfortable foyer and lounge, and there are two bars. Well-maintained bedrooms–those in the main building are best–have simple decor and functional fittings; compact bathrooms are adequate. Guide dogs only.

Rooms 170	*Room phone* Yes	*Confirm by* 6	*Parking* Ample
with bath/shower 152	*Room TV* Yes	*Last dinner* 9.15	*Banquets* 220/24

Map 20 D3
2 Camden Passage *N1 8ED*
01–226 5353
Manager Mr Luis Navarrete

● **Set L** £11·50 & £17
Set D £12·65 & £19·55
About £60 for two

⊖ Tube Angel

Carrier's ★ ♕ ♕

Gunther Schlender's cooking skills remain undiminished at this stylish restaurant, but lack of inspiration and the occasional lapse in service can detract from the enjoyment of a meal. There's something for everyone on the interesting menus, from simple grills and calf's liver with avocado to unusual and successful combinations like our charcoal-grilled marinated duck breast served on a bed of spinach and garnished with lime segments. There are some delicious desserts, too, and presentation is excellent. **Specialities** Japanese beef with sesame and fresh ginger, Roquefort cream quiche, carpetbag of salmon with oysters, les fraises chaudes au poivre vert
🍷 *SUPERIOR. Credit* Amex, Barclaycard, Diners

Lunch 12.30–2.30 *Dinner* 7.30–11.30
Closed Sun & Bank Holidays

Map 7 B5
129 Rushey Green, Catford *SE6 4AA*
01–697 2314
Proprietor Mr David Cominetti
About £24 for two
⊖ Buses 1, 2, 36, 36b, 47, 108b, 180, 185

Casa Cominetti

Favourite dishes at this long-established restaurant include grills, home-made pasta cooked al dente and a really excellent trifle. Cooking is capable and consistent, service is conscientious. *Credit* Access, Amex, Barclaycard, Diners *Lunch* 12–2, Sun 12–2.30 *Dinner* 7–10 **Closed** L Sat, D Sun, 25 & 26 December & L Good Friday *Banquets* 40/10   ♿

Map 21 A6
30 Putney High Street
SW15 1SQ
01–788 8668
Manager Mr Tony Colossi
French cooking

● **Set L & Set D** £6·75
About £25 for two
Banquets 25/2
⊖ Buses 14, 22, 30, 37, 39, 74

Cassis

This unpretentious bistro has a loyal following of regulars who come to savour reliable French provincial cooking in simple surroundings. Our highly enjoyable snails with basil and garlic in puff pastry and breast of duck with blackcurrant sauce were prepared from the finest raw materials and perfectly seasoned, while fresh strawberry flan made a deliciously light finish.   ♿

Lunch 12–2 *Dinner* 7–11
Closed L Sat, all Sun & Bank Holidays

Cavendish Hotel 68% £B

Map 25 B4
Jermyn Street *SW1Y 6JF*
01–930 2111
Telex 263187

Credit Access, Amex,
Barclaycard, Diners
Ө Tube Green Park

A marble-floored foyer covered with cheerful carpets sets the tone of this smart modern hotel near Piccadilly, which also has a panelled bar and a bright upstairs lounge-bar with live music most evenings. Double-glazed bedrooms (including eight comfortable suites) have contemporary furniture, mini-bars and fully tiled, well-equipped bathrooms..

Rooms 255	*Room phone* Yes	*Confirm by* 6	*Parking* Ample
with bath/shower 255	*Room TV* Yes	*Last dinner* 11	*Banquets* 80/–

Cecconi's ♛♛ Ⓢ

Map 24 B3
5 Burlington Gardens *W1X 1LE*
01–434 1509
Italian cooking
About £55 for two
Ө Buses 3, 6, 12, 13, 15, 23, 53, 88, 159

A fashionable restaurant with elegant modern decor where Italian dishes plus a few French specialities (such as fish soup and eggs Benedict) are generally well prepared. Enjoyable sweets. *Credit* Access, Amex, Diners *Lunch* 12–2.30 *Dinner* 7–11 **Closed** L Sat, all Sun & Bank Holidays *Banquets* 16/–

Central Park Hotel 56% £D/E

Map 22 B2
49 Queensborough Terrace *W2 3SS*
01–229 2424
Telex 27342

Credit Access, Amex,
Barclaycard, Diners
Ө Tube Queensway

Across the road from Kensington Gardens and conveniently close to the West End, this bright, modern hotel provides cheerful accommodation for short-stay visitors. Open-plan public areas include a striking lounge and a busy coffee shop and bar. Compact bedrooms are neatly fitted and all have gleaming, fully tiled bathrooms (most with shower only).
Amenities sauna, coffee lounge (11am–1am).

Rooms 291	*Room phone* Yes	*Confirm by* By arrang.	*Parking* Limited
with bath/shower 291	*Room TV* Yes	*Last dinner* 10.30	*Banquets* 100/–

Chanterelle ♧ Ⓢ

Map 23 B5
119 Old Brompton Road
SW7 3RN
01–373 5522

About £30 for two
Ө Buses 30, 49

A pleasant restaurant whose menu offers straightforward dishes ranging from eggs florentine and steak au poivre, to bacon-wrapped scallops and some enjoyable desserts. Capable cooking, friendly service. *Credit* Access, Amex, Barclaycard, Diners *Lunch* 12–2.30, Sun 12.30–3 *Dinner* 7–12 **Closed** 4 days Christmas & last 3 weeks Aug ● **Set L** £5, Sun £7 *Banquets* 20/–

Chaopraya Ⓢ

Map 22 D1
22 St Christopher's Place *W1M 5HD*
01–486 0777

Thai cooking

● **Set L & Set D** from £6·90
About £25 for two
Ө Tube Bond Street

Charming waitresses help you choose from the long menu of authentic Thai specialities served in this elegant restaurant with pretty cane chairs. Charcoal-grilled satay makes an excellent start, and you could go on to delicious clear tom yum soup, followed perhaps by crisp-fried mackerel topped with garlic and chilli. Try coconut milk and green jelly among cooling desserts. *Credit* Access, Amex, Barclaycard, Diners

Lunch 12–3 *Dinner* 6.30–11
Closed Sun & Bank Holidays

Charing Cross Hotel 63% £D

Map 25 C4
Strand *WC2N 5HX*
01–839 7282
Telex 261101
Credit Access, Amex,
Barclaycard, Diners
Closed 24–30 December
Ө Tube Charing Cross

Businessmen form the major part of the clientele at this fine railway hotel. Large mirrors give the foyer a feeling of spaciousness, and there are two new bars in contrast to the quiet Victorian residents' lounge. Comfortable bedrooms have built-in units, tea-makers and well-equipped modern bathrooms (smaller annexe rooms have showers only). Room service no longer available. *Amenities* sauna, gentlemen's hairdressing. &

Rooms 206	*Room phone* Yes	*Confirm by* 6	*Parking* Difficult
with bath/shower 206	*Room TV* Yes	*Last dinner* 10.15	*Banquets* 120/2

Le Chef 🎩 Ⓢ

Map 22 C2
41 Connaught Street *W2 2BB*
01–262 5945
Proprietor Mr Alan King
French cooking

● **Set L** £7 **Set D** Sat only £8·75
About £26 for two
🚌 Buses 6, 7, 8, 12, 15, 16, 16A, 23, 36B, 88

Wine posters, gingham tablecloths and casually dressed staff give an informal bistro feel to this friendly, popular restaurant, which offers a short choice of French regional dishes. Fish soup with rouille makes a rich, tasty starter, and main courses could include pepper steak, veal provençale and herb-stuffed pork chop topped with ham and cheese. Set meals only on Saturday evening. Booking advisable. *Credit* Access

Lunch 12.30–2.30 *Dinner* 7–11.30, Sat 7–11
Closed Sun, Mon, Bank Holidays & last 2 weeks August

We do not necessarily recommend the cooking at hotels whose restaurants are not separately listed.

Chesterfield Hotel   70%   £B

Map 25 A4
34 Charles Street *W1X 8LX*
01–491 2622
Telex 269394

Rooms 82
with bath/shower 82
Room phone Yes
Room TV Yes
Confirm by 6
Last dinner 10.30
Parking Difficult
Banquets 90/2

Credit Access, Amex, Barclaycard, Diners
🚇 Tube Green Park

Built in the 18th century as the London home of the fourth Earl of Chesterfield, this fine house is a model of discreet luxury and Georgian elegance. A finely proportioned entrance hall with pillars and a black and white marble floor sets the tone; there's also an intimate panelled library-lounge where you can take afternoon tea, and a Victorian-style cocktail bar opening on to a charming terrace. Bedrooms are beautifully furnished with period-style units, heavy drapes, comfortable armchairs and well-lit writing desks. Neat, marble-lined bathrooms have good modern fittings and are fully equipped with everything from expensive soap to bathrobes. *Amenities* garden.

Chez Franco Ⓢ

Map 22 A2
3 Hereford Road *W2 4AB*
01–229 5079
Proprietor Mr A. Bruno Cenzolo

About £26 for two
🚌 Buses 7, 15, 23, 27, 28, 31

A lively bistro-style restaurant where Bruno and Carlo offer reliably prepared dishes such as caneton à l'orange and sole bonne femme, along with Italian favourites like minestrone, fettuccine and steak pizzaiola. *Lunch* 12.30–2.30 *Dinner* 7–11 **Closed** L Sat, all Sun, Bank Holiday Mons & August
● **Set L & Set D** £4·50 incl. service

Chez Gerard Ⓢ

Map 24 B2
5 Charlotte Street *W1P 1HD*
01–636 4975
Manager Mr C. Bellone
French cooking
About £28 for two
🚇 Tube Goodge Street

Pretty French waitresses greet you at this endearing bistro, whose short menu offers pâtés, soups, charcoal grills and daily specials like moules marinière. End a splendid meal with a fruit tart or chocolate mousse.
Credit Access, Barclaycard *Lunch* 12.30–2.30 *Dinner* 6.30–11
Closed L Sat, D 24 and all 25–27 December & 1 January *Banquets* 40/15

Chez Moi 🎩 👑 Ⓢ

Map 21 A4
3 Addison Avenue *W11 4QS*
01–603 8267
Proprietors Mr Richard Walton & Mr Colin Smith

About £35 for two
🚇 Tube Shepherd's Bush

Gilt-framed mirrors, embossed wallpaper and oil paintings give this little restaurant an air of elegance. Highly enjoyable French-inspired dishes like onion soup, grilled lamb cutlets with mint béarnaise and turbot quenelles with creamy lobster sauce feature on the menu, along with crisp vegetables and sweets such as a wonderful chocolate truffle cake. Booking advisable.
🍷 *ABOVE AVERAGE. Credit* Amex, Barclaycard, Diners

Lunch 12.30–2.30 *Dinner* 7–11.30
Closed L Sat, all Sun, Bank Hols, last 2 weeks Aug & 2 weeks Christmas

Chez Nico ★

Map 21 C6
129 Queenstown Road *SW8 3RH*
01–720 6960
Proprietor Nico Ladenis

French cooking

The two comfortable dining rooms of Nico Ladenis' popular Battersea restaurant are a very pretty setting for his well-conceived and often brilliantly executed French dishes. Richly textured mousse de foies de canard, pink-cooked noisettes d'agneau à la crème de persil, chicken breast with foie gras and a superb girolle sauce–all show great skill and imagination, and Armagnac-flavoured parfait with chestnut purée is a sublime dessert. Excellent coffee and friandises.
Specialities soupe de poissons avec sa rouille, suprême de canard grillé aux herbes de Provence à la purée de poireaux, selection of sorbets.
Credit Access, Barclaycard

About £48 for two

⊖ Bus 137

Lunch 12.30–2 *Dinner* 7.15–10.45
Closed L Sat, all Sun, Bank Holidays, 10 days Christmas & 3 weeks August

Chez Solange

Map 25 C6
35 Cranbourn Street *WC2H 7AD*
01–836 5886

Proprietors M & Mme Rochon
French cooking

After 23 years at the helm, the Rochons still attract a wide following at their cheerful, bustling restaurant just off Charing Cross Road. Making the most of market-fresh produce, the menu offers a good choice of French dishes ranging from appetising mousse d'avocats and omelettes to sole, coq au vin and mignon de veau. Lovely crunchy vegetables and refreshing desserts.
Credit Access, Amex, Barclaycard, Diners

About £35 for two
Banquets 40/25
⊖ Tube Leicester Square

Lunch 12–3.15 *Dinner* 5.30–12.30am
Closed Sun & Bank Holidays

Chinatown

Map 7 B4
795 Commercial Road
Limehouse *E14 7HG*
01–987 2330
Proprietor Mrs G. Farmer
Chinese cooking

Situated near London's dockland (the home of the city's first Chinese restaurants), this pleasant place is family run. Cooking is mainly Cantonese, with authentic dishes like delicate lemon chicken, steamed mullet in black bean sauce and outstanding beef and salt cabbage soup, supplemented by a few Malaysian and Singaporean specialities. Booking essential.
Credit Access, Amex, Barclaycard, Diners

About £21 for two
⊖ Buses 5, 15, 23, 40, 56, 106, 225, 277

Meals noon–10.30, Fri & Sat noon–11
Closed 25 & 26 December

Churchill Hotel   80%   *E*   £ A

Map 22 D1
Portman Square *W1A 4ZX*
01–486 5800
Telex 264831
Manager Mr Richard Garland

Rooms 489
with bath/shower 489
Room phone Yes
Room TV Yes
Confirm by 6
Last dinner 11
Parking Limited
Banquets 200/20

Credit Access, Amex, Barclaycard, Diners
⊖ Buses 1, 2, 2B, 13, 30, 74, 113, 159

Standards remain consistently high at this smart modern hotel dominating Portman Square. The lofty entrance hall with its gleaming marble floor, sparkling chandeliers and ornamental pillars has a relaxed, inviting atmosphere which extends to the elegant Regency-style lounge, where guests can take afternoon tea to the accompaniment of a tinkling piano. There are also varied function facilities and a cosy intimate bar with Oriental sporting prints decorating the walls. Bedrooms are also in Regency style, with luxurious patterned bedspreads and matching curtains. Well-equipped bathrooms have extras like bathrobes. *Amenities* coffee shop (7am–1am), valeting, shopping arcade, hairdressing, in-house movies.

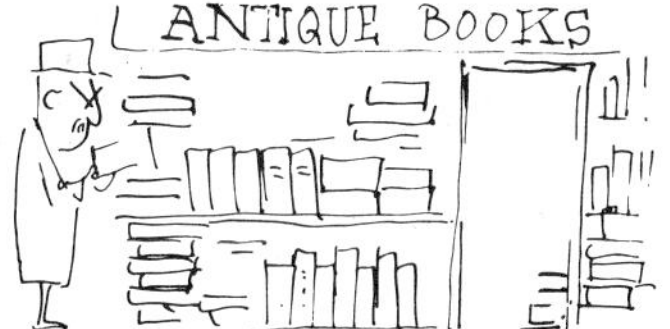

We publish annually, so make sure you use the current edition. It's worth it!

Churchill Hotel, No. 10 Restaurant ♔ Ⓢ

Map 22 D1
Portman Square *W1A 4ZX*
01–486 5800
Manager Sergio Filotrani

This elegant dining room recalls the tented campaign headquarters of Napoleon and Wellington. An ambitious, classically based menu offers a good choice of tasty dishes ranging from pâté en croûte to veal escalopes stuffed with rice, truffles and foie gras and a beautifully garnished and sauced suprême de turbot. Simpler dishes also at lunchtime. Service is polite and friendly. *Credit* Access, Amex, Barclaycard, Diners

About £50 for two
⊖ Buses 1, 2, 2B, 13, 30, 74, 113, 159

Lunch 12–3 *Dinner* 6–11

Clarendon Court Hotel   57%   £ D/E

Map 20 B3
Edgware Road *W9 1AG*
01–286 8080
Telex 27374

Credit Access, Amex, Barclaycard, Diners
⊖ Tube Warwick Avenue

Popular with tourists and cricket enthusiasts, this sturdy red-brick hotel near Lord's provides clean, comfortable accommodation. The pillared entrance hall suggests an air of former grandeur, whereas the aptly named Sportsman's Bar and meeting rooms are more up to date in style. Simply equipped bedrooms have fitted white units and modern bathrooms.
Amenities sauna, beauty centre, solarium, 12-hour laundry service.

Rooms 145	*Room phone* Yes	*Confirm by* 6	*Parking* Difficult
with bath/shower 140	*Room TV* Yes	*Last dinner* 10.30	*Banquets* 130/4

Claridge's   92%   £ A

Map 24 A3
Brook Street *W1A 2JQ*
01–629 8860
Telex 21872
Manager Mr B. Lund Hansen

Rooms 205
with bath/shower 205
Room phone Yes
Room TV Yes
Confirm by By arrang.
Last dinner 11
Parking Difficult
Banquets 200/12

Credit Access, Barclaycard

⊖ Tube Bond Street

Faultless, exemplary service, with the emphasis on personal comfort and privacy, is the hallmark of this unique hotel. A lofty hallway with arches and chandeliers sets the tone, and the tastefully elegant style is continued in the quiet reading room and the comfortable lounge, where resident musicians play. There's no bar, but you can have drinks served in the room of your choice. Spacious bedrooms are fitted out in traditional or Art Deco style, and many lovely pieces of china, prints, clocks and books help to create a truly homely atmosphere. Large bathrooms have fascinating original fittings. No dogs. *Amenities* 24-hour laundry service, hairdressing, 24-hour lounge service, valeting.

Claridge's Causerie   ♔♔ Ⓢ

Map 24 A3
Brook Street *W1A 2JQ*
01–629 8860

Manager Mr Peter Mand

Pastel colours and impeccable table settings give this intimate restaurant a very elegant air. The à la carte features a varied choice of grills and well-prepared French-inspired dishes like chicken Kiev and trout with almonds. There's also a tempting smörgåsbord, the price of which includes one drink and unlimited helpings from the dishes on offer. Book for lunch.
🍷 *OUTSTANDING. Credit* Access, Barclaycard

● **Set L** from £5·75
About £38 for two
⊖ Tube Bond Street

Lunch 12–3, Sun 12.30–3 *Dinner* 6–11, Sun 7–11
Closed Sat & 24 & 25 December

Claridge's Restaurant   ♔♔ Ⓢ

Map 24 A3
Brook Street *W1A 2JQ*
01–629 8860

Courteous waiters in tails grace this opulent restaurant. Daily-changing menus offer a wide choice of mainly French-inspired dishes like our tasty terrine maison and enjoyable poached turbot with smooth hollandaise sauce, plus grills and a cold buffet. Prime-quality ingredients are used throughout, and the standard of cooking is generally acceptable.
🍷 *OUTSTANDING. Credit* Access, Barclaycard

About £45 for two
⊖ Tube Bond Street

Lunch 12.30–2.30 *Dinner* 7–11
Closed 26 & 27 December

Map 22 D1

47 Welbeck Street *W1M8DN*
01–486 6600
Telex 22569

Credit Access, Amex,
Barclaycard, Diners
⊖ Tube Bond Street

Rooms 228
with bath/shower 228

Clifton-Ford Hotel   64%   £ C/D

Redecoration of the public areas has given a facelift to this modern hotel located in a quiet street conveniently near the West End shops. The spacious entrance hall has a smart lounge area and there is an attractive, welcoming bar decorated with heraldic devices. Well-equipped bedrooms have restful decor and excellent bathrooms.
Amenities 24-hour laundry service, valeting.

| *Room phone* Yes | *Confirm by* 6 | *Parking* Limited |
| *Room TV* Yes | *Last dinner* 10.15 | *Banquets* 100/– |

Our inspectors are our full-time employees; they are professionally trained by us.

Map 22 A2

129 Bayswater Road *W2 4RT*
01–229 3654
Telex 268235
Manager Mr E. E. Gray
Credit Access, Amex,
Barclaycard, Diners
⊖ Tube Queensway

Rooms 125
with bath/shower 65

Coburg Hotel   62%   £ D

There are pleasant views of Kensington Gardens from the double-glazed front rooms of this well-maintained, three-domed hotel. Bedrooms are furnished in simple modern style and equipped with tea-making facilities and trouser presses. The best bathrooms are fully tiled. Public areas include a foyer and a spacious bar-lounge with cane furniture. Friendly, helpful staff.

| *Room phone* Yes | *Confirm by* 6 | *Parking* Ample |
| *Room TV* Yes | *Last dinner* 9.30 | *Banquets* 120/10 |

Map 23 D5

22 Holbein Pl, Pimlico Rd *SW1W8NL*
01–730 2954
Proprietor Mr A. Bellini
Italian cooking
About £22 for two
⊖ Tube Sloane Square

Como Lario

Home-made gnocchi and well-sauced tagliatelle are among the favourites on a menu of familiar, acceptably cooked Italian specialities at this light and airy restaurant. For afters there are ices, sorbets, perhaps a smooth crème caramel. *Lunch* 12.15–2.30 *Dinner* 6.30–11.30
Closed Sun, Bank Holidays & 7–29 August

Map 22 D2

Carlos Place *W1Y 6AL*
01–499 7070

Manager P. Zago

Rooms 90
with bath/shower 90
Room phone Yes
Room TV Yes
Confirm by By arrang.
Last dinner 10.15
Parking Difficult
Banquets 20/8

Credit Access
⊖ Buses 2, 1B, 16, 30, 36B, 73, 74, 137

Connaught Hotel   92%   £ A

There's an unfussy elegance about this renowned Mayfair hotel, where standards of service and housekeeping remain exceptionally high. Public rooms are warm and relaxing: the two beautifully appointed lounges are the last word in traditional civilised comfort, and there's a cosy bar with fine oak panelling, Victorian prints and mounted hunting trophies. A handsome carved wooden staircase leads from the pillared entrance hall to the spacious bedrooms, many of which are filled with splendid antique furniture. Others have attractive built-in units, and all are decorated with impeccable taste. The suites are quite magnificent, and fully tiled bathrooms positively sparkle. No dogs. *Amenities* 24-laundry service, valeting.

Map 22 D2

Carlos Place *W1Y 6AL*
01–499 7070
Manager Mr J. P. Chevallier

French cooking

● **Set L** £14 **Set D** £18·50
About £60 for two

☻ Buses 2, 2B, 16, 30, 36B, 73, 74, 137

Connaught Hotel Restaurant ★  

If the Connaught didn't exist, it would have to be invented, as the saying goes. Stately, dignified and affluent, its restaurant is like a particularly civilised and perfectly maintained gentlemen's club without the noble patina of wear. The progression into the crystal-chandeliered, panelled room accompanied by ministering headwaiters is a worthwhile experience on its own, and much, though not all, of the food lives up to all this. **Specialities** croustade d'œufs de caille Maintenon, zéphyr de filets de sole 'Tout Paris', salmi de canard strasbourgeoise en surprise, bread and butter pudding.
🍷 *SUPERIOR. Credit* Access

Lunch 12.30–2.30 *Dinner* 6.30–10.30

Our inspectors never book in the name of the Egon Ronay Organisation; they disclose their identity only after paying their bills.

Map 20 C3

Upper Woburn Place *WC1H 0HT*
01–387 5111
Telex 261591
Credit Access, Amex,
Barclaycard, Diners
☻ Tube Russell Square

Cora Hotel 56% £D

Part of an 18th-century terrace, this cheerful, informal hotel has been attractively modernised inside. The roomy reception area leads to a small residents' lounge with writing desks and there's another lounge (with TV), a cosy cocktail bar and several function rooms. Bright bedrooms of various sizes have simple contemporary furnishings; bathrooms are reasonably well equipped. *Amenities* games room.

Rooms 133	*Room phone* Yes	*Confirm by* 7	*Parking* Difficult
with bath/shower 50	*Room TV* Yes	*Last dinner* 9	*Banquets* 130/2

Map 24 C2

56 St Giles High Street
WC2H 8LH
01–836 7235
Proprietor Mr Choy
Korean cooking

● **Set L & Set D** from £4·50
About £19 for two
☻ Tube Tottenham Court Road

La Corée

Spicy but not necessarily fiery, the dishes served in this simple Korean restaurant are notable for their freshness, careful preparation and visual appeal. Koo jeul pan makes an excellent starter, offering a varied selection of nine tasty hors d'oeuvre, and we much enjoyed chicken breasts fried in crisp batter coated with sesame seeds, as well as bulgogi–tender slices of beef cooked at the table. *Credit* Access, Amex, Barclaycard, Diners

Lunch 12–2.30 *Dinner* 6–10.30
Closed Sun & Bank Holidays

Map 23 B6

362 King's Road *SW3 5UZ*
01–352 0074

La Corse

An enjoyable selection of French-style dishes is served at this smart little bistro, whose white walls are adorned with mementoes of Corsica. Grills are always on the menu, along with lunchtime dishes such as pork escalope or navarin of lamb and some evening specials–perhaps estouffade de bœuf or cassoulet. Everything is prepared from good fresh ingredients, including the desserts, which feature sorbets and fruit tartlets.

● **Set L** £4·50 **Set D** £8
About £24 for two
☻ Buses 11, 19, 22, 31, 45, 49

Lunch 12–2.30 *Dinner* 7–11.30
Closed Sun & Bank Holidays

Map 26 C2

Bucklersbury House
Cannon Street *EC4N 8EL*
01–248 4735

About £32 for two
☻ Tube Cannon Street

Cotillion Room 👑 Ⓢ

This quietly luxurious basement restaurant, a popular place for business lunches, offers a familiar selection of capably prepared dishes, main courses being based mainly on sole, steak and veal. Formal, efficient service.
Credit Access, Amex, Barclaycard, Diners *Lunch only* 12–3
Closed Sat, Sun & Bank Holidays *Banquets* 20/6

Essential equipment for eating out in style.

Diners Card.
Accepted without question in good restaurants everywhere.

Diners Club House, Kingsmead, Farnborough, Hants.

La Croisette   Ⓢ

Map 23 A6
168 Ifield Road *SW10 9AF*
01–373 3694

Seafood

● **Set L & Set D** £14
About £38 for two
⊖ Bus 31

Enjoy a complimentary glass of kir, some prawns and little canapés in the bar of this bustling restaurant. Wonderfully fresh seafood is the mainstay of the set menu, with oysters, mussels, crab and scallops supplemented by a marvellous tomato-based fish soup and daily specialities like our excellent salmon in puff pastry with shredded leeks. There are some meat dishes too, and fruit tarts for dessert. *Credit* Amex

Lunch 1–2.30 *Dinner* 8–11.30, Sun 8–10
Closed L Mon & Tues & 20 December–5 January

Crystal Palace   Ⓢ

Map 23 A5
10 Hogarth Place
Hogarth Road *SW5 0QT*
01–373 0754

Chinese cooking

● **Set L & Set D** £17 for two
About £22 for two
Banquets 50/20
⊖ Tube Earl's Court

A fresh, modern restaurant specialising in popular Peking dishes as well as the more fiery Szechuan cuisine. Friendly staff provide help with the menus: there's an extensive à la carte, or you could settle down to a set meal such as the Szechuan feast of nine different dishes, including spicy bang-bang chicken, king prawns with piquant sauce and deliciously tender pork with crunchy peppers. *Credit* Access, Amex, Barclaycard, Diners

Lunch 12–3 *Dinner* 7–11.45
Closed 3 days Christmas

Cumberland Hotel   69%   £ B

Map 22 D2
Marble Arch *W1A 4RF*
01–262 1234
Telex 22215

Credit Access, Amex,
Barclaycard, Diners
⊖ Tube Marble Arch

This hotel—one of London's largest—is ideally placed for visitors to the West End. A marble-lined entrance hall leads to the comfortable lounge and two distinctive bars. Older-style bedrooms are well equipped, with trouser presses and mini-bars; all have fully tiled bathrooms. There are also nine attractive modern suites. *Amenities* sauna, hairdressing, beauty salon, 24-hour laundry service, coffee shop (10.30am–1am), shops, valeting.

Rooms 910	*Room phone* Yes	*Confirm by* 6	*Parking* Difficult
with bath/shower 910	*Room TV* Yes	*Last dinner* 10.30	*Banquets* 350/4

Cunard International Hotel   66%   £ C

Map 21 A5
Shortlands *W6 8DR*
01–741 1555
Telex 934539

Credit Access, Amex,
Barclaycard, Diners
⊖ Tube Hammersmith

This large modern hotel alongside the Hammersmith flyover is efficiently run and offers extensive conference facilities. Escalators from the car park lead to the bright, luxurious first-floor foyer, and there's a gallery lounge and opulent bar. Fair-sized bedrooms are decorated and furnished to a high standard; bathrooms are well equipped. *Amenities* carvery (7am–10pm), in-house movies, 24-hour lounge service.   ♿

Rooms 640	*Room phone* Yes	*Confirm by* 6	*Parking* Ample
with bath/shower 640	*Room TV* Yes	*Last dinner* 11	*Banquets* 900/50

Curzon Hotel   68%   £ C/D

Map 22 D3
Stanhope Row, Park Lane *W1Y 7HE*
01–493 7222
Telex 291855
Credit Access, Amex,
Barclaycard, Diners
⊖ Buses 2, 16, 30, 36B, 73, 74, 137

A marble-floored foyer with a beautiful chandelier and comfortable arm-chairs sets the elegant, relaxed tone of this modern hotel in a convenient position just off Park Lane. There's a stylish note, too, about the Cathay Bar, with its striking Oriental decor, and the tastefully decorated bedrooms, which have attractive pine furnishings and neat, well-lit shower or bathrooms.
Closed 4 days Christmas

Rooms 70	*Room phone* Yes	*Confirm by* 6	*Parking* Limited
with bath/shower 70	*Room TV* Yes	*Last dinner* 10	

Dan's   Ⓢ

Map 23 C5
119 Sydney Street *SW3 6NR*
01–352 2718

Phillip Britten is an adventurous chef who is prepared to take risks to create really unusual dishes. Mistakes can occur, but there are also unqualified successes like ravioli of crab and wild mushrooms in smooth champagne sauce and steamed paupiettes of sole stuffed with broccoli. Vegetables are beautifully presented and sweets are imaginative. Shorter lunch menu. *Credit* Amex, Barclaycard

Continued

About £41 for two
Banquets 12/6
Buses 11, 19, 22, 49

Lunch 12.30–2.30 *Dinner* 7.30–11.30
Closed L Sat, all Sun & Bank Holidays

Map 23 C5
112 Draycott Avenue *SW3 3AE*
01–589 4257
Proprietors Mr G. Ponticelli &
Mr Julian Tennant
French cooking

Daphne's ★ 

Chandeliers, velvet banquettes and crisp napery impart a discreet smartness to this '50s-style restaurant. The short à la carte and plats du jour menus offer superb French dishes such as beautifully tender médaillons de bœuf, and good-quality meat is complemented by crisp, well-cooked vegetables. Desserts include a delicious hot banane Martinique with butterscotch sauce. **Specialities** grilled lobster, carré d'agneau paloise, game in season, soufflé Grand Marnier.
SUPERIOR.
Credit Access, Amex, Barclaycard, Diners

About £38 for two
Tube South Kensington

Dinner only 7.30–12
Closed Sun & Bank Holidays

Map 22 C1
114 Crawford Street *W1H 1AG*
01–935 5736

Del Monico's

Stylish modern decor and formal service set the tone for this attractive restaurant. The menu offers skilfully cooked dishes like minestrone and fritto misto along with specialities ranging from stuffed roast veal to chicken in a creamy Marsala sauce with oranges, celery and cucumber. Nicely prepared vegetables.
Credit Access, Amex, Barclaycard

About £26 for two
Banquets 54/–
Tube Baker Street

Meals noon–midnight, Sat 7.30pm–midnight
Closed L Sat, all Sun & Bank Holidays

Map 25 C6
23 Lisle Street *WC2H 7BA*
01–437 2517

Chinese cooking

● **Set L & Set D** from £5
About £23 for two
Banquets 40/10
Tube Leicester Square

Diamond

First-class Cantonese cuisine brings the crowds flocking to this modest little Chinatown restaurant, so be prepared to queue. The long menu offers tasty treats ranging from steaming wun tun soup and plump prawns in a sweet-sharp sauce to the really delicious chicken and vegetables fried in a paper bag. Tea comes automatically, and an excellent meal ends with refreshing sliced orange.

Meals noon–3.30am

Map 21 B4
5 Warwick Place *W9 2PX*
01–286 7484

Proprietor
Mr Richard William-Ellis

About £28 for two
Banquets 30/10
Tube Warwick Avenue

Didier 

Capable cooking and a happy atmosphere make it a treat to visit this pleasantly informal restaurant. A simple menu of salads, spicy sausages, omelettes and grills is supplemented by daily specials such as creamy leek and potato soup, saffron chicken and bœuf en daube, and to finish there are homely desserts like apple and quince tart or rhubarb fool.
Credit Amex

Lunch 12.30–2.30 *Dinner* 7.30–10.30
Closed L Sat, all Sun & Bank Holidays

Map 22 C1
30 Connaught Street *W2 2AF*
01–258 3947

Le Dodo Gourmand 

Bernard de Rosnay is the charming host at this simply decorated little restaurant. The menu features a small choice of French-style dishes like poussin in cider sauce and steak with mushrooms and wine sauce, supplemented by Créole specialities such as curry or cod marinated in saffron, coriander and mustard. Sweets include tasty banana tart. Generally acceptable cooking. *Credit* Access, Amex, Barclaycard, Diners

About £29 for two
Buses 6, 7, 8, 15, 16, 36B

Lunch 12.30–2.30 *Dinner* 7–10.30
Closed Sun, 1 January & 25 December

Stars in this Guide stand for the quality of the cooking only–
our overriding criterion, irrespective of price, luxury or service.

Dorchester   92% *E*   £A

Map 22 D3
Park Lane *W1A 2HJ*
01–629 8888
Telex 887704

Rooms 285
with bath/shower 285
Room phone Yes
Room TV Yes
Confirm by 6
Last dinner 11.30
Parking Difficult
Banquets 550/2

Credit Access, Amex,
Barclaycard, Diners
Buses 2, 2B, 16, 30, 36B,
73, 74, 137

A lavish programme has given this fine and justly famous hotel a new lease of life, and it exudes an air of unashamed luxury sustained by really first-class service. The fashionable Promenade with its rows of pillars and lovely furniture is a popular meeting place; there's also a modern split-level bar and a new library, which serves as a residents' lounge. Attractive bedrooms are impeccably maintained and have pretty matching fabrics and deep velvet armchairs, while many of the spacious bathrooms retain their original hand-painted Dutch tiles. There are also a number of sumptuous suites. No dogs.
Amenities patio, dinner dance (Mon–Sat), hairdressing, shopping arcade. &

Dorchester Grill Room

Map 22 D3
Park Lane *W1A 2HJ*
01–629 8888
Manager Mr John Curry
English cooking
● **Set L** £12·50 incl. wine &
service
Set D £15·50 incl. service
About £38 for two
Buses 2, 2B, 16, 30,
36B, 73, 74, 137

The traditional English menus in this spacious, elegant room are proving a great success, and every lunchtime there's a regional speciality such as honey-baked Oxfordshire ham or roast Norfolk turkey. Roast beef from the trolley is a great favourite, too, and to finish there are classic English puddings and savouries. Service is smart and efficient.
ABOVE AVERAGE. Credit Access, Amex, Barclaycard, Diners &

Lunch 12.30–3, Sun 12.30–2.30 *Dinner* 6.30–11, Sun 7–11

Dorchester, The Terrace ★

Map 22 D3
Park Lane *W1A 2HJ*
01–629 8888
Manager Mr Lorenzo Susini
French cooking

● **Set D** £17
About £48 for two

Buses 2, 2B, 16, 30, 36B, 73,
74, 137

A most attractive new restaurant, where the French interior decorator has created a quietly luxurious atmosphere, and where chef Anton Mosimann and maître d'hôtel Lorenzo Susini have together devised a splendid menu along nouvelle cuisine lines. Lightness is the watchword, with superbly fresh ingredients, delicate sauces and beautifully prepared tiny crisp vegetables. Great care and finesse are shown at every stage, from the perfectly poached oysters in champagne to the exquisite passion fruit soufflé. Presentation and service are outstanding, too. **Specialities** rendez-vous de fruits de mer, consommé de homard aux feuilles de coriandre, suprême de canard Nossi Bé. *ABOVE AVERAGE. Credit* Access, Amex, Barclaycard, Diners

Dinner only 6–11.30
Closed Sun

Drakes

Map 23 C5
2a Pond Place
Fulham Road *SW3 6QJ*
01–584 4555

About £32 for two
Tube South Kensington

An attractive basement restaurant, where the menu offers capably cooked dishes ranging from lobster and prawn mousse to grilled plaice, spit roasts and individual steak Wellington. *Credit* Access, Amex, Barclaycard, Diners *Lunch* 12.30–2.15, Sun 12.30–2.45 *Dinner* 7.30–11, Sun 7.30–10.15 **Closed** Bank Holidays ● **Set L** £5·95, Sun £7·95 **Set D** Tues–Fri £7·95 *Banquets* 75/–

Map 24 C2
10 Drury Lane
High Holborn *WC2B 5RE*
01–836 6666
Telex 8811395

Rooms 130
with bath/shower 130
Room phone Yes
Room TV Yes
Confirm by 6
Last dinner 10
Parking Limited
Banquets 80/8

Credit Access, Amex,
Barclaycard, Diners
♔ Buses 8, 19, 22, 25, 38, 55

Drury Lane Hotel   71%   *E*   £ B/C

Part of a concrete and glass office block in the heart of theatreland, this excellent modern hotel is well maintained and efficiently run. Attractive cane furniture and luxuriant greenery give a fresh, light feel to the relaxing foyer-lounge, and Maudie's Bar, warmly decorated and comfortably furnished, features many original cartoons of Sir Osbert Lancaster's well-loved character Maudie Littlehampton. Fair-sized bedrooms, with cheerful cream, green and beige colour schemes, have attractive darkwood unit furniture and plenty of storage space. Fully tiled bathrooms are equipped with little luxuries like bath foam and sewing kits.
Amenities patio.

Map 24 C2
10 Drury Lane
High Holborn *WC2B 5RE*
01–836 6666

Drury Lane Hotel, Maudie's Restaurant   Ⓢ

Sir Osbert Lancaster's famous heroine can be admired in the original cartoons in this comfortable modern dining room, which also features an appetising serve-yourself hors d'œuvre table. The short seasonal menu has an up-to-date flavour, with dishes like duck in a red wine sauce or crayfish tails with chicken breasts, and cooking by the English chef is skilled and careful. *Credit* Access, Amex, Barclaycard, Diners

● **Set L & Set D** from £7·75
About £27 for two
♔ Buses 8, 19, 22, 25, 38, 55

Lunch 12.30–2.30, Sun 12.30–2 *Dinner* 6–10, Sun 6.30–9.30
Closed 5 days Christmas

Map 25 B4
35 St James's Place *SW1A 1NY*
01–491 4840
Telex 28283

Rooms 42
with bath/shower 42
Room phone Yes
Room TV Yes
Confirm by By arrang.
Last dinner 10
Parking Difficult
Banquets 55/10

Credit Access, Amex,
Barclaycard, Diners
♔ Tube Green Park

Dukes Hotel   74%   £ A

Nestling in the peace and quiet of a courtyard just off St James's Place, this splendid Edwardian red-brick hotel maintains old-fashioned standards of personal service in dignified, civilised surroundings. Fresh flowers and antique pieces grace the carpeted entrance hall and comfortable little residents' lounge, and the cosy, dimly lit bar is hung with oil paintings of dukes. Dukes also give their names to the compact bedrooms, which have cheerful colour schemes, tasteful reproduction furniture and luxurious brocade bedspreads; modernised bathrooms, most of them tiled, are thoughtfully equipped. No dogs.
Amenities valeting.

Map 25 B4
35 St James's Place *SW1A 1NY*
01–491 4840

Dukes Hotel, St James's Room Restaurant   ♛

A stylish, relaxing restaurant, whose menu ranges from potted shrimps and tasty chicken consommé to lamb cutlets, châteaubriand and tender calf's liver alla veneziana. Capable cooking and fast, efficient service.

About £39 for two
♔ Tube Green Park

♟ *ABOVE AVERAGE. Credit* Access, Amex, Barclaycard, Diners
Lunch 12.30–2 *Dinner* 6.30–10, Sun 7–10

Map 22 D1
26 George Street *W1H 6BJ*
01–935 8131
Telex 894919
Proprietor Mr R. C. Miller

Credit Access, Amex, Diners
♔ Buses 1, 2, 13, 30, 74, 113, 159

Durrants Hotel   63%   Ⓜ   £ D

This owner-run hotel with a handsome Regency facade is solidly and delightfully British. Public rooms like the spacious residents' lounge and the cosy bar have the dignified appeal of a private club, with oak panelling, writing desks and comfortable leather armchairs. Cheerfully decorated bedrooms of various sizes have simple contemporary furnishings; modernised bathrooms are adequately equipped. No dogs.

Continued

Continued
Rooms *104*
with bath/shower 80

Room phone Yes
Room TV Yes

Confirm by 6
Last dinner 10

Parking Difficult
Banquets 60/10

Map 23 D5
49 Elizabeth Street *SW1W 9PP*
01–730 0074

Proprietors Shayne Pope,
Dieter Vagtz & Santosh Bakshi

Eatons

Careful cooking and cheerful, efficient service have enabled the three partners to build up a strong following at their smart Belgravia restaurant. Blinis with smoked salmon make a popular starter, while main courses on the short menu range from plain grills to chicken brochette or the interesting pork escalope stuffed with red cabbage and raisins. Tempting sweet trolley. *Credit* Access, Amex, Barclaycard, Diners

About £27 for two
Buses 11, 39

Lunch 12–2 *Dinner* 7–11.15
Closed Sat, Sun & Bank Holidays

Map 25 A6
26 Ebury Street *SW1W 0LU*
01–730 8147

Proprietors
Mr & Mrs R. Topham
Credit Access, Barclaycard
Tube Victoria

Ebury Court Hotel   50%   Ⓜ   £ C/D

Loyal regulars and overseas visitors like the quiet English charm of this small hotel not far from Victoria Station. Four of the compact bedrooms have four-posters, and all are prettily decorated in pastel shades. Bathrooms are simply fitted. There are two pleasant little lounges. Drinks are served in rooms, or temporary membership is available for guests wishing to use the Club Bar.

Rooms *39*
with bath/shower 11

Room phone Yes
Room TV No

Confirm by 6
Last dinner 9

Parking Difficult

Map 23 B6
11 Park Walk *SW10 0AJ*
01–352 3449
Proprietors
Giuliano Movio, Salvatore Livesi
& Franco Zanellato
Italian cooking

Eleven Park Walk   Ⓢ

An interesting selection of carefully prepared Italian dishes attracts a lively clientele to this elegantly cool tiled restaurant just off Fulham Road. There are excellent salads and pasta dishes to start, and main courses include poussin with rosemary, saltimbocca and lovely poached turbot with sage. Our Amaretto-doused crêpes with Strega ice cream made a delectable sweet. Friendly, polished service. *Credit* Amex

About £32 for two
Buses 14, 45

Lunch 12.30–3 *Dinner* 7–12
Closed Sun & Bank Holidays

Map 23 A4
162 Cromwell Road *SW5 0TT*
01–370 4282
Telex 918978

Credit Access, Amex,
Barclaycard, Diners
Tube Earl's Court

Elizabetta Hotel   65%   £ D/E

Behind a modern concrete and glass facade, this well-run hotel is fitted out in delightful classical French style. The charming foyer-lounge has a pink marble floor and is furnished, like the cocktail bar, with elegant reproduction chairs and tables. The French influence extends to the compact, comfortable bedrooms, which all have smart, up-to-date bathrooms with showers. No dogs.

Rooms *84*
with bath/shower 84

Room phone Yes
Room TV Yes

Confirm by 6
Last dinner 10

Parking Limited

Map 23 B4
31 Queen's Gate *SW7 5JA*
01–584 7222
Telex 8813387

Credit Access, Amex,
Barclaycard, Diners
Tube Gloucester Road

Embassy House Hotel   58%   £ D/E

Outwardly this stylish hotel retains the pillared features of its 19th-century town-house neighbours, but inside it's completely modernised. Bright colour schemes add to the appeal of the public rooms, which include the open-plan reception-lounge area and a cheerful basement bar. Bedrooms, too, are pleasantly decorated; all have neat fitted units, tea/coffee-makers and gleaming tiled bathrooms.

Rooms *72*
with bath/shower 72

Room phone Yes
Room TV Yes

Confirm by 6
Last dinner 9.30

Parking Difficult

English Garden ♔ ⑤

Map 23 C5
10 Lincoln Street *SW3 2TS*
01–584 7272

English cooking

About £36 for two
Banquets 28/6
⊖ Tube Sloane Square

Fresh, delicate flavours and attractive, colourful presentation are features of the traditional English dishes served in this comfortable, civilised restaurant. English Garden terrine (puréed turbot layered with scallops) is a delicious starter, and tasty main courses could include juicy home-made sausages, herbed veal chop or richly sauced chicken vol-au-vent.
Credit Access, Amex, Barclaycard, Diners

Lunch 12.30–2.30 *Dinner* 7.30–11.30, Sun 7.30–10
Closed 25 December

English House ♔ ⑤

Map 23 C4
3 Milner Street *SW3 2QA*
01–584 3002

English cooking

● **Set L** £5·75
About £42 for two
Banquets 10/6
⊖ Buses 19, 22, 137

For a real taste of Olde England, make sure you book for this charming little restaurant in a quiet town house. The menu is based on 18th-century court and country cooking, and you can travel back in time with delights like galantine of rabbit served with sage and apple jelly, succulent collops of venison and darkly rich chocolate pie. Coffee or tea is served with English fudge. ♟ *ABOVE AVERAGE. Credit* Access, Amex, Barclaycard, Diners

Lunch 12.30–2.15 *Dinner* 7.30–11.30
Closed Sun & Bank Holidays

Changes in data may occur in establishments after the Guide goes to press. Prices should be taken as indications rather than firm quotes.

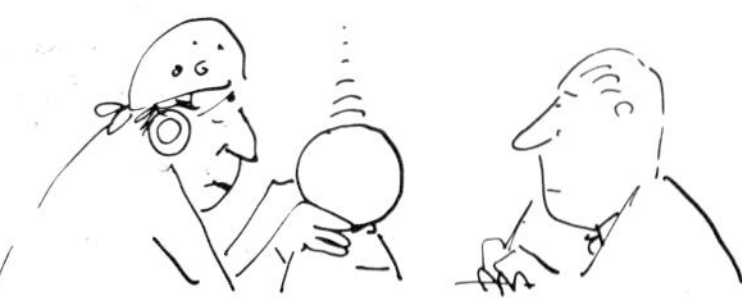

Equatorial ☘ ⑤

Map 25 C5
37 Old Compton Street *W1V 5PL*
01–437 6112

Singapore cooking
● **Set L** £3·90 **Set D** £7
incl. service
About £23 for two
Banquets 40/–
⊖ Buses 14, 19, 22, 24, 29, 38, 55

Enticing and subtle flavour combinations are a feature of the authentic Singapore dishes served at this simple, modern restaurant. After succulent satay you could choose a delicately spiced chicken curry, beef in a delicious coconut-flavoured sauce or superb fresh crab in a hot chilli sauce. End with a refreshing syrupy sweet. Friendly waitress service.
Credit Access, Amex, Barclaycard, Diners

Lunch 12–2.45, Sat & Sun 12–11.15pm *Dinner* 6–11.15
Closed 25 & 26 December

L'Escargot ♔ ⑤

Map 25 C5
48 Greek Street *W1V 5LQ*
01–437 2679

About £36 for two
Banquets 40/10
⊖ Buses 14, 19, 22, 24, 29, 38, 55

In the heart of Soho, this smart upstairs restaurant is a relaxing, informal place. Monthly-changing menus offer capably prepared specialities like snails in garlic sauce, sea bass with fennel and smooth cream of lettuce soup. There are several plats du jour, a good cheeseboard and tempting sweets such as French strawberry tart. ♟ *OUTSTANDING.*
Credit Access, Amex, Barclaycard, Diners

Lunch 12.30–2.30 *Dinner* 6.30–11.15
Closed L Sat, all Sun & Bank Holidays

Estoril da Luigi e Roberto ⑤

Map 24 B3
3 Denman Street *W1V 7RH*
01–437 8700

Proprietor Mr L. Musetti
Italian cooking

About £31 for two
⊖ Tube Piccadilly Circus

A change of name has done nothing to diminish the reliability of the cooking in this cosy Italian restaurant. The menu offers a good choice of traditional favourites, from well-cooked macaroni and prosciutto to saltimbocca, chicken cacciatora and our succulent veal chop with a creamy mushroom and red pepper sauce. Simple sweets are mainly gâteaux and fruit. Service with a smile. *Credit* Access, Amex, Barclaycard, Diners

Lunch 12–2.30 *Dinner* 6–11.30, Sun 6–11
Closed 24–26 December

Map 22 D2
Grosvenor Square *W1A 4AW*
01–493 1232
Telex 268101

Rooms 275
with bath/shower 275
Room phone Yes
Room TV Yes
Confirm by 6
Last dinner 10.30
Parking Limited
Banquets 550/10

Credit Access, Amex,
Barclaycard, Diners
⊖ Tube Bond Street

Europa Hotel   73% *E*   £B

Conveniently placed for the West End shops, this luxurious hotel enjoys a peaceful position overlooking Grosvenor Square. A large, business-like lobby leads into a charming lounge with a tent-like roof supported by bamboo poles. There's also a strikingly elegant panelled bar whose walls are hung with old prints, and a wide range of conference and banqueting rooms. Fair-sized bedrooms (many with attractive views over the square or gardens) are comfortable and practical, with high-quality fabrics and furnishings; bathrooms are simpler and have plenty of good thick towels. No dogs.
Amenities coffee shop (noon–1am), valeting.

Map 22 D2
Grosvenor Square *W1A 4AW*
01–493 1232

● **Set L & Set D** £8·25
About £43 for two
⊖ Tube Bond Street

Europa Hotel, Diplomat Restaurant ♕♕ 

An inviting and stylish restaurant, whose menu offers an interesting selection of nicely prepared, mainly French-inspired dishes. Evergreens like escargots and grills stand alongside less usual choices such as tasty coquilles St Jacques with a puff pastry top or tender entrecôte steak served with sweetbreads and a lovely rich port sauce. Tempting sweet trolley. Excellent, polished service. *Credit* Access, Amex, Barclaycard, Diners

Lunch 12.30–2.30, Sun 12–2 *Dinner* 6.30–10.30, Sun 6.30–10

Map 23 B6
7 Langton Street *SW10 0JL*
01–351 0761
Proprietor Mr Alvaro Maccioni
Italian cooking

About £27 for two
⊖ Buses 11, 22, 31

La Famiglia   

Crowds flock to this lively, fashionable restaurant, where the atmosphere matches the authentically Italian flavour of the food. Unusual home-made pasta dishes precede well-prepared specialities like mussels in a pungent tomato and garlic sauce or cold veal with tuna-flavoured mayonnaise, while chicken and beef entrées, simple grills and excellent vegetables complete the picture. *Credit* Access, Amex, Barclaycard, Diners

Lunch 12–3 *Dinner* 7–12
Closed Bank Holidays

Map 20 B2
250 Finchley Road *NW3 6DJ*
01–435 8622

English cooking

● **Set L** £3·95
About £25 for two
Banquets 25/12
⊖ Buses 2B, 13, 113

Finches   ♀ 

Traditional English fare is the order of the day in this pretty restaurant, where Terry Farr offers skilfully prepared, uncomplicated dishes like devilled baby chicken, jugged hare and poached halibut with butter sauce along with lightly cooked vegetables. Sweets have an old-fashioned flavour, too. Set lunches feature daily specials such as casserole of veal with ginger wine. *Credit* Access, Amex, Barclaycard, Diners

Lunch 12–2.15 *Dinner* 7–11.15
Closed Sun, Mon, Bank Holidays & 3 weeks summer

Map 24 D3
19 Tavistock Street *WC2E 7PA*
01–836 3925

Seafood

● **Set D** £6·75
(5.30pm–7.30pm only)
About £34 for two
⊖ Tube Covent Garden

Flounders   Ⓢ

Excellent fresh seafood is the main attraction at this smart, stylish restaurant, with a choice of dishes ranging from perfect grilled herrings and succulent scallops Thermidor to deep-fried haddock and skate. There are also a few meat items like grilled sirloin steak, and sweets such as rich chocolate mousse. Pre-theatre suppers are very popular. Informal, friendly service. *Credit* Access, Amex, Barclaycard, Diners

Lunch 12.30–3 *Dinner* 5.30–11.30, Sat 5.30–12
Closed Sun & Bank Holidays

Four Seasons

Map 20 D3
69 Barnsbury Street *N1 1EJ*
01–607 0857

French cooking

● Set L £9·80
About £38 for two
Banquets 20/10
✆ Buses 4, 19, 30, 43, 104, 279

Robust French cooking is the attraction in this friendly little restaurant with a courtyard at the back. The hot tartlet filled with mushrooms and snails is a perennial favourite on the short menu, and other dishes range from suprême of chicken garnished with wild mushrooms to pork fillet flambéed with Calvados. Sauces are rich, vegetables are crisp and there are lovely sweets to finish. *Credit* Access, Barclaycard

Lunch 12.30–2.30 *Dinner* 7–11
Closed L Sat, all Sun & L Bank Holidays

Frederick's

Map 20 D3
Camden Passage *N1 8ED*
01–359 2888

● Set L Sat only £5·95
incl. service
About £31 for two
Banquets 85/50
✆ Tube Angel

The menu changes fortnightly at this smart, spacious restaurant where it's possible to eat outdoors in fine weather. An imaginative choice of French-inspired dishes may include specialities like loin of pork with charcutière sauce or turbot poached in white wine with green peppercorns, cream and tarragon. There are also grills, plus excellent al dente vegetables. *ABOVE AVERAGE. Credit* Access, Amex, Barclaycard, Diners

Lunch 12.30–2.30 *Dinner* 7.30–11.30
Closed Sun, 1 January & 26 December

Fuji

Map 24 B3
36 Brewer Street *W1R 3HP*
01–734 0957

Manager Mr Senda
Japanese cooking
● Set L from £5·90
Set D from £9 incl. service
About £32 for two
Banquets 80/–
✆ Tube Piccadilly Circus

Attractive, eye-catching decor sets the scene in this long-established Japanese restaurant, where food is characteristically subtle and beautifully presented. Set menus are based on familiar tempura, sukiyaki and teriyaki, and there's a long à la carte featuring perfectly prepared sushi, sashimi and exquisite combinations like vinegared seafood with glass noodles and vegetables. *Credit* Access, Amex, Barclaycard, Diners

Lunch 12.30–2.30 *Dinner* 6–10.45, Sun 6–10.15
Closed L Sat, Sun & Bank Holidays

Any person using our name to obtain free hospitality is a fraud. Proprietors, please inform the police and us.

Gallant

Map 25 C6
5 Macclesfield Street *W1V 7LE*
01–437 2930

Chinese cooking

● Set D from £5
About £24 for two
✆ Buses 14, 19, 22, 38, 55

Cleverly placed spotlights illuminate this smart Chinese restaurant furnished with modern cane chairs. The long menu has a varied choice of Cantonese dishes ranging from wun tun soup and roast crab with ginger and spring onion to less familiar items such as stuffed bean curd and chicken roasted in salt. Ingredients are first class and cooking is very reliable. *Credit* Access, Amex, Barclaycard, Diners

Meals noon–11.30pm
Closed 25 December

Le Gamin

Map 26 B1
32 Old Bailey *EC4M 7HS*
01–236 7931

French cooking

● Set L £14·75 incl. wine
& service
About £29·50 for two
✆ Buses 4, 6, 9, 11, 15, 18, 23, 141

Enjoyable French provincial cooking in informal surroundings draws the crowds to this pleasant restaurant near St Paul's. Three-course set lunches (price includes aperitif, wine, coffee and petits fours) offer starters like cream of artichoke soup, followed perhaps by salmon with sorrel, rack of lamb with herbs or fillet of beef in a cream sauce. Sweets or French cheeses to finish. *Credit* Access, Amex, Barclaycard, Diners

Lunch only 12–2.30
Closed Sat, Sun & Bank Holidays

Le Gavroche ★ ★  

Map 22 D2
43 Upper Brook Street *W1Y 1PE*
01–408 0881

Proprietors Messrs Roux
French cooking

● **Set L** £19·80
About £70 for two

Albert Roux reigns at what is one of the three or four best restaurants in London; his brother Michel's kingdom, the unsurpassed Waterside Inn, is at Bray in Berkshire. We are lucky in Britain to have such a pair of perfectionists. At Le Gavroche everything is very high powered: cooking, presentation and service; and perhaps one will be made a little less aware of it when this suddenly successful place becomes more relaxed. Albert is very much given to nouvelle cuisine and its typically pretty presentation. **Specialities** mousseline de homard en champagne, bressoles de barbue Silvano, caneton Gavroche, sablé aux fraises.
OUTSTANDING. Credit Access, Amex, Barclaycard, Diners

Lunch 12–2 *Dinner* 7–10
Closed Sat, Sun, Bank Hols, 27 Aug–9 Sept & 24 Dec–9 Jan

⊖ Tube Marble Arch

Gavvers 

Map 23 D5
61 Lower Sloane Street *SW1W 8DH*
01–730 5983

French cooking

● **Set D** £14·75
incl. wine & service
About £29·50 for two
⊖ Tube Sloane Square

Booking is essential at this luxurious brasserie owned by the Roux brothers. The daily-changing fixed-price menu covers everything from a kir aperitif to wine and coffee, and the cooking is imaginative and artistic: carefully prepared and beautifully presented dishes include ragout of snails, calf's liver, bacon and artichoke in flaky pastry, or beef strips with a creamy basil sauce. Delightful sweets, too. 

Dinner only 7–11
Closed Sun, Bank Holidays & 2 weeks August/September

Gay Hussar ★

Map 24 C2
2 Greek Street *W1Y 6NB*
01–437 0973
Managers Stephen Droppa &
Gabor Csapo
Hungarian cooking

● **Set L** £7
About £31 for two
Banquets 10/-

A long-established and very popular little restaurant where friendly waiters are eager to explain the vast choice of Hungarian dishes available on the menu. Authentic specialities such as ragout of beef and pork in sour cream sauce and minced goose with pungent smoked beans have strong well-defined flavours and come with interesting side dishes like thimble egg dumplings. Most, but not all, Hungarian dishes are starworthy, and the restaurant is at its best at lunchtime.
Specialities szegedi halkocsonya, füstölt liba sólettel, vagdalt borjuhus tök fözelékkel, bogrács gulyás.
SUPERIOR.

Lunch 12.30–2.30 *Dinner* 5.30–11
Closed Sun & Bank Holidays

⊖ Tube Tottenham Court Road

Gaylord 

Map 24 B2
79 Mortimer Street *W1N 7TB*
01–580 3615
Manager Mr M. Lamba
Indian cooking
About £28 for two
⊖ Tube Oxford Circus

Elegance and reliability are the hallmarks of this attractive restaurant. Popular North Indian dishes, from chicken tikka to masalas and dopiazas, are subtle, but strongly flavoured; side dishes are also well represented.
Credit Access, Amex, Barclaycard, Diners
Lunch 12–3 *Dinner* 6–11.30 ● **Set L & Set D** £6·45

Our inspectors are our full-time employees; they are professionally trained by us.

Ginnan

Map 26 B1
5 Cathedral Place *EC4M 7EA*
01–236 4120
Japanese cooking
Manager Mr Kazuo Dotai
About £20 for two
⊖ Tube St Paul's

A simply decorated Japanese restaurant where lunch features set meals based on tempura, grills, steaks and—of course—raw fish, skilfully prepared and beautifully presented. More elaborate dinner menu. *Credit* Access, Amex, Barclaycard, Diners *Lunch* 12–2.30 *Dinner* 6–10 **Closed** Sat, Sun & Bank Holidays ● **Set L** from £3·30 **Set D** from £8 *Banquets* 25/4

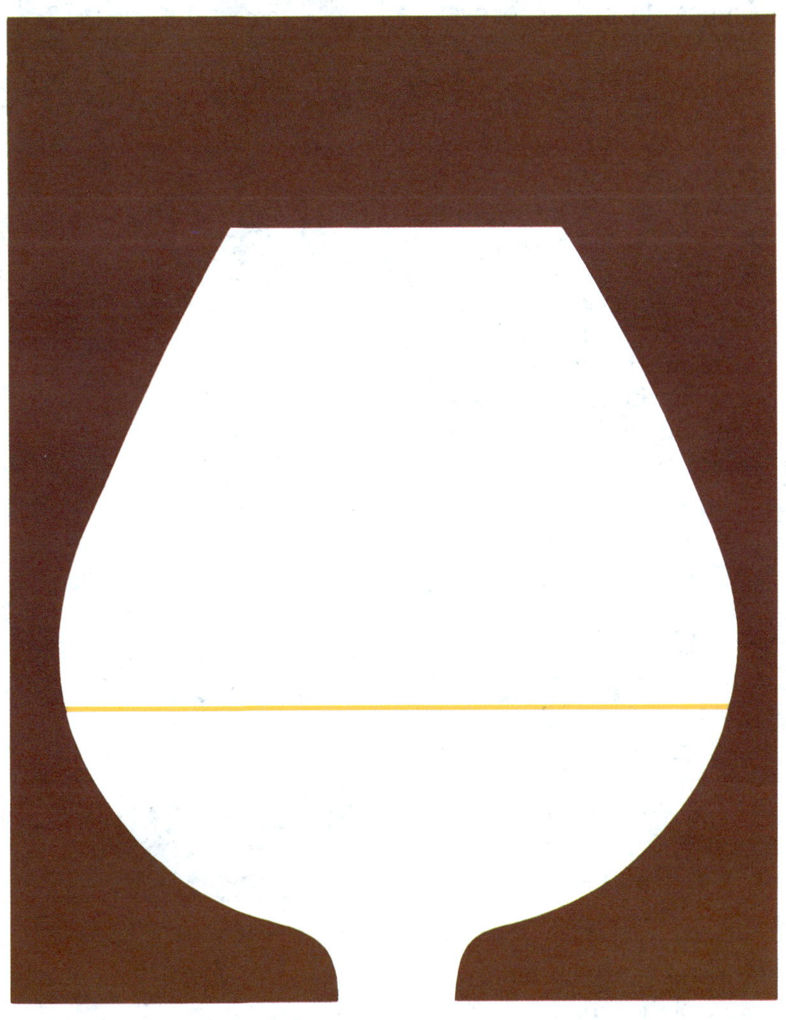

Armagnac
Not the best known, but known by the best.

What is Armagnac?

Armagnac is France's oldest brandy. It's been distilled in Gascony, land of the famous Musketeers, for over 500 years. Deliciously impregnated with the fragrance of the forest and native soil of Gascony, Armagnac acquires a distinctive aroma which has been enjoyed almost exclusively by the French for centuries.

Recently, however, the British discovered the joys of Armagnac for themselves and now this subtle, gently aromatic brandy is available here in Britain.

Where does Armagnac come from?

Armagnac can be produced only in an area of France which includes part of the 'departements' of Gers, Landes and Lot-et-Garonne. This is the heart of Gascony.

Armagnac is an appellation d'origine contrôlée brandy. Each of the three growing areas, Bas-Armagnac, Haut-Armagnac and Ténarèze, produces its own characteristic, subtle fragrance.

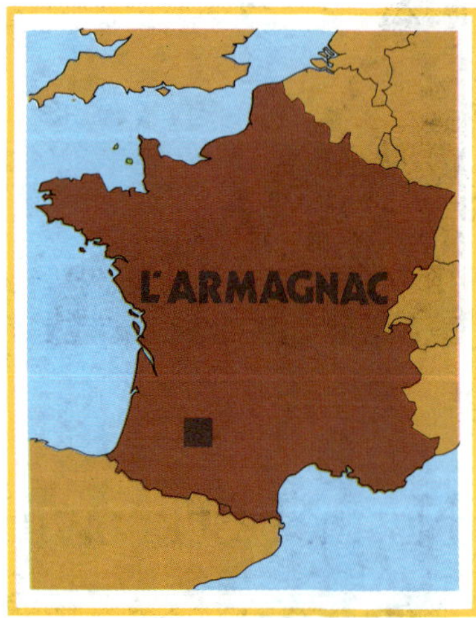

What makes Armagnac different?

The character of Armagnac comes from the soil of Gascony, the method of production and the type of wood used for the casks.

The light soil produces a white wine that is left in contact with the sediment and then distilled. The brandy is then placed in handmade oaken casks from the local forest of Monlezun. When fully matured, the brandy is transferred to older casks.

No Armagnac may be less than three years old. If designated V.O., V.S.O.P. or Reserve, it cannot be less than four years old. All Armagnac called Extra, Napoleon or Vieille Reserve must have been matured for five or more years.

How to enjoy Armagnac.

As you come to the end of a good meal, just ask the waiter for an Armagnac. Then savour the aroma and taste of the oldest brandy of France.

Not the best known, but known by the best.

Gloucester Hotel   77%   *E*   **£B**

Map 23 B5
Harrington Gardens *SW7 4LH*
01–373 6030
Telex 91 7505
Manager
Mr Michael Holland
Rooms 551
with bath/shower 551
Room phone Yes
Room TV Yes
Confirm by 6
Last dinner 10.30
Parking Limited
Banquets 120/2

Credit Access, Amex,
Barclaycard, Diners
⊖ Tube Gloucester Road

A stylish galleried foyer-lounge, with marble pillars, elegant greenery and plenty of relaxing sofas and armchairs, creates a welcoming first impression at this well-run modern hotel just off Cromwell Road. That impression continues throughout the public areas, which include a bright coffee shop, a 24-hour cocktail bar and a popular tavern serving real ale. Bedrooms, too, are attractive and comfortable, with smart darkwood tables, writing desks, fitted wall units, mini-bars and luxurious easy chairs; all have excellent bathrooms. The hotel has a comprehensive range of conference and banqueting rooms. *Amenities* sauna, shopping arcade, hairdressing, coffee shop (6.30am–1am), in-house movies.   &

Golden Duck

Map 23 B6
6 Hollywood Road *SW10 9HY*
01–352 3500
Manager Mr George Lee
Chinese cooking
About £24 for two
⊖ Buses 14, 31

A large, modern Chinese restaurant, where Pekinese and Szechuan specialities like griddle-fried dumplings and crispy aromatic duck are acceptably prepared. *Credit* Access, Amex, Barclaycard, Diners
Lunch Sat & Sun only 1–3 *Dinner* 7–12 **Closed** 3 days Christmas
● **Set L & Set D** from £8·50

Gondoliere   Ⓢ

Map 23 B4
3 Gloucester Road *SW7 4PP*
01–584 8062

Proprietor Mrs E. Moulton
Italian cooking

● **Set L** £4·90 **Set D** £7·85
About £29 for two
Banquets 10/–
⊖ Tube Gloucester Road

This ornately decorated Italian restaurant offers a wide choice of familiar dishes like fettuccine and spaghetti alle vongole, plus specialities such as veal, chicken and ham with olives and brandy sauce baked in a paper bag. Vegetables are carefully handled, and sweets include individually whisked zabaglione. Mrs Moulton's friendly presence adds to the pleasure of a meal here. *Credit* Access, Barclaycard

Lunch 12–2.30 *Dinner* 6–11
Closed L Sat, all Sun & Bank Holidays

Good Earth   ♔ Ⓢ

Map 7 B4
143 The Broadway
Mill Hill *NW7 4RN*
01–959 7011

Chinese cooking
● **Set L & Set D** from £7·95
About £25 for two
Banquets 35/20
⊖ Buses 52, 113, 140, 221, 240, 251

Potted palms and Chinese paintings give this friendly restaurant a most pleasing atmosphere, and the wide range of Cantonese and Pekinese dishes appeals to both eye and palate. Sesame prawns or subtle steamed dumplings make a delicious start, sliced lamb and spring onions arrives sizzling hot on an iron plate, and crispy fragrant duck is cooked to perfection. *Credit* Access, Amex, Barclaycard, Diners

Lunch 12–2.30, Sun 12.30–3 *Dinner* 6–11
Closed 24–26 December

Good Earth   Ⓢ

Map 23 C5
91 King's Road *SW3 4PA*
01–352 9231

Chinese cooking

● **Set L** £5·50 **Set D** £7·50
About £28 for two
Banquets 75/–
⊖ Buses 11, 19, 22

A relaxing atmosphere pervades this cosy Chinese restaurant with its subdued beige decor offset by large paintings. The menu offers authentic Cantonese and Pekinese dishes to tempt Western palates: deep-fried mustard chicken and pork patties with water chestnuts are most enjoyable, while the imperial hors d'œuvre is a feast of mixed meats, abalone and sweet pickled ginger. *Credit* Access, Amex, Barclaycard, Diners

Meals 12.30pm–11.45pm, Sun 12.30pm–11pm
Closed 25 & 26 December

Map 7 B4
139 Salmon Lane
Stepney *E14 7PG*
01–987 5541

Proprietor Mr W. M. Chung
Chinese cooking

About £17 for two
⊖ Tube Stepney Green

Good Friends

Whatever the hour, booking is advisable at this brisk, friendly Chinese restaurant. The mainly Cantonese menu offers a long and varied selection, from superb soups to a range of tempting specialities such as suckling pig or stuffed duckling, for which two days' notice is needed. Dishes like chicken in a tangy lemon sauce are carefully prepared, and vegetables are deliciously crisp. *Credit* Access, Amex, Barclaycard, Diners

Meals noon–11pm, Sat noon–11.30pm
Closed D 24 & all 25 & 26 December

Map 22 B3
189 Queen's Gate *SW7 5EX*
01–584 6601
Telex 296244
Proprietors
Mr & Mrs Dale-Thomas

⊖ Buses 9, 33, 49, 52, 73

Rooms 59
with bath/shower 59

Gore Hotel   53%   Ⓜ   £D

Mr and Mrs Dale-Thomas' converted Victorian town house offers a friendly welcome and adequate comforts for short-stay guests. Bedrooms vary from those with plain modern units to superior newer rooms with pastel decor, smart cane and bamboo furniture and bright, well-appointed bathrooms. The comfortable bar has a pleasing traditional atmosphere, and there's a useful coffee shop. *Credit* Access, Amex, Barclaycard, Diners

Room phone Yes   *Confirm by* 6   *Parking* Difficult
Room TV Yes   *Last dinner* None

Map 25 A6
15 Beeston Place
Grosvenor Gardens *SW1W 0JW*
01–834 8211
Telex 919166
Manager Mr W. A. Cowpe
Rooms 100
with bath/shower 100
Room phone Yes
Room TV Yes
Confirm by By arrang.
Last dinner 9.30
Parking Limited
Banquets 60/2

Credit Access, Amex,
Barclaycard, Diners
⊖ Tube Victoria

Goring Hotel   73%   £B/C

Built in 1910, the Goring still epitomises all the virtues traditionally associated with a fine hotel: courteous personal service, friendliness, charm and impeccable maintenance. An arched entrance hall with its Wedgwood-blue walls and sparkling chandeliers sets the tone of gracious elegance, and there are two spacious lounge areas (one with its own bar) overlooking the attractive garden. Bedrooms vary in shape and size but are kept in excellent order with pastel colour schemes, pretty patterned bedspreads and matching curtains; those facing the road are double-glazed. Spotlessly clean bathrooms are well equipped. No dogs.
Amenities valeting.

Map 25 A6
15 Beeston Place
Grosvenor Gardens *SW1W 0JW*
01–834 8211

About £31 for two
⊖ Tube Victoria

Goring Hotel Restaurant

This handsome restaurant offers a varied menu of acceptably prepared dishes like stuffed trout poached in white wine, chicken breast cooked in cider and simple grills. Soups are particularly good. Booking advisable for weekday lunches. 🍷 *ABOVE AVERAGE. Credit* Access, Amex, Barclaycard, Diners *Lunch* 12.30–2.30 *Dinner* 6–9.30 ● **Set L** £8·50 **Set D** £10

Map 25 B6
52 Wilton Road *SW1V 1DE*
01–828 5818
Proprietor Mr Sandro
Italian cooking

About £24 for two
Banquets 22/–
⊖ Tube Victoria

Gran Paradiso

Near Victoria Station, a busy restaurant with spotlights, oil paintings and comfortable cane chairs. The menu offers a good choice of Italian dishes, including many of the evergreens and some appetising specials like mussels in tomato sauce or our excellent sautéed chicken livers in a fragrant wine and herb sauce. Dependable cooking, attractive presentation, brisk service.
Credit Access, Amex, Barclaycard, Diners   ♿

Lunch 12.30–2.30 *Dinner* 6.30–11.30
Closed L Sat, all Sun, Bank Holidays & 10–31 August

The Grange ♛ Ⓢ

Map 25 D6
39 King Street *WC2E 8JS*
01–240 2939
Manager Dominic Francini

● **Set L & Set D** from £11.10
incl. wine
About £29 for two
⊖ Tube Covent Garden

A sophisticated atmosphere pervades this simply decorated restaurant. The monthly-changing set menus (two, three or four courses) feature a well-balanced selection of dishes ranging from pigeon pie and lamb Shrewsbury to spiced brochette of sole and poached salmon with hollandaise sauce. Vegetables are perfectly timed and tempting sweets include cranberry tart and crème brûlée. Booking advisable. *Credit* Amex

Lunch 12.30–2.30 *Dinner* 7.30–11.30, Sat 6.45–11.30
Closed L Sat, all Sun, Bank Holidays & August

Grapes

Map 20 D3
The Mall
Camden Passage *N1 0PD*
01–359 4960

About £36 for two
⊖ Tube Angel

Choose between two dining areas (one slightly more formal than the other) and two menus at this bright, lively restaurant. Dishes like poached salmon with champagne sauce are competently prepared, and vegetables are very good. *Credit* Access, Barclaycard *Lunch* 12–3, Sat noon–midnight *Dinner* 6–12 **Closed** Bank Holidays *Banquets* 110/–

Great Eastern Hotel   61%   £ C/D

Map 26 D1
Liverpool Street *EC2M 7QN*
01–283 4363
Telex 886812

Credit Access, Amex,
Barclaycard, Diners
⊖ Tube Liverpool Street

Recent cleaning of its handsome red brickwork has given a facelift to this imposing old railway hotel, popular with businessmen for its extensive banqueting and conference facilities. Public rooms like the ornate Abercorn Bar retain their Victorian grandeur, and there's also a convivial coffee shop with its own little bar. Well-furnished bedrooms (all with tea-makers) are bright, cheerful and comfortably spacious.

Rooms 150	*Room phone* Yes	*Confirm by* 6	*Parking* Limited
with bath/shower 127	*Room TV* Yes	*Last dinner* 10	*Banquets* 400/4

Great Mughal   ♛ Ⓢ

Map 22 C2
2 Hyde Park Square *W2 2JY*
01–258 3507

Indian cooking

● **Set L & Set D** £5·95
About £30 for two
Banquets 150/15
⊖ Tube Lancaster Gate

Marvellously courteous service makes eating in this luxurious Indian restaurant a real pleasure, and the food is absolutely authentic. Seasoning and marinating are faultless, and everthing is prepared with care and attention to detail. We particularly enjoyed tandoori fish and quails in a subtly flavoured sauce, with spicy dahl, excellent pilau rice and fresh nan.
Credit Access, Amex, Barclaycard, Diners   &

Lunch 12–3 *Dinner* 6.30–11.30
Closed 25 & 26 December

Great Northern Hotel   63%   £ D

Map 20 C3
King's Cross *N1 9AN*
01–837 5454
Telex 299041
Credit Access, Amex,
Barclaycard, Diners
Closed 4 days Christmas
⊖ Tube King's Cross

Standing alongside King's Cross Station, this crescent-shaped Victorian hotel still retains its large windows and high ceilings, but has been brought up to date with extensive refurbishment. The wood-panelled lounge and bar have been completely redecorated, and attractively papered bedrooms have modern freestanding furniture. Bathrooms are well equipped.
Amenities coffee shop (7am–10am & 11am–10pm).   &

Rooms 69	*Room phone* Yes	*Confirm by* 6	*Parking* Limited
with bath/shower 42	*Room TV* Yes	*Last dinner* 10	*Banquets* 65/–

Great Western Royal Hotel   64%   £ D

Map 22 B1
Praed Street *W2 1HE*
01–723 8064
Telex 263972
Manager Mr Anthony A. Short
Credit Access, Amex,
Barclaycard, Diners
⊖ Tube Paddington

Brunel built this large hotel next to Paddington Station in 1854 as the starting point for a route to America via Bristol. The lounge remains a vast pillared room of splendid proportions, and the Brunel Bar shows tastefully how the place has kept up with the times. Comfortable bedrooms are traditionally furnished, and the best have fine white marble bathrooms.
Amenities 24-hour laundry service.   &

Rooms 160	*Room phone* Yes	*Confirm by* 6	*Parking* Limited
with bath/shower 135	*Room TV* Yes	*Last dinner* 9.30	*Banquets* 300/–

Hilton International Kensington, Hiroko Rest. ⑤

Map 21 A4
179 Holland Park Avenue *W11 4UL*
01–603 5003

Manager Mr Shoji
Japanese cooking

● **Set L** £6·50 **Set D** £10·50
About £38 for two
⊖ Tube Shepherd's Bush

A tranquil restaurant with lacquered tables and wooden screens arranged around a central cooking area. The set meals offer an excellent range of dishes—fragrant soups, beautifully presented sashimi, tempura and specialities like superb cod in teriyaki sauce; there's also a varied à la carte. The cooking shows a typically Japanese blend of skill and artistry. Charming service. *Credit* Access, Amex, Barclaycard, Diners ♿

Lunch 12–2.30 *Dinner* 6–10
Closed L Mon, May Day, August Bank Holiday & 1–4 January

Hilton International London   81%   *E*   **£ A**

Map 22 D3
22 Park Lane *W1A 2HH*
01–493 8000
Telex 24873

Manager M Jean-Pierre Piquet
Rooms 509
with bath/shower 509
Room phone Yes
Room TV Yes
Confirm by 6
Last dinner 12.30am
Parking Ample
Banquets 1,000/10

Credit Access, Amex,
Barclaycard, Diners
⊖ Tube Hyde Park Corner

Flourishing as a monument to the virtues of good living, the Hilton maintains its enviable reputation for excellent facilities and superb service thanks to highly professional, assured staff. Numerous elegantly furnished meeting rooms and suites cater for the needs of business visitors, while for relaxation there are many attractions, including a vast ballroom and the St George's Bar, designed like a gentleman's club with brown leather armchairs and sporting prints. Comfortable bedrooms are very well appointed with elegant reproduction furniture, pretty soft furnishings and compact, marble-lined bathrooms. *Amenities* dinner dance (Mon–Sat), valeting, 24-hour laundry service, hairdressing, shopping arcade, beauty salon. ♿

Hogarth Hotel   58%   **£ E**

Map 23 A5
Hogarth Road *SW5 0QQ*
01–370 6831
Telex 8951994
Manager Mr M. Dawson
Credit Access, Amex, Diners
Closed 4 days Christmas
⊖ Tube Earl's Court

A clean-lined, five-storey brick building, this modern, purpose-built hotel stands in a quiet street off Earl's Court Road. Everything is simple and bright, from the spacious reception hall, residents' lounge and bar hung with Hogarth prints to the cheerfully decorated bedrooms, which have well-designed fitted furniture, tea/coffee-making facilities and neat bathrooms with patterned tiles. No dogs.

Rooms 86
with bath/shower 86

Room phone Yes   *Confirm by* 6   *Parking* Limited
Room TV Yes   *Last dinner* 8.30   *Banquets* 20/–

Holiday Inn (Chelsea)   79%   *E*   **£ B**

Map 23 D4
Sloane Street *SW1X 9NU*
01–235 4377
Telex 919111

Rooms 217
with bath/shower 217
Room phone Yes
Room TV Yes
Confirm by 6
Last dinner 10.30
Parking Ample
Banquets 180/6
Credit Access, Amex,
Barclaycard, Diners

⊖ Tube Knightsbridge

A striking split-level foyer-lounge, with chandeliers, marble floor and comfortable leather chesterfields, is one of the features of this luxurious modern hotel, which stands in fashionable Knightsbridge just a short walk from Harrods. Other attractions include an elegant swimming pool with a roof that slides back in summer, and, overlooking it, a leafy restaurant and the intimate, club-like Bohemian Bar. Bright bedrooms have high-quality built-in furnishings, extra large beds, ornate velvety chairs and mini-bars. Compact, sumptuously fitted bathrooms are thoughtfully equipped. Staff are particularly friendly and efficient. *Amenities* indoor/outdoor swimming pool, in-house movies, hairdressing.

Map 22 C1

134 George Street *W1H 6DN*
01–723 1277
Telex 27983

Rooms 241
with bath/shower 241
Room phone Yes
Room TV Yes
Confirm by 6
Last dinner 12
Parking Ample
Banquets 120/–

Credit Access, Amex,
Barclaycard, Diners
⊖ Tube Marble Arch

Holiday Inn (Marble Arch) 72% *E*   £A

One attraction of this modern 12-storey hotel is the private car park in the basement, from which guests have access into the airy reception hall with its polished marble floor. The comfortable lounge area has potted plants and glass-topped tables and there's a smart cocktail bar fitted out with cane furniture. Refurbished bedrooms have pretty matching curtains and bedspreads, deep-pile carpets and good-quality contemporary freestanding furniture, including extra-large beds. Bathrooms are fully tiled and well equipped.
Amenities sauna, indoor swimming pool, solarium, brasserie (7.30am–10.30pm), in-house video.   &

Map 20 B3

128 King Henry's Road
NW3 3ST
01–722 7711
Telex 267396
Manager Mr E. van Empel
Rooms 291
with bath/shower 291
Room phone Yes
Room TV Yes
Confirm by 6
Last dinner 10.15
Parking Ample
Banquets 300/20

Credit Access, Amex,
Barclaycard, Diners

⊖ Tube Swiss Cottage

Holiday Inn (Swiss Cottage) 76% *E*   £C

Handily placed for the main road out of London to the North yet in a peaceful residential area, this attractive modern hotel is noted for its pleasant, friendly atmosphere. Cool, relaxing decor is a feature of the spacious foyer-reception and the lounge-bar with its distinctive central fireplace and comfortable armchairs. Immaculately maintained bedrooms have extra-large double beds and beautifully warm, well-equipped bathrooms. There is a drink dispenser on each floor.
Amenities garden, sauna, indoor swimming pool, dinner dance (Sat), Prestel, Ceefax, keep-fit equipment, solarium, in-house movies, 12-hour laundry service, hairdressing, valeting.   &

Map 22 A3

38c Kensington Church Street
W8 4LL
01–937 2005

Indian cooking

About £28 for two
⊖ Tube High Street Kensington

Holy Cow   Ⓢ

A cool, relaxed atmosphere pervades this softly lit basement restaurant, where the menu offers an interesting choice of dishes based on North Indian recipes. Herbs and spices are used with care and balance to create authentic tandoori specialities and curries such as prawn masala and chicken dhansak. Excellent nan bread and sundries. Service is informal and friendly.
Credit Access, Amex, Barclaycard, Diners

Lunch 12–2.45 *Dinner* 6–11.45
Closed L Sun

Map 20 B1

30 Temple Fortune Parade
Finchley Road *NW11 0QX*
01–455 9444

Chinese cooking

● **Set L & Set D** from £4·20
About £22 for two
Banquets 60/–
⊖ Buses 13, 26, 102, 260

Hongs   Ⓢ

Mr Wong delights customers at this smart, efficiently run Chinese restaurant with his capable and reliable cooking. The long menu, which features popular dishes representing several regional cuisines, ranges from crispy spring rolls and braised bean curd to steamed spareribs and nicely sauced duck with pineapple and sweet ginger. Service is very helpful.
Credit Access, Amex, Barclaycard, Diners   &

Lunch 12–3 *Dinner* 6–11

Map 24 D3

Temple Place
Strand *WC2R 2PR*
01–836 3555
Telex 268047

Rooms 136
with bath/shower 136
Room phone Yes
Room TV Yes
Confirm by 6
Last dinner 11
Parking Ample
Banquets 120/10

Credit Access, Amex,
Barclaycard, Diners
⊖ Tube Temple

Howard Hotel   81%   *E*   **£ A**

Despite its striking concrete and glass exterior, this modern hotel has all the elegance and sumptuous decor of the past. Italian marble pillars, Adam-style colour schemes and fine period furniture suggest the spirit of the 18th century, and this theme is continued in the cosy Temple Bar overlooking the court-yard garden. Bedrooms are superb-ly furnished, with velvet-covered beds and French tables and chairs. All are provided with mini-fridges. Marble bathrooms are fully equipped with everything from bidets to bath oil. There are also seven lovely penthouse suites with balconies. No dogs. *Amenities* valeting.

Map 24 D3

Temple Place *WC2R 2PR*
01–836 3555
Manager Mr E. Hokke

About £42 for two
⊖ Tube Temple

Howard Hotel, Quai d'Or Restaurant   👑👑 Ⓢ

A comfortable, dignified restaurant, with crystal chandeliers and elegant table settings. The talented German chef uses superb materials for classic dishes ranging from fish terrine and œufs en cocotte to specialities like poulet sauté au champagne or the excellent beef fillet in puff pastry. At lunch time, a trolley circulates with the day's roast. 🍷 *ABOVE AVERAGE.*
Credit Access, Amex, Barclaycard, Diners   ♿

Lunch 12–2.45, Sun 12–2.30 *Dinner* 6.30–11

Map 23 D5

51 Pimlico Road *SW1W 8NE*
01–730 5712

Chinese cooking

● **Set L & Set D** from £10
About £28 for two
⊖ Buses 11, 39, 137

Hunan   Ⓢ

You can nibble spiced nuts and pickled cucumber while perusing the menu in this simply decorated Chinese restaurant. Most of the food has the hot, spicy character of the south-west provinces, and there are exciting combina-tions like deep-fried king prawns wrapped in laver (seaweed) and scallops with straw mushrooms in sweet Hunan sauce. Accurate, subtle cooking and knowledgeable service. *Credit* Access, Amex, Barclaycard, Diners

Lunch 12–2.30 *Dinner* 6–11.30
Closed Sun & Bank Holidays

Map 22 B2

54 Queensway *W2 3RY*
01–727 6017
Proprietor Mr Cheung Tang
Chinese cooking
About £18 for two
⊖ Tube Bayswater

Hung Toa   Ⓢ

Magnificent crispy roast duck is the crowning glory of this popular little restaurant, which is much loved by Chinese locals and Western diners. Other authentic Cantonese specialities like full-flavoured wun tun soup and char-siu pork are also skilfully prepared. *Lunch* 12–2.30 *Dinner* 6–12
Closed Sun & 25 & 26 December ● **Set L & Set D** £5 *Banquets* 28/20

Map 23 B6

196 Fulham Road *SW10 9PN*
01–352 7757

Manager Nino Martines
English cooking

● **Set L** from £4·45
About £26 for two
Banquets 16/–
⊖ Buses 14, 45

Hungry Horse   Ⓢ

Combining the informal atmosphere of a bistro with unpretentious, tradi-tionally English food, this little restaurant has great appeal. As well as familiar grills and roasts, there are some unusual dishes such as North Sea cod with caper mayonnaise and *hot* veal, ham and sage pie, plus an enterprising selection of sweets (why not try Yorkshire pudding with golden syrup?).
Credit Access, Barclaycard, Diners

Lunch 12.30–2.30, Sun 12.30–3 *Dinner* 6.30–12, Sun 7–11
Closed L Sat, all Good Friday & 25 December

Map 23 D4

2 Cadogan Place *SW1X 9PY*
01–235 5411
Telex 21944

Rooms 244
with bath/shower 244
Room phone Yes
Room TV Yes
Confirm by 6
Last dinner 11.15
Parking Ample
Banquets 270/4

Credit Access, Amex,
Barclaycard, Diners
Buses 19, 22, 137

Hyatt Carlton Tower 88% *E* £ A

Exceptionally high standards of comfort, elegance, service and maintenance are the hallmarks of this impressive 17-storey modern hotel overlooking Cadogan Place. The superb lobby is dominated by a central chandelier and glorious, eye-catching flower displays, and there's a busy, convivial bar-lounge adjoining the Chelsea Room. Bedrooms are extremely comfortable with good-quality modern furniture and matching fabrics and soft furnishings; all are fitted with double glazing and air conditioning, Bathrooms are superbly equipped, too, with everything from telephones to hairdryers. No dogs. *Amenities* 24-hour lounge service, men's hairdressing, in-house movies, hotel car, 12-hour laundry service.

Map 23 D4

2 Cadogan Place *SW1X 9PY*
01–235 5411
Manager Jean Quéro

French cooking

About £60 for two

Buses 19, 22, 137

Hyatt Carlton Tower, Chelsea Rm ★ ★ ♔ ♔ Ⓢ

We must start with Bernard Gaume, the star of this marvellous restaurant, his cooking as good as the best in London. His lightness of touch combines with respect for robust flavours. He is haute cuisine, without abstract culinary feats you cannot get your teeth into. Just try the three-sauced, very lightly poached oysters or the fabulous fillet of lamb with a garlicky red wine sauce. Jean Quéro represents him most discreetly and ably in a spacious dining room.

Specialities salade nouvelle, fricassée de turbot et homard aux concombres, filet d'agneau au basilic et tomate, gratin de fraises.
SUPERIOR. *Credit* Access, Amex, Barclaycard, Diners

Lunch 12.30–2.45 *Dinner* 7–11, Sun 7–10.15
Closed Easter Monday

Map 23 D4

Cadogan Place *SW1X 9PY*
01–235 5411
Manager Mr N. Bondenno

About £42 for two
Buses 19, 22, 137

Hyatt Carlton Tower, Rib Room ♔ ♔ Ⓢ

Freshly made hamburgers are a big attraction in this highly dignified restaurant, but the star of the show is undoubtedly the splendid roast Aberdeen Angus beef, carved in thick slices from the trolley, and served American-style with Yorkshire 'popovers', jacket potatoes and sour cream dressing. Starters are equally enjoyable. Very busy at lunch time.
SUPERIOR. *Credit* Access, Amex, Barclaycard, Diners

Lunch 12.30–2.45 *Dinner* 6.30–10.45, Sun 7–10.15
Closed Good Friday & $3\frac{1}{2}$ days Christmas or New Year

Map 22 C3

Knightsbridge *SW1Y 7LA*
01–235 2000
Telex 262057

Rooms 179
with bath/shower 179
Room phone Yes
Room TV Yes
Confirm by 6
Last dinner 10
Parking Limited
Banquets 275/-

Credit Access, Amex,
Barclaycard, Diners
Tube Knightsbridge

Hyde Park Hotel 82% *E* £ A

The Victorian splendour of this fashionably situated hotel is apparent as soon as you step inside the impressive foyer with its crystal chandeliers and ornate moulded ceiling. The small Cavalry Bar, the magnificent ballroom and the club-like lounges are all examples of discreet luxury. Well-carpeted corridors lead to stylish bedrooms with elegant antiques, huge mahogany wardrobes and handsome beds. The spacious bathrooms are attractively decorated, too, and are comprehensively fitted with bidets, telephones and radios.
Amenities valeting, hairdressing.

COURVOISIER
VSOP Fine Champagne Cognac
'The Cognac of Napoleon'

Hyde Park Hotel, Grill Room ♔ Ⓢ

Map 22 C3
Knightsbridge *SW1Y 7LA*
01–235 2000

A formal yet relaxing room with oak panels, an ornate moulded ceiling and elegant table settings. High-quality ingredients are generally handled with skill and care, producing enjoyable dishes like our crème Malakoff–a richly flavoured tomato and potato soup–and suprême de volaille Amaretto, plus fish dishes, grills and roasts from the trolley.
Credit Access, Amex, Barclaycard, Diners

● **Set L** £10 incl. service
About £37 for two
Tube Knightsbridge

Lunch 12.30–2.30 *Dinner* 7–11, Sun 7–10
Closed Sat & Bank Holidays

Ikeda ♧ Ⓢ

Map 24 A3
30 Brook Street *W1Y 1AG*
01–629 2730
Proprietor Shigereu Ikeda
Japanese cooking

Cooking in full view of his customers, hard-working Mr Ikeda produces a particularly tasty selection of Japanese dishes in his tiny, welcoming restaurant. Helpful, smiling girls explain details of the menu, which offers delights like salmon roe with radishes, a good choice of sushi, and grilled turbot, superbly sauced and garnished with shredded spring onions.
Credit Access, Amex, Barclaycard, Diners

● **Set L** £5·60 **Set D** £20
About £50 for two
Tube Bond Street

Lunch 12–2.30 *Dinner* 6.30–10.30, Sun 6–10
Closed L Sun, all Sat & Bank Holidays

Imperial Hotel 57% £ D

Map 24 C1
Russell Square *WC1B 5BB*
01–837 3655
Telex 263951
Proprietors Walduck family
Credit Access, Amex,
Barclaycard, Diners
Tube Russell Square

A modern hotel of glass and concrete, the Imperial has a central courtyard (with ornamental fountain) and a useful underground car park. Accommodation is neat and practical, all rooms having their own compact, tiled bathrooms. There are several conference rooms, and the roomy bar-lounge overlooks the square. Guide dogs only. *Amenities* in-house movies, coffee shop (10am–2.30am), shopping arcade, ladies' hairdressing, bank.

Rooms 460	*Room phone* Yes	*Confirm by* 6	*Parking* Ample
with bath/shower 460	*Room TV* Yes	*Last dinner* 10	*Banquets* 300/–

Inigo Jones ♔ Ⓢ

Map 25 D6
14 Garrick Street *WC2E 9BJ*
01–836 6456
Proprietor Mr Peter Ward

Eye-catching decor and smartly clad waiters help to give this stylish restaurant a sophisticated atmosphere matching the assured cooking of Marc Legros. The menu is a blend of ambitious French dishes such as boned quail in tangerine and liqueur aspic and pink trout with saffron butter, plus simple grills. Tempting sweets to finish. There is a shorter menu at lunchtime.
🍷 *SUPERIOR. Credit* Access, Amex, Barclaycard, Diners

About £50 for two
Tube Leicester Square

Lunch 12.30–2.30 *Dinner* 6–11.45
Closed L Sat, all Sun & Bank Holidays

Inn on the Park 90% *E* £ A

Map 22 D3
Hamilton Place
Park Lane *W1A 1AZ*
01–499 0888
Telex 22771
Manager Mr R. Pajares
Rooms 228
with bath/shower 228
Room phone Yes
Room TV Yes
Confirm by 6
Last dinner 12
Parking Ample
Banquets 360/15

Mr Pajares and his excellent team ensure that standards of service in this towering modern hotel attain new heights while remaining as personal as you could wish for. The spacious marble-floored foyer and its comfortable lounge areas set the tone with superb decor and soft furnishings, and the theme of tasteful luxury continues in the stunning first-floor bar with its marble-topped counter and tables. Bedrooms are beautifully designed with mahogany furniture, good lighting and quiet, relaxing colour schemes. Bathrooms, too, are first class, with marble floors and comprehensive fittings that include telephones. There are also several elegantly furnished suites. *Amenities* garden, valeting, shopping arcade, 12-hour laundry service.

Credit Access, Amex,
Barclaycard, Diners
Tube Hyde Park Corner

Map 22 D3

Hamilton Place
Park Lane *W1A 1AZ*
01–499 0888
Manager Mr Luigi Zambon

● **Set L** £12·50 **Set D** £18·50
About £60 for two
✚ Tube Hyde Park Corner

Inn on the Park, Four Seasons Restaurant   ♛ ⑤

Cut glass, silverware and plant-filled urns give this restaurant an air of opulent elegance. The menu of French-inspired dishes ranges from delicate quail terrine and silky smooth vichyssoise to trout poached in white wine. Cooking is generally competent and presentation is attractive. Smartly dressed waiters provide skilled, attentive service.
♟ *OUTSTANDING. Credit* Access, Amex, Barclaycard, Diners   ♿

Lunch 12–3 *Dinner* 7–11

Map 22 D3

Hamilton Place
Park Lane *W1A 1AZ*
01–499 0888

Managers Mr R. Gemelli &
Mr P. Romerio

● **Set L** from £10·85 incl. wine
About £33 for two
✚ Tube Hyde Park Corner

Inn on the Park, Lanes Restaurant   ♛♛

A splendid cold buffet is the main attraction in this elegant restaurant. At lunch time (when the set-meal price includes wine throughout the meal) there are succulent cold cuts, seafood, attractive terrines and appetising salads supplemented by hot dishes like Dover sole or steak and kidney pie. Grills, sauced main courses and a smaller buffet in the evening.
♟ *OUTSTANDING. Credit* Access, Amex, Barclaycard, Diners   ♿

Lunch 12–3 *Dinner* 6–12
Closed D Sun

Map 22 D3

1 Hamilton Place *W1V 0QY*
01–409 3131
Telex 25853
Manager Mr G. Jeffery

Rooms 500
with bath/shower 500
Room phone Yes
Room TV Yes
Confirm by 6
Last dinner 11.30
Parking Ample
Banquets 850/–

Credit Access, Amex,
Barclaycard, Diners
✚ Tube Hyde Park Corner

Inter-Continental Hotel   85%   *E*   **£ A**

This impressive modern hotel on Hyde Park Corner offers the international traveller a very high standard of luxury, comfort and service. The gleaming marble-floored foyer leads to a cool, contemporary lounge area with tubular chrome seating and splendid flower displays. There's also an intimate cocktail bar, a relaxing coffee shop and a top-floor bar with spectacular views. Opulent bedrooms, all air-conditioned and double-glazed, have high-quality reproduction furniture and sumptuous bathrooms. No dogs. *Amenities* sauna, dancing (Sat), discothèque (Mon–Sat), hairdressing, massage, plunge pool, in-house movies, coffee house (7am–midnight, Fri–Sun 7am–2am), 24-hour laundry service, valeting, hotel car.   ♿

Map 22 D3

1 Hamilton Place *W1V 0QY*
01–409 3131

French cooking

● **Set L** £13
Set D Sat only £21
About £48 for two

✚ Tube Hyde Park Corner

Inter-Continental Hotel, Le Soufflé   ★   ♬ ♛ ⑤

Savoury and sweet soufflés (from oysters with chervil to glorious hazelnut) are indeed a noteworthy speciality of this striking Art Deco restaurant, but chef Peter Kromberg's scope is much wider. He offers a varied range of French dishes, carefully prepared from prime ingredients and often showing the imaginative influence of the nouvelle cuisine. Special menus for Sunday brunch and Saturday evening dinner dance. Skilled friendly service.
Specialities fricassée de petits gris aux pleurottes, papillote de Saint Jacques au foie gras et au basilic, noisettes d'agneau à l'ail doux en chemise, soufflé aux châtaignes sabayon au Kirsch.
♟ *OUTSTANDING. Credit* Access, Amex, Barclaycard, Diners   ♿

Lunch 12.30–3, Sun 12.30–3.30 *Dinner* 7–11.30, Sun 7–11
Closed L Sat, D 25 & 26 December & all Good Friday

Map 25 D5

7 Bow Street *WC2E 7AH*
01–379 6473

French cooking

Interlude de Tabaillau   ★ ★   ♬ ♛ ⑤

A most civilised, simple but attractive little restaurant, developed around the exceptional talents of the young chef-patron. His strong point is light cooking with delightfully blended flavours. Hot savoury mousses, simple sauces with fish, an outstanding duck dish, excellent sorbets are some of the many dishes to go for, not forgetting London's best French cheese selection,

Continued

Continued
● **Set L** £16·50 **Set D** £21
incl. wine & service
About £38 for two

perfectly kept and ably explained. (Note the 'all-in' pricing for food, wine, coffee, service and VAT.)
Specialities feuilleté d'agneau à la moelle, filet de barbue karpinski, suprême de caneton juliette.
Credit Access, Amex, Barclaycard, Diners

Lunch 12.30–2 *Dinner* 7–11.30 **Closed** L Mon & Sat, D Sun, Bank Holidays, 1 week Easter, 2 weeks August & 1 week Christmas

✆ Tube Covent Garden

Map 21 B6
12 York Road *SW11 3QA*
01–228 8519
Proprietor Mr Jack King

Jack's Place

Jack King and his family run this delightfully informal bistro, welcoming all comers and offering them enormous portions of simple fare. Prime Scotch beef, seafood and market-fresh vegetables feature on the daily-changing blackboard menu, where choices range from coarse garlicky pâté to grills and entrées like chicken chasseur. Sweets include home-made gâteaux.
Credit Access

About £18 for two
Banquets 50/30
✆ Buses 19, 39, 44, 45, 49, 170

Lunch 12–3 *Dinner* 6.30–11
Closed Sun, Mon, Easter, Whit Monday & August

Map 22 B3
4 Queen's Gate *SW7 5EH*
01–581 3011
Telex 8813397

Rooms 32
with bath/shower 32
Room phone Yes
Room TV Yes
Confirm by 6
Last dinner 10.15
Parking Limited

John Howard Hotel   78%   *E*   **£ B**

The handsome Regency facade of this fine hotel near the Albert Hall hides a fully refurbished interior with excellent facilities and an air of quiet luxury. The welcoming foyer has a little lounge area with potted plants and comfortable modern armchairs, and the Captain's Bar features a wall-length mural of Lloyd's insurance offices. Bedrooms ranging from compact singles to large studios are modern and comprehensively equipped, with minibars, trouser presses and smart modern furnishings. Bathrooms, too, are of a high standard, with attractive coloured tiles and suites (most have bidets) and nice touches like luxury soap and ready-pasted toothbrushes. No dogs. No children under 12. *Amenities* patio, transport for airport. 

Credit Access, Amex,
Barclaycard, Diners
✆ Buses 9, 33, 49, 52, 73

Map 20 D3
39 Upper Street
Islington *N1 0PN*
01–226 4380
Proprietor Mr Julius Oberegger

Julius's

Julius Oberegger can be seen working in the kitchen of this smart bow-fronted restaurant, preparing enjoyable dishes ranging from stuffed crêpes and sautéed veal cutlet flambéed with Calvados to salmon trout with flaked almonds; he also features seasonal specialities and a choice of charcoal grills. Vegetables are crisp, and sweets like apple flan come from a well-presented trolley. *Credit* Access, Amex, Barclaycard, Diners

About £30 for two
✆ Buses 4, 19, 30, 43, 104, 279

Lunch 12.30–2.30 *Dinner* 7.30–11.45
Closed L Sat, all Sun & Bank Holidays

Map 24 B3
22 Dean Street *W1V 5AL*
01–437 6630
Korean cooking

About £28 for two
✆ Buses 1, 7, 8, 25, 73

Kaya

A smart, friendly restaurant where Korean specialities are freshly prepared (many of them at the table) and artistically presented. Set menus are a good introduction to this interesting cuisine. *Credit* Access, Amex, Barclaycard, Diners *Lunch* 12–3 *Dinner* 6–10.30 **Closed** L Sat, all Sun, Bank Holidays, last week Aug & 2 weeks Christmas ● **Set L** £5·75 **Set D** £9·80 *Banquets* 12/4

Map 20 B2
3 Downshire Hill *NW3 1NR*
01–435 3544
Proprietor Aron Misan
French cooking

Keats

Paintings and bookshelves line the walls of this welcoming restaurant with purple velvet seating. French staff offer most attentive service and the cooking, if not always consistent, produces enjoyable results in dishes like calf's liver provençal or gratin of sole and langoustines. Now open for a table d'hôte lunch, the restaurant also features a menu gastronomique in the

Continued

● **Set L** £9·80 **Set D** £15
About £48 for two
Banquets 20/–
Θ Tube Hampstead

evening. *Credit* Access, Amex, Barclaycard, Diners

Lunch 12.30–2.15 *Dinner* 7–11, Sat 7–11.30
Closed L Sat, all Sun, Bank Holidays & 3 weeks August

Map 25 A6
67 Ebury Street *SW1W 0NZ*
01–730 7734

Chinese cooking

● **Set L** from £7·60
Set D from £12·10
About £36 for two

Θ Tube Victoria

Ken Lo's Memories of China ★

It pays to take some advance trouble about your meal here. A brief discussion on the telephone will ensure full attention in the kitchen, which is capable of turning out masterpieces but can also make the very occasional slip. The legendary Ken Lo, equally adept with pen and wok (not to speak of his beloved tennis racket!), names dishes clearly and cleverly on an understandable menu. The dining room—coolly tasteful and comfortable—is efficiently run by Anne Lo.
Specialities Peking duck, 'Simulation of lobster', boneless duck, Shanghai long-cooked knuckle of pork.
🍷 *ABOVE AVERAGE. Credit* Access, Amex, Barclaycard, Diners

Lunch 12–2.30 *Dinner* 7–11
Closed Sun & Bank Holidays

Map 20 C3
43 Cardington Street *NW1 2LP*
01–387 4400
Telex 28250
Manager Mr A. Allen
Credit Access, Amex,
Barclaycard, Diners
Θ Tube Euston

Rooms 324
with bath/shower 324

Kennedy Hotel   65%   £D

Close to Euston Station, this large, modern and well-maintained hotel is a popular stopping place for both businessmen and tourists. Steps lead down from the airy, marble-floored foyer to the sunken lounge, which, like the pleasant cocktail bar, is decorated in elegant contemporary style. Smart, well-furnished bedrooms have neat tiled bathrooms. No dogs.
Amenities restaurant (7am–10.30pm).

Room phone Yes	*Confirm by* 6	*Parking* Ample
Room TV Yes	*Last dinner* 10.30	

Map 23 A4
Wright's Lane *W8 5SP*
01–937 8170
Telex 23914

Credit Access, Amex,
Barclaycard, Diners
Θ Tube High Street Kensington

Rooms 530
with bath/shower 530

Kensington Close Hotel   65%   £D

Just off Kensington High Street, this large hotel (originally a block of service flats) boasts many recreational facilities. Public areas include a long lounge, spacious cocktail bar and a charming patio with greenery and a pool. The attractive bedrooms have well-fitted bathrooms; there are also 19 penthouses and four suites. *Amenities* patio, sauna, indoor swimming pool, squash, coffee shop (7.30am–midnight), keep-fit equipment.

Room phone Yes	*Confirm by* 6	*Parking* Limited
Room TV Yes	*Last dinner* 10	*Banquets* 250/5

Map 22 B3
De Vere Gardens *W8 5AF*
01–937 8121
Telex 262422

Credit Access, Amex,
Barclaycard, Diners
Θ Buses 9, 33, 49, 52, 73

Rooms 318
with bath/shower 318

Kensington Palace Hotel   68%   £C

Conveniently situated for the Royal Albert Hall and Kensington's shops, this friendly, well-run hotel is a fine example of elegant modern design. Public rooms like the spacious foyer, bars and bright coffee shop are stylishly contemporary, and double-glazed bedrooms (front ones overlooking Kensington Gardens) have comfortable velvet-clad armchairs, solid built-in units and well-fitted bathrooms. *Amenities* coffee house (7am–midnight).

Room phone Yes	*Confirm by* 6	*Parking* Difficult
Room TV Yes	*Last dinner* 10.30	*Banquets* 250/5

Map 24 C2
Bloomsbury Way *WC1A 2SD*
01–242 5881
Telex 21157
Manager Mr J. B. Stewart
Credit Access, Amex,
Barclaycard, Diners
Θ Tube Holborn

Rooms 169
with bath/shower 123

Kingsley Hotel   57%   £D

Built as a hotel at the turn of the century, this unusual red-brick building with turrets at its two front corners is situated close to the British Museum. An arched and pillared entrance/reception hall leads to a large, comfortable residents' lounge and a plush bar. Bedrooms have practical fitted furniture and tea/coffee-makers; most also have compact, tiled bathrooms.

Room phone Yes	*Confirm by* 6	*Parking* Difficult
Room TV Yes	*Last dinner* 9	*Banquets* 100/12

Map 24 C1
50 Woburn Place *WC1H0JZ*
01–580 1188

Chinese cooking
About £29 for two
✆ Tube Russell Square

Kites   ♛ Ⓢ

This smart Chinese restaurant offers a large selection of Cantonese and Pekinese dishes. Cooking reaches consistently high standards, and really excellent sauces accompanied our succulent prawns, sliced aromatic duck and deliciously tender beef with Chinese vegetables. *Credit* Access, Amex, Barclaycard, Diners *Lunch* 12–2.45 *Dinner* 6–11.30 *Banquets* 50/–

Map 21 C5
3 Horseferry Road *SW1P2AN*
01–834 3434

Proprietor Mr Nayab Abbasi
Indian & Pakistani cooking

About £34 for two
Banquets 130/–
✆ Buses 3, 10, 77, 77A, 88, 149, 159, 168, 507

Kundan   ♛ Ⓢ

The emphasis is on authentic North Indian and Pakistani dishes in this smartly decorated basement restaurant. Tandoori specialities, kebabs and curries like our fragrant prawn masala show skilful use of spices to enhance rather than mask natural flavours; pilau rice is nicely cooked and rich kulfi topped with pistachio nuts makes a refreshing finale.
Credit Access, Amex, Barclaycard, Diners

Lunch 12–3 *Dinner* 7–12.30
Closed Sun & Bank Holidays

Map 20 A3
217 High Rd, Willesden *NW102NX*
01–459 2297
Proprietor Mr B. C. Wu
Chinese cooking
About £21 for two
✆ Tube Dollis Hill

Kuo Yuan

This simple restaurant specialises in Pekinese food, including aromatic crispy duck. Whet your appetite with fried seaweed, smoked fish or preserved eggs, and finish with Chinese toffee apples dotted with sesame seeds.
Lunch Sat & Sun only 12–2.30 *Dinner* 6–11
● **Set D** from £6 *Banquets* 24/6

Our inspectors never book in the name of the Egon Ronay Organisation; they disclose their identity only after paying their bills.

Map 20 C3
Primrose Hill Road *NW33NA*
01–588 2233
Telex 22759
Credit Access, Amex, Barclaycard, Diners
Closed 6 days Christmas
✆ Tube Chalk Farm

Ladbroke Clive Hotel   66%   £ C

Combining up-to-date accommodation with a comprehensive banqueting and conference centre, this purpose-built modern hotel is popular with business people. The thickly carpeted open-plan bar and lounge are pleasant meeting places, while well-equipped bedrooms have radios, tea-makers and trouser presses; there are also luxurious Gold Star rooms. Fully tiled bathrooms. No dogs. *Amenities* garden.

| *Rooms* 83 | *Room phone* Yes | *Confirm by* 6 | *Parking* Limited |
| *with bath/shower* 83 | *Room TV* Yes | *Last dinner* 9.45 | *Banquets* 240/– |

Map 20 B3
18 Lodge Road
St John's Wood *NW87JT*
01–722 7722
Telex 23101

Rooms 347
with bath/shower 347
Room phone Yes
Room TV Yes
Confirm by 6
Last dinner 10
Parking Ample
Banquets 150/–
Credit Access, Amex, Barclaycard, Diners

✆ Buses 2B, 13, 74, 113

Ladbroke Westmoreland Hotel   75%   £ C

There are views of Lord's cricket ground from the upper floors of this large modern hotel, and the main public bar–the Nursery End–takes as its theme the sport of leather and willow. Elsewhere the emphasis is purely on comfort, especially in the relaxing lounge with its deep modern settees and the open-plan cocktail bar. The best bedrooms are the sumptuous Gold Star rooms, which are superbly furnished and fitted with thick carpets, quilted bedspreads and all manner of thoughtful extras including fresh fruit and miniatures of sherry; standard rooms are more modest but equally pleasant. Fully tiled, well-equipped bathrooms.
Amenities café bar (10.30am–1am).   ♿

Lafayette ♔ Ⓢ

Map 25 B4
32 King Street *SW1Y 6RJ*
01–930 1131

The menu in this elegantly appointed restaurant is, naturally enough, a blend of French and American dishes. The choice ranges from subtly flavoured hot fish terrine with lobster sauce and tender duck with blackcurrant sauce to New England clam chowder. Raw materials are generally quite acceptable, although vegetables may disappoint.
Credit Access, Amex, Barclaycard, Diners ♿

● **Set L & Set D** £8·50
About £38 for two
⊖ Tube Green Park

Lunch 12.15–2.30 *Dinner* 6.30–11.30
Closed Sat, Sun & Bank Holidays

Langan's Bistro

Map 24 A1
26 Devonshire Street *W1N 1RJ*
01–935 4531

A sibling to Langan's Brasserie, this stylishly cheerful, bustling bistro offers weekly changing menus of simple, skilfully cooked dishes like brill in prawn sauce or pork chops with apples and cider. Home-made puddings are enjoyable too. *Lunch* 12.30–2.30 *Dinner* 7–11.15
Closed L Sat, all Sun & Bank Holidays

About £23 for two
⊖ Tube Regent's Park

Langan's Brasserie

Map 25 A4
Stratton Street *W1X 5FE*
01–493 6437
Proprietors Messrs Langan,
Caine & Shepherd

Richard Shepherd offers well-chosen international favourites at this fashionable, relaxed restaurant. Cooking standards are generally high throughout a long menu that could range from stuffed artichokes and salmon coulibiac to navarin of lamb and roast duck with a very tasty sage and onion stuffing. Good choice of desserts like sherry trifle and crème brûlée.
Credit Access, Amex, Barclaycard, Diners

About £37 for two
⊖ Tube Green Park

Lunch 12.30–2.45 *Dinner* 7–11.45, Sat 8–12.45am
Closed L Sat, all Sun & Bank Holidays

Last Days of the Raj ♧ Ⓢ

Map 24 C2
22 Drury Lane *WC2B 5RH*
01–836 1628

Indian cooking

Eight partners run this comfortable Indian restaurant staffed by smart, knowledgeable waiters. The cooking reaches a high standard, with careful use of fresh herbs and spices, and the choice ranges from tandoori specialities to curries like mild creamy chicken korma. Good side dishes and breads. Try the thali—well-planned and nicely varied assortments of meat or vegetables. *Credit* Access, Amex, Barclaycard, Diners

● **Set L & Set D** from £6·50
About £18 for two
⊖ Buses 8, 19, 22, 25, 38, 55

Lunch 12–2.30 *Dinner* 6–11.30, Sun 6.30–11.30
Closed L Sun, L Bank Holidays & all 25 & 26 December

Legends ♔ Ⓢ

Map 24 B3
29 Old Burlington Street
W1X 1LB
01–437 9933

Standards of cooking and presentation are high at this popular restaurant, where the menu offers enjoyable, uncomplicated dishes ranging from beef bourguignonne and coq au vin to poached salmon with hollandaise sauce; there are also grills, well-prepared vegetables and a tempting sweet trolley. Added attractions are a cocktail bar and a disco downstairs in the evening.
Credit Access, Amex, Barclaycard, Diners

● **Set L** £10
Set D Mon–Thurs £7·50
About £38 for two
Banquets 75/–
⊖ Buses 3, 6, 12, 13, 15, 23,
53, 88, 159

Lunch 12.30–2.45 *Dinner* 7.30–12.30am, Sat 8.30–1.30am
Closed L Sat, D Sun & L Bank Holidays

Leith's ♔ Ⓢ

Map 21 B4
92 Kensington Park Road *W11 2PN*
01–229 4481
Manager Mr J. B. Reynaud

Delicate flavours and attractive presentation are the hallmarks of the food in this smart, very distinctive restaurant. The short fixed-price menu features a range of enjoyable French-inspired dishes, from special dry-roasted duckling and grilled baby chicken with mustard and cumin to veal steak with cream and watercress sauce. Hors d'œuvre and sweet trolleys are especially eye-catching. ♗ *SUPERIOR. Credit* Access, Amex, Barclaycard, Diners

● **Set D** £21 incl. service
About £49 for two
Banquets 30/8
⊖ Tube Notting Hill Gate

Dinner only 7.30–12
Closed Notting Hill Gate Carnival & 4 days Christmas

Ley-On's Ⓢ

Map 24 B3
56 Wardour Street *W1V 3HN*
01–437 6465
Chinese cooking

About £21 for two
🚌 Buses 14, 19, 22, 38, 55

A busy, roomy and colourful restaurant, where you'll find all the Cantonese favourites (including a wide range of dim sum) on the extensive menu.
Credit Access, Amex, Barclaycard, Diners
Meals 11.30am–11.15pm, Sun 11am–10.45pm **Closed** 25 & 26 December
● **Set meals** from £5

London Belgravia 67% £ B

Map 23 D4
20 Chesham Place *SW1X 8HQ*
01–235 6040
Telex 919020

Credit Access, Amex,
Barclaycard, Diners
🚌 Buses 19, 22, 137

Refurbishment continues at this well-run tower-block hotel in Belgravia. Public rooms include a foyer with a few sofas and armchairs, and a smart bar in various shades of green. Well-furnished bedrooms, most of them now redecorated in attractive pastels, have thick carpeting, high-quality bed linen and pretty prints. Elegant bathrooms include telephone extensions among their many extras. No dogs.

Rooms 107	*Room phone* Yes	*Confirm by* 6	*Parking* Difficult
with bath/shower 107	*Room TV* Yes	*Last dinner* 11	*Banquets* 40/4

London Embassy Hotel 66% £ C

Map 22 A2
150 Bayswater Road *W2 4RT*
01–229 1212
Telex 27727

Credit Access, Amex,
Barclaycard, Diners
🚇 Tube Queensway

Staff are smartly attired at this modern hotel. The functional marble-floored foyer leads to the attractively refurbished bar and lounge; there's also a popular terrace set with tables and chairs. Compact bedrooms have simple built-in units, armchairs, writing areas and well-equipped bathrooms; some also have pleasant views overlooking Kensington Gardens. Entry is from St Petersburgh Place. ♿

Rooms 193	*Room phone* Yes	*Confirm by* 6	*Parking* Ample
with bath/shower 193	*Room TV* Yes	*Last dinner* 10.15	*Banquets* 120/2

London International Hotel 66% £ D

Map 23 A4
147 Cromwell Road *SW5 0TH*
01–370 4200
Telex 27260

Credit Access, Amex,
Barclaycard, Diners
🚇 Tube Gloucester Road

Knightsbridge and the Earl's Court Exhibition centre are within easy reach of this modern glass and marble hotel. The bar-lounge is cosy and club-like, and panoramic windows enhance the cheerful Aviary Coffee House. Bedrooms, recently redecorated, have well-designed fitted units and neat bathrooms. *Amenities* coffee shop (7am–midnight), hotel coach, 24-hour laundry service, 24-hour lounge service. ♿

Rooms 415	*Room phone* Yes	*Confirm by* 6	*Parking* Limited
with bath/shower 415	*Room TV* Yes	*Last dinner* 11	*Banquets* 150/10

London Metropole 66% £ B

Map 22 C1
Edgware Road *W2 1JU*
01–402 4141
Telex 23711

Credit Access, Amex,
Barclaycard, Diners
🚇 Tube Edgware Road

This large modern hotel is popular with tour parties, and its extensive conference facilities appeal to the business community. There's a busy, marble-walled foyer and a small lounge with comfortable bamboo seating, as well as an intimate cocktail bar. Double-glazed bedrooms have functional fitted units and well-equipped bathrooms with showers. No dogs.
Amenities in-house movies, coffee shop (7am–11.45pm), hairdressing. ♿

Rooms 588	*Room phone* Yes	*Confirm by* 6	*Parking* Ample
with bath/shower 588	*Room TV* Yes	*Last dinner* 10.30	*Banquets* 200/20

London Penta Hotel 60% £ D

Map 23 B4
97 Cromwell Road *SW7 4DN*
01–370 5757
Telex 919663
Manager Mr Charles Gorman
Credit Access, Amex,
Barclaycard, Diners
🚇 Tube Gloucester Road

This busy hotel makes the most of modern technology in catering for guests. Spacious public rooms include a huge reception area, the sleek Zodiac bar-lounge and an Edwardian-style pub. Bedrooms (many with excellent views) are bright, neat and well fitted, with mini-bars and even tiny ovens for heating breakfast croissants. *Amenities* garden, coffee shop (noon–1am), hairdressing, Prestel, 12-hour laundry service. ♿

Rooms 914	*Room phone* Yes	*Confirm by* 6	*Parking* Ample
with bath/shower 914	*Room TV* Yes	*Last dinner* 10.30	*Banquets* 300/20

1983 is the Findus 25th anniversary year.
So we are joining with Egon Ronay in a Silver Jubilee
Celebration - 25 successful years of quality from
people who know what good food is.

Findus make it a great...
family occasion

FINDUS ®

We always catch them …
at their best

FINDUS ®

Map 23 A4
Scarsdale Place
Wright's Lane *W8 5SR*
01-937 7211
Manager Mr E. Dillon
Credit Access, Amex,
Barclaycard, Diners
⊖ Tube High Street Kensington

London Tara Hotel   67%   **£ C/D**

Uninhibited colour characterises the decor of this huge modern yellow-brick hotel run by friendly staff. From the vivid green chairs in the marble and chrome foyer to the pillarbox-red cocktail bar and blue and beige plant-filled lounge there's a bold, refreshing stylishness. Attractive bedrooms have fitted furniture and well-equipped bathrooms.
Amenities nightclub, coffee shop (7am–11pm).   ᕼ

Rooms 843	*Room phone* Yes	*Confirm by* 6	*Parking* Limited
with bath/shower 843	*Room TV* Yes	*Last dinner* 1am	*Banquets* 500/50

Map 22 D3
19 Park Lane *W1Y 8AP*
01-493 7292
Telex 263292

Credit Access, Amex,
Barclaycard, Diners
⊖ Tube Hyde Park Corner

LONDONDERRY HOTEL   **£ A**

At the time of our researches, a major programme of redecoration and refurbishment was well under way throughout this modern luxury hotel by Hyde Park Corner (1981 rating was 73%). Management hoped that everything would be completed by Christmas 1982, and it's business as usual as the work continues. No dogs. *Amenities* in-house movies, discothèque, coffee shop.

Rooms 141	*Room phone* Yes	*Confirm by* 6	*Parking* Limited
with bath/shower 141	*Room TV* Yes	*Last dinner* 10.30	*Banquets* 60/–

Map 22 D1
Welbeck Street *W1M 8HS*
01-935 4442
Telex 894630

Credit Access, Amex,
Barclaycard, Diners
⊖ Tube Bond Street

Londoner Hotel   60%   **£ D**

This narrow-fronted hotel within easy reach of Oxford Street provides comfortable accommodation and good standards of service. A spacious, tastefully furnished open-plan foyer-lounge leads into a very attractive bar with elegant decor and chesterfield amchairs. Uniform bedrooms have simple modern furniture, colourful bedspreads and compact, fully tiled bathrooms.

Rooms 142	*Room phone* Yes	*Confirm by* 6	*Parking* Difficult
with bath/shower 142	*Room TV* Yes	*Last dinner* 10	

Map 25 C6
37 Gerrard Street *W1V 7LP*
01-437 5429

Chinese cooking

● **Set L & Set D**
for two from £11
About £25 for two
Banquets 40/–
⊖ Tube Leicester Square

Loon Fung

New owners have completely revamped this spacious, popular Chinese restaurant, where dim sum trolleys circulate between 11 and 5. At all times there's an excellent choice of capably prepared, generously served dishes ranging from succulent rainbow shredded eel and spicy Szechuan prawns to Cantonese fried chicken and noodles with pork and chilli sauce. Service is polite and attentive. *Credit* Access, Amex, Barclaycard, Diners

Meals 11am–2am, Sun 10am–1am
Closed 25 December

Map 23 D4
Lowndes Street *SW1X 9ES*
01-235 6020
Telex 919065

Rooms 80
with bath/shower 80
Room phone Yes
Room TV Yes
Confirm by 6
Last dinner 10.15
Parking Ample

Credit Access, Amex,
Barclaycard, Diners
⊖ Tube Knightsbridge

Lowndes Hotel   79%   **£ B**

The facade may be modern, but chandeliers, marble floors and moulded ceilings create an elegant Regency style inside this small luxury hotel in peaceful Belgravia. Equally impressive is the genuinely personal service provided by courteous staff. There's a comfortable little lounge off the entrance hall and a pleasantly relaxing bar with striking Chinese Chippendale decor and modern paintings on the walls. Bedrooms have attractive patterned wallpaper and matching curtains, deep armchairs and smart Regency-style darkwood furnishings. Well-equipped bathrooms are particularly appealing, with white marble walls and telephone extensions. Immaculate housekeeping. *Amenities* 12-hour laundry service (weekdays only).   ᕼ

Ma Cuisine ★ ★

Map 23 C4
113 Walton Street *SW3 2HP*
01–584 7585
Proprietor Guy Mouilleron

French cooking

● **Set L & Set D** £13
About £50 for two

Chef-patron Guy Mouilleron, a warm and outgoing man, is such a wonderful chef that one is torn between the wish for him to find bigger premises and the anxiety to keep everything tiny and manageable. He swings like a pendulum between kitchen and dining room and is a master of true, big flavours, without exaggerated refinements, manifest in superb terrine, skilfully cooked ham, marvellously sauced duck, delightful shellfish and a good choice of unusual desserts full of flavour.
Specialities terrine de poisson aux algues, croustade de champignons à la Chartres, casserolette de turbot Doria, civet de canard à la française.
Credit Amex, Diners

Lunch 12.30–2 *Dinner* 7.30–11
Closed Sat, Sun, Bank Holidays & 15 July–15 August

✆ Tube South Kensington

Mandarin Kitchen

Map 22 B2
14 Queensway *W2 3RX*
01–727 9012
Manager Miss Helen Lee
Chinese cooking
About £20 for two
✆ Tube Queensway

A roomy and popular Chinese restaurant, where well-prepared dishes range from tasty soups and steamed fish to crispy roast duck and sliced beef with seasonal vegetables. *Credit* Amex, Barclaycard, Diners
Meals noon–1.30am
● **Set L** £2·85 **Set D** £4·95

Manzi's ⓢ

Map 25 C6
1 Leicester Street *WC2H 7BL*
01–734 0224
Proprietor Louis G. Manzi
Seafood
About £26 for two
✆ Tube Leicester Square

Go for the simple fresh fish dishes at this long-established, popular restaurant. A wide choice ranges from flavoursome fish soup and fried scampi to halibut joinville. *Credit* Access, Amex, Barclaycard, Diners
Lunch 12–2.40 *Dinners* 5.30–11.40, Sat & Sun 6–11.40
Closed L Sun & all 25 & 26 December

Marzi's ⓢ

Map 21 A5
95 Fulham Palace Road *W6 8JA*
01–748 1180
Indian cooking

About £20 for two
✆ Tube Hammersmith

Parsee specialities like well-seasoned patia and lamb with ginger and garlic are the best bets in this basement Indian restaurant. Excellent rice and vegetarian dishes too. *Credit* Access, Amex, Barclaycard, Diners
Lunch 12–2.45 *Dinner* 6–11.30 **Closed** 25 & 26 December *Banquets* 20/10 ● **Set L** £2·75

Masako ♛

Map 22 D1
6 St Christopher's Place *W1M 5HB*
01–935 1579
Manager Mr Yamamoto
Japanese cooking

● **Set L** £4·50 **Set D** £11
About £50 for two
Banquets 20/4
✆ Tube Bond Street

A comfortable, stylish Japanese restaurant, with black lacquered tables and rolled rattan blinds. Set dinners and lighter set lunches are centred around tempura, sushi or sukiyaki, or you can build up your own meal from the extensive à la carte menu. Ingredients are beautifully fresh, cooking is careful and precise, and great care is taken over attractive presentation.
Credit Access, Amex, Barclaycard, Diners

Lunch 12–2 *Dinner* 6–10
Closed Sun, 3 days New Year & 2 days Christmas

May Fair Hotel 79% *E* £B

Map 25 A4
Stratton Street *W1A 2AN*
01–629 7777
Telex 262526
Manager
Mr Herbert Striessnig
Rooms 391
with bath/shower 391
Room phone Yes
Room TV Yes
Confirm by 6
Last dinner 10.30
Parking Difficult
Banquets 60/–

Traditional standards of comfort, service and housekeeping are maintained at this long-established hotel in the heart of Mayfair. The splendid foyer, with its marble pillars, sweeping staircase and magnificent chandelier, sets the stylish tone of the public rooms, which include an intimate, richly furnished lounge, the plush May Fair Bar with its amusing '20s prints and the Aloha Bar with flamboyant South Seas decor and its own resident

Continued

Credit Access, Amex, Barclaycard, Diners
☎ Tube Green Park

parrot. Attractively appointed bedrooms are very roomy and comfortable; the best are quite sumptuous, with elegant classical furnishings and comprehensively equipped marble-clad bathrooms. *Amenities* dinner dance (Mon–Sat), coffee shop (7am–11.30pm, Sun 8am–11.30pm), valeting. &

Map 7 B5
47 Greenwich Church Street
SE10 9BL
01–858 8705

Mean Time

All the staff of this unpretentious restaurant only yards away from the *Cutty Sark* are Spanish, and Spanish specialities–including an authentic paella Valenciana–are the strongpoint of a regular menu of familiar international dishes, capably prepared from good ingredients. A frequently changing seasonal menu also features venison, jugged hare, and tasty game birds.
Credit Access, Amex, Barclaycard, Diners

About £29 for two
Banquets 30/8
☎ Buses 108b, 177, 180, 188

Lunch 12–2.30 *Dinner* 6.30–11, Sat 6.30–11.30
Closed L Sat, all Sun & Bank Holidays

Map 24 B3
21 Great Windmill Street *W1V 9PH*
01–437 2745

South-East Asian cooking
About £18 for two
☎ Tube Piccadilly

Melati

This cheerful, bustling restaurant, sister to the Peter Street Melati, offers a good choice of popular and traditional south-east Asian dishes notable for their fresh preparation and attractive presentation. *Credit* Access, Amex, Barclaycard, Diners *Lunch* 12–2.45 *Dinner* 6–11.30 **Closed** Sun & Bank Holidays ● **Set L** £3 **Set D** £17 for two incl. wine *Banquets* 40/–

Map 24 B3
31 Peter Street *W1V 3RQ*
01–437 2011

South-East Asian cooking

● **Set D** £17 for two
About £21 for two
☎ Buses 14, 19, 22, 38, 55

Melati

Refined South-East Asian cooking is the attraction in this simply decorated, unpretentious little restaurant. Flavours are completely authentic, and the subtle blending of ingredients creates dishes to delight jaded Western palates. Particularly delicious are the excellent satay, the spicy Singapore noodles with prawns, and rendang (fried beef with coconut).
Credit Access, Amex, Barclaycard, Diners

Lunch 12–2.30 *Dinner* 6–11.30
Closed Sun & Bank Holidays

Map 23 C4
14 Beauchamp Place *SW3 1NQ*
01–589 4252

French cooking

About £35 for two
Banquets 35/–
☎ Tube Knightsbridge

Ménage à Trois

The menu is strikingly original at this smart, popular new restaurant: it consists of 33 starters, and you can have just one dish or make a full meal from the imaginative specialities, which range from vegetable terrine to light oyster and scallop mille-feuille or luxurious truffle en croûte. The capable chef achieves most enjoyable results right through to his delicious sweets.
Credit Access, Amex, Barclaycard, Diners

Lunch 11.30–2.30 *Dinner* 5.30–12.15am
Closed Sun & 23 December–4 January

Map 23 C5
169 Fulham Road *SW3 6SP*
01–589 8815
Manager Pasquale
Italian cooking

Meridiana

Standards remain high at this elegant restaurant, where in summer you can eat al fresco on the roof terrace. A wide range of authentic Italian dishes, prepared from really fresh ingredients, includes a colourful hors d'œuvre display, pasta cooked al dente, delicious sea bass and specialities such as involtini, grilled calf's liver and peppered fillet steak. 🍷 *ABOVE AVERAGE.*
Credit Access, Amex, Barclaycard, Diners

About £40 for two
☎ Tube South Kensington

Lunch 12.30–3 *Dinner* 7–12
Closed Bank Holidays

Map 23 C4
31 Basil Street *SW3 1BB*
01–584 4484
Proprietor Mr J. Parnes
French cooking
About £36 for two
☎ Tube Knightsbridge

Mes Amis

Service is delightfully attentive in this bright bistro-style restaurant. The menu offers starters such as terrine, or a superb fish soup, followed by main courses like sea bream with fennel or garlic-laden chicken. Simple grills, too.
Credit Access, Amex, Barclaycard, Diners *Lunch* 12.15–2.30, Sat 12.15–3 *Dinner* 7.15–11 **Closed** 25 Dec ● **Set L** £8·95 *Banquets* 30/10

Mijanou ★   🔔 Ⓢ

Map 23 D5
143 Ebury Street *SW1W 9QN*
01–730 4099

French cooking

● **Set L £7·95 Set D £16·95**
About £40 for two

🚌 Buses 11, 39

Sonia Blech's innovative approach to French cuisine is responsible for the popularity of this smart little restaurant, one of whose rooms is reserved for non-smokers. The short menu offers some delightfully different choices, from a tasty warm mousseline of quail livers to superb loin of lamb baked in a herby brioche and a rich, crisp chocolate and hazelnut gâteau. Charming, professional service.
Specialities le gâteau aux trois délices de veau, les médaillons de chevreuil au sureau et à l'eau de vie de genièvre, les cailles au riz sauvage de mon amie Pearl, le fromage glacé aux pruneaux à l'Armagnac. 🍷 *OUTSTANDING.*
Credit Access, Amex, Diners

Lunch 12.30–2 *Dinner* 7.30–10, Fri 7.30–11
Closed Sat, Sun, Bank Holidays, August & 2 weeks Christmas

Mimmo d'Ischia

Map 23 D4
61 Elizabeth Street *SW1W 9PP*
01–730 5406
Proprietor Sig. Mimmo Mattera
Italian cooking
About £29 for two
🚌 Buses 11, 39

Flamboyant owner Mimmo Mattera almost steals the show in this lively Italian restaurant, where dishes ranging from lentil soup to spaghetti carbonara and osso bucho have a robust, authentic flavour. Ample portions.
Credit Access, Amex, Barclaycard, Diners *Lunch* 12.30–3 *Dinner* 7–11.30
Closed Sun & Bank Holidays *Banquets* 30/10

Mirabelle ★ ★   👑👑👑 Ⓢ

Map 25 A4
56 Curzon Street *W1Y 7PE*
01–499 4636

Manager Victor Sonvico
French cooking

● **Set L £11**
About £60 for two
Banquets 32/12

🚇 Tube Green Park

We can never understand why the Mirabelle should have its few detractors: it has been the most consistently superb restaurant for decades and described as such in all our 25 editions. This is mainly due to chef Drees, in charge for all these years. Not for him the new-fangled fashion of overpraised nouvelle cuisine. Everything remains classic: if Escoffier were alive, he would thoroughly approve. Service is rigidly formal, in keeping with the old-world cuisine.
Specialities quenelles de homard, côte de bœuf Villette, noisettes d'agneau Edouard VII, timbale Elysée.
🍷 *OUTSTANDING. Credit* Access, Amex, Barclaycard, Diners

Lunch 12.30–2.30 *Dinner* 7–11
Closed Sun & Bank Holidays

M'sieur Frog   🔔 Ⓢ

Map 20 D3
31 a Essex Road *N1 2SE*
01–226 3495
Proprietors
Howard & Tina Rawlinson
& Philip Snuggs

About £28 for two
🚌 Buses 38, 73, 171, 277

Informality reigns in this friendly, pine-walled bistro, where the short menu is full of interesting ideas. Cooking is of an admirably high standard, with French-style dishes such as veal normande, pork and apricot casserole and braised rabbit with tarragon. Vegetables are splendid—absolutely fresh and superbly prepared—while simple sweets range from sorbets to chocolate and raisin cake.

Dinner only 7–11.30
Closed Sun, Easter Mon, 3 weeks August & 1 week Christmas

Monsieur Thompsons   Ⓢ

Map 21 B4
29 Kensington Park Road
W11 2EU
01–727 9957
Proprietor Mr Rocher
French cooking

About £28 for two
Banquets 40/12
🚇 Tube Notting Hill Gate

Authentic and enjoyable French cooking is the main attraction in this informal restaurant on two floors. The menu, supplemented by a few specialities, ranges from delicious tomato-based fish soup with crisp croûtons to tender veal cutlet encased in crisp pastry and monkfish baked with garlic. Puddings and pastries like mille-feuille are all made on the premises. Friendly service. *Credit* Amex, Barclaycard

Lunch 12.30–2.30 *Dinner* 7.30–10.30
Closed Bank Holidays

Montcalm Hotel   77%   *E*   **£ A/B**

Map 22 D1
Great Cumberland Place *W1A 2LF*
01–402 4288
Telex 28710

Rooms 116
with bath/shower 116
Room phone Yes
Room TV Yes
Confirm by 6
Last dinner 11
Parking Limited
Banquets 20/4

Credit Access, Amex,
Barclaycard, Diners
✆ Tube Marble Arch

Built in 1973 behind a handsome Georgian facade, this stylish modern hotel exudes an air of tasteful luxury. Reception is at an antique gilt table and guests can relax in the restful bar-lounge with its suede-covered walls and smart leather armchairs. Bedrooms vary in size and style, from simple twins and singles to a lavish penthouse suite complete with its own sauna. All have attractive mahogany furniture and are fully equipped with everything from mini-bars to writing paper. Excellent, fully tiled bathrooms are provided with iced drinking water, bathrobes and hairdryers as well as telephones.

Montcalm Hotel, La Varenne   ♔ ⑤

Map 22 D1
Great Cumberland Place
W1A 2LF
01–402 4288

Elegant decor and nicely paced, professional service make this restaurant a relaxed setting for an enjoyable meal. The short à la carte features carefully prepared dishes like breast of duckling with green peppercorn sauce and veal with lemon and butter sauce, as well as simple items such as steak and Dover sole, all based on excellent raw materials. 🍷 *OUTSTANDING.*
Credit Access, Amex, Barclaycard, Diners

About £35 for two
✆ Tube Marble Arch

Lunch 12.30–2.30 *Dinner* 7–11
Closed L Sat & Sun, & L Bank Holidays

Montpeliano   ⑤

Map 23 C4
13 Montpelier Street *SW7 1HQ*
01–589 0032
Proprietors Claudio Pulze,
Antonio Trapani &
Luigi Reghenzani
Italian cooking

About £32 for two
Banquets 20/10
✆ Tube Knightsbridge

The three proprietors have built up a loyal following of regulars in this friendly restaurant serving well-prepared, tasty Italian food. Seasonal specialities like pheasant and crab supplement starters like mozzarella salad, veal dishes, steaks and specialities such as sweetbreads with ham. Vegetables are reliably cooked and there's a delicious choice of sweets, plus hot strong coffee. Booking essential.

Lunch 12.30–3 *Dinner* 7–12
Closed Sun & Bank Holidays

Motcombs   ⑤

Map 23 D4
26 Motcomb Street *SW1X 8JU*
01–235 6382

Proprietor Donald Phillips

Situated beneath a wine bar, this intimate beamed restaurant provides a cosy setting for capably prepared and well-presented food. The menu features specialities such as our tender roast partridge served on a croûton and sea bass grilled with herbs and lemon, as well as sautéed kidneys and veal escalope. Vegetables are skilfully handled, and there's an impressive sweet trolley. *Credit* Access, Amex, Barclaycard, Diners

About £28 for two
✆ Tube Knightsbridge

Lunch 12–3 *Dinner* 7–11
Closed Sat, Sun, Bank Holidays & 1 week Christmas

Mount Royal Hotel   60%   **£ D**

Map 22 D2
Bryanston Street *W1A 4UR*
01–629 8040
Telex 23355
Manager Mr Rios
Credit Access, Amex,
Barclaycard, Diners
✆ Tube Marble Arch

Visitors to the West End make good use of this large modern hotel just behind Marble Arch. Public rooms, which are all on the first floor, include a reception-foyer, a beautifully panelled bar and a plain lounge. Sizeable bedrooms have built-in units and matching soft furnishings, as well as walk-in dressing rooms and fully tiled bathrooms.
Amenities hairdressing, coffee shop (7am–11.30pm).

Rooms 705	*Room phone* Yes	*Confirm by* By arrang.	*Parking* Ample
with bath/shower 705	*Room TV* Yes	*Last dinner* 9.30	*Banquets* 400/–

Engineering for World Transport

In Europe and America, diesel cars are growing in popularity – and in sophistication. Lucas CAV, a company famous for its diesel fuel injection systems, has mirrored this trend by developing a number of specialised products, latest of which is a fast start aid.

The CAV Micronova system eliminates the cold-start delay associated with glowplugs and allows the motorist to key-start his diesel car in 2–3 seconds, even at sub-zero temperatures.

Nanten Yakitori   Ⓢ

Map 22 D1
6 Blandford Street *W1H 3HA*
01–935 6319

Japanese cooking

You can sit at the street-level bar of this Japanese restaurant and enjoy skewered specialities like chicken hearts with a teriyaki glaze, as well as selections from the long menu such as fragrant miso soup, sashimi and grilled mackerel marinated in soy sauce and saké. There are also private dining rooms downstairs, where prices are higher and booking is essential. *Credit* Access, Amex, Barclaycard, Diners

About £32 for two
Banquets 20/4
⊖ Buses 1, 2, 13, 30, 74, 113, 159

Lunch 12–2 *Dinner* 6–10
Closed L Sat, all Sun, Bank Holidays & 1–4 January

Neal Street Restaurant

Map 25 D5
26 Neal Street *WC2H 9PS*
01–836 8368

Designed in smart contemporary style, this friendly Covent Garden restaurant offers varied, tasty dishes ranging from mussel and saffron soup to roast wild duck. Vegetables are treated particularly well. *Credit* Access, Amex, Barclaycard, Diners *Lunch* 12.30–2.30 *Dinner* 7.30–11

About £45 for two
⊖ Tube Covent Garden

Closed Sat, Sun, Bank Holidays & last 2 weeks August *Banquets* 25/–

New Berners Hotel   68%   £B

Map 24 B2
Berners Street *W1A 3BE*
01–636 1629
Telex 25759
Manager Mr Clayton Joyce
Credit Access, Amex,
Barclaycard, Diners
⊖ Tube Tottenham Court Road

A galleried entrance lounge with a magnificent carved ceiling is just one of the superb original features that grace this busy, well-run hotel just off Oxford Street. Other public areas include three elegant function rooms and a handsome panelled bar. Bedrooms in various shapes and sizes (including 12 for disabled guests) have excellent furnishings and bright, fully tiled bathrooms. No dogs.   ♿

Rooms 237	*Room phone* Yes	*Confirm by* 6	*Parking* Difficult
with bath/shower 237	*Room TV* Yes	*Last dinner* 9.30	*Banquets* 300/–

New Mandeville Hotel   66%   £B

Map 22 D1
Mandeville Place *W1M 6BE*
01–935 5599
Telex 269487
Manager Mr Charles Serrand
Credit Access, Amex,
Barclaycard, Diners
⊖ Tube Bond Street

Handily situated just north of Wigmore Street, this well-maintained hotel is run by particularly welcoming and efficient staff. The Victorian-style Boswell's Lounge Bar is a popular lunchtime rendezvous and residents can get a drink at anytime in the attractive Studio Lounge. Compact, well-designed bedrooms have attractive fitted furniture and sleek tiled bathrooms. *Amenities* coffee shop (7am–11.30pm).

Rooms 165	*Room phone* Yes	*Confirm by* 6	*Parking* Difficult
with bath/shower 165	*Room TV* Yes	*Last dinner* 10.30	

New Rasa Sayang

Map 25 C6
3 Leicester Place *WC2H 7BP*
01–437 4556
Proprietor M. Kee
South-east Asian cooking

● **Set L & Set D** £19 for two
incl. wine
About £22 for two
Banquets 30/4
⊖ Tube Leicester Square

A good choice of authentic Indonesian and Malaysian food is served in this informal restaurant, whose interior is brightened by tropical murals. Start with the popular satay—tender skewers of chicken and beef with a thick peanut sauce—then take advice, as spicing produces effects varying from the gentle glow of a chicken korma to the full-blooded fieriness of an aubergine sambal.

Lunch 12–2.45, Sat noon–11.45pm, Sun noon–10.45pm *Dinner* 6–10.45
Closed Bank Holidays

Newports   Ⓢ

Map 22 C3
Knightsbridge Green
22 Brompton Road *SW1X 7QN*
01–589 8772

Split-level flooring divides this stylish restaurant into three comfortable eating areas, where diners choose from a short set menu of English and French dishes such as steak, grilled mackerel with gooseberry sauce and pigeon and juniper casserole (the selection changes every few weeks to make the best of seasonal produce). Delicious sweets include various sorbets and crème brûlée. *Credit* Access, Amex, Barclaycard, Diners

● **Set L** £6·50
Set D £7·50
About £20 for two
Banquets 100/–
⊖ Tube Knightsbridge

Lunch 12–3 *Dinner* 6–11.30
Closed Sun & Bank Holidays

Map 21 B6
143 St Johns Hill *SW11 1TQ*
01–228 3043

French cooking

● Set L £5·75
About £26 for two
Banquets 40/25
⊖ Buses 45, 77, 77a

No Name Place

A bistro-style restaurant, whose distinctive decor uses wood rescued from demolished buildings. The straightforward French menu, changed every fortnight, offers tasty well-prepared dishes that could include refreshing cucumber mousse, coq au vin and lovely tender calf's liver with avocado. Pommes de terre bretonne and ratatouille are the genuine articles, and there are some pleasant desserts. *Credit* Access, Barclaycard

Lunch Sun only 1–2.45 *Dinner* 7.30–11
Closed D Sun, Mon, 26–31 December & 2 weeks August

Map 20 C3
130 Regent's Park Road *NW1 8XL*
01–586 5486
Proprietor Mrs S. Green

Odette's ★

Regulars keep coming back to this cosy attractive restaurant to sample Tino Guardini's superb specialities. His menu is full of marvellous contrasts, from the robustness of leek and potato soup to the subtlety and refinement of a creamy smoked salmon-trout mousse, from fillet steak with a selection of mustards to calf's liver with sage and avocado or scallops perfumed with limes and oranges. Vegetables are faultless, and sweets include a truly outstanding chocolate cake soaked in sherry. Affable, attentive service. **Specialities** deep-fried Camembert with gooseberry preserve, gravad lax, lamb in leaf pastry, wet chocolate cake.
Credit Access, Amex, Barclaycard, Diners

About £30 for two
⊖ Bus 74

Lunch 12.30–2.30 *Dinner* 7.30–10.30
Closed L Sat, all Sun, Bank Hols, 2 weeks Aug/Sept & 10 days Christmas

---

Map 24 A1
27 Devonshire Street *W1N 1RJ*
01–935 7296

Manager Mr Michael Brown

● Set L £8·25
About £42 for two

Odin's ★

Bruce Wass continues to maintain the highest culinary standards in this intimate, sophisticated restaurant bedecked with paintings and prints. His menu, which changes regularly, makes the best use of prime produce and displays real flair and imagination, particularly in the choice of starters. There is true brilliance in speciality dishes like our velvety smooth red mullet pâté and a light, beautifully flavoured chocolate and Armagnac loaf, and main courses include original delights such as turbot fricassée served with fresh chanterelles and spinach. Excellent Columbian coffee is the perfect finishing touch. **Specialities** duck breast with glazed turnips and green peppercorns, three sorbets.

⊖ Tube Regent's Park

Lunch 12.30–2.30 *Dinner* 7–11.15
Closed L Sat, all Sun & Bank Holidays

Map 21 C5
44 Hugh Street *SW1V 4EP*
01–828 1486

Portuguese cooking

Os Arcos

Authentic Portuguese cooking and a lively atmosphere contribute to the popularity of this pretty little Pimlico restaurant. The emphasis is on seafood, with a wide choice ranging from spicy squid with garlic and lemon juice to grilled grouper, fresh sardines and salt cod. There are also meat dishes such as veal in brandy sauce, plus a few simple sweets.
🍷 *ABOVE AVERAGE. Credit* Access, Amex, Barclaycard, Diners

About £28 for two
⊖ Tube Victoria

Lunch 12.30–2.30 *Dinner* 7.30–11.30
Closed L Sat, all Sun & Bank Holidays

Map 20 B3
215 Sutherland Avenue *W9 1TN*
01–289 2562

Chinese cooking

About £32 for two
Banquets 120/6
⊖ Tube Warwick Avenue

Pangs

High-quality Cantonese cooking is the attraction in this elegantly appointed Chinese restaurant, and friendly young waiters provide helpful service. Dishes like king prawns with vegetables and chilli sauce and perfectly matched duckling with ginger and pineapple show the chef's reliability, deftness and skill. Rice, too, is cooked to perfection.
Credit Access, Amex, Barclaycard, Diners

Lunch 12–2.45 *Dinner* 6.30–10.45
Closed Mon

Paper Tiger

Map 23 C4
10 Exhibition Road *SW7 2HF*
01–584 3737
Chinese cooking

About £22 for two
⊖ Tube South Kensington

A smart basement restaurant specialising in excellent hot, spicy Szechuan cuisine. The interesting menu also offers Peking-style dishes and well-planned set meals. Willing, helpful service. *Credit* Access, Amex, Barclaycard, Diners *Lunch* Sat & Sun only 12–2.30 *Dinner* 7–1
Closed Bank Holidays ● **Set L & Set D** £9 *Banquets* 40/2

Park Lane Hotel   74%   £B

Map 25 A4
Piccadilly *W1A 4UA*
01–499 6321
Telex 21533

Rooms 300
with bath/shower 300
Room phone Yes
Room TV Yes
Confirm by 6
Last dinner 10.45
Parking Ample
Banquets 630/2

Credit Access, Amex, Barclaycard, Diners
⊖ Tube Green Park

Still firmly rooted in the 1920s, but with tasteful concessions to the 1980s here and there, this fine hotel overlooking Green Park combines classic decor with very friendly, attentive service. The evocative Palm Court lounge has been stylishly refurbished. The Art Deco ballroom and Harry's Bar are smart, luxurious rooms and many of the sizeable bedrooms boast double glazing, and all have attractively patterned curtains and upholstery, as well as mini-bars. Fully tiled bathrooms with good-quality fittings are spotlessly clean.
Amenities shopping arcade, hairdressing.

Parkes

Map 23 C4
5 Beauchamp Place *SW3 1NG*
01–589 1390

Proprietor Tom Benson

● **Set D** £22·50
About £55 for two
⊖ Tube Knightsbridge

Beautiful fresh flowers, adorning not only the room but some of the dishes, remain a feature of this stylish modern restaurant. After 20 years, Tom Benson's skill and inventiveness are still apparent in dishes like delicate avocado soup, boned chicken with · spinach, quail with apricots and chestnuts and a splendid Roquefort pâté. Service is at once friendly and professional. *Credit* Access, Amex, Barclaycard, Diners

Lunch 12.30–2.45 *Dinner* 7.30–11
Closed L Sat, all Sun, 4 days Easter & 4 days Christmas

Pastoria Hotel   56%   Ⓜ   £C/D

Map 25 C6
St Martin's Street,
Leicester Square *WC2H 7HL*
01–930 8641
Telex 25538
Credit Access, Amex, Barclaycard, Diners
⊖ Tube Leicester Square

Conveniently situated right next to Leicester Square, this pleasant hotel provides adequate accommodation for visiting tourists and businessmen. A small reception area leads to the compact, traditionally furnished lounge, which has a bar attached. Most of the smallish, simply fitted bedrooms have bathrooms with fairly modern suites. (Best rooms are on the upper floors.) dogs. **Closed** 3 days Christmas.

Rooms 54	*Room phone* Yes	*Confirm by* 6	*Parking* Difficult
with bath/shower 40	*Room TV* Yes	*Last dinner* 10	

Our inspectors never book in the name of the Egon Ronay Organisation; they disclose their identity only after paying their bills.

Map 24 D3
28 Wellington Street *WC2E 7DA*
01–240 1919

Brazilian cooking

● **Set L & Set D** £4·95
About £26 for two
Banquets 90/50
✆ Tube Covent Garden

Paulos' ⑤

Enjoy Brazilian cooking to the sound of sambas in the large cellar room of this colourful, family-run restaurant. Begin with a potent cocktail and then choose from starters like herby chicken croquettes with a fiery chilli sauce and main dishes such as beef pot roast or vatapa (a spicy blend of nuts and prawns), accompanied by fried spring greens.
Credit Access, Amex, Barclaycard, Diners

Lunch 12.30–2.30 *Dinner* 6–11.30
Closed Sun & Bank Holidays

Map 22 D1
5 Blandford Street *W1H 3AF*
01–486 9696

Italian cooking

● **Set L & Set D** £9·75
About £38 for two
✆ Buses 1, 2, 13, 30, 74, 113, 159

La Pavona ⑤

A varied selection of seafood specialities dominates the menu in this stylishly decorated Italian restaurant. Choices range from baked sea bass to poached halibut in lobster sauce; there are also some unusual pasta-based starters as well as familiar meat dishes, all prepared with an authentic touch and full of flavour. Sweets range from gâteaux to fresh fruit.
Credit Access, Amex, Barclaycard, Diners

Lunch 12–2.30 *Dinner* 7–11.15
Closed L Sat all Sun & Bank Holidays

Map 20 B2
205 Haverstock Hill *NW3 4QG*
01–435 6744
Proprietor Sally Kimbell
French cooking

About £26 for two
✆ Tube Belsize Park

Peachey's ⑤

French provincial dishes are prepared with skill at this pleasantly relaxed restaurant, whose walls are adorned with mirrors, prints and photographs. The à la carte menu (with daily specials) offers dishes ranging from tasty cauliflower soup and savoury spinach flan to grilled steak, monkfish in sorrel sauce and a very enjoyable suprême de volaille Vallée d'Auge.
🍷 *ABOVE AVERAGE. Credit* Access, Amex, Barclaycard, Diners ♿

Lunch 12–3 *Dinner* 5.30–11.30
Closed L Sat, all Sun, Bank Holidays & 2 weeks August

Map 20 B3
65 Fairfax Road *NW6 4EE*
01–624 5804

Proprietor Peter Simonyi

● **Set L** £4·95
About £30 for two
Banquets 60/8
✆ Tube Swiss Cottage

Peter's ♫ ⑤

Paris of the Belle Epoque is conjured up by the garlanded arches of this pretty little restaurant where a pianist plays at night. The Algerian chef prepares an enjoyable menu of French-style dishes, with a succulent joint of roast lamb–that takes two to demolish–as the house speciality. Friendly Italian waiters serve with relish and aplomb.
🍷 *ABOVE AVERAGE. Credit* Access, Amex, Barclaycard, Diners ♿

Lunch 12–2.30, Sun 12–3 *Dinner* 6.30–11.30
Closed L Sat, D Sun, & 1 January

Map 22 D1
15 Marylebone Lane *W1M 5FE*
01–935 9226
Manager Mr M. Souto

About £31 for two
✆ Tube Bond Street

Le P'tit Montmartre

Parisian posters enliven this intimate restaurant, where classic French dishes like quenelles de brochet, filet de bœuf oriental and crêpes suzette are prepared with skill and care. Good assertive flavours and well-made sauces.
Credit Access, Amex, Barclaycard, Diners *Lunch* 12–2.30 *Dinner* 6–11
Closed L Sat, all Sun & Bank Holidays

Map 25 B4
Piccadilly *W1V 0BH*
01–734 8000
Telex 25795
Manager Mr Fitzgerald
Credit Access, Amex,
Barclaycard, Diners
✆ Tube Piccadilly Circus

Rooms 294
with bath/shower 294

Piccadilly Hotel   66% £ B

Right in the heart of the capital, this fine Victorian building is notable for the elegance of its public areas. Carved wood panelling, embossed wallpaper and ornate gilt mouldings give the lounge a touch of grandeur, while the Press Bar has an air of plush intimacy. Traditionally decorated bedrooms have attractive wood furniture and warm colour schemes. Well-equipped bathrooms. *Amenities* hairdressing, 24-hour laundry service. ♿

| *Room phone* Yes | *Confirm by* 6 | *Parking* Difficult |
| *Room TV* Yes | *Last dinner* 9.30 | *Banquets* 500/– |

Pollyanna's   Ⓢ

Map 21 C6
2 Battersea Rise *SW11 1ED*
01–228 0316

This lively, bistro-style restaurant attracts a young clientele with good food in informal surroundings–music is loud but not oppressive. The interesting menu reflects enthusiasm in the kitchen. Imaginative starters and home-made sweets back up nicely sauced meat and fish specialities, and there's a carrot mousse or cheese and vegetable pancakes for vegetarians.
♟ *SUPERIOR. Credit* Access, Amex, Barclaycard, Diners

● **Set L** £5·95
About £28 for two
Banquets 85/10
⊖ Buses 19, 37, 49, 77, 249

Lunch Sun only 1–3 *Dinner* 7–12
Closed 25 & 26 December

Stars in this Guide stand for the quality of the cooking only– our overriding criterion, irrespective of price, luxury or service.

Pomegranates   Ⓢ

Map 21 C5
94 Grosvenor Road *SW1V 3LF*
01–828 6560
Proprietor
Patrick Gwynn-Jones

The array of cold dishes displayed at the entrance to this friendly basement restaurant provides a mouthwatering introduction to Patrick Gwynn-Jones' imaginative choice of dishes from all over the world. From Turkish, Scandinavian, Mexican and Szechuan specialities to grilled sole and farmhouse cheddar, everything is delicious and presented with flair.
♟ *OUTSTANDING. Credit* Access, Amex, Barclaycard, Diners

● **Set L** £11 incl. service
About £40 for two
Banquets 12/–
⊖ Bus 24

Lunch 12.30–2.15 *Dinner* 7.30–11.15
Closed L Sat, all Sun & Bank Holidays

Poons   ♧ Ⓢ

Map 25 C6
4 Leicester Street *WC2H 7BL*
01–437 1528

Chinese cooking

The latest addition to the Poon family of restaurants echoes the simple style of its forerunner in Lisle Street. The menu offers a wide choice of authentic, deliciously flavoured Cantonese dishes ranging from fried king prawns with green peppers and black beans to spiced beef with mixed noodles, but the real highlight is the range of wind-dried meats and unusual specialities like chicken and pork liver hotpot.

● **Set L & Set D**
from £6·80 for two
About £16 for two
Banquets 35/–
⊖ Tube Leicester Square

Meals noon–11.30pm
Closed Sun

Poons & Co.   ♧ Ⓢ

Map 25 C6
27 Lisle Street *WC2H 7BA*
01–437 1528
Proprietor Miss Shirley Poon
Chinese cooking
About £14 for two
⊖ Tube Leicester Square

Informality is the hallmark of this very busy little restaurant, where Cantonese specialities such as delicious wind-dried meats feature on the interesting menu. Cooking is subtle and authentic.
Meals noon–11.30pm
Closed Sun & 25 & 26 December

Poons of Covent Garden   ♧ 👑 Ⓢ

Map 25 D6
41 King Street *WC2E 8JS*
01–240 1743

Chinese cooking

Attractive cane furniture, brightly painted walls and concealed lighting give this modern restaurant a very striking atmosphere. The long menu of Cantonese dishes ranges from fried king prawns with pineapple to steamed bean curd with oyster sauce, as well as the famous selection of wind-dried meats. You can watch the chefs at work behind the glass partition of the kitchen. *Credit* Amex, Diners   &

● **Set L** £6
About £31 for two
Banquets 70/–
⊖ Tube Covent Garden

Meals noon–11.30pm
Closed Sun & Christmas

Map 22 D1
22 Portman Square *W1H 9FL*
01–486 5844
Telex 261526

Rooms 276
with bath/shower 276
Room phone Yes
Room TV Yes
Confirm by 6
Last dinner 11
Parking Ample
Banquets 400/4

Credit Access, Amex,
Barclaycard, Diners
✆ Buses 1, 2, 2B, 13, 30,
74, 113, 159

Portman Inter-Continental Hotel   79%   *E*   £ A/B

Extensive refurbishment of bedrooms and suites has added still further to the attractions of this notably friendly and efficiently run hotel, which has all the amenities required by the modern tourist or businessman. Bright bedrooms, their walls tastefully decorated in eye-catching stripes or lattice patterns, have campaign-style chests, relaxing armchairs and sparkling bathrooms, all equipped with telephone extensions. Brass chandeliers light the spacious lobby, which has polished wood walls and plenty of comfortable chairs, and other public areas include a pleasantly nautical bar and coffee shop and a large number of function rooms. No dogs.
Amenities in-house movies, valeting, coffee shop (7am–11pm).   &

Map 21 B4
22 Stanley Gardens *W11 2NG*
01–727 2777   Telex 21879
Manager Miss Eva Lofstad
Credit Access, Amex,
Barclaycard, Diners
Closed 5 days Christmas
✆ Tube Notting Hill Gate

Rooms 25
with bath/shower 25

Portobello Hotel   60%   £ D

Potted plants, military chests and canvas folding chairs produce a distinctly colonial atmosphere at this friendly hotel in a quiet Victorian terrace. The little foyer leads to a delightfully comfortable lounge, and there's a charming basement bar. Neat, compact bedrooms are well equipped, and thoughtful extras like mini-bars and fresh croissants add to the appeal of this well-run establishment. *Amenities* restaurant (24 hours).

| *Room phone* Yes | *Confirm by* By arrang. | *Parking* Difficult |
| *Room TV* Yes | *Last dinner* Any time | |

Map 22 B2
104 Bayswater Road *W2 3HL*
01–262 4461
Telex 22667

Credit Access, Amex,
Barclaycard, Diners
✆ Tube Queensway

Rooms 175
with bath/shower 175

Post House Hotel (Bayswater)   57%   £ D

Bedrooms at this pleasant, modern hotel have smart fitted furniture, useful mini-bars and practical tiled bathrooms. Views over Kensington Gardens provide an extra appeal in the large double-glazed rooms at the front. There's an attractive bar-cum-lounge on the first floor, and a further asset is the free garage in the basement.   &

| *Room phone* Yes | *Confirm by* 6 | *Parking* Ample |
| *Room TV* Yes | *Last dinner* 10.15 | *Banquets* 30/2 |

Map 20 B2
215 Haverstock Hill *NW3 4RB*
01–794 8121
Telex 262494

Credit Access, Amex,
Barclaycard, Diners
✆ Tube Belsize Park

Rooms 140
with bath/shower 140

Post House Hotel (Hampstead)   55%   £ D

On the edge of Hampstead Village, this compact modern hotel is popular with visiting businessmen looking for unfussy accommodation. Public areas include a brightly decorated foyer-cum-lounge and a bar with large picture windows. Most bedrooms are of good size and have fitted units, mini-bars and tea/coffee-making facilities. Tiled bathrooms are adequate.   &

| *Room phone* Yes | *Confirm by* 6 | *Parking* Ample |
| *Room TV* Yes | *Last dinner* 10.30 | |

Map 26 B2
45 Cheapside *EC2V 6AR*
01–236 4379
Manager Mr Jean Cottard
French cooking

● **Set L** £14·50 incl. service
About £38 for two

Le Poulbot   ★

A favourite place for discussing City business deals, this plush basement restaurant offers the privacy of high-backed booths, discreet, efficient service and the excellent French cuisine of Christopher Oakley. Set menus provide a range of artistically presented dishes–including perhaps oysters à la nage, braised veal tongues and steak béarnaise–notable for the quality of their ingredients and the superb balance of their flavours. Desserts are delicious, too, and there's a fine choice of prime French cheeses.
Specialities boudin blanc sauce périgueux, filets de sole Léonora, grenadins de veau Vallée d'Auge.

Continued

Continued

Credit Access, Amex, Barclaycard, Diners

Lunch only 12–3
Closed Sat, Sun, Bank Holidays & 24 December–2 January

⊖ Tube St Paul's

Map 7 B5
78 East Dulwich Grove *SE22 8TW*
01–693 0372
Proprietor Mr Sami Youssef
French cooking

Pyramid

Egyptian-born Sami Youssef is the proprietor and able chef in this simple little restaurant in a shopping parade. His French-style menu offers some interesting dishes like mackerel fillets in a mustard sauce or fillet of veal with cream and brandy, and his skilful cooking produces flavoursome results. Continental cheeses and tempting home-made sweets like pear sorbet or chocolate mousse to finish.

About £32 for two
⊖ Bus 37

Dinner only 7–10
Closed Sun, Mon, Bank Hols except 25 Dec, 1 week Easter & 2 weeks Aug

---

Map 23 A4
7 Stratford Road *W8 6RF*
01–937 6388

Seafood

Le Quai St Pierre

Like its sister establishments La Croisette and Le Suquet, this bright, cheerful restaurant with a bustling French atmosphere bases its menu on super-fresh seafood. The simplest dishes are the best—mussels, scallops and the impressive plateau de fruits de mer—and there are also salads, fish soup, daily specials like raie au beurre noir or loup bordelaise, and a couple of meat dishes.

About £36 for two
⊖ Buses 31, 74

Lunch 12.30–2.30 *Dinner* 7.30–11.30
Closed L Tues, all Mon & 2 weeks Christmas

Map 24 A1
Carburton Street *W1P 8EE*
01–388 2300
Telex 22453

Credit Access, Amex,
Barclaycard, Diners
⊖ Tube Great Portland Street

Regent Crest Hotel   64%   £C

Extensive refurbishment has improved this modern hotel (formerly the Regent Centre), which is efficiently geared to the needs of the business community. There is an attractive bar, and the open-plan lounge areas are smartly contemporary. Well-equipped bedrooms range from simple standard and more luxurious executive rooms to spacious suites. Guide dogs only. *Amenities* in-house movies, coffee shop (7am–12.30am).

Rooms 322	*Room phone* Yes	*Confirm by* 6	*Parking* Limited
with bath/shower 322	*Room TV* Yes	*Last dinner* 10.30	*Banquets* 600/2

Map 25 A4
17b Curzon Street *W1Y 7FA*
01–499 7595

French cooking

Relais des Amis

French cooking is the inspiration for the menu in this smart tiled restaurant with mirrored brick arches. Starters such as a delicate herb terrine and main courses like succulent lamb chops wrapped in pastry are very ably prepared, as are sweets like our excellent grape tart. Waiters in businesslike aprons offer attentive service.
Credit Access, Amex, Barclaycard, Diners

About £38 for two
Banquets 50/10
⊖ Tube Hyde Park Corner

Lunch 12.15–3 *Dinner* 7.15–midnight
Closed 25 December

Map 23 C4
11 Thurloe Place *SW7 2RS*
01–589 8100
Telex 295828

Credit Access, Amex,
Barclaycard, Diners
⊖ Tube South Kensington

Rembrandt Hotel   60%   £D

Friendly, courteous staff add to the pleasures of a stay in this solidly built hotel, whose position right opposite the Victoria and Albert Museum and near the Knightsbridge shops makes it a popular base for tourists. Smartly carpeted public rooms are spacious and comfortable, and most of the bedrooms have good fitted units and neat tiled bathrooms. Some are more traditional in style. No dogs.

Rooms 190	*Room phone* Yes	*Confirm by* 6	*Parking* Difficult
with bath/shower 151	*Room TV* Yes	*Last dinner* 9.30	*Banquets* 150/6

Map 25 B4
Piccadilly *W1V 9DG*
01–493 8181
Telex 267200

Rooms 139
with bath/shower 139
Room phone Yes
Room TV Yes
Confirm by 6
Last dinner 11
Parking Ample
Banquets 40/15

Credit Access, Amex,
Barclaycard, Diners

⊖ Tube Green Park

Ritz Hotel   88%   *E*   £ A

The best features of the Ritz are its beautiful Palm Court and restaurant. The historically plush atmosphere still lingers on here and there, but things aren't quite what they used to be. One doesn't entirely feel the magic and smooth touch of perfection to be expected in luxurious grand hotels. Also, filling the beautiful, generous entrance corridor with tables for tea satisfies the hotel accountant, not the seeker of luxury. Not all rooms are of the same standard yet and one hopes that efficiency, from reception (you can be kept waiting) to housekeeping will improve. No dogs.
Amenities dinner dance (Fri, Sat), men's hairdressing, valeting.

Map 25 B4
Piccadilly *W1V 9DG*
01–493 8181

About £50 for two
⊖ Tube Green Park

Ritz Hotel, Louis XVI Restaurant   ♕ ♕ ♕ Ⓢ

One of London's most beautiful dining rooms – luxurious, dainty, spacious and light. The ambitious new kitchen brigade is trying hard, but still has some way to go. Service is formal and friendly, but somewhat erratic. ♉ *OUT-STANDING. Credit* Access, Amex, Barclaycard, Diners *Lunch* 12.30–2.30 *Dinner* 6.30–11, Sun 7–10.30 ● **Set L & Set D** £18 incl. service

---

Map 21 A6
5 White Hart Lane
Barnes *SW13 0PX*
01–876 3335

Italian cooking

● **Set L** Sun only £4·50
About £30 for two
Banquets 45/6
⊖ Buses 9, 33, 37

Rose

A cosy unpretentious little restaurant, partly owned by a butcher-cum-fishmonger, so you are sure of good meat and fresh fish. The competent Spanish chef prepares simple Italian dishes featuring chicken, veal and steak, and there's an authentic Mediterranean flavour to his superb crab chowder. Portions are generous, and you're guaranteed a friendly welcome.
Credit Access, Amex, Barclaycard, Diners

Lunch 12.30–2.45, Sun 12.30–3 *Dinner* 6.30–11.45
Closed D Sun

Map 20 B3
23 Ordnance Hill *NW8 6PR*
01–722 7141
Manager Mr Biguzzi
Italian cooking

About £26 for two
⊖ Tube St John's Wood

Rossetti   Ⓢ

Booking is advisable at this lively restaurant with its rustic seating and enlarged photographs of the doyen of the Pre-Raphaelites. The food is unmistakably Italian, with an impressive selection of hors d'œuvre, carefully cooked pasta, grills and specialities like baby squid sautéed with garlic or veal cutlet with white wine and rosemary. There's also a tempting sweet trolley. *Credit* Access, Amex, Barclaycard, Diners

Lunch 12.30–2.45 *Dinner* 7–11.30, Sun 7–11
Closed 25 & 26 December

Map 25 C6
39 Coventry Street *W1V 8EL*
01–930 4033

Credit Access, Amex,
Barclaycard, Diners
⊖ Tube Piccadilly Circus

Rooms 92
with bath/shower 92

Royal Angus Hotel   59%   £ C/D

Right in the heart of the West End between Piccadilly Circus and Leicester Square, this is a popular base for tourists and visiting businessmen. There's a large welcoming foyer, as well as a popular bar and coffee shop in the basement. Bedrooms are well designed, with fitted furniture and theatrical prints on the walls. Tiled bathrooms are spacious. No dogs.
Amenities coffee shop (7.30am–3pm & 5pm–10pm).   ⎸♿

| *Room phone* Yes | *Confirm by* 6 | *Parking* Difficult |
| *Room TV* Yes | *Last dinner* 9.45 | |

Royal Garden Hotel 78% *E* £C

Map 22 A3
Kensington High Street *W8 4PT*
01–937 8000
Telex 263151
Manager Mr James A. Brown

Rooms 434
with bath/shower 434
Room phone Yes
Room TV Yes
Confirm by 6
Last dinner 12.30am
Parking Ample
Banquets 600/10

Credit Access, Amex,
Barclaycard, Diners
⊖ Tube High Street Kensington

Designed with excellent facilities for the executive and the tourist alike, this stylish modern hotel on the edge of Kensington Gardens is a model of luxurious comfort. The elegant foyer with tall pillars and a white marble floor leads to the beautifully decorated Garden Bar; there's also an intimate pub-style bar. Bedrooms have tasteful furnishings and pleasing decor, the quietest being those with balconies overlooking the Gardens. Many of the well-equipped, fully tiled bathrooms have bidets. There are also 56 attractively appointed suites. Guide dogs only.
Amenities dancing (Mon–Sat), coffee shop (7am–11pm), hairdressing, valeting.

Royal Horseguards Hotel 65% £C

Map 25 C4
Whitehall Court *SW1A 2EJ*
01–839 3400
Telex 917096

Credit Access, Amex,
Barclaycard, Diners
⊖ Tube Embankment

Flamboyantly designed like a French château, this hotel has pleasing views of the Thames. There's a tasteful blend of traditional and contemporary in the plush Grenadier Bar (fitted with a division bell for the benefit of MPs) and the lounge with its patio leading to the Embankment Gardens. Compact bedrooms have military-style units and simple tiled bathrooms. No dogs.
Amenities garden, in-house movies.

Rooms 280	*Room phone* Yes	*Confirm by* 6	*Parking* Difficult
with bath/shower 280	*Room TV* Yes	*Last dinner* 11	*Banquets* 120/10

Royal Lancaster Hotel 78% *E* £B

Map 22 B2
Lancaster Terrace *W2 2TY*
01–262 6737
Telex 24822

Rooms 434
with bath/shower 434
Room phone Yes
Room TV Yes
Confirm by 6
Last dinner 11
Parking Ample
Banquets 1,000/2

Credit Access, Amex,
Barclaycard, Diners
⊖ Tube Lancaster Gate

The higher you go, the better the view at this well-run modern hotel right above Lancaster Gate Station, so that the 'superior' rooms and the luxurious air-conditioned suites on the upper floors enjoy superb vistas of Hyde Park and the Serpentine. Good-sized rooms in varying styles and colour schemes are all well furnished, with excellent tiled bathrooms. A small arcade leads to the welcoming reception-lounge area, above which there's an elegant, comfortable lounge. The mirror-lined bar with a tented ceiling and rich maroon decor has an exotic air, and there are extensive conference facilities.
Amenities coffee shop (7am–10.45pm), 8-hour laundry service, hairdressing, valeting. ♿

Royal National Hotel 61% £D/E

Map 24 C1
Bedford Way *WC1H 0DG*
01–637 2488
Telex 263951
Manager Mr S. Walduck
Credit Access, Amex,
Barclaycard, Diners
⊖ Tube Russell Square

This vast modern hotel near King's Cross Station caters well for tourists and travelling businessmen. Public rooms, including a large foyer and a functional bar, are contemporary in style, and a patio provides a pleasant touch of greenery. Well-designed bedrooms have practical furniture and plenty of writing space. Spotless, fully equipped bathrooms. No dogs.
Amenities patio, coffee shop (10am–2am), hairdressing. ♿

Rooms 1,028	*Room phone* Yes	*Confirm by* 6	*Parking* Ample
with bath/shower 1,028	*Room TV* Yes	*Last dinner* 10	*Banquets* 420/12

ONLY DELTA HAS ONE-AIRLINE SERVICE FROM LONDON TO OVER 80 U.S.A. CITIES.

Delta flies nonstop every day to Atlanta, Georgia. You leave from Gatwick Airport. And you can fly Delta from Atlanta to 80 cities in the continental United States. No other transatlantic carrier offers as many connections with no change of airline.

You fly to Atlanta aboard Delta's Wide-Ride™ Lockheed L-1011 TriStar. You enjoy superb dining, current-release films, 7-channel stereo. (There is a small charge for headsets in Economy.)

Compare Delta's thrifty London—Atlanta fares. There's one to fit every budget — from our regular Medallion First Class to Economy, with a choice of thrifty discount fares. There's also Medallion Service Class for business travel.

Book reservations for complete itineraries through our Deltamatic® computer. It's linked to the U.S.A. for instant facts on flights to over 90 cities.

For information and reservations, call your Travel Agent. Or call Delta in London on (01) 668-0935 or (01) 668-9135, Telex 87480. Or call Crawley (0293) 517600. Or visit Delta Ticket Office at 140 Regent Street, London W1R 6AT.

All fares and schedules are subject to change without notice.

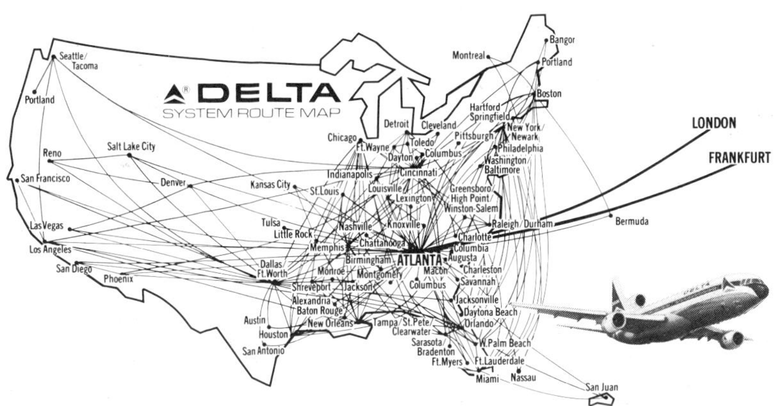

DELTA. THE AIRLINE RUN BY PROFESSIONALS.

Royal Scot Hotel 58% £ C

Map 20 D3
100 King's Cross Road *WC1X 9DT*
01–278 2434
Telex 27657

Credit Access, Amex,
Barclaycard, Diners
⊖ Tube King's Cross

This modern businessman's hotel is a short walk from King's Cross and St Pancras Stations. There's a comfortable, contemporary air about the public areas, which include a welcoming foyer, a smart coffee shop and the relaxing Charlie's Bar. Bedrooms (two floors are reserved for non-smokers) are simply furnished with built-in units, and compact bathrooms are well equipped. No dogs. *Amenities* sauna, coffee shop (10.30am–11pm).

Rooms 349	*Room phone* Yes	*Confirm by* 6	*Parking* Limited
with bath/shower 349	*Room TV* Yes	*Last dinner* 9.30	*Banquets* 100/2

Royal Trafalgar Hotel 70% £ C/D

Map 25 C4
Whitcomb Street *WC2H 7HG*
01–930 4477
Telex 298564
Manager Mr M. S. Charman

Rooms 108
with bath/shower 108
Room phone Yes
Room TV Yes
Confirm by 6
Last dinner 10.30
Parking Difficult

Closed Christmas

Credit Access, Amex,
Barclaycard, Diners
⊖ Tube Piccadilly Circus

Tucked away in a quiet side street, this efficiently run hotel has a most congenial, relaxed atmosphere. The elegant reception leads to a subtly lit open-plan foyer with deep sofas, and there's a small cocktail bar as well as a traditionally furnished pub. Bedrooms are fitted with smart, elegant dark-wood units complemented by attractive wallcoverings and lush carpeting. Fully tiled bathrooms are adequately equipped. ♿

Royal Westminster Hotel 69% £ C

Map 25 A6
Buckingham Palace Rd *SW1W 0QT*
01–834 1302
Telex 916821
Credit Access, Amex,
Barclaycard, Diners
Closed 5 days Christmas
⊖ Tube Victoria

This fine modern hotel near Victoria Station is a comfortable and well-equipped base for businessmen and tourists alike. Public rooms like the two bars combine subtle sophistication with a relaxed atmosphere, and luxurious bedrooms have elegant modern furniture, deep carpets and neat tiled bathrooms. A special feature is the 18 suites, opulently fitted in distinctive styles such as Victorian and Spanish. No dogs.

Rooms 135	*Room phone* Yes	*Confirm by* 6	*Parking* Difficult
with bath/shower 135	*Room TV* Yes	*Last dinner* 11	*Banquets* 120/4

Hotel Russell 67% £ C

Map 24 C1
Russell Square *WC1B 5BE*
01–837 6470
Telex 24615

Credit Access, Amex,
Barclaycard, Diners
⊖ Tube Russell Square

This turn-of-the-century hotel, with its distinctive red-stone and brick facade, retains much of its original grandeur. The foyer is resplendent in Italian marble, and the King's Bar panelled in oak; there's also a huge lounge and magnificent ballroom. Well-equipped bedrooms are traditionally furnished (those facing the central quadrangle are quietest). Spacious modern bathrooms. *Amenities* dancing (Sat May–Sept), coffee shop (7am–10.30pm).

Rooms 318	*Room phone* Yes	*Confirm by* 6	*Parking* Difficult
with bath/shower 318	*Room TV* Yes	*Last dinner* 10	*Banquets* 350/–

St Ermin's Hotel 66% £ C/D

Map 25 B5
Caxton Street *SW1H 0QW*
01–222 7888
Telex 917731
Manager John Ellerington
Credit Access, Amex,
Barclaycard, Diners
⊖ Tube St James's Park

Built at the turn of the century, this impressive red-brick hotel is remarkable for its ornate, galleried entrance lounge and opulent two-tier pillared ballroom. In contrast, the Caxton Bar, with its panelled walls and leather armchairs, has a more subdued, club-like atmosphere. Neat bedrooms have functional furniture and simple modern bathrooms. Efficient staff. *Amenities* valeting.

Rooms 245	*Room phone* Yes	*Confirm by* 6	*Parking* Limited
with bath/shower 245	*Room TV* Yes	*Last dinner* 10.30	*Banquets* 250/–

St George's Hotel   69%   £C

Map 24 A2
Langham Place
Oxford Circus *W1N 8QS*
01–580 0111
Telex 27274
Credit Access, Amex,
Barclaycard, Diners
✆ Tube Oxford Circus

Occupying the top of a tower block in the heart of the West End, this smart modern hotel has been designed with the businessman in mind. Five floors of comfortable bedrooms (either studios or twins) have solid built-in furniture and bold colour schemes, plus mini-bars and fully tiled bathrooms with showers. On the top floor there's an elegant open-plan lounge and bar area.

Rooms 85
with bath/shower 85

Room phone Yes *Confirm by* 6 *Parking* Difficult
Room TV Yes *Last dinner* 10 *Banquets* 20/–

St Moritz

Map 24 B3
161 Wardour Street *W1V 3TA*
01–734 3324
Proprietor Mr A. Loetscher

● **Set L** £6·75
About £26 for two
Banquets 28/–
✆ Buses 14, 19, 22, 38, 55

Strings of onions and Continental sausages hang inside the door of this cosy Tyrolean-style restaurant on two floors. The menu features many Swiss specialities like Grisons air-dried beef, fondues and veal in various guises, as well as grills, seasonal items and some French-style dishes. The delicious sweets are made by Mr Loetscher himself, a pâtissier from Lucerne.
Credit Access, Amex, Barclaycard, Diners

Lunch 12–2.30 *Dinner* 6–11.30, Fri & Sat 6–12.30am
Closed L Sat, all Sun & Bank Holidays

Salloos

Map 22 D3
62 Kinnerton Street *SW1X 8ER*
01–235 4444
Pakistani cooking

About £34 for two
✆ Tube Knightsbridge

Authentic Pakistani cooking and pleasing ethnic decor are features of this smart modern restaurant. The short menu ranges from flavoursome tandoori dishes and curries to specialities like marinated, deep-fried chicken taimuri.
🍷 *ABOVE AVERAGE. Credit* Access, Amex, Barclaycard, Diners
Lunch 12–3 *Dinner* 7–12 **Closed** Sun & Bank Holidays

San Carlo

Map 20 C2
2 Highgate High Street
N6 5JL
01–340 5823
Manager Mr C. H. Renzo
Italian cooking

About £26 for two
Banquets 30/12
✆ Tube Archway

An impressive hors d'œuvre trolley greets visitors to this spacious, modern restaurant, and smoked meats hang from the ceiling. The Italian menu offers familiar favourites as well as a few dishes based on the new Italian cuisine. There's a lunchtime roast and an attractive sweet trolley. Cooking is skilled and imaginative, service cheerful and enthusiastic.
Credit Access, Amex, Barclaycard, Diners

Lunch 12.30–3 *Dinner* 7–11.30
Closed Mon, 2 days Easter & 25 & 26 December

San Lorenzo Fuoriporta

Map 7 A5
38 Worple Road Mews
Wimbledon *SW19 4DB*
01–946 8463
Proprietors
Mr L. R. Berni & Mr Vilardo
Italian cooking

About £33 for two
Banquets 50/25
✆ Tube Wimbledon

Approached via a little Wimbledon mews, this charming Italian restaurant is as popular as ever. It's neat and bright, with crisp table linen and large potted plants, and in summer you can eat on the leafy terrace. The varied menu offers some enjoyably different dishes like fettuccine with sweet basil and pine kernel sauce or leg of lamb with green peppercorn sauce.

Lunch 12.30–3 *Dinner* 7–11, Sun 7–10
Closed Bank Holidays & 24 December

San Ruffillo

Map 23 D4
8 Harriet Street *SW1X 9JW*
01–235 3969

Italian cooking

About £24 for two
✆ Tube Knightsbridge

Simplicity is the hallmark of both the decor and the food in this cheerful Italian restaurant. There's a choice of accurately cooked pasta, uncomplicated dishes like skewered giant prawns and more unusual specialities such as chicken escalope stuffed with spinach and Bel Paese cheese. Sweets on the trolley range from peach flan to sherry trifle, with fresh strong coffee to finish. *Credit* Access, Amex, Barclaycard, Diners

Lunch 12–2.30 *Dinner* 7–11
Closed Sun & Bank Holidays

Savoy Hotel 87% *E* £A

Map 24 D3
Strand *WC2R 0EU*
01–836 4343
Telex 24234

Rooms 200
with bath/shower 200
Room phone Yes
Room TV Yes
Confirm by 6
Last dinner 11.30
Parking Ample
Banquets 500/–

Credit Access, Amex, Barclaycard
⊖ Tube Temple

Highly professional staff maintain traditional standards of courteous, efficient service at this renowned hotel, whose public rooms are models of style and elegance. The Thames Foyer with its ornamental gazebo and intricate friezes, the strikingly modern American Bar, the peaceful, dignified reading room, the vast Wedgwood-blue Lancaster room–each has its own distinctive character and appeal. Large, well-equipped bedrooms are furnished in a harmonious blend of styles, and bathrooms are sumptuous, some retaining their splendid original fittings and marble surfaces. Maintenance and housekeeping are of a very high order. No dogs. *Amenities* dancing (Mon–Sat), shopping arcade, ladies' hairdressing, barber shop.

Savoy Hotel, Grill Room ♔ Ⓢ

Map 24 D3
Strand *WC2R 0EU*
01–836 4343
Manager Mr Aldo Fiorentini

About £44 for two
⊖ Tube Temple

Classic French dishes, plus tasty daily specials like roasts or steak and kidney pudding, comprise the menu at this superbly elegant restaurant. Service is appropriately stylish and sophisticated. ♟ *OUTSTANDING.*
Credit Access, Amex, Barclaycard *Lunch* 12.30–2.30 *Dinner* 6.30–11.30
Closed Sat, Sun & some Bank Holidays ♿

Savoy Hotel, River Room ♔ ♔

Map 24 D3
Strand *WC2R 0EU*
01–836 4343
Manager Mr Antonio

Diners at one end of this magnificently ornate room can enjoy fine views across the river, and wherever you sit you can enjoy capably prepared classic dishes from the extensive menu. The choice ranges from simple terrine maison or roast beef carved from the trolley to côtes d'agneau Reform and tasty pilaff de coquilles St Jacques with a well-seasoned cream sauce. ♟ *OUTSTANDING. Credit* Access, Amex, Barclaycard

● **Set L** £10·75 **Set D** £13·50
About £44 for two
⊖ Tube Temple

Lunch 12.30–2.30 *Dinner* 7.30–12, Sun 7.30–11

Scott's ♔ ♔ Ⓢ

Map 22 D2
20 Mount Street *W1Y 5RB*
01–629 5248
Manager Mr Tino Paissino
About £45 for two
⊖ Buses 2, 2B, 16, 30, 36B, 73, 74, 137

Not merely a restaurant but an institution, this luxurious establishment prides itself on beautifully fresh seafood, including superb plump oysters and succulent lobster. A few grills for meat-eaters. Service is faultless. ♟ *OUTSTANDING. Credit* Access, Amex, Barclaycard, Diners *Lunch* 12.30–3 *Dinner* 6–10.45, Sun 7–10 **Closed** L Sun & Bank Holidays *Banquets* 10/–

Selfridge Hotel 81% *E* £B

Map 22 D1
Orchard Street *W1A 1AB*
01–408 2080
Telex 22361

Rooms 298
with bath/shower 298
Room phone Yes
Room TV Yes
Confirm by By arrang.
Last dinner 10
Parking Ample
Banquets 220/20

Credit Access, Amex, Barclaycard, Diners
⊖ Tube Bond Street

Behind Oxford Street's famous department store, this marvellous hotel provides welcome relief from the hectic pace of the world outside, combining modern comforts with old-fashioned elegance. A fine marble staircase leads to the first-floor public rooms, including a really delightful lounge with cedar wood panelling, marble walls and brown leather club chairs creating an atmosphere of utter serenity; in contrast, beams and Windsor chairs give the Stoves Bar the feel of a rustic country pub. Most bedrooms have reproduction furniture, attractive dusky-blue soft furnishings and ultra-modern bedside controls. Fully tiled, streamlined bathrooms.
Amenities valeting, in-house movies, coffee shop (7am–12.30am). ♿

Map 22 D1

Orchard Street *W1A 1AB*
01–408 2080
Manager Mr George Batz

● **Set L** from £11·75 incl. wine
Set D from £11·50
About £46 for two
✆ Tube Bond Street

Selfridge Hotel, Fletchers Restaurant ♔

Prints of London by Geoffrey Fletcher line the walls of this luxurious restaurant, where the extensive carte features a wide choice of mainly classic French-style dishes. Reliably cooked favourites like baked red mullet with fennel and noisettes of lamb with fresh herbs are supplemented by grills and flambéed specialities, all prepared from excellent raw materials. 🍷 *ABOVE AVERAGE. Credit* Access, Amex, Barclaycard, Diners ♿

Lunch 12.30–2.30 *Dinner* 6.30–10, Sat 6.30–10.30
Closed L Sat, all Sun & 25 & 26 December

Map 23 B6

457 Fulham Road *SW10 9UZ*
01–352 0206

Proprietors R. McCallum,
U. Gutierrez & G. Mole

● **Set L** £7·75
About £34 for two
✆ Buses 14, 31

September ♧ Ⓢ

A leafy central conservatory gives a pleasant garden atmosphere to this popular, bustling restaurant. Cooking is capable and imaginative, and standard favourites like roast beef share the menu with more unusual dishes such as Stilton mousse, duck crêpes with peach sauce and filet de porc Esterhazy. Desserts include a classic crème brûlée. Attentive, courteous service. *Credit* Access, Amex, Barclaycard, Diners

Lunch Sun only 12.30–2.30 *Dinner* 7.30–11.45, Sun 7–11
Closed Good Friday & 25 & 26 December

Map 26 C2

12 Lime Street *EC3M 7AA*
01–623 1843

● **Set L** £12 & £13·50
About £34 for two
Banquets 50/20
✆ Buses 15, 23, 25

Shares ♧ Ⓢ

Occupying the ground floor of a new building in the City, this mirrored restaurant makes an elegant setting for Terry Boyce's fixed-price menus. You might start with brandade of smoked eel or fine-textured veal pâté with herbs and spinach, and follow with, say, delicate saffron soup. Main courses range from simple grills to specialities like the perfectly cooked duck breast with cherry sauce. *Credit* Access, Amex, Barclaycard, Diners

Lunch only 11.30–3
Closed Sat, Sun & Bank Holidays

Map 25 C6

28 St Martin's Court *WC2N 4AL*
01–240 2565

Seafood

About £20 for two
Banquets 50/10
✆ Tube Leicester Square

Sheekeys ♔ Ⓢ

The Dickensian decor of the former Sheekeys has given way to a smart theatrical setting in which to enjoy excellent seafood. Sole, scallops, oyster and lobster are all represented, as well as plaice, haddock and skate, and their freshness is well served by careful cooking and perfect sauces. Grills and a daily special for meat-eaters too.
Credit Access, Amex, Barclaycard, Diners ♿

Lunch 12.30–2.30 *Dinner* 5.30–11.30
Closed Sun & Bank Holidays

Map 22 D3

101 Knightsbridge *SW1X 7RN*
01–235 8050
Telex 917222
Manager Mr E. N. Behard

Rooms 295
with bath/shower 295
Room phone Yes
Room TV Yes
Confirm by 6
Last dinner 11
Parking Limited
Banquets 70/10

Credit Access, Amex,
Barclaycard, Diners
✆ Tube Knightsbridge

Sheraton Park Tower 86% *E* £A

A 17-storey-high circular building, this luxurious modern hotel provides some spectacular views over London from the sumptuous suites on the top floor. All bedrooms are beautifully furnished in traditional style, with pale colour schemes, some fine antiques and original paintings. Space and lighting are thoughtfully planned, and large bathrooms are comprehensively equipped. Main public rooms include the splendidly relaxing rotunda lounge and a delightful bar divided into alcoves by glass screens. There's also a charming, summery coffee shop. Uniformed staff offer most attentive service. No dogs. *Amenities* in-house movies, beauty salon, valeting, barber shop, coffee shop (7am–midnight). ♿

Sheraton Park Tower, The Trianon 👑👑

Map 22 D3
101 Knightsbridge *SW1X 7RN*
01–235 8050
Manager Mr E. N. Behard

A colourful cold table is the focal point of this ornately elegant first-floor dining room with a large bow window. English specialities like baked lamb and even fish and chips appear on a classical menu which also features adventurous choices such as quail's eggs barquettes and sea bass en papillote. Ingredients are first class and service is impeccable.
Credit Access, Amex, Barclaycard, Diners

● **Set** L £8·75 **Set D** £14·50
About £48 for two
⊖ Tube Knightsbridge

Lunch 12.30–2.30 *Dinner* 7–11
Closed L Sat & D 25 December

Shezan ★ 👑 Ⓢ

Map 23 C4
16 Cheval Place *SW7 1ES*
01–589 7918
Proprietor Mr Shah Nawaz
Pakistani cooking

This coolly elegant restaurant, simply decorated in restful creams and browns, has a long-established reputation as a centre of first-class Pakistani cuisine. Service, too, is excellent, and attentive waiters will take you through the menu, which leans towards lamb and chicken dishes. You could try juicy murgh tikka Lahori, chicken marinated in gentle aromatic spices and barbecued over charcoal, or perhaps karahi kebab Khyberi, spicy diced chicken and vegetables served piping hot in a cast-iron pot. Bread and rice are superb, too, and there are some refreshingly light desserts. **Specialities** grilled prawns, gosht kata masala, pulao hijazi.
Credit Access, Amex, Barclaycard, Diners

● **Set D** £35 for two
About £38 for two

⊖ Tube Knightsbridge

Lunch 12–2.30 *Dinner* 7–11.30
Closed Sun & Bank Holidays

Shireen 👑 Ⓢ

Map 21 A4
270 Uxbridge Road *W12 7JA*
01–749 5927

Indian cooking

The accent is on subtle spicing, variety and really individual flavours in this stylish Indian restaurant. Tandoori specialities, appetisers like marinated lamb's liver and masala aubergine, plus an interesting choice of unusual curries, are all prepared with skill and understanding, without relying on fieriness for effect. Vegetables are particularly crisp and fresh-tasting.
Credit Access, Amex, Barclaycard, Diners   ♿

About £28 for two
⊖ Tube Shepherd's Bush

Lunch 12–3 *Dinner* 6–11.30
Closed Sun & 25 & 26 December

Shogun Ⓢ

Map 22 D2
Adams Row *W1A 3AN*
01–493 1877

Japanese cooking

At the back of the Britannia Hotel, this basement restaurant with its Japanese pictures and bric-à-brac has an atmosphere as authentically Nippon as the menu. Flavours are delicate and subtle–as in the superb clam soup–and first-class ingredients are served with sophisticated sauces, crisp vegetables and well-cooked rice. Don't miss the delightful green tea ice cream.
Credit Access, Amex, Barclaycard, Diners

● **Set D** from £14
About £30 for two
Banquets 40/15
⊖ Tube Bond Street

Dinner only 6–11.30
Closed Easter & Christmas

Shu Shan Ⓢ

Map 25 C6
36 Cranbourn Street *WC2H 7AD*
01–836 7501

Chinese cooking

Aromatic Szechuan duck, smoked over camphor wood and tea, is one of the highlights in this simply decorated Chinese restaurant, and other Szechuan specialities like thinly sliced pork with chilli sauce and garlicky fried aubergine are skilfully prepared and authentically spicy. More familiar items such as sliced beef with oyster sauce and sweet and sour fish are equally successful. *Credit* Access, Amex, Barclaycard, Diners

About £22 for two
Banquets 30/8
⊖ Tube Leicester Square

Meals noon–11pm
Closed 25 & 26 December

Shu Shan II 

Map 23 B5
53 Old Brompton Road *SW7 3JS*
01–589 3149

Chinese cooking
About £22 for two
Tube South Kensington

This is the younger sister of the Cranbourn Street restaurant, offering the same menu. Cooking is chiefly Szechuan in style, with a wide choice of well-prepared dishes. Friendly service.
Credit Access, Amex, Barclaycard, Diners *Meals* noon–11pm
Closed 3 days Christmas *Banquets* 100/–

Siam 

Map 23 B4
12 St Albans Grove *W8 5PN*
01–937 8765
Proprietors
Mr & Mrs K. Chareonying
Thai cooking

● **Set L** £5·50 **Set D** £7·50
About £27 for two
Banquets 45/–
Tube High Street Kensington

For a truly authentic experience, make for the basement room of this Thai restaurant, where, sitting on plush cushions, you can watch classical dancing and enjoy spicy food served by beautiful waitresses. Dishes like sliced pork in a sweet soya sauce and fried chicken with mint and chillis show a subtle blend of different flavours. The ground-floor room is more Western in style. *Credit* Access, Amex, Barclaycard, Diners

Lunch 12.30–2.30, Sun 12–2.30 *Dinner* 6.15–11.15, Sun 6–10.30
Closed L Mon & Sat & all Bank Holidays

Sidi Bou Said 

Map 22 C1
9 Seymour Place *W1H 5AG*
01–402 9930

Tunisian cooking
● **Set L** £3·95
Set D £4·95 incl. service
About £22 for two
Banquets 60/20
Tube Marble Arch

You can nibble spicy appetisers while perusing the short menu in this family-run Tunisian restaurant. Piquant salads, various kinds of tagine (savoury stews named after the earthenware pot in which they are cooked) and couscous have an authentic flavour, while fresh dates, pastries and strong coffee perfumed with orange water make a delightful finale.
Credit Access, Amex, Barclaycard, Diners

Lunch 12–3 *Dinner* 6–11.30
Closed Sun & Bank Holidays

Simpson's-in-the-Strand

Map 24 D3
100 The Strand *WC2R 0EW*
01–836 9112

English cooking
● **Set D** (6–7.30pm) £11·50
incl. wine & service
About £30 for two
Banquets 150/70
Buses 1, 6, 9, 11, 13, 15, 23, 77, 77A, 170, 172, 176

Dating back to 1828, Simpson's is still very much an institution, with a sedate, almost Victorian, atmosphere and food that is uncompromisingly English. The real highlights are the traditional roasts, which are wheeled round on heated trolleys by long-serving retainers. Other favourites like tripe and onions, bubble and squeak and chunky apple pie are also deservedly popular. *Credit* Access, Barclaycard

Lunch 12–3 *Dinner* 6–10
Closed Sun & Bank Holidays

We welcome complaints and bona fide recommendations on the tear-out pages for readers' comments. They are followed up by our professional team. Please also complain to the management instantly.

Spread Eagle 

Map 7 B5
2 Stockwell Street
Greenwich *SE10 9JN*
01–853 2333

Proprietors R. Mouf & M. Heap

About £32 for two
Banquets 40/2
Buses 108, 108B, 177, 180

Mr Heap is the capable and imaginative chef at this pleasant restaurant near the National Maritime Museum. His interesting menus offer something for everyone, from simple pâté maison or excellent, authentic moules marinière to more exotic choices like hot Guinness and oyster soup and duck–pink-cooked breast as well as crisp-roasted leg served with a sauce made of three citrus fruits. *Credit* Access, Amex, Barclaycard, Diners

Lunch 12–2.30, Sun 12–3 *Dinner* 6.30–10.45, Sat 6.30–11
Closed L Sat, D Sun & Bank Holidays except 25 December

Stafford Hotel 78% £ A

St James's Place *SW1A 1NJ*
01–493 0111
Telex 28602

Manager Mr Terry Holmes
Rooms 60
with bath/shower 60
Room phone Yes
Room TV Yes
Confirm by By arrang.
Last dinner 10.30
Parking Difficult
Banquets 50/2

Credit Amex

✆ Tube Green Park

Standing in a peaceful cul-de-sac off St James's Street, this civilised hotel offers the discreet elegance, quiet comfort and friendly personal service that guests would expect in a club or private house. The long, narrow lounge, with its relaxing sofas, polished tables and pretty lamps, is a popular place for afternoon tea, and for cocktails there's an intimate bar looking out over a little cobbled patio with log benches and plant-filled tubs. Newly decorated bedrooms, each with its own individual charm, have fine reproduction furniture, excellent lighting and attractive tiled bathrooms. There are several rooms available for banquets or conferences. No dogs. *Amenities* valeting.

Standard

Map 23 D5
62 Lower Sloane Street *SW1W 8BP*
01–730 1110

Indian cooking

Formerly Clive's India, this smartly furnished restaurant now has new owners. The menu has a good choice of familiar Indian dishes from tandoori chicken to lamb pasanda and vegetarian selections. Spicing is subtle and delicate and flavours are excellent. Starters like prawn pakora or vegetable cutlass (fritters) are delicious, and Basmati rice is perfectly cooked. *Credit* Access, Amex, Barclaycard, Diners

● **Set L** £3
About £18 for two
✆ Tube Sloane Square

Lunch 12–3 *Dinner* 6–11.30
Closed 25 December

Strand Palace Hotel 62% £ C/D

Map 24 D3
369 Strand *WC2R 0JJ*
01–836 8080
Telex 24208
Credit Access, Amex, Barclaycard, Diners
✆ Buses 1, 6, 9, 11, 13, 15, 23, 77, 77A, 170, 172, 176

This imposing greystone building is a convenient and comfortable base for exploring the city's sights. There's a bright, modern foyer and two smart, spacious bars. Improvements continue in the cheerful bedrooms, some having been completely restyled to provide delightfully furnished and well-equipped accommodation. Older rooms are functionally fitted. *Amenities* coffee shop (24 hours), hairdressing, shopping arcade.

Rooms 760
with bath/shower 760

| *Room phone* Yes | *Confirm by* 6 | *Parking* Difficult |
| *Room TV* Yes | *Last dinner* 9.30 | *Banquets* 240/– |

Stratford Court Hotel 54% £ D

Map 24 A3
350 Oxford Street *W1N 0BY*
01–629 7474
Telex 22270
Manager David Bull
Credit Access, Amex, Barclaycard, Diners
✆ Tube Bond Street

Literally on top of the Oxford Street shops, this useful tourist hotel offers a friendly welcome and modest, comfortable accommodation. Bedrooms of various sizes have well-coordinated carpets and curtains, practical fitted furniture and compact bathrooms. Public rooms include a cheerful coffee shop and a relaxing cocktail bar with prints of Stratford and Shakespearian actors. No dogs. *Amenities* coffee shop (7am–10.30pm).

Rooms 139
with bath/shower 139

| *Room phone* Yes | *Confirm by* 6 | *Parking* Difficult |
| *Room TV* Yes | *Last dinner* None | |

Suntory

Map 25 B4
72 St James's Street *SW1A 1PH*
01–409 0201

Japanese cooking

There's a sense of theatre about eating at this comfortable, cleverly lit Japanese restaurant. In one room you can order shabu-shabu, thinly sliced beef and vegetables cooked in steaming broth at your table; in the other, the attraction is teppan-yaki, steaks and seafood lightly grilled on a hot plate by your own personal chef. Other choices range from sashimi to tempura. *Credit* Access, Amex, Barclaycard, Diners

● **Set L & Set D** from £10·35
About £54 for two
Banquets 18/4
✆ Tube Green Park

Lunch 12–2.20 *Dinner* 7–10.20
Closed Sun, Bank Holidays & 1 week August

Map 23 C5

104 Draycott Avenue *SW3 3AE*
01–581 1785

Seafood

About £42 for two
Tube South Kensington

Le Suquet ★ ⑤

This delightful and popular seafood restaurant has all the bustle and charm of a French quayside eating place, with its fishing tackle, French coastal scenes on the walls and enthusiastic French staff. One of the star attractions is the plateau de fruits de mer, a beautifully presented assortment of mussels, winkles, oysters, crabs and langoustines all accompanied by lovely thick mayonnaise. Everything is perfectly fresh and expertly prepared, and many of the daily specials feature delicate buttery sauces. A few meat dishes are also available.
Specialities turbot au Champagne, loup grillé au fenouil.
Credit Amex

Lunch 12.30–2.30 *Dinner* 7.30–11.30
Closed L Tues, all Mon & 2 weeks Christmas

Changes in data may occur in establishments after the Guide goes to press. Prices should be taken as indications rather than firm quotes.

Map 25 C6

2 New Coventry Street *W1V 3HG*
01–734 1291

About £29 for two
Tube Piccadilly Circus

Swiss Centre, Chesa ⑤

Elegant table settings enhance the simple decor of this spotless basement restaurant. Choose between light Swiss dishes such as a creamy chowder with fish dumplings or air-dried meats, and more solid French-style dishes served perhaps with rösti potatoes and a generous side salad. Don't miss the delicious sorbets and mousses. Wide choice of Swiss wines.
Credit Access, Amex, Barclaycard, Diners

Lunch 12–2.30 *Dinner* 6–12
Closed 25 December

Map 20 B3

4 Adamson Road *NW3 3HP*
01–722 2281
Telex 27950

Credit Access, Amex,
Barclaycard, Diners
Tube Swiss Cottage

Rooms 65
with bath/shower 60

Swiss Cottage Hotel 64% Ⓜ £ D/E

This smart, family-run hotel is part of an imposing Victorian terrace. Paintings and antiques give an air of opulence to the public rooms, each with its own distinctive colour scheme. Bedrooms, too, have much traditional elegance, the larger ones having especially stylish furnishings. Modern bathrooms have attractive coloured suites. No dogs.
Amenities garden, sauna, 24-hour laundry service.

| *Room phone* Yes | *Confirm by* 6 | *Parking* Ample |
| *Room TV* Yes | *Last dinner* 9 | *Banquets* 25/– |

Map 24 C1

8 Brunswick Centre
Bernard Street *WC1N 1AE*
01–837 9397

Indian cooking

● **Set L** £3·45
About £22 for two
Banquets 60/10
Tube Russell Square

Tagore 

Part of a modern shopping complex, this brightly decorated restaurant offers a good choice of excellent Indian dishes, including several prepared in the tandoor. There are curries ranging from mild to fiery, Kashmiri specialities (usually based on lamb) and thalis, both meat and vegetarian. Good fresh ingredients and a subtle blending of flavours produce very tasty results.
Credit Access, Amex, Barclaycard, Diners ♿

Lunch 12–3 *Dinner* 6–11.30
Closed L Sun & Christmas

Map 23 C4

8 Egerton Garden Mews *SW3 2EH*
01–589 8287

Chinese cooking
About £44 for two
Buses 14, 30, 74

Tai-Pan ♔

Hot and pungently spicy Hunan and Szechuan dishes dominate the menu in this smart basement restaurant with cool, elegant decor. Traditional recipes are enhanced by the use of excellent raw materials. 🍷 *ABOVE AVERAGE. Credit* Access, Amex, Barclaycard, Diners *Lunch* 12–2.30 *Dinner* 7–11.30 **Closed** L Bank Hols & all 25 Dec ● **Set L** from £10 for two **Set D** from £24 for two

Map 23 C5
153 Fulham Road *SW3 6SN*
01–589 7617

Indian cooking

About £27 for two
☻ Buses 14, 45, 49

Tandoori of Chelsea   Ⓢ

A turbaned doorman greets visitors to this intimate basement restaurant decorated with batik fabrics and Eastern artefacts. Excellent tandoori dishes and accurately spiced North Indian curries are consistently reliable and nicely complemented by fluffy Basmati rice, well-cooked vegetables and sundries. Finish with fresh mangoes in season.
Credit Access, Amex, Barclaycard, Diners

Lunch Sun only 12.30–3 *Dinner* 6.30–12.30am, Sun 6.30–11.30
Closed 25 & 26 December

Map 23 C6
68 Royal Hospital Road *SW3 4HP*
01–352 6045

French cooking

● **Set L** £10·50
About £55 for two

☻ Bus 39

La Tante Claire ★ ★ ★   ♁ ♔ Ⓢ

The self-effacing, invisible chef Koffmann is a true artist. His creations as well as his execution of the classics have lent this small, narrow, civilised room the well-deserved aura of a gastronomic temple. Connoisseurs seeking to be delighted, not those seeking to be seen, flock to it. Pig's trotters stuffed with morel mushrooms are a fabulous achievement; the handling of fresh goose liver on a thin bed of caramelised potatoes shows consummate skill; all the textures and sauces are perfection itself.
Specialities andouillette de la mer au vinaigre de cassis, foie de veau au citron vert, biscuit glacé avec son coulis. ♙ *OUTSTANDING.*
Credit Amex

Lunch 12.30–2 *Dinner* 7–11 **Closed** Sat, Sun, Bank Holidays, 2 weeks Easter, 3 weeks August & 2 weeks Christmas

Map 21 C5
30 Winchester Street *SW1V 4NF*
01–828 3366

About £33 for two
Banquets 50/25
☻ Bus 24

Tapas   ♔ Ⓢ

A cosmopolitan, eclectic choice of dishes from all parts of the world draws customers to this smart basement restaurant. Chinese pancake rolls, Indonesian satay, pastelitos (giant prawns in paper-thin pastry with an almond sauce spiced with chilli) and baked crab with rice all show a capable touch and are full of flavour. Limited sweets include honey and cognac ice cream.
Credit Access, Amex, Barclaycard, Diners

Dinner only 6–11.30
Closed Sun & Bank Holidays

Map 24 D3
36 Tavistock Street *WC2E 7PB*
01–240 3972

Proprietors
Kevin Jones & Luigi Wegrzynek

About £42 for two
Banquets 50/12
☻ Tube Covent Garden

Thomas de Quincey's

Inventiveness is the key to the menu in this attractive, dimly lit restaurant. André Cluzeau creates many complex dishes like turbot stuffed with a scallop mousse and served with a creamy orange sauce, and there are more straightforward grills as well. Vegetables are elaborately prepared and standards of cooking are generally very creditable.
Credit Access, Amex, Barclaycard, Diners   ♿

Lunch 12.30–3 *Dinner* 6–11.15, Sat 7–11.30
Closed L Sat, all Sun, Bank Holidays & last 3 weeks August

Map 25 A4
22 Queen Street *W1X 7PJ*
01-629 3561

Manager Basilio de Colle
Italian cooking

About £36 for two
☻ Tube Green Park

Tiberio   ♔ Ⓢ

A wide staircase leads down to this sophisticated basement restaurant, where friendly, smartly dressed waiters serve well-prepared Italian dishes. The extensive menu ranges from Parma ham and pasta to braised oxtail, petto di pollo and our very tasty roast duckling with a light orange and Curaçao-flavoured sauce. Piano in the evening, and dancing late at night.
♙ *ABOVE AVERAGE. Credit* Access, Amex, Barclaycard, Diners

Lunch 12–2.30 *Dinner* 7–1
Closed L Sat, all Sun & Bank Holidays

Map 23 A5
251 Old Brompton Road *SW5 9HP*
01–370 2323
Chinese cooking

About £36 for two
Banquets 20/8
☻ Tube Earl's Court

Tiger Lee　　　♕ Ⓢ

Excellent, imaginative cooking, attractive presentation and smart, informed service all make it very worth while visiting this elegantly modern Chinese restaurant. There's always a wide choice of seafood–fish are on display in tanks– and other interesting and delicious choices include pan-fried beef fillets with fresh mango and beautifully prepared chicken fillets with a tangy lemon sauce. *Credit* Amex, Diners

Dinner only 6–11.30
Closed 25 & 26 December

Map 22 A2
39 Uxbridge Street *W8 7TQ*
01–727 5813

Proprietor Mr G. Giornandi
Italian cooking

About £25 for two
Banquets 22/6
☻ Tube Notting Hill Gate

Topo d'Oro　　　Ⓢ

A menu of popular Italian dishes, cooked with care and served with cheerful efficiency, ensures a regular following at Mr Giornandi's roomy basement restaurant. As well as the usual range of appetisers, pasta, fish and meat dishes, there are specials based on the pick of the morning market–perhaps asparagus, salmon trout or roast veal–and desserts featuring fresh fruits. *Credit* Access, Amex, Barclaycard, Diners

Lunch 12–3, Sun 12–2.30 *Dinner* 6–11.30, Sun 6–11
Closed 25 & 26 December

Map 26 D3
St Katharine's Way *E1 9LD*
01–481 2575
Telex 885934

Rooms 826
with bath/shower 826
Room phone Yes
Room TV Yes
Confirm by 9
Last dinner 9.30
Parking Limited
Banquets 200/10

Credit Access, Amex,
Barclaycard, Diners
☻ Buses 23, 42, 78

Tower Hotel　76%　*E*　　　£C

This impressive riverside hotel has superb views of the Thames, Tower Bridge and a busy marina. Plenty of greenery and elegant leather seating bring an air of luxury to the vast foyer with its massive pillars, and other public areas are equally attractive. Colourful bedrooms, handsomely equipped with all modern comforts, have smart compact bathrooms. No dogs.
Amenities in-house movies, coffee shop (7.30am–1am), valeting.

Map 26 D3
St Katharine's Way *E1 9LD*
01–481 2575

● **Set L & Set D** from £10·75
incl. wine
About £43 for two
☻ Buses 23, 42, 78

Tower Hotel, Princes Room　　　♕

Gentlemen must wear jacket and tie at this elegant restaurant with a magnificent view of the Thames and Tower Bridge (book a window table). The short menu is based mainly on French classical dishes, with one or two unusual items such as a leek and clam soup and peppered swordfish steak. There are charcoal-grilled steaks, too, and crisp, carefully cooked vegetables. *Credit* Access, Amex, Barclaycard, Diners

Lunch 12.30–3 *Dinner* 6.30–9.30
Closed L Sat

Map 22 D3
Hilton Hotel
22 Park Lane *W1A 2HH*
01–493 7586
Manager
Mr Jacky Laugenie

About £50 for two
Banquets 35/20
☻ Tube Hyde Park Corner

Trader Vic's　　　♕

Park Lane's answer to Polynesia, with South Seas decor and bamboo furniture. The menu is an interesting blend of the familiar–melon and Parma ham, Dover sole, grilled steaks–and the exotic–Tahitian fish soup served in a giant shell, tasty crab Rangoon and intriguing bongo bongo. Cooking is expert, with subtle spicing and carefully combined flavours. Superb cheesecake, too. *Credit* Access, Amex, Barclaycard, Diners

Lunch 12–3 *Dinner* 6.30–11.30, Sun 7–11.30
Closed L Sat & all 25 December

Vasco & Piero's Pavilion   Ⓢ

Map 24 B2
167 Oxford Street *W1R 1TA*
01-437 8774
Proprietors Vasco Matteuci
& Piero Orazietti
Italian cooking

Blue and gold pillars and wrought-iron chairs make the decor of this Italian restaurant a little different, and the food is refreshingly out of the ordinary, too. Specialities like seafood lasagne, fillets of bream and breast of chicken with lemon and sage are typical of the uncomplicated, enjoyable dishes on the short, daily-changing menu, and there are also some simple sweets.
Credit Access, Amex, Barclaycard, Diners

About £32 for two
◿ Tube Oxford Circus

Lunch 12–3 *Dinner* 6–11
Closed L Sat, all Sun & Bank Holidays

Viceroy of India   ♕ Ⓢ

Map 21 C4
3 Glentworth Street *NW1 5PG*
01-486 3515

Indian cooking

● **Set L** £5·95
Set D £5·75 & £6·95
About £28 for two
Banquets 20/10
◿ Tube Baker Street

Rippling fountains and soft Indian music set the tone in this luxurious restaurant where the tandoors are on open view. A short, interesting menu features specialities like marinated quail, grilled prawns, and a range of tempting vegetable dishes, as well as more familiar kebabs, curries and biryanis. Careful preparation extends to the rice and fresh, tasty breads.
Credit Access, Amex, Barclaycard, Diners

Lunch 12–3 *Dinner* 6–11.30, Sun 6–11
Closed 25 December

Vijay   ♧ Ⓢ

Map 20 B3
49 Willesden Lane *NW6 7RF*
01-328 1087
Proprietor Mr Ramanthan
Indian cooking

Authentic South Indian dishes are a feature of this intimate corner-shop restaurant just off Kilburn High Road. There's a reliable quality about the cooking, from the carefully spiced mild lamb korma or more pungent beef Madras to specialities like dosais (pancakes filled with vegetables) and avial (vegetables in a rich coconut and yoghurt sauce). Service is friendly and efficient.

About £19 for two
Banquets 14/–
◿ Buses 8, 16, 32, 176

Lunch 12–2.45 *Dinner* 6–10.45, Fri & Sat 6–11.45
Closed 25 & 26 December

Villa dei Fiori   Ⓢ

Map 20 B2
38 North End Road
Golders Green *NW11 7PT*
01-458 6344
Italian cooking
About £25 for two
◿ Tube Golders Green

Friendly waiters serve in this inviting Italian restaurant, where standard dishes like stracciatella and fettuccine are capably prepared from good raw materials. *Credit* Access, Amex, Barclaycard, Diners
Lunch 12–2.30 *Dinner* 6–11.30, Sun 6–11
Closed 25 & 26 December   ♿

Waldorf Hotel   77%   *E*   **£B/C**

Map 24 D3
Aldwych *WC2B 4DD*
01-836 2400
Telex 24574

Rooms 310
with bath/shower 310
Room phone Yes
Room TV Yes
Confirm by 6
Last dinner 11
Parking Difficult
Banquets 400/6

Credit Access, Amex,
Barclaycard, Diners
◿ Buses 1, 6, 9, 11, 13, 15, 23,
77, 77A, 170, 172, 176

An enduring monument to the Edwardian era, this grand crescent-shaped hotel is immaculately maintained, and combines old-fashioned elegance with modern comforts. Polished stone stairs lead to a marble-floored reception, but the main feature of the ground floor is the lovely sunken Palm Court with its vast skylight and giant potted plants; there's also the darkly panelled Club Bar and the Edwardian-styled Footlights Bar. Comfortable bedrooms have good freestanding furniture, while suites are fitted out with antiques. Spacious, well-equipped bathrooms. *Thé dansant* on Friday afternoons. *Amenities* in-house video, barber's shop, lounge service (10am–2am), thé dansant (Fri 3.30pm–6pm), 24-hour laundry service, valeting.   ♿

Map 24 D3

Aldwych *WC2B 4DD*
01–836 2400

● **Set L** £9·25
Set D from £10·25
incl. service
About £25 for two
♿ Buses 1, 6, 9, 11, 13, 15, 23, 77

Waldorf Hotel, Wellington Restaurant ♔ Ⓢ

Chandeliers, moulded ceilings and classical pillars give this Edwardian restaurant a very elegant air. The menu features imaginative starters like king prawns with chervil sauce, skilfully prepared entrées such as entrecôte Armagnac, grills and cold dishes. Vegetables are crisp, and attractive sweets range from delicate walnut mousse to fruit roly-poly. Popular business lunches. *Credit* Access, Amex, Barclaycard, Diners

Lunch 12.30–3, Sun 12.30–2.30 *Dinner* 6–11, Sun 6–10
Closed L Sat

Map 20 B1

8 Monkville Parade
Finchley Road *NW11 0AL*
01–458 5317

● **Set L** £5·95 **Set D** £7·95
About £32 for two
♿ Buses 13, 26, 102, 260

Walkers Ⓢ

Night-time brings candlelight to this pleasant arched restaurant with its own little bar. Fish and shellfish dishes predominate, composed of first-class fresh ingredients lightly sauced. Competently cooked vegetables are crisp and flavoursome, and there are home-made sweets and excellent coffee. Friendly waiters in shirt-sleeves and waistcoats provide skilful service.
Credit Access, Amex, Barclaycard, Diners

Lunch 12–2.30 *Dinner* 6.30–10.30, Sat 6.30–11
Closed L Sat, D Sun & all Mon

Map 23 C4

121 Walton Street *SW3 2HP*
01–584 0204

Manager Mr Rolf Ambergi

● **Set L** £6·90, Sun £13·80
Set D from £20·13
About £58 for two
Banquets 12/10
♿ Tube South Kensington

Walton's ♔♔ Ⓢ

Standards are consistently high at this elegant, comfortable restaurant, where dishes on the set menus are carefully prepared and artistically presented. First and second courses range from simple mushroom salad to glazed pancakes stuffed with spinach and chicken, while interesting main dishes include delicate suprême of brill and richly sauced breast of pheasant. 🍷 *OUTSTANDING. Credit* Access, Amex, Barclaycard, Diners

Lunch 12.30–2.30, Sun 12–2 *Dinner* 7.30–11.30, Sun 7.30–10.30
Closed Bank Holidays

Map 25 A4

Curzon Street *W1Y 8DT*
01–499 7030
Telex 24540

Credit Access, Amex,
Barclaycard, Diners
♿ Buses 9, 14, 19, 22, 25, 38, 55

Washington Hotel   62%   £ C/D

This comfortably modernised hotel stands in the heart of Mayfair just near Berkeley Square. Its welcoming public areas include a marble-floored entrance hall, a roomy pastel-decorated lounge and the smart, convivial 4th Hussars Bar, which is filled with military paraphernalia. Well-maintained bedrooms have bright, cheerful colour schemes, patterned bedspreads, and neat, tiled bathrooms. *Amenities* 24-hour laundry service. ♿

Rooms 160	*Room phone* Yes	*Confirm by* By arrang.	*Parking* Difficult
with bath/shower 160	*Room TV* Yes	*Last dinner* 9.30	*Banquets* 200/–

Our inspectors are our full-time employees; they are professionally trained by us.

Map 23 A6

47 Lillie Road *SW6 1UQ*
01–385 1255
Telex 917728

Credit Access, Amex,
Barclaycard, Diners
♿ Tube West Brompton

West Centre Hotel   52%   £ C/D

Situated right by Earl's Court Exhibition Centre, this large concrete and glass hotel has extensive conference facilities. There's a choice of two bars (an especially stylish one for residents only), as well as a large coffee shop. Bedrooms have functional fitted units, tea/coffee-makers and radio alarms, plus well-equipped, fully tiled bathrooms. *Amenities* in-house movies, coffee house (10am–11.30pm). ♿

Rooms 510	*Room phone* Yes	*Confirm by* 6	*Parking* Ample
with bath/shower 510	*Room TV* Yes	*Last dinner* 10.30	*Banquets* 1500/–

Map 24 A3
New Bond Street *W1Y 0PD*
01–629 7755
Telex 24378

Rooms 254
with bath/shower 254
Room phone Yes
Room TV Yes
Confirm by 6
Last dinner 11
Parking Limited
Banquets 120/–

Credit Access, Amex,
Barclaycard, Diners
⊖ Bus 25

Westbury Hotel   75%   £ A/B

Built in the heart of the West End in 1955, this impressive hotel has a truly international clientele of businessmen and tourists who appreciate its excellent standards of service and maintenance. The spacious foyer sets the tone of restrained, traditional elegance with its gilt mirrors, oil paintings and sparkling crystal light fittings. There's also a comfortable cocktail bar leading to the lovely panelled lounge, which is a very popular spot for afternoon tea. Comfortable double-glazed bedrooms have attractive darkwood furniture and large up-to-date bathrooms. There are also numerous sumptuously appointed function suites. No dogs. *Amenities* valeting, men's hairdressing.

We publish annually, so make sure you use the current edition. It's worth it!

Map 22 B3
17 Kensington High Street *W8 5NP*
01–937 1443
Manager Mr René Guano
Seafood
About £34 for two
⊖ Tube High Street Kensington

Wheeler's Alcove

A plush restaurant offering a wide choice of fresh seafood – from scallops and halibut to lobster and Dover sole (in 23 ways) – plus a few grills. Cooking is generally acceptable, simplest dishes being the best.
Credit Access, Amex, Barclaycard, Diners *Lunch* 12–2.30 *Dinner* 6–11
Closed Sun & Bank Holidays *Banquets* 35/12

Map 24 A1
Albany Street *NW1 3UP*
01–387 1200
Telex 24111

Rooms 587
with bath/shower 587
Room phone Yes
Room TV Yes
Confirm by 6
Last dinner 11.30
Parking Limited
Banquets 120/6

Credit Access, Amex,
Barclaycard, Diners
⊖ Tube Great Portland Street

The White House   71%   £ B/C

Standing by the south-east corner of Regent's Park, this handsome white-stone hotel was built in the 1930s as a block of flats. Delightful flower arrangements abound in the public rooms, which include a cool marble-floored reception hall with pillars and a central lounge area. There are two bars also, a wine bar and a bright, cheerful coffee shop. Bedrooms vary in size and style from refurbished twins with smart white furniture and deep carpets to studio rooms and luxury suites; all have double glazing, bedside TV and radio controls and well-equipped, tiled bathrooms. Maintenance and housekeeping are excellent. *Amenities* coffee shop (7am–10.30pm), hairdressing, shopping arcade, valeting. ♿

Map 24 A1
Albany Street *NW1 3UP*
01–387 1200

French cooking

● **Set L & Set D** £9 incl. wine
About £39 for two
⊖ Tube Great Portland Street

The White House Restaurant   

An intimate, relaxing restaurant, where elegant surroundings are matched by excellent cooking and friendly, assured service. Standards are consistently high throughout an interesting range of French dishes, from starters like tasty truffled game pâté to deliciously sauced main courses served with an eye-catching selection of lightly cooked vegetables, and some really lovely desserts. *Credit* Access, Amex, Barclaycard, Diners ♿

Lunch 12.30–3 *Dinner* 6.30–11.30
Closed L Sat, all Sun & Bank Holidays

Map 24 B2
1 Percy Street *W1P 9FA*
01–636 8141
Proprietors
Mr & Mrs J. P. Stais
Greek cooking

About £31 for two
Banquets 16/4
✆ Tube Goodge Street

White Tower

Long established as a centre of authentic Greek cuisine, the White Tower offers excellent cooking, elegant surroundings and efficient, friendly service. Most of the favourites are on the menu, plus less usual dishes like courgettes stuffed with rice, lamb with avgolemono sauce or fried chicken with banana and aubergines, as well as seasonal specials such as suprême of hare smitane. Simple grills, too. *Credit* Access, Amex, Barclaycard, Diners

Lunch 12.30–2.30 *Dinner* 6.30–10.30
Closed Sat, Sun, Bank Holidays, 3 weeks August & 1 week Christmas

Any person using our name to obtain free hospitality is a fraud. Proprietors, please inform the police and us.

Map 22 B2
90 Lancaster Gate *W2 3NR*
01–262 2711
Telex 23922

Credit Access, Amex,
Barclaycard, Diners
✆ Tube Lancaster Gate

White's Hotel   57%   £ C/D

Front bedrooms with balconies overlooking Kensington Gardens are a feature of this handsome, white-painted Victorian hotel, popular with businessmen as well as tourists. Comfortable, roomy lounge areas flank the reception desk, and there's a smart little cocktail bar. Cheerful, good-sized bedrooms (most with mini-bars) have practical built-in furniture, attractive brocade bedspreads and simple tiled bathrooms.

Rooms 61
with bath/shower 61

| *Room phone* Yes | *Confirm by* 6 | *Parking* Limited |
| *Room TV* Yes | *Last dinner* 10.15 | *Banquets* 50/2 |

Map 23 D4
1 Wilbraham Place
Sloane Street *SW1X 9AE*
01–730 8296
Proprietors
Monique von Kospoth &
L. E. S. Ffytche
✆ Tube Sloane Square

Wilbraham Hotel   55% Ⓜ   £ D

Three handsome Victorian terraced houses make up this pleasant, privately owned hotel, which manages to recapture some of the style and quiet charm of days gone by. Modest public rooms include two peaceful lounges and a cosy panelled bar; three fine oak staircases lead to the individually styled bedrooms, some of them quite small, which are tastefully decorated and furnished. Bathrooms are neat and tidy. No dogs.

Rooms 50
with bath/shower 36

| *Room phone* Yes | *Confirm by* 6 | *Parking* Difficult |
| *Room TV* Some | *Last dinner* 9.45 | |

Map 21 A6
96 Felsham Road *SW15 1DQ*
01–789 3323

Proprietor
Commander R. Herbert Smith

About £26 for two
Banquets 28/–
✆ Buses 14, 22, 30, 39, 74, 85, 93, 220, 264

Wild Thyme

Among the closely packed tables of this bustling bistro, Commander Herbert Smith enthusiastically explains the inventive and unusual menu to his customers. Starters like mushrooms stuffed with brains and main courses such as noisette de chevreuil or gougère de dinde are prepared with skill and imagination, and there are some delicious desserts, including rhubarb brûlée and iced honey cheesecake. *Credit* Access, Barclaycard

Lunch 12–2.30 *Dinner* 7.30–11
Closed L Sat, all Sun, 2 days Easter, 2 weeks August & 5 days Christmas

Map 23 B5
140 Fulham Road *SW10 9PY*
01–373 5534

Proprietor George Tabet

About £24 for two
✆ Buses 14, 45

William F

It's best to book at this informal little restaurant, where the Lebanese owner-chef prepares a range of tasty, mainly French-style dishes. Starters vary from simple avocado with prawns to an excellent croustade de saumon Thermidor, while main courses include moussaka, fish pie and a perfectly prepared lamb steak with fennel stuffing and red wine sauce. Fresh vegetables are flavoursome and desserts tempting.

Dinner only 6–12
Closed Sun, Good Friday & 25 & 26 December

Map 25 B4
27 Bury Street *SW1Y 6AL*
01–930 8391

Manager Mrs L. Marks
English cooking

About £50 for two
⊖ Tube Green Park

Wilton's ♛♛ Ⓢ

Very much an institution, this plush, well-ordered dining room behind an oyster bar is a bastion of traditional English cooking, presided over by soberly dressed, long-serving staff. The choicest raw materials are used for basically simple dishes like dressed crab, York ham, chump chops and roast woodcock, and the oysters are superb. Fresh fruit, cheese and savouries on toast complete the picture. *Credit* Amex, Diners

Lunch 12.30–2.30 *Dinner* 6.30–10.30
Closed D Fri, all Sat & Sun, Bank Holidays & 23 July–16 August

Map 24 B3
16 Beak Street *W1R 3HA*
01–437 2236
Proprietor Miss Y. Fujii
Japanese cooking

● **Set D** from £12
About £65 for two
Banquets 20/–
⊖ Buses 3, 6, 12, 13, 15, 23, 53, 88, 159

Yamaju ♛♛ Ⓢ

This beautiful restaurant is a study in simple sophistication, and the cooking has all the delicate artistry and finesse of authentic Japanese cuisine. Sit shoeless in one of the intimate private dining rooms and enjoy a leisurely set dinner of five, seven or nine courses which will both delight the eye and excite the palate. Smiling waitresses serve with tact, charm and discretion. *Credit* Access, Amex, Barclaycard, Diners

Dinner only 6–10.30
Closed Sun, Bank Holidays & 10 days Christmas

Map 23 A4
Troy Court
222 Kensington High Street
W8 7RG
01–937 8938
Manager Mr Tom Leung
Chinese cooking
Set meals from £6·50
About £20 for two
Banquets 40/12
⊖ Tube High Street Kensington

Yangtze ♛ Ⓢ

A bright, comfortable Chinese restaurant, where special set menus allow diners to sample a wide variety of enjoyable Pekinese dishes. There's also a lengthy à la carte (including a few Cantonese items), and our excellent meal included stuffed crab claws, tasty pork dumplings and nicely sauced sliced duck with Chinese mushrooms. Jasmine tea is a refreshing accompaniment. *Credit* Access, Amex, Barclaycard, Diners

Lunch 12–2.45, Sat noon–11.15pm, Sun noon–10.45pm *Dinner* 6–11.15
Closed 25 & 26 December

Gatwick Hilton International   76%   *E*   Ⓜ   £C

Map 7 B5 Surrey
Horley *RH6 0LL*
Gatwick (0293) 518080
Telex 877021

Rooms 333
with bath/shower 333
Room phone Yes
Room TV Yes
Confirm by 6
Last dinner 11
Parking Ample
Banquets 350/10

Credit Access, Amex,
Barclaycard, Diners

Built within the airport perimeter, this ultra-modern concrete and glass hotel is linked by covered walkway to the terminals. Public areas on two floors include a spacious lobby with a relaxing lounge-bar, the pubby Jockey Bar and numerous function rooms. There's also a health club and a comprehensively equipped secretarial and courier service. Well-lit, double-glazed bedrooms with smart fitted units are full of up-to-the-minute features such as individual climate control, electronic doorlocks and flight information on the TV screens. Roomy, tiled bathrooms have excellent fittings. *Amenities* sauna, indoor swimming pool, gymnasium, in-house movies, 24-hour lounge service, hairdressing.   &

Gatwick Moat House   58%   £D

Map 7 B5 Surrey
Longbridge Roundabout
Horley *RH6 0AB*
Horley (029 34) 5599
Telex 877138

Credit Access, Amex,
Barclaycard, Diners

New owners have taken over this modern hotel, formerly called the Europa Lodge. Public areas are on the first floor and include a 1930s-style bar, a coffee shop and a lounge. Simple, well-kept bedrooms are air-conditioned and double-glazed; bathrooms are spotless.
Amenities 24-hour laundry service, in-house movies, long-term parking, transport for airport.   &

| *Rooms* 120 | *Room phone* Yes | *Confirm by* 6 | *Parking* Ample |
| *with bath/shower* 120 | *Room TV* Yes | *Last dinner* 9.45 | *Banquets* 180/– |

Gatwick Penta Hotel   73%   *E*   £C/D

Map 7 B5 Surrey
Povey Cross Road
Horley *RH6 0BE*
Horley (029 34) 5533
Telex 87440

Rooms 260
with bath/shower 260
Room phone Yes
Room TV Yes
Confirm by 6
Last dinner 11
Parking Ample
Banquets 180/–

Credit Access, Amex,
Barclaycard, Diners

Designed with the business executive as well as the tourist in mind, this modern, rectangular brick building has numerous self-contained function rooms. The spacious reception lounge with its shining marble floor and square pillars is sleek and luxurious, while the Brighton Belle Bar, which evokes a nostalgic atmosphere enhanced by old railway mementoes, has French windows opening out on to an attractive terrace. Large, double-glazed bedrooms are well equipped, with darkwood fitted units, and some of the more elegant study rooms also have fridges and trouser presses. Ultra-modern bathrooms are spotlessly clean.
Amenities garden, transport for airport, in-house movies.

Post House Hotel   62%   £C/D

Map 7 B5 Surrey
Povey Cross Road
Horley *RH6 0VA*
Horley (029 34) 71621
Telex 877351

Credit Access, Amex,
Barclaycard, Diners

A stone's throw from the passenger terminals, this five-storey hotel with its own pool offers very comfortable accommodation. Bedrooms all have colour TV, tea/coffee-makers and mini-bars and many have been smartly refurbished. There's a relaxing lounge and a welcoming bar in traditional style.
Amenities garden, outdoor swimming pool, coffee shop (10.30am–11pm), transport for airport, 24-hour laundry service.   &

| *Rooms* 149 | *Room phone* Yes | *Confirm by* 7 | *Parking* Ample |
| *with bath/shower* 149 | *Room TV* Yes | *Last dinner* 10.30 | *Banquets* 40/– |

Map 7 B5 West Sussex
Lowfield Heath
Crawley *RH11 0PQ*
Crawley (0293) 33441
Telex 87287

Credit Access, Amex,
Barclaycard, Diners

Saxon Inn   67%   **£ D**

Formerly the Gatwick Hickmet, this modern hotel is now under new ownership. Statues and plants give the pink-carpeted reception a distinctive style, which continues in the smart open-plan lounge and the sleek panelled bar. Double-glazed bedrooms have coordinated fabrics, whitewood furniture and well-designed bathrooms. There's also a luxurious honeymoon suite. *Amenities* transport for airport, 24-hour laundry service (Mon–Fri).

| *Rooms* 94 | *Room phone* Yes | *Confirm by* 6 | *Parking* Ample |
| *with bath/shower* 94 | *Room TV* Yes | *Last dinner* 10.30 | *Banquets* 100/– |

HEATHROW AIRPORT

Map 5 E2 Middlesex
Bath Road, Hayes *UB3 5AJ*
01–759 2552   Telex 21777
Manager Mr J. Fitzgerald
Credit Access, Amex,
Barclaycard, Diners
⊖ Buses 81, 98, 105, 111, 140, 222, 285

Ariel Hotel   58%   **£ C**

Built around an attractive patio in a distinctive circular design, this four-storey hotel offers pleasant and comfortable facilities. Open-plan public areas include a spacious reception-lounge, a cocktail bar and the pub-like Circle Bar which overlooks the patio. Well-equipped bedrooms (including some studio-style) have plenty of storage space and compact, fully tiled bathrooms. *Amenities* patio, transport for airport.

| *Rooms* 178 | *Room phone* Yes | *Confirm by* 6 | *Parking* Ample |
| *with bath/shower* 178 | *Room TV* Yes | *Last dinner* 10.30 | *Banquets* 40/– |

Our inspectors never book in the name of the Egon Ronay Organisation; they disclose their identity only after paying their bills.

Map 5 E2 Middlesex
Bath Road, Cranford *TW5 9QE*
01–897 2121
Telex 935728
Manager Mr T. C. Bruce
Credit Access, Amex,
Barclaycard, Diners
⊖ Buses 81, 105, 110, 111, 222

Berkeley Arms Hotel   62%   **£ D**

On the A4 two miles east of the airport, this turreted hotel has a delightful garden containing a dovecote. The comfortable lounge has pleasant views and there is a welcoming, softly lit cocktail bar. Neatly fitted, double-glazed bedrooms have radio-alarms, tea/coffee-makers and well-fitted bathrooms. *Amenities* garden, transport for airport, 12-hour laundry service (Mon–Fri). **Closed** 25 & 26 December

| *Rooms* 42 | *Room phone* Yes | *Confirm by* 6 | *Parking* Ample |
| *with bath/shower* 42 | *Room TV* Yes | *Last dinner* 10.15 | *Banquets* 80/– |

Map 5 E2 Middlesex
Bath Road
West Drayton *UB7 0DU*
01–759 6611
Telex 24525
Credit Access, Amex,
Barclaycard, Diners
⊖ Buses 81, 105, 222

Excelsior Hotel   66%   **£ C**

A smart foyer-lounge and three convivial bars provide ample scope for relaxation at this vast hotel on the A4, while more active guests will enjoy the new health and fitness centre. Well-designed, air-conditioned bedrooms have pleasing soft colour schemes and excellent bathrooms. *Amenities* garden, sauna, outdoor swimming pool, transport for airport, health centre, solarium, hairdressing, coffee shop (24 hours).   ♿

| *Rooms* 662 | *Room phone* Yes | *Confirm by* 6 | *Parking* Ample |
| *with bath/shower* 662 | *Room TV* Yes | *Last dinner* 10.45 | *Banquets* 600/– |

Map 5 E2
Bath Road, Hounslow *TW6 2AQ*
01–897 6363
Telex 934660

Rooms 670
with bath/shower 670
Room phone Yes
Room TV Yes
Confirm by 6
Last dinner 10.30
Parking Ample
Banquets 500/–
Credit Access, Amex,
Barclaycard, Diners

✆ Buses 81, 98, 105, 111,
140, 222, 285

Heathrow Penta Hotel   70%   *E*   £ C

It's a short walk from the passenger terminal to this sophisticated concrete and glass building, where aviation buffs will feel at home in the Flying Machine Bar, which overlooks the main runway. The vast foyer-lounge is attractively furnished with black stone floor tiles, red armchairs and modern lighting systems. Bedrooms have all modern comforts, from double glazing and air conditioning to mini-bars and sparkling, well-equipped bathrooms. Excellent conference facilities.
Amenities sauna, indoor swimming pool, transport for airport, in-house movies, gymnasium, solarium, valeting, hairdressing, 24-hour laundry service, coffee shop (24 hours).   &

Map 5 E2 Middlesex
Stockley Road
West Drayton *UB7 9NA*
West Drayton (089 54) 45555
Telex 934518

Rooms 401
with bath/shower 401
Room phone Yes
Room TV Yes
Confirm by 6
Last dinner 10.30
Parking Ample
Banquets 100/8

Credit Access, Amex,
Barclaycard, Diners

✆ Bus 222

Holiday Inn   70%   *E*   £ C

Situated just off the M4, this friendly modern hotel has wide appeal with its extensive range of sports and conference facilities. Public areas include an attractive open-plan foyer, a mock-Tudor beamed bar and a pleasantly decorated coffee shop, with lots of plants throughout. Neat, double-glazed bedrooms have fitted units, large beds and trouser presses, plus compact well-equipped bathrooms.
Amenities garden, sauna, indoor swimming pool, tennis, 9-hole golf course, 12-hour laundry service, gymnasium, helipad, transport for airport, coffee shop (6.30am–midnight), in-house movies, solarium.   &

We welcome complaints and bona fide recommendations on the tear-out pages for readers' comments. They are followed up by our professional team. Please also complain to the management instantly.

Map 5 E2 Middlesex
366 Great West Road
Hounslow *TW5 0BA*
01–570 6261

Credit Access, Amex,
Barclaycard, Diners
✆ Tube Hounslow West

Rooms 63
with bath/shower 63

Master Robert Motel   55%   £ E

Situated on the Great West Road not far from Heathrow, this modern motel is popular with air travellers. Double-glazed bedrooms (six with spacious dressing rooms) are equipped with built-in units and tea-makers, and bathrooms are fully tiled. Public areas in a separate block include a plush cocktail bar and a traditional public bar. *Amenities* garden, coffee shop (7am–11pm), transport for airport.   &

| *Room phone* Yes | *Confirm by* 6 | *Parking* Ample |
| *Room TV* Yes | *Last dinner* 10.30 | *Banquets* 70/10 |

You may not know which restaurant you're going to yet, but you certainly know the best way to get there.

A little prestige and comfort did no business relationship any harm, so why not arrive and depart in style in a Godfrey Davis Chauffeur Driven car?

You can choose from the Granada saloon, the Dorchester Limousine, the Daimler Limousine or the Rolls-Royce saloon. Each one is driven by one of our team of highly qualified and experienced chauffeurs, all of which goes to make us Britain's largest and most prestigious chauffeur driven service. To reserve your chauffeur driven car phone 01-834 6701.

Map 5 E2 Middlesex
Sipson Road
West Drayton *UB70JU*
01–759 2323
Telex 934280
Credit Access, Amex,
Barclaycard, Diners
♿ Bus 222

Rooms 594
with bath/shower 594

Post House Hotel   58%   £ D

Standing conveniently close to the M4 and the airport, this large modern hotel has a pleasant, relaxed atmosphere. There's a smart, open-plan foyer and two attractive modern bars. Comfortable, double-glazed bedrooms are all uniform in style, with good fitted furniture and compact, fully tiled bathrooms.
Amenities transport for airport, helipad, buttery (11am–11pm).

Room phone Yes	*Confirm by* 6	*Parking* Ample
Room TV Yes	*Last dinner* 10.30	*Banquets* 166/10

Map 5 E2 Middlesex
West Drayton *UB70HJ*
01–759 2424
Telex 934331
Manager Mr Fred Wakelin

Rooms 440
with bath/shower 440
Room phone Yes
Room TV Yes
Confirm by 6
Last dinner 10.30
Parking Ample
Banquets 100/–

Credit Access, Amex,
Barclaycard, Diners

♿ Buses 81, 223

Sheraton-Heathrow Hotel   72% *E*   £ C

Geared towards the needs of the travelling business person, this concrete and glass hotel on the A4 boasts lavishly equipped conference and meeting rooms. Public areas, which include a relaxing lounge and a charming cocktail bar with intimate alcoves, have an air of modern luxury. Brightly decorated, double-glazed bedrooms are well fitted with excellent lighting, plenty of writing space and trouser presses. Bathrooms have good-quality fittings. There are also four executive suites.
Amenities garden, sauna, indoor swimming pool, transport for airport & London, coffee shop (6am–midnight), in-house movies, beauty salon, hairdressing. ♿

Map 5 E2 Middlesex
West Drayton *UB70HJ*
01–759 2424

Manager Mr Fred Wakelin

● Set L £6·80
About £35 for two
♿ Buses 81, 223

Sheraton-Heathrow Hotel, Ascot Grill   ♔ ⑤

Pictures of Ascot winners line the walls of this restful, intimate restaurant, where the chef successfully blends the adventurous with the familiar. Guests can choose dishes like boned roast duckling with a prune and Grand Marnier sauce or settle for prime beef carved from the trolley. The real highlight is perhaps the superb array of delectable sweets.
Credit Access, Amex, Barclaycard, Diners

Lunch 12–2.30 *Dinner* 7–11
Closed Bank Holidays (except Easter Monday & 25 December)

Map 5 E2 Middlesex
Bath Road, Hayes *UB35BP*
01–759 2535
Telex 934254

Rooms 355
with bath/shower 355
Room phone Yes
Room TV Yes
Confirm by 6
Last dinner 11
Parking Ample
Banquets 400/–

Sheraton Skyline   77% *E*   £ B/C

The indoor poolside garden with its luxuriant tropical plants is a popular attraction of this striking modern hotel on the A4, close to the airport

                                        Continued

Credit Access, Amex,
Barclaycard, Diners

⊖ Buses 81, 98, 105, 111, 140,
222, 285

entrance. There are nightly floor shows in Diamond Lil's Klondyke Saloon,
while the Colony Bar offers cosy Edwardian nostalgia. The double-glazed,
air-conditioned bedrooms, with their quality modern furnishings and pleasing spaciousness, are maintained to a high standard; some overlook the pool.
Spotless bathrooms are thoughtfully equipped, many with hairdryers.
Amenities patio, sauna, indoor swimming pool, dancing (nightly), transport
for airport & central London, hairdressing, shopping arcade, in-house
movies, coffee shop (6am–2am), 24-hour laundry service. &

Map 5 E2 Middlesex
Bath Road, Hayes *UB3 5BP*
01–759 2535
Manager Mr A. Gonzalez Rua

● **Set L & Set D** £14
About £42 for two
⊖ Buses 81, 98, 105, 111, 140,
222, 285

Sheraton Skyline, Colony Room 👑👑 Ⓢ

Beautifully finished dark mahogany enhances the sense of period splendour
in this sumptuously appointed restaurant. The lavish menu is full of
adventurous creations like broccoli terrine with fresh goose liver and
poached turbot with raspberries and cucumber, alongside simpler grills and
roasts, while the superb sweet trolley promises a glorious finale.
🍷 *ABOVE AVERAGE. Credit* Access, Amex, Barclaycard, Diners &

Lunch 12.30–2.30 *Dinner* 7–11, Fri & Sat 7–11.30
Closed L Sat & Sun, 1 January & 26 December

Map 5 E2 Middlesex
Bath Road, Hayes *UB3 5AW*
01–759 6311
Telex 23935
Credit Access, Amex,
Barclaycard, Diners
⊖ Buses 81, 98, 105, 111, 140,
222, 285

Skyway Hotel 62% £ C/D

Situated on the A4, not far from the airport, this low modern hotel has a
pleasant atmosphere. Public areas include a plant-filled foyer with a few
armchairs, an attractively decorated coffee lounge and a split-level bar. Neat
bedrooms have good-quality built-in units, well-coordinated soft furnishings and functional bathrooms. *Amenities* outdoor swimming pool,
transport for airport, coffee lounge (10.30am–midnight), hairdressing. &

Rooms 445	*Room phone* Yes	*Confirm by* 6	*Parking* Ample
with bath/shower 445	*Room TV* Yes	*Last dinner* 10	*Banquets* 275/10

Carlsberg
LAGER DE LUXE
What to expect when you ask
the best wine waiters for lager.

ENGLAND

Abberley

Map 10 B4 Hereford & Worcester
Near Worcester *WR6 6AT*
Great Witley (029 921) 666
Telex 337105
Manager Miss R. T. Mooney
Rooms 21
with bath/shower 21
Room phone Yes
Room TV Yes
Confirm by 6
Last dinner 9
Parking Ample
Banquets 40/–

Credit Access, Amex,
Barclaycard, Diners

Elms Hotel 76% £C

At the end of a tree-lined avenue in beautiful grounds (including a marvellous herb garden), this splendid Queen Anne house makes a most peaceful retreat. A spacious reception hall leads to the superbly furnished public rooms like the library bar, with its original mantelpiece and fine old mahogany bookcases, and the Gallery Room, which serves as a writing room. Spacious bedrooms are individually furnished with antiques and reproduction pieces, and they are fully equipped with everything from trouser presses to wall safes for jewellery. Large, carpeted bathrooms are equally well supplied and fitted.
Amenities garden, tennis, croquet, putting, 24-hour laundry service.

Abberley

Map 10 B4 Hereford & Worcester
Near Worcester *WR6 6AT*
Great Witley (029 921) 666
Manager Miss R. T. Mooney

● **Set L** £7·50, Sun £8·25
Set D from £12·50
About £37 for two

Elms Hotel, Brooke Room Restaurant ★ 

Chef Murdo McSween is now giving full rein to his culinary talents, and his ambitious menu is perfectly suited to the elegant surroundings of this lofty, Regency-style restaurant. Dishes like our superbly flavoured chicken mousse in pastry with a delicate tarragon sauce and poached salmon with incomparable hollandaise show a complete mastery of modern and classical cooking in the French style. Everything is prepared with the fullest attention to detail, and presentation is marvellous. Simpler dishes like fried plaice and cold meat salad at lunch time. **Specialities** terrine de coquilles St Jacques au beurre blanc, noisette de veau ciboulette.
ABOVE AVERAGE. Credit Access, Amex, Barclaycard, Diners

Lunch 1–2, Sun 12.30–2 *Dinner* 7.30–9

Acton Bridge

Map 10 B2 Cheshire
Near Northwich *CW8 3QB*
Weaverham (0606) 852310

Proprietors Watson family

● **Set L** £5, Sun £5·50
Set D from £7
About £23 for two
Banquets 114/17

Rheingold Riverside Inn 

Standing on the A49 alongside the river Weaver, this roomy, purpose-built restaurant has smart contemporary decor and a friendly, welcoming atmosphere. Stephen Watson offers a straightforward menu of carefully prepared dishes; grilled steaks are popular choices, and there are plenty of other favourites such as coq au vin, deep-fried scampi and barbecued loin of lamb. Fresh, crisp vegetables and an eyecatching sweet trolley.

Lunch 12–2 *Dinner* 7–9.30
Closed D Sun, all Mon, 25 December & 1 January

Alcester

Map 4 C1 Warwickshire
Stratford Road *B49 6LN*
Alcester (0789) 762505

Credit Access, Barclaycard

Cherrytrees Hotel 53% Ⓜ £E/F

This well-kept, welcoming motel just east of Alcester on the A422 offers comfortable accommodation arranged in a single storey around a courtyard. Chalet-style bedrooms panelled in varnished pine have a Scandinavian air, and are thickly carpeted, with attractive darkwood furniture and spacious, well-equipped bathrooms. In the main building there's a roomy open-plan bar-lounge. *Amenities* garden, dancing (Sat in winter).

| *Rooms* 22 | *Room phone* Yes | *Confirm by* 6 | *Parking* Ample |
| *with bath/shower* 22 | *Room TV* Yes | *Last dinner* 8.30 | *Banquets* 120/– |

Aldborough
Map 6 C1 Norfolk
Near Norwich *NR11 7AA*
Hanworth (026 376) 451

● **Set L** from £6·50
About £29 for two
Banquets 30/–

Old Red Lion   ♧ Ⓢ

The two young partners put a tremendous amount of thought and care into every aspect of the decor and food in this attractive red-brick building alongside the village green. Superbly fresh ingredients, subtle sauces and unusual combinations of flavours are evident in dishes like crab claws in a herby mustard sauce and pigeon breast with a sauce of spinach purée, cream and tomatoes. Interesting vegetables and excellent light sweets.

Lunch 12.30–2.30 *Dinner* 7–9
Closed D Sun, all Mon, 25 & 26 Dec, last 2 weeks Feb & last 2 weeks Oct

Aldeburgh
Map 6 D3 Suffolk
The Parade *IP15 5BU*
Aldeburgh (072 885) 2071

Credit Access, Amex,
Barclaycard, Diners

Rooms 47
with bath/shower 47

Brudenell Hotel   58%   £ D

In fine weather guests can gaze out over the North Sea from the patio of this modernised Victorian hotel, which caters well for family holidays. Bright, pleasantly decorated public rooms all have large picture windows, and there are fine views, too, from many of the spacious bedrooms, which are furnished in attractive contemporary style. *Amenities* patio, sea fishing, board sailing, boat trips, bicycles, table tennis.   ♿

Room phone Yes	*Confirm by* 6	*Parking* Ample
Room TV Yes	*Last dinner* 9	*Banquets* 30/–

Aldeburgh
Map 6 D3 Suffolk
Victoria Road *IP15 5DX*
Aldeburgh (072 885) 2420

Credit Access, Amex,
Barclaycard, Diners
Closed February

Rooms 19
with bath/shower 7

Uplands Hotel   55%   Ⓜ   £ E

Once the home of physician and feminist Elizabeth Garrett Anderson, this attractive Queen Anne house is now a cosy, welcoming hotel. A small entrance hall leads to the neatly furnished cocktail bar, and there's a homely, old-fashioned residents' lounge with colour TV. Bedrooms in the house are traditional in style, while seven modern chalets in the garden have traditional fittings and private bathrooms. *Amenities* garden.   ♿

Room phone No	*Confirm by* 6	*Parking* Ample
Room TV Some	*Last dinner* 9	

Aldeburgh
Map 6 D3 Suffolk
IP15 5BD
Aldeburgh (072 885) 2312

Proprietor Mr Michael Pritt
Credit Diners
Closed January

Rooms 33
with bath/shower 20

Wentworth Hotel   60%   Ⓜ   £ D/E

The Pritt family have run this welcoming hotel beside the beach since the 1920s. Downstairs are two lounges, one chintzy and traditional, the other modern with sea views through wide windows. There's also a cosy little bar. Bedrooms have pretty wallpapers and fabrics. Private bathrooms are thoroughly up to date, while public ones are perfectly adequate. *Amenities* garden.

Room phone Some	*Confirm by* 6	*Parking* Limited
Room TV No	*Last dinner* 8.45	*Banquets* 100/50

Aldeburgh
Map 6 D3 Suffolk
IP15 5BD
Aldeburgh (072 885) 2312
Proprietor Mr Michael Pritt

● **Set L** £5 **Set D** £6·75
About £27 for two

Wentworth Hotel Restaurant   Ⓢ

White linen creates a formal effect in this bright modern dining room overlooking the sea. Fish is the obvious choice here—beautifully fresh cod in a mushroom and white wine sauce or juicy local prawns with aïoli. The frequently changed menu also offers tempting meat dishes, including grills and local game. Cooking is very capable, and sauces are notably tasty.
Credit Diners

Lunch 12.30–2 *Dinner* 7.30–8.45
Closed L Mon–Fri in winter & January

Alderley Edge
Map 10 B2 Cheshire
Macclesfield Road *SK9 7BJ*
Alderley Edge (0625) 583033

Credit Access, Amex,
Barclaycard, Diners

Edge Hotel   57%   £ E

Three acres of garden surround this Victorian mansion which has pleasant views over the town. Inside are two bars, including a large, plush cocktail bar. Bedrooms in both the main house and the newer extension are comfortably furnished in modern style with shag-pile carpets and duvets. There's also a honeymoon suite with a four-poster. Private bathrooms are especially colourful. *Amenities* garden.

Continued

Continued
Rooms 26
with bath/shower 21   *Room phone* Yes   *Confirm by* By arrang.   *Parking* Ample
    Room TV Yes   *Last dinner* 9.45   *Banquets* 60/10

Alderley Edge   Le Rabelais   Ⓢ

Map 10 B2 Cheshire
75 London Road *SK9 7DY*
Alderley Edge (0625) 584848

French cooking

A change in owners has not affected the high standards of French cuisine offered at this elegant first-floor restaurant. Prime ingredients are used for an interesting choice of skilfully prepared dishes like fillet of sole in pastry with a creamy Chablis sauce, veal normande and duck bourguignonne. Vegetables are good, and sweets include an authentic, full-flavoured French apple tart. *Credit* Access, Amex, Diners

About £27 for two

Lunch 12–2 *Dinner* 7–10, Sat 7–10.30
Closed L Mon & Sat, all Sun & 25 & 26 December

Alfold Crossways   Chez Jean   ⌘ Ⓢ

Map 5 E3 Surrey
Near Cranleigh *GU6 8JE*
Loxwood (0403) 752357
Proprietors M & Mme J. Clemaron
French cooking

Jean Clemaron, proprietor for 17 years, does the cooking, while his wife directs operations in the dining room with its central fireplace, warm red decor and velvet-covered chairs. Cooking is reliable and competent, with an ample choice of largely familiar French dishes, including moules marinière, mixed meat terrine, tournedos with subtle écrevisse sauce and some appealing sweets. *Credit* Access, Amex, Barclaycard, Diners   ♿

● **Set L** £4 **Set D** £7·30
About £30 for two

Lunch 12–1.45 *Dinner* 7–10
Closed D Sun, all Mon & Bank Holidays

Alfriston   Moonrakers   ⌘ Ⓢ

Map 7 B6 East Sussex
High Street *BN26 5TD*
Alfriston (0323) 870472

New owners Elaine and Barry Wilkinson provide a warm welcome in this cosy little high street restaurant with beams and low ceilings. Elaine's simple three-course menu changes monthly and includes dishes such as watercress soup, tasty lamb cassoulet and tenderloin of pork with black cherry and redcurrant sauce, all prepared from good-quality raw materials. Finish with meringue or lemon cheesecake. *ABOVE AVERAGE.*

● **Set D** £9·75
About £28 for two

Dinner only 7–9.45
Closed Sun, Mon, 1 January, 25 December & 11 January–14 February

---

Alnwick   Hotspur Hotel   55%   Ⓜ   £E

Map 14 B3 Northumberland
Bondgate Without *NE66 1PR*
Alnwick (0665) 602924
Proprietors
Mr & Mrs G. M. Williamson
Credit Access, Barclaycard
Closed Christmas

This old stone house, which stands a short walk away from the centre of town, has been much extended over the years. Bedrooms in two wings are neat and modern, and bathrooms are warm, clean and adequately fitted. Locals and residents meet in the cheerful first-floor Harry's Bar, which has a fine collection of toby jugs, and there are two peaceful lounges, including one with TV.

Rooms 28
with bath/shower 18   *Room phone* Yes   *Confirm by* 6   *Parking* Ample
    Room TV No   *Last dinner* 9

Alnwick   White Swan Hotel   63%   £E

Map 14 B3 Northumberland
Bondgate Within *NE66 1TD*
Alnwick (0665) 602109

Credit Access, Amex,
Barclaycard, Diners

This coaching inn stands in the town centre. There's a roomy cocktail bar and a cosy residents' lounge, but the outstanding public room is the ballroom, with magnificent carved panelling from the *Titanic*'s sister ship. Bedrooms are attractively decorated (traditional ones in the original building, modern in the extension), and bathrooms are well kept. *Amenities* garden, dancing (monthly in winter), buttery (10am–7pm, 10am–5.30pm in winter)

Rooms 41
with bath/shower 40   *Room phone* Yes   *Confirm by* 6   *Parking* Ample
    Room TV Yes   *Last dinner* 9   *Banquets* 140/–

Egon Ronay's...
pub dish of the year

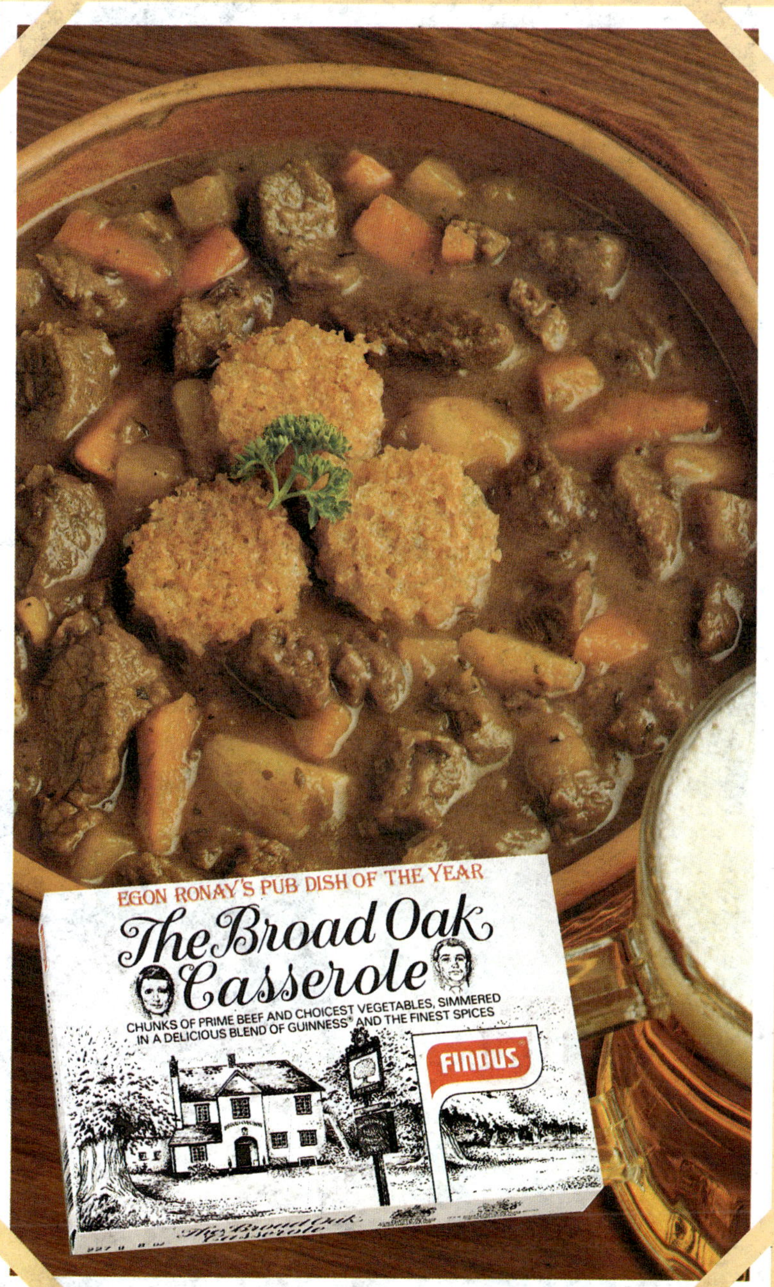

EGON RONAY'S PUB DISH OF THE YEAR
The Broad Oak
Casserole
CHUNKS OF PRIME BEEF AND CHOICEST VEGETABLES, SIMMERED
IN A DELICIOUS BLEND OF GUINNESS® AND THE FINEST SPICES
FINDUS

A Great British favourite

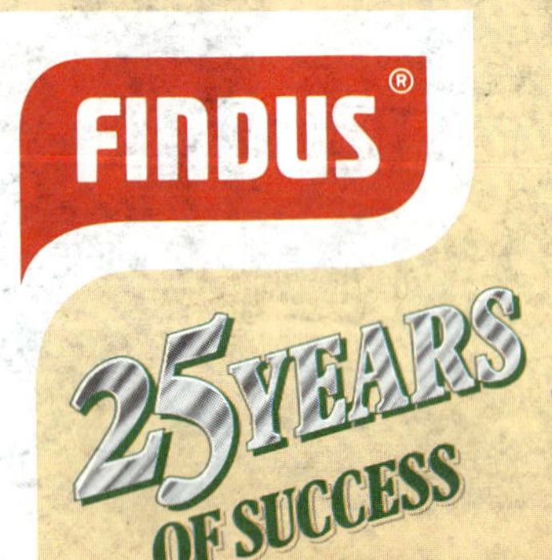

Alsager

Map 10 B3 Cheshire
Audley Road
Near Stoke-on-Trent *ST7 2QQ*
Alsager (093 63) 78013

Credit Access, Amex,
Barclaycard, Diners

Rooms 9
with bath/shower 9

Manor House *(Inn)* £E

Originally a group of farm buildings, this comfortable inn still retains some original brickwork and beams, which blend pleasantly with modern fittings in the large lounge and cosy upstairs cocktail bar. Bedrooms are compact and nicely appointed, with mahogany furniture and pretty floral fabrics. Bathrooms (showers only) are spotlessly clean and well equipped.

Room phone Yes	*Confirm by* By arrang.	*Parking* Ample
Room TV Yes	*Last dinner* 9.30	*Banquets* 35/15

Alston

Map 13 D4 Cumbria
Hexham Road *CA9 3JX*
Alston (0498) 81230

Closed 31 October–end April

Rooms 11
with bath/shower 8

Lowbyer Manor Hotel   55%   Ⓜ   £E

Pleasantly situated among the moors and fells of the North Pennines, this converted 17th-century manor house provides simple comforts in cheerful surroundings. Residents can relax in the large TV lounge or choose the more rustic atmosphere of the small bar. Compact bedrooms (including some newer ones in converted outbuildings) have practical modern units and adequate bathrooms. No dogs. *Amenities* garden.

Room phone No	*Confirm by* 6	*Parking* Ample
Room TV No	*Last dinner* 8.15	*Banquets* 20/–

Alton

Map 5 D3 Hampshire
Holybourne *GU34 4EG*
Alton (0420) 86565

Credit Access, Amex,
Barclaycard, Diners

Rooms 10
with bath/shower 10

Grange Hotel   60%   Ⓜ   £E

Small is comfortable at this inviting, well-run hotel, a nicely converted period house just outside town. All the public areas – lounge, bar and function room – are modest in size, with attractive decor and smart furnishings that make them most appealing. Cottagy bedrooms, with simple, freestanding furniture and neat pleated curtains, have compact, adequately equipped bathrooms. *Amenities* garden, badminton, putting.

Room phone Yes	*Confirm by* By arrang.	*Parking* Ample
Room TV Yes	*Last dinner* 9.15	*Banquets* 30/–

Alton

Map 5 D3 Hampshire
High Street *GU34 1AT*
Alton (0420) 83777
Telex 858875
Manager Mr J. H. Dewey
Credit Access, Amex,
Barclaycard, Diners

Rooms 38
with bath/shower 38

Swan Hotel   63%   £E

With a history stretching back to the 16th century, this former coaching inn still retains echoes of the past, while providing good modern facilities. Downstairs there are two distinctive bars and an elegant lounge, where a huge old clock provides character. Comfortable bedrooms with radios and tea-makers are stylishly fitted out with reproduction furniture, and attractive bathrooms are well equipped.

Room phone Yes	*Confirm by* 6	*Parking* Ample
Room TV Yes	*Last dinner* 9.15	*Banquets* 65/20

Altrincham

Map 10 B2 Greater Manchester
Langham Road,
Bowdon *WA14 2HT*
061–928 8825
Manager Mr Bernard Kilcoyne
Credit Access, Amex,
Barclaycard, Diners

Rooms 41
with bath/shower 38

Bowdon Hotel   58%   £D/E

An extension to this large Victorian mansion provides excellent conference and banqueting facilities, as well as comfortable accommodation. Both the original and the new bedrooms are fitted to the same standard, with neat built-in units and colourful patterned wallpapers; bathrooms are very well equipped. The small lounge and bar are smartly furnished in contemporary style. *Amenities* dancing (Sat).

Room phone Yes	*Confirm by* 6	*Parking* Ample
Room TV Yes	*Last dinner* 10	*Banquets* 100/15

Our inspectors never book in the name of the Egon Ronay Organisation; they disclose their identity only after paying their bills.

Altrincham
Map 10 B2 Greater Manchester
Church Street *WA14 4DP*
061–928 8017
Telex 667242
Manager Mr David Roe
Credit Access, Amex,
Barclaycard, Diners

Rooms 135
with bath/shower 135

Cresta Court Hotel   55%   Ⓜ   £E

Conferences are a speciality at this modern brick-built hotel, whose prominent position on the A56 near the town centre make it convenient for businessmen and travellers alike. There's a small residents' lounge and three relaxing bars, and smartly furnished, double-glazed bedrooms have tea-makers, trouser presses, good writing space and neat, well-equipped bathrooms. *Amenities* 12-hour laundry service.

Room phone Yes	*Confirm by* 6	*Parking* Ample
Room TV Yes	*Last dinner* 11	*Banquets* 350/–

Altrincham
Map 10 B2 Greater Manchester
22 Manchester Road *WA14 4PH*
061–928 9933

Credit Access, Amex,
Barclaycard, Diners

Rooms 50
with bath/shower 46

George & Dragon Hotel   58%   £E

Situated in the centre of town alongside the A56, this well-kept hotel is convenient for travellers. A carpeted reception leads to the smart cocktail bar and the comfortable lounge bar; there's also a popular public bar. Neatly equipped bedrooms vary from freshly decorated ones in the original building to compact fitted ones in the extension. Most now have spotlessly clean bath or shower rooms.

Room phone Yes	*Confirm by* 6	*Parking* Ample
Room TV Yes	*Last dinner* 9.45	*Banquets* 60/10

Alveston
Map 4 B2 Avon
Near Bristol *BS12 2LJ*
Thornbury (0454) 415050
Telex 449683

Credit Access, Barclaycard

Rooms 16
with bath/shower 16

Alveston House Hotel   55%   £E

This distinctive white Georgian house with an annexe stands high in its pleasant garden alongside the A38. Public rooms are modestly furnished, and there are well-equipped conference facilities. Bedrooms of varying sizes have functional built-in units and tea/coffee-makers. Some bathrooms have showers only, but there is a large public bathroom for those who prefer a bath tub. No dogs. *Amenities* garden.

Room phone Yes	*Confirm by* 6	*Parking* Ample
Room TV Yes	*Last dinner* 9.30	*Banquets* 75/50

Alveston
Map 4 B2 Avon
Thornbury Road *BS12 2LL*
Thornbury (0454) 412521
Telex 444753

Credit Access, Amex,
Barclaycard, Diners

Rooms 75
with bath/shower 75

Post House Hotel   60%   £D

Modern wings blend surprisingly well with the genuine Tudor inn at the heart of this hotel just off the A38. Locals favour the public bar, and the Old Ship Bar is plush and comfortable. Glassed-in corridors lead to neat, functional bedrooms with simple bathrooms. Cricket fans can have rooms overlooking W. G. Grace's home ground. *Amenities* garden, outdoor swimming pool, dinner dance (Sat November–March), putting.

Room phone Yes	*Confirm by* 6	*Parking* Ample
Room TV Yes	*Last dinner* 10.15	*Banquets* 100/–

Amberley
Map 4 B2 Gloucestershire
Near Stroud *GL5 5AF*
Amberley (045 387) 2565

Manager Mrs Sue Ash
Credit Access, Amex,
Barclaycard

Rooms 16
with bath/shower 5

Amberley Inn   56%   £E

A programme of improvements is under way at this solid stone-built inn perched high up in the Cotswolds. Central heating has been installed, and many of the homely, unpretentious bedrooms have been redecorated. There are five rooms in the charming cottage annexe. Public rooms include a quaint little reception area, a cosy panelled bar-lounge and a residents' lounge with TV. *Amenities* garden.

Room phone Yes	*Confirm by* By arrang.	*Parking* Ample
Room TV No	*Last dinner* 9.30	*Banquets* 30/4

Ambleside
Map 13 D5 Cumbria
Borrans Road *LA22 0EN*
Ambleside (096 63) 3476
Proprietor Roger Stones

About £34 for two

Galava Gate   ⚘ Ⓢ

The Stones provide a warm welcome at their cosy, rustic little restaurant on the site of a Roman fort. Enthusiastically prepared dishes range from a creamy pâté to a tasty marinade of pigeon and attractive sweets.
Lunch Sun only 12–2.30 *Dinner* 7.15–10 **Closed** Sun October–June
● **Set L** £5 **Set D** £13 *Banquets* 30/–

Ambleside

Map 13 D5 Cumbria
Kirkstone Pass Road *LA22 9EH*
Ambleside (096 63) 2232
Proprietors Mr & Mrs Bateman
Credit Access, Amex,
Barclaycard, Diners
Closed 1 November–25 March

Rooms 12
with bath/shower 12

Kirkstone Foot Country House Hotel   61%   Ⓜ £F

Originally a manor house, this pretty whitewashed hotel is enthusiastically run by Jane and Simon Bateman. Public rooms, which include a cosy bar and a comfortable residents' lounge, have a traditional welcoming atmosphere, while bedrooms are bright and cheerful, with simple modern furniture and patterned wallpaper. Compact carpeted bathrooms. Inclusive terms only. No dogs. *Amenities* garden, croquet

Room phone No	*Confirm by* 5.30	*Parking* Ample
Room TV No	*Last dinner* 8	

Ambleside

Map 13 D5 Cumbria
Kirkstone Pass Road *LA22 9EH*
Ambleside (096 63) 2232
Proprietors Mr & Mrs Bateman
English cooking

● **Set D** £8·25
About £24 for two

Kirkstone Foot Country House Hotel Rest.   ♧ Ⓢ

Jane Bateman's cooking has a traditional English flavour, and her five-course dinner menu (no choice except for pudding and cheese) is highly enjoyable. You might begin with pears Marie Rose followed by a soup such as cream of turkey and leek. The main course is usually a roast, while to finish there's the sweet trolley and a varied English cheeseboard.
Credit Access, Amex, Barclaycard, Diners

Dinner only at 8
Closed 1 November–25 March

Ambleside

Map 13 D5 Cumbria
Rothay Bridge *LA22 0EH*
Ambleside (096 63) 3605
Proprietors Mrs Bronwen Nixon &
Messrs Nigel & Stephen Nixon
Rooms 12
with bath/shower 12
Room phone Yes
Room TV Yes
Confirm by By arrang.
Last dinner 9
Parking Ample
Banquets 40/6
Closed mid January–
early February
Credit Amex, Diners

Rothay Manor   70%   Ⓜ   £C

A friendly, civilised atmosphere prevails at this attractive Regency house, which stands in colourful, secluded grounds just half a mile from Lake Windermere. Inside all is traditional grace and elegance, and the two drawing rooms, with their comfortable sofas and armchairs, are ideal settings for a relaxing drink or a superb afternoon tea. Bright, cheerful bedrooms (some with large balconies) have good-quality furnishings and lots of thoughtful touches like fresh fruit and iced water, as well as hairdryers and sewing kits. Up-to-date carpeted bathrooms are also lavishly equipped. *Amenities* garden, croquet, 24-hour laundry service.

Ambleside

Map 13 D5 Cumbria
Rothay Bridge *LA22 0EH*
Ambleside (096 63) 3605
Proprietors
Mrs Bronwen Nixon &
Messrs Nigel & Stephen Nixon

● **Set L** Sun only £6·50
Set D £13
About £34 for two

Rothay Manor Restaurant   ♧ ♔ Ⓢ

Five-course dinners are prepared with skill and flair at this charming restaurant, where friendly, courteous service is an additional delight. Pork and pepper terrine, creamy asparagus soup and traditional oxtail casserole are typical flavour-packed dishes, and there are some equally appealing desserts and prime English cheeses. Buffet lunch except Sunday. No smoking in dining room. ♟ *SUPERIOR. Credit* Amex, Diners   ⓑ

Lunch 12.30–2 *Dinner* 7.30–9
Closed mid January–early February

Ambleside

Map 13 D5 Cumbria
Borrans Road *LA22 0EP*
Ambleside (096 63) 2332
Proprietors
J. D. & N. B. Scott
Credit Access
Closed November–March

Wateredge Hotel   58%   Ⓜ   £D

Converted from two pebbledash fishermen's cottages overlooking Lake Windermere, this charming hotel has a very homely atmosphere. Besides a beamed bar with exposed stone walls there are two cheerful lounges. Compact, smartly decorated bedrooms have a mixture of antique and modern furniture; half also have simple private bathrooms. Inclusive terms only in high season. *Amenities* garden, jetty, hotel boats.

Continued

Continued
Rooms 18
with bath/shower 9

| | **Room phone** No | **Confirm by** 5 | **Parking** Ample |
| | **Room TV** No | **Last dinner** 8 | **Banquets** 40/12 |

Ambleside

Map 13 D5 Cumbria
Borrans Road *LA22 0EP*
Ambleside (096 63) 2332
Proprietors J. D. & N. B. Scott

About £28 for two

Wateredge Hotel Restaurant ⓢ

Two beamed, candlelit dining rooms make a relaxing setting for Sally Collier's enjoyable five-course dinners, which might include wholesome pea and mint soup and carefully prepared pork fillet with a creamy mushroom sauce. Good sweets, too. *Credit* Access *Dinner only* 7–8
Closed November–March ● **Set D** £9·90

Ampfield

Map 5 D3 Hampshire
Near Romsey *SO5 9ZF*
Chandler's Ford (042 15) 66611

Manager Mr A. J. Flemming
Credit Access, Amex,
Barclaycard, Diners

Rooms 42
with bath/shower 42

Potters Heron Hotel   62%   £ E

This thatched and whitewashed pub, much extended, offers an agreeable and harmonious mixture of old and new. The Long Bar in the original part is solidly traditional, with heavy beams and gleaming copperware, while the spacious foyer-lounge is strikingly modern, a charming blend of exposed brickwork and polished pine, with comfortable armchairs. Bedrooms and bathrooms are cheerful, contemporary and sparklingly clean. *Amenities* garden.

| **Room phone** Yes | **Confirm by** 6 | **Parking** Ample |
| **Room TV** Yes | **Last dinner** 10 | **Banquets** 150/10 |

Andover

Map 4 C3 Hampshire
90 High Street *SP10 1NE*
Andover (0264) 64033

About £24 for two
Banquets 30/20

Forius   ♟ ⓢ

Young John Rolland obviously enjoys cooking, and delights customers with his skill and talent for invention. We began with cold stuffed peppers and a mild curry sauce, followed by delicious jugged duck in a creamy white wine sauce; vegetables were crisp and full of flavour, and a light home-made gâteau provided the perfect finish. The beamed 15th-century house makes a congenial setting. *Credit* Access, Barclaycard, Diners

Lunch 12–2 *Dinner* 7–10
Closed L Sat, all Sun, Bank Holidays & 2 weeks mid September

Andover

Map 4 C3 Hampshire
Bridge Street *SP10 1BH*
Andover (0264) 52266

Credit Access, Amex,
Barclaycard, Diners

Rooms 21
with bath/shower 21

White Hart Hotel *(Inn)*   £ E

A White Hart has stood on this town-centre site for more than 300 years and the present inn, a handsome red-brick and stone Georgian building, offers visitors a friendly welcome, comfortable accommodation and conscientious service. The beamed foyer-lounge and bar are warm and relaxing, and centrally heated bedrooms have pleasant floral wallpaper and contemporary furnishings. Well-fitted bathrooms.

| **Room phone** Yes | **Confirm by** 6 | **Parking** Limited |
| **Room TV** Yes | **Last dinner** 9.15 | **Banquets** 65/15 |

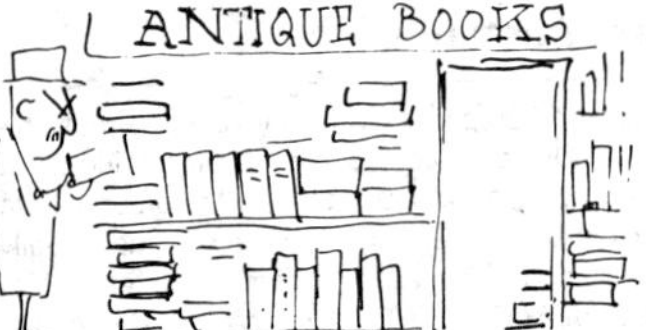

We publish annually, so make sure you use the current edition. It's worth it!

Andoversford

Map 4 C1 Gloucestershire
Shipton
Near Cheltenham *GL54 4HT*
Andoversford (024 282) 547
Proprietor Mr John Young
Credit Amex
Closed 25 December

Rooms 15
with bath/shower 7

Frogmill Inn *(Inn)* Ⓜ   £ E

Mellow stone walls, blackened beams and lattice windows preserve a sense of history in the bar of John Young's friendly inn, whose public rooms also include a residents' lounge with TV and extensive conference facilities in a harmonious modern extension. Cheerful, well-maintained bedrooms have attractive carpets and curtains and smart white furniture; adequately fitted bathrooms are equally bright. No dogs. *Amenities* garden.

| **Room phone** Yes | **Confirm by** 6 | **Parking** Ample |
| **Room TV** No | **Last dinner** 10 | **Banquets** 250/10 |

Arundel

Map 5 E4 West Sussex
High Street *BN18 9AD*
Arundel (0903) 882101

Credit Access, Amex,
Barclaycard, Diners

Rooms 35
with bath/shower 26

Norfolk Arms Hotel   59%   £ E

Built by the Duke of Norfolk in 1787, this coaching inn retains much of its original charm. Antiques abound in the public rooms, which include an elegant lounge and two cosy panelled bars. Comfortable, cheerfully appointed bedrooms range from some with four-posters to especially good ones with fitted modern units in the courtyard block. Well-equipped bathrooms. *Amenities* pool table, table tennis.

Room phone Yes	*Confirm by* 6	*Parking* Limited
Room TV Yes	*Last dinner* 10	*Banquets* 100/–

Ascot

Map 5 E2 Berkshire
Bagshot Road *SL5 9JA*
Ascot (0990) 23311
Telex 847707

Credit Access, Amex,
Barclaycard, Diners

Rooms 90
with bath/shower 90

Berystede Hotel   65%   £ C/D

This turreted Victorian building standing in wooded grounds has modern extensions housing its conference facilities and most of the bedrooms. The graceful reception hall doubles as a lounge, and there's a cosy bar. Bedrooms range from contemporary in the extension to more traditional in the original building. *Amenities* garden, outdoor swimming pool, dancing (Fri, Sat), putting, croquet, 24-hour laundry service, games room.

Room phone Yes	*Confirm by* 6	*Parking* Ample
Room TV Yes	*Last dinner* 10	*Banquets* 140/10

Ashburton

Map 3 D3 Devon
Tavistock Road *TQ13 7NS*
Poundsgate (036 43) 471
Proprietors
Mr & Mrs K. M. Bromage
Credit Access, Amex,
Barclaycard, Diners

Rooms 15
with bath/shower 10

Holne Chase Hotel   54%   Ⓜ   £ E

Homely, traditional comforts and a lovely, peaceful location are the main attractions of the Bromages' delightful old hunting lodge, which stands on the B3357 west of Ashburton. Log fires warm the cosy drawing room and pretty little lounge-bar, and simple bedrooms (three in an annexe) are modestly furnished. All have tea/coffee-making facilities. Shower and bathrooms are adequate. *Amenities* garden, game fishing.   &

Room phone Yes	*Confirm by* By arrang.	*Parking* Ample
Room TV No	*Last dinner* 8.30	*Banquets* 40/2

Ashford

Map 7 C5 Kent
Eastwell Park *TW25 4HR*
Ashford (0233) 35751
Telex 966281

Rooms 20
with bath/shower 20
Room phone Yes
Room TV Yes
Confirm by 6
Last dinner 9.30
Parking Ample
Banquets 25/4
Closed 25 December

Credit Access, Amex,
Barclaycard, Diners

Eastwell Manor   86%   Ⓜ   £ C

Built on a Saxon site, rebuilt and added to over the centuries, this palatial manor house is now a superbly comfortable and luxurious hotel, with housekeeping and service to match. Richly carved panelling, ornate plasterwork, mullioned windows and big open fireplaces recall the grandeur of bygone days in the public rooms, which are filled with massive chesterfields and relaxing armchairs. Vast bedrooms, individually decorated and furnished with elegant reproduction and period pieces, overlook the beautiful gardens; equally spacious bathrooms are sleek, modern and sumptuous. No children under seven. Dogs in kennels only.
Amenities garden, tennis, game fishing, croquet, snooker.   &

Ashford

Map 7 C5 Kent
Eastwell Park *TN25 4HR*
Ashford (0233) 35751

French cooking

Eastwell Manor Restaurant   ★   ♛ Ⓢ

The setting is classically English – a large open fireplace, fine panelling and stone-mullioned windows overlooking the beautifully laid-out gardens– but Ian McAndrew's imaginative menus are based firmly on French nouvelle cuisine. Scallop pâté, salmon trout with a cucumber and dill sauce and suprême of duck with raspberries are among dishes notable for their subtle,

Continued

Continued

● **Set L** £9 incl. service
About £46 for two

delicate flavours, light sauces and artistic presentation. Service is excellent, too. **Specialities** mousseline de saumon et champignons de bois, filet d'agneau sur lit d'artichauts, cœur de lotte au foie gras et basilic, soupe de cerises glacée à la menthe. 🍷 *SUPERIOR.*
Credit Access, Amex, Barclaycard, Diners

Lunch 12.30–2 *Dinner* 7.30–9.30
Closed D 25 December

Ashford

Map 5 E2 Middlesex
45 Church Road *TW15 2TY*
Ashford (078 42) 44887
Proprietors Attilio Cepollina
& Emanuele Maffi
Italian cooking

Terrazza ⓢ

Colourful displays of seafood and antipasti greet visitors to this cheerful trattoria, whose long menu makes excellent use of prime ingredients. Sauces are particularly successful–smooth mayonnaise with hors d'œuvre, delicate pesto with al dente spaghettini, creamy Marsala with veal. Vegetables are excellent and there's an alluring trolleyload of rich desserts. Charming, attentive service. *Credit* Access, Amex, Barclaycard

● **Set L** £5·70
About £32 for two

Lunch 12–2.30 *Dinner* 7–11
Closed L Sat, all Sun & Bank Holidays

Askham

Map 13 D5 Cumbria
Near Penrith *CA10 2PF*
Hackthorpe (093 12) 225

Queen's Head Inn *(Inn)* Ⓜ £E/F

For over 300 years this charming inn has been offering hospitality to travellers, and it is still noted for its really cosy atmosphere. The two bars are full of splendid collections of copper kettles and brass, and there's a luxurious lounge to relax in. Compact bedrooms are prettily decorated, and the two public bathrooms are excellent. John Askew's model railway is worth seeing. No children under five. No dogs.

Rooms 8
with bath/shower 1

Room phone No
Room TV No

Confirm by 6.30
Last dinner 8

Parking Ample
Banquets 42/10

Aston Clinton

Map 5 E2 Buckinghamshire
HP22 5HP
Aylesbury (0296) 630252
Telex 826715
Proprietor Mr Michael Harris
Rooms 21
with bath/shower 21
Room phone Yes
Room TV Yes
Confirm by By arrang.
Last dinner 9.45
Parking Ample
Banquets 250/–

Credit Access, Barclaycard

Bell Inn 73% Ⓜ £C/D

Charmingly run by the Harris family for more than 40 years, this attractive old coaching inn is a model of warmth and hospitality. A small, welcoming reception hall leads to the mellow bar with its flagstone floor, and there's also an elegant panelled lounge with a roaring log fire. Spacious bedrooms, in the main house and in the Courtyard (a converted brewery across the road), are splendidly fitted out with matching fabrics, antique furniture and mini-bars. This high standard extends to the bathrooms, which are fully carpeted and superbly equipped with everything from bath salts to hairdryers and weighing scales.
Amenities garden, helipad. ♿

Aston Clinton

Map 5 E2 Buckinghamshire
HP22 5HP
Aylesbury (0296) 630252
Proprietor Mr Michael Harris

Bell Inn Restaurant ♛ ⓢ

Young staff provide very helpful service in this large, elegant restaurant. The French-inspired menu features dishes like smooth salmon mousse and succulent local duckling with a tasty cream and green peppercorn sauce. Vegetables are imaginative, and there are rich, tempting sweets as well as an excellent cheeseboard. A six-course gourmet menu only is available Saturday evenings. 🍷 *OUTSTANDING. Credit* Access, Barclaycard ♿

● **Set D** £16·50 incl. service
About £37 for two

Lunch 12.30–1.45 *Dinner* 7.30–9.45

Avening

Map 4 B2 Gloucestershire
High Street
Near Tetbury *GL8 8NF*
Nailsworth (045 383) 3070

About £26 for two

Four Seasons

In this charming little Cotswold restaurant the talented young Michael Mowles produces a short menu of carefully prepared and very enjoyable dishes. Starters might include salmon mousse or œufs pochés à la bourguignonne, and main courses – perhaps sweetbreads or entrecôte Charlemagne – are served with lovely fresh vegetables. Finish with cheese or a deliciously light dessert. Friendly, attentive service. *Credit* Access, Amex, Barclaycard, Diners

Lunch 12–2 by arrangement only *Dinner* 7–11
Closed L Sat, all Sun, Mon & 1st 2 weeks January

Stars in this Guide stand for the quality of the cooking only – our overriding criterion, irrespective of price, luxury or service.

Axbridge

Map 4 A3 Somerset
The Square *BS26 2AP*
Axbridge (0934) 732444
Proprietors Mrs R. Barrington &
Mr N. Barrington
Credit Amex, Diners
Closed 1 week Christmas

Rooms 12
with bath/shower 8

Oak House Hotel   57%   Ⓜ   £ E

There's a warm welcome from the proprietors at this pleasant market-square hotel, whose history can be traced back to the 14th century. The cosy lounge-bar is full of period charm, with an open hearth, stone walls and blackened beams, and there's a homely residents' lounge with colour TV. Modernised bedrooms offer simple, adequate comforts; bathrooms are up to date and well maintained.

Room phone No	*Confirm by* By arrang.	*Parking* Limited	
Room TV No	*Last dinner* 9.30	*Banquets* 60/8	

Axbridge

Map 4 A3 Somerset
The Square *BS26 2AP*
Axbridge (0934) 732444
Proprietors Mrs R. Barrington
& Mr N. Barrington

● **Set L** £3·60, Sun £4·95
About £24 for two

Oak House Restaurant   Ⓢ

A cosy restaurant with exposed stone walls and wheelback chairs. The short menu features an interesting selection of dishes ranging from robust vegetable soup and steak and kidney pie to tabbouleh (Lebanese cracked wheat salad) and Nicholas Fry's Delight, a 17th-century recipe for veal casserole with lemon and chervil sauce. Sweets include home-made raisin pie. Generally acceptable cooking. *Credit* Amex, Diners

Lunch 12.15–2 *Dinner* 7–9.30, Sat 7–10
Closed D Sun & 1 week Christmas

Aylesbury

Map 5 D2 Buckinghamshire
Market Square *HP20 1TX*
Aylesbury (0296) 89835

Credit Access, Amex,
Barclaycard, Diners

Rooms 17
with bath/shower 17

Bell Hotel   58%   £ D

Park your car at the civic centre and walk the short distance to this welcoming town-centre hotel. Built around 1800, it still has fine old beams, pillars and a splendid fireplace in the relaxing lounge. There are two bars. Good-sized bedrooms are uniformly furnished with neat fitted units and attractive carpets. All have tea-makers and well-equipped modern bathrooms.

Room phone Yes	*Confirm by* 6	*Parking* Difficult	
Room TV Yes	*Last dinner* 9.30		

Bagshot

Map 5 E3 Surrey
1 London Road *GU19 5HR*
Bagshot (0276) 73196

Credit Access, Amex,
Barclaycard, Diners

Rooms 26
with bath/shower 12

Henekey's Hotel   54%   £ E

Formerly known as the Cricketer's, this whitewashed hotel draws much of its trade from businessmen seeking a pleasant overnight stay. The cocktail bar doubles as a lounge and there's also a public bar decorated with prints of cricketers. Well-maintained bedrooms (including eight in the annexe) are furnished in functional modern style and have tea-makers. Bathrooms are adequate. *Amenities* garden.   ♿

Room phone Yes	*Confirm by* 6	*Parking* Ample	
Room TV Yes	*Last dinner* 10.30	*Banquets* 40/–	

Bagshot
Map 5 E3 Surrey
College Ride *GU19 5ET*
Bagshot (0276) 71774
Telex 858334

Rooms 34
with bath/shower 34
Room phone Yes
Room TV Yes
Confirm by 6
Last dinner 10.30
Parking Ample
Banquets 80/8

Credit Access, Amex,
Barclaycard, Diners

Pennyhill Park Hotel   77%   *E*   Ⓜ   £C

Turn off the A30 down a small lane to find this magnificent country mansion, which forms the centrepiece of a carefully maintained 100-acre estate. A small reception hall hung with tapestries and oil paintings leads to two finely furnished lounges and a mock-Tudor bar. Upstairs, ample bedrooms furnished with antiques have well-equipped modernised bathrooms; the vast Hayward Suite is particularly luxurious. Bedrooms in the converted stables are more up to date in style, with compact bathrooms.
Amenities garden, sauna, outdoor swimming pool, tennis, 9-hole golf course, coarse fishing, clay-pigeon shooting, putting, riding, croquet, helipad, table tennis.

Bagshot
Map 5 E3 Surrey
13 London Road *GU19 5HJ*
Bagshot (0276) 75114
Proprietor Mr Ouzoum Ahmed
Turkish cooking

About £22 for two
Banquets 40/25

Sultan's Pleasure

Eating in this attractively laid out Turkish restaurant is indeed a pleasure, with Mr Ahmed and his wife acting as friendly, attentive hosts. To begin there are appetising dishes like stuffed aubergine, followed by a choice of ten kinds of superbly cooked kebabs (our mixed meat one was a really tasty feast), and for the perfect finish there's strong coffee and Turkish delight.

Dinner only 6.30–10.30
Closed Sun, Mon, 25 & 26 December & last 2 weeks August

Bakewell
Map 10 C2 Derbyshire
The Square *DE4 1BT*
Bakewell (062 981) 2812

Credit Access, Amex,
Barclaycard, Diners

Rooms 36
with bath/shower 36

Rutland Arms Hotel   62%   £D/E

Renowned as the birthplace of the famous Bakewell pudding, this 19th-century hotel still retains many of its period features, with graceful archways dividing the bar and chintzy lounge and a handsome black and white floor in reception. Well-equipped bedrooms (including those in a converted stable block across the road) have mainly fitted units, and modern bathrooms are fully tiled.

Room phone Yes   *Confirm by* 6   *Parking* Limited
Room TV Yes   *Last dinner* 9.45

Bamburgh
Map 14 B2 Northumberland
Front Street *NE69 7BL*
Bamburgh (066 84) 243
Proprietors
Mr & Mrs Brian R. Holland

Closed November–Easter

Rooms 26
with bath/shower 12

Lord Crewe Arms Hotel   55%   Ⓜ   £E

There are magnificent views of the castle from this pleasant hotel, which makes a good base for sightseeing. Old settles and oil paintings in reception create an atmosphere of period charm, and there are two traditional lounges, a cosy cocktail bar with a real fire, and a locals' bar. Bedrooms in the main building and the extension have modern fitted units. Bathrooms are adequate. No children under five. *Amenities* garden.

Room phone No   *Confirm by* 6   *Parking* Ample
Room TV No   *Last dinner* 8.30

Banbury
Map 5 D1 Oxfordshire
27 Oxford Road *OX16 9AH*
Banbury (0295) 59361

Credit Access, Amex,
Barclaycard, Diners

Banbury Moat House   66%   £E

This striking three-storey Georgian building, which combines elegance with modern facilities, is kept in a good state of repair. The spacious reception-lounge has a touch of grandeur, with pillars, Regency furniture and a deep-blue carpet; there's also a plush, dimly lit bar. Well-equipped bedrooms have fitted units, matching colour schemes, radios and tea-makers. Bathrooms are particularly luxurious. *Amenities* baby listening.

Continued

Rooms 30	*Room phone* Yes	*Confirm by* 6	*Parking* Ample
with bath/shower 30	*Room TV* Yes	*Last dinner* 9.30	*Banquets* 175/10

Banbury
Map 5 D1 Oxfordshire
By Banbury Cross *OX16 0AN*
Banbury (0295) 3451
Telex 837149

Credit Access, Amex,
Barclaycard, Diners

Whately Hall Hotel   64%   £ D

A fine stone facade gives way to a comfortable, traditional interior at this town-centre hotel which dates back in part to 1632. Bedrooms vary between handsome beamed rooms with dark furniture and pleasant modern ones fitted with simple units; all have spotless modern bathrooms. Two penthouse suites enjoy fine views from picture windows. *Amenities* garden, dinner dance (Sat), croquet, miniature golf. &

Rooms 71	*Room phone* Yes	*Confirm by* 6	*Parking* Ample
with bath/shower 71	*Room TV* Yes	*Last dinner* 9.30	*Banquets* 180/2

Barham
Map 7 C5 Kent
Elham Valley Road
Near Canterbury *CT4 6LN*
Barham (022 782) 241
Props Mr Warden & Mrs Allen
About £25 for two

Dolls House

A friendly welcome awaits visitors to this cosy, cottage restaurant, where the menus offer a choice of straightforward dishes making generally enjoyable use of good ingredients. *Credit* Access, Barclaycard *Lunch* 12.30–2.30 *Dinner* 7.30–9.30 **Closed** D Sun, all Mon except Bank Hols, 1 Jan, Good Friday, 26 Dec & 3 wks Feb ● **Set L** £3·90 **Set D** £6·50 *Banquets* 60/14 &

Barnard Castle
Map 15 B5 Co. Durham
The Bank *DL12 8PN*
Teesdale (0833) 37668
Proprietors
Neil & Josie Davidson

Blagraves House

A fine bow-fronted Elizabethan house is the setting for Josie Davidson's enjoyable cooking. Portions are generous, and the menu changes daily: you might start with a robust, flavoursome soup or seafood pancake, and follow with leg of lamb with almond and apricot stuffing or beef fillet with a pepper and mushroom sauce. Excellent vegetables, too, and delicious sweets. Booking essential. *ABOVE AVERAGE. Credit* Amex, Barclaycard

● **Set D** £10·50
About £27 for two

Dinner only 7.30–9.30
Closed Sun, Mon, Bank Holidays & 2 weeks October

Barnby Moor
Map 11 D2 Nottinghamshire
Near Retford *DN22 8QS*
Retford (0777) 705121

Credit Access, Amex,
Barclaycard, Diners

Ye Olde Bell Hotel   55%   £ D

This historic creeper-clad coaching inn has useful conference facilities. The cosy little bar with its comfortable old Windsor chairs has a fine moulded ceiling, and there's some handsome panelling in the ballroom. Simple traditional bedrooms have old-fashioned brass beds; one or two have been updated with more elegant, Edwardian-style furnishings. Well-kept modern bathrooms. *Amenities* garden, dinner dance (Sat September–May).

Rooms 55	*Room phone* Yes	*Confirm by* 6	*Parking* Ample
with bath/shower 44	*Room TV* Yes	*Last dinner* 9.45	*Banquets* 250/–

Barnham Broom
Map 6 C1 Norfolk
Near Norwich *NR9 4DD*
Barnham Broom (060 545) 393
Telex 975568

Credit Access, Amex,
Barclaycard, Diners

Barnham Broom Hotel   61%   £ D

There's always plenty to do at this low, modern hotel standing in 120 acres of pleasant Norfolk countryside. Businessmen appreciate the well-fitted conference and meeting rooms, and everyone can enjoy the spacious, lively Club Bar and the impressive sports and country club facilities. Bedrooms are of an unfussy contemporary design, with neat fitted furniture, radios and tea-making facilities. They're all roomy, and several are of family size. Sparklingly clean bathrooms are also equipped with radios! Excellent maintenance throughout.
Amenities garden, sauna, covered outdoor swimming pool, tennis, squash, golf course, game fishing, solarium, snack bar (9.30am–9.30pm). &

Rooms 30	*Room phone* Yes	*Confirm by* By arrang.	*Parking* Ample
with bath/shower 30	*Room TV* Yes	*Last dinner* 9.30	*Banquets* 120/–

Barnsdale Bar

Map 11 D1 West Yorkshire
Near Pontefract *WF8 3JB*
Pontefract (0977) 620711
Telex 557457
Manager Mrs. E. Wilson
Credit Access, Amex,
Barclaycard, Diners

TraveLodge 53% £E

This well-run purpose-built complex is located on the southbound carriage-way of the A1. Adequate comforts for a short stay are provided by the identically furnished bedrooms, which have good work and luggage space and compact, well-equipped bathrooms. Continental breakfast is available, and other meals may be taken in an adjacent building with a cafeteria and bar-lounge. *Amenities* petrol pumps, cafeteria (24 hours).

| *Rooms* 72 | *Room phone* Yes | *Confirm by* 6 | *Parking* Ample |
| *with bath/shower* 72 | *Room TV* Yes | *Last dinner* None | |

Barnsley

Map 10 C2 South Yorkshire
Doncaster Road *S71 5EH*
Barnsley (0226) 89401
Telex 547762
Manager Mr J. Gibson
Credit Access, Amex,
Barclaycard, Diners

Ardsley House Hotel 63% £C/D

On the eastern edge of Barnsley, this Georgian house has been considerably altered over the years. Bedrooms vary from lofty and traditional in the original building to simple ones in the modern wing, and bathrooms are well equipped. Downstairs there's a foyer-lounge, and the contemporary-style bar retains its attractive plasterwork ceiling. No dogs.
Amenities garden, dancing (Fri), dinner dance (Sat Nov–Jan).

| *Rooms* 63 | *Room phone* Yes | *Confirm by* 6 | *Parking* Ample |
| *with bath/shower* 63 | *Room TV* Yes | *Last dinner* 10.30 | *Banquets* 200/4 |

Barnstaple

Map 3 D2 Devon
Braunton Road *EX31 1LE*
Barnstaple (0271) 76221
Managers
Mr & Mrs D. L. Hastings
Credit Access, Amex,
Barclaycard, Diners

Barnstaple Motel 54% £E/F

This purpose-built motel on the A361 offers modest standards of accommodation for short stays. There's a modern reception area, a spacious, airy bar-lounge and a TV lounge well stocked with reading matter, as well as a popular ballroom and function suite. Bedrooms in an L-shaped wing are functional and unpretentious, with simple fitted units and compact bathrooms. *Amenities* garden, indoor swimming pool.

| *Rooms* 60 | *Room phone* Yes | *Confirm by* By arrang. | *Parking* Ample |
| *with bath/shower* 60 | *Room TV* Most | *Last dinner* 10 | *Banquets* 200/– |

Barnstaple

Map 3 D2 Devon
Taw Vale Parade *EX32 8NB*
Barnstaple (0271) 5861

Manager Mr B. D. Gates
Credit Access, Amex,
Barclaycard, Diners

Imperial Hotel 58% £D

Furnishings are modern, but the public rooms of this imposing town-centre hotel have the proportions of a loftier age and retain a few period features like the lovely polished wooden staircase. There are two cheerful bars and an airy residents' lounge. Bedrooms of varying sizes provide comfortable, up-to-date accommodation, with attractive fabrics, lightwood furniture and simple, well-kept bathrooms. &

| *Rooms* 56 | *Room phone* Yes | *Confirm by* 6 | *Parking* Ample |
| *with bath/shower* 56 | *Room TV* Yes | *Last dinner* 8.45 | *Banquets* 100/10 |

Basildon

Map 7 B4 Essex
Cranes Farm Road *SS14 3DG*
Basildon (0268) 3955
Telex 995141

Credit Access, Amex,
Barclaycard, Diners

Crest Hotel 59% £D

Geared to the needs of the business community, this modern red-brick hotel (formerly the Essex Centre) offers pleasant accommodation in spotlessly clean surroundings. The smart reception is festooned with greenery, and there's a mock-Elizabethan bar as well as several meeting rooms. Functional bedrooms have adequate fitted units, unassuming decor and well-equipped modern bathrooms. *Amenities* garden, coarse fishing. &

| *Rooms* 116 | *Room phone* Yes | *Confirm by* 6 | *Parking* Ample |
| *with bath/shower* 116 | *Room TV* Yes | *Last dinner* 9.45 | *Banquets* 220/– |

Basingstoke

Map 5 D3 Hampshire
Venture Roundabout
Alton Road *RG21 3EE*
Basingstoke (0256) 68181
Telex 858501
Credit Access, Amex,
Barclaycard, Diners

Crest Hotel 69% £D

This well-maintained hotel alongside the A30 combines sophisticated modern decor with a high degree of comfort. Exposed brick walls, smoked glass and luxurious plants are features of the foyer-lounge and cocktail bar, and there's an informal pub-style bar. Good-sized bedrooms are bright, simple and practical, with built-in lightwood furniture and well-fitted, up-to-date bathrooms. &

Continued

| Rooms 85 | Room phone Yes | Confirm by 6 | Parking Ample |
| with bath/shower 85 | Room TV Yes | Last dinner 10 | Banquets 200/10 |

Basingstoke
Map 5 D3 Hampshire
Aldermaston Road Roundabout
RG24 9NU
Basingstoke (0256) 20212
Telex 858223
Credit Access, Amex,
Barclaycard, Diners

Ladbroke Mercury Hotel   60%   £ C/D

With its well-designed accommodation and extensive conference facilities, this efficiently run red-brick hotel appeals especially to the business community. Open-plan public areas include a bright foyer-lounge and a cocktail bar with smart cane furniture. Comfortable bedrooms have plenty of room, excellent writing surfaces and bedside control panels. Neat tiled bathrooms. *Amenities* garden, dinner dance (Sat), cinema. **Closed** Christmas

| Rooms 82 | Room phone Yes | Confirm by 6 | Parking Ample |
| with bath/shower 82 | Room TV Yes | Last dinner 9.55 | Banquets 150/10 |

Basingstoke
Map 5 D3 Hampshire
24 London Street *RG21 1NY*
Basingstoke (0256) 28525
Telex 27120
Manager Mr A. C. Wadkins
Credit Access, Amex,
Barclaycard. Diners

Red Lion Hotel   55%   £ D/E

Starting life as a coaching inn in 1601, this whitewashed town-centre hostelry has been comfortably modernised. There's no lounge, but guests can relax in the bar or in the pleasant coffee shop. Bedrooms vary from a new wing of stopover singles with built-in units and shower rooms to more traditionally furnished older rooms with simple, adequate bathrooms. *Amenities* coffee shop (9.30am–9.45pm).   &

| Rooms 64 | Room phone Yes | Confirm by 6 | Parking Ample |
| with bath/shower 64 | Room TV Yes | Last dinner 9.45 | |

Baslow
Map 10 C2 Derbyshire
Bakewell *DE4 1SP*
Baslow (024 688) 2311

Proprietor Eric Marsh
Rooms 13
with bath/shower 13
Room phone Yes
Room TV Yes
Confirm by By arrang.
Last dinner 10
Parking Ample
Banquets 10/–

Credit Amex, Barclaycard

Cavendish Hotel   73%      £ C/D

Part of the Chatsworth estate, this handsome stone-built former inn is a well-run, friendly and relaxing hotel where visitors are made to feel like guests in a private house. Rooms like the splendidly comfortable residents' lounge are tastefully furnished in a style befitting the building's character, and some of the pieces actually come from Chatsworth. Equally inviting is the bar, which has a brick floor and a fine mahogany counter. Attractively decorated bedrooms, which vary in style from traditional to more modern, have high-quality furnishings and thoughtful extras like books, radio-alarms and mini-bars. Carpeted bathrooms are well equipped. No dogs. *Amenities* garden, game fishing, putting.

Baslow
Map 10 C2 Derbyshire
Bakewell *DE4 1SP*
Baslow (024 688) 2311
Proprietor Eric Marsh

About £32 for two

Cavendish Hotel Restaurant   ♕ ⑤

Nick Buckingham offers enjoyably different dishes in this smartly redesigned restaurant. Chatsworth game is a seasonal feature, and there's a good choice of seafood, grills and imaginatively sauced entrées like pork fillets with peppercorns. *Credit* Amex, Barclaycard
Lunch 12.30–2 *Dinner* 7–10

Bassenthwaite Lake
Map 13 C5 Cumbria
Near Cockermouth *CA13 9YE*
Bassenthwaite Lake
(059 681) 234
Proprietor
Mr W. E. Barrington-Wilson
Closed 25 December

Pheasant Inn   58%      £ E

Visitors looking for traditional comfort and hospitality flock to this charming whitewashed inn just off the A66. There's nothing to disturb the peace in the three prettily furnished lounges or in the rustic bar with its smoke-darkened walls. Bedrooms are bright and cheerful with either traditional or good modern fitted furniture, and compact bathrooms are spotlessly clean. No dogs. *Amenities* garden.

| Rooms 20 | Room phone No | Confirm by By arrang. | Parking Ample |
| with bath/shower 12 | Room TV No | Last dinner 8.15 | |

LÖWENBRÄU
seit 1383
DIAT
Pils
LAGER
STRONG IN ALCOHOL
MÜNCHEN

LÖWENBRÄU PILS.

THE PILS TO BE TAKEN
SERIOUSLY.

Map 4 B3
Town plan opposite

Population 84,000

The Romans settled in Bath because of the waters and built baths used for therapy and recreation. In the 18th century spa treatment reached the peak of fashion and Bath was greatly enlarged at this time. Being wholly built within the space of a century, all its buildings are of the same classic, elegant style. Its Georgian character and charm remained unchanged until very recently. Yet Bath has become the centre of much environmental controversy: should the face of Bath be gradually eroded to develop it as a 20th-century commercial city, or should it be enshrined for ever as a masterpiece of urban architecture?

Annual Events
Bath Festival (music and drama)
2nd May–6th June
Royal Bath and West Show
2nd–5th June

Sights Outside City
Cheddar Gorge, Wookey Hole Caves, Wells Cathedral, Glastonbury Abbey, Longleat House and Lion Reserve, Castle Combe Village, Lacock Abbey and Village, Stourhead House and gardens, Avebury Circles, Corsham Court

Information Centre
Abbey Churchyard
Telephone Bath 62831
Accommodation Enquiries 60521

Fiat Dealer
Motor Services (Bath) Ltd.
Margaret's Buildings, Circus Place, Bath
Avon BA1 2LP
Tel. Bath 27328

Bath

1	Abbey *15th c*	B4
2	American Museum at Claverton Manor $2\frac{1}{2}$ miles, *life in the New World from 17th c to 1860*	C3
3	Assembly Rooms *Finely restored Georgian suite, also houses world-famous Museum of Costume*	A2
4	Bath Carriage Museum	A2
5	Bath Spa Station	B5
6	Botanical Gardens in Victoria Park	A3
7	Burrows Toy Museum	B4
8	The Circus, Royal Crescent and Lansdown Crescent *superb examples of Georgian town-planning*	A2
9	Guildhall Banqueting Room *fine Adam-style room*	B3
10	Herschel House	A3
11	Holburne of Menstrie Museum *paintings, silver, objets d'art*	C2
12	Lansdown Race-course	A1
13	Museum of Bookbinding	B4
14	National Museum of Photography	B3
15	Postal Museum	C3
16	Pulteney Bridge *Adam bridge lined with shops*	B3
17	Pump Room and Roman Baths *the heart of Bath, includes Britain's finest Roman remains*	B4
18	Sham Castle *18th-c folly and viewpoint*	C3
19	Theatre Royal	A3
20	Tourist Information Centre	B4
21	University	C3
22	Victoria Art Gallery *works by mainly West Country artists; glass; Delft; horology*	B3

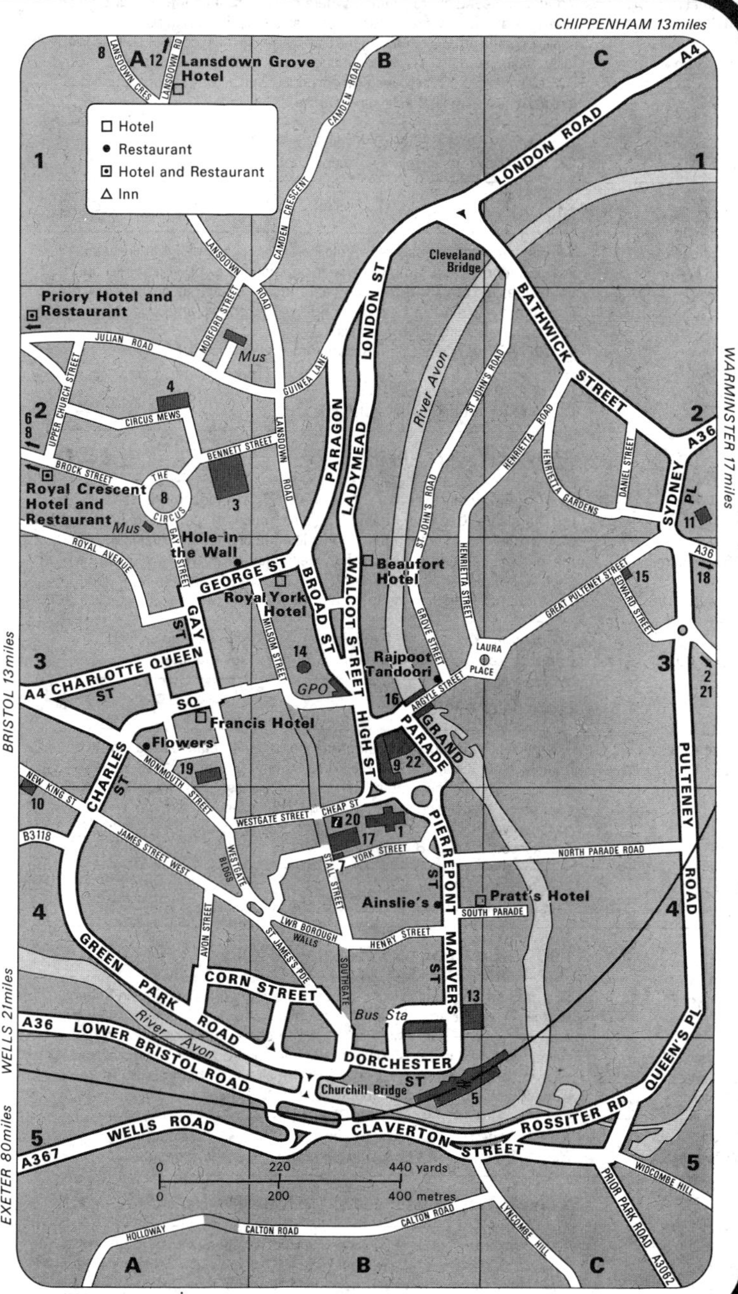

© 1982 Egon Ronay's Guides

Bath   Ainslie's   Ⓢ

Town plan B4 Avon
12 Pierrepont Street *BA1 1LA*
Bath (0225) 61745
Proprietors
Dick & Ainslie Ensom

An intimate candlelit restaurant, where diners can tuck into a well-chosen selection of capably prepared dishes. Salade niçoise, scallops mornay and snails in garlic butter are among the starters, while main courses (served with tasty fresh vegetables) could include sole meunière, steaks and nicely sauced calf's liver. Our enjoyable meal ended with a fruity summer pudding.
Credit Access, Amex, Barclaycard, Diners

● **Set D** £9·30
About £30 for two

Dinner only 6.30–11.30, Sat 7–11.30, Sun 7–10.30
Closed Mon & Bank Holidays except Good Friday

Bath   Flowers   ♣ Ⓢ

Town plan A3 Avon
27 Monmouth Street *BA1 2AP*
Bath (0225) 313774

Teresa Lipin's set menus offer simple, carefully cooked delights like cream of leek and fennel soup, lamb with garlic and wine or a superb cheese soufflé. Vegetables are crisp and colourful, and puddings such as pear sponge hot from the oven make an excellent finish. The bright, attractive restaurant stands in a row of terraced cottages.
🍷*ABOVE AVERAGE. Credit* Access, Amex, Barclaycard, Diners

● **Set L** £5·25 **Set D** £7·25
About £25 for two
Banquets 20/12

Lunch 12–2 *Dinner* 7–10.30
Closed Sun, Mon & 10 days Christmas

Bath   Francis Hotel   68%   £ C/D

Town plan A3 Avon
Queen Square *BA1 2HH*
Bath (0225) 24257
Telex 449162
Manager Mr R. W. Palmer
Credit Access, Amex,
Barclaycard, Diners

Occupying virtually the whole of the south side of handsome Queen Square, this imposing Georgian building retains much of its period style and elegance in comfortable public rooms like the charming pastel lounge and the intimate, relaxing bars. Tastefully decorated bedrooms–including compact, well-lit ones in the extension–have attractive traditional-style furniture and thoughtfully equipped, up-to-date bathrooms.   ♿

Rooms 90	*Room phone* Yes	*Confirm by* 6	*Parking* Limited
with bath/shower 90	*Room TV* Yes	*Last dinner* 9.30	*Banquets* 140/–

Bath   Hole in the Wall   ♣ Ⓢ

Town plan A3 Avon
16 George Street *BA1 2EN*
Bath (0225) 25242

A large table loaded with colourful hors d'œuvre catches the eye in this homely little restaurant, where Tim Cumming produces an interesting selection of very enjoyable French-style dishes. Fish soup with garlic croûtons is a satisfying starter, and main courses are served with beautifully prepared vegetables. End with lovely home-made ice cream. 🍷*SUPERIOR.*
Credit Access, Amex, Barclaycard, Diners   ♿

About £36 for two
Banquets 40/–

Lunch 12.30–2 *Dinner* 7–10
Closed Sun, Mon, Bank Holidays & 25 & 26 December

Bath   Ladbroke Beaufort Hotel   68%   £ C/D

Town plan B3 Avon
Walcot Street *BA1 5BJ*
Bath (0225) 63411
Telex 449519
Manager Mr G. A. Dalling
Credit Access, Amex,
Barclaycard, Diners

This modern stone-faced hotel stands in the city centre overlooking Pulteney Bridge. A bright, marble-floored reception area leads to the roomy and attractive lounge bar, which has bamboo chairs and glass-topped tables. Crisp, functional decor is common to all the bedrooms, which have trouser presses, tea-makers and compact, well-maintained bathrooms. There are extensive meeting and conference facilities. No dogs.

Rooms 123	*Room phone* Yes	*Confirm by* 6	*Parking* Ample
with bath/shower 123	*Room TV* Yes	*Last dinner* 9.30	*Banquets* 200/–

Bath   Lansdown Grove Hotel   61% Ⓜ   £ D

Town plan A1 Avon
Lansdown Road *BA1 5EH*
Bath (0225) 315891

A sturdy Georgian building perched on a hill overlooking the town. Bedrooms are large and traditionally furnished, all with TV and tea-makers, and bathrooms are tiled and decently fitted. There's a peaceful residents' lounge and an attractive cocktail bar with white wrought-iron furniture and an elaborate fairground mural. Some redecoration would be welcome.
Amenities garden, croquet.

Credit Access, Amex,
Barclaycard, Diners

      Continued

Rooms 41 *with bath/shower* 38	*Room phone* Yes *Room TV* Yes	*Confirm by* 6 *Last dinner* 9.30	*Parking* Limited *Banquets* 100/–

Bath

Town plan C4 Avon
South Parade *BA2 4AB*
Bath (0225) 60441
Telex 47439
Manager Mr D. B. Meakin
Credit Access, Amex,
Barclaycard, Diners

Pratt's Hotel   56%   £ D/E

This mellow Georgian hotel in a cul-de-sac offers a friendly welcome and traditional comforts. Two roomy lounges with chintzy furnishings are ideal for relaxing, and there's also a small cocktail bar. Bedrooms are homely and comfortable, with darkwood furniture and tea/coffee-makers. Bathrooms range from old-fashioned and adequate to modern and well equipped. *Amenities* dinner dance (Sat autumn–spring), table tennis.

Rooms 48 *with bath/shower* 46	*Room phone* Yes *Room TV* Yes	*Confirm by* By arrang. *Last dinner* 9	*Parking* Difficult *Banquets* 90/2

Changes in data may occur in establishments after the Guide goes to press. Prices should be taken as indications rather than firm quotes.

Bath

Town plan A2 Avon
Weston Road *BA1 2XT*
Bath (0225) 331922
Telex 44612

Rooms 15
with bath/shower 15
Room phone Yes
Room TV Yes
Confirm by By arrang.
Last dinner 9.30
Parking Ample
Banquets 26/–
Closed 1–10 January

Credit Access, Amex,
Barclaycard

Priory Hotel   78%   Ⓜ   £ B

Built of Bath stone in 1835 and set in very attractive gardens, this lovely house is the pride and joy of its owners, who greet guests with all the warmth and enthusiasm of old friends. The handsome drawing room is typical of the place, with antiques, flower arrangements and silk-covered walls blending with the soft colour schemes of the settees and armchairs; there's also a very comfortable bar. Elegant bedrooms are individually decorated and tastefully furnished, and useful extras include hairdryers and sewing kits. Excellent modern bathrooms. No children under ten. No dogs.
Amenities garden, outdoor swimming pool, croquet.

Bath

Town plan A2 Avon
Weston Road *BA1 2XT*
Bath (0225) 331922

● **Set L** Sun only £12
Set D from £12·50
About £39 for two

Priory Hotel Restaurant   ★   ♛ Ⓢ

Chef Michael Collom brings a special quality to this dignified restaurant, and his French-inspired menu reflects sophisticated talents. His skill and imagination show up best in lightly sauced, intricate dishes such as featherlight mousseline of scallops with smooth beurre blanc, or succulent salmon layered in puff pastry with a piquant dill sauce, but there are also more conventional items like beef Stroganoff. Vegetables are excellent and superb sweets include rich chocolate gâteau served with a passion fruit sorbet. Buffet lunches except on Sunday. **Specialities** mousseline de coquilles St Jacques sauce beurre blanc, tournedos bambos, gratin de fraises en surprise. ♟ *SUPERIOR. Credit* Access, Amex, Barclaycard

Lunch 12.45–2 *Dinner* 7.30–9.30
Closed 1–10 January

Bath

Town plan B3 Avon
4 Argyle Street *BA2 4BA*
Bath (0225) 66833

Indian cooking
About £26 for two

Rajpoot Tandoori

This smart restaurant in a converted cellar has a quietly exotic atmosphere and offers familiar tandoori dishes and subtly spiced North Indian curries all prepared with great skill and attention to detail. *Credit* Access, Amex, Barclaycard, Diners *Lunch* 12–2.45 *Dinner* 6–11.15 **Closed** Mon (Jan–March) & 25 December ● **Set L & Set D** from £5·75 *Banquets* 20/–

Bath

Town plan A2 Avon
Royal Crescent *BA1 2LS*
Bath (0225) 319090
Telex 444251

Rooms 29
with bath/shower 29
Room phone Yes
Room TV Yes
Confirm by 6
Last dinner 10
Parking Limited
Banquets 25/–

Credit Access, Amex,
Barclaycard, Diners

Royal Crescent Hotel 88% £C

The graceful sweep of the famous Royal Crescent makes an appropriate setting for this exquisite hotel, and the combination of attentive service with sumptuous decor makes staying here a delight. The marble floor of the entrance hall, the curving staircase with its 16th-century tapestry and the luxurious soft furnishings throughout show that every effort has been made to complement the classical style of the building. Bedrooms are breathtaking, with beautiful moulded ceilings, sparkling chandeliers and elaborate drapes helping to create a feeling of splendour, which is echoed in the superbly equipped bathrooms. The suites (some with four-posters) have open log fires in winter. *Amenities* garden, valeting. &

Bath

Town plan A2 Avon
Royal Crescent *BA1 2LS*
Bath (0225) 319090

About £36 for two

Royal Crescent Hotel Restaurant

Comfortable and quietly dignified, this basement restaurant offers fixed-price menus (smaller lunchtime choice) of French-inspired dishes, for which the cooking is not always consistent. Polite, formal service.
 *SUPERIOR. Credit* Access, Amex, Barclaycard, Diners *Lunch* 12.30–2 *Dinner* 7–10 ● **Set L** £10 **Set D** £16

Bath

Town plan B3 Avon
George Street *BA1 2DY*
Bath (0225) 61541
Telex 23241

Credit Access, Amex,
Barclaycard, Diners

Rooms 52
with bath/shower 41

Royal York Hotel 55% £D

A large foyer with oak-panelled walls and ornate plaster ceiling sets the tone for this city-centre Georgian hotel, where Queen Victoria stayed just before her coronation. There's also a quiet writing room, a little TV lounge and a comfortable bar. Some bedrooms are simple and traditional, others more modern with attractive contemporary furnishings and fully tiled bathrooms. Conference facilities. &

Room phone Yes *Confirm by* 6 *Parking* Difficult
Room TV Yes *Last dinner* 9.15 *Banquets* 40/–

Battle

Map 7 B6 East Sussex
Netherfield *TN33 9PP*
Battle (042 46) 4455

Rooms 11
with bath/shower 11
Room phone Yes
Room TV Yes
Confirm by By arrang.
Last dinner 10.30
Parking Ample
Banquets 50/–

Credit Access, Amex,
Barclaycard, Diners

Netherfield Place 79% Ⓜ £C/D

The latest venture of the Katnic family, who for many years ran an excellent restaurant in St John's Wood, this Georgian-style mansion stands in 30 acres of beautiful gardens and parkland. The relaxing atmosphere of a fine country house is evident in the comfortably furnished public rooms, which include a traditional lounge and a plush bar. Open fires and pretty flower arrangements make them particularly inviting. At the rear of the hotel there's a bright, airy sun lounge. Spacious bedrooms, individually decorated with great good taste, have high-quality reproduction furniture and many thoughtful extras. Bathrooms are beautifully appointed. No dogs.
Amenities garden, dinner dance (monthly).

Battle
Map 7 B6 East Sussex
Netherfield *TN33PP*
Battle (042 46) 4455

● **Set L** Sun only £7·50
Set D £11
About £30 for two

Netherfield Place Restaurant ★

Many of the splendid Greek and Balkan dishes that made the Katnics' London establishment so popular have travelled with them to this elegant panelled restaurant. Cooking standards remain consistently excellent, with great emphasis on prime raw materials and superbly balanced sauces. Crab La Rochelle, a herby mixture in featherlight puff pastry, is a delicious starter and main courses include moussaka, sautéed kidneys and crisp-roast duck with duck livers, pine kernels and cherry sauce. Chocolate pots and cream-cheese pancakes are among the tempting desserts. **Specialities** crab Joinville, duck Bosnaka, venison Podgorski, raspberry soufflé. *OUTSTANDING. Credit* Access, Amex, Barclaycard, Diners

Lunch Sun 12.30–2.30, Mon–Sat by reservation only *Dinner* 7–10.30
Closed D Sun to non-residents

Bawtry
Map 11 D2 South Yorkshire
Market Place *DN10 6JW*
Doncaster (0302) 710341

Manager Mr P. H. Keary
Credit Access, Amex, Barclaycard, Diners

Rooms 57
with bath/shower 57

Crown Hotel   62%   £E

An elegant white-painted exterior with window shutters distinguishes this long, low former posting house. Inside, prints of coaching scenes hang in the main lounge bar, and there's another, smaller bar at the rear. Newly decorated bedrooms have coordinated colour schemes and pretty prints; older-style rooms are simpler in character. Well-kept bathrooms are mostly carpeted. *Amenities* garden.

Room phone Yes	*Confirm by* 6.30	*Parking* Limited
Room TV Yes	*Last dinner* 9.45	*Banquets* 120/20

Beaconsfield
Map 5 E2 Buckinghamshire
Oxford Road *HP9 2XE*
Gerrards Cross (028 13) 87211
Telex 848719
Manager Mr H. Waser
Credit Access, Amex, Barclaycard, Diners

Rooms 126
with bath/shower 126

Bellhouse Hotel   64%   £D

Situated on the A40 midway between Beaconsfield and Gerrards Cross, this modern hotel has been designed to cater for businessmen, with extensive function facilities including a ballroom. There's a spacious reception and a bar decked out like a pirate ship with figureheads and cannon. Well-equipped bedrooms have fitted units and fully tiled bathrooms. *Amenities* garden, dancing (Fri, Sat), pool table, 24-hour laundry service, baby listening.

Room phone Yes	*Confirm by* 6	*Parking* Ample
Room TV Yes	*Last dinner* 10	*Banquets* 350/–

Beaconsfield
Map 5 E2 Buckinghamshire
43 Aylesbury End *HP9 1LU*
Beaconsfield (049 46) 6806

Italian cooking

● **Set L** £5
About £28 for two

Santella

The menu's Italian, but French fashion sketches line the walls of this stylish restaurant. Familiar favourites are supplemented by daily specials, and the cooking is careful and reliable. Pasta is home-made, and commendable attention to detail is shown in dishes like scaloppina di vitello 'Casa Nostra' – lightly cooked veal in a delicate suprême sauce, with sliced avocado and truffle. *Credit* Access, Amex, Barclaycard, Diners

Lunch 12.30–2.30 *Dinner* 7–11
Closed D Sun, all 26 December & most Bank Holidays

We publish annually, so make sure you use the current edition. It's worth it!

Beaconsfield
Map 5 E2 Buckinghamshire
7 The Broadway
Penn Road *HP9 2PD*
Beaconsfield (049 46) 4580
Indian cooking
About £20 for two

Tropical Curry Centre

Elegant decor and careful cooking are equally noteworthy features of this smart Indian restaurant, where delicious, freshly spiced tandoori dishes are highlights of the varied menu. *Credit* Access, Amex, Barclaycard, Diners
Lunch 12–2.30 *Dinner* 6–11.30
Closed 25 & 26 December *Banquets* 50/20

Beanacre

Map 4 B2 Wiltshire
Near Melksham *SN12 7PU*
Melksham (0225) 703700

Rooms 8
with bath/shower 8
Room phone Yes
Room TV Yes
Confirm by By arrang.
Last dinner 9
Parking Ample
Banquets 50/–

Credit Access, Amex,
Barclaycard, Diners

Beechfield House   75%   Ⓜ   £ D/E

An impressive driveway leads from the Chippenham–Melksham road to this well-proportioned Victorian mansion, run with efficiency and charm by Peter Crawford-Rolt and his helpful team. Arched windows and marble fireplaces are among the attractive features of the elegant, relaxing public rooms, which also have comfortable armchairs and some fine antiques. There are period pieces, too, in the spacious bedrooms, which have large brass beds and lots of little extras like bowls of fruit and sewing kits. Bathrooms are particularly attractive, and here as elsewhere original fittings combine harmoniously with more modern features to preserve the character of the house. *Amenities* garden, tennis, coarse fishing, croquet.

Beanacre

Map 4 B2 Wiltshire
Near Melksham *SN12 7PU*
Melksham (0225) 703700

● **Set L** £5·95
About £34 for two

Beechfield House Restaurant   ♀ ♔ Ⓢ

In a dignified country-house setting you can enjoy the beautifully presented dishes that make up the chef-patron's interesting menus. Cream of water-cress soup and plump scallops sautéed with lime butter make enjoyable starters, while main courses like lamb noisettes arranged round crisp French beans delight both the eye and the palate. Delicious desserts, too.
*OUTSTANDING. Credit* Access, Amex, Barclaycard, Diners   ♿

Lunch 12.30–1.45 *Dinner* 7–9, Sat 7–9.30, Sun 7–8
Closed May Day & August Bank Holiday

Beaulieu

Map 4 C4 Hampshire
Near Brockenhurst *SO4 7ZL*
Beaulieu (0590) 612324

Credit Access, Amex,
Barclaycard, Diners

Rooms 26
with bath/shower 26

Montagu Arms Hotel   65%   £ D/E

Originally used as a hostelry by monks from the nearby abbey, this hotel still retains much of its traditional style and character. The panelled hall with its open log fire and grandfather clock sets the tone of the place, and there are two bars plus two comfortable lounges. The bedrooms have solid, old-fashioned furniture (there are a few four-posters) and adequate tiled bathrooms. *Amenities* garden.

Room phone Yes	*Confirm by* By arrang.	*Parking* Ample
Room TV Yes	*Last dinner* 10	*Banquets* 110/–

Beccles

Map 6 D2 Suffolk
Puddingmoor *NR34 9PL*
Beccles (0502) 712270

Proprietors Mr & Mrs S. Strong
Credit Access, Amex,
Barclaycard, Diners

Rooms 14
with bath/shower 12

Waveney House Hotel   59%   Ⓜ   £ D

A log fire blazing in the foyer-lounge welcomes winter visitors to this handsome hotel on the river Waveney. The pub-like bar offers fine river views, as do several of the attractively decorated, well-furnished bedrooms; rooms in the attics are smaller, with quaint beams and sloping roofs. Bathrooms are neat and compact, and there's a self-contained chalet for two. *Amenities* coarse fishing, mooring.

Room phone Yes	*Confirm by* By arrang.	*Parking* Ample
Room TV Yes	*Last dinner* 9.30	*Banquets* 120/20

Bedford

Map 5 E1 Bedfordshire
St Mary's Street *MK42 0AR*
Bedford (0234) 55131
Telex 825243

Credit Access, Amex,
Barclaycard, Diners

Rooms 117
with bath/shower 117

Bedford Moat House   62%   £ D/E

An imposing, modern hotel, standing on the banks of the Ouse overlooking the old town. Bright, airy bedrooms have functional fitted furniture, comfortable armchairs and tea/coffee-making facilities, and bathrooms are neat and compact. A small residents' lounge with river views is a pleasant place to relax, and there are two bars off the open-plan foyer. No dogs.
Amenities dinner dance (Sat), pool table.   ♿

Room phone Yes	*Confirm by* 6	*Parking* Ample
Room TV Yes	*Last dinner* 9.45	*Banquets* 365/2

Bedford

Map 5 E1 Bedfordshire
Green Lane, Clapham *MK41 6EP*
Bedford (0234) 63281

Proprietor Mr Richard Lee
Credit Access, Amex,
Barclaycard

Rooms 18
with bath/shower 18

Woodlands Manor   69%   Ⓜ   £ D

Set in over three acres of woodland and two miles north of the town, this handsome Regency-style manor house offers peace and spacious comfort. Traditional elegance is the keynote in the impressive entrance hall-cum-lounge and in the cocktail bar, and attractive, well-appointed bedrooms all have spotlessly clean, carpeted bathrooms. No children under seven. No dogs. *Amenities* garden.

Room phone Yes	*Confirm by* 6	*Parking* Ample
Room TV Yes	*Last dinner* 10	*Banquets* 80/6

Beeston

Map 10 B2 Cheshire
Near Tarporley *CW6 9NW*
Bunbury (0829) 260309
Telex 61455

Credit Access, Amex,
Barclaycard, Diners

Rooms 30
with bath/shower 30

Wild Boar Motor Lodge Inn   63%   £ D

Originally a girls' school, this is now a smart motel-restaurant complex. Spacious, boldly decorated bedrooms (and a small TV lounge) are in one block, and have fitted units, armchairs, tea-makers and radios plus well-equipped bathrooms. Two attractive bars and the restaurant are in a separate building with a distinctive black and white facade.

Room phone Yes	*Confirm by* By arrang.	*Parking* Ample
Room TV Yes	*Last dinner* 10	*Banquets* 60/10

Belford

Map 14 B2 Northumberland
Market Square *NE70 7NE*
Belford (066 83) 543
Telex 53168

Credit Access, Amex,
Barclaycard, Diners

Rooms 15
with bath/shower 6

Blue Bell Hotel *(Inn)*   £ E

There's a friendly welcome for visitors to this pleasant old coaching inn, whose ivy-clad facade dominates the market square. The smart Moorland Bar is a popular meeting place, and there's a roomy, relaxing lounge. Individually decorated bedrooms have easy chairs and offer acceptable comforts in traditional style. Private bathrooms are modern. *Amenities* garden, discothèque (twice monthly in summer), putting.

Room phone Yes	*Confirm by* 6	*Parking* Ample
Room TV Yes	*Last dinner* 9	*Banquets* 80/20

Belper

Map 10 C3 Derbyshire
84 Bridge Street *DE5 1PP*
Belper (077 382) 2246

French cooking

About £31 for two

Rémy's   ♔ Ⓢ

Elegant and stylish in appearance, Rémy Bopp's attractive first-floor restaurant is an oasis of imaginative French cooking. Dishes like fresh salmon aspic with lemon and green peppercorns and best end of lamb in a tomato and basil sauce employ the best possible ingredients, and there's more than a hint of nouvelle cuisine in preparation and presentation.
 *ABOVE AVERAGE. Credit* Amex, Barclaycard

Lunch 12.30–1.30 *Dinner* 7.30–9.30
Closed Sun, Mon, Bank Hols, $2\frac{1}{2}$ weeks Jan/Feb & $2\frac{1}{2}$ weeks July/Aug

Belstone

Map 3 D2 Devon
Near Okehampton *EX20 1RD*
Sticklepath (083 784) 243
Proprietors
Mr & Mrs P. A. Barsby
Closed 1 October–week before
Easter

Rooms 7
with bath/shower 1

Skaigh House Hotel   54%   Ⓜ   £ D

A cheery welcome greets visitors to Mr and Mrs Barsby's peaceful little country hotel which stands in terraced gardens within Dartmoor National Park. Public rooms like the hall and lounge are warm and relaxing, with traditional decor and furnishings, while bedrooms offer modest, homely comforts. The whole house is very neat and tidy. No dogs.
Amenities garden, outdoor swimming pool.

Room phone No	*Confirm by* By arrang.	*Parking* Ample
Room TV No	*Last dinner* 9	

Our inspectors never book in the name of the Egon Ronay Organisation; they disclose their identity only after paying their bills.

CLEMENS XII PON

Engineering for World Transport

An increasingly familiar sight in European cities, Britain's sprightly Metro is one of many cars relying on Lucas electrical and electronic equipment.

Lucas Electrical has grown up with the automotive industry and, through a policy of innovative product development, has helped to engineer today's electronics revolution, with sophisticated microprocessor-controlled engine management systems, computer designed lighting equipment and an extensive range of electronic aids to better and safer motoring.

Lucas Electrical

Bembridge
Map 5 D4 Isle of Wight
Lane End Road *PO35 5SU*
Bembridge (098 387) 2838
Proprietors Mr & Mrs Cobb
Credit Access, Amex,
Barclaycard, Diners
Closed 3 weeks Oct & 24–28 Dec

Highbury Hotel 62% Ⓜ £E

Ask for directions when booking at this attractive little family-run hotel. There's a fascinating selection of bric-à-brac in the public rooms, which include two elegant lounges (one like a Victorian drawing room) and an intimate bar. Pretty bedrooms have modern fitted units and a host of thoughtful extras from games to hairdryers. Bathrooms are well equipped.
Amenities garden, sauna, outdoor swimming pool, croquet.

Rooms 9	*Room phone* Yes	*Confirm by* By arrang.	*Parking* Ample
with bath/shower 8	*Room TV* Yes	*Last dinner* 10	

Berkhamsted
Map 5 E2 Hertfordshire
139 High Street *HP4 3HJ*
Berkhamsted (044 27) 71451

Proprietors Mr & Mrs P. Caro
Credit Amex, Barclaycard

Swan Hotel *(Inn)* Ⓜ £E

A distinctive salmon-pink facade highlights this centuries-old town-centre hostelry. The bar with its heavy timbers and flagstone floor is a lively and popular meeting place, and there's a cosy TV lounge for residents. Narrow corridors lead to the traditionally furnished bedrooms (those with private bath are the best). Public bathrooms have simple modern suites.
Amenities sauna, dinner dance (Fri, Sat).

Rooms 18	*Room phone* Some	*Confirm by* 6	*Parking* Limited
with bath/shower 4	*Room TV* Yes	*Last dinner* 10	*Banquets* 20/–

Berwick-upon-Tweed
Map 14 B2 Northumberland
Castlegate *TD15 1LF*
Berwick-upon-Tweed
(0289) 6471

Credit Access, Amex,
Barclaycard, Diners

Castle Hotel *(Inn)* Ⓜ £F

This friendly little family-run hotel on the edge of town near the railway station offers adequate comforts for a short stay. Freestanding pine furniture is standard throughout the homely bedrooms, which share three simple, well-kept bathrooms. The roomy lounge bar, warmed in winter by a cheerful open fire, is a popular local rendezvous, and there's a cosy sitting room.

Rooms 15	*Room phone* No	*Confirm by* 6	*Parking* Ample
with bath/shower None	*Room TV* Some	*Last dinner* 9.30	

Berwick-upon-Tweed
Map 14 B2 Northumberland
Hide Hill *TD15 1EU*
Berwick-upon-Tweed
(0289) 7454
Telex 8811232
Credit Access, Amex,
Barclaycard, Diners

King's Arms Hotel 56% £E

Traditional comfort is the order of the day in this friendly Georgian hotel. Locals gather in the rustic public bar, and you can relax in the lounge with its marble-topped tables and modern sofas, or in the cosy cocktail bar. Bedrooms vary from small singles to spacious twins and family rooms; all are centrally heated and have freestanding furniture. Adequate bathrooms.
Amenities garden, dinner dance (Fri or Sat in season).

Rooms 39	*Room phone* Yes	*Confirm by* 6	*Parking* Ample
with bath/shower 21	*Room TV* Yes	*Last dinner* 10	*Banquets* 150/35

Beverley
Map 11 E1 Humberside
North Bar Within *HU17 8DD*
Hull (0482) 869241

Credit Access, Amex,
Barclaycard, Diners

Beverley Arms Hotel 61% £D

This fine hotel, steeped in history, still contains many echoes of its past. Warm comfortable public areas include two bars (one celebrating the dastardly deeds of Dick Turpin) and two cosy lounges. Double-glazed bedrooms range from large and traditional in the main building to more functional ones in the modern wing. Compact, well-fitted bathrooms.
Amenities coffee shop (9.30am–9.30pm, Sun 10am–6pm).

Rooms 61	*Room phone* Yes	*Confirm by* 6	*Parking* Ample
with bath/shower 61	*Room TV* Yes	*Last dinner* 10	*Banquets* 60/10

Bibury
Map 4 C2 Gloucestershire
GL7 5NW
Bibury (028 574) 204
Proprietor
Mr Colin T. Morgan

Credit Access, Barclaycard

Swan Hotel 55% Ⓜ £D

Across the road from a stone humpback bridge over the river Coln, this creeper-clad hotel has a beguiling country atmosphere enhanced by log fires, a grandfather clock and comfortable, well-used seating in the various lounges. Cosy bedrooms with attractively coordinated soft furnishings are traditional in style, and compact bathrooms are up to date.
Amenities garden, game fishing.

Continued

Rooms 24	*Room phone* Most	*Confirm by* 6	*Parking* Limited
with bath/shower 24	*Room TV* Yes	*Last dinner* 8.30	

Biddenden

Map 7 C5 Kent
High Street *TN27 8AL*
Biddenden (0580) 291306
Proprietors Mr & Mrs Daniels

Ye Maydes Ⓢ

Old-world charm, a friendly atmosphere and an enterprising menu ensure no shortage of regulars at this charming little village restaurant. The choice ranges from scallops that melt in the mouth to creamy stuffed leg of chicken and generous portions of roast duckling or bœuf bourguignonne. The young chef's cooking is skilled and robust, with flavoursome sauces a strong point.
Credit Access

● **Set L** £4·85
About £32 for two
Banquets 20/8

Lunch 12–1.45 *Dinner* 7.30–9.30, Sat 7–9.30
Closed Sun, Mon & Bank Holidays

Bideford

Map 2 C2 Devon
Heywood Road
Northam *EX39 3QB*
Bideford (023 72) 2361
Manager Mr J. G. Starke
Credit Access, Amex,
Barclaycard, Diners

Durrant House Hotel 62% £ E

A Georgian building forms the core of this modern hotel on the outskirts of town. Six bedrooms in the original part retain their traditional charm and character, although most of the rooms are stylishly contemporary. All have tea-makers and functional up-to-date bathrooms. Public rooms include an attractive lounge and three bars. *Amenities* garden, sauna, outdoor swimming pool, dancing (twice weekly), table tennis, games room.

Rooms 58	*Room phone* Yes	*Confirm by* By arrang.	*Parking* Ample
with bath/shower 58	*Room TV* Yes	*Last dinner* 9.30	*Banquets* 200/–

Bideford

Map 2 C2 Devon
Durrant Lane
Northam *EX39 2RL*
Bideford (023 72) 4400
Proprietors Chris & Judi Fulford
Credit Access, Amex,
Barclaycard, Diners

Yeoldon House 61% Ⓜ £ D

A warm welcome awaits visitors to the Fulfords' well-kept house, which stands in landscaped gardens. The entrance hall retains much of its Victorian elegance, and there's also a traditionally furnished lounge and a cosy bar. Most of the bright, cheerful bedrooms have simple white units, and modern bathrooms are compact. No dogs.
Amenities garden. **Closed** 2 weeks January/February, 4 days Christmas

Rooms 10	*Room phone* No	*Confirm by* 4	*Parking* Ample
with bath/shower 10	*Room TV* Yes	*Last dinner* 8.30	*Banquets* 40/–

Bilbrook

Map 3 E1 Somerset
Near Minehead *TA24 6HQ*
Washford (0984) 40215
Credit Access, Amex,
Barclaycard, Diners
Closed November–mid March
except 5 days Christmas

Dragon House Hotel 63% Ⓜ £ E

Tony and Valerie Wright take excellent care of their charming rose-covered, stone inn. The homely lounge and cosy little bar are attractive with period pieces and big stone fireplaces, and there's a delightful courtyard for summer drinks. Beamed bedrooms are prettily furnished (one with a half-tester), and bathrooms are smart and carpeted.
Amenities garden, game fishing, games room, croquet, stabling, riding. ♿

Rooms 11	*Room phone* No	*Confirm by* By arrang.	*Parking* Ample
with bath/shower 8	*Room TV* Some	*Last dinner* 9.15	*Banquets* 35/–

Bilbrook

Map 3 E1 Somerset
Near Minehead *TA24 6HQ*
Washford (0984) 40215

Dragon House Hotel Restaurant ♊ Ⓢ

Charming young waitresses provide the service in this attractive little dining room. A simple lunchtime menu offers mainly grills, while the short evening carte features some interesting dishes like fresh local trout with a white wine sauce or veal escalope in a deliciously smooth hazelnut and Stilton sauce. Rich fresh cream trifle makes an excellent finish.
🍷 *ABOVE AVERAGE. Credit* Access, Amex, Barclaycard, Diners

● **Set L** Sun only £5·50
Set D £8
About £29 for two

Lunch 12–1.45 *Dinner* 7–9.15, Sun 7–9
Closed November–mid March except 5 days Christmas

Map 10 C4
Town plan opposite

Population 1,006,948

Birmingham is the centre of one of Britain's most dynamic regions. It achieved industrial fame as a result of a fine tradition of craftsmanship. Today the city is noted for its production of motor cars, electrical equipment, machine tools and plastics. It has a splendid tradition in metal ware, including gold and silver work. Birmingham sponsored the £20m plus National Exhibition Centre at Bickenhill, just nine miles north-east of the city. This exhibition centre is Britain's first ever purpose-designed centre and ranks among the most modern in the world.

Sights Outside City
Airport, Coughton Court, Ragley Hall, Packwood House, Warwick Castle, West Midland Safari Park, Arbury Hall, Charlecote Park

Information Office
110 Colmore Row, Birmingham
Telephone 021–235 3411/2

Lancia Dealers

Colmore Depot
Sutton New Road
Erdington
Birmingham
Tel. 021–350 1301

Colmore Depot
Stratford Road
Hall Green
Birmingham
Tel. 021–777 6181

Birmingham

1	Alexandra Theatre	C3
2	Aston Hall *Jacobean masterpiece open to public*	D1
3	Baskerville House	B2
4	Botanical Gardens	A3
5	Bull Ring Shopping Centre *rotunda, multi-level shopping centre and market*	C/D3
6	Cannon Hill Park	C3
7	Central Libraries	B2
8	Chamber of Commerce	A3
9	Council House	B2
10	Hall of Memory	B2
11	Hippodrome Theatre	C3
12	Lickey Hills *500 beautiful acres with views from Beacon Hill of ten counties*	C3
13	Midland Red Bus Station	C3
14	Museum and Art Gallery *from Veronese to Picasso via Hogarth and Constable*	B2
15	Museum of Science and Industry *a link with the Industrial Revolution*	B1
16	Repertory Theatre	A2
17	New Street Station	C3
18	Night Out Theatre Club	C3
19	Post Office Tower	B1
20	St Chad's Cathedral *first English Roman Catholic Cathedral since Reformation*	C1
21	St Philip's Cathedral *18th-c Palladian with later Burne-Jones windows*	C2
22	Town Hall *meeting-place and home of Symphony orchestra*	B2
23	University of Aston	D1
24	University of Birmingham	C3

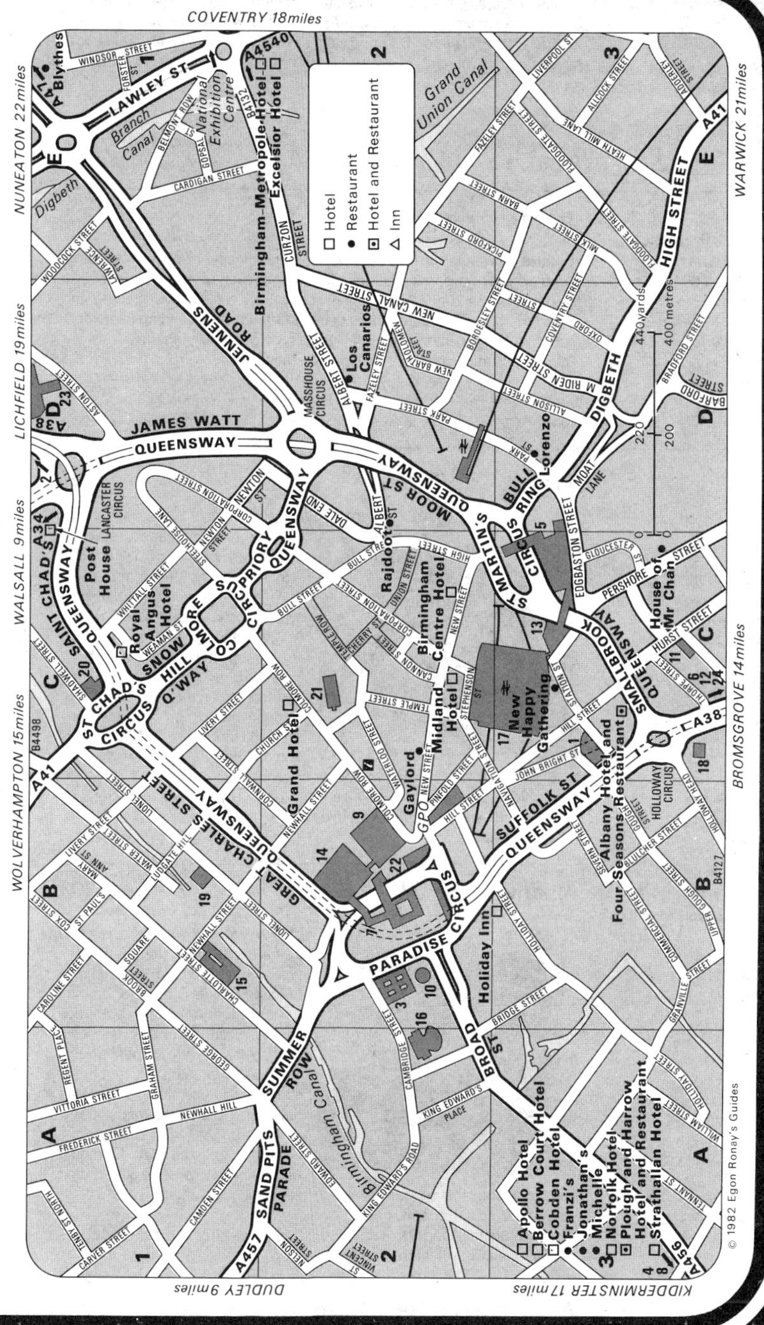

Birmingham
LANCIA
LANCIA

COVENTRY 18 miles

Hotel
Restaurant
Hotel and Restaurant
Inn

NUNEATON 22 miles
LICHFIELD 19 miles
WALSALL 9 miles
WOLVERHAMPTON 15 miles

WARWICK 21 miles
BROMSGROVE 14 miles

DUDLEY 9 miles
KIDDERMINSTER 17 miles

Grand Union Canal
HIGH STREET
DIGBETH
Digbeth
Branch Canal
Blythes
WINDSOR STREET
FORSTER STREET
LAWLEY ST
BELMONT ROW
GOSTA GREEN
National Exhibition Centre
Birmingham Metropole Hotel
Excelsior Hotel
CURZON STREET
CARDIGAN STREET
WOODCOCK STREET
LAWRENCE STREET
ASTON STREET
JAMES WATT QUEENSWAY
JENNENS ROAD
MASSHOUSE CIRCUS
ALBERT STREET
Los Canarios
NEW CANAL STREET
FAZELEY STREET
PARK STREET
BARTHOLOMEW STREET
NEW BARTHOLOMEW STREET
BORDESLEY STREET
ALLISON STREET
MOAT LANE
BULL RING
Lorenzo
FLOODGATE STREET
MILK STREET
BARN STREET
PICKFORD STREET
COVENTRY STREET
OXFORD STREET
HEATH MILL LANE
ALLCOCK STREET
LIVERPOOL STREET
FAZELEY STREET
ADDERLEY STREET
BARFORD STREET
BRADFORD STREET
PERSHORE STREET
GLOUCESTER ST
EDGBASTON STREET
440 yards
400 metres
220
200
QUEENSWAY
NEWTON STREET
CORPORATION STREET
STEELHOUSE LANE
LANCASTER CIRCUS
Post House
PRIORY QUEENSWAY
DALE END
MOOR ST QUEENSWAY
ST MARTIN'S
CIRCUS RING
HURST STREET
SMALLBROOK QUEENSWAY
House of Mr Chan
Royal Angus Hotel
WHITTALL STREET
WEAMAN ST
SNOW HILL Q'WAY
COLMORE
BULL STREET
UNION STREET
NEW STREET
HIGH STREET
Rajdoot
Birmingham Centre Hotel
ST CHAD'S QUEENSWAY
SHADWELL STREET
ST CHAD'S CIRCUS
LIVERY STREET
CHURCH STREET
CORNWALL STREET
EDMUND STREET
NEWHALL STREET
TEMPLE ROW
CHERRY STREET
CANNON STREET
TEMPLE STREET
CORPORATION STREET
STEPHENSON ST
New Happy Gathering
HILL STATION ST
Midland Hotel
Grand Hotel
Gaylord
GPO
NEW STREET
HILL STREET
PINFOLD STREET
NAVIGATION STREET
JOHN BRIGHT ST
SUFFOLK ST QUEENSWAY
Albany Hotel and Four Seasons Restaurant
HOLLOWAY CIRCUS
HOLLOWAY HEAD
SEVERN STREET
GOUGH STREET
BLUCHER STREET
GREAT CHARLES STREET QUEENSWAY
LIONEL STREET
WATER STREET
LUDGATE HILL
MARY ANN ST
LIVERY STREET
ST PAULS SQUARE
COX STREET
BROOK STREET
CHARLOTTE STREET
NEWHALL STREET
GEORGE STREET
GRAHAM STREET
CAROLINE STREET
REGENT PLACE
VITTORIA STREET
NEWHALL HILL
FREDERICK STREET
CAMDEN STREET
CARVER STREET
TENBY ST NORTH
SAND PITS PARADE
SUMMER ROW
EDWARD STREET
KING EDWARD'S ROAD
Birmingham Canal
CAMBRIDGE STREET
KING EDWARD'S PLACE
BROAD ST
BRIDGE STREET
GRANVILLE STREET
COMMERCIAL STREET
UPPER GOUGH STREET
HOLLIDAY STREET
PARADISE CIRCUS
Holiday Inn
ST VINCENT STREET
NELSON STREET
GEORGE STREET
NEWHALL STREET
Apollo Hotel
Berrow Court Hotel
Cobden Hotel
Franzi's
Jonathan's
Michelle
Norfolk Hotel
Plough and Harrow Hotel and Restaurant
Strathallan Hotel
WILLIAM STREET
TENNANT ST
HOLLIDAY STREET
© 1982 Egon Ronay's Guides

Billingham

Map 15 C5 Cleveland
Town Square *TS23 2HD*
Stockton-on-Tees
(0642) 553661
Telex 587746
Credit Access, Amex,
Barclaycard, Diners

Rooms 64	
with bath/shower 55	

Billingham Arms Hotel   57%   £ D/E

Built in 1958 as part of a town-centre shopping precinct, this popular hotel boasts five separate bars and a huge ballroom; residents have a peaceful lounge on the first floor. Bedrooms are neatly fitted and all have radios, tea-makers and welcoming baskets of fresh fruit. Twelve singles have shower rooms.

Room phone Yes	*Confirm by* 6	*Parking* Ample
Room TV Yes	*Last dinner* 10.15	*Banquets* 350/5

Bingley

Map 10 C1 West Yorkshire
Bradford Road *BO16 1TV*
Bradford (0274) 567123

Manager Mr C. D. Galbraith
Credit Access, Amex,
Barclaycard, Diners

Rooms 74	
with bath/shower 58	

Bankfield Hotel   60%   £ E

An attractive panelled foyer with a fine old staircase suggests the rather grand origins of this Victorian house, although much of the hotel now bears the marks of the 20th century. There is a hessian-walled residents' bar, and bedrooms range from traditionally decorated in the main building to 48 more modern ones with fitted units and tiled bathrooms in the wing.
Amenities garden, dancing (Sat October–May).

Room phone Yes	*Confirm by* 6	*Parking* Ample
Room TV Yes	*Last dinner* 9.15	*Banquets* 250/10

Birkenhead

Map 10 A2 Merseyside
2 Talbot Road, Oxton *L43 2HH*
051–652 4931

Manager Mr R. Gatti
Rooms 29
with bath/shower 29
Room phone Yes
Room TV Yes
Confirm by By arrang.
Last dinner 9.45
Parking Ample
Banquets 100/20

Credit Access, Amex,
Barclaycard, Diners

Bowler Hat Hotel   71%   £ C/D

Elegant comfort is the hallmark of this fine Victorian mansion set high above the town overlooking the Dee estuary with the Welsh mountains beyond. Inside, a charming little reception leads to the bar and a really delightful lounge with velvet settees and an array of nautical bric-à-brac. Bedrooms vary from old-fashioned and spacious in the main building to compact modern ones in the extension, all being beautifully furnished and superbly equipped with thoughtful extras ranging from trouser presses to bowls of fresh fruit. Bathrooms are equally well fitted and are provided with telephone extensions, as well as hairdryers and bathrobes. No dogs.
Amenities garden.

Birmingham

Town plan C3 West Midlands
Smallbrook
Queensway *B5 4EW*
021–643 8171
Telex 337031
Rooms 254
with bath/shower 254
Room phone Yes
Room TV Yes
Confirm by 6
Last dinner 11
Parking Ample
Banquets 560/–

Credit Access, Amex,
Barclaycard, Diners

Albany Hotel   71%   *E*   £ C

This well-designed 12-storey hotel in the heart of the city offers practical modern comforts, extensive function facilities and a good range of sports and leisure activities (residents are automatic members of the Albany Club). Public rooms are stylishly contemporary, from the streamlined reception area to the little open-plan residents' lounge, with its bright red sofas, and the dimly lit cocktail bar. Compact bedrooms, all double-glazed and air-conditioned, have simple pastel decor, practical fitted furniture and well-equipped tiled bathrooms.
Amenities sauna, indoor swimming pool, squash, dancing (Sat in autumn & winter), billiards, solarium, gymnasium.   &

Birmingham

Town plan C3 West Midlands
Smallbrook

Albany Hotel, Four Seasons Restaurant   ♛ Ⓢ

Three set lunchtime menus and an evening carte provide an excellent choice

Continued

Queensway *B5 4EW*
021–643 8171

● **Set L** from £7·25 incl. wine & service
About £40 for two

Birmingham

Town plan A3 West Midlands
243 Hagley Road *B16 9RA*
021–455 0271
Telex 336759
Credit Access, Amex, Barclaycard, Diners
Closed 2 days Christmas

Rooms 130
with bath/shower 130

Apollo Hotel   60%   £ D/E

Designed as a motel, this low brick building with striped window awnings is a convenient base for businessmen. Public areas have been refurbished in modern style, and there are good function and banqueting facilities. Most bedrooms are in a separate block and have well-designed fitted furniture, tea-makers, radios and compact, partly tiled bathrooms.
Amenities 24-hour laundry service.

Room phone Yes	*Confirm by* By arrang.	*Parking* Ample
Room TV Yes	*Last dinner* 10	*Banquets* 100/–

Birmingham

Town plan A3 West Midlands
Westfield Road
Edgbaston *B15 3UD*
021–454 1488
Proprietor Mr G. E. Morris
Credit Amex, Barclaycard
Closed 24 Dec for 1 week

Rooms 16
with bath/shower None

Berrow Court Hotel   55%   Ⓜ   £ F

Set in a quiet residential area two miles from the city centre, this large red-brick mansion has a peaceful, welcoming atmosphere. There's an oak-panelled entrance hall with a fine wooden staircase as well as two lounges (one with TV). Very large, spotlessly clean bedrooms have sturdy furniture, and public bathrooms retain their splendid original fittings. No meals at weekends. *Amenities* garden.

Room phone No	*Confirm by* By arrang.	*Parking* Ample
Room TV No	*Last dinner* 7.30	*Banquets* 100/10

Birmingham

Town plan C2 West Midlands
New Street *B2 4RX*
021–643 2747
Telex 338331

Credit Access, Amex, Barclaycard, Diners

Rooms 200
with bath/shower 200

Birmingham Crest Hotel   62%   £ D

This well-kept modern hotel (formerly the Birmingham Centre) stands right in the heart of the city. There's a comfortable, streamlined reception area, and the softly lighted cocktail bar on the ninth floor has panoramic city views. Air-conditioned bedrooms have attractive darkwood fitted furniture and neat, well-equipped bathrooms.
Amenities coffee shop (10am–4.30pm Mon–Sat), 12-hour laundry service.

Room phone Yes	*Confirm by* 6	*Parking* Ample
Room TV Yes	*Last dinner* 9.45	*Banquets* 200/–

Birmingham

Town plan E1 West Midlands
19 High Street
Coleshill *B46 1AY*
Coleshill (0675) 62266

● **Set D** £9·95
About £27 for two
Banquets 30/10

Blythes   ♎ Ⓢ

The Martins have created an attractive restaurant with an interesting homely menu based on quality ingredients. The lunchtime carte includes light dishes like tasty shellfish pancake; the four-course set dinner could start with prawn and haddock mousse, followed by rich beef chasseur with carefully cooked vegetables. Don't miss the delectable fudge sweet. Booking essential. No pipes. *Credit* Access, Barclaycard

Lunch 12.30–2 *Dinner* 7.30–9.45 **Closed** L Sat, D Mon, all Sun, Bank Holiday Mon, 2 days after Christmas & 2 weeks August

---

Birmingham

Town plan D2 West Midlands
105 Albert Street
Digbeth *B5 5JY*
021–236 3495
Proprietor F. Pancho Garcia
Spanish cooking

About £24 for two
Banquets 70/2

Los Canarios   ♎ Ⓢ

Authentic food and a colourfully flamboyant atmosphere bring this friendly Spanish restaurant to life. Pancho Garcia prepares some enjoyable, strongly flavoured dishes like fillet steak mexicana (with a peppery tequila sauce) and deep-fried squid, as well as favourites such as paella and kidneys in sherry sauce.
Credit Access, Amex, Diners

Lunch 12–2.30 *Dinner* 7.30–12
Closed L Sat, all Sun & Bank Holidays

---

at this comfortable, sophisticated restaurant. A selection from the hors d'œuvre trolley makes a tasty starter, and main courses include cuisine minceur dishes as well as more substantial specialities like medallions of venison in a rich game sauce with wild mushrooms. Super profiteroles to finish. ♟ *ABOVE AVERAGE. Credit* Access, Amex, Barclaycard, Diners

Lunch 12.30–2.30 *Dinner* 7.30–11
Closed L Sat, all Sun & most Bank Holidays

Birmingham

Town plan A3 West Midlands
166 Hagley Road
Edgbaston *B16 9NZ*
021–454 6621
Manager Mr A. J. Colley
Credit Access, Amex,
Barclaycard

Rooms 210
with bath/shower 156

Cobden Hotel 57% £E

Recently completed improvements at this well-run hotel have added a spacious, airy reception-lounge and a residents' lounge overlooking the attractive garden. Bedrooms range from modern ones in the newest wing, with cheerful fabrics and tiled shower rooms, to plainer, more traditional ones in the original building. Adequate bathrooms. The hotel is unlicensed. *Amenities* garden, putting. **Closed** 4 days Christmas

Room phone Yes	*Confirm by* 6	*Parking* Ample
Room TV Most	*Last dinner* 9	*Banquets* 50/–

Birmingham

Town plan A3 West Midlands
151 Milcote Road
Bearwood *B67 5BN*
021–429 7920
Austrian cooking

About £24 for two
Banquets 35/20

Franzl's

Everything about this restaurant is decidedly Austrian, from the chalet-style decor to the choice of food and wines. Adolf Geiregger uses good produce to prepare not only familiar dishes like wiener schnitzel but also specialities such as medallions of fillet steak in a creamy kümmel sauce. Vegetables are excellent and there are gorgeous sweets. *ABOVE AVERAGE.*
Credit Access, Barclaycard

Dinner only 7–10.30
Closed Sun, Mon & August

Birmingham

Town plan C2 West Midlands
61 New Street *B2 4DU*
021–632 4500

Indian cooking
About £25 for two

Gaylord

Spicy lamb, chicken and fish main courses, interesting tandoori specialities and some unusual vegetable dishes are all capably prepared in this stylish upstairs restaurant. *Credit* Access, Amex, Barclaycard, Diners *Lunch* 12–3 *Dinner* 6–11.30 **Closed** Sun & 25 & 26 December ● **Set L** £4·50 **Set D** from £4·50 *Banquets* 50/2

Birmingham

Town plan C2 West Midlands
Colmore Row *B3 2DA*
021–236 7951
Telex 338174
Credit Access, Amex,
Barclaycard, Diners
Closed 4 days Christmas

Rooms 190
with bath/shower 190

Grand Hotel 69% £D

Victorian style combines happily with modern comfort in this well-run city-centre hotel. The roomy reception-lounge area is attractively furnished, and there are several appealing bars; the star of the 15 function rooms is undoubtedly the magnificently ornate Grosvenor Suite. Attractive, spacious bedrooms have well-designed modern fittings, as do the carpeted bathrooms. *Amenities* 12-hour laundry service, restaurant (7am–10pm)

Room phone Yes	*Confirm by* 6	*Parking* Difficult
Room TV Yes	*Last dinner* 10	*Banquets* 500/8

Birmingham

Town plan B2 West Midlands
Holliday Street *B1 1HH*
021–643 2766
Telex 337272

Rooms 304
with bath/shower 304
Room phone Yes
Room TV Yes
Confirm by By arrang.
Last dinner 10.30
Parking Ample
Banquets 200/–

Credit Access, Amex,
Barclaycard, Diners

Holiday Inn 72% E £C/D

There's a distinct air of an ocean liner in the decor of the foyer and other public areas of this impressive modern hotel right in the city centre. There's a poolside Deck Bar with luxuriant tropical greenery, and the West End Bar recalls Victorian days with its plush alcoves and a pianola (live music, too). Bedrooms are large and attractively decorated, all with the Holiday Inn trademark of two double beds, and immaculately kept bathrooms feature a plentiful supply of thick, soft towels.
Amenities sauna, indoor swimming pool, keep-fit equipment, in-house movies, coffee shop (7am–11pm), entertainment (Sun).

Birmingham
Town plan C3 West Midlands
167 Bromsgrove Street *B5 6NU*
021–622 1725

Chinese cooking

● **Set L & Set D** £9 for two
About £20 for two
Banquets 40/–

House of Mr Chan   Ⓢ

A jokily presented booklet (*The Thoughts of Chairman Chan*) details the wide range of Cantonese and other dishes available in this pleasantly simple restaurant. Dim sum, eight kinds of soup, and specialities like steamed whole fish, char-siu pork and shredded beef Szechuan style are all freshly cooked to a consistently high standard. Service is friendly and helpful.
Credit Access, Amex, Barclaycard, Diners

Meals noon–midnight
Closed 25 & 26 December

Birmingham
Town plan A3 West Midlands
16 Wolverhampton Rd *B68 0LH*
021–429 3757
Proprietors Mr Jonathan Baker
& Mr Jonathan Bedford
English cooking
● **Set D** Sat only £12·90
incl. service
About £31 for two
Banquets 45/–

Jonathans'   Ⓢ

Two Jonathans–Baker and Bedford–run this splendid Victorian-style restaurant, which specialises in traditional (and excellent) English cooking. The menu changes frequently, offering delights like mace-flavoured minced pork, lamb cutlets with Cumberland sauce and our superb salmon and prawn pie. Beautifully cooked vegetables, and some lovely old-fashioned puddings. Post-theatre suppers. *Credit* Access, Amex, Barclaycard, Diners

Lunch 12–2 *Dinner* 7–11
Closed L Sat, all Sun & 26 December

Birmingham
Town plan D3 West Midlands
3 Park Street, Digbeth *B5 5JD*
021–643 0541
Proprietor Lorenzo Ferrari
Italian cooking

● **Set L** £4·50
About £24 for two
Banquets 80/30

Lorenzo   Ⓢ

A rustic oak table loaded with wine and fruit forms the centrepiece of this elegant Italian restaurant. The menu offers mainly well-known dishes such as cannelloni, risotto, saltimbocca alla romana and bistecca alla pizzaiola which are served with delicious vegetables. Tempting sweets include chocolate gâteau and trifle. Book.
Credit Access, Amex, Barclaycard, Diners

Lunch 12–2.15 *Dinner* 6.30–11
Closed L Sat, all Sun, Bank Holidays & mid July–mid August

Birmingham
Town plan E1 West Midlands
National Exhibition Centre
B40 1PP
021–780 4242
Telex 336129
Rooms 709
with bath/shower 709
Room phone Yes
Room TV Yes
Confirm by By arrang.
Last dinner 10.30
Parking Ample
Banquets 1200/–

Credit Access, Amex,
Barclaycard, Diners

Metropole & Warwick Hotel   81%   *E*   £B

Situated right next to the National Exhibition Centre, this impressive building has all the sophistication, elegance and style of a modern executive hotel, and it boasts a vast range of conference facilities. Automatic doors open on to the spectacular foyer with its huge chandeliers, and there's a large, open-plan lounge furnished with comfortable bamboo armchairs and deep sofas, as well as an elegant cocktail bar. Well-appointed, sizeable bedrooms all have good-quality fitted units and attractively coordinated colour schemes. Bathrooms are also large and fully equipped.
Amenities garden, sauna, squash, coffee shop (7am–10.30pm), hairdressing, solarium, cinema.   ♿

Birmingham
Town plan A3 West Midlands
182 High Street
Harborne *B17 9PP*
021–426 4133
Proprietor Mrs Michelle Vale
French cooking
● **Set L** from £2·65

Michelle   Ⓢ

This charming restaurant has the welcoming atmosphere of a genuine French bistro, and the cooking is typically Gallic to match. The à la carte and daily set menus include attractively presented pâtés and rillettes and dishes like herby salmon en croûte, beef Stroganoff and steak au poivre. Vegetables are prepared with care and sweets include a deliciously rich chocolate mousse.   ♿

Continued

Continued
Set D from £5·75 incl. service
Banquets 60/10

Lunch 12–2 *Dinner* 7–10, Sat 7–10.30
Closed Sun & Bank Holidays

Birmingham

Town plan C2 West Midlands
New Street *B2 4JT*
021–643 2601
Telex 338419
Manager Mr P. W. Gravett
Credit Access, Amex,
Barclaycard, Diners

Midland Hotel   67%   **£ D**

This traditional hotel has been busy updating its appearance: the impressive pillared entrance hall-cum-lounge has had a facelift, and refurbished bedrooms with restful decor are individually styled and have smart bathrooms. Bars range from a pubby one dedicated to real ale to a panelled cocktail bar, and there's a useful buttery. *Amenities* dancing (Sat October–end April), buttery (Mon–Sat 10am–10pm).

Rooms 116
with bath/shower 116

Room phone Yes
Room TV Yes

Confirm by 6
Last dinner 10.30

Parking Ample
Banquets 200/–

Birmingham

Town plan C3 West Midlands
43 Station Street *B5 4DY*
021–643 5247

Chinese cooking

● **Set L** from £2
About £17 for two
Banquets 140/40

New Happy Gathering

A roomy first-floor restaurant with Chinese decor and a long menu which includes dim sum and well-cooked Cantonese dishes like our tender, tasty stuffed crispy duck with crabmeat sauce. Other tempting specialities are steamed scallops in garlic dressing, shredded pork in lettuce and sizzling chicken in black bean sauce. Light, fluffy steamed lotus paste buns make a delicious sweet. *Credit* Amex, Diners

Meals noon–midnight
Closed 3 days Christmas

Birmingham

Town plan A3 West Midlands
257 Hagley Road *B16 9NA*
021–454 8071
Telex 339715
Manager Mr S. H. Barlow
Credit Access, Amex,
Barclaycard

Norfolk Hotel   54%   **£ E**

This friendly, well-run hotel was originally a couple of large Victorian houses, which have been converted and considerably extended. Public rooms include a spacious entrance hall and a TV lounge with contemporary seating. Bedrooms are neatly furnished in simple modern style, and bath or shower rooms are adequate. Unlicensed. *Amenities* garden, 12-hour laundry service, 24-hour lounge service. **Closed** 3 days Christmas

Rooms 190
with bath/shower 80

Room phone Yes
Room TV Some

Confirm by 7
Last dinner 9

Parking Ample
Banquets 35/–

Birmingham

Town plan A3 West Midlands
Hagley Road
Edgbaston *B16 8LS*
021–454 4111
Telex 338074
Rooms 44
with bath/shower 44
Room phone Yes
Room TV Yes
Confirm by By arrang.
Last dinner 10.30
Parking Ample
Banquets 60/2

Credit Access, Amex,
Barclaycard, Diners

Plough & Harrow Hotel   80%   *E*   **£ B/C**

Situated a mile from the city centre, this handsomely decorated hotel is superbly maintained and offers excellent facilities for business executives. A stylish, brightly lit reception hall leads to the sumptuous residents' lounge with hessian-covered walls, oil paintings and elegant armchairs; there are also two comfortable bars. Decor in the bedrooms (most are in the modern extension) is especially pleasing. All are well designed and equipped with polished wooden cupboards and chesterfield armchairs; compact, fully tiled bathrooms have gold-plated fittings and coloured suites. Very professional management. Guide dogs only. *Amenities* sauna.

Birmingham

Town plan A3 West Midlands
Hagley Road
Edgbaston *B16 8LS*
021–454 4111

Plough & Harrow Hotel Restaurant   ★ ♕♕ ⓢ

John Sweeney produces meals to remember in this elegant restaurant overlooking a lawned courtyard. French-inspired dishes are prepared with great skill and care, from simple onion soup and chicken liver pâté to pike mousse stuffed with spinach, veal sweetbreads with cream and pink-roasted magret de canard. Game and fish make seasonal appearances, and the

Continued

● **Set L** £12·50 **Set D** £17·10
incl. service
About £44 for two

special *menu gastronomique* is particularly imaginative. A colourful sweet trolley offers delights like pineapple sponge gâteau. Less choice Sunday evening. **Specialities** goujonettes de sole aux oranges et au poivre vert, canette aux baies de cassis, médaillons de filet de bœuf 'Stephane', soufflé chaud aux framboises. *Credit* Access, Amex, Barclaycard, Diners

Lunch 12.30–2 *Dinner* 7.30–10.30
Closed Bank Holidays

Birmingham
Town plan C1 West Midlands
Chapel Lane
Great Barr *B43 7BG*
021–357 7444
Telex 338497
Credit Access, Amex,
Barclaycard, Diners

Post House Hotel   59%   £ D

A popular overnight stop for business people, this low-rise modern hotel is located near junction 7 of the M6. Brightly contemporary public areas include a streamlined reception, a comfortable lounge and two bars. Well-equipped bedrooms have built-in units giving ample storage and work space; bathrooms are neat and tidy. Extensive conference facilities. *Amenities* garden, outdoor swimming pool, coffee shop (7.30am–10.30pm).　　　　　&

Rooms 204
with bath/shower 204

| *Room phone* Yes | *Confirm by* 6 | *Parking* Ample |
| *Room TV* Yes | *Last dinner* 10.30 | *Banquets* 140/6 |

Birmingham
Town plan C2 West Midlands
12 Albert Street *B4 7UD*
021–643 8805

Indian cooking

● **Set L** from £3·30
Set D from £6·50
About £25 for two

Rajdoot ★   

In this luxurious restaurant, with its subdued lighting and soothing background music, authentic North Indian dishes, including many tandoori specialities, are served by friendly, helpful waiters in colourful traditional dress. Superb fresh ingredients are used, and the careful balancing of herbs and spices produces some really mouthwatering delights like mild chicken bhuna with spring onions and mushrooms or richly sauced fish masala. Vegetables, breads and basmati rice are all excellent, too. The à la carte range is extensive, and set menus give an opportunity to sample several dishes. **Specialities** chicken shashlik, shish kebab, lamb pasanda, makhan chicken. *Credit* Access, Amex, Barclaycard, Diners

Lunch 12–2.15 *Dinner* 6.30–12
Closed Bank Holidays

We welcome complaints and bona fide recommendations on the tear-out pages for readers' comments. They are followed up by our professional team. Please also complain to the management instantly.

Birmingham
Town plan C1 West Midlands
St Chad's Queensway *B4 6HY*
021–236 4211
Telex 336889

Credit Access, Amex,
Barclaycard, Diners

Royal Angus Hotel   61%   £ D

This centrally situated modern hotel makes a useful base for visitors to the city. It has a spacious reception hall with a patterned ceramic-tiled floor, while on the second floor (which has access to the multi-storey car park) there's a smart open-plan lounge area leading to a pleasant bar. Compact bedrooms are double-glazed and well equipped with practical built-in units, and bathrooms are fully tiled.

Rooms 140
with bath/shower 140

| *Room phone* Yes | *Confirm by* 6 | *Parking* Ample |
| *Room TV* Yes | *Last dinner* 10 | *Banquets* 180/– |

Birmingham
Town plan A3 West Midlands
225 Hagley Road
Edgbaston *B16 9RY*
021–445 9777
Telex 336680
Credit Access, Amex,
Barclaycard, Diners

Strathallan Hotel   60%   £ D

This distinctive circular hotel, just outside the city centre, is built over its own car park. The spacious reception-lounge has plenty of restful armchairs, and there is a cocktail bar with a safari-style decor and a more pubby bar that resembles a log cabin. Compact bedrooms have simple fitted units and adequate bathrooms. *Amenities* dancing (Fri, Sat), jazz (Sun), solarium, 12-hour laundry service.　　　　　&

Rooms 171
with bath/shower 171

| *Room phone* Yes | *Confirm by* 6 | *Parking* Ample |
| *Room TV* Yes | *Last dinner* 10.30 | *Banquets* 230/– |

Birmingham Airport
Town plan E2 West Midlands
Coventry Road *B26 3QW*
021–743 8141
Telex 338005

Credit Access, Amex,
Barclaycard, Diners

Rooms 141
with bath/shower 141

Excelsior Hotel   63%   £ C/D

This comfortable modern airport hotel is built around a 1930s pub. Among its public rooms are an eye-catching foyer-lounge, a coachhouse-style bar and a cosy cocktail bar; there are also extensive conference facilities. Cheerfully decorated, double-glazed bedrooms have smart fitted furniture, tea-makers, mini-bars and well-equipped bathrooms. A refurbishment programme is under way. *Amenities* patio, transport for airport.

Room phone Yes	*Confirm by* 6	*Parking* Ample
Room TV Yes	*Last dinner* 10	*Banquets* 200/10

Birtle
Map 10 B1 Greater Manchester
Elbut Lane
Near Bury *BL9 6UT*
061–764 3869

About £36 for two

Normandie Hotel Restaurant

Decorated in classical French style, this elegant hotel restaurant offers enjoyable cooking: sauces are light, vegetables are carefully cooked and overall presentation is excellent. Friendly service. *ABOVE AVERAGE.*
Credit Access, Amex, Barclaycard, Diners *Lunch* 12.30–2 *Dinner* 7–9
Closed L Sat, all Sun, 1 January & 26 December

Bishop's Cleeve
Map 4 B1 Gloucestershire
Evesham Road
Near Cheltenham *GL52 4SA*
Bishop's Cleeve (024 267) 2585
Proprietors Marfell family

● **Set L** Sun only £7·50
About £31 for two
Banquets 30/–

Cleeveway Hotel Restaurant

An old stone manor house with pretty gardens is the setting for this attractive restaurant where Mr Marfell offers ably prepared dishes like beef Stroganoff, roast duckling with lemon sauce, and sole Thermidor, plus a tempting cold buffet and delicious sweets. Three comfortable bedrooms with private bath are available for overnight guests. *SUPERIOR.*
Credit Access

Lunch 12–1.45, Sun at 1 *Dinner* 7–9.45
Closed L Mon, D Sun, Easter & Christmas

Bishop's Stortford
Map 6 B3 Hertfordshire
Hadham Road *CM23 2QD*
Bishop's Stortford (0279) 52289

Credit Amex, Diners
Closed 1 week January

Rooms 14
with bath/shower 4

Dane House Hotel   57%   £ E/F

Situated about one mile west of the town centre on the A1250, this converted private house offers peace and relaxation in simple yet attractive surroundings. The spacious lounge and bar will benefit from planned redecoration. Bedrooms with radios are attractively fitted out with pretty wallpapers, matching fabrics and built-in units, and bathrooms are well maintained. *Amenities* garden.

Room phone No	*Confirm by* 6	*Parking* Ample
Room TV No	*Last dinner* 9.30	

Blackburn
Map 10 B1 Lancashire
Yew Tree Drive
Preston New Road *BB2 7AJ*
Blackburn (0254) 64441
Telex 63271
Credit Access, Amex,
Barclaycard, Diners

Rooms 98
with bath/shower 98

Saxon Inn Motor Hotel   60%   £ D

This pleasant, efficiently run motel—a gabled, Scandinavian-style building—stands above the road between the M6 (junction 31) and Blackburn. The streamlined reception hall has a comfortable lounge area, and there are also two relaxing bars and a self-contained banqueting suite. Bedrooms have well-designed fitted furniture and neat, sparkling bathrooms.
Amenities garden, outdoor swimming pool, dancing (Fri, Sat), pool table.

Room phone Yes	*Confirm by* 6	*Parking* Ample
Room TV Yes	*Last dinner* 10.15	*Banquets* 400/–

Blackheath

Bardon Lodge Hotel

See under London Economy Hotels

Blackpool
Map 10 A1 Lancashire
Talbot Square *FY1 1ND*
Blackpool (0253) 21481

Manager Mr S. W. Johnston
Credit Access, Amex,
Barclaycard, Diners

Clifton Hotel   58%   £ E

This handsome modernised Victorian hotel occupies a corner site overlooking North Pier. A central wooden staircase dominates the airy entrance hall, and other public areas include a traditionally styled lounge and no less than five bars. Bedrooms are comfortable and well fitted, the best being the de luxe rooms, with attractively patterned wallpaper, smart darkwood furniture and spacious modern bathrooms. *Amenities* dancing (Fri, Sat).

Continued

Rooms 76	*Room phone* Yes	*Confirm by* By arrang.	*Parking* Difficult
with bath/shower 66	*Room TV* Some	*Last dinner* 9	*Banquets* 120/–

Blackpool

Mayflower

Map 10 A1 Lancashire
118 Promenade *FY1 1NX*
Blackpool (0253) 27368
Chinese cooking

About £20 for two

Perennial Cantonese favourites like meaty roast duck, spareribs and chicken with black bean sauce dominate the long menu in this friendly, family-run Chinese restaurant right on the seafront. *Credit* Access, Amex, Barclaycard, Diners *Lunch* 12–2 *Dinner* 5–12
● **Set L** £1·90 **Set D** £4·50

Blackpool

Savoy Hotel 56% £D/E

Map 10 A1 Lancashire
Queen's Promenade *FY2 9SJ*
Blackpool (0253) 52561
Telex 67570

Credit Access, Amex,
Barclaycard, Diners

Public rooms are first in line for the renovation programme planned by new owners at this large red-brick hotel on the seafront. These include a well-proportioned entrance hall with a moulded plasterwork ceiling, several bars and lounges and the spacious ballroom. Compact bedrooms have simple whitewood units and tea/coffee-makers; those at the front have fine sea views. *Amenities* dancing (Sat), jazz (Mon).

Rooms 135	*Room phone* Yes	*Confirm by* 7	*Parking* Ample
with bath/shower 100	*Room TV* Yes	*Last dinner* 8.45	*Banquets* 320/–

Blagdon

Mendip Hotel 62% Ⓜ £D/E

Map 4 A3 Avon
Near Bristol *BS18 6TS*
Blagdon (0761) 62688

Manager Mr G. Holloway
Credit Access, Amex,
Barclaycard, Diners

Spread along a hillside, this modern building has splendid views over the village and Blagdon Lake, and huge picture windows are a spectacular feature of the airy, open-plan reception and bar. Most of the bedrooms also overlook the lake and have bright, up-to-date fittings. Bathrooms–which include four shower rooms–are especially well appointed. The hotel has good conference facilities. *Amenities* garden.

Rooms 37	*Room phone* No	*Confirm by* 6	*Parking* Ample
with bath/shower 37	*Room TV* Yes	*Last dinner* 10	*Banquets* 270/80

We do not necessarily recommend the cooking at hotels whose restaurants are not separately listed.

Blakeney

Blakeney Hotel 61% Ⓜ £D

Map 6 C1 Norfolk
Quayside *NR25 7AU*
Cley (0263) 740797
Telex 975465
Proprietor Mr Ralph Murfitt
Credit Access, Amex,
Barclaycard, Diners

This popular brick and flint holiday hotel enjoys fine views over the harbour towards Blakeney Point conservation area. There are two comfortable lounges (one with picture windows), several bars and a galleried function room. Well-maintained bedrooms are decorated in a variety of styles; downstairs ones in the modern granary annexe have their own patios. *Amenities* garden, sauna, indoor swimming pool, games room.

Rooms 54	*Room phone* Yes	*Confirm by* 8	*Parking* Ample
with bath/shower 36	*Room TV* Most	*Last dinner* 9.30	*Banquets* 120/5

Blakeney

Manor Hotel 58% £E

Map 6 C1 Norfolk
Near Holt
Cley (0263) 740376
Manager Mr G. E. Murray

Closed 2 weeks November &
9 days Christmas

A 16th-century farmhouse is at the core of this delightfully rambling flint building overlooking marshes and saltings. A paved entrance leads to a comfortable bar and an attractive lounge with deep sofas and armchairs. Some bedrooms are in the main house, others in the converted stables; all have smart white units, tea/coffee-makers and compact, well-fitted bathrooms. *Amenities* garden.

Rooms 22	*Room phone* No	*Confirm by* By arrang.	*Parking* Ample
with bath/shower 22	*Room TV* No	*Last dinner* 8.45	

Blanchland
Map 15 B4 Northumberland
Near Consett, Co. Durham
DH8 9SP
Blanchland (043 475) 251
Telex 53168
Credit Access, Amex,
Barclaycard, Diners

Rooms 17
with bath/shower 10

Lord Crewe Arms Hotel   56%   Ⓜ   **£E**

Improvements continue at this interesting moorland inn. Many of the traditionally furnished bedrooms (12 are in an annexe across the road) have a bright, fresh look, and three private bathrooms have been added. Flagstone floors and superb stone fireplaces add considerable charm to the public rooms, which include the popular Crypt Bar and a TV lounge.
Amenities garden. **Closed** Sun–Thurs early Jan–early March

Room phone Yes	*Confirm by* By arrang.	*Parking* Limited
Room TV No	*Last dinner* 9	

Blandford Forum
Map 4 B4 Dorset
Whitecliff Mill Street *DT11 7BP*
Blandford (0258) 52842

About £24 for two

La Belle Alliance   🦢 Ⓢ

Teamwork is the key to the success of the Harrisons' homely *restaurant avec chambres*, and the emphasis is very much on fresh produce. The short menu –handwritten daily–has a French flavour, with main courses like delicious lamb's kidneys in Calvados sauce and fillet steak bordelaise capably prepared by the man of the house, Tony. His wife takes care of starters such as delicate prawn and smoked salmon terrine, along with the superb sweets like rich, rum-soaked gâteau paradis. Overnight guests can enjoy the comfort of the four delightfully furnished bedrooms, which have colour TVs and carpeted modern bathrooms.
Credit Access, Diners

Lunch by arrangement only *Dinner* 7–9.30
Closed Sun, 25 & 26 December & 2 weeks January

Bletchingley
Map 7 B5 Surrey
36 High Street *RH1 4PA*
Godstone (0883) 843130

● **Set L** £3·85
About £28 for two

King Charles   🦢 Ⓢ

A charming old cottage is the setting for this delightfully cosy little restaurant. The welcoming Mr and Mrs Streit offer an eclectic menu which ranges from Hungarian goulash soup and steak pizzaiola to grills, shaslik and chicken Maryland, with a fair sprinkling of specialities from Mr Streit's native Switzerland. Good ingredients are carefully cooked, and sauces are especially tasty. *Credit* Access, Amex, Barclaycard, Diners

Lunch 12–2 *Dinner* 7–10.30 **Closed** D Sun, all Mon, Bank Holidays, last 2 weeks April, last 2 weeks August & Christmas week

Blindley Heath
Map 7 B5 Surrey
Tandridge Lane *RH7 6LL*
Lingfield (0342) 834272

About £32 for two

Red Barn Inn

A charming beamed restaurant in a lovely old tile-clad building. Simple, carefully prepared dishes range from chicken basquaise to grills and coquilles St Jacques. *Credit* Access, Amex, Barclaycard, Diners
Lunch 12–2.30, Sun 12.30–2.15 *Dinner* 7.30–10, Sat 7.30–10.30
Closed L Sat & D Sun ● **Set L** Sun only £5·50 *Banquets* 120/–

Blockley
Map 4 C1 Gloucestershire
Near Moreton-in-Marsh
GL56 9DS
Blockley (0386) 700286

Credit Access, Barclaycard
Closed 1st 3 weeks January

Rooms 8
with bath/shower 6

Lower Brook House   60%   Ⓜ   **£D**

A hospitable atmosphere fills this 17th-century stone house in a peaceful Cotswold village. Guests can relax in the delightful lounge with its exposed timbers and huge open fireplace, or gather in the cosy bar. A steep staircase leads to the pretty little bedrooms, which are smartly furnished in modern style. Sizeable bathrooms are well fitted. Inclusive terms only. No children under five. No dogs. *Amenities* garden.

Room phone No	*Confirm by* 6.30	*Parking* Ample
Room TV No	*Last dinner* 9	

Bodiam
Map 7 C6 East Sussex
Robertsbridge *TN32 5UY*
Hurst Green (058 086) 272

Curlew Inn   🦢 Ⓢ

Julian Caffyn's short menu is supplemented by daily specials which might include robust shellfish bisque, deep-fried mushrooms stuffed with pâté, and perhaps melon and raspberry sorbet for dessert. His meat is of excellent quality and sauces are well flavoured and hearty. Flowery wallpaper lends a summery touch to this homely, friendly pub dining room.
Credit Access, Amex, Barclaycard, Diners

Continued

● **Set L** £6
About £30 for two
Banquets 40/-

Lunch 12.30–2 *Dinner* 7–9.30
Closed Mon

Bodymoor Heath

Map 10 C4 Warwickshire
Near Sutton Coldfield
West Midlands *B76 0EA*
Tamworth (0827) 872133

Credit Access, Amex,
Barclaycard, Diners

Rooms 17
with bath/shower 17

Marston Farm Hotel   62%   Ⓜ   £E

This attractively converted farmhouse in a peaceful rural setting is approached down a narrow road leading off the A4091. The small reception area and traditionally furnished lounges and bar have a delightfully homely air, as do the compact, nicely coordinated bedrooms, most of which have shower rooms. No dogs. *Amenities* garden, outdoor swimming pool, tennis, coarse fishing, dancing (Wed), canal mooring.

Room phone Yes	*Confirm by* 6	*Parking* Ample
Room TV Yes	*Last dinner* 10	*Banquets* 60/20

Bognor Regis

Map 5 E4 West Sussex
The Esplanade *PO21 2LH*
Bognor Regis (0243) 826222

Credit Access, Amex,
Barclaycard, Diners

Rooms 53
with bath/shower 39

Royal Norfolk Hotel   64%   £D/E

Standing in grounds dotted with palm trees, this distinctive seafront hotel has fine views over the nearby beaches. Public areas are liberally adorned with pictures, brass ornaments and large mirrors, while spacious bedrooms– attractively decorated and pleasantly furnished–are well equipped, and bathrooms are large. *Amenities* garden, outdoor swimming pool, tennis, dinner dance (Sat), putting, croquet.

Room phone Yes	*Confirm by* 6	*Parking* Ample
Room TV Yes	*Last dinner* 9.30	*Banquets* 250/-

Bolton

Map 10 B1 Greater Manchester
Beaumont Road *BL3 4TA*
Bolton (0204) 651511
Telex 635527

Credit Access, Amex,
Barclaycard, Diners

Rooms 100
with bath/shower 100

Crest Hotel   57%   £D

This modern red-brick hotel, situated on the outskirts of town not far from the M61 (junction 5), is a useful and comfortable overnight stopping place. Decor throughout the public rooms is bright and cheerful, contemporary red and brown wall tiles blending harmoniously with the carpeting. Compact, well-decorated bedrooms have tea/coffee-makers, electric trouser presses and good tiled bathrooms. *Amenities* garden.   ♿

Room phone Yes	*Confirm by* By arrang.	*Parking* Ample
Room TV Yes	*Last dinner* 9.45	*Banquets* 100/-

Bolton

Map 10 B1 Greater Manchester
Bromley Cross *BL7 9PZ*
Bolton (0204) 591131
Telex 635322

Credit Access, Amex,
Barclaycard, Diners

Rooms 69
with bath/shower 69

Last Drop Hotel   66%   £D

This stone-built hotel with a clock tower stands at the entrance to a village complex complete with its own pub, tea shop and crafts centre. It has a welcoming reception area, a comfortable modern lounge and a rustic bar. Well-designed bedrooms have smart fitted units, hairdryers, trouser presses and tea-makers. Excellent bathrooms.
Amenities garden, dancing (Sat), tea shop (10am–5.30pm), hairdressing.

Room phone Yes	*Confirm by* 3	*Parking* Ample
Room TV Yes	*Last dinner* 10.30	*Banquets* 250/6

Bolton

Map 10 B1 Greater Manchester
Nelson Square
Bradshawgate *BL1 1DP*
Bolton (0204) 27261
Telex 635168
Credit Access, Amex,
Barclaycard, Diners

Rooms 80
with bath/shower 80

Packhorse Hotel   54%   £D/E

Comfortable overnight accommodation is just one of the facets of this friendly, red-brick hotel in the town centre: two of the bars are popular local meeting places (the other is for residents only), and there are also several banqueting and conference rooms. Cheerful bedrooms have practical fitted furniture, bedside controls and tea-makers; newest bathrooms are especially attractive. *Amenities* pool table.   ♿

Room phone Yes	*Confirm by* 6	*Parking* Ample
Room TV Yes	*Last dinner* 10	*Banquets* 220/-

Bolton Abbey
Map 15 B6 North Yorkshire
BD23 6AJ
Bolton Abbey (075 671) 441
Telex 51218

Rooms 38
with bath/shower 38
Room phone Yes
Room TV Yes
Confirm by 6
Last dinner 9.30
Parking Ample
Banquets 100/–

Credit Access, Barclaycard

Devonshire Arms Hotel   78%   £ D

Half a mile from the ruins of Bolton Abbey, this splendid hotel has been created round an old roadside inn. Decor throughout is most impressive, combining contemporary style with fine oil paintings and many lovely pieces of furniture from Chatsworth House. The entrance hall has a hunting theme, with antlers on the walls and stuffed pheasants in glass cases; the spacious lounge bar and an intimate cocktail bar are decorated with impeccable taste. Bedrooms vary from large rooms in the original house to smaller ones in the extension, but all are superbly appointed with brass bedsteads, delightful soft furnishings and silk wallpapers. Excellent, well-equipped bathrooms.
Amenities garden.

Bonchurch
Map 5 D4 Isle of Wight
Near Ventnor *PO38 1RJ*
Ventnor (0983) 852019
Proprietors
Mr & Mrs J. Wolfenden

● **Set L** £8
Set D £11·50 incl. service
About £28 for two
Banquets 20/12

Peacock Vane Restaurant

Home of the Wolfenden family for many years, this attractive *restaurant avec chambres* offers excellent fare and comfortable accommodation. In the mellow dining room the short set menus offer satisfying soups, main courses like seafood, beef pudding or roast pheasant and simple sweets. Seven homely bedrooms have Victorian furnishings and bright modern bathrooms. Garden and swimming pool. *Credit* Access, Amex, Barclaycard, Diners

Lunch 1–1.45 *Dinner* 8–9.30
Closed Mon & Tues to non-residents, May Day Mon & 1 Jan–14 Feb

---

Bonchurch
Map 5 D4 Isle of Wight
Near Ventnor *PO38 1RQ*
Ventnor (0983) 852535
Proprietors Mr R. G. Henderson &
Mr R. W. Hoskins
Rooms 19
with bath/shower 17
Room phone No
Room TV Yes
Confirm by By arrang.
Last dinner 8.30
Parking Limited

Closed mid November–mid January
Credit Access, Amex, Barclaycard, Diners

Winterbourne Hotel   70%   Ⓜ   £ D

With beautiful sloping lawns, a little stream and tiny waterfalls, not to mention steps leading right down to the beach, this lovely house makes a most delightful retreat. The hotel has strong Dickensian connections and many of the rooms are named after characters from his novels. There's a charming drawing room on the first floor with comfortable fireside chairs, fine ornaments and paintings, as well as an intimate little ground-floor bar. Bedrooms (including some cottagy ones in a converted coach house) are all large and attractively decorated. Most have modern, well-equipped bathrooms. No children under seven.
Amenities garden, outdoor swimming pool, putting.

Bonchurch
Map 5 D4 Isle of Wight
Near Ventnor *PO38 1RQ*
Ventnor (0983) 852535
Proprietors Mr R. G. Henderson
& Mr R. W. Hoskins
About £26 for two

Winterbourne Hotel, Copperfield Room

There are pleasant views from the bay windows of this elegant first-floor dining room. Dishes on the set menu (four courses plus cheese) are prepared from prime ingredients and cooking is consistent and enjoyable.
Credit Access, Amex, Barclaycard, Diners *Lunch* at 1 *Dinner* 7–9
Closed mid November–mid January ● **Set L** £5·20 **Set D** £8·50

Boreham Street
Map 7 B6 East Sussex
Near Hailsham *BN27 4SE*
Herstmonceux (032 181) 2355

Proprietors Baker family
Credit Access, Amex,
Barclaycard, Diners

Rooms 21
with bath/shower 17

White Friars Hotel 61%  £ D/E

Set in four acres of lovely garden alongside the A271, this hotel is charmingly run by the Baker family, who ensure good standards of maintenance. Two chintzy lounges have a welcoming, homely feel, and there's a convivial alcoved bar in the basement. Bedrooms (including modern ones in an adjacent cottage) provide solid comfort.
Amenities garden.

Room phone Yes	*Confirm by* 4	*Parking* Ample
Room TV Yes	*Last dinner* 9.15	*Banquets* 55/–

Borehamwood
Map 5 E2 Hertfordshire
Barnet By-pass *WD6 5PU*
01–953 1622

Credit Access, Amex,
Barclaycard, Diners

Rooms 60
with bath/shower 60

Elstree Moat House 54% £ D/E

Situated beside the A1, this white-painted mock-Tudor building centred round the outdoor swimming pool is popular with travelling businessmen. There's a traditional cottage public bar and a more stylish cocktail bar, as well as a pleasant lounge. Bedrooms have functional modern furniture and cheerful soft furnishings. Bathrooms are adequate. *Amenities* garden, outdoor swimming pool, dinner dance (Sat October–April).

Room phone Yes	*Confirm by* 6	*Parking* Ample
Room TV Yes	*Last dinner* 10	*Banquets* 180/–

Boroughbridge
Map 15 C6 North Yorkshire
Horsefair *YO5 9LB*
Boroughbridge (090 12) 2328

Rooms 43
with bath/shower 43
Room phone Yes
Room TV Yes
Confirm by 9
Last dinner 9.15
Parking Ample
Banquets 40/–

Credit Access, Amex,
Barclaycard, Diners

Crown Hotel 72% £ E

This fine old coaching inn has been gradually transformed into an excellent hotel offering very comfortable accommodation. Attractively furnished public areas include a relaxing residents' lounge and a choice of three distinctive bars. Bedrooms are of three types: standard rooms have pleasantly co-ordinated decor and are equipped with tea/coffee-makers, as well as miniatures of sherry and fresh fruit; five executive rooms are more luxurious and have good mahogany furniture, while the best rooms are superbly furnished with antiques. Bathrooms are carpeted and fully tiled, and the whole hotel is spotlessly maintained.
Amenities sauna, solarium.

Boroughbridge
Map 15 C6 North Yorkshire
Horsefair *YO5 9LL*
Boroughbridge (090 12) 2245

Credit Access, Amex,
Barclaycard, Diners
Closed 2 days Christmas

Rooms 18
with bath/shower 9

Three Arrows Hotel 55% £ E

Standing in a pleasant garden close to the centre of town yet minutes from the A1, this former manor house is gradually being converted to standards befitting its handsome Victorian exterior. The lounge is smartly decorated in pastel shades, and the main bedrooms are being individually restyled. Other rooms are smaller and have simple modern furnishings. Bathrooms are adequate. *Amenities* garden, dinner dance (Sat).

Room phone Yes	*Confirm by* 6	*Parking* Ample
Room TV Yes	*Last dinner* 9	

Borrowdale
Map 13 C5 Cumbria
Near Keswick *CA12 5UY*
Borrowdale (059 684) 224

Proprietor Mr Gunter Fidrmuc

Closed January

Rooms 37
with bath/shower 35

Borrowdale Hotel 59%  £ E

Surrounded by spectacular Lakeland scenery, this Victorian building on the B5289 is a popular, well-managed hotel. The carpeted reception leads to a comfortably furnished TV lounge and a simple modern bar. Bedrooms in the original building are large and traditional, while those in the extension are compact and fitted with functional units. Adequate bathrooms. Inclusive terms only. *Amenities* garden, launderette.

Room phone No	*Confirm by* By arrang.	*Parking* Ample
Room TV No	*Last dinner* 8.15	*Banquets* 55/20

Bosham

Map 5 E4 West Sussex
Bosham Lane, Old Bosham
PO18 8HL
Bosham (0243) 573234
Proprietors Wild family
Credit Access, Amex,
Barclaycard, Diners

Rooms 22
with bath/shower 19

Millstream Hotel   68%      £ E

A charming, relaxed atmosphere pervades every corner of this attractive red-brick hotel, where the Wild family maintain exemplary standards of housekeeping. There's a comfortable lounge and a bar with a log fire, while tastefully furnished bedrooms (including six in an extension) are equipped with tea/coffee-makers and trouser presses. Excellent bathrooms. No children under eight. *Amenities* garden.

Room phone Yes	*Confirm by* By arrang.	*Parking* Ample
Room TV Most	*Last dinner* 9.15	*Banquets* 35/–

Botallack

Map 2 A4 Cornwall
Near Penzance *TR19 7QQ*
Penzance (0736) 788588
Proprietors
Mr & Mrs Ian Long

● **Set L** £4·50
About £27 for two

Count House   

Set in a lovingly restored 19th-century workshop with an eerie backdrop of disused tin mines, this clifftop restaurant is a showcase for Ann Long's splendid cooking. In the best tradition of self-taught chefs she is enthusiastic, dedicated and skilful, drawing her inspiration from a wide range of sources. Unusual broad bean and hazelnut soup and crabmeat with raw mushrooms show her feeling for simple dishes, while a marvellously intricate ballotine of duck cooked in honey displays her talents at full stretch. Excellent seasonal vegetables, too, and delightful sweets like raspberry oatmeal meringue.
Credit Access, Amex, Barclaycard, Diners

Lunch Sun only 12.30–1.45 *Dinner* 7.30–9.45
Closed D Mon, Tues & Sun & 25 December

Botley

Map 5 D3 Hampshire
The Square *SO3 2EA*
Botley (048 92) 2068
Proprietors
Charles & Lucie Skipwith
French cooking

● **Set L** £7·50
About £28 for two
Banquets 12/8

Cobbett's   

French-born Lucie Skipwith is the talented chef, while her husband Charles sees to the front of the house at this delightfully relaxed and friendly country restaurant. Fine ingredients are used in French dishes like ham soufflé or leg of lamb with flageolet beans, and the short, frequently changed menu is always tempting and well balanced.
Credit Access

Lunch 12–2 *Dinner* 7.30–10, Sat 7–10
Closed L Sat & Mon, all Sun, Bank Hols, 2 weeks summer & 2 weeks winter

Bournemouth

Map 4 C4 Dorset
East Overcliff
Meyrick Road *BH1 3DN*
Bournemouth (0202) 22011
Telex 41244
Rooms 80
with bath/shower 80
Room phone Yes
Room TV Yes
Confirm by By arrang.
Last dinner 11
Parking Ample
Banquets 180/–

Credit Access, Amex,
Barclaycard, Diners

Carlton Hotel   77%      £ B

Friendly, efficient staff keep things running smoothly at this striking Edwardian hotel, whose clifftop position affords splendid sea views. Public rooms are stylish and relaxing: the luxuriously appointed lounge areas overlook the swimming pool and there's a plush cocktail bar. Bedrooms are spacious, comfortable and well furnished, whether in the newer wing–many have seating areas; all have lovely views–or in the original building. Fully tiled bathrooms have comprehensive equipment. *Amenities* garden, outdoor swimming pool, dinner dance (Sat April–Christmas), bank, in-house movies, 12-hour laundry, baby sitting, baby listening, valeting, billiards, games room, solarium, hairdressing, 24-hour lounge service.   &

Bournemouth

Map 4 C4 Dorset
Meyrick Road, The Lansdowne
BH1 2PR
Bournemouth (0202) 23262
Telex 41232
Credit Access, Amex,
Barclaycard, Diners

Crest Hotel   56%   £ D

Conveniently situated close to the town centre, this distinctive circular building is a popular business hotel, offering good facilities and unfussy accommodation. There's a stylish open-plan foyer and bar with ample seating, as well as a public bar in more traditional style. Bedrooms have neat fitted units, colourful fabrics and extras like tea-makers, radios and trouser presses. Bathrooms are nicely appointed.   &

Continued

Rooms 102	*Room phone* Yes	*Confirm by* 6	*Parking* Ample
with bath/shower 102	*Room TV* Yes	*Last dinner* 9.45	*Banquets* 100/–

Bournemouth

Crust

Map 4 C4 Dorset
The Square *BH2 5AE*
Bournemouth (0202) 21430
Proprietor Mr Paul Harper

Situated in the bus station complex, this cheerful bistro makes an informal setting for an enjoyable meal. Good-quality ingredients are skilfully used for unusual dishes like seafood soup with saffron or venison, grape and burgundy pie. There are also straightforward choices such as grilled plaice and a nice selection of home-made puddings.
Credit Access, Amex, Barclaycard, Diners

● **Set L** £4·50
About £22 for two
Banquets 70/–

Lunch 12–2.30 *Dinner* 6.30–11, Sat 6.30–11.30, Sun 6.30–10.30
Closed L Sun Christmas–Easter & 25 & 26 December

Bournemouth

Durley Hall Hotel   54%   **£ D**

Map 4 C4 Dorset
Durley Chine Road *BH23 5JS*
Bournemouth (0202) 766886

Conveniently placed for beach and town centre, this sturdy red-brick Victorian hotel is popular with holiday-makers. There's a spacious reception area, plus a lounge, bar and ballroom; centrally heated bedrooms are neatly painted and solidly furnished, and bathrooms are adequate. *Amenities* garden, outdoor swimming pool, dancing (nightly May–October, Thurs–Sat November–April), games room, putting, laundry room, children's playground.

Credit Access, Amex,
Barclaycard, Diners

Rooms 84	*Room phone* Yes	*Confirm by* 6	*Parking* Ample
with bath/shower 54	*Room TV* Yes	*Last dinner* 8.30	*Banquets* 200/–

Bournemouth

East Cliff Court Hotel   61%   **£ E**

Map 4 C4 Dorset
East Overcliff Drive *BH1 3AN*
Bournemouth (0202) 24545

There's a traditional air about this comfortable clifftop hotel, whose lounges and conference rooms feature fine pillars and mouldings. The same atmosphere extends to the spacious, airy bedrooms, though furniture is mainly of the modern unit variety. Many rooms have fine sea views, and all have spotless bathrooms. *Amenities* garden, outdoor swimming pool, dinner dance (Sat), entertainment (nightly in season), solarium, sauna.

Credit Access, Amex,
Barclaycard, Diners

Rooms 70	*Room phone* Yes	*Confirm by* 6	*Parking* Ample
with bath/shower 70	*Room TV* Yes	*Last dinner* 9	*Banquets* 200/–

Bournemouth

Highcliff Hotel   63%   **£ C/D**

Map 4 C4 Dorset
St Michael's Road
West Cliff *BH2 5DU*
Bournemouth (0202) 27702
Telex 417153
Credit Access, Amex,
Barclaycard, Diners

Latest improvements at this clifftop hotel (a lift provides direct access to the beach) include additional bathrooms and a delightful new bar-lounge with a sun terrace. Most of the spacious neatly furnished bedrooms command sea views.
Amenities garden, sauna, outdoor swimming pool, tennis, nightclub (Mon–Sat), solarium, putting, games room, children's playroom.

Rooms 100	*Room phone* Yes	*Confirm by* By arrang.	*Parking* Ample
with bath/shower 96	*Room TV* Yes	*Last dinner* 8.45	*Banquets* 170/8

Bournemouth

Ladbroke Savoy Hotel   61%   **£ D/E**

Map 4 C4 Dorset
West Hill Rd, West Cliff *BH2 5EJ*
Bournemouth (0202) 20347
Telex 418220
Credit Access, Amex,
Barclaycard, Diners
Closed 2 weeks January

Front bedrooms have sunny balconies at this sturdy red-brick hotel with lawns running to the cliff's edge. Rooms are solidly furnished and all have tea/coffee-makers. The cocktail bar opens on to a pleasant glass-enclosed verandah, and there's a large, relaxing lounge.
Amenities garden, outdoor swimming pool, dancing (Wed & Sat June–September), pitch & putt, games room (in summer)

Rooms 89	*Room phone* Yes	*Confirm by* 6	*Parking* Ample
with bath/shower 83	*Room TV* Yes	*Last dinner* 9	*Banquets* 150/–

Bournemouth
Map 4 C4 Dorset
42e Poole Road *BH4 9DW*
Bournemouth (0202) 763704
Proprietor Mrs Verna Standish

About £21 for two

Mrs T's Supper Room ♕

Lace tablecloths and candelabra give this unusual restaurant a quaint Victorian atmosphere. Dinner is a leisurely six-course feast including tasty hors d'œuvre, freshly prepared soup, marvellous roasts and gorgeous sweets. *Dinner only* 7.45–8.45 **Closed** Sun, Mon & 25 & 26 December
● **Set D** £6·50, Sat £7·80 *Banquets* 50/40

Bournemouth
Map 4 C4 Dorset
Manor Road
East Cliff *BH1 3HL*
Bournemouth (0202) 22246

Credit Access, Amex,
Barclaycard, Diners

Hotel Normandie 64% Ⓜ £D

A popular hotel for family holidays, which, though brightly modernised, retains some elegant pillars and a splendid staircase. Good-sized bedrooms have attractive fitted furniture and well-equipped bathrooms. No dogs. *Amenities* garden, sauna, outdoor swimming pool, dinner dance (Sat), dancing (nightly in season), beauty salon, children's playground, gymnasium, hairdressing, 24-hr laundry, games room, golf driving range, putting.

Rooms 71
with bath/shower 71

Room phone Yes	*Confirm by* 6	*Parking* Ample
Room TV Yes	*Last dinner* 9	*Banquets* 40/–

Bournemouth
Map 4 C4 Dorset
Westover Road *BH1 3B7*
Bournemouth (0202) 27681
Telex 418451
Manager Mr G. C. Ronco
Credit Access, Amex,
Barclaycard, Diners

Palace Court Hotel 69% Ⓜ £D

This large 1930s hotel close to the seafront has benefited from extensive refurbishment. A sedate, sophisticated air pervades the plushly carpeted foyer; the large lounge and the cocktail bar and bedrooms are just as stylish. Spacious bedrooms are tastefully furnished with fitted units, while bathrooms are well equipped. *Amenities* sauna, dinner dance (Sat in summer), solarium, keep-fit equipment, games room, 24-hour laundry service.

Rooms 108
with bath/shower 108

Room phone Yes	*Confirm by* By arrang.	*Parking* Ample
Room TV Yes	*Last dinner* 10.45	*Banquets* 350/–

Bournemouth
Map 4 C4 Dorset
Meyrick Rd, East Cliff *BH1 3DL*
Bournemouth (0202) 24415
Telex 262180
Manager Mr A. M. Thom
Credit Access, Amex,
Barclaycard, Diners

Queen's Hotel 55% £E

A firm favourite with holiday-making families, this friendly, white-painted hotel stands on the East Cliff close to the sea. Accommodation ranges from standard fitted twins in the wing to more traditionally furnished and individually decorated rooms in the older part. Private bathrooms are the best. Two spacious lounges overlook the pleasant garden.
Amenities garden, games room, laundry room.

Rooms 116
with bath/shower 80

Room phone Yes	*Confirm by* 5	*Parking* Limited
Room TV Yes	*Last dinner* 8	*Banquets* 140/–

Bournemouth
Map 4 C4 Dorset
Bath Road *BH1 2EW*
Bournemouth (0202) 25555
Telex 41375
Manager Mr D. R. Lloyd-Jones
Rooms 135
with bath/shower 135
Room phone Yes
Room TV Yes
Confirm by By arrang.
Last dinner 10.30
Parking Ample
Banquets 550/–

Credit Access, Amex,
Barclaycard, Diners

Royal Bath Hotel 79% £B/C

This luxurious white-painted hotel overlooking the sea is a harmonious blend of the traditional and the modern. The comfortable main lounge, with its Doric columns and fine plaster ceiling, is a splendid example of elegance on the grand scale, while the warmly decorated bars have a bright, more contemporary appeal. Bedrooms are spacious and stylish, with carefully coordinated colour schemes, smart whitewood furniture and gleaming, well-equipped bathrooms. Many rooms overlook the pool and gardens and some have their own sitting areas. Staff are welcoming and efficient. *Amenities* garden, sauna, outdoor swimming pool, dinner dance (Sat), gymnasium, putting, games room, nanny, hairdressing. ♿

Bournemouth
Map 4 C4 Dorset
43 Charminster Road *BH8 8UE*
Bournemouth (0202) 291019

Sophisticats

Bernard Calligan's imaginative menu makes for enjoyable meals at this pleasant little restaurant. Subtle and unusual combinations of flavours are the basis of dishes such as sole and salmon strips marinated in lime juice, or veal with a mustardy tarragon sauce plus vegetables like carrots and mushrooms with almonds. End with a refreshing sorbet or a spirited Viennese chocolate dessert.

● **Set L** £4·95
About £24 for two

Lunch 12–1.30 *Dinner* 7–10
Closed Sun & Mon

Bournemouth
Map 4 C4 Dorset
148 Holdenhurst Road *BH8 8AS*
Bournemouth (0202) 21132
Proprietor Mr E. Longi

About £27 for two

Trattoria San Marco

At this friendly trattoria you'll find a varied menu of steaks and Italian dishes, which range from scallops to veal escalopes in various guises. Food is capably prepared and served in generous portions. *Credit* Access, Amex, Barclaycard, Diners *Lunch* 12–2 *Dinner* 7–11.30
Closed Mon & Bank Holidays

Bourton-on-the-Water
Map 4 C1 Gloucestershire
Riverside *GL54 2BX*
Bourton-on-the-Water
(0451) 20635
Proprietors
Jane Mann & Iain Gaylor

● **Set L** £8·50
Set D £11·50 incl. service
About £30 for two

Rose Tree

Jane Mann produces an interesting selection of French-inspired dishes in this attractive little Queen Anne house on the banks of the Windrush. Between crunchy crudités with mayonnaise dip and home-made mints with coffee you could enjoy smooth aubergine pâté, followed perhaps by coulibiac de saumon or suprême de volaille. Some cuisine minceur dishes, too, and eye-catching desserts. 🍷 *OUTSTANDING. Credit* Amex, Diners

Lunch Sun only 12.30–3 *Dinner* 7.30–10
Closed D Sun, all Mon & end January–February

Bowness on Windermere — Belsfield Hotel   62%   £ D
Map 13 D5 Cumbria
Kendal Road *LA23 3EL*
Windermere (096 62) 2448
Telex 65238

Credit Access, Amex,
Barclaycard, Diners

Refurbishment is in progress at this fine Georgian house overlooking Lake Windermere. Public rooms include a spacious reception lounge area and a smart bar with lake views. Pastel-decorated bedrooms of various sizes have fitted furniture; bathrooms are up to date. *Amenities* garden, indoor/outdoor swimming pool, dancing (Sat), badminton, clock golf, children's play area, games room, table tennis, pool table.

Rooms 71	*Room phone* Yes	*Confirm by* 6	*Parking* Ample
with bath/shower 59	*Room TV* Yes	*Last dinner* 9.30	*Banquets* 150/–

Bowness on Windermere — Burnside Hotel   57%   £ D
Map 13 D5 Cumbria
Kendal Road *LA23 3EP*
Windermere (096 62) 2211
Telex 65238

Credit Access, Amex,
Barclaycard, Diners

A pleasant, comfortable hotel on a hillside overlooking the lake. Public rooms, many with fine views, include a welcoming reception-lounge area, another lounge and a bar which leads to the sun lounge. Bedrooms in the main building have solid, traditional furnishings, while those in the extension are compact and more modern. Well-kept bathrooms. *Amenities* garden, putting, table tennis.

Rooms 31	*Room phone* Yes	*Confirm by* 6	*Parking* Ample
with bath/shower 26	*Room TV* Yes	*Last dinner* 9.10	*Banquets* 120/40

Bowness on Windermere — Old England Hotel   68%   £ C/D
Map 13 D5 Cumbria
Church Street *LA23 3DF*
Windermere (096 62) 2444
Telex 65194

Credit Access, Amex,
Barclaycard, Diners

Antiques and displays of china grace the splendid entrance hall of this fine old lakeside mansion. There's a cheerful modern cocktail bar and a superbly comfortable lounge opening on to a paved terrace. Well-furnished bedrooms (many with lovely lake views) include some in a modern extension. Neat bathrooms. *Amenities* garden, outdoor swimming pool, games room, mooring, table tennis, 24-hour laundry service.

Rooms 84	*Room phone* Yes	*Confirm by* 6	*Parking* Ample
with bath/shower 84	*Room TV* Yes	*Last dinner* 9.30	*Banquets* 215/–

Bowness on Windermere

Map 13 D5 Cumbria
3 Ash Street *LA23 3EB*
Windermere (096 62) 2793
Proprietors Judy & Gianni Berton
Italian cooking

● **Set D** Oct & Nov only £10
About £29 for two
Banquets 34/12

Porthole Eating House

Authentic Italian cooking by Gianni Berton draws a regular following to this friendly, informal little restaurant in the centre of Bowness. A short carte of largely familiar pasta, fish and meat dishes is supplemented each week by some less usual choices like our tasty potted trout or tender calf's liver with an enjoyable grape and vinegar sauce. Booking advisable.
☕ *OUTSTANDING. Credit* Access, Amex, Barclaycard

Dinner only 7–10.30
Closed Tues & December–February

Bradfield Combust

Map 6 C3 Suffolk
Near Bury St Edmunds *IP30 0LR*
Sicklesmere (028 486) 301

English cooking
About £27 for two

Bradfield House Restaurant

Excellent terrines, garden fresh vegetables and enjoyable dishes like sautéed Suffolk lamb with japonica jelly are typical offerings on the well-chosen English menu at this charming 17th-century house.
Credit Barclaycard, Diners *Lunch* 12.30–2.30 *Dinner* 7–10.30 **Closed** L Sat, D Sun, all Mon & 1st 2 weeks January ● **Set L** £5·75 *Banquets* 24/–

Bradford

Map 10 C1 West Yorkshire
Highfield Road
Idle *BD10 8QH*
Bradford (0274) 611914
Telex 517229
Proprietor Mr J. Maron
Credit Amex, Diners

Baron Hotel   62%   Ⓜ   £E

A modern, stone-faced hotel just a short drive away from the city centre. A sweeping staircase leads from the main public area–reception, lounge and bar–where vivid colours predominate. Spacious bedrooms with sitting areas are also decorated in lively style; all have tiled bathrooms with bidets. *Amenities* sauna, indoor swimming pool, discothèque (Sat & all December), solarium.

Rooms 65	*Room phone* Yes	*Confirm by* 8	*Parking* Ample
with bath/shower 65	*Room TV* Yes	*Last dinner* 10	*Banquets* 150/–

Bradford

Map 10 C1 West Yorkshire
Hall Ings *BD1 5SH*
Bradford (0274) 34733
Telex 517573

Credit Access, Amex,
Barclaycard, Diners

Norfolk Gardens Hotel   64%   £D

Standing right in the middle of the city, this modern, seven-storey hotel provides smart accommodation for businessmen, including extensive conference facilities. Spacious public areas include two stylish bars. Well-equipped bedrooms are furnished in simple contemporary style; all have tiled bathrooms with showers. *Amenities* discothèque (weekends except August), dancing (Fri, Sat October–March).

Rooms 125	*Room phone* Yes	*Confirm by* 6.30	*Parking* Ample
with bath/shower 125	*Room TV* Yes	*Last dinner* 10.30	*Banquets* 600/10

Bradford

Map 10 C1 West Yorkshire
Euroway Trading Estate
Merrydale Road *BD4 6SA*
Bradford (0274) 683683
Telex 517312
Credit Access, Amex,
Barclaycard, Diners

Novotel   60%   £D/E

This well-designed modern hotel stands just off the M606 about ten minutes' drive from the city centre. Wooden screens and potted plants divide the bright, open-plan public areas, which include a reception, bar and lounge. Studio-style bedrooms have white unit furniture, central heating controls and well-equipped bathrooms with bidets. *Amenities* garden, outdoor swimming pool, pool table, coffee shop (6am–midnight).

Rooms 136	*Room phone* Yes	*Confirm by* 6	*Parking* Ample
with bath/shower 136	*Room TV* Yes	*Last dinner* 11.30	*Banquets* 350/15

Bradford

Map 10 C1 West Yorkshire
Bridge Street *BD1 1JX*
Bradford (0274) 28706
Telex 517456
Manager Mr A. McGuigan
Credit Access, Amex,
Barclaycard, Diners

Victoria Hotel   57%   £D

Just across the road from the bus and railway terminal, this town-centre Victorian hotel boasts splendidly proportioned public rooms. The foyer-lounge has a comfortable air with its sofas, classical columns and potted palms, and there are two bars. Bedrooms are gradually being refurbished; newly decorated ones have attractive, pastel colour schemes, light wood units and brass lamps; all have tea/coffee-makers. Simple, adequate bathrooms.

Rooms 58	*Room phone* Yes	*Confirm by* 6	*Parking* Ample
with bath/shower 45	*Room TV* Yes	*Last dinner* 10	*Banquets* 200/–

Braintree

Map 6 C3 Essex
3 Rayne Road *CM7 7QA*
Braintree (0376) 24319
Proprietor Mr Kim Sing Man
Chinese cooking
About £20 for two

Braintree Chinese Restaurant Ⓢ

An unassuming first-floor restaurant, whose long menu of Chinese favour-ites includes some enjoyable Pekinese specialities. Pleasant decor, friendly service. *Credit* Barclaycard, Diners *Meals* noon–11.30pm, Fri & Sat noon–midnight **Closed** 25 & 26 December ● **Set L** £2·50 **Set D** £6·50 *Banquets* 120/4

Braintree

Map 6 C3 Essex
Bocking End *CM7 6AB*
Braintree (0376) 21401

Credit Access, Amex,
Barclaycard, Diners

Rooms 35
with bath/shower 30

White Hart Hotel 56% £ E

This old coaching inn with a black and white half-timbered facade has been considerably updated inside. The reception area and cocktail bar have bold modern colour schemes. Bedrooms in the original building are cosy and traditional, while the majority, which are in the modern brick-built extension, are fitted out in contemporary style. Bathrooms are adequate.

Room phone Yes	*Confirm by* 6	*Parking* Ample
Room TV Yes	*Last dinner* 11.30	*Banquets* 70/–

Braithwaite

Map 13 C5 Cumbria
Keswick *CA12 5SD*
Braithwaite (059 682) 338

Credit Access, Amex,
Barclaycard, Diners
Closed November–February

Rooms 9
with bath/shower 6

Ivy House Hotel 61% Ⓜ £ D/E

A warm welcome awaits visitors to the Mulliners' peaceful hotel in the centre of Braithwaite. Public rooms include an inviting beamed bar-lounge and a pleasant residents' lounge with TV and French windows opening on to the gardens. Bedrooms have bold bright wallpaper and traditional furnishings; like the carpeted bathrooms, they are very well maintained. No dogs. *Amenities* garden.

Room phone No	*Confirm by* By arrang.	*Parking* Ample
Room TV Some	*Last dinner* 8.30	

Bramhope

Map 10 C1 West Yorkshire
Otley Road
Near Leeds *LS16 8AG*
Leeds (0532) 672551

Credit Access, Barclaycard,
Diners

Rooms 46
with bath/shower 13

Parkway Hotel 56% £ E

Six miles north of Leeds on the A660, not far from the airport, this mock-Tudor hotel is popular with travelling businessmen. The foyer doubles as a lounge and there's a choice of two spacious bars. Bedrooms are simply furnished in modern style and equipped with radios and tea-makers; those facing the road are also double-glazed. Bathrooms are old-fashioned but adequate. *Amenities* garden.

Room phone Yes	*Confirm by* 6	*Parking* Ample
Room TV Yes	*Last dinner* 9.30	*Banquets* 250/8

Bramhope

Map 10 C1 West Yorkshire
Near Leeds *LS16 9JJ*
Leeds (0532) 842911
Telex 556367

Credit Access, Amex,
Barclaycard, Diners

Rooms 120
with bath/shower 120

Post House Hotel 60% £ D

This modern hotel on the A660 is popular with tourists and business visitors alike. Sheep form the decorative theme of the Fleece Bar, and there is a comfortable foyer-lounge. Fitted bedrooms are bright and well maintained, with plenty of storage space; all have tea/coffee-makers, mini-bars and compact, well-equipped bathrooms. *Amenities* garden, dancing (Fri April–October), coffee shop (7.30am–10.30pm). &

Room phone Yes	*Confirm by* 6	*Parking* Ample
Room TV Yes	*Last dinner* 10.15	*Banquets* 120/2

Bramley

Map 5 E3 Surrey
High Street *GU5 0HB*
Guildford (0483) 893392
Proprietors Antonio Orlando
& Giuliano Matteucci
Italian cooking

● **Set L** £4·95
About £28 for two
Banquets 14/–

La Baita ♀ ♛ Ⓢ

A really cheerful atmosphere fills this cosy, attractively decorated Italian restaurant. The menu offers a good choice of tasty, skilfully prepared items such as veal in a rich cream and brandy sauce with peppers, mushrooms and Parma ham. Sweets range from zabaglione to cheesecake. *Credit* Access, Amex, Barclaycard, Diners

Lunch 12–2 *Dinner* 7–10
Closed Sun & Bank Holidays

Bramley

Map 5 E3 Surrey
Horsham Road
Near Guildford *GU5 0BL*
Guildford (0483) 893434
Proprietors Mr & Mrs K. W. Taylor
Credit Amex, Diners

Bramley Grange Hotel **60%** Ⓜ **£ D**

There is a fine view of the attractive grounds from the cosy bar of this rambling mock-Tudor hotel. The recently added grill room has its own bar, and major improvements have been made to the bedrooms. All now have smart modern bathrooms and many have been refurbished with cheerful decor, white laminated furniture and new carpets. Rooms facing the road are double-glazed. *Amenities* garden, tennis, squash, putting. ♿

Rooms 22	*Room phone* Yes	*Confirm by* By arrang.	*Parking* Ample
with bath/shower 22	*Room TV* Yes	*Last dinner* 9.15	

Brampton

Map 13 D4 Cumbria
Hallbankgate *CA8 2NG*
Hallbankgate (069 76) 234

Proprietors Quinion family
Credit Access, Amex

Farlam Hall **65%** Ⓜ **£ D**

The Quinion family's attractive manor house stands on the A689 just east of Brampton, in four acres of mature gardens. There are fine views from most of the public rooms, which include a bar and several lounges, and all the bedrooms are brightly decorated. These are roomy and comfortable, with floral wallpapers and traditional furnishings. *Amenities* garden.
Closed Feb, 1st 2 weeks Nov & Christmas, also Mon & Tues Nov–Jan

Rooms 11	*Room phone* No	*Confirm by* 6	*Parking* Ample
with bath/shower 6	*Room TV* No	*Last dinner* 8	*Banquets* 50/–

Brampton

Map 13 D4 Cumbria
Hallbankgate *CA8 2NG*
Hallbankgate (069 76) 234
Proprietors Quinion family

Farlam Hall Restaurant ♧ ♔ Ⓢ

A lovely room overlooking the gardens, friendly service and Barry Quinion's capable cooking add up to a fine dinner in most pleasant surroundings. After soup or a light mousse, you could choose between monkfish provençale, roast pork or tender veal escalope, served with plenty of beautifully cooked vegetables. English cheese and some tempting desserts to finish. Table d'hôte only. *Credit* Access, Amex

● **Set L** £7
Set D £9·50, Sat £10
About £29 for two

Lunch Sun only at 1 *Dinner* at 8
Closed D Mon & Tues Nov–Jan, 25 & 26 Dec, Feb & 1st 2 weeks Nov

Brandon

Map 11 D4 Warwickshire
Near Coventry *CV8 3FW*
Coventry (0203) 542571
Telex 31472

Credit Access, Amex,
Barclaycard, Diners

Brandon Hall Hotel **58%** **£ D**

Set in 17 acres of parkland, but conveniently placed for the industrial centres of the Midlands, this impressive Victorian house has been usefully updated. Chesterfields blend with original trappings in the reception-lounge and cocktail bar, while bedrooms range from spacious and traditional in the main building to more compact ones in the modern wing. Well-fitted bathrooms. *Amenities* garden, squash, children's playground, games room.

Rooms 68	*Room phone* Yes	*Confirm by* 6	*Parking* Ample
with bath/shower 44	*Room TV* Yes	*Last dinner* 9.30	*Banquets* 100/2

Branscombe

Map 3 E2 Devon
Near Seaton *EX12 3DJ*
Branscombe (029 780) 300

Proprietor Mrs J. Inglis

Masons Arms *(Inn)* Ⓜ **£ D**

Nestling in an unspoilt village near the sea, this quaint old inn dates back to the 14th century. The lovely first-floor sitting room is full of antiques and flower displays, and there's a popular bar with beams, flagstones and settles; another comfortable lounge has TV. Bedrooms, most of them charmingly traditional, are either in the main building or in nearby cottages. *Amenities* garden, sea fishing.

Rooms 21	*Room phone* No	*Confirm by* By arrang.	*Parking* Ample
with bath/shower 13	*Room TV* Some	*Last dinner* 9	

Branscombe

Map 3 E2 Devon
Near Seaton *EX12 3DJ*
Branscombe (029 780) 300
Proprietor Mrs J. Inglis

Masons Arms Restaurant Ⓢ

The Austrian chef makes excellent use of fresh local produce at this picturesque old country inn. Set menus (changed daily) might offer home-made soup, mackerel pâté or perhaps creamed mushrooms to start, followed by dressed crab salad, plump sautéed scallops, steak hongroise or succulent roast duckling flamande served with nicely prepared vegetables. And his apple strudel provides a magnificent finale. ♿

  Continued

● **Set L** £4·50
Set D from £7·50
About £25 for two

Lunch Sun only 12–1.30 *Dinner* 7.15–9, Sat 7.15–9.15

Bransgore
Map 4 C4 Dorset
Lyndhurst Road *BH23 8JZ*
Bransgore (0425) 72064

Harrow Lodge Country House Hotel   65%   Ⓜ   **£ D**

Fourteen acres of grounds provide a beautiful setting for this handsome Victorian hotel owned and run by the Shutler family. Ancient tomes line the bookshelves in the plush sitting room, and there's also a tiny cocktail bar with pleasant views. Centrally heated bedrooms vary in size and decor, but all are attractive and have very well-equipped bathrooms. No children under ten. No dogs. *Amenities* garden, croquet, laundry room.

| *Rooms* 12 | *Room phone* Yes | *Confirm by* 6 | *Parking* Ample |
| *with bath/shower* 12 | *Room TV* Yes | *Last dinner* 9.30 | *Banquets* 30/10 |

Bray-on-Thames
Map 5 E2 Berkshire
Ferry Road *SL1 6AT*
Maidenhead (0628) 20691
Proprietors Messrs Roux
French cooking

● **Set L** £15
About £70 for two
Banquets 85/–

Waterside Inn   ★ ★ ★

Michel Roux is on the pinnacle of British gastronomy, his appeal enhanced by a restlessly innovative mind and an obsessive attention to detail. Could one, for instance, imagine a combination of skate and raspberries? It takes Michel to turn it into a tour de force. And so it goes from start to finish: imagination, superb skill and presentation of Japanese artistry. It would be unfair to all his other masterpieces to single out a dish. A ravishingly beautiful place on the riverside and more than worth the drive.
Specialities pâté de poisson à la Guillaume Tirel, côte de veau boucanière, lapereau grillé aux marrons glacés, soufflé chaud aux framboises.
🍷 *OUTSTANDING. Credit* Access, Amex, Barclaycard, Diners

Lunch 12.30–2 *Dinner* 7.30–10 **Closed** L Tues (after 1/2/83), all Mon also D Sun in winter, Bank Holidays & from D 25 Dec–31 Jan

---

Bredwardine
Map 4 A1 Hereford & Worcester
HR3 6BU
Moccas (098 17) 303

Proprietors Mr & Mrs Stockwell

Red Lion Hotel *(Inn)*   Ⓜ   **£ E**

Excellent shooting and fishing are the chief attractions of this red-brick inn in a peaceful rural setting close to the river Wye. It's easy to unwind in the comfortable lounge, and bedrooms–some in well-converted outbuildings– are roomy and cheerful, with a homely blend of modern units and farmhouse antiques. Well-maintained shower or bathrooms. No dogs.
Amenities garden, coarse & game fishing, shooting.

| *Rooms* 14 | *Room phone* No | *Confirm by* By arrang. | *Parking* Ample |
| *with bath/shower* 6 | *Room TV* No | *Last dinner* 8 | |

Brentwood
Map 7 B4 Essex
London Road *CM14 4NR*
Brentwood (0277) 225252
Telex 995182
Manager Mr S. Pearson
Credit Access, Amex,
Barclaycard, Diners

Moat House Hotel   67%   **£ D**

Stone lions stand guard at this beautifully preserved timbered building, where Henry VIII was a frequent visitor. Moulded ceilings, panelled walls and leaded windows grace the public rooms, and beamed bedrooms are full of old-fashioned charm. Most rooms are in the modern chalet-style extension, with attractive fitted units, seating areas and well-equipped private bathrooms. *Amenities* garden, sauna, pool table, 24-hour laundry service.

| *Rooms* 24 | *Room phone* Yes | *Confirm by* 6 | *Parking* Ample |
| *with bath/shower* 18 | *Room TV* Yes | *Last dinner* 9.30 | *Banquets* 60/– |

Brentwood
Map 7 B4 Essex
Brook Street *CM14 5NF*
Brentwood (0277) 210888
Telex 995379
Manager Mr Paul Murray-Smith
Credit Access, Amex,
Barclaycard, Diners

Post House Hotel   57%   **£ D**

This long, low, red-brick hotel alongside the A12 offers comfortable modern accommodation and comprehensive conference facilities. The foyer-lounge is brightly attractive, and there's a coffee shop, an appealing cocktail bar and the Oak Bar, a popular meeting place. Good-sized bedrooms have smart fitted units, tea-makers, mini-bars and compact, tiled bathrooms. *Amenities* garden, outdoor swimming pool, coffee shop (7.15am–10.30pm).

| *Rooms* 120 | *Room phone* Yes | *Confirm by* 6 | *Parking* Ample |
| *with bath/shower* 120 | *Room TV* Yes | *Last dinner* 10 | *Banquets* 100/– |

Map 7 B6
Town Plan opposite

Population 153,700

Brighton is Regency Squares and terraces, the maze of art and junk shops called the Lanes, the beach and piers, the conferences and entertainments, the milling crowds in Brighton, and the quiet lawns of Hove, a day out for Londoners, a holiday and retirement centre, a commuter's town and a university town. The person most responsible for all this was George IV, who made it the vogue and commissioned his unique palace, the Royal Pavilion.

Annual Events
Brighton Boat Show *May*
Brighton Festival *1st–16th May*
Glyndebourne *May–Aug*
London to Brighton veteran car run *Nov*

Sights Outside Town
Arundel Castle, Petworth House, Bluebell Railway

Information Centres
Marlborough House, Old Steine and Sea-front opp. West Street
Telephone Brighton 23755
Weekends Brighton 26450

Lancia Dealers

Keen & Betts
Brighton Road
Shoreham-by-Sea
Tel: 079–17 61333

Brighton

1	Aquarium and Dolphinarium	D3
2	Booth Bird Museum *British birds in natural surroundings*	B1
3	Brighton & Hove Albion F.C.	A1
4	Brighton Conference & Exhibition Centre	C3
5	Churchill Square	C3
6	County Cricket Ground	A2
7	Devil's Dyke *4 miles, Sussex beauty spot*	B1
8	Information Centres	C3
9	The Lanes *network of old fishermen's cottages, now world centre for antiques*	C3
10	Marina	E3
11	Palace Pier	D3
12	Preston Park and Preston Manor *18th c*	C1
13	Race-course	E1
14	Rottingdean *2½ miles, toy museum, Rudyard Kipling's house*	E3
15	Royal Pavilion *Regency exhibition, art gallery and museum*	C/D3
16	Station	C2
17	Sussex University *4 miles*	E1
18	Theatre Royal	C3
19	Volks Railway *first electric railway; on seafront*	D3

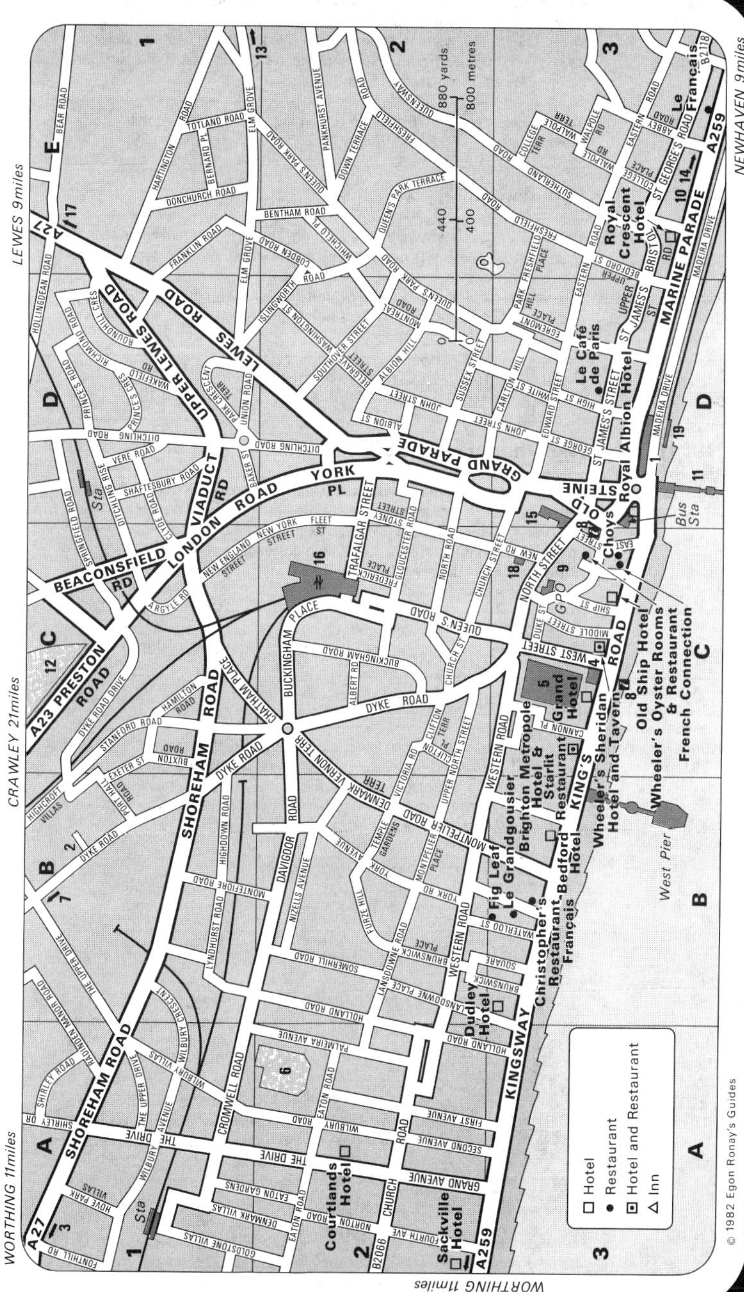

Brighton LANCIA
LANCIA
Hotel
Restaurant
Hotel and Restaurant
Inn
© 1982 Egon Ronay's Guides
LEWES 9miles
WORTHING 11miles
CRAWLEY 21miles
NEWHAVEN 9miles
WORTHING 11miles
Royal Crescent Hotel
Le Café de Paris
Royal Albion Hotel
Choys
Old Ship Hotel
Wheeler's Oyster Rooms & Restaurant
French Connection
Wheeler's Sheridan Hotel and Tavern
Grand Hotel
Brighton Metropole Hotel & Starlit Restaurant
Bedford Hotel
Le Grandgousier
Fig Leaf
Christopher's Restaurant Français
Dudley Hotel
Courtlands Hotel
Sackville Hotel
West Pier
Bus Sta
OLD STEINE
GRAND PARADE
MARINE PARADE
KINGSWAY
SHOREHAM ROAD
A23 PRESTON ROAD
BEACONSFIELD RD
LONDON ROAD
UPPER LEWES ROAD
LEWES ROAD
VIADUCT RD
YORK PL
WEST STREET
KING'S ROAD
DYKE ROAD
CHATHAM PLACE
DENMARK VERNON TERR
BUCKINGHAM PLACE
WESTERN ROAD
MONTPELIER ROAD
A259
A27
A23
880 yards
800 metres
440
400

Bridgwater

Map 3 E1 Somerset
Cornhill *TA6 3AT*
Bridgwater (0278) 55196
Manager Mr J. E. Lloyd

Credit Access, Barclaycard

Royal Clarence Hotel   63%   Ⓜ   £E

This handsome early 19th-century coaching house, with tall windows and an elegant portico, stands in the centre of historic Bridgwater. Guests can relax in the peaceful, well-furnished residents' lounge or chat with the locals in the cheerful Edwardian-style bar. Boldly decorated, well-lit bedrooms have contemporary fitted units and tea/coffee-makers. Bathrooms are modern. Excellent housekeeping and maintenance.

Rooms 28
with bath/shower 15

Room phone Yes
Room TV Yes

Confirm by By arrang.
Last dinner 9.15

Parking Ample
Banquets 120/–

Bridlington

Map 15 D6 Humberside
North Marine Drive *YO15 2LS*
Bridlington (0262) 75347
Proprietors
Mr & Mrs A. F. Seymour
Credit Access, Amex,
Barclaycard

Expanse Hotel   59%   Ⓜ   £E

This popular seafront hotel has been run by the Seymour family for over 30 years. The Marine Bar is popular with locals, and there are fine sea views from the traditionally furnished panelled lounge. Bedrooms are individually decorated, with functional modern units; some have compact bathrooms, and the public bathrooms, though more old-fashioned, are adequate. No dogs. *Amenities* laundry room.

Rooms 48
with bath/shower 30

Room phone Yes
Room TV Yes

Confirm by By arrang.
Last dinner 8.30

Parking Ample
Banquets 100/–

Brighton (Hove)

Town plan A3 East Sussex
42 Brunswick Terrace *BN3 1HA*
Brighton (0273) 202722
Telex 877159

Credit Access, Amex,
Barclaycard, Diners

Alexandra Hotel   58%   £D

Once the home in exile of Austrian diplomat Prince Metternich, this handsome Regency terrace hotel on the seafront is a listed building. Period charm has been preserved in the Earl Grey Tea Parlour, and the popular basement cocktail bar is bright and airy. Comfortable, attractive bedrooms have simple brown and white decor and modern bathrooms. Swimming pool and health club facilities available nearby.

Rooms 62
with bath/shower 62

Room phone Yes
Room TV Yes

Confirm by 7
Last dinner 7.30

Parking Ample
Banquets 50/–

Brighton

Town plan B3 East Sussex
King's Road *BN1 2JF*
Brighton (0273) 29744
Telex 877245

Credit Access, Amex,
Barclaycard, Diners

Bedford Hotel   68%   £C

Extensive refurbishment has taken place at this smart modern hotel on the seafront. The relaxing foyer-lounge is enlivened by potted plants, and the little Dickens Bar is plush and cosy. Bedrooms are most attractively fitted, those at the front being a little larger and having bathrooms with showers and bidets. Guests can use amenities at the nearby Metropole Hotel.

Rooms 126
with bath/shower 126

Room phone Yes
Room TV Yes

Confirm by 6
Last dinner 9

Parking Ample
Banquets 300/–

Brighton

Town plan C3 East Sussex
King's Road *BN1 2FU*
Brighton (0273) 775432
Telex 877245
Manager Mr F. Hutchings
Rooms 333
with bath/shower 333
Room phone Yes
Room TV Yes
Confirm by By arrang.
Last dinner 11
Parking Ample
Banquets 1,200/–

Credit Access, Amex,
Barclaycard, Diners

Brighton Metropole Hotel   71%   £B

Top-hatted commissionaires set the tone at this grand seaside hotel, which a major refit has largely restored to its former splendour. High-ceilinged banqueting and conference rooms have impressive chandeliers and ornate plasterwork, and other public areas include a comfortable lounge and the beautiful Victorian-style Cannon Bar, with its cast-iron tables, brass wall-lights, and a Continental-style terrace. Modernised bedrooms, many overlooking the sea, have attractive pastel decor, good-quality built-in furniture and comprehensively equipped, up-to-date bathrooms.
Amenities sauna, health centre, buttery (10am–11pm), hairdressing.   ♿

Brighton
Town plan C3 East Sussex
King's Road *BN1 2FU*
Brighton (0273) 775432

French cooking

● **Set L** £8·25 **Set D** £9·50
About £44 for two

Brighton Metropole Hotel, Starlit Room Ⓢ

An elegant, stylishly decorated restaurant where the menu promises ambitious and inventive French cooking that's decidedly slanted towards nouvelle cuisine. We particularly enjoyed king prawns steamed with Noilly Prat and wild mushrooms, also sautéed veal, lamb and beef fillets served with full-bodied red wine sauce. Raw materials are excellent and service is professional. *Credit* Access, Amex, Barclaycard, Diners ♿

Lunch 12.30–2.30 *Dinner* 7–10.30
Closed L Sat, all Sun, Mon, 1 January & 25 December

Brighton
Town plan D3 East Sussex
40 St James's Street *BN2 1RG*
Brighton (0273) 603740

French cooking

● **Set L** £4·25 **Set D** £7·90
About £26 for two

Le Café de Paris Ⓢ

Huge wooden platters of crudités and assorted charcuterie precede the three-course fixed-price menu in this modest basement restaurant. The food is authentically French in style with dishes like sole normande and skilfully prepared stuffed leg of lamb in crisp puff pastry. Vegetables are unusually varied, and tempting sweets include delicious tarte tatin. Friendly, helpful service. *Credit* Amex, Barclaycard, Diners

Lunch 12–2.30 *Dinner* 7–11
Closed L Sat & D Sun

Brighton
Town plan C3 East Sussex
2 Little East Street *BN1 1HT*
Brighton (0273) 25305

Chinese cooking

● **Set L & Set D** £5
About £20 for two

Choys Ⓢ

The Tang family run this charming little Chinese restaurant tucked away in one of the small streets of the town. Good-quality produce is used to prepare a comprehensive selection of mainly Cantonese specialities. Tastily sauced dishes range from beef with oyster sauce to baked crab with ginger and spring onions; there are also plenty of noodle, rice and vegetable choices. *Credit* Access, Amex, Barclaycard, Diners

Lunch 12–2.30, Sat & Sun noon–midnight *Dinner* 5.30–11.30
Closed 25 & 26 December

Brighton
Town plan B3 East Sussex
24 Western Street *BN1 2PG*
Brighton (0273) 775048
Proprietors
Messrs Keys & Jackson

About £24 for two

Christopher's Restaurant Français Ⓢ

The menu changes every four months at this tiny, cheerful restaurant in a side street. Donald Keys offers friendly service while his partner Donald Jackson cooks a range of enjoyable, imaginative dishes such as chicken with lemon and ginger in a creamy wine sauce or pork chops with prawns and asparagus. There's always a home-made soup, and the sweet trolley is especially appealing. *ABOVE AVERAGE. Credit* Access, Amex

Dinner only 7–10.45, Sun 7–10 **Closed** Wed, Bank Holidays except Good Friday, 24 December, last 2 weeks March & last 2 weeks October

Brighton (Hove)
Town plan A2 East Sussex
19 The Drive *BN3 3JE*
Brighton (0273) 731055
Telex 87574
Manager Mr G. Messina
Credit Access, Amex, Barclaycard, Diners

Rooms 64
with bath/shower 58

Courtlands Hotel 64% £E

Several Victorian houses close to the seafront make up this friendly hotel. The converted coach house holds bright, spacious bedrooms with their own sitting areas and mini-bars; those in the main building vary in style, and all are well kept. There's a large cocktail bar and a welcoming lounge with comfortable sofas and an open fire.
Amenities garden, children's playground, pool table, games room.

Room phone Yes	*Confirm by* 6	*Parking* Ample
Room TV Yes	*Last dinner* 9.30	*Banquets* 25/6

Brighton (Hove)
Town plan B2 East Susssex
Lansdowne Place *BN3 1HQ*
Brighton (0273) 736266
Telex 87537

Credit Access, Amex, Barclaycard, Diners

Dudley Hotel 66% £C/D

Four houses were converted at the turn of the century to make up this attractive hotel with its bay windows and wrought-iron balcony. Inside are a welcoming foyer, two bars–one opening on to a patio in summer–and a series of pretty, comfortable lounges. Bedrooms, which are mostly furnished in traditional style, vary in size; all have well-equipped bathrooms.

Continued

Continued
Rooms 78
with bath/shower 78 | *Room phone* Yes
Room TV Yes | *Confirm by* 6
Last dinner 10 | *Parking* Ample
Banquets 150/6

Brighton
Town plan B3 East Sussex
37 Waterloo Street *BN3 1AY*
Brighton (0273) 732383

The Fig Leaf

David Stott does all the cooking in this cosy, bistro-style restaurant, where he offers a fixed-price dinner menu of four enjoyable, skilfully prepared courses. You might begin with leek and bacon au gratin, followed by a home-made soup and then a main course like veal escalope in ginger sauce. To finish there are a few sweets such as gâteaux and sorbets.
Credit Access, Amex, Barclaycard

● **Set D** £6·95
About £22 for two
Banquets 22/10

Dinner only 7.30–9.30
Closed Sun, Mon, Bank Holidays & Christmas week

Brighton
Town plan E3 East Sussex
1 Paston Place, Kemp Town
BN2 1HA
Brighton (0273) 680716
French cooking

Le Français ★

John Brunner, chef here for four years, and his charming wife now own this tastefully appointed restaurant and are raising still further the high standards of cooking and service. Only the best ingredients are used, and dishes are prepared with great skill and finesse. Sauces, like the delicate cream and sorrel one that accompanied our paillard de saumon, are masterly. Strawberry tart is irresistible, and home-made truffles are served with the excellent coffee.
Specialities crevettes roses à la mayonnaise avocat, loup de mer flambé au Pernod sauce fenouil, gigot d'agneau à la beaumanière.
Credit Access, Amex, Barclaycard, Diners

About £56 for two

Dinner only 7–11.30
Closed Bank Holidays

Brighton
Town plan C3 East Sussex
11 Little East Street *BN1 1NT*
Brighton (0273) 24454

French Connection

There's classical music in the smart basement dining room, and in warmer weather you can enjoy your meal on the tiny patio. The menu, which changes every three months, features a good choice of familiar French and English dishes. Local seafood and lamb are put to good use and everything is carefully prepared. Finish with zabaglione or home-made ice cream.
Credit Access, Amex, Barclaycard, Diners

● **Set L & Set D** £4·95
About £31 for two
Banquets 36/–

Lunch 12–2.15 *Dinner* 6–11
Closed Sun & 25 December

Brighton
Town plan C3 East Sussex
King's Road *BN1 2FW*
Brighton (0273) 26301
Telex 877410
Manager Mr Paul Boswell
Rooms 166
with bath/shower 166
Room phone Yes
Room TV Yes
Confirm by By arrang.
Last dinner 9.30
Parking Ample
Banquets 300/20

Credit Access, Amex,
Barclaycard, Diners

Grand Hotel 77%   £ C

The beautiful facade of this elegant hotel has dominated the Brighton seafront since 1864, and the interior still retains much of its original dignity and splendour. Fine plaster ceilings and marble pillars are features of the lofty public rooms, and a spectacular wrought-iron staircase surmounted by a glass dome catches the eye in the plush foyer-lounge. Spacious bedrooms are fitted with modern units, armchairs and matching curtains and bedspreads; there are also several attractive suites. Tiled bathrooms are spotlessly clean. The hotel has first-class banqueting and conference facilities.
Amenities dancing (Sat), buttery (11.30am–midnight).

Brighton

Town plan B3 East Sussex
15 Western Street *BN1 2PG*
Brighton (0273) 772005
Proprietor Mr Lewis Harris

● **Set L & Set D** £6·45 incl. wine
About £15·50 for two
Banquets 40/–

Le Grandgousier   Ⓢ

There's a six-course set menu for both lunch and dinner at this cosy, bustling little restaurant. Help yourself to crudités, salami and home-made pâté before going on to the main course of your choice—poached trout, perhaps, or pepper steak or the chef's daily special. A hunk of Brie and a selection of sweets such as chocolate mousse make an enjoyable finish. Booking essential. *Credit* Amex

Lunch 12.30–1.30 *Dinner* 7.30–9.30, Fri & Sat 7.30–10.45
Closed L Sat, all Sun & 24 December–3 January

Brighton

Town plan C3 East Sussex
King's Road *BN1 1NR*
Brighton (0273) 29001
Telex 877101
Manager Mr J. M. Richards
Credit Access, Amex,
Barclaycard, Diners

Rooms 152
with bath/shower 134

Old Ship Hotel   65%   £ D

Despite extensive modernisation, this famous seafront hotel still retains many splendid Regency features in its public rooms—ornate ceilings, chandeliers, and wood panelling in the large Tattersalls Bar. Comfortable, attractively decorated bedrooms (some in a modern wing) have up-to-date furnishings and fittings; many have balconies overlooking the sea. Spotlessly clean bathrooms. No dogs.

Room phone Yes	*Confirm by* 6	*Parking* Ample
Room TV Yes	*Last dinner* 10	*Banquets* 250/–

Brighton

Town plan D3 East Sussex
Old Steine *BN1 1NT*
Brighton (0273) 29202

Credit Access, Amex,
Barclaycard, Diners

Rooms 115
with bath/shower 115

Royal Albion Hotel   59%   £ C/D

This imposing Victorian hotel occupies a town-centre corner site just a stone's throw from the beach and the Palace Pier. Public areas include the intimate bar and a spacious, comfortably furnished lounge which overlooks the seafront. Bright bedrooms, many also with sea views, have practical modern furniture and well-kept bathrooms. *Amenities* dinner dance (Sat), games room, 24-hour laundry, baby listening.

Room phone Yes	*Confirm by* 6	*Parking* Difficult
Room TV Yes	*Last dinner* 9	*Banquets* 150/–

Brighton

Town plan D3 East Sussex
100 Marine Parade *BN2 1AX*
Brighton (0273) 606311

Credit Access, Amex,
Barclaycard, Diners

Rooms 66
with bath/shower 66

Royal Crescent Hotel   65%   Ⓜ   £ D

This handsome hotel, once two private residences, offers style, comfort and a pleasant and convenient situation overlooking the sea. Spacious Regency public rooms, with bold colour schemes and ornate plasterwork, have plenty of relaxing chairs, and the bedrooms, reached by a fine stone and wrought-iron staircase, are individually furnished and attractively decorated. Warm, well-equipped bathrooms.

Room phone Yes	*Confirm by* 6	*Parking* Limited
Room TV Yes	*Last dinner* 9.45	*Banquets* 24/10

Brighton (Hove)

Town plan A2 East Sussex
189 Kingsway *BN3 4GU*
Brighton (0273) 736292
Telex 877830
Manager Mike Bevans
Credit Access, Amex,
Barclaycard, Diners

Rooms 49
with bath/shower 49

Sackville Hotel   60%   £ D/E

This pleasant seafront hotel offers a friendly welcome, comfortable surroundings and a comprehensive room service. The panelled bar and lounge areas have plenty of relaxing chairs, and some of the larger, traditionally furnished bedrooms have balconies overlooking the beach. Most rooms have modern fitted units. Bathrooms also vary in style and fittings.

Room phone Yes	*Confirm by* By arrang.	*Parking* Ample
Room TV Yes	*Last dinner* 9	*Banquets* 100/8

Brighton

Town plan C3 East Sussex
17 Market Street *BN1 1HH*
Brighton (0273) 25135
Manager Mr A. Tully
Seafood
About £35 for two

Wheeler's Oyster Rooms & Restaurant   ♕

A plushly traditional seafood restaurant, where the long menu offers oysters, scallops, plaice and 25 ways with Dover sole. All the fish is good and fresh, and for meat-eaters there are a few grills. *Credit* Access, Amex, Barclaycard, Diners *Lunch* 12.15–2.15, Sun 12.15–2 *Dinner* 6.30–10.30, Sun 7–10
Closed 1 January & 25 & 26 December *Banquets* 30/–

Brighton
Town plan C3 East Sussex
64 King's Road *BN1 1NA*
Brighton (0273) 23221
Manager Mrs Rumbold
Credit Access, Amex,
Barclaycard, Diners
Closed 25 & 26 December

Rooms 56
with bath/shower 56

Wheeler's Sheridan Hotel   67%   £D

High standards of service and housekeeping are maintained by Mrs
Rumbold and her industrious team at this tall Edwardian hotel facing the sea.
Public rooms are elegant and comfortable, with lots of relaxing armchairs
and settees, and spacious bedrooms are thoughtfully appointed. Ten
tastefully furnished new bedrooms include two with private sitting rooms,
and bathrooms are excellent throughout. No dogs.

| *Room phone* Yes | *Confirm by* 6 | *Parking* Difficult |
| *Room TV* Yes | *Last dinner* 10.30 | |

Brighton
Town plan C3 East Sussex
64 King's Road *BN1 1NA*
Brighton (0273) 28372

Seafood
About £34 for two

Wheeler's Sheridan Tavern

A panelled, club-like restaurant, where the menu offers a comprehensive
range of seafood dishes, with particular emphasis on sole. Fish is deliciously
fresh and carefully prepared. Good vegetables, too, and simple sweets.
Credit Access, Amex, Barclaycard, Diners *Lunch* 12–2.30, Sun 12–2 *Dinner*
6.30–10.30, Sun 7–10 **Closed** Bank Holidays

Bristol
Town plan E1 Avon
Filton Road, Hambrook *BS16 1QX*
Bristol (0272) 564242
Telex 449376
Manager Mr H. B. R. F. Bangert
Credit Access, Amex,
Barclaycard, Diners

Rooms 151
with bath/shower 151

Crest Hotel   65%   £C/D

Situated on the outskirts of the city close to the M4 and the M32, this
modern purpose-built hotel is popular with businessmen. The smart reception area doubles as a lounge and there's a neat bar. Refurbished bedrooms
have lightwood fitted units and attractive matching fabrics, plus tea-makers
and trouser presses. Compact bathrooms.
Amenities garden, dancing (Fri, Sat), helipad, buttery (9am–4pm).

| *Room phone* Yes | *Confirm by* By arrang. | *Parking* Ample |
| *Room TV* Yes | *Last dinner* 10 | *Banquets* 400/– |

Bristol
Town plan C2 Avon
Broad Street *BS1 2EL*
Bristol (0272) 291645
Telex 449889

Rooms 178
with bath/shower 178
Room phone Yes
Room TV Yes
Confirm by 6
Last dinner 10.30
Parking Difficult
Banquets 500/–

Credit Access, Amex,
Barclaycard, Diners

Grand Hotel   70%   £D

This Victorian city-centre hotel has
undergone a real transformation
and now offers most attractive, up-
to-date facilities. A plush foyer with
a splendid crystal chandelier sets
the tone, but the striking contemporary theme is highlighted in the
smart new cocktail bar with its
panelled walls, mirrored ceiling and
leather-backed chairs; there's also a
cheerful basement public bar. Bedrooms, which are smartly fitted out
in traditional style with matching
fabrics, freestanding furniture and top-quality deep-pile carpets, are also
equipped with tea/coffee-makers and trouser presses. Modern bathrooms
have excellent fittings including hairdryers.
Amenities dancing (Sat), in-house movies.

Bristol
Town plan B2 Avon
12a Denmark Street *BS1 5DQ*
Bristol (0272) 277665
Manager Mr F. Sanfiz
French cooking

About £42 for two
Banquets 50/10

Harveys

Originally used by Harveys for storing casks of sherry and wine, these cellars
now form a splendidly luxurious restaurant. The extensive menu of elaborately presented French dishes includes a wide choice of starters like game
pâté en croûte, fish and entrées such as tournedos basquaise. The sweet
trolley is loaded with popular creations like charlotte russe.
OUTSTANDING. Credit Access, Amex, Barclaycard, Diners

Lunch 12–2.30 *Dinner* 7–11.30
Closed L Sat, all Sun & Bank Holidays

Bristol
Town plan D2 Avon
Lower Castle Street *BS1 3AD*
Bristol (0272) 294281
Telex 449720

Rooms 274
with bath/shower 274
Room phone Yes
Room TV Yes
Confirm by 6
Last dinner 10.45
Parking Ample
Banquets 400/–

Credit Access, Amex,
Barclaycard, Diners

Holiday Inn 72% *E* £C

Overlooking Castle Park in the centre of Bristol, this large modern hotel has an extensive range of amenities and service appealing to executives and tourists alike. The airy public rooms are designed in open-plan style with lots of deep sofas, glass-topped tables and potted plants, while the cocktail bar has particularly refreshing decor. Double-glazed bedrooms are all superbly fitted with solid-looking dark furniture and shag-pile carpets; there are also four luxury suites. Compact bathrooms are fully tiled and equipped with many thoughtful touches.
Amenities sauna, indoor swimming pool, gymnasium, solarium, in-house movies, hotel mini bus, restaurant (7am–11pm), baby listening.

Our inspectors never book in the name of the Egon Ronay Organisation; they disclose their identity only after paying their bills.

Bristol
Town plan A1 Avon
6 Chandos Road
Redland *BS6 6PF*
Bristol (0272) 734901

● **Set L** £10 **Set D** £13·50
About £32 for two

Keith Floyd's

It's wise to ask for directions when booking at this appealing little restaurant tucked away in a back street. Owner-chef Keith Floyd offers a small choice of well-cooked dishes mainly reflecting his years in France: tasty starters like onion quiche and pâté-stuffed mushrooms, meat and fish served with delicate sauces, palate-reviving salads, excellent cheeses and tempting sweets. ● *ABOVE AVERAGE.*

Lunch Sun 12–3, Mon–Sat by arrangement only *Dinner* 7.30–9.30
Closed Tues, Wed, Bank Holidays, last 2 weeks Aug & 1st 2 weeks Sept

Bristol
Town plan D3 Avon
Redcliffe Way *BS1 6NJ*
Bristol (0272) 20044
Telex 449240

Rooms 210
with bath/shower 210
Room phone Yes
Room TV Yes
Confirm by By arrang.
Last dinner 10.30
Parking Ample
Banquets 400/–

Credit Access, Amex,
Barclaycard, Diners

Ladbroke Dragonara Hotel 74% *E* £B/C

Eighty bedrooms at this well-run city-centre hotel have benefited from a recent refurbishment programme, and now feature the latest designs in elegant soft furnishings. All rooms are comprehensively equipped, with smart fitted units, tea-makers and neat, tiled bathrooms. Spacious public rooms include the handsome foyer/lounge, two distinctive bars and excellent conference facilities. *Amenities* dancing (Thurs–Sat).

Bristol
Town plan A3 Avon
129 Hotwell Road *BS8 4RU*
Bristol (0272) 276190
Proprietor Michael McGowan

About £30 for two

Michael's

In an ornately Victorian setting Michael McGowan offers imaginative and enjoyable meat and game dishes, outstanding vegetables, hot home-made bread and irresistible desserts like kiwi Pavlova. Smoking in bar only. *Credit* Access *Lunch* Sun only 1–4.30 *Dinner* 6–12 **Closed** D Sun also L Sun in summer, Mon & 1 January ● **Set L** £5·95 *Banquets* 40/–

Map 4 B2
Town plan opposite

Population 410,000

The Birthplace of America–the Cabots sailed from here to discover Newfoundland in 1497. This and later voyages brought Bristol prosperity, largely in sugar, tobacco, rum and the slave trade. Architecture surviving the 1940 war damage ranges over the 13th-century Lord Mayor's Chapel, St Mary Redcliffe Church, England's oldest theatre (Theatre Royal–now completely renovated), and Clifton's Georgian terraces.

Sights Outside City
Severn Bridge, Berkeley Castle, Wells Cathedral, Cheddar Gorge, Severn Wildfowl Trust, Castle Combe Village

Information Centre (City)
Colston House, Colston Street
Telephone Bristol 293891

Bristol

1	Airport *6 miles*	A3
2	Arnolfini (Arts Centre)	C3
3	Ashton Court Estate and Mansion *beautiful parklands*	A1
4	Blaise Castle House Folk Museum *Henbury*	A1
5	National Lifeboat Museum	C3
6	Bristol Cathedral *dates from 12th c*	B3
7	Bristol Tapestry and Permanent Planning Exhibition	D1
8	Cabot Tower *Brandon Hill*, built 1897	A2
9	Central Library	B3
10	Chatterton House *Chatterton's birthplace*	D3
11	Christmas Steps *antique shops*	C1
12	City Museum & Art Gallery *fine & applied arts*	B1
13	Clifton suspension bridge	A1
14	Colston Hall concert hall	B2
15	Council House *modern architecture*	B2
16	Entertainment Centre	B2
17	Georgian House *late 18th-c showpiece*	B2
18	Hippodrome	B2
19	Information Centre	B2
20	John Wesley Chapel *first Methodist Chapel*	D1
21	Little Theatre	C2
22	Lord Mayor's Chapel *13th c*	B2
23	Nails and the Exchange *'pay on the nail' originated here*	C2
24	Norman Arch	B3
25	Observatory, Clifton Down	A1
26	Red Lodge *late 16th-c showpiece*	B2
27	Royal York Crescent *Regency*	A2
28	St Mary Redcliffe Church *dates from 13th c*	D3
29	St Nicholas Church Museum	C2
30	St Peter and St Paul *R.C. Cathedral*	A1
31	S.S. 'Great Britain' *first ocean-going propeller ship, launched Bristol 1843 Great Britain Dock, Gasferry Road*	A3
32	Temple Meads Station	E3
33	Theatre Royal *home of the Bristol Old Vic*	C2
34	Zoo *including flowers and rare trees*	A1

Bristol LANCIA

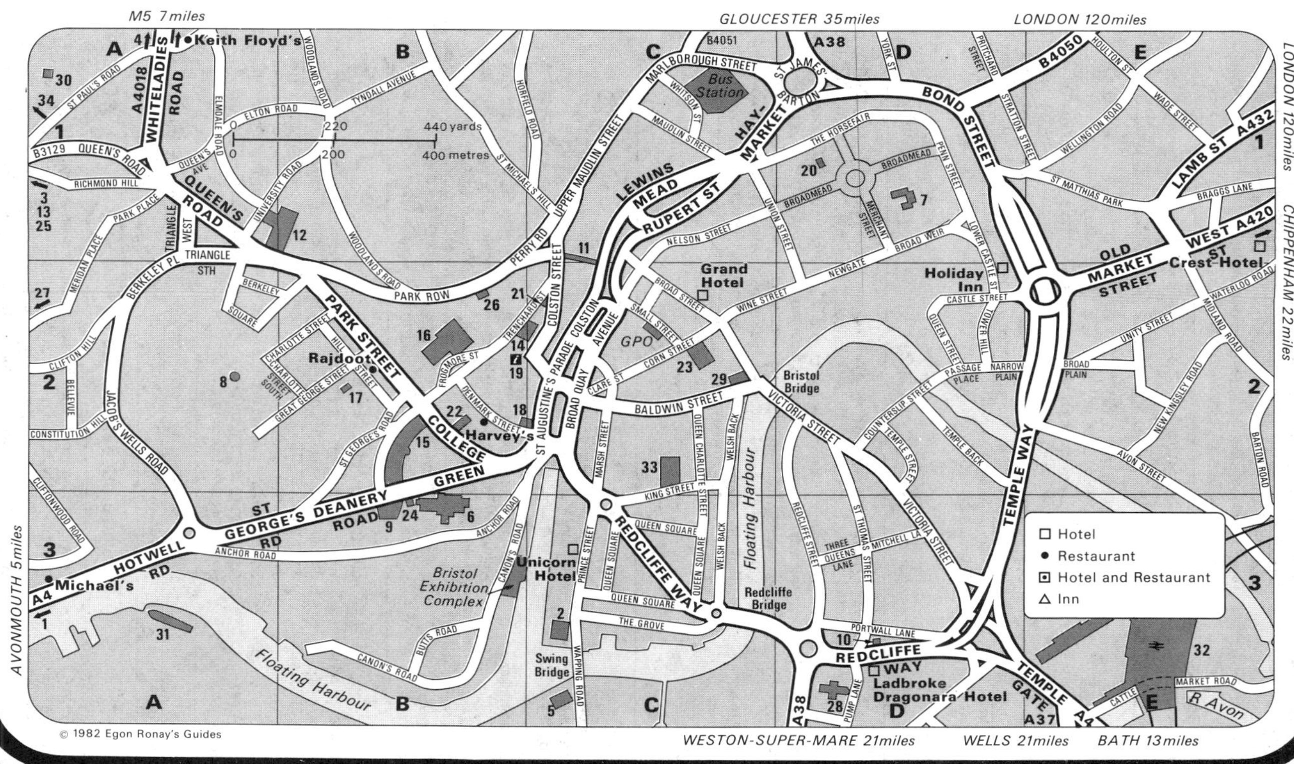

Bristol
Town plan B2 Avon
83 Park Street *BS1 5PJ*
Bristol (0272) 28033
Proprietor S. D. Sharma
Indian cooking

● **Set L** £3·50 **Set D** £6·50
About £25 for two
Banquets 60/–

Rajdoot ♛

Waiters in full Indian costume and the scent of burning joss sticks give this restaurant a truly authentic atmosphere. There's a widely ranging menu including excellent, delicately spiced tandoori specialities like chicken tikka and shish kebab, but some dishes may be uncharacteristically bland. Accompaniments like rice and nan bread are delicious.
Credit Access, Amex, Barclaycard, Diners

Lunch 12–2.15 *Dinner* 6.30–11.30
Closed L Sun & Bank Holidays

Bristol
Town plan C3 Avon
Prince Street *BS1 4QF*
Bristol (0272) 294811
Telex 44315
Manager John D. Mills
Credit Access, Amex, Barclaycard, Diners

Rooms 192
with bath/shower 192

Unicorn Hotel 66% £ D

Situated close to the city centre, this large modern hotel has its own multi-storey car park with access to each floor of the building. Two bars (the Unicorn and the Waterfront overlooking the river) are smart and very comfortable, while tastefully designed bedrooms are carefully fitted out with modern units and tea/coffee-makers. Spacious, well-equipped bathrooms. *Amenities* 24-hour lounge service. &

Room phone Yes	*Confirm by* 6	*Parking* Ample
Room TV Yes	*Last dinner* 10	*Banquets* 300/24

Brixham
Map 3 D3 Devon
King Street *TQ5 9TJ*
Brixham (080 45) 55751
Telex 42962

Credit Access, Amex, Barclaycard, Diners

Rooms 32
with bath/shower 25

Quayside Hotel 61% Ⓜ £ C/D

New owners have greatly improved this friendly hotel, a conversion of six period cottages overlooking the harbour. Housekeeping is excellent throughout, from the cosy lounge and two bars–one in Edwardian style, the other with a nautical flavour–to the compact, simply furnished bedrooms. These have pretty matching fabrics and good carpets; most have modern bathrooms. *Amenities* sea fishing, dancing (Sat except high season).

Room phone Yes	*Confirm by* 4	*Parking* Limited
Room TV Yes	*Last dinner* 9.30	*Banquets* 60/–

Brixham
Map 3 D3 Devon
3 The Strand *TQ5 8EH*
Brixham (080 45) 3357
Proprietors
Mr & Mrs John Brunker

● **Set D** from £6·50
About £32 for two
Banquets 50/5

Randall's ♧ Ⓢ

Run very much as a family affair, with mother and daughter in the kitchen, this quayside restaurant has a bias towards fresh seafood. The pick of the day's catch appears in French-style dishes such as plump coquilles St Jacques en brochette; there's fillet steak and duck, too, and it's all enthusiastically prepared with generally commendable results. Simpler lunches. ♟*ABOVE AVERAGE. Credit* Access, Amex, Barclaycard, Diners

Lunch 12–2 *Dinner* 7–11
Closed Mon, also L October–March & 2 weeks November

Broadway
Map 4 C1 Hereford & Worcester
The Green *WR12 7AA*
Broadway (0386) 852401

Credit Access, Amex, Barclaycard, Diners

Rooms 24
with bath/shower 22

Broadway Hotel 58% £ D

Built in 1575 and rich in history, this Cotswold-stone and timber hostelry is well maintained. The flagstoned entrance hall, the beamed lounge (with a gallery) and the simple bar with leaded windows all retain echoes of the past. Some bedrooms are also traditional in style, while others (particularly in the garden wing) are more modern and equipped with fitted units. No dogs. *Amenities* garden, putting.

Room phone Yes	*Confirm by* 6	*Parking* Ample
Room TV Some	*Last dinner* 9	

Broadway
Map 4 C1 Hereford & Worcester
Collin Lane *WR12 7PB*
Broadway (0386) 858354
Credit Access, Amex, Barclaycard
Closed 2 weeks January & 25 & 26 December

Collin House Hotel 65% Ⓜ £ D/E

New owners extend a friendly welcome at this stone-built 17th-century farmhouse, which stands in secluded gardens north-west of Broadway. There's a TV lounge and a charming bar-lounge with an inglenook fireplace and chintzy furniture. Bedrooms have bold patterned wallpaper, solid traditional furnishings and duvets; carpeted bathrooms have smart coloured suites. No dogs. *Amenities* garden, outdoor swimming pool.

Continued

Rooms 7	*Room phone* No	*Confirm by* By arrang.	*Parking* Ample
with bath/shower 7	*Room TV* No	*Last dinner* 9	*Banquets* 30/–

Broadway
Map 4 C1 Hereford & Worcester
Collin Lane *WR127PB*
Broadway (0386) 858354

Collin House Hotel Restaurant   ⑤

Prime fresh ingredients and enthusiastic home cooking produce excellent results at this cosy beamed restaurant down a country lane. Simple starters like soup, pâté and garlic mushrooms are followed by generously served main courses such as coq au vin or sirloin steak with Stilton and horseradish cream. To finish there's a really splendid traditional bread and butter pudding. *Credit* Access, Amex, Barclaycard   ♿

● **Set D** from £8·50
About £26 for two

Lunch by arrangement only *Dinner* 7–9
Closed D Sun, all 25 & 26 December & 2 weeks January

Broadway
Map 4 C1 Hereford & Worcester
Copgrove, West End *WR127JP*
Broadway (0386) 852690
Proprietors
Mr & Mrs John Foster

The Dining Room   ♛ ⑤

Parties of six to ten people can enjoy a memorable dinner at this beautiful Cotswold manor house, provided they book and order well in advance. There's a wide choice of starters ranging from smoked eel to lasagne, while main courses feature perfectly cooked roasts and dishes like fillet of beef in puff pastry. Vegetables are fresh and tasty, and there are light creamy sweets to finish.

● **Set D** £15
About £16·50 per head

Dinner only by arrangement from 7.30
Closed Christmas week

Broadway
Map 4 C1 Hereford & Worcester
Willersey Hill *WR127LF*
Broadway (0386) 852711
Telex 338571

Credit Access, Amex,
Barclaycard, Diners

Dormy House   67%   Ⓜ   £ C/D

A lovely hilltop position and excellent conference facilities make this mellow and welcoming complex (a converted farmhouse and outbuildings) equally popular for business and holiday trips. The reception area is bright and elegant, and there's a cosy lounge as well as two convivial bars. Attractive, individually styled bedrooms (some with French windows opening on to the garden) have well-equipped bathrooms. *Amenities* garden, sauna.

Rooms 50	*Room phone* Yes	*Confirm by* By arrang.	*Parking* Ample
with bath/shower 50	*Room TV* Yes	*Last dinner* 10.30	*Banquets* 150/–

Broadway
Map 4 C1 Hereford & Worcester
Willersey Hill *WR127LF*
Broadway (0386) 852711

Dormy House Restaurant   ⑤

A dining room full of charm and character, with exposed brick walls, fresh flowers and friendly, attentive service. The capable new chef offers traditional English dishes on his set meals, whereas the à la carte is mainly French-inspired, with dishes like escalope de barbue à la menthe and flavoursome coq au vin. Excellent sweets such as apricot crumble. 🍷 *ABOVE AVERAGE.*
Credit Access, Amex, Barclaycard, Diners

● **Set L** £7·50, Sun £5·50
Set D £10·50
About £26 for two

Lunch 12.30–2.15, Sun 12.30–2.30 *Dinner* 7–10.30

Broadway
Map 4 C1 Hereford & Worcester
High Street *WR127DT*
Broadway (0386) 853247

Hunter's Lodge   ⑤

This Cotswold-stone house makes a lovely setting for the Friedlis' charming restaurant. Lunchtime brings simple fare like braised oxtail, smoked trout and grills, while in the evening, seasonal fish and game figure in elaborate French-style dishes such as mousseline of scallops with lobster sauce and breast of chicken en croûte. Delicious treats like hazelnut meringue to finish. *Credit* Access, Amex, Barclaycard, Diners   ♿

About £32 for two
Banquets 45/–

Lunch 12.30–2 *Dinner* 7.30–9.30
Closed D Sun, all Mon & 2–27 January

Broadway

Map 4 C1 Hereford & Worcester
High Street *WR12 7DU*
Broadway (0386) 852255
Telex 338260
Proprietor Mr D. Barrington
Rooms 67
with bath/shower 63
Room phone Yes
Room TV Yes
Confirm by 6
Last dinner 9.15
Parking Ample
Banquets 100/–

Credit Access, Amex,
Barclaycard, Diners

Lygon Arms 77%  £B

One of the best-known–and most frequently photographed–hotels in the country, this fine, 600-year-old Cotswold-stone hostelry still maintains high standards of professional service and a charming atmosphere. A welcoming flagstoned reception leads to a series of delightfully cosy lounges with lovely antiques and open fires; there's also a rustic bar and an attractive first-floor drawing room. Many bedrooms have oak panelling and traditional fittings (four have four-posters); rooms in the two wings are rather more modern in style. Superb, fully equipped bathrooms. Excellent breakfasts.
Amenities garden, tennis, 24-hour lounge service, 24-hour laundry service, hotel car.

Broadway

Map 4 C1 Hereford & Worcester
High Street *WR12 7DU*
Broadway (0386) 852255
Proprietor
Mr D. Barrington

● **Set L** £7 **Set D** £12
About £38 for two

Lygon Arms Restaurant

Home-grown herbs feature in capably prepared dishes like saddle of lamb with sorrel sauce and salmon trout with chervil, and there's also game in season. Vegetables are crisp, the cheeseboard features English varieties and sweets are delightful. The vaulted Great Hall makes a resplendent setting for a meal except in winter months, when a more intimate room is used.
 SUPERIOR. *Credit* Access, Amex, Barclaycard, Diners

Lunch 12.30–2 *Dinner* 7.30–9.30

Brockdish

Map 6 C2 Norfolk
Near Diss *IP21 4JY*
Hoxne (037 975) 316
Proprietor
Sqn Ldr F. Pichel-Juan

About £30 for two
Banquets 16/9

Sheriff House ★

The Pichel-Juans prefer guests to book and order well in advance at their simple, elegant restaurant, with everyone in the same party having the same dishes (there's a short menu for casual callers). Starters include superb rillettes, pâtés and terrines (a house speciality), croustade de fruits de mer and gnocchi à la parisienne, while main courses range through coq au vin, couscous and steaks to our exquisite civet de chevreuil in a dark, rich and flavoursome sauce. Vegetables and desserts are delicious, too; preparation is first class, and flavours perfectly balanced.
Specialities quenelles de brochet, gigot en croûte, crêpe soufflée.

Lunch 12–2 *Dinner* 7–9
Closed Wed

Brockenhurst

Map 4 C4 Hampshire
New Forest *SO47RH*
Lymington (0590) 23551
Telex 47442
Manager Mr C. Biggin
Credit Access, Amex,
Barclaycard, Diners

Rooms 57
with bath/shower 57

Carey's Manor Hotel 63% £D/E

On the outskirts of the village, this handsome Victorian house still retains echoes of its past in the panelled reception hall. By contrast, the smart cocktail bar and conference rooms are much more up to date. Bedrooms in the main house are furnished in sophisticated traditional style, while those in the garden annexe are more streamlined and modern.
Amenities garden, dancing (Fri, Sat).

| *Room phone* Yes | *Confirm by* 7 | *Parking* Ample |
| *Room TV* Yes | *Last dinner* 10 | *Banquets* 120/– |

Brockenhurst

Map 4 C4 Hampshire
Balmer Lawn Road *SO47ZB*
Lymington (0590) 23116

Credit Access, Amex,
Barclaycard, Diners
Closed 1st 2 weeks January

Ladbroke Balmer Lawn Hotel 59% £D/E

Visitors are drawn to this imposing hotel as much by its considerable sports facilities as by its location in the heart of the New Forest. Public areas like the foyer-lounge and cocktail bar have plush, attractive decor, while bedrooms, all pleasantly furnished, vary considerably in style and size. Simple bathrooms. *Amenities* garden, outdoor swimming pool, tennis, squash, games room, laundry room.

Continued

| Rooms 60 | Room phone Yes | Confirm by 6 | Parking Ample |
| with bath/shower 52 | Room TV Yes | Last dinner 8.45 | Banquets 70/– |

Bromley

Map 7 B5 Kent
Bromley Hill *BR1 4JD*
01–464 5011
Telex 896310

Credit Access, Amex,
Barclaycard, Diners

Bromley Court Hotel   67%   £D/E

A handsome period house has been modernised and extended into this comfortable, very well-maintained hotel. A roomy, elegant bar-lounge overlooks the garden, and there's a little residents' lounge, a cocktail bar and a useful coffee shop. Some bedrooms are traditionally styled but the majority are pleasantly modern; all have neat, compact bathrooms. *Amenities* garden, dinner dance (Sat), coffee shop (10am–midnight), putting.

| Rooms 130 | Room phone Yes | Confirm by 6 | Parking Ample |
| with bath/shower 130 | Room TV Yes | Last dinner 9.45 | Banquets 160/12 |

Bromley

Map 7 B5 Kent
9 Simpsons Road *BR2 3RS*
01–464 8036
Proprietors Mr Cane & Mr Serra
Italian cooking
About £26 for two

Capisano's

Behind the shopping centre, a cheerful trattoria offering tasty, well-prepared dishes ranging from minestrone and spaghetti to calf's liver fried in butter with sage. Good vegetables and desserts, too. Booking advisable.
Credit Access, Amex, Barclaycard *Lunch* 12–2.30 *Dinner* 7–11
Closed Sun, Mon, Bank Holidays & 3 weeks August/September

Bromsgrove

Map 10 C4 Hereford & Worcester
Grafton Lane *B61 7HA*
Bromsgrove (0527) 31525

Grafton Manor Restaurant

John Morris uses home-grown herbs in many of the dishes on his imaginative set menus, and capable preparation and careful presentation produce very enjoyable results in choices which range from delicately flavoured carrot and coriander soup and asparagus crêpes with orange hollandaise to noisettes of spring lamb with mint béarnaise. The splendid baronial house is on the A38. *Credit* Access, Amex, Barclaycard, Diners

● **Set L** £7·50 **Set D** £12·50
About £34 for two

Lunch Sun only 12.30–2 *Dinner* 7.30–9
Closed D Sun & Bank Holiday Mons

Bucklow Hill

Map 10 B2 Cheshire
Near Knutsford *WA16 6RN*
Bucklow Hill (0565) 830295
Telex 666911

Credit Access, Amex,
Barclaycard, Diners

Swan Hotel   58%   £D

Ideally situated close to the motorway network, this modernised coaching inn is a useful hotel for visiting businessmen. There are two bars, one of which serves as a lounge. Bedrooms in the original building are the nicest, with traditional furnishings and attractive bathrooms; motel-style chalets have functional fitted units and adequate bathrooms (some with showers only). *Amenities* discothèque (Sat in winter).

| Rooms 74 | Room phone Yes | Confirm by 6 | Parking Ample |
| with bath/shower 74 | Room TV Yes | Last dinner 10 | Banquets 30/– |

Stars in this Guide stand for the quality of the cooking only – our overriding criterion, irrespective of price, luxury or service.

Bude

Map 2 C2 Cornwall
The Strand *EX23 8RA*
Bude (0288) 3222

Credit Access, Amex,
Barclaycard, Diners

Strand Hotel   58%   £D

Holiday-makers and business people alike appreciate the simple modern comforts of this well-maintained hotel overlooking the river Neet. Public rooms include a bright upstairs residents' lounge, a smart coffee shop and a cocktail bar with striking red decor. Cheerful, well-kept bedrooms have practical fitted furniture and neat, up-to-date bathrooms.
Amenities coffee shop (8am–9pm).

| Rooms 40 | Room phone Yes | Confirm by 6 | Parking Ample |
| with bath/shower 40 | Room TV Yes | Last dinner 9 | Banquets 120/– |

Budock Vean

Map 2 B4 Cornwall
Near Falmouth *TR11 5LG*
Mawnan Smith (0326) 250288
Proprietors
Mr P. H. & Mr J. Whiteside
Rooms 54
with bath/shower 54
Room phone Yes
Room TV No
Confirm by By arrang.
Last dinner 9
Parking Ample
Banquets 120/10
Closed January & February
Credit Access, Amex,
Barclaycard, Diners

Budock Vean Hotel   72%   Ⓜ   £ D

Almost a self-contained mini-resort, the Whitesides' extended manor house offers elegance, comfort and a wide range of recreational facilities. The lofty lounges (one for non-smokers) are furnished in a mixture of traditional and more modern styles, and command fine views of the hotel's well-kept grounds. There's also a flowery sun lounge and a choice of several bars. Spacious bedrooms are bright and cheerful, bathrooms neat and well cared for. No children under five. No dogs. Inclusive terms only.
Amenities garden, indoor swimming pool, tennis, 9-hole golf course, sea fishing, dancing (Sat Easter–October), discothèque (Wed in summer), games room, billiards.

Burbage

Map 4 C3 Wiltshire
Near Marlborough *SN8 3AY*
Marlborough (0672) 810206

Credit Access, Amex,
Barclaycard, Diners

Rooms 13
with bath/shower 5

Savernake Forest Hotel   58%   Ⓜ   £ E

Lovers of the great outdoors will particularly appreciate the delightful, tranquil setting of this red-brick Victorian building on the edge of Savernake Forest. The comfortable bar and a functionally furnished residents' lounge have a homely, unpretentious air, while bedrooms are neat and tidy, modestly decorated and equipped with simple freestanding furniture and tea-makers. Modern bathrooms. *Amenities* garden, coarse fishing.

Room phone No	*Confirm by* 6	*Parking* Ample
Room TV No	*Last dinner* 9	*Banquets* 26/–

Burford

Map 4 C2 Oxfordshire
Sheep Street *OX8 4LW*
Burford (099 382) 3137
Proprietor Miss Sylvia Gray

Closed 4 days late January

Rooms 24
with bath/shower 18

Bay Tree Hotel   58%   Ⓜ   £ E

Comfort and charm are the keynotes of this old Cotswold-stone hotel in a quiet side street. There's a beamed bar overlooking the pretty walled garden, and three restful lounges with open fires and leather armchairs. Comfortable bedrooms (some in a cottage across the courtyard) are traditionally furnished, with some nice antiques, and bathrooms are adequate. No children under four. *Amenities* garden.

Room phone No	*Confirm by* 6	*Parking* Ample
Room TV No	*Last dinner* 8.45	

Burford

Map 4 C2 Oxfordshire
High Street *OX8 4RJ*
Burford (099 382) 3223

Proprietor Mr W. Ellse
Credit Access, Amex,
Barclaycard, Diners

Rooms 12
with bath/shower 12

Golden Pheasant Hotel *(Inn)*   Ⓜ   £ E

One of the oldest buildings in Burford, this lovely little Cotswold inn retains much of its original character although a great deal of modernisation has taken place. A small reception leads to the elegant, tastefully furnished lounge, and there are a few antiques in the small bar. Except for two beamed rooms boasting splendid four-posters, most bedrooms are simply furnished in modern style. Compact bathrooms are carpeted.

Room phone Yes	*Confirm by* 7	*Parking* Limited
Room TV Yes	*Last dinner* 9.30	

We do not necessarily recommend the cooking at hotels whose restaurants are not separately listed.

Burford

Map 4 C2 Oxfordshire
The Barringtons
Gloucestershire *OX8 4TN*
Windrush (045 14) 324

Credit Amex
Closed 1 week Christmas

Rooms 9			
with bath/shower 9			

Inn for all Seasons *(Inn)* Ⓜ £E

New owners have taken over at this delightful Cotswold-stone inn on the A40. A little reception hall leads to the traditionally furnished residents' lounge and the attractive, luxuriously appointed lounge-bar. Cosy, individually decorated bedrooms have mainly antique furniture and carpeted modern bathrooms. Good standards of housekeeping throughout. No children under ten. No dogs. *Amenities* garden.

Room phone Yes	*Confirm by* By arrang.	*Parking* Ample
Room TV Yes	*Last dinner* 9.45	*Banquets* 40/–

Burghfield

Map 5 D2 Berkshire
Near Reading *RG3 3XE*
Reading (0734) 52366

● **Set D** £9·75
About £25 for two
Banquets 24/8

Knights Farm ♧ Ⓢ

Ask for directions when booking dinner at the Trevor-Ropers' converted farmhouse. The four-course fixed-price menu features natural flavours in abundance, and dishes show a keen eye for attractive presentation. We particularly enjoyed a thin wholewheat pancake filled with smoked haddock, well-hung venison in a distinctive wine and juniper sauce, and a superbly dressed salad. ♗ *ABOVE AVERAGE. Credit* Access, Barclaycard

Dinner only 7.30–9.30
Closed Sun, Mon, 1st 2 weeks August & 25 December–1 January

Burley

Map 4 C4 Hampshire
Ringwood Road, near Ringwood
BH24 4BS
Burley (042 53) 3314
Telex 47439
Credit Access, Amex,
Barclaycard, Diners

Rooms 22			
with bath/shower 22			

Burley Manor Hotel 59% £D/E

A long drive through parkland leads to this 19th-century house. The foyer and open-plan lounge are reached through a massive oak doorway, and there's the attractively rustic Barn Bar across the courtyard. Pleasant bedrooms vary in size and style but all have radios, tea-makers and well-equipped, fully tiled bathrooms. *Amenities* garden, outdoor swimming pool, dinner dance (Sat), riding, hairdressing, games room (in season), badminton, croquet.

Room phone No	*Confirm by* By arrang.	*Parking* Ample
Room TV Yes	*Last dinner* 10	*Banquets* 40/–

Burnham

Map 5 E2 Buckinghamshire
Grove Road *SL1 8DP*
Burnham (062 86) 3333

Manager Michael D. Milnes
Credit Amex, Barclaycard,
Diners

Rooms 54			
with bath/shower 54			

Burnham Beeches Hotel 56% £D

Forty acres of parkland make a peaceful setting for this Georgian hotel, which is popular for conferences. Public rooms include a lofty lounge with garden views and two panelled bars. Bedrooms vary from comfortably traditional rooms in the main building to more modern ones in the extension. Some refurbishment would be welcome. *Amenities* garden, tennis, squash, putting, billiards, table tennis, croquet, 24-hour laundry service.

Room phone Yes	*Confirm by* 6	*Parking* Ample
Room TV Yes	*Last dinner* 9.30	*Banquets* 150/–

Burnham

Map 5 E2 Buckinghamshire
Taplow Common Road *SL1 8LP*
Burnham (062 86) 3131

Proprietors Mr & Mrs Don Hall
Credit Access, Amex,
Barclaycard, Diners

Rooms 8			
with bath/shower 4			

Grovefield Hotel 59% Ⓜ £E

A three-storey gabled building standing in several acres of grounds, the Grovefield is a peaceful and friendly little place to stay. Bedrooms of varying shapes and sizes are traditionally furnished, and bathrooms are adequately equipped. Residents have a small, comfortable lounge and there's a cosy, tartan-carpeted cocktail bar. The hotel is $1\frac{1}{2}$ miles from the M4 (junction 7). *Amenities* garden. **Closed** Sun nights & Christmas night.

Room phone Yes	*Confirm by* By arrang.	*Parking* Ample
Room TV Yes	*Last dinner* 9.30	*Banquets* 44/6

Burnham-on-Crouch

Map 7 C4 Essex
80 High Street *CM0 8AA*
Maldon (0621) 782139

Proprietor Mr R. T. Walton

● **Set L** £3·50
About £28 for two
Banquets 35/10

Contented Sole

After over 17 years at this cottage restaurant, Roy Walton still delights in creating tasty dishes based on seasonal produce. Although there's an obvious bias towards seafood (we enjoyed delicious moules marinière and strips of sole with lobster sauce in a perfect puff pastry case), there are meat dishes, too, such as carpetbag steak and pheasant braised with chestnuts. Sweets like orange norvégienne are also notable.

Lunch 12–2 *Dinner* 7–9.30
Closed Sun, Mon, last 2 weeks July & 4 weeks December/January

Burnham Market

Map 6 C1 Norfolk
Market Place
Near King's Lynn *PE31 8HD*
Burnham Market (032 873) 588
Proprietor Gillian Cape
Seafood

● **Set L** £4·75
About £24 for two
Banquets 20/3

Fishes

Rich crab soup, oysters and home-smoked fish are among the delights of this simple, excellent seafood restaurant. There are also scallops and mussels, along with succulent *fresh* sardines on toast, Norfolk trout with almonds and bananas and perfectly cooked mackerel with a tangy lemon sauce. And, to round off a most enjoyable meal, lovely home-made ice creams and gâteaux. *Credit* Access, Amex, Barclaycard, Diners

Lunch 12–2 *Dinner* 7–9.30
Closed D Sun October–July, all Mon & 25 & 26 December

Changes in data may occur in establishments after the Guide goes to press. Prices should be taken as indications rather than firm quotes.

Burnley

Map 10 B1 Lancashire
Keirby Walk *BB11 2DH*
Burnley (0282) 27611
Telex 63119

Credit Access, Amex,
Barclaycard, Diners

Crest Hotel 63% £ D

Good conference facilities make this modern town-centre hotel attractive to businessmen, who are well catered for by good-sized bedrooms equipped with tea-makers and trouser presses. The spacious foyer serves as an open-plan lounge. Enterprising bar decor, including a display of counterfeit coins in the Coiners Bar, goes down well with the locals.

Rooms 49	*Room phone* Yes	*Confirm by* 6	*Parking* Limited
with bath/shower 49	*Room TV* Yes	*Last dinner* 9.45	*Banquets* 250/–

Burton upon Trent

Map 10 C3 Staffordshire
Riverside Drive
Branston *DE14 3EP*
Burton upon Trent (0283) 63117
Proprietors Mr & Mrs Pumphrey
Credit Access, Barclaycard

Riverside Inn 58% Ⓜ £ F

In a residential area yet conveniently placed for the surrounding industrial centres, this extended and modernised inn retains some older features such as a fine 14th-century fireplace and the beams in the cottage bar overlooking the river. Brightly decorated bedrooms are fitted with practical units, and bathrooms are up to date. No dogs.
Amenities garden.

Rooms 22	*Room phone* Yes	*Confirm by* 10	*Parking* Ample
with bath/shower 20	*Room TV* Yes	*Last dinner* 10	*Banquets* 100/20

Burton upon Trent

Map 10 C3 Staffordshire
Ashby Road East, Bretby *DE15 0PU*
Burton upon Trent
(0283) 217954
Proprietors J. H. Staley & sons

Closed 24–26 December

Stanhope Arms Hotel 55% Ⓜ £ F

Two miles south of Burton on the A50, this welcoming old roadside inn has been owned by the Staley family for 45 years. Original beams and stone walls are features of public rooms like the relaxing pub-style bar, while bedrooms have fitted modern furniture and useful writing space. Front rooms are double-glazed; rear ones overlook pleasant fields. Bathrooms are adequate. *Amenities* garden.

Rooms 19	*Room phone* Yes	*Confirm by* By arrang.	*Parking* Ample
with bath/shower 17	*Room TV* Yes	*Last dinner* 9.30	*Banquets* 165/–

VISIT AN ENGLISH GARDEN

The English Tourist Board have again produced the booklet to help you make your visits to English gardens a real joy.

Visit an English Garden '83 includes details of over 200 gardens you can visit with lots of useful information including descriptions, opening times, events, tours and excursions.

English gardens are - grand classical landscapes, modest cottage borders, botanic gardens, water gardens, woodland gardens, alpine and rock gardens.

Follow the seasons. Go south and west for springtime colour and see the gardens before the summer crowds.

In the early summer gardens are coming to their peak in the south and east of England with dazzling displays of colour.

Peak summer is the time to explore the great northern estates and in autumn the trees are in all their glory at parks and arboretums throughout the country.

Visit an English Garden '83 is a handy pocket size available from many Tourist Information Centres and bookshops price 70p or by post (plus 25p postage) from:

The English Tourist Board,
Dept. VAEG, 4 Grosvenor Gardens,
London SW1W 0DU.

Map 6 B3
Town plan opposite

Population 102,300

Unexcelled as a centre of learning and research, settled by the Romans as a trading bridgehead. Cambridge was a place of scholarship even before the first college, Peterhouse, was founded. Entrance to University buildings and gardens (but not up staircases without permission) is generally allowed until dusk. Ideal punting round Backs of colleges for beauty rivalling Venice and Bruges. King's College Chapel has Britain's most celebrated boys' choir.

Annual Events
Cambridge Festival of Arts *July*
Festival of Nine Carols *Christmas Eve*
May Week *first two weeks June*

Sights Outside City
Ely Cathedral, Audley End, Grantchester, Wimpole Hall, Anglesey Abbey, American Cemetery, Cromwell Museum at Huntingdon, Wicken Fen

Information Centre
Wheeler Street
CB2 3QD
Telephone Cambridge 358977
Weekends Telephone Cambridge 353363

Cambridge

1	Arts Theatre	B3
2	Botanic Gardens	C5
3	Church of the Holy Sepulchre *12th-c round church*	B2
	Colleges	
4	*Clare 1326*	A3
5	*Corpus Christi 1362*	B3
6	*Emmanuel 1584, Wren Chapel*	B/C3
7	*King's 1441 and Chapel*	A3
8	*Magdalene 1542*	A2
9	*Pembroke 1347, Wren Chapel*	B3/4
10	*Peterhouse 1284, oldest college*	B4
11	*Queens' 1448*	A3/4
12	*St John's 1511 and Bridge of Sighs*	A2
13	*Trinity 1546*	A3
14	Fitzwilliam Museum *manuscripts, statuary, tapestry and archaeology*	B4
15	Folk Museum *furniture, cooking equipment, clothes and tools*	A2
16	Great St Mary's Church *University Church*	B3
17	St Bene't's Church *oldest in county*	B3
18	Tourist Information Centre	B3
19	University Arts Faculties	A4

Fiat Dealer

F. H. Motors (Duchy's Corner) Ltd.
Coldhams Lane, Cambridge CB1 3EX
Tel: Cambridge 67777

Cambridge

FIAT

ELY 16 miles
HUNTINGDON 16 miles
HISTON B1049 ROAD
A604
BEDFORD 29 miles
A1303
SANDY 22 miles
A603
ELY 16 miles
NEWMARKET 13 miles
COLCHESTER 48 miles
LONDON 60 miles

A
B
C

VICTORIA ROAD
VICTORIA ROAD
CLARE STREET
ST LUKE'S STREET
HERTFORD STREET
ALPHA ROAD
HOLLAND STREET
CARLYLE ROAD
CARLISLE ROAD
HERBERT ST
MONTAGUE ROAD
PRETORIA ROAD
KIMBERLEY ROAD
DE FREVILLE AVENUE
AYLESTONE ROAD

CHESTERTON ROAD
CHESTERTON ROAD

Cunard
Cambridgeshire
Hotel

Arundel
House
Hotel

Victoria
Bridge

River Cam

PLEASANT ROW
SHELLY ROW
MOUNT PLEASANT
LADY MARGARET ROAD
ALBION ROW
ST PETER'S ST
POUND HILL

CASTLE STREET
CHESTERTON LANE
MAGDALENE STREET
BRIDGE STREET

THOMPSON'S LANE
PARK PARADE
PARK STREET

QUEEN'S ROAD

15
8
3
12
13
4
7
11
16
1
18
17
5
9
10
14
19
6
2

ST JOHN'S ST
SIDNEY STREET
TRINITY ST
GREEN ST
MARKET STREET
KING'S PARADE
BENET ST
TRUMPINGTON STREET
CORN EXCHANGE ST
PEMBROKE STREET
DOWNING STREET
SILVER STREET

JESUS LANE
JESUS LANE
MALCOLM ST
KING STREET
MAID'S CAUSEWAY
BRUNSWICK WALK
BRUNSWICK TERRACE
FAIR ST
NEW SQUARE
Peking
FITZROY STREET
NEW SQUARE
EDEN STREET
CITY ROAD
JOHN ST
PROSPECT ROW
WARKWORTH ST
ORCHARD ST
CLARENDON STREET
WARKWORTH TERRACE
EMMANUEL ROAD
EMMANUEL ST
PARKER ST
PARKSIDE

Bus
Station

Guildhall
GPO

ST ANDREWS STREET
HOBSON STREET

University Arms
Hotel

Garden
House
Hotel

River Cam

WEST ROAD
SIDGWICK AVENUE

TENNIS COURT ROAD
FITZWILLIAM STREET
TRUMPINGTON STREET
REGENT STREET
PARK TERRACE

GONVILLE PLACE A603
GRESHAM ROAD
HARVEY ROAD
Gonville
Hotel

LENSFIELD ROAD
HILLS ROAD
ST PAUL'S ROAD
UNION ROAD
PANTON STREET
CORONATION STREET
ST PAUL'S ROAD
GLISSON RD
NORWICH STREET
BATEMAN STREET
FEN CAUSEWAY
NEWNHAM ROAD
TRUMPINGTON ROAD A1309

A1309
VICTORIA AVENUE

0   220   440 yards
0   200   400 metres

Hotel
Restaurant
Hotel and Restaurant
Inn

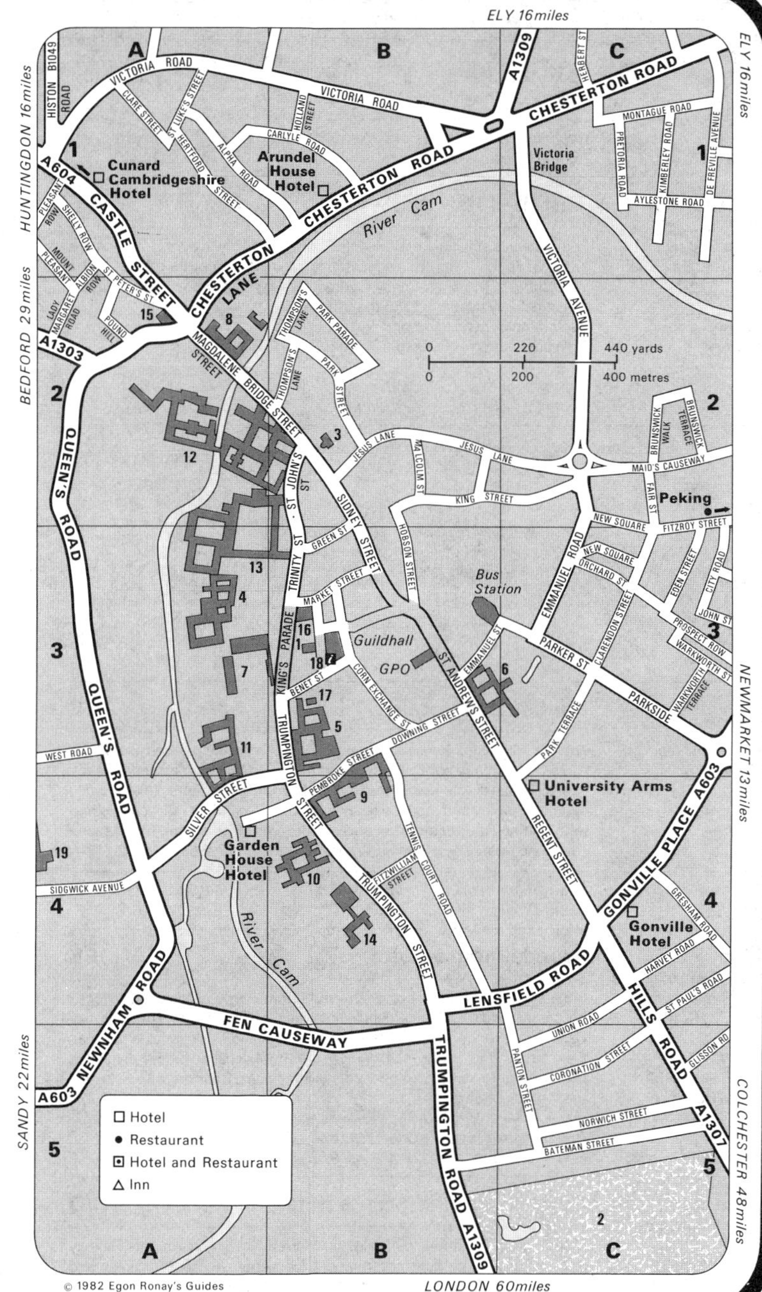

Bury St Edmunds

Map 6 C2 Suffolk
Angel Hill *IP33 1LT*
Bury St Edmunds (0284) 3926
Telex 81630
Managers Mr & Mrs Donovan
Credit Access, Amex,
Barclaycard, Diners

Rooms 43
with bath/shower 36

Angel Hotel   64%   £ D

Facing the gateway to the Norman abbey, this handsome, creeper-clad hotel offers a friendly welcome and high standards of comfort and service. Public rooms include an elegant residents' lounge and two popular bars. Roomy, well-equipped bedrooms are furnished in a variety of styles; three have four-posters. Good, well-maintained bathrooms. *Amenities* dinner dance (Sat monthly October–March), 12-hour laundry service.

| *Room phone* Yes | *Confirm by* 6.30 | *Parking* Ample |
| *Room TV* Yes | *Last dinner* 10.30 | *Banquets* 140/– |

Bury St Edmunds

Map 6 C2 Suffolk
Buttermarket *IP33 1DC*
Bury St Edmunds (0284) 3995

Credit Access, Amex,
Barclaycard, Diners

Rooms 41
with bath/shower 13

Suffolk Hotel   55%   £ D/E

The buttery is strikingly designed in Scandinavian style at this town-centre hotel, while the Viking Bar is pleasantly adorned with military prints and a brass ship's bell in the chimney. Bedrooms—all with radios and tea-makers—are attractively decorated and thoughtfully designed, and private as well as public bathrooms are neat and well kept.
Amenities buttery (10.30am–10.30pm, Sun 10.30am–7.30pm).

| *Room phone* Yes | *Confirm by* 6 | *Parking* Limited |
| *Room TV* Yes | *Last dinner* 9.30 | *Banquets* 30/– |

We do not necessarily recommend the cooking at hotels whose restaurants are not separately listed.

Camberley

Map 5 E3 Surrey
Portsmouth Road *GU15 2BG*
Camberley (0276) 28321
Telex 858446

Credit Access, Amex,
Barclaycard, Diners

Rooms 71
with bath/shower 71

Frimley Hall Hotel   64%   £ E

This fine old manor house stands in four acres of lovely gardens just off the A325. Some of the public rooms are in the grand Victorian manner, like the imposing panelled entrance hall with its carved wooden staircase, while others are more contemporary in style. Work is in hand on redecorating and refurbishing the bedrooms and bathrooms. The hotel has several conference/banqueting rooms. *Amenities* garden, dinner dance (Sat).

| *Room phone* Yes | *Confirm by* 6.30 | *Parking* Ample |
| *Room TV* Yes | *Last dinner* 10 | *Banquets* 100/2 |

Cambridge

Town plan B1 Cambridgeshire
53 Chesterton Road *CB4 3AN*
Cambridge (0223) 67701

Manager Mr D. Clark
Credit Access, Barclaycard
Closed 25 & 26 December

Rooms 66
with bath/shower 39

Arundel House Hotel   57%   Ⓜ   £ E

Converted and developed over the years from a row of Victorian terraced houses, Mr and Mrs Clark's friendly hotel enjoys pleasant views over the river Cam. Public rooms include a neat foyer-lounge and a comfortable little bar; there are also two conference rooms in the new extension. Simply decorated bedrooms are furnished with functional fitted units. Bathrooms have up-to-date coloured suites.

| *Room phone* Yes | *Confirm by* 6 | *Parking* Ample |
| *Room TV* Yes | *Last dinner* 9.30 | *Banquets* 30/10 |

Cambridge

Town plan A1 Cambridgeshire
Bar Hill *CB3 8EU*
Crafts Hill (0954) 80555
Telex 817141

Credit Access, Amex,
Barclaycard, Diners

Cunard Cambridgeshire Hotel   59%   £ C/D

Standing on the A604 four miles north-west of Cambridge, this capably run hotel offers modern accommodation, plenty of sports facilities and numerous conference and syndicate rooms. Public areas are decorated in old-world style, and bright, neat bedrooms are well equipped.
Amenities garden, sauna, indoor swimming pool, tennis, squash, golf course, dinner dance (Sat), laundry room, putting, children's playground. ♿

Continued

Rooms 100	*Room phone* Yes	*Confirm by* 6	*Parking* Ample
with bath/shower 100	*Room TV* Yes	*Last dinner* 10.30	*Banquets* 250/–

Cambridge

Town plan A4 Cambridgeshire
Granta Place
Off Mill Lane *CB2 1RT*
Cambridge (0223) 63421
Telex 81463
Manager Mr Paul Breen

GARDEN HOUSE HOTEL £C

As we go to press, substantial improvements are near completion at this attractive modern hotel, which was graded at 64% last year. It will be doubled in size, with completely new public areas overlooking its lovely, well-kept gardens by the river Cam. Existing bedrooms are also to be refurbished. No dogs. *Amenities* garden, coarse fishing, hotel punts.
Credit Access, Amex, Barclaycard, Diners

Rooms 117	*Room phone* Yes	*Confirm by* 6	*Parking* Ample
with bath/shower 117	*Room TV* Yes	*Last dinner* 9.30	

Cambridge

Town plan C4 Cambridgeshire
Gonville Place *CB1 1LY*
Cambridge (0223) 66611
Manager Mrs E. Hooper
Credit Access, Amex,
Barclaycard
Closed 3/4 days Christmas

Gonville Hotel 62% £D/E

Mrs Hooper is responsible for the pleasant atmosphere and spotless appearance from top to bottom of this Victorian house that has been modernised over the years. Public areas include a lively bar and a cheerful lounge overlooking a large green. Spacious bedrooms are colourfully decorated and have good-quality fitted furniture, plus compact, up-to-date bathrooms. *Amenities* patio, dinner dance (Sat).

Rooms 62	*Room phone* Yes	*Confirm by* 6	*Parking* Ample
with bath/shower 62	*Room TV* Yes	*Last dinner* 8.45	*Banquets* 40/–

Cambridge

Town plan C2 Cambridgeshire
21 Burleigh Street *CB1 1DG*
Cambridge (0223) 354755
Proprietors Mr & Mrs C. C. Mao
Chinese cooking

Peking

Crisp-skinned Peking duck is a must at this unpretentious pine-panelled Chinese restaurant, where Mr Mao and his friendly team offer a varied choice of authentic, fresh-tasting dishes, including many regional specialities. Portions are generous, and half-portions are available for those wanting to try a wide selection from the menu. Booking is advisable.

● **Set L** £1·80 **Set D** £7
About £18 for two
Banquets 30/–

Lunch 12–2.15 *Dinner* 6–10.45
Closed Mon & Bank Holidays

Cambridge

Town plan C4 Cambridgeshire
Regent Street *CB2 1AD*
Cambridge (0223) 51241
Telex 817311
Proprietors Bradford family
Credit Access, Amex,
Barclaycard, Diners

University Arms Hotel 64% Ⓜ £D/E

Traditional standards of service prevail at this family-run Edwardian hotel, with its smartly uniformed porters and tea served from gleaming silver in the cosy, octagonal lounge. Three bars include one with an impressive range of whiskies, and there are extensive meeting facilities. Well-maintained bedrooms have neat fitted furniture, ample writing space and tiled bathrooms. *Amenities* dancing (Sat October–March), laundry room.

Rooms 114	*Room phone* Yes	*Confirm by* 6	*Parking* Ample
with bath/shower 114	*Room TV* Yes	*Last dinner* 9.45	

Canterbury

Town plan D3 Kent
52 Dover Street *CT1 3HD*
Canterbury (0227) 61126
Proprietor Mr M. Garcia Gomez

Beehive

Three cottage rooms make up this restaurant in a pleasant little 16th-century building. Prime ingredients, including fish and lobsters from Broadstairs and beef from Smithfield, are cooked by the capabale chef-patron, and well-known dishes with a French influence like our veal à la crème are made even more enjoyable by helpful, polite service.
Credit Access, Amex, Barclaycard

● **Set L** from £3·80
About £24 for two
Banquets 50/6

Lunch 12–2.30 *Dinner* 7–10.30, Sat 7–11
Closed Sun & Bank Holidays

Map 7 C5
Town plan opposite

Population 36,290

The Metropolitan City of the English Church (since 602), where St Augustine preached (597), and Archbishop Thomas à Becket was martyred in the Cathedral (1170). Canterbury was successfully settled by the Belgae, the Romans, the Saxons and the Normans. It has been a town of pilgrim-tourists since 1008 and the Cathedral, medieval buildings and archives well repay a lingering visit. It is strong in literary association through Chaucer and Marlowe.

Sights Outside City
Bodiam Castle, Chilham, Dover Castle, Herne Bay, Leeds Castle, Lympne Castle, Reculver Towers, Rye and Winchelsea, Walmer Castle, Whitstable Castle and Grounds

Information Office
St Peter's Street
Telephone Canterbury 66567

Canterbury

1	Blackfriars *13th-c Friary*	C1
2	Cathedral *11th–15th c*	D2
3	Christchurch Gate and Buttermarket	C2
4	Conquest House	C1
5	Dane John Garden *a memorial to Marlowe*	C3
6	East Station	B3
7	Greyfriars *first Franciscan settlement*	B2
8	Martyrs' Memorial *to Bloody Mary's victims*	B3
9	Norman Castle *large Norman keep*	B3
10	Norman Staircase *very fine roofed steps* and King's School *originally Priory hostel*	D1
11	Queen Elizabeth's Guest Chamber	C2
12	Roman Pavement and hypocaust	C2
13	Royal Museum	C2
14	St Augustine's Abbey *layered monastic remains*	D2
15	St Dunstan's church *contains head of Sir Thomas More*	A1
16	St George's Tower	D2
17	St Martin's Church *oldest in use*	E2
18	St Peter's Church *Anglo-Saxon*	C2
19	St Peter's Street *typical medieval street*	C2
20	St Thomas's (Eastbridge Hospital) *collection of 12th-c–17th-c buildings, beautiful Norman crypt*	C2
21	Sir John Boys's House *ancient lopsided house*	C1
22	The Weavers *16th-c weavers' houses*	C2
23	Tower House	B2
24	University and Gulbenkian Theatre	A1
26	West Station	B1
26	Westgate Tower *arms and armour museum*	B1

The new
Lancia HPE 2000 IE.

LANCIA–the drivers' car. 

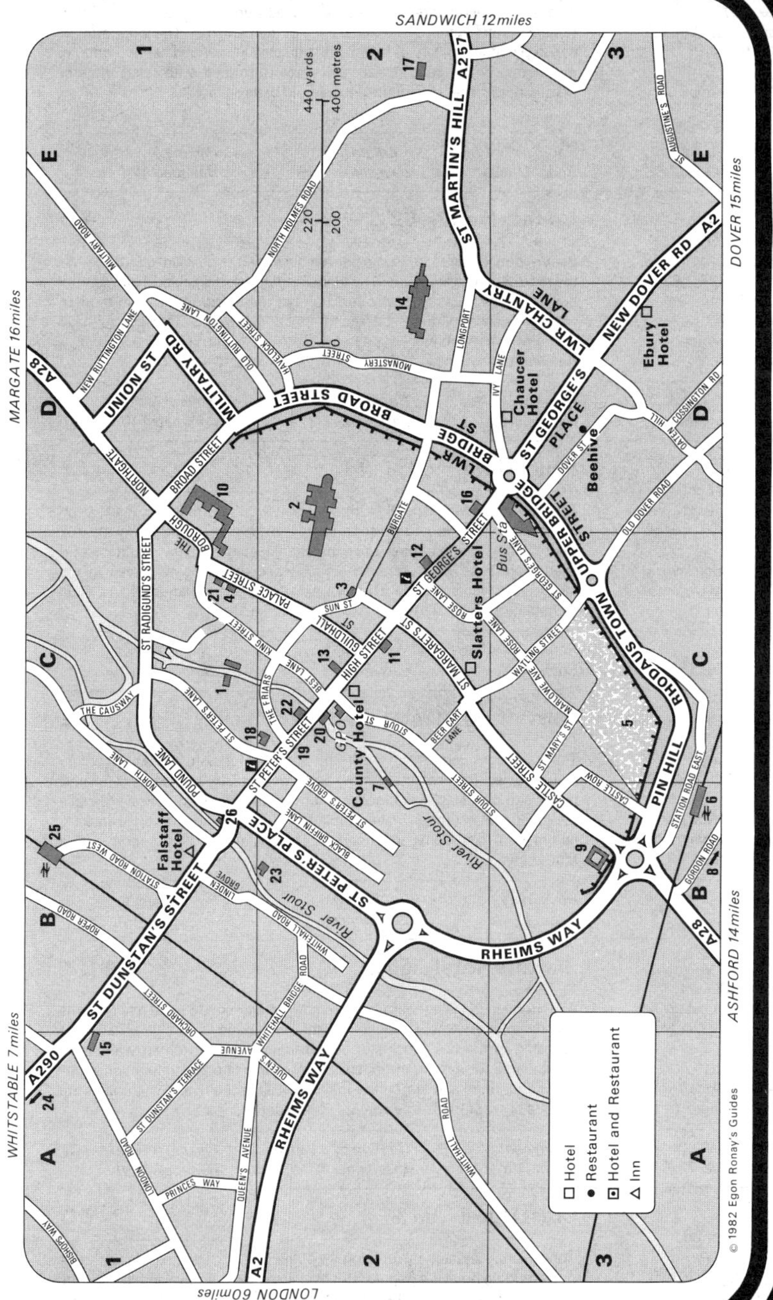
SANDWICH 12 miles
440 yards
400 metres
220
200
MARGATE 16 miles
A28
MILITARY RD
NEW RUTTINGTON LANE
OLD RUTTINGTON LANE
NORTH HOLMES ROAD
UNION ST
NORTHGATE
BROAD STREET
BROAD STREET
THE BOROUGH
ST RADIGUND'S STREET
HAVELOCK STREET
MONASTERY STREET
LONGPORT
ST MARTIN'S HILL
A257
LWR CHANTRY LANE
ST AUGUSTINE'S ROAD
NEW DOVER RD A2
DOVER 15 miles
OATEN HILL
COSSINGTON RD
IVY LANE
Chaucer Hotel
ST GEORGE'S PLACE
Ebury Hotel
DOVER ST
Beehive
LWR BRIDGE ST
BRIDGE ST
BURGATE
ST GEORGE'S STREET
Slatters Hotel
Bus Sta
ST GEORGE'S LANE
ROSE LANE
WATLING STREET
UPPER STREET
OLD DOVER ROAD
RHODAUS TOWN
PIN HILL
PALACE STREET
SUN ST
GUILDHALL ST
KING STREET
BEST LANE
HIGH STREET
ST MARGARET'S ST
County Hotel
GPO
THE FRIARS
ST PETER'S LANE
THE CAUSEWAY
NORTH LANE
POUND LANE
ST PETER'S STREET
ST PETER'S GROVE
BLACK GRIFFIN LANE
STOUR ST
BEER CART LANE
STOUR STREET
CASTLE STREET
ST MARY'S ST
CASTLE ROW
STATION ROAD EAST
GORDON ROAD
A28
ASHFORD 14 miles
River Stour
Falstaff Hotel
ST PETER'S PLACE
ST DUNSTAN'S STREET
STATION ROAD WEST
ROPER ROAD
ORCHARD STREET
ST DUNSTAN'S TERRACE
LINDEN GROVE
WHITEHALL ROAD
WHITEHALL BRIDGE ROAD
River Stour
QUEEN'S AVENUE
RHEIMS WAY
RHEIMS WAY
A290
LONDON ROAD
PRINCES WAY
BISHOP'S WAY
A2
LONDON 60 miles
WHITSTABLE 7 miles
□ Hotel
● Restaurant
▣ Hotel and Restaurant
△ Inn
© 1982 Egon Ronay's Guides

Canterbury
Town plan D3 Kent
Ivy Lane *CT1 1TT*
Canterbury (0227) 64427
Telex 965096

Credit Access, Amex,
Barclaycard, Diners

Rooms 51
with bath/shower 32

Chaucer Hotel   60%   £ D

Extensive redecoration has greatly improved public areas of this red-brick, Regency hotel within walking distance of the cathedral. The lounge-cum-bar, in particular, is very pleasant with attractively arranged period furniture. Bedrooms, which vary in size, are simply furnished with fitted units or freestanding pieces. Adequate, modernised bathrooms.

Room phone Yes	*Confirm by* 6	*Parking* Ample
Room TV Yes	*Last dinner* 9.45	*Banquets* 120/–

Canterbury
Town plan C2 Kent
High Street *CT1 2RX*
Canterbury (0227) 66266
Telex 965076

Credit Access, Amex,
Barclaycard, Diners

Rooms 74
with bath/shower 74

County Hotel   62%   £ D

Beams, potted plants and some fine antiques create a pleasant atmosphere in the reception area and superb residents' lounge of this gabled 16th-century building, which has extensive function facilities. Bedrooms are in modern style, with cheerful decor, baskets of fruit and tea/coffee-makers. All have neat private bathrooms.
Amenities coffee shop (11am–11pm), 24-hour laundry service.

Room phone Yes	*Confirm by* 6	*Parking* Ample
Room TV Yes	*Last dinner* 8.30	*Banquets* 140/–

Canterbury
Town plan E3 Kent
65 New Dover Road *CT1 3DX*
Canterbury (0227) 68433

Credit Access, Barclaycard
Closed 2 weeks December–
January

Rooms 15
with bath/shower 15

Ebury Hotel   57%   Ⓜ   £ F

This well-maintained hotel–a three-storey Victorian building that's been modernised from top to bottom–stands in its own grounds on the A2. Bright, cheerful bedrooms have functional contemporary furniture and adequately fitted bathrooms. There's no bar, drinks being served in the spacious residents' lounge. The reception area sports a handsome polished mahogany staircase. No dogs. *Amenities* garden.

Room phone Yes	*Confirm by* 6	*Parking* Ample
Room TV Yes	*Last dinner* 8.30	*Banquets* 30/6

Canterbury
Town plan B1 Kent
St Dunstan's Street *CT2 8AF*
Canterbury (0227) 62138
Managers
Mr & Mrs A. D. Mackintosh
Credit Access, Amex,
Barclaycard, Diners

Rooms 16
with bath/shower 10

Falstaff Hotel *(Inn)*   £ E

Thanks to the friendliness of Mr and Mrs MacKintosh, this 15th-century half-timbered inn remains a most welcoming place to visit. Oak beams, rafters and panelling make the small lounge and bar most appealing, while the functional bedrooms have simple built-in units and tea/coffee-makers, and modern bathrooms are adequate. There is one lovely old room with a four-poster.

Room phone No	*Confirm by* 6	*Parking* Ample
Room TV Yes	*Last dinner* 9	

Canterbury
Town plan C2 Kent
St Margaret's Street *CT1 1AA*
Canterbury (0227) 63271
Telex 966227

Credit Access, Amex,
Barclaycard, Diners

Rooms 30
with bath/shower 23

Slatters Hotel   55%   £ D/E

Although externally modern, this welcoming city-centre hotel retains some historic interior features like the wattle and daub wall and Elizabethan panelling in the cosy cocktail bar and the section of Roman wall in the basement. Bedrooms in the extension are simply fitted, with functional, up-to-date furniture and tea/coffee-making facilities. Fully tiled bathrooms are adequately equipped. *Amenities* 24-hour laundry service.

Room phone Yes	*Confirm by* By arrang.	*Parking* Ample
Room TV Yes	*Last dinner* 9	*Banquets* 100/–

Carlisle
Map 13 D4 Cumbria
Kingstown *CA4 0HR*
Carlisle (0228) 31201
Telex 64201

Credit Access, Amex,
Barclaycard, Diners

Crest Hotel   55%   £ D

Conveniently situated by junction 44 of the M6 (the last going north), this smart modern hotel is a popular stopover for tourists. A travelling theme runs through public areas like the foyer, lounge and bar, with mementoes of early railway and motoring days. Compact, well-fitted bedrooms are double-glazed and have tea-makers, trouser presses and neat tiled bathrooms.
Amenities garden, coffee shop (9am–6pm).

Continued

| Rooms 98 | Room phone Yes | Confirm by 6 | Parking Ample |
| with bath/shower 98 | Room TV Yes | Last dinner 10 | Banquets 40/10 |

Carlisle
Map 13 D4 Cumbria
English Street *CA3 8HZ*
Carlisle (0288) 25491
Telex 64183

Credit Access, Amex,
Barclaycard, Diners

Crown & Mitre Hotel   60%   £ D/E

Old-fashioned standards of service and housekeeping are maintained at this imposing Edwardian hotel, whose public rooms range from the pillared foyer and elegant residents' lounge to the two cheerfully modern bars and coffee shop. Well-fitted bedrooms with plenty of working space provide good comfort; 20 compact rooms in the wing have excellent bathrooms. *Amenities* coffee shop (9am–10.30pm).   &

| Rooms 96 | Room phone Yes | Confirm by 6 | Parking Limited |
| with bath/shower 95 | Room TV Yes | Last dinner 10 | Banquets 400/6 |

Carlisle
Map 13 D4 Cumbria
London Road *CA1 2PQ*
Carlisle (0228) 29255
Telex 64292

Credit Access, Amex,
Barclaycard, Diners

Swallow Hilltop Hotel   60%   £ D/E

Standing alongside the A6 on the outskirts of town, this modern hotel, with its practical accommodation and conference facilities, caters well for the needs of businessmen. Refurbished bars and lounges are smart, relaxing places and bedrooms are also being improved: most now have excellent lighting, well-designed fitted units, tea/coffee-makers and neat bathrooms. *Amenities* dancing (Sat), pool table, in-house movies.   &

| Rooms 112 | Room phone Yes | Confirm by 6 | Parking Ample |
| with bath/shower 99 | Room TV Yes | Last dinner 9.45 | Banquets 400/– |

Carlton Colville
Map 6 D2 Suffolk
Chapel Road
Near Lowestoft *NR33 8BL*
Lowestoft (0502) 60772
Telex 975592
Credit Access, Amex,
Barclaycard, Diners

Hedley House Park Hotel   57%   Ⓜ   £ E

Set in nine acres of parkland, this pleasant, homely hotel is popular for both family holidays and business conferences. There's a large modern bar and a residents' lounge. Bright, spacious bedrooms are neatly fitted and carpeted bathrooms well equipped. Rooms without private baths have shower units. *Amenities* garden, discothèque (Tues, Thurs, Fri), hairdressing, putting, children's playground, games room, in-house movies.   &

| Rooms 17 | Room phone Yes | Confirm by By arrang. | Parking Ample |
| with bath/shower 14 | Room TV Yes | Last dinner 11 | Banquets 180/15 |

Carlyon Bay
Map 2 B3 Cornwall
Near St Austell *PL25 3RD*
Par (072 681) 2304

Credit Access, Amex,
Barclaycard, Diners

Carlyon Bay Hotel   62%   £ C/D

This large 1920s hotel, popular with golfers and holiday-makers, enjoys a clifftop position overlooking the bay. There are lovely sea views from the spacious lounge, which has lots of comfortable armchairs and plenty to read. Most of the simply decorated bedrooms have bathrooms with colourful suites. *Amenities* garden, outdoor swimming pool, tennis, golf course, dancing (2–3 nights weekly in summer), putting, croquet, games room.   &

| Rooms 78 | Room phone Yes | Confirm by By arrang. | Parking Ample |
| with bath/shower 70 | Room TV Yes | Last dinner 8.45 | Banquets 180/– |

Carlyon Bay
Map 2 B3 Cornwall
Near St Austell *PL25 3SG*
Par (072 681) 2802
Proprietors Mr & Mrs H. D. Stow
Credit Access, Amex,
Barclaycard, Diners
Closed 2 weeks Christmas

Porth Avallen Hotel   62%   Ⓜ   £ E

Homely comfort and attentive service are the hallmarks of this converted 1930s house overlooking Carlyon Bay. Guests can relax in the plush panelled lounge or enjoy a drink in the smartly refurbished cocktail bar. Bedrooms vary in size and decor, some having modern fitted or freestanding units, while others are more traditional in style. Compact, well-kept bathrooms. No dogs. *Amenities* garden, children's playground, putting.   &

| Rooms 25 | Room phone Yes | Confirm by By arrang. | Parking Ample |
| with bath/shower 19 | Room TV Most | Last dinner 9 | Banquets 120/6 |

Cartmel
Map 13 D6 Cumbria
Near Grange-over-Sands
LA11 6HH
Cartmel (044 854) 276

Credit Access
Closed 1st 3 weeks January

Rooms 15	*Room phone* No	*Confirm by* 6	*Parking* Ample
with bath/shower 13	*Room TV* Some	*Last dinner* 8.30	

Aynsome Manor Hotel   58%   Ⓜ   £ D/E

New owners Tony and Margaret Varley are welcoming hosts at this peaceful manor house. A log fire burns in the entrance hall, and there's a rustic bar as well as a first-floor lounge. Sizeable bedrooms have solid Victorian furniture (one has a four-poster) and attractive bath or shower rooms. There are two modern bedrooms and a TV lounge in the annexe. Inclusive terms only in high season. *Amenities* garden.   &

Any person using our name to obtain free hospitality is a fraud. Proprietors, please inform the police and us.

Castle Combe
Map 4 B2 Wiltshire
Near Chippenham *SN14 7HR*
Castle Combe (0249) 782206
Telex 44220
Proprietor O. R. Clegg
Rooms 34
with bath/shower 32
Room phone Yes
Room TV Yes
Confirm by 6
Last dinner 9.30
Parking Ample
Banquets 125/4

Credit Access, Amex,
Barclaycard, Diners

Manor House Hotel   71%   Ⓜ   £ C

The enchanting village of Castle Combe is the setting for this welcoming hotel, a fine old manor house standing in 26 acres of superb gardens and parkland. The large oak-panelled lounge with its open fireplace and deep armchairs paints an immediate picture of traditional charm and comfort, and a second similar room has a splendid 18th-century Italian frieze. The lounges, corridors and small panelled bar are enlivened by antiques, gleaming brassware and interesting prints of local scenes. Bedrooms are bright and roomy, with pretty matching fabrics, traditional furnishings and attractive plant arrangements. Carpeted bathrooms are adequate.
Amenities garden, outdoor swimming pool, tennis, game fishing, croquet.

Catford

Casa Cominetti

See under London

Cauldon Lowe
Map 10 C3 Staffordshire
Waterhouses *ST10 3EX*
Waterhouses (053 86) 338
Proprietor Jean Pierre Champeau
French cooking

About £30 for two
Banquets 12/2

Jean Pierre   Ⓖ   Ⓢ

Book before venturing forth to Jean Pierre Champeau's charmingly rustic restaurant, which stands high in the hills on the A52 between Ashbourne and Froghall. The amiable chef-patron uses only the freshest of ingredients in his well-prepared French dishes, which range from tasty onion soup and assiette de pâtés maison to lamb cutlets or roast wild duck served with excellent vegetables.   &

Lunch 12–1.30 *Dinner* 7.30–9.30
Closed L Sat, all Sun, 1 January, 14 July & 25 December

Chagford
Map 3 D2 Devon
Easton Cross *TQ12 8JL*
Chagford (064 73) 3469

Credit Access, Amex,
Barclaycard, Diners

Rooms 8	
with bath/shower 8	

Easton Court Hotel   57%   Ⓜ   £ E/F

Original beams and open fireplaces preserve the old-world character of this thatched 15th-century hostelry standing about a mile from Chagford on the A382. Public rooms include a delightful lounge, a cosy bar and a charming little library. Simply fitted bedrooms offer modest, homely comforts. New owners are cordial hosts. No children under ten.
Amenities garden.

Room phone No	*Confirm by* By arrang.	*Parking* Limited
Room TV No	*Last dinner* 8.30	

Chagford

Map 3 D2 Devon
TQ13 8HH
Chagford (064 73) 2367
Proprietors
Paul & Kay Henderson
Rooms 11
with bath/shower 11
Room phone Yes
Room TV Yes
Confirm by By arrang.
Last dinner 9
Parking Ample
Banquets 16/4

Gidleigh Park Hotel   77%   Ⓜ   £ C

Americans Paul and Kay Henderson maintain very high standards at their delightful mock-Tudor country house, which stands in wooded grounds on the banks of the North Teign River (it's difficult to find, so check directions when booking). Open log fires, fine panelling and comfortable chintz-covered settees create a warm, homely atmosphere in public rooms like the foyer and lovely bright lounge, and there's a charming bar in similar style. Individually decorated bedrooms have a pleasing combination of antiques and more modern furniture, including relaxing armchairs. Carpets and soft furnishings are of excellent quality, and bathrooms are luxurious. Children by arrangement only. *Amenities* garden, tennis (grass), game fishing, croquet.

Chagford

Map 3 D2 Devon
TQ13 8HH
Chagford (064 73) 2367
Proprietors
Paul & Kay Henderson

● **Set D** £19·55
About £49 for two

Gidleigh Park Hotel Restaurant   ★   

It's reservations only at this splendid panelled restaurant, where Kay Henderson and John Webber combine perfectly to plan and prepare a short selection of French-inspired dishes notable for their beautifully balanced flavours and textures. Our lobster with puréed spinach was a mouthwatering prelude to the superb veal medallions and veal kidneys with two subtle sauces. Glorious sweets include melon and mint sorbet and a classic tarte Tatin. Service is appropriately skilled and well informed.
Specialities onion 'tart' wrapped in a lettuce leaf, salmon with sorrel sauce, Scotch sirloin steak with red and green peppercorns, pastry cup with vanilla ice cream and apricot sauce.  *OUTSTANDING*.

Lunch 12.30–1.30 *Dinner* 7–9

Chagford

Map 3 D2 Devon
Sandy Park *TQ13 8JS*
Chagford (064 73) 2491

Credit Access, Amex,
Barclaycard, Diners

Rooms 14
with bath/shower 14

Great Tree Hotel   69%   Ⓜ   £ C/D

This immaculately maintained former hunting lodge stands in beautiful gardens and woodland in Dartmoor National Park. There's a spacious raftered lounge with plenty of comfortable armchairs, and the panelled bar, with antiques and a wall tapestry, is an elegant little retreat. Traditionally furnished bedrooms have pretty floral curtains, dozens of thoughtful extras and neat bathrooms. Friendly, helpful staff. *Amenities* garden, croquet, putting.

Room phone No	*Confirm by* 6	*Parking* Ample
Room TV Yes	*Last dinner* 9	*Banquets* 50/–

Chagford

Map 3 D2 Devon
Sandy Park *TQ13 8JS*
Chagford (064 73) 2491

About £33 for two

Great Tree Hotel Restaurant   Ⓢ

A pleasantly traditional dining room, whose long carte offers well-prepared dishes ranging from smooth chicken liver pâté to goujons of sole, and pork fillet with delicious apple and chestnut purées. Simpler set menus.
Credit Access, Amex, Barclaycard, Diners
Lunch 12–2 *Dinner* 7–9 ● **Set L** £5·17 **Set D** £8·62

Chagford

Map 3 D2 Devon
Sandy Park *TQ13 8JN*
Chagford (064 73) 2282
Props Mr & Mrs D. N. Craddock
Credit Access, Amex,
Barclaycard, Diners
Closed 10 days Christmas

Rooms 17
with bath/shower 14

Mill End Hotel   62%   Ⓜ   £ D/E

The charming Craddocks maintain excellent standards of housekeeping in this converted mill on the banks of the Teign. There's an atmosphere of traditional comfort in the public rooms with their good period furniture and chintzy chairs. This theme continues in some of the bedrooms, which are very tastefully decorated; other rooms are simpler and more modern in style. Compact, up-to-date bathrooms. *Amenities* garden, game fishing.

Room phone Yes	*Confirm by* 6	*Parking* Ample
Room TV No	*Last dinner* 9	

Chagford

Map 3 D2 Devon
Sandy Park *TQ13 8JN*
Chagford (064 73) 2282
Proprietors
Mr & Mrs D. N. Craddock

● **Set L** £7
Set D £10·50

Mill End Hotel Restaurant ⑤

This low-ceilinged dining room makes a pleasant setting for a carefully prepared meal. Seafood chowder, roast duckling with mint and Marsala sauce and noisettes of lamb garnished with hot cucumber and spring onions are typical dishes on the daily-changing set menus, and there are also some delicious sweets such as caramelised oranges with brandy snaps.
🍷 *ABOVE AVERAGE. Credit* Access, Amex, Barclaycard, Diners

Lunch 12.45–1.30 *Dinner* 7.30–9
Closed 10 days Christmas

Our inspectors are our full-time employees; they are professionally trained by us.

Chalford

Map 4 B2 Gloucestershire
Near Stroud *GL6 8NW*
Brimscombe (045 388) 3555

Credit Amex, Barclaycard, Diners
Closed January

Springfield House Hotel 66% Ⓜ £ E/F

This handsome Georgian building stands in well-kept grounds on the A419 just outside Chalford. The grand flagstoned reception hall is dominated by a sweeping stone staircase, and there's also a large lounge with original plasterwork and fine antiques, as well as a comfortable little bar. Spacious bedrooms are traditionally furnished, and bathrooms are up to date. Maintenance could perhaps be improved. *Amenities* garden.

| *Rooms* 7 | *Room phone* Most | *Confirm by* By arrang. | *Parking* Ample |
| *with bath/shower* 5 | *Room TV* Most | *Last dinner* By arrang. | *Banquets* 30/– |

Charnock Richard

Map 10 A1 Lancashire
Mill Lane, nr Chorley *PR7 5LQ*
Coppull (0257) 791746
Telex 67315
Manager Mrs E. A. Chadwick
Credit Access, Amex, Barclaycard, Diners

TraveLodge 56% £ E/F

At the Charnock Richard service area on the M6 (between junctions 27 and 28), this hospitable motel offers quiet, peaceful accommodation. Well-planned bedrooms have smart darkwood furniture, and tiled bathrooms are neat and compact. Self-service breakfast is available in the bar-lounge, and other meals can be taken in the service centre cafeteria. *Amenities* patio, 24-hour cafeteria, petrol pumps. ♿

| *Rooms* 107 | *Room phone* Yes | *Confirm by* 6 | *Parking* Ample |
| *with bath/shower* 107 | *Room TV* Yes | *Last dinner* None | |

Chartham Hatch

Map 7 C5 Kent
Howfield Lane
Near Canterbury *CT4 7HQ*
Chartham (022 773) 294
Props Frank & Moreen Pardoe
Credit Access, Amex, Barclaycard
Closed 2 weeks January

Howfield Manor Hotel 65% Ⓜ £ D/E

The tranquil rural setting and the charm of the Pardoe family make it a real pleasure to stay at this attractive gabled hotel, which stands two miles south of the M2. Fine antiques and deep, relaxing armchairs grace the public rooms, and the individually decorated bedrooms are particularly homely and comfortable. Pretty, carpeted bathrooms. No children under eight. No dogs. *Amenities* garden, 24-hour laundry service.

| *Rooms* 6 | *Room phone* No | *Confirm by* By arrang. | *Parking* Ample |
| *with bath/shower* 4 | *Room TV* No | *Last dinner* 8 | *Banquets* 18/4 |

Cheam

Map 7 B5 Surrey
52 Upper Mulgrave Road *SM2 7AJ*
01–661 9763

● **Set D** £8·75
About £24 for two

Jardin ♧ ⑤

Booking is essential at this bright, unpretentious little restaurant, where the fixed-price dinner menu (two courses plus dessert, cheese and coffee) offers good value for money. Simple starters include lemony tuna and caper pâté and mushrooms in port, while carefully cooked main courses range from baked trout to chilli beef or chicken breast braised with Calvados, apple and onion. *Credit* Access, Barclaycard

Dinner only 7.30–10.30
Closed Sun, Easter Mon, 24–26 December & 2 weeks summer

Chedington

Map 4 A4 Dorset
Beaminster *DT8 3HY*
Corscombe (093 589) 265

Rooms 8
with bath/shower 8
Room phone Yes
Room TV Yes
Confirm by By arrang.
Last dinner 9.15
Parking Ample
Banquets 35/–

Credit Amex

Chedington Court   70%   Ⓜ   £ D

Built high on a ridge with views across the border to Somerset, this lovely Jacobean-style mansion combines old-fashioned elegance with solid comfort. Heavy brass door handles, leaded lights in stone mullions and a magnificent oak staircase set the tone for the whole house; especially noteworthy are the superb drawing room (where drinks are served) and the peaceful library. Large bedrooms are individually furnished – one has an antique four-poster, another an opulent 1930s suite from the stateroom of the *Queen Mary*; all are equipped with tea-makers and radios. Bathrooms are modern and well equipped. No dogs.
Amenities garden, croquet, putting, billiards, helipad.

Chedington

Map 4 A4 Dorset
Beaminster *DT8 3HY*
Corscombe (093 589) 265

● **Set D** £11·50
About £31 for two

Chedington Court Restaurant   ♧ ♔ Ⓢ

Hilary Chapman changes her four-course menu each day to make the best use of excellent seasonal fare. In summer there's avocado and grapefruit salad and juicy lemon sole on a bed of spinach, while winter might bring creamy leek soup or roast partridge with Calvados. Vegetables show touches of ingenuity, and tempting sweets include a marvellous strawberry Pavlova.
🍷 *OUTSTANDING. Credit* Amex   &

Lunch Sun 12.30–1.45, Mon–Fri by arrangement only *Dinner* 7–9

Cheltenham

Map 4 C1 Gloucestershire
Southam *GL52 3NH*
Cheltenham (0242) 37771
Telex 43232

Credit Access, Amex,
Barclaycard, Diners

Rooms 29
with bath/shower 25

Hotel de la Bere   66%   £ D

Two miles north of the town, this splendid Tudor mansion has all the trappings of a bygone age: stone-mullioned windows, oak panelling and even a minstrels' gallery. Public areas are elegant and luxuriously furnished, while bedrooms in period style have modern amenities and neat bathrooms. *Amenities* garden, sauna, tennis, outdoor swimming pool, squash, dancing (Fri, Sat), pitch & putt, gymnasium, riding.

Room phone Yes	*Confirm by* 6	*Parking* Ample
Room TV Yes	*Last dinner* 9.45	*Banquets* 180/4

Cheltenham

Map 4 C1 Gloucestershire
Parabola Road *GL50 3AQ*
Cheltenham (0242) 514453

Credit Access, Amex,
Barclaycard

Rooms 50
with bath/shower 50

Carlton Hotel   58%   Ⓜ   £ D/E

Situated in a quiet tree-lined road near the Promenade, this fine Regency building still retains echoes of its past, in particular the fine moulded ceilings which are a feature of the lofty foyer and the main lounge. The bar and a second lounge are simpler in style. Bedrooms are quite large and in good order, all with fitted furniture, radios and tea/coffee-makers. Compact bathrooms are adequately equipped. *Amenities* garden.

Room phone Yes	*Confirm by* 6	*Parking* Ample
Room TV Yes	*Last dinner* 9	*Banquets* 180/10

Cheltenham

Map 4 C1 Gloucestershire
Imperial Lane *GL50 1PT*
Cheltenham (0242) 38001
Proprietor
Mr Henry Forrest-Hampson
About £17 for two

Forrest Wine Bar   ♧ Ⓢ

Mrs Forrest-Hampson's honest home cooking is the main attraction in this cheerful, intimate wine bar. Dishes range from tasty soups and quiches to lasagne and grilled rump steak. Pleasant sweets too.
Lunch 12.30–2.15 *Dinner* 7–10.15, Fri & Sat 7–10.45
Closed Sun & Bank Holidays

Cheltenham

Map 4 C1 Gloucestershire
Gloucester Road *GL51 0TS*
Cheltenham (0242) 32691
Telex 43410
Manager Mr P. K. Hawkes
Credit Access, Amex,
Barclaycard, Diners

Golden Valley Hotel   67%   **£D**

Conveniently placed close to junction 11 of the M5, this modern hotel offers guests up-to-date facilities. In addition to a smart open-plan foyer-bar, public areas include a cheerful lounge designed like a sunken garden. Uniform bedrooms have simple fitted units, well-coordinated colour schemes plus radios and tea-makers. Compact bathrooms.
Amenities garden, putting, buttery (7.30am–6pm, Sun 8am–6pm).

Rooms 103	*Room phone* Yes	*Confirm by* 6.30	*Parking* Ample
with bath/shower 103	*Room TV* Yes	*Last dinner* 10	*Banquets* 300/4

Cheltenham

Map 4 C1 Gloucestershire
Cirencester Road
Charlton Kings *GL53 8EA*
Cheltenham (0242) 25861

Credit Access, Amex,
Barclaycard, Diners

Lilleybrook Hotel   60%   **£D/E**

Improvements continue at this handsome Edwardian hotel, whose imposing colonnaded foyer features a splendid white marble fireplace. Other public rooms include a cocktail lounge and a cellar bar. Best bedrooms have either prettily traditional or stylishly contemporary decor, neat modern furniture and compact, well-maintained bathrooms. Other rooms will benefit from planned refurbishment. *Amenities* garden, sauna, solarium, nightclub.

Rooms 40	*Room phone* Yes	*Confirm by* By arrang.	*Parking* Ample
with bath/shower 40	*Room TV* Yes	*Last dinner* 10	*Banquets* 110/–

Cheltenham

Map 4 C1 Gloucestershire
Cleeve Hill *GL52 3PR*
Bishops Cleeve (024 267) 2017
Proprietors
Mr & Mrs W. P. E. Sparks

Closed 3 weeks Christmas

Malvern View Hotel   63%   Ⓜ   **£E**

Situated on the A46 four miles north of Cheltenham, this immaculately maintained hotel has fine views of the distant Malvern Hills. Attentive, friendly staff ensure that guests are made to feel very much at home in the cosy lounges and cocktail bar of the pleasant stone building. Comfortable, traditionally furnished bedrooms have compact, fully tiled bathrooms. No children under five. No dogs. *Amenities* garden.

Rooms 7	*Room phone* No	*Confirm by* By arrang.	*Parking* Ample
with bath/shower 7	*Room TV* Yes	*Last dinner* 9.30	*Banquets* 20/12

Cheltenham

Map 4 C1 Gloucestershire
Cleeve Hill *GL52 3PR*
Bishops Cleeve (024 267) 2017
Proprietors
Mr & Mrs W. P. E. Sparks

Malvern View Hotel Restaurant   🗲 Ⓢ

Owner Mr Sparks is a talented and enthusiastic cook, whose fixed-price menu features a wide choice of skilfully prepared dishes with an international slant. Our crab and cucumber mousse made a refreshing starter, and the best end of lamb in puff pastry was perfectly executed. Excellent ingredients are used throughout, and the charming restaurant is staffed by attentive, courteous waitresses. 🍷 *SUPERIOR*.

● **Set D** £10·50
About £29 for two

Dinner only 7.30–9.30, Sun at 7.30
Closed D Sun to non-residents & 3 weeks Christmas

We welcome complaints and bona fide recommendations on the tear-out pages for readers' comments. They are followed up by our professional team. Please also complain to the management instantly.

Cheltenham

Map 4 C1 Gloucestershire
The Burgage *GL52 3DN*
Cheltenham (0242) 29533
Proprietors Mr & Mrs G. W. Gorrie

Closed 4 days Easter, Bank
Holidays & Christmas

Prestbury House Hotel   57%   Ⓜ   **£E**

Dating from the early 19th century, this converted private house two miles north of the town now offers modest accommodation, while retaining some of its former elegance, especially in the comfortable cocktail bar with its huge fireplace and in the panelled residents' lounge. Enormous bedrooms are plainer in style with simple freestanding furniture.
Amenities garden.

Rooms 10	*Room phone* Yes	*Confirm by* By arrang.	*Parking* Ample
with bath/shower 5	*Room TV* No	*Last dinner* 9	*Banquets* 40/–

Cheltenham

Map 4 C1 Gloucestershire
Promenade *GL50 1NN*
Cheltenham (0242) 514724
Telex 43381

Credit Access, Amex,
Barclaycard, Diners

Rooms 77
with bath/shower 77

Queen's Hotel   69%   £ C/D

Built in 1838 overlooking the Imperial Gardens, this imposing hotel has an extraordinary facade with magnificent colonnades in the manner of a Roman temple, and there's a feeling of opulence in the elegant foyer and the grand Regency lounge. Some bedrooms echo this lavish style with exquisite decor and soft furnishings, but most have simple freestanding furniture and more modest fittings. Simple bathrooms. *Amenities* garden.

| *Room phone* Yes | *Confirm by* 6 | *Parking* Ample |
| *Room TV* Yes | *Last dinner* 10 | *Banquets* 200/– |

Cheltenham

Map 4 C1 Gloucestershire
12 Suffolk Parade *GL50 2AB*
Cheltenham (0242) 584544

About £25 for two
Banquets 30/6

Twelve Suffolk Parade

Norman Young is the chef-patron of this pleasant restaurant, whose dining room is dominated by a huge hanging basket of greenery. The short menu offers standards like steak au poivre or a most enjoyable beef Stroganoff alongside less familiar dishes such as rabbit with prunes or delicious halibut kebabs with a yoghurt and cucumber sauce. To finish there's a magnificent crème brûlée. *Credit* Access, Barclaycard

Dinner only 7.30–10.30
Closed Sun, Bank Holidays & 2 weeks July

We do not necessarily recommend the cooking at hotels whose restaurants are not separately listed.

Chenies

Map 5 E2 Buckinghamshire
Near Rickmansworth, Herts
WB3 6EQ
Chorleywood (092 78) 3301
Telex 893939
Credit Access, Amex,
Barclaycard, Diners

Rooms 10
with bath/shower 10

Bedford Arms Hotel   68%   £ C

A garden with a pond is an attractive feature of this small Elizabethan-style red-brick hotel. Two bars with their own entrances are used by locals, while residents can enjoy the comfort of the cocktail bar and the lounge. An oak staircase leads to the bedrooms (including one for non-smokers), which have traditional darkwood furniture, deep-pile carpets and pretty wallpapers, plus trouser presses. Well-equipped bathrooms. *Amenities* garden.

| *Room phone* Yes | *Confirm by* 6 | *Parking* Ample |
| *Room TV* Yes | *Last dinner* 10 | *Banquets* 20/4 |

Chenies

Map 5 E2 Buckinghamshire
Near Rickmansworth, Herts
WB3 6EQ
Chorleywood (092 78) 3301

About £24 for two

Bedford Arms Hotel Restaurant

An air of quiet elegance pervades this oak-panelled dining room. The extensive à la carte menu features French classical dishes, with excellent seasonal specialities such as venison, lobster and partridge very much to the fore. A particularly wide choice of fresh vegetables ranges from mange-touts to sweet potatoes, and preparation is careful. Booking advisable. *Credit* Access, Amex, Barclaycard, Diners

Lunch 12.30–2 *Dinner* 7.30–10

Chester

Town plan C4 Cheshire
Whitchurch Road
Christleton *CH3 5QL*
Chester (0244) 32121
Telex 61561
Credit Access, Amex,
Barclaycard, Diners

Rooms 138
with bath/shower 138

Abbots Well Motor Lodge   62%   £ D

Set well back from the busy main road, this modern hotel complex is surrounded by four acres of grounds, which include a large car park. The welcoming foyer has bold decor and an abundance of plants, and there are two bars. Comfortable bedrooms with attractively coordinated colour schemes are well equipped, and bathrooms are smartly fitted. No dogs. *Amenities* garden, pool table.

| *Room phone* Yes | *Confirm by* 7 | *Parking* Ample |
| *Room TV* Yes | *Last dinner* 10 | *Banquets* 300/4 |

Map 10 A2
Town plan opposite

Population 117,300

Nowhere in Britain are history and architectural beauty better preserved: especially this may be seen in the Roman remains, the complete two-mile circuit of medieval walls and towers, and in the unique shopping Rows.
Add to this the charms of the River Dee, Canal and the Castle, the Tudor buildings, and the Cathedral. Chester was once a port, but fortunately for today's tourists the mouth of the Dee silted up in the 15th century, so that Chester's sea-trade passed to Liverpool. Probably fortunate for Chester too.

Sights Outside City
Beeston Castle, Chirk Castle, Hawarden Castle and Park, Eccleston, Llangollen, Tatton Park

Information Office
Town Hall
Telephone Chester 40144 Ext 2111

Chester

1	Bishop Lloyd's House	B4
2	British Heritage Exhibition	C4
3	Chester Castle and Regimental Museum	B5
4	Chester Cathedral	B3
5	Chester Heritage Centre	B4
6	Gamul House	B4
7	Gateway Theatre	A3
8	General Station	C2
9	Grosvenor Museum	B4
10	Guildhall and Museum	A4
11	Information Centre, Town Hall	B3
12	Northgate Arena	A1
13	St John's Church	C4
14	The Groves *for river trips*	C4
15	The Rows	B4
16	Watergate Street	A/B4
17	Zoo	A1

The new Lancia Coupé.

LANCIA – the drivers' car.

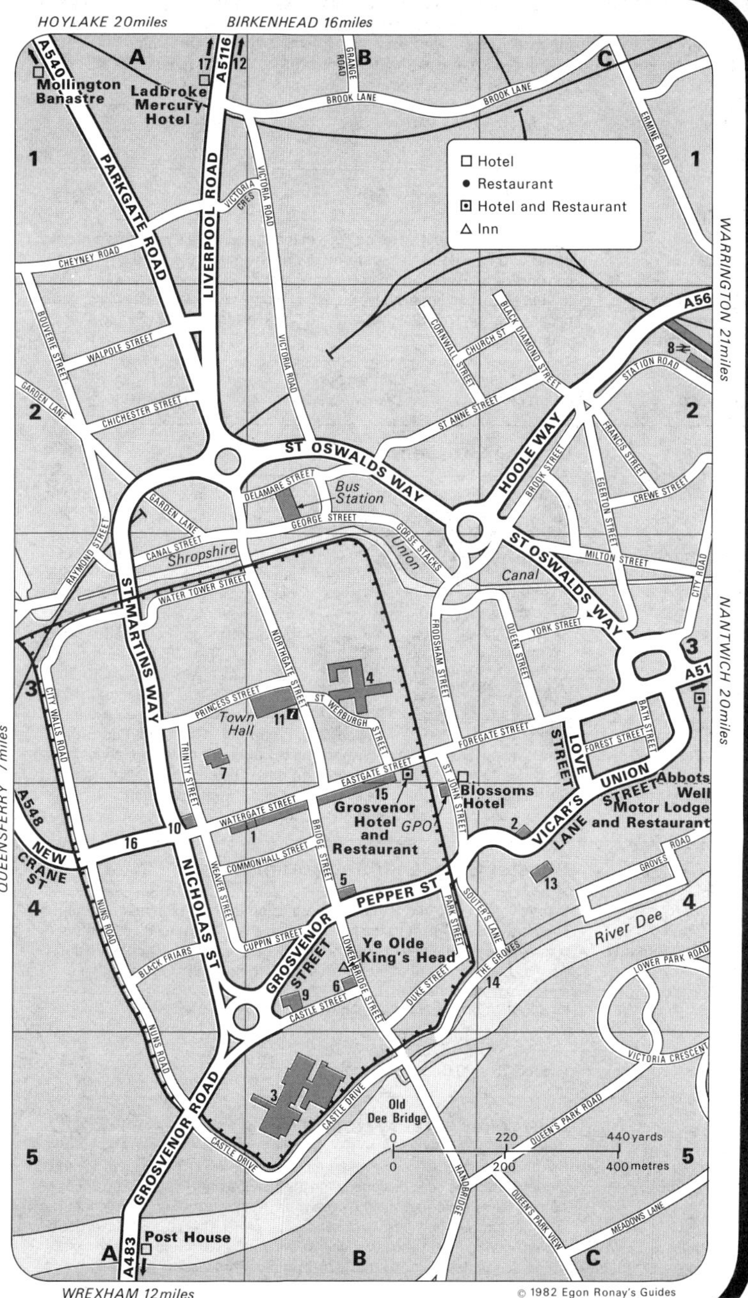

Chester LANCIA

HOYLAKE 20miles
BIRKENHEAD 16miles
WARRINGTON 21miles
NANTWICH 20miles
QUEENSFERRY 7miles
WREXHAM 12miles

Hotel
Restaurant
Hotel and Restaurant
Inn

Mollington Banastre
Ladbroke Mercury Hotel
Post House
Grosvenor Hotel and Restaurant
Blossoms Hotel
Abbots Well Motor Lodge and Restaurant
Ye Olde King's Head

A540
A5116
A56
A51
A548
A483

PARKGATE ROAD
LIVERPOOL ROAD
ST MARTINS WAY
ST OSWALDS WAY
HOOLE WAY
WARRINGTON
NANTWICH
GROSVENOR ROAD
NICHOLAS ST
GROSVENOR STREET
PEPPER ST
LOVE STREET
VICAR'S LANE
UNION STREET

CHEYNEY ROAD
BOUVERIE STREET
WALPOLE STREET
GARDEN LANE
CHICHESTER STREET
VICTORIA CRES
VICTORIA ROAD
GRANGE ROAD
BROOK LANE
BROOK LANE
ERMINE ROAD
CORNWALL STREET
CHURCH ST
BLACK DIAMOND STREET
ST ANNE STREET
STATION ROAD
FRANCIS STREET
CREWE STREET
EGERTON STREET
MILTON STREET
CITY ROAD
RAYMOND STREET
GARDEN LANE
CANAL STREET
DELAMARE STREET
GEORGE STREET
GORSE STACKS
Bus Station
Shropshire Union Canal
WATER TOWER STREET
CITY WALLS ROAD
PRINCESS STREET
NORTHGATE STREET
ST WERBURGH STREET
FOREGATE STREET
FRODSHAM STREET
QUEEN STREET
YORK STREET
BATH STREET
FOREST STREET
Town Hall
TRINITY STREET
EASTGATE STREET
ST JOHN STREET
WATERGATE STREET
BRIDGE STREET
COMMONHALL STREET
WEAVER STREET
PARK STREET
SOUTER'S LANE
GROVES ROAD
NEW CRANE ST
NUNS ROAD
BLACK FRIARS
CUPPIN STREET
CASTLE STREET
LOWER BRIDGE STREET
DUKE STREET
THE GROVES
River Dee
LOWER PARK ROAD
VICTORIA CRESCENT
CASTLE DRIVE
Old Dee Bridge
QUEEN'S PARK ROAD
QUEEN'S PARK VIEW
HANDBRIDGE
MEADOWS LANE
GPO

0   220   440 yards
0   200   400 metres

© 1982 Egon Ronay's Guides

Chester — Abbots Well Motor Lodge Restaurant ⓢ

Town plan C4 Cheshire
Whitchurch Road
Christleton *CH3 5QL*
Chester (0244) 32121

Tables are well spaced and attractively laid in this large, Regency-style dining room. Without being over-ambitious, the menu offers a good range of classical dishes, as well as house specialities which include fish straight from the market, succulent local poussin and tasty duckling terrine. There are grills, too, and perhaps a light cheesecake to round off an enjoyable meal.
Credit Access, Amex, Barclaycard, Diners

● **Set L** from £6·70
Set D from £8·95
About £24 for two

Lunch 12–2 *Dinner* 7–10

Chester — Blossoms Hotel   60%   £ D

Town plan B4 Cheshire
St John Street *CH1 1HL*
Chester (0244) 23186
Telex 61113
Credit Access, Amex,
Barclaycard, Diners
Closed 2 days Christmas

This sturdy brick-built Victorian hotel in the city centre still retains its original grand wrought-iron staircase rising the full height of the building. Guests can choose between the smart cocktail bar and the Snooty Fox public bar in the basement. Bedrooms have either traditional or modern furnishings and decor, and all are provided with tea-makers and radios. Simply fitted bathrooms.

Rooms 70
with bath/shower 70

Room phone Yes	*Confirm by* 6	*Parking* Difficult
Room TV Yes	*Last dinner* 9.30	*Banquets* 100/–

Chester — Chester Grosvenor   80%   *E*   £ C

Town plan B4 Cheshire
Eastgate Street *CH1 1LT*
Chester (0244) 24024
Telex 61240
Manager Mr Richard Edwards
Rooms 100
with bath/shower 100
Room phone Yes
Room TV Yes
Confirm by 6
Last dinner 10
Parking Ample
Banquets 200/–
Closed 25 & 26 December

Credit Access, Amex,
Barclaycard, Diners

Situated in the city's fashionable shopping centre, this splendid half-timbered building exudes style and elegance from top to bottom, the jewels on the crown undoubtedly being the magnificent public rooms with their glittering chandeliers, marble facings, colonnades and antiques. The lovely lounge is popular for afternoon tea, while the Arkle Bar with its racing theme provides a formal setting for drinks. Tastefully decorated bedrooms, which vary in size, are superbly appointed with pretty matching fabrics and good furniture. Excellent modern bathrooms. There are four luxury suites. Golf and game fishing can be arranged. *Amenities* dancing (Sat September–April), hairdressing, shopping arcade.

Chester — Chester Grosvenor Restaurant   ♛♛ ⓢ

Town plan B4 Cheshire
Eastgate Street *CH1 1LT*
Chester (0244) 24024
Manager Mr Richard Edwards
French cooking

Stylish French cooking is the main attraction in this luxurious restaurant. There's a classical slant to the menu, with dishes like sautéed chicken with lobster sauce and entrecôte béarnaise alongside imaginative combinations such as braised fillet of salmon garnished with broccoli mousse. Buffet or a shorter carte at lunchtime.
🍷 *SUPERIOR. Credit* Access, Amex, Barclaycard, Diners

● **Set L** £5·50
About £33 for two

Lunch 12.30–2.15 *Dinner* 7–10
Closed 25 & 26 December

Chester — Ladbroke Mercury Hotel   60%   £ C/D

Town plan A1 Cheshire
Backford Cross *CH1 6PE*
Chester (0244) 851551
Telex 61552

Credit Access, Amex,
Barclaycard, Diners

Six miles north of Chester at the junction of the A5117 and the A41, this modern hotel has been designed with the businessman in mind. Streamlined public rooms include a small bar and the reception-lounge with attractive sofas. Bedrooms are freshly decorated in pastel shades and have good bathrooms. There are also ten spacious, well-equipped 'Gold Star' rooms.
Amenities garden, dancing (Sat), 24-hour laundry service.

Rooms 122
with bath/shower 122

Room phone Yes	*Confirm by* 6	*Parking* Ample
Room TV Yes	*Last dinner* 10	*Banquets* 150/6

Chester — Mollington Banastre Hotel 60% Ⓜ £ D

Town plan A1 Cheshire
Parkgate Road
Great Mollington *CH1 6NN*
Chester (0244) 851471
Telex 61686
Credit Access, Amex, Barclaycard
Closed 25 & 26 December

Situated on the A540 only two miles from the city centre, this converted Victorian mansion is much favoured by businessmen. A comfortable lounge area adjoins the spacious foyer, and there are many function rooms, as well as a pub, the Good Intent. Bedrooms (including some luxurious ones with four-posters) have neat fitted units and compact, well-equipped bathrooms. *Amenities* garden, sauna, games room, children's play area.

Rooms 50	*Room phone* Yes	*Confirm by* By arrang.	*Parking* Ample
with bath/shower 47	*Room TV* Yes	*Last dinner* 9.30	*Banquets* 200/–

Chester — Post House Hotel 58% £ D

Town plan A5 Cheshire
Wrexham Road *CH4 9DL*
Chester (0244) 674111
Telex 61450

Credit Access, Amex,
Barclaycard, Diners

This modern, purpose-built hotel just outside the city is a popular stopover place for businessmen and tourists alike. There's an airy, spacious foyer-lounge with cheerful contemporary furnishings, and the main staircase leading from this features a spectacular ceramic-tiled mural depicting the history of Chester. Bedrooms have bright coordinated fabrics, modern fitted units and up-to-date tiled bathrooms. *Amenities* garden.

Rooms 62	*Room phone* Yes	*Confirm by* 6	*Parking* Ample
with bath/shower 62	*Room TV* Yes	*Last dinner* 9.45	*Banquets* 150/2

Chester — Ye Olde Kings Head *(Inn)* £ F

Town plan B4 Cheshire
48 Lower Bridge Street *CH1 1RS*
Chester (0244) 24855
Telex 629462
Manager Mr W. Sharp
Credit Access, Amex,
Barclaycard, Diners

Built as a private residence for a prominent Chester family in 1520, and licensed in 1717, this striking half-timbered inn is still rich in character and history. Heavy oak beams abound in the rustic, dimly lit bar (popular with locals) and in the residents' TV lounge. Charming old-fashioned bedrooms are simply furnished and equipped with washbasins, razor points and radios.

Rooms 11	*Room phone* No	*Confirm by* By arrang.	*Parking* Limited
with bath/shower None	*Room TV* Some	*Last dinner* 8.45	*Banquets* 80/–

Chester-le-Street — Lumley Castle Hotel 56% £ E

Map 15 B4 Co. Durham
DH3 4NX
Chester-le-Street
(0385) 885326
Telex 537433
Credit Access, Amex,
Barclaycard, Diners

New owners plan long-term improvements at this impressive castle dating from the 13th century and much altered in the 18th century. Public rooms include a simple reception and bar as well as several splendid function suites. Bedrooms in the castle itself are grandly traditional, while those in the converted stables have fitted modern units. Bathrooms are up to date. *Amenities* garden, sauna, outdoor swimming pool, helipad.

Rooms 50	*Room phone* Yes	*Confirm by* 6	*Parking* Ample
with bath/shower 50	*Room TV* Yes	*Last dinner* 9	*Banquets* 180/–

Chester-le-Street — Lumley Castle Hotel, Black Knight Restaurant

Map 15 B4 Co. Durham
DH3 4NX
Chester-le-Street (0385) 885326

About £31 for two

An intriguing medieval-style vaulted dining room, where the extensive menu ranges from simple starters and soups to seafood, sauced entrées, grills, roasts and a colourful sweet trolley.
Credit Access, Amex, Barclaycard, Diners
Lunch 12.30–2 *Dinner* 7–9 ● **Set L** £5·50 **Set D** £6·75 incl. service

Chesterton — Woods Farmhouse Restaurant ♀ Ⓢ

Map 5 D1 Oxfordshire
Near Bicester *OX6 8UE*
Bicester (086 92) 41444

● **Set L & Set D** from £7·85
About £25 for two
Banquets 40/25

Mr and Mrs Wood are now at the helm in this spacious beamed restaurant, formerly called Kinchs. Three-course set menus (lighter lunches also available) offer a selection of interesting, well-prepared dishes ranging from tasty stuffed mushrooms and spiced spareribs to local game, traditional fish pie and our beautifully roasted duck with grape sauce. Delicious sweets, too.
Credit Access, Amex, Barclaycard, Diners

Lunch 12–2.30 *Dinner* 7–11
Closed L Sat, D Sun, all Mon & August

Chichester

Map 5 E4 West Sussex
Westhampnett *PO19 4UL*
Chichester (0243) 786351
Proprietor Mr B. W. Hammett

Credit Access, Amex,
Barclaycard

Chichester Lodge   57%   Ⓜ   £ D/E

Next door to the popular White Swan pub, this modern hotel stands a mile from the town centre on the A27. The spacious reception area leads to a smart cocktail bar with plenty of chairs and sofas. Bedrooms, including ten family rooms, are warm and comfortably furnished, all with modern units, radios and tea-makers. Good bathrooms, newest ones being fully tiled. *Amenities* garden.

Rooms 43	*Room phone* Yes	*Confirm by* 6	*Parking* Ample
with bath/shower 43	*Room TV* Yes	*Last dinner* 9.30	*Banquets* 120/20

Chichester

Map 5 E4 West Sussex
149 St Pancras *PO19 1SH*
Chichester (0243) 788724

● **Set L** £5
About £25 for two
Banquets 30/10

Christopher's      Ⓢ

Victor and Patricia Theokritoff run this attractive modern restaurant with a large, comfortable bar area upstairs. The varied menu offers mainly French-style dishes which are very carefully prepared, with sauces especially showing Victor's skilful touch, and his home-made sweets like our crème brûlée providing a delightful finish.
Credit Access, Amex, Barclaycard, Diners

Lunch 12–2 *Dinner* 7–10
Closed Sun, Mon, Bank Holidays & 3 weeks winter

Chichester

Map 5 E4 West Sussex
Guildhall Street *PO19 1NJ*
Chichester (0243) 789915
Proprietors Mr & Mrs T. Clinch

Credit Access, Amex,
Barclaycard

Clinchs' Hotel   64%   Ⓜ   £ E

The Clinchs run this charming little town-centre hotel along the lines of a private house. There's no bar, but guests can enjoy a drink in the cheerful lounge or in their rooms. Bedrooms are very tastefully furnished with good fitted units and attractive curtains, and bathrooms are fully equipped. Dinner served only by arrangement. No children under ten. No dogs.
Amenities garden.

Rooms 9	*Room phone* Yes	*Confirm by* 5	*Parking* Limited
with bath/shower 9	*Room TV* Yes	*Last dinner* By arrang.	

Chichester

Map 5 E4 West Sussex
West Street *PO19 1QE*
Chichester (0243) 785121

Credit Access, Amex,
Barclaycard, Diners

Dolphin & Anchor Hotel   65%   £ D

Formerly two separate inns, this attractively modernised hotel opposite the cathedral retains plenty of character. The lounge is especially welcoming, with its deep sofas and handsome antiques. There are also two bars and an elegant ballroom. A maze of corridors leads to varying sized bedrooms, all comfortably equipped with good modern units, tea-makers and private bathrooms. *Amenities* buttery (10am–10pm).

Rooms 54	*Room phone* Yes	*Confirm by* 6	*Parking* Ample
with bath/shower 54	*Room TV* Yes	*Last dinner* 10	*Banquets* 180/10

Chichester

Map 5 E4 West Sussex
Little London *PO19 1PL*
Chichester (0243) 784899

Proprietor Mr Philip Stroud

● **Set L** from £3·35 incl. wine
Set D £6·50 & £10·50
About £24 for two
Banquets 14/6

Little London Restaurant

Behind the bow-windowed facade of a little 18th-century house you'll find the modern decor, crisp pink linen and spotlit tables of this immaculate restaurant. You'll also enjoy carefully prepared dishes, both familiar and less usual: baked avocado with curried chicken is a starter with a difference, and main courses could include plaice, veal or a splendid duck en croûte.
🍷 *ABOVE AVERAGE. Credit* Access, Amex, Barclaycard, Diners

Lunch 12–2 *Dinner* 7–10 (later in Festival season)
Closed Sun, Mon & Bank Holidays

Any person using our name to obtain free hospitality is a fraud. Proprietors, please inform the police and us.

Chiddingfold

Map 5 E3 Surrey
Near Godalming *GU8 4TX*
Wormley (042 879) 2255

Proprietor Mr Angus Lamont
Credit Amex, Diners

Rooms 5	
with bath/shower 5	

Crown Inn *(Inn)* Ⓜ **£ D/E**

The main part of this delightful inn, run in welcoming fashion, is 700 years old and there are beams, quaint passageways and even wattle and daub to prove it. Public rooms have deep plush armchairs and the bar is very cosy. Charmingly furnished bedrooms with comfortable beds are equipped with tea-making facilities, and bathrooms are adequate.

Room phone Yes	*Confirm by* By arrang.	*Parking* Ample
Room TV Yes	*Last dinner* 10	*Banquets* 100/6

Chiddingfold

Map 5 E3 Surrey
Near Godalming *GU8 4TX*
Wormley (042 879) 2255
Proprietor Mr Angus Lamont

About £21 for two

Crown Inn Bistro Ⓢ

In this attractive beamed and panelled room, choose from snacks like cheese and crusty bread, a cold buffet or hearty enjoyable dishes such as braised ox-tongue with Madeira sauce and lovely fresh vegetables. *Credit* Amex, Diners
Lunch 12–2.15, Sun 12–2 *Dinner* 7–10
● **Set L & Set D** £4·95

Chiddingfold

Map 5 E3 Surrey
Near Godalming *GU8 4TX*
Wormley (042 879) 2255
Proprietor Mr Angus Lamont

● **Set L** from £7·90
Set D from £14·90
About £36 for two

Crown Inn Restaurant ♕ ♕ Ⓢ

A beautifully proportioned dining room with an unmistakably English atmosphere. The simple à la carte featuring grills and seafood is supplemented by a monthly fixed-price *menu gastronomique* with more ambitious French regional dishes like fillet of pork with Calvados sauce or suprême of pheasant with chanterelles. Generally competent cooking.
🍷 *OUTSTANDING. Credit* Amex, Diners

Lunch 12–2 *Dinner* 7–10
Closed Mon, last 2 weeks January & middle 2 weeks August

Chiddingstone

Map 7 B5 Kent
Near Edenbridge *TN8 7AH*
Penshurst (0892) 870247
Proprietors Lucas family

● **Set L** £6·65 & £14·50
incl. service
Set D £14·50 incl. service
About £35 for two
Banquets 15/8

Castle Inn Ⓢ

Set in a lovely old tile-clad inn, this beamed restaurant has a really traditional atmosphere, and the Lucas family are charming hosts. High-quality raw materials are used to excellent advantage in roasts, grills and fish dishes, and there's local game in season, too. Vegetables are nicely cooked and there are a few sweets like lemon pancakes. 🍷 *ABOVE AVERAGE.*
Credit Access, Amex, Barclaycard, Diners

Lunch 12–2 *Dinner* 7.30–9.30
Closed L Wed, all Tues & January

We publish annually, so make sure you use the current edition. It's worth it!

Chideock

Map 4 A4 Dorset
Near Bridport *DT6 6JN*
Chideock (029 789) 242
Proprietors Mr & Mrs A. Way &
Mr & Mrs K. Davies
Credit Access, Barclaycard,
Diners

Rooms 9	
with bath/shower 3	

Chideock House Hotel 58% Ⓜ **£ F**

Once the local headquarters of the Roundheads, this 15th-century stone house now enjoys more peaceful times as a friendly, welcoming hotel. Massive beams feature in the comfortable cocktail bar, and there's a cosy residents' lounge with TV. Bright bedrooms, furnished in various styles, have lots of little extras like fresh flowers and tissues. Good modern bathrooms.
Amenities garden. **Closed** 2 weeks January/February

Room phone No	*Confirm by* By arrang.	*Parking* Ample
Room TV Some	*Last dinner* 9.30	*Banquets* 50/20

Chilgrove

Map 5 E3 West Sussex
Near Chichester *PO18 9HX*
East Marden (024 359) 219
Proprietors Dorothea &
Barry Phillips

● **Set L** £4·95
About £35 for two
Banquets 30/10

White Horse Inn

A long, low country pub where you can enjoy Adrian Congdon's first-class cooking in warm, relaxing surroundings. After some prawns with lemon mayonnaise or a bowl of rich, creamy crab soup, you might go on to rack of English lamb, fried calf's liver or the very tasty veal escalope filled with chopped snails. Mouthwatering desserts, too, and excellent coffee.
🍷 *OUTSTANDING. Credit* Access, Amex, Barclaycard, Diners   ♿

Lunch 12.15–1.45 *Dinner* 7.15–9.15
Closed Sun, Mon, 25 & 26 Dec, 3 weeks Jan–Feb & 2 weeks Nov

Chipping Campden

Map 4 C1 Gloucestershire
The Square *GL55 6AW*
Evesham (0386) 840256
Proprietors
Mr & Mrs V. Willmott
Credit Access, Amex,
Barclaycard, Diners

Rooms 14
with bath/shower 2

Kings Arms Hotel   58%   Ⓜ   **£ D**

This welcoming Cotswold-stone hotel on the market square has warmth and character. Public rooms leading off the entrance hall include a charming bar dominated by an open stone fireplace and a comfortable panelled lounge which looks out over the pretty garden. Simply furnished bedrooms have a cheerful, homely appeal, and bathrooms are adequate. *Amenities* garden.
Closed January & February except weekends   ♿

Room phone No	*Confirm by* 6	*Parking* Ample
Room TV No	*Last dinner* 9	*Banquets* 22/6

Chipping Campden

Map 4 C1 Gloucestershire
The Square *GL55 6AW*
Evesham (0386) 840256
Proprietors
Mr & Mrs V. Willmott

● **Set D** from £8·75
About £27 for two

Kings Arms Hotel Restaurant   ♉ Ⓢ

Hunting prints decorate the walls of this panelled dining room, where Rosemary Willmott's four-course fixed-price menu is full of interest and variety. A basket of crudités is followed by dishes like flaked turbot in aïoli with prawns or calf's liver with avocado, lemon and cream, accompanied by lightly cooked vegetables. To finish there are sweets like Pavlova or English cheeses. *Credit* Access, Amex, Barclaycard, Diners

Lunch Sun only 1–2 *Dinner* 7.30–9, Sat 7.30–9.30
Closed January & February except weekends

Chipping Campden

Map 4 C1 Gloucestershire
High Street *GL55 6AT*
Evesham (0386) 840317
Proprietors
Mr & Mrs R. P. Sargent

Rooms 19
with bath/shower 13

Noel Arms Hotel   58%   Ⓜ   **£ D/E**

Behind the handsome facade of this family-run inn, an impressive array of antiques and prints helps to create a marvellous sense of history, especially in the foyer and the two charming lounges (one with TV). The period atmosphere extends to most of the pretty, comfortably furnished bedrooms, two of which have four-posters. There are modern rooms in one wing. No dogs. *Amenities* garden, bowling green.

Room phone No	*Confirm by* By arrang.	*Parking* Ample
Room TV No	*Last dinner* 9	

Chipstead

Map 7 B5 Surrey
Outwood Lane *CR3 3NP*
Downland (073 75) 52661

● **Set L** £8·75, Sun from £7·15
About £40 for two
Banquets 85/–

Dene Farm   Ⓢ

A charming beamed restaurant standing among attractive gardens. The chef is full of enthusiasm, and although not every dish on the French menu is completely successful, standards are generally high. We enjoyed our beautifully fresh poached turbot with a tomato and mustard sauce followed by a feuilleté aux bananes; good French cheeses, too. Friendly, professional service. 🍷 *SUPERIOR. Credit* Access, Amex, Barclaycard, Diners

Lunch 12.15–1.45 *Dinner* 7.15–9.45
Closed L Sat, D Sun & Bank Holidays except Good Friday & 25 December

Chittlehamholt

Map 3 D2 Devon
Near Umberleigh *EX37 9HD*
Chittlehamholt (076 94) 248

Proprietors Mr & Mrs H. Neil

Highbullen Hotel   63%   Ⓜ   **£ E**

There are fine views of Exmoor from this lovely Victorian house. Stone arches, leaded windows and a marble fireplace lend character to the public areas, and bedrooms are traditionally furnished. Cottage rooms are smartly modern. No children under 13. No dogs. Inclusive terms only.
Amenities garden, sauna, indoor & outdoor swimming pools, tennis, squash, 9-hole golf course, game fishing, solarium, gymnasium, croquet, table tennis.

Continued

Rooms 28	Room phone No	Confirm by By arrang.	Parking Ample
with bath/shower 28	Room TV Yes	Last dinner 9	

Chittlehamholt

Map 3 D2 Devon
Near Umberleigh *EX37 9HD*
Chittlehamholt (076 94) 561
Proprietors Mr & Mrs H. Neil

Highbullen Hotel Restaurant

The great virtue of the cooking in this cleverly conceived cellar restaurant is its commendable simplicity in handling choice ingredients. The fixed-price dinner menu features very competently prepared dishes like smooth crab mousse, tender calf's liver with bordelaise sauce and local trout meunière, followed by delicious sweets such as creamy lemon soufflé. Residents only in high season. No smoking. 🍷*SUPERIOR.*

● **Set D** £8
About £25 for two

Dinner only *7.30–9*

Chollerford

Map 15 B4 Northumberland
Humshaugh
Near Hexham *NE46 4EW*
Humshaugh (043 481) 205

Credit Access, Amex,
Barclaycard, Diners

George Hotel   57%   £ D

Separated from the river by terraced gardens, this pleasant hotel has developed over the years round a Georgian inn. The Fisherman's Bar retains its pub atmosphere, and there's a modern cocktail bar and an attractive lounge. Well-equipped bedrooms vary between those in the old building and smart modern ones in the newest wing. *Amenities* garden, coarse & game fishing, dancing (Sat October–May), putting, children's playground.

Rooms 54	Room phone Yes	Confirm by 6	Parking Ample
with bath/shower 54	Room TV Yes	Last dinner 9	Banquets 150/10

Christchurch

Map 4 C4 Dorset
Castle Street *BH23 1DT*
Christchurch (0202) 484117

Manager Mr C. J. Astin
Credit Access, Amex,
Barclaycard, Diners

King's Arms Hotel   58%   £ D/E

A traditional hotel with a fine Georgian facade and pillared entrance, this former coaching inn with its own bowling green overlooks the ruins of the priory. There's a comfortable little bar in plush red, and the bright, airy lounge gives you plenty of space to relax. Comfortable bedrooms (six in the annexe) have neat fitted units, good mirrors and trouser presses; bathrooms are warm and functional. *Amenities* garden, bowling green.

Rooms 32	Room phone Yes	Confirm by 6	Parking Ample
with bath/shower 32	Room TV Yes	Last dinner 10	Banquets 250/12

Christchurch

Map 4 C4 Dorset
12 Church Street *BH23 1BW*
Bournemouth (0202) 483454
Proprietors Jua & John Carter &
Peter Hornsby

Splinters

Over the years this cosy restaurant has established a reputation for competent cooking and friendly informal service. Choose from the main dinner menu or the plats du jour, which might include poached salmon with hollandaise sauce and turkey breast in orange and Dubonnet sauce. Vegetables are full of flavour, and there are some pleasant sweets like lemon syllabub. 🍷*SUPERIOR. Credit* Amex

About £27 for two
Banquets 20/16

Dinner only 6.30–10.30
Closed Sun & 25 & 26 December

Church Stretton

Map 10 A4 Shropshire
All Stretton *SY6 6HG*
Church Stretton (0694) 723224

Credit Amex, Barclaycard,
Diners

Stretton Hall Hotel   61%   Ⓜ   £ F

This pleasant, inviting Georgian manor house stands in sheltered grounds in the shadow of the ancient Long Mynd ridge. Fine antiques, and wood panelling in the bar and residents' lounge (some superb linenfold here) are among the noteworthy features, and there's also a handsome staircase. Comfortable bedrooms are furnished in traditional style, and bathrooms are well fitted. *Amenities* garden, outdoor swimming pool, laundry room, Prestel.

Rooms 12	Room phone Yes	Confirm by By arrang.	Parking Ample
with bath/shower 6	Room TV Yes	Last dinner 9.15	Banquets 50/12

Churt

Map 5 E3 Surrey
Near Farnham *GU102QB*
Frensham (025 125) 3175

Credit Access, Amex,
Barclaycard, Diners

Frensham Pond Hotel   **69%**   Ⓜ   **£ D/E**

There's a pleasantly relaxed air about this white-painted hotel, which stands by the beautiful Great Pond. Tastefully furnished public rooms, though not large, are comfortable and welcoming. Seven spacious, well-equipped bedrooms are in the main building, while 12 are in a modern bungalow annexe across the lawn; both types have neat, well-maintained bathrooms. No dogs. *Amenities* garden, coarse fishing, dinner dance (Sat), helipad.

Rooms 19	*Room phone* Yes	*Confirm by* By arrang.	*Parking* Ample
with bath/shower 19	*Room TV* Yes	*Last dinner* 9.30	*Banquets* 120/–

Churt

Map 5 E3 Surrey
Near Farnham *GU102QB*
Frensham (025 125) 3175

About £30 for two

Frensham Pond Hotel, Fountain Restaurant   Ⓢ

A bright, smartly furnished restaurant offering simple set meals and a long carte of mainly French-style dishes. Generally good cooking, though vegetables can disappoint; affable, attentive service. 🍷 *ABOVE AVERAGE.* *Credit* Access, Amex, Barclaycard, Diners *Lunch* 12.30–2 *Dinner* 7.30–9.30 ● **Set L** £6·50, Sun £6·95 **Set D** £7·50

Churt

Map 5 E3 Surrey
Near Farnham *GU102LE*
Hindhead (042 873) 5799

Credit Access, Amex,
Barclaycard, Diners

Pride of the Valley Inn *(Inn)*   **£ D**

Surrounded by woods on the Tilford road off the A287, this old brick and pebbledash inn is especially welcoming in winter, when a fire blazes in the comfortable panelled lounge. There are also two friendly bars to relax in. Compact, cheerful bedrooms (all with radios and tea-makers) are neatly furnished in modern style, and bathrooms are warm and smartly tiled. *Amenities* garden.

Rooms 10	*Room phone* Yes	*Confirm by* 6	*Parking* Ample
with bath/shower 9	*Room TV* Yes	*Last dinner* 10	*Banquets* 45/10

Cirencester

Map 4 C2 Gloucestershire
Market Place *GL72NR*
Cirencester (0285) 3322
Telex 43470
Proprietor Mr M. Haigh-Gannon
Credit Access, Amex,
Barclaycard, Diners

King's Head Hotel   **60%**   Ⓜ   **£ D/E**

Dating back to the 14th century, this fine inn has had a most eventful history, and a magnificent painting in the spacious cocktail bar depicts a famous Civil War incident. Public rooms also include a panelled public bar and two plush lounges. Attractively coordinated soft furnishings now feature in most of the bedrooms, which are simply furnished. Compact, colourful bathrooms. *Amenities* skittle alley, pool table, table tennis.   ♿

Rooms 70	*Room phone* Yes	*Confirm by* 6	*Parking* Limited
with bath/shower 65	*Room TV* Yes	*Last dinner* 9.30	*Banquets* 300/–

Cirencester

Map 4 C2 Gloucestershire
GL72LE
Cirencester (0285) 61761
Proprietor Mrs Anne
Manley-Walker
Credit Access, Amex,
Barclaycard, Diners

Stratton House Hotel   **68%**   Ⓜ   **£ D**

Paintings and antiques in the lounge, Persian rugs in the beamed bar and displays of fine porcelain throughout public areas—all add up to a picture of refined elegance and gracious living in Mrs Manley-Walker's Queen Anne house. Bedrooms are warm and homely, with pleasing colour schemes and relaxing easy chairs (eight in the extension are more functional in style). *Amenities* garden, croquet.   ♿

Rooms 28	*Room phone* Yes	*Confirm by* 6	*Parking* Ample
with bath/shower 22	*Room TV* No	*Last dinner* 9.45	*Banquets* 110/20

Clanfield

Map 4 C2 Oxfordshire
OX82RG
Clanfield (036 781) 223

About £22 for two
Banquets 60/8

Clanfield Tavern Restaurant   Ⓢ

A delightfully rustic little restaurant set in a charming village pub. The menu is sensibly short and uncomplicated, with appealing starters like stuffed mushrooms or Stilton pancakes and main courses such as beef Stroganoff, grills and baked trout with prawn and lemon sauce. You can finish an enjoyable meal with delicious lemon meringue pie or a gâteau. *Credit* Access, Barclaycard

Lunch Sun only 12–1.30 *Dinner* 7.30–9.45, Fri & Sat 7.30–10.15 **Closed** D Sun & Mon

Clanfield   Plough Hotel   64%   (M)   £ D/E

Map 4 C2 Oxfordshire
OX8 2RB
Clanfield (036 781) 222
Proprietors
Mr & Mrs A. R. Barnes
Credit Amex, Diners

Caring owners maintain this delightful Elizabethan manor house in pristine condition and it has lost nothing of its bewitching character. The bar has splendid oak beams, pillars and an original fireplace, and there's a cheerful little TV lounge upstairs. Cosy bedrooms (including one with a four-poster) are traditionally furnished, and public bathrooms are up to date. No children under ten. No dogs. *Amenities* garden.

Rooms 6	*Room phone* No	*Confirm by* By arrang.	*Parking* Ample
with bath/shower 1	*Room TV* Yes	*Last dinner* 9.30	*Banquets* 36/–

Clanfield   Plough Hotel Restaurant    (S)

Map 4 C2 Oxfordshire
OX8 2RB
Clanfield (036 781) 222
Proprietors
Mr & Mrs A. R. Barnes

Care and attention to detail are the hallmarks of the cooking in this cosy, elegant little restaurant, The international menu based on first-class ingredients features dishes like salmon mousse with avocado relish and roast duck with a delicate Cointreau-flavoured sauce. Vegetables are skilfully prepared, and sweets include a delicious lemon cheesecake.
Credit Amex, Diners

About £32 for two
Banquets 35/6

Lunch 12–1.45 *Dinner* 7.30–9.30
Closed D 25 December

Clare   Bell Hotel *(Inn)*   (M)   £ E

Map 6 C3 Suffolk
Near Sudbury *CO10 8NN*
Clare (078 727) 7741
Proprietors
Mr & Mrs Hugh Jones
Credit Access, Amex,
Barclaycard, Diners

Once an ale house, this timbered 16th-century building still dispenses hospitality and old-world charm. There are beams and open fireplaces in the lounge and bar, and Mr Jones' hunting trophies lend a personal touch. Bedrooms in the main house are simply decorated, while the skilfully converted stables provide large, comfortable double rooms with colour TV and fully tiled, well-equipped bathrooms. *Amenities* garden   &

Rooms 21	*Room phone* Most	*Confirm by* 6	*Parking* Ample
with bath/shower 13	*Room TV* Most	*Last dinner* 9.30	*Banquets* 80/25

Claygate   The Gallery   (S)

Map 5 E3 Surrey
The Green *KT10 0JQ*
Esher (0372) 65125

Pictures (for sale) cover the walls of this pleasant restaurant, where the menu offers a varied choice of reliably cooked dishes like monkfish with a Ricard and tarragon sauce and honey-baked chicken. *Credit* Access, Amex, Barclaycard, Diners *Lunch* 12.30–2 *Dinner* 7–9.45, Sat 7–10.30

About £25 for two

Closed D Sun & all Mon ● **Set L** from £5·50   &

Clayton-le-Woods   Pines Hotel   65%   (M)   £ E

Map 10 B1 Lancashire
Near Chorley *PR6 7ED*
Preston (0772) 38551
Telex 677584
Proprietors Mr & Mrs J. M. Duffin
Credit Access, Amex,
Barclaycard, Diners

A new wing of luxury bedrooms is the latest addition to the Duffins' well-organised hotel. A fine panelled hall, splendid carved staircase and lofty public rooms are reminders of the original Victorian mansion, which benefits from bold modern colour schemes. Bedrooms, individually decorated, are very comfortable and bathrooms are thoroughly modern. No dogs. *Amenities* garden, squash, dancing (Fri). **Closed** 25 & 26 December   &

Rooms 26	*Room phone* Yes	*Confirm by* By arrang.	*Parking* Ample
with bath/shower 25	*Room TV* Yes	*Last dinner* 9.30	*Banquets* 164/24

Cleadon   French Blackboard   (S)

Map 15 C4 Tyne & Wear
63 Front Street *SR6 7PG*
Boldon (0783) 367397
Proprietor Mr Stanley James
French cooking

It's advisable to book for this cheerful little French bistro, which has a reputation for good value and charming service. The menu is short but varied, ingredients are first class and portions generous. The robust choice might include spicy spareribs, braised venison, a winy beef stew and duckling in puff pastry disarmingly described as robe de chambre. For a sweet, try home-made sorbet or blackberry and apple meringue.   &

About £24 for two
Banquets 75/20

Dinner only 7–10
Closed Sun, 1 January & 25 & 26 December

Clearwell

Map 4 B2 Gloucestershire
Near Coleford *GL168ST*
Dean (0594) 33666
Proprietors
John & Rosemary Stanford

● **Set L & Set D** £10·50
About £29 for two
Banquets 20/–

Wyndham Arms Restaurant   Ⓢ

In the charming main dining room of this friendly old inn, the fixed-price menu offers an interesting choice of dishes from flavour-packed mushroom soup or omelette Arnold Bennett to lobster salad, roast baby chicken and the Wyndham version of tournedos Rossini. Finish with a delicious dessert like rich chocolate, walnut and brandy cake. Simpler grill-room menu.
Credit Access, Amex

Lunch 12–2 *Dinner* 7–10, Sun 7–9.30
Closed Mon & 25 & 26 December

Cleethorpes

Map 11 F2 Humberside
Kingsway *DN350AE*
Cleethorpes (0472) 601122

Proprietor Mr Harris
Credit Access, Amex,
Barclaycard, Diners

Rooms 56
with bath/shower 43

Kingsway Hotel   59%   Ⓜ   £ D/E

Right on the seafront overlooking the Humber Estuary, this cheerful family-run hotel offers comfortable accommodation to suit both businessman and tourist. Public rooms like the lounges and bar have good sea views, as do some of the bright, well-furnished bedrooms; 12 others look out on to a pleasant roof garden complete with ornamental pond. Guide dogs only.
Amenities garden.

Room phone Yes	*Confirm by* By arrang.	*Parking* Ample
Room TV Yes	*Last dinner* 9.30	*Banquets* 36/4

Clevedon

Map 4 A2 Avon
1 Wellington Terrace *BS21 7BL*
Clevedon (0272) 874253

Proprietor Mr R. P. B. Curtis

Credit Access, Barclaycard

Rooms 38
with bath/shower 21

Walton Park Hotel   52%   Ⓜ   £ D

Situated not far from junction 20 of the M5, with splendid views across the Bristol Channel to the South Wales coast, this is a friendly, popular seaside hotel with a steady conference trade too. The large lounge and bar are furnished in contemporary style, while bedrooms vary in decor, all having ample cupboard space, tea/coffee-makers and radios. Simple bathrooms are adequate. *Amenities* garden.

Room phone No	*Confirm by* 6	*Parking* Ample
Room TV Yes	*Last dinner* 8.30	*Banquets* 150/20

Climping

Map 5 E4 West Sussex
Near Littlehampton *BN175RW*
Littlehampton (090 64) 23511

Rooms 19
with bath/shower 19
Room phone Yes
Room TV Yes
Confirm by By arrang.
Last dinner 9.30
Parking Ample
Banquets 60/4
Closed January
Credit Access, Amex,
Barclaycard, Diners

Bailiffscourt Hotel   76%   Ⓜ   £ D

Built in the 1930s on the site of a Norman house and chapel not far from the sea, this imposing country house incorporates architectural features from a number of medieval buildings. Great stone fireplaces, oak-beamed ceilings and flagstoned passages lend character and charm, and the bedrooms (some in the adjoining Thatched House) are superb. All have fine oak furniture, rich carpeting and warming log fires, and seven have four-posters. Bathrooms are equally impressive. Three sitting areas and a little bar have a cosy, inviting air, emphasised by friendly, helpful staff. No children under ten.
Amenities garden, outdoor swimming pool, tennis, croquet, games room.

Climping

Map 5 E4 West Sussex
Near Littlehampton *BN175RW*
Littlehampton (090 64) 23511

● **Set L** Sun only £9·25

Bailiffscourt Hotel Restaurant   Ⓢ

Two stone-walled rooms with mullioned windows form this appealing little restaurant, where Tim Dalglish offers daily-changing dinner menus and simpler à la carte lunches. An imaginative choice could include appetising pâtés and terrines, tasty venison and chestnut pie, local lobster and crunchy fresh vegetables. Refreshing sorbets and good coffee with petits fours make a nice finish. ♟ *ABOVE AVERAGE. Credit* Access, Amex, Barclaycard, Diners

     Continued

Set D from £11·25
About £30 for two
Banquets 60/4

Lunch 12.30–2 *Dinner* 7.30–9.30
Closed D Sun to non-residents & January

Coatham Mundeville

Map 15 B5 Co. Durham
Near Darlington *DL1 3LU*
Aycliffe (0325) 313333
Proprietors Mrs J. L. Crocker &
Mr E. Williamson
Rooms 19
with bath/shower 19
Room phone Yes
Room TV Yes
Confirm by By arrang.
Last dinner 9.15
Parking Ample
Banquets 12/–
Closed 10 days Christmas

Hall Garth   71%   Ⓜ   £ D

Dating back to Tudor times, this listed country house is now a charming hotel, lovingly maintained by its welcoming owners. The three comfortable lounges are spick and span, with antiques, bric-à-brac and comfortable armchairs helping to create a really cosy atmosphere. Well-appointed bedrooms in the original house feature fine paintings and prints, and four have four-posters; there are also smart new rooms in a tastefully converted stable block with stylish modern furniture, pastel colour schemes and tea-making facilities. All rooms have colourful modern bathrooms. Also in the new block is an attractive rustic-style pub.
Amenities garden, putting, croquet.

Coatham Mundeville

Map 15 B5 Co. Durham
Near Darlington *DL1 3LU*
Aycliffe (0325) 313333
Proprietors Mrs J. L. Crocker
& Mr E. Williamson

● **Set L** from £6·50
Set D from £9·25
About £27 for two

Hall Garth Restaurant   

There's a delightful homely atmosphere in this pretty dining room, where Janice Crocker's enjoyable cooking makes good use of fresh produce, including vegetables from the hotel's kitchen garden. The short four-course set menu starts with a hearty soup, followed perhaps by pâté or Stilton mousse and well-prepared main courses such as chicken breast with mushrooms in cream sauce. Simple sweets. No smoking. 🍷 *ABOVE AVERAGE.*

Lunch 12.15–1.30 *Dinner* 7.15–9.15
Closed Sun, 1st Mon May & 10 days Christmas

Cobham

Map 5 E3 Surrey
48 High Street *KT11 3EF*
Cobham (093 26) 21 21

Italian cooking
About £32 for two

La Capanna

Full-bodied fish soup and veal with creamy tarragon sauce typify the authentic Italian specialities offered in this barn-like restaurant. Well-chosen hors d'œuvre and pasta dishes, too. *Credit* Access, Amex, Barclaycard *Lunch* 12.15–2.15 *Dinner* 7–10.45 **Closed** Sun & 25 & 26 Dec
● **Set L** £4·95 *Banquets* 26/6

Cobham

Map 5 E5 Surrey
Seven Hills Road South
KT11 1EW
Cobham (093 26) 4471
Telex 929196
Credit Access, Amex,
Barclaycard, Diners

Ladbroke Seven Hills Hotel   60%   £ C

Check directions when booking at this modern hotel just off the A3. Although it is geared towards functional, streamlined accommodation, it has the added attraction of extensive sports and banqueting facilities. There are two cheerfully decorated bars, and bedrooms in a separate block have fitted furniture and compact bathrooms. *Amenities* garden, sauna, outdoor swimming pool, tennis, squash, dinner dance (Fri, Sat), helipad.

| *Rooms* 92 | *Room phone* Yes | *Confirm by* 6 | *Parking* Ample |
| *with bath/shower* 92 | *Room TV* Yes | *Last dinner* 10 | *Banquets* 200/– |

Cobham

Map 5 E3 Surrey
Portsmouth Road *KT11 1EL*
Cobham (093 26) 3006
Manager Mr Roberto Castagni
Italian cooking

About £34 for two
Banquets 50/15

San Domenico

On the A3 just south of the A245 roundabout, this airy restaurant with crisp yellow table linen overlooks a wooded garden. Fish is well represented on the Italian menu, and there are home-made pastas, charcoal grills and tempting daily specials, too. Superb materials are used, and fresh herbs enhance enjoyable flavours. Gloriously rich trifle is among the irresistible sweets. *Credit* Access, Amex, Barclaycard, Diners   ♿

Lunch 12.30–2.30, Sun 12.30–3 *Dinner* 7–11
Closed D Sun & Bank Holidays

Cockfield

Map 6 C3 Suffolk
Cross Green
Near Bury St Edmunds *IP30 0LG*
Cockfield Green (0284) 828246
Proprietor C. S. Ingram
About £25 for two

Thatchers

A charming thatched cottage is the setting for Mrs Ingram's enjoyable cooking. Dishes range from soups and pâté to roast duckling, saddle of venison and tournedos Rossini, with perhaps a sundae or fruit pie to finish. *Lunch* Sun only 12–2 *Dinner* 7–9.30 **Closed** D Sun, all Mon, 25 & 26 December & 2 weeks May/June ● **Set L** £4·75

Coggeshall

Map 6 C3 Essex
Market End *CO6 1NH*
Coggeshall (0376) 61654
Proprietor Mr R. Pluck
Credit Access, Amex,
Barclaycard, Diners
Closed Aug & 1 week Christmas

White Hart Hotel   65%   Ⓜ   £ D/E

Raymond Pluck's beautifully restored 15th-century hostelry—once the guildhall—retains much of its former charm and appeal. The delightful bar is full of antiques and copperware, but the star of the public rooms is the splendid residents' lounge, which features original sweet chestnut beams and a huge brick fireplace. Prettily decorated bedrooms have fitted modern units, and compact bathrooms are well equipped. Guide dogs only.

Rooms 23	*Room phone* Yes	*Confirm by* By arrang.	*Parking* Ample
with bath/shower 23	*Room TV* Yes	*Last dinner* 10	*Banquets* 60/12

Coggeshall

Map 6 C3 Essex
Market End *CO6 1NH*
Coggeshall (0376) 61654
Proprietor Mr R. Pluck

About £35 for two

White Hart Hotel Restaurant   ♕

A charming beamed restaurant, whose well-planned menu offers seafood and seasonal game alongside grills and tasty dishes like ham and potato bake or nicely sauced pork fillets. ♟ *OUTSTANDING. Credit* Access, Amex, Barclaycard, Diners *Lunch* 12.30–2 *Dinner* 7.30–10 **Closed** L Mon & Sat, D Sun, August & 1 week Christmas ● **Set L** Sun only £5·95

Colchester

Map 6 C3 Essex
116 High Street *CO1 0NJ*
Colchester (0206) 78494

Credit Access, Amex,
Barclaycard, Diners

George Hotel   57%   £ E

The attractive white-painted facade is Georgian but the origins of this pleasant, well-run inn go back 500 years. Fine panelling and sturdy beams give a homely appeal to public rooms like the lounge and bar, while modernised bedrooms with attractively patterned wallpapers have dark-wood furniture and well-equipped tiled bathrooms.
Amenities 24-hour laundry service.

Rooms 47	*Room phone* Yes	*Confirm by* 6	*Parking* Ample
with bath/shower 40	*Room TV* Yes	*Last dinner* 10	*Banquets* 80/–

Colchester

Map 6 C3 Essex
London Road
Marks Tey *CO6 1DU*
Colchester (0206) 210001
Telex 987176
Credit Access, Amex,
Barclaycard, Diners

Marks Tey Hotel   60%   £ E

Built alongside the A12, five miles south of Colchester, this modern two-storey hotel has extensive conference and banqueting facilities. There's also a functional open-plan reception lounge and a bright cocktail bar dominated by a striking mural. Cheerfully decorated bedrooms have whitewood furniture, good writing areas and spacious, carefully designed bathrooms.

Rooms 106	*Room phone* Yes	*Confirm by* 8	*Parking* Ample
with bath/shower 106	*Room TV* Yes	*Last dinner* 9.45	*Banquets* 160/–

Colchester

Map 6 C3 Essex
East Gates *CO1 2TZ*
Colchester (0206) 866677

Credit Access, Amex,
Barclaycard, Diners

Rose & Crown Hotel   57%   Ⓜ   £ E/F

This half-timbered historic posting house exudes charm, with its leaded windows, beamed ceilings and uneven floors. Public rooms include the welcoming reception area with exposed brick and rough plaster walls, and two comfortable bars. There are 12 bedrooms in a modern annexe, but the more attractive ones, with fine traditional furnishings, are in the main building. Shower or bathrooms are adequate.

Rooms 27	*Room phone* Yes	*Confirm by* By arrang.	*Parking* Ample
with bath/shower 18	*Room TV* Yes	*Last dinner* 10	*Banquets* 25/6

Coleford

Map 4 B2 Gloucestershire
Forest of Dean *GL16 7EL*
Dean (0594) 22607

Credit Access, Amex,
Barclaycard, Diners

Rooms 14
with bath/shower 3

Speech House Hotel *(Inn)* £D

Two miles from Coleford in the heart of the Forest of Dean, this splendidly preserved 17th-century house is full of atmosphere. A fine oil portrait sets the decorative tone in reception, and there are two bars (one with a fireplace dated 1883). Spacious first-floor bedrooms have handsome furniture (three have magnificent four-posters), while those on the top floor are smaller and more modern. *Amenities* garden.

Room phone Yes	*Confirm by* 6	*Parking* Ample	
Room TV Yes	*Last dinner* 9.30	*Banquets* 60/–	

Our inspectors never book in the name of the Egon Ronay Organisation; they disclose their identity only after paying their bills.

Cooden Beach

Map 7 B6 East Sussex
Near Bexhill-on-Sea *TN39 4TT*
Cooden (042 43) 2281

Proprietor Mr A. G. Shields
Credit Access, Amex,
Barclaycard, Diners

Rooms 38
with bath/shower 38

Cooden Beach Hotel 65% Ⓜ £D/E

Guests here can use the adjacent Cooden Beach golf club as well as the hotel's own extensive facilities. The 1930s building has been well modernised, with comfortable, airy lounge and bar areas. Bedrooms are individually decorated, some in smart modern style, others pleasantly traditional. Demi-pension terms only. *Amenities* garden, outdoor swimming pool, game fishing, ladies' hairdressing, croquet, games room.

Room phone Yes	*Confirm by* By arrang.	*Parking* Ample	
Room TV Yes	*Last dinner* 10.30	*Banquets* 120/10	

Cookham

Map 5 E2 Berkshire
19 Station Hill Parade
SL6 9BR
Bourne End (062 85) 25775

French cooking

About £26 for two
Banquets 25/12

Le Radier ♧ Ⓢ

Situated in a small shopping precinct near the railway station, this modest restaurant specialises in uncomplicated French provincial cooking. M Voisin hails from Marseilles and brings an authentic Gallic touch to the enjoyable dishes, like pork fillets in a green peppercorn and brandy sauce and pheasant bourguignonne, which feature on his short menu. Booking advisable. ♿

Dinner only 7.30–9
Closed Sun, Mon, 1 January, 25 & 26 December & 2 weeks late August

Copdock

Map 6 C3 Suffolk
Near Ipswich *IP8 3JD*
Copdock (047 386) 444
Telex 987207
Manager Miss Judith Coleman
Credit Access, Amex,
Barclaycard, Diners

Rooms 47
with bath/shower 39

Ipswich Moat House 59% £D/E

Good conference facilities are a major attraction of this thoroughly modernised hotel, formerly the Copdock. As well, there's a spacious foyer lounge with plenty of relaxing chairs, and a pleasant buffet/bar. The best bedrooms (in the extension) have attractive pine fitted units with generous writing space, double glazing, and tea-makers. Tiled bathrooms are well kept. *Amenities* garden, sauna, dinner dance (Sat), croquet.

Room phone Yes	*Confirm by* 6	*Parking* Ample	
Room TV Yes	*Last dinner* 9.20	*Banquets* 400/–	

Corbridge

Map 15 B4 Northumberland
Tinklers Bank
Farnley *NE45 3RN*
Corbridge (043 471) 2424
Proprietors
Heinrich & Jennifer Herrmann

About £27 for two
Banquets 40/–

Ramblers of Corbridge ♧ Ⓢ

After eight years in Corbridge itself the Herrmanns have moved to this peaceful white-painted mansion on the outskirts. They continue to offer enjoyable French-inspired dishes, cooked with care and served with a smile. Avocado filled with smoked cod roe mousse makes a very tasty starter, and generously served main courses come with excellent seasonal vegetables. There's a splendid sweet trolley. *Credit* Access, Barclaycard ♿

Dinner only 7–10
Closed Sun, Mon & Bank Holidays

Cornhill-on-Tweed

Map 14 B2 Northumberland
Main Street *TD12 4UH*
Coldstream (0890) 2424

Credit Access, Barclaycard
Closed for accommodation
24 & 25 December

Collingwood Arms Hotel *(Inn)*  £E

Bill and Doreen McRae ensure that visitors receive the friendliest of welcomes in this charming Georgian inn. A blazing fire warms the entrance hall in winter, and there are two comfortable bars as well as a little lounge upstairs. Prettily decorated bedrooms are warm, cosy and comfortably furnished; all have tea-makers and excellent bedside lights. Good bathrooms. *Amenities* garden, solarium.

| *Rooms* 17 | *Room phone* Yes | *Confirm by* By arrang. | *Parking* Ample |
| *with bath/shower* 7 | *Room TV* Some | *Last dinner* 10 | *Banquets* 100/20 |

Cornhill-on-Tweed

Map 14 B2 Northumberland
TD12 4UU
Coldstream (0890) 2255

Credit Access, Amex,
Barclaycard, Diners

Tillmouth Park Hotel 61% £D

This grandiose Victorian mansion built of stone has an air of old-fashioned elegance. There are two vast lounges with chandeliers and great fireplaces, a simple TV lounge and two bars. Bedrooms leading off an oak gallery are very well furnished, whether a grand chamber with two four-posters or a compact little room. Bathrooms are adequate. *Amenities* garden, coarse & game fishing, dancing (most Sats), putting, croquet.

| *Rooms* 16 | *Room phone* Yes | *Confirm by* 6 | *Parking* Ample |
| *with bath/shower* 7 | *Room TV* No | *Last dinner* 8.45 | *Banquets* 110/20 |

Corse Lawn

Map 4 B1 Gloucestershire
Near Tirley *GL19 4LZ*
Tirley (045 278) 479

● **Set L** £6·95 **Set D** £9·75
incl. service
About £33 for two
Banquets 32/8

Corse Lawn House ★ 

A Queen Anne house in a quiet village on the B4211 is the attractive setting for this splendid *restaurant avec chambres*. Baba Hine shows great skill and a fine respect for fresh natural flavours in producing her memorable meals: clams, scallops and lobster are seasonal favourites, and other choices might include kidneys, steak, game or salmon with an incomparable hollandaise sauce. Desserts are just as delicious, and there's home-made fudge with the excellent coffee. Accommodation consists of four comfortable rooms with private bathrooms. **Specialities** hot shrimps en croustade, prawn and courgette pancake, stuffed chicken breast with tarragon sauce.
Credit Access, Amex, Barclaycard, Diners

Lunch 12.30–2 *Dinner* 7–10
Closed D Sun, all Mon & 1 week January

Corsham

Map 4 B2 Wiltshire
Leafy Lane *SN13 0PA*
Hawthorn (0225) 810555

Credit Access, Diners

Rudloe Park Hotel 61% Ⓜ £D/E

Beautifully maintained gardens surround this substantial 19th-century house built of Portland stone which has been lavishly updated throughout in flamboyant style with bold wallpapers and floral fabrics. Comfortable bedrooms all have radios, tea-makers and compact bathrooms. Downstairs, there's a traditionally furnished lounge bar and a cheerful public bar.
Amenities garden, dancing (Sat), croquet.

| *Rooms* 8 | *Room phone* Yes | *Confirm by* By arrang. | *Parking* Ample |
| *with bath/shower* 8 | *Room TV* Yes | *Last dinner* 10 | *Banquets* 120/– |

Coventry

Map 10 C4 West Midlands
London Road, Willenhall *CV3 4EQ*
Coventry (0203) 303398
Telex 311993
Manager Mr I. L. Johnston
Credit Access, Amex,
Barclaycard, Diners

Chace Hotel 60% £D

The Victorian origins of this part-timbered hotel show in the massive staircase and the lofty panelled entrance hall, which also serves as a comfortable residents' lounge. There's a pleasant little cocktail bar, and the bedrooms, brightly and charmingly decorated, have practical fitted furniture. Rooms in the extension are similarly equipped, and all have spotless bathrooms. *Amenities* garden.

| *Rooms* 68 | *Room phone* Yes | *Confirm by* 6 | *Parking* Ample |
| *with bath/shower* 68 | *Room TV* Yes | *Last dinner* 9.45 | *Banquets* 90/2 |

Coventry

Map 10 C4 West Midlands
Hinckley Road
Walsgrave *CV2 2HP*
Coventry (0203) 613261
Telex 311292
Credit Access, Amex,
Barclaycard, Diners

Rooms 160
with bath/shower 160

Crest Hotel   60%   £D

Situated at junction 2 of the M6, this large modern hotel with 13 acres of grounds has been designed with the business person in mind. Bold contemporary decor is a feature of the foyer-lounge and the smart bar, while uniform bedrooms are neatly fitted with built-in units, tea-makers and trouser presses. Attractive half-tiled bathrooms. *Amenities* garden, dinner dance (Sat), games room, bar buffet (Mon–Fri 9am–5pm).

Room phone Yes	*Confirm by* 6	*Parking* Ample
Room TV Yes	*Last dinner* 10	*Banquets* 450/2

Coventry

Map 10 C4 West Midlands
Cathedral Square *CV1 5RP*
Coventry (0203) 51851
Telex 31380
Manager David Selby
Rooms 215
with bath/shower 215
Room phone Yes
Room TV Yes
Confirm by 7
Last dinner 10.30
Parking Ample
Banquets 460/–

Credit Access, Amex,
Barclaycard, Diners

De Vere Hotel   74%   £ C/D

Built right next to the famous cathedral, this imposing seven-storey hotel has been thoughtfully designed to provide the best in modern comfort and facilities. An impressive canopied entrance leads to the handsome marble-lined foyer, and public rooms include a large ground-floor lounge with tapestry-hung walls, as well as a choice of attractive bars (one luxuriously smart, the other more cosy). Double glazed bedrooms, which range from executive rooms and suites to studio rooms, are beautifully decorated and furnished with stylish rosewood units, writing desks, bedside consoles and ample seating. Streamlined bathrooms are equally well appointed.
Amenities coffee shop (7.30am–9.30pm, Fri & Sat 7.30am–10.30pm).

Coventry

Map 10 C4 West Midlands
King Richard Street *CV2 4GU*
Coventry (0203) 27053
Manager Mr A. R. Caluori

About £25 for two
Banquets 120/40

Grandstand   Ⓢ

A friendly team runs this spacious restaurant at Coventry City Football Club. The undoubted star of the lunch menu is the superb roast rib of beef, carved to order at your table, and alternatives include variations on scampi and sole and a number of steaks and grills. Kick off with terrine or rich onion soup, and end with a dessert from the trolley.
Credit Access, Amex, Barclaycard, Diners

Lunch only 12–2.30
Closed Sat, Sun & Bank Holidays

Coventry

Map 10 C4 West Midlands
Broadgate *CV1 1LZ*
Coventry (0203) 21371
Telex 311193
Credit Access, Amex,
Barclaycard, Diners
Closed Christmas

Rooms 90
with bath/shower 90

Hotel Leofric   68%   £ D

Situated right in the city centre, this well-kept modern hotel with good function facilities is a popular place for business people. There's a simply furnished, open-plan reception-lounge area and a choice of three bars. Compact, cheerfully decorated bedrooms have bright, patterned bedspreads and partly tiled bathrooms. Suites are attractive and particularly comfortable.
Amenities hairdressing, coffee shop (10am–7pm) .

Room phone Yes	*Confirm by* 6	*Parking* Ample
Room TV Yes	*Last dinner* 10	*Banquets* 600/6

Coventry

Map 10 C4 West Midlands
Wilsons Lane *CV6 6HL*
Coventry (0203) 365000
Telex 31545

Credit Access, Amex,
Barclaycard, Diners

Rooms 100
with bath/shower 100

Novotel   62%   £ D

This low, modern hotel (just off exit 3 of the M6) boasts an attractive garden and a self-contained sports unit. Hanging plant baskets adorn the strikingly simple reception lounge and bar, while the studio-style bedrooms are spacious and uncluttered, and have well-fitted bathrooms. *Amenities* garden, sauna, outdoor swimming pool, squash, dancing (Sat monthly), 24-hour laundry service, restaurant (6am–midnight), gymnasium, solarium.

Room phone Yes	*Confirm by* 7	*Parking* Ample
Room TV Yes	*Last dinner* 11.30	*Banquets* 200/10

Coventry

Map 10 C4 West Midlands
Rye Hill, Allesley *CV5 9PH*
Coventry (0203) 402151
Telex 31427

Credit Access, Amex,
Barclaycard, Diners

Rooms 196
with bath/shower 196

Post House Hotel   58%   £ D

Convenient for businessmen and travellers alike, this tower-block hotel stands on the A45, a short drive from Birmingham Airport and the National Exhibition Centre. Among public areas are a spacious reception-lounge, a bar, and various conference rooms. Double-glazed bedrooms have built-in furniture, tea/coffee-makers, mini-bars and compact tiled bathrooms. *Amenities* dancing (Fri, Sat), restaurant (7.30am–10.15pm).

Room phone Yes	*Confirm by* 6	*Parking* Ample
Room TV Yes	*Last dinner* 10.15	*Banquets* 120/–

Cranleigh

Map 5 E3 Surrey
High Street *GU6 8RF*
Cranleigh (0483) 274900
Proprietor Mr R. Mazzotta
Italian cooking
About £20 for two

La Scala

A simple upstairs restaurant where the menu offers a comprehensive range of Italian specialities. Home-made pasta is properly cooked, meat is tender and sauces are tasty. Finish with a gâteau or zabaglione. *Lunch* 12–1.45 *Dinner* 6.30–10.45, Fri & Sat 6.30–11.15
Closed Sun, Mon & 1–30 August *Banquets* 25/15

Crawley

Map 5 D3 Hampshire
Near Winchester *SO21 2PR*
Sparsholt (096 272) 285
Proprietors
Mrs J. Marsden & family
About £29 for two

Fox & Hounds

Mrs Marsden offers good ingredients and careful cooking in this simple, relaxing pub dining room. The menu features mainly grills, supplemented by daily specials such as crab mousse and pheasant normande. Delicious vegetables and sweets, too. *Lunch* 12–2 *Dinner* 7.30–9.45 **Closed** D Sun, all Mon & 24–31 December ● **Set L** Sun only £6 *Banquets* 32/25

Crawley

Map 7 B5 West Sussex
High Street *RH10 1BS*
Crawley (0293) 24215
Telex 87385

Credit Access, Amex,
Barclaycard, Diners

Rooms 76
with bath/shower 76

George Hotel   58%   £ D

A gallows sign runs across the street from this fine old building, an inn since 1615. Heavy beams, oak panels and antique furnishings grace the foyer and popular George Bar, and there's a plush cocktail bar and useful buttery. Most of the attractive, practically furnished bedrooms are in a modern wing. Bathrooms are adequate. *Amenities* dancing (Sat in December), buttery (10am–10.30pm, Sun 10am–7pm), baby listening.

Room phone Yes	*Confirm by* 6	*Parking* Ample
Room TV Yes	*Last dinner* 9.30	*Banquets* 220/4

Crawley

See also under London Airports

Cressage

Map 10 B4 Shropshire
Near Shrewsbury *SY5 6AD*
Cressage (095 289) 298

Proprietor Mr Michael Richings

● **Set L** £5·46 **Set D** £9·48
About £26 for two
Banquets 40/12

Old Hall Hotel Restaurant

Fixed-price menus feature enjoyable dishes ranging from local salmon with prawn and sweet pepper sauce to grilled gammon with apricots; vegetables are nicely cooked, and simple sweets carefully prepared. The timber-framed building stands in the centre of Cressage overlooking the Severn, and there are a few, large, simply furnished bedrooms for overnight accommodation. *Credit* Access

Lunch 12.15–1.30 *Dinner* 7.30–9.15
Closed D Sun & all Mon

Crick

Map 11 D4 Northamptonshire
NN6 7XR
Crick (0788) 822101
Telex 311107

Credit Access, Amex,
Barclaycard, Diners

Rooms 96
with bath/shower 96

Post House Hotel   63%   £ D

Neatly kept gardens surround this low modern hotel conveniently close to junction 18 of the M1. The open-plan foyer with its picture windows and deep chairs is pleasantly relaxing, and there are two cosy bars and good conference facilities. Colourful, functional bedrooms have tea-makers, mini-bars and good spacious bathrooms. *Amenities* garden, coffee shop (7am–11pm), children's playground, helipad.

Room phone Yes	*Confirm by* 6	*Parking* Ample
Room TV Yes	*Last dinner* 10	*Banquets* 150/10

Crick

Map 11 D4 Northamptonshire
NN6 7XR
Crick (0788) 822101

● **Set L & Set D** £6·50
About £30 for two

Post House Hotel, Turnpike Restaurant ⑤

Attractive modern furnishings provide a pleasant contrast to the plain brick walls of this hotel dining room. The short, interesting menu offers traditional favourites and imaginative variations. For something different try the unusual mushroom and sweetbread starter, followed by Rutland venison pie or the flamed mixed kebabs. Mouthwatering sweets, too. ♥*ABOVE AVERAGE.*
Credit Access, Amex, Barclaycard, Diners &

Lunch 12.30–2 *Dinner* 7–10
Closed L Sat & D Sun

Crondall

Map 5 D3 Surrey
Odiham Road
Near Farnham *GU105RJ*
Aldershot (0252) 850328
Proprietor Mr Robin Neale
About £28 for two

La Piperade ⑤

Simple French-inspired dishes like medallions of beef in Madeira sauce feature on the menu of this cottage little restaurant. Reliable cooking and friendly service. *Credit* Access, Amex, Barclaycard, Diners
Lunch 12–2 *Dinner* 7–9.30
Closed L Mon & Sat, all Sun, Bank Holidays & 1st week January

---

Crooklands

Map 13 D6 Cumbria
Near Milnthorpe *LA7 7NW*
Crooklands (044 87) 432

Credit Access, Amex,
Barclaycard

Rooms 15
with bath/shower 15

Crooklands Hotel 59% £ D/E

This much-extended 17th-century building stands near junction 36 of the M6. Public areas include an attentively staffed reception and three cheerful bars. Bedrooms (including a family room) have pretty flowered wallpaper and practical modern white units; bathrooms are smart and well equipped. *Amenities* garden, game fishing, dinner dance (Sat), buttery (7.30am–3pm, also 6.30pm–10.30pm in summer), clay-pigeon shooting, canoeing.

Room phone Yes	*Confirm by* 6	*Parking* Ample
Room TV Yes	*Last dinner* 9.30	*Banquets* 120/30

Crosby-on-Eden

Map 13 D4 Cumbria
Near Carlisle *CA6 4QZ*
Crosby-on-Eden (022 873) 618
Proprietors
Michael & Patricia Sedgwick
Credit Amex, Diners
Closed 24 Dec–mid Jan

Rooms 11
with bath/shower 9

Crosby Lodge Hotel 63% Ⓜ £ D/E

There are fine views of the surrounding countryside from this impressive red-brick Georgian building on the B6264. A large reception hall leads to the spacious bar and the welcoming, bay-windowed residents' lounge, which has TV and comfortable sofas. Good-sized bedrooms have sturdy antique furniture and adequate bathrooms; two rooms in the converted stable block are modern. *Amenities* garden.

Room phone No	*Confirm by* By arrang.	*Parking* Ample
Room TV No	*Last dinner* 9	*Banquets* 40/6

Crosby-on-Eden

Map 13 D4 Cumbria
Near Carlisle *CA6 4QZ*
Crosby-on-Eden (022 873) 618
Proprietors
Michael & Patricia Sedgwick

● **Set L** £6·25 **Set D** £9·25
About £27 for two

Crosby Lodge Hotel Restaurant ♧ ⑤

An elegant atmosphere pervades this friendly hotel restaurant, where Mr Sedgwick's cooking reaches a reliably high standard. The simple à la carte features grills, salads and omelettes, and there are also more enterprising fixed-price menus with dishes like crêpe bolognese and roast guinea fowl with Calvados-flavoured sauce. Interesting sweet trolley, too.
Credit Amex, Diners

Lunch 12.30–1.45, Sun 12.30–1.15 *Dinner* 7.30–9
Closed D Sun, Easter Mon, Aug Bank Holiday & 24 Dec–mid Jan

Croxdale

Map 15 B4 Co. Durham
DH1 3SP
Durham (0385) 780524
Telex 538156
Credit Access, Amex,
Barclaycard, Diners
Closed 10 days Christmas

Rooms 54
with bath/shower 46

Crest Hotel 54% £ D

South of Durham alongside the A167, this friendly hotel is very convenient for travellers. The combination of natural stone and pine gives the public rooms an attractive Scandinavian air, and the charming bar-lounge has an unusual Swedish fireplace. Bedrooms in the bright motel-style extension have well-fitted bathrooms; those in the original building have been modernised and share good public facilities. *Amenities* game fishing.

Room phone Yes	*Confirm by* 6	*Parking* Ample
Room TV Yes	*Last dinner* 10	

Darlington
Map 15 B5 Co. Durham
38 Coniscliffe Road *DL3 7RG*
Darlington (0325) 286666

● **Set L** from £4·95
Set D from £8·75
About £27 for two
Banquets 20/12

Bishop's House

The enthusiastic Lees work hard at their elegant restaurant, whose walls are adorned with their own paintings and collages. Anne is a caring and capable chef, whose fixed-price menus offer tasty starters like delicious cream of courgette soup or ham and chicken terrine, entrées such as trout with almonds or nicely sauced sirloin steak, and a few tempting desserts.
Credit Access, Amex, Barclaycard

Lunch 12–2.15 *Dinner* 7–9.30, Sat 7–9.45
Closed L Sat, all Sun, Bank Holidays & last week July/1st week August

Darlington
Map 15 B5 Co. Durham
Blackwell Grange *DL3 8QH*
Darlington (0325) 60111
Telex 587272

Credit Access, Amex,
Barclaycard, Diners

Blackwell Grange Moat House   65%   £ E

This 17th-century red-brick mansion stands in parkland just outside the town and not far from the A1. Handsome fireplaces and oil paintings grace the welcoming public rooms, and a grand staircase leads to the spacious, traditionally furnished bedrooms with lounge areas. Other bedrooms, in an extension, are crisply modern, with fitted furniture and tiled bathrooms.
Amenities garden, tennis, coarse fishing, dancing (Sat in winter).

Rooms 96	*Room phone* Yes	*Confirm by* By arrang.	*Parking* Ample
with bath/shower 96	*Room TV* Yes	*Last dinner* 10	*Banquets* 160/–

Darlington
Map 15 B5 Co. Durham
Priestgate *DL1 1NW*
Darlington (0325) 67612

Credit Access, Amex,
Barclaycard, Diners

King's Head Hotel   60%   £ E

Combining modern comforts with Victorian decor, this town-centre hotel is popular with locals and visiting businessmen. There's a convivial lounge bar and a spacious cocktail bar as well as a number of function rooms. Cheerfully decorated bedrooms in the main building and the extension have neat fitted furniture, tea-makers and radios, plus smart, fully tiled bathrooms.
Amenities coffee shop (9am–4.30pm).

Rooms 86	*Room phone* Yes	*Confirm by* 6	*Parking* Limited
with bath/shower 86	*Room TV* Yes	*Last dinner* 9.30	*Banquets* 230/–

Changes in data may occur in establishments after the Guide goes to press. Prices should be taken as indications rather than firm quotes.

Darlington
Map 15 B5 Co. Durham
Harrowgate Hill *DL1 3AD*
Darlington (0325) 487111

Credit Access, Amex,
Barclaycard, Diners

Stakis White Horse Hotel   61%   £ E

The modern, well-equipped bedrooms are in a recent extension to this old pub on the outskirts of town. All are extremely comfortable, with shag-pile carpets, colour TV, radios, tea/coffee-makers, fruit and pretty fabrics. Tiled bathrooms are spotless, and provided with hairdryers. There's a striking red and green bar-lounge, and two other bars.
Amenities dancing (Fri), discothèque (Wed, Thurs).

Rooms 40	*Room phone* Yes	*Confirm by* 7	*Parking* Ample
with bath/shower 40	*Room TV* Yes	*Last dinner* 10.30	*Banquets* 70/–

Darrington
Map 11 D1 West Yorkshire
Great North Road
Near Pontefract *WF8 3BL*
Pontefract (0977) 71458

Credit Access, Amex,
Barclaycard

Darrington Hotel *(Inn)*   £ E

Friendly, helpful staff make it a pleasure to stay at this solid brick pub, which stands at the junction of the A1 and M62. A simple foyer leads to the popular bar, and there are extensive conference facilities. Bedrooms have functional modern furnishings, the best being those in the rear wing, which have neat shower or bathrooms. *Amenities* garden, dinner dance (Sat September–April, nightly during December).

Rooms 31	*Room phone* Yes	*Confirm by* 6	*Parking* Ample
with bath/shower 24	*Room TV* Yes	*Last dinner* 9.45	*Banquets* 70/20

Dartmouth
Map 3 D3 Devon
2 South Embankment *TQ6 9BB*
Dartmouth (080 43) 2465
Proprietors Tom Jaine &
Joyce Molyneux

● **Set L** Sun only £12
Set D from £11·50
About £38 for two
Banquets 15/–

Carved Angel ★ 

Joyce Molyneux is the guiding light of this delightful waterfront restaurant with its bustling open-plan kitchen, and everything she does bears the mark of a truly dedicated cook. Regularly changing menus take full advantage of local seafood and seasonal produce, and there's a deceptive simplicity about many of the dishes. Ragout of lobster and turbot with a subtle and delicately flavoured lobster sauce, and plump roast quail with grapes and brandy show Joyce's talents at their best, while julienne of carrots in cider sauce is typical of her imaginative way with vegetables.
Specialities Provençal fish soup, Dartmouth pie, salmon in pastry with ginger and currants. ♟*OUTSTANDING.*

Lunch *12.30–1.45* Dinner *7.30–10, Sat 6.30–10*
Closed *L Mon, D Sun, Bank Hols except Good Fri, 4 days Christmas & Jan*

Dartmouth
Map 3 D3 Devon
11 The Quay *TQ6 9PS*
Dartmouth (080 43) 2397

Credit Access, Amex,
Barclaycard, Diners

Rooms 20
with bath/shower 9

Royal Castle Hotel   55%   £ D/E

This delightful quayside hostelry is full of historical interest and old-world charm: timbers from wrecked Armada ships are said to have been used in the Galleon Bar, and throughout the public rooms assorted period pieces provide reminders of its colourful past. Compact bedrooms (one with a four-poster) are traditionally decorated and furnished; all have TV, radios and tea/coffee-makers.

| *Room phone* No | *Confirm by* 6.30 | *Parking* Limited |
| *Room TV* Yes | *Last dinner* 8.45 | |

Dartmouth
Map 3 D3 Devon
8 The Quay *TQ6 9DH*
Dartmouth (080 43) 2748
Proprietor Mrs Diana Taylor

● **Set D** from £7·75
About £28 for two

Taylor's

The tent-like decor may be inspired by the Arabian desert, but the menu here owes more to the proximity of the harbour. Mussels, lobster, sole and whiting are popular choices, and there are also grills, steak, kidney, mushroom and oyster pies and chicken dishes with interesting sauces such as horseradish, cream, wine and walnuts. Fresh seasonal produce is capably prepared. *Credit* Access, Amex, Barclaycard, Diners

Lunch 12–2 *Dinner* 7–10.30
Closed Tues, 1 January, 25 & 26 December & mid January–mid February

Dedham
Map 6 C3 Essex
Near Colchester *CO7 6HW*
Colchester (0206) 322273

Credit Access, Amex,
Barclaycard, Diners

Rooms 6
with bath/shower 6

Dedham Vale Hotel   69%   £ C/D

A major programme of improvements has completely transformed this charming early 19th-century house in Constable country. Bedrooms in particular have benefited, and their beautiful summery decor shows great attention to detail. Bathrooms are gleaming white. Public rooms include a peaceful, traditional lounge and a bar featuring hand-painted Chinese wallpaper. No dogs. *Amenities* garden.

| *Room phone* Yes | *Confirm by* By arrang. | *Parking* Ample |
| *Room TV* Yes | *Last dinner* 10 | *Banquets* 100/– |

Dedham
Map 6 C3 Essex
Near Colchester *CO7 6HW*
Colchester (0206) 322273

About £27 for two

Dedham Vale Hotel, Terrace Restaurant   

It's summer all year round at this enchantingly lovely glass-roofed restaurant, with its fresh decor and garden views. Simplicity is the keynote of the menu, which features excellent spit roasts, charcoal grills and steak tartare, tasty soups and pâtés, and a selection of tempting sweets. Enjoyable, down-to-earth cooking by Terry Barber, and charming waitress service. ♟*SUPERIOR. Credit* Access, Amex, Barclaycard, Diners

Lunch Sun only 12.30–2 *Dinner* 7–10

Dedham

Map 6 C3 Essex
Stratford Road
Near Colchester *CO7 6HN*
Colchester (0206) 322367
Proprietor G. M. W. Milsom
Rooms 10
with bath/shower 10
Room phone Yes
Room TV Yes
Confirm by By arrang.
Last dinner 9
Parking Ample

Credit Access, Amex,
Barclaycard, Diners

Maison Talbooth 79% Ⓜ £C

There's a thoroughly English air to this solid Victorian mansion in the heart of Constable country. Two lounges overlooking the lawns have heavy tweed sofas, carved fireplaces and even a grand piano to complete the picture of traditional elegance. Bedrooms are individually decorated, with bold colour schemes, luxurious matching soft furnishings and well-chosen period furniture in keeping with the rest of the hotel; each room is provided with a mini-bar as well as welcoming fresh fruit and flowers. Bathrooms are palatial with stylish modern suites. Breakfast is served in your room, and Le Talbooth restaurant is a short walk away. No dogs.
Amenities garden, tennis.

Dedham

Map 6 C3 Essex
Gun Hill
Near Colchester *CO7 6HP*
Colchester (0206) 323150
Proprietor G. M. W. Milsom

● Set L £9·25
About £46 for two

Le Talbooth ★

Set on the banks of the river Stour, this beguiling half-timbered restaurant makes a fine traditional setting for Sam Chalmers' robust and very skilful cooking. He uses superb ingredients and gives his dishes a distinctive, forthright flavour: chicken liver and mushroom stew is full of natural goodness, Finnan haddock soufflé (a speciality) is both featherlight and rich, and casserole of calf's sweetbreads and kidneys with a dark Madeira sauce is deliciously mellow. Sweets such as Grand Marnier parfait end the meal in appropriate style. **Specialities** game and oysters in season, soufflé Talbooth, breast of duckling in green pepper sauce, brandy snaps.
🍷 *OUTSTANDING. Credit* Access, Amex, Barclaycard, Diners

Lunch 12.30–2 *Dinner* 7–9
Closed D 25 December

Denton

Map 10 B2 Greater Manchester
Meadow Lane
Haughton Green *M34 1GD*
061–336 7516
Telex 668615
Proprietors
Challenor-Chadwick family

Old Rectory Hotel 61% Ⓜ £E

Check directions when booking at this friendly, family-run hotel, which stands in a quiet, tree-lined cul-de-sac. There's a neat reception hall, a restful panelled cocktail bar, and a pleasant first-floor residents' lounge furnished in traditional style. Well-designed bedrooms have smart fitted units, tea-makers and fridges. Modern tiled bathrooms with bidets. No dogs.
Amenities garden. **Closed** 25–30 December & Bank Holidays

Rooms 26	*Room phone* Yes	*Confirm by* By arrang.	*Parking* Ample
with bath/shower 26	*Room TV* Yes	*Last dinner* 9	*Banquets* 70/10

Any person using our name to obtain free hospitality is a fraud. Proprietors, please inform the police and us.

Derby

Map 10 C3 Derbyshire
119 London Road *DE1 2QR*
Derby (0332) 40633

Manager Mrs Bridge

Closed Christmas week

Gables Hotel 53% £F

This red-brick Victorian hotel is a popular place offering modest comfort and straightforward facilities. There's no bar, but drinks can be enjoyed round the fire in the comfortably furnished lounge. Bedrooms—mostly in a wing at the back of the original building—are neatly fitted with functional wooden units. Bathrooms are simply equipped and well maintained.

Rooms 60	*Room phone* No	*Confirm by* 6	*Parking* Ample
with bath/shower 17	*Room TV* No	*Last dinner* 9.45	

the new System One gas cooker.

The man at the bottom does just as nicely as the man at the top.

left don't get browned off either.

They can thank Gyroflo® for that, a unique system which not only makes heat

rise but flow down and around corners as well. In other words, everything cooks perfectly.

Something that also happens under

The first built-in gas cooker to treat all men as equals.

our unique Sola® grill. The pork chop at the end of the grill does just as well as the piggy in the middle, whatever the setting.

It's all quite simple really but no other cooker can do it.

All·this comes with the built-in elegance and style you've never seen in a gas cooker before.

So look for System One at your nearest gas showroom.

It's the only way to kiss the half-baked men in your life goodbye.

Derby

Map 10 C3 Derbyshire
Midland Road *DE1 2SQ*
Derby (0332) 45894

Credit Access, Amex,
Barclaycard, Diners

Rooms 63
with bath/shower 26

Midland Hotel   64%   £E

Visitors to this sturdy red-brick hotel by the railway station will be pleasantly surprised to find that it has a delightful little walled garden. Lofty, spacious public areas include a long reception hall stretching almost the entire length of the building, plus a large bar and a lounge, both in contemporary style. Warm, cosy bedrooms have traditional furnishings, and bathrooms are adequate. *Amenities* garden, putting.

Room phone Yes	*Confirm by* 6	*Parking* Limited
Room TV Yes	*Last dinner* 9	*Banquets* 180/10

Diss

Map 6 C2 Norfolk
84 Victoria Road *IP22 3JG*
Diss (0379) 4738

● **Set D** £12
About £32 for two
Banquets 14/6

Salisbury House

An artist's eye has created a stunning overall effect with a perfect blend of antique and modern artefacts (including a superb collection of fans) in this most elegant *restaurant avec chambres*. Eye appeal is important to the chef, too, whose set dinner menu offers an inventive selection of generally well-prepared, beautifully presented dishes—perhaps avocado terrine and then soup, followed by sole goujons with mussels, julienne of carrots and a fine creamy sauce. Vegetables are especially interesting, and sweets enjoyable. Lunchtime bookings can be arranged in advance for parties of six or more. Three delightfully appointed bedrooms offer comfortable, civilised accommodation.

Dinner only 7.30–9.30
Closed Sun, Mon & 1 week Christmas

Our inspectors are our full-time employees; they are professionally trained by us.

Ditton Priors

Map 10 B4 Shropshire
Near Bridgnorth *WV16 6SQ*
Ditton Priors (074 634) 200
Proprietors
Mr & Mrs R. P. H. Marsh

● **Set L** £6 **Set D** £10
About £28 for two
Banquets 35/10

Howard Arms Hotel Restaurant

Excellent country cooking, good presentation and a friendly atmosphere add up to very enjoyable meals at the Marshs' welcoming restaurant set in a 14th-century stone building. Standards are consistent throughout, from plump moules au gratin or galantine of pork as starters, to beef goulash, richly sauced wild duck and homely sweets like fruit trifle or creamy chocolate mousse. Traditional roast for Sunday lunch. *SUPERIOR.*

Lunch Sun only 12–1.45 *Dinner* 7.15–9.30
Closed D Sun, all Mon & 4 weeks late August–September

Stars in this Guide stand for the quality of the cooking only— our overriding criterion, irrespective of price, luxury or service.

Doncaster

Map 11 D2 South Yorkshire
Bennetthorpe *DN2 6AD*
Doncaster (0302) 61371

Credit Access, Amex,
Barclaycard, Diners

Rooms 57
with bath/shower 57

Earl of Doncaster Hotel   57%   £D/E

Friendly staff make guests instantly welcome at this modernised 1920s-style hotel just over half a mile from the famous racecourse. Accommodation is simple and comfortable, with the popular restaurant bar doubling as a lounge. Double-glazed, well-kept bedrooms have fitted units, tea-makers, and compact tiled bathrooms. The hotel has a ballroom and a range of conference rooms.

Room phone Yes	*Confirm by* 6	*Parking* Ample
Room TV Yes	*Last dinner* 10	*Banquets* 270/–

Doncaster
Map 11 D2 South Yorkshire
Bawtry Road
Bessacarr *DN4 7BS*
Doncaster (0302) 535235

Credit Access, Amex,
Barclaycard, Diners

Rooms 25
with bath/shower 15

Punch's Hotel   60%   £E

Designed to resemble the head of Mr Punch from the air, this '30s hotel has benefited from recent refurbishment. The spacious open-plan foyer-lounge has comfortable fireside chairs and settees, and there are two attractive bars. Bedrooms have lightwood units, nicely matched soft furnishings and tea-makers. Private bathrooms have modern white suites, whereas public ones are more old-fashioned. *Amenities* garden.

Room phone Yes   *Confirm by* 6   *Parking* Ample
Room TV Yes   *Last dinner* 9.15   *Banquets* 90/–

Donyatt
Map 3 E2 Somerset
Near Ilminster *TA19 0RG*
Ilminster (046 05) 3210
Proprietors
Pamela & Michael Smith

● **Set L** £6·50 **Set D** £7
About £21 for two
Banquets 30/25

Thatcher's Pond

A lovingly converted thatched farmhouse makes a delightful setting for Pamela and Michael Smith's sumptuous cold buffet. You'll find it hard to choose from dressed lobster and crab, fresh salmon with home-made mayonnaise, succulent rare roast beef, and an impressive array of crisp, colourful salads. The sweet trolley, with Pamela's own Pavlovas, soufflés, trifles and gâteaux, is equally irresistible.

Lunch 12–2 *Dinner* 7 for 7.30 & 8.30 for 9
Closed D Sun, all Mon & 25 December–1 February

Dorchester
Map 4 B4 Dorset
30 High East Street
DT1 1HF
Dorchester (0305) 65353
Manager Mr R. A. Charlton
Credit Access, Amex,
Barclaycard

Rooms 27
with bath/shower 21

King's Arms   56%   £E

Thomas Hardy set parts of his novel *The Mayor of Casterbridge* in this fine old town-centre coaching inn. Nowadays there are two bars with panelled walls, as well as two large lounges on the first floor. Well-appointed bedrooms (including one with a four-poster) have good fitted units, pretty fabrics and tea-making facilities. Most have large bright bathrooms. Helpful staff. *Amenities* solarium.

Room phone Yes   *Confirm by* 10   *Parking* Limited
Room TV Yes   *Last dinner* 8.30   *Banquets* 75/6

Dorking
Map 5 E3 Surrey
Burford Bridge *RH5 6BX*
Dorking (0306) 884561
Telex 859507

Rooms 52
with bath/shower 52
Room phone Yes
Room TV Yes
Confirm by 6
Last dinner 9.30
Parking Ample
Banquets 200/–

Credit Access, Amex,
Barclaycard, Diners

Burford Bridge Hotel   70%   £C

This rambling black and white hotel in the shadow of Box Hill offers high standards of comfort and service. Public areas are informal and relaxing, with luxurious sofas and fine antiques. Bedrooms in a new wing have tasteful modern fittings and sun terraces overlooking the delightful garden; other rooms are more traditional. Bathrooms throughout are modern, compact and well equipped. *Amenities* garden, outdoor swimming pool.

Dorking
Map 5 E3 Surrey
Reigate Road *RH4 1QB*
Dorking (0306) 889335
Telex 858875

Credit Access, Amex,
Barclaycard, Diners

Rooms 29
with bath/shower 29

Punch Bowl Hotel   55%   £D/E

Situated at the foot of Box Hill just outside Dorking, this useful hotel is based around a modernised stone building containing a contemporary cocktail bar-cum-residents' lounge and a homely pub-style bar. Good-sized bedrooms in a separate two-storey block are cheerfully decorated. Bathrooms (no showers) are partly tiled and have plenty of shelf space. *Amenities* garden.

Room phone Yes   *Confirm by* 6   *Parking* Ample
Room TV Yes   *Last dinner* 9.15   *Banquets* 70/15

Dorking
Map 5 E3 Surrey
Hig' Street *RH4 1BE*
Dorking (0306) 881138

Credit Access, Amex,
Barclaycard, Diners

Rooms 70
with bath/shower 70

White Horse Hotel   58%   £ D

Parts of this former coaching inn date back to 1500, and its charm has been well preserved through careful modernisation. There's a cosy beamed cocktail bar and a lounge with a welcoming fire. Cheerful bedrooms vary considerably from simple ones in the original building to purpose-built studio rooms, and bathrooms are adequate.
Amenities outdoor swimming pool, 24-hour laundry service (Mon–Fri).

Room phone Yes	*Confirm by* 6	*Parking* Ample
Room TV Yes	*Last dinner* 9.30	*Banquets* 40/–

Dovedale
Map 10 C3 Derbyshire
Near Ashbourne *DE6 2AY*
Thorpe Cloud (033 529) 261

Credit Access, Amex,
Barclaycard, Diners

Rooms 27
with bath/shower 26

Izaak Walton Hotel   59%   £ D/E

Izaak Walton, the 'Compleat Angler' himself, was a visitor to this converted farmhouse in the 17th century, and arrangements can be made for today's fishermen to enjoy their sport on the nearby river Dove. There are three comfortable lounges and a rustic bar with carved oak settles. Bedrooms range from lovely old beamed rooms to more modern ones with fitted units. Simple, up-to-date bathrooms. *Amenities* garden, dinner dance (Sat). &

Room phone Yes	*Confirm by* By arrang.	*Parking* Ample
Room TV Yes	*Last dinner* 9.30	

Dovedale
Map 10 C3 Derbyshire
Thorpe
Near Ashbourne *DE6 2AW*
Thorpe Cloud (033 529) 333

Credit Access, Amex,
Barclaycard, Diners

Rooms 41
with bath/shower 41

Peveril of the Peak Hotel   60%   £ D

Tactful modernisation, with well-grouped extensions, has transformed a rambling old rectory set in delightful gardens into a most attractive hotel. Warm, cheerful public rooms include the cosy Peveril Bar with its tweedy decor. Bright bedrooms, furnished with pine or darkwood units, have compact modern bathrooms.
Amenities garden, tennis.

Room phone Yes	*Confirm by* 6	*Parking* Ample
Room TV Yes	*Last dinner* 9.30	*Banquets* 200/–

We welcome complaints and bona fide recommendations on the tear-out pages for readers' comments. They are followed up by our professional team. Please also complain to the management instantly.

Dover
Map 7 D5 Kent
Townwall Street *CT16 1SZ*
Dover (0304) 203270
Telex 96458

Rooms 83
with bath/shower 83
Room phone Yes
Room TV Yes
Confirm by 6
Last dinner 10.30
Parking Ample
Banquets 120/10

Credit Access, Amex,
Barclaycard, Diners

Holiday Inn   72%   *E*   £ C/D

Standards continue to improve at this modern executive hotel thanks to a programme of refurbishment backed up by good maintenance. There's a very comfortable, traditionally furnished bar with burgundy-coloured decor adjoining the sumptuous lounge with its chesterfields and leather wing chairs. Bedrooms (including some with king-size beds) are very well equipped with everything from alarm clocks to mini-bars. Bathrooms are rather functional, but sensibly planned and nicely fitted. Staff are friendly and helpful.
Amenities indoor swimming pool, in-house movies, keep-fit equipment. &

Dover
Map 7 D5 Kent
Seafront *CT17 9BW*
Dover (0304) 203633
Telex 965422
Manager Mrs Pamela Gibbons
Credit Access, Amex,
Barclaycard, Diners

Rooms 63
with bath/shower 27

White Cliffs Hotel   57%   £E

There are fine views of the harbour from the sun lounge of this attractive and spotlessly clean seafront hotel. Public areas also include a small foyer, two lounges (one with TV) and a well-carpeted bar. Bedrooms vary in size and furnishings (the largest have comfortable armchairs) but all offer adequate facilities; those with private bathrooms have TV. Friendly, helpful staff.

Room phone Yes	*Confirm by* 7	*Parking* Ample
Room TV Some	*Last dinner* 9.30	*Banquets* 75/6

Droitwich
Map 4 B1 Hereford & Worcester
WR9 0BN
Droitwich (0905) 774411
Telex 336673
Proprietor Mr. Z. S. Raguz
Rooms 68
with bath/shower 68
Room phone Yes
Room TV Yes
Confirm by By arrang.
Last dinner 10.30
Parking Ample
Banquets 300/12
Closed for accommodation
25 & 26 December
Credit Access, Amex,
Barclaycard, Diners

Château Impney Hotel   76%   *E*      £C

This impressive Victorian building, standing in parkland near the M5, was the brainchild of engineer John Corbett, who designed it in the style of a French château. Converted to a hotel, it offers high standards of comfort and elegance, as well as excellent banqueting and conference facilities. Handsome marble pillars are a feature of the well-maintained public areas, and the lofty hallway has a magnificent staircase and some fine stained glass. Traditionally furnished bedrooms are spacious and comfortable, especially the first-floor ones, some of which have balconies and sitting areas. Modern rooms in a wing are smaller; all have well-fitted bathrooms. *Amenities* garden, sauna, tennis, coarse fishing, dancing (Sat), solarium.

Droitwich
Map 4 B1 Hereford & Worcester
St Andrews Road *WR9 8DU*
Droitwich (0905) 772224

Credit Access, Amex,
Barclaycard, Diners

Rooms 55
with bath/shower 55

Raven Hotel   59%   £D

Continuing improvements and helpful staff add to the pleasure of staying at this historic timbered hotel, whose oak-panelled reception hall once formed part of the Old Manor of Wyche. Other public rooms include a beamed bar, a relaxing lounge bar and several banqueting rooms. Bedrooms offer simple modern comforts. Guests may use the facilities of nearby Château Impney. *Amenities* dancing (3 Sats per month), 24-hour laundry service.

Room phone Yes	*Confirm by* By arrang.	*Parking* Ample
Room TV Yes	*Last dinner* 10	*Banquets* 230/–

Dulverton
Map 3 D2 Somerset
TA22 9AE
Dulverton (0398) 23302
Proprietor Mrs T. Jones

Closed Christmas

Rooms 27
with bath/shower 16

Carnarvon Arms Hotel   58%      £E/F

Guests return year after year to enjoy the peace and quiet of this friendly creeper-clad hotel and its wide range of sporting activities. The lounges are ideal places for relaxing, and there are two cheerful bars. Individually furnished bedrooms have pretty decor; bathrooms are bright and spacious. *Amenities* garden, outdoor swimming pool, game fishing, billiards, games room, clay-pigeon shooting, stables, hairdressing, fishing tuition.

Room phone No	*Confirm by* By arrang.	*Parking* Ample
Room TV No	*Last dinner* 8.30	*Banquets* 70/–

Dulwich

Pyramid

See under London

Dunchurch
Map 11 D4 Warwickshire
The Green
Near Rugby *CV22 6NJ*
Rugby (0788) 810233
Telex 312242
Credit Access, Amex,
Barclaycard, Diners

Dun Cow Hotel *(Inn)*   Ⓜ   £D/E

Standing at a busy crossroads in the middle of the village, this friendly, black-and-white-fronted hotel retains much of the character and charm of its days as an important coaching inn. Oak beams, wood panelling and gleaming brassware are features of the two bars and lounge, and bedrooms are furnished with fine, solid antiques. Most have their own neat, modern bathrooms. *Amenities* garden, coarse fishing.

                    Continued

Continued
Rooms 20
with bath/shower 15   *Room phone* No   *Confirm by* 6   *Parking* Ample
   Room TV Yes   *Last dinner* 10.30   *Banquets* 220/6

Dunkirk
Map 4 B2 Avon
Near Badminton *GL9 1AF*
Didmarton (045 423) 361

Credit Access, Amex,
Barclaycard, Diners

Petty France Hotel   63%   £ D

This charming 18th-century house stands beside the A46 in pleasant grounds complete with an ornamental pond. The long lounge, with plenty of comfortable chairs, is a peaceful, relaxing room and the bar features a collection of antique corkscrews. Spacious, traditionally furnished bedrooms in the main house and neatly converted, modern ones in the stable block are fresh and bright. *Amenities* garden, croquet.

Rooms 16
with bath/shower 16   *Room phone* Yes   *Confirm by* 6   *Parking* Ample
   Room TV Yes   *Last dinner* 9.45   *Banquets* 60/–

Dunstable
Map 5 E1 Bedfordshire
Church Street *LU5 4RT*
Dunstable (0582) 62201
Manager Rico Saccoccio
Credit Access, Amex,
Barclaycard, Diners
Closed 26 December

Old Palace Lodge Hotel   55%   £ E

Echoes of an illustrious past linger on in the fine panelled entrance hall of this spotlessly clean, creeper-clad hotel. Elsewhere, the bright little bar and the delightful lounge with its inviting armchairs and log fire offer genuine warmth and comfort. Bedrooms vary from compact and modern to more spacious older rooms with beams and antique furniture. Adequate bathrooms. No dogs. *Amenities* garden.

Rooms 18
with bath/shower 18   *Room phone* Yes   *Confirm by* noon   *Parking* Ample
   Room TV No   *Last dinner* 10   *Banquets* 20/–

Dunster
Map 3 E1 Somerset
High Street
Near Minehead *TA24 6SG*
Dunster (064 382) 555
Managers Mr & Mrs R. A. Mann
Credit Access, Amex,
Barclaycard, Diners

Luttrell Arms Hotel   59%   Ⓜ   £ D

Modern comforts blend invitingly with historic atmosphere in this mellow stone building. Impressive public rooms include a Gothic beamed bar with a huge fireplace, and a lofty lounge furnished with comfortable antiques. Attractively decorated bedrooms are neat and cheerful; many have well-designed modern units, while the best period ones with four-posters are luxuriously appointed. *Amenities* garden.

Rooms 21
with bath/shower 21   *Room phone* Yes   *Confirm by* 6   *Parking* Limited
   Room TV Yes   *Last dinner* 9   *Banquets* 60/–

Durham
Map 15 B4 Co. Durham
Carville *DH1 1TD*
Durham (0385) 65282

Credit Access, Amex,
Barclaycard, Diners

Ramside Hall Hotel   57%   £ E

Towers and battlements lend a touch of bravura to this Victorian pile which stands in 80 acres of parkland three miles north-east of the city on the A690. The lofty public rooms include a vast bar that's a favourite haunt of local revellers. Bedrooms have simple traditional furnishings; those without private bathrooms have shower cubicles.
Amenities garden, dancing (Wed–Sat).

Rooms 11
with bath/shower 5   *Room phone* Yes   *Confirm by* By arrang.   *Parking* Ample
   Room TV Yes   *Last dinner* 9.30   *Banquets* 300/–

Durham
Map 15 B4 Co. Durham
Old Elvet *DH1 3JN*
Durham (0385) 66821
Telex 538238
Manager Mr B. F. Hawley
Credit Access, Amex,
Barclaycard, Diners

Royal County Hotel   67%   £ D/E

Parts of this city-centre hotel date back several hundred years, although it now bears all the hallmarks of tasteful modernisation with only a few features to remind one of its past. Public areas include a comfortable, open-plan foyer-lounge and a split-level bar. Bedrooms are attractively fitted in functional style and have spotlessly clean bathrooms. *Amenities* sauna, hairdressing, coffee shop (10am–8pm, Sun 10am–5.30pm).   ♿

Rooms 120
with bath/shower 120   *Room phone* Yes   *Confirm by* 6   *Parking* Ample
   Room TV Yes   *Last dinner* 10.15   *Banquets* 120/–

Durham

Map 15 B4 Co. Durham
72 Claypath *DH1 1QT*
Durham (0385) 65370

About £30 for two

Travellers Rest   Ⓢ

This charming restaurant above a quaint little pub makes a nice cottage setting for an enjoyable dinner. The short, regularly changed menu shows enterprising use of fresh ingredients, with dishes ranging from game pâté and quiche to hearty Pickwick pie (beef, kidney, oysters and Guinness) and tastily sauced chicken breast sautéed in butter. *ABOVE AVERAGE.*
Credit Access, Amex, Barclaycard, Diners

Dinner only 7.30–9.30
Closed Sun & Bank Holidays

Dursley

Map 4 B2 Gloucestershire
Stinchcombe *GL11 6BQ*
Dursley (0453) 2538
Proprietors Mrs P. Spyvee &
Mr Colin Russell
Credit Access, Amex,
Barclaycard, Diners

Rooms 16
with bath/shower 16

Stinchcombe Manor   64%   Ⓜ   £E

This handsome late-Georgian manor house stands in a quiet village west of Dursley. There are splendid views from the public rooms, which include an inviting cocktail bar and a relaxing lounge dotted with antiques. Thoughtfully equipped bedrooms range from traditional (a few four-posters) to more modern in style. Well-fitted bathrooms throughout. *Amenities* garden, outdoor swimming pool, tennis, dinner dance (Fri, Sat), croquet, putting.

Room phone Yes	*Confirm by* By arrang.
Room TV Yes	*Last dinner* 9

Parking Ample
Banquets 100/–

Ealing

Carnarvon Hotel, Gino's & New Leaf Restaurant

See under London and London Economy Evening Meals

Earl Stonham

Map 6 C3 Suffolk
Near Stowmarket *IP14 5DW*
Stonham (044 971) 206

● **Set L** £7·25 **Set D** £10·95
About £31 for two

Mr Underhill's   ♿ Ⓢ

Tolkien experts will recognise the name of this charming little restaurant on the A140, south of the A1120 junction. Christopher Bradley is an accomplished young chef with a leaning towards nouvelle cuisine. His set menus offer little choice, but an imaginative soup, perfectly cooked vegetables and a crisp salad accompany, say, a steak and oyster pie or king prawns in pastry. Booking essential. *ABOVE AVERAGE. Credit* Diners

Lunch 12–1.45, Sun 12–2 *Dinner* 7.30–9.45
Closed L Sat, D Sun, all Mon, 1 January & Good Friday

East Dereham

Map 6 C1 Norfolk
Church Street *NR19 1DL*
Dereham (0362) 2276

Manager Mr Tim Ireson
Credit Access, Amex,
Barclaycard, Diners

Rooms 28
with bath/shower 17

Phoenix Hotel   56%   £D/E

Built in 1966, this plain red-brick hotel has a cheerful, welcoming interior. Open-plan public areas include two bars, one a popular local meeting place; a modern ballroom adjoins the rear of the hotel. Bedrooms are bright and neatly furnished, all with radios and tea-makers. Simple bathrooms are adequately fitted.
Amenities dinner dance (Sat September–April).

Room phone Yes	*Confirm by* 6
Room TV Yes	*Last dinner* 9

Parking Ample
Banquets 50/–

East Grinstead

Map 7 B5 West Sussex
RH19 4LJ
Sharpthorne (0342) 810567
Telex 957239
Proprietor Mr Peter Herbert
Rooms 14
with bath/shower 14
Room phone Yes
Room TV Yes
Confirm by By arrang.
Last dinner 9.30
Parking Ample
Banquets 16/10

Gravetye Manor   80%   Ⓜ   £C

This glorious 16th-century manor house is surrounded by magnificent gardens laid out by the famous gardener William Robinson, who lived here for more than 50 years. Inside, the house is marvellously preserved, with polished wood floors, superb panelling and fine plaster ceilings helping to create a richly historic atmosphere in this wonderfully peaceful country retreat. Most of the individually decorated bedrooms have views of the gardens through

Continued

mullioned windows as well as light modern-style furnishings, but three have retained their sturdy traditional character. Bathrooms are luxuriously equipped. To reach the hotel, which is set in extensive wooded grounds, take the West Hoathly road off the B2110 between East Grinstead and Turners Hill. No children under seven. No dogs.
Amenities garden, game fishing, clock golf, croquet.

East Grinstead
Map 7 B5 West Sussex
West Hoathly *RH194LJ*
Sharpthorne (0342) 810567
Proprietor Mr Peter Herbert

About £50 for two

Gravetye Manor Restaurant ★ ★   ⑤

Dining in this panelled restaurant is a sublime experience, offering the perfect combination of opulence, considerate service and unforgettable food. Chef Allan Garth is continuing where his predecessor Michael Quinn left off, cooking with brilliant flair and producing exquisite dishes like tender scallops in a perfectly judged leek and saffron sauce, and suprême of guinea fowl, its superb wild mushroom sauce garnished with a mousse of sweetbreads. The marvellous assortment of delicate green vegetables is beyond criticism, while sweets such as marquise au champagne or strawberries perfumed with tarragon are pure inspiration. **Specialities** parfait de foie de volaille, salmon trout Beaulieu, entrecôte Inez, crêpe Kircher. 🍷*OUTSTANDING.*

Lunch *12.30–2* Dinner *7.30–9.30*

East Grinstead
Map 7 B5 West Sussex
London Road *RH192BH*
East Grinstead (0342) 26992
Telex 95156
Manager Clive Tee
Credit Access, Amex,
Barclaycard, Diners

Rooms 50
with bath/shower 50

YE OLDE FELBRIDGE HOTEL £E

This mock-Tudor hotel, still undergoing renovation after a fire, has a well-equipped country club and a glittering space-age disco bar in the former ballroom, popular with the young. Bedrooms in separate blocks have smart fitted units and streamlined bathrooms. *Amenities* garden, sauna, indoor & outdoor swimming pools, discothèque (Thurs–Sat), roller discothèque (Mon, Tues, Fri, Sat), gymnasium, beauty salon, snooker, in-house movies. ♿

Room phone Yes	*Confirm by* 6	*Parking* Ample
Room TV Yes	*Last dinner* 10	*Banquets* 120/–

East Horsley
Map 5 E3 Surrey
Epsom Road *KT246TB*
East Horsley (048 65) 4291

French cooking

● Set D £7
About £30 for two

Thatchers Hotel Restaurant  ⑤

John Mann displays skill and enterprise with his interesting menu at this elegant beamed restaurant. Dishes like grilled entrecôte steak and delicately sauced chicken breast stuffed with Parma ham and Brie are most attractively presented, vegetables are well handled and there are some delicious sweets to finish. Friendly service. Cold buffet only on Sunday evening.
Credit Access, Amex, Barclaycard, Diners

Lunch 12.30–2 *Dinner* 7.30–9.30, Sat 7.30–10, Sun 7.30–9

East Molesey
Map 5 E2 Surrey
107 Walton Road *KT80DR*
01–979 7150
Proprietors
Messrs L. & C. Dioli
French cooking

Set L £4·50
About £34 for two
Banquets 40/–

Le Chien Qui Fume 🍴 ⑤

Although two Italian brothers run this attractive restaurant, the menu is as unmistakably Gallic as the name. Alongside pâté, frogs' legs and escargots you'll find beautifully sauced meat dishes, flavoursome seasonal mussels, shellfish and game, and excellent vegetables–crisp, plentiful and piping hot. Presentation, too, is first class, and service pleasant. 🍷*ABOVE AVERAGE.*
Credit Access, Amex, Barclaycard, Diners ♿

Lunch 12–2 *Dinner* 7.30–11
Closed L Sat, all Sun & Bank Holidays

East Molesey
Map 5 E2 Surrey
20 Bridge Road *KT89HA*
01–979 1531
Proprietors Mr & Mrs P. Morphew
French cooking

Lantern 🍴 ⑤

A warm and welcoming restaurant, with attractive decor, friendly staff and Peter Morphew's excellent choice of familiar French dishes. After a simple, tasty starter–perhaps pâté de campagne or soupe à l'oignon gratinée–you could go on to entrecôte with three butters (mustard, parsley and anchovy) or tender breast of chicken served with a tarragon-flavoured cream sauce and nice fresh vegetables. *Credit* Access, Amex, Barclaycard, Diners

Continued

● **Set D** £10·35
About £30 for two

Dinner only 7–11
Closed Sun, Easter, August & Christmas week

East Molesey
Map 5 E2 Surrey
160 Walton Road *KT8 0HP*
01–979 5072
Indian cooking

About £19 for two

New Anarkali 

A pleasantly decorated modern restaurant, offering a standard Indian menu (from nan and dahl soup to prawn biryani) with some tasty tandoori specialities. Recommended both for the excellent cooking and the polite, efficient service. *Credit* Access, Amex, Barclaycard, Diners *Lunch* 12–2.30 *Dinner* 6–11.15 **Closed** 25 & 26 December ● **Set L & Set D** from £4·95

East Molesey
Map 5 E2 Surrey
57 Bridge Road *KT8 9ER*
01–979 5490
Proprietors Mr Tony Dimichele & Mr Adolfo Fiore
Italian cooking

● **Set L** £5·25
About £29 for two
Banquets 100/80

Vecchia Roma

A ceramic-tiled floor and murals of ancient Rome help to create the atmosphere in this modern restaurant offering a wide choice of authentic Italian fare. Enjoyable home-made pasta, veal and chicken dishes are supplemented by daily specialities like sea bass baked with Pernod and garlic; vegetables are expertly handled and there are some gorgeous sweets. *Credit* Access, Amex, Barclaycard, Diners

---

Lunch 12–2.15, Sun 12–2.30 *Dinner* 7–11
Closed L Sat

East Stoke
Map 4 B4 Dorset
Near Wareham *BH20 6AL*
Bindon Abbey (0929) 462563

Credit Access, Amex, Barclaycard, Diners
Closed 4 days Christmas

Rooms 8
with bath/shower 5

Kemps Country House Hotel   61%   Ⓜ   £ F

There are pleasant views of the Purbeck Hills from this homely little hotel. Public rooms leading off the informal hallway include a spacious bar-lounge with a mixture of traditional and contemporary furniture and a small TV lounge. Spotlessly clean bedrooms have modern freestanding units, pretty fabrics and tea-makers. There are also several self-contained suites in the converted coach house. No dogs.

| *Room phone* No | *Confirm by* By arrang. | *Parking* Ample |
| *Room TV* No | *Last dinner* 10.30 | *Banquets* 30/10 |

East Stoke
Map 4 B4 Dorset
Near Wareham *BH20 6AL*
Bindon Abbey (0929) 462563

● **Set D** £8·50
About £23 for two

Kemps Country House Hotel Restaurant

Homely surroundings, friendly service and capable cooking make it a real pleasure to dine in this attractive, candlelit restaurant. The short set menu changes frequently and offers interesting starters such as creamy green pepper soup or baked egg lorraine, and splendid sweets might include tasty lemon mousse, delicate Paris-Brest or rich chocolate brandy flan. *Credit* Access, Amex, Barclaycard, Diners

Dinner only 7–10.30
Closed Sun & Mon to non-residents, Bank Holidays & 4 days Christmas

---

We do not necessarily recommend the cooking at hotels whose restaurants are not separately listed.

Eastbourne
Map 7 B6 East Sussex
Grand Parade *BN21 3YN*
Eastbourne (0323) 22724
Telex 87591

Credit Access, Amex, Barclaycard

Rooms 135
with bath/shower 125

Burlington Hotel   65%   £ D/E

Refurbishment continues at this elegant, white-painted seafront hotel. The ornate plasterwork and sober decor of the open-plan foyer-lounge contrasts with the modern style of the two bars. Bedrooms have functional fitted units, plenty of storage space and tea-makers; most have smart, prettily decorated bathrooms. Extensive conference facilities. *Amenities* dancing (Wed, Sat), games room, laundry room.

| *Room phone* Yes | *Confirm by* 7 | *Parking* Limited |
| *Room TV* Yes | *Last dinner* 9 | *Banquets* 200/– |

Eastbourne   Byrons

Map 7 B6 East Sussex
6 Crown Street, Old Town
BN21 1NX
Eastbourne (0323) 20171
Proprietors Mr & Mrs S. Scrutton
About £28 for two

Simon Scrutton offers a simple dinner menu of tasty French regional dishes like lamb cooked with garlic and herbs in this cosy, informal bistro. Light lunches too. *Credit* Amex, Barclaycard
Lunch 12.30–2 *Dinner* 7.30–10.30
Closed L Sat, all Sun, Bank Holidays, Christmas & Easter *Banquets* 16/8

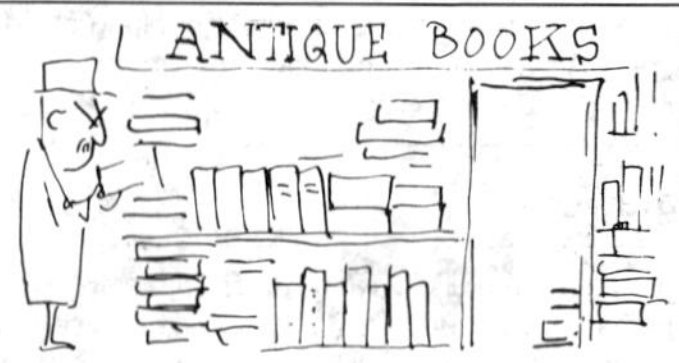

We publish annually, so make sure you use the current edition. It's worth it!

Eastbourne   Cavendish Hotel   76%   £ C

Map 7 B6 East Sussex
Grand Parade *BN21 4DH*
Eastbourne (0323) 27401
Telex 87579
Manager Mr Rodney Phelps
Rooms 115
with bath/shower 115
Room phone Yes
Room TV Yes
Confirm by By arrang.
Last dinner 9.30
Parking Limited
Banquets 250/2

Credit Access, Amex, Barclaycard, Diners

Partly modern, with balconies and picture windows, and partly traditional, with a gabled central tower, this impressive building is a familiar landmark on the Eastbourne seafront. Public rooms like the foyer, long sun lounge and sophisticated bar are roomy and relaxing, and extensive conference facilities make it a popular place with businessmen as well as holiday-makers. Bedrooms range from traditional in style, with freestanding furniture, to large rooms with agreeable contemporary decor and furnishings and their own balconies. Fully tiled, modern bathrooms are well equipped.
Amenities dinner dance (Sat, also Wed May–September), nanny, games room.

Eastbourne   Chatsworth Hotel   62%   Ⓜ   £ E

Map 7 B6 East Sussex
Grand Parade *BN21 3YR*
Eastbourne (0323) 30327
Proprietors
Mr & Mrs V. Benzmann

Closed January–mid March

A firm favourite with families, who return year after year, this seafront hotel offers a warm welcome, traditional comforts and friendly service. Public rooms are cosy and inviting, with soft carpeting and relaxing velvety armchairs. Bedrooms vary from large front ones with attractive white furniture and spacious, well-equipped bathrooms to smaller ones with simpler fittings and shower rooms.

Rooms 46	*Room phone* Yes	*Confirm by* By arrang.	*Parking* Difficult
with bath/shower 46	*Room TV* Yes	*Last dinner* 8	*Banquets* 70/–

Eastbourne   Eastbourne Motel   55%   £ E

Map 7 B6 East Sussex
Pevensey Bay Road *BN23 6JG*
Eastbourne (0323) 764188

Credit Access, Amex, Barclaycard, Diners

Just outside Eastbourne on the road to Pevensey Bay, this purpose-built motel with a modern and functional air offers practical overnight accommodation and a very high standard of housekeeping. Spacious public rooms, including reception hall, bar and lounge, are open plan. Well-equipped bedrooms have sensibly designed fitted furniture and adequate bathrooms (singles have shower only).

Rooms 80	*Room phone* Yes	*Confirm by* 6	*Parking* Ample
with bath/shower 80	*Room TV* Yes	*Last dinner* 9.30	*Banquets* 175/50

Eastbourne

Map 7 B6 East Sussex
King Edward's Parade *BN21 4EQ*
Eastbourne (0323) 22611
Telex 87332
Manager Mr J. Welsh
Rooms 178
with bath/shower 178
Room phone Yes
Room TV Yes
Confirm by By arrang.
Last dinner 9.30
Parking Ample
Banquets 460/2

Credit Access, Amex,
Barclaycard, Diners

Grand Hotel   80%   £ C

Approached by a sweeping drive, this vast Victorian hotel overlooking the sea is an impressive sight. The foyer is splendidly ornate, with its pillars and chandeliers, as is the intricately moulded plasterwork of the ballroom. Lounges have comfortable modern chairs and there's a smart American-style bar. Individually decorated bedrooms have good fitted furniture and attractive colour schemes, and most enjoy delightful views over the sea or garden. Bathrooms are all large and very well equipped. Dedicated staff create a most welcoming atmosphere.
Amenities garden, outdoor swimming pool, dancing (Fri, Sat), putting, snooker, games room, hairdressing.

Eastbourne

Map 7 B6 East Sussex
Grand Parade *BN21 3YS*
Eastbourne (0323) 27411

Credit Access, Amex,
Barclaycard, Diners

Rooms 103
with bath/shower 52

Mansion Hotel   59%      £ D

This impressive, white-painted Victorian building occupies a prime position right on the seafront. A traditionally furnished foyer leads to the comfortable residents' lounge and smart open-plan bar, and a sun terrace runs all the way along the front. Pleasantly appointed bedrooms, which vary considerably in size and shape, have mostly neat fitted units, and bathrooms are adequate. No dogs. *Amenities* dancing (twice weekly in summer).

| *Room phone* Yes | *Confirm by* 6 | *Parking* Difficult |
| *Room TV* Yes | *Last dinner* 8.30 | *Banquets* 150/– |

Eastbourne

Map 7 B6 East Sussex
Marine Parade *BN21 3DY*
Eastbourne (0323) 22822
Telex 877736
Manager Peter Hawley
Rooms 108
with bath/shower 108
Room phone Yes
Room TV Yes
Confirm by By arrang.
Last dinner 9
Parking Ample
Banquets 250/20

Credit Access, Amex,
Barclaycard, Diners

Queen's Hotel   71%   £ D

Old-fashioned personal service still distinguishes this grand seafront hotel, and constant maintenance has ensured that it has lost none of its Victorian splendour. Ornate plasterwork and magnificent pillars give the lounge a feeling of dignified opulence, and there's the elegant, stylishly furnished Queen's Bar in addition to the more informal Hunting Lodge Bar. Most bedrooms have sea views and are equipped with sumptuous soft furnishings and smart fitted units. Excellent bathrooms.
Amenities dancing (Wed in summer), dinner dance (Sat in summer), cabaret (Wed in summer), snooker, children's playroom with nanny (in summer), games room, laundry room, film show (Mon in summer).

Eastbourne

Map 7 B6 East Sussex
Park Gates
Chiswick Place *BN21 4BE*
Eastbourne (0323) 33056

Chinese cooking

● **Set meals** from £4
About £20 for two

Summer Palace   

The food's definitely the thing at this Chinese restaurant in a block of flats just off the seafront. Go for the Pekinese specialities, which include sole in rice wine, hot cucumber and pork soup, minced prawns with seaweed and the excellent Shangsoo duckling–beautifully tender, crisp-skinned pieces served with pancakes, spring onions and a tasty yellow bean sauce.
Credit Amex, Barclaycard, Diners

Lunch 12–2 *Dinner* 6–11, Sat 6–11.30
Closed 25 & 26 December

Eastbourne
Map 7 B6 East Sussex
King Edward's Parade *BN21 4EB*
Eastbourne (0323) 22676

Credit Access, Amex,
Barclaycard, Diners

Rooms 74			
with bath/shower 40			

Wish Tower Hotel   58%   **£ D**

The lounge has picture windows to take advantage of the views from this neatly painted hotel on a corner site overlooking the sea, and there is also a simple bar. Bedrooms vary between small ones at the back of the building which have private bathrooms, and larger ones, without bath, at the front. All are bright, cheerful and well kept.
Amenities film show (Wed in summer).

Room phone Yes	*Confirm by* 6	*Parking* Limited
Room TV Yes	*Last dinner* 8.30	*Banquets* 120/10

Eggleston
Map 15 B5 Co. Durham
Near Barnard Castle *DL12 0AH*
Teesdale (0833) 50289
Proprietors
Mr & Mrs James Dykes

● **Set L** £6·25
About £23 for two
Banquets 40/–

Three Tuns Inn   

A flagstone-floored room with heavy beams is the delightfully rustic setting for Christine Dykes' dependable home cooking. After a tasty pâté or hearty soup you could enjoy local game in season, double lamb chop with onion sauce or beautifully succulent roast duckling with a fruity orange sauce. Simple mouthwatering desserts include home-made ice cream and a smooth, creamy treacle mousse. Booking essential.   &

Lunch Sun only at 12.30 for 1 *Dinner* 7.30–9.30
Closed D Sun, all Mon & 25 December

Our inspectors never book in the name of the Egon Ronay Organisation; they disclose their identity only after paying their bills.

Egham
Map 5 E2 Surrey
Stroude Road *TW20 9UR*
Egham (0784) 33822

Manager Mr John E. Baumann
Rooms 44
with bath/shower 44
Room phone Yes
Room TV Some
Confirm by 6
Last dinner 9.30
Parking Ample
Banquets 220/8

Credit Access, Amex,
Barclaycard, Diners

Great Fosters   72%   **£ D**

Formal gardens and wooded parkland surround this splendid Tudor mansion near Virginia Water. Behind the great front door, topped with the arms of Elizabeth I, are tapestries, antiques, ornate ceilings and fine panelling to recall 400 years of history. Eight sumptuous bedrooms combine modern comforts with impressive antique furniture and hangings; other rooms in the main house are more modest, with neat modern fittings and small, well-equipped bathrooms. The former stable block, which has been converted into a conference centre, contains compact functional bedrooms that are adequately fitted for short visits. No dogs.
Amenities garden, outdoor swimming pool, tennis, dancing (Sat).

Egham
Map 5 E2 Surrey
Windsor Road *TW20 0AG*
Egham (0784) 36171
Telex 934900

Credit Access, Amex,
Barclaycard, Diners

Rooms 90			
with bath/shower 90			

Runnymede Hotel   65%   **£ D**

Standing in ten acres of grounds on the banks of the Thames, this smart modern hotel has extensive function facilities. There are two bars and a colourful open-plan lounge. Bright bedrooms are well equipped, with sensible furnishings and trouser presses. Compact, carpeted bathrooms.
Amenities garden, coarse fishing, discothèque (Fri, Sat), 24-hour laundry service (Mon–Fri), pitch & putt, helipad.

Room phone Yes	*Confirm by* 6	*Parking* Ample
Room TV Yes	*Last dinner* 9.45	*Banquets* 120/–

Elstree

Map 5 E2 Hertfordshire
Edgwarebury Lane
Off Barnet Lane *WD6 3RE*
01–953 8227
Manager Mr Franco Lombardo

● **Set L** £8 **Set D** £8
About £36 for two
Banquets 140/–

Edgwarebury Restaurant ♛

A pleasantly intimate atmosphere pervades this oak-panelled dining room, which offers a very wide-ranging menu. Seafood figures prominently among the starters, while main courses are based around steak, veal, duckling and chicken, mostly served with well-made sauces. Vegetables are expertly handled and there's an eye-catching sweet trolley.
Credit Access, Amex, Barclaycard, Diners

Lunch 12.30–2 *Dinner* 7–10
Closed D Sun

Ely

Map 6 B2 Cambridgeshire
Lynn Road *CB7 4EJ*
Ely (0353) 3574

Credit Access, Amex,
Barclaycard, Diners

Rooms 32
with bath/shower 32

Lamb Hotel   54%   £ E/F

Public rooms have been considerably brightened up at this friendly town-centre hotel, popular with locals and travellers alike. Bedrooms are comfortable and attractively furnished, all with good fitted furniture, TVs, radios and simple modern bathrooms. Some rooms have views across the town to the cathedral, and those overlooking the square are efficiently double-glazed.

Room phone Yes	*Confirm by* 6	*Parking* Ample
Room TV Yes	*Last dinner* 9	*Banquets* 75/–

Epping

Map 7 B4 Essex
Bell Common *CM16 4DG*
Epping (0378) 73137
Telex 81617

Credit Access, Amex,
Barclaycard, Diners

Rooms 82
with bath/shower 82

Post House Hotel   55%   £ D

Situated on the outskirts of the town, this roadside hotel offers pleasantly comfortable motel-style accommodation. Bedrooms in three separate blocks are all similar in style with soft autumnal colour schemes and up-to-date fittings including tea-makers and mini-bars. Bathrooms, too, are modern. In the main building there's a smart reception-lounge plus the intimate Turpin's Bar. *Amenities* garden.

Room phone Yes	*Confirm by* 6	*Parking* Ample
Room TV Yes	*Last dinner* 10.15	*Banquets* 24/–

Eskdale

Map 13 C5 Cumbria
Holmrook *CA19 1TD*
Eskdale (094 03) 244

Closed 5 days early January

Rooms 14
with bath/shower 8

Bower House Inn *(Inn)*   £ F

Visitors cannot fail to be charmed by this pretty whitewashed inn, which enjoys a tranquil setting in the beautiful Eskdale Valley. The chintzy lounge and beamed cocktail bar are splendidly cosy and traditional, as are the bedrooms in the main building. Eight cheerful rooms in the annexe have practical built-in furniture, colour TV and modern bathrooms. All rooms have a welcoming glass of sherry. *Amenities* garden.

Room phone No	*Confirm by* Noon	*Parking* Ample
Room TV Most	*Last dinner* 8.45	*Banquets* 30/6

Ettington

Map 4 C1 Warwickshire
Near Stratford-upon-Avon
CV37 7NZ
Stratford-upon-Avon
(0789) 740000
English cooking

● **Set L** £5·95
Set D from £7·95
About £28 for two

Chase Country House Hotel Restaurant

A feast of traditional English fare awaits visitors to this attractive, formal dining room. The fixed-price dinner menu changes monthly, and features intriguing dishes like 'wallfish' (snails) and mushroom patties, venison and steak pie and baked Lowestoft plaice with bacon rolls. Delicious vegetables, fine English cheeses and lovely sweets complete the picture. Simpler lunch menu. *Credit* Access, Amex, Barclaycard

Lunch 12–2, Sun 12.30–1.30 *Dinner* 7.30–9
Closed D Sun to non-residents, 1 January & 24–30 December

Evershot

Map 4 B4 Dorset
Summer Lane *DT2 0JR*
Evershot (093 583) 424

Credit Access, Amex,
Barclaycard, Diners
Closed 1 December–31 January

Summer Lodge Hotel   68%   Ⓜ   £ D/E

An atmosphere of peace and tranquillity pervades this friendly hotel in the heart of Thomas Hardy's Wessex. There's a spacious, homely lounge with interesting curios and attractive antiques, as well as a pleasant little bar and a simple TV room. Spacious bedrooms are traditionally furnished and prettily decorated; all have well-equipped, carpeted bathrooms. No children under eight. *Amenities* garden, tennis.

Continued

Continued
Rooms 9   *Room phone* No   *Confirm by* By arrang.   *Parking* Ample
with bath/shower 9   *Room TV* No   *Last dinner* 7.30

Evershot

Map 4 B4 Dorset
Summer Lane *DT2 0JR*
Evershot (093 583) 424

Summer Lodge Hotel Restaurant   ⑤

Margaret Corbett delights visitors to her beguiling little dining room with a simple set menu making the best of home-grown produce. Dishes like beef en croûte and roast lamb with garlic and rosemary are complemented by perfectly cooked vegetables, sweets range from treacle sponge to lemon and lime syllabub, and there are fine local cheeses, too.
Credit Access, Amex, Barclaycard, Diners

● **Set D** £9·25
About £24 for two

Dinner only at 7.30
Closed 1 December–31 January

Evesham

Map 4 C1 Hereford & Worcester
Coopers Lane *WR11 6DA*
Evesham (0386) 6344
Telex 339342
Proprietors Jenkinson family
Credit Access, Amex,
Barclaycard, Diners

Evesham Hotel 62% Ⓜ   **£ D**

Built in 1540 and modernised in the early 19th century, this hotel still retains some of the grandeur of a Georgian manor house. A flagstoned hallway leads to the plush modernised bar and the panelled sitting room which has French windows opening on to the lawns. Bedrooms are simpler in style, with modern fitted units and tea/coffee-makers. Carpeted bathrooms are adequate. *Amenities* garden, putting.

Rooms 18   *Room phone* Yes   *Confirm by* 6   *Parking* Ample
with bath/shower 17   *Room TV* Yes   *Last dinner* 9.30

Evesham

Map 4 C1 Hereford & Worcester
Coopers Lane *WR11 6DA*
Evesham (0386) 6344
Proprietors Jenkinson family

Evesham Hotel, Cedar Restaurant

An impressive cedar tree dominates the view from the bay windows of this attractive hotel restaurant. The dinner menu features an imaginative choice of skilfully prepared French-inspired dishes like galantine of guinea fowl and calf's liver provençale, plus crunchy vegetables. At lunchtime there's a cold buffet and a selection of grills.
Credit Access, Amex, Barclaycard, Diners   &

● **Set L** £4·15 & £7·15
Set D £8·50 inc. service
About £27 for two

Lunch 12.30–2 *Dinner* 7–9.30

Ewen

Map 4 C2 Gloucestershire
Near Cirencester *GL7 6BY*
Kemble (028 577) 310

Credit Access, Barclaycard,
Diners

Wild Duck Inn *(Inn)* Ⓜ   **£ D**

Built of Cotswold stone in 1563, this peaceful, friendly village inn not far from Cirencester is full of character. The bar has oak beams, a stone fireplace and a fine collection of firearms on its walls, and the residents' lounge is equally cosy. Cheerfully decorated bedrooms, all in the modern extension, have colour TVs, tea/coffee-makers and neat little carpeted bathrooms. *Amenities* garden.

Rooms 7   *Room phone* No   *Confirm by* By arrang.   *Parking* Ample
with bath/shower 7   *Room TV* Yes   *Last dinner* 9.45   *Banquets* 40/8

Exeter

Map 3 D2 Devon
Topsham Road *EX2 4SQ*
Exeter (0392) 52451

Credit Access, Amex,
Barclaycard, Diners

BUCKERELL LODGE HOTEL   **£ D**

At the time of our researches, building and refurbishment are transforming this hotel, whose attractive Regency lines will remain unspoiled. The most important part of the work is the construction of a new wing of fitted bedrooms, each with its own fully tiled bathroom. Older rooms will be updated in traditional style, and public areas will receive attention as well. *Amenities* garden.   &

Rooms 54   *Room phone* Yes   *Confirm by* 6   *Parking* Ample
with bath/shower 54   *Room TV* Yes   *Last dinner* 9.45   *Banquets* 30/8

Exeter
Map 3 D2 Devon
Topsham Road *EX2 6HE*
Topsham (039 287) 5441

Credit Access, Amex,
Barclaycard, Diners

Rooms 44
with bath/shower 44

Exeter Moat House   52%   £E

This hotel by a roundabout on the A38, formerly the Countess Wear Lodge, offers adequate overnight accommodation in motel-style blocks at the rear. Rooms are functional in appearance, with tea-makers, trouser presses, bedside controls and well-equipped tiled bathrooms. Among the public rooms are the Ploughboy Bar, popular with locals, the residents' own comfortable Quarterdeck Bar and a conference suite.   &

Room phone Yes	*Confirm by* 6	*Parking* Ample
Room TV Yes	*Last dinner* 9.45	*Banquets* 150/30

Exeter
Map 3 D2 Devon
Queen Street *EX4 3SP*
Exeter (0392) 54982
Telex 42455

Credit Access, Amex,
Barclaycard, Diners

Rooms 63
with bath/shower 63

Rougemont Hotel   62%   £E

This four-storey Victorian building is conveniently placed for St David's station and the shops. Public rooms include a pleasant foyer, a smart cocktail bar with comfortable modern armchairs and numerous function rooms (the large ballroom has its own bar). Bedrooms of quite good size have identical flowered decor with matching curtains and covers, and functional fitted units. Half-tiled, wallpapered bathrooms.

Room phone Yes	*Confirm by* By arrang.	*Parking* Limited
Room TV Yes	*Last dinner* 9.45	*Banquets* 208/2

Exeter
Map 3 D2 Devon
South Street *EX1 1EE*
Exeter (0392) 79897

Manager Mr B. Wilkinson
Credit Access, Amex,
Barclaycard, Diners

Rooms 65
with bath/shower 51

White Hart Hotel   56%   Ⓜ   £E

Built in the 14th century, this is one of the town's oldest hostelries, and it wears its age well. Visitors have a choice of three charming beamed bars with antiques, stone fireplaces and collections of pewter and copper; there are also three peaceful lounges. Bedrooms in the main building are cosy and traditional, those in the extension modern. Adequate bathrooms. No dogs. **Closed** for accommodation 25 & 26 December.

Room phone Yes	*Confirm by* 6.30	*Parking* Ample
Room TV Most	*Last dinner* 9.45	*Banquets* 45/8

Exford
Map 3 D1 Somerset
Near Minehead *TA24 7PP*
Exford (064 383) 554

Credit Access, Amex,
Barclaycard, Diners

Rooms 18
with bath/shower 18

Crown Hotel   64%   Ⓜ   £D

Enthusiastic new owners extend a warm welcome at this attractive village hotel, which is very popular with the riding and hunting fraternity. Two lounge areas have comfortable chairs and plenty of reading matter, and there's a rustic bar with stone hearth. Neat, smartly furnished bedrooms have pretty colour schemes, tea-makers and modern bathrooms. Children under ten by arrangement. *Amenities* garden, riding, stabling.

Room phone No	*Confirm by* By arrang.	*Parking* Ample
Room TV Yes	*Last dinner* 9.30	*Banquets* 60/–

Exmouth
Map 3 E3 Devon
Douglas Avenue *EX8 2EX*
Exmouth (039 52) 72277

Proprietor Mr D. E. Gibbons

Rooms 68
with bath/shower 68

Devoncourt Hotel   62%   Ⓜ   £E

Standing in four acres of secluded grounds with its own access to the beach, this purpose-built 1930s hotel is a pleasant spot for holiday-makers. There are sea views from the two traditionally furnished lounges, the bar and the book-filled library. Bedrooms (some with balconies) have functional furniture, radios and compact bathrooms. *Amenities* garden, outdoor swimming pool, tennis, games room, putting, croquet, table tennis.

Room phone Yes	*Confirm by* By arrang.	*Parking* Limited
Room TV No	*Last dinner* 9.30	*Banquets* 120/5

Failand
Map 4 B2 Avon
Beggar Bush Lane
Near Bristol *BS8 3TG*
Long Ashton
(027 580) 3901
Credit Access, Amex,
Barclaycard, Diners

Redwood Lodge Hotel   60%   £D/E

Designed particularly for the sports- and leisure-minded, this vast development is also a popular conference centre. Seven bars cater well for healthy outdoor thirsts, and practically fitted bedrooms have compact bathrooms en suite (mostly showers only). *Amenities* garden, sauna, indoor & outdoor swimming pools, tennis, squash, dinner dance (Sat), discothèque (4 nights weekly), bistro (9.30am–11.30pm), badminton, snooker, cinema.

Continued

Continued

Rooms 72	*Room phone* Yes	*Confirm by* 6	*Parking* Ample
with bath/shower 72	*Room TV* Yes	*Last dinner* 10	*Banquets* 250/10

Fairford

Map 4 C2 Gloucestershire
Market Place *GL7 4AA*
Cirencester (0285) 712535

Credit Access, Amex,
Barclaycard, Diners

Bull Hotel 60%   £ E

This fine old Cotswold-stone inn, which has 1½ miles of fishing rights on the river Coln, dominates one side of the market place. Its public rooms centre around an open-plan bar-lounge area to which heavy oak beams and rustic furniture add charm and character. Bedrooms provide good comfort, most being very attractively decorated and furnished. Bathrooms are neat and modern. *Amenities* garden, game fishing.   &

Rooms 19	*Room phone* No	*Confirm by* By arrang.	*Parking* Limited
with bath/shower 15	*Room TV* Yes	*Last dinner* 9	*Banquets* 80/–

Fairy Cross

Map 2 C2 Devon
Near Bideford *EX39 5BX*
Horn's Cross (023 75) 262

Closed January–February

Portledge Hotel 65% Ⓜ   £ D

History looms large in this family-run hotel, a fine mansion with parts dating back to Norman times. Through a stone archway is a lovely foyer-lounge boasting a magnificent gallery; there's also a simple bar and a beamed TV room. Bedrooms are traditionally furnished, and bathrooms are adequate. No children under five. *Amenities* garden, outdoor swimming pool, tennis, sea fishing, private beach, putting, croquet, games room.

Rooms 32	*Room phone* No	*Confirm by* By arrang.	*Parking* Ample
with bath/shower 21	*Room TV* No	*Last dinner* 9	*Banquets* 60/20

Falmouth

Map 2 B4 Cornwall
Sea Front *TR11 4NU*
Falmouth (0326) 312094
Telex 45617
Manager Mr G. E. Fields
Credit Access, Amex,
Barclaycard, Diners

Bay Hotel 61%   £ D/E

Overlooking a sandy cove, this Edwardian building is set in delightfully lush gardens. The lounge and bar have an air of solid comfort and there's a pleasant sun terrace facing the sea. Bedrooms, including several family rooms, are cheerfully decorated and have well-designed modern units. Guests can use the swimming pool at the nearby Falmouth Hotel. *Amenities* garden, sauna, games room, solarium, putting. **Closed** October–April

Rooms 39	*Room phone* Yes	*Confirm by* By arrang.	*Parking* Ample
with bath/shower 25	*Room TV* Yes	*Last dinner* 9.30	*Banquets* 100/–

Falmouth

Map 2 B4 Cornwall
Sea Front *TR11 4NZ*
Falmouth (0326) 312671

Credit Access, Amex,
Barclaycard, Diners
Closed 1 week Christmas

Falmouth Hotel 61%   £ D/E

Surrounded by palm trees and luxuriant gardens, this imposing Victorian hotel on the sea front still retains its aura of grandeur. Public rooms leading off the foyer include a sunny lounge and two plush bars. Spacious, colourful bedrooms have modern built-in units and well-fitted bathrooms. *Amenities* garden, outdoor swimming pool, dancing (Wed, Sat May–September), solarium, games room, snooker, putting, croquet, in-house movies.   &

Rooms 73	*Room phone* Yes	*Confirm by* By arrang.	*Parking* Ample
with bath/shower 73	*Room TV* Yes	*Last dinner* 8.45	*Banquets* 200/–

Falmouth

Map 2 B4 Cornwall
Harbourside *TR11 2SR*
Falmouth (0326) 312440
Telex 45240
Credit Access, Amex,
Barclaycard, Diners
Closed 4 days Christmas

Greenbank Hotel 64%   £ E

Updated over the years, this 18th-century building overlooking the harbour still has strong nautical associations. There are seafaring memorabilia in the public rooms, which include two tasteful lounges (one with bamboo chairs) and two bars. Most bedrooms have pretty fabrics and modern furniture, although a few retain their traditional style. Bathrooms are spotlessly clean. *Amenities* garden, sea fishing.

Rooms 40	*Room phone* Yes	*Confirm by* By arrang.	*Parking* Ample
with bath/shower 40	*Room TV* Yes	*Last dinner* 10	*Banquets* 40/–

Farnham

Map 5 E3 Surrey
The Borough *GU9 7NN*
Farnham (0252) 715237
Telex 858764
Manager Mr Peter Kelsey
Credit Access, Amex,
Barclaycard, Diners

Bush Hotel   60%   £D

This old coaching inn with records dating back to 1618 manages to combine the best of old and new. There's a lovely lounge with interesting 18th-century frescoes, and one of the two bars has coaching mementoes. Cheerfully furnished bedrooms in the main building and smart modern ones in the annexe are all well equipped, and bathrooms are compact. A marvellous cobbled courtyard and large garden are further assets. *Amenities* garden.

Rooms 76	*Room phone* Yes	*Confirm by* 6	*Parking* Ample
with bath/shower 57	*Room TV* Yes	*Last dinner* 10	*Banquets* 70/10

Farnham

Map 5 E3 Surrey
69 Castle Street *GU9 7LP*
Farnham (0252) 721133

French cooking

Latour   ⑤

Originally the Farnham Theatre, this lofty, barn-like restaurant now draws the crowds thanks to David Leuchars' highly enjoyable French cooking. The dinner à la carte has a varied choice of dishes like loin of pork stuffed with prunes alongside quite ambitious creations such as poached chicken on a bed of watercress topped with grilled almonds. The sweet trolley is very tempting. ♟*ABOVE AVERAGE. Credit* Access, Amex, Barclaycard

About £33 for two

Dinner only 7.30–10.30, Fri & Sat till 11 **Closed** Sun, Bank Holidays except 25 December, 1 week New Year, 1 week Easter & 2 weeks end August

Farnham Common

Map 5 E2 Buckinghamshire
6 The Broadway *SL2 3PQ*
Farnham Common (028 14) 6211

French cooking

Oscar's   ⚲ ⑤

Enjoy a bowl of crudités while perusing the menu in this cosy little bistro. Uncomplicated but interesting French dishes, like lightly poached fillets of lemon sole with white wine sauce and veal escalope flambéed in Calvados, are reliably prepared and served with very good vegetables. Sweets such as crème brûlée come with a glass of dessert wine. Booking essential.
Credit Access, Amex, Barclaycard, Diners

About £26 for two
Banquets 14/6

Lunch 12–2 *Dinner* 7–9.30, Sat 7–10
Closed L Sat & Bank Holidays, all Sun & 3 days after Christmas

Farrington Gurney

Map 4 B3 Avon
Near Bristol *BS18 5UB*
Temple Cloud (0761) 52211
Proprietors
Mr & Mrs W. E. Gofton Watson

Old Parsonage Hotel Restaurant   ⚲ ⑤

Mrs Gofton Watson produces delicious meals for guests to enjoy in the intimate surroundings of this elegant dining room. Simple starters like soup, fish pâté or mushrooms in garlic precede tempting choices such as whole Dover sole, sautéed guinea fowl or succulent noisettes of lamb with herb butter. Vegetables are beautifully prepared and delectable sweets could include gooseberry ice cream or chestnut cream meringue   ♿

● **Set L** Sun only £7·75
About £32 for two

Lunch 12–2, Sun 1–2 *Dinner* 7.30–10
Closed D Sun & all Mon to non-residents & 25–28 December

Faugh

Map 13 D4 Cumbria
Heads Nook, near Carlisle *CA4 9EG*
Hayton (022 870) 297
Proprietors
Ann & Eric Tasker
Credit Access, Amex,
Barclaycard, Diners

String of Horses Inn   65%   Ⓜ   £D/E

The Taskers have devoted ten years to turning their 17th-century village pub into a luxurious hotel. The bars have great period appeal with their beams, panelling, brassware and antique settles, and there's a charming residents' lounge. Superbly decorated and furnished bedrooms are full of little comforts, but pride of place must go to the sumptuously appointed shower and bathrooms. *Amenities* sauna, outdoor swimming pool, solarium.

Rooms 13	*Room phone* Yes	*Confirm by* By arrang.	*Parking* Ample
with bath/shower 13	*Room TV* Yes	*Last dinner* 10.30	

Felixstowe

Map 6 D3 Suffolk
Hamilton Road *IP11 7DX*
Felixstowe (039 42) 5511

Manager Mr N. A. Button
Credit Access, Amex,
Barclaycard, Diners

Orwell Moat House   67%   Ⓜ   £D

A gabled, red-brick hotel, whose spacious, well-used public rooms include a comfortable, traditionally furnished lounge and three bars, one truly evocative of its name, the Garden Bar. Newly decorated bedrooms have pleasantly coordinated pink carpets and bedspreads and white-painted built-in furniture. Roomy bathrooms are well equipped.
Amenities garden, dinner dance (Sat), hairdressing, 12-hour laundry service.

Continued

Continued
Rooms 63
with bath/shower 53

Room phone Yes	*Confirm by* 6	*Parking* Ample
Room TV Yes	*Last dinner* 10	*Banquets* 200/10

Felsted
Map 7 B4 Essex
Near Great Dunmow *CM6 3DH*
Great Dunmow (0371) 820279

● **Set L** £6·50 **Set D** £11·75
About £32 for two
Banquets 36/12

Boote House   Ⓢ

Part of a beamed Elizabethan house, this panelled restaurant is pleasantly run by Christine and Robert Marsello. The fixed-price menu (three or four courses) features dishes like deep-fried sweetbreads, grilled Dover sole, and roast duckling with apricot sauce, and there are some delicious sweets such as chocolate roulade. Sunday lunch brings a choice of three roasts.
🍷 *ABOVE AVERAGE. Credit* Access, Amex, Barclaycard, Diners

Lunch Sun only 12.30–2.30 *Dinner* 7.30–9.30
Closed D Sun & Mon

Ferndown
Map C4 Dorset
New Road *BH22 8ES*
Ferndown (0202) 872121

Credit Access, Amex,
Barclaycard, Diners

Rooms 90
with bath/shower 90

Dormy Hotel   69%   £ C

Set in verdant grounds next to a championship golf course, this large, well-run hotel has a lot to offer. There are several plush lounges, two elegant bars and a club room. Refurbished bedrooms have been tastefully furnished in traditional style; there are also studio rooms in the new wing and charming detached cottages in the grounds. *Amenities* garden, outdoor swimming pool, tennis, dinner dance (Sat), driving nets, pool table, table tennis.

Room phone Yes	*Confirm by* By arrang.	*Parking* Ample
Room TV Yes	*Last dinner* 9.30	*Banquets* 300/2

Fleet
Map 5 D3 Hampshire
Church Road *GU13 8NA*
Fleet (025 14) 28555

Proprietors Mr & Mrs Jones
Credit Access, Amex,
Barclaycard, Diners

Rooms 42
with bath/shower 25

Lismoyne Hotel   56%   Ⓜ   £ E

A short drive lined with rhododendron bushes leads to this quiet, well-maintained hotel, an attractive red-brick building surrounded by trim lawns. Traditionally furnished public rooms are comfortable and relaxing, and there's a little sun lounge off the bar. The best bedrooms are the modern ones in the new wing; those in the main house vary in size and style. Adequate bathrooms. *Amenities* garden, dinner dance (Sat).

Room phone Yes	*Confirm by* By arrang.	*Parking* Ample
Room TV Yes	*Last dinner* 9.30	*Banquets* 120/20

Flitton
Map 5 E1 Bedfordshire
1 Brook Lane *MK45 5EJ*
Silsoe (0525) 60403
Proprietor Somerset Moore
Seafood

● **Set L** from £7
About £32 for two
Banquets 20/10

White Hart Inn   ♣ Ⓢ

Amiable Somerset Moore presides over this immaculate village pub with pride and affection. Seafood obtained direct from his own fishing company dominates the quarterly changing menu, which has interesting, highly enjoyable dishes ranging from home-smoked North Sea prawns with horseradish sauce to baked lemon sole with lobster butter. There are a few meat dishes, too. *Credit* Access, Barclaycard

Lunch 12–2 *Dinner* 7.30–9.30
Closed Sun & Bank Holidays except Good Friday

Folkestone
Map 7 C5 Kent
Earls Avenue *CT20 2HR*
Folkestone (0303) 55301
Telex 96215

Credit Access, Amex,
Barclaycard

Rooms 56
with bath/shower 56

Burlington Hotel   64%   £ D

Friendly, professional staff create a happy relaxed atmosphere at this large red-brick hotel near the seafront. Some of its Edwardian style remains in the comfortably furnished lounge which overlooks the gardens, though other public areas like the reception and bar are more contemporary. Bright, cheerful bedrooms decorated in pastel shades have simple modern furnishings, and bathrooms are well equipped. *Amenities* garden.

Room phone Yes	*Confirm by* By arrang.	*Parking* Ample
Room TV Yes	*Last dinner* 9.30	*Banquets* 120/10

Folkestone

Map 7 C5 Kent
91 Sandgate High Street
Sandgate *CT20 3BY*
Folkestone (0303) 38420
Italian cooking

About £27 for two
Banquets 50/10

Caverna 91

This unpretentious restaurant has a family atmosphere, with Giorgio Rossi doing all the cooking and his wife and son running the bar and supervising the service. The menu features many Sicilian specialities alongside more familiar Italian dishes; sauces are well made and intriguingly herby, and there's an impressive selection of fresh vegetables. Delicious sweets.
Credit Access

Dinner only 7–11, Sun 7–9
Closed Mon & January

Folkestone

Map 7 C5 Kent
2a Bouverie Road West *CT20 2RX*
Folkestone (0303) 59697

About £24 for two
Banquets 50/10

Paul's

A stylish and popular restaurant, with pastel-coloured walls, crisp table linen and smart cane chairs. Fine fresh ingredients and Paul Hagger's sure touch are a winning combination, and the short, frequently changing menu offers appealing choices like creamy leek soup with nutmeg, pheasant pie with sherry and prime turbot in a sophisticated cream sauce with prawns. A few delicious desserts. Booking advisable. *Credit* Access.

Lunch 12.30–2, Sat by arrangement only *Dinner* 7.30–9.30
Closed Sun, Mon, Bank Holidays & 2 weeks August/September

Folkestone

Map 7 C5 Kent
Leaside Court
Clifton Gardens *CT20 2ED*
Folkestone (0303) 54955
Proprietors R. Bocchi
& F. Puricelli
Italian cooking

● **Set L** £4·40
About £22 for two

La Tavernetta

Eating's a pleasure and cooking is always reliable at this popular restaurant on the ground floor of a block of flats. The menu offers a good choice of familiar Italian dishes, well prepared from excellent raw materials, and Signor Puricelli, chef and joint owner, rings the changes with some seasonal fish and game specialities. Smart, friendly service and a lively, happy atmosphere.
Credit Access, Amex, Barclaycard, Diners

Lunch 12–2.30 *Dinner* 6–10.30
Closed Sun & Bank Holidays

Stars in this Guide stand for the quality of the cooking only—
our overriding criterion, irrespective of price, luxury or service.

Fordwich

Map 7 C5 Kent
Near Canterbury *CT2 0BX*
Canterbury (0227) 710661

Credit Access, Amex,
Barclaycard, Diners

Rooms 13
with bath/shower 5

George & Dragon *(Inn)* £E

Standing on the banks of the river Stour, this attractive little inn offers pleasant accommodation in a quiet village setting. Several beamed, cottage rooms form the bar, and there's a comfortable TV lounge for residents. Bedrooms in the main building are full of character and charm, and there are also four modern rooms with private bath in a converted boathouse overlooking the river. No dogs. *Amenities* garden, boating.

| *Room phone* Yes | *Confirm by* By arrang. | *Parking* Ample |
| *Room TV* Some | *Last dinner* 9.45 | *Banquets* 35/– |

Fowey

Map 2 C3 Cornwall
Passage Street *PL23 1DE*
Fowey (072 683) 2275
Proprietor
Mr T. B. Featherstone

Credit Access

Rooms 14
with bath/shower 6

Riverside Hotel 56% Ⓜ £E

Lovers of boats and rivers are in their element at the Featherstones' cheerful, well-run hotel, whose chintzy residents' lounge and charming cocktail bar extend out over the beautiful river Fowey, offering fine views from their picture windows. Shipshape bedrooms are colourfully decorated, and there's a pastel-pink honeymoon suite with a four-poster. Bright, well-fitted bathrooms. *Amenities* sea fishing, slipway, mooring.

| *Room phone* No | *Confirm by* By arrang. | *Parking* Limited |
| *Room TV* Some | *Last dinner* 9 | |

Framlingham
Map 6 D2 Suffolk
Market Hill *IP13 9HN*
Framlingham (0728) 723521

Credit Access, Amex,
Barclaycard, Diners

Rooms 15
with bath/shower 4

Crown Hotel 56% £D/E

Overlooking the market square, this 16th-century coaching inn has several comfortable little lounges with beams and open fires, as well as a cosy bar. A fine curving staircase leads up to the bedrooms, which have more beams and pleasant traditional furnishings; one room has a four-poster and another a half-tester. Bathrooms are adequately equipped, and there are washbasins in the bedrooms.

Room phone Yes	*Confirm by* 6	*Parking* Ample
Room TV Yes	*Last dinner* 9.15	*Banquets* 40/10

Frant
Map 7 B5 East Sussex
35 High Street *TN3 9DT*
Frant (089 275) 635

● **Set L** £6·75
Set D £6·75 & £7·75
About £24 for two

Bassetts

Gerald and Susan Campion make the perfect team in this charming village restaurant. He delights guests with a short set menu of imaginative dishes, and she ensures that service is most friendly and attentive. The choice ranges from mussels with garlic and Pernod butter and duckling braised with port, celery and walnuts, to lovely vegetables and sublime orange and chestnut mousse. *Credit* Access, Amex, Barclaycard

Lunch Sun only 12.30–2 *Dinner* 6.30–8.30, Sat 6.30–8.45
Closed D Sun, all Mon & Tues, most Bank Holidays & June

Frenchbeer
Map 3 D2 Devon
Near Chagford *TQ13 8EX*
Chagford (064 73) 3355

Closed 3 weeks January

Rooms 9
with bath/shower 9

Teignworthy 66% Ⓜ £D

South-west of Chagford (ask for directions when booking), this fine old granite house has a charming, homely atmosphere. Books and comfortable settees make the lounge a relaxing place, and there's a pleasant bar. Bedrooms (including three in the Hayloft) have simple modern fittings attractive soft furnishings and well-equipped bathrooms. No children under 14. No dogs. *Amenities* garden, sauna, tennis, game fishing.

Room phone Yes	*Confirm by* By arrang.	*Parking* Ample
Room TV Yes	*Last dinner* 9	

Frenchbeer
Map 3 D2 Devon
Near Chagford *TQ13 8EX*
Chagford (064 73) 3355

● **Set D** £12
About £33 for two

Teignworthy Restaurant

This simply decorated restaurant makes a pleasant setting for John Newell's capable cooking. The fixed-price dinner menu features carefully prepared and presented dishes like noisettes of lamb with mushroom sauce and fillet of brill with fennel hollandaise, and home-made sweets such as treacle tart are delicious. The lunchtime à la carte is replaced by a cold buffet on Sundays. Booking essential.  *ABOVE AVERAGE.*

Lunch 12.30–2, Sun 1–2 *Dinner* 7.30–9
Closed 3 weeks January

Freshford
Map 4 B3 Avon
Hinton Charterhouse
Near Bath *BA3 6BB*
Limpley Stoke (022 122) 2643

Rooms 8
with bath/shower 8
Room phone Yes
Room TV Yes
Confirm by By arrang.
Last dinner 9.30
Parking Ample
Banquets 30/2
Closed 25 December–14 January

Credit Access, Barclaycard

Homewood Park Hotel 77% Ⓜ £D

This delightful country-house hotel stands in ten acres of pleasant, rambling gardens on the A36 between Bath and Warminster. A carved stone archway leads into the reception-foyer area, where the highly polished floor and flower-bedecked antique tables set the style of the interior. There are antiques, too, in the lounge and bar, which also feature open stone fireplaces and comfortable settees. All public rooms have restful pastel colour schemes. At the top of a handsome staircase are the beautifully furnished bedrooms, most of which have fine views across the gardens and valley. Individually decorated with impeccable good taste, they all have spacious, well-equipped bathrooms. No dogs. *Amenities* garden, tennis, riding.

Freshford
Map 4 B3 Avon
Hinton Charterhouse *BA3 6BB*
Limpley Stoke (022 122) 2643

French cooking

● **Set L** £7·50
Set D Thurs only £9·50
About £32 for two

Homewood Park Restaurant ★ 

This attractive modern dining room has a relaxed atmosphere which admirably complements the expert cooking of Stephen Ross and Antony Pitt. Everything is prepared with care in the classical manner to produce dishes that are subtly flavoured and highlighted by delicate sauces. Perfectly marinated gravad lax, delightful tomato and anchovy salad with basil and plump stuffed chicken breast roasted with tarragon are typical of the short menu; vegetables are superb and sweets like hot chocolate soufflé are irresistible. Special fish dinner on Thursdays. **Specialities** timbale de coquilles St Jacques, salad of frisée, smoked chicken and scallops, gooseberry and elderflower sorbet. ♟ *ABOVE AVERAGE.* **Credit** Access, Barclaycard

Lunch 12–2 *Dinner* 7–9.30, Sun 7–8.30
Closed 25 December–14 January

Freshwater
Map 4 C4 Isle of Wight
Bedbury Lane *PO40 9PE*
Freshwater (0983) 752500
Credit Access, Amex,
Barclaycard, Diners
Closed end October–
beginning April

Rooms 38
with bath/shower 38

Farringford Hotel   59%   £ E/F

Once Tennyson's home, this 200-year-old stone mansion retains echoes of the past, especially in the three traditional lounges. Accommodation ranges from simple rooms in the main house to modern cottage-style chalets in the grounds. The hotel would benefit from some repair and redecoration. *Amenities* garden, outdoor swimming pool, tennis, dancing (Wed, Sat, May–September), 9-hole golf course, croquet, putting, games room.

Room phone Yes	*Confirm by* By arrang.	*Parking* Ample
Room TV Most	*Last dinner* 9.30	

Fressingfield
Map 6 D2 Suffolk
Near Diss, Norfolk *IP21 5PB*
Fressingfield (037 986) 247
Proprietors Clarke family

About £35 for two

Fox & Goose ★

Marvellous seasonal produce (from pheasant to pike caught in the Waveney) figures strongly on the menu of this delightful cottage restaurant, so diners should book and order well in advance. Adrian Clarke's selection of the finest, freshest raw materials helps to elevate basically simple dishes like king prawns with mayonnaise and beef en croûte to new heights, while the array of creamy, liqueur-based sweets makes a perfect finale. Most dishes are available for a minimum of two people, and casual callers can choose from a short menu featuring smoked fish, steak and chicken. **Specialities** coquilles St Jacques avec sauce homard, escalopes de veau à l'estragon, fruits de mer Rachael, trio of ice creams. ♟ *OUTSTANDING.*

Lunch 12–1.30 *Dinner* 7–9
Closed Tues & 21–28 December

Frinton-on-Sea
Map 7 C4 Essex
32 The Esplanade *CO13 9HL*
Frinton-on-Sea (025 56) 4391

Credit Access, Amex,
Barclaycard, Diners

Rooms 26
with bath/shower 18

Frinton Lodge Hotel   64%   £ D/E

A pleasant seaside hotel, built at the turn of the century and once a peer's residence. Dutch oak panels and a 16th-century fireplace grace the reception area, and there are plenty of comfortable chairs in the panelled bar and residents' lounge. Pleasantly decorated bedrooms have modern fitted furniture giving lots of storage space, and bathrooms are adequate. Many rooms have fine sea views.

Room phone Yes	*Confirm by* 6	*Parking* Ample
Room TV Yes	*Last dinner* 9	*Banquets* 120/10

Frome
Map 4 B3 Somerset
Bath Road *BA11 2HP*
Frome (0373) 63223
Telex 44832
Proprietor Mr Charles Worz
Credit Access, Amex,
Barclaycard, Diners

Rooms 40
with bath/shower 40

Mendip Lodge Hotel   60%   Ⓜ   £ E

Fine views of the hills are a feature of this cheerful whitewashed hotel on the outskirts of Frome. Public rooms in modern open-plan style include a pleasant lounge and two simple bars, and there are also conference facilities. Bedrooms, many attractively refurbished, are in a chalet-style extension and offer ample comfort and space; bathrooms are adequately equipped. *Amenities* garden.

Room phone Yes	*Confirm by* 6	*Parking* Ample
Room TV Yes	*Last dinner* 9.45	*Banquets* 80/10

Chris Lord
Lucas
Lucas
Lucas
Lucas
Lucas
Luca
GAO 601X

Engineering for World Transport

A constant stream of international rally and racing successes is tangible proof of Lucas engineering ability and stirring evidence of the company's innovative skills. For ten-tenths competitive motoring is a test of endurance in which only the finest and fittest equipment survives.

Against this sporting background, Lucas Electrical offers you, the motorist, a world-beating range of systems and components, many embodying advanced electronics and all built to endure.

Gateshead

Map 15 B4 Tyne & Wear
High West Street *NE8 1PE*
Gateshead (0622) 771105
Telex 53534

Credit Access, Amex,
Barclaycard, Diners

Rooms 106
with bath/shower 106

Five Bridges Hotel 64%   **£E**

Most of the bedrooms in this modern town-centre hotel have wide windows giving splendid panoramic views across the Tyne; all are cheerful and neatly fitted. There are two bars off the large, busy foyer, as well as an attractive cocktail bar on the first floor. The hotel has numerous well-equipped conference and exhibition rooms.
Amenities dancing (Sat).

Room phone Yes   *Confirm by* By arrang.   *Parking* Ample
Room TV Yes   *Last dinner* 9.45   *Banquets* 350/6

Gateshead

Map 15 B4 Tyne & Wear
High West Street *NE8 1PE*
Gateshead (0632) 771105
Manager Mr C. Garcia

● **Set L** from £3·75 **Set D** £6·75,
Sat £7·75 incl. service
About £27 for two

Five Bridges Hotel, King Edward Restaurant   ⑤

A wide choice of mostly standard favourites is offered in this spacious modern dining room, where cooking by the French chef is very capable and portions are hearty. Start with a seafood pancake or a deliciously garnished poached egg, and go on to steak, pork cordon bleu or a flavoursome bœuf bourguignonne. You can finish with a filling fruit pie.
Credit Access, Amex, Barclaycard, Diners

Lunch 12.30–2 *Dinner* 7–9.45, Fri & Sat 8–10
Closed L Sat, D Fri & all Sun

Changes in data may occur in establishments after the Guide goes to press. Prices should be taken as indications rather than firm quotes.

Gateshead

Map 15 B4 Tyne & Wear
Durham Road *NE9 5PT*
Gateshead (0632) 774121

Credit Access, Amex,
Barclaycard, Diners

Rooms 40
with bath/shower 40

Springfield Hotel 56%   **£E**

A major rebuilding programme is adding to the attractions of this 1930s hotel. A new side entrance leads to a roomy foyer-lounge and there's a smart circular cocktail bar as well as a well-equipped conference room. The fine Italian marble staircase remains and leads to good-sized bedrooms which have colourful, comfortable furnishings, radios, tea-makers and modern bathrooms. No dogs. *Amenities* garden.

Room phone Yes   *Confirm by* 6   *Parking* Ample
Room TV Yes   *Last dinner* 9.30

Gatwick Airport

See under London Airports

Gerrards Cross

Map 5 E2 Buckinghamshire
Oxford Road *SL9 7PA*
Gerrards Cross (028 13) 85995

Manager Mr D. B. Oldham
Credit Access, Amex,
Barclaycard, Diners

Rooms 40
with bath/shower 40

Bull Hotel 61%   **£D**

Old-world charm and modern comforts combine happily in this attractive whitewashed building, parts of which date back to 1688. Sturdy beams enhance the period atmosphere of the reception area and lounge bar, and there's a relaxing cocktail bar with fine wood panels. Bedrooms—some in the original building, the rest in a modern block—are all well furnished, with spacious, up-to-date bathrooms. *Amenities* garden.

Room phone Yes   *Confirm by* By arrang.   *Parking* Ample
Room TV Yes   *Last dinner* 9.30   *Banquets* 126/6

Gillingham

Map 4 B3 Dorset
High Street *ST8 4QT*
Gillingham (074 76) 3512

About £22 for two

Pepper's   ✄ ⑤

Photographs of film stars line the walls of this cheerful restaurant, whose chef-proprietors use fresh local produce in enjoyably different dishes like mushroom ratatouille, chicken liver kebabs and roast mallard.
Lunch 12.30–2 *Dinner* 7.30–10.30
Closed L Mon, all Sun & 1st 2 weeks February *Banquets* 40/20

Gittisham

Map 3 E2 Devon
Near Honiton *EX14 0AD*
Honiton (0404) 2756
Proprietors
Mr & Mrs J. R. D. Boswell
Rooms 13
with bath/shower 11
Room phone No
Room TV Yes
Confirm by 6
Last dinner 9.30
Parking Ample
Banquets 42/10

Credit Access, Amex,
Barclaycard, Diners

Combe House Hotel   74%   Ⓜ   £ D

Beautifully situated in extensive grounds, this charming Elizabethan mansion retains the atmosphere of an elegant country house with its ornate moulded ceilings, large stone fireplaces and antiques. Family portraits hang on the varnished, oak-panelled walls of the entrance hall and the two comfortable lounges, while the club-like bar is decorated with hunting prints and photographs. Comfortable bedrooms are nicely furnished in traditional style, all featuring duvets and lots of thoughtful extras like sewing kits, soda water and barrels of home-made biscuits. Public and private bathrooms are old-fashioned but well equipped.
Amenities garden, game fishing, croquet, clock golf, table tennis.

Gittisham

Map 3 E2 Devon
Near Honiton *EX14 0AD*
Honiton (0404) 2756
Proprietors
Mr & Mrs J. R. D. Boswell
About £30 for two

Combe House Hotel Restaurant    Ⓢ

Two charming dining rooms are the setting for enjoyably prepared steaks, fish (including Dover sole in several guises) and tempting daily specialities. Finish with petits fours in the lounge. 🍷 *SUPERIOR. Credit* Access, Amex, Barclaycard, Diners *Lunch* Sun only at 1 *Dinner* 7.30–9.30
● **Set L** Sun only from £7

Glastonbury

Map 4 A3 Somerset
High Street *BA6 9DP*
Glastonbury (0458) 31146
Proprietors
Major & Mrs J. C. Richardson
Credit Access, Amex,
Barclaycard, Diners

Rooms 14
with bath/shower 7

George & Pilgrims Hotel *(Inn)*   Ⓜ   £ E

A handsome stone facade distinguishes this ancient inn, which was *re*-built by Abbot John de Selwood in 1475! A flagstoned entrance leads to the charming beamed bars, and upstairs there's a chintzy TV lounge. Large bedrooms in the main house have fine antique furniture (some with four-posters), while those in the extension are smaller and more modern. Owners and staff are particularly friendly and helpful.

Room phone No
Room TV No
Confirm by 6
Last dinner 9.30
Parking Ample

Gloucester

Map 4 B1 Gloucestershire
Crest Way, Barnwood *GL4 7RX*
Gloucester (0452) 63311
Telex 437273

Credit Access, Amex,
Barclaycard, Diners

Rooms 100
with bath/shower 100

Crest Hotel   62%   £ D

Functional, bright and crisply contemporary, this well-run hotel is situated about three miles from Gloucester, not far from junction 11 of the M5. Attractive brickwork and good-quality carpeting are features of the public rooms, and there are plenty of easy chairs in well-coordinated soft-coloured fabrics. Bedrooms are light and modern, with practical fitted furniture and excellent bathrooms. *Amenities* buttery (9.30am–6pm).

Room phone Yes
Room TV Yes
Confirm by 6
Last dinner 9.45
Parking Ample
Banquets 80/10

Gloucester

Map 4 B1 Gloucestershire
Upton Hill, Upton St Leonards
GL4 8DE
Gloucester (0452) 67412
Proprietor Richard E. Crown
Credit Access, Amex,
Barclaycard, Diners

Rooms 22
with bath/shower 15

Tara Hotel   63%   Ⓜ   £ D

This Cotswold-stone hotel, three miles outside Gloucester, enjoys fine views over the Severn Valley. Run by the hospitable Crown family, it's a warm and pleasant place, with plenty of relaxing chairs in the foyer-lounge and a blazing fire in the bar in winter. Double-glazed bedrooms are comfortable, with good-quality furnishings, and bathrooms are well equipped. No dogs. *Amenities* garden, outdoor swimming pool. **Closed** 27–29 December

Room phone Yes
Room TV Yes
Confirm by 6
Last dinner 9.45
Parking Ample
Banquets 120/6

Goathland

Map 15 C5 North Yorkshire
Near Whitby *YO22 5AN*
Goathland (094 786) 206
Proprietor Mrs J. Heslop

Credit Amex
Closed December & January

Mallyan Spout Hotel   60%      £E

Built in 1892, this handsome ivy-clad building standing in the heart of the North Yorkshire moors offers traditional comfort in pleasant surroundings. Public rooms, which include two bars and a relaxing lounge, are dominated by vivid tartan carpeting. Leaded windows lend character to some of the bedrooms, all of which have simple furniture and are bright with floral patterns. Bathrooms are spacious. *Amenities* garden, sauna.

Rooms 24
with bath/shower 15

Room phone No
Room TV Yes

Confirm by By arrang.
Last dinner 9

Parking Ample
Banquets 120/–

Godalming

Map 5 E3 Surrey
Ockford Road *GU7 1RH*
Godalming (048 68) 5575

Credit Amex, Barclaycard, Diners

Lake Hotel   57%   Ⓜ   £E/F

This part-Georgian hotel with a lake at the bottom of its lovely garden is well cared for. An elegant little lounge has attractive wood panelling, and the bay-windowed bar is warmed by an open fire. Matching wallpaper and bedspreads are features of the attractive bedrooms, which have fitted whitewood units. Five have shower cubicles, and there are three adequate public bathrooms. No dogs. *Amenities* garden.

Rooms 12
with bath/shower 1

Room phone No
Room TV No

Confirm by By arrang.
Last dinner 10

Parking Ample
Banquets 60/–

Golant

Map 2 C3 Cornwall
Near Fowey *PL23 1LL*
Fowey (072 683) 3426
Proprietors Mrs Jo Henderson & Mr Stephen Henderson

Cormorant Hotel   61%   Ⓜ   £E

Jo Henderson and her son Stephen are the charming hosts at this comfortable modern hotel, which commands sensational river views from its hillside position. Best vantage points are the elegant lounge and the swimming pool, which has a sliding roof and bar service. Ten bedrooms in an extension have modern units and neat bathrooms, the rest have more traditional furnishings. *Amenities* garden, indoor/outdoor swimming pool, table tennis.

Rooms 14
with bath/shower 10

Room phone No
Room TV No

Confirm by By arrang.
Last dinner 8.30

Parking Ample
Banquets 30/–

Goodwood

Map 5 E4 West Sussex
Waterbeach *PO18 0QB*
Chichester (0243) 775537

Credit Access, Amex, Barclaycard, Diners

Richmond Arms Hotel   60%   £D/E

Close to the gates of Goodwood House about a mile from the A27, this flintstone hotel is popular with followers of the Turf. Inside, striking contemporary decor prevails in open-plan public areas like the comfortable Goodwood Bar and lounge; there's also a separate public bar. Bedrooms are functional and modern in style with fitted units, tea-makers and radios. Adequate tiled bathrooms. *Amenities* garden.

Rooms 18
with bath/shower 18

Room phone Yes
Room TV Yes

Confirm by 6
Last dinner 10

Parking Ample
Banquets 120/6

Goudhurst

Map 7 B5 Kent
High Street *TN17 1AL*
Goudhurst (0580) 211512
Manager Mr T. Hussey
Credit Access, Amex, Barclaycard, Diners
Closed 3 days Christmas

Star & Eagle *(Inn)*   £F

This lovely old 14th-century timbered inn has lost nothing of its character despite improvements over the years. The bar still has great charm, and elsewhere exposed beams and leaded windows (with gorgeous views of the Weald) add to the atmosphere of the place. Bedrooms have been tastefully modernised with cheerful colour schemes, fitted units, radios and tea/coffee-makers. Bathrooms are well equipped.

Rooms 11
with bath/shower 9

Room phone No
Room TV Yes

Confirm by By arrang.
Last dinner 9.30

Parking Ample
Banquets 60/20

Grantham

Map 11 E3 Lincolnshire
High Street *NG31 6NN*
Grantham (0476) 3286

Credit Access, Amex, Barclaycard, Diners

George Hotel   57%      £E/F

Right in the centre of town, this attractive Georgian hotel still has some original features, including the fine circular windows on the stairs, and the moulding and fluted pillars of the classical Corinthian Bar. Residents have a welcoming lounge, and the good-sized bedrooms are pleasantly furnished in simple modern style. Some redecoration in public areas would be beneficial.

Continued

Rooms 43 *with bath/shower* 30	*Room phone* Yes *Room TV* Yes	*Confirm by* 6 *Last dinner* 9.45	*Parking* Ample *Banquets* 135/–

Grasmere
Map 13 C5 Cumbria
Near Ambleside *LA22 9RP*
Grasmere (096 65) 496

Proprietor Mr R. S. E. Gifford
Rooms 10
with bath/shower 10
Room phone Yes
Room TV Yes
Confirm by By arrang.
Last dinner 8.30
Parking Ample
Banquets 30/–

Michael's Nook   74%   Ⓜ   £ D

Ring the bell to gain admittance to Reg Gifford's delightfully secluded country house and you'll be personally greeted and offered a welcoming pot of tea: everything here enhances the feeling that you are visiting an impeccably kept private house. Beautiful antiques, fine furnishings and fresh flowers adorn every corner, from the entrance hall to the sumptuous drawing room. Bedrooms are prettily decorated with delicate pastel shades and floral prints, while bathrooms are large and thoughtfully equipped–one has a splendid Victorian bath tub and shower with a plethora of pipes and taps. Children by arrangement. Inclusive terms only.
Amenities garden.

Grasmere
Map 13 C5 Cumbria
Near Ambleside *LA22 9RP*
Grasmere (096 65) 496
Proprietor Mr R. S. E. Gifford

● **Set L** £10·95 **Set D** £13·50
About £36 for two

Michael's Nook Restaurant   ★   ♛ Ⓢ

Meals are generally served at one sitting in this beautifully furnished dining room, so booking is essential. Nigel Marriage uses the finest seasonal produce for his four-course, fixed-price menus and his faultlessly seasoned dishes have well-defined flavours. Skilfully executed individual creations like thick cream of mushroom and mustard soup appear alongside traditional English specialities such as game pie and a rich casserole of beef with chestnuts; vegetables are crisp, and sweets like gorgeous chocolate and rum meringues make an excellent finale. **Specialities** salmon and sole terrine with lobster mayonnaise, chicken liver and flageolet soup, hare pudding, chocolate and chestnut roulade.   

Lunch 12.30 for 1 *Dinner* 7.30 for 8, Sat 7 for 7.15 & 8.45 for 9

Grasmere
Map 13 C5 Cumbria
Broadgate *LA22 9RH*
Grasmere (096 65) 334
Proprietors Mr & Mrs T. Towler
Credit Access, Amex,
Barclaycard
Closed November–March

Rothay Bank Hotel   56%   Ⓜ   £ F

Tidy and well maintained, this 19th-century granite hotel on the outskirts of Grasmere is a useful touring base. The residents' lounge, bar and small reception area are all bright and airy, with comfortable modern furnishings. Bedrooms of varying shapes and sizes, decorated in pastel shades and sensibly furnished, include two family rooms. No children under five.
Amenities garden.

Rooms 15 *with bath/shower* 4	*Room phone* No *Room TV* No	*Confirm by* 5.30 *Last dinner* 7.30	*Parking* Ample

Grasmere
Map 13 C5 Cumbria
Near Ambleside *LA22 9RF*
Grasmere (096 65) 551

Credit Access, Amex,
Barclaycard, Diners

Swan Hotel   64%   £ D

An open-plan foyer with a winter log fire and comfortable old armchairs is a welcoming sight for visitors to this charming hotel, which stands alongside the A591. The lounges–one of which contains Wordsworth's chair–and bar are equally cosy and inviting, and neatly fitted bedrooms are prettily papered and well furnished. Adequate, compact bathrooms.
Amenities garden.

Rooms 41 *with bath/shower* 25	*Room phone* Yes *Room TV* Yes	*Confirm by* 6 *Last dinner* 9	*Parking* Ample *Banquets* 120/6

Grasmere

Map 13 C5 Cumbria
Rydal Water *LA22 9SE*
Grasmere (096 65) 295

Proprietors
Mr & Mrs J. A. Butterworth
Closed early Nov–mid Mar

Rooms 7
with bath/shower 7

White Moss House 68% Ⓜ £C

Overlooking Rydal Water, this family-run hotel makes a wonderfully tranquil retreat, where you can relax with a good book in the comfortable lounge. No TVs or telephones disturb the peace in the luxuriously appointed bedrooms, which have modern fitted units and well-equipped bathrooms; there are also two simpler rooms in a cottage 1½ miles away. Inclusive terms only. No children under 15. No dogs. *Amenities* garden.

| *Room phone* No | *Confirm by* By arrang | *Parking* Ample |
| *Room TV* No | *Last dinner* 7.30 | |

Grasmere

Map 13 C5 Cumbria
Rydal Water *LA22 9SE*
Grasmere (096 65) 295
Proprietors
Mr & Mrs J. A. Butterworth

● **Set D** £12·50
About £34 for two

White Moss House Restaurant ♧ Ⓢ

Mrs Butterworth's cooking has a genuine English character, and her dinner menu (four courses plus English cheese; no choice except sweets) is highly enjoyable. You might begin with celery and almond soup and smoked mackerel soufflé, go on to roast rack of lamb with an interesting array of vegetables, and finish with raspberry shortcake. The menu changes daily to make the best use of fresh products. Booking essential.

Dinner only at 7.30 for 8
Closed early November–mid March

Grasmere

Map 13 C5 Cumbria
Near Ambleside *LA22 9SW*
Grasmere (096 65) 592
Telex 65329

Rooms 35
with bath/shower 35
Room phone Yes
Room TV Yes
Confirm by 6
Last dinner 9.30
Parking Ample
Banquets 130/–

Credit Access, Amex,
Barclaycard, Diners

Wordsworth Hotel 76% £D

This gabled greystone building has been skilfully converted into a luxurious, comfortable hotel. Public rooms range from the traditional, like the roomy entrance hall or the large, antique-filled residents' lounge, to the more contemporary, such as the cane-furnished cocktail bar with its own sun-lounge area. There are also purpose-built banqueting and conference facilities. Well-designed bedrooms, each with its own attractive colour scheme, have high-quality soft furnishings and smart whitewood furniture. Spacious bathrooms with modern coloured suites are comprehensively equipped. No dogs. *Amenities* garden, sauna, indoor swimming pool, coarse fishing, games room, solarium.

Grasmere

Map 13 C5 Cumbria
Near Ambleside *LA22 9SW*
Grasmere (096 65) 592

About £30 for two

Wordsworth Hotel, Prelude Restaurant ♔ Ⓢ

A large, smartly laid-out restaurant where cooking is skilful and reliable. Dishes range from stuffed rack of lamb coated with honey and almonds to simple grills. Good vegetables and an attractive sweet trolley.
Credit Access, Amex, Barclaycard, Diners *Lunch* 12.30–2 *Dinner* 7–9. Fri & Sat 7–9.30 ● **Set L** £6·50 **Set D** £9·50

Grassington

Map 15 B6 North Yorkshire
Threshfield, Skipton *BD23 5EL*
Grassington (0756) 752666
Telex 517357
Manager Simon Briggs
Credit Access, Amex,
Barclaycard, Diners

Rooms 28
with bath/shower 28

Wilson Arms Hotel 59% £D

Set in its own pleasant grounds in the Yorkshire Dales National Park, this is a relaxing hotel. There are several traditionally furnished bars and lounges (one with TV). Simply decorated bedrooms equipped with radios are well maintained, and all have good modern bathrooms (the newest are fully tiled and fitted with showers).
Amenities garden, dinner dance (Sat November–March).

| *Room phone* Yes | *Confirm by* 6 | *Parking* Ample |
| *Room TV* Some | *Last dinner* 8.30 | |

Grayshott
Map 5 E3 Hampshire
Headley Road
Near Hindhead, Surrey *GL26 6LE*
Hindhead (042 873) 5555

About £28 for two

Woods 

The hardworking couple who run this charming little restaurant in a converted fishmonger's shop look after their guests well. The brief menu is full of interesting, reliably prepared dishes like duck liver mousse and turbot stuffed with crabmeat and pike mousse. Bread is home-baked, vegetables are tasty and sweets include a creamy vanilla parfait served with strawberry purée. *Credit* Access, Barclaycard, Diners

Dinner only 7–12
Closed Sun, Mon & 23–30 December

Great Driffield
Map 11 E1 Humberside
Market Place *YO25 7AN*
Driffield (0377) 46661
Proprietor Mr G. A. F. Riggs

Credit Access, Amex, Barclaycard

Rooms 16
with bath/shower 16

Bell Hotel *(Inn)* Ⓜ £F

An impressive bell hangs above the entrance to this white-painted 18th-century inn, among whose public rooms are a welcoming bar and a pleasant glass-covered seating area. Comfortable bedrooms have good-quality traditional furnishings complemented by attractive floral wallpaper, and bathrooms are well equipped. Friendly staff keep the whole place spotless. Guide dogs only; no children under 14. *Amenities* squash.

Room phone Yes	*Confirm by* 6	*Parking* Limited
Room TV Yes	*Last dinner* 9.30	*Banquets* 200/20

Great Dunmow
Map 6 B3 Essex
Braintree Road *CM6 1HU*
Great Dunmow (0371) 3338

● **Set D** £12·50 incl. wine
About £27·50 for two
Banquets 40/20

Ford Farm House

Fresh local produce is the basis for the menus at this converted Georgian farmhouse, where the welcome is friendly and the atmosphere relaxing. You could start your meal with a robust pea and ham soup or smoked fish pâté, and main courses like fillets of plaice with prawn stuffing and steak chasseur are well prepared and generously served. Good coffee and petits fours. *Credit* Access, Amex, Barclaycard, Diners

Lunch 12–2 *Dinner* 7–9.30, Sat 7–10
Closed D Sun

Great Dunmow
Map 6 B3 Essex
High Street *CM6 1AG*
Great Dunmow (0371) 3901

Credit Access, Amex, Barclaycard, Diners

Rooms 34
with bath/shower 23

Saracen's Head 57% £D

This delightful hotel opposite the Old Market Place has an 18th-century facade hiding some earlier features. There's a charmingly traditional air about the beamed foyer-lounge with its tiny bar, and upstairs there's a comfortable residents' lounge. The best bedrooms are in the newly built wing; roomy and nicely furnished, they all have spotless tiled bathrooms. Other rooms are simpler. *Amenities* garden.

Room phone Yes	*Confirm by* 6	*Parking* Ample
Room TV Yes	*Last dinner* 9.30	*Banquets* 36/–

Great Dunmow
Map 6 B3 Essex
Market Place *CM6 1AX*
Great Dunmow (0371) 4321

● **Set L** £11
About £38 for two

The Starr Ⓢ

Set in a lovingly converted 15th-century inn, this beamed restaurant makes a charming setting for Paul Barnard's highly accomplished cooking. Dishes chalked on the blackboard vary with the seasons and range from veal escalope and marinated hare to perfectly roasted partridge splendidly garnished with peeled white grapes, sliced green apples and orange zest in a Calvados sauce. Flavours throughout are subtle and well defined, vegetables crisp and garden fresh. Enjoyable sweets include home-made ice cream, sorbets and hot puddings like citrus soufflé. Enthusiastic and helpful young staff. *Credit* Access, Amex, Barclaycard, Diners

Lunch Sun only 12–2 *Dinner* 7–10
Closed D Sun, all Mon & 3 weeks August

Great Wakering

Map 7 C4 Essex
7 Silchester Corner
Southend Road *SS3 0PX*
Southend-on-Sea
(0702) 585479
Proprietor Mr Metaxas Kaye

● **Set L & Set D £7**
About £32 for two

Tex

⑤

The long international menu at this smart neo-Tudor restaurant contains many house specialities which owner Tex Kaye describes to diners over a drink in the cocktail lounge. Cooking is careful and consistent, whether it's a simple grill or something as elaborate as prawn-stuffed chicken breast with a tasty mushroom and lobster sauce and a garnish of fresh asparagus. Charming service. *Credit* Access, Amex, Barclaycard, Diners

Lunch 12–2 *Dinner* 7.30–10
Closed L Sat, all Sun, 25 & 26 December & 2 weeks summer

Great Yarmouth

Map 6 D1 Norfolk
Marine Parade *NR30 3JE*
Great Yarmouth (0493) 55234
Telex 97249
Manager Mr Grahame Tinnion
Credit Access, Amex,
Barclaycard, Diners

Rooms 96
with bath/shower 65

Carlton Hotel   54%

£D

On the seafront opposite Wellington Pier, this friendly, old-fashioned hotel offers accommodation in four grades ranging from compact singles to roomy suites with sea views. Public rooms include several comfortable lounges and bars–among them the Victorian-style Penny Farthing–and a number of function rooms. Continuing refurbishment is welcome. *Amenities* dinner dance (Sat Oct–June), entertainment (June–Oct nightly).

Room phone Yes	*Confirm by* 6	*Parking* Ample
Room TV Yes	*Last dinner* 9.30	*Banquets* 200/10

Greenwich

Mean Time, Spread Eagle & Le Premier Cru

See under London and London Economy Evening Meals

Greta Bridge

Map 15 B5 Co. Durham
Rokeby, Near Barnard Castle
DL12 9SE
Teesdale (0833) 27232
Proprietors Mr S. R. Waldron &
Mr N. Chandley
Credit Access, Diners

Rooms 24
with bath/shower 13

Morritt Arms Hotel   54%   Ⓜ

£E

A Georgian house, close by the graceful bridge over the river Greta, and next to the site of a Roman settlement. The large lounge is comfortable and relaxing, and other public rooms include a TV lounge and the Dickens Bar with its amusing murals. Bedrooms vary from compact modern singles to larger ones in period style; adequate bathrooms. *Amenities* garden, game & coarse fishing, putting, croquet, children's playground.

Room phone No	*Confirm by* By arrang.	*Parking* Ample
Room TV No	*Last dinner* 9	*Banquets* 200/20

Grimsby

Map 11 F1 Humberside
St James' Square *DN31 1EP*
Grimsby (0472) 59771
Telex 527741

Credit Access, Amex,
Barclaycard, Diners

Rooms 132
with bath/shower 132

Grimsby Crest Hotel   57%

£D

Right in the heart of town, this red-brick hotel is popular with business people. There's a comfortable, welcoming bar and a busy public bar. Good-sized bedrooms include six rooms especially designed for women, with pretty curtains and extras such as magazines and make-up stools; all rooms have tea/coffee-makers and well-kept tiled bathrooms. *Amenities* sauna, coffee shop (Mon–Sat 10am–5.30pm). ♿

Room phone Yes	*Confirm by* 6	*Parking* Ample
Room TV Yes	*Last dinner* 9.45	*Banquets* 30/10

Grimsby

Map 11 F1 Humberside
Littlecoates Road *DN34 4LX*
Grimsby (0472) 50295
Telex 537776
Manager Mr Stuart Smith
Credit Access, Amex,
Barclaycard, Diners

Rooms 52
with bath/shower 52

Humber Royal Hotel   65%

£C/D

This five-storey hotel just off the A18 has benefited from extensive improvements, and most bedrooms have been attractively refurbished to a high standard and equipped with reclining armchairs, tea-makers and trouser presses. Fully tiled bathrooms are excellent. Public rooms include an open-plan foyer-lounge and two attractive bars. *Amenities* garden, dancing (Sat Oct–Mar), dinner dance (Sat monthly in summer), 24-hour laundry service.

Room phone Yes	*Confirm by* 6	*Parking* Ample
Room TV Yes	*Last dinner* 10	*Banquets* 300/6

Grimsthorpe

Map 11 E3 Lincolnshire
Near Bourne *PE10 0LY*
Edenham (077 832) 247
Proprietors Mr & Mrs K. S. Fisher
Credit Access, Amex,
Barclaycard
Closed Sun & 25 December

Rooms 5
with bath/shower 1

Black Horse Inn *(Inn)* Ⓜ £D

Full of old-world character and charm, this attractive early Georgian coaching inn near Grimsthorpe Castle is run by the friendly and hospitable Fishers. Original stone walls, roaring winter fires and fresh flower displays provide a homely atmosphere in public rooms like the bar and residents' lounge, and the cosy, cheerful bedrooms include a few antiques among their simple, cottage furnishings. *Amenities* garden.

Room phone No
Room TV No
Confirm by By arrang.
Last dinner 9.30
Parking Ample
Banquets 35/6

Grimsthorpe

Map 11 E3 Lincolnshire
Near Bourne *PE10 0LY*
Edenham (077 832) 247
Proprietors
Mr & Mrs K. S. Fisher
English cooking

● **Set L & Set D** £9·95
About £26 for two

Black Horse Inn Restaurant Ⓢ

The atmosphere and menu are both traditionally English at this delightfully rustic inn. Careful preparation of fresh ingredients makes tasty treats of dishes like grilled Lincolnshire sausages with fruity chutney, cream of vegetable soup, richly sauced Abbot John's beef and the deliciously light old English syllabub. Set menu only in the evening. *ABOVE AVERAGE.*
Credit Access, Amex, Barclaycard

Lunch 12–2 *Dinner* 7.30–9.30, Sat 7.30–10
Closed Sun & 25 December

Grizedale

Map 13 D5 Cumbria
Near Ambleside *LA22 0QH*
Hawkshead (096 66) 532

Closed January & February

Rooms 6
with bath/shower 6

Ormandy Hotel 55% Ⓜ £E

An air of peace pervades this friendly hotel, which stands in a position of unrivalled tranquillity in the middle of Grizedale Forest between Lake Windermere and Coniston Water. There's a welcoming little reception hall, a residents' lounge with TV and a contemporary-style bar – all spotlessly clean and very well maintained. Bedrooms, too, are neat and tidy, with sensible furnishings and shower rooms. *Amenities* garden.

Room phone No
Room TV No
Confirm by 7
Last dinner 8.30
Parking Ample
Banquets 25/10

Grizedale

Map 13 D5 Cumbria
Near Ambleside *LA22 0QH*
Hawkshead (096 66) 532

French cooking

About £22·50 for two

Ormandy Hotel Restaurant Ⓢ

French provincial dishes are cooked with skill and care at this delightful restaurant in beautiful Grizedale Forest. Starting with snails or creamy vegetable soup you could go on to trout meunière, followed by a main course such as steak au poivre or tender grouse in a rich, tasty sauce. To finish there are simple sweets like apple tart. Pre-theatre dinners at weekends.

Lunch 12.30–2 *Dinner* 7–8.30
Closed Wed, January & February

Guildford

Map 5 E3 Surrey
High Street *GU1 3DR*
Guildford (0483) 64555

Manager Mr B. A. Mortali
Credit Access, Amex,
Barclaycard, Diners

Rooms 24
with bath/shower 24

Angel Hotel 56% £D

This old coaching inn facing the High Street still retains its picturesque courtyard and a superb copper-hung inglenook fireplace in the foyer-lounge. Bedrooms of varying sizes – including two family rooms – are comfortably furnished, and styles vary from antique to modern. All have small, neatly fitted bathrooms. *Amenities* coffee shop (Mon–Thurs 7.30am–3pm, Fri–Sun 8am–3pm & 6pm–10pm).

Room phone Yes
Room TV Yes
Confirm by By arrang.
Last dinner 9.45
Parking Difficult

Guiseley

Map 10 C1 West Yorkshire
White Cross *LS20 8LZ*
Guiseley (0943) 74641

Seafood
About £7·50 for two

Harry Ramsden's Ⓢ

The crowds never stop flocking to this world-famous chippy to enjoy the simplest menu in the land: superb fried fish, terrific chips, bread and butter and a cup of tea. Unlicensed.
Meals 11.30am–11.30pm.
Closed 25 & 26 December

Guist

Map 6 C1 Norfolk
Near East Dereham *NR205AJ*
Foulsham (036 284) 359
Proprietors
William & Glynis Stark

● **Set L** £5
About £28 for two
Banquets 40/3

Tollbridge 

The menu varies with the seasons at William and Glynis Stark's charmingly converted 18th-century tollhouse. Excellent moules marinière and fluffy mousseline of pike benefit from prime local supplies, and main courses like pink-cooked duck with blackcurrants and cassis, partridge with cider and rack of lamb with garlic are prepared with skill and care. Imaginative selection of vegetables, too. ♟ *ABOVE AVERAGE. Credit* Barclaycard

Lunch 12.30–1.45 *Dinner* 7–9.30 **Closed** Sun, Mon (except D Bank Holiday Mons), 25 & 26 Dec, last 3 weeks Jan & 1st week Oct

Gulworthy

Map 2 C3 Devon
Tamar View House
Near Tavistock *PL19 8JD*
Tavistock (0822) 832528
Proprietors
Sonia & Patrick Stevenson

● **Set L** £12 **Set D** £20
incl. wine
About £47 for two
Banquets 35/–

Horn of Plenty ★ ★ ★ 

A quite outstanding restaurant, with lovely views over the Tamar Valley, welcoming staff under the genial, larger-than-life Patrick Stevenson and, above all, the renowned cooking talents of his wife Sonia. Her exciting menus include seafood, robust country dishes and 'Culinary Specialities', many of which are accompanied by beautifully balanced sauces, rich and of great refinement. Starters range from straightforward egg mayonnaise to our sublime asparagus croquettes, and sweets are simple—perhaps ginger sorbet or spiced oranges in Grand Marnier. Set menus offer excellent value. **Specialities** quenelles de saumon à la crème, venison with pine kernel sauce, lamb en croûte with mint béarnaise sauce. ♟ *SUPERIOR.*

Lunch 12–2 *Dinner* 7–9.15
Closed L Fri, all Thurs & 25 December

Hackness

Map 15 D6 North Yorkshire
Near Scarborough *YO13 0JW*
Scarborough (0723) 69966
Proprietors
Mr & Mrs K. R. Horncastle
Credit Access, Amex,
Barclaycard, Diners

Rooms 28
with bath/shower 28

Hackness Grange Country Hotel   69%   Ⓜ   £ C/D

Alongside the river Derwent this carefully restored 19th-century house is set in lovely country. Past and present blend happily in the public rooms, while thoughtfully designed bedrooms (half in the stable block) have tasteful fitted furniture and tiled bathrooms. No children under five. Dogs in kennels only. *Amenities* garden, indoor swimming pool, tennis, game fishing, pitch & putt, bowling green, laundry room.

Room phone Yes	*Confirm by* 6	*Parking* Ample
Room TV Yes	*Last dinner* 8.30	

Hadley Wood

Map 7 B4 Hertfordshire
Cockfosters Road *EN4 0YP*
01–440 8311

Manager Mr J. S. Phillips
Credit Access, Amex,
Barclaycard, Diners

Rooms 53
with bath/shower 53

West Lodge Park   69%   £ C/D

This stately mansion set in rolling parkland is a popular retreat for businessmen and weekenders. Public areas, including the lounge and meeting rooms, are elegantly appointed with antiques and well-chosen reproduction furniture. Individually decorated bedrooms are stylish and have attractively coordinated soft furnishings. Bathrooms have good-quality fittings. No dogs. *Amenities* garden, croquet, badminton, putting, helipad.

Room phone Yes	*Confirm by* By arrang.	*Parking* Ample
Room TV Yes	*Last dinner* 9.30	*Banquets* 65/2

Hadley Wood

Map 7 B4 Hertfordshire
Cockfosters Road *EN4 0PY*
01–440 8311
Manager Mr J. S. Phillips

● **Set L** Sun only £7·75
About £25 for two
Banquets 63/2

West Lodge Park Restaurant   Ⓢ

An attractive modern dining room where the monthly-changing menu makes good use of seasonal produce. Dishes like baked gammon with Madeira sauce are skilfully prepared and most attractively presented, and there are also steaks in various guises, simple items such as rabbit and mushroom pie and an excellent selection of fresh vegetables. Nice sweets and fresh coffee to finish. *Credit* Access, Amex, Barclaycard, Diners

Lunch 12.30–2 *Dinner* 7–9.30, Fri & Sat 7.30–10

Noilly Prat.
French. Dry. Different.
And now free.

Enjoy a Noilly Prat on the Rocks at recommended establishments listed in this guide. You'll be offered 2 FREE GLASSES of NOILLY PRAT on the Rocks when you order a meal for two in the hotels and restaurants which have agreed to participate in our scheme.

FRENCH EXTRA DRY
NOILLY NP PRAT

NOILLY PRAT
REG STERED TRADE MARK
EXTRA DRY VERMOUTH
NOILLY PRAT & Cie
ANCIENNE MAISON Lᵉ NOILLY FILS & Cⁱᵉ
MAISON FONDEE EN 1813
MARSEILLE
PRODUCE OF FRANCE
BOTTLED IN FRANCE
NOT LESS THAN 17% VOL
RUTHERFORD OSBORNE & PERKIN LTD
LONDON SW1Y 4TG
FRENCH EXTRA DRY

This voucher entitles you to enjoy 2 glasses of Noilly Prat on the Rocks with our compliments.

To the Diner: This voucher entitles you to 2 FREE glasses of Noilly Prat on the Rocks in hotels and restaurants participating in this promotion when you purchase a main meal for two. Make a reservation for a meal at any establishment from Egon Ronay's Lucas Guide 1983 to Hotels and Restaurants and when you telephone them enquire whether they are participating in the Noilly Prat promotion. If so, they have undertaken to accept this voucher as payment for 2 glasses of Noilly Prat on the Rocks when you settle your bill. NOTE: Please hand the voucher to the waiter when you ask for your bill.

To the Establishment Manager: Please accept this voucher as payment for 2 glasses of Noilly Prat on the Rocks. The Agent will redeem it for £1 plus refund of postage provided it has been accepted for such a purpose, but reserves the right to refuse payment if they believe the voucher has been exchanged for any other product.

For reimbursement, send voucher to Rutherford, Osborne & Perkin, P.O. Box 3, Diss, Norfolk IP22 3HH.

Noilly Prat.
French. Dry. Different.

What precise quality is it that makes Noilly Prat so stubbornly different and yet so distinctly French? The near perfect blend of two dry French white wines and a rare bouquet of forty aromatic herbs, perhaps. Or the agonisingly slow process of maturing in ancient oak casks. The possibilities are legion. The speculation grows by the day. And the mystery, as yet, remains unsolved.

Here are just a few ways of enjoying Noilly Prat, one of the world's most distinctive drinks.

ON THE ROCKS

A good measure
of Noilly Prat
with plenty of ice.

DIPLOMAT

2/3 measure Noilly Prat
1/3 measure
Martini Extra Dry
2 dashes Maraschino
1 Maraschino cherry.

GIN & FRENCH

A good measure of
Noilly Prat plus an
equal measure of Gin

EL PRESIDENTE

3 measures light rum
1 measure Curacao
1 measure Noilly Prat
2 dashes Grenadine
Ice cubes.

MERRY WIDOW

1/2 measure Noilly Prat
1/2 measure Byrrh
Lemon Zest
Serve very cool.

GLOOM RAISER

8 measures or more
Dry Gin
1 measure Noilly Prat
2 dashes Pernod
2 dashes Grenadine.

NOILLY FIZZ (long Summer drink)

Juice of half a lemon
Powdered sugar to taste
One wineglass Noilly Prat
Pour into tumbler and add cold soda.
Beaten white or yolk of egg can be
added with a shot of Cognac.

NOILLY CUP (for eight to ten)

Cut seasonal fruit into pieces and steep in a large bowl with 1 liqueur glass Cointreau and 2 liqueur glasses Cognac, lemon juice and orange juice in equal proportions–Sugar and ice to taste–Add a bottle of Noilly Prat and a bottle of Champagne– Stir until well mixed and cold–Serve in wineglasses garnished with fruit.

Why not enjoy a meal for two at a fine restaurant and accept a Noilly Prat on the Rocks with our compliments?

SEE PREVIOUS PAGE FOR FULL DETAILS.

Hale Barns

Map 10 B2 Greater Manchester
14 The Square *WA15 8ST*
061–980 5331
Proprietor Dominique Mooney
French cooking

About £27 for two
Banquets 40/15

Borsalino

Dishes from her native France dominate the blackboard menu at Dominique Mooney's popular bistro. Simple starters like tasty onion soup and crêpes au jambon are authentically prepared, and our tender paupiettes de veau were served with an excellent creamy sauce, a liberal sprinkling of fresh parsley and some nicely cooked vegetables. Delicious desserts, too, and good strong coffee. *Credit* Access, Amex, Barclaycard, Diners

Dinner only 7.30–10.30, Fri & Sat 7.30–11
Closed Sun, Mon & Bank Holidays

Halesworth

Map 6 D2 Suffolk
London Road *IP19 8LS*
Halesworth (098 67) 3154
Proprietor Mr Bassett

● **Set D** £9·10
About £24 for two

Bassett's

A converted bakehouse with exposed beams and rustic furnishings is just the place to enjoy some tasty home cooking. Using prime local meat, fish and vegetables on his regularly changing menu, chef/patron Stuart Bassett produces all sorts of flavoursome dishes ranging from cream of artichoke soup and moules marinière to chicken in white wine with lardons and mushrooms. *SUPERIOR. Credit* Access, Barclaycard

Dinner only 7.30–10
Closed Sun, 1 January & 25 & 26 December

Halifax

Map 10 C1 West Yorkshire
Holmfield *HX2 9TQ*
Halifax (0422) 244270

Proprietors Mr & Mrs F. Pearson
Rooms 30
with bath/shower 30
Room phone Yes
Room TV Yes
Confirm by By arrang.
Last dinner 10
Parking Ample
Banquets 100/18

Credit Access, Amex,
Barclaycard, Diners

Holdsworth House 71%  £D

Mr and Mrs Pearson, enthusiastic owners for nearly 20 years, have turned this lovely 17th-century country house just off the A629 into a delightfully comfortable and relaxing hotel. Throughout the resplendent public rooms–the whole place is maintained in tip-top condition–there are oil paintings, fine antiques and displays of fresh flowers; the traditional Cromwell Bar has splendid Windsor chairs and a wealth of brass and pewter, and an open gallery leads from the elegant lounge to the bedrooms. These, and another 18 in a separate block, are pleasantly decorated and tastefully furnished in a variety of styles. Well-lighted bathrooms are comprehensively equipped. *Amenities* garden, snooker.

Halifax

Map 10 C1 West Yorkshire
Holmfield *HX2 9TQ*
Halifax (0422) 244270
Proprietors
Mr & Mrs F. Pearson

● **Set L** from £5
Set D from £8·50
About £32 for two

Holdsworth House Restaurant

The main dining area here is a splendid panelled room with mullioned windows, gateleg tables and some lovely oak chairs. Carefully prepared and attractively presented dishes include many specialities such as pea, pear and watercress soup, gougère aux fromages and noisettes of lamb with onion purée. Sauces are particularly successful, and there are a few delicious desserts. *SUPERIOR. Credit* Access, Amex, Barclaycard, Diners

Lunch 12.30–2 *Dinner* 7.30–10
Closed L Sat, all Sun, Good Friday & Easter Monday & 24–31 December

Halstead

Map 6 C3 Essex
73 Head Street *CO9 2AU*
Halstead (0787) 476271

Indian cooking

About £23 for two

Halstead Tandoori

Authentic Indian cooking in pleasant, unobtrusive surroundings is the highlight of this modern, family-run restaurant. Aromatic tandoori dishes and a choice of freshly spiced curries ranging from mild, creamy kormas to rich dhansaks can be enjoyed with yoghurt-based raita, nan bread, delicious vegetables and a selection of pickles. Smartly uniformed waiters provide excellent service. *Credit* Access, Barclaycard

Lunch 12–1.45 *Dinner* 6–10.45
Closed 25 & 26 December

Hamble

Map 5 D4 Hampshire
The Quay *SO35HA*
Hamble (042 122) 4314

French cooking

● **Set L & Set D** £6·95 & £9·50
About £28 for two
Banquets 45/10

Beth's 

A charming Queen Anne building is the setting for this splendid waterfront restaurant, where Beth Cockburn-Smith offers an imaginative menu based on classical French recipes. Every dish is prepared with loving care, from a simple omelette to lemon sole with parsley and caper sauce or lamb en croûte with an excellent sauce soubise and beautifully crisp vegetables. Sweets are delicious, too. *Credit* Access, Amex, Barclaycard, Diners

Lunch 12.30–2.30 *Dinner* 7.30–9.30
Closed D Sun, all Mon, 25 & 26 December & Tues January & February

Handforth

Map 10 B2 Cheshire
Near Wilmslow *SK93LD*
061–437 0511
Telex 666358
Proprietors Beech family
Rooms 92
with bath/shower 92
Room phone Yes
Room TV Yes
Confirm by By arrang.
Last dinner 10
Parking Ample
Banquets 180/–

Credit Access, Amex,
Barclaycard, Diners

Belfry Hotel   70%   Ⓜ   £D

The Beech family run this well-designed modern hotel with the help of friendly, efficient staff, and its position about three miles from Manchester Airport makes it popular with business people. The pink-marble-floored reception area leads to a comfortable lounge lit by chandeliers, and other public areas include a smart split-level cocktail bar, the beamed Belfry Bar and several function rooms. Quietly decorated bedrooms, many featuring oil paintings by Mrs Beech, have good solid furnishings, plenty of storage space and very comfortable beds (some with duvets); bathrooms are well equipped and neatly maintained. The pleasant grounds include lawns, a pool and a fountain. No dogs. *Amenities* garden, dancing (Tues–Sat).

Handforth

Map 10 B2 Cheshire
Near Wilmslow *SK93LD*
061–437 0511
Proprietors Beech family

About £26 for two

Belfry Hotel Restaurant 

A smart modern restaurant offering well-prepared international favourites. The choice ranges from moules marinière to tournedos Rossini and richly sauced roast partridge. Excellent desserts. Must book.
Credit Access, Amex, Barclaycard, Diners
Lunch 12.30–2 *Dinner* 7–10 ● **Set L** £7·25 **Set D** £7·95

Handforth

Map 10 B2 Cheshire
180 Wilmslow Road *SK93LG*
Wilmslow (0625) 529211

Credit Access, Amex,
Barclaycard, Diners

Rooms 64
with bath/shower 64

Pinewood Hotel   62%   £D

Once a private house, this red-brick hotel surrounded by well-maintained gardens is popular with conference visitors. Public areas include a marble-floored reception and a large, comfortably furnished bar-lounge. Bedrooms have neat fitted units and pleasant views. Adequate bathrooms, some with showers.
Amenities garden, indoor swimming pool, dancing (Thurs, Sun).

Room phone Yes	*Confirm by* By arrang.	*Parking* Ample
Room TV Yes	*Last dinner* 10	*Banquets* 160/–

Harbertonford

Map 3 D3 Devon
Old Road
Near Totnes *TQ97TA*
Harbertonford (080 423) 441
Proprietors Mr & Mrs B. Jefferies
About £27 for two

Hungry Horse 

An unpretentious riverside restaurant, where Mr Jefferies offers some imaginative dishes like salmon quenelles with prawn and green peppercorn sauce on his regularly changing menu. Nice sweets, too. *Credit* Access, Amex, Diners *Dinner only* 7–10 **Closed** Sun (except before Bank Holidays), Mon, 25 & 26 December, February & 2 weeks end September

Harlow

Map 7 B4 Essex
Southern Way *CM187BA*
Harlow (0279) 22441
Telex 81658
Manager Mr N. Moore
Credit Access, Amex,
Barclaycard, Diners

Saxon Inn   56%   £D

Built beside a roundabout close to junction 7 of the M11, this single-storey hotel has simple modern decor and a pleasantly informal atmosphere. Potted plants and chesterfields lend character to the lounge, and there's a large bar with a games room attached. Bedrooms are furnished in attractive contemporary style and have compact, well-maintained bathrooms.
Amenities garden, dinner dance (Sat), games room.

Continued

Rooms 120	*Room phone* Yes	*Confirm by* 6	*Parking* Ample
with bath/shower 120	*Room TV* Yes	*Last dinner* 10.30	*Banquets* 200/–

Harnham
Map 4 C3 Wiltshire
Harnham Road
Near Salisbury *SP2 8JQ*
Salisbury (0722) 27908

Credit Access, Amex,
Barclaycard, Diners

Rose & Crown Hotel   56%   £ D

This half-timbered 13th-century inn with a garden sloping down to the banks of the Avon has charm and character in abundance. Two heavily beamed bars are popular with locals and residents alike, and there's also a plush cocktail bar. Comfortable bedrooms range from traditional in the original building to well-equipped modern ones in the two extensions at the back. Fully tiled bathrooms. *Amenities* garden.

Rooms 26	*Room phone* Yes	*Confirm by* 6	*Parking* Ample
with bath/shower 26	*Room TV* Yes	*Last dinner* 9.30	*Banquets* 80/60

Harpenden
Map 5 E2 Hertfordshire
1 Luton Road *AL5 2PX*
Harpenden (058 27) 60271
Telex 925859
Proprietor Mr O. B. Hemmens
Credit Access, Amex,
Barclaycard, Diners

Glen Eagle Hotel   61%   Ⓜ   £ D

Originally a private house, this hotel at the end of the High Street has an air of quiet luxury. The huge cocktail bar doubles as a lounge and has French windows opening on to a paved pergola. An oak staircase leads to the bedrooms which are double-glazed and have solid freestanding furniture; the best rooms also have trouser presses. Well-equipped modern bathrooms. *Amenities* garden.

Rooms 50	*Room phone* Yes	*Confirm by* 7	*Parking* Ample
with bath/shower 50	*Room TV* Yes	*Last dinner* 10	*Banquets* 70/4

Any person using our name to obtain free hospitality is a fraud. Proprietors, please inform the police and us.

Harpenden
Map 5 E2 Hertfordshire
18 Southdown Road *AL5 1PE*
Harpenden (058 27) 64111

Manager Mr Luigi Bellorini
Rooms 35
with bath/shower 35
Room phone Yes
Room TV Yes
Confirm by 6
Last dinner 10
Parking Ample
Banquets 90/–

Credit Access, Amex,
Barclaycard, Diners

Moat House Hotel   77%   £ D

Standing alongside the A6 overlooking the common, this elegant, red-brick Georgian house offers really luxurious comfort in dignified surroundings. The spacious foyer opens out into the splendid lounge with its tall pillars, moulded plasterwork and comfortable reproduction furniture, and there's also a striking cocktail bar dominated by a mural depicting the Battle of Gibraltar. Bedrooms in the main building are most tastefully designed with pleasing colour schemes, heavy drapes and thick carpets. Equally luxurious rooms in the extension have striking modern decor and stunning bathrooms fully tiled in black. There are also three self-contained family apartments, each with two bedrooms. *Amenities* garden.

Harpenden
Map 5 E2 Hertfordshire
18 Southdown Road *AL5 1PE*
Harpenden (058 27) 64111
Manager Mr Luigi Bellorini

Moat House Hotel Restaurant   ♕ ♕

Dominated by a handsome chandelier hanging from the magnificent painted ceiling, this charming dining room makes a most elegant setting for a meal. The menu offers a wide choice from grills and fish to more elaborate dishes like turkey escalope cordon bleu. Vegetables are excellent, and you'll find trifle and fruit salad on the beautifully laid-out sweet trolley.
Credit Access, Amex, Barclaycard, Diners

● **Set L** £7·48 **Set D** £11·03
About £32 for two

Lunch 12.30–2.30, Sun 12.30–2 *Dinner* 7.30–10, Sun 7.30–9

Harrogate — Burdekins ♨ Ⓢ

Map 15 C6 North Yorkshire
21 Cheltenham Crescent *HG1 1DH*
Harrogate (0423) 502610

English cooking

Kathleen Burdekin is in charge of the kitchen, while her husband presides in the friendliest fashion over the neat, simple dining room. The theme is traditional British cooking, with some recipes going back centuries, and dishes like Yorkshire vegetable soup or chicken with brandy-soaked apricots are very tasty and appealing. Sweets such as the Grand Marnier cream should not be missed. *Credit* Access, Barclaycard

● **Set D** from £6·60
About £23 for two

Dinner only 7–10
Closed some Sun in winter, most Mon & 25 & 26 December

Our inspectors are our full-time employees; they are professionally trained by us.

Harrogate — Cairn Hotel   63%   £ D

Map 15 C6 North Yorkshire
Ripon Road *HG1 2JD*
Harrogate (0423) 504005
Telex 57992

Credit Access, Amex,
Barclaycard, Diners

Situated close to the town centre, this large late-Victorian hotel combines traditional style and elegance with modern comfort and convenience. Marble pillars and arches grace the lofty foyer and lounge and numerous conference rooms are equally splendid. Well-lit bedrooms have modern fitted furniture and tea-makers; the best have excellent tiled bathrooms. *Amenities* garden, tennis, croquet, games room, helipad.

Rooms 140	*Room phone* Yes	*Confirm by* 6	*Parking* Ample
with bath/shower 119	*Room TV* Yes	*Last dinner* 9.15	*Banquets* 850/6

Harrogate — Crown Hotel   64%   £ D

Map 15 C6 North Yorkshire
Crown Place *HG1 2RZ*
Harrogate (0423) 67755
Telex 57652

Credit Access, Amex,
Barclaycard, Diners

Victorian elegance has returned to the public areas of this spacious hotel close to the town centre. The refurbished foyer is resplendent with classical pillars, high moulded ceilings, handsome palms and deep, comfortable chairs, and there are two bars and a wide choice of function rooms. Bedrooms are furnished in a more contemporary style, with attractive light oak units. Cheerful bathrooms are well equipped.

Rooms 120	*Room phone* Yes	*Confirm by* 6	*Parking* Limited
with bath/shower 120	*Room TV* Yes	*Last dinner* 9.30	*Banquets* 300/–

Harrogate — Drum & Monkey ♨

Map 15 C6 North Yorkshire
5 Montpellier Gardens *HG1 2TF*
Harrogate (0423) 502650

Seafood

You can dine in the comfortable bar or the plush upstairs room of this bustling little restaurant. Excellent, carefully chosen seafood is the mainstay of the menu, and dishes like moules marinière and poached turbot with hollandaise sauce are prepared to consistently high standards. Oven-fresh granary bread and lovely sweets add to the pleasure of a meal. Less choice at lunch time. *Credit* Access, Barclaycard

About £25 for two

Lunch 12–2.30 *Dinner* 7–10.15
Closed Sun & 24 December–2 January

Harrogate — Granby Hotel   67%   £ D

Map 15 C6 North Yorkshire
Granby Road *HG1 4SR*
Harrogate (0423) 503046
Telex 23241

Credit Access, Amex,
Barclaycard, Diners

High standards of housekeeping are maintained at this imposing hotel, popular with tourists and also offering good conference facilities. Public rooms vary in style from the traditionally furnished foyer-lounge to the cocktail bar and bright modern buttery. Wide hallways lead to the very comfortable bedrooms, which have attractively coordinated furnishings and well-fitted bathrooms. *Amenities* garden, games room, putting.

Rooms 101	*Room phone* Yes	*Confirm by* 6	*Parking* Ample
with bath/shower 101	*Room TV* Yes	*Last dinner* 10	*Banquets* 230/10

Harrogate
Map 15 C6 North Yorkshire
Ripon Road *HG1 2HU*
Harrogate (0423) 68972
Telex 57918

Rooms 151
with bath/shower 151
Room phone Yes
Room TV Yes
Confirm by 6
Last dinner 9.15
Parking Ample
Banquets 500/–
Credit Access, Amex,
Barclaycard, Diners

Hotel Majestic   70%   £ C/D

Built in the grand style at the turn of the century, this massive red-brick hotel combines flamboyant splendour with the best in modern comfort. Wonderfully restored moulded ceilings, pillars and glittering chandeliers blend with luxurious contemporary furnishings in the lofty public rooms: the cocktail bar, in particular, with its chesterfields and velvet-covered banquettes, is an especially superb room. Spacious, cheerfully decorated bedrooms have built-in furniture and plenty of writing space. Bathrooms are adequate. There are also ten sumptuous suites.
Amenities garden, indoor swimming pool, tennis, squash, dancing (Sat September–April), games room, billiards.

Harrogate
Map 15 C6 North Yorkshire
6 Ripon Road *HG1 2JB*
Harrogate (0423) 502908
Proprietors
M. A. & F. Di Silvestro

● **Set D** from £8·55
About £34 for two
Banquets 24/8

Number Six

There's a warm welcome for friend and stranger alike at this smart family-run restaurant in a Victorian house. The chef makes full use of excellent produce and his variable-price set menus range from simple starters to roast pheasant with cranberry sauce, seasonal Scotch salmon and French classics like quails en cocotte. Nice sweets from the trolley. Swift, assured service.
OUTSTANDING. Credit Access, Amex

Dinner only 7.30–10
Closed Mon, Bank Holidays & last week July/1st 2 weeks August

Harrogate
Map 15 C6 North Yorkshire
Swan Road *HG1 2SR*
Harrogate (0423) 504051
Telex 57922

Credit Access, Amex,
Barclaycard, Diners

Rooms 143
with bath/shower 143

Old Swan Hotel   67%   Ⓜ   £ C

This elegant spa hotel, dating from the 18th century, stands among attractive lawns and gardens close to the city centre. Spacious public rooms are benefiting from refurbishment, and the lounge/bar, with its pale grey walls, palms, mirrors and comfortable modern seating, is particularly pleasing. Next in line for redecoration are the conference rooms and traditionally styled bedrooms. *Amenities* garden, tennis, croquet, putting.

Room phone Yes   *Confirm by* 6   *Parking* Ample
Room TV Yes   *Last dinner* 10   *Banquets* 375/6

Harrogate
Map 15 C6 North Yorkshire
24 King's Road *HG1 5JW*
Harrogate (0423) 68600

● **Set D** from £12
About £35 for two
Banquets 45/20

Oliver

A pleasantly formal restaurant, where the four-course menu offers a choice of carefully cooked and nicely seasoned dishes. Appetisers like snails in puff pastry with garlic butter are followed by a soup or sorbet, plus a main course such as steak Wellington or delicious salmon with beurre blanc. Vegetables are perfectly timed and there are simple sweets to finish.
ABOVE AVERAGE. Credit Access, Amex, Barclaycard

Dinner only 7–10.30
Closed Sun, Bank Holidays & 3 days Easter & Christmas

Harrogate
Map 15 C6 North Yorkshire
Valley Drive *HG2 0JP*
Harrogate (0423) 503134

Credit Access, Amex,
Barclaycard

Russell Hotel   58%   Ⓜ   £ E

Delightfully friendly and helpful staff make it a pleasure to stay at this family-run hotel, part of a late-Victorian terrace overlooking Valley Gardens. Public rooms include a warmly decorated lounge and two cheerful bars, one with beaten copper tables and canopy. Attractive bedrooms, all now with TV, are quietly decorated and well furnished; bathrooms are simple and tidy.

Continued

Continued
Rooms 40
with bath/shower 20

| *Room phone* Yes | *Confirm by* 6 | *Parking* Limited |
| *Room TV* Yes | *Last dinner* 10.30 | |

Harrogate

Russell Hotel, Hodgson's Restaurant

Map **15 C6** North Yorkshire
Valley Drive *HG2 0JP*
Harrogate (0423) 5031 26

From the tasty soups to the petits fours, meals are most enjoyable in this charming panelled dining room, with its romantically laid tables. Five-course set menus including delights like duck and orange terrine and fillets of trout in Pernod sauce demonstrate chef Richard Hodgson's culinary skill—he has a particularly delicate touch with sauces. Polite, friendly service.
Credit Access, Amex, Barclaycard

● **Set D** from £9·90
About £30 for two

Dinner only 7.30–10.30
Closed Sun & Mon to non-residents

Harrogate

Hotel St George   60%   **£ C/D**

Map **15 C6** North Yorkshire
1 Ripon Road *HG1 2SY*
Harrogate (0423) 61431
Telex 57995

Credit Access, Amex,
Barclaycard, Diners

Conveniently situated opposite one of the town's conference centres, this solid 19th-century hotel provides adequate overnight accommodation. Brightly decorated bedrooms, equipped with tea-makers, have mainly simple white units, and modern bathrooms are carpeted. There are two bars, one contemporary, the other Victorian in style. Some refurbishment would be welcome. *Amenities* garden, sauna.

Rooms 82
with bath/shower 82

| *Room phone* Yes | *Confirm by* 6 | *Parking* Limited |
| *Room TV* Yes | *Last dinner* 9.30 | *Banquets* 300/– |

Harrogate

Studley Hotel   64%   Ⓜ   **£ D**

Map **15 C6** North Yorkshire
Swan Road *HG1 2SE*
Harrogate (0423) 60425
Telex 57506
Proprietors Mr & Mrs G. Dilasser
Credit Access, Amex,
Barclaycard, Diners

A friendly atmosphere pervades this little hotel conveniently situated near the town centre. The reception-cum-bar and the upstairs residents' lounge have a pleasant mixture of old and new furniture, and there's an abundance of plants everywhere. Bedrooms are provided with fitted units, tea/coffee-makers and trouser presses, and all have excellent, fully tiled bathrooms. No children under seven.

Rooms 30
with bath/shower 30

| *Room phone* Yes | *Confirm by* 6 | *Parking* Ample |
| *Room TV* Yes | *Last dinner* 10.30 | |

Harrow Weald

Grims Dyke Hotel   66%   Ⓜ   **£ E**

Map **5 E2** Middlesex
Old Redding *HA3 6SH*
01–954 4227
Manager Mr Paul Fanchini

Credit Access, Amex,
Barclaycard, Diners

Devotees of *The Mikado* will adore this splendid old house surrounded by woodland. For 20 years it was the home of W. S. Gilbert, and the lofty hall with its minstrels' gallery is the scene of regular Gilbert and Sullivan evenings. Accommodation is mainly in a new block of contemporary-style bedrooms, with good-quality fittings and compact modern bathrooms; original rooms are large and traditional. *Amenities* garden.

Rooms 49
with bath/shower 49

| *Room phone* Yes | *Confirm by* 6 | *Parking* Ample |
| *Room TV* Yes | *Last dinner* 10 | *Banquets* 120/20 |

Hartford

Hartford Hall Hotel   59%   **£ E**

Map **10 B2** Cheshire
School Lane *CW8 1PW*
Northwich (0606) 75711

Credit Access, Amex,
Barclaycard, Diners

Parts of this attractive gabled hotel date from 1630, and it still retains much of its original character, while benefiting from present-day comforts. Old beams and wooden shutters blend with modern soft furnishings in the open-plan public areas. Bedrooms (all situated in the extension) have duvets, radios and tea/coffee-makers, and functional bathrooms have showers. *Amenities* garden.

Rooms 21
with bath/shower 21

| *Room phone* Yes | *Confirm by* By arrang. | *Parking* Ample |
| *Room TV* Yes | *Last dinner* 9.45 | *Banquets* 35/10 |

Hartlepool
Map 15 C5 Cleveland
Swainson Street *TS24 8AA*
Hartlepool (0429) 66345

Credit Access, Amex,
Barclaycard, Diners

Rooms 46
with bath/shower 21

Grand Hotel   60%
£ D

Built in the grand manner at the turn of the century, this handsome red-brick hotel in the town centre still retains a certain dignity in lofty public rooms like the reception hall and function suites. There are also two bars, including the comfortable contemporary Reef Bar. Bedrooms of various sizes have simple modern furnishings; bathrooms are adequate.

Room phone Yes	*Confirm by* 8	*Parking* Limited
Room TV Yes	*Last dinner* 9.30	*Banquets* 200/–

Harwich
Map 6 D3 Essex
The Quay *CO12 3HH*
Harwich (025 55) 3363

Seafood

● **Set L** Sun only £6·85
About £24 for two
Banquets 100/10

Pier at Harwich
Ⓢ

Murals and decor reflect the maritime history of Harwich at this cheerful quayside restaurant. Seafood dominates the menu (a few meat dishes are available) and excellent ingredients combined with careful preparation guarantee the success of everything from creamy mussel soup or cheese and prawn fritters to simple fish and chips or poached turbot in a tasty cider sauce. ♟ *ABOVE AVERAGE. Credit* Access, Amex, Barclaycard, Diners

Lunch 12.30–2 *Dinner* 6.30–10, Sun 7–10

Hascombe
Map 5 E3 Surrey
Near Godalming *GU8 4JA*
Hascombe (048 632) 258
Proprietor Mr John Keen

● **Set L** from £5·25
About £29 for two

White Horse, La Petite Auberge
Ⓢ

It's obvious that food comes high on John Keen's list of priorities. He uses the finest meat and beautifully fresh fish in dishes like veal Vallée d'Auge or sole meunière, and seasoning and sauces are just right. Vegetables are excellent, too, and there are scrumptious home-made sweets. Service is informal and friendly in this cosy, beamed pub dining room.
Credit Access, Amex, Barclaycard, Diners

Lunch 12–2 *Dinner* 7–10
Closed Sun, 25 & 26 December & 2 weeks end August

Haslemere
Map 5 E3 Surrey
14 Petworth Road *GU27 2HR*
Haslemere (0428) 52625

● **Set L** £2·95 **Set D** £6·95
About £32 for two
Banquets 36/12

Fourteen Petworth Road
Ⓢ

Eileen Bamford is the hard-working chef-proprietor at this smart, contemporary restaurant. From the best and freshest materials she produces imaginative, monthly-changing menus, and her skill and flair are obvious right from delicate cucumber soup to well-sauced roast duck and crisp, flavoursome vegetables. Delicious desserts, too.
Credit Access, Amex, Barclaycard, Diners

Lunch 12–2 *Dinner* 7.30–10
Closed L Mon & Sat, all Sun, 2 weeks January & 2 weeks August

We welcome complaints and bona fide recommendations on the tear-out pages for readers' comments. They are followed up by our professional team. Please also complain to the management instantly.

Haslemere
Map 5 E3 Surrey
High Street *GU27 2JY*
Haslemere (0428) 51555
Proprietors
Mrs D. H. Godfrey & sons
Credit Access, Amex,
Barclaycard, Diners

Rooms 22
with bath/shower 13

Georgian Hotel   56% Ⓜ
£ E

The Godfrey family are making changes to the public rooms of this gracious Queen Anne house in the High Street. A new bar has already been completed, and further improvements are planned. A garden annexe contains the largest of the well-equipped bedrooms, all of which have tea/coffee-makers. Private bathrooms are modern and well fitted; public ones more old-fashioned. *Amenities* garden, sauna, squash.

Room phone Yes	*Confirm by* By arrang.	*Parking* Ample
Room TV No	*Last dinner* 9.15	*Banquets* 100/–

Haslemere

Map 5 E3 Surrey
Petworth Road *GU27 3BQ*
Haslemere (0428) 51251
Telex 858402
Manager Mr P. W. Ford
Rooms 34
with bath/shower 32
Room phone Yes
Room TV Yes
Confirm by 4
Last dinner 9.15
Parking Ample
Banquets 120/12

Credit Access, Amex,
Barclaycard, Diners

Lythe Hill Hotel 75% *E*  £D

A half-timbered 14th-century house and a group of smartly converted farm buildings make up this handsome hotel, which is set in 14 acres of lovely grounds and overlooking National Trust countryside. Among public rooms are the splendid Italian garden full of plants, an impressive split-level lounge furnished with antiques, and a comfortable modern bar overlooking the hotel lake. Bedrooms in the old house have beams and appealing odd shapes, whereas newer rooms are light, airy and stylishly modern. Carpeted bathrooms are very well equipped. The hotel is popular for small meetings and seminars. *Amenities* garden, sauna, tennis, coarse fishing, dancing (Sat), croquet, helipad, clay-pigeon shooting.

Haslemere

Map 5 E3 Surrey
Petworth Road *GU27 3BQ*
Haslemere (0428) 51251
Manager Mr P. W. Ford
French cooking

About £37 for two

Lythe Hill Hotel, Auberge de France ★  

French classical dishes dominate the menu at this welcoming restaurant, whose two dining rooms offer a choice of traditional—beams, panelling and an open brick fireplace—and simpler, more modern surroundings. The new chef uses high-quality fresh ingredients, with good sauces and excellent crisp vegetables, in producing main courses such as poularde à la moutarde de Meaux and mignon de bœuf forestière. Simple starters and desserts. Service is helpful and courteous.
Specialities caneton aux baies de cassis, paupiette de saumon en feuilleté, côte de veau aux girolles, brochette de royales au Ricard.
ABOVE AVERAGE. Credit Access, Amex, Barclaycard, Diners

Lunch 12.15–2.15 *Dinner* 7.30–10.30
Closed L Tues, all Mon & 2–3 weeks after Christmas

Haslemere

Map 5 E3 Surrey
Petworth Road *GU27 3BQ*
Haslemere (0428) 51251
Manager Mr P. W. Ford

● **Set L** £5·50 **Set D** £7·50
About £28 for two

Lythe Hill Hotel, Entente Cordiale  

Smart waiters offer skilful service in this elegant modern dining room. Menus list mostly French-style dishes, including tasty gratinée lyonnaise, crêpes mornay, plump sole in a white wine sauce, and a variety of sauced meat dishes. Excellent ingredients are carefully handled and vegetables are beautifully fresh. Smooth lemon syllabub is a delightful dessert.
SUPERIOR. Credit Access, Amex, Barclaycard, Diners

Lunch 12.30–2.15 *Dinner* 7.30–9.15, Sat 7.30–9.45

Haslemere

Map 5 E3 Surrey
25 Lower Street *GU27 2NY*
Haslemere (0428) 51462

French cooking

● **Set D** £6·95
About £25 for two
Banquets 20/–

Morels ★ 

Jean-Yves Morel is the gastronomic inspiration behind this simply decorated restaurant, and his cooking reaches heights of all-round excellence. He is a master of French haute cuisine, although he also has an eye for modern trends which are reflected in his quarterly-changing menu. Ingredients are chosen with the utmost care, soufflés beautifully light, sauces exquisitely delicate and dishes such as pig's trotter stuffed with sweetbreads and chocolate marquise with coffee bean sauce are, quite simply, masterpieces.
Specialities quenelles de poisson sauce langoustine, feuilleté de crustacés aux épinards et au beurre blanc.
ABOVE AVERAGE. Credit Access, Amex, Barclaycard, Diners

Dinner only 7–10
Closed Sun, Bank Holidays & September

Haslemere
Map 5 E3 Surrey
2 Grove Cottages, Midhurst Road
Kingsley Green *GU27 3AL*
Haslemere (0428) 3539
Proprietors Ron & Beryl Keeley

About £27 for two
Banquets 22/10

Shrimpton's

Set back from the A286, one mile south of Haslemere, this cosy beamed restaurant is part of a row of cottages. The menu offers a variety of familiar, well-prepared dishes ranging from trout with almonds to beef Stroganoff and chicken Kiev, highlighted by excellent vegetables. Sweets include light pancakes with lemon or butterscotch sauce. Booking advisable. *Credit* Access, Amex, Barclaycard, Diners

Lunch Tues–Sat 12–2 by arrangement only *Dinner* 6.30–10 **Closed** Sun, Mon, Bank Holidays except Good Friday, 20 June–5 July & 12 Sept–4 Oct

Hatch Beauchamp
Map 3 E2 Somerset
Near Taunton *TA3 6SG*
Hatch Beauchamp (0823) 480664

Rooms 6
with bath/shower 5
Room phone Yes
Room TV Yes
Confirm by By arrang.
Last dinner 9.30
Parking Ample
Banquets 30/8

Credit Access, Amex, Barclaycard

Farthings Country House Hotel 70% Ⓜ £D/E

The Coopers are the pleasant hosts at this handsome Georgian country house set in three acres of pretty gardens. A well-ordered, traditional atmosphere prevails throughout the hotel: comfortable armchairs are clustered round the fire in the cosy reception-lounge, which is decorated with signed prints, and there's an elegantly furnished bar-lounge. Individually designed bedrooms vary in size and decor, but all overlook the garden and are nicely furnished with antiques or freestanding units; rooms are equipped with TV and tea/coffee-makers and compact bathrooms are carpeted and modern. *Amenities* garden.

Hatch End
Map 5 E2 Middlesex
302 Uxbridge Road *HA5 4HR*
01–428 4232
Italian cooking

About £29 for two

Canaletto 2 Ⓢ

A bright, attractive restaurant, where standard Italian dishes (including a wide choice of antipasti and fresh seafood) are capably prepared, colourfully presented and cheerfully served. *Credit* Access, Amex, Barclaycard, Diners *Lunch* 12–3 *Dinner* 7–11
Closed L Sat, all Sun & Bank Holidays *Banquets* 60/10

Hatfield
Map 7 B4 Hertfordshire
St Albans Road West *AL10 9RH*
Hatfield (070 72) 65411

Credit Access, Amex, Barclaycard, Diners
Closed 25 & 26 December

Rooms 45
with bath/shower 35

Comet Hotel 58% £E

Standing at a roundabout on the A1, this '30s-style hotel, named after the locally built De Havilland Comet Racer, attracts a mainly business and conference clientele. Attractive public rooms include the plushly comfortable cocktail bar. Motel-style bedrooms have cheerful decor and smart modern built-in units; compact bathrooms, like the rest of the hotel, are very well maintained. *Amenities* garden.

Room phone Yes	*Confirm by* 6	*Parking* Ample	
Room TV Yes	*Last dinner* 9.45		

Hatherleigh
Map 3 D2 Devon
EX20 3JN
Hatherleigh (083 781) 454
Proprietors Mr & Mrs M. E. F. Giles

Credit Amex, Barclaycard, Diners

Rooms 12
with bath/shower 10

George Hotel *(Inn)* Ⓜ £E

Mary and Martin Giles are the cheerful hosts at this lovely old thatched hotel, whose ancient cobbled courtyard attests to its days as a coaching inn. Oak beams, panelled walls and huge open fireplaces give an old-fashioned charm to the public rooms, and comfortable bedrooms, too, are quaint and appealing; two have four-posters. Compact, modern bathrooms. *Amenities* garden, outdoor swimming pool, croquet.

Room phone No	*Confirm by* By arrang.	*Parking* Ample
Room TV No	*Last dinner* 9.30	*Banquets* 50/–

Havant

Map 5 D4 Hampshire
Northney Road
Hayling Island *PO11 0NQ*
Hayling Island (070 16) 5011
Telex 86620
Credit Access, Amex,
Barclaycard, Diners

Rooms 96	
with bath/shower 96	

Post House Hotel   64%   £ D

Curving round its own kidney-shaped pool, this modern two-storey hotel stands alongside the estuary. Wide windows in the busy Mast Bar provide splendid views, and the smart foyer overlooks the pool. Bedrooms are bright and attractive, with neatly fitted units, mini-bars, tea-makers and well-fitted bathrooms. *Amenities* garden, outdoor swimming pool, keep-fit equipment, games room, children's playground, helipad.

Room phone Yes	*Confirm by* 6	*Parking* Ample
Room TV Yes	*Last dinner* 11	*Banquets* 126/40

Hawkchurch

Map 3 E2 Devon
Near Axminster *EX13 5TX*
Hawkchurch (029 77) 349
Proprietors
Mr & Mrs P. L. Fairfield
Credit Access
Closed 1 November–mid March

Rooms 14	
with bath/shower 14	

Fairwater Head Hotel   60%   Ⓜ   £ D/E

A quiet, secluded position and a friendly welcome from the Fairfields are just two of the attractions of this pleasant holiday hotel. The foyer and lounges (one has TV) are neat and homely, and there's a simple modern bar with fine views. Chintzy bedrooms have practical fitted furniture and compact bathrooms. No dogs.
Amenities garden, game fishing, clock golf, bowling green, badminton.

Room phone No	*Confirm by* By arrang.	*Parking* Ample
Room TV Some	*Last dinner* 8.30	*Banquets* 70/12

We do not necessarily recommend the cooking at hotels whose restaurants are not separately listed.

Haydock

Map 10 B2 Merseyside
Lodge Lane
Newton-le-Willows *WA12 0JG*
Haydock (0942) 717878
Telex 677672
Credit Access, Amex,
Barclaycard, Diners

Rooms 98	
with bath/shower 98	

Post House Hotel   65%   £ D

Clever siting of this modern red-brick hotel at the intersection of the M6 and A580 attracts travellers, while racegoers will appreciate the splendid view of the racecourse. Leather chesterfields form a luxurious lounge area within the pleasant open-plan foyer, and there's a welcoming cocktail bar. Spacious, well-equipped bedrooms, in a separate block, have compact tiled bathrooms. *Amenities* garden, coffee shop (10am–6pm).

Room phone Yes	*Confirm by* 6	*Parking* Ample
Room TV Yes	*Last dinner* 10.15	*Banquets* 50/–

Heald Green

Map 10 B2 Cheshire
224 Finney Lane *SK8 3QA*
061–437 5701
Proprietors Boutinot family
French cooking

● **Set L** £4·50 incl. service
About £25 for two
Banquets 35/10

La Bonne Auberge

This immaculate little restaurant is bright with check curtains and crisp cloths on the large, well-spaced tables. Roger Boutinot's menus offer mainly straightforward French dishes (set lunch, evening à la carte) carefully prepared from good raw materials; the choice ranges from pâté and snails to Dover sole, roast duckling in a port and cherry sauce, and steaks.
🍷 *SUPERIOR. Credit* Access, Amex, Diners

Lunch 12–1.45 *Dinner* 6.45–9.45
Closed D Mon, all Sun & Bank Holidays

Heddon's Mouth

Map 3 D1 Devon
Near Parracombe *EX31 4PY*
Parracombe (059 83) 230

Credit Access, Barclaycard

Rooms 12	
with bath/shower 6	

Hunter's Inn *(Inn)*   Ⓜ   £ E/F

Watch for the signs as you drive down winding lanes to this picturesque inn set in a beautiful valley and surrounded by ornamental lakes and strutting peacocks. Public rooms include a plush, welcoming bar and a comfortable little TV lounge. Bedrooms are simply furnished in a variety of styles, and half have colourful, adequate bathrooms. Some refurbishment would be welcome. *Amenities* garden, game fishing.

Room phone No	*Confirm by* By arrang.	*Parking* Ample
Room TV No	*Last dinner* 9	*Banquets* 90/20

Ooo la la! French Recipe Crêpes from Findus

Another delicious offer you can't refuse – Findus Lasagne

Helford

Map 2 B4 Cornwall
Near Helston *TR12 6JU*
Manaccan (032 623) 443
Proprietors Heather Crosbie
& George Perry-Smith

● **Set D** £16
About £40 for two
Banquets 35/–

Riverside ★

A scenic drive through winding lanes brings the hungry visitor to this welcoming *restaurant avec chambres* in a delightful setting by the Helford estuary. The reward is a superb dinner showing all the skill gained over the years by George Perry-Smith. The interesting menu ranges from sorrel soup and guinea fowl terrine to baked brill and the simple but magnificent lamb cutlets with kidneys, tomatoes provençale and deliciously fruity chutney. Overnight guests have a choice of six tastefully appointed bedrooms in cottages overlooking the estuary. **Specialities** terrine of salmon, lobster and mushrooms, salmon baked in pastry with currants and ginger, St Emilion au chocolat. *SUPERIOR.*

Dinner only 7.30–9.30
Closed 1 November–mid March

Hellandbridge

Map 2 B3 Cornwall
Near Bodmin *PL30 4QS*
St Mabyn (020 884) 262
Proprietors
Mr & Mrs A. S. Vernoit

Rooms 11
with bath/shower 11

Tredethy Country Hotel   60%   Ⓜ   £ E/F

Standing in nine acres of lovely gardens and parkland overlooking a wooded valley, this sturdy manor house is admirably run by the Vernoit family. Massive oak doors separate the elegant public rooms, where log fires burn in winter. Bedrooms vary in size but all have fine traditional furniture and cheerfully decorated bathrooms. Children under 12 by arrangement only. No dogs. *Amenities* garden, outdoor swimming pool.

Room phone No
Room TV No
Confirm by By arrang.
Last dinner 8
Parking Ample

Helmsley

Map 15 C6 North Yorkshire
Market Place *YO6 5BJ*
Helmsley (0439) 70466

Manager Mrs J. Hopper
Credit Access, Amex,
Barclaycard, Diners

Rooms 38
with bath/shower 38

Black Swan Hotel   60%   £ D

Part Tudor and part Georgian, the facade of this friendly hotel overlooks the market square. A great open fireplace dominates the beamed lounge, and there's a second lounge with views of the walled garden. Well-equipped bedrooms in the original building have attractive furniture made by a local craftsman, while those in the modern extension have fitted units. Bathrooms are spacious. *Amenities* garden, dancing (Sat December–January).

Room phone Yes
Room TV Yes
Confirm by By arrang.
Last dinner 9.15
Parking Ample
Banquets 100/10

Helmsley

Map 15 C6 North Yorkshire
Market Place *YO6 5BH*
Helmsley (0439) 70275
Proprietor Mr J. Feather
Credit Access, Amex,
Barclaycard, Diners
Closed Christmas

Rooms 18
with bath/shower 13

Feathers Hotel *(Inn)*   Ⓜ   £ E

Family-run and full of character, this friendly country inn consists of an old stone house and an adjoining cottage. Public rooms include two rustic bars with locally carved oak fittings and a comfortable residents' lounge with TV and writing desks. Cottage bedrooms are traditional and heavily beamed, while those in the main house have smart modern unit furniture. Neat, practical bathrooms. *Amenities* garden.

Room phone No
Room TV No
Confirm by 6
Last dinner 8.30
Parking Ample
Banquets 160/12

Helmsley

Map 15 C6 North Yorkshire
1 High Street *YO6 5AG*
Helmsley (0439) 70766
Proprietors Mr & Mrs G. Aragues

Credit Access, Barclaycard
Closed 24–31 December

Rooms 15
with bath/shower 15

Feversham Arms Hotel   65%   Ⓜ   £ E

A warm, friendly atmosphere prevails in this attractive Yorkshire-stone hotel, run with charm and efficiency by Spanish-born Gonzalo Aragues and his English wife. Embossed wallpapers and exposed stone are features of the stylish public rooms, while similar wallpaper combines with freestanding furniture in the bedrooms. Comprehensive equipment in the bathrooms includes bidets and hairdryers. *Amenities* garden, tennis.   &

Room phone Yes
Room TV Yes
Confirm by 6
Last dinner 9.30
Parking Ample

Hemel Hempstead

Map 5 E2 Hertfordshire
London Road
Bourne End *HP1 2RJ*
Berkhamsted (044 27) 71241

Credit Access, Amex,
Barclaycard, Diners

Rooms 39
with bath/shower 39

Hemel Hempstead Moat House   54%   (M)   £E

New owners are making gradual improvements to this attractive modern hotel built on the site of an old flour mill. Simple open-plan public areas include a bar and a comfortable lounge. Motel-style bedrooms on two floors are usefully equipped with colour TVs, radios, trouser presses and tea/coffee-making facilities, and all have well-fitted private bathrooms.

Room phone Yes	*Confirm by* 6.30	*Parking* Ample
Room TV Yes	*Last dinner* 9.45	*Banquets* 100/10

Hemel Hempstead

Map 5 E2 Hertfordshire
Brakespear Way *HP2 4UA*
Hemel Hempstead (0442) 51122
Telex 826902

Credit Access, Amex,
Barclaycard, Diners

Rooms 107
with bath/shower 107

Post House Hotel   56%   £D

Situated just off junction 8 of the M1, this purpose-built hotel offers up-to-date facilities and well-maintained accommodation. An attractive plant-filled foyer leads to the comfortable lounge, and there's also a spacious cocktail bar. Pleasant motel-style bedrooms, some overlooking a courtyard with a well-kept garden, have fitted units, mini-bars and compact bathrooms. *Amenities* garden, coffee shop (10am–10.30pm).

Room phone Yes	*Confirm by* 6	*Parking* Ample
Room TV Yes	*Last dinner* 10	*Banquets* 100/6

Hemel Hempstead

Map 5 E2 Hertfordshire
30 High Street *HP1 3AE*
Hemel Hempstead (0442) 42458
Proprietors
Mrs Vasey & Mr & Mrs Bullock
English cooking

About £22 for two

White Hart Inn

There's a warm welcome at this delightful old inn, where the daily-changing menu offers mainly traditional English dishes such as roast lamb, pheasant with bacon rolls and Parson Woodforde's rabbit and onions. Cooking is first class, with faultless seasoning and excellent sauces. Lovely vegetables (including the special potato fritters) and mouthwatering desserts. Essential to book. *Credit* Access, Amex, Barclaycard, Diners

Lunch only 12.30–2.30
Closed Sat, Sun, Bank Holidays & last 2 weeks August

Henley-in-Arden

Map 10 C4 Warwickshire
Birmingham Road *B95 5QR*
Henley-in-Arden (056 42) 2675

● **Set L** £5·95 **Set D** £7·50
About £28 for two
Banquets 65/12

Beaudesert

New owners have created a friendly atmosphere in this pleasant restaurant, where Simon Smith is the skilful, painstaking cook. The short menu features beautifully presented dishes like crab bisque (served with a crab claw and hollandaise sauce) and tender medallions of pork with kiwi fruit and limes. Vegetables are imaginative and there's an impressive sweet trolley.
SUPERIOR. Credit Access, Amex, Barclaycard, Diners

Lunch Sun only 12.30–2 *Dinner* 7.30–10.30
Closed D Sun, Mon & 26–31 December

Henley-in-Arden

Map 10 C4 Warwickshire
64 High Street *B95 5BX*
Henley-in-Arden (056 42) 2700
Proprietors M & Mme Guerrot
French cooking

About £32 for two

Le Filbert Cottage

A little beamed dining room with velvet drapes and shining brassware is the attractive setting for M Guerrot's tasty French cooking. His interesting menu offers seasonal produce prepared with care to enhance fresh, natural flavours: featherlight trout mousse with a piquant American sauce is a typical delight, and vegetables and desserts show the same skilled, assured handling. Service is delightfully French.

Dinner only 7.30–9.30 **Closed** Sat, Sun, Bank Holidays, 3 weeks July/August & 3 weeks Christmas

Henley-on-Thames

Map 5 D2 Oxfordshire
Hart Street *RG9 2AR*
Henley-on-Thames
(049 12) 2161
Proprietor Mr Charles Ractliff
Credit Amex, Barclaycard

Red Lion Hotel   57%   (M)   £E

Built in 1531 right alongside the river, this distinctive red-brick hotel has seen more than its share of famous guests over the years. The split-level lounge is a popular spot for morning coffee, and there's also a small cocktail bar. Bedrooms are mainly traditional and simply furnished (those facing the street are the most spacious and comfortable). Bathrooms have coloured modern suites.

                                        Continued

Rooms 28 *with bath/shower* 19	*Room phone* Yes *Room TV* Yes	*Confirm by* 6 *Last dinner* 10	*Parking* Limited *Banquets* 70/25

Hereford
Map 4 A1 Hereford & Worcester
Broad Street *HR4 9BG*
Hereford (0432) 272506
Telex 35491

Credit Access, Amex,
Barclaycard, Diners

Green Dragon Hotel   64%   £ E

Georgian elegance is still apparent in this handsome city-centre hotel a minute or so from the cathedral. Spacious public rooms include a panelled lounge, plush cocktail bar and the smart Offa Bar. Comfortable, well-fitted bedrooms boast crisp linen, easy chairs and central heating. Bathrooms include some with coloured suites.
Amenities dancing (Sat November–February)

Rooms 88 *with bath/shower* 88	*Room phone* Yes *Room TV* Yes	*Confirm by* 6 *Last dinner* 9.15	*Parking* Limited *Banquets* 200/2

Hereford
Map 4 A1 Hereford & Worcester
Belmont Road *HR2 7BP*
Hereford (0432) 54301

Credit Access, Amex,
Barclaycard, Diners
Closed 5 days after Christmas

Hereford Moat House   59%   £ E/F

A steep red-tiled roof distinguishes this contemporary brick-built hotel, which stands on the Abergavenny road just outside the city centre. The reception area and roomy lounge-bar are in the main building, while spacious, comfortable bedrooms are in attractive chalets. Bright and fresh, they all have alarm clocks, tea-makers and smart blue-and-white bathrooms. There are good banqueting and conference facilities. *Amenities* garden.

Rooms 32 *with bath/shower* 32	*Room phone* Yes *Room TV* Yes	*Confirm by* 6 *Last dinner* 9.45	*Parking* Ample *Banquets* 230/8

Herne
Map 7 C5 Kent
Herne Common
Herne Bay *CT6 7LE*
Herne Bay (022 73) 4849
Proprietors Mr & Mrs G. Morgan

Fox & Hounds Restaurant

During the week an extensive buffet is laid out in this rustic weatherboarded pub, and in a convivial atmosphere visitors can enjoy home-baked meats, plentiful fresh salads, cheeses, soups and a few pies and hot dishes. On Saturday evening there is an à la carte menu featuring items like roast duckling, steak, and crown of lamb. Tempting home-made sweets, too.

● **Set L** £6·50 **Set D** £7·50
About £21 for two

Lunch 12.30–2 *Dinner* 8–9.30, Sat 7.30–9
Closed D Mon, all Sun & 25 & 26 December

Herne Bay
Map 7 C5 Kent
Charles Street *CT6 8HS*
Herne Bay (022 73) 61126

La Chandelle

This smart modern restaurant has a special bar area where you can study Robin Gundry's varied menu. Very good raw materials are used to prepare a selection of mainly French-inspired dishes ranging from coquilles St Jacques mornay to duckling bigarade and coq au vin, all distinguished by excellent sauces. There's also an attractive sweet trolley with gâteaux and cheesecake. *Credit* Access, Barclaycard

● **Set L** £4·25 **Set D** from £4·30
About £27 for two
Banquets 70/–

Lunch 12–2 *Dinner* 7–10.30
Closed D Sun & all Mon

Herstmonceux
Map 7 B6 East Sussex
BN27 4LA
Herstmonceux (0323) 832217
Proprietors Mr & Mrs L. G. Bertoli
French cooking

Sundial ★

Enthusiastic Giuseppe Bertoli gives visitors to his immaculate little restaurant a memorable taste of classical French cuisine. His concern with the freshness and quality of raw materials is a suitable foundation for the imaginative flair that is the hallmark of his cooking and is manifest in such main courses as baby crawfish sautéed with sliced artichoke hearts or saddle of lamb roasted with thyme. Sweets are exquisite as well. (Many dishes are available for a minimum of two people.) **Specialities** la petite bouillabaisse à la rouille, la terrinette de crabe frais, le suprême de caneton au délice de fraises, le petit pot blanc glacé au Grand Marnier.
SUPERIOR. *Credit* Barclaycard, Diners

● **Set L** £6·75 **Set D** £10·75
About £33 for two
Banquets 50/–

Lunch 12.30–2.30 *Dinner* 7.30–10
Closed D Sun, all Mon, Bank Hols, 25 Dec–20 Jan & last 3 weeks Aug

Hertingfordbury

Map 7 B4 Hertfordshire
SG14 2LB
Hertford (0992) 56791

Credit Access, Amex,
Barclaycard, Diners

Rooms 30
with bath/shower 30

White Horse Inn   60%   £D

Efficient maintenance ensures that this whitewashed roadside inn is in good order. Polished brass and gold-coloured chairs dominate the comfortable reception-lounge, and the same colour theme continues in the little bar. Bedrooms in a modern block are attractively decorated in light pine and well equipped with trouser presses and hairdryers. Fully tiled bathrooms. *Amenities* garden, dancing (Fri monthly).

Room phone Yes	*Confirm by* 6	*Parking* Ample
Room TV Yes	*Last dinner* 9.45	*Banquets* 20/–

We publish annually, so make
sure you use the current
edition. It's worth it!

Hethersett

Map 6 C2 Norfolk
Near Norwich *NR9 3DL*
Norwich (0603) 810264

Proprietors Mr & Mrs Gowing
Credit Access, Amex,
Barclaycard, Diners

Rooms 17
with bath/shower 9

Park Farm Hotel   62%   Ⓜ   £F

Set well back from the A11 amid gardens and farmland, this pleasant country hotel with good facilities for families offers a choice of motel-style accommodation or traditional bedrooms in the original Georgian building. Furnishings and decor throughout are tastefully coordinated, and maintenance is good. Guide dogs only. *Amenities* garden, sauna, indoor swimming pool, tennis, games room, putting, croquet, solarium.   &

Room phone No	*Confirm by* 6	*Parking* Ample
Room TV No	*Last dinner* 9	*Banquets* 25/10

Heversham

Map 13 D6 Cumbria
Milnthorpe *LA7 7EE*
Milnthorpe (044 82) 3159

Proprietor Mr J. Chew
Credit Access, Barclaycard

Rooms 28
with bath/shower 17

Blue Bell Hotel   60%   Ⓜ   £E/F

Mr Chew has made a delightful establishment out of his old country inn three miles from junction 36 of the M6. There's a traditional bar with carved oak benches and rough stone walls, and a choice of three comfortable lounges. Bedrooms are well maintained, with light oak furniture and quilted bedspreads, plus radios and tea-makers; simple bathrooms are spotless. Guide dogs only. *Amenities* garden.

Room phone No	*Confirm by* By arrang.	*Parking* Ample
Room TV No	*Last dinner* 9.15	

Hexham

Map 15 B4 Northumberland
Beaumont Street *NE46 3LT*
Hexham (0434) 602331
Proprietors Mr & Mrs. W. Goff
Credit Access, Barclaycard
Diners
Closed 24–26 December

Rooms 22
with bath/shower 17

Beaumont Hotel   54%   Ⓜ   £F

This friendly stone-built hotel near the abbey has been run by the Goff family for the past 12 years. The well-furnished reception/lounge is a popular spot for morning coffee, and there are also two bars and a function room. Brightly decorated bedrooms have freestanding modern furniture and efficient central heating; most have up-to-date shower rooms. *Amenities* dancing (Sat monthly September–April).

Room phone Some	*Confirm by* By arrang.	*Parking* Limited
Room TV Yes	*Last dinner* 9.45	*Banquets* 120/15

High Easter

Map 7 B4 Essex
Near Chelmsford *CM1 4AW*
Good Easter (024 531) 222
Proprietors Brian & Liz Clark

● **Set L** £6·25
Set D Tues–Thurs £12·95
incl. wine
About £32 for two

Punch Bowl   Ⓢ

Starters like creamy Roquefort quiche, main courses such as roast duck with a peach sauce or Indonesian lamb with rice, and a well-laden sweet trolley all add up to a most pleasant meal at this smart, cottage restaurant near the church. Everything is soundly and colourfully prepared by Brian Clark, while his wife Liz provides a friendly welcome.
Credit Access, Amex, Barclaycard, Diners

Lunch Sun only 12–2.30 *Dinner* 7.30–10.30
Closed D Sun, Mon & Bank Holidays except 1 January & Good Friday

High Halden
Map 7 C5 Kent
Durrant Green
Near Ashford *TN26 3NE*
High Halden (023 385) 522

Credit Amex

Rooms 6
with bath/shower 2

Hookstead House   59%   **£ E/F**

This 15th-century Kentish manor house has an atmosphere full of unspoilt country charm. A grandfather clock stands watch in the beamed entrance hall, and there are two nicely furnished lounges, one of which serves as the bar. Bedrooms (one with a four-poster) have cheerful decor, and there's also a well-appointed suite. Compact, modernised bathrooms. No children under seven. No dogs. *Amenities* garden, outdoor swimming pool.

Room phone No   *Confirm by* By arrang.   *Parking* Ample
Room TV Yes   *Last dinner* 9.30   *Banquets* 30/–

Hillingdon
Map 5 E2 Middlesex
Western Avenue
Hillingdon Circus *UB10 9BR*
Uxbridge (0895) 51199
Manager Mr A. C. P. Walton
Credit Access, Amex,
Barclaycard, Diners

Rooms 64
with bath/shower 64

Master Brewer Motel   54%   **£ D/E**

This well-designed motel is located at the junction of Long Lane and Western Avenue. Public areas include an open-plan foyer/lounge and a popular bar. A separate block contains the fair-sized bedrooms, each with a balcony or patio; all have fitted units, tea/coffee-makers and fully tiled bathrooms. Some redecoration would be welcome. *Amenities* garden, coffee shop (7.30am–11am), transport for airport, children's playground. &

Room phone Yes   *Confirm by* 6   *Parking* Ample
Room TV Yes   *Last dinner* 11   *Banquets* 200/50

Hintlesham
Map 6 C3 Suffolk
Near Ipswich *IP8 3NS*
Hintlesham (047 387) 268
Manager Mr Lewis

● **Set L** £10 & £16
Set D £12 & £18·50 incl. service
About £45 for two
Banquets 100/10

Hintlesham Hall   ★ ★   ♛♛ Ⓢ

Robert Carrier is justly proud of his splendid 16th-century country house, a comfortable, civilised setting for some really superb cooking, with presentation and service to match. Prime ingredients (including home-grown herbs and vegetables) are handled with great skill and respect, producing excellent dishes ranging from salade paysanne and smoked leg of lamb with two mousses to grilled sirloin or calf's liver with blackcurrants. For diners staying overnight there are two spacious, boldly decorated bedrooms with TVs and good modern bathrooms. **Specialities** rillettes d'anguille aux petits légumes, diplomate aux grenouilles, charcoal-grilled guinea fowl.
🍷*OUTSTANDING. Credit* Access, Amex, Barclaycard, Diners   &

Lunch 12.30–2.30 *Dinner* 7.30–10.30
Closed 1 & 2 January

Hollingbourne
Map 7 C5 Kent
Ashford Road
Near Maidstone *ME17 1RE*
Maidstone (0622) 30022
Telex 96198
Credit Access, Amex,
Barclaycard, Diners

Rooms 128
with bath/shower 128

Great Danes Hotel   65%   **£ C**

Standing in 20 acres of grounds at the end of the M20, this hotel has ample amenities and conference facilities for the businessman. Bedrooms vary from simple studio-style ones to luxurious 'superior' rooms and vast 'de luxe' rooms. *Amenities* garden, indoor swimming pool, coarse fishing, dinner dance (Sat), pitch & putt, helipad, coffee shop (2pm–11pm), croquet, golf practice area, 9-hour laundry service (Mon–Fri).

Room phone Yes   *Confirm by* 6   *Parking* Ample
Room TV Yes   *Last dinner* 10.30   *Banquets* 425/–

Hollingbourne
Map 7 C5 Kent
Ashford Road *ME17 1PG*
Hollingbourne (062 780) 377

About £28 for two

Park Gate Inn   Ⓢ

A charming panelled restaurant, where top-quality ingredients are used to prepare familiar dishes like duck à l'orange, some of which are flambéed at the table. Honest, capable cooking. *Credit* Access, Amex, Barclaycard, Diners *Lunch* 12–2 *Dinner* 7–10.15
Closed D Sun & 25 & 26 December ● **Set L** Sunday only £5·25

Holywell Green
Map 10 C1 West Yorkshire
Near Halifax *HX4 9AW*
Elland (0422) 79721

Credit Access, Amex,
Barclaycard, Diners

Rock Inn *(Inn)* Ⓜ   **£ D/E**

This friendly 17th-century country pub with modern extensions nestles at the foot of a hill about a mile from junction 24 of the M62. Behind the long white facade everything is bright and cheerful, from the two roomy, comfortable bars to the attractive bedrooms with their pretty pink and white decor. They all have tea/coffee-making facilities and compact shower rooms. Guide dogs only.

Continued

Continued
Rooms 18
with bath/shower 18

| *Room phone* Yes | *Confirm by* By arrang. | *Parking* Ample |
| *Room TV* Yes | *Last dinner* 10 | *Banquets* 100/– |

Hope

Map 10 C2 Derbyshire
Castleton Road *S30 2RD*
Hope Valley (0433) 20380
Proprietors
Anton & Barbara Singleton
Credit Access, Amex,
Barclaycard, Diners

House of Anton 59% Ⓜ £E

Ex-farmer Anton Singleton and his wife Barbara are the delightful hosts at this spick-and-span modern roadside hotel. A sunny bar with picture windows overlooks the patio, and upstairs there's a cosy little lounge with easy chairs and a large period writing desk. Neatly fitted bedrooms have radio/clocks, tea-makers and immaculate bathrooms with plenty of towels. *Amenities* garden. **Closed** 1 January

Rooms 5
with bath/shower 5

| *Room phone* Yes | *Confirm by* 6 | *Parking* Ample |
| *Room TV* Yes | *Last dinner* 9.30 | *Banquets* 80/4 |

Hope

Map 10 C2 Derbyshire
Castleton Road *S30 2RD*
Hope Valley (0433) 20380
Proprietors
Anton & Barbara Singleton

● **Set L** from £3·95
Set D from £4·50
About £34 for two

House of Anton Restaurant 🍴 Ⓢ

Anton does much of the cooking at this elegant restaurant, but still finds time to shoot game for the kitchen! Wild rabbit casserole and pheasant in cider are typical specialities, but the menu changes weekly and can range from grilled trout and eggs florentine to chicken Kiev, fried lamb's liver and roast beef. Good reliable cooking, generous portions and smart, professional service. *Credit* Access, Amex, Barclaycard, Diners ♿

Lunch 12–2 *Dinner* 7–9.30
Closed 1 January

Hope Cove

Map 3 D3 Devon
Near Kingsbridge *TQ7 3HJ*
Galmpton (0548) 561555
Proprietors J. K. & J. Ireland

Closed 2 January–1 February

Cottage Hotel 54% Ⓜ £D

Perched above a craggy beach, this is the perfect base for a family holiday. The cosy sitting rooms have a delightfully traditional atmosphere; there's also a little bar and a TV room. Four refurbished bedrooms with smart shower rooms offer the best accommodation; other rooms provide simpler, but perfectly adequate comforts. Inclusive terms in high season. *Amenities* garden, dancing (Sat July/August), games room, laundry room. ♿

Rooms 36
with bath/shower 14

| *Room phone* Some | *Confirm by* 6 | *Parking* Ample |
| *Room TV* No | *Last dinner* 8.45 | *Banquets* 85/– |

Hope Cove

Map 3 D3 Devon
Galmpton
Near Kingsbridge *TQ7 3HE*
Galmpton (0548) 561280

Credit Amex, Barclaycard
Closed January & February

Lantern Lodge Hotel 59% Ⓜ £E

High on the cliffs overlooking the cove, this attractive, well-run hotel is a friendly and relaxing place to stay. The two comfortable, tastefully decorated lounges have some fine pieces of antique furniture and there are antiques, too, in the bedrooms, three of which have four-posters. All have neat, well-fitted bathrooms. No children under 12. No dogs. *Amenities* garden, sauna, indoor swimming pool, putting, solarium.

Rooms 15
with bath/shower 15

| *Room phone* No | *Confirm by* 6 | *Parking* Ample |
| *Room TV* No | *Last dinner* 9 | |

Horning

Map 6 D1 Norfolk
Lower Street *NR12 8PF*
Horning (0692) 630741

Credit Access, Amex,
Barclaycard, Diners

Petersfield House Hotel 53% Ⓜ £E

A peaceful and pleasant base for exploring the Norfolk Broads, this privately owned Edwardian hotel stands in landscaped gardens close to the river Bure. The traditionally furnished bar and lounge areas are homely and relaxing, and simply fitted bedrooms, some with attractive views, offer ample space and comfort. Bathrooms are adequate. *Amenities* garden, coarse fishing, dinner dance (Sat), mooring, hotel launches.

Rooms 16
with bath/shower 13

| *Room phone* Yes | *Confirm by* 6 | *Parking* Ample |
| *Room TV* Yes | *Last dinner* 9.30 | *Banquets* 110/– |

Horn's Cross
Map 2 C2 Devon
Near Bideford *EX39 5PJ*
Horn's Cross (023 75) 325

Credit Barclaycard

Foxdown Manor   65%   Ⓜ   £E

Extensive amenities and immaculate housekeeping distinguish this sturdy Victorian house, which has been improved by new owners. Public rooms are charmingly traditional in style, as are the tastefully decorated bedrooms. (There's also simple accommodation in six nearby cottages.) Inclusive terms only. *Amenities* garden, sauna, outdoor swimming pool, tennis, solarium, pitch & putt, games room, croquet, laundry room, hotel car.   &

Rooms 8	*Room phone* No	*Confirm by* By arrang.	*Parking* Ample
with bath/shower 6	*Room TV* Yes	*Last dinner* 9.30	*Banquets* 60/–

Horton
Map 4 C4 Dorset
Cranborne Road
Near Wimborne *BH21 5AD*
Witchampton (0258) 840252
Manager Mr Chisnall
Credit Access, Amex,
Barclaycard, Diners

Horton Inn *(Inn)*   £E

Situated about half a mile outside the village, this popular, well-managed Georgian inn has a most welcoming and friendly atmosphere. A vast inglenook dominates the comfortable lounge bar, and there's also a cosy cocktail bar. Spacious, pleasantly decorated bedrooms have sturdy traditional furniture and tea-making facilities. Old-fashioned bathrooms are well kept. *Amenities* garden, game fishing. **Closed** 25 December

Rooms 6	*Room phone* Yes	*Confirm by* By arrang.	*Parking* Ample
with bath/shower 3	*Room TV* Most	*Last dinner* 9.30	*Banquets* 40/–

Horton
Map 5 D1 Northamptonshire
Newport Pagnell Road *NN7 2AP*
Northampton (0604) 870033
Proprietors Mr & Mrs Partridge
French cooking

● **Set D** £10·50
About £28 for two
Banquets 20/10

French Partridge    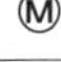 Ⓢ

Waitresses in long dresses enhance the elegant Victorian atmosphere of this thriving restaurant. Mr Partridge cooks to high standards, and his short four-course fixed-price menu features delightfully presented French dishes like tender pheasant normande and monkfish in a creamy, green peppercorn sauce. Sweets such as pineapple Pavlova or home-made ices complete an enjoyable meal. Booking essential.

Dinner only 7.30–9.30 **Closed** Sun, Mon, Tues after Bank Holidays, 3 weeks summer & 2 weeks Christmas

Horton-cum-Studley
Map 5 D2 Oxfordshire
Near Oxford *OX9 1AZ*
Stanton St John (086 735) 203
Telex 847777
Proprietor Mr J. R. Parke
Credit Access, Amex,
Barclaycard, Diners

Studley Priory Hotel   61%   Ⓜ   £E

This impressive Elizabethan manor house is surrounded by 13 acres of splendid grounds. There are period furnishings and an open fireplace in the foyer, and the bar is richly panelled in oak. Bedrooms vary from the large, oak-panelled Elizabethan suite with a half-tester bed to very modest singles. All have adequate shower or bathrooms. *Amenities* garden, tennis, clay-pigeon shooting.   &

Rooms 19	*Room phone* Yes	*Confirm by* 6	*Parking* Ample
with bath/shower 19	*Room TV* Yes	*Last dinner* 9.30	*Banquets* 55/6

Hoveton
Map 6 D1 Norfolk
Broads Centre *NR12 8AJ*
Wroxham (060 53) 2061

Credit Access, Amex,
Barclaycard, Diners

Hotel Wroxham   56%   Ⓜ   £E

Popular with business people and holiday-makers lured by the pleasures of the Broads, this modern hotel makes the most of its location on the river Bure. There's an informal bar-lounge with access to a riverside terrace. Bedrooms (the eight with balconies overlooking the river are especially nice) are brightly decorated and well maintained, and bathrooms are adequate. *Amenities* coarse fishing, dinner dance (Sat), mooring.

Rooms 19	*Room phone* No	*Confirm by* By arrang.	*Parking* Ample
with bath/shower 14	*Room TV* Yes	*Last dinner* 9.30	*Banquets* 150/–

Hovingham
Map 15 C6 North Yorkshire
Near York *YO6 4LA*
Hovingham (065 382) 234

Proprietor Mr Timothy Rowe
Credit Access, Barclaycard
Closed 25 & 26 December

Worsley Arms Hotel   60%   Ⓜ   £E

Timothy Rowe is a welcoming host at this straightforward village hotel, which has an attractive walled garden at one side. A fire burns in the comfortable entrance hall in winter and there are two other lounges to choose from, as well as two bars. Modest bedrooms have plain, practical furniture, and carpeted bathrooms are well maintained. *Amenities* garden.

Continued

Continued
Rooms 14
with bath/shower 14 | Room phone No | Confirm by By arrang. | Parking Ample
Room TV No | Last dinner 9

Howden
Map 11 D1 Humberside
Bridgegate *DN14 7JJ*
Howden (0430) 30805

Manager Mr F. Cunajo
Credit Access, Barclaycard

Bowmans Hotel *(Inn)* £E

This friendly inn halfway between Doncaster and Hull and just off the M62 offers adequate comforts for an overnight stop. Compact bedrooms with duvets are simply furnished and bathrooms are modern. No lounge as such, but there's a choice of three bars whose bare stone walls give them an agreeably rustic air. Guide dogs only.

Rooms 13	Room phone Yes	Confirm by Noon	Parking Ample
with bath/shower 10	Room TV Yes	Last dinner 10	

Huddersfield
Map 10 C1 West Yorkshire
St George's Square *HD1 1JA*
Huddersfield (0484) 25444

Credit Access, Amex,
Barclaycard, Diners

George Hotel   57% £D

This substantial Victorian hotel, built 130 years ago, stands in the centre of town right beside the railway station. It has two bars, a bright modern buttery and a comfortable foyer-lounge. Potted plants lend a homely touch to the practical bedrooms, which are gradually being refurbished. Simple bathrooms are adequate. *Amenities* dinner dance (Sat September–March), coffee shop (11am–7pm, Sun 11am–9pm).

Rooms 60 | Room phone Yes | Confirm by 6 | Parking Ample
with bath/shower 36 | Room TV Yes | Last dinner 10 | Banquets 140/–

Huddersfield
Map 10 C1 West Yorkshire
Ainley Top *HD3 3RH*
Elland (0422) 75431
Telex 517346
Credit Access, Amex,
Barclaycard, Diners
Closed Christmas

Ladbroke Mercury Hotel   64% £C/D

This eye-catching modern hotel situated near junction 24 of the M62 commands fine views of the Pennines. A spacious open-plan reception area leads to the relaxing lounge, which is stylishly furnished with luxurious leather sofas and armchairs; there's also a sophisticated bar. Well-designed bedrooms all have good-quality built-in units, tea-makers and trouser presses. Bright modern bathrooms. *Amenities* dancing (Sat).

Rooms 120 | Room phone Yes | Confirm by By arrang. | Parking Ample
with bath/shower 120 | Room TV Yes | Last dinner 10 | Banquets 350/10

Hull
Map 11 E1 Humberside
Ferriby High Road *HU14 3LG*
Hull (0482) 645212
Telex 52558
Manager Mr Chris Tomkinson
Credit Access, Amex,
Barclaycard, Diners

Crest Hotel   59% £D

Situated on the A63 five miles west of Hull, this modern riverside hotel offers splendid views of the Humber Bridge. Relaxing public areas like the two bars are attractively contemporary in style, and bedrooms, too, provide up-to-date comforts. Older rooms have bright fitted units, and newer rooms are especially pleasant, with oatmeal-coloured carpets and light pine furniture. Compact, tiled bathrooms. *Amenities* garden. &

Rooms 102 | Room phone Yes | Confirm by 6 | Parking Ample
with bath/shower 102 | Room TV Yes | Last dinner 9.45 | Banquets 70/4

Hull
Map 11 E1 Humberside
Ferensway *HU1 3UF*
Hull (0482) 25087   Telex 52450
Credit Access, Amex,
Barclaycard, Diners
Closed 4 days Easter & 5 days
Christmas

Royal Station Hotel   58% £D

Once visited by Queen Victoria, this large railway hotel is a blend of old and new. There's a spacious glass-ceilinged lounge and two bars smartly decked out in Victorian style. Most bedrooms and bathrooms are very large, and have slightly old-fashioned fittings. There is a measure of wear and tear. *Amenities* dancing (Fri or Sat May–September), hairdressing, 12-hour laundry service. &

Rooms 106 | Room phone Yes | Confirm by 6 | Parking Limited
with bath/shower 84 | Room TV Yes | Last dinner 10.15 | Banquets 350/–

Hull

Map 11 E1 Humberside
Dagger Lane, Old Town *HU1 2LS*
Hull (0482) 227222
Manager Ms Carol Hagan
Credit Access, Amex,
Barclaycard, Diners
Closed 4 days Christmas

Rooms 32
with bath/shower 25

Waterfront Hotel   59%   £ D

This popular city-centre hotel retains many features from its days as a Victorian warehouse. Cast-iron columns, beams and flagstone floors have been integrated into the reception/lounge area, and upstairs there's a pleasantly rustic bar with a roof terrace. Bedrooms have shag-pile carpets and attractive pine fittings; top-floor rooms are quite small.
Amenities dinner dance (Fri), nightclub (Tues–Sat).

Room phone Yes *Confirm by* 6.30   *Parking* Limited
Room TV Yes   *Last dinner* 9.45

Hungerford

Map 4 C2 Berkshire
Charnham Street *RG17 0EL*
Hungerford (048 86) 2512

Credit Access, Amex,
Barclaycard, Diners

Rooms 28
with bath/shower 24

Bear at Hungerford   60% Ⓜ   £ E

Friendly staff extend a warm welcome at this well-kept, brick-built inn, whose sturdy beams and open fireplaces attest to its great age. The pretty foyer-lounge is a comfortable and relaxing area, and there's a cheerful panelled bar. Large bedrooms in the main house are full of traditional charm and character, while those in the converted stables have a more modest appeal. *Amenities* garden.

Room phone Yes *Confirm by* 6   *Parking* Ample
Room TV Yes   *Last dinner* 9.30   *Banquets* 20/2

Hungerford

Map 4 C2 Berkshire
RG17 0EL
Hungerford (048 86) 2512

About £25 for two

Bear at Hungerford Restaurant   Ⓢ

Set menus in this attractive beamed restaurant offer a good choice of enjoyable, well-prepared dishes ranging from stuffed mussels to local trout, roast rack of lamb and medallions of venison. 🍷 *SUPERIOR.*
Credit Access, Amex, Barclaycard, Diners *Lunch* 12.30–2 *Dinner* 7.30–9.30, Sat 7.30–10 **Closed** 25 & 26 December ● **Set L** £7·45 **Set D** £8·50   &

Hunstrete

Map 4 B3 Avon
Chelwood
Near Bristol *BS18 4NS*
Compton Dando (076 18) 578
Telex 449540
Proprietors Mr & Mrs Dupays
Rooms 20
with bath/shower 20
Room phone Yes
Room TV Yes
Confirm by By arrang.
Last dinner 9.30
Parking Ample
Banquets 24/-
Closed 2 weeks January
Credit Amex, Barclaycard

Hunstrete House   81% Ⓜ   £ C

Mr and Mrs Dupays have created an exceptionally comfortable hotel in this 18th-century manor house, which stands in 90 acres of parkland. The entrance hall, with its handsome antiques and beautiful flower displays, sets the civilised, welcoming tone of the whole place, and everywhere there are lovely ornaments and paintings. Elegant traditional furnishings create a peaceful atmosphere in the library and drawing room, while a contemporary note is struck by the poster-adorned bar. Luxurious bedrooms are decorated and furnished to a very high standard, with immaculate, sumptuously equipped bathrooms. No children under nine. Guide dogs only.
Amenities garden, outdoor swimming pool, tennis, croquet.   &

Hunstrete

Map 4 B3 Avon
Chelwood
Near Bristol *BS18 4NS*
Compton Dando (076 18) 578
Proprietors Mr & Mrs Dupays

● **Set L** from £5·75
Set D from £11·50
About £45 for two

Hunstrete House Restaurant   ♔ Ⓢ

Classically based menus offer something to please all tastes at this elegant restaurant. A good choice of starters–asparagus soup, Brie and chive quiche, terrine of scallop mousse–precedes well-prepared main courses such as poached turbot, venison cutlet and our tender sliced fillet steak with an excellent mushroom sauce. Lots of delicious desserts. Soup and cold buffet for lunch. 🍷 *SUPERIOR. Credit* Amex, Barclaycard   &

Lunch 1–2, Sun 12.30–2 *Dinner* 7.30–9.30
Closed 2 weeks January

Huntingdon

Map 6 A2 Cambridgeshire
1 High Street *PE18 6TQ*
Huntingdon (0480) 52681
Telex 32706

Credit Access, Amex,
Barclaycard, Diners

Rooms 26	*Room phone* Yes	*Confirm by* 6	*Parking* Ample
with bath/shower 14	*Room TV* Yes	*Last dinner* 10.30	*Banquets* 40/–

Old Bridge Hotel   62%   £ D/E

Overlooking the river Ouse, this handsome, ivy-clad Georgian building offers a homely atmosphere and pleasantly old-fashioned service. Downstairs is a relaxing lounge with antique pieces and floral settees, as well as a friendly, comfortable bar decorated with bird prints. Cheerful bedrooms have neat fitted units and the plain bathrooms have modern fittings.
Amenities garden, coarse fishing, boating, mooring.

Huntingdon

Map 6 A2 Cambridgeshire
1 High Street *PE18 6TQ*
Huntingdon (0480) 52681

About £28 for two

Old Bridge Hotel Restaurant   ♛

Succulent roast joints carved on the trolley are popular in this handsome panelled dining room. There's also fish (smoked and fresh), fillet of beef in pastry, venison casserole and roast duckling with black cherry sauce. Imaginative starters include baked avocado with crispy bacon and cheese, and sweets are tempting. Cooking is competent and enjoyable.
🍷 *ABOVE AVERAGE. Credit* Access, Amex, Barclaycard, Diners

Lunch 12.15–2.30 *Dinner* 7.15–10.30

Hurley

Map 5 D2 Berkshire
High Street *SL6 5LX*
Littlewick Green (062 882) 4244
Telex 847035
Proprietors Mr & Mrs S. Alder
Credit Access, Amex,
Barclaycard, Diners

Rooms 19	*Room phone* Yes	*Confirm by* 6	*Parking* Ample
with bath/shower 19	*Room TV* Yes	*Last dinner* 10	*Banquets* 40/–

Ye Olde Bell Hotel   65%   Ⓜ   £ D/E

Said to be the oldest inn in England, this delightful whitewashed 12th-century hostelry is marvellously preserved, with its leaded windows and timber frame, and, inside, blackened beams and log fires in the cosy bar and lounge. Bedrooms in the main building are cottage and traditional, while those in the Bell Lodge across the road are more compact and modern. Adequate bathrooms. No dogs. *Amenities* garden.

Hurley

Map 5 D2 Berkshire
High Street *SL6 5LX*
Littlewick Green (062 882) 4244
Proprietors Mr & Mrs S. Alder

● **Set L** £9 **Set D** £12
About £44 for two

Ye Olde Bell Hotel Restaurant   Ⓢ

This large beamed dining room makes an attractive, traditional setting for an enjoyable selection of classical dishes. There's a wide choice including seasonal game, various ways with sole, grills and elaborate specialities like veal garnished with aubergines, mushrooms and palm hearts. Vegetables are well prepared and sweets include soufflés and mousses. 🍷 *SUPERIOR. Credit* Access, Amex, Barclaycard, Diners

Lunch 12.30–2.30 *Dinner* 7.30–10

Hurst Green

Map 10 B1 Lancashire
Near Whalley *BB6 9QJ*
Stonyhurst (025 486) 208

Proprietors Mr & Mrs Almonti
Credit Barclaycard

Rooms 12	*Room phone* Yes	*Confirm by* By arrang.	*Parking* Ample
with bath/shower 7	*Room TV* Yes	*Last dinner* 9.30	*Banquets* 45/10

Shireburn Arms *(Inn)*   Ⓜ   £ E

This attractive country inn, whose origins are in the 17th century, is run with charm and efficiency by Mr and Mrs Almonti. The bar and lounge are cosy and comfortable, with lots of brass and copper, antique furniture and interesting knick-knacks. Bedrooms, individually furnished to a high standard, have appealing colour schemes, good beds and some lovely old chairs. Bathrooms are adequately equipped. *Amenities* garden.

Hurstbourne Tarrant

Map 4 C3 Hampshire
Near Andover *SP11 0ER*
Hurstbourne Tarrant
(026 476) 444

Credit Access, Amex,
Barclaycard, Diners

Esseborne Manor   60%   Ⓜ   £ E

Joyce Goble has transformed this Regency house in its wooded garden into a peaceful and appealing hotel with a decor of soft pale colours and pretty wallpapers. The small bar and sunny sitting room are perfect for relaxation, while the spacious bedrooms have comfortable beds, carefully chosen furniture and attractive fabrics. Bathrooms are well equipped.
Amenities garden.

Continued

| Rooms 6 | Room phone Yes | Confirm by By arrang. | Parking Ample |
| with bath/shower 6 | Room TV Yes | Last dinner 9.30 | Banquets 45/– |

Hurstbourne Tarrant

Map 4 C3 Hampshire
Near Andover *SP11 0ER*
Hurstbourne Tarrant
(026 476) 444

Esseborne Manor Restaurant Ⓢ

Fresh flowers, dainty napkins and dark polished tables give this dining room a charming traditional atmosphere. Joyce Goble uses good fresh ingredients for her short, regularly changing menu, which includes dishes like pork with juniper berries and trout with almonds and lime butter. Vegetables are excellent and sweets light and delectable. Sunday lunch is a set meal.
Credit Access, Amex, Barclaycard, Diners

● **Set L** Sun only £5·50
About £25 for two

Lunch Sun 12–2, Mon–Sat by arrangement only *Dinner* 7.30–9.30
Closed D Sun to non-residents

Husbands Bosworth

Map 11 D4 Leicestershire
Berridges Lane *LE17 6LE*
Market Harborough
(0858) 880551
Proprietors Mr & Mrs R. J. Speight

Fernie Lodge  Ⓢ

Friendly waitresses serve in this elegant airy dining room in a large Georgian house. The fixed-price menus offer a remarkably wide choice of dishes all prepared to a consistently high standard from the finest raw materials, and ranging from Cotswold trout stuffed with crab to oxtail braised in Burgundy. There are some luscious sweets, too. Book well in advance. Gentlemen are requested to wear ties.

● **Set L** from £5 **Set D** £9·50
About £26 for two

Lunch 12.15–1.15 *Dinner* 7–9.30
Closed L Sat, all Sun, Mon, Bank Hols, 2 weeks July & 10 days Christmas

Hythe

Map 7 C6 Kent
Prince's Parade *CT21 6AE*
Hythe (0303) 67441
Telex 965082

Credit Access, Amex,
Barclaycard, Diners

Hotel Imperial 64% Ⓜ £C/D

Space, comfort and excellent leisure facilities attract holiday-makers to this seafront hotel, whose public rooms include a relaxing lounge and two popular bars. Large bedrooms have built-in furniture and fine views. No dogs. *Amenities* garden, sauna, indoor swimming pool, squash, tennis, 9-hole golf course, coarse & sea fishing, dancing (most Sats Sept–Easter), croquet, putting, bowls, snooker, table tennis, pool table, riding, solarium.

| Rooms 86 | Room phone Yes | Confirm by 6 | Parking Ample |
| with bath/shower 86 | Room TV Yes | Last dinner 9 | Banquets 200/– |

Hythe

Map 7 C6 Kent
West Parade *CT21 6DT*
Hythe (0303) 68263

Manager Mr A. J. Hall
Credit Access, Amex,
Barclaycard, Diners

Stade Court Hotel 55% £D/E

Pleasant staff and access to the extensive leisure facilities at the nearby Hotel Imperial make this unassuming seafront hotel ideal for a family holiday. Functional public areas include a small bar, and a sun lounge and TV room on the first floor. Simple bedrooms are similar in style, with coordinated soft furnishings and practical fitted units. Bathrooms are modern.

| Rooms 32 | Room phone Yes | Confirm by By arrang. | Parking Ample |
| with bath/shower 26 | Room TV Most | Last dinner 9 | Banquets 100/30 |

Ilkley

Map 10 C1 West Yorkshire
Church Street *LS29 9DR*
Ilkley (0943) 608484
Proprietors
Malcolm Reid & Colin Long
French cooking

● **Set D** (low season) £9·95
About £52 for two
Banquets 30/8

Box Tree Restaurant ★ ★ 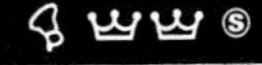 Ⓢ

A veritable Aladdin's cave of paintings and objets d'art, this is also an exceptional eating place. Michael Lawson's faultless technique–superb flavours, textures and sauces and outstanding presentations–makes for meals to remember, based on classical French recipes and including such delights as salmon and sole mousseline and brilliantly simple lamb fillets accompanied by perfect vegetables. Grapefruit sorbet makes a tangy bridge between starter and main course, and there are some luscious desserts.
Specialities mousseline de volaille au Roquefort, mélodie de poissons de mer, biscuit glacé aux trois parfums et son coulis.
🍷 *OUTSTANDING. Credit* Access, Amex, Barclaycard, Diners

Dinner only 7.30–9.30
Closed Sun, Mon, 1 January & 25 & 26 December

Ilkley
Map 10 C1 West Yorkshire
Cowpasture Road *LS29 8RQ*
Ilkley (0943) 607676
Telex 51137

Credit Access, Amex,
Barclaycard, Diners

Rooms 76	Room phone Yes	Confirm by 6	Parking Ample
with bath/shower 52	Room TV Yes	Last dinner 9.30	Banquets 350/10

Craiglands Hotel 64% £ D

Originally built as a spa hotel, this imposing Victorian building has pleasantly spacious public rooms including a foyer-lounge with splendid views across the gardens to the Yorkshire Dales. Homely bedrooms are gradually being refurbished with smart fitted units and bedside consoles. Bathrooms are adequate. *Amenities* garden, tennis, dancing (Fri, Sat), pitch & putt, croquet, games room.

Inglesham
Map 4 C2 Wiltshire
Highworth
Near Swindon *SN6 7QY*
Faringdon (0367) 52298
French cooking

About £28 for two
Banquets 35/28

Inglesham Forge

Silky smooth terrine maison, light, airy soufflés and home-made sorbets help to give the menu here an unmistakably Gallic flavour. Seamus O'Kelly is an accomplished chef who selects ingredients with great care, and specialities like our excellent salmon coulibiac show a truly professional touch. Friendly waitresses add to the pleasant atmosphere in this cosy restaurant.
Credit Access, Amex, Barclaycard, Diners

Lunch 11.30–3 *Dinner* 6–12
Closed L Mon & Sat, all Sun & 25–30 December

Ipswich
Map 6 C3 Suffolk
Belstead Road *IP2 9HB*
Ipswich (0473) 684241
Telex 987674
Proprietors Hatfield family
Credit Access, Amex,
Barclaycard, Diners

Rooms 26	Room phone Yes	Confirm by By arrang.	Parking Ample
with bath/shower 26	Room TV Yes	Last dinner 9.30	Banquets 50/2

Belstead Brook Hotel 67% Ⓜ £ D/E

Set two miles out of the town in attractive gardens complete with peacocks and a running brook, this charming hotel has been in the Hatfield family for more than 25 years. Mellow oak panelling, beams and an open fire set the tone in the bar-lounge, while tastefully decorated bedrooms in the extension have modern fitted units, tea/coffee-makers and trouser presses. Compact bathrooms. No dogs. *Amenities* garden.

Ipswich
Map 6 C3 Suffolk
Tavern Street *IP1 3AH*
Ipswich (0473) 56558

Credit Access, Amex,
Barclaycard, Diners

Rooms 56	Room phone Yes	Confirm by 6	Parking Difficult
with bath/shower 7	Room TV Yes	Last dinner 9.15	Banquets 185/–

Great White Horse Hotel 53% £ D

Charles Dickens stayed at this friendly hotel when he worked as a reporter on the *Ipswich Chronicle*, and the Pickwick bedroom lovingly preserves the flavour of his time. Other rooms are in simpler traditional style, all with tea-makers and radios, and bathrooms are modern. There is a popular bar on the ground floor and a larger cocktail bar upstairs.
Amenities buttery (10am–10pm).

Ipswich
Map 6 C3 Suffolk
73 Henley Road *IP1 3SP*
Ipswich (0473) 57677
Telex 81630
Managers Mr & Mrs D. A. Brooks
Credit Access, Amex,
Barclaycard, Diners

Rooms 25	Room phone Yes	Confirm by By arrang.	Parking Ample
with bath/shower 21	Room TV Yes	Last dinner 9	Banquets 85/–

Marlborough Hotel 64% £ D

A pleasing, comfortable atmosphere pervades this converted Victorian house away from the centre of town. The warmly inviting foyer-lounge with well-placed reading lamps and comfortable sofas leads to a cosy cocktail bar. There are a few traditionally furnished bedrooms in the main building, but most are in a modern extension at the rear and have carefully chosen decor and nicely equipped bathrooms. *Amenities* garden.

Ipswich
Map 6 C3 Suffolk
73 Henley Road *IP1 3SP*
Ipswich (0473) 57677
Managers
Mr & Mrs D. A. Brooks

Marlborough Hotel Restaurant Ⓢ

This charmingly laid-out dining room overlooking a garden is a lovely setting in which to enjoy a wide-ranging menu of established favourites like roast duckling (with ginger and lemon stuffing) and more unusual items such as pork fillet and scampi in a cream and brandy sauce. Vegetables are imaginatively handled, and there's an attractive sweet trolley.
🍷 *SUPERIOR. Credit* Access, Amex, Barclaycard, Diners

Continued

● **Set L** Sun only £6·75
Set D £8
About £31 for two

Lunch 12.30–2 *Dinner* 7–9

Ipswich
Map 6 C3 Suffolk
London Road *IP2 0UA*
Ipswich (0473) 212313
Telex 987150

Credit Access, Amex,
Barclaycard, Diners

Post House Hotel   59%   **£ D**

This two-storey brick and glass building lies south of Ipswich on the A12. A life-size carving of a Suffolk Punch horse stands in the foyer, which leads to the bright, comfortable bars and lounges. Bedrooms are cheerfully decorated and all have colour TV, tea-makers, mini-bars and well-fitted bathrooms with showers. *Amenities* garden, outdoor swimming pool, laundry room, buttery (11am–10.30pm).

Rooms 118	*Room phone* Yes	*Confirm by* 6	*Parking* Ample
with bath/shower 118	*Room TV* Yes	*Last dinner* 10	*Banquets* 120/4

Ipswich
Map 6 C3 Suffolk
200 St Helen's Street *IP4 2LH*
Ipswich (0473) 55236
Proprietor Rosemarie Farrell
English cooking

● **Set D** £8·50
About £25 for two
Banquets 16/–

Rosie's Place

Trailing greenery now fills the windows of this former butcher's shop, and the atmosphere within is very cosy. Rosemarie Farrell's short menu is thoroughly English, from smoked Cornish mackerel and mashed parsnips to steak and kidney pie (with optional oysters) or devilled pork chops, and there are sweets such as syllabub and treacle tart. Everything is lovingly prepared and served in the friendliest fashion. *Credit* Amex

Dinner only 7–10 Sat 7–10.30
Closed Sun, 25 December & 3 weeks summer

Ivinghoe
Map 5 E1 Buckinghamshire
Near Leighton Buzzard *LU7 9EB*
Cheddington (0296) 668388
Manager Georges de Maison

● **Set L & Set D** £8·50
About £32 for two
Banquets 80/12

King's Head

An attractive beamed restaurant with dark oak pillars in a creeper-clad 17th-century building. The à la carte and fixed-price menus offer a varied choice of competently prepared French and traditional English dishes—from flambéed medallions of beef, coated with cream and green peppercorns, to jugged hare—made all the more enjoyable by careful seasoning.
Credit Access, Amex, Barclaycard, Diners

Lunch 12.30–2 *Dinner* 7.30–10, Sun 7.30–9.30
Closed D Sun January & February & D 25 December

Our inspectors never book in the name of the Egon Ronay Organisation; they disclose their identity only after paying their bills.

Jervaulx
Map 15 B6 North Yorkshire
Near Masham
Ripon *HG4 4PH*
Bedale (0677) 60235

Rooms 8
with bath/shower 5
Room phone No
Room TV No
Confirm by By arrang.
Last dinner 8
Parking Ample
Banquets 30/–
Closed January & February

Credit Access, Barclaycard

Jervaulx Hall Country House Hotel   71%   Ⓜ   **£ E**

Approached through an archway by a circular gravel drive, this fine 19th-century house stands in eight acres of beautiful grounds by the ruins of Jervaulx Abbey, a Cistercian house dissolved by Henry VIII. The warmly decorated entrance hall has some elegant Victorian furnishings, a wood-burning stove in the fireplace and Chinese rugs on the floor, and a sunny lounge in pale blue has French windows which open on to the gardens. Attractive pictures and prints are a feature throughout. Good-sized bedrooms, all with lovely views, are furnished in a mixture of antique and modern styles; bathrooms are roomy and well equipped.
Amenities garden, croquet.

White Arrow
BEDFORD
ELECTRIC
CON 160V

Engineering for World Transport

Most of Britain's vehicles start life with a Lucas battery. High on technology, these compact power packs ensure first time starting in all weathers, with the added bonus of a long and trouble-free life.

Lucas advanced battery expertise is quietly demonstrated by the traffic-compatible Bedford CF electric van, powered by Lucas batteries, equipped with Lucas electric drive and developed as a system by Lucas over more than a decade.

Jevington

Map 7 B6 East Sussex
Near Eastbourne *BN26 5QF*
Polegate (032 12) 2178
Proprietors
Nigel & Sue Mackenzie

● **Set L** £8 **Set D** £9·15
About £27 for two

Hungry Monk ⑤

Nigel and Sue Mackenzie's cheerfully decorated country restaurant makes a cosy setting for daily-changing set menus based on a varied choice of local produce, seasonal fish and game. Individual flavours are brought out well, as in our venison and pigeon pie, and vegetables are nicely judged. Tempting sweets include sorbets and cheesecake, and a glass of port comes with all meals. Booking essential.

Lunch Sun only 12–2 *Dinner* 7–10
Closed 24 & 25 December

Kendal

Map 13 D5 Cumbria
26 Wildman Street *LA9 6EN*
Kendal (0539) 21170
Proprietors Elaine Wright &
Avril Leigh

● **Set D** £9·50
About £29 for two

Castle Dairy ♧ ⑤

Diners should book and arrive on time at this cosy old-world restaurant where Elaine Wright recites the splendid five-course set menu. Local delicacies ranging from Windermere char and tender smoked chicken to roast venison with fresh horseradish sauce are served with commendably simple vegetables; sweets include enjoyable strawberry Pavlova, and there's superb Stilton to finish.

Dinner only at 8
Closed Sun–Tues, 25 & 26 December, 1st week January & August

Kendal

Map 13 D5 Cumbria
Station Road *LA9 6BT*
Kendal (0539) 22461

Credit Access, Amex,
Barclaycard, Diners

Rooms 30
with bath/shower 26

County Hotel   59% £E

Behind an unassuming facade this is a well-run, comfortable and friendly hotel. The small reception area has showcases displaying local wares, and one of the two bars, the Parr Lounge, has Tudor-style decor. Upstairs, there's a pleasant little residents' lounge. Bright, fully carpeted bedrooms have contemporary fitted furniture and plenty of storage space. Compact bathrooms are well kept. *Amenities* discothèque (Sat October–March).

Room phone Yes	*Confirm by* 6	*Parking* Limited
Room TV Yes	*Last dinner* 9	*Banquets* 75/10

Kendal

Map 13 D5 Cumbria
Stricklandgate *LA9 4ND*
Kendal (0539) 23852
Telex 53168

Credit Access, Amex,
Barclaycard, Diners

Rooms 58
with bath/shower 58

Woolpack Hotel   59% £E

Skilful modernisation has increased the accommodation of this 18th-century coaching inn near the market place. Rooms in the spacious wing have modern units and colour schemes; those in the main building are pretty and more traditional, some with shower rooms only. Public rooms include a fine old bar once used for wool auctions. *Amenities* coffee shop (June–October 10am–10pm, November–May 10am–4pm).

Room phone Yes	*Confirm by* By arrang.	*Parking* Ample
Room TV Yes	*Last dinner* 9	*Banquets* 100/6

Kenilworth

Map 10 C4 Warwickshire
97a Warwick Road *CV8 1HP*
Kenilworth (0926) 52463

French cooking

● **Set L & Set D** £9
About £32 for two
Banquets 26/–

Restaurant Bosquet ♧ ⑤

As intimate in style as a private drawing room, this cosy restaurant has maintained its reputation for capable French cooking thanks to the efforts of its new owners. Dishes like calf's liver and kidneys with juniper sauce or turbot with salmon mousse in a rich morel sauce show imagination and lovely presentation, while sweets such as lime mousse set on jellied muscat wine also delight the eye and palate. 🍷*ABOVE AVERAGE.*

Lunch by arrangement only *Dinner* 7–10
Closed L Sat & Sun all Bank Holidays, 2 weeks August & 1 week Christmas

Kenilworth

Map 10 C4 Warwickshire
High Street *CV8 1LZ*
Kenilworth (0926) 57668

Proprietor Mr Martin Lea
Credit Access, Amex,
Barclaycard, Diners

Clarendon House Hotel *(Inn)* Ⓜ £E

Martin Lea generates an atmosphere of warmth and hospitality in this fine old 16th-century inn. There's a brightly decorated split-level bar as well as a homely TV lounge with carved mahogany furniture and comfortable settees. Compact bedrooms—some in the original house, some in the extension—are neat and cheerful, two with four-posters. Good modern bath or shower rooms. *Amenities* garden.

Continued

Rooms 14	*Room phone* No	*Confirm by* 6.30	*Parking* Limited
with bath/shower 9	*Room TV* No	*Last dinner* 9	

Kenilworth

Map 10 C4 Warwickshire
The Square *CV8 1ED*
Kenilworth (0926) 55944
Telex 311012
Manager Mr Patrick Griffin
Credit Access, Amex,
Barclaycard, Diners

De Montfort Hotel   65%   £ D

Extensive conference facilities make this modern red-brick hotel popular with the business community. There's also a bright, contemporary foyer and lounge, two bars and a cheery coffee shop. Sixty bedrooms have been redecorated in pleasing pastel shades, with smart fitted furniture and new curtains and bedspreads. Well-equipped bathrooms. *Amenities* garden, discothèque (Fri), pool table, croquet, coffee shop (10am–10pm Mon–Sat).

Rooms 100	*Room phone* Yes	*Confirm by* By arrang.	*Parking* Ample
with bath/shower 100	*Room TV* Yes	*Last dinner* 9.30	*Banquets* 200/–

Kenilworth

Map 10 C4 Warwickshire
121 Warwick Road *CV8 1HP*
Kenilworth (0926) 53763

French cooking

● **Set L** £4·20
Aboutr £30 for two
Banquets 45/12

Restaurant Diment   Ⓢ

French-inspired dishes dominate the weekly changing menu at this pleasant corner restaurant, where the service is friendly and the ambience warm and relaxing. Enjoyable standards are maintained throughout a range which could include smooth tomato soup with tarragon, breast of wild duck with blackcurrants and deliciously rich desserts like chocolate cream with coffee sauce. *Credit* Access, Amex, Barclaycard, Diners

Lunch 12–2 *Dinner* 7–10, Sat 7–10.30 **Closed** L Sat, all Sun, Mon (except during N.E.C. exhibitions), 26 December, 1st January & 1st 3 weeks August

Keston

Map 7 B5 Kent
6 Commonside
Near Bromley *BR2 6BP*
Farnborough (0689) 56410
Proprietor G. Artini
Italian cooking

● **Set L** £5·75
About £30 for two

Giannino's   Ⓢ

Crowds flock to this friendly little restaurant so it's wise to book. The menu has a varied choice of well-prepared Italian dishes distinguished by really excellent ingredients, from gigantic scampi to superb tender veal. Vegetables are nicely handled and there's a carefully chosen selection of tempting home-made sweets.
Credit Access, Barclaycard, Diners

Lunch 12–2.30 *Dinner* 7–10 **Closed** Sun, Mon, Bank Holidays, 1st 3 weeks August & 24 December–3 January

Keswick

Map 13 C5 Cumbria
Station Road *CA12 4NQ*
Keswick (0596) 72020
Telex 64200

Credit Access, Amex,
Barclaycard, Diners

Keswick Hotel   62%   £ D

Set in four acres of attractive grounds, this imposing, turreted Victorian building enjoys a peaceful hillside setting above the town. Lofty public rooms boast some fine antiques, and there is a comfortable cocktail bar and residents' lounge, plus a well-stocked conservatory. Bedrooms have good modern furniture and armchairs, and well-equipped bathrooms are beautifully kept. *Amenities* garden, putting, croquet, games room.   ♿

Rooms 64	*Room phone* Yes	*Confirm by* 6	*Parking* Ample
with bath/shower 64	*Room TV* Yes	*Last dinner* 9.30	*Banquets* 120/8

Keswick

Map 13 C5 Cumbria
Borrowdale *CA12 5UX*
Borrowdale (059 684) 285
Telex 64305
Proprietors England family
Rooms 72
with bath/shower 72
Room phone Yes
Room TV Yes
Confirm by By arrang.
Last dinner 9
Parking Ample

Closed November–March

Lodore Swiss Hotel   76%   Ⓜ   £ C/D

Marvellously situated in 40 acres of grounds overlooking Derwent Water, this superbly modernised 17th-century granite building makes a splendid holiday centre for families. Fresh flowers, deep leather armchairs, some lightwood panelling and even an ornamental fountain help to create an impression of relaxed luxury in the spacious public rooms. All the bedrooms have good views and are individually styled with tasteful coordinated fabrics; bathrooms are very well equipped and fully tiled. No dogs.

Continued

Continued

Amenities garden, sauna, indoor & outdoor swimming pools, tennis, squash, dancing (Sat), massage, children's playground, games room, ladies' hair-dressing, solarium, nursery.

Keswick
Map 13 C5 Cumbria
Borrowdale *CA12 5UX*
Borrowdale (059 684) 285
Proprietors England family

Lodore Swiss Hotel Restaurant

Chef Kurt Hartmann's adventurous menu features dishes like duck breast with mushroom purée, or monkfish with leeks, alongside more familiar items such as Dover sole meunière and partridge, plus, of course, the occasional Swiss speciality like émincé de veau zurichoise. Cooking is reliable, and the magnificent views add to the pleasure of a meal in the handsome modern dining room. ☕ *SUPERIOR.*

● **Set L** £6 **Set D** £8
About £30 for two

Lunch 1–2 *Dinner* 7–9
Closed November–March

Keswick
Map 13 C5 Cumbria
Borrowdale *CA12 5UU*
Borrowdale (059 684) 223

Closed 2 weeks mid December

Mary Mount Country House Hotel   61%   £ D/E

Attentive personal service adds to the pleasure of a stay at this well-maintained hotel on the shores of beautiful Derwent Water. Public rooms like the bar and lounge are comfortable and relaxing in contemporary style, as are the well-furnished bedrooms (the biggest are in the annexe), which have good modern bathrooms. Guests may use the amenities of the Lodore Swiss Hotel. No dogs. *Amenities* garden.

Rooms 15
with bath/shower 15

Room phone Yes	*Confirm by* 6	*Parking* Ample
Room TV Yes	*Last dinner* 8.30	*Banquets* 50/15

Kew

Le Provence

See under London Economy Evening Meals

Kildwick
Map 10 C1 West Yorkshire
Near Keighley *BD20 9AE*
Cross Hills (0535) 32244

Rooms 12
with bath/shower 12
Room phone Yes
Room TV Yes
Confirm by By arrang.
Last dinner 9.30
Parking Ample
Banquets 64/4

Credit Access, Amex,
Barclaycard, Diners

Kildwick Hall   77%   Ⓜ   £ C/D

Superlatives are in order to describe this handsome Jacobean stone manor house on the wooded slopes of the Aire Valley. It has been lovingly restored by John and Julia Sharpe, who are now at work on the 200-year-old garden. The entrance hall with its heavy beams, fine oak panelling and enormous fireplace makes an impressive lounge bar, and there is also a delightfully relaxing residents' lounge. The sumptuous bedrooms—one still has its original 17th-century four-poster—combine the antique charm of mullioned windows with every modern comfort, including luxurious bathrooms.
Amenities garden, putting, croquet.

Kingham
Map 4 C1 Oxfordshire
OX7 6UH
Kingham (060 871) 255

Credit Amex, Barclaycard,
Diners

Rooms 11
with bath/shower 8

Mill Hotel   55%   Ⓜ   £ D/E

The Barnetts have worked hard to improve standards of comfort throughout this converted mill situated on the B4450 in tranquil countryside. Original features include flagstone floors in the tastefully furnished lounge and a splendid stone hearth in the rustic bar. There's a TV lounge, too. Bedrooms have attractive floral fabrics and modern furniture. No children under five.
Amenities garden, game fishing, clay pigeon shooting, golf driving range.

Room phone No	*Confirm by* 6	*Parking* Ample
Room TV No	*Last dinner* 8.30	*Banquets* 50/–

King's Lynn

Map 6 B1 Norfolk
Tuesday Market Place *PE30 1JS*
King's Lynn (0553) 4996
Telex 817349
Manager Mr F. Shone
Credit Access, Amex,
Barclaycard, Diners

Rooms 72
with bath/shower 72

Duke's Head Hotel   66%   £D

Overlooking the market square, this comfortably modernised inn, whose origins go back to the 17th century, is a lively, cheerful place. Its large panelled lounge is warmly welcoming, with plenty of comfortable armchairs, and there are two popular bars. Pleasantly decorated bedrooms, furnished mainly in contemporary style, have tea-makers and bedside controls. Well-fitted modern bathrooms. *Amenities* buttery (9.45am–10.30pm)

Room phone Yes	*Confirm by* 6	*Parking* Ample
Room TV Yes	*Last dinner* 9.30	*Banquets* 230/3

Kingsbridge

Map 3 D3 Devon
Goveton *TQ7 2DS*
Kingsbridge (0548) 3055
Props Mr & Mrs V. E. Shepherd
Credit Access, Amex,
Barclaycard
Closed 1 December–1 March

Rooms 13
with bath/shower 13

Buckland-Tout-Saints Hotel   69%   Ⓜ   £D

This fine 18th-century manor house looks out on to beautiful landscaped gardens and acres of parkland. Elegant public rooms include a large entrance hall and comfortable lounge with lovely pine panelling, polished wood floors and mahogany doors. Spacious bedrooms are attractively furnished in traditional style, and well-kept bathrooms (two with showers only) are modern. *Amenities* garden, croquet, putting.

Room phone Yes	*Confirm by* 4	*Parking* Ample
Room TV Some	*Last dinner* 8.45	

Kingsland

Map 4 A1 Hereford & Worcester
Near Leominster *HR6 9QS*
Kingsland (056 881) 355

● **Set L** Sun only £4·25
About £20 for two

Angel Inn

Solid oak beams and rough plaster walls make a delightfully rustic setting for enjoying some excellent cooking. Dinner menus on Tuesday to Saturday could include flavoursome pork and tomato soup, smoked prawns with aïoli, pheasant in red wine, and lamb cutlets with tomato and garlic sauce. Tempting sweets, too. At other times the menu is simpler (grills, etc.).
Credit Access, Barclaycard, Diners

Lunch 12.30–1.30 *Dinner* 7.15–9, Sat 7.15–9.30
Closed L Sat & 25 December

Kingston

Map 5 E2 Surrey
Canbury Gardens
Lower Ham Road *KT2 5BD*
01–546 6562

● **Set L** from £3·50
Set D from £8
About £36 for two
Banquets 60/2

Down by the Riverside

As its name suggests, a lovely position right on the banks of the Thames is part of the attraction of this pleasant restaurant, where the menu features a wide choice of international dishes plus a few Swiss specialities. Our thick French onion soup was delicious with a home-baked roll, the saddle of venison tender, and the chocolate walnut gâteau light and creamy.
Credit Access, Amex, Diners

Lunch 11.45–3 *Dinner* 7–11.30
Closed L Sat & all 24 December

Kintbury

Map 4 C2 Berkshire
Near Newbury *RG15 0UT*
Kintbury (048 85) 263
Proprietors
Mr & Mrs D. A. Dalzell-Piper

● **Set D** from £12·50
About £36 for two

Dundas Arms Restaurant

Mrs Dalzell-Piper takes the orders at this charming country restaurant, while husband David beavers away in the kitchen. The three-course dinner menu offers a good selection of interesting dishes like smooth, subtle terrine of scallops and salmon fillet with tomato coulis and noisettes of lamb with kidneys and béarnaise sauce. Excellent puddings, too.
🍷*SUPERIOR. Credit* Access, Amex, Barclaycard, Diners

Dinner only 7.30–9.15
Closed Sun, Mon & Royal Ascot week

Kinver

Map 10 B4 West Midlands
High Street
Near Stourbridge *DY7 6HG*
Kinver (038 483) 3679

Berkleys Restaurant, Piano Room   Ⓢ

A pianist plays, and Andrew Mortimer presides over the kitchen of this light, friendly restaurant above a bistro. His imaginative set dinner menus range from soup with croûtons and delicate mousseline of sole with spinach to fillet steak, veal with morels and our deliciously sauced suprême of chicken coated with hazelnuts and served with a selection of really excellent vegetables. *Credit* Access, Amex, Barclaycard, Diners

                                                   Continued

Continued
● **Set D** £12·50
About £34 for two
Banquets 30/12

Dinner only 7–10, Sat 7–10.30
Closed 25 & 26 December

Kirkby
Map 10 A2 Merseyside
Cherryfield Drive *L32 8SB*
051–546 4355

Credit Access, Amex,
Barclaycard, Diners
Closed 25 December–2 January

Rooms 70
with bath/shower 70

Golden Eagle Hotel   57%   £E

A modern town-centre hotel offering comfortable accommodation for business people and short-stay guests. Good-sized bedrooms–some in studio style–have pleasant pastel decor, neat built-in furniture units and tea/coffee-making facilities. The cocktail bar has been refurbished in a cool, modern manner, and there are plans to redecorate other public rooms. *Amenities* 24-hour laundry service.

Room phone Yes	*Confirm by* 6	*Parking* Ample
Room TV Yes	*Last dinner* 9.30	*Banquets* 35/–

Kirkby Fleetham
Map 15 B5 North Yorkshire
Northallerton *DL7 0SU*
Northallerton (0609) 748226

Rooms 11
with bath/shower 11
Room phone Yes
Room TV Yes
Confirm by By arrang.
Last dinner 9.15
Parking Ample
Banquets 25/–
Closed 2 weeks January

Credit Amex, Barclaycard,
Diners

Kirkby Fleetham Hall   78%      £E

Mr and Mrs Grant continue to lavish much care on this substantial Georgian manor set in 30 peaceful acres not far from the A1. A fine lounge with leather chesterfields overlooks the lake, and drinks are served in a delightfully homely library. Large bedrooms with pleasant views have good antique and reproduction furniture and carpeted bathrooms are thoughtfully equipped. Friendly and efficient service. *Amenities* garden.

Kirkbymoorside
Map 15 C6 North Yorkshire
Market Place *YO6 6AA*
Kirkbymoorside (0751) 31637
Proprietors Mr & Mrs Curtis &
Mr & Mrs Austin
Credit Access, Barclaycard
Closed 25 & 26 December

Rooms 17
with bath/shower 15

George & Dragon *(Inn)*      £E

Looking out on to the cobbled market square, this immaculate, family-run coaching inn has plenty of old-world charm, particularly in the delightful beamed bar with its horse brasses and open fireplace. Most of the bright, spotless bedrooms are across the courtyard in a converted granary that also contains a pretty lounge. Compact, carpeted bathrooms. Guide dogs only. *Amenities* garden.   &

Room phone No	*Confirm by* 5	*Parking* Ample
Room TV No	*Last dinner* 8.30	

Knaresborough
Map 15 C6 North Yorkshire
Bond End *HG5 9AL*
Harrogate (0423) 863302

Credit Access, Barclaycard
Closed 25 & 26 December

Rooms 20
with bath/shower 18

Dower House Hotel   62%   Ⓜ   £D/E

A handsome 16th-century red-brick building forms the main part of this friendly owner-run hotel. A cosy bar and a modern lounge are in this section, while the smart foyer is in the newer wing. Older bedrooms, many with cottage oak beams, are decorated in a variety of styles; those in the extension have shag-pile carpets and attractive modern fittings. Good bathrooms throughout. *Amenities* garden.

Room phone Yes	*Confirm by* By arrang.	*Parking* Ample
Room TV Yes	*Last dinner* 9.30	*Banquets* 85/40

Knutsford
Map 10 B2 Cheshire
60 King Street *WA16 2DT*
Knutsford (0565) 3060
Proprietors
Mr & Mrs K. Mooney
Credit Access, Amex,
Barclaycard, Diners

La Belle Epoque Hotel   56%   Ⓜ   £F

An essentially Edwardian ambience characterises this fascinating hotel, which enshrines many examples of the Art Nouveau style. The reception-lounge (which doubles as a bar and breakfast room) has a remarkable mosaic floor of Venetian glass, an Art Nouveau fireplace and many sepia prints. Bedrooms provide adequate comfort, and share a single public bathroom. No children under seven. No dogs. Accommodation Mon–Fri only.

Continued

Rooms 5	Room phone No	Confirm by By arrang.	Parking Difficult
with bath/shower None	Room TV Yes	Last dinner 10	Banquets 100/10

Knutsford
Map 10 B2 Cheshire
60 King Street *WA16 2DT*
Knutsford (0565) 3060
Proprietors Mr & Mrs K. Mooney
French cooking

La Belle Epoque Hotel Restaurant ♕ Ⓢ

Original Art Nouveau decor complements the authentic French cooking in this charming restaurant. Dishes like chicken breast with champagne sauce and stuffed quail with wild rice and Madeira sauce are nicely flavoured and served with skilfully cooked fresh vegetables, while the sweet trolley has some deliciously light creations. ♟*ABOVE AVERAGE.*
Credit Access, Amex, Barclaycard, Diners

● **Set L & Set D** £5·90
About £31 for two

Dinner only 7–10
Closed Sun & Bank Holidays

Lacock
Map 4 B2 Wiltshire
6 Church Street *SN15 2LB*
Lacock (024 973) 230

Proprietors Levis family
Closed 23 December–
1 January

Sign of the Angel *(Inn)* Ⓜ £E

The charm of this ancient inn owes much to the Levis family, who have loved and cared for it for nearly 30 years. An enchanting half-timbered facade gives way to an equally pleasing interior, typified by the upstairs lounge full of beams, panelling and polished antiques. Quaint whitewashed bedrooms have pretty bed coverings and thoroughly modern little bathrooms. No children under ten. *Amenities* garden.

Rooms 6	Room phone No	Confirm by 6.30	Parking Limited
with bath/shower 6	Room TV No	Last dinner 8	Banquets 25/8

Lacock
Map 4 B2 Wiltshire
6 Church Street *SN15 2LB*
Lacock (024 973) 230
Proprietors Levis family
English cooking

Sign of the Angel Restaurant ♞ Ⓢ

The beamed, rustic setting is just right for the best of simple, straightforward English cooking. The main course is always a roast–perhaps duck or superb rare roast beef with all the trimmings–and there's a choice of starters such as devilled kidneys and creamy salmon mousse. Irresistible sweets range from home-made ice cream or profiteroles to the deliciously unusual treacle lick. ♟*ABOVE AVERAGE.*

● **Set L** £8·50, Sun £12·50
Set D £12·50
About £34 for two

Lunch 1–1.30 *Dinner* 7.30–8
Closed L Sat, D Sun & 23 December–1 January

Lamorna Cove
Map 2 A4 Cornwall
Near Penzance *TR19 6XH*
Mousehole (073 673) 411
Proprietors
Mr & Mrs G. S. Bolton & family
Credit Access, Amex,
Barclaycard, Diners

Lamorna Cove Hotel 66% Ⓜ £D

Fine views are a feature of this tastefully modernised, family-run hotel on the wooded slopes of the cove. Modern furnishings and antiques blend happily in the lounges, and the neat bedrooms have melamine furniture, comfortable beds and centrally heated bathrooms. Additional accommodation in two cottages is ideal for families. *Amenities* garden, sauna, outdoor swimming pool. **Closed** December & January.

Rooms 18	Room phone Some	Confirm by 6	Parking Limited
with bath/shower 18	Room TV Yes	Last dinner 9.45	

Lamorna Cove
Map 2 A4 Cornwall
Near Penzance *TR19 6XH*
Mousehole (073 673) 411
Proprietors
Mr & Mrs G. S. Bolton & family

Lamorna Cove Hotel Restaurant Ⓢ

A light, airy restaurant where a typical evening table d'hôte choice might be fresh salmon salad, sole with mushrooms and prawns, or lamb chops. The carte offers more adventurous dishes such as cheese and ham profiteroles, and delicious local seafood, all competently prepared. Nicely varied puddings like savarin, croquenbouche or pears in red wine.
Credit Access, Amex, Barclaycard, Diners

● **Set L** Sun only £5·25
Set D £7·95
About £29 for two

Lunch 12.30–2 *Dinner* 7.30–9.45
Closed December & January

Langham
Map 11 E3 Leicestershire
Near Oakham *LE15 7HU*
Oakham (0572) 2931

Noel Arms Ⓢ

A peaceful place in the heart of rolling countryside, this homely pub restaurant offers a varied range of well-loved English dishes. Start with a

Continued

Continued
English cooking

home-made soup of the day, and go on to a roast, a country pie, tender baked ham or perhaps Dover sole. Ingredients are of excellent quality, and there's an enterprising choice of fresh vegetables. ♟*ABOVE AVERAGE.*
Credit Access, Amex, Barclaycard, Diners

Lunch 12.30–2 *Dinner* 7.15–9.45

About £29 for two

Lanreath

Map 2 C3 Cornwall
Near Looe *PL13 2NX*
Lanreath (0503) 20218
Proprietors
Mr & Mrs T. C. Mansfield

Closed November–1 April

Punch Bowl Inn *(Inn)* Ⓜ £E

Formerly a courthouse, coaching inn and smugglers' haunt, this charming old hostelry in a peaceful Cornish village is now a popular holiday hotel. The flagstoned bars are favourite local meeting places, and there's a bright modern residents' lounge overlooking the little garden. Bedrooms vary in size, decor and furnishings: some have modern fitted units, and a few feature splendid four-posters. *Amenities* garden.

Rooms 20	*Room phone* No	*Confirm by* 6	*Parking* Ample
with bath/shower 13	*Room TV* Most	*Last dinner* 9.30	

Lavenham

Map 6 C3 Suffolk
High Street *CO10 9QA*
Lavenham (0787) 247477

Credit Access, Amex,
Barclaycard, Diners

Swan Hotel 62% £D

Tourists appreciate the old-world charm of this carefully modernised and very welcoming hotel. The heavily beamed lounges are furnished in cosy traditional style, and the quarry-tiled Old Bar has plenty of character; another bar has pleasant views over the garden. Bedrooms, too, are beamed and traditional, with good beds and efficient central heating providing up-to-date comfort. Bathrooms are large and well equipped. *Amenities* garden.

Rooms 42	*Room phone* Yes	*Confirm by* 6	*Parking* Ample
with bath/shower 42	*Room TV* Yes	*Last dinner* 9.30	*Banquets* 100/6

Leamington Spa

Map 10 C4 Warwickshire
Harbury Lane
Bishop's Tachbrook *CV33 9QB*
Leamington Spa (0926) 30214
Proprietors Jeremy Mort
& Allan Holland
Rooms 7
with bath/shower 5
Room phone Yes
Room TV Yes
Confirm by By arrang.
Last dinner 9.30
Parking Ample
Banquets 30/20
Closed 1 January &
25–30 December
Credit Access, Barclaycard

Mallory Court 80% Ⓜ £C

Standing in ten acres of meticulously maintained formal gardens two miles south of Leamington Spa, this immaculate country mansion is the epitome of elegance, good taste and civilised comfort. Two beautiful lounges with deep sofas or leather chesterfields and roaring winter fires are ideal places to relax over a book or a drink. Luxurious, spacious bedrooms, each with its own colour scheme, have high-quality period furnishings and deep-pile carpets which extend into the bathrooms. These are thoughtfully equipped and sumptuously appointed (the Blenheim suite even boasts twin baths!). Breakfasts are superb. No children under 12. No dogs. *Amenities* garden, outdoor swimming pool, squash, croquet.

Leamington Spa

Map 10 C4 Warwickshire
Harbury Lane
Bishop's Tachbrook *CV33 9QB*
Leamington Spa (0926) 30214
Proprietors Jeremy Mort &
Allan Holland
French cooking
● **Set L** £8·50 incl service
About £46 for two

Mallory Court Restaurant ★ ♟ ♔♔♔ Ⓢ

Allan Holland is a self-taught perfectionist whose skill and artistry are evident in every dish on his French-inspired dinner menus, from simple grilled Dover sole to whole roast partridge with a supremely light orange and champagne sauce. Add to this the splendour of the oak-panelled dining room and the charm of the young staff, and you have the recipe for a memorable occasion. Luncheon (less elaborate) is a set meal.
Specialities terrine chaude de sole et saumon aux asperges, soufflé au saumon fumé et à l'avocat, sauce à l'oseille au vinaigre de cassis, filet d'agneau au basilic et aux tomates, crème brûlée à l'orange.
♟*ABOVE AVERAGE. Credit* Access, Barclaycard

Lunch 12.30–1.45 by arrangement *Dinner* 7.30–9.30, Sun at 7.30
Closed L Sat, D Sun to non-residents, 1 January & 25–30 December

The one first class service for which no claims, clichés or superlatives are necessary.

British airways

We'll take more care of you.

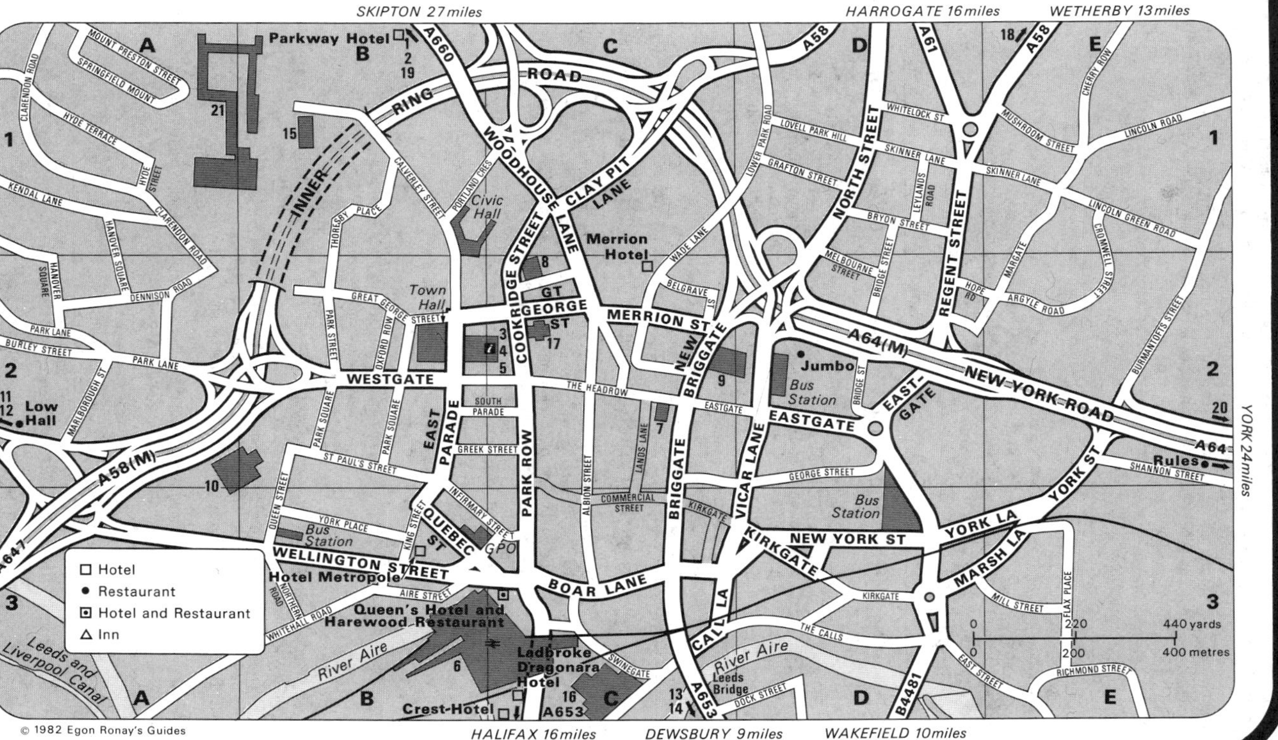
SKIPTON 27 miles
HARROGATE 16 miles
WETHERBY 13 miles
YORK 24 miles
WAKEFIELD 10 miles
DEWSBURY 9 miles
HALIFAX 16 miles
BRADFORD 9 miles
Parkway Hotel
RING ROAD
A660
A58
A61
A58
A64(M)
A64
A58(M)
A647
A653
B4481
NEW-YORK-ROAD
WOODHOUSE LANE
CLAY PIT LANE
COOKRIDGE STREET
INNER
Mount Preston Street
Springfield Mount
Clarendon Road
Hyde Terrace
Hyde Street
Kendal Lane
Hanover Square
Hanover Square
Dennison Road
Clarendon Road
Park Lane
Burley Street
Marlborough St
Park Lane
Calverley Street
Thoresby Place
Portland Cres
Civic Hall
Lower Park Road
Lovell Park Hill
Grafton Street
NORTH STREET
Whitelock St
Skinner Lane
Skinner Lane
Leylands Road
Bryon Street
Melbourne Street
Bridge Street
REGENT STREET
Cherry Row
Mushroom Street
Lincoln Road
Lincoln Green Road
Cromwell Street
Margate
Hope Rd
Argyle Road
Burmantofts Street
Merrion Hotel
Wade Lane
Belgrave St
MERRION ST
GT GEORGE ST
Town Hall
Great George Street
Oxford Row
Park Street
WESTGATE
EAST PARADE
South Parade
Greek Street
St Paul's Street
Park Square
PARK ROW
THE HEADROW
Lands Lane
Albion Street
Commercial Street
NEW BRIGGATE
BRIGGATE
Jumbo
Bus Station
Bridge St
Eastgate
EASTGATE
EAST-GATE
A64(M)
NEW-YORK-ROAD
VICAR LANE
George Street
Bus Station
NEW YORK ST
YORK LA
YORK ST
MARSH LA
Rules
Shannon Street
Flax Place
Mill Street
East Street
Richmond Street
KIRKGATE
Kirkgate
Kirkgate
CALL LA
The Calls
River Aire
Leeds Bridge
Swinegate
Dock Street
BOAR LANE
Low Hall
A58(M)
QUEBEC ST
Queen Street
York Place
Bus Station
King Street
Infirmary Street
GPO
WELLINGTON STREET
Hotel Metropole
Northern Road
Whitehall Road
Aire Street
Queen's Hotel and Harewood Restaurant
River Aire
Ladbroke Dragonara Hotel
Crest-Hotel
A653
Leeds and Liverpool Canal
Hotel
Restaurant
Hotel and Restaurant
Inn
0   220   440 yards
0   200   400 metres
© 1982 Egon Ronay's Guides

Leamington Spa

Map 10 C4 Warwickshire
The Parade *CV32 4AX*
Leamington Spa (0926) 27231

Manager Mr Vernon May
Credit Access, Amex,
Barclaycard, Diners

Rooms 80
with bath/shower 80

Regent Hotel   63%   £ D/E

Royalty and other distinguished guests once favoured this solid Georgian hotel, and today's visitors will still find traditional services like turning-down of beds. Tradition reigns, too, in the classically proportioned public rooms— and an elegant staircase leads to the spacious bedrooms. Most of these have simple, contemporary furnishings, and all have modern bathrooms.

Room phone Yes   *Confirm by* 6   *Parking* Ample
Room TV Most   *Last dinner* 10.45   *Banquets* 250/4

Stars in this Guide stand for the quality of the cooking only— our overriding criterion, irrespective of price, luxury or service.

Ledbury

Map 4 B1 Hereford & Worcester
Hope End *HR8 1JQ*
Ledbury (0531) 3613
Credit Access, Amex,
Barclaycard, Diners
Closed beginning December– end February

Rooms 7
with bath/shower 7

Hope End Country House Hotel   69%   Ⓜ   £ D/E

Once the home of Elizabeth Barrett Browning, this secluded hotel is run along very friendly lines by Patricia and John Hegarty. Natural colours, beautiful fabrics and hand-made furniture give the sitting rooms a distinctive style, while bedrooms are wonderfully peaceful (no radios or TV) and comfortably furnished. Gleaming bathrooms are well equipped. Inclusive terms only. No children under 12. Guide dogs only. *Amenities* garden.   &

Room phone Yes   *Confirm by* By arrang.   *Parking* Ample
Room TV No   *Last dinner* 9

Ledbury

Map 4 B1 Hereford & Worcester
Hope End *HR8 1JQ*
Ledbury (0531) 3613

English cooking

● **Set D** £11
About £30 for two

Hope End Country House Hotel Restaurant   ♌ 

The natural decor of this dining room matches the traditional character of Patricia Hegarty's cooking, which makes imaginative use of local produce. The set dinner might begin with delicate lovage soup, followed by devilled chicken or roast Ledbury lamb stuffed with apricots in perry sauce. A salad and unusual English cheeses precede sweets like damson tart. Book.
🍷 *ABOVE AVERAGE. Credit* Access, Amex, Barclaycard, Diners   &

Dinner only 7.30–9
Closed beginning December–end February

Leeds

Town plan B3 West Yorkshire
The Grove
Oulton Roundabout *LS26 8EJ*
Leeds (0532) 826201
Telex 557646
Credit Access, Amex,
Barclaycard, Diners

Rooms 40
with bath/shower 40

Crest Hotel   54%   £ D

You'll find this compact, modern hotel about five miles south-east of Leeds near junction 30 of the M62. Functional bedrooms in a motel-style block offer adequate comforts for a short stay, with good lighting, tea-makers, trouser presses and neat, tidy bathrooms. Public rooms include a small foyer-lounge, the pubby Falstaff Bar and a cocktail bar which overlooks a large goldfish pond. *Amenities* garden. **Closed** 25–30 December

Room phone Yes   *Confirm by* 6   *Parking* Ample
Room TV Yes   *Last dinner* 10

Leeds

Town plan D2 West Yorkshire
120 Vicar Lane *LS2 7NL*
Leeds (0532) 458324
Proprietor Tony Kwan
Chinese cooking
About £15 for two

Jumbo Chinese Restaurant   ♌

A well-liked, well-run basement restaurant where you can enjoy skilfully prepared favourites like beef chow mein and Peking duck, along with unusual delights like brown mushrooms in prawn meat stuffing and some excellent dim sum. *Meals* noon–midnight.
Closed 25 & 26 December

Leeds

Town plan C3 West Yorkshire
Neville Street *LS1 4BX*
Leeds (0532) 442000
Telex 557143
Manager Mr Tim Latty
Rooms 236
with bath/shower 236
Room phone Yes
Room TV Yes
Confirm by 6
Last dinner 10
Parking Limited
Banquets 350/6

Credit Access, Amex,
Barclaycard, Diners

Ladbroke Dragonara Hotel   70%   *E*   £B/C

Built in the mid-'70s, this smart modern hotel provides a wide choice of bars and conference rooms. The busy, comfortable foyer with its tartan-covered armchairs is on the first floor, along with the convivial Brigantes Bar. Large bedrooms have shag-pile carpets, functional fitted units and tea/coffee-makers, and bathrooms are well equipped.
Amenities dancing (Fri, Sat), men's hairdressing.

Leeds

Town plan A2 West Yorkshire
Calverley Lane
Horsforth *LS18 4EF*
Leeds (0532) 588221
Proprietor Mr Kenneth Monkman

● **Set L** £6 incl. service
Set D £12 incl. service
About £32 for two
Banquets 110/4

Low Hall

Yorkshire pudding and Barnsley chop are two local specialities at this attractively restored Elizabethan hall just off the A6120. Lunchtime also sees roast beef and grills, while in the evening you'll find a wider choice which could include Dutch veal or a seafood medley with Thermidor sauce and saffron rice. Food is well prepared and enjoyable, service friendly and efficient. *Credit* Access, Barclaycard

Lunch 12.30–2 *Dinner* 7.30–10
Closed L Sat, all Sun, Mon, Bank Holidays & 1 week end August

---

Leeds

Town plan C1 West Yorkshire
Merrion Centre *LS2 8NH*
Leeds (0532) 39191
Telex 55459
Manager Mr David Barber
Credit Access, Amex,
Barclaycard, Diners

Rooms 120
with bath/shower 120

Merrion Hotel   65%   £D

This modern hotel next to a multi-storey car park in the city centre has a relaxing lounge and a lovely cocktail bar with a music-hall theme. Two other bars in an adjoining pub provide a nautical choice between the Captain's Cabin and the Gun Deck. Fair-sized bedrooms with attractively coordinated colour schemes have benefited from recent refurbishment.
Amenities dinner discothèque (Fri, Sat).

Room phone Yes	*Confirm by* By arrang.	*Parking* Ample
Room TV Yes	*Last dinner* 10.30	*Banquets* 70/10

Leeds

Town plan B3 West Yorkshire
King Street *LS1 2HQ*
Leeds (0532) 450841
Teiex 557755
Manager Mr Richard Lay
Credit Access, Amex,
Barclaycard, Diners

Rooms 110
with bath/shower 75

Hotel Metropole   60%   £D

This handsome Victorian hotel, whose city-centre position and impressive conference facilities make it popular with businessmen, has an imposing carved facade and a lofty foyer with marble pillars, potted plants and plenty of comfortable chairs. There are also two bars, including the warmly decorated Gaslight Bar. Refurbishment is adding to the character and cheerfulness of the spacious bedrooms and bathrooms.

Room phone Yes	*Confirm by* 6	*Parking* Limited
Room TV Yes	*Last dinner* 10.15	*Banquets* 150/–

Leeds

Town plan B3 West Yorkshire
City Square *LS1 1PL*
Leeds (0532) 31323
Telex 55161
Credit Access, Amex,
Barclaycard, Diners
Closed 4 days Christmas

Rooms 193
with bath/shower 173

Queen's Hotel   68%   £D

This solid 1930s hotel dominating City Square caters well for travellers and business people. Impressive conference facilities are very much a feature, and besides a popular coffee shop there's a modern bar and a comfortable lounge. Spacious bedrooms, furnished in traditional style, include six suites with their own sitting rooms. Mainly old-fashioned bathrooms are well kept.
Amenities sauna, hairdressing, coffee shop (7am–9pm).

Room phone Yes	*Confirm by* 6	*Parking* Ample
Room TV Yes	*Last dinner* 10.30	*Banquets* 600/–

Leeds

Town plan B3 West Yorkshire
City Square *LS1 1PL*
Leeds (0532) 31323

About £34 for two

Queen's Hotel, Harewood Restaurant ♕

An elegant 30s-style sunken dining room makes a splendid setting for well-prepared and attractively presented dishes ranging from simple grills and roasts to more elaborate French-style specialities.
Credit Access, Amex, Barclaycard, Diners *Dinner only* 7–10.30
Closed Sat, Sun, Bank Hols & 4 days Christmas ● **Set D** £8·75 incl. service

Leeds

Town plan E2 West Yorkshire
188 Selby Road *LS15 0LF*
Leeds (0532) 604564

About £24 for two

Rules

You'll find this neat, cosy little restaurant in a small shopping parade out on the A63 Selby Road. A French-style menu offers tempting starters like mushrooms in garlic butter and duck liver pâté, and main courses such as lamb with rosemary or venison in claret. Everything is very fresh and appetising, and sweets like chocolate brandy cake are generously served.
Credit Access, Amex, Barclaycard, Diners

Dinner only 7.30–11
Closed Sun, Mon, Bank Holidays & 1st 2 weeks August

Leicester

Map 11 D4 Leicestershire
Humberstone Road *LE5 3AT*
Leicester (0533) 20471
Telex 341460

Credit Access, Amex,
Barclaycard, Diners

Crest Hotel, Leicester   60%   £ D/E

Formerly known as the Leicester Centre Hotel, this modern seven-storey hotel, which boasts extensive conference and banqueting facilities, is under new ownership. Public areas include a spacious entrance hall-cum-lounge and two bars in contrasting styles. Compact bedrooms have darkwood fitted furniture, radios and tea/coffee-makers plus well-equipped bathrooms.

| *Rooms* 222 | *Room phone* Yes | *Confirm by* 6 | *Parking* Limited |
| *with bath/shower* 222 | *Room TV* Yes | *Last dinner* 10 | *Banquets* 250/8 |

Leicester

Map 11 D4 Leicestershire
Abbey Street *LE1 3TE*
Leicester (0533) 50666
Telex 342434
Manager Mr Martin Puljic
Credit Access, Amex,
Barclaycard, Diners

Eaton Bray Hotel   65%   £ D

This city-centre hotel is built on top of a multi-storey car park. A fast lift whisks pedestrian visitors up to the reception area, which leads to a smart, well-furnished lounge and bar with rooftop views of the city. Compact, comfortable bedrooms have restful colour schemes, attractive fitted furniture and fully equipped tiled bathrooms with modern suites. *Amenities* roof garden. **Closed** 1 week after Christmas

| *Rooms* 72 | *Room phone* Yes | *Confirm by* Midnight | *Parking* Ample |
| *with bath/shower* 72 | *Room TV* Yes | *Last dinner* 10.30 | *Banquets* 220/5 |

Changes in data may occur in establishments after the Guide goes to press. Prices should be taken as indications rather than firm quotes.

Leicester

Map 11 D4 Leicestershire
Granby Street *LE1 6ES*
Leicester (0533) 555599
Manager Mr P. B. Kemp
Credit Access, Amex,
Barclaycard, Diners
Closed 3–4 days Christmas

Grand Hotel   62%   £ D/E

This Victorian hotel in the city centre retains many fine period features and its original grand proportions. Bedrooms are comfortable and spacious with built-in units, tea/coffee-makers and well-fitted, fully tiled bathrooms. Public areas, including the lofty glass-domed lounge, would benefit from some refurbishment.
Amenities dinner dance (Sat October–April). ♿

| *Rooms* 93 | *Room phone* Yes | *Confirm by* 6 | *Parking* Ample |
| *with bath/shower* 93 | *Room TV* Yes | *Last dinner* 9.30 | *Banquets* 300/5 |

Leicester

Map 11 D4 Leicestershire
St Nicholas Circle *LE1 5LX*
Leicester (0533) 531161
Telex 341281

Rooms 190
with bath/shower 190
Room phone Yes
Room TV Yes
Confirm by 6
Last dinner 10
Parking Ample
Banquets 250/10

Credit Access, Amex,
Barclaycard, Diners

Holiday Inn   76%   *E*   £ **C/D**

This modern hotel on a roundabout just outside the city centre offers high standards of service and comfort, extensive conference and banqueting facilities and a good range of leisure activities. Public rooms are smart and comfortable: the lounge has contemporary brown and beige decor, potted plants and brass table lamps, while the rustic Red Fox Bar sports a wealth of beams and farming implements as decoration. Bedrooms have mini-bars, trouser presses and attractive built-in furniture providing ample storage and work space. Spotlessly maintained bathrooms have abundant thick towels. Room service is excellent. *Amenities* sauna, indoor swimming pool, dinner dance (Fri, Sat), coffee shop (11am–11pm), keep-fit equipment.

Leicester

Map 11 D4 Leicestershire
Wigston Road, Oadby *LE2 5QE*
Leicester (0533) 719441

Credit Access, Amex,
Barclaycard, Diners

Rooms 29
with bath/shower 29

Leicestershire Moat House   58%   £ **E**

Situated just off the A6, three miles south-east of the city, this converted private house has been designed to cater for businessmen. The spacious foyer opens into a cheerful little cocktail bar, and there's another bar with a pub atmosphere, as well as a residents' lounge. Bedrooms—whether in the original building or the extension—have functional fitted furniture, tea-makers and compact modern bathrooms.

Room phone Yes	*Confirm by* 6	*Parking* Ample
Room TV Yes	*Last dinner* 9	*Banquets* 220/-

Leicester

Map 11 D4 Leicestershire
Braunstone Lane East *LE3 2FW*
Leicester (0533) 896688
Telex 341009

Credit Access, Amex,
Barclaycard, Diners

Rooms 179
with bath/shower 179

Post House Hotel   60%   £ **D**

Extensive conference and function facilities set the tone of this low modern hotel near junction 21 of the M1. There is plenty of seating in the pleasant open-plan public areas, and the nearby Grand Union Canal provides a barge theme for the cheerful coffee shop. Bedrooms—some in bold, others subtle, colours—have fitted units, tea/coffee-makers and thoughtfully equipped bathrooms. *Amenities* coffee shop (7.30am–10pm).

Room phone Yes	*Confirm by* 6	*Parking* Ample
Room TV Yes	*Last dinner* 9.45	*Banquets* 220/-

Leigh

Map 10 B2 Greater Manchester
Warrington Road *WN7 3XQ*
Leigh (0942) 671256

Credit Access, Amex,
Barclaycard, Diners
Closed 25 December

Rooms 64
with bath/shower 64

Greyhound Motor Hotel   56%   £ **D**

Just south of Leigh at the junction of the A574 and the A580, this converted pub is a useful spot for an overnight stay. In the original building there's a carpeted reception hall and lounge area plus two bars. Bedrooms in a block at the rear have sensible built-in units, tea-makers and radios. Well-maintained, tiled bathrooms. Some refurbishment is planned. *Amenities* discothèque (Sat).

Room phone Yes	*Confirm by* By arrang.	*Parking* Ample
Room TV Yes	*Last dinner* 9.45	*Banquets* 30/-

Letchworth

Map 6 A3 Hertfordshire
Broadway *SG6 3NZ*
Letchworth (046 26) 5651

Credit Access, Amex,
Barclaycard, Diners
Closed 1 week Christmas

Rooms 37
with bath/shower 22

Broadway Hotel   57%   £ **D/E**

Businessmen appreciate the unfussy accommodation offered by this unassuming red-brick hotel in the town centre. Spotlessly clean bedrooms have modern unit furniture, trouser presses and tea-makers (there's no room service), while fully carpeted bathrooms are well maintained. Public rooms include a large, attractively decorated public bar and another pleasant bar for residents, as well as a small lounge.

Room phone Yes	*Confirm by* 6	*Parking* Ample
Room TV Yes	*Last dinner* 9.15	*Banquets* 250

Lewes

Map 7 B6 East Sussex
Pipe Passage
151a High Street *BN7 1XU*
Lewes (079 16) 2343

English cooking

● **Set D** £6·25
About £24 for two

Kenwards

John and Caroline Kenward's cooking has gone from strength to strength since they moved to this converted warehouse. Their unusual menu, which changes weekly, offers game, a vegetarian savoury, and perhaps bass, gurnet or deliciously sauced grey mullet. Skilful use is made of fresh herbs and simple vegetables, and for afters there are homely puds, choice English cheeses and superb coffee. ♟*ABOVE AVERAGE.*

Lunch by arrangement only *Dinner* 7.30–10
Closed D Sun, all Mon, 1st week November & 1 week Christmas

Lewes

Map 7 B6 East Sussex
High Street *BN7 1XS*
Lewes (079 16) 2361

Credit Access, Amex,
Barclaycard, Diners

Rooms 21
with bath/shower 21

Shelleys Hotel   58%   £ D

This solid, well-cared-for hotel on the High Street is a popular stop for businessmen and summer visitors alike. Older bedrooms are attractively furnished with antique pieces–there's even one with a four-poster; the smaller modern rooms are very bright and cheerful. Oils and watercolours adorn the comfortable, pleasantly Victorian lounge and panelled bar. *Amenities* garden.

Room phone Yes	*Confirm by* 6	*Parking* Ample
Room TV Yes	*Last dinner* 9.15	*Banquets* 50/–

Lewes

Map 7 B6 East Sussex
55 High Street *BN7 1XE*
Lewes (079 16) 6694

Proprietor Mr R. Simmonds
Credit Access, Amex,
Barclaycard, Diners

Rooms 32
with bath/shower 20

White Hart Hotel   58%   Ⓜ   £ E/F

Wigs and gowns are much in evidence in the two mellow bars of this old hostelry opposite the law courts. Bedrooms in the annexe across the car park are large, with neat units and colourful soft furnishings; those in the main building vary in size but are equally comfortable. Bathrooms are well fitted, and residents have a bright, relaxing lounge. *Amenities* garden.

Room phone Yes	*Confirm by* 6	*Parking* Ample
Room TV Some	*Last dinner* 10.15	*Banquets* 90/–

Leyland

Map 10 A1 Lancashire
Leyland Way
Near Preston *PR5 2JX*
Leyland (077 44) 22922
Telex 677651
Credit Access, Amex,
Barclaycard, Diners

Rooms 93
with bath/shower 93

Ladbroke Mercury Hotel   65%   £ D

This recently built red-brick hotel just off junction 28 of the M6 has extensive conference facilities. The spacious open-plan area comprising reception, lounge and cocktail bar is especially well designed in stylish modern fashion. Smart bedrooms with fitted units have carefully coordinated colour schemes, and spotless bathrooms are equipped with radio extensions.
Amenities dancing (Sat), helipad. **Closed** 24–31 December.

Room phone Yes	*Confirm by* 6	*Parking* Ample
Room TV Yes	*Last dinner* 10	*Banquets* 180/10

Lifton

Map 2 C2 Devon
PL16 0AA
Lifton (056 684) 244
Proprietor Mrs Anne Voss-Bark
Credit Access, Amex,
Barclaycard
Closed 1 week Christmas

Rooms 27
with bath/shower 21

Arundell Arms   60%   Ⓜ   £ D/E

With 20 miles of its own water, a tackle shop and a resident instructor, this charming creeper-clad hotel is a fisherman's paradise. The cheerful Long Bar doubles as the village pub, and there's also a smart flagstoned lounge, a TV room and a cocktail bar. Attractive bedrooms are furnished mainly in contemporary style; bathrooms are neat and compact.
Amenities garden, game fishing, snipe shooting, games room, skittle alley.

Room phone No	*Confirm by* By arrang.	*Parking* Ample
Room TV No	*Last dinner* 9	*Banquets* 110/–

Lifton

Map 2 C2 Devon
PL16 0AA
Lifton (056 684) 244
Proprietor Mrs Anne Voss-Bark

About £31 for two

Arundell Arms Restaurant   Ⓢ

Locally caught fish is a popular choice at this welcoming restaurant, and our salmon was served with a lovely champagne sauce. The choice is nicely varied, and cooking is most enjoyable. Pleasant service. ♟*ABOVE AVERAGE.*
Credit *Access, Amex, Barclaycard* Lunch *12.30–2* Dinner *7.30–9* **Closed** *1 week Christmas* ● **Set L** Sun only £5·50 **Set D** £8·50 *Banquets* 110/–

Limehouse

Chinatown

See under London

Limpley Stoke
Map 4 B3 Wiltshire
Near Bath, Avon *BA3 6HY*
Limpley Stoke (022 122) 3226

Credit Access, Amex,
Barclaycard, Diners

Rooms 10
with bath/shower 8

Cliffe Hotel   62%   Ⓜ   **£ D**

Standing in terraced grounds high above the beautiful Avon Valley, this converted house makes a charming and relaxing hotel. Everywhere there's a friendly, homely appeal, from the public rooms like the airy, chintzy lounge or the intimate little bar, to the individually styled bedrooms, which vary from cosy singles to spacious de luxe ones. No children under two. No dogs.
Amenities garden, outdoor swimming pool.

Room phone Yes	*Confirm by* By arrang.	*Parking* Ample
Room TV Yes	*Last dinner* 8.30	*Banquets* 60/–

Limpley Stoke
Map 4 B3 Wiltshire
The Bridge
Near Bath *BA3 6EU*
Limpley Stoke (022 122) 3150
French cooking

● **Set L** Sun only from £7·50
Set D from £10·50
About £29 for two

Danielle

A gorgeous tarte tatin (caramelised upside-down apple tart) is typical of the simple, perfectly prepared treats at this delightful French restaurant, where charming Danielle runs the front while her husband sees to the cooking. Dishes on the fixed-price menu like vegetable soup or lamb steak with herbs use prime ingredients, carefully handled to keep all their natural flavours.
Credit Access, Amex, Barclaycard, Diners

Lunch Sun 1–2.30, Mon–Sat by arrangement *Dinner* 7.30–10, Sat 7.30–11
Closed D Sun & Mon October–Easter & 3 weeks January

Limpsfield
Map 7 B5 **Surrey**
High Street *RH8 0DR*
Oxted (088 33) 2996

● **Set L** £10·50 **Set D** £11·50
About £40 for two
Banquets 16/4

Old Lodge   ★

Manager Brian Clivaz and chef David Nicholls, both in their 20s, are determined to make a name for themselves at this smart panelled restaurant in an 18th-century weatherboarded lodge. The cooking's very good indeed, and materials first class: from the menu of French-inspired dishes we especially enjoyed beautifully cooked fillets of sole and tender beef medallions, both accompanied by brilliant sauces, delicious wild mushrooms and lovely crisp vegetables. There are some superb sweets, too. **Specialities** mousseline de volaille Cimiez aux jeunes pommes et aux raisins secs, paupe de truite de Bassin Rouge farcie, ris de veau sauté au Gevrey-Chambertin, terrine de cassis. *Credit* Access, Amex, Barclaycard, Diners

Lunch 12.30–2.30 *Dinner* 7.30–10.30
Closed D Sun & all Mon

Lincoln
Map 11 E2 Lincolnshire
Eastgate *LN2 1PN*
Lincoln (0522) 20341
Telex 56316

Credit Access, Amex,
Barclaycard, Diners

Rooms 71
with bath/shower 71

Eastgate Post House Hotel   65%   **£ D**

Overlooking the magnificent cathedral, this converted Victorian house is a pleasant and comfortable place to stay. It has a spacious open-plan foyer-lounge as well as two attractive bars. Bedrooms in the original building have pretty decor, while those in the extension are more functional in style with fitted furniture. Bathrooms are modern.
Amenities coffee shop (noon–10pm, Sun noon–7pm).

Room phone Yes	*Confirm by* 6	*Parking* Ample
Room TV Yes	*Last dinner* 9.45	*Banquets* 70/–

Lincoln
Map 11 E2 Lincolnshire
Branston *LN4 1HU*
Lincoln (0522) 791366

Proprietor Mr M. G. Downey
Credit Access, Amex,
Barclaycard, Diners

Rooms 34
with bath/shower 16

Moor Lodge Hotel   55%   Ⓜ   **£ E/F**

Situated on the B1188, four miles south-east of Lincoln, this extended Edwardian house is popular with travelling businessmen. Inside, there's a cottage residents' lounge with comfortable sofas and armchairs, as well as a Gunroom Bar with a fine collection of old firearms. Simple modern bedrooms have functional fitted units, and a number also have carpeted private bathrooms.

Room phone No	*Confirm by* By arrang.	*Parking* Ample
Room TV Yes	*Last dinner* 9.30	*Banquets* 240/12

Lincoln

Map 11 E2 Lincolnshire
St Paul's Lane
Bailgate *LN1 3AL*
Lincoln (0522) 41359

Seelys   ⏰ Ⓢ

The first floor of a converted warehouse, with exposed brick walls and heavy roof trusses, is the unusual but comfortable setting for enjoying Robert Etty's repertoire of imaginative, well-cooked dishes. The menu offers a home-made soup, and other choices might include mushrooms in garlic butter, tasty cockles and mussels marinière, poulet Vallée d'Auge and plain grilled steaks. *Credit* Access

About £27 for two
Banquets 80/12

Lunch 12–2 *Dinner* 7.30–10, Sat 7.30–11
Closed Sun & 1 January

Lincoln

Map 11 E2 Lincolnshire
Bailgate *LN1 3AR*
Lincoln (0522) 26222
Telex 56304

Credit Access, Amex,
Barclaycard, Diners

Rooms 68
with bath/shower 57

White Hart Hotel   65%   £ C/D

Standing between castle and cathedral, this historic old inn still has links with the past, and many of its well-appointed public rooms are filled with antiques and displays of silverware and lovely porcelain. In contrast, the glass-domed orangery is strikingly contemporary in style, with bamboo furniture. Bedrooms range from traditional to 12 more modern ones with simple fitted units. Most bathrooms have sturdy old-fashioned suites.

Room phone Yes	*Confirm by* 6	*Parking* Ample
Room TV Yes	*Last dinner* 9.45	*Banquets* 110/–

Lincoln

Map 11 E2 Lincolnshire
Jews House
15 The Strait *LN2 1JD*
Lincoln (0522) 24851

About £30 for two

White's   ⏰ Ⓢ

Set in a 12th-century stone house, this friendly, informal restaurant makes an admirable setting for Colin White's very able cooking. The menu is not extensive but features an interesting selection of attractively presented dishes such as pheasant with celery in a rich port and cream sauce served with excellent vegetables. Sweets like hazelnut meringues make a delightful finale. *Credit* Amex

Lunch 11.30–2.30 *Dinner* 7.30–10
Closed L Mon, all Sun, Bank Holidays, 2 weeks Aug & 1 week Dec

Little Sutton

Map 10 A2 Cheshire
Berwick Road *L66 4PS*
051–339 5121
Proprietors Mr A. V. Wilding &
Mr G. Vickers
Credit Access, Amex,
Barclaycard, Diners

Rooms 28
with bath/shower 27

Woodhey Hotel   57%   Ⓜ   £ E

Conveniently situated on the A550 within easy reach of the industrial centres of the north-west, this converted and extended private house is a popular businessman's hotel with modest facilities including a large function suite and a comfortable bar-lounge. Bedrooms are simply furnished in modern style, and tiled bathrooms are adequate. *Amenities* garden, dinner dance (Fri, Sat), supper dance (Wed). **Closed** 26 December   ♿

Room phone Yes	*Confirm by* By arrang.	*Parking* Ample
Room TV Yes	*Last dinner* 10	*Banquets* 300/–

Little Weighton

Map 11 E1 Humberside
Near Hull *HU20 3XR*
Hull (0482) 848248

Credit Access, Amex,
Barclaycard, Diners
Closed Christmas

Rooms 16
with bath/shower 12

Rowley Manor Hotel   66%   Ⓜ   £ E

This handsome Georgian manor house stands in attractive parkland next to the parish church. A flagstoned entrance hall leads to the lovely panelled lounge, and in the library (which doubles as a bar) you can enjoy a drink and gaze out across the garden. Bedrooms are furnished with either good built-in units or antiques (two have four-posters). Bathrooms of varying sizes are adequately equipped. *Amenities* garden.

Room phone Yes	*Confirm by* By arrang.	*Parking* Ample
Room TV Yes	*Last dinner* 9	*Banquets* 60/10

Any person using our name to obtain free hospitality is a fraud.
Proprietors, please inform the police and us.

4 PACK
All Beef
Beef
Burgers
FINDUS
10 COD
Fish
Fingers
FINDUS
EXTRA COD
LESS CRUMB

Quarter Pounder with a Blue Cheese Dressing

1 packet of 2 Findus All Beef
Quarter Pounders
50g/2oz Blue Cheese, grated
1 x 170g/7oz can cream
2 bap rolls   2 lettuce leaves
Tomato   Salt and Pepper

Cook Quarter Pounders according to directions. Meanwhile, mix cheese, cream and seasoning together. Place mixture onto cooked beefburgers and grill until cheese melts and begins to bubble. Place in roll with lettuce and tomato to garnish.

Indian Style Beefburgers with Coconut Rice

1 packet x 6 Findus All Beef Beefburgers
50g/2oz flour   15ml/1 tbsp tomato purée
500ml/1 pint chicken stock
30ml/2 tbsp mango chutney
4 pieces of preserved stem ginger, chopped or
2.5ml/½ level tsp ground ginger
170g/7oz tin of tomatoes, chopped
Coconut Rice
225g/8oz long grain rice   30ml/2 tbsp oil
50g/2oz dessicated coconut Pinch of saffron powder

Fry burgers in oil for 3 minutes turning once. Remove from pan and stir in the flour. Cook for one minute. Remove from heat and stir in tomato purée, stock, chutney, chopped ginger and tomatoes. Bring to the boil stirring continuously. Add burgers to mixture. Cover and simmer gently for 20-30 minutes. Meanwhile, fry rice in oil for 2 minutes stirring continuously. Add coconut, saffron and 500ml/1 pint water. Bring up to the boil, then simmer gently until rice is just tender. Drain rice and arrange on serving dish. Place burgers in sauce in centre of rice. Serve.

Celery and Cucumber Dip for Fish Fingers

2.5cm/1 inch of cucumber, cubed
2 sticks of celery, chopped
2 x small cartons of natural yoghurt
5ml/1 tsp tomato purée
5ml/1 tsp lemon juice
Seasoning

Cube cucumber and chop celery. Blend yoghurt with tomato purée, lemon juice and seasoning. Add vegetables and mix thoroughly.
Chill before serving.

Fish Finger Kebabs

10 Haddock or Cod Fish Fingers
1 Large green pepper, sliced
into 1" squares
6 tomatoes, halved
Oil for brushing

If frozen cook fish fingers for 2-3 minutes, until defrosted. Cut in half. Place ingredients onto skewers alternating the vegetables and fish fingers. Brush lightly with oil and grill for 6 minutes turning kebab frequently.
Remove skewer to serve.

New family favourites

Little Wymondley
Map 6 A3 Hertfordshire
Near Hitchin *SG4 7JR*
Stevenage (0438) 729500

Proprietor Peter Butterfield
Credit Amex, Barclaycard
Closed 10 days Christmas

Rooms 10
with bath/shower 4

Redcoats Farmhouse Hotel 55% Ⓜ £F

Hidden away down a winding road off the A602, this charming hotel still resembles a farmhouse, and Mrs Butterfield makes guests feel really at home. Downstairs there's a pleasant TV lounge and a delightful beamed bar. Characterful bedrooms with exposed brick walls and casement windows offer traditional comfort; there are also rooms with private bath or shower in two converted outbuildings. *Amenities* garden.

Room phone No	*Confirm by* By arrang.	*Parking* Ample
Room TV No	*Last dinner* 9	*Banquets* 26/2

Liverpool
Town plan E4 Merseyside
Ranelagh Place *L3 5UL*
051–709 7200   Telex 629644
Manager Mr R. J. Pearce
Credit Access, Amex,
Barclaycard, Diners
Closed 2 days Christmas

Rooms 168
with bath/shower 146

Adelphi Hotel 68% £D

A handsome greystone hotel with the grand proportions of the early 19th century. There's a spacious entrance hall, and the enormous lounge has classical statues in its alcoves. There's also a modern cocktail bar, the refurbished Radley's Bar and many function rooms. Large, lofty bedrooms are traditionally furnished; bathrooms are splendidly old-fashioned. *Amenities* sauna, indoor swimming pool, squash, hairdressing, valeting.

Room phone Yes	*Confirm by* 6	*Parking* Limited
Room TV Yes	*Last dinner* 10	*Banquets* 670/6

Liverpool
Town plan B3 Merseyside
Chapel Street *L3 9RE*
051–227 4444
Telex 627070

Rooms 226
with bath/shower 226
Room phone Yes
Room TV Yes
Confirm by 6
Last dinner 10
Parking Ample
Banquets 120/6

Credit Access, Amex,
Barclaycard, Diners

Atlantic Tower Hotel 71% *E* £C/D

Towering over the Mersey docks like a gigantic liner, this impressive concrete and glass hotel has an elegant and very comfortable interior. The Tradewinds Bar has a distinctly below-decks air with its wood-panelled walls and ceiling, and the Club Bar with its summer terrace is an effective evocation of a Pullman car. Bedrooms are large and colourful, with fitted units and deep-pile carpets; all have air conditioning, tea/coffee-makers, bedside radio and TV controls, and excellent, fully tiled bathrooms with telephone extensions. Ten penthouse suites are sumptuously furnished in Regency, Georgian or Spanish styles. *Amenities* dancing (Thurs–Sat), hairdressing, coffee shop (10am–10pm).

Liverpool
Town plan D4 Merseyside
Paradise Street *L1 8JD*
051–709 0181
Telex 627270
Manager Mr J. Ferguson
Rooms 273
with bath/shower 273
Room phone Yes
Room TV Yes
Confirm by 6
Last dinner 10.15
Parking Ample
Banquets 450/6

Credit Access, Amex,
Barclaycard, Diners

Holiday Inn 73% *E* £C/D

High standards of comfort and service are being maintained and improved at this large business hotel in the city centre. Leisure and conference facilities have been expanded, and the luxurious Spyglass Bar has been doubled in size. Other public rooms include a tiled reception area, an open-plan lounge area with comfortable chesterfields and potted plants, and a coffee shop modelled on a dockside warehouse. Smartly decorated bedrooms have carefully matched furnishing fabrics, air conditioning, trouser presses and king-size beds. *Amenities* garden, sauna, indoor swimming pool, keep-fit equipment, solarium, in-house movies, coffee shop (11am–8.30pm), 24-hour laundry service, Prestel.

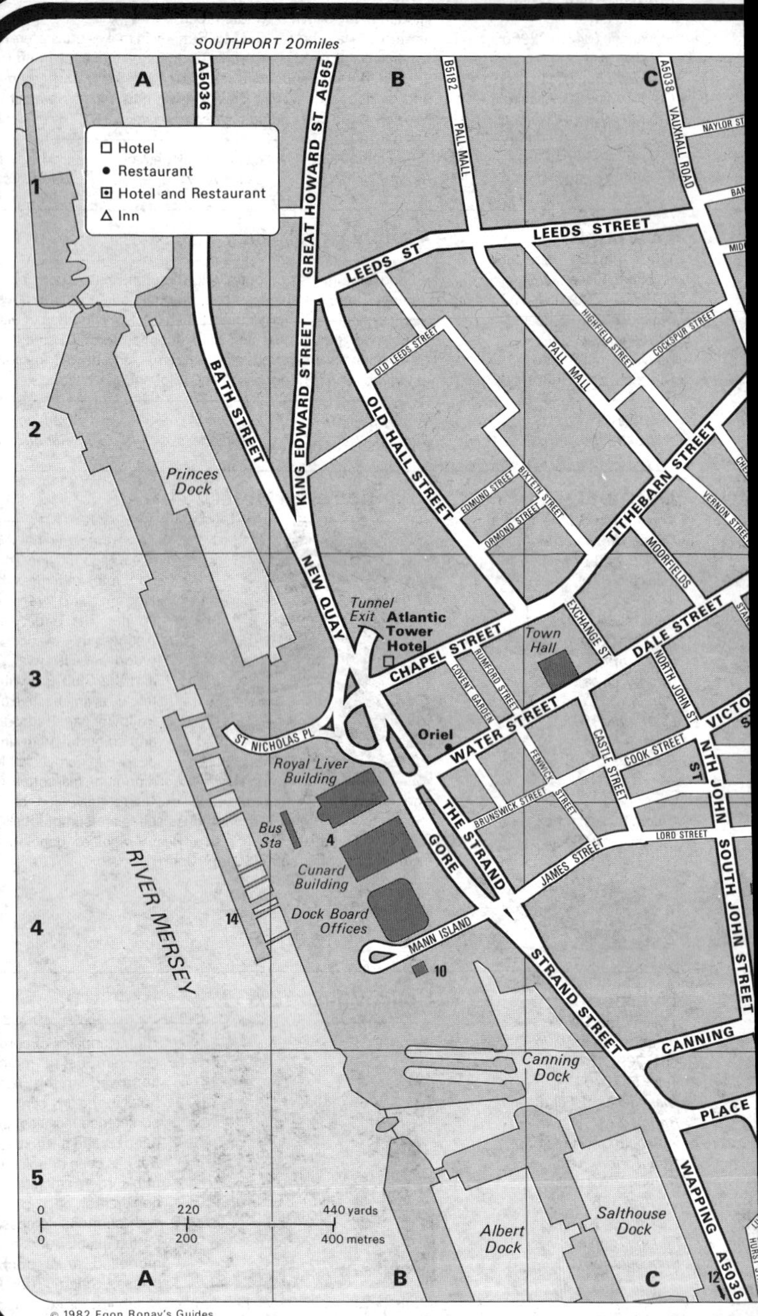

LANCIA
LANCIA
Liverpool
SOUTHPORT 20miles
Hotel
Restaurant
Hotel and Restaurant
Inn
A
B
C
1
2
3
4
5
A5036
GREAT HOWARD ST A565
B5182
PALL MALL
A5038 VAUXHALL ROAD
NAYLOR ST
LEEDS STREET
LEEDS ST
BATH STREET
KING EDWARD STREET
OLD HALL STREET
OLD LEEDS STREET
HIGHFIELD STREET
COCKSPUR STREET
PALL MALL
TITHEBARN STREET
VERNON STREET
EDMUND STREET
BIXTETH STREET
ORMOND STREET
MOORFIELDS
Princes
Dock
NEW QUAY
Tunnel
Exit
Atlantic
Tower
Hotel
CHAPEL STREET
Town
Hall
EXCHANGE ST
DALE STREET
NORTH JOHN ST
ST NICHOLAS PL
Royal Liver
Building
RUMFORD STREET
COVENT GARDEN
Oriel
WATER STREET
FENWICK STREET
CASTLE STREET
COOK STREET
NTH JOHN ST
VICTO
RIVER MERSEY
Bus
Sta
4
Cunard
Building
14
Dock Board
Offices
BRUNSWICK STREET
GORE
THE STRAND
JAMES STREET
LORD STREET
SOUTH JOHN STREET
MANN ISLAND
10
STRAND STREET
Canning
Dock
CANNING
PLACE
0   220   440 yards
0   200   400 metres
Albert
Dock
Salthouse
Dock
WAPPING
A5036
12
A
B
C
© 1982 Egon Ronay's Guides

LANCIA

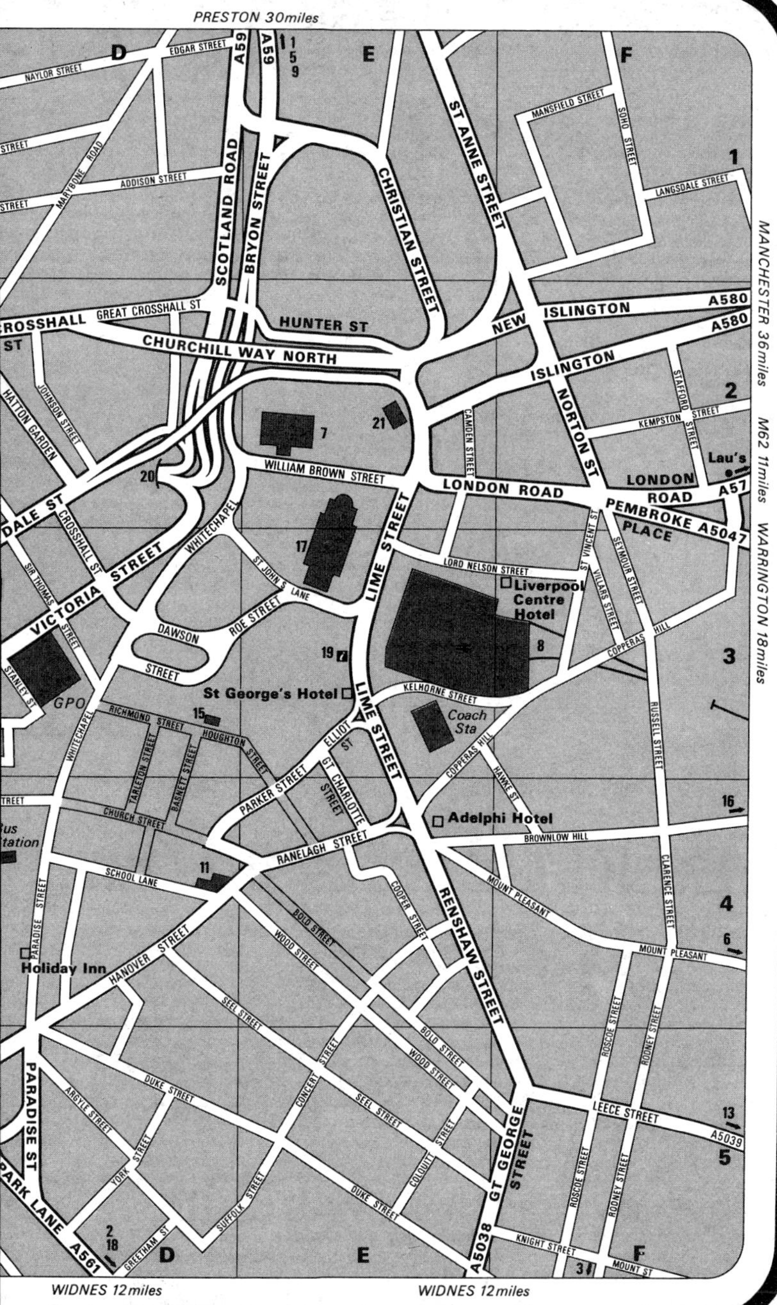

PRESTON 30 miles
MANCHESTER 36 miles
M62 11 miles
WARRINGTON 18 miles
WIDNES 12 miles
WIDNES 12 miles
D
E
F
1
2
3
4
5
6
NAYLOR STREET
EDGAR STREET
A59
A59
ADDISON STREET
MARYBONE ROAD
STREET
SCOTLAND ROAD
BRYON STREET
CHRISTIAN STREET
ST ANNE STREET
MANSFIELD STREET
SOHO STREET
LANGSDALE STREET
GREAT CROSSHALL ST
CROSSHALL ST
HUNTER ST
CHURCHILL WAY NORTH
NEW ISLINGTON
ISLINGTON
A580
A580
NORTON ST
STAFFORD STREET
KEMPSTON STREET
HATTON GARDEN
JOHNSON STREET
7
21
WILLIAM BROWN STREET
CAMDEN STREET
LONDON ROAD
LONDON ROAD
LAU'S
A57
PEMBROKE A5047
PLACE
DALE ST
CROSSHALL ST
WHITECHAPEL
20
LIME STREET
LORD NELSON STREET
ST VINCENT ST
VILLARS STREET
SEYMOUR STREET
COPPERAS HILL
VICTORIA STREET
17
ST JOHN'S LANE
Liverpool Centre Hotel
8
3
DAWSON
ROE STREET
STREET
19
KELHORNE STREET
RUSSELL STREET
STANLEY ST
GPO
St George's Hotel
LIME STREET
Coach Sta
COPPERAS HILL
HAWKE ST
16
RICHMOND STREET
HOUGHTON STREET
15
ELLIOT ST
GT CHARLOTTE STREET
Adelphi Hotel
BROWNLOW HILL
CLARENCE STREET
WHITECHAPEL
TARLETON STREET
BASNETT STREET
PARKER STREET
CHURCH STREET
RANELAGH STREET
MOUNT PLEASANT
SCHOOL LANE
11
COOPER STREET
MOUNT PLEASANT
4
6
PARADISE STREET
Bus Station
Holiday Inn
HANOVER STREET
BOLD STREET
WOOD STREET
RENSHAW STREET
ROSCOE STREET
RODNEY STREET
SEEL STREET
BOLD STREET
WOOD STREET
LEECE STREET
13
A5039
PARADISE ST
ARGYLE STREET
DUKE STREET
YORK STREET
CONCERT STREET
SEEL STREET
GT GEORGE STREET
A5038
ROSCOE STREET
RODNEY STREET
PARK LANE A561
GREETHAM ST
SUFFOLK STREET
DUKE STREET
COLQUITT STREET
KNIGHT STREET
MOUNT ST
2 18
3
5

Map 10 A2
Town plan on preceding page

Population 539,700

Since King John granted its Charter in 1207, Liverpool has taken increasing advantage of its sheltered Merseyside position to become England's leading Atlantic port and an industrial magnet, while the Arts are as vigorously pursued as football. The Philharmonic Orchestra, the Walker Art Gallery, the University's music-making, and the city's five theatres are at least as important to it as pop.

Annual Events
Grand National at Aintree
Lord Mayor's Parade *June*

Sights Outside City
Aintree, Hoylake, Chester, Mersey trip to New Brighton

Information Office
Lime Street
Liverpool 1
Telephone 051–709 3631/8681

Liverpool

1	Aintree Race-course	E1
2	Airport	D5
3	Anglican Cathedral *20th-c Gothic, complete after 75 years*	F5
4	Cunard Building, Dock Board office, and Royal Liver Building *waterfront landmarks*	B4
5	Everton Football Club	E1
6	Everyman Theatre	F4
7	Library and Museum *Hornby library has outstanding prints and first editions. Museum houses aquarium, ivories, jewellery, birds, shipping gallery*	E2
8	Lime Street Station	E/F3
9	Liverpool Football Club	E1
10	Maritime Museum	B4
11	Neptune Theatre	D4
12	Otterspool Promenade	C5
13	Philharmonic Hall	F5
14	Pier Head	A4
15	Playhouse Theatre	D3
16	Roman Catholic Cathedral *space-age architecture*	F4
17	St George's Hall *Assize Courts and concert hall*	E3
18	Speke Hall *Elizabethan house with beautiful gardens on the Mersey*	D5
19	Tourist Information Centre	E3
20	Tunnel Entrance	D2
21	Walker Art Gallery *England's largest collection outside London*	E2

Liverpool
Town plan F2 Merseyside
358 Prescot Road *L133AP*
051–228 6447
Proprietors Lau family
Chinese cooking

● **Set D** from £15 for two
incl. service
About £21 for two
Banquets 200/50

Lau's

This large restaurant has a strong following, so booking is advisable. Mr Lau makes his own egg noodles and offers an extensive range of Peking specialities from dried scallops and greens to crispy duck. Dishes are carefully prepared and service is friendly. The restaurant is moving to 44 Ullet Road, Sefton Park.

Dinner only 6–11
Closed Sun, Good Friday, 25 & 26 Dec & Tues after Bank Holiday Mons

Liverpool
Town plan F3 Merseyside
Lord Nelson Street *L35QB*
051–709 7050
Telex 627954
Credit Access, Amex,
Barclaycard, Diners
Closed Christmas

Rooms 170
with bath/shower 170

Liverpool Centre Hotel   60%   £E

With its practical accommodation and versatile conference and function rooms, this modern hotel next to Lime Street Station is a popular place with businessmen. The spacious foyer has plenty of comfortable settees, and two bars include one with a quiet lounge area. Double-glazed bedrooms, with views over the city, have neat contemporary fittings and roomy, well-equipped bathrooms.

Room phone Yes   *Confirm by* 6   *Parking* Ample
Room TV Yes   *Last dinner* 9.45   *Banquets* 450/15

Liverpool
Town plan B3 Merseyside
Oriel Chambers
Water Street *L28TH*
051–236 4664
Manager Mr A. Coticelli

● **Set L & Set D** £8·95
About £35 for two
Banquets 40/10

Oriel

There's an air of confidence about this comfortable, softly lit restaurant, and the cooking fully lives up to expectations. Fresh seafood like our superb sea bass with fennel and Pernod sauce features prominently on the menu, along with a few game dishes and specialities such as Aylesbury duckling terrine with pistachios and walnuts. Vegetables are excellent and there are lovely sweets. *Credit* Access, Amex, Barclaycard, Diners

Lunch 12–2.15 *Dinner* 7–10.15
Closed L Sat, all Sun & Bank Holidays except 25 December

Liverpool
Town plan E3 Merseyside
St John's Precinct
Lime Street *L11NQ*
051–709 7090
Telex 627630
Credit Access, Amex,
Barclaycard, Diners

Rooms 155
with bath/shower 155

St George's Hotel   64%   £D

This tall, slim modern hotel towers above a city-centre shopping precinct and offers convenient overnight parking. Smart, colourful bedrooms on seven floors have panoramic views, neat fitted units, message warning lights and tea-makers, as well as full room service. All have well-equipped bathrooms. Public areas include a relaxing bar-lounge with a delightful tapestry. *Amenities* coffee shop (10am–10pm).

Room phone Yes   *Confirm by* 6   *Parking* Ample
Room TV Yes   *Last dinner* 10.15   *Banquets* 250/–

Llanfair Waterdine
Map 10 A4 Shropshire
Knighton, Powys *LD71TU*
Knighton (0547) 528214
Proprietors Mr & Mrs S. J. Rhodes

● **Set L & Set D** £8·65
About £29 for two

Red Lion Inn Restaurant

There are only four tables in the tiny dining room of this friendly country pub, so you need to book and give Mrs Rhodes 24-hours' notice. Everything is freshly prepared, and the set menu includes home-made soup, superb pâté, tender steaks, and maybe roast duck or chicken suprême, with lovely vegetables. There are simple fruit tarts and delicious soufflés for afters, and good coffee.

Meals by arrangement only
Closed 25 December

Loftus
Map 15 C5 Cleveland
Near Saltburn-by-the-Sea
TS134UB
Guisborough (0287) 40515

Credit Access, Amex,
Barclaycard, Diners

Grinkle Park Hotel   60%   £E/F

A rhododendron-lined drive leads to this splendid Victorian mansion set in 400 acres of parkland. Lofty public rooms include two comfortable bars, an elegant residents' lounge and a warm sun lounge festooned with plants. Large bedrooms (most with fine views) are traditionally furnished and have extras like trouser presses and tea-makers. Modern bathrooms. *Amenities* garden.

Continued

Continued
Rooms 20 | *Room phone* Yes | *Confirm by* By arrang. | *Parking* Ample
with bath/shower 17 | *Room TV* Yes | *Last dinner* 9.30 | *Banquets* 70/10

London Airports

See pages 313–21

Long Melford
Bull Hotel 66%
£ D

Map **6 C3** Suffolk
Hall Street *CO10 9JG*
Sudbury (0787) 78494

The atmosphere of old England lives on in this friendly half-timbered roadside inn, whose charming lounge and two bars are graced by attractive period furnishings, massive open fireplaces and splendid carved beams (some dating back to the 15th century). Bedrooms, also beamed, have smart built-in units; tiled bathrooms with modern white suites are well maintained. *Amenities* dinner dance (Fri November–April).

Credit Access, Amex,
Barclaycard, Diners

Rooms 27 | *Room phone* Yes | *Confirm by* 6 | *Parking* Ample
with bath/shower 27 | *Room TV* Yes | *Last dinner* 10 | *Banquets* 120/20

Longframlington
Besom Barn

Map **14 B3** Northumberland
NE65 8EN
Longframlington (066 570) 627
Proprietors
Andrew & Sue Shilton

Andrew Shilton's restaurant–converted from old farm buildings–makes an apt setting for robust, interesting fare which successfully combines quality with quantity. Dishes like baked crabmeat with whisky sauce, pork and venison pie laced with Guinness and chicken Cordon Bleu are carefully prepared and full of flavour. There are also grills, plenty of crisp fresh vegetables and a few simple home-made sweets.

About £27 for two
Banquets 40/10

Lunch Sun only 12–1 *Dinner* 7–9.30
Closed D Sun & Mon, Bank Holidays & 5 weeks from 25 December

Longhorsley
Linden Hall Hotel 81% *E*
£ E/F

Map **14 B3** Northumberland
Near Morpeth *NE65 5XF*
Morpeth (0670) 56611
Telex 538224

Rooms 45
with bath/shower 45
Room phone Yes
Room TV Yes
Confirm by By arrang.
Last dinner 9.30
Parking Ample
Banquets 200/10

This early 19th-century mansion is an exceptionally stylish hotel. Through the splendid pillared arch is a welcoming foyer, where guests sit at a desk to register. There are comfortable armchairs and sofas in the huge galleried hall with a domed ceiling; and the air of opulence extends to the lofty residents' lounge and the elegant suede-walled bar. There's also a plant-filled conservatory. Attractive fitted furniture and coordinated fabrics make the bedrooms especially luxurious, while bathrooms have mosaic-tiled floors and excellent fittings.

Credit Access, Amex,
Barclaycard, Diners

Amenities garden, sauna, tennis, dancing (Sat in winter), solarium, hairdressing, table tennis, billiards, children's play area, putting, croquet.

Looe
Talland Bay Hotel 62% Ⓜ
£ D

Map **2 C3** Cornwall
Talland Bay *PL13 2JB*
Polperro (0503) 72667
Proprietors Major & Mrs Mayman
Credit Access, Amex,
Barclaycard, Diners
Closed mid Dec–early Feb

This smart whitewashed building stands high above a Cornish cove in well-kept gardens with sub-tropical plants. Public rooms are furnished as if in an elegant private house, and the charming lounge has a sun terrace overlooking the pool. Good-sized bedrooms are bright, airy and cheerfully decorated. Children under five by arrangement only. *Amenities* garden, outdoor swimming pool, solarium, putting, games room, croquet.

Rooms 24 | *Room phone* Yes | *Confirm by* By arrang. | *Parking* Ample
with bath/shower 16 | *Room TV* Yes | *Last dinner* 9 | *Banquets* 25/–

Lostwithiel

Map 2 C3 Cornwall
20 Castle Hill *PL22 0DD*
Lostwithiel (0208) 872223

Proprietor Mr R. T. Hanson
Credit Access, Amex,
Barclaycard, Diners

Rooms 32
with bath/shower 32

Carotel Motel   53%   Ⓜ   £ E/F

Mr Hanson and his friendly team make guests very welcome at this modestly appointed modern hotel, a popular place with businessmen as well as holiday-makers. The residents' lounge and adjacent bar have a simple, cheerful appeal, and bedrooms (including three family rooms) are bright and comfortable, with practical fitted units and compact bathrooms.
Amenities garden, pool table, solarium, laundry room, in-house movies.   ♿

Room phone No	*Confirm by* By arrang.	*Parking* Ample
Room TV Yes	*Last dinner* 9.30	*Banquets* 80/–

Loughborough

Map 11 D3 Leicestershire
High Street *LE11 2QL*
Loughborough (0509) 214893

Manager Mr E. Johnston
Credit Access, Amex,
Barclaycard, Diners

Rooms 82
with bath/shower 69

King's Head Hotel   58%   £ E

Only three miles from the M1 (junction 23), this town-centre hotel is a convenient stopping place for businessman or tourist. Public rooms include a small lounge and two bars, one of which overlooks an attractive courtyard with a fountain and fishpond. A modern wing contains most of the bedrooms, which are bright, roomy and well equipped, with good tiled bathrooms. *Amenities* 24-hour laundry service.

Room phone Yes	*Confirm by* 6	*Parking* Ample
Room TV Yes	*Last dinner* 8.30	*Banquets* 60/–

Louth

Map 11 F2 Lincolnshire
5 Eve Street *LN11 0JJ*
Louth (0507) 602021
Proprietors
Maureen & Clive Rhodes

● Set L £3·50
About £34 for two

Forbidden Fruits   ★ 

Changing the short menus according to the market and the seasons, Maureen Rhodes delights visitors with dishes whose delicate preparation and simple visual appeal match the fresh, contemporary decor of this lovely little restaurant. Exquisitely light flavours and beautifully balanced sauces are features of her memorable meals, and perfect crisp vegetables are noteworthy, as are sweets. Husband Clive is a charming host.
Specialities petit cassoulet de pêcheurs aux flageolets, salade de palombes aux noix et au mesclun, tronçons de barbue à la crème au citron vert et aux petits légumes, aiguillettes de canard aux mangues.
Credit Access, Amex, Barclaycard

Lunch by arrangement 12–2 *Dinner* 7.30–10 **Closed** L Sat & Sun, D Mon, all Bank Holidays, 1st 2 weeks September & 1 week Christmas

Lower Beeding

Map 5 E3 West Sussex
Sandygate Lane *RH13 6NF*
Lower Beeding (040 376) 216

French cooking

About £30 for two
Banquets 25/–

Cisswood House Restaurant   

After years of experience in Vienna, Paris, London and Billingshurst, Austrian Othmar Illes now runs this traditionally beamed and panelled restaurant with his charming wife Elizabeth. He's a very accomplished chef, and his French menu includes excellent fish dishes as well as classics like chicken Kiev, duck à la bigarade and steak au poivre. To finish, sorbets or treats from the colourful trolley. *Credit* Access, Amex, Barclaycard, Diners

Lunch 12–2.15 *Dinner* 7–10.15
Closed L Sat, all Sun, Mon, 1 week Christmas & last 2 weeks May

Lower Peover

Map 10 B2 Cheshire
Near Knutsford *WA16 9PZ*
Lower Peover (056 581) 2269
Proprietors Mr & Mrs C. Fisher

● Set L £4·50 Set D £8·50
About £26 for two

Bells of Peover   

Just off the A50, this wonderful old whitewashed pub makes the perfect setting for a fine wholesome meal. Much of the food has a traditional English flavour, with excellent soups, natural gravies and firm fresh vegetables complementing roasts (like our tender Cheshire chicken), grills and dishes such as beef Stroganoff. Old-fashioned sweets range from blackcurrant pie to cream caramel. *Credit* Diners

Lunch 12.30–2 *Dinners* 7–9
Closed D Sun, all Mon, 25 December & 3 weeks August

Lower Slaughter

Map 4 C1 Gloucestershire
Near Cheltenham *GL54 2HP*
Bourton-on-the-Water
(0451) 20456

Credit Access, Amex,
Barclaycard, Diners

Manor Hotel   63%   Ⓜ   £D

Well-kept grounds and a charming village setting add to the appeal of this handsome Cotswold-stone house. The reception area and lounge are very welcoming, with their fine fireplaces and comfortable armchairs, and there's a pleasant bar. Spacious bedrooms have traditional furniture and pretty floral decor, and bathrooms are thoroughly up to date. No dogs.
Amenities garden, indoor swimming pool, tennis, game fishing, croquet.

Rooms 12
with bath/shower 12

Room phone Yes
Room TV Yes

Confirm by 6
Last dinner 9.30

Parking Ample
Banquets 40/–

Lower Swell

Map 4 C1 Gloucestershire
Near Stow-on-the-Wold *GL54 1LF*
Stow-on-the-Wold
(0451) 30232

Credit Access, Barclaycard
Closed January

Old Farmhouse Hotel *(Inn)*   Ⓜ   £E

Built as a farmhouse in the 16th century, this charming Cotswold-stone inn has kept its rustic appeal, and it offers all the simple comforts of home. A delightful little bar leads to the comfortable TV lounge, while bedrooms are traditionally furnished in cottage style. Bathrooms are bright and cheerful. No dogs.
Amenities garden.

Rooms 8
with bath/shower 2

Room phone No
Room TV Yes

Confirm by By arrang.
Last dinner 9.30

Parking Ample

Lowestoft

Map 6 D2 Suffolk
Kirkley Cliff *NR33 0BZ*
Lowestoft (0502) 4433
Telex 97129

Credit Access, Amex,
Barclaycard, Diners

Victoria Hotel   55%   £E

A sheltered garden separates this red-brick Victorian hotel from the promenade. The much-modernised ground floor holds a number of conference rooms as well as a smart, relaxing cocktail bar with fine sea views. Bedrooms, including many family rooms, are traditionally furnished, all with radios and tea-makers, and bathrooms are adequate.
Amenities garden, outdoor swimming pool.   ♿

Rooms 52
with bath/shower 32

Room phone Yes
Room TV Most

Confirm by By arrang.
Last dinner 9

Parking Ample
Banquets 180/–

Ludlow

Map 10 B4 Shropshire
Bull Ring *SY8 1AA*
Ludlow (0584) 2919

Managers Mr & Mrs P. R. Nash
Rooms 35
with bath/shower 35
Room phone Yes
Room TV Yes
Confirm by 6
Last dinner 8.45
Parking Ample
Banquets 80/10

Credit Access, Amex,
Barclaycard

Feathers Hotel   70%   £D

Dating back to 1603, this friendly, well-run hotel is known far and wide for its truly magnificent half-timbered facade–complete with balcony, gables and leaded windows. Its beamed and panelled interior is equally striking. Fine antiques fill the bars and the James I lounge, which also features a superb carved mantelpiece and an ornate plaster ceiling. Another highlight is the splendid baronial banqueting room. Comfortable bedrooms range from standard to luxury, the latter being particularly spacious, some with beautiful furniture in oak or African hardwood, others with fitted pine units. All rooms have radio-alarms, mineral water, fruit and well-fitted, up-to-date bathrooms. No dogs. *Amenities* 24-hour laundry service.

Lustleigh

Map 3 D3 Devon
Near Newton Abbot *TQ13 9SN*
Lustleigh (064 77) 341
Proprietors Mr & Mrs M. T. Harris

Moorwood Cottage   ♣   Ⓢ

A little thatched cottage on the A382 north of Lustleigh makes a charming setting for enjoying Mr Harris's splendidly homely dinners. Unusual soups such as nettle or chicken with red wine are a speciality, and fish, poultry and meat dishes are accompanied by excellent sauces (using fresh garden herbs) and nicely prepared vegetables. Good home-made desserts, too. Friendly, attentive service.

Lunch Sun only 12–2 *Dinner* 7–9.30
Closed D Sun, Mon & 25 December

About £23 for two

Luton   Chiltern Hotel   64%   £D

Map 5 E1 Bedfordshire
Waller Ave, Dunstable Rd *LU4 9RU*
Luton (0582) 55911
Telex 825048
Manager Mr H. A. Bodtenberg
Credit Access, Amex,
Barclaycard, Diners

This purpose-built businessman's hotel near the M1 is professionally run and immaculately maintained throughout. The sleek open-plan foyer-lounge opens into the popular bar with equally smart furnishings. Attractively decorated bedrooms (including some very luxurious executive ones) are modern and comfortable, with fitted furniture, excellent carpets and tea-makers. *Amenities* dinner dance (Sat monthly September–June).

Rooms 99	*Room phone* Yes	*Confirm by* 6	*Parking* Ample
with bath/shower 99	*Room TV* Yes	*Last dinner* 10	*Banquets* 250/20

Luton   Crest Motor Hotel   55%   £D

Map 5 E1 Bedfordshire
641 Dunstable Road LU4 8RQ
Luton (0582) 55955
Telex 826283
Manager Mr Peter Harrison
Credit Access, Amex,
Barclaycard, Diners

Businessmen make ample use of this functional hotel that is handily placed 100 yards from junction 11 of the M1. There's a neat little bar off the reception-lounge, plus a number of conference rooms. Practical bedrooms are simply fitted with built-in darkwood units and plain soft furnishings; all have well-equipped private bathrooms. *Amenities* garden.
Closed Christmas–New Year

Rooms 139	*Room phone* Yes	*Confirm by* 6.30	*Parking* Ample
with bath/shower 139	*Room TV* Yes	*Last dinner* 9.45	*Banquets* 100/–

Luton   Strathmore Hotel   67%   £D

Map 5 E1 Bedfordshire
Arndale Centre *LU1 2TR*
Luton (0582) 34199
Telex 825763
Manager Mr R. Finlay
Credit Access, Amex,
Barclaycard, Diners

There is much use of boldly patterned wallpaper throughout this modern hotel next to the Arndale Centre. The panelled foyer leads to a smart, softly lit cocktail bar, and there are also public and saloon bars. Good-sized bedrooms have fitted units and small, well-equipped bathrooms. One floor is set aside for non-smokers. Guide dogs only.
Amenities coffee shop (10am–10pm Mon–Fri, 10am–5pm Sat).

Rooms 151	*Room phone* Yes	*Confirm by* 6	*Parking* Ample
with bath/shower 151	*Room TV* Yes	*Last dinner* 10	*Banquets* 200/2

Lymington   Limpets

Map 4 C4 Hampshire
9 Gosport Street *SO4 9BG*
Lymington (0590) 75595

Robust French-inspired dishes like onion soup, smoked haddock brandade and honey-roast duck are capably prepared in this simple restaurant. Good vegetables, too, and the orange syllabub is delicious. 🍷 *SUPERIOR. Credit* Access, Amex *Dinner only* 6.30–10.30 **Closed** Sun & Mon December–

About £29 for two — May, 25 & 26 December & November *Banquets* 16/–

Lymington   Marlo's Barge

Map 4 C4 Hampshire
Bridge Yard *SO4 9DA*
Lymington (0590) 72237

The atmosphere is relaxed and friendly in this converted French barge at the end of a boatyard. Marlo Johnston offers a short menu of robust dishes like sliced sausage with chick pea salad, cream-sauced sweetbreads or pheasant with sauerkraut. Main courses come with carefully prepared fresh vegetables, and there are delicious meringues and iced soufflés to finish. Book. *Credit* Access, Barclaycard, Diners

Dinner only 7.30–10.30
About £24 for two — **Closed** Mon, Tues, 25 & 26 December & 4 weeks October/November

Lymington   Passford House Hotel   68% Ⓜ   £D

Map 4 C4 Hampshire
Mount Pleasant *SO4 8LS*
Lymington (0590) 682398

Proprietor Mr Patrick Heritage
Credit Amex

Signposts from the A337 lead you to this attractive house standing in nine acres of woodland and paddocks. The highlight of the public rooms is the splendid main lounge with its velvet-covered chairs, fine wood panelling and open log fire. Comfortable bedrooms are tastefully appointed in various styles, with well-equipped tiled bathrooms. *Amenities* garden, sauna, outdoor swimming pool, tennis, putting, croquet, children's playground, games room.

Rooms 50	*Room phone* Yes	*Confirm by* 6	*Parking* Ample
with bath/shower 50	*Room TV* Yes	*Last dinner* 8.30	*Banquets* 150/–

Lymington

Map 4 C4 Hampshire
High Street *SO4 9AA*
Lymington (0590) 77123
Proprietors Willcock family
Credit Access, Amex,
Barclaycard, Diners
Closed 25–28 December

Rooms 22
with bath/shower 16

Stanwell House Hotel   59%   Ⓜ   £E

Two Georgian houses on the High Street make up this informal little hotel. Inside, everything is cosy and homely, from the welcoming foyer and cocktail bar to the plush, elegant lounge. There are antiques on the landings, and bedrooms, including a four-postered bridal suite, are individually furnished in bright, tasteful style. The hotel's daily weather reports are much appreciated by sailing patrons! *Amenities* garden.

Room phone Yes	*Confirm by* By arrang.	*Parking* Difficult
Room TV Yes	*Last dinner* 9.30	

Lymington

Map 4 C4 Hampshire
High Street *SO4 9AA*
Lymington (0590) 77124

Proprietors Willcock family

● **Set L** from £5·50
Set D from £8·25
About £31 for two

Stanwell House Hotel, Railings Restaurant   Ⓢ

This comfortable dining room overlooks a pretty walled garden, which is floodlit at night. There's a table d'hôte menu at lunch time, and the longer evening menu offers tempting grills and roasts, as well as a few more unusual dishes like Arbroath smokies with Pernod and cream. It's all carefully cooked and accompanied by appetising fresh vegetables. ♟ *OUTSTANDING.*
Credit Access, Amex, Barclaycard, Diners

Lunch 12.30–2 *Dinner* 7–9.30, Sat 7–10.30
Closed 1 January & 25–28 December

Lyndhurst

Map 4 C4 Hampshire
High Street *SO4 7NF*
Lyndhurst (042 128) 2722
Telex 85778

Credit Access, Amex,
Barclaycard, Diners

Rooms 42
with bath/shower 42

Crown Hotel   66%   £D

This imposing, creeper-clad building is an agreeable and convenient base for discovering the beauty of the New Forest. Public rooms featuring fine panelling and sombre, elegant furnishings preserve all the charm of a 19th-century inn. Well-equipped bedrooms offer abundant comfort, ample seating and useful writing surfaces. Neat, compact bedrooms, many with bidets. *Amenities* garden, dinner dance (Sat).

Room phone Yes	*Confirm by* By arrang.	*Parking* Ample
Room TV Yes	*Last dinner* 9.30	*Banquets* 70/–

Our inspectors are our full-time employees; they are professionally trained by us.

Lyndhurst

Map 4 C4 Hampshire
High Street *SO4 7BJ*
Lyndhurst (042 128) 2823
Telex 47439

Credit Access, Amex,
Barclaycard, Diners

Rooms 68
with bath/shower 64

Lyndhurst Park Hotel   58%   £E

A smart new bar with rich leather seating is among recent extensive improvements to this large New Forest hotel. Bedrooms, too, are being redecorated, and nearly all now have private bathrooms; rooms in the modern wing are especially bright and cheerful. Guests can use the leisure facilities of two nearby sister hotels. *Amenities* garden, outdoor swimming pool, tennis, dinner dance (Sat), hotel boat.

Room phone Yes	*Confirm by* 7	*Parking* Ample
Room TV Yes	*Last dinner* 9.45	*Banquets* 300/20

Lyndhurst

Map 4 C4 Hampshire
Beaulieu Road *SO4 7FZ*
Lyndhurst (042 128) 2944
Proprietors Mr P. T. Ames & family

Credit Access, Amex,
Barclaycard, Diners

Rooms 18
with bath/shower 18

Parkhill Hotel   68%   Ⓜ   £C

Nine acres of parkland surround this handsome Georgian house set half a mile back from the road. Elegantly proportioned public rooms have fine antique furniture and tasteful colour schemes. Traditionally furnished bedrooms on the first floor are large, others being smaller and more modern in style; all have carpeted, up-to-date bathrooms. *Amenities* garden, outdoor swimming pool, coarse fishing. **Closed** 1 week January

Room phone Yes	*Confirm by* By arrang.	*Parking* Ample
Room TV Yes	*Last dinner* 9.30	*Banquets* 45/10

Lynmouth

Map 3 D1 Devon

EX35 6NA
Lynton (059 85) 3236

Credit Access, Amex,
Barclaycard, Diners
Closed November–March

Rooms 39
with bath/shower 32

Tors Hotel 60% £E

Perched on a wooded hillside above the picturesque town and the sea, this white-painted gabled hotel is a popular place for family holidays. Comfortable public rooms make the most of the panoramic views, and there's a sunny terrace. Many of the modest bedrooms with pretty floral wallpaper and built-in units also have fine views. Adequate bathrooms. *Amenities* garden, outdoor swimming pool, dancing (Fri, Sat), games room.

| *Room phone* No | *Confirm by* By arrang. | *Parking* Limited |
| *Room TV* No | *Last dinner* 9 | *Banquets* 110/– |

Lynton

Map 3 D1 Devon

North Walk Hill *EX35 6ED*
Lynton (059 85) 2342
Proprietors R. J. & P. J. Green
& H. R. & P. M. Parkins
Credit Access, Barclaycard, Diners
Closed end Oct–beginning Mar

Rooms 22
with bath/shower 12

Lynton Cottage Hotel 58% Ⓜ £E/F

A pleasant, family-run hotel high on the cliffs above the bay. Through the spacious reception area, there's a sunny lounge, a second lounge–comfortably furnished, with TV as an alternative to the lovely views–and a snug bar with a splendid collection of toby jugs. Fair-sized bedrooms are smartly decorated and furnished with modern pieces. Neat, well-appointed bathrooms. *Amenities* garden.

| *Room phone* No | *Confirm by* By arrang. | *Parking* Ample |
| *Room TV* No | *Last dinner* 8.30 | *Banquets* 70/10 |

Lyonshall

Map 4 A1 Hereford & Worcester

Kington *HR5 3LH*
Kington (0544) 230720
Proprietor Daphne Lambert

About £25 for two

Penrhos Court

Part of a complex of rustic old buildings which now includes a brewery, this unpretentious restaurant makes a delightful setting for Daphne Lambert's wholesome cooking. Her short, daily-changing menu makes good use of seasonal produce with dishes like baked bonito tuna, tarragon chicken and beef carbonnade. There are also delicious sweets such as rum and chocolate charlotte. *Credit* Barclaycard

Lunch By arrangement *Dinner* 7.30–9.30, Sat 7.30–10
Closed Sun, Mon, 25 & 26 December, January & February

Lytham St Anne's

Map 10 A1 Lancashire

West Beach *FY8 5QT*
Lytham (0253) 739898
Telex 677463
Manager Mr H. J. Thompson
Credit Access, Amex,
Barclaycard

Rooms 49
with bath/shower 47

Clifton Arms Hotel 65% £E

This handsome Victorian hotel on the seafront has extensive banqueting and function facilities. A smart entrance hall leads to the comfortable lounge with high-backed settles, and there's also a pleasant bar. Spacious bedrooms in the main building have freestanding furniture, while those in the wing are smaller and more modern in style. Well-equipped bathrooms.

| *Room phone* Yes | *Confirm by* By arrang. | *Parking* Ample |
| *Room TV* Yes | *Last dinner* 10.15 | *Banquets* 200/2 |

Maidenhead

Map 5 E2 Berkshire

Shoppenhangers Road *SL6 2PZ*
Maidenhead (0628) 35934
Telex 848443
Proprietors Mr & Mrs Lösel
Credit Access, Amex,
Barclaycard, Diners

Rooms 34
with bath/shower 29

Aldingham House Hotel 69% Ⓜ £D

The Lösels continue to improve standards at this attractive gabled hotel standing in two acres of gardens next to the local golf course. Sofas and armchairs fill the small reception area, panelled lounge and two bars. Well-designed bedrooms have matching soft fabrics and most also have nicely fitted bathrooms with coloured suites. A smart new bedroom block is especially attractive. No dogs. *Amenities* garden.

| *Room phone* Yes | *Confirm by* 6 | *Parking* Ample |
| *Room TV* Yes | *Last dinner* 9.45 | *Banquets* 100/10 |

Maidenhead

Map 5 E2 Berkshire

Shoppenhangers Road *SL6 2PZ*
Maidenhead (0628) 35934
Proprietors Mr & Mrs Lösel

Aldingham House Hotel, Fredrick's Rest.

Oriental tapestries and pretty pictures decorate this smart, well-run restaurant, where the fixed-price menu offers an intriguing blend of the familiar and the unexpected–from baked mushrooms and grilled Dover sole to avocado with scallops in hot lime butter and suprême of pheasant in raspberry sauce. Home-made sorbets provide a delightful finale.

Continued

Continued

     🍷 *ABOVE AVERAGE. Credit* Access, Amex, Barclaycard, Diners

● **Set L** £13·50 **Set D** £19·50
About £42 for two

Lunch 12.30–2.15 *Dinner* 7.30–9.45
Closed L Sat, all Sun & Bank Holidays

Maidenhead
Map 5 E2 Berkshire
St Mary's Walk *SL6 1QZ*
Maidenhead (0628) 36638
Proprietor Mrs Lieserach

Swiss cooking

Bacchus Swiss Restaurant   🍷 Ⓢ

The decor of this friendly restaurant resembles an Alpine chalet, so it's fitting that the menu offers a choice of skilfully prepared, authentic Swiss dishes to match. As well as various fondues and raclette, there are specialities like our tender veal zurichoise in a creamy wine sauce and excellent rösti potatoes. Sweets such as rich chestnut vermicelles are delicious, too.
Credit Access, Amex, Barclaycard, Diners   ♿

About £25 for two

Lunch 12–2.30 *Dinner* 7–10.30 Sat 7–11
Closed Sun & Bank Holidays

Maidenhead
Map 5 E2 Berkshire
Manor Lane *SL6 2RA*
Maidenhead (0628) 23444
Telex 847502

Credit Access, Amex,
Barclaycard, Diners

Crest Hotel   63%   £ D

Conveniently close to the M4, this three-storey brick and glass hotel provides pleasant, comfortable accommodation. The bar overlooks an attractive duck pond, and there are ample, relaxing lounge areas. Smartly decorated bedrooms are double-glazed and well carpeted; all have tea-making facilities as well as radio-alarms, trouser presses and small tiled bathrooms with bidets and showers. *Amenities* garden, pool table.   ♿

Rooms 190	*Room phone* Yes	*Confirm by* 6	*Parking* Ample
with bath/shower 190	*Room TV* Yes	*Last dinner* 11	*Banquets* 320/2

Maidenhead
Map 5 E2 Berkshire
Manor Lane
Off Shoppenhangers Rd *SL6 2QW*
Maidenhead (0628) 23444
Manager David Blackford
English cooking

● **Set L & Set D** £8·50
About £42 for two
Banquets 100/2

Shoppenhangers Manor   ♛ Ⓢ

The oak-panelled dining room of a handsome manor house is a suitably traditional setting for some authentic English fare. First-class seasonal ingredients are carefully handled to produce tempting dishes ranging from potted pigeon and salmon pâté to scallops with leeks, beef Wellington and roast lamb with rosemary-flavoured gravy. Lovely old-fashioned sweets.
🍷 *SUPERIOR. Credit* Access, Amex, Barclaycard, Diners

Lunch 12.30–2.15 *Dinner* 8–10.45
Closed Sun, Bank Holidays, D 25 December & 26 December–3 January

---

Maidstone
Map 7 B5 Kent
London Road
Larkfield *ME60 6HJ*
West Malling (0732) 846858
Telex 957420
Credit Access, Amex,
Barclaycard, Diners

Larkfield Hotel   58%   £ D/E

Popular with travellers using the Channel ports, this converted rectory is well designed for short stays. The pub-style King's Bar is a popular meeting place, and there are a few seats in the foyer, as there is no lounge. Bedrooms (most are in the modern extension) are attractively decorated and fitted with freestanding furniture. Compact, fully tiled bathrooms.
Amenities garden, in-house video.

Rooms 52	*Room phone* Yes	*Confirm by* 6	*Parking* Ample
with bath/shower 52	*Room TV* Yes	*Last dinner* 9.45	*Banquets* 90/12

Maidstone
Map 7 B5 Kent
High Street *ME14 1JA*
Maidstone (0622) 55721

Credit Access, Amex,
Barclaycard, Diners

Royal Star Hotel   53%   £ E

A favourite haunt of Benjamin Disraeli when he was the local MP, this former coaching inn now gains much of its trade from large conferences and banquets. But there are still links with the past in the first-floor lounge with its beamed ceiling and wood-panelled walls; there are also two bars. Cheerful bedrooms are furnished in simple modern style, and bathrooms are adequate.

Rooms 31	*Room phone* Yes	*Confirm by* 5	*Parking* Ample
with bath/shower 14	*Room TV* Yes	*Last dinner* 9.30	*Banquets* 600/10

Maldon
Map 7 C4 Essex
3 Silver Street *CM9 7QE*
Maldon (0621) 52681

Credit Access, Amex,
Barclaycard, Diners

Rooms 26		
with bath/shower 26		

Blue Boar Hotel   57%   £D/E

The facade of this town-centre hotel is Georgian, but parts of it date back to the 14th century. The three bars have plenty of character, and upstairs is a splendid banqueting room. Bedrooms, in contrast, are modern, all with practical fitted units, radios and tea-makers, and well-equipped bathrooms are up to date as well.

Room phone Yes	*Confirm by* 6	*Parking* Ample
Room TV Yes	*Last dinner* 9.30	*Banquets* 25/–

Malmesbury
Map 4 B2 Wiltshire
Easton Grey *SN16 0RB*
Malmesbury (066 62) 2888

Rooms 15
with bath/shower 15
Room phone Yes
Room TV Yes
Confirm by By arrang.
Last dinner 9.30
Parking Ample
Banquets 65/–

Credit Access, Amex,
Barclaycard

Whatley Manor Hotel   75%   Ⓜ   £D

New owners have taken over this impressive Cotswold-stone manor house set in peaceful countryside just outside Malmesbury. Two large panelled lounges with big log fires, antiques and deep armchairs and sofas are wonderfully relaxing, and there is an attractive bar (in what was once the library) with bamboo furniture. Comfortable bedrooms are individually decorated in traditional style, and nearly all enjoy fine views over the extensive gardens. Bathrooms are very well equipped, mostly with smart modern suites; one or two have enormous period fittings. No dogs. No children under seven. *Amenities* garden, outdoor swimming pool, game fishing, croquet, helipad, 12-hour laundry service.   ♿

Malmesbury
Map 4 B2 Wiltshire
Easton Grey *SN16 0RB*
Malmesbury (066 62) 2888

● **Set L** £5·50, Sun £7·50
Set D £10
About £29 for two

Whatley Manor Restaurant   Ⓢ

Tables are elegantly laid in this attractive dining room overlooking the grounds. Short set menus concentrate on capably prepared roasts, grills and game in season, with a few more elaborate specialities like pork dijonnaise or succulent pheasant with mandarins. Vegetables such as beetroot mornay are tasty, too, and there are some unusual sweets like tempting melon and port sorbet. *Credit* Access, Amex, Barclaycard

Lunch 12.30–2 *Dinner* 7–9.30

We welcome complaints and bona fide recommendations on the tear-out pages for readers' comments. They are followed up by our professional team. Please also complain to the management instantly.

Malvern
Map 4 B1 Hereford & Worcester
Abbey Rd, Great Malvern *WR14 3ET*
Malvern (068 45) 3325
Telex 335008
Manager Mr Cave-Brown-Cave
Credit Access, Amex,
Barclaycard, Diners

Rooms 106		
with bath/shower 85		

Abbey Hotel   54%   £D

This ivy-covered hotel standing near Abbey Gate is very popular for conferences. Public areas include two old-fashioned lounges and a functional cocktail bar with views of the famous priory. Bedrooms in the original building and in the annexe are simply furnished in modern style, and bathrooms are adequately equipped.
Amenities garden. **Closed** 25 & 26 December

Room phone Yes	*Confirm by* By arrang.	*Parking* Ample
Room TV Yes	*Last dinner* 8.30	

Malvern

Map 4 B1 Hereford & Worcester
Holywell Road
Malvern Wells *WR14 4LG*
Malvern (068 45) 3487
Proprietor Mr Michael Ross

Credit Access, Barclaycard

Rooms 20
with bath/shower 17

Cottage in the Wood Hotel   67%   Ⓜ   £ D

This splendid Georgian house high in the Malvern Hills enjoys spectacular views across the Severn Plain towards the Cotswolds. The reception area, with its interesting mixture of cane and antique furniture, has a fresh green decor which contrasts with the bold red of the bar. Pleasant, individually styled bedrooms include eight compact modern ones in the coach house. Bathrooms are well equipped. No dogs. *Amenities* garden.

Room phone Yes	*Confirm by* 6	*Parking* Ample
Room TV Yes	*Last dinner* 8.30	

Malvern

Map 4 B1 Hereford & Worcester
Holywell Road
Malvern Wells *WR14 4LG*
Malvern (068 45) 3487
Proprietor Mr Michael Ross

● **Set L** £6·75 **Set D** £10·75
incl. service
About £31 for two

Cottage in the Wood Hotel Restaurant

Unusual combinations like beef slices in dill jelly or hare pâté with greengage relish are a feature of the daily-changing set menus in this brightly decorated restaurant. Main courses, including seasonal seafood and game, are served with lovely crunchy vegetables, and there are some really mouthwatering desserts such as apple and rum meringue and light, subtle almond soufflé. *Credit* Access, Barclaycard   &

Lunch 12.30–2 *Dinner* 7–9

Malvern

Map 4 B1 Hereford & Worcester
221 Wells Road
Malvern Wells *WR14 4HF*
Malvern (068 45) 65612

French cooking

● **Set L** £8·80 **Set D** £12·50
About £38 for two

Croque-en-Bouche   ★   

Marion Jones' culinary enthusiasm continues unabated at this charming Victorian-style restaurant, where both cooking and service are in true French style, with serving dishes brought to your table. The fixed-price dinner menu might include superb gazpacho, skate with a butter and red wine sauce, and plump chicken with pistou. Unusual garden herbs transform a simple green salad, and there's a marvellous selection of French cheeses followed by delicious sweets like grape tart to ensure a perfect meal from start to finish. No pipes or cigars. **Specialities** soupe de poisson, lemon sole with crab sauce, pheasant 'truffé' with bacon and thyme, bavarois aux fraises des bois.  *OUTSTANDING. Credit* Access, Barclaycard

Lunch Sun only 12.30–1.45 *Dinner* 7.45–9.15 **Closed** D Sun, Mon, Tues, also Wed after Bank Holidays & Bank Holidays except Good Friday

Malvern

Map 4 B1 Hereford & Worcester
14 Worcester Road
Great Malvern *WR14 2QS*
Malvern (068 45) 3397

Credit Access, Amex,
Barclaycard, Diners

Rooms 26
with bath/shower 22

Foley Arms Hotel   61%   Ⓜ   £ D/E

Spectacular views over the Severn Valley are one of the attractions of this well-preserved Regency hotel in the town centre. Oil paintings, prints and porcelain add period charm to the two lounges, and there's a comfortable bar with stained-glass windows and plush seating. Traditionally decorated bedrooms feature handsome Victorian wardrobes and chests of drawers; all have tea/coffee-makers. *Amenities* garden.

Room phone Yes	*Confirm by* 6	*Parking* Ample
Room TV Yes	*Last dinner* 9.15	*Banquets* 115/–

Manchester

Town plan D3 Greater Manchester
Clarence Street *M2 4FW*
061–236 6657
Manager Mr W. W. Hannah

● **Set L** £3·40 **Set D** £8·75
About £31 for two

Blinkers Bijou

An attractive city-centre restaurant with terrazzo flooring, pillars and mural-covered alcoves. The menu features popular French-inspired dishes: onion soup, seafood, grills, loin of lamb and more elaborate entrées like roast duckling with orange sauce. Vegetables are fresh, and there's a nice choice of familiar sweets such as profiteroles and pears in red wine. *Credit* Access, Amex, Barclaycard, Diners

Lunch 12–2.30 *Dinner* 7.15–11.15, Sat 7.15–11.30
Closed L Sat, all Sun & Bank Holidays

Manchester
Town plan D3 Greater Manchester
16 Princess Street M1 4NB
061–228 2503
Manager Mr W. W. Hannah

Blinkers French

Like the Bijou, this smart basement restaurant with a colourful mural makes a feature of fresh produce obtained direct from Manchester's excellent market. Game, seafood (including salmon and lobster) and carefully selected vegetables are used for a good range of French-inspired dishes, and there's a well-stocked dessert trolley.
Credit Access, Amex, Barclaycard, Diners

● **Set L** £4·30
About £33 for two

Lunch 12–2.30 *Dinner* 7.15–11.15, Sat 7.15–11.30
Closed L Sat, all Sun & Bank Holidays

Manchester
Town plan E3 Greater Manchester
Portland Street M1 3LA
061–228 2288
Telex 665007

Credit Access, Amex,
Barclaycard

Britannia Hotel   68%   £E

Painstaking conversion has transformed this 130-year-old textile warehouse into a comfortable and luxuriously appointed hotel. The splendid entrance hall-lounge with a giant Italian chandelier and gold-painted pillars is equipped with deep leather chesterfields, and the vast central staircase is a most impressive structure. There's an ample choice of bars. Well-designed bedrooms have smart darkwood furniture, beautifully soft bed linen and a host of extras. Fully carpeted bathrooms are comprehensively equipped.
Amenities sauna, indoor swimming pool, dancing (Fri, Sat), disco (Mon–Sat), gymnasium, solarium, turkish baths, baby listening, 24-hour laundry service, nightclub.

Rooms 180	*Room phone* Yes	*Confirm by* 6	*Parking* Ample
with bath/shower 180	*Room TV* Yes	*Last dinner* 10.30	*Banquets* 100/–

Manchester
Town plan C2 Greater Manchester
Royal Exchange Building,
Cross Street M2 7BY
061–832 9924
Manager Mr. Aksel Nielsen
Danish cooking
● **Set L** £4·95 & £6·50
Set D £8·50
About £22 for two
Banquets 200/5

Danish Food Centre, Copenhagen Restaurant   Ⓢ

A spotlit cold table laden with meats, fish, salads and cheese is the chief attraction of this bright, stylish restaurant. It all looks colourful, fresh and tempting, and you can help yourself to as much as you can eat. If you prefer, choose a hot meal from the à la carte—fish soup, perhaps, followed by a roast or veal in dill sauce.
Credit Access, Amex, Barclaycard, Diners

Lunch 12–2.30 *Dinner* 6–10.30, Sat 6-11
Closed Sun & Bank Holidays

Manchester
Town plan E3 Greater Manchester
Aytoun Street M1 3DR
061–236 9559
Telex 667580
Manager Mr A. C. Drummond
Credit Access, Amex,
Barclaycard, Diners

Grand Hotel   64%   £C

Situated in the heart of the city, this large stone hotel offers good facilities for businessmen and tourists. A spacious pillared entrance hall features an ornamental fountain, and there are two attractive bars (one with a Victorian theme), plus a relaxing lounge. Bedrooms have darkwood fitted units, smart patterned bedspreads and well-equipped bath or shower rooms.
Amenities 24-hour laundry service, baby listening.

Rooms 146	*Room phone* Yes	*Confirm by* 6	*Parking* Difficult
with bath/shower 146	*Room TV* Yes	*Last dinner* 11	*Banquets* 500/–

Manchester
Town plan D3 Greater Manchester
6a Booth Street M2 4AW
061–236 6417
Proprietor Mr E. Barbieri
Italian cooking

Isola Bella   Ⓢ

A canopied entrance leads to this stylish basement restaurant, whose decor features terrazzo flooring, lots of greenery and smart wicker chairs. Chicken and veal dishes are popular choices on the authentically Italian menu, along with pasta and seafood; there's an eye-catching display of cold meats and salads, as well as a tempting sweet trolley. Cooking is assured, service amiable and efficient. *Credit* Amex, Barclaycard, Diners

About £27 for two

Lunch 12.30–2.30 *Dinner* 7–11
Closed Sun & Bank Holidays

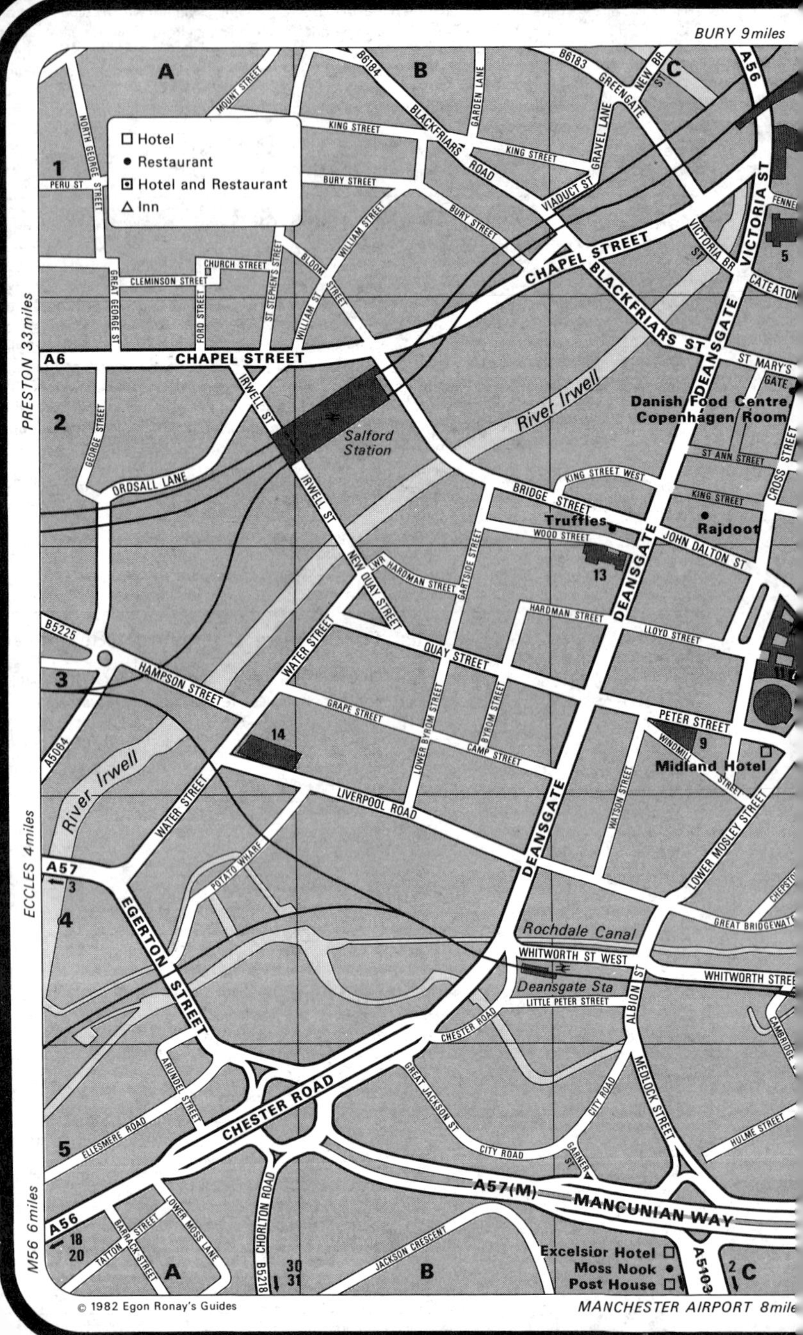

FIAT Manchester
BURY 9 miles
□ Hotel
• Restaurant
⊡ Hotel and Restaurant
△ Inn
A
B
C
1
2
3
4
5
PRESTON 33miles
ECCLES 4miles
M56 6miles
PERU ST
NORTH GEORGE STREET
MOUNT STREET
KING STREET
KING STREET
BLACKFRIARS ROAD
B6184
B6183
GARDEN LANE
GREENGATE
GRAVEL LANE
NEW BR ST
A56
VICTORIA ST
FENNE
BURY STREET
BURY STREET
WILLIAM STREET
BLOOM STREET
CHAPEL STREET
VIADUCT ST
BLACKFRIARS ST
VICTORIA BR
VICTORIA ST
CATEATON
5
CHURCH STREET
CLEMINSON STREET
GREAT GEORGE ST
FORD STREET
ST STEPHEN'S STREET
WILLIAM ST
DEANSGATE
ST MARY'S GATE
A6
CHAPEL STREET
IRWELL ST
River Irwell
Danish Food Centre
Copenhágen Room
ST ANN STREET
CROSS STREET
GEORGE STREET
ORDSALL LANE
IRWELL ST
Salford Station
BRIDGE STREET
KING STREET WEST
Truffles •
WOOD STREET
KING STREET
Rajdoot
JOHN DALTON ST
DEANSGATE
2
B5225
NEW QUAY STREET
LWR HARDMAN STREET
GARTSIDE STREET
HARDMAN STREET
HARDMAN STREET
LLOYD STREET
13
A5064
River Irwell
HAMPSON STREET
WATER STREET
GRAPE STREET
QUAY STREET
LOWER BYROM STREET
BYROM STREET
CAMP STREET
PETER STREET
WINDMILL STREET
9
Midland Hotel
3
14
WATSON STREET
DEANSGATE
LOWER MOSLEY STREET
A57
3
4
WATER STREET
POTATO WHARF
LIVERPOOL ROAD
Rochdale Canal
WHITWORTH ST WEST
Deansgate Sta
LITTLE PETER STREET
ALBION ST
WHITWORTH STREET
GREAT BRIDGEWAT
CHEPSTO
EGERTON STREET
ARUNDEL STREET
CHESTER ROAD
CHESTER ROAD
GREAT JACKSON ST
CITY ROAD
MEDLOCK STREET
A56
18
20
TATTON STREET
BARRACK STREET
LOWER MOSS LANE
CHORLTON ROAD
B5218
30
31
JACKSON CRESCENT
CITY ROAD
GARNER
A57(M)
MANCUNIAN WAY
HULME STREET
CAMBRIDGE
Excelsior Hotel □
Moss Nook •
Post House □
A5103
2
C
© 1982 Egon Ronay's Guides
MANCHESTER AIRPORT 8 mile

FIAT

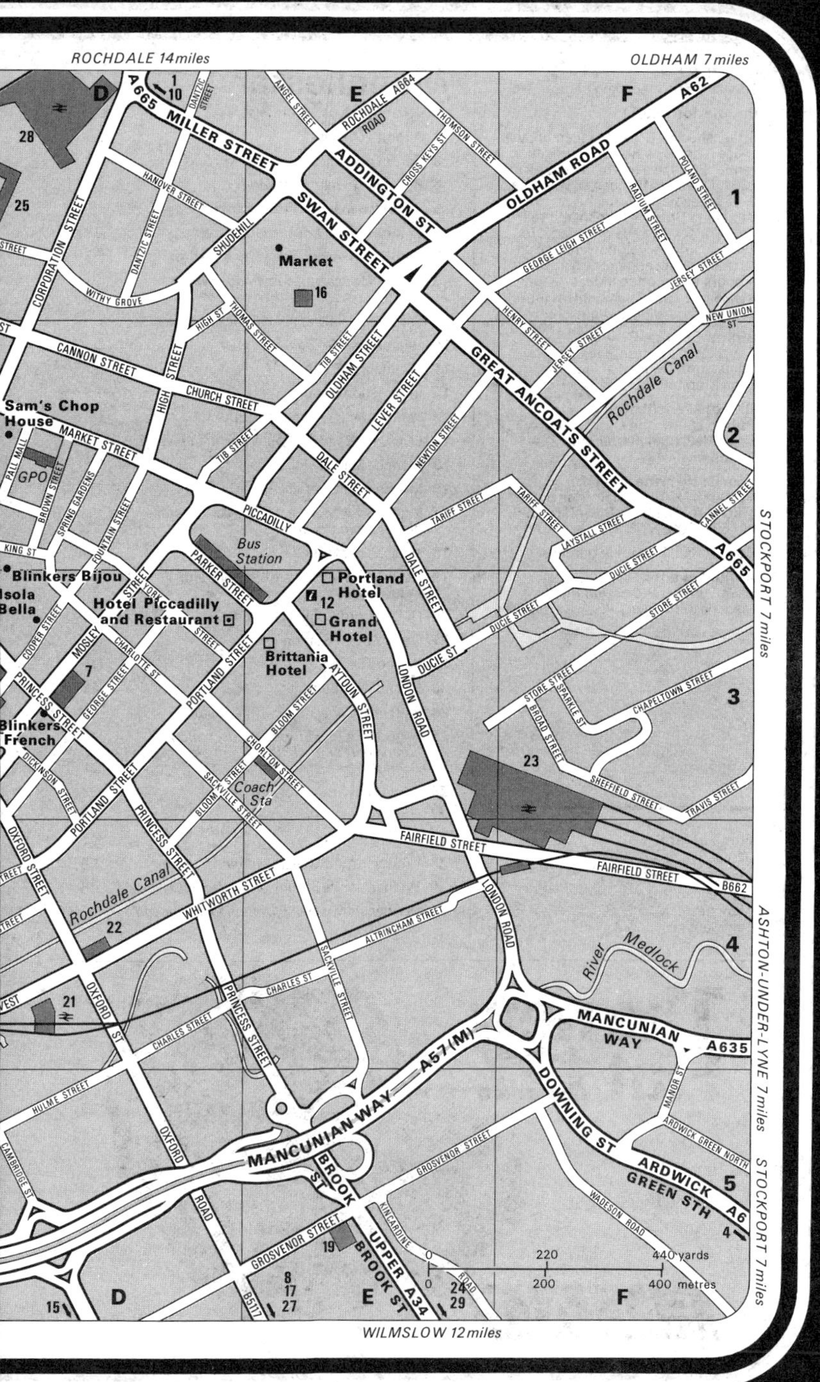

ROCHDALE 14 miles
OLDHAM 7 miles
D
E
F
A 665
A664
A62
MILLER STREET
ADDINGTON ST
OLDHAM ROAD
SWAN STREET
Rochdale A664 ROAD
THOMSON STREET
ANGEL STREET
CROSS KEYS ST
1
28
DANTZIC STREET
HANOVER STREET
GEORGE LEIGH STREET
POLAND STREET
RADIUM STREET
25
DANTZIC STREET
SHUDEHILL
Market
HENRY STREET
JERSEY STREET
JERSEY STREET
16
NEW UNION ST
STREET
WITHY GROVE
HIGH ST
THOMAS STREET
TIB STREET
GREAT ANCOATS STREET
CANNON STREET
OLDHAM STREET
CHURCH STREET
HIGH ST
LEVER STREET
NEWTON STREET
Rochdale Canal
2
Sam's Chop House
TIB STREET
DALE STREET
TARIFF STREET
TARIFF STREET
CANNEL STREET
PALL MALL
MARKET STREET
LAYSTALL STREET
GPO
SPRING GARDENS
BROWN STREET
FOUNTAIN STREET
PICCADILLY
DUCIE STREET
DUCIE STREET
STORE STREET
A665
KING ST
Bus Station
DALE STREET
DUCIE STREET
Blinkers Bijou
YORK STREET
PARKER STREET
Portland Hotel
STORE STREET
Isola Bella
Hotel Piccadilly and Restaurant
12
Grand Hotel
STORE STREET
SPARKLE ST
CHAPELTOWN STREET
3
COOPER STREET
CHARLOTTE ST
PORTLAND STREET
Brittania Hotel
AYTOUN STREET
BROAD STREET
MOSLEY
7
BLOOM STREET
LONDON ROAD
23
PRINCESS STREET
GEORGE STREET
STREET
CHORLTON STREET
SHEFFIELD STREET
TRAVIS STREET
Blinkers French
DICKINSON STREET
PORTLAND STREET
SACKVILLE STREET
Coach Sta
BLOOM STREET
PRINCESS STREET
DUCIE ST
FAIRFIELD STREET
OXFORD STREET
WHITWORTH STREET
FAIRFIELD STREET
B662
Rochdale Canal
22
ALTRINCHAM STREET
LONDON ROAD
River Medlock
4
OXFORD ST
SACKVILLE STREET
21
CHARLES ST
MANCUNIAN WAY
A635
WEST
CHARLES STREET
PRINCESS STREET
A57(M)
DOWNING ST
MANOR ST
HULME STREET
OXFORD ROAD
BROOK ST
GROSVENOR STREET
ARDWICK GREEN NORTH
5
CAMBRIDGE ST
MANCUNIAN WAY
UPPER BROOK ST A34
KINCARDINE
GROSVENOR STREET
WADESON ROAD
ARDWICK GREEN STH A6
B5117
GROSVENOR STREET
19
0
220
440 yards
8
17
27
0
200
400 metres
15
D
E
BROOK ST
24
29
F
4
WILMSLOW 12 miles
STOCKPORT 7 miles
ASHTON-UNDER-LYNE 7 miles
STOCKPORT 7 miles

Map 10 B2
Town plan on preceding page

Population 488,511

Established 38 BC as Mancenion, the 'place of tents', a Roman fortification centre. Became a free market town in 1301. Opened Manchester Ship Canal in 1894 leading to Manchester becoming Britain's third inland seaport. The textile trade prepared it for the Industrial Revolution and the city prospered with engineering skills brought to its cotton industry. Apart from night-spot entertainment the city is noted for the Hallé Orchestra.

Sights Outside City
Jodrell Bank, Tatton Hall, Chatsworth House, Haddon Hall, Little Moreton Hall, Bramall Hall

City of Manchester
Public Relations Dept. PO Box 532 Town Hall, Manchester M60 2LA Telephone 061–236 3377

Tourist Information Offices
PO Box 532, Town Hall, Manchester M60 2LA Telephone 061–236 1606, 251697, 2035

County Hall, Piccadilly Gardens

Annual Events
Hallé Summer Proms *June–July*
Manchester Show *July*

Fiat Dealers

Knibbs (Manchester) Ltd, Midland Street Garage, Ashton Old Road, Manchester M12 6LB Tel: Manchester 273 4411

Manchester

1	Abraham Moss Centre *leisure facilities*	D1
2	Airport *10 miles*	C5
3	Barton Aqueduct *swing trough bridge*	A4
4	Belle Vue *exhibitions, sports*	F5
5	Cathedral *mainly 15th-c. fine carvings*	C1
6	Central Library *houses 11 libraries*	C3
7	City Art Gallery *mostly early British art*	D3
8	Fletcher Moss Museum *English water-colours*	E5
9	Free Trade Hall *home of Hallé Orchestra*	C3
10	Heaton Hall *Georgian museum*	D1
11	Information Centre	C3
12	Information Centre	E3
13	John Rylands Library *rare books*	C3
14	Liverpool Road Station *oldest in the world*	A3
15	Manchester City F.C.	D5
16	Manchester Craft Village	E1
17	Manchester Museum *Egyptology; natural history; coins; stamps*	E5
18	Manchester United F.C.	A5
19	North West Museum of Science and Industry	E5
20	Old Trafford Cricket Ground	A5
21	Oxford Road Station	D4
22	Palace Theatre	D4
23	Piccadilly Station	F3
24	Platt Hall *Gallery of English Costume*	E5
25	Schools Library *Europe's oldest public library; part of the 13th-c Chetham Hospital School*	D1
26	Town Hall *Gothic revival*	C3
27	University Theatre	E5
28	Victoria Station	D1
29	Whitworth Art Gallery *paintings; textiles*	E5
30	Wythenshawe Forum *leisure facilities*	A5
31	Wythenshawe Hall *Elizabethan manor and art gallery*	A5

Manchester
Town plan E1 Greater Manchester

30 Edge Street *M4 1HN*
061–834 3743

Market ♫ Ⓢ

This charming little bistro really buzzes with life. The weekly-changing menu is a cosmopolitan affair including many of Mary-Rose Edgecombe's personal favourites like chicken véronique, Hungarian pork goulash and spiced lamb with almonds and yoghurt, as well as some vegetarian dishes. Delightful sweets can vary from watermelon milk sherbet to Elizabeth Raffald's orange custard–an 18th-century English recipe. Book.

Dinner only 7–10.30
About £21 for two **Closed** Sun, Mon, 25 & 26 December, 2 weeks spring & all August

---

Manchester
Town plan C3 Greater Manchester

Peter Street *M60 2DS*
061–236 3333
Telex 667797
Manager Mr H. A. Berry
Credit Access, Amex,
Barclaycard, Diners

Midland Hotel 66% £B/C

Traditional standards of service have been maintained at this handsome red-brick hotel, where Mr Rolls first met Mr Royce. There's a comfortable elegant lounge, several bars and some magnificent banqueting rooms. Bedrooms have well-designed fitted units and good modern bathrooms. Six suites are decorated in various national styles. *Amenities* sauna, 24-hour lounge service, coffee shop (7.30am–10.30pm), 24-hour laundry service, hairdressing.

Rooms 302
with bath/shower 274

Room phone Yes	*Confirm by* 6	*Parking* Difficult
Room TV Yes	*Last dinner* 11	*Banquets* 430/–

Manchester
Town plan D3 Greater Manchester

Piccadilly Plaza *M60 1QR*
061–236 8414
Telex 668765
Manager Mr D. Mercer
Rooms 250
with bath/shower 250
Room phone Yes
Room TV Yes
Confirm by 6
Last dinner 10.30
Parking Ample
Banquets 700/–
Closed 25 & 26 December

Credit Access, Amex,
Barclaycard, Diners

Hotel Piccadilly 77% *E* £C

This large glass and concrete hotel stands above a modern shopping complex in the heart of the city. Comprehensive facilities for banquets, conferences and exhibitions make it a firm favourite with businessmen, and it's also a popular place for socialising, with a cane-furnished coffee shop leading off the streamlined reception area and a choice of three bars. There's also a very large residents' lounge with comfortable, contemporary seating and 24-hour service. Attractive bedrooms have smart fitted furniture, plenty of writing and storage space and well-equipped, mosaic-floored bathrooms. Most rooms have panoramic city views. *Amenities* dancing (Sat), hairdressing, valet, 24-hour lounge service, coffee shop (10am–midnight).

Manchester
Town plan D3 Greater Manchester

Piccadilly Plaza *M60 1QR*
061–236 8414
Manager Mr. D. Mercer

About £25 for two

Hotel Piccadilly, Ambassador Restaurant ♕ Ⓢ

A smart modern restaurant, whose two fixed-price menus centre round an enticing hors d'œuvre selection that serves either as a main course or as a starter on the more expensive menu. *Credit* Access, Amex, Barclaycard, Diners *Lunch* 12.30–2.30 *Dinner* 6.30–10.30 **Closed** 25 & 26 December
● **Set L & Set D** £7·75 & £10·45 incl. wine & service ♿

Manchester
Town plan E3 Greater Manchester

3 Portland Street
Piccadily *M1 6DP*
061–228 3400
Telex 669157
Credit Access, Amex,
Barclaycard, Diners

Portland Hotel 67% £C/D

This well-designed modern hotel, which is set behind a Victorian facade, has excellent facilities for the businessman. Conference and banqueting rooms are lavishly equipped, and two attractive bars include one with Edwardian decor. Compact bedrooms are very well fitted, with comfortable armchairs, radios and tea-makers, and the particularly smart bathrooms boast the luxury of radio and telephone extensions. *Amenities* coffee shop (7am–midnight).

Rooms 221
with bath/shower 221

Room phone Yes	*Confirm by* 6	*Parking* Ample
Room TV Yes	*Last dinner* 10.15	*Banquets* 350/10

Manchester — Post House Hotel 60% £D

Town plan C5 Greater Manchester

Palatine Road
Northenden *M22 4FH*
061–998 7090
Telex 669248
Credit Access, Amex,
Barclaycard, Diners

Well placed for motorway travellers, this modern eight-storey hotel woos businessmen with comprehensive banqueting and conference facilities. There's a pleasant, open-plan reception-lounge, as well as two attractively appointed bars. Cheerful, double-glazed bedrooms have fitted pine units and spacious writing areas. Small bathrooms make effective use of space. *Amenities* coffee shop (10.30am–10.30pm).

Rooms 201
with bath/shower 201

Room phone Yes — *Confirm by* 6 — *Parking* Ample
Room TV Yes — *Last dinner* 10.30

Manchester — Rajdoot

Town plan C2 Greater Manchester

St James' House
South King Street *M2 6DW*
061–834 2176
Indian cooking

● **Set L** from £3·30
Set D from £6·50
About £23 for two
Banquets 100/30

Waiters in colourful Indian costumes provide helpful service in this large elegant restaurant. Ingredients are excellent, herbs and spices are carefully balanced, and dishes are attractively presented. The choice ranges from marinated tandoori dishes to familiar curries like tender chicken moghlai and rich, spicy, bhuna gosht served with carefully cooked basmati rice. *Credit* Access, Amex, Barclaycard, Diners

Lunch 12–2.15 *Dinner* 6.30–11.30
Closed L Sun, L Bank Holidays & all 25 & 26 December

Manchester — Sam's Chop House

Town plan D2 Greater Manchester

Back Pool Fold
Chapel Walks *M2 1HE*
061–834 1526
Grills
About £21 for two

Lunch in this bustling grill room is a highly enjoyable experience. Steaks, chops and roasts are amply served with delicious fresh vegetables and there's soup or fish to start and simple sweets to round things off. Book.
Credit Access, Amex, Barclaycard, Diners *Lunch only* 12–3
Closed Sat, Sun & Bank Holidays *Banquets* 100/50

Manchester — Truffles

Town plan C2 Greater Manchester

63 Bridge Street *M3 3BQ*
061–832 9393

● **Set L** £3·50 **Set D** £9·95,
also pre- & post-theatre
£7 incl. wine
About £28 for two
Banquets 20/20

There's a relaxed Victorian atmosphere in this friendly restaurant, where two set menus are reliably prepared from the finest ingredients. Dishes like creamy Stilton and garlic soup and lamb's kidneys with chestnut and sherry sauce show a fondness for imaginative English cooking, while sweets range from jam roly-poly to delicious lime and chocolate cheesecake. Lighter lunches. *Credit* Access, Amex, Barclaycard, Diners

Lunch 12–2 *Dinner* 5.30–11.30
Closed L Sat, all Sun, Mon & Bank Holidays except Good Friday

Manchester Airport — Excelsior Hotel 68% £C

Map 10 B2 Greater Manchester

Wythenshawe *M22 5NS*
061–437 5811
Telex 668721
Manager Mr E. T. Jones
Credit Access, Amex,
Barclaycard, Diners

Stopover travellers are well served by this modern hotel just opposite the airport. The cleverly designed lounge areas in the open-plan foyer are ideal for business chats, and there is a smart bar. Compact, double-glazed bedrooms are nicely appointed, with neat fitted units and relaxing chairs. Good bathrooms. *Amenities* garden, outdoor swimming pool, coffee shop (10.30am–1.30am), transport for airport.

Rooms 304
with bath/shower 304

Room phone Yes — *Confirm by* 7 — *Parking* Ample
Room TV Yes — *Last dinner* 10.15 — *Banquets* 235/–

Manchester Airport — Moss Nook

Map 10 B2 Greater Manchester

Ringway Road *M22 5NA*
061–437 4778
Proprietors
Pauline & Derek Harrison

A refined Edwardian atmosphere pervades this smart restaurant. Seasonal items such as Maryland soft shell crabs supplement the main menu, which has some ingenious creations like scampi wrapped in Parma ham, grilled and served with fingers of fresh mango. There are also familiar dishes such as noisettes of lamb sautéed with rosemary. Vegetables are excellent and sweets inviting. ♟ *ABOVE AVERAGE. Credit* Access, Amex, Barclaycard

● **Set L** £9·50 **Set D** £13·50
About £38 for two

Lunch 12–2 *Dinner* 7–10.30
Closed L Mon & Sat, all Sun, Bank Holidays & 1 week Christmas

Margate
Map 7 D5 Kent
36 Arlington Square *CT9 1XN*
Margate (0843) 22626
Italian cooking

About £21 for two

Al Gatto Bianco

Enrico Harkin, the friendly owner-chef at this simple little restaurant by the seafront, offers tasty, nicely presented Italian dishes like cannelloni or tender saltimbocca alla romana. Enjoyable sweets.
Credit Access, Barclaycard *Lunch* 12–2.30, Sun 12–3 *Dinner* 6–11
Closed D Sun, all Mon & November–March

Market Harborough
Map 11 D4 Leicestershire
21 High Street *LE16 7NJ*
Market Harborough
(0838) 66644
Proprietor Mr W. Knauf
Credit Access, Amex,
Barclaycard, Diners

Three Swans Hotel   55%   Ⓜ   £E

There's a solid, traditional air about this former coaching inn, parts of which date back to the 14th century. Two cheerful bars are popular local meeting places, and residents can relax in the cocktail bar or lounges (one with TV). Some of the spotlessly maintained bedrooms have antique furnishings (two with four-posters) but most are more modern in style; immaculate, up-to-date bathrooms.

Rooms 20	*Room phone* Yes	*Confirm by* 7.30	*Parking* Ample
with bath/shower 20	*Room TV* Yes	*Last dinner* 10	*Banquets* 80/8

Marlow
Map 5 E2 Buckinghamshire
Marlow Bridge *SL7 1RG*
Marlow (062 84) 4444
Telex 848644

Rooms 42
with bath/shower 42
Room phone Yes
Room TV Yes
Confirm by 6
Last dinner 10
Parking Ample
Banquets 120/–
Credit Access, Amex,
Barclaycard, Diners

Compleat Angler Hotel   78%   £B/C

Smooth lawns running down to the edge of a weir, hanging baskets of flowers in summer and a lovely verandah make this a most alluring hotel. Inside, antique furniture sets off the fine white marble floor of the foyer, and an L-shaped lounge with deep armchairs and chintzy curtains offers relaxation. The panelled cocktail bar opens on to the terrace. Traditionally furnished bedrooms with pretty colour schemes live up to expectations, recently redecorated ones being especially attractive. Bathrooms (some featuring splendid antique tiles) are thoughtfully equipped. Friendly, efficient staff add to the enjoyment of a stay here.
Amenities garden, tennis, coarse fishing, mooring, 24-hour laundry service.

Marston Trussell
Map 11 D4 Northamptonshire
Near Market Harborough *LE16 9TY*
Market Harborough
(0858) 65531

Credit Amex, Barclaycard,
Diners

Sun Inn Hotel   59%   £F

This friendly whitewashed hotel provides good comfort. Guests can relax in the plush little cocktail bar, and there's also a simple TV lounge. Neat bedrooms have modern fitted furniture, pretty matching fabrics, duvets, radios and tea/coffee-makers, plus carpeted, up-to-date bathrooms. Two bedrooms in the annexe are simpler in style. No dogs.
Amenities garden.

Rooms 12	*Room phone* Yes	*Confirm by* By arrang.	*Parking* Ample
with bath/shower 12	*Room TV* No	*Last dinner* 10	*Banquets* 40/6

Matlock
Map 10 C2 Derbyshire
Riber *DE4 5JU*
Matlock (0629) 2795
Proprietors
Alex & Gill Biggin
Credit Access, Amex,
Barclaycard, Diners

Riber Hall   69%   Ⓜ   £D

Nestling beneath the ruins of Riber Castle, this beautifully restored Elizabethan manor house conjures up strong echoes of the past. Handsome carved antique furniture and leaded windows add character to the public rooms, and most of the bedrooms (across the courtyard) have four-posters—plus mini-bars, tea-makers and smart modern bathrooms. No children under ten. No dogs. *Amenities* garden, helipad.

Rooms 8	*Room phone* Yes	*Confirm by* By arrang.	*Parking* Ample
with bath/shower 8	*Room TV* Yes	*Last dinner* 9.30	*Banquets* 34/6

Matlock

Map 10 C2 Derbyshire
Riber *DE45JU*
Matlock (0629) 2795
Proprietors
Alex & Gill Biggin

● **Set L** £5·50
About £33 for two

Riber Hall Restaurant   Ⓢ

Ken Parker, who trained under Robert Carrier, offers a wide-ranging dinner menu in this simple, charming dining room. Dishes like turbot Nantua, jugged hare and the more unusual fried veal with peach, banana and hollandaise sauce are characterised by well-judged seasoning and balanced flavours; vegetables are carefully cooked and sweets show a light touch. ♉ *SUPERIOR. Credit* Access, Amex, Barclaycard, Diners

Lunch 12–1.30 *Dinner* 7–9.30, Sun 7–8

Matlock Bath

Map 10 C2 Derbyshire
New Bath Road *DE43PX*
Matlock (0629) 3275

Manager Mr G. Youssef
Credit Access, Amex,
Barclaycard, Diners

New Bath Hotel   58%   £D

This handsome Georgian hotel, set in elevated gardens overlooking the river Derwent, blends period charm with modern comfort in its attractive public rooms. Bedrooms in the wing have balconies overlooking the pool, and like the somewhat larger rooms in the main building, feature radios, tea/coffee-makers and well-fitted bathrooms. *Amenities* garden, indoor & outdoor swimming pools, tennis, solarium, children's playground.

Rooms 56	*Room phone* Yes	*Confirm by* 6	*Parking* Ample
with bath/shower 56	*Room TV* Yes	*Last dinner* 9.30	*Banquets* 200/–

Mawnan Smith

Map 2 B4 Cornwall
Near Falmouth *TR11 5HT*
Falmouth (0326) 250541
Proprietors Mr & Mrs H. Pilgrim
Credit Access, Amex,
Barclaycard, Diners
Closed January & early February

Meudon Hotel   66%   Ⓜ   £B

Beautiful sub-tropical gardens are part of the attraction of this enlarged private house with its own beach. Public areas, including a comfortable cocktail bar and two lounges, are solidly traditional. Bedrooms, all in the newer extensions, are modern and have well-designed fitted units. Attractive bathrooms. Residents are temporary members of Falmouth Golf Club. *Amenities* garden, sea fishing, private beach.

Rooms 38	*Room phone* Yes	*Confirm by* By arrang.	*Parking* Ample
with bath/shower 30	*Room TV* Yes	*Last dinner* 8.45	*Banquets* 80/2

Mayfield

Map 7 B6 East Sussex
High Street *TN20 6AG*
Mayfield (043 55) 2342

● **Set D** from £9·65 incl. service
About £28 for two

Old Brew House   ♧ Ⓢ

Dinner in this delightful restaurant is a highly enjoyable experience, thanks to Geoff Allinson's hospitality and his wife's imaginative cooking. Although steaks and plain fish are available, it pays to be adventurous and try something like swordfish Andalusian-style, chicken breasts stuffed with smoked fish or creamy Nepalese lamb curry. Equally inventive starters and sweets on the fixed-price menus. ♉ *ABOVE AVERAGE.*

Dinner only 7.30–9.30
Closed Sun, Mon & 1 week January

Meal Bank

Map 13 D5 Cumbria
Kendal *LA8 9DJ*
Kendal (0539) 23082

Proprietors Mr & Mrs W. Taylor
Credit Diners

High Laverock House Hotel   57%   Ⓜ   £F

Friendly Mr and Mrs Taylor run this welcoming hotel, which stands two miles out of Kendal on the Penrith road. A small vestibule with a display of old bottles leads to the open-plan lounge and bar area which provides attractive views over undulating countryside, and there's also a little TV room. Well-kept bedrooms have cheerful modern furnishings and adequate tiled bathrooms. *Amenities* garden.

Rooms 8	*Room phone* No	*Confirm by* By arrang.	*Parking* Ample
with bath/shower 8	*Room TV* No	*Last dinner* 9	*Banquets* 60/20

Melksham

Map 4 B3 Wiltshire
26 Church Street *SN12 6LS*
Melksham (0225) 705242

Japanese cooking

Chikako's Japanese Restaurant   ♧ Ⓢ

Japanese restaurants outside London are very much a rarity, and this one, enthusiastically run by Scotsman Duncan Cameron and his charming wife Chikako, attracts clientele from a large area. Set meals featuring perhaps flavoursome onion soup followed by beef teriyaki, gingery pork fillet or various meats grilled at table are truly enjoyable. To finish there's deliciously

Continued

light cheesecake or fresh fruit cocktail.

● **Set D** from £5·90
About £20 for two
Banquets 14/–

Lunch Tues–Fri by arrangement only *Dinner* 6.30–11
Closed L Sat & Sun, all Mon & 25 December

Melton Mowbray
Map 11 D3 Leicestershire
Burton Street *LE13 1AF*
Melton Mowbray (0664) 60121

Manager Mr Chris Dyson
Credit Access, Amex,
Barclaycard, Diners

Harboro' Hotel   56%   £E

This classically styled 18th-century coaching inn stands just out of the town centre on the Oakham road. An extensive programme of alterations has added to its attractions, and there's now a comfortable little lounge as well as a popular panelled bar. Bedrooms are decorated and furnished to a high contemporary standard, and overnight guests can look forward to a splendid, cheerfully served English breakfast.   ♿

| *Rooms* 29 | *Room phone* Yes | *Confirm by* 6 | *Parking* Ample |
| *with bath/shower* 29 | *Room TV* Yes | *Last dinner* 9.30 | *Banquets* 95/– |

Mere
Map 4 B3 Wiltshire
Castle Street *BA12 6JE*
Mere (0747) 860258

Proprietors John & Jean Doyle
Credit Access, Amex,
Barclaycard, Diners

Old Ship Hotel *(Inn)* Ⓜ   £E

The beamed bar of this 200-year-old hostelry in the centre of town provides a cosy rendezvous for locals, and there's a comfortable little lounge bar, too. Bedrooms in the main building are attractively decorated, with pretty floral wallpaper and a smattering of beams and antiques; the bright, neat rooms and baths in the wing are more modern.   ♿

| *Rooms* 24 | *Room phone* Yes | *Confirm by* 6 | *Parking* Ample |
| *with bath/shower* 17 | *Room TV* Yes | *Last dinner* 9 | |

Meriden
Map 10 C4 West Midlands
Main Road *CV7 7NH*
Meriden (0676) 22735
Telex 311011
Manager Mr J. Portman
Credit Access, Amex,
Barclaycard, Diners

Manor Hotel   64%   £D/E

Originally the manor house in Meriden, this Georgian building has been tastefully extended to form a useful businessman's hotel. It has a comfortable foyer-lounge and two bars (one public, one for residents). Bedrooms are all studio-style and have fitted units and half-tiled bathrooms.
Amenities garden, outdoor swimming pool, dinner dance & cabaret (Sat).

| *Rooms* 32 | *Room phone* Yes | *Confirm by* 6 | *Parking* Ample |
| *with bath/shower* 32 | *Room TV* Yes | *Last dinner* 9.45 | *Banquets* 275/2 |

Mickleton
Map 4 C1 Gloucestershire
Near Chipping Campden *GL55 6SB*
Mickleton (038 677) 231
Proprietors
Hutchinson family
Credit Access, Amex,
Barclaycard

Three Ways Hotel   60% Ⓜ   £E

Extensive refurbishment has greatly improved this Cotswold-stone hotel, where the decor is up to date yet in keeping with the character of the building. The bright, modern reception is dominated by elegant chesterfield sofas, and there's a spacious bar as well as a sun lounge which doubles as a TV room. Bedrooms have fitted furniture and colourful bedspreads. Bathrooms are spotlessly clean. *Amenities* garden.   ♿

| *Rooms* 39 | *Room phone* No | *Confirm by* By arrang. | *Parking* Ample |
| *with bath/shower* 36 | *Room TV* Yes | *Last dinner* 9 | *Banquets* 100/– |

Middle Wallop
Map 4 C3 Hampshire
Near Stockbridge *SO20 8EG*
Wallop (026 478) 565
Proprietor Mrs Leigh Taylor
Credit Access, Amex,
Barclaycard, Diners
Closed 2 wks Christmas–New Year

Fifehead Manor   66% Ⓜ   £D/E

This manor house with attractive gardens has great charm and character, thanks to the efforts of Mrs Leigh Taylor. Public rooms, grouped around the entrance hall, include a homely lounge and a small meeting room. Bedrooms are most welcoming, with fresh flowers, pretty fabrics and freestanding furniture, plus good modern bathrooms; those in a converted barn are more compact and have shower rooms. *Amenities* garden, croquet.

| *Rooms* 12 | *Room phone* Yes | *Confirm by* By arrang. | *Parking* Ample |
| *with bath/shower* 12 | *Room TV* Yes | *Last dinner* 9.30 | *Banquets* 38/– |

Middle Wallop

Map 4 C3 Hampshire
Near Stockbridge *SO20 8EG*
Wallop (026 478) 565
Proprietor Mrs Leigh Taylor

About £27 for two

Fifehead Manor Restaurant

Margaret Leigh Taylor delves into cookery books to get many of the ideas for her regularly changing menu, and she features imaginative specialities like orange and lemon pork alongside more familiar dishes such as veal escalope in a cream sauce, all prepared from good-quality local produce. There are some delightfully unusual sweets on the trolley.
Credit Access, Amex, Barclaycard, Diners

Lunch 12–2, Sun 12.30–2 *Dinner* 7.30–9.30
Closed L Sat, D Sun & 2 weeks Christmas–New Year

Middlesbrough

Map 15 C5 Cleveland
250 Marton Road *TS4 2EZ*
Middlesbrough (0642) 224111

Credit Access, Amex,
Barclaycard, Diners

Hotel Baltimore   66%   £ D/E

High standards of decor and comfort prevail at this tastefully refurbished red-brick hotel. Elegant chesterfields add a touch of luxury to the reception area, and there's a roomy bar-lounge decorated in striking contemporary style. Compact bedrooms with restful colour schemes have practical fitted furniture, radio-alarms, tea/coffee-makers and spotless up-to-date tiled bathrooms. No dogs.

Rooms 31	*Room phone* Yes	*Confirm by* By arrang.	*Parking* Ample
with bath/shower 31	*Room TV* Yes	*Last dinner* 11	*Banquets* 70/–

Middlesbrough

Map 15 C5 Cleveland
Fry Street *TS1 1JH*
Middlesbrough (0642) 248133
Telex 58266

Rooms 140
with bath/shower 140
Room phone Yes
Room TV Yes
Confirm by By arrang.
Last dinner 10.30
Parking Ample
Banquets 400/–

Credit Access, Amex,
Barclaycard, Diners

Ladbroke Dragonara Hotel   72%   *E*   £ C/D

Fresh, contemporary decor is a feature of this tall modern hotel in the centre of town. There's a welcoming air about the spacious reception-lounge which has shag-pile carpeting and comfortable leather chairs; and the luxuriously appointed bar-lounge, complete with an ornamental fountain, is a relaxing place to enjoy a drink. There are also thick carpets in the bedrooms, which have restful decor and smart fitted or freestanding furniture. All are equipped with tea/coffee-makers, and the Gold Star rooms offer many extras, including trouser presses and sewing kits. Modern bathrooms are compact. There are several attractive suites and extensive conference facilities. *Amenities* dancing (Fri, Sat), transport for airport.

Middleton Stoney

Map 5 D1 Oxfordshire
Near Bicester *OX6 8SE*
Middleton Stoney (086 989) 234
Proprietor Mr Robert F. Ansell

Credit Access, Amex, Barclaycard
Closed 4 days Christmas

Jersey Arms *(Inn)* Ⓜ   £ E/F

Bedrooms are efficiently double-glazed at this 16th-century stone inn on the busy A43. Beamed and cosy, with antique furniture and pretty fabrics, all now have their own bathrooms. Downstairs, there's a charming, friendly bar with an open fire and a homely residents' lounge. Converted stables across the courtyard offer self-contained suites with private sitting rooms. No dogs.

Rooms 11	*Room phone* No	*Confirm by* 6	*Parking* Ample
with bath/shower 11	*Room TV* Yes	*Last dinner* 9.30	

Middleton in Teesdale

Map 15 B5 Co. Durham
DL12 0QG
Middleton in Teesdale
(083 34) 264
Proprietors
Mr & Mrs D. P. J. Streit
Credit Barclaycard

Teesdale Hotel   59%   Ⓜ   £ E/F

You can expect a warm welcome from Mr and Mr Streit when you arrive at this stone-built 18th-century coaching inn. Oil paintings of circus clowns animate the reception, as well as the convivial bar-lounge, and there is a comfortable TV lounge. Bedrooms are furnished with good reproduction pieces and attractive matching fabrics. Bathrooms have good carpets and modern suites.

Rooms 14	*Room phone* No	*Confirm by* 6	*Parking* Ample
with bath/shower 6	*Room TV* No	*Last dinner* 8.30	*Banquets* 50/–

Middlewich

Map 10 B2 Cheshire
51 Wheelock Street *CW109AB*
Middlewich (060 684) 3204
Proprietor Francesco Larosa
Italian cooking

About £25 for two

Franco's

Franco Larosa produces some very enjoyable Italian food in his unpretentious little restaurant, which he runs with his wife and son. Apart from evergreens like lasagne verdi, Parma ham and steak pizzaiola, there are some less usual choices like veal with fennel or pork fillet with mustard sauce; at 48 hours' notice, Franco will organise special regional dishes for parties of four or more.

Lunch by arrangement only *Dinner* 7–10
Closed D Mon (except for bookings), all Sun & Bank Holidays

Midhurst

Map 5 E3 West Sussex
Knockhundred Row *GU29 9DQ*
Midhurst (073 081) 3712

● **Set D** £12·45
About £33 for two

Knockers

Q ⓢ

The Phipps take good care of visitors to their cosy restaurant, where Mary is in charge of the cooking. Her short, fixed-price dinner menu shows style and imagination, with dishes ranging from robust cassoulet to sautéed chicken with horseradish, accompanied by expertly handled vegetables. Puddings are mainly ice creams and gâteaux. Light lunches.
Credit Access, Amex, Barclaycard, Diners

Lunch 12–2.30 *Dinner* 7.30–10.30
Closed D Sun & 25–30 December

Midhurst

Map 5 E3 West Sussex
South Street *GU29 9NH*
Midhurst (073 081) 2211
Telex 86853
Manager Brian Tonks
Credit Access, Amex,
Barclaycard, Diners

Spread Eagle Hotel   66%

£E

Dating back to 1430, this beautifully preserved hostelry continues to offer charming hospitality. Polished wooden floors, inglenooks and old beams are features of the comfortable lounge, and there's also the popular Coal Hole Bar in the basement. Most bedrooms have traditional freestanding furniture, and two superb panelled rooms also have four-posters. Adequate bathrooms. *Amenities* garden.

Rooms 27	*Room phone* Yes	*Confirm by* 7	*Parking* Ample
with bath/shower 23	*Room TV* Yes	*Last dinner* 9.15	*Banquets* 120/10

Milford

Map 5 E3 Surrey
Near Godalming *GU8 5HJ*
Godalming (048 68) 7227

Credit Access, Amex,
Barclaycard, Diners

Milford House Hotel   65%   

£E

Set in five acres of grounds, with open fields at the back, this well-kept Georgian building is delightfully peaceful. Handsome public rooms include the plush lounge bar, an elegant panelled lounge and the vaulted cellar bar. Comfortable bedrooms with white furniture and pretty bedspreads all have colour TV, radio-alarms, tea-making facilities and gleaming modern bathrooms. *Amenities* garden, sauna, squash, solarium.

Rooms 18	*Room phone* Yes	*Confirm by* By arrang.	*Parking* Ample
with bath/shower 18	*Room TV* Yes	*Last dinner* 10.15	*Banquets* 110/20

Milford on Sea

Map 4 C4 Hampshire
Lymington Road *SO40RF*
Milford on Sea (059 069) 3911

Proprietor Mr E. D. Barten
Credit Access,
Closed Christmas

South Lawn Hotel   65%   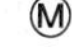

£D/E

This attractive mock-Tudor hotel surrounded by beautifully kept lawns is a peaceful country retreat. Vivid red carpeting dominates all the public areas, from the spacious, comfortably furnished lounge area and cosy bar to the large function room. Bedrooms are well designed with good fitted units, plenty of storage space and stylish bathrooms. No children under seven. No dogs. *Amenities* garden.

Rooms 17	*Room phone* Yes	*Confirm by* By arrrang.	*Parking* Ample
with bath/shower 17	*Room TV* Yes	*Last dinner* 9	*Banquets* 70/–

Milford on Sea

Map 4 C4 Hampshire
Lymington Road *SO40RF*
Milford on Sea (059 069) 3911
Proprietor Mr E. D. Barten

About £24 for two

South Lawn Hotel Restaurant

Q

Pretty garden views add to the charm of this spacious hotel dining room, where the fixed-price menu ranges from tasty coarse pâté and prawn cocktail to chicken Maryland and well-flavoured pork hongrois.
Credit Access *Lunch* Sun only 12.30–1.30 *Dinner* 7–9 **Closed** D Sun, all Mon & Christmas ● **Set L** £4·75 **Set D** £6·75

Mill Hill

Good Earth

See under London

Milton Damerel
Map 2 C2 Devon
Near Holsworthy *EX22 7LL*
Milton Damerel (040 926) 481
Proprietors
Mr & Mrs R. M. Vincent

Woodford Bridge Hotel   66%   Ⓜ   £ D

The Vincents have modernised their 15th-century thatched inn without losing any of its period appeal; there are three chintzy lounges (one with TV) and two bars, plus charmingly appointed bedrooms with compact modern bathrooms. In the grounds are nine self-contained suites and an impressive leisure complex. *Amenities* garden, sauna, solarium, indoor swimming pool, tennis, squash, game fishing, stables, games room, skittles.   &

Rooms 34	*Room phone* Yes	*Confirm by* By arrang.	*Parking* Ample
with bath/shower 28	*Room TV* Some	*Last dinner* 8.45	*Banquets* 120/–

Milton Damerel
Map 2 C2 Devon
Near Holsworthy *EX22 7LL*
Milton Damerel (040 926) 481
Proprietors
Mr & Mrs R. M. Vincent

● **Set L** Sun only £5·50
Set D £8·50
About £38 for two

Woodford Bridge Hotel Restaurant   Ⓢ

Cheerful girls provide pleasant service in this spacious two-roomed restaurant. The extensive à la carte and set menus are based on prime local produce, and dishes like hot Devon smokie, tender calf's liver with orange and Dubonnet sauce and sea bass with lobster sauce are capably prepared and served in very generous portions. There's also a good choice of seasonal game ranging from mallard to woodcock. 🍷 *ABOVE AVERAGE.*   &

Lunch Sun 12–2, Mon–Sat by arrangement only *Dinner* 7–8.45

Minster Lovell
Map 4 C2 Oxfordshire
Near Witney *OX8 5RN*
Witney (0993) 75614

Credit Access, Amex,
Barclaycard

Old Swan Hotel *(Inn)*   £ E

Follow the signs for *Old* Minster Lovell to find this historic, creeper-clad inn set in eight acres of grounds. Oak beams, a lovely stone hearth and a flagstone floor add to the character of the bar, and there's also a comfortable TV lounge for residents. A wooden spiral staircase leads to the cottage bedrooms, which have simple freestanding furniture, matching fabrics and washbasins. *Amenities* garden.

Rooms 5	*Room phone* No	*Confirm by* By arrang.	*Parking* Ample
with bath/shower None	*Room TV* No	*Last dinner* 9.30	*Banquets* 20/2

Monk Fryston
Map 11 D1 North Yorkshire
Near Leeds *LS25 5DU*
South Milford (0977) 682369
Manager Mrs J. M. Dodd

Monk Fryston Hall Hotel   64%   £ E

Handsome family portraits and stags' heads remind one of the origins of this greystone manor house, which is now an efficiently run hotel with attractive public areas. Most bedrooms have chintzy soft furnishings and good-quality built-in units, plus radios and tea-makers; rooms in the extension are more modern. Well-fitted bathrooms.
Amenities garden, dinner dance (Sat October–March).   &

Rooms 24	*Room phone* Yes	*Confirm by* By arrang.	*Parking* Ample
with bath/shower 24	*Room TV* Yes	*Last dinner* 9.30	*Banquets* 100/10

Montacute
Map 4 A3 Somerset
17 The Borough *TA15 6XB*
Martock (0935) 823823
Proprietors
Mr & Mrs C. Donovan

● **Set D** incl. service
About £27 for two
Banquets 24/10

Milk House   ♧ Ⓢ

A charming old stone building houses this attractive restaurant, where Charles Donovan does the cooking while his wife provides friendly, helpful service. High-quality ingredients are enjoyably prepared, and the menu offers tasty starters like haddock à la crème and main courses ranging from grilled steak to brochette of lamb or crisp roast duck with Grand Marnier sauce. Book. 🍷 *ABOVE AVERAGE. Credit* Access, Amex, Barclaycard

Dinner only 7–9.30
Closed Sun, Mon, 25 & 26 December, 2 weeks January & 2 weeks October

Morecambe
Map 13 D6 Lancashire
Marine Road *LA4 4BZ*
Morecambe (0524) 417180
Manager Mr J. L. Latty

Credit Access, Amex,
Barclaycard, Diners

Rooms 46
with bath/shower 46

Midland Hotel   60%   £ D

This seafront hotel in typical 1930s style has an impressive circular staircase dominating the reception area. Splendid uninterrupted views across the bay are a feature of both the delightful sun lounge and plush, panelled cocktail bar. Plain, comfortably furnished bedrooms are a good size and all have colour TV, radios and tea/coffee-makers; bathrooms of varying ages are adequate.

Room phone Yes   *Confirm by* By arrang.   *Parking* Ample
Room TV Yes   *Last dinner* 9   *Banquets* 150/–

Moreton-in-Marsh
Map 4 C1 Gloucestershire
High Street *GL56 0AZ*
Moreton-in-Marsh
(0608) 50251
Proprietor Mr Ian MacKenzie

● **Set L & Set D** from £6
About £36 for two
Banquets 60/8

Lamb's   ♔ Ⓢ

Young chef David Cappendell cooks with flair and skill in this charming, thoughtfully designed restaurant. His short à la carte menu offers sophisticated French-inspired dishes like our excellent calf's liver with sage and avocado, or pork tenderloin baked in pastry with apple and prune stuffing, supplemented by seasonal game and steaks. Lighter set meals are available in the reception area. *Credit* Access, Barclaycard

Lunch 12.30–2 *Dinner* 7.30–10.30
Closed D Sun, 1 January & D 25 December

Moreton-in-Marsh
Map 4 C1 Gloucestershire
High Street *GL56 0LJ*
Moreton-in-Marsh (0608) 50501
Telex 837151

Credit Access, Amex,
Barclaycard, Diners

Rooms 41
with bath/shower 31

Manor House Hotel   69%   Ⓜ   £ D

Mr and Mrs Fentum take obvious pride in running this old Cotswold manor house, which has a most friendly atmosphere. Inside, there's a comfortable reception-lounge with portraits and leather armchairs, and the stone-walled bar overlooks the garden. Bedrooms range from charming and traditional in the original building to more modern ones in the wing. Bathrooms are well equipped. No dogs. *Amenities* garden, sauna, putting, croquet.   

Room phone Yes   *Confirm by* By arrang.   *Parking* Limited
Room TV Yes   *Last dinner* 9   *Banquets* 60/–

Moreton-in-Marsh
Map 4 C1 Gloucestershire
High Street *GL56 0AW*
Moreton-in-Marsh (0608) 50308

Credit Access, Amex,
Barclaycard, Diners

Rooms 14
with bath/shower 5

Redesdale Arms   55%   £ E

Now privately owned, this modest Cotswold-stone coaching inn offers simple comforts and traditional hospitality, especially in its two cosily furnished bars. Bedrooms in the original building are pleasantly old-fashioned in style, while those in the annexe are more up to date. All have tea/coffee-makers and trouser presses. Bathrooms are modern and fully tiled. Dogs in the annexe only.

Room phone No   *Confirm by* By arrang.   *Parking* Ample
Room TV Yes   *Last dinner* 10

Moretonhampstead
Map 3 D3 Devon
TQ13 8RE
Moretonhampstead (064 74) 355
Telex 42794

Rooms 66
with bath/shower 66
Room phone Yes
Room TV Yes
Confirm by By arrang.
Last dinner 9
Parking Ample
Banquets 180/–
Closed 6 days Christmas

Manor House Hotel   74%   £ D

This superb mock-Jacobean manor house stands in 270 acres of beautiful Devon countryside complete with trout streams and its own private golf

Continued

Continued

course. Fine panelling is a feature of the spacious reception hall and the comfortable main lounge, which also boasts a handsome timbered ceiling and a massive, ornately carved stone fireplace. Bright bedrooms ranging from compact singles to roomy doubles and twins have solid traditional furnishings and pleasant decor; many of the bathrooms retain their original enormous tubs. Conference facilities are available. Staff are courteous and attentive. *Amenities* garden, tennis, squash, golf course, game fishing, pitch & putt, billiards, table tennis. &

Credit Access, Amex, Barclaycard, Diners

Morpeth
Map 14 B3 Northumberland
Bridge Street *NE61 1NB*
Morpeth (0670) 512083

Queen's Head Hotel   56%   £E

Function rooms are kept busy at this modernised town-centre coaching inn, where the cheerful Buffet Bar is a popular meeting place. Residents have a quiet lounge bar with a splendid 17th-century fireplace, as well as a first-floor TV lounge. Fitted bedrooms are neatly furnished and equipped with tea/coffee-makers, and plain bathrooms are acceptable. *Amenities* buttery (9am–8pm, winter 9am–4pm).

Credit Access, Amex, Barclaycard, Diners

| *Rooms* 23 | *Room phone* Yes | *Confirm by* By arrang. | *Parking* Limited |
| *with bath/shower* 10 | *Room TV* Yes | *Last dinner* 9.45 | *Banquets* 120/20 |

Mortehoe
Map 2 C1 Devon
Near Woolacombe *EX34 7EG*
Woolacombe (0271) 870347

Rockham Bay Hotel   57%   Ⓜ   £F

Extensive amenities make this hotel converted from three terraced houses ideal for family holidays. Comfortable public rooms are attractively decorated, while compact bedrooms have functional built-in furniture and well-equipped bathrooms. *Amenities* garden, sauna, outdoor swimming pool, dancing (Mon, Fri June–Sept), discothèque (Tues), children's playroom, solarium, laundry room, games room, video show (nightly).

Credit Amex, Diners
Closed November–February

| *Rooms* 34 | *Room phone* Yes | *Confirm by* 6 | *Parking* Ample |
| *with bath/shower* 34 | *Room TV* Yes | *Last dinner* 9 | |

Mottram St Andrew
Map 10 B2 Cheshire
Near Prestbury *SK10 4QT*
Prestbury (0625) 828135
Telex 668181
Manager Mr J. M. Smith
Credit Access, Amex, Barclaycard, Diners

Mottram Hall Hotel   67%   £D

A tree-lined drive leads to this fine Georgian house set in well-kept grounds of 120 acres that include a lake. Public areas retain many attractive period features, although furnishings are mainly contemporary. Comfortable bedrooms include 28 modern rooms in the wing and four large, elegant studio rooms on the ground floor with particularly smart bathrooms. *Amenities* garden, coarse fishing, dancing (Sat September–May), pitch & putt, snooker.

| *Rooms* 72 | *Room phone* Yes | *Confirm by* 6 | *Parking* Ample |
| *with bath/shower* 72 | *Room TV* Yes | *Last dinner* 10 | *Banquets* 130/8 |

Moulton
Map 15 B5 North Yorkshire
Near Richmond *DL10 6QJ*
Barton (032 577) 289
Proprietors
Mr & Mrs Pagendam

Black Bull Inn   Ⓢ

A tankful of live lobsters is just one of the attractions of this popular village pub, one of whose dining rooms is Hazel, a converted Brighton Belle Pullman car (book for this). The chef makes good use of local produce, and besides a large variety of delicious seafood you can get meat dishes, Yorkshire game and charcoal grills. To finish, lovely desserts and excellent English cheese. ♟*ABOVE AVERAGE.*

About £32 for two
Banquets 30/6

Lunch 12–2 *Dinner* 7–10.15, Sat 7–10.45
Closed L Sat, all Sun, L Good Friday & all 24–31 December

Mousehole
Map 2 A4 Cornwall
Near Penzance *TR19 6QX*
Penzance (0736) 731251
Proprietors
Major & Mrs J. T. Kelly
Closed mid November–end February

Lobster Pot   56%   Ⓜ   £D

This delightful family-run hotel, converted from a row of fishermen's cottages, occupies a lovely position right on the harbour wall. Homely public rooms like the lounge and bar enjoy splendid views, and there's also a TV lounge. Steep stairs lead up to the neat, cosy bedrooms, which have simple modern furnishings. Some rooms are in nearby houses. Compact bathrooms are well fitted. *Amenities* sea fishing.

| *Rooms* 24 | *Room phone* No | *Confirm by* By arrang. | *Parking* Difficult |
| *with bath/shower* 21 | *Room TV* No | *Last dinner* 9.45 | |

Much Birch
Map 4 A1 Hereford & Worcester
Near Hereford *HR2 8HJ*
Golden Valley (0981) 540742

Credit Access, Amex,
Barclaycard, Diners

Rooms 15
with bath/shower 15

Pilgrim Hotel *(Inn)*  £ D/E

Once used by pilgrims on their way to Hereford, this large inn still offers accommodation for travellers. Black beams, brass ornaments and highly polished tables give the spacious bar and lounge a traditional atmosphere, while well-maintained bedrooms (mostly in a wing) are more modern and have fully tiled bathrooms. No children under 12. No dogs.
Amenities garden, game fishing.

Room phone Yes	*Confirm by* 6	*Parking* Ample
Room TV Yes	*Last dinner* 9.30	

Mudeford
Map 4 C4 Dorset
Near Christchurch *BH23 3NT*
Christchurch (0202) 483434

Manager Mr E. Buffa
Credit Access, Amex,
Barclaycard, Diners

Rooms 41
with bath/shower 41

Avonmouth Hotel   58%   £ D

On the edge of Christchurch harbour, this hotel offers excellent amenities for families on holiday. Open-plan lounges and bar have fine views and a relaxed atmosphere, while simply furnished bedrooms are comfortable; those in the annexe are in modern studio-style. *Amenities* garden, outdoor swimming pool, sea fishing, discothèque (Sat in season), games room, laundry room, golf-practice nets, children's playground, slipway.

Room phone Yes	*Confirm by* 6	*Parking* Ample
Room TV Yes	*Last dinner* 8.45	*Banquets* 50/–

Mullion
Map 2 A4 Cornwall
Polurrian *TR12 7EN*
Mullion (0326) 240421
Proprietors Francis family

Credit Access, Barclaycard
Closed 7 Oct–1st week May

Rooms 45
with bath/shower 33

Polurrian Hotel   55%      £ D

There are fine views of the sea from this clifftop hotel, which has been run by the Francis family since 1948. Public areas include a spacious bar lounge and two cosy little lounges. Bright bedrooms are furnished in simple, up-to-date style, while bathrooms have colourful suites. *Amenities* garden, outdoor swimming pool, tennis, squash, dancing (twice weekly), solarium, table tennis, laundry room, pool table, croquet, badminton, putting.

Room phone No	*Confirm by* By arrang.	*Parking* Ample
Room TV Yes	*Last dinner* 9.30	*Banquets* 145/–

Nantwich
Map 10 B3 Cheshire
Worleston *CW5 6DQ*
Nantwich (0270) 626866

Rooms 12
with bath/shower 12
Room phone Yes
Room TV Yes
Confirm by 4
Last dinner 8.30
Parking Ample
Banquets 42/12
Closed Bank Holidays,
2 weeks July/August
& 24–30 December
Credit Access, Amex,
Barclaycard, Diners

Rookery Hall   84%      £ B

Standing in 28 acres of beautifully maintained gardens complete with terrace, fountain and lake, this wonderful English château is a most gracious and thoughtfully run hotel where Harry and Jean Norton ensure that guests feel completely at home. Two lounge areas with moulded plaster ceilings and friezes are tastefully arranged with antiques and contemporary furniture. A massive oak staircase leads to the bedrooms, which are individually furnished and superbly equipped with everything from champagne to sewing kits, plus luxurious bathrooms. Inclusive terms only. No children under ten. Guide dogs only. *Amenities* garden, tennis, coarse fishing, helipad, croquet, putting, 24-hour laundry service, rowing boats.

Nantwich
Map 10 B3 Cheshire
Worleston *CW5 6DQ*
Nantwich (0270) 626866

● **Set L** £4·95 & £16·25
Set D £16·25
About £45 for two

Rookery Hall Restaurant   ★   

Jean Norton's excellent six-course dinners are matched by the splendour of the room, with its handsome panelling, ornate plasterwork and well-spaced antique tables. High-quality raw materials, subtle, delicate sauces and attractive presentation are features of the French-style dishes, which range from the lightest of quiches to trout en papillote and casseroled quail. Beautifully cooked vegetables, too, and delicious, refreshing desserts. English lunchtime menu. No smoking in dining room.
Specialities striade de saumon, turbot et épinards en mousse, aiguillettes de caneton sur duxelle, deux sauces, croûte de veau et ris d'agneau.

Continued

Continued

🍷*ABOVE AVERAGE. Credit* Access, Amex, Barclaycard, Diners   ♿

Lunch 12–1.30 *Dinner* 7–8.30 **Closed** L Sat & all Sun & Mon to non-residents, Bank Holidays, 2 weeks July/August & 24–30 December

---

Nayland
Map 6 C3 Suffolk
Bear Street
Near Colchester *CO6 4HX*
Nayland (0206) 262204
Proprietors Gerard & Jane Ford

● **Set L & Set D** £7·25
About £28 for two
Banquets 40/12

Bear Country Restaurant

Hospitality, care and attention to detail are very much in evidence the moment you step inside the Fords' handsome half-timbered restaurant. They produce everything on the interesting menus, and dishes such as garlic-stuffed mussels, sauté de bœuf, seafood vol-au-vent and jugged hare are bound to please. You'll find crunchy vegetables and enjoyable desserts, as well as home-made after-dinner mints served with excellent coffee. ♿

Lunch Sun only 12.30–2 *Dinner* 7.15–9.30 **Closed** D Sun, all Mon, Tues, 1 week spring, 2 weeks late summer & 25 Dec–2 Jan

---

Neasham
Map 15 B5 Co. Durham
Newbus Grange
Near Darlington *DL2 1PE*
Darlington (0325) 721071

Credit Access, Amex,
Barclaycard, Diners

Rooms 19
with bath/shower 10

Newbus Grange Hotel   65%   Ⓜ   £ E

A handsome ivy-clad facade and a wealth of oak panelling and ornate plasterwork throughout the public rooms distinguish this sturdily built 17th-century house, where Eddie and Jean Irwin are the welcoming hosts. Good-sized bedrooms have bright, cheerful wallpapers and curtains and smart reproduction furniture; modern carpeted bathrooms are well fitted. *Amenities* garden, squash, dancing (Sat).

Room phone Yes	*Confirm by* By arrang.	*Parking* Ample
Room TV Yes	*Last dinner* 10	*Banquets* 80/–

Needingworth
Map 6 B2 Cambridgeshire
Overcote Ferry *PE17 3TW*
St Ives (0480) 63336

Manager Mr J. Fernandez
Credit Access, Barclaycard,
Diners

Rooms 11
with bath/shower 2

Pike & Eel *(Inn)*   £ E/F

True to its name, this 17th-century inn on the banks of the Great Ouse is a popular fisherman's haunt, and the main bar has displays of the ones that *didn't* get away! There's also a cosy, traditionally furnished lounge-bar and a first-floor TV lounge in similar style. Bedrooms have simple built-in units. Private bathrooms are modern, as is one of the two public bathrooms. Guide dogs only. *Amenities* garden, coarse fishing, mooring.

Room phone No	*Confirm by* By arrang.	*Parking* Ample
Room TV No	*Last dinner* 10	

We do not necessarily recommend the cooking at hotels whose restaurants are not separately listed.

New Milton
Map 4 C4 Hampshire
Christchurch Road *BH25 6QS*
Highcliffe (042 52) 5341
Telex 41456
Proprietors Skan family
Rooms 47
with bath/shower 47
Room phone Yes
Room TV Yes
Confirm by By arrang.
Last dinner 9.30
Parking Ample
Banquets 80/4

Credit Access, Amex,
Barclaycard, Diners

Chewton Glen Hotel   88%   £ B

Surrounded by 30 acres of woodland close to the New Forest, this luxurious hotel is a model of country house elegance, where friendly staff ensure that guests feel completely at ease. A long entrance hall leads to the wonderfully appointed public rooms, which include a lovely lounge with comfortable armchairs and access to the patio; there's also the peaceful little Oak Room, a sun lounge and an intimate bar. Spacious bedrooms (including some coach-house suites) are individually decorated with imaginative colour schemes, and the impressive bathrooms are superbly equipped. No children under seven. Guide dogs only. *Amenities* garden, outdoor swimming pool, tennis, billiards, croquet, putting, helipad. ♿

New Milton
Map 4 C4 Hampshire
Christchurch Road *BH25 6QS*
Highcliffe (042 52) 5341
Manager David Brockett
French cooking

● **Set L** from £8 **Set D** £16·50
About £50 for two

Chewton Glen Hotel, Marryat Room ★ ★ ♕ Ⓢ
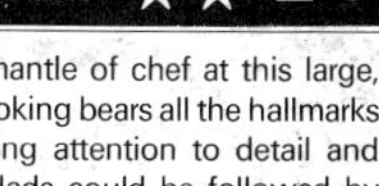

Young Pierre Cheviallard has taken over the mantle of chef at this large, formal restaurant, and it fits him perfectly. His cooking bears all the hallmarks of a true artist: faultless preparation, painstaking attention to detail and delicate presentation. A brilliant trio of tiny salads could be followed by scallops with sliced leeks in perfect puff pastry or roast guinea fowl in thyme sauce, accompanied by an excellent selection of vegetables. And, to finish, the rich chocolate marquise is in a class of its own. No pipes or cigars.
Specialities salade de canard aux betteraves et foie gras, coquilles St Jacques au gingembre, gratinée de pamplemousse.
♟ *OUTSTANDING. Credit* Access, Amex, Barclaycard, Diners   ♿

Lunch 12.30–2 *Dinner* 7.30–9.30

Newbury
Map 5 D2 Berkshire
Oxford Street *RG13 1JB*
Newbury (0635) 43666

Credit Access, Amex,
Barclaycard, Diners

Rooms 69
with bath/shower 51

Chequers Hotel 60% £ D

Once a posting house on the London–Bath road, this three-storey hotel still provides a comfortable haven. Bedrooms in the main house and the wing are neat and well designed, and bathrooms are carefully kept. Downstairs are a relaxing modern lounge, a cocktail bar, the smart John Porter Bar adorned with horsy prints, and several conference and function rooms.
Amenities garden, dancing (Sat November–April).

Room phone Yes	*Confirm by* 6	*Parking* Ample
Room TV Yes	*Last dinner* 9	*Banquets* 50/4

Newbury
Map 5 D2 Berkshire
RG16 8NJ
Kintbury (0488) 58100
Proprietors
Mr & Mrs Harold Sterne
Credit Access, Amex,
Barclaycard, Diners

Rooms 22
with bath/shower 19

Elcot Park Hotel 59% Ⓜ £ D/E

Five miles west of Newbury, just off the A4, this converted country mansion stands in 16 acres of mature gardens. Inside there's an antique-filled reception hall, a large lounge and a simple cocktail bar. Attractive bedrooms are in a good state of repair, some having solid traditional furniture, others more modern pieces, and bathrooms are well fitted.
Amenities garden, tennis, croquet, table tennis, helipad.   ♿

Room phone Yes	*Confirm by* 6	*Parking* Ample
Room TV Yes	*Last dinner* 9.30	*Banquets* 125/6

Newbury
Map 5 D2 Berkshire
Cedars, Enborne *RG15 0JS*
Newbury (0635) 41237
Proprietors
Mr & Mrs Basil Jones

● **Set L** £7·25 **Set D** £7·75
About £28 for two
Banquets 30/12

Enborne Dining Club & Restaurant ♿ ♕ Ⓢ

Basil Jones abandoned the stage to open this delightful restaurant, and he now runs the front of the house in charming style. His wife cooks very capably, offering dishes like veal escalope with a subtle Calvados sauce, beef bourguignonne and salmon with parsley sauce. Vegetables come fresh from the garden, and there's an eye-catching sweet trolley. Book.
Credit Access, Amex, Barclaycard, Diners   ♿

Lunch 12.30–2 *Dinner* 7.30–10
Closed L Sat, D Sun & all Bank Holidays

Newby Bridge
Map 13 D6 Cumbria
Near Ulverston *LA12 8NB*
Newby Bridge (0448) 31681

Manager Mr J. Bertlin
Credit Access, Amex,
Barclaycard, Diners

Rooms 36
with bath/shower 36

Swan Hotel 58% £ D

Extended and modernised in recent years, this old coaching inn has a fine position beside a stone bridge over the river Leven. There's a traditional lounge/reception area with beams and panelling, plus three pleasant bars in various styles. Bedrooms (some newly refurbished) have neat, well-equipped bathrooms and most have trouser presses. *Amenities* garden, coarse fishing, country & western dancing (Fri), moorings, baby listening.

Room phone Yes	*Confirm by* By arrang.	*Parking* Ample
Room TV Yes	*Last dinner* 9	*Banquets* 60/–

Map 15 B4
Town plan opposite

Population 270,000

Newcastle was founded in Roman times and later became a fortress against the Scots. Its commercial influence began with the mining of coal, but today rests on engineering and other industries. The coast and hinterland of Northumberland are areas of outstanding natural beauty. The theatres, Northern Sinfonia Orchestra, and the University, provide some of the many cultural activities.

Annual Events
The Hoppings (travelling fair) *last week in June*
Newcastle Festival *October*
Tyneside Summer Exhibition *End July–August*

Sights Outside City
Hadrian's Wall, Hexham Abbey, Durham Cathedral, Alnwick, Seaton Delaval, Northumberland National Park

City Information Service
Central Library, PO Box IMC, Princess Square
Newcastle-upon-Tyne NE99 1MC
Telephone Newcastle 610691

Fiat Dealers

Benfield Motors Ltd
Railway Street
Newcastle-upon-Tyne
Tyne and Wear NE4 7AD
Tel: Newcastle 732131

Newcastle-upon-Tyne

1	Airport	A1
2	Bessie Surtees House *fine 17th-c timbered house*	B5
3	Blackfriars Heritage and Interpretation Centre	A4
4	Castle, Black Gate Museum	B5
5	Central Library and Information Bureau	B3
6	Central Station	A5
7	Civic Centre *outstanding modern architecture including Carillon Tower*	B2
8	Gosforth Park Race-course	B1
9	Grey's Monument	B3
10	Guildhall *17th-c with Georgian facade*	B5
11	Hancock Museum *natural history of area*	B1/2
12	Jesmond Dene Park	C1
13	John George Joicey Museum *history, furniture, Northumberland Fusiliers Museum*	C4
14	Laing Art Gallery	B3
15	Museum of Science and Engineering *exhibits of Newcastle's great engineers*	A5
16	Newcastle Playhouse Theatre	A2
17	Newcastle United F.C. *St James's Park*	A3
18	Northumberland County C.C.	B1
19	Plummer Tower *museum in rebuilt tower of old walls*	B3
20	Quayside *open-air market on Sunday mornings*	C4/5
21	St Nicholas's Cathedral *mainly 14th & 15th c*	B4
22	Theatre Royal	B4
23	Town Moor *nearly 1,000 acres of free grazing, sport and recreation*	A1
24	Tyne Bridge	C5
25	University and Museum of Antiquities	A2

Newcastle upon Tyne

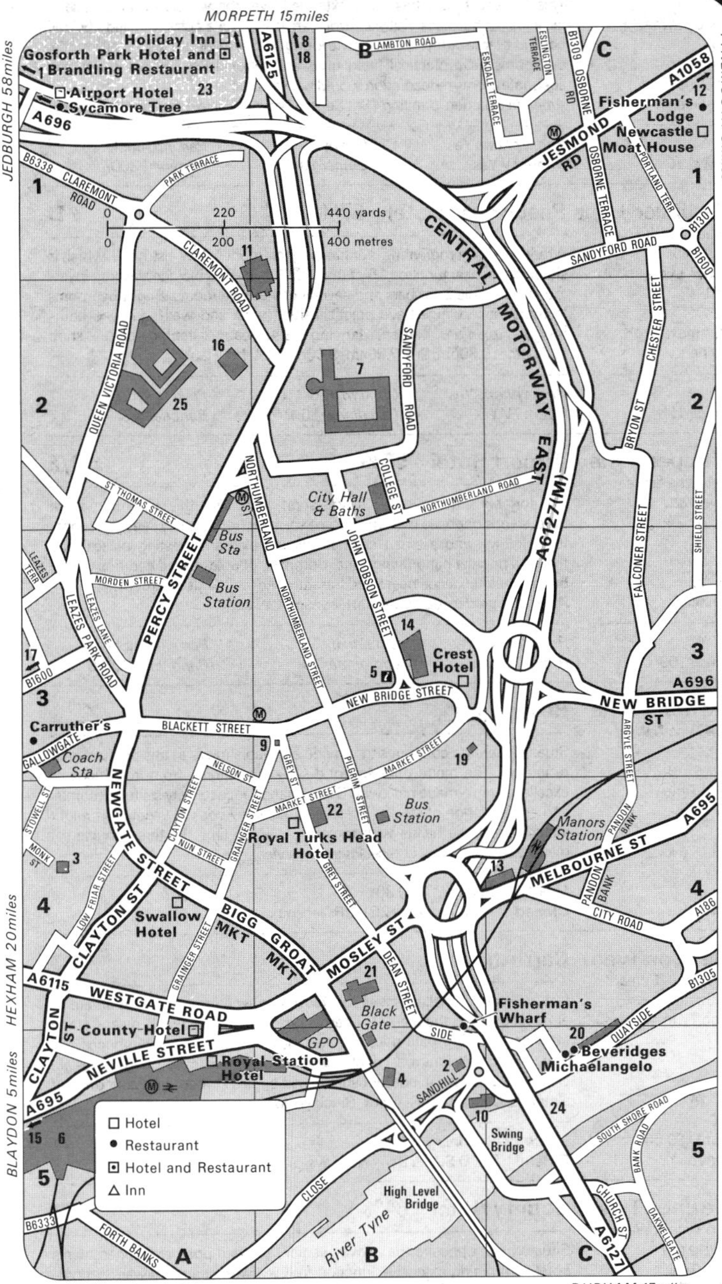

Newcastle-under-Lyme   Clayton Lodge Hotel   57%   £E

Map 10 B3 Staffordshire
Clayton Road *ST5 4AF*
Newcastle-under-Lyme
(0782) 613093

Credit Access, Amex,
Barclaycard, Diners

This turreted house has been extended over the years to provide useful facilities for business visitors. Public areas include a cosy panelled cocktail bar and a large contemporary-style lounge bar, as well as a residents' lounge. Bedrooms have practical fitted units and tea-makers, and bathrooms are adequate. Some redecoration would be welcome.
Amenities garden, dancing (Sat September–April), 24-hour laundry service.

| *Rooms* 51 | *Room phone* Yes | *Confirm by* 6 | *Parking* Ample |
| *with bath/shower* 40 | *Room TV* Yes | *Last dinner* 10 | *Banquets* 300/– |

Newcastle-under-Lyme   Post House Hotel   57%   £D

Map 10 B3 Staffordshire
Clayton Road *ST5 4DL*
Newcastle-under-Lyme
(0782) 625151
Telex 36531
Credit Access, Amex,
Barclaycard, Diners

A redecoration programme is enhancing this modern low-rise hotel, which is situated just near junction 15 of the M6. Public areas include a roomy foyer-lounge, two pleasant bars and several conference rooms. Bright bedrooms in motel-style wings have practical fitted units and well-equipped bath-rooms. *Amenities* garden, dancing (Sat), baby listening, coffee shop (7.30am–10.30pm, Sun 7.30am–9.30pm), 24-hour laundry service.

| *Rooms* 126 | *Room phone* Yes | *Confirm by* 6 | *Parking* Ample |
| *with bath/shower* 126 | *Room TV* Yes | *Last dinner* 10.15 | *Banquets* 65/– |

Newcastle upon Tyne   Airport Hotel   58%   £D/E

Town plan A1 Tyne & Wear
Woolsington *NE13 8DJ*
Ponteland (0661) 24911
Telex 537121

Credit Access, Amex,
Barclaycard, Diners

Comfortable and convenient for the short-stay visitor, this well-run modern hotel stands opposite the airport some six miles from the city centre. A roomy foyer/lounge and a smart cocktail bar are pleasant meeting places, and there's a popular banqueting suite. Compact, double-glazed bedrooms have bright, cheerful decor, neat fitted furniture and well-kept bathrooms.
Amenities garden, dancing (Sat), transport for airport.

| *Rooms* 100 | *Room phone* Yes | *Confirm by* 6 | *Parking* Ample |
| *with bath/shower* 100 | *Room TV* Yes | *Last dinner* 10 | *Banquets* 400/30 |

Newcastle upon Tyne   Beveridges

Town plan C4 Tyne & Wear
Sandgate
Quayside *NE1 2NG*
Newcastle upon Tyne
(0632) 23114

Stuart Beveridge continues to provide enjoyable meals at this pleasant pub restaurant. The menu offers a good selection ranging from frogs' legs or excellent home-made pâté with Cumberland sauce to tasty seafood mornay and a wide range of steaks. Interesting, carefully cooked vegetables might include artichoke hearts with tomato. At lunch time the three-course set menu provides further choice. Friendly service.

● **Set L** £3·50
About £26 for two

Lunch 12–2 *Dinner* 7–10.30
Closed L Sat, D Sun & all 25 & 26 December

Newcastle upon Tyne   Carruther's

Town plan A3 Tyne & Wear
52 St Andrew Street *NE1 5SF*
Newcastle upon Tyne
(0632) 617027

Natural wood panelling gives this recently opened restaurant an attractive atmosphere, and the menu is international in style. Enjoyable dishes range from fresh-tasting pâté maison and moules marinière to saltimbocca alla romana and delicious roast duckling with a rich cherry sauce. Vegetables are crisp, and sweets include unusual baked apples stuffed with apricots and almonds. *Credit* Access, Amex, Barclaycard, Diners

● **Set L** £5 **Set D** £9·50
About £32 for two

Lunch 12–2 *Dinner* 7–11
Closed L Sat, D Sun & Bank Holidays

Newcastle upon Tyne   County Hotel   64%   £D

Town plan A5 Tyne & Wear
Neville Street *NE99 1AH*
Newcastle upon Tyne
(0632) 322471   Telex 537873
Manager Mr G. Stephenson
Credit Access, Amex,
Barclaycard, Diners

Situated just opposite the railway station, this is a popular businessman's hotel, combining extensive function facilities with straightforward accom-modation. Attractively papered bedrooms have simple fitted units, tea-makers and radios, plus tiled bathrooms with showers. Public areas include a plush foyer and two distinctive bars. *Amenities* coffee lounge (10am–5pm), 24-hour laundry service (Mon–Fri).

Continued

Rooms 115	*Room phone* Yes	*Confirm by* 8	*Parking* Ample
with bath/shower 115	*Room TV* Yes	*Last dinner* 9.45	*Banquets* 120/8

Newcastle upon Tyne — Crest Hotel 60% £D

Town plan B3 Tyne & Wear
New Bridge Street *NE1 8BS*
Newcastle upon Tyne
(0632) 326191
Telex 53467
Credit Access, Amex,
Barclaycard, Diners

Formerly the Newcastle Centre, this cheerful modern hotel with comprehensive conference facilities caters well for the needs of the businessman. The reception area incorporates a roomy, comfortable lounge and there's a choice of three bars to suit all moods. Warm, double-glazed bedrooms have practical fitted furniture, tea-makers and well-equipped tiled bathrooms. *Amenities* sauna, solarium, bistro (9.30am–9.45pm). &

Rooms 180	*Room phone* Yes	*Confirm by* 6	*Parking* Ample
with bath/shower 180	*Room TV* Yes	*Last dinner* 9.45	*Banquets* 500/–

Newcastle upon Tyne — Fisherman's Lodge ♛ ⓢ

Town plan C1 Tyne & Wear
Jesmond Dene *NE7 7BQ*
Newcastle upon Tyne
(0632) 813281
Seafood

In a Victorian house alongside the Ouse Burn, this elegant restaurant specialises in excellent seafood, which ranges from fish terrine and fresh mussel soup to grilled halibut and poached scallops in a creamy Pernod and saffron sauce, accompanied by lovely fresh vegetables. There are also a few steak and chicken dishes, as well as some delicious sweets.
Credit Access, Amex, Barclaycard, Diners

● **Set L** £6·50
About £32 for two
Banquets 60/–

Lunch 12–2 *Dinner* 7–11
Closed L Sat, all Sun, Bank Holidays & 25 December–1 January

Newcastle upon Tyne — Fisherman's Wharf ⓢ

Town plan C4 Tyne & Wear
15 The Side *NE1 3JE*
Newcastle upon Tyne
(0632) 321057
Proprietors Mr & Mrs Cetolini
Seafood

Wood panelling, faded murals and formal waiters give this seafood restaurant the dignified atmosphere of an Edwardian gentlemen's club. Locally landed fish is deliciously fresh, and we enjoyed a splendid bouillabaisse à la maison, plus turbot in a wine sauce. Other specialities feature swordfish, salmon, mussels and oysters, all capably prepared, and there are grills for meat-eaters. *Credit* Access, Amex, Barclaycard, Diners

● **Set L** £6·50
About £31 for two

Lunch 12–1.45 *Dinner* 7–10.45
Closed L Sat, all Sun, Bank Holidays & 1 week Christmas

Newcastle upon Tyne — Gosforth Park Hotel 76% *E* £C

Town plan A1 Tyne & Wear
High Gosforth Park *NE3 5HN*
Newcastle upon Tyne
(0632) 364111
Telex 53655
Rooms 178
with bath/shower 178
Room phone Yes
Room TV Yes
Confirm by 6
Last dinner 10.30
Parking Ample
Banquets 550/4

Credit Access, Amex,
Barclaycard, Diners

Standing in wooded parkland four miles north of the city centre, this large modern hotel complex combines comfortable accommodation and high standards of service with an extensive range of leisure activities and impressive conference facilities. Rectangular marble columns add a touch of elegance to the roomy foyer-lounge, and the cosy late-night Cabin Bar is one of two pleasant drinking spots. Bedrooms (including several suites) have stylish modern decor, smart fitted furniture and up-to-the-minute bathrooms whose comprehensive equipment includes radio and telephone. *Amenities* garden, sauna, indoor swimming pool, squash, dancing (Tues–Sat), hotel coach, helipad, hairdressing, solarium, gymnasium. &

Newcastle upon Tyne
Town plan A1 Tyne & Wear
High Gosforth Park *NE3 5HN*
Newcastle upon Tyne
(0632) 364111

● **Set L** from £5·95 **Set D** £9·25
incl. service
About £39 for two

Gosforth Park Hotel, Brandling Restaurant   ♔

An elegant modern restaurant, where you can enjoy French-inspired dishes prepared with consistent care by chef Jacques Molinari. The menus range from simple hors d'œuvre and omelettes to seafood, grills, roasts and sauced entrées. Vegetables enjoy the same skilful handling, and to finish there's a choice between sweets, cheese and savouries. ♟*ABOVE AVERAGE.*
Credit Access, Amex, Barclaycard, Diners

Lunch 12.30–2.30 *Dinner* 7–10.30
Closed L Sat

Newcastle upon Tyne
Town plan A1 Tyne & Wear
Great North Road
Seaton Burn *NE13 6BP*
Newcastle upon Tyne
(0632) 365432   Telex 53271
Rooms 150
with bath/shower 150
Room phone Yes
Room TV Yes
Confirm by 6
Last dinner 11
Parking Ample
Banquets 340/–

Credit Access, Amex,
Barclaycard, Diners

Holiday Inn   74%   *E*   £ **C/D**

A major programme of refurbishment is under way at this modern brick and glass hotel beside the Great North Road. The open-plan foyer leads to a luxuriously comfortable lounge area, and there's a glass-walled cocktail bar overlooking the heated indoor swimming pool. Good conference facilities attract a business clientele, while spacious, colourful bedrooms are equally well suited to the needs of families. All rooms have radios, TV, air condition-ing, and fully tiled bathrooms complete with showers and thick, fluffy towels. *Amenities* garden, sauna, indoor swimming pool, coffee shop (7am–11pm), gymnasium, solarium, games room, discothèque (Thurs–Sat), baby listening, hotel car.

Newcastle upon Tyne
Town plan C5 Tyne & Wear
25 King Street *NE1 3UQ*
Newcastle upon Tyne
(0632) 614415

● **Set L** £4·45
About £28 for two

Michelangelo   ♧ ⓢ

Situated on the waterfront, in the shadow of the Tyne Bridge, this comfortable modern restaurant features an enjoyable mixture of French and Italian specialities, ranging from deep-fried Camembert and fillet of turbot in red wine sauce to cannelloni and saltimbocca alla romana. Vegetables are excellent and there are some tempting sweets such as lemon sorbet and chocolate roulade. *Credit* Access, Amex, Barclaycard, Diners

Lunch 12.30–2.30 *Dinner* 7–11
Closed L Sat, all Sun & Bank Holidays

Newcastle upon Tyne
Town plan C1 Tyne & Wear
Coast Road
Wallsend *NE28 9NH*
Newcastle upon Tyne
(0632) 628989   Telex 53583
Credit Access, Amex,
Barclaycard, Diners

Newcastle Moat House   64%   £ **E**

A convenient position alongside the A1, friendly, efficient staff, excellent conference facilities and carefully designed accommodation make this modern brick-and-glass hotel (formerly the Europa Lodge) a popular place with businessmen. The spacious foyer-lounge is cheerful and relaxing, and there are two convivial bars. Bright, compact bedrooms have neat built-in units and well-planned bathrooms. *Amenities* dancing (Fri, Sat).

Rooms 182
with bath/shower 182

Room phone Yes	*Confirm by* 7	*Parking* Ample
Room TV Yes	*Last dinner* 9.45	*Banquets* 300/–

Newcastle upon Tyne
Town plan A5 Tyne & Wear
Neville Street *NE99 1DW*
Newcastle upon Tyne
(0632) 320781
Telex 53681
Credit Access, Amex,
Barclaycard, Diners

Royal Station Hotel   66%   £ **D**

A classic 19th-century railway hotel that succeeds in combining Victorian elegance with up-to-date comforts. It has a magnificent entrance hall dominated by a wrought-iron staircase, a fine panelled lounge and a stylish bar. Bedrooms range from large and traditional to compact and modern. Neat bathrooms are well equipped. *Amenities* dancing (alternate Sats October–April). **Closed** 4 days Christmas.

                                          Continued

Rooms 128	*Room phone* Yes	*Confirm by* 6	*Parking* Difficult
with bath/shower 101	*Room TV* Yes	*Last dinner* 10	*Banquets* 200/–

Newcastle upon Tyne
Town plan B4 Tyne & Wear
Grey Street *NE99 6EG*
Newcastle upon Tyne
(0632) 326111

Credit Access, Amex,
Barclaycard, Diners

Royal Turks Head Hotel   55%   £ D

Converted from a 19th-century coaching inn, this city-centre hotel still retains some original features such as its superb mahogany staircase. There are three bars, including one restored in Victorian style. Bedrooms, which are decorated in warm autumnal colours, have fitted units, plenty of writing space and good lighting, plus tea-makers. Well-equipped bathrooms have shower attachments. *Amenities* pool table.

Rooms 91	*Room phone* Yes	*Confirm by* By arrang.	*Parking* Difficult
with bath/shower 80	*Room TV* Yes	*Last dinner* 9.30	*Banquets* 100/–

Newcastle upon Tyne
Town plan A4 Tyne & Wear
Newgate Street *NE1 5SX*
Newcastle upon Tyne
(0632) 325025

Credit Access, Amex,
Barclaycard, Diners

Swallow Hotel   63%   £ E

Towering above a shopping precinct, this modern seven-storey hotel has access to its rooftop car park from Clayton Street. Off the pleasant reception area is the cheerfully decorated coffee shop, and the top-floor lounge-cum-cocktail bar offers fine views of the city. Smart bedrooms have neat fitted furniture, tea/coffee-makers and fully tiled bathrooms.
Amenities dancing (Sat), coffee shop (9am–5pm).

Rooms 92	*Room phone* Yes	*Confirm by* 6	*Parking* Ample
with bath/shower 92	*Room TV* Yes	*Last dinner* 9.30	*Banquets* 80/10

Newcastle upon Tyne
Town plan A1 Tyne & Wear
78 High Street
Gosforth *NE3 1HB*
Gosforth (0632) 844088

Sycamore Tree   ⑤

Behind a row of shops, this is a friendly restaurant where Chef Ken Elliott whets the appetites with a constantly changing choice of interesting dishes. Highlights of our meal were a superb game terrine and a generously served rack of lamb, although the sauce was less successful. Other choices could include duck pancakes and skewered scampi with garlic butter. Smaller lunchtime choice. *Credit* Access, Barclaycard, Diners   &

About £35 for two

Lunch 12–2 *Dinner* 7–10
Closed L Sat, all Sun & Bank Holidays

Newgate Street Village
Map 7 B4 Hertfordshire
Ponsbourne Park
Near Cuffley *SG13 8QZ*
Cuffley (070 787) 5221
Telex 299912

Credit Access, Amex,
Barclaycard, Diners

Ponsbourne Hotel   66%   £ D

Present owners have completely refurbished this fine Victorian house, which stands in 30 acres of beautiful parkland. Spacious, comfortable public rooms, all of which overlook the grounds, include two restful lounges and a cocktail bar, and there are also several attractive conference and banqueting rooms. Bedrooms offer a high degree of comfort and elegance, with tasteful decor, high-quality furnishings and excellent bathrooms. Good room service and pleasant staff add further to the enjoyment of a stay here.
Amenities garden, outdoor swimming pool, tennis, pitch & putt, dinner dance (Fri January–May), discothèque (Fri May–August), games room, croquet.   &

Rooms 32	*Room phone* Yes	*Confirm by* By arrang.	*Parking* Ample
with bath/shower 32	*Room TV* Yes	*Last dinner* 10	*Banquets* 75/–

Newmarket
Map 6 B2 Suffolk
High Street *CB8 8JP*
Newmarket (0638) 663051

Manager Mr R. J. Jobson
Credit Access, Amex,
Barclaycard, Diners

White Hart Hotel   55%   £ D

Racing is the dominant topic of conversation in the large Rous Bar of this red-brick hotel right opposite the Jockey Club. Residents have a peaceful, comfortable lounge. Bedrooms of different shapes and sizes, including several family rooms, have neat built-in units, radios and tea-makers; bathrooms are modern and well fitted. Rooms without baths have wash-basins.

Rooms 21	*Room phone* Yes	*Confirm by* 6	*Parking* Ample
with bath/shower 10	*Room TV* Yes	*Last dinner* 9	*Banquets* 120/–

Newport Pagnell

Map 5 E1 Buckinghamshire
18 St Johns Street *MK16 8HJ*
Goldcrest (090 862) 6398
Proprietors Mr & Mrs West

● **Set L & Set D** from £8·50
About £27 for two
Banquets 36/–

Glovers

A pleasantly intimate little restaurant with exposed stone walls and polished, well-spaced tables. The menu offers two- or three-course set meals, prepared by Mr West, whose sure touch is evident in enjoyable dishes like moules marinière, pheasant alsacienne and spirited tipsy cake. Other choices might be pipérade, steak, kidney and mushroom pie and Dover sole with oyster stuffing. *Credit* Access, Amex, Barclaycard, Diners

Lunch 12.15–1.45 *Dinner* 7–9.30
Closed L Sat, all Sun, Mon, 2 weeks beginning Aug & 1 week after Christmas

Newport Pagnell

Map 5 E1 Buckinghamshire
Service Area 3, M1 Motorway
MK16 8D5
Newport Pagnell (0908) 610878
Telex 826186
Credit Access, Amex,
Barclaycard, Diners

Rooms 100
with bath/shower 100

TraveLodge   56%   £ E

Travellers will find comfortable accommodation at this functional modern hotel situated in the Newport Pagnell Service Area. Pleasant bedrooms have good carpets, hessian-covered walls and fitted units, plus extras like tea/coffee-makers. Bathrooms with showers are equally well equipped. There's also a bar and a lounge where continental breakfast is served (no restaurant). *Amenities* garden, petrol pumps, cafeteria (24 hours).

Room phone Yes	*Confirm by* 6	*Parking* Ample
Room TV Yes	*Last dinner* None	

Newquay

Map 2 B3 Cornwall
Dane Road *TR7 1EN*
Newquay (063 73) 2244
Proprietors Mr & Mrs W. J. Pascoe
& Mr B. Longworth
Credit Access, Amex,
Barclaycard, Diners

Rooms 80
with bath/shower 68

Atlantic Hotel   62%   Ⓜ   £ D

Extensive recreational facilities and fine sea views add to the attraction of this pleasant, family-run hotel. Public areas are spacious, while bedrooms and bathrooms offer simple comfort in modern style. *Amenities* garden, sauna, indoor & outdoor swimming pools, squash, sea fishing, dancing (Mon–Tues, Thurs–Sat), billiards, solarium, pitch & putt, games room, children's playground, films, laundry room, keep-fit equipment. **Closed** 5 Oct–Easter

Room phone Yes	*Confirm by* 6	*Parking* Ample
Room TV No	*Last dinner* 8.45	*Banquets* 200/–

Newquay

Map 2 B3 Cornwall
Narrowcliff *TR7 2PG*
Newquay (063 73) 5181
Proprietors Young family

Credit Access, Amex,
Barclaycard, Diners

Rooms 105
with bath/shower 65

Hotel Bristol   65%   Ⓜ   £ D

Standing above a sandy beach, this long-established family-run hotel offers a friendly, welcoming environment and a good range of leisure activities. There's a choice of comfortable lounges and bars, and bedrooms are bright, airy and spacious. Well-kept modern bathrooms. *Amenities* sauna, indoor swimming pool, dancing (Tues–Thurs, Sat May–September), games room, billiards, in-house video, hairdressing, solarium, laundry room.

Room phone Yes	*Confirm by* By arrang.	*Parking* Ample
Room TV Most	*Last dinner* 8.30	*Banquets* 260/–

Newquay

Map 2 B3 Cornwall
Headland Road *TR7 1EW*
Newquay (063 73) 2211

Closed mid November–
mid March

Rooms 110
with bath/shower 110

Headland Hotel   62%   Ⓜ   £ E

Catering for the whole family, this friendly hotel of vast late-Victorian proportions stands on a private headland jutting out into the Atlantic. Bright, spacious public areas include a foyer with a grand staircase, a simply furnished lounge and bar and two peaceful little sitting rooms with antique pieces. Bedrooms of varying sizes and styles are comfortable, and bathrooms offer adequate facilities.
Amenities garden, sauna, indoor & outdoor swimming pools, tennis, 9-hole golf course, dancing (Mon, Wed, Fri), discothèque (Thurs, Sat), coffee shop (10am–12.15am), solarium, putting, games room, billiards, table tennis, laundry room, children's playground, gymnasium.

Room phone Yes	*Confirm by* By arrang.	*Parking* Ample
Room TV Yes	*Last dinner* 9	*Banquets* 450/6

Newquay

Map 2 B3 Cornwall
TR7 3AA
Newquay (063 73) 4251
Proprietors Mr & Mrs D. C. Nixon
& Mr & Mrs D. E. Moret
Credit Access, Barclaycard
Closed 3 days Christmas

Hotel Riviera 63% Ⓜ £D

A range of leisure activities keeps guests busy at this friendly seafront hotel, and those who want to relax have a quiet lounge and several bars. Bedrooms are cheerful and comfortable, bathrooms modern. *Amenities* garden, sauna, outdoor swimming pool, squash, sea fishing, dancing (Mon–Sat in summer, Sat in winter), yacht, games room, badminton, laundry room, putting, coffee shop (10am–7pm), in-house movies, children's room.

Rooms 53 | *Room phone* Yes | *Confirm by* By arrang. | *Parking* Ample
with bath/shower 40 | *Room TV* Yes | *Last dinner* 10 | *Banquets* 150/–

Newquay

Map 2 B3 Cornwall
TR7 3AA
Newquay (063 73) 4251
Proprietors Mr & Mrs Nixon &
Mr & Mrs Moret
About £29 for two

Hotel Riviera, La Corniche Restaurant ♧ Ⓢ

A spacious, convivial restaurant, whose menu offers favourites such as onion soup and grills alongside enterprising, capably cooked dishes like sole with almonds and asparagus or piquantly sauced sauté de bœuf. *Credit* Access, Barclaycard *Lunch* Sun only 12.45–2 *Dinner* 8–10 **Closed** D Sun & 3 days Christmas ● **Set L** £4·50 **Set D** £7   &

Newton

Map 11 D4 Warwickshire
Newton Grange
Near Rugby *CV23 0DR*
Swinford (078 885) 348
Proprietors
Mr & Mrs Tabuteau-Harrison

● **Set D** £9·50
About £27 for two
Banquets 26/–

Tabuteau's ♧ Ⓢ

This elegant restaurant is run in polite, orderly fashion by Mr Tabuteau-Harrison, who likes diners to book in advance and arrive on time. His wife does the cooking and offers an interesting four-course fixed-price menu featuring dishes ranging from smoked tunny tartlets to roast duck with brandy and apricot sauce. Tempting sweets might include meringue Chantilly. 🍷 *ABOVE AVERAGE. Credit* Access, Barclaycard

Dinner only at 7.30 for 8.30
Closed Sun

Newton Solney

Map 10 C3 Derbyshire
Near Burton upon Trent *DE15 0SS*
Burton upon Trent
(0283) 703568
Manager Ms J. D. Ansell
Credit Access, Amex,
Barclaycard, Diners

Newton Park Hotel 65% £E

Three acres of pleasant gardens surround this converted country mansion, which still retains much of its original character, with panelled walls and fine stained-glass windows enhancing the charm of the public areas. In contrast, bedrooms are mostly modern in style, with good-quality built-in units, radios and well-equipped, up-to-date bathrooms.
Amenities garden.

Rooms 26 | *Room phone* Yes | *Confirm by* By arrang. | *Parking* Ample
with bath/shower 26 | *Room TV* Yes | *Last dinner* 9 | *Banquets* 100/–

North Petherton

Map 3 E2 Somerset
Near Bridgwater *TA6 6QA*
North Petherton (0278) 662255
Proprietors
Mr & Mrs G. R. Goulden
Credit Access, Amex,
Barclaycard, Diners

Walnut Tree Inn *(Inn)* Ⓜ £E

Painted a cheerful primrose, this former coaching inn offers a homely welcome in its comfortable little entrance lounge and cottage lounge bar with wall brasses and a stone fireplace. Pretty bedrooms in the main building (including four new ones) and simpler modern rooms in a motel-style extension have shag-pile carpets, tea/coffee-makers and smart tiled bathrooms. No dogs. *Amenities* garden.   &

Rooms 12 | *Room phone* No | *Confirm by* By arrang. | *Parking* Ample
with bath/shower 12 | *Room TV* Yes | *Last dinner* 10 | *Banquets* 60/–

North Stifford

Map 7 B4 Essex
Cuckoo Lane
Near Grays *RM16 1UE*
Grays Thurrock (0375) 71451

Credit Access, Amex,
Barclaycard, Diners

Stifford Moat House 64% £D/E

This converted Georgian house in six acres of gardens is a useful businessman's hotel. Neat bedrooms, all in the extension, are especially bright and cheerful, with fitted furniture, tea/coffee-makers and compact, well-equipped bathrooms. There's a small reception area, a traditional-style bar and good function facilities. *Amenities* garden, tennis, dinner dance (Sat), pitch & putt, pétanque, croquet, 24-hour laundry service.

Rooms 64 | *Room phone* Yes | *Confirm by* 6 | *Parking* Ample
with bath/shower 64 | *Room TV* Yes | *Last dinner* 9.15 | *Banquets* 100/–

North Stoke

Map 5 D2 Oxfordshire
Wallingford Road *OX9 6BE*
Wallingford (0491) 36687
Telex 849794

Rooms 22
with bath/shower 22
Room phone Yes
Room TV Yes
Confirm by By arrang.
Last dinner 10
Parking Ample
Banquets 85/–

Credit Access, Amex,
Barclaycard, Diners

Springs Hotel   77%   £C

Taking its name from the picturesque lake in the grounds, this splendid mock-Tudor country house enjoys a secluded position set back from the B4009 Goring to Wallingford road. There's a warm welcome in the comfortable panelled reception lounge, which sets the tone for other public rooms like the cocktail bar and the library (used for functions). Spacious bedrooms are individually decorated and furnished in the best of traditional good taste, and their comprehensive equipment includes tissues, sewing kits and information folders. Spruce carpeted bathrooms have excellent modern fittings and lots of luxurious extras. *Amenities* garden, sauna, outdoor swimming pool, tennis, putting, croquet, helipad, bicycles.   &

North Stoke

Map 5 D2 Oxfordshire
Wallingford Road
Near Oxford *OX9 6BE*
Wallingford (0491) 36687

● **Set L** £6·50, Sun £7·50
Set D £8·50
About £36 for two
Banquets 85/–

Springs Hotel, Lakeview Restaurant   Ⓢ

There are enchanting views from this lovely lakeside restaurant, whose menu offers a choice of competently prepared, attractively presented dishes. Starters include a tasty duck liver pâté with ginger sauce, and main courses range from Dover sole or grilled sirloin to sweetbreads with lime juice and crisp-skinned, honey-glazed duck. Good selection of crunchy vegetables, too.
🍷 *ABOVE AVERAGE. Credit* Access, Amex, Barclaycard, Diners

Lunch 12.30–2.30 *Dinner* 7–10

Northallerton

Map 15 C5 North Yorkshire
High Street *DL7 8PG*
Northallerton (0609) 774918
Proprietors Toni Pala &
Giovanni Collu
About £26 for two

Romanby Court   ♧ Ⓢ

The attractive dining rooms here make a delightful setting for a delicious four-course dinner. Top-quality ingredients are skilfully handled in dishes with an Italian slant. 🍷 *ABOVE AVERAGE. Dinner only* 7.30–9.30
Closed Sun, Mon, Bank Holidays, 1 week February & 3 weeks August
● **Set D** from £8·50 *Banquets* 20/8   &

Northampton

Map 5 D1 Northamptonshire
Ashley Way
Weston Favell *NN3 3EA*
Northampton (0604) 406262

Credit Access, Amex,
Barclaycard, Diners

Northampton Moat House   60%   £E

This handsome mansion with modern bedroom wings stands peacefully among lawns and trees just outside town. There's a bright, modernised reception area, and the warmly decorated bar-lounge offers plenty of comfortable seats. Most bedrooms have attractive decor and smart fitted furniture; all have tea-makers and trouser presses. *Amenities* garden, dinner dance (Sat in winter, alternate Sats in summer), putting, croquet.

| *Rooms* 64 | *Room phone* Yes | *Confirm by* 7 | *Parking* Ample |
| *with bath/shower* 64 | *Room TV* Yes | *Last dinner* 9.45 | *Banquets* 170/– |

Northampton

Map 5 D1 Northamptonshire
Silver Street *NN1 2TA*
Northampton (0604) 22441
Telex 311142

Credit Access, Amex,
Barclaycard, Diners

Saxon Inn   66%   £D

Overlooking the ring road near the city centre, this tall modern hotel is geared mainly towards the business trade. The large foyer-lounge has comfortable leather chesterfields and there's a spacious, panelled bar. Double-glazed bedrooms have fitted units, tea-makers and trouser presses plus up-to-date bathrooms. Some redecoration would be welcome.
Amenities dinner dance (Sat), coffee shop (10am–10pm, 2pm–10pm Sun).

| *Rooms* 130 | *Room phone* Yes | *Confirm by* 6 | *Parking* Ample |
| *with bath/shower* 130 | *Room TV* Yes | *Last dinner* 10.30 | *Banquets* 450/– |

Northampton

Map 5 D1 Northamptonshire
7 Derngate *NN1 1TU*
Northampton (0604) 33978

Vineyard

Deserting the groves of Academe for the world of the gourmet, Jim Ainsworth runs this smart town-centre restaurant with great enthusiasm and vitality. He has devised a novel, frequently changing menu of dishes in the French provincial style, and results are generally most enjoyable, from a light, fluffy asparagus custard through to a gorgeous chestnut and orange roulade. *Credit* Access, Barclaycard, Diners.

● **Set L** £5·25
About £27 for two

Lunch 12–2 *Dinner* 7.30–10.30
Closed L Sat, D Mon, all Sun, Bank Holidays & 23 December–3 January

---

Northiam

Map 7 C6 East Sussex
Village Green *TN31 6NN*
Northiam (079 74) 3142
Credit Access, Amex,
Barclaycard, Diners
Closed Jan & mid Nov–
mid Dec

Hayes Arms *(Inn)* Ⓜ

£ D

Visitors receive a really warm welcome in this charming Elizabethan inn with Georgian additions. The bar and lounge boast a profusion of beams and huge open fireplaces, while bedroom furnishings range from traditional to more modern in the Georgian section. Neat, up-to-date bathrooms. Demi-pension only in high season. Children under 12 by arrangement only. No dogs. *Amenities* garden.

Rooms 7	*Room phone* Yes	*Confirm by* By arrang.	*Parking* Ample
with bath/shower 7	*Room TV* No	*Last dinner* 9	*Banquets* 20/10

Northiam

Map 7 C6 East Sussex
Village Green *TN31 6NN*
Northiam (079 74) 3142

Hayes Arms Restaurant

Carol Jackson blends the familiar with the unconventional in her daily five-course fixed-price menu. You could begin with hot mushroom tartlets followed by smoked haddock chowder and then perhaps cucumbers in turmeric. Main courses might include rack of lamb with herb and tomato stuffing, while banana and toffee pie makes a good finish. Roast lunch on Sundays. ▼ *ABOVE AVERAGE. Credit* Access, Amex, Barclaycard, Diners

● **Set L** £7 **Set D** £11
About £27 for two

Lunch Sun only 12.30–2 *Dinner* 7.30–9.30
Closed D Sun & Mon to non-residents, Jan & mid Nov–mid Dec

Northleach

Map 4 C2 Gloucestershire
Market Place *GL54 3EJ*
Northleach (045 16) 421

Country Friends

A rustic atmosphere pervades this delightful little restaurant, where Pauline Whittaker offers an appealing choice of imaginative dishes. The regularly changing menu features unusual soups, and main courses such as pork fillet with sage and Emmenthal sauce or fillets of sole with smoked salmon mousse, all prepared with great attention to detail. Vegetables are crisp and there are some delicious puddings.

● **Set L** £5·60
About £28 for two

Lunch Sun 12.30–2, Mon–Sat by arrangement only *Dinner* 7.30–9.30
Closed D Sun, all Mon & 25 & 26 December

Northleach

Map 4 C2 Gloucestershire
The Square *GL54 3EE*
Northleach (045 16) 366
Proprietors
M & Mme Jacques Astic
French cooking

Old Woolhouse ★

Dinner is at 8.15 sharp in this simple little beamed restaurant, and the reputation established by Lyonnais Jacques Astic means that it's essential to book. His set menus, explained over an aperitif by his charming wife Jenny, feature outstanding sauces: fish dishes like crab tartlets and red mullet with a Pernod-based sauce dominate the starters, while main courses, served with creamy gratin dauphinois and a well-dressed salad, could include kidneys, veal with sweetbreads, wild duck (game is a seasonal speciality) and wing rib of beef. Glorious desserts such as prune tart or chocolate gâteau precede coffee and home-made petits fours.

● **Set D** £13·50
About £32 for two

Dinner only at 8.15
Closed Sun, 3 weeks May/June & 2 weeks Christmas

Norwich

Map 6 C1 Norfolk
Castle Meadow *NR1 3PZ*
Norwich (0603) 611511
Telex 975582
Manager Mr G. V. Du Bois
Credit Access, Amex,
Barclaycard, Diners

Rooms 76
with bath/shower 26

Castle Hotel   54%   £E

A distinctive marble porchway leads to this otherwise unobtrusive hotel opposite the castle in the city centre. Adequately furnished public rooms include two bars and a residents' lounge. Fair-sized bedrooms are simply furnished and equipped with TV and radio. About a third have private baths; there are also plenty of well-kept public bathrooms. *Amenities* dinner dance (Sat October–January, monthly February–September).

Room phone Yes	*Confirm by* By arrang.	*Parking* Difficult
Room TV Yes	*Last dinner* 9	*Banquets* 120/6

Norwich

Map 6 C1 Norfolk
19 Fye Bridge Street *NR3 1LJ*
Norwich (0603) 21825

Italian cooking
About £25 for two

Hobbs   ⓢ

You'll find a warm welcome at this cosy little restaurant near the city centre. There's a wide range of mainly Italian dishes, which are ably cooked and enjoyable. Save room for a delicious sweet.
Credit Access, Amex, Barclaycard, Diners *Lunch* 12–2 *Dinner* 7–11.30
Closed Sun & Bank Holidays ● **Set L** £3·65

Norwich

Map 6 C1 Norfolk
116 Thorpe Road *NR1 1RU*
Norwich (0603) 20302

Credit Access, Amex,
Barclaycard, Diners

Rooms 45
with bath/shower 24

Lansdowne Hotel   55%   £E

Not far from the city centre, this modern three-storey hotel is a popular place with businessmen. A roomy bar and first-floor residents' lounge are furnished in contemporary style, and there's a ballroom as well as some well-equipped meeting rooms. Compact bedrooms in warm colours have space-saving fitted furniture, radio-alarms and tea-makers; bathrooms are adequately fitted. Staff are friendly and helpful.

Room phone Yes	*Confirm by* 6	*Parking* Ample
Room TV Yes	*Last dinner* 8.30	*Banquets* 126/–

Norwich

Map 6 C1 Norfolk
Tombland *NR3 1LB*
Norwich (0603) 28821
Telex 975080
Manager Mr D. B Cooke
Credit Access, Amex,
Barclaycard, Diners

Rooms 82
with bath/shower 78

Maid's Head Hotel   64%   £D

This delightful old inn, whose history can be traced back over 700 years, occupies a central position just opposite the cathedral. Its focal point is an attractive glassed-in courtyard, off which are two comfortable bars and a traditionally furnished lounge. Bright bedrooms of various sizes have bedside controls and trouser presses; like the bathrooms, they are very well maintained. *Amenities* lounge service (10.30am–10.30pm Mon–Sat).

Room phone Yes	*Confirm by* 6	*Parking* Ample
Room TV Yes	*Last dinner* 9.45	*Banquets* 130/2

Norwich

Map 6 C1 Norfolk
17 Pottergate *NR2 1DS*
Norwich (0603) 24044
Proprietor Marco Vessalio
Italian cooking
About £30 for two

Marco's   ♧ ⓢ

Genial Marco Vessalio is the enthusiastic chef in this simply furnished restaurant, and offers a well-balanced menu of enjoyable Italian fare, highlighted by home-made pasta and prime veal.
Credit Access, Amex, Barclaycard, Diners *Lunch* 12.30–2 *Dinner* 7.30–10
Closed Sun, Mon, Bank Holidays & August ● **Set L** £6 *Banquets* 15/–

Norwich

Map 6 C1 Norfolk
Prince of Wales Road *NR1 1DX*
Norwich (0603) 28612
Telex 975203

Credit Access, Amex,
Barclaycard, Diners

Rooms 94
with bath/shower 94

Hotel Nelson   61%   £E

This modern, efficiently run hotel, a popular place with businessmen, stands by the river Wensum near the city centre. It has a bright, cheerful reception-lounge area, and one of its bars has mementoes of the locally born naval hero. Bedrooms (many overlooking the river) are roomy and practical, and there are hairdryers in all the sensibly designed tiled bathrooms. No dogs. *Amenities* garden, sauna, coarse fishing.

Room phone Yes	*Confirm by* 6	*Parking* Ample
Room TV Yes	*Last dinner* 9.45	*Banquets* 70/24

Norwich

Map 6 C1 Norfolk
121 Boundary Road *NR3 2BA*
Norwich (0603) 410431
Telex 975337

Credit Access, Amex,
Barclaycard, Diners

Rooms 102
with bath/shower 102

Hotel Norwich   62%   £D/E

This modern brick-built hotel on the city's ring road offers good conference facilities and bright, comfortable accommodation. Spacious bedrooms include 18 in a new wing, and are well equipped with radio, TV, message lights and tea/coffee-makers. There are two lounges and a bar with its own games room. Guide dogs only. *Amenities* garden, dinner dance (Sat), coffee shop (10am–7.30pm), 12-hour laundry service.   ♾

Room phone Yes	*Confirm by* 6	*Parking* Ample
Room TV Yes	*Last dinner* 9.45	*Banquets* 300/2

Norwich

Map 6 C1 Norfolk
Ipswich Road *NR4 6EP*
Norwich (0603) 56431
Telex 975106

Credit Access, Amex,
Barclaycard, Diners

Rooms 120
with bath/shower 120

Post House Hotel   62%   £D

Set in pleasant grounds, this low modern hotel lies just south of the city on the A140. Bedroom blocks, with convenient nearby parking, have bright, practical modern rooms, all with mini-bars, tea-makers and neat, well-fitted bathrooms. The main block contains two cheerful bars and a large lounge overlooking the swimming pool. *Amenities* garden, outdoor swimming pool, buttery (7.30am–10.30pm).   ♾

Room phone Yes	*Confirm by* 6	*Parking* Ample
Room TV Yes	*Last dinner* 9.45	

Nottingham

Map 11 D3 Nottinghamshire
St James's Street *NG1 6BN*
Nottingham (0602) 40131
Telex 37211

Rooms 160
with bath/shower 160
Room phone Yes
Room TV Yes
Confirm by 6
Last dinner 11
Parking Ample
Banquets 450/8

Credit Access, Amex,
Barclaycard, Diners

Albany Hotel   70% *E*   £C

Right in the city centre, with multi-storey car parks nearby, this towering modern hotel is noted for its sophisticated comfort, and it is equally popular with business executives and families alike. There's a bar on the ground floor, as well as a complete floor given over to conference and function facilities. A translucent blue screen divides the attractive little cocktail bar from the relaxing lounge area, which is lined with contemporary paintings. Bedrooms are quite large, streamlined and comfortably furnished in modern style with plenty of writing space. Well-equipped, fully tiled bathrooms.

Nottingham

Map 11 D3 Nottinghamshire
32 Lenton Boulevard *NG7 2ES*
Nottingham (0602) 411088
Proprietor Mr Yves Bouanchaud

About £22 for two

La Grenouille   ♧ Ⓢ

A busy, cheerful little place, where Yves Bouanchaud produces a good range of simple Gallic favourites, from terrine and salade niçoise to porc dijonnaise and steak bordelaise. Be prepared for good strong flavours, and enormous portions. *Lunch* 12.30–2.30 *Dinner* 7.30–9.30 **Closed** L Sat, all Sun, Bank Holidays, 1 week Aug & 24 Dec–4 Jan ● **Set** L £5·10 *Banquets* 26/–

Nottingham

Map 11 D3 Nottinghamshire
Bostock Lane *NG10 4EP*
Long Eaton (060 76) 60106
Telex 377585
Manager Mr M. J. H. Dubois
Credit Access, Amex,
Barclaycard, Diners

Rooms 112
with bath/shower 112

Novotel   59%   £D

Potted palms and pine furniture lend a Continental air to the reception-bar-lounge area of this functional modern hotel. The various conference rooms are popular with businessmen and there is a cheerful public bar. Comfortable bedrooms are airy and colourful, and all have compact, well-fitted bathrooms. *Amenities* garden, outdoor swimming pool, grill room, (6am–10am, noon–11.30pm), pétanque, pool table.   ♾

Room phone Yes	*Confirm by* 7	*Parking* Ample
Room TV Yes	*Last dinner* 12	*Banquets* 300/–

Nottingham
Map 11 D3 Nottinghamshire
Bostocks Lane
Sandiacre *NG10 5NJ*
Nottingham (0602) 397800
Telex 377378
Credit Access, Amex,
Barclaycard, Diners

Post House Hotel   59%   £ D

A refurbishment programme is under way at this modern low-rise hotel near junction 25 of the M1. Public rooms like the foyer, lounge and bar are smart and comfortable, and the best bedrooms have pleasantly coordinated decor and neat black-stained units. All rooms have mini-bars and tea-makers. *Amenities* garden, discothèque (alternate Sats July–August), coffee shop (10.30am–10.30pm), children's play area, riding.   &

| *Rooms* 106 | *Room phone* Yes | *Confirm by* 6 | *Parking* Ample |
| *with bath/shower* 106 | *Room TV* Yes | *Last dinner* 10.30 | *Banquets* 60/20 |

Nottingham
Map 11 D3 Nottinghamshire
Mansfield Road
Carrington *NG5 2BT*
Nottingham (0602) 602621
Telex 377429
Credit Access, Amex,
Barclaycard, Diners

Savoy Hotel   65%   £ D

Not far from the centre of the city, this modern hotel combines traditional features with a contemporary setting. Brown leather chesterfields and mirrored walls characterise the spacious lounge, while the intimate Fagin's Bar has Victorian overtones. Attractively decorated bedrooms have fitted units, comfortable armchairs and tea-makers. Well-equipped bathrooms. *Amenities* in-house movies, coffee lounge (24 hours). **Closed** 25 Dec

| *Rooms* 125 | *Room phone* Yes | *Confirm by* 6 | *Parking* Ample |
| *with bath/shower* 125 | *Room TV* Yes | *Last dinner* 11 | |

Nottingham
Map 11 D3 Nottinghamshire
44 Derby Road *NG1 5FT*
Nottingham (0602) 48501
Telex 377185
Manager Peter Robinson
Credit Access, Amex,
Barclaycard, Diners

Strathdon Hotel   58%   £ D

A convenient base for businessmen, with modern comforts and facilities. Most public areas are devoted to the hotel's considerable conference and function business, but the nautical-style Mariner's Bar is a popular local meeting place and there's also a colourful cocktail bar. Double-glazed bedrooms–compact and simple, with neat fitted furniture–include some for non-smokers. Colourful contemporary bathrooms.

| *Rooms* 64 | *Room phone* Yes | *Confirm by* 6.30 | *Parking* Difficult |
| *with bath/shower* 64 | *Room TV* Yes | *Last dinner* 10 | *Banquets* 120/– |

Oakham
Map 11 E3 Leicestershire
Hambleton *LE15 8TH*
Oakham (0572) 56991
Telex 341995

Rooms 15
with bath/shower 15
Room phone Yes
Room TV Yes
Confirm by By arrang.
Last dinner 9.30
Parking Ample
Banquets 30/–

Credit Access, Amex,
Barclaycard, Diners

Hambleton Hall   82%      £ C/D

On a peninsula in the middle of Rutland Water and surrounded by acres of fine gardens, this tile-clad Victorian mansion is an enchanting place to visit, thanks to the care and dedication of young owners Tim and Stefa Hart and their staff. Public rooms, including a luxurious drawing room and a cosy bar, are most gracefully appointed and comfortably furnished in traditional style, while bedrooms are individually designed with attractively patterned wallpaper and lovely soft furnishings. Bathrooms are superbly equipped with good carpets and washbasins with marble surrounds. Children under nine and dogs by arrangement only.
Amenities garden, tennis, 12-hour laundry service.

Oakham
Map 11 E3 Leicestershire
Hambleton *LE15 8TH*
Oakham (0572) 56991

Hambleton Hall Restaurant   ♔ ⑤

Nicholas Gill worked at Maxim's in Paris before becoming chef at this elegant hotel restaurant. His fixed-price menus (four courses for lunch, five for dinner) show considerable talent and artistry, with dishes ranging from garlicky snails cooked with fennel and Pernod to noisette of venison with juniper berries. There are also delightful sweets such as raspberry charlotte.

Continued

● **Set L** £11 incl. service
Set D £17·50 incl. service
About £40 for two
Banquets 30/–

💬 *OUTSTANDING. Credit* Access, Amex, Barclaycard, Diners

Lunch 12.30–2 *Dinner* 7.30–9.30

Ockley
Map 5 E3 Surrey
Stane Street *RH5 5TH*
Oakwood Hill (030 679) 430

Old School House

Chianti bottles and vine leaves adorn this attractive pub restaurant which serves some really enjoyable food. The choice of soups and hors d'œuvre is excellent, and main courses include six ways with sole as well as grills and favourites like chicken Maryland or veal escalope Holstein. Vegetables are carefully prepared and there's a good selection of sweets.
Credit Amex, Barclaycard, Diners

● **Set L** £4·25, Sun £5
About £26 for two
Banquets 64/50

Lunch 12–1.45 *Dinner* 7–9.45, 7–10
Closed D Sun & all Mon

Odstock
Map 4 C3 Wiltshire
Near Salisbury *SP5 4JE*
Salisbury (0722) 29786
Proprietor Mrs Ginette Gould

Yew Tree Inn

As French-born Ginette Gould presides over the kitchen of this delightfully rustic and cosy pub restaurant, the menu has a distinctly Gallic slant. Seasonal variations might include grilled fresh sardines or lamb with ratatouille, while frogs' legs, snails and steak au poivre are among regular features. Finish a carefully prepared, flavoursome meal with rich chocolate and orange mousse. *Credit* Access, Amex, Barclaycard, Diners

About £23 for two

Lunch 12.30–2 *Dinner* 7–10
Closed Sun, Mon & Bank Holidays

Old Harlow
Map 7 B4 Essex
Mulberry Green *CM17 0ET*
Harlow (0279) 442521
Telex 817972
Managers Mr & Mrs P. J. Smith
Credit Access, Amex,
Barclaycard, Diners

Green Man Hotel   63%   £E

Be sure to ask for directions when booking at this hotel, whose origins can be traced back to the 15th century. There are some well-preserved oak beams in the public areas, which include two welcoming bars, whereas pristine bedrooms in a separate block are absolutely up to date; roomy, attractively decorated and smartly furnished, they all have well-equipped carpeted bathrooms. *Amenities* garden.

| *Rooms* 55 | *Room phone* Yes | *Confirm by* 6.30 | *Parking* Ample |
| *with bath/shower* 55 | *Room TV* Yes | *Last dinner* 10 | *Banquets* 85/12 |

Orford
Map 6 D3 Suffolk
Front Street
Near Woodbridge *IP12 2LW*
Orford (039 45) 271
Proprietors Mrs Phyll Shaw &
Mr Alistair Shaw

King's Head Inn Restaurant

Fresh local seafood is very much to the fore at this delightful 13th-century inn. Alistair Shaw offers Colchester oysters, Aldeburgh sprats in oatmeal, lobster, crab and cockles (tossed in butter) along with Norfolk duckling, pheasant and dishes like beef Stroganoff. The home-baked bread is delicious, vegetables are excellent and there are some interesting sweets like pears in red wine served hot.

About £27 for two

Lunch 12–2 *Dinner* 7–9
Closed D Sun, all Mon except Bank Holidays & 3–27 January

Ormesby St Margaret
Map 6 D1 Norfolk
Decoy Road *NR29 3LG*
Great Yarmouth (0493) 730910

Credit Access, Amex,
Barclaycard, Diners

Ormesby Lodge Hotel   62% Ⓜ   £E

A peaceful garden surrounds this attractive white house, where bedrooms are notably comfortable and welcoming. All have thick carpeting, pleasing decor and good modern furniture, as well as radios and tea/coffee-makers. Large bathrooms have pretty patterned tiles. Downstairs is a relaxing bay-windowed bar-cum-lounge overlooking the garden. No dogs.
Amenities garden.

| *Rooms* 8 | *Room phone* Yes | *Confirm by* By arrang. | *Parking* Ample |
| *with bath/shower* 7 | *Room TV* Yes | *Last dinner* 10.30 | *Banquets* 65/– |

Orton
Map 13 D5 Cumbria
Penrith
Orton (058 74) 351

Credit Access, Amex,
Barclaycard, Diners

Rooms 30
with bath/shower 30

Tebay Mountain Lodge Motel   59%   £ E

Just north of junction 38 on the northbound carriageway of the M6, this modern motel provides useful facilities for travellers. Potted plants and wood panelling adorn the open-plan public areas which enjoy pleasant moorland views. Spacious studio-style bedrooms have fitted furniture, tea/coffee-makers and fully tiled bathrooms. There is also one family room.
Amenities petrol pump, 24-hour cafeteria.

Room phone Yes	*Confirm by* By arrang.	*Parking* Ample
Room TV Yes	*Last dinner* 10	

Oswestry
Map 10 A3 Shropshire
Church Street *SY11 2SZ*
Oswestry (0691) 5261

Credit Access, Amex,
Barclaycard, Diners

Rooms 31
with bath/shower 17

Wynnstay Hotel   55%   £ D

Once a coaching inn, this imposing red-brick building near the town centre has a handsome pillared entrance. Cheerful furnishings give a welcoming warmth to the bar, and the airy lounge overlooks an ancient bowling green. The size and decor of the bedrooms varies, but all have modern furniture, colour TV and tea-makers.
Amenities garden, bowling green.

Room phone Yes	*Confirm by* 6	*Parking* Ample
Room TV Yes	*Last dinner* 9.30	*Banquets* 70/–

Otterburn
Map 14 B3 Northumberland
NE19 1NR
Otterburn (0830) 20261

Credit Access, Amex,
Barclaycard, Diners

Rooms 33
with bath/shower 17

Percy Arms Hotel   56%   £ E

This former coaching inn makes a comfortable retreat for anglers, and shooting can also be arranged. Refurbished public areas include three elegant Regency-style lounges as well as three bars. Large, individually decorated bedrooms have matching soft furnishings with pretty colour schemes, and bathrooms are perfectly adequate. The hotel is beautifully warm and clean. *Amenities* garden, coarse & game fishing, croquet, putting.

Room phone Yes	*Confirm by* By arrang.	*Parking* Limited
Room TV No	*Last dinner* 8.45	*Banquets* 120/–

Ottery St Mary
Map 3 E2 Devon
17 Silver Street *EX11 1DB*
Ottery St Mary (040 481) 2356
Proprietors
Mr & Mrs Freeman-Cowen

● **Set D** from £9·50
About £22 for two
Banquets 21/6

The Lodge

Anne Freeman-Cowen is the able chef at this elegant, tastefully furnished little restaurant, and her two fixed-price menus (which change every few weeks) make excellent use of prime-quality local produce. Dishes ranging from smoked mackerel mousse with carrot marinade to Elizabethan pork or mixed seafood casserole flavoured with fennel show skilful preparation and plenty of imagination; there's also a selection of tempting home-made sweets like iced chocolate and orange soufflé. Not far from the restaurant is a charming mews cottage with a comfortable sitting room, two cosy bedrooms and a compact modern bathroom. Booking essential.
SUPERIOR.

Lunch *by arrangement only* Dinner *7.30–9.30* **Closed** D Sun, all Mon, Bank Holidays, 2 weeks January/February, 1 week June & 1 week November

Ottery St Mary
Map 3 E2 Devon
EX11 1RQ
Ottery St Mary (040 481) 2310

Proprietor Mr N. Svendsen
Credit Access, Amex,
Barclaycard, Diners

Rooms 35
with bath/shower 25

Salston Hotel   55%   Ⓜ   £ D

Once the home of the Coleridge family, this large manor house offers extensive leisure facilities. The lounge and bars are spacious and comfortable, though here and in the older bedrooms some redecoration would be welcome. Best bedrooms (in the extension) have neat contemporary furnishings and well-equipped bathrooms. *Amenities* garden, sauna, indoor swimming pool, squash, game fishing, dancing (Sat fortnightly), putting, croquet, helipad.

Room phone Yes	*Confirm by* 6	*Parking* Ample
Room TV Yes	*Last dinner* 10	*Banquets* 90/20

Savour the flavour of England

England is almost unique in the wide selection of foods it can produce, all due to our largely equable climate and our varied topography with a wide range of differing soils.

The quality and abundance of our raw ingredients, particularly meat, fish, fruit and vegetables, ensures good eating no matter what part of the country you visit. Follow this guide to the true flavour of England's great food-producing regions . . .

ENGLAND'S CAPITAL

Though no longer a food-producing region, London, our capital city, continues to contribute much to the overall flavour of English food and English cookery.

Fine fish from Billingsgate, superb meat from Smithfield and fruit and vegetables from the New Covent Garden market provide the basic ingredients for the 'classic' English fare you'll find at traditional pubs and restaurants throughout the city. Here you may sample nourishing soups, huge roast joints, fine chops, steak and kidney puddings and pies, hot-pots and casseroles, grilled sole, plaice or turbot, all served with fresh vegetables.

Aldermen's banquets and gentlemen's clubs provided the good food inspiration – to say nothing of the drinks such as Buck's Fizz and Black Velvet – at one end of the eating scale while the local stalls and snack bars provided more instant, but equally delicious dishes at the other end. For centuries, the Cockneys have loved their jellied eels and eel pies, their oysters, cockles, mussels and whelks. Sometimes, the two traditions became combined and it is interesting to note that Pimm's, that long, cucumber-topped drink, was invented by James Pimm in 1857 – as a drink to sell in his fish bars!

START IN THE SOUTH AND SOUTH EAST

Kent, the Garden of England, Sussex, home of the famous South|Down sheep, the rich acres of market gardens and horticulture under glass within easy reach of London, the rolling green pastures of Hampshire and Eastern Dorset – the South of England is one of the country's most important and varied food producing areas.

Three times more land is used for fruit production in Kent than in any other county. Apples, pears, plums, cherries and all kinds of soft fruit from loganberries to gooseberries and redcurrants have been grown here since the Middle Ages. At first they were concentrated in the gardens of the large manor houses, but today's planned orchards and fields were well-established by the middle of the 17th century.

Hops, the county's other famous crop, need no introduction to serious beer-drinkers. But, the acres of vines strung in their regimented rows, interspersed with warm, red-brick, conical oast houses, are worth seeing, looking much the same today as they did 200 years ago.

Intensive horticulture exists all over this region,

HOPS

We owe a debt to the Romans . . . it was they who introduced hops to England. But not for beer-making! They used the young shoots of the plant as a vegetable. Today, you can occasionally find a restaurant serving these May-picked shoots hot, covered in melted butter.

from the Thames river terraces to the Vale of Sussex, inland from Worthing. Both field vegetables and salad crops such as lettuce and tomatoes are widely grown. The region abounds with Farm Shops selling supremely fresh fruit and vegetables at farm prices, or, farms offering 'pick your own' facilities. You can be sure of getting best quality produce.

To the west of this region lies Hampshire, famous for its succulent strawberries. The clear waters of the rivers here produce an abundance of fine, fresh watercress, used not only in salads but in soups and stuffings, too.

MORELLO CHERRIES

Kent's famous black Morello cherries are used locally in delicious Cherry Batter Pudding and a reminder of our often shared cooking tradition with France is that there, 'Clafoutis' – pastry topped with black cherries – is a popular dessert today.

Poultry, particularly in East Sussex, home of that tender table bird, the Light Sussex, is important, and, throughout the area, the weekend motorist or holiday-maker can buy really fresh eggs direct from many farms.

The coast is a lure for the good food lovers. Whitstable, home of some of the world's finest oysters, Dover, renowned for those succulent soles, vie with other resorts famed for their fresh fish, from dabs at Deal, whiting in Brighton, mullet from Arundel Bay and crabs, mackerel and haddock around Southampton Water. In many coastal towns, fishermen sell their catch direct from the beach.

Specialities? It's a rich region for them. Look out, in particular, for veal or pork cooked with apples and cider, prime roast chicken, game pies and casseroles in the Ashdown Forest area, venison around the New Forest, Sussex or Kent Pond Puddings – a suet pudding filled with currants, butter and lemon juice – and mullet cooked in red wine. Country wines and cider are produced throughout this area which also has a thriving English wine industry. The southern-facing slopes of Hampshire and the Isle of Wight, in particular, are famous for their vineyards producing fine light, dry white wines.

FROM ANGLIA INTO THE SHIRES

With more grass and crops than any other region of England, today grown on large, highly-mechanised farms, this region has rightly been called the 'Granary of England'

But, to the searcher for fine food, the important factor is that the grain production supports a higher proportion of pigs and poultry than elsewhere in the country.

As long ago as 1740, nine thousand geese and turkeys set out from Norfolk, from one farm alone, for the long walk to London's market – the Marquess of Queensberry lost 1,000 guineas to Lord Oxford whose geese beat his turkeys to St Paul's by two days!

Today, Norfolk still boasts Europe's largest turkey producing organisation, in addition to its famous ducks, raised on the sandlands of Breckland. Usefully, the county also produces everything to go with them, from potatoes to carrots, cabbages, peas and beans.

The old, reclaimed silt soils of the coastal areas are the most fertile in England with varied vegetable field crops, delicious asparagus, and strawberries and other soft fruits produced for canning or freezing at centres such as King's Lynn and Wisbech, but also sold fresh from farms and in the local shops.

Suffolk is famous for its hams and home-cured bacon. Locally-smoked fish – kippers, bloaters, mackerel, trout and salmon – is another important feature of this region. Don't leave the coast without sampling such delicacies as Cromer crabs which are widely available, Norfolk trout, Colchester oysters and mussels, cockles and whelks.

North Lincolnshire is 'pea country' with nearly 40,000 acres devoted to pea growing. Watch the huge pea viners cut and shell the peas in almost one motion and deliver them for freezing within minutes. Or, on small farms, try your hand at pea-picking and take home a harvest of sweet young peas to enjoy with your roast lamb.

Stop off in Leicestershire, heart of the Shires, situated between the arable east and the livestock producing west. Sheep and cattle are sent from the

SAMPHIRE

Look out for samphire – also known as glasswort, saltwort or crab grass – around the North Norfolk coast. Similar in taste to asparagus (Norfolk asparagus is plentiful and cheap in season too), this marsh plant is tradi-tionally served hot with local lamb, or fish, such as dabs, but the young shoots can be used raw in salads. Some restaurants in the area serve it and you can buy it from fish stalls at Norwich market.

Melton Mowbray pies – their production isn't limited to the town of that name though it still produces some of the finest – were formerly made in gigantic proportions to celebrate civic and national events.

Latest recorded 'giant' was the 30lb Melton Mowbray pie baked in 1973 to send to the citizens of Dieppe to celebrate the 'twinning' of the two towns.

west to the county's famous fattening pastures, so meat has long been plentiful. Dairy herds thrive and the whey from cheese production provides excellent food for pig rearing.

The local sport – hunting – has strongly influenced eating habits. Regional specialities reflect the stamina and appetites of the huntsmen – huge joints, delicious brawns, fine pies and great cheeses.

Taste Stilton cheese, thought by many to be 'King' of all England's famous hard cheeses. Originally made at Quenby Hall and sold to hungry travellers at an Inn, in Stilton, on the Great North Road, it is now widely made in Leicestershire, Derbyshire, and Nottinghamshire. Sample the unique Red Leicester and Sage Derby

Enjoy a baked apple, apple pie or apple snow with England's finest cooking apple – the Bramley. It was first grown in Nottinghamshire by innkeeper and butcher Matthew Bramley and, though now nationally available, it is the favourite choice in the Shires where it is often used with pork in main course dishes, too.

cheeses, try a hand-raised Melton Mowbray pork pie, taste the wide range of locally-made sausages, polonies and faggots that decorate the local butchers' shops or take home a butter-covered tub of the flavoursome potted meat. Although formal Hunt Breakfasts are held only occasionally today, some restaurants still serve the huge joints of hunt beef, baked or boiled in beer.

WEST TO THE SEVERN

Follow the road from Oxfordshire to Wiltshire and the name Swindon, (Swine-don) alone, gives you the clue to the foods you'll find here. Black puddings, white puddings, brawns, sausages, lard – and cakes and pastries made from it – you can eat your way round on pork and pork products. Oxfordshire boasts, in addition to those flaky, currant-filled Banbury cakes and chunky Oxford marmalade, its own speciality sausages made from veal and pork, and Oxford brawn, a cold, pressed pig-meat.

Wiltshire, rightly called the Kingdom of the Pig, is the place to sample fine hams, excellent, locally cured bacon and Wiltshire faggots.

Elvers from the Severn river are a traditional speciality here. The young of the eel, the needle-like elvers were considered a delicacy for centuries. They flood into the river in their hundreds of thousands at the end of a three year journey from the breeding grounds in the Sargasso Sea. Daniel Defoe, in 1784, mentioned the fame of the elver cakes made at Keynsham. Today, around Epney, they are still fished in large quantities for a few weeks in the early spring. Occasionally restaurants serve them fried, like whitebait. If you are lucky you can get them on one or two Saturdays at Gloucester market, or you can persuade fishermen to sell you some.

Moving west towards the Welsh border, you come to gentle pastoral lands, some of our finest meat-producing areas.

The white-faced Hereford cattle, considered by many to be the best beef cattle in England, are 'at home' here, though their breed, which does so well in a wide variety of conditions, has spread round the world. The old, local breeds of sheep – the grey-faced, sharp-nosed Radnor, the hardy Clun and Kerry Hill, graze the pastures as they have done for centuries.

The richly fertile Vale of Evesham is a huge market garden of open air vegetables, and a paradise of apple, plum and pear blossom every spring. Succulent asparagus (known locally as

Don't be confused by an Oldbury Tart. The hand-raised, hot crust pastry used makes them look extremely like raised meat pies – but the filling is quite different. You'll find it full of sweet, soft gooseberries and rich juice from the Demarara sugar mixed in with them. They can be found at local bakers, but only in season.

'Evesham Grass' though less widely grown today, is still available here.

Locally-made cider and perry can be found around Hereford and Worcester – and, for a true local flavour, drink them with a ploughman's lunch of home-made crusty bread and creamy, delicately-flavoured Double Gloucester cheese. If too much of the local brew causes problems the morning after, then the cure is local, too – Mr Lea and Mr Perrin's recipe for Worcestershire Sauce has been a closely guarded secret since they first made it in 1835, but, mixed with a raw egg or tomato juice, it is still a fine cure for a hangover!

Linger a while at the towns and villages around the Severn estuary and enjoy freshly-caught salmon, eels and elvers, the young of the eel, considered a delicacy for centuries. They are fished for a few weeks in early spring. Move down

Our over-indulgent, 18th century ancestors went to Bath to cure their systems by taking the water and limiting themselves to plain food. Dr Oliver produced his famous biscuits to be nibbled while drinking the mineral water. Today, these simple biscuits, made from butter, flour, yeast and milk are a perfect partner for cheese – and you can tell you are eating one made to the original recipe as you'll find Dr Oliver's face on one side.

to Bath to try Bath Chaps, the pickled, smoked cheek pieces of a pig, cooked in breadcrumbs and eaten cold with pickles and mustard or hot with pease pudding and parsley sauce. Other specialities of this fine city are Bath Olivers, thin plain biscuits superb with cheese, sugar-topped Bath Buns, Sally Lunns, hot buns filled with whipped cream and Lardy Cakes flavoured with nutmeg, cinnamon and allspice.

THE SOUTH WEST

The 'Green Gold' of England's West Country, from the Mendips through to Land's End, is its lush

West Country clotted cream has been a popular 'treat' for centuries. In the 19th century, Mrs Beeton, herself, felt called upon to comment: 'this cream is so much esteemed that it is sent to the London markets in small square tins and jars and is exceedingly delicate eaten with fresh fruit.' Today's visitors to Devon and Cornwall will certainly agree and, if not feeling 'delicate,' will enjoy clotted cream in those famous cream teas when it is served with freshly-baked scones and strawberry jam.

grasslands. Here, there are more acres of permanent grass and grass leys than anywhere else in the country and the herds of black and white Friesians, the big Red Devon and the soft beige-brown Jersey or Guernsey cows provide milk in abundance.

Cream production has been recorded since the 13th century and the Devon and Cornish 'clotted' cream has proved so popular with visitors that it is sent by post all over the world.

Cider is the local drink from Somerset (original home of that great English cheese, Cheddar) through to Cornwall. You'll find a few farms and pubs that still brew their own, but beware . . . the true 'scrumpy' can be devastatingly more potent than the commercially-produced varieties.

The moist, mild climate of the South West of England makes it ideal for growing early fruit and market garden crops. Visit in spring, and early summer to enjoy delicious potatoes, carrots, spring greens, broccoli, in fact vegetables of every variety, and, a little later, early soft fruit such as raspberries and strawberries.

The coastal villages and towns offer a range of delicious seafood from freshly-caught mackerel, turbot and sole to crabs, lobsters and prawns. Many rivers boast trout and salmon. Sample mackerel with gooseberry sauce, buckling (smoked herring),

Why do they say 'the Devil never crosses the Tamar'? The answer is for fear of ending up chopped and cooked in pastry – so long-established is the Cornish tradition of turning everything into pasties or pies . . .

There are no rules about what goes into a Cornish Pasty – the filling should be meat, potatoes, turnips or carrots and perhaps a little onion. But the secret of their success is that, while the vegetables are pre-cooked, the meat should be put in raw so its juices flavour the whole of the contents.

hot buttered crab as well as the other fine foods of this region from Cornish Pasties, chicken cooked in cider and cream, Dartmoor honey and Dartmoor Apple Cake to creamy Devon Junket, a light milk-based dessert, or Helston Pudding, a steamed pudding of currants, breadcrumbs, suet, sugar and ground rice.

GOING NORTH

Local food traditions are strong throughout the North of England where the heritage of farm cooking has been greatly influenced by industrial development.

The picture many people have of farming in this region – of hardy sheep on windswept moors or craggy Pennine slopes – does not represent its true wealth and variety.

The Fylde, the flat coastal lands between the Lune and Ribble rivers, is, for example, an area of intensive horticulture. Here you'll find salad and vegetable crops of all kinds, plus locally-reared poultry and pigs.

Further north, the Lyth Valley is famous for its damsons – used in pies and puddings and also for jam, wine, punch and damson gin. The rich fertile plain that runs from South West Lancashire to the Lake District has large dairy and beef herds. Inland, the fell farms run north into Cumbria supporting the flocks of hardy Herdwick sheep on the slopes and dairy cattle in the more sheltered valleys. Pork and bacon pigs are widely reared, fed on the whey left from the making of those crumbly, fine-flavoured cheeses, Cheshire and Lancashire.

Throughout the north, butchers' shops are full of sausages, pies, meat pastes and brawns, black puddings, pressed tongues and corned beef as well as locally-produced lamb, beef and pork.

Cumberland Sausage made from pork and herbs, comes in long lengths and hangs coiled in the butchers' shop windows. Other Lake District specialities include Rum Butter and Rum Nickies, similar to small mince pies, well soused with rum, which recall the days when Whitehaven was one of the leading ports in the rum trade with the West Indies.

Other 'delicacies' in the North West include lamb's kidneys traditionally grilled with their surrounding white fat which cooks to a crisp golden-brown, bacon so 'streaky' that only the faintest tinge of pink veins the clear white fat, jellied veal, tripe and onions, cow heel and tasty pig's fry.

It's an area where you'll find a wide selection of excellent, locally-caught fish. Salmon, from the river Esk, is served both fresh and made into a delicious salmon paste. Around the windy sweep of Morecambe Bay you can sample freshly-netted shrimps or shrimps potted in butter, now widely available throughout the seaside towns of Lancashire and the Lake District.

Coastal towns such as Fleetwood offer fine fresh hake, halibut and salmon trout. Char, a lake fish from Cumbria, is rare but occasionally available at restaurants and is similar to salmon, while Flookburgh Flukes, flat fish with long tails and a plaice-like flavour, are caught with stake nets on the sands around Flookburgh.

EAST OVER THE PENNINES

The farming tradition here is similar, though the local foods vary. Pork and bacon are widely popular – Holderness boasts one of the country's largest pig-breeding and fattening units. The Large White is the famous breed of pig here, traditionally the producer of the well-known York hams, still oak-smoked.

It's the area where no weekend is complete

Sheep Dog Trials are a local event not to miss in the Yorkshire Dales, the Fell country of Lancashire and the Lake District. They happen frequently and it is a joy to watch the skill of dogs and shepherds moving the flocks so efficiently over the rugged terrain. The predominance of sheep in these areas is reflected in the fact that they are one of the last strongholds of mutton.

GO AWAY TO ENGLAND English Tourist Board **GO AWAY TO ENGLAND**

Thin and floppy or thicker and chewy, oatcakes are found in many parts of the North. They are delicious eaten warmed through, with butter or cheese or served at breakfast with bacon.

without a 'proper' roast, either beef, with, of course, Yorkshire Pudding, or lamb from the excellent Cheviot sheep.

Wensleydale is the cheese to sample here, often eaten with dark fruit cake, apple pie or the locally-made oatcakes. Curd tarts, fruit pies, spiced breads and parkin, a treacle-based dark cake traditionally eaten on bonfire-night, are just some of the foods to appeal to those with a sweet tooth.

The Humberside and Yorkshire coasts produce superb fish from Scarborough plaice and Grimsby haddock to shellfish such as Whitby crab, Bridlington Bay prawns plus whelks and oysters.

Local markets abound, selling not only meat and fish but regional specialities from pressed and potted meats, puddings and sausages to sweet and savoury pies and locally-made cakes, biscuits and sweets.

Superb fried fish and chips – served with mushy peas – is a traditional part of good fare here and,

True Yorkshire Pudding isn't just a puff of crispy batter. It should be thick and cooked under a joint secured on a jack so that the meat juices run into the pudding giving a tasty, moist centre with crisp golden edges. It doesn't just go with beef. In Yorkshire they eat it with any roast meat, in Durham with duck or goose and, in parts of Lancashire, at the end of the meal served with sugar or syrup.

north, towards the border country, don't miss Craster kippers cured in the smoke from oak chips, locally-caught crab and lobster in the Seahouses area and fine salmon from the Tweed.

Buyers from all over England come to Northumbria to select the quality beef calves Northumberland rears. In summer, over one million sheep – the famous Cheviots and Border Leicesters – graze on the hillside pastures. The county is renowned, also, for its fine choice of game: pheasant, partridge and grouse from the woods and moors and venison from the Kielder Forest, the largest man-made forest in Europe. Venison steaks are served with a sauce made from Lindisfarne Mead and visitors to St. Aidan's Winery Showrooms can buy jams, curds, marmalades, cakes and fudge, all flavoured with the honey mead. Northumbrian game pie is delicious, particularly eaten out in the open as part of a picnic lunch.

While soft fruits and vegetables are grown everywhere, one vegetable is 'special' – the leek. There's enormous rivalry between Northumbria and Wales about whose leeks are the larger! Leeks are not only cooked as a vegetable here but are also used in a variety of appetising puddings, pies and other made-up dishes, as well as in soups.

The true flavour of England is deliciously wide and varied and, no matter what part of the country you visit, you'll find high-quality, locally-produced food, exciting regional dishes – and a warm welcome in the pubs, teashops and restaurants of each part.

If you like browsing round markets, Lancashire is the county to visit. Almost every town has its own, the smaller ones having regular 'street market' days. Although the mouth-watering foods you'll find there may be your prime target you'll also discover 'seconds' and 'ends of lines' from the mills. There are plenty of cut price bargains in clothes, sheets, towels, curtains, fabric lengths, children's wear and anoraks for keen-eyed shoppers to select from.

Oundle
Map 6 A2 Northamptonshire
New Street *PE8 4EA*
Oundle (0832) 73621

Credit Access, Amex,
Barclaycard, Diners

Rooms 40
with bath/shower 38

Talbot Hotel   61%   £ D

Stones from Fotheringhay Castle were used to build the frontage of this impressive 17th-century hostelry, where the solidly traditional public areas, with panelling, engravings, armour and a lovely oak staircase, are very simply furnished. Bedrooms, in contrast, are quite stylish, especially those in the recent extension, with pretty fabrics and good-quality furniture. Fully carpeted bathrooms. *Amenities* garden.

| *Room phone* Yes | *Confirm by* 6 | *Parking* Ample |
| *Room TV* Yes | *Last dinner* 9.30 | *Banquets* 100/2 |

Oxford
Town plan B1 Oxfordshire
Bardwell Road *OX2 6SR*
Oxford (0865) 52746
Manager Dudley Winterbottom

● **Set L** £7·30 **Set D** £7·70
About £23 for two

Cherwell Boathouse   ⓢ

Book and arrive as early as possible if you want the best choice at this charming converted boathouse at the water's edge. The two fixed-price menus have some interesting dishes like cream of celeriac soup, chicken in leek and cream sauce, and sweets such as hazelnut torte. Cooking is consistent and flavours are excellent. ▼ *SUPERIOR.*
Credit Access, Amex, Barclaycard, Diners

Lunch Sun only 1–2 *Dinner* 8–10
Closed Christmas–New Year

Oxford
Town plan B4 Oxfordshire
84 St Aldgate's *OX1 1RA*
Oxford (0865) 42230
Proprietor Antonio F. Lopez

About £40 for two
Banquets 40/10

Restaurant Elizabeth   ♀ ♔ ⓢ

Long established on the Oxford scene, this friendly, intimate restaurant attracts a large following with some well-executed dishes. Popular starters include pipérade and a beautifully delicate mussel soup, while main courses like poulet au porto or trout stuffed with a shellfish mousse are served with superb sauces. Simple, delicious desserts and excellent coffee. ▼ *OUTSTANDING. Credit* Access, Amex, Barclaycard

Lunch Sun only 12.30–2.30 *Dinner* 6.30–11, Sun 7–10.30
Closed Mon, Good Friday, 24–26 December & last 3 weeks August

We publish annually, so make
sure you use the current
edition. It's worth it!

Oxford
Town plan B1 Oxfordshire
Linton Road *OX2 6UJ*
Oxford (0865) 53461
Telex 837093

Credit Access, Amex,
Barclaycard, Diners

Rooms 72
with bath/shower 66

Ladbroke Linton Lodge   64%   £ C

Close to the city centre, yet away from the noise and bustle, this well-run hotel offers a warm welcome, helpful service and very comfortable accommodation. The spacious modern foyer-lounge has bamboo tub chairs, while the bar is decorated in Edwardian style. Bedrooms are bright and neatly fitted, 'Gold Star' rooms being quite luxurious. Bathrooms are compact and well equipped. *Amenities* garden, croquet.

| *Room phone* Yes | *Confirm by* 6 | *Parking* Ample |
| *Room TV* Yes | *Last dinner* 9.30 | *Banquets* 120/– |

Oxford
Town plan C4 Oxfordshire
146 London Road
Headington *OX3 9ED*
Oxford (0865) 62587

French cooking
● **Set L** £4·25, Sun £5·95
Set D £6·95
About £30 for two
Banquets 45/–

Michel's Bistro   ♀ ⓢ

Uncomplicated French cooking is the attraction in Michel Sardones' charming little bistro. The regularly changing, fixed-price menu features a simple choice of competently prepared dishes ranging from trout with tarragon sauce to coq au vin and lamb's liver provençale. Tempting sweets include chocolate mousse and lemon sorbet. Roast lunch on Sundays. *Credit* Access, Barclaycard, Diners

Lunch 12–2.30, Sun 12–2 *Dinner* 7.30–11
Closed Bank Holidays, last week July–1st week Aug & 24–31 Dec

Map 5 D2
Town plan opposite

Population 127,000

Despite the encroachment of industry, Oxford remains incomparable—except with Cambridge—as a centre of learning for 1,000 years, interrupted only by the disturbance of the Civil War siege in the 1640s. No city has more to offer the sightseer in its own architectural glories and the beauty of its surroundings—the Thames Valley, the Cotswolds and so much besides.

Sights Outside City
Blenheim Palace
Burford Village
Dorchester-on-Thames
Chipping Campden
Sulgrave Manor
Waddesdon Manor

Information Centre
St Aldate's, Oxford OX1 1DY
Telephone Oxford 726871/2
Accommodation 727873/4

Annual Events
St Giles Fair *6th–7th Sept*

Lancia Dealers

J. D. Barclay
Botley Road
Oxford
Tel: 0865 722444

Oxford

1	Ashmolean Museum *art and archaeology treasures*	B3
2	Botanic Garden *one of the oldest in the country*	C4
3	Carfax Tower *viewpoint open in summer*	B4
4	Christ Church Meadow	C5
5	Divinity School *15th-c fine vaulted ceiling*	B3
6	Folly Bridge	B5
7	Information Centre	B4
8	Martyrs' Memorial	B3
9	Museum of the History of Science	B3
10	New Theatre	B3
11	Playhouse Theatre	B3
12	Sheldonian Theatre *Wren building for conferment of degrees*	B3
13	Station	A3
14	Town Hall	B4
15	University Museum	B2
16	University Parks	B/C1/2

A true 4-seat, 4-door businessman's express.

LANCIA TREVI

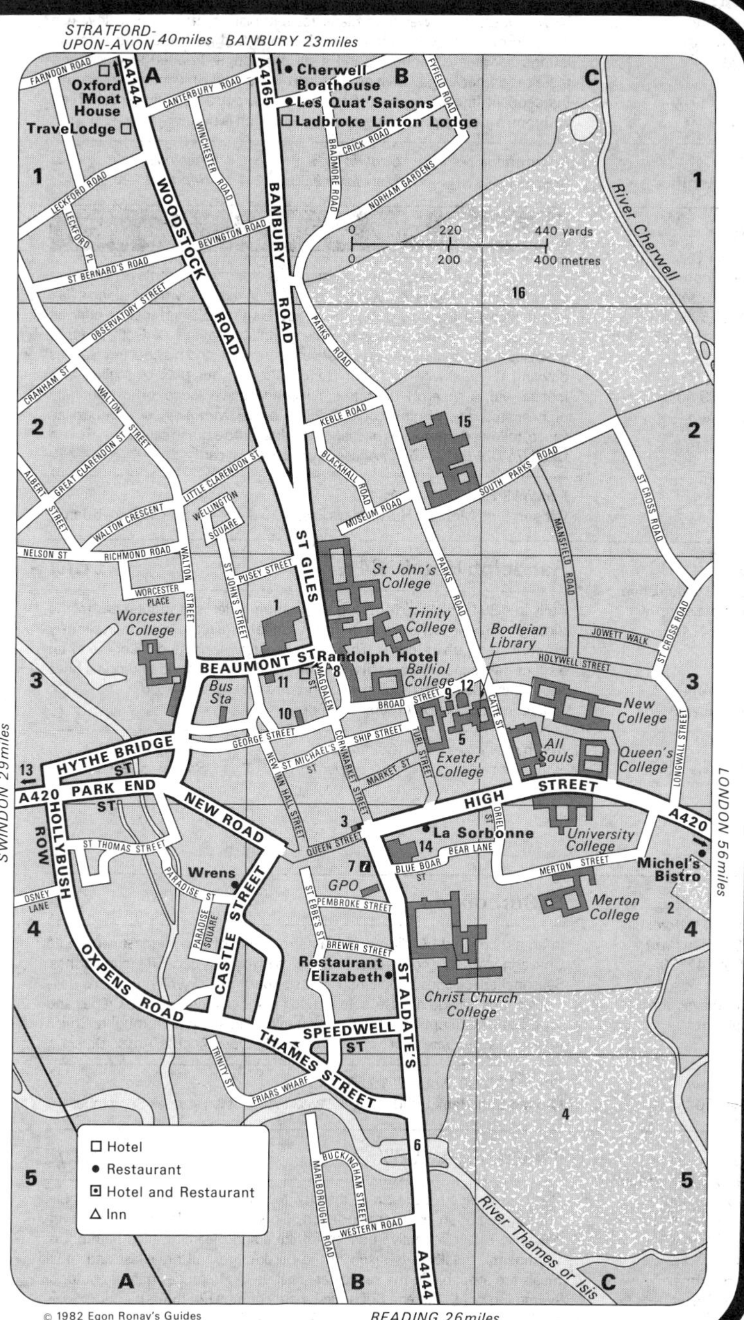

Oxford LANCIA
LANCIA
STRATFORD-UPON-AVON 40miles BANBURY 23miles
FARNDON ROAD
A4144
A
A4165
Cherwell Boathouse
B
Les Quat'Saisons
Ladbroke Linton Lodge
C
Oxford Moat House
TraveLodge
CANTERBURY ROAD
LECKFORD ROAD
LECKFORD PL
WINCHESTER ROAD
BEVINGTON ROAD
BANBURY ROAD
FYFIELD ROAD
CRICK ROAD
BRADMORE ROAD
NORHAM GARDENS
River Cherwell
1
ST BERNARD'S ROAD
WOODSTOCK ROAD
PARKS ROAD
220   440 yards
0
200   400 metres
0
16
OBSERVATORY STREET
CRANHAM ST
WALTON STREET
GREAT CLARENDON ST
LITTLE CLARENDON ST
KEBLE ROAD
BLACKHALL ROAD
MUSEUM ROAD
15
SOUTH PARKS ROAD
MANSFIELD ROAD
ST CROSS ROAD
2
ALBERT STREET
WALTON CRESCENT
NELSON ST
RICHMOND ROAD
WALTON STREET
ST GILES
PARKS ROAD
St John's College
Trinity College
Bodleian Library
JOWETT WALK
ST CROSS ROAD
3
Worcester College
WORCESTER PLACE
PUSEY STREET
ST JOHN'S STREET
1
BEAUMONT ST
Randolph Hotel
8
Balliol College
HOLYWELL STREET
New College
LONGWALL STREET
Bus Sta
11
MAGDALEN ST
Broad
9 12
STREET
CATTE ST
All Souls
Queen's College
10
GEORGE STREET
NEW INN HALL STREET
ST MICHAEL'S ST
CORNMARKET STREET
SHIP STREET
TURL STREET
5
Exeter College
HYTHE BRIDGE
ST
13
PARK END
ST
NEW ROAD
MARKET ST
HIGH   STREET
A420
LONDON 56miles
SWINDON 29miles
A420
HOLLYBUSH ROW
ST THOMAS STREET
Queen Street
3
ORIEL STREET
La Sorbonne
University College
Michel's Bistro
Wrens
PARADISE ST
14
BEAR LANE
MERTON STREET
OSNEY LANE
PARADISE SQUARE
CASTLE STREET
BLUE BOAR ST
7
GPO
ST EBBE'S ST
PEMBROKE STREET
Merton College
2
4
BREWER STREET
Restaurant Elizabeth
ST ALDATE'S
Christ Church College
4
OXPENS ROAD
SPEEDWELL ST
THAMES STREET
TRINITY ST
FRIARS WHARF
Hotel
Restaurant
Hotel and Restaurant
Inn
BUCKINGHAM STREET
MARLBOROUGH STREET
WESTERN ROAD
6
River Thames or Isis
5
A4144
A
B
C
5
© 1982 Egon Ronay's Guides
READING 26miles

Oxford

Town plan A1 Oxfordshire
Wolvercote Roundabout *OX2 8AL*
Oxford (0865) 59933
Telex 837926

Credit Access, Amex,
Barclaycard, Diners

Rooms 156
with bath/shower 156

Oxford Moat House   56%   £ D

New owners have welcome plans for refurbishing this modern low-rise hotel, formerly known as the Oxford Europa Lodge. The spacious foyer-lounge-bar area is centred round a striking copper-hooded fireplace, and there's another large, inviting bar and a variety of conference rooms. Functionally fitted bedrooms offer plenty of storage and writing space. Tiled bathrooms are adequate. *Amenities* garden, pitch & putt.

Room phone Yes	*Confirm by* 6	*Parking* Ample
Room TV Yes	*Last dinner* 9.30	*Banquets* 120/10

Oxford

Town plan B1 Oxfordshire
272 Banbury Road
Summertown *OX2 8ED*
Oxford (0865) 53540
Proprietors M & Mme R. Blanc
French cooking

● **Set L** from £9·50
About £55 for two

Les Quat' Saisons   ★ ★

For the student of gastronomy, a visit to this charmingly simple restaurant in a modern shopping precinct is an education in itself. Raymond Blanc's flair and dedication are truly exceptional, and his long French menus offer all that's best and freshest season by season. Brilliant sauces, perfectly textured mousses and stunning desserts captivate the visitor, and his cooking reaches dizzying heights with memorable creations like our pâté of scallop and lobster with a superbly delicate crayfish and chive sauce, or a beautifully orchestrated dish of pink-cooked duck's breast with a sweet Monbazillac sauce, followed by morsels of crisp skin folded into a green salad.
🍷 *OUTSTANDING. Credit* Access, Amex, Barclaycard

Lunch 12.15–2 *Dinner* 7.15–10
Closed Sun, Mon, Bk Hols, 4 days Easter, 19 July–4 Aug & 24 Dec–6 Jan

Oxford

Town plan B3 Oxfordshire
Beaumont Street *OX1 2LN*
Oxford (0865) 47481
Telex 83446

Credit Access, Amex,
Barclaycard, Diners

Rooms 109
with bath/shower 109

Randolph Hotel   64%   £ C/D

Built in 1864, this solid-looking city-centre hotel is a monument to the Victorian Gothic style, with a fine wooden staircase and marvellously proportioned public rooms. There's an ornately appointed lounge and an elegant oak-panelled cocktail bar. Many of the good-sized bedrooms have been freshly decorated. Compact bathrooms are well equipped.
Amenities coffee shop (10am–11.15pm)

Room phone Yes	*Confirm by* 6	*Parking* Limited
Room TV Yes	*Last dinner* 10.15	*Banquets* 280/12

Oxford

Town plan B4 Oxfordshire
130 High Street *OX1 4DH*
Oxford (0865) 41320
Proprietor
M André P. Chavagnon
French cooking

About £35 for two
Banquets 40/10

La Sorbonne

In an old beamed building down a narrow lane off the High Street, André Chavagnon offers a comprehensive choice of expertly cooked French dishes. Seasonal specialities supplement the standard menu which includes delicious soups, salade niçoise, sole bonne femme and coq au vin. Crêpes and soufflés make tempting sweets, or you might finish on a thoroughly British note with Welsh rarebit or Scotch woodcock. *Credit* Access, Amex, Diners

Lunch 12–2.30 *Dinner* 7–10.30, Sat 7–11
Closed Sun, Bank Holidays, last 2 weeks August & 1st week September

Oxford

Town plan A1 Oxfordshire
Peartree Roundabout
Woodstock Road *OX2 8JZ*
Oxford (0865) 54301
Telex 83202
Credit Access, Amex,
Barclaycard, Diners

Rooms 102
with bath/shower 102

TraveLodge   58%   £ D/E

Part of a service area north of the city, the TraveLodge offers comfortable, unfussy motel-style accommodation. Good-sized bedrooms (some with balconies) have attractive built-in furniture and gleaming tiled bathrooms. Continental breakfast is taken in the bar-lounge; full breakfast and other meals are available in the service area cafeteria. *Amenities* garden, outdoor swimming pool, cafeteria (24 hours), petrol pumps (24 hours).

Room phone Yes	*Confirm by* 6	*Parking* Ample
Room TV Yes	*Last dinner* None	

WORTHINGTON'S WHITE SHIELD

Pale by name, but not by nature, Worthington's White Shield is no ordinary beer; it matures in the bottle. This continuous fermentation gives White Shield its distinctively smooth taste and sets it apart from ordinary pale ales.

Keep a look out for Worthington's White Shield —

IT'S NOT TO BE TAKEN LIGHTLY

Oxford

Town plan A4 Oxfordshire
29 Castle Street *OX1 1LJ*
Oxford (0865) 42944

French cooking

● **Set D** from £7·75
About £30 for two
Banquets 50/10

Wrens   ♀ ⑤

This charming little French restaurant is noted for its attractively presented food. The set menus (three, four and five courses) are strong in seafood dishes like fish soup and cod provençale, and there are also some meat specialities such as chicken with cream and tarragon. Simple sweets and fine French cheeses, with coffee and petits fours to finish.
Credit Access, Amex, Barclaycard, Diners   ♿

Dinner only 7–11
Closed Sun & Bank Holidays

Padstow

Map 2 B3 Cornwall
Riverside *PL28 8BY*
Padstow (0841) 532485
Proprietor Mr Richard Stein
Seafood

● **Set L & Set D** £7·65
About £33 for two

Seafood Restaurant   ♀ ⑤

The pick of the day's catch arrives fresh at this cheerful quayside restaurant, forming the basis of some really enjoyable dishes. Crème de moules à la fleur de safran is a lovely delicate soup, and main courses include lobster (hot and cold), seafood Thermidor and grilled sole. There's steak or duck for meat-eaters, and a selection of excellent desserts. ▼ *ABOVE AVERAGE.*
Credit Access, Amex, Barclaycard, Diners   ♿

Lunch 12.30–2 *Dinner* 7.30–10.30
Closed L Sat, all Sun, 1 May & 20 October–2 weeks before Easter

Padstow

Map 2 B3 Cornwall
Constantine Bay *PL28 8JH*
Padstow (0841) 520727
Proprietors Mr & Mrs E. H. Barlow
Credit Access
Closed mid November–
mid March

Treglos Hotel   68%   Ⓜ   £C

Golfers and holiday-makers particularly appreciate this seaside hotel, where the friendly Barlows give everyone the warmest of welcomes. Guests can relax in one of several comfortable sitting rooms or in the convivial atmosphere of the bar-lounge. Cheerful bedrooms have modern fitted or freestanding units, and bathrooms are well equipped. *Amenities* garden, indoor swimming pool, solarium, croquet, water skiing, yachting, surfing. ♿

Rooms 43	Room phone Yes	Confirm by By arrang.	Parking Ample
with bath/shower 43	Room TV No	Last dinner 9.30	Banquets 20/–

Paignton

Map 3 D3 Devon
59 Torquay Road *TQ3 3DT*
Paignton (0803) 556185
Proprietor Mr Luigi Randi
Italian cooking

● **Set L** from £3 **Set D** £7·25
About £28 for two

Luigi   ⑤

Genial Luigi Randi presides over this simply decorated restaurant where thoroughly enjoyable Italian cooking is the order of the day. Dishes like plump scallops in a tasty wine and cheese sauce and tender peppered steak are skilfully prepared from first-class ingredients, vegetables are good and plentiful, and sweets like light, creamy zabaglione make a delightful finale. Book. *Credit* Barclaycard

Lunch 12.30–2 *Dinner* 7–11
Closed 25 & 26 December

Paignton

Map 3 D3 Devon
Esplanade *TQ4 6BJ*
Paignton (0803) 555121

Manager Mrs A. Renshaw
Credit Access, Amex,
Barclaycard, Diners

Palace Hotel   63%   £D

This imposing white hotel retains many reminders of its grand Victorian origins. The splendid Singer Room, with its original fireplace and ornate ceiling, is the star of the public rooms, which also include a restful reception-lounge and a panelled bar. Pleasantly decorated bedrooms have practical furnishings and compact modern bathrooms. *Amenities* garden, outdoor swimming pool, tennis, dancing (Wed June–September), putting, games room.

Rooms 54	Room phone Yes	Confirm by 6	Parking Ample
with bath/shower 54	Room TV Yes	Last dinner 9	Banquets 40/–

Paignton

Map 3 D3 Devon
4 Marine Drive *TQ3 2NL*
Paignton (0803) 526397

Credit Amex

Redcliffe Hotel   63%   Ⓜ   £D/E

This seafront building has been greatly extended and modernised since it was built by a colonel for his Indian bride in 1902. It's very much a family place, with comfortable public rooms, including TV rooms, bars and a lofty lounge. Simply appointed bedrooms have radios and adequate bathrooms. *Amenities* garden, outdoor swimming pool, tennis, dancing (3 nights weekly in summer), putting, croquet, hairdressing, games room.

Continued

Rooms 65	*Room phone* Yes	*Confirm by* By arrang.	*Parking* Ample
with bath/shower 65	*Room TV* No	*Last dinner* 8.30	*Banquets* 200/–

Painswick

Map 4 B2 Gloucestershire
New Street *GL6 6XA*
Painswick (0452) 813564
Proprietors
Jane & Michael Medforth

Country Elephant

Jane Medforth changes her menu daily at this friendly little restaurant, where the service is as charming as the decor. An interesting choice of starters could include cold curried apple soup or our delicious avocado mousse with prawn and green peppercorn dressing, while main courses range from chicken Kiev to pork fillets served with good vegetables. Sweets can sometimes disappoint. *Credit* Barclaycard

● **Set L** £5·45
About £29 for two

Lunch Sun only 12.30–2.30 *Dinner* 7–11 **Closed** D Sun, Mon, Bank Holidays, 1 week Easter, mid August–mid September & 1 week Christmas

Painswick

Map 4 B2 Gloucestershire
Kemps Lane *GL6 6YB*
Painswick (0452) 812160

Credit Access, Amex,
Barclaycard, Diners
Closed 1 week Dec–Jan

Painswick Hotel   65%   Ⓜ   £D

Major improvements have changed the bedrooms at this friendly hotel, which stands on a hillside below the church. Whether in the main Georgian building or in the modern extension, they are decorated and furnished to a high standard, and up-to-date bathrooms are equally well fitted. Public rooms include a cheerful bar-lounge with a winter log fire and a terrace for warmer days. *Amenities* garden, croquet.

Rooms 16	*Room phone* Yes	*Confirm by* By arrang.	*Parking* Ample
with bath/shower 14	*Room TV* Yes	*Last dinner* 9.30	*Banquets* 60/–

Pangbourne

Map 5 D2 Berkshire
Church Road *RG8 7AR*
Pangbourne (073 57) 2244

Proprietor Mr A. W. Hampton
Credit Access, Amex,
Barclaycard, Diners

Copper Inn   65%   Ⓜ   £D/E

This popular town-centre hotel consists of an early 19th-century half-timbered building and a harmonious modern bedroom block. The refurbished reception-foyer has pleasing pink wallpaper and stylish low sofas, and there's also a relaxing residents' lounge and a popular rustic bar. All bedrooms are decorated and furnished to a high standard, and bathrooms in the garden wing are especially attractive. No dogs. *Amenities* garden.

Rooms 21	*Room phone* Yes	*Confirm by* By arrang.	*Parking* Ample
with bath/shower 21	*Room TV* Yes	*Last dinner* 9.30	*Banquets* 50/–

Parkgate

Map 10 A2 Cheshire
The Parade, Wirral *L64 6SA*
051–336 3931

Credit Access, Amex,
Barclaycard, Diners

Ship Hotel *(Inn)*   £E

This narrow, stucco-fronted hotel provides a welcome refuge from the blustery winds that blow across the marshy estuary of the river Dee, and the hills of Clwyd can be admired from the snug Birdwatcher's Bar. Steep stairs lead to small, simply furnished bedrooms with comfortable beds, central heating and carpeted modern bathrooms. Friendly, helpful staff. No dogs.

Rooms 26	*Room phone* Yes	*Confirm by* 6	*Parking* Ample
with bath/shower 26	*Room TV* Yes	*Last dinner* 9	

Pendoggett

Map 2 B3 Cornwall
St Kew, nr Port Isaac *PL30 3HH*
Port Isaac (020 888) 263
Proprietors Nigel Pickstone &
Alan & Margaret Wainwright
Credit Access, Amex,
Barclaycard, Diners

Cornish Arms *(Inn)*   Ⓜ   £E/F

This lovely old ivy-clad inn on the B3314 is a well-preserved haven of traditional comfort. The two bars have open fires, low beams and flagstone floors, and the little TV room is full of cosy armchairs and settees. Bedrooms, too, are solidly furnished, and, like the rest of the inn, are kept in gleaming condition. No children under 14. *Amenities* garden, dancing (Sat fortnightly). **Closed** for accommodation Christmas

Rooms 7	*Room phone* No	*Confirm by* 6	*Parking* Ample
with bath/shower 4	*Room TV* No	*Last dinner* 8.45	

Penshurst

Map 7 B5 Kent
Smart Hill *TN11 8EE*
Penshurst (0892) 870253

● **Set L** £5·75 **Set D** from £7·50
About £29 for two
Banquets 45/25

Spotted Dog

Enjoyable eating in very pleasant surroundings rewards visitors to this cottage pub restaurant, whose beamed dining room looks out over attractive terraced gardens. The fixed-price menus offer an ample choice of starters—pâté and soup such as a flavoursome seafood chowder—and well-prepared main dishes based on prime chicken, duck, steak and game in season. Vegetables are handled with similar care. *Credit* Amex, Barclaycard, Diners

Lunch 12.30–2 *Dinner* 7.30–10
Closed D Sun

Penzance

Map 2 A4 Cornwall
Abbey Street *TR18 4AW*
Penzance (0736) 2541
Proprietor Mr Ian Morris

About £26 for two

Berkeley

Striking '30s-style decor is a feature of this stylish restaurant, where genial Ian Morris is in charge of the cooking. Specialities like home-made tagliatelle and escalope of pork fillet in a creamy Marsala sauce show his fondness for Italian food, and there are also simple dishes like grilled Dover sole and steak and kidney pie. Excellent vegetables and delicious sweets, too.
Credit Amex, Barclaycard

Dinner only 7.30–10.30
Closed Sun, 1 January & 25 & 26 December

Penzance

Map 2 A4 Cornwall
46 New Street *TR18 2LZ*
Penzance (0736) 4408
Proprietors
Mr & Mrs Roger Harris

About £27 for two

Harvis's

In the intimate surroundings of his charming little bistro, Roger Harris offers a short selection of capably cooked dishes, including seasonal game and shellfish. French onion soup is a tasty alternative to pâté or hot mushrooms to start, and main courses could include sautéed kidneys, entrecôte cacciatora or our succulent caneton au porto, served with excellent ratatouille. Delicious sweets, too. *Credit* Amex, Barclaycard, Diners

Lunch 12–2 *Dinner* 7–10
Closed Sun, also D Mon in winter & 25 December

Peterborough

Map 6 A2 Cambridgeshire
Norman Cross *PE7 3TB*
Peterborough (0733) 240209
Telex 32576

Credit Access, Amex,
Barclaycard, Diners

Crest Hotel   60%   £ D

Some five miles out of the city alongside the A1, this smart modern hotel, which has very good facilities for meetings and seminars, is popular with business people. Public rooms include a spacious foyer and a bright bar with a terrace. Nicely proportioned bedrooms have fitted units, plenty of writing space, tea-makers and trouser presses. Well-designed bathrooms. *Amenities* garden, coffee shop (9.30am–9.30pm).

| *Rooms* 97 | *Room phone* Yes | *Confirm by* 6 | *Parking* Ample |
| *with bath/shower* 97 | *Room TV* Yes | *Last dinner* 10 | *Banquets* 60/– |

Peterborough

Map 6 A2 Cambridgeshire
Station Road *PE1 1QL*
Peterborough (0733) 52331
Telex 32822

Credit Access, Amex,
Barclaycard, Diners

Great Northern Hotel   60%   £ E

Situated right by the railway station, this Victorian hotel has a reputation for friendliness and personal service. A small foyer leads to the homely bar and a pleasant residents' lounge overlooking the garden. Bedrooms range from cheerfully decorated and traditional in the main building to well-designed modern ones with practical fitted furniture in the extension.
Amenities garden, 24-hour laundry service.

| *Rooms* 50 | *Room phone* Yes | *Confirm by* 6 | *Parking* Ample |
| *with bath/shower* 27 | *Room TV* Yes | *Last dinner* 9.30 | *Banquets* 180/– |

Peterborough

Map 6 A2 Cambridgeshire
Thorpe Wood *PE3 6SG*
Peterborough (0733) 260000
Telex 32708

Credit Access, Amex,
Barclaycard, Diners

Saxon Inn Motor Hotel   64%   £ D

Opened in March 1981, this eye-catching yellow-brick hotel beside the ring road is set in pleasantly landscaped grounds. In addition to numerous conference and meeting rooms, it has a luxuriously furnished lounge area and an attractive bar with a huge stone fireplace. Bedrooms on three floors are spacious, all with neatly fitted furniture, comfortable beds and fully tiled bathrooms. *Amenities* dancing (Sat).

Continued

Rooms 98	*Room phone* Yes	*Confirm by* 7	*Parking* Ample
with bath/shower 98	*Room TV* Yes	*Last dinner* 10.30	*Banquets* 350/–

Petersfield
Map 5 D3 Hampshire
Langrish *GU32 1RN*
Petersfield (0730) 66941

Credit Amex, Diners
Closed possibly 3 weeks August

Langrish House 68% Ⓜ £E

This delightful country retreat stands in the tiny village of Langrish (three miles west of Petersfield on the A272) on a site once occupied by a 15th-century manor house. Bedrooms are spacious and most attractive, with fabric wall panels, elegant unit furniture and excellent bathrooms. Public rooms in the well-converted cellars include a cosy little bar and a lounge with a small grotto. No dogs. *Amenities* garden.

Rooms 10	*Room phone* Yes	*Confirm by* By arrang.	*Parking* Ample
with bath/shower 10	*Room TV* Yes	*Last dinner* 10	*Banquets* 50/12

Pett Bottom
Map 7 C5 Kent
Bridge
Near Canterbury *CT4 5PB*
Bridge (0227) 830354
Proprietors John & Ulla Laing

● **Set L** £8·60
About £36 for two
Banquets 20/10

Duck Inn Ⓖ Ⓢ

John and Ulla Laing create a delightfully restful atmosphere in the gracious dining room of their charming country pub. Ulla's skilful cooking ranges capably from starters like watercress and vegetable soup to main courses such as seasonal game and spring chicken with cream and mustard sauce, accompanied by crisp, colourful vegetables. There are mouthwatering sweets, too, including rich chocolate pot. *Credit* Amex, Diners

Lunch 12.30–1.45 *Dinner* 7.30–9.30
Closed Mon, Tues, 25 December, 2 weeks March & 2 weeks October

Petworth
Map 5 E3 West Sussex
East Street *GU28 0AB*
Petworth (0798) 43149

About £27 for two

Paddington's Table Ⓖ Ⓢ

Cartoons of the famous bear line the bar of this unpretentious restaurant, where Susie Smith is the capable chef and husband Peter serves. The interesting menu features French-inspired dishes like pâté-stuffed chicken breast, but you'll also find traditional English fare and even satay from Indonesia. Excellent fresh vegetables and delicious desserts, like rich chocolate brandy cake. *Credit* Access, Amex, Barclaycard, Diners

Lunch 12–2 *Dinner* 7–10.45 **Closed** D Wed & Sun, Easter Mon, 25 & 26 December & 2 weeks September

Pewsey
Map 4 C3 Wiltshire
River Street *SN9 5DB*
Pewsey (067 26) 3226

● **Set D** from £9
About £24 for two
Banquets 26/–

Close Ⓖ

A long drive leads to this charming country restaurant where Rhona Aitken offers an enjoyable, highly individual brand of home cooking. The daily-changing set dinner menu might range from rich braised oxtail to Edwardian lamb with caper sauce. Lunch menus during the week are more limited, but on Sunday there are exotic dishes like Nigerian groundnut chicken. Please book. *Credit* Access, Amex, Barclaycard, Diners

Lunch 12.30–1.30, Sun 1–2 *Dinner* from 7.30
Closed D Sun, all Mon, 1 January, 31 December & last 2 weeks October

Pickering
Map 15 C6 North Yorkshire
Malton Road *YO18 7DL*
Pickering (0751) 72722

Credit Access, Barclaycard
Closed 2 days Christmas

Forest & Vale Hotel 56% Ⓜ £E

This renovated Georgian manor house makes a convenient base for exploring the North Yorkshire Moors National Park. The gleaming little foyer strikes a cheerful note, and there are two bars and a residents' TV lounge. Bedrooms (some are in a courtyard annexe) have simple melamine furniture, tea/coffee-makers and all but one now have a bathroom.
Amenities garden.

Rooms 23	*Room phone* No	*Confirm by* By arrang.	*Parking* Ample
with bath/shower 22	*Room TV* No	*Last dinner* 9	*Banquets* 140/–

Piercebridge

Map 15 B5 Co. Durham
Near Darlington *DL2 3SW*
Piercebridge (032 574) 576
Proprietors Mr Ray Wade &
Mr Ralph Wilkinson
Credit Access, Amex,
Barclaycard, Diners

Rooms 5
with bath/shower None

George Hotel *(Inn)*  £ F

This rambling 17th-century inn by the banks of the Tees is a hostelry of great charm and character. The long Highwayman's Bar is full of exposed beams, settles and old photographs, and there's a traditional feel, too, about the residents' lounge and cheerfully decorated bedrooms. These are furnished in a variety of styles, and all of them have teamakers and radios. No dogs. *Amenities* garden.

Room phone No	*Confirm by* By arrang.	*Parking* Ample
Room TV No	*Last dinner* 10	*Banquets* 190/–

Plymouth

Map 2 C3 Devon
14 Elliot Street
The Hoe *PL1 2PS*
Plymouth (0752) 25511
Credit Access, Amex,
Barclaycard, Diners
Closed 25 & 26 December

Rooms 58
with bath/shower 58

Astor Hotel 59% £ D

Traditional decor gives a feeling of comfortable elegance to this late-Victorian hotel in the heart of historic Plymouth. Potted palms, oil paintings, chandeliers and velvet drapes adorn the foyer-lounge and cocktail bar, and the spacious, well-furnished bedrooms warmly decorated in browns and creams are attractive. Gleaming modern bathrooms are well maintained, and service throughout is friendly. No dogs.

Room phone Yes	*Confirm by* 6	*Parking* Limited
Room TV Yes	*Last dinner* 9.30	*Banquets* 120/12

Plymouth

Map 2 C3 Devon
13 Frankfort Gate *PL1 1QA*
Plymouth (0752) 266793
Proprietor Mr J. Marchal
French cooking

● **Set L & Set D** £10
About £32 for two
Banquets 25/12

Chez Nous  Ⓢ

This simple little bistro makes a pleasant setting for Jacques Marchal's careful cooking. The French menu changes with the seasons, and mussels, snails and frogs' legs rub shoulders with beautifully prepared steaks, lamb and duck dishes. To finish, as well as good coffee, there are exotic sorbets, crème brûlée and a superb chocolate mousse. ♟*ABOVE AVERAGE.*
Credit Access, Amex, Barclaycard, Diners

Lunch 12.30–2 *Dinner* 7–10.30
Closed Sun, Bank Holidays, 1st 10 days February & 1st 10 days September

Plymouth

Map 2 C3 Devon
Millbay Road *PL1 3LG*
Plymouth (0752) 266256
Telex 45424
Man. Mr L. MacDermott Brown
Credit Access, Amex,
Barclaycard, Diners

Rooms 70
with bath/shower 70

Duke of Cornwall Hotel 60%  £ E

An imposing Victorian Gothic building, convenient for the ferry services and right opposite the exhibition centre. Guests have a choice of three bars, including the Spider's Web in the cellar, and there's also a bright panelled lounge. Bedrooms vary in style, but most are quite roomy, with simple, practical furniture and neat bathrooms. *Amenities* dancing (Sat), discothèque (Sat October–April). **Closed** 3–4 days Christmas.

Room phone Yes	*Confirm by* 6	*Parking* Ample
Room TV Yes	*Last dinner* 9.45	*Banquets* 300/4

Plymouth

Map 2 C3 Devon
Armada Way *PL1 2HJ*
Plymouth (0752) 662866
Telex 45637

Rooms 222
with bath/shower 222
Room phone Yes
Room TV Yes
Confirm by 6
Last dinner 11
Parking Ample
Banquets 300/–

Credit Access, Amex,
Barclaycard, Diners

Holiday Inn 75% *E* £ C/D

Public rooms and most bedrooms at this towering modern hotel have benefited from a recent expensive refit. The roomy foyer/lounge is bright and attractive, and three distinctive bars include the smart black-walled Poonah Bar, which offers spectacular views over the harbour from its rooftop position. There's also a coffee shop and full conference facilities. Spacious bedrooms have neat, practical fitted furniture, trouser presses, bedside

Continued

controls and compact modern bathrooms. Staff are friendly and efficient.
Amenities sauna, indoor swimming pool, coffee shop (7am–10.30pm), in-house movies, gymnasium, games room, hotel car, laundry room.   ♿

Plymouth

Map 2 C3 Devon
The Hoe *PL1 3DL*
Plymouth (0752) 662828
Telex 45442

Credit Access, Amex,
Barclaycard, Diners

Mayflower Post House Hotel 57%   £ D

Right on Plymouth Hoe, with splendid views of the Sound, this modern glass and concrete hotel caters well for both businessmen and tourists. Public rooms include an open-plan reception-lounge and an airy public bar. Bedrooms have practical fitted units and pleasant soft furnishings; bathrooms are compact. An extensive programme of refurbishment is planned.
Amenities outdoor swimming pool, coffee shop (7am–10.30pm). ♿

Rooms 104	*Room phone* Yes	*Confirm by* 6	*Parking* Ample
with bath/shower 104	*Room TV* Yes	*Last dinner* 10.30	*Banquets* 80/–

Plymouth

Map 2 C3 Devon
Marsh Mills
Plymouth Road *PL6 8NH*
Plymouth (0752) 21422
Telex 45711
Credit Access, Amex,
Barclaycard, Diners

Novotel Plymouth 64%   £ D

This well-designed, recently completed hotel on the outskirts of the city is thoroughly modern and functional in style. There's a large, smart open-plan reception and a bar with a pleasant Victorian theme. Bright bedrooms have dazzling white walls and fitted units, plus gleaming bathrooms with ingenious fittings. Extensive conference facilities.
Amenities garden, outdoor swimming pool, dancing (once a month). ♿

Rooms 101	*Room phone* Yes	*Confirm by* 7	*Parking* Ample
with bath/shower 101	*Room TV* Yes	*Last dinner* 12	*Banquets* 300/–

Pocklington

Map 11 E1 Humberside
Market Place *YO4 2UN*
Pocklington (075 92) 3155

Credit Access, Amex,
Barclaycard

Feathers Hotel *(Inn)*   £ E/F

This former coaching inn in the market place offers the traveller a friendly welcome, efficient service and comfortable, well-kept accommodation. There's a large, cheerful bar with stone walls and simple oak tables, and a comfortably furnished TV lounge. Bright bedrooms have smart fitted furniture and well-equipped bathrooms, whether in the main building or the motel-style annexe. No dogs.

Rooms 12	*Room phone* No	*Confirm by* By arrang	*Parking* Ample
with bath/shower 12	*Room TV* No	*Last dinner* 9.30	*Banquets* 45/2

Pool-in-Wharfedale

Map 10 C1 West Yorkshire
Pool Bank
Near Otley *LS21 1EH*
Arthington (0532) 842288
Proprietors Hanni & Michael Gill

● **Set D** £10 & from £13·50
About £44 for two
Banquets 30/12

Pool Court ★   ♛ Ⓢ

Dinner at this smart, well-run restaurant in the Dales really is an occasion to remember, with meticulous presentation and service playing major roles in the occasion. Roger Grime's frequently changing menus based on classical French recipes are full of interest, ranging from vegetable timbale and samosas to saddle of lamb en croûte and crisp-skinned roast duckling with a lovely fruity sauce. Vegetables and desserts are delicious, too, and the petits fours served on a huge silver salver more than live up to visual promise.
Specialities médaillons de veau Anton Mosimann, cassoulet de cuisse de canard, suprême de volaille avec crustacés, terrine of fruits.
☟ *OUTSTANDING. Credit* Amex, Barclaycard, Diners

Dinner only 7–10
Closed Sun, Mon, 2 weeks July/August & 2 weeks from 25 December

Our inspectors never book in the name of the Egon Ronay Organisation; they disclose their identity only after paying their bills.

Poole

Map 4 C4 Dorset
The Quay *BH15 1HJ*
Poole (0202) 671200
Telex 418374

Rooms 68
with bath/shower 68
Room phone Yes
Room TV Yes
Confirm by 6
Last dinner 10.30
Parking Ample
Banquets 60/10

Credit Access, Amex,
Barclaycard, Diners

Quay Hotel   74%   *E*   £ D

Standing right on the quay, this modern red-brick hotel has been designed to suit both businessmen and tourists. Exposed brick and pine woodwork give an attractive rustic air to the public areas, which include the smart foyer, the Anchor Bar with its nautical theme and the comfortable first-floor American Bar, which also serves as a lounge. Identically furnished bedrooms are well fitted, with bedside consoles, tea-makers and thoughtful extras like embossed writing paper. Compact tiled bathrooms also show great attention to detail. No dogs.
Amenities dinner dance (Sat).

Portloe

Map 2 B3 Cornwall
Near Truro *TR2 5RD*
Veryan (087 250) 322
Proprietors Powell family
Credit Access, Amex,
Barclaycard, Diners
Closed 1 Nov–late Feb

Rooms 21
with bath/shower 21

Lugger Hotel   56%   Ⓜ   £ E

Set in a tiny fishing cove, this quaint old inn offers visitors homely comforts in peaceful surroundings. The residents' lounge is warm and welcoming, and the bar has French windows opening on to a sun terrace. Bedrooms in the annexe have modern fittings, while those in the original building are more traditionally furnished. No children under 12. No dogs.
Amenities sauna, solarium.

| *Room phone* No | *Confirm by* 6 | *Parking* Ample |
| *Room TV* No | *Last dinner* 9 | |

Portsmouth

Map 5 D4 Hampshire
North Harbour *PO6 4SH*
Portsmouth (0705) 383151
Telex 86611

Rooms 170
with bath/shower 170
Room phone Yes
Room TV Yes
Confirm by 6
Last dinner 11
Parking Ample
Banquets 300/5

Credit Access, Amex,
Barclaycard, Diners

Holiday Inn   78%   *E*   £ C/D

On the A3 just north of the city, this recently built hotel boasts the first 'Holidome' in Europe, an impressive glass and steel construction containing a kidney-shaped pool and sauna. Overlooking the pool is a cocktail bar and lounge area, with classical pillars and an abundance of tropical plants; Oliver's Bar offers nightly dancing and entertainment. Large bedrooms have deep shag-pile carpets, comfortable beds and attractive modern furniture, and smartly fitted bathrooms are well endowed with thick, fluffy towels.
Amenities garden, sauna, indoor swimming pool, squash, dancing (Mon–Sat), games room, in-house movies, keep-fit equipment, health centre.   &

Poundsgate

Map 3 D3 Devon
Leusdon, Lower Town
Near Ashburton *TQ13 7PE*
Poundsgate (036 43) 304
Proprietors Mr & Mrs Hutchins
English cooking

● **Set L** £3·95 **Set D** from £5·85
About £27 for two

Leusdon Lodge Restaurant   ♀ Ⓢ

A simple panelled restaurant in a guest house on the edge of Dartmoor. Cooking is delightfully and traditionally English, and Neelia Hutchins uses fresh local produce whenever possible. Follow soup or flavoursome pâté with trout, pork in cider or perhaps succulent roast quail with a rich wine sauce. Well-kept English cheeses or homely sweets to finish. Friendly, attentive service. *Credit* Access, Amex, Barclaycard, Diners   &

Lunch 12.30–2 *Dinner* 7–9
Closed Mon & October–March except by arrangement

Poynings
Map 7 B6 West Sussex
2 The Street
Near Brighton *BN4 7AQ*
Poynings (079 156) 346
French cooking

● **Set L** from £3·25
About £25 for two
Banquets 20/8

Au Petit Normand

It's best to book at this cheerful little restaurant, as the talented chef-patron from Normandy has built up a strong local following. His birthplace features strongly on the weekly changing menu in dishes like cassolette de moules normande, and you'll also find French provincial favourites like soupe de poissons, lobstor Thermidor and roast duck with pears. Simple sweets from the trolley. *Credit* Access, Amex, Barclaycard

Lunch Sun only 12.15–1.45 *Dinner* 7–9
Closed D Sun, Mon, 1 Jan, 25 & 26 Dec, Feb & 1 week Sept

Praa Sands
Map 2 A4 Cornwall
Near Penzance *TR20 9TX*
Germoe (073 676) 2325

Credit Access, Amex,
Barclaycard, Diners

Rooms 26
with bath/shower 13

Lesceave Cliff Hotel 62% Ⓜ £ D/E

Close to a sandy beach, this cheerful clifftop hotel is a popular choice for family holidays. Public rooms include a smart lounge with luxurious modern settees, the appealing Zambesi Bar and a comfortable sun terrace. Bedrooms (nine in an annexe) are light, airy and crisply contemporary, all with colour TV. Bathrooms are well fitted. *Amenities* garden, sea fishing, games room, children's play area, baby listening.

Room phone Some	*Confirm by* By arrang.	*Parking* Ample
Room TV Yes	*Last dinner* 9	*Banquets* 80/–

Prestbury
Map 10 B2 Cheshire
Near Macclesfield *SK10 4DQ*
Prestbury (0625) 829326
Proprietors Mr & Mrs Whiteside
& Mrs E. Grange
Credit Access, Amex,
Barclaycard, Diners

Rooms 6
with bath/shower 4

Bridge Hotel *(Inn)* Ⓜ £ E

Converted from a group of 17th-century cottages close to the river Bollin, this charming inn has a flagstoned entrance hall and a comfortable bar with pleasing modern decor. Well-equipped bedrooms have matching fabrics and good reproduction furniture plus tea-makers, radios and complimentary fruit. Smart carpeted bathrooms (some with showers only). Friendly staff. No dogs. *Amenities* garden, dancing (Fri, Sat). **Closed** 3 days Easter

Room phone Yes	*Confirm by* By arrang.	*Parking* Ample
Room TV Yes	*Last dinner* 9.30	*Banquets* 20/–

Prestbury
Map 10 B2 Cheshire
Near Macclesfield *SK10 4DQ*
Prestbury (0625) 829326
Proprietors Mr & Mrs Whiteside
& Mrs E. Grange
French cooking

● **Set L** £4·50
Set D £7·50, Sat £9·50
About £31 for two

Bridge Hotel Restaurant

Chef Michel Loyeau offers enjoyable, capably prepared French dishes in this spacious, modern restaurant. The à la carte offers a good choice, ranging from sole véronique and duckling bigarade to loin of lamb with herbs. Vegetables are skilfully handled and there's a large choice of sweets, including Grand Marnier soufflé. Simpler set menus feature grills and roasts.
Credit Access, Amex, Barclaycard, Diners

Lunch 12.30–2 *Dinner* 7–9.30
Closed Sun & 3 days Easter

Prestbury
Map 10 B2 Cheshire
Near Macclesfield *SK10 4DG*
Prestbury (0625) 829130
Proprietor Mr Otto Polyanszky

● **Set L** £4·95
About £31 for two
Banquets 25/10

Legh Arms & Black Boy Restaurant Ⓢ

The menu offers ample choice in ths cosy pub dining room: starters range from soups and tasty terrine to moules marinière and coquilles de volaille, while main courses include grills, six ways with sole, and our tender, nicely sauced duck à la bigarade. To finish, there's an impressive sweet trolley. Capable cooking is matched by smart, polite service.  *ABOVE AVERAGE.*
Credit Access, Amex, Barclaycard, Diners

Lunch 12.30–2, Sun 12.30–3 *Dinner* 7–10, Sat 7–10.30
Closed D 25 December

Preston
Map 10 A1 Lancashire
The Ring Way *PR1 3AU*
Preston (0772) 59411
Telex 677147
Manager Mr B. Edwards
Credit Access, Amex,
Barclaycard, Diners

Crest Hotel 63% £ D

This curved red-brick hotel stands in the centre of town opposite a multi-storey car park. Function rooms and a smart pub-style bar are at ground level, while the reception hall and an open-plan bar-lounge are on the first floor. Well-equipped bedrooms have attractive fitted units and neat tiled bathrooms. *Amenities* dancing (Fri & Sat fortnightly in winter) 24-hour laundry service.

Continued

Continued
Rooms 133
with bath/shower 133

Room phone Yes	*Confirm by* 6	*Parking* Ample
Room TV Some	*Last dinner* 9.45	*Banquets* 110/8

Puddington
Map 10 A2 Cheshire
Parkgate Road
South Wirral *L66 9PB*
051–339 3111
Proprietors Mr & Mrs M. Petranca
Credit Access, Amex,
Barclaycard, Diners

Craxton Wood Hotel 68% Ⓜ £E

Secluded in attractive wooded grounds, the Petrancas' rambling ivy-clad house combines traditional and modern features. There's a comfortable TV lounge for residents, and a bright cocktail bar-lounge with a terrace overlooking the trim lawns. Tastefully decorated and furnished bedrooms are light and spacious, bathrooms adequate. *Amenities* garden. **Closed** for accommodation Sun nights; also last 2 weeks Aug & 2 weeks Christmas &

Rooms 15
with bath/shower 12

Room phone Yes	*Confirm by* By arrang.	*Parking* Ample
Room TV Some	*Last dinner* 10	*Banquets* 24/–

Puddington
Map 10 A2 Cheshire
Parkgate Road
South Wirral *L66 9PB*
051–339 3111
Proprietors
Mr & Mrs M. Petranca
French cooking

About £32 for two

Craxton Wood Hotel Restaurant ♛ Ⓢ

Four interconnecting rooms with luxurious purple and pink decor make up the elegant *mise en scène* for a classical French menu that ranges from snails and shrimp pancakes to poached salmon, poussin with apples and Calvados, and herby loin of lamb. There's a deft touch with sauces, vegetables are fresh, crisp and perfectly seasoned, and the sweet trolley is irresistible. ♟ *SUPERIOR*. *Credit* Access, Amex, Barclaycard, Diners &

Lunch 12.30–2 *Dinner* 7.30–10
Closed Sun, Bank Holidays, last 2 weeks August & 2 weeks Christmas

---

Pulborough
Map 5 E3 West Sussex
Church Place *RH20 1AD*
Pulborough (079 82) 2486

Proprietors Searancke family
Credit Access, Amex,
Barclaycard, Diners

Chequers Hotel 56% Ⓜ £F

For 22 years the Searancke family have run this friendly, informal little hotel opposite the church. Drinks are served in the sitting rooms, one of which has a TV; plants, magazines and chintzy furniture create the cosy air of a private house. Cheerful, well-kept bedrooms have pleasing traditional decor, and larger ones have relaxing chairs. Adequate carpeted bathrooms.
Amenities garden.

Rooms 9
with bath/shower 7

Room phone No	*Confirm by* 6	*Parking* Limited
Room TV No	*Last dinner* 8.30	

Pulborough
Map 5 E3 West Sussex
Codmore Hill *RH20 1BG*
Pulborough (079 82) 2819
Proprietors Ann & René Kaiser

● Set L £3·15
About £25 for two
Banquets 24/12

Stane Street Hollow Restaurant ♧ Ⓢ

René Kaiser and his wife have created a truly Swiss atmosphere in their charming country restaurant. Cowbells hang on the walls, and the menu has a distinctly national flavour, too, with rich dishes such as lamb's sweetbreads poached in cream and wine, veal escalopes and stuffed chicken wrapped in bacon. Garden-fresh vegetables are lightly cooked, and sweets like home-made cheesecake are tempting.

Lunch 12.30–1.15 *Dinner* 7.15–9.15 **Closed** L Sat & Tues, all Sun & Mon, 2 weeks spring, 2 weeks autumn & 2 weeks from 24 December

---

Reading
Map 5 D2 Berkshire
Basingstoke Road *R62 0SL*
Reading (0734) 85485
Telex 849160
Manager Mr A. J. Gatt
Credit Access, Amex,
Barclaycard, Diners

Post House Hotel 59% £D

Built around a central quadrangle with a garden, this modern, red-brick hotel on the A33 is equally popular with businessmen and families. Pleasantly decorated public areas include an open-plan lounge and a cocktail bar, plus the Great Western Bar designed to look like a railway carriage. Simple bedrooms have fitted units and well-equipped bathrooms.
Amenities garden, outdoor swimming pool, buttery (7.30am–10.30pm). &

Rooms 143
with bath/shower 143

Room phone Yes	*Confirm by* 6	*Parking* Ample
Room TV Yes	*Last dinner* 10.30	*Banquets* 110/5

Redbourn

Map 5 E2 Hertfordshire
Hemel Hempstead Road
AL3 7AF
Redbourn (058 285) 2105

Credit Access, Amex,
Barclaycard, Diners

Rooms 57
with bath/shower 57

Aubrey Park Hotel   56%   £E

Standing in six acres of grounds close to junction 9 of the M1, this popular
hotel is used a great deal for conferences. The main block contains the bright,
airy foyer and a cocktail bar-cum-lounge, while a covered walkway leads
through the well-kept garden to the motel-style bedrooms, which have fitted
furniture and fully tiled bathrooms with showers.
Amenities garden, outdoor swimming pool, tennis, games room.

Room phone Yes	*Confirm by* 6	*Parking* Ample
Room TV Yes	*Last dinner* 10	*Banquets* 70/–

Richmond

Map 5 E2 Surrey
15 Hill Rise *TW10 6UQ*
01–940 3002

Italian cooking

About £28 for two
Banquets 40/–

Gino's

You can read the daily papers in the bar while waiting for your meal at this
smart, tiled restaurant. The Italian menu offers tempting dishes like squid and
shrimp salad, fettuccine and spaghetti with clams, as well as house
specialities such as tastily stuffed veal escalopes. Cooking is careful and
robust, and there are simple sweets and excellent coffee to finish.
Credit Access, Amex, Barclaycard, Diners

Lunch 12.30–2.30, Sun 12.30–3 *Dinner* 7–11.30, Fri & Sat 7–12
Closed Mon & Bank Holidays

Richmond

Map 5 E2 Surrey
11 Kew Green *TW9 3AA*
01–940 3987
Proprietor P. Carvosso

● **Set L & Set D** £7·50
About £25 for two
Banquets 30/10

Jasper's Bun in the Oven

This charming restaurant is made up of a series of neat little rooms, where
you'll find a good selection of interesting dishes, ranging from grilled Dover
sole and salmon trout with hollandaise sauce to spinach-stuffed crêpes (a
tasty speciality) and roast duckling with apple purée. Vegetables are carefully
handled, and there are varied sweets.
Credit Access, Amex, Barclaycard, Diners

Lunch 12.30–3, Sat 12.30–2.30 *Dinner* 7–11
Closed Sun & Bank Holidays

Richmond

Map 5 E2 Surrey
110 Kew Road *TW9 2PQ*
01–948 4343
Manager Joseph Yeung
Chinese cooking

● **Set L** £8 **Set D** £9
About £29 for two
Banquets 60/10

Kew Rendezvous

This popular Chinese restaurant on three floors has won considerable local
approval, both for its cool, modern decor and for its enjoyable Peking
cuisine. You'll find lots of familiar favourites on the extensive menu, from
sesame shrimp toasts to sole in wine sauce and very good aromatic crispy
duck. There's also a variety of set meals and banquet meals.
Credit Access, Amex, Barclaycard, Diners

Lunch 12–2.30 *Dinner* 6–11.30
Closed Bank Holidays

Richmond

Map 5 E2 Surrey
Lichfield Terrace
Sheen Road *TW9 1AS*
01–940 5236

● **Set L** £9
About £40 for two

Lichfield's

Stephen Bull attracts a large following to his civilised restaurant with a menu
full of imaginative dishes. Richly-sauced chicken-liver mousse makes a fine
starter, and among main courses there are delights like medallions of veal
with Stilton or chicken breast stuffed with sweetbreads served with a superb
tarragon sauce. Beautifully prepared vegetables have a menu to themselves.
Book for dinner. ♉ *SUPERIOR. Credit* Access, Amex

Lunch 12.15–2 *Dinner* 7.15–10.45 **Closed** L Sat, all Sun, Mon, 25
December, 1 week Whitsun, 2 weeks September & 1 week Christmas

Richmond

Mrs Beeton

See under London Economy Evening Meals

Richmond

Map 5 E2 Surrey
Richmond Hill *TW10 6RP*
01–940 7471
Telex 928556

Petersham Hotel 62% Ⓜ £D

Overlooking the Thames from Richmond Hill, this early 19th-century building provides comfortable accommodation in stately high-ceilinged bedrooms as well as neat modern ones in the wing. All have small colour TVs and plain, up-to-date bathrooms. The foyer has a wide staircase and some fine original frescoes, and there are two plush lounges and a bar to relax in. No dogs. *Amenities* garden.

| *Rooms* 60 | *Room phone* Yes | *Confirm by* 6 | *Parking* Ample |
| *with bath/shower* 60 | *Room TV* Yes | *Last dinner* 9.15 | *Banquets* 130/8 |

Richmond

Map 5 E2 Surrey
6 Church Walk *TW9 1SN*
01–940 6264
Proprietors
Roger & Mary Kingsley
English cooking

● **Set D** £7·85
About £22 for two
Banquets 50/12

Refectory Ⓢ

Mary Kingsley is a dedicated enthusiastic cook who specialises in imaginative English food, and this homely, friendly restaurant is a pleasant setting in which to enjoy a delicious set dinner. You could begin with crab mousse, followed by spiced lamb with apricots (served with a crunchy mixture of brown rice and nuts) and finish with a nice sweet such as praline syllabub. Light lunches only. Booking essential.

Lunch 12–2.15 *Dinner* 7.30–8.30
Closed D Sun, Tues & Wed, all Mon & Bank Holidays

Ripon

Map 15 C6 North Yorkshire
Park Street *HG4 2BU*
Ripon (0765) 2172
Telex 57780
Manager Mrs G. M. Curry
Credit Access, Amex,
Barclaycard

Ripon Spa Hotel 65% Ⓜ £E

A pleasant, family-run hotel, where old-fashioned service includes efficient porterage and the turning down of beds. Impressive wooden columns and large windows are features of public rooms like the two comfortable lounges, and there are also two bars. Spacious bedrooms are prettily decorated and traditionally furnished; bathrooms, both old and new, are very well maintained. *Amenities* garden, dancing (last Sat in month).

| *Rooms* 41 | *Room phone* Yes | *Confirm by* 6 | *Parking* Ample |
| *with bath/shower* 41 | *Room TV* Yes | *Last dinner* 9 | *Banquets* 200/15 |

Ripponden

Map 10 C1 West Yorkshire
Millfold *HX6 4DF*
Halifax (0422) 823722
Proprietor Mr Ian Beaumont

● **Set D** £12
About £31 for two

Over the Bridge ♛ Ⓢ

It's wise to book at Ian Beaumont's comfortable, attractive restaurant standing near an old stone footbridge. The four-course set dinners show most capable presentation and an artistic eye: you might start with smoked salmon roulade or délice de Gruyère and then, after an excellent soup, enjoy sautéed kidneys, juicy noisettes of lamb or seasonal game. Nice vegetables, delectable desserts and good fresh coffee. *Credit* Amex

Dinner only 7.30–9.30
Closed Sun & Bank Holidays

Rochford

Map 7 C4 Essex
1 South Street *SS4 1BL*
Southend (0702) 544393

● **Set L & Set D** £6·60
About £29 for two

Renouf's Ⓢ

Derek Renouf has an intense love of cooking, and his tireless enthusiasm remains undiminished. His long, varied menu features mainly French-inspired dishes from suprême of chicken with Calvados to bass in white wine sauce, and duckling à la presse is a speciality. Raw materials are the best available, and presentation (including the superb sweet trolley) shows enviable artistry. *Credit* Access, Amex, Barclaycard, Diners

Lunch 12.30–2.30 *Dinner* 7.30–10
Closed L Sat, all Sun, Mon, Good Friday, 26 Dec, 1–21 Jan & 13–21 June

Romaldkirk

Map 15 B5 Co. Durham
Near Barnard Castle *DL12 9EB*
Teesdale (0833) 50213
Proprietors David & Jill Jackson
Credit Access, Amex,
Barclaycard, Diners
Closed 25 December

Rose & Crown Hotel *(Inn)* Ⓜ £F

David and Jill Jackson continue to make improvements to their delightful village inn, a popular spot with country-loving tourists. There are two cosy bars, and a comfortable residents' lounge with TV. Existing bedrooms, many of them featuring attractive stone walls and original woodwork, have good carpets and traditional furnishings. Five new rooms, with fitted darkwood units and bathrooms en suite, are being built.

Continued

Rooms 11	*Room phone* No	*Confirm by* By arrang.	*Parking* Ample
with bath/shower 2	*Room TV* Some	*Last dinner* 10	*Banquets* 50/–

Romsey
Map 4 C3 Hampshire
21 Palmerston Street *SO5 8GF*
Romsey (0794) 517353

Old Manor House ♦ ♛ Ⓢ

A delightful little beamed restaurant, where the food is enjoyably different and the service attentive and friendly. Mauro Bregoli's frequently changing menu features home-prepared Italian and French specialities such as fettuccine or smoked fillet of beef, along with plaice and sole, pleasantly sauced meat dishes and game in season. Excellent home-made ice creams are among the tempting desserts. *Credit* Access, Amex, Barclaycard, Diners

● **Set L** £4·95
About £30 for two

Lunch 12–2.30 *Dinner* 7–10.30
Closed D Sun, all Mon & 25 & 26 December

Romsey
Map 4 C3 Hampshire
Market Place *SO5 8ZJ*
Romsey (0794) 512431

Credit Access, Amex,
Barclaycard, Diners

White Horse Hotel   59%   £ D

Bedrooms in this old coaching inn vary from quaint, traditionally furnished rooms in the original part of the building to practical modern ones in the recent extension; all have bright, up-to-date bathrooms. Converted stables provide three family rooms. Handsomest of the public areas is the beamed Tudor lounge, with solid period furniture; there is also a cheerful bar. *Amenities* garden.

Rooms 33	*Room phone* Yes	*Confirm by* 6	*Parking* Ample
with bath/shower 33	*Room TV* Yes	*Last dinner* 9.30	*Banquets* 40/6

Rosedale Abbey
Map 15 C5 North Yorkshire
Near Pickering *YO18 8RA*
Lastingham (075 15) 312
Tenants
Mr & Mrs J. T. Horsley-Scott
Credit Diners

Milburn Arms Hotel   56%   Ⓜ   £ F

This small, friendly hotel with good views of the North Yorkshire moors makes a useful base for exploring the area. The rustic beamed bar of the old stone building has bench seating, and the spacious residents' lounge offers quiet, cosy comfort. Bedrooms have simple freestanding furniture and good carpets; one also has its own private bathroom. No children under 12. *Amenities* garden, badminton.

Rooms 8	*Room phone* No	*Confirm by* 9	*Parking* Ample
with bath/shower 1	*Room TV* No	*Last dinner* 8.30	*Banquets* 45/2

Ross-on-Wye
Map 4 B1 Hereford & Worcester
HR9 6LL
Harewood End (098 987) 211
Proprietor Mr Andrew Sime

Credit Access, Amex,
Barclaycard, Diners

Pengethley Hotel   60%   Ⓜ   £ D

Lovely grounds surround this converted Georgian house just off the A49. An oak-panelled reception hall leads to the homely cocktail bar, and there's also a cosy TV lounge. Bedrooms vary and may be large with antique furniture or compact and modern, with bathrooms to match. There's also up-graded accommodation in the elegant Coach House and simpler Stable Rooms. *Amenities* garden, outdoor swimming pool, 24-hour laundry service.   ♿

Rooms 22	*Room phone* Yes	*Confirm by* 6	*Parking* Ample
with bath/shower 16	*Room TV* Yes	*Last dinner* 9	*Banquets* 96/–

Rosthwaite
Map 13 C5 Cumbria
Borrowdale
Near Keswick *CA12 5XB*
Borrowdale (059 684) 280
Manager Mr M. Lopez
Closed end October–week
before Easter

Scafell Hotel   59%   £ E

This pleasant whitewashed hotel, which enjoys a tranquil position in the heart of beautiful Borrowdale, is a popular base for holiday-makers. Residents have a traditionally furnished lounge and separate sun lounge, and there's a choice of two bars. Well-maintained bedrooms have whitewood units; five refurbished rooms are especially attractive, with luxurious carpeting and excellent new bathrooms. *Amenities* garden, game fishing.   ♿

Rooms 21	*Room phone* No	*Confirm by* 6	*Parking* Ample
with bath/shower 14	*Room TV* No	*Last dinner* 10	*Banquets* 70/–

Rotherham

Map 11 D2 South Yorkshire
Moorgate Road *S60 2BG*
Rotherham (0709) 64902
Telex 547810

Credit Access, Amex,
Barclaycard, Diners

Carlton Park Hotel   75%   £D

Situated just over two miles from junction 33 of the M1, this sparkling new red-brick hotel is an oasis of comfort and elegance. Marble-tiled floors, potted palms and luxurious jade-green wallpaper give the public areas an exotic atmosphere; the superb Pavilion Bar features an ornate central fountain, and there's also a cocktail bar in the open-plan lounge. Well-equipped bedrooms have huge comfortable beds, bamboo furniture and deep carpets, as well as mini-bars and tea-makers. Smart, gleaming bathrooms are fitted with excellent coloured suites.
Amenities garden, sauna, dinner dance (Fri, Sat), discothèque (Sat), solarium, in-house movies, helipad.

Rooms 64
with bath/shower 64

Room phone Yes	*Confirm by* 6	*Parking* Ample
Room TV Yes	*Last dinner* 10	

Rothley

Map 11 D3 Leicestershire
Westfield Lane *LE7 7LG*
Leicester (0533) 374141

Credit Access, Amex,
Barclaycard, Diners
Closed 25 & 26 December

Rothley Court   64%   £D/E

This 13th-century stone manor house bears its age well, and great care has been taken with restoration over the years. It has a lovely oak-panelled lounge and a mellow bar with fine views of the peaceful gardens. Many bedrooms in the main building have been attractively refurbished with contemporary fittings and coordinated colour schemes; those in the stable block are cheerfully modern in style. *Amenities* garden.

Rooms 36
with bath/shower 31

Room phone Yes	*Confirm by* By arrang.	*Parking* Ample
Room TV Yes	*Last dinner* 9.30	*Banquets* 96/–

Rothley

Map 11 D3 Leicestershire
Westfield Lane *LE7 7LG*
Leicester (0533) 374141

Rothley Court Restaurant   ♛ Ⓢ

This attractively laid out dining room makes an elegant setting for a menu of skilfully prepared classical dishes. Our fillets of sole stuffed with salmon and served with two beautifully composed sauces was very enjoyable; other items range from duckling à l'orange to grills and flambéed specialities. Vegetables are outstanding in variety and presentation. Efficient service.
Credit Access, Amex, Barclaycard, Diners

● **Set L** £5·50 **Set D** £6·75
About £30 for two

Lunch 12.30–2 *Dinner* 7–9.30, Sat 7–10
Closed L Sat, D Sun & all Bank Holidays

Rowsley

Map 10 C2 Derbyshire
Near Matlock *DE4 2EB*
Darley Dale (062 983) 3518

Manager Mr G. M. Gillson
Credit Access, Amex,
Barclaycard, Diners

Peacock Hotel   65%   £E

The peacock theme runs through the public areas of this welcoming 17th-century hotel. A lovely ceramic bird and some fine antiques feature in the entrance hall; the lounge has a brass incense burner in the shape of a peacock, and there's a modern mural in the bar. Best bedrooms (the 14 in the main house) have comfortable, traditional furnishings and neat, tiled bathrooms. *Amenities* garden, game fishing.

Rooms 20
with bath/shower 15

Room phone Yes	*Confirm by* 6	*Parking* Ample
Room TV Yes	*Last dinner* 9	*Banquets* 20/–

Rugby

Map 11 D4 Warwickshire
Sheep Street *CV21 3BX*
Rugby (0788) 4585

Credit Access, Amex,
Barclaycard, Diners

Three Horse Shoes Hotel   57%   £C/D

A well-preserved and charming old coaching inn standing in the centre of town. It has a comfortable reception-bar area which doubles as the residents' lounge when the upstairs lounge is in use as a function room. Neat, cheerful bedrooms, all with tea-makers, hairdryers and trouser presses, offer a host of thoughtful little extras, and the spotless, compact bathrooms are fully equipped. *Amenities* dancing (Sat except August).

Rooms 32
with bath/shower 32

Room phone Yes	*Confirm by* By arrang.	*Parking* Difficult
Room TV Yes	*Last dinner* 9.45	*Banquets* 30/–

Runcorn
Map 10 B2 Cheshire
Wood Lane, Beechwood *WA7 3HA*
Runcorn (0928) 714000
Telex 627426
Credit Access, Amex,
Barclaycard, Diners
Closed 4 days Christmas

Rooms 128
with bath/shower 128

Crest Hotel   60%   £ D

Designed with the businessman in mind, this modern red-brick hotel has
extensive function facilities. There's also a spacious foyer with plenty of room
to relax in and a choice of two up-to-date bars. Bedrooms are uniform in
style with fitted furniture, tea-makers, trouser presses and compact bathrooms. The hotel would benefit from refurbishment.
Amenities garden, dancing (Sat), pool table, 24-hour laundry service.

Room phone Yes	*Confirm by* 6	*Parking* Ample
Room TV Yes	*Last dinner* 9.45	*Banquets* 400/–

Rushlake Green
Map 7 B6 East Sussex
Near Heathfield *TN21 9RG*
Rushlake Green (0435) 830553

Proprietors Mr & Mrs P. Dunn
Rooms 12
with bath/shower 12
Room phone Yes
Room TV Yes
Confirm by 4
Last dinner 9
Parking Ample
Banquets 16/12
Closed 22 December–16 January

Priory Hotel   73%   Ⓜ   £ D/E

It would be hard to find a more
peacefully situated hotel than this
delightful 15th-century former
monastery, approached by a long
drive that winds through unspoilt
downland. The heavily beamed interior has been lovingly restored by
the welcoming Dunns, and the
massive woodwork of the bedrooms is offset by white walls and
tasteful summery fabrics that match
right down to the hot-water-bottle
covers! Bathrooms are modern and
spotless. The two lounges have huge fireplaces and plenty of inviting
armchairs from which to admire the green countryside outside the quaint
mullioned windows. No children under nine. *Amenities* garden, game
fishing, croquet, rough shooting, clay pigeon shooting.

Rushlake Green
Map 7 B6 East Sussex
Near Heathfield *TN21 9RG*
Rushlake Green (0435) 830553
Proprietors Mr & Mrs P. Dunn

● **Set L** £6·85 **Set D** £11·45
About £32 for two

Priory Hotel Restaurant   ♛ Ⓢ

Heavy beams and mullioned windows give the dining rooms of this country
house restaurant a mini-baronial air. Jane Dunn's young staff make good
use of local produce in ably cooked, well-sauced dishes. The mushrooms
with cream, gruyère and garlic are an outstanding starter, and mouthwatering desserts include a superb chocolate marquise. Excellent English
cheeses, too. No pipes or cigars. 🍷 *OUTSTANDING*.

Lunch 12.30–1.30 *Dinner* 7.30–9
Closed 22 December–16 January

Rusper
Map 5 E3 West Sussex
Near Horsham *RH12 4PX*
Rusper (029 384) 571

Rooms 10
with bath/shower 8
Room phone Yes
Room TV Yes
Confirm by By arrang.
Last dinner 10
Parking Ample
Banquets 60/6

Credit Access, Amex,
Barclaycard, Diners

Ghyll Manor   70%   £ E

Small conferences and seminars
play an important part in the life of
this beautifully restored manor
house, parts of which date back to
Elizabethan times. The lounge has
some fine linenfold panelling and
comfortable velvet-covered chesterfields, and there's also a neat little
bar which opens on to the courtyard. Bedrooms vary greatly in style
from one grand room with a four-
poster and an onyx bathroom to a
simpler, more modern one on the
ground floor, but all are thoughtfully designed and equipped with fridges,
trouser presses and clock-radios. No dogs.
Amenities garden, outdoor swimming pool, tennis, riding.

Rusper

Map 5 E3 West Sussex
High Street
Near Horsham *RH12 4PX*
Rusper (029 384) 571

● **Set L** Sun only £9·50
About £34 for two
Banquets 60/6

Ghyll Manor Restaurant

Chef Regner's comprehensive menu includes some adventurous choices in the restaurant of this delightful hotel. The range includes pâté en croûte flavoured with juniper berries, tenderloin of pork wrapped in cabbage leaves and salt pork, and sea bass with champagne sauce. Good ingredients are competently prepared and everything is most attractively presented.
Credit Access, Amex, Barclaycard, Diners

Lunch 12–2.30 *Dinner* 7–10
CLosed L Mon & D Sun

Rye

Map 7 C6 East Sussex
Mermaid Street *TN31 7EY*
Rye (079 73) 3065
Telex 957141
Proprietor Mr M. K. Gregory
Credit Amex, Barclaycard,
Diners

Rooms 30
with bath/shower 21

Mermaid Inn   60%      £ E

Re-built in 1420, and once notorious as a smugglers' haunt, this marvellous hostelry still boasts medieval timbers, leaded windows and narrow, twisting corridors. Two snug sitting rooms are full of carefully restored carvings and murals, and there's a giant inglenook in the bar. Lovely old beamed bedrooms are fully in keeping with the rest of the place, while bathrooms are plain but adequate. No children under five. No dogs.

Room phone Some	*Confirm by* 6	*Parking* Limited
Room TV No	*Last dinner* 9.15	*Banquets* 90/25

Saddleworth

Map 10 C2 Greater Manchester
Huddersfield Road *OL16 3TJ*
Saddleworth (045 77) 2659

About £32 for two
Banquets 75/15

Moorcock

An attractive stone-built restaurant high up in the moors between New Hey and Denshaw. Interesting menus, with the emphasis on market-fresh ingredients, offer a choice of well-prepared dishes which could include creamy asparagus soup, poached salmon or rack of lamb served with crunchy vegetables. Hors d'œuvre, sweets and cheeses are displayed on eye-catching trolleys. *Credit* Access, Amex, Barclaycard, Diners

Lunch 12–2 *Dinner* 7–9.30
Closed L Sat & D Sun

St Albans

Map 5 E2 Hertfordshire
17 Heritage Close *AL3 4EB*
St Albans (0727) 66067
Proprietor Mr M. Charalambous
Greek cooking
About £27 for two

Aspelia

Beautifully arranged fresh flowers adorn this smart Greek restaurant in a shopping precinct, and the menu features robust, carefully prepared authentic dishes like avgolemono, afelia and moussaka.
Credit Access, Amex, Barclaycard, Diners *Lunch* 12–3 *Dinner* 6.30–11
Closed Sun & Bank Holidays

St Albans

Map 5 E2 Hertfordshire
Watford Road *AL2 3DS*
St Albans (0727) 54252
Telex 893834

Credit Access, Amex,
Barclaycard, Diners

Rooms 57
with bath/shower 57

Noke Hotel   63%   £ D

Helpful, friendly staff make it a pleasure to stay at this much-extended Victorian house, not far from junction 6 of the M1. Excellent conference facilities are popular with businessmen, as are the bright bedrooms with neat built-in furniture and warm, spacious bathrooms. Public rooms include a fine panelled entrance hall, two lively bars and a cosy little cocktail bar.
Amenities garden.

Room phone Yes	*Confirm by* 6	*Parking* Ample
Room TV Yes	*Last dinner* 9.45	*Banquets* 90/–

St Albans

Map 5 E2 Hertfordshire
Fishpool Street *AL3 4RY*
St Albans (0727) 64444
Manager Mr Martin Richardson
Credit Access, Amex,
Barclaycard
Closed Christmas night

Rooms 22
with bath/shower 14

St Michael's Manor Hotel   63%   £ D

Although only a short walk from the city centre, this charming building–a manor house of many styles–has an air of great peace and tranquillity. Fine panelling, antiques and chandeliers grace the elegant public rooms, and there are fresh flowers everywhere. Neat bedrooms in restful pastel shades have matching modern units, and bathrooms are adequate. No children under six. No dogs. *Amenities* garden,

Room phone Most	*Confirm by* By arrang.	*Parking* Ample
Room TV Yes	*Last dinner* 9.30	*Banquets* 80/6

St Annes-on-Sea

Map 10 A1 Lancashire
South Promenade *FY8 1NP*
St Annes (0253) 720061
Proprietors Mrs. E. A. Corbett
& Mr M. Corbett
Credit Access, Amex,
Barclaycard, Diners

Rooms 60
with bath/shower 60

Chadwick Hotel   58%   Ⓜ   £ E/F

Families return year after year to the Corbetts' friendly hotel, whose public rooms include an attractive sun lounge overlooking the sea and a pleasant little bar. Bright, spacious bedrooms have simple whitewood furniture and well-fitted modern bathrooms. *Amenities* garden, dancing (3 Sats monthly in winter, Thurs in summer), children's playroom, solarium, baby listening, games room, table tennis, laundry room, exercise room.   ♿

Room phone Yes	*Confirm by* By arrang.	*Parking* Ample
Room TV Yes	*Last dinner* 8	*Banquets* 140/–

St Austell

Map 2 B3 Cornwall
Church Street *PL25 4AT*
St Austell (0726) 2100

Credit Access, Amex,
Barclaycard
Closed 25 & 26 December

Rooms 21
with bath/shower 4

White Hart Hotel *(Inn)*   £ F

Dating back in parts to the 16th century, this solidly built inn stands in the town centre right opposite the parish church. Attractively refurbished public rooms include a reception-lounge and two relaxing bars with plush modern seating. Compact bedrooms are furnished in a variety of styles and offer simple comforts; some have a foldaway shower unit. Bathrooms are neat and well cared for.

Room phone No	*Confirm by* By arrang.	*Parking* Difficult
Room TV Yes	*Last dinner* 8.30	*Banquets* 40/–

St Helens

Map 5 D4 Isle of Wight
Upper Green Road *PO33 1UQ*
Bembridge (098 387) 2014

Proprietor Caroline Brooks

● **Set D** from £6
About £20 for two
Banquets 20/–

Hayloft   ♧ Ⓢ

Booking is essential at this lively, bistro-style restaurant, which is just the place to enjoy local produce prepared in imaginative ways. Blackboards list the day's choice of fresh-tasting dishes, which may range from seafood such as lobster, crab or plaice to meat specialities like lamb cooked with rosemary and haricot beans. There's also a good selection of simple sweets

Dinner only 7.30–9.15
Closed Sun (except August) & October–May

St Ives

Map 6 B2 Cambridgeshire
Ramsey Road *PE17 4RB*
St Ives (0480) 63122
Proprietors Peter & Maggie Scott
Credit Access, Amex,
Barclaycard, Diners
Closed 25 & 26 December

Rooms 14
with bath/shower 9

Slepe Hall Hotel   65%   Ⓜ   £ E

Follow the signs from the A1123 to the recreation centre to find this converted Victorian mansion, which is impeccably maintained by the Scotts. There's ample seating in the cosy, tastefully decorated lounge, while the bar is dominated by a striking wrought-iron gazebo. Pretty bedrooms have freestanding furniture and well-coordinated colour schemes. Bathrooms have simple modern fittings. *Amenities* garden.

Room phone Yes	*Confirm by* By arrang.	*Parking* Ample
Room TV Yes	*Last dinner* 10	*Banquets* 200/10

St Ives

Map 2 A3 Cornwall
Burthallan Lane *TR26 3AA*
Penzance (0736) 796199
Proprietors Mr & Mrs Kilby
Credit Access, Amex,
Barclaycard, Diners
Closed mid October–Easter

Rooms 17
with bath/shower 10

Garrack Hotel   59%   Ⓜ   £ E

Standing in two acres of attractive gardens, this friendly family-run hotel enjoys magnificent views across the bay. Public rooms include a comfortable lounge with TV and a cosy bar. Neat, tidy bedrooms vary from traditional in the main building to bright and modern in the extension, which has a large sun terrace. Bathrooms are well equipped. A garden cottage is popular for family letting. *Amenities* garden, baby listening.

Room phone No	*Confirm by* By arrang.	*Parking* Ample
Room TV Some	*Last dinner* 8.30	

St Ives

Map 2 A3 Cornwall
Carthew Terrace *TR26 1EB*
Penzance (0736) 795707
Credit Access, Amex,
Barclaycard
Closed October–March except
by arrangement

Trecarrell Hotel   57%   Ⓜ   £ E

Just a few minutes' walk from the centre of town, this well-maintained little holiday hotel overlooking St Ives Bay has a friendly, welcoming feel. Public rooms like the lounge and bar are delightfully homely, and neat, cheerfully decorated bedrooms have practical modern units, clock radios and duvets. Carpeted shower and bathrooms have up-to-date fittings. No dogs. *Amenities* garden.

Continued

Continued
Rooms 17
with bath/shower 8   *Room phone* No   *Confirm by* By arrang.   *Parking* Limited
   Room TV No   *Last dinner* 7.45

St Ives

Map 2 A3 Cornwall
TR26 2DE
Penzance (0736) 795254
Telex 45128

Rooms 83
with bath/shower 67
Room phone Yes
Room TV Yes
Confirm by By arrang.
Last dinner 9
Parking Ample
Banquets 350/2

Credit Access, Amex,
Barclaycard, Diners

Tregenna Castle Hotel   74%   £E

Set in attractive grounds, this ivy-covered miniature castle offers high standards of service and housekeeping, comfortable accommodation and a host of leisure activities. Traditional lounges include a delightfully chintzy one with picture windows overlooking the grounds, and there's a well-appointed cocktail bar. Spacious bedrooms are furnished in tasteful style; bathrooms (some with original marble fittings) are large and luxurious. *Amenities* garden, outdoor swimming pool, tennis, squash, golf course, dancing (Thurs, Sat in summer), riding, putting, sailing, table tennis, badminton, cinema (in summer), clay-pigeon shooting, croquet, pool table, children's playground, 24-hour laundry service.   &

St Mary's

Map 2 A2 Isles of Scilly
(Cornwall)
Church Street *TR21 0JR*
Scillonia (0720) 22316
Proprietors Mumford family

Closed 15 October–mid March

Rooms 31
with bath/shower 22

Hotel Godolphin   60%   Ⓜ   £E

A luxuriant sub-tropical garden with palm trees is one of the attractions of this comfortable, family-run hotel. Well-maintained public areas include three lounges with a mixture of traditional and modern furniture and a simple cocktail bar. Pleasant bedrooms have freestanding units and functional bathrooms. Inclusive terms only in high season. No dogs. *Amenities* garden, games room, laundry room.

Room phone No   *Confirm by* By arrang.   *Parking* Ample
Room TV Yes   *Last dinner* 8.15

St Mawes

Map 2 B4 Cornwall
Tredenham Road *TR2 5AN*
St Mawes (0326) 270771
Proprietors Powell family
Credit Access, Amex,
Barclaycard, Diners
Closed late October–late March

Rooms 22
with bath/shower 22

Idle Rocks Hotel   62%   Ⓜ   £E

Right on the water's edge this white-painted, blue-shuttered hotel enjoys splendid views across the harbour to the sea beyond. The cheerful reception area leads to a comfortable lounge and plush bar, both with French windows opening on to a sun terrace. Simply decorated bedrooms (six in an annexe) have practical furnishings and neat carpeted bathrooms. No children under six. Inclusive terms only.

Room phone No   *Confirm by* 6   *Parking* Limited
Room TV No   *Last dinner* 8.30   *Banquets* 100/60

St Mawes

Map 2 B4 Cornwall
Near Truro *TR2 5DT*
St Mawes (0326) 270233
Tenant
Mrs Campbell Marshall
Credit Access, Amex,
Diners

Rooms 20
with bath/shower 13

Rising Sun Inn   60%   Ⓜ   £E

This convivial little hotel is lovingly maintained and furnished with a delightful mixture of curios and antiques. The lounge is homely and comfortable, and there's a snug cocktail bar. Small cottage bedrooms are simply fitted; those in the annexe right on the water's edge have the best sea views. There are also two superior double bedrooms in a house just up the hill. No children under 12.

Room phone No   *Confirm by* 6   *Parking* Ample
Room TV No   *Last dinner* 8.45

St Mawes

Map 2 B4 Cornwall
Near Truro *TR2 5DT*
St Mawes (0326) 270233
Tenant Mrs Campbell Marshall

About £27 for two

Rising Sun Inn Restaurant

Dinner menus in this bright, neat hotel restaurant offer a good choice of capably cooked dishes, from richly sauced meat to excellent local seafood and carefully prepared vegetables. Light meals only at lunchtime.
Credit Access, Amex, Diners *Dinner only* 7.30–8.45
Closed New Year & Christmas ● **Set D** from £6·50

St Mawes

Map 2 B4 Cornwall
TR2 5DR
St Mawes (0326) 270544
Proprietor
Mrs E. Y. Farquharson Oliver
Rooms 21
with bath/shower 21
Room phone Some
Room TV No
Confirm by 6
Last dinner 8.45
Parking Ample

Closed 1 November–1 April

Credit Barclaycard

Hotel Tresanton 79% Ⓜ £ B/C

Secluded among terraced gardens overlooking the sea, this immaculately kept hotel is a stylish model of civilised elegance. Reception and three bedrooms are in the original house, while other rooms are in two buildings reached along an attractive flowery pathway. The lounge is particularly appealing, with deep armchairs and the odd antique, and the tastefully decorated bar has its own sun terrace. Traditionally furnished bedrooms have pretty pastel fabrics and lots of little extras like books, sewing kits, tissues and torches. Each room has its own well-fitted, spotless bathroom, but it may be situated immediately across the corridor. No children under 12.
Amenities garden, sailing, water skiing.

St Mawes

Map 2 B4 Cornwall
TR2 5DR
St Mawes (0326) 270544
Manager Miss M. McAndrew

● **Set D** £10
About £34 for two

Hotel Tresanton Restaurant ♔ Ⓢ

An elegantly simple restaurant, with gleaming white paint and masses of greenery. The long-serving chef features plenty of local seafood on his menus, which may include fresh lobster bisque, prawn and crab cocktails and vol-au-vents filled with scallops. There are meat dishes too, served with enjoyable sauces and excellent vegetables. Good simple desserts. Friendly and efficient service. *Credit* Barclaycard

Lunch 1–1.45 *Dinner* 7.30–8.45
Closed 1 November–1 April

St Michael's on Wyre

Map 10 A1 Lancashire
Near Preston *PR3 0UB*
St Michael's (099 58) 267

Proprietor Mrs M. A. Fielding
Credit Access
Closed 24 Dec–1 Feb

Rivermede Country House Hotel 66% Ⓜ £ D/E

The river winds past this converted Victorian vicarage, which is now a delightful little hotel with the intimate atmosphere of a private house. It has a wonderfully peaceful drawing room complete with a small library, and there is an elegant bar. Stylish bedrooms are individually decorated. All have well-equipped carpeted bathrooms.
Amenities garden, outdoor swimming pool, coarse fishing.

Rooms 4	*Room phone* Yes	*Confirm by* By arrang.	*Parking* Ample
with bath/shower 4	*Room TV* Yes	*Last dinner* 9	*Banquets* 50/20

St Michael's on Wyre

Map 10 A1 Lancashire
Near Preston *PR3 0UB*
St Michael's (099 58) 267
Proprietor Mrs M. A. Fielding

● **Set D** £10·50
About £27 for two

Rivermede Country House Hotel Restaurant ♔ Ⓢ

The choicest ingredients are used to prepare enjoyable, satisfying fare in this elegant hotel dining room, and guests can choose from the set three-course menu or the regularly changing carte. Dishes like ballotine of lamb or pork schnitzel with mushroom sauce are served with reliably cooked vegetables, and there are some tempting sweets such as banana and hazelnut meringue.
Credit Access

Dinner only 7–9
Closed Tues, Bank Holidays & 24 December–1 February

Salcombe

Map 3 D3 Devon
Cliff Road *TQ8 8JH*
Salcombe (054 884) 2251
Telex 45185
Proprietors Mr & Mrs T. P. Andrew
& Mr W. J. Northcott
Rooms 51
with bath/shower 51
Room phone Yes
Room TV Yes
Confirm by By arrang.
Last dinner 9.15
Parking Ample
Banquets 120/2
Closed December–February
Credit Access, Amex,
Barclaycard, Diners

Marine Hotel 75% Ⓜ £C

Run in friendly fashion by the same family for 20 years, this comfortable hotel has lovely views of the estuary from its cliff-side position. The reception leads into a smart open-plan lounge-bar area with stylish contemporary furniture and attractive colour schemes. Spacious bedrooms are fitted out in simple modern style with good-quality built-in units and nicely co-ordinated carpets and curtains. (Those in the front have balconies overlooking the sea.) Well-appointed bathrooms are half-tiled. No children under seven. No dogs.
Amenities garden, indoor & outdoor swimming pools, sea fishing, dancing (Sat), solarium, hairdressing, games room, slipway, sauna.

Salcombe

Map 3 D3 Devon
Sandhills Road
North Sands *TQ8 8JR*
Salcombe (054 884) 2233

Credit Access, Barclaycard
Closed early October–Easter

St Elmo Hotel 59% Ⓜ £D/E

Tim and Janet Tremellen offer a friendly welcome at their well-kept Edwardian house, which stands in attractive terraced gardens overlooking the sea. Public rooms like the homely lounge and bar are invitingly relaxing, and there's a separate TV room. Sunny bedrooms (some with balconies and most with pleasant views) have simple decor and up-to-date units; modern bathrooms. *Amenities* garden, croquet, games room.

Rooms 24	*Room phone* No	*Confirm by* By arrang.	*Parking* Ample
with bath/shower 21	*Room TV* No	*Last dinner* 8.30	

Salcombe

Map 3 D3 Devon
South Sands *TQ8 8LL*
Salcombe (054 884) 2791

Credit Access, Amex,
Barclaycard, Diners

South Sands Hotel 60% Ⓜ £D/E

Recent redecoration has added to the appeal of this friendly holiday hotel, which enjoys a splendid position by a sandy beach. Comfortable public rooms command lovely views of the bay, and the sun terrace is a popular spot for tea or an evening drink. Compact, simply equipped bedrooms are neat and bright, and modern bathrooms are well fitted.
Amenities sea fishing, board sailing, hotel motor boats, in-house movies.

Rooms 20	*Room phone* No	*Confirm by* 6	*Parking* Limited
with bath/shower 20	*Room TV* Yes	*Last dinner* 9.30	*Banquets* 60/–

Salcombe

Map 3 D3 Devon
South Sands *TQ8 8LJ*
Salcombe (054 884) 3466
Proprietors Edwards family

Rooms 40
with bath/shower 40
Room phone Yes
Room TV Yes
Confirm by By arrang.
Last dinner 9.30
Parking Ample
Banquets 100/–
Closed 1 December–1 March

Credit Access, Amex,
Barclaycard, Diners

Tides Reach Hotel 71% Ⓜ £D/E

Narrow lanes wind down to the Edwards family's holiday hotel set beside a beautiful sandy cove. Refurbishment in a highly individual style has transformed the public areas and bedrooms, and the leisure facilities have been extended. Off the colourful reception area are a leafy sun lounge, the roomy main lounge and an inviting cocktail bar. Most of the comfortable bedrooms have eye-catching colour schemes, excellent furnishings and spectacular views. Modern bathrooms are compact. Inclusive terms in high season. No children under seven. *Amenities* garden, sauna, indoor swimming pool, squash, sea fishing, games room, board sailing, health & beauty centre, solarium, sailing, canoes, hairdressing.

Salisbury

Map 4 C3 Wiltshire
90 Crane Street *SP1 2QD*
Salisbury (0722) 3471

● **Set D** £9·25
About £25 for two
Banquets 20/4

Crane's

Tom Geary takes care to ensure that guests are content in his simple, cosy little restaurant. He offers a tempting choice of French-inspired dishes like scallops with puréed leeks or breast of chicken Vallée d'Auge, followed by delicious sweets such as chocolate mousse or home-made ice cream. Don't miss the excellent New Orleans fish chowder. *ABOVE AVERAGE.*
Credit Access, Amex, Barclaycard, Diners

Lunch 12–2, Sat 12–1.30 *Dinner* 6.30–10 **Closed** Sun, also D Mon in winter, Bank Holidays except 25 December & 1st 2 weeks October

Salisbury

Map 4 C3 Wiltshire
14 Ox Row, Market Place
SP1 1EU
Salisbury (0722) 28923
French cooking
Proprietors Edward &
Geraldine Moss
● **Set L** from £5 **Set D** £8·50
About £29 for two
Banquets 20/10

Provençal

Choose from the daily table d'hôte or from a short carte at this simple restaurant overlooking the busy market place. Starters may include a well-flavoured onion soup, and you can go on to moules marinière or perhaps a grilled spring chicken with olives or crab claws with garlic butter. Dark, rich venison casserole is a delicious seasonal speciality. No children under seven.
Credit Amex, Barclaycard, Diners

Lunch 12–1.30 *Dinner* 6–10.30
Closed L Sat, all Sun and Bank Holidays

Salisbury

Map 4 C3 Wiltshire
St John Street *SP1 2SD*
Salisbury (0722) 27476

Credit Access, Amex,
Barclaycard, Diners

Rooms 72
with bath/shower 56

White Hart Hotel   58%   £ D

A fine pillared portico surmounted by a stone hart dominates the facade of this city-centre hotel. Inside, there's a warm, roomy reception-lounge area with a model of Stonehenge, and two bars, one of which overlooks a pleasant little courtyard. Bedrooms, identically equipped with built-in furniture, radios, TVs and tea-makers, range from singles to family size. Those at the front are double-glazed. Adequate bathrooms.

| *Room phone* Yes | *Confirm by* 6 | *Parking* Ample |
| *Room TV* Yes | *Last dinner* 9.45 | *Banquets* 70/10 |

Samlesbury

Map 10 B1 Lancashire
Preston New Road *PR5 0UJ*
Samlesbury (077 477) 671
Telex 629706

Credit Access, Amex,
Barclaycard, Diners

Rooms 66
with bath/shower 66

Tickled Trout   58%   £ D/E

Standing just off junction 31 of the M6 close to the river Ribble, this two-storey hotel is much favoured by businessmen. There are several conference rooms, and other public areas include a flagstoned reception hall and a comfortable bar-lounge. Well-designed bedrooms with ample shelf and writing space have tea-makers, trouser presses and sparkling tiled bath-rooms. *Amenities* game fishing, dancing (Sat), discothèque (Fri).

| *Room phone* Yes | *Confirm by* 7 | *Parking* Ample |
| *Room TV* Yes | *Last dinner* 10.15 | *Banquets* 140/– |

Sandbach Heath

Map 10 B2 Cheshire
CW11 0ST
Sandbach (093 67) 4141
Telex 666971
Manager Mr A. I. Nardi
Credit Access, Barclaycard

Rooms 23
with bath/shower 23

Chimney House Hotel   62%   £ E/F

Nestling in its own secluded grounds not far from the M6 (junction 17) this former rectory has a mock-Tudor facade and a pleasantly modernised interior. The open-plan public areas have simple decor and deep, comfort-able seating. Well-carpeted bedrooms are equipped with practical contemporary furniture (fitted or freestanding), armchairs and colour TV, and all have colourful, luxurious bathrooms. No dogs. *Amenities* garden.

| *Room phone* Yes | *Confirm by* By arrang. | *Parking* Ample |
| *Room TV* Yes | *Last dinner* 9.45 | |

Sanderstead

Map 7 B5 Surrey
Addington Road *CR2 8TA*
01–657 8811
Telex 945003
Proprietor Mr B. A. Sanderson
Credit Access, Amex,
Barclaycard, Diners

Selsdon Park Hotel   68% Ⓜ   £ C

Run by the same family for over 50 years. this much-extended Tudor mansion standing in 200 acres of grounds provides a high degree of comfort in its gracious public rooms and large bedrooms with well-fitted modern bathrooms. Excellent conference facilities. *Amenities* garden, sauna, outdoor swimming pool, tennis, golf, dancing (Sat), children's playground, helipad, croquet, transport to station, solarium, riding, billiards.

Continued

Continued
Rooms 160
with bath/shower 160 | Room phone Yes
Room TV Yes | *Confirm by* By arrang.
Last dinner 9 | *Parking* Ample
Banquets 220/10

Sandown
Map 5 D4 Isle of Wight
Melville Street *PO36 9DH*
Sandown (0983) 403794

Proprietor Mr Alan Smith

Closed October–April

Melville Hall Hotel   55%   Ⓜ    £ E

Just a few minutes' walk from the beach and shops, this extended and modernised Victorian house is a friendly, relaxing holiday hotel. Public areas like the lounge and bar are bright and roomy, while simply furnished bedrooms offer adequate comforts and plenty of storage space. Bathrooms are compact. No children under three. No dogs. *Amenities* garden, outdoor swimming pool, dancing (Tues, Sat in summer), putting.

Rooms 38
with bath/shower 16 | Room phone No
Room TV No | *Confirm by* By arrang.
Last dinner 8.30 | *Parking* Limited
Banquets 180/70

Saunton
Map 2 C1 Devon
Near Braunton *EX33 1LQ*
Croyde (0271) 890212
Proprietors Brend family

Credit Access, Amex,
Barclaycard, Diners

Saunton Sands Hotel   63%   Ⓜ   £ C/D

This '30s hotel overlooking miles of sandy beach is a marvellous place for holidays. There are superb leisure facilities, various bars and lounges with fine views and nicely furnished bedrooms with colourful bathrooms. No dogs. *Amenities* garden, sauna, indoor swimming pool, tennis, squash, dancing (5 nights weekly), solarium, putting, games room, surfing, cinema (Sun), in-house movies, table tennis, billiards, hairdressing.

Rooms 112
with bath/shower 112 | Room phone Yes
Room TV Yes | *Confirm by* By arrang.
Last dinner 9 | *Parking* Ample
Banquets 300/–

Scarborough
Map 15 D6 North Yorkshire
The Esplanade *YO11 2AG*
Scarborough (0723) 73491
Telex 52580
Manager Mr M. J. P. Mort
Credit Access, Amex,
Barclaycard, Diners

Crown Hotel   66%   Ⓜ   £ C/D

Built in Regency times, this imposing hotel overlooking South Bay has been restored to something like its original grandeur. The foyer, with its tall columns and moulded ceilings, is particularly ornate, and there are two attractive bars. Most bedrooms retain their original proportions although furnishings are modern in style. Compact bathrooms. No dogs. *Amenities* garden, dancing (Sat Oct–Jan), solarium, hairdressing, billiards, table tennis.   &

Rooms 80
with bath/shower 80 | Room phone Yes
Room TV Yes | *Confirm by* By arrang.
Last dinner 8.45 | *Parking* Limited
Banquets 210/–

Scarborough
Map 15 D6 North Yorkshire
Sea Cliff Road *YO11 2XX*
Scarborough (0723) 74374

Credit Access
Closed January & February

Holbeck Hall Hotel   66%   Ⓜ   £ D

Perched high on a cliff, this mock-Tudor hotel with its own path to the beach has superb views over South Bay. The splendidly ornate entrance hall with its magnificent fireplace leads to an elegant lounge opening on to a conservatory; there are also two smart modern bars. The best bedrooms are at the front, but all are attractively furnished in traditional style and have compact, carpeted bathrooms. *Amenities* garden.

Rooms 31
with bath/shower 31 | Room phone Yes
Room TV Yes | *Confirm by* By arrang.
Last dinner 8.45 | *Parking* Ample
Banquets 120/–

Scarborough
Map 15 D6 North Yorkshire
33 Queen Street *YO11 1HQ*
Scarborough (0723) 63616
Proprietor
Gian Luigi Arecco
Italian cooking

Lanterna Ristorante   

Everything is cooked to order at this simply furnished restaurant with brown and red decor. And it's certainly worth waiting for, as Gian Luigi Arecco produces thoroughly enjoyable Italian dishes with excellent sauces. You could start with a hearty plate of spaghetti alla carbonara, and go on to a tasty main course based on steak, veal, scampi or chicken. Coffee is served with delicious sweet fritters. *Credit* Barclaycard

About £28 for two | *Dinner only* 7–9.30
Closed Sun, Mon & Bank Holidays

Scarborough

Map 15 D6 North Yorkshire
St Nicholas Cliff *YO11 2ES*
Scarborough (0723) 68161

Credit Barclaycard

Palm Court Hotel 62% Ⓜ £ D

A charming atmosphere pervades this family-run hotel. Warmly decorated public rooms include a delightful foyer-lounge and cocktail bar, and a ballroom overlooking the pool. Bedrooms of varying size and decor are colourful and thoughtfully fitted. Neat, compact bathrooms. No dogs.
Amenities sauna, indoor swimming pool, dinner dance (Sat, also Wed & Fri Easter–September), coffee shop (Mon–Sat 9–5), in-house movies.

Rooms 60	*Room phone* Yes	*Confirm by* By arrang.	*Parking* Limited
with bath/shower 60	*Room TV* Yes	*Last dinner* 9	*Banquets* 160/–

Scarborough

Map 15 D6 North Yorkshire
St Nicholas Street *YO11 2HE*
Scarborough (0723) 64333

Manager Mr Michael Court
Rooms 137
with bath/shower 137
Room phone Yes
Room TV Yes
Confirm by By arrang.
Last dinner 11.30
Parking Difficult
Banquets 400/–

Credit Access, Amex,
Barclaycard, Diners

Royal Hotel 75% £ E/F

The 19th-century grandeur of this impressive seafront hotel has been carefully preserved, and it caters handsomely for both holiday and conference visitors. A grand staircase leads to the galleried upper floors with their classical pillars, and there are two smartly comfortable bars (one decorated with theatrical costume designs) as well as a large, relaxing lounge. Bedrooms range from the sumptuous Churchill suite to simpler rooms with white-painted units and candlewick bedspreads. Bathrooms are fully tiled and well equipped. Guide dogs only. *Amenities* sauna, dinner dance (twice weekly October–May, thrice weekly June–September), table tennis, billiards, coffee shop (9.30am–11pm, 9.30am–5.30pm in winter).

Stars in this Guide stand for the quality of the cooking only – our overriding criterion, irrespective of price, luxury or service.

Scarborough

Map 15 D6 North Yorkshire
St Nicholas Cliff *YO11 2EU*
Scarborough (0723) 64101
Telex 52351
Proprietor Mrs J. Craig-Tyler
Credit Access, Amex,
Barclaycard, Diners

Hotel St Nicholas 60% Ⓜ £ D/E

Fine views across the harbour are a feature of this most pleasant and welcoming Victorian hotel. A smart modern bar, several lounges and a splendid ballroom are among the stylish public rooms, and the cheerfully decorated, well-fitted bedrooms include some suites and family rooms. *Amenities* dancing (Sat in winter, 3 nights weekly in summer), discothèque (Fri in winter, 3 nights weekly in summer), games room. &

Rooms 166	*Room phone* Yes	*Confirm by* By arrang.	*Parking* Ample
with bath/shower 102	*Room TV* Yes	*Last dinner* 9	*Banquets* 600/10

Isles of Scilly

See under St Mary's and Tresco

Seavington St Mary

Map 4 A4 Somerset
Near Ilminster *TA19 0QE*
South Petherton (0460) 40502
Credit Access, Amex,
Barclaycard, Diners
Closed 1 January &
25 & 26 December

Pheasant Hotel 61% Ⓜ £ E

A charming traditional atmosphere still lingers in this tastefully converted 17th-century farmhouse in a quiet village. Public areas include a quaint lounge bar with a huge original fireplace, while bedrooms in the main house and in nearby buildings are compact and simply decorated with practical modern furniture, tea-makers and radios. Spotlessly clean bathrooms. No dogs. *Amenities* garden. &

Rooms 10	*Room phone* Yes	*Confirm by* By arrang.	*Parking* Ample
with bath/shower 10	*Room TV* Yes	*Last dinner* 9.30	

Seavington St Mary
Map 4 A4 Somerset
Near Ilminster *TQ190QE*
South Petherton (0460) 40502

Pheasant Hotel Restaurant

Friendly local ladies provide pleasant service in this charming beamed restaurant. The menu of reliably prepared dishes ranges from delicious tenderloin of pork normande and popular grills to specialities like lasagne and bistecca pizzaiola from chef Paoloni's native Italy. Our creamy strawberry surprise was an outstanding choice from the superb sweet trolley.
🍷 *SUPERIOR. Credit* Access, Amex, Barclaycard, Diners

● **Set L** £5·70
About £27 for two

Lunch Sun only 12–2 *Dinner* 7.30–9.30
Closed D Sun to non-residents, 1 January & 25 & 26 December

Sedlescombe
Map 7 C6 East Sussex
The Green *TN330QA*
Sedlescombe (042 487) 253

Proprietors Mr & Mrs Lanaway
Credit Access, Amex, Diners
Closed January

Brickwall Hotel   55%   Ⓜ   £E

Mr and Mrs Lanaway's charming 16th-century beamed house is a perfect retreat for those seeking peace and tranquillity. Log fires blaze in the rustic bar, and there are two cosy lounges (one with TV). Older bedrooms in the main building are traditionally furnished, while those in the extension are more modern and compact. Bathrooms are spotlessly clean.
Amenities garden, outdoor swimming pool, putting, croquet.

Rooms 16
with bath/shower 10

Room phone No
Room TV No

Confirm by By arrang.
Last dinner 8.15

Parking Ample

Seend
Map 4 B3 Wiltshire
Near Melksham *SN126RY*
Seend (038 082) 534

Seend Bridge Farm

Jolly Mrs Podger runs this highly popular farmhouse restaurant, where you must book and order well in advance. She is an enthusiastic, if slightly unorthodox, cook, whose seasonal three-course set menu features wholesome traditional fare like home-made soup and steak and kidney pie alongside her versions of dishes such as beef Stroganoff and kidneys Turbigo. Unlicensed, so bring your own.

● **Set D** £4·95
About £11·50 for two
Banquets 30/20

Dinner only by arrangement
Closed Sun, Tues, 25 & 26 December & 1 week autumn

Selmeston
Map 7 B6 East Sussex
Church Farm
Near Lewes *BN266TL*
Ripe (032 183) 343
Proprietors Geoff & Mary Corin
About £26 for two

Corins

This beautiful old cottage makes a charming setting for Geoff Corin's enthusiastic cooking. Dishes like rich lovage soup and tasty sliced beef in creamy mustard sauce are typical of a varied, regularly changing set menu.
Credit Access, Amex, Barclaycard *Lunch* Sun at 1, Tues–Sat by arrangement only *Dinner* 7.30–11 **Closed** D Sun, all Mon & 25 December ● **Set D** £9

Sennen
Map 2 A4 Cornwall
Near Penzance *TR197BE*
Sennen (073 687) 408

Credit Access, Barclaycard
Closed November–February except Christmas

Tregiffian Hotel   57%   Ⓜ   £E

Homely comforts and excellent housekeeping are features of this sturdy old Cornish farmhouse, which enjoys a tranquil moorland position looking out towards Sennen Cove and the Atlantic. Public areas include three traditional lounges and an intimate bar with an impressive granite fireplace. The cosy bedrooms have mostly white-painted stone walls; neat bathrooms are up to date. No children under five. *Amenities* garden.

Rooms 8
with bath/shower 4

Room phone No
Room TV No

Confirm by By arrang.
Last dinner 8.30

Parking Ample

Shaftesbury
Map 4 B3 Dorset
The Commons *SP78JA*
Shaftesbury (0747) 2282

Credit Access, Amex,
Barclaycard, Diners

Grosvenor Hotel   60%   Ⓜ   £D/E

This handsome hotel of Georgian character has an attractive pillared portico. The most striking of the public rooms is the stately Chevy Chase lounge, which features a magnificent carved oak sideboard. There's also a pleasant cocktail bar and a cheerful TV lounge. Most of the bedrooms are simply decorated with modern units, the best having small sitting areas and chintzy soft furnishings. Neat bathrooms are well kept.

Rooms 48
with bath/shower 42

Room phone Yes
Room TV Yes

Confirm by 6
Last dinner 9

Parking Difficult
Banquets 110/10

Shaftesbury
Map 4 B3 Dorset
Royal Chase Roundabout *SP7 8DB*
Shaftesbury (0747) 3355

Proprietor Mr George F. Hunt
Credit Access, Amex,
Barclaycard, Diners

Rooms 20
with bath/shower 14

Royal Chase Hotel 55%  £ D

Situated on the edge of the town, this imposing Georgian house offers cheerful hospitality and comfortable accommodation. You can relax in the cosy lounge or enjoy a drink in the cottagy bar, with its fine old kitchen range. Most bedrooms have modern units and colourful soft furnishings, and all are provided with radios and tea-makers. Well-equipped bathrooms with showers. *Amenities* garden, pool table.

Room phone Yes *Confirm by* 6 *Parking* Ample
Room TV Yes *Last dinner* 9.30 *Banquets* 90/10

Shanklin
Map 5 D4 Isle of Wight
Park Road *PO33 6BB*
Shanklin (098 386) 3262

Manager Mr D. R. Beckett
Credit Access, Amex,
Barclaycard, Diners

Rooms 110
with bath/shower 99

Cliff Tops Hotel 61% £ E

Holiday-makers and conference delegates alike appreciate the extensive amenities of this aptly named hotel. Public rooms include two convivial bars and a vast modern lounge highlighted by marvellous sea views. Bedrooms have functional furniture and adequate bathrooms. *Amenities* garden, sauna, outdoor swimming pool, dancing (twice weekly May–Sept), solarium, hairdressing (May–Sept), nightclub (June–Sept), coffee shop (9am–6.30pm).

Room phone Yes *Confirm by* 7 *Parking* Ample
Room TV Yes *Last dinner* 8.45 *Banquets* 160/–

Shedfield
Map 5 D4 Hampshire
Sandy Lane
Near Southampton *SO32 HQ*
Wickham (0329) 833455
Telex 86272
Credit Access, Amex,
Barclaycard, Diners

Rooms 54
with bath/shower 54

Meon Valley Hotel, Golf & Country Club 56% £ D

In the middle of a golf course, this modern complex combines comfortable accommodation with a wide range of sporting activities and conference facilities. There are two spacious bars, a reception lounge, and bright, simply furnished bedrooms with compact bathrooms. *Amenities* garden, sauna, indoor swimming pool, tennis, squash, golf course, dinner & discothèque (Sat fortnightly), snooker, pool table, club room (9am–10.30pm).

Room phone Yes *Confirm by* By arrang. *Parking* Ample
Room TV Yes *Last dinner* 9.45 *Banquets* 140/–

Sheffield
Map 10 C2 South Yorkshire
Charter Square *S1 3EH*
Sheffield (0742) 20041
Telex 54312

Credit Access, Amex,
Barclaycard, Diners

Rooms 120
with bath/shower 101

Grosvenor House Hotel 65% £ C/D

Conveniently situated in the heart of the city, this towering modern hotel offers functional, up-to-date facilities. Well-maintained public rooms, including the cocktail bar and lounge, have attractive colour schemes, while neat bedrooms are equipped with practical fitted furniture and tea/coffee-makers. Bathrooms are fully tiled.
Amenities dancing (Sat), hairdressing, coffee shop (11am–11.45pm).

Room phone Yes *Confirm by* 6 *Parking* Ample
Room TV Yes *Last dinner* 9.45 *Banquets* 500/2

Sheffield
Map 10 C2 South Yorkshire
Manchester Road *S10 5DX*
Sheffield (0742) 686031
Telex 547293

Credit Access, Amex,
Barclaycard, Diners

Rooms 135
with bath/shower 135

Hallam Tower Post House Hotel 67% £ D

Perched high on a hill near the university, this modern hotel provides a high standard of accommodation. Attractive public areas are open-plan, and the decor of the Vulcan Bar pays homage to Sheffield's lifeblood, the steel industry. Neat bedrooms have white unit furniture, mini-bars, radios and smartly fitted bathrooms. There are two luxury suites.
Amenities garden, baby listening, 24-hour laundry service.

Room phone Yes *Confirm by* 6 *Parking* Ample
Room TV Yes *Last dinner* 9.45 *Banquets* 250/10

Shelton Lock
Map 10 C3 Derbyshire
Derby *DE2 9EE*
Derby (0332) 700112

About £29 for two

Golden Pheasant

A pleasant mock-Tudor restaurant outside Derby on the A514. Sidney Williams is a capable chef who offers classic favourites from duckling à l'orange to crème brûlée. Excellent sweets. *Credit* Access, Amex, Barclaycard, Diners *Lunch* 12–2 *Dinner* 7–10 **Closed** D Sun, all Bank Hols (except 25 & 26 Dec) & 1 week Spring Bank Hol ● **Set L** from £4·25 **Set D** from £6 &

Shepperton

Map 5 E2 Middlesex
Felix Lane *TW17 8NP*
Walton-on-Thames
(093 22) 41404
Telex 928170
Credit Access, Amex,
Barclaycard, Diners

Rooms 180			
with bath/shower 180			

Shepperton Moat House   60%   £D

Situated in 11 acres of grounds two miles from junction 1 of the M3, this three-storey hotel with extensive conference facilities caters mainly for businessmen. Public rooms include an open-plan reception-lounge and a bar. Comfortable bedrooms have fitted furniture, radio-alarms and compact modern bathrooms. *Amenities* garden, dancing (Sat), games room, helipad, landing stage, keep-fit equipment, target golf.

Room phone Yes	*Confirm by* By arrang.	*Parking* Ample
Room TV Yes	*Last dinner* 10	*Banquets* 300/4

Changes in data may occur in establishments after the Guide goes to press. Prices should be taken as indications rather than firm quotes.

Shepperton

Map 5 E2 Middlesex
Church Square *TW17 9JZ*
Walton on Thames
(093 22) 42972   Telex 8954665
Proprietor Mr D. J. S. Gordon
Credit Access, Amex,
Barclaycard, Diners

Rooms 45			
with bath/shower 45			

Warren Lodge Hotel *(Inn)* Ⓜ   £E

Situated almost on the banks of the Thames, this quaint whitewashed inn has a series of modern bedroom extensions at the back. Rooms are compact and simply fitted, some with mini-bars. Most bathrooms have showers only. For those wanting a drink there are two bars, one small and cosy in traditional style, the other a larger room overlooking the garden. No dogs. *Amenities* garden.

Room phone Yes	*Confirm by* By arrang.	*Parking* Ample
Room TV Yes	*Last dinner* 10	*Banquets* 18/–

Shepton Mallet

Map 4 B3 Somerset
29 Waterloo Road *BA4 5HH*
Shepton Mallet (0749) 3648
Proprietor Mr Bill Austin

About £27 for two

Blostin's

Booking is advisable at this smart, intimate little restaurant. Owner Bill Austin offers tempting dishes like beef bourguignonne or roast pheasant with port, and his cooking is tasty and enjoyable. 🍷*ABOVE AVERAGE. Credit* Access, Barclaycard *Dinner only* 7.30–9.30, Sat 7–10 **Closed** Sun, 1 January & 25 & 26 December ● **Set D** from £5·95 *Banquets* 28/22

Shepton Mallet

Map 4 B3 Somerset
Wells Road *BA4 5JD*
Shepton Mallet (0749) 2022
Proprietor Mr Brian Jordan

● **Set D** £17 & £22 for two
About £26 for two

Bowlish House Restaurant

Set menus offer excellent value for money at this welcoming *restaurant avec chambres* in a splendid Georgian mansion, where Brian Jordan and his enthusiastic staff are welcoming, informative hosts. Cauliflower and chive soup and pork and chicken liver pâté with apricot relish are excellent starters, and generously served main courses like our sautéed medallions of pork with a deliciously rich sauce are accompanied by an abundance of well-prepared vegetables. Victorian brown bread ice cream is a scrumptious way to round off a most enjoyable meal. Overnight accommodation is provided by four simple rooms with private bathrooms.
🍷*OUTSTANDING.*

Dinner only 7–10.30
Closed 4 days Christmas

Sherborne

Map 4 B3 Dorset
Horsecastles Lane *DT9 6BB*
Sherborne (093 581) 3191
Telex 46522

Credit Access, Amex,
Barclaycard, Diners

Rooms 60			
with bath/shower 60			

Post House Hotel   61%   £D

Just off the A30, this unpretentious modern hotel makes a convenient stopping point for travellers to the West Country. The pleasant open-plan reception, lounge and bar area has exposed brick walls and a pine ceiling, and there's a popular function room. Bedrooms are spacious and bright, with practical natural wood units; all have mini-bars and well-kept, businesslike bathrooms. *Amenities* garden.

Room phone Yes	*Confirm by* 6	*Parking* Ample
Room TV Yes	*Last dinner* 9.45	*Banquets* 80/–

Shifnal

Map 10 B4 Shropshire
Park Street
Near Telford *TF11 9BA*
Telford (0952) 460128
Telex 35438
Proprietors
Nicholas & Julie Hollinshead
Rooms 21
with bath/shower 21
Room phone Yes
Room TV Yes
Confirm by 6
Last dinner 9.45
Parking Ample
Banquets 130/–
Credit Access, Amex,
Barclaycard, Diners

Park House Hotel   75%   Ⓜ   £ E

Converted from two interconnected buildings (one 17th, the other 18th century), this luxurious hotel is like a private house, and it is run with thoughtfulness, care and dedication by Nicholas and Julie Hollinshead. Elegant, tastefully chosen antique furniture and fine moulded ceilings give the public rooms an air of grandeur, the restful lounge and split-level cocktail bar, in particular, are absolutely delightful. Bedrooms are also most attractively fitted, with traditional furniture and thoughtful extras ranging from bowls of fresh fruit to trouser presses. Excellent bathrooms are carpeted.
Amenities garden, sauna (May–Sept), outdoor swimming pool, dancing (Wed, also Sat Sept–May).

Shinfield

Map 5 D2 Berkshire
Church Lane
Near Reading *RG2 9BY*
Reading (0734) 883783

● **Set D** £13·75 incl. service
About £34 for two
Banquets 12/8

Milton Sandford   

Set in a charming country mansion, this restaurant is decorated in simple modern style. The fixed-price dinner menu changes regularly to make the best use of fresh ingredients: you might begin with garlicky scallop tarts or artichokes and almond soup followed by, say, marinated duck or stuffed saddle of lamb. To finish there's cheese, then some simple sweets.
🍷 *SUPERIOR. Credit* Access, Amex, Barclaycard, Diners

Dinner only 7–9
Closed Sun & 25 & 26 December

Any person using our name to obtain free hospitality is a fraud. Proprietors, please inform the police and us.

Shipdham

Map 6 C2 Norfolk
Near Thetford *IP25 7LX*
Dereham (0362) 820303

Rooms 5
with bath/shower 5
Room phone Yes
Room TV No
Confirm by By arrang.
Last dinner By arrang.
Parking Ample

Closed 19 December–
mid March (except
Thurs–Sun in January)

Shipdham Place   70%   Ⓜ   £ E

For anyone who wants to enjoy homely comforts in peaceful surroundings, Justin and Melanie de Blank's characterful converted 17th-century rectory is just the place. Guests can relax in the spacious, comfortable lounge, where Victorian pieces combine happily with modern furniture and paintings, or in the panelled drawing room (with TV), and when the weather's right the garden and terrace are pleasant spots for a drink. Bedrooms of various sizes, again with a mixture of traditional and more modern furnishings, are tastefully decorated and thoughtfully equipped. Excellent bathrooms have marble washbasin surrounds and sparkling white suites.
Amenities garden.

Shipdham

Map 6 C2 Norfolk
Near Thetford *IP25 7LX*
Dereham (0362) 820303

● **Set D** £11
About £30 for two

Shipdham Place Restaurant ★  

Melanie de Blank maintains such high standards in this attractively rustic restaurant that her occasional absence from the kitchen may cause disappointment. But the daily-changing five-course dinner menu is still a well-balanced, imaginative affair, with starters like fresh tomato and basil soup followed by a main course such as juicy lamb and veal brochette with a minty béarnaise sauce. Then comes a crisp salad dressed with walnut oil, the cheeseboard and finally a sweet such as chocolate mousse. Book.
Specialities salade tiède of veal kidney and French mushrooms, steamed beef fillet with baby vegetables and béarnaise sauce, chicken turbot with champagne sauce. *ABOVE AVERAGE.*

Dinner only at 8
Closed 19 December–mid March (except Thurs–Sun in January)

Shipton-u-Wychwood   Lamb Inn *(Inn)* Ⓜ   £E

Map 4 C1 Oxfordshire
High Street *OX7 6DQ*
Shipton-u-Wychwood
(0993) 830465
Credit Access, Amex,
Barclaycard, Diners
Closed 5 days after Christmas

Hugh and Lynne Wainwright continue to make improvements at their welcoming little Cotswold-stone inn, whose traditionally furnished bedrooms, each with its own compact bathroom, have been redecorated in pleasant pastel shades. Public rooms consist of a small reception area, a charming restaurant and a cosy beamed bar with sturdy old settles and a polished wooden floor. No children under 14. *Amenities* garden.

Rooms 4	*Room phone* No	*Confirm by* 6	*Parking* Ample
with bath/shower 4	*Room TV* No	*Last dinner* 9.15	*Banquets* 30/12

Shipton-u-Wychwood   Lamb Inn Restaurant   Ⓢ

Map 4 C1 Oxfordshire
High Street *OX7 6DQ*
Shipton-u-Wychwood
(0993) 830465

A delightfully rustic dining room, with exposed oak beams, an open stone fireplace and polished wooden tables, is the charming setting for Keith Baker's enjoyable cooking. The menu offers tasty, simply prepared treats such as cream of vegetable soup and braised duck with apples, with a few mouthwatering desserts like the moist, darkly rich chocolate gâteau.
Credit Access, Amex, Barclaycard, Diners

● **Set D** from £5·25
About £29 for two

Lunch Sun only 12.30–1.45 *Dinner* 7.30–9.15
Closed D Sun & 5 days after Christmas

Shipton-u-Wychwood   Shaven Crown Hotel *(Inn)* Ⓜ   £D

Map 4 C1 Oxfordshire
High Street *OX7 6BA*
Shipton-u-Wychwood
(0993) 830330
Proprietor Mr Norman Gee
Credit Access, Amex,
Barclaycard, Diners

Once a hospice for the monks of Bruern Abbey, this Cotswold-stone inn retains great charm. The beamed foyer-lounge has a huge stone fireplace, as does the attractive bar. Bedrooms, furnished in traditional style, offer modern amenities such as colour TV, radios, and tea/coffee-makers, and simple bathrooms are well kept. No dogs.
Amenities garden, bowling green.

Rooms 7	*Room phone* No	*Confirm by* 6	*Parking* Ample
with bath/shower 2	*Room TV* Yes	*Last dinner* 9.30	*Banquets* 60/20

Shorne   Inn on the Lake   61%   £D/E

Map 7 B5 Kent
Near Gravesend *DA12 3HB*
Shorne (047 482) 3333

Manager Mr R. J. Roger
Credit Access, Amex,
Barclaycard, Diners

Set just back from the A2, this low, brick-built motel stands in handsome grounds. Public rooms, which make the most of the lakeside setting, include a modern reception area and two stylish bars, and there are extensive banqueting and conference facilities. Bright, colourful bedrooms are spacious and well equipped, with neat, tiled bathrooms. No dogs.
Amenities garden, coarse fishing, dinner dance (Sat), lake swimming.

Rooms 78	*Room phone* Yes	*Confirm by* 6	*Parking* Ample
with bath/shower 78	*Room TV* Yes	*Last dinner* 9.30	*Banquets* 400/10

Shrawley

Map 4 B1 Hereford & Worcester
Near Worcester *WR6 6TB*
Worcester (0905) 620229
Proprietors Mr & Mrs Michael Bendall
Credit Access, Amex, Barclaycard, Diners

Rooms 7
with bath/shower 5

Lenchford Hotel *(Inn)* Ⓜ £E

A day's fishing or sailing, a quiet riverside walk or a drink in the pleasant lounge bar—the choice is yours at this charming inn on a peaceful stretch of the Severn beside the B4196. Comfortable accommodation is provided by bright, well-furnished bedrooms in a modern wing; some of them have balconies, and most have excellent carpeted bathrooms.
Amenities garden, outdoor swimming pool, coarse fishing, sailing.

Room phone Yes   *Confirm by* By arrang.   *Parking* Ample
Room TV Yes   *Last dinner* 9.30

Shrewsbury

Map 10 A3 Shropshire
Wyle Cop *SY1 1UY*
Shrewsbury (0743) 53107
Telex 35648

Credit Access, Amex, Barclaycard, Diners

Rooms 60
with bath/shower 60

Lion Hotel   61% £D

Traces of the 15th-century origins are still visible in this delightful city-centre inn patronised by De Quincey, Disraeli and Dickens. As well as an elegant Adam-style ballroom, there are two traditional bars and two lounge areas, one with a fine stone fireplace. Attractive bedrooms, refurbished to a high standard, have well-equipped modern bathrooms.
Amenities 24-hour laundry service, baby listening.

Room phone Yes   *Confirm by* 6   *Parking* Limited
Room TV Yes   *Last dinner* 9.30   *Banquets* 180/15

Shrewsbury

Map 10 A3 Shropshire
23 Abbey Foregate *SY2 6AE*
Shrewsbury (0743) 56119
Proprietors Greenhow family

About £31 for two

Penny Farthing Ⓢ

This smart little oak-panelled restaurant in the shadow of the abbey offers a daily-changing selection of interesting dishes capably prepared by Chris Greenhow. Starters like onion and sherry soup or mushrooms baked in cream and garlic could precede lamb Shrewsbury or generously served fillets of sole with prawns and a delicate white wine sauce. Good vegetables and sweets, too. *Credit* Access, Amex, Diners

Lunch by arrangement only *Dinner* 7–9.30, Sat 7–10
Closed Sun, Mon, Bank Holidays, 2 weeks February & 2 weeks June

---

Shrewsbury

Map 10 A3 Shropshire
Butcher Row *SY1 1UQ*
Shrewsbury (0743) 52461
Telex 35438

Credit Access, Amex, Barclaycard, Diners

Rooms 64
with bath/shower 47

Prince Rupert Hotel   57% Ⓜ £E

The Morris-Joneses have undertaken some discreet refurbishment in this atmospheric 15th-century building, while preserving its original character. It has a comfortably furnished bar dominated by a huge tapestry and a really peaceful lounge. Winding corridors lead to the cheerful bedrooms, most of which have fitted units. Bathrooms are well equipped. There's a large parking area nearby. *Amenities* games room.

Room phone Yes   *Confirm by* By arrang.   *Parking* Ample
Room TV Yes   *Last dinner* 10.15   *Banquets* 45/20

Shurdington

Map 4 B1 Gloucestershire
Near Cheltenham *GL51 5UG*
Cheltenham (0242) 862352
Telex 437216

Rooms 12
with bath/shower 12
Room phone Yes
Room TV Yes
Confirm by 6
Last dinner 9.30
Parking Ample
Banquets 22/6
Closed 1 week from 28 December
Credit Access, Amex, Barclaycard, Diners

Greenway Hotel   72% Ⓜ £C

Tony and Maryan Elliott's hard work and artistic flair have turned this 16th-century manor house into a charming, comfortable and peaceful hotel, whose attractions are enhanced by splendid views to the Cotswolds. In the spacious entrance hall and lounge overlooking the gardens there are open fireplaces, paintings and antiques, which create a homely, traditional atmosphere. Bedrooms on three floors are individually decorated in beautifully coordinated colours, and most of them have their own little sitting areas. Well-equipped bathrooms are carpeted and partly tiled. Friendly helpful staff. No children under seven. No dogs.
Amenities garden, croquet.

Shurdington

Map 4 B1 Gloucestershire
Near Cheltenham *GL51 5UG*
Cheltenham (0242) 862352

French cooking

● **Set L** £7·50 **Set D** £11·50
About £31 for two

Greenway Hotel Restaurant ♛ Ⓢ

Fixed-price menus are the order of the day at this elegant restaurant and at lunch time the choice is supplemented by a buffet—cold in summer, hot in winter. From crab en cocotte and deep-fried mushrooms to creamily sauced veal escalope and a lovely light chocolate mousse, cooking is capable although standards vary. Excellent friendly service.
Credit Access, Amex, Barclaycard, Diners   ♿

Lunch 12.30–2 *Dinner* 7.30–9.30
Closed L Sat, D Sun, L Bank Holiday Mons & 1 week from 28 December

---

Sidmouth

Map 3 E2 Devon
The Esplanade *EX10 8RX*
Sidmouth (039 55) 2555

Proprietor Mr B. E. Fitzgerald

Belmont Hotel   61%   Ⓜ   £ D

This pleasant Victorian hotel stands in its own trim-lawned grounds just back from the sea. Lovely sea views are features of the light, airy public rooms, which are most inviting, with their comfortable chairs, and attractive moulded ceilings. Upstairs, besides a little TV room, are the well-kept, quietly decorated bedrooms; some have balconies, all have adequately equipped bathrooms. No children under two. *Amenities* garden. ♿

Rooms 50	*Room phone* Yes	*Confirm by* By arrang.	*Parking* Ample
with bath/shower 50	*Room TV* Yes	*Last dinner* 8.30	*Banquets* 150/–

Sidmouth

Map 3 E2 Devon
Station Road *EX10 8NU*
Sidmouth (039 55) 2403

Proprietors Mr & Mrs Doddrell
Credit Access, Amex,
Barclaycard, Diners

Fortfield Hotel   60%   Ⓜ   £ D

There are lovely views of the sea from the sun terrace of this attractive red-brick hotel, and a relaxed atmosphere pervades the airy public rooms, which boast fine oak panelling and some interesting antiques. Comfortable, centrally heated bedrooms range in style from old-fashioned to modern; all have radios and tea-makers. Bathrooms are well equipped.
Amenities garden, solarium, putting, games room. ♿

Rooms 60	*Room phone* No	*Confirm by* By arrang.	*Parking* Ample
with bath/shower 32	*Room TV* Some	*Last dinner* 8.30	*Banquets* 140/50

Sidmouth

Map 3 E2 Devon
Peak Hill *EX10 8RY*
Sidmouth (039 55) 2651

Credit Access, Amex,
Barclaycard, Diners

Victoria Hotel   67%   £ C/D

General refurbishment has enlivened this classic Edwardian hotel, whose public rooms range from the elegant, spacious lounge and peaceful writing room to the cheerfully modern bars. Well-maintained bedrooms offer good standards of comfort. Willing, courteous service. *Amenities* garden, sauna, indoor & outdoor swimming pools, tennis, dancing (Sat), mini-golf, in-house movies, games room, hairdressing, solarium. ♿

Rooms 62	*Room phone* Yes	*Confirm by* 6	*Parking* Ample
with bath/shower 62	*Room TV* Yes	*Last dinner* 9	*Banquets* 150/–

Silchester

Map 5 D3 Hampshire
Near Reading, Berks *RG7 2PN*
Silchester (0734) 700421
Proprietor Zelma Myers
Credit Access, Amex,
Barclaycard, Diners
Closed 2 weeks Aug & Christmas

Romans Hotel   67%   Ⓜ   £ D/E

An attractive country house, designed early this century by Lutyens and standing peacefully in its own well-kept grounds. Fine antiques and elegant furniture grace the oak-panelled lounge and intimate cocktail bar, and individually decorated bedrooms in the main building have the same traditional charm. Rooms in the annexe are modern, with smart fitted units.
Amenities garden, outdoor swimming pool, tennis, putting. ♿

Rooms 24	*Room phone* Some	*Confirm by* 10	*Parking* Ample
with bath/shower 24	*Room TV* No	*Last dinner* 8.45	*Banquets* 60/–

Silchester

Map 5 D3 Hampshire
Nr Reading, Berks *RG7 2PN*
Silchester (0734) 700421
Proprietor Zelma Myers

Romans Hotel Restaurant ♛ Ⓢ

Talented young chef Shelley May keeps the customers happy in this pleasant dining room with his imaginative, daily-changing set menus. Following starters such as herrings soused in cider or tasty Russian croquettes, you might find bœuf à la bourguignonne, roast duckling with brandy and apricot sauce or jugged hare. Carefully prepared vegetables, too,

Continued

and some delicious desserts. *Credit* Access, Amex, Barclaycard, Diners

● **Set L** £7 **Set D** £9, Sat £11
About £25 for two

Lunch 12.30–1.15 *Dinner* 7.30–8.45, Sat 7.30–9
Closed L Sat, D Sun, Bank Holidays, 2 weeks August & Christmas

---

Simonsbath
Map 3 D1 Somerset
Near Minehead *TA24 7SH*
Exford (064 383) 259

Credit Access, Amex,
Barclaycard, Diners

Rooms 9
with bath/shower 6

Simonsbath House Hotel   68%   Ⓜ   £C

There are fine views over the river Barle to the hills beyond from this whitewashed stone building on Exmoor. It has a snug little bar and a spacious lounge with panelling and chesterfields combining to create a relaxed atmosphere. Attractive, individually decorated bedrooms have sturdy darkwood furniture, and bathrooms are fully modernised. No children under ten. No dogs. *Amenities* garden, squash, games room.

Room phone No	*Confirm by* 6.30	*Parking* Ample
Room TV Yes	*Last dinner* 9.30	

Simonsbath
Map 3 D1 Somerset
Near Minehead *TA24 7SH*
Exford (064 383) 259

Simonsbath House Hotel Restaurant    Ⓢ

Mrs Brown offers a varied three-course, fixed-price menu each day in this prettily decorated hotel dining room. She uses good-quality ingredients for dishes like roast duckling with honey and mead or Dover sole meunière and takes particular care with vegetables, which are often imaginatively prepared. Sweets may include ginger syllabub or rhubarb crumble.
Credit Access, Amex, Barclaycard, Diners

● **Set L** £7 **Set D** £10·50
About £29 for two

Lunch Sun only 12.30–2 *Dinner* 7.30–9.30, Sun 7.30–8.30

Sindlesham
Map 5 D2 Berkshire
Mill Lane
Near Wokingham *RG11 5DF*
Reading (0734) 666551

● **Set L** £9·75 **Set D** £12·75
About £42 for two
Banquets 75/–

Sindlesham Mill Restaurant   ♔ Ⓢ

Historic Sindlesham Mill is now a complex which includes this handsome restaurant with an interesting French-inspired menu. Cooking is generally excellent, and we much enjoyed smooth pâté en croûte and fricassee of turbot and lobster, served with a delicate chervil-flavoured sauce and lovely crunchy vegetables. Immaculate table settings and friendly, helpful service are additional attractions. *Credit* Access, Amex, Barclaycard, Diners   

Lunch 12–2, Sun 11.45–2 *Dinner* 7–11.30
Closed L Sat, D Sun & 1 January

Six Mile Bottom
Map 6 B3 Cambridgeshire
Near Newmarket, Suffolk
CB8 0UQ
Six Mile Bottom (063 870) 234
Proprietor Ian Bryant
Rooms 12
with bath/shower 12
Room phone Yes
Room TV Yes
Confirm by 6
Last dinner 9
Parking Ample
Banquets 50/–

Credit Access, Amex,
Barclaycard, Diners

Swynford Paddocks   76%   Ⓜ   £C/D

In 1813, this gabled white-painted house was the scene of Byron's affair with his half-sister Augusta Leigh, but these days it's known as a serene and comfortable hotel surrounded by a mature 40-acre stud. The elegant entrance hall filled with fine antiques is dominated by a magnificent carved oak staircase, and there's also a lovely drawing room with views over the garden, plus a cheerful bar. Bedrooms are impressively large, with immaculate individual colour schemes and excellent modern furniture. Bathrooms are equally spacious, fully carpeted and very well equipped.
Amenities garden, tennis, mini-golf, croquet, 24-hour laundry service.

Skipton
Map 10 C1 North Yorkshire
Chapel Hill *BD23 1NL*
Skipton (0756) 3604

Oats

Smart contemporary decor is a feature of this bustling restaurant, where the dinner menu offers generous portions of freshly prepared dishes ranging from poached halibut with shrimp sauce to roast pheasant or sautéed calf's liver with Dubonnet sauce. Vegetables are nicely judged and there are some interesting sweets such as plum and port fool. Simpler menu at lunchtime.

Continued

Continued

ABOVE AVERAGE. *Credit* Barclaycard

Lunch 12.15–2 *Dinner* 7.30–9
Closed Sun, Mon & Bank Holidays

About £32 for two

Slough
Map 5 E2 Berkshire
Ditton Road
Langley *SL3 8PR*
Slough (0753) 44244
Telex 848646
Rooms 239
with bath/shower 239
Room phone Yes
Room TV Yes
Confirm by 6
Last dinner 10.30
Parking Ample
Banquets 350/12

Credit Access, Amex,
Barclaycard, Diners

Holiday Inn 71% *E* £ C

Right beside junction 5 of the M4 and only about ten minutes' drive from Heathrow, this large modern hotel provides sophisticated comforts and a comprehensive range of business and leisure facilities. Red-brick walls and pillars are used to stylish effect in the tiled foyer and in the split-level bar-lounge, which has an eye-catching central open fireplace surrounded by comfortable armchairs and sofas. The bar overlooks the heated swimming pool. Smart, well-equipped bedrooms include eight executive studios which are suitable for small meetings. Excellent bathrooms. *Amenities* garden, sauna, indoor swimming pool, tennis, dancing (Fri, Sat), in-house movies, hairdressing, transport to airport, games room.

Solihull
Map 10 C4 West Midlands
The Square *B91 3RF*
021–704 1241

Credit Access, Amex,
Barclaycard, Diners
Closed 1 week Christmas

George Hotel 60% £ E

This old coaching inn has been modernised and extended with the needs of the businessman much in mind. Bedrooms in the extension are neatly furnished, with well-designed fitted units, colour TV, radios and tea/coffee-makers; bedrooms in the original house, without private bathrooms, are charmingly beamed and traditional. There are two comfortable bars and a residents' lounge. *Amenities* bowling green.

| *Rooms* 47 | *Room phone* Yes | *Confirm by* 6 | *Parking* Ample |
| *with bath/shower* 41 | *Room TV* Yes | *Last dinner* 9.15 | *Banquets* 180/10 |

Solihull
Map 10 C4 West Midlands
651 Warwick Road *B91 1AT*
021–705 6777
Telex 339352
Manager Mr M. Duffy
Credit Access, Amex,
Barclaycard, Diners

St John's Hotel 61% £ E

With its extensive conference facilities and a convenient position near the M42, this privately owned hotel–a Victorian town house with modern extensions–is particularly popular with businessmen. Fair-sized bedrooms, whether in the original building or the newer wings, are well fitted in studio-style; all have tea/coffee-making facilities and fully tiled bathrooms. There's a choice of five bars.

| *Rooms* 210 | *Room phone* Yes | *Confirm by* 7 | *Parking* Ample |
| *with bath/shower* 210 | *Room TV* Yes | *Last dinner* 9.30 | *Banquets* 850/10 |

Somerton
Map 4 A3 Somerset
Broad Street *TA11 7NJ*
Somerton (0458) 72339

Credit Access, Barclaycard,
Diners

Red Lion Hotel 61% Ⓜ £ E

Thoroughly renovated to provide up-to-date comforts, this handsome old coaching inn retains plenty of character with its cheerful courtyard and panelled public rooms. A log fire burns in the cosy bar-lounge and there's a restful residents' lounge with a writing desk. Bedrooms range from a sumptuous suite or a four-poster bedroom to comfortable but simpler modern rooms. *Amenities* dinner dance (Tues, Fri, Sat), helipad.

| *Rooms* 18 | *Room phone* Yes | *Confirm by* By arrang. | *Parking* Ample |
| *with bath/shower* 18 | *Room TV* Yes | *Last dinner* 9.30 | *Banquets* 200/– |

Sonning-on-Thames
Map 5 D2 Berkshire
RG4 0UT
Reading (0734) 692277

Credit Access, Amex,
Barclaycard, Diners

White Hart Hotel 62% £ D

This riverside hotel consisting of delightful old half-timbered cottages clustered round a courtyard is full of character. The foyer-lounge has original beams and antique furniture, and there are two bars. The best bedrooms are the smart, modern Palace Yard ones, which have very pretty bathrooms. Other rooms, which have been attractively refurbished, have old-world charm. *Amenities* garden, discothèque (Sat), mooring.

Continued

Rooms 25	*Room phone* Yes	*Confirm by* By arrang.	*Parking* Ample
with bath/shower 25	*Room TV* Yes	*Last dinner* 9.45	*Banquets* 100/–

South Godstone

Map 7 B5 Surrey
Tilburston Hill *RH9 8JY*
South Godstone (034 285) 3184
Proprietor Antoine Jalley
French cooking

● **Set L** from £6·80
Set D from £9 incl. service
About £35 for two
Banquets 100/–

La Bonne Auberge

This charming restaurant has the relaxed atmosphere of a country house. The menu is an interesting blend of classic and inventive dishes from noisettes of lamb with tarragon to veal kidneys in raspberry vinegar sauce, while sweets include a variety of sorbets, creams and pastries. Cooking achieves some outstanding results, and presentation is most attractive.
SUPERIOR. Credit Access, Amex, Barclaycard, Diners

Lunch 12–2 *Dinner* 7–10
Closed D Sun & all Mon

South Milford

Map 11 D1 North Yorkshire
Near Leeds *LS25 5LF*
South Milford (0977) 682711
Telex 557074
Manager Mr J. McNamara
Credit Access, Amex,
Barclaycard, Diners

Selby Fork Hotel   64%   £ D

Situated just off the A1, this modern business hotel boasts extensive conference and recreational facilities. The nicest of the public areas is the plushly refurbished Rosedale Bar, while spacious bedrooms are functionally fitted and have tiled bath or shower rooms.
Amenities garden, sauna, indoor swimming pool, tennis, helipad, buttery (9am–7pm, Sat & Sun 10am–6pm), pitch & putt, children's play area.

Rooms 117	*Room phone* Yes	*Confirm by* 6	*Parking* Ample
with bath/shower 117	*Room TV* Yes	*Last dinner* 10	*Banquets* 150/6

South Mimms

Map 5 E2 Hertfordshire
Bignells Corners
Potters Bar *EN6 3NH*
Potters Bar (0707) 43311
Telex 299162
Credit Access, Amex,
Barclaycard, Diners

Crest Hotel   60%   £ D

Situated on the B197 at the junction of the A1 and A6, this is a comfortable, well-equipped modern business hotel. Recently redecorated public rooms are cheerful, bright and contemporary, and bedrooms in restful beige and brown have practical built-in furniture, tea-makers, trouser presses and neat tiled bathrooms.
Amenities buffet bar (7am–10pm, Sundays 7am–9.30pm).

Rooms 120	*Room phone* Yes	*Confirm by* 6	*Parking* Ample
with bath/shower 120	*Room TV* Yes	*Last dinner* 10	*Banquets* 130/60

South Molton

Map 3 D2 Devon
134 East Street *EX36 3BU*
South Molton (076 95) 3683

Stumbles

The dinner menu at this pleasant *restaurant avec chambres* features acceptably cooked dishes ranging from strongly flavoured gazpacho and moussaka to poached salmon trout with champagne sauce. For overnight guests there are four smart panelled bedrooms with tasteful bamboo furniture, colour TV and luxurious bathrooms. *ABOVE AVERAGE.*
Credit Access, Amex, Barclaycard, Diners

Dinner only 7.30–10
Closed Sun, Mon in winter & 25 & 26 December

About £22 for two

South Normanton

Map 11 D3 Derbyshire
Carter Lane East *DE55 2EH*
Ripley (0773) 812000
Telex 377264

Rooms 123
with bath/shower 123
Room phone Yes
Room TV Yes
Confirm by 6
Last dinner 10
Parking Ample
Banquets 200/–

Swallow Hotel   72%   *E*   £ D

Close to junction 28 of the M1, this modern brick hotel has been designed to cater for business executives. The spacious, open-plan entrance hall adjoins

Continued

Continued
Credit Access, Amex, Barclaycard, Diners

a smart bar-lounge with shelves of leatherbound books lining the walls and deep sofas and chairs. There are also numerous function facilities. Stylish double-glazed bedrooms have comfortable beds, good-quality fitted units and matching fabrics; they are also provided with mini-bars. All have tiled bathrooms with up-to-date fittings.
Amenities garden, in-house movies, coffee shop (7am–11pm). &

South Walsham

Map 6 D1 Norfolk
Norwich *NR136DQ*
South Walsham (060 549) 378

Credit Access, Amex, Barclaycard, Diners

South Walsham Hall Hotel   65%   Ⓜ   £E

A magnificent 17th-century staircase dominates the entrance hall of this red-brick manor house, which also has a spacious, traditionally furnished lounge and bar. Bedrooms range from the luxurious London Room to seven in a converted outhouse with smart fitted furniture, duvets and tiled bathrooms. No dogs. *Amenities* garden, outdoor swimming pool, tennis, squash, coarse fishing, badminton, pétanque.

Rooms 15	*Room phone* Yes	*Confirm by* 7	*Parking* Ample
with bath/shower 10	*Room TV* Yes	*Last dinner* 10	*Banquets* 100/4

Southampton

Map 5 D4 Hampshire
High Street *SO92DS*
Southampton (0703) 26178
Telex 477735

Credit Access, Amex, Barclaycard, Diners

Dolphin Hotel   57%   £D

Built in 1751, this hotel on the High Street has huge bay windows and retains much old-fashioned charm. Ornately plastered ceilings have been carefully preserved, and there is an elegant panelled lounge, as well as the pleasant Nelson's Bar. Bedrooms range from small singles with modern fitted units and shower rooms to some very large, traditionally furnished ones.

Rooms 72	*Room phone* Yes	*Confirm by* 6	*Parking* Ample
with bath/shower 72	*Room TV* Yes	*Last dinner* 9.45	*Banquets* 60/5

Southampton

Map 5 D4 Hampshire
Cumberland Place *SO94GD*
Southampton (0703) 26401
Telex 47175

Credit Access, Amex, Barclaycard, Diners

Polygon Hotel   65%   £D

Close to the centre of town, this large red-brick hotel with extensive conference facilities is a popular choice for businessmen. Bedrooms are bright and practical, all with colour TVs, radios, tea-makers and mini-bars; bathrooms are large and well fitted. There are two bars decorated in modern style and a comfortable lounge.
Amenities dancing (Sat in winter).

Rooms 119	*Room phone* Yes	*Confirm by* 6	*Parking* Ample
with bath/shower 119	*Room TV* Yes	*Last dinner* 9.45	*Banquets* 500/–

Southampton

Map 5 D4 Hampshire
Herbert Walker Avenue *SO1 0HJ*
Southampton (0703) 28081
Telex 477368

Credit Access, Amex, Barclaycard, Diners

Post House Hotel   61%   £D

You can see the berth of the *QE2* from this tall modern hotel overlooking Southampton Water. Smart settees and coffee tables feature in the refurbished foyer, while the intimate Harbour Bar has suitably nautical decor. Pleasant bedrooms have large picture windows and contemporary furniture plus tea-makers, radios and mini-bars. Compact, well-equipped bathrooms.
Amenities outdoor swimming pool, baby listening service.

Rooms 132	*Room phone* Yes	*Confirm by* 6	*Parking* Ample
with bath/shower 132	*Room TV* Yes	*Last dinner* 10	*Banquets* 300/–

Southampton

Map 5 D4 Hampshire
Cumberland Place *SO94NY*
Southampton (0703) 23467
Telex 47439

Credit Access, Amex, Barclaycard, Diners

Southampton Park Hotel   62%   £E

Built in solid pre-war style, this large, square hotel with ample parking is conveniently close to the town centre. The interior is very warm and welcoming, with a comfortable, chintzy lounge on the ground floor and a cosy panelled bar downstairs. Improvements continue on the bedrooms, which are smartly fitted with modern white units; most have handsome, fully tiled bathrooms. *Amenities* dinner dance (once a month).

Rooms 87	*Room phone* Yes	*Confirm by* 8.30	*Parking* Ample
with bath/shower 84	*Room TV* Yes	*Last dinner* 11	*Banquets* 160/10

Southport

Map 10 A1 Merseyside
Lord Street *PR9 0BE*
Southport (0704) 32578

Credit Access, Amex,
Barclaycard

Rooms 28
with bath/shower 12

Bold Hotel 55% Ⓜ £E

Situated on a corner in the main street of the town, this white-painted former coaching inn is a popular business hotel. There's a choice of two pleasant bars, one with a vivid tartan carpet, as well as a traditionally furnished lounge and a useful banqueting room. Attractively redecorated bedrooms have tea/coffee-makers and radios. Tiled bathrooms are carpeted and well maintained.

Room phone Yes   *Confirm by* 6   *Parking* Limited
Room TV Yes   *Last dinner* 10   *Banquets* 250/–

Southport

Map 10 A1 Merseyside
1b Seabank Road *PR9 0EW*
Southport (0704) 37803
Proprietors Mr & Mrs Garcia
Spanish cooking
About £25 for two

Don Quijote Ⓢ

Dony Garcia is the capable chef at this popular little town-centre restaurant. There are enjoyable daily specialities including fish and game, as well as authentic Spanish dishes like paella and zarzuela (fish stew). Charming service. *Dinner only* 7–10.30 **Closed** Sun, Mon, 1 January, 26 December & 2 weeks August–September

---

Southport

Map 10 A1 Merseyside
Lord Street *PR8 1JS*
Southport (0704) 36688
Telex 67415

Credit Access, Amex,
Barclaycard, Diners

Rooms 96
with bath/shower 86

Prince of Wales Hotel 65% £D

High standards of personal service still prevail at this fine red-brick hotel, built in the 1880s and standing in the centre of town. Elegant public rooms include a spacious, well-furnished foyer-lounge, two relaxing bars (one hung with a collection of clocks) and numerous function rooms. Good-sized bedrooms are comfortable and well furnished, bathrooms neat and modern. *Amenities* garden, 24-hour laundry service.

Room phone Yes   *Confirm by* 7   *Parking* Ample
Room TV Yes   *Last dinner* 10.30   *Banquets* 400/–

Southport

Map 10 A1 Merseyside
78 King Street *PR8 1LG*
Southport (0704) 30046

About £28 for two

Squires Ⓢ

A warmly decorated town-centre restaurant, whose menus offer capably prepared dishes ranging from soups and terrines to fresh salmon and steak au poivre. Service is helpful and courteous. 🍷*ABOVE AVERAGE.*
Credit Access, Amex, Barclaycard, Diners *Dinner only* 7–10.30 **Closed** Sun
● **Set D** Mon–Fri £8·25   ♿

Southsea

Map 5 D4 Hampshire
Clarence Parade *PO5 2HY*
Portsmouth (0705) 823201
Telex 86376

Credit Access, Amex,
Barclaycard, Diners

Rooms 58
with bath/shower 37

Pendragon Hotel 57% £D

There are fine views over the Solent from the top floors of this Victorian building facing Southsea Common. The hotel has two comfortable bars and a high-ceilinged residents' lounge. Warm, attractively decorated bedrooms have simple wooden units, radios, colour TVs and tea-makers. Partly tiled bathrooms are adequate. Extensive conference facilities.
Amenities dancing (Sat in winter).

Room phone Yes   *Confirm by* 6   *Parking* Ample
Room TV Yes   *Last dinner* 9   *Banquets* 80/–

Southsea

Map 5 D4 Hampshire
South Parade *PO4 0RN*
Portsmouth (0705) 731281

Manager Mr A. Marchesi
Credit Access, Amex,
Barclaycard, Diners

Rooms 111
with bath/shower 111

Royal Beach Hotel 59% £E/F

This large, white-painted hotel with black wrought-iron balconies overlooking the sea offers excellent accommodation. All bedrooms are very acceptable, the best ones having rich deep-pile carpeting, high-quality fitted furniture and attractive, comprehensively equipped bathrooms. Public areas include two comfortable lounges and four bars.
Amenities dinner dance (Sat).

Room phone Yes   *Confirm by* By arrang.   *Parking* Ample
Room TV Yes   *Last dinner* 9.45   *Banquets* 250/–

Southwell
Map 11 D3 Nottinghamshire
Market Place *NG25 0HE*
Southwell (0636) 812701
Telex 858875
Managers Mr & Mrs R. F. Koomen
Credit Access, Amex,
Barclaycard, Diners

Rooms 23
with bath/shower 23

Saracen's Head Hotel   60%   £ D/E

For centuries this impressive half-timbered hostelry has been a welcome stopping place for travellers, and its public rooms with their heavy beams, exposed stonework and antiques still bear witness to the age of the building. In contrast, attractive bedrooms (most of which are in the red-brick extension at the rear) have elegant modern furniture, pretty fabrics and simple, well-fitted bathrooms.

Room phone Yes   *Confirm by* 5.30   *Parking* Ample
Room TV Yes   *Last dinner* 9.45   *Banquets* 100/10

Southwold
Map 6 D2 Suffolk
Market Place *IP18 6EG*
Southwold (0502) 722186

Manager Mr E. C. Bath-Jones
Credit Access, Amex,
Barclaycard, Diners

Rooms 53
with bath/shower 28

Swan Hotel   60%      £ D

The origins of this popular ivy-clad hotel lie in the 17th century, but its facade and character are Georgian. There's ample comfortable seating in the spacious panelled lounge and smart, well-appointed bar, and residents also have a first-floor TV lounge. Good-sized bedrooms have a fresh, bright appeal, the 18 in the garden quadrangle being especially attractive.
Amenities garden.   &

Room phone Yes   *Confirm by* By arrang.   *Parking* Ample
Room TV Most   *Last dinner* 8.30   *Banquets* 130/–

Speldhurst
Map 7 B5 Kent
Near Tunbridge Wells *TN3 0NN*
Langton (089 286) 3125
Proprietors Sankey family

About £38 for two

George & Dragon, Oak Room   

Heavy beams, polished tables and wheelback chairs give an old-fashioned charm to this popular restaurant in a country inn. The long menu ranges from duckling soup and potted salmon to charcoal-grilled steaks and superb suprême de volaille with a dill and truffle sauce. Presentation is attractive and service friendly and professional, but cooking can occasionally disappoint. *OUTSTANDING. Credit* Access, Amex, Barclaycard, Diners

Lunch 12–1.30 *Dinner* 7–10
Closed L Sat, all Sun & Bank Holidays

Staddle Bridge
Map 15 C5 North Yorkshire
Near Northallerton *DL6 3JB*
East Harlsey (060 982) 207
Proprietors McCoy brothers

Credit Access, Amex,
Barclaycard, Diners

Rooms 5
with bath/shower 5

Cleveland Tontine Inn *(Inn)*      £ E

Noted for its warmth and friendly hospitality, this inn is owned by the McCoy brothers and houses their restaurant. As well as a popular cellar bar there's a cocktail bar decked out with woven chairs and potted plants and reminiscent of the '20s. Spacious bedrooms are tastefully equipped, with nicely co-ordinated colour schemes and well-maintained bathrooms. Superb breakfasts. *Amenities* garden. **Closed** Bank Holidays except Good Friday

Room phone No   *Confirm by* By arrang.   *Parking* Ample
Room TV Yes   *Last dinner* 11

Staddle Bridge
Map 15 C5 North Yorkshire
Near Northallerton *DL6 3JB*
East Harlsey (060 982) 207
Proprietors McCoy brothers

About £40 for two

McCoy's Restaurant   ★      

The unconventional is the norm at this extraordinary restaurant, where the showmanship of the McCoy brothers, the amazing decor–paper parasols, potted palms and silvery wallpaper–and a menu full of interest and imagination combine to produce an occasion to remember. Most important, the brothers' culinary skills are very evident throughout, from starters like delicious poached langoustines wrapped in cabbage leaves to superbly sauced main dishes and some mouthwatering desserts. **Specialities** light chicken mousse with lemon sabayon sauce on a bed of watercress purée, grilled guinea fowl with shallot, red pepper, Chablis and tarragon sauce, fresh fruit terrine. *SUPERIOR. Credit* Access, Amex, Barclaycard, Diners

Lunch by arrangement only *Dinner* 7–11
Closed Sun & Bank Holidays except Good Friday

YOUR GUIDE TO BRITAIN'S FIRST COLOUR KITCHEN RANGE.

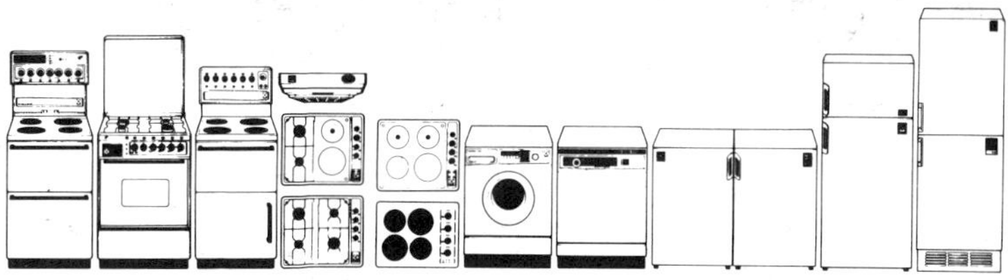

Brighten up your surroundings as well as your taste-buds with a perfectly matched kitchen range.

Electrolux offer you cookers, hobs, hoods, refrigerators, freezers, dishwashers and washing machines in Poppy Red, Coppertone, Almond and White.

See the newest ideas in kitchen technology. From Electrolux naturally.

ELECTROLUX LTD · LUTON · BEDS

Stafford

Map 10 B3 Staffordshire
Eccleshall Road *ST16 1JJ*
Stafford (0785) 53531
Telex 36566
Manager Mr Ian Taylor Brett
Credit Access, Amex,
Barclaycard, Diners

Rooms 94			
with bath/shower 94			

Tillington Hall Hotel   58%   £ E

Originally a large private house, gradually extended and modernised over the years, this substantial whitewashed hotel near the M6 (junction 14) offers conference facilities as well as comfortable accommodation. The bars and lounge are relaxing places, and bedrooms have well-designed fitted furniture and neat tiled bathrooms. *Amenities* garden, discothèque (Thurs), 24-hour laundry service, baby listening, pool table. **Closed** 1 week Christmas

Room phone Yes	*Confirm by* By arrang.	*Parking* Ample
Room TV Yes	*Last dinner* 10	*Banquets* 170/–

Stamford

Map 11 E4 Lincolnshire
St Martin's High Street *PE9 2LB*
Stamford (0780) 55171
Telex 32578
Manager Mr Richard Gorrie
Credit Access, Amex,
Barclaycard, Diners

Rooms 48			
with bath/shower 33			

George of Stamford   66%   £ D

This historic coaching inn meets the needs of the modern traveller while retaining all its delightful character; a well-equipped business centre is the latest addition. Stone walls, beams and antiques grace the lounge and bars, and the garden lounge, with its plants and wrought-iron tables and chairs, is particularly attractive. Comfortable, spacious bedrooms have pretty floral wallpapers and smart darkwood furniture. Good bathrooms. *Amenities* garden.

Room phone Yes	*Confirm by* 6	*Parking* Ample
Room TV Yes	*Last dinner* 9.30	*Banquets* 120/5

Stamford

Map 11 E4 Lincolnshire
St Martin's High Street *PE9 2LB*
Stamford (0780) 55171

About £30 for two

George at Stamford Restaurant   ♕ ⑤

Traditional roasts, carved from the trolley, are the highlights of the food in this handsome panelled dining room. Excellent fresh vegetables and enjoyable sweets, too. Careful, consistent cooking and polite service. *Credit* Access, Amex, Barclaycard, Diners

Lunch 12.30–2.30 *Dinner* 7.30–10.30 ● **Set L** from £4

Our inspectors are our full-time employees; they are professionally trained by us.

Steeple Aston

Map 5 D1 Oxfordshire
South Street *OX5 3RY*
Steeple Aston (0869) 40225
Proprietors
Colin & Margaret Mead

● **Set D** from £9
About £26 for two

Red Lion   ♧ ⑤

Genial Colin Mead takes the orders in this tiny pub restaurant, while his wife Margaret takes the greatest care preparing her lovely set dinners. Creamy celery soup with Stilton or robust liver pâté could precede roast quail or our delicious pork tenderloin with Highland herbs accompanied by perfectly cooked vegetables. Good, hearty home cooking and pleasant, informal service. Booking essential. *Credit* Access, Barclaycard

Dinner only 7.30–9.30
Closed Sun, Mon & Bank Holidays except Good Friday

Stepney

Good Friends

See under London

Stevenage

Map 6 B3 Hertfordshire
Old London Road
Broadwater *SG2 8DS*
Stevenage (0438) 65444
Telex 825505
Credit Access, Amex,
Barclaycard, Diners

Rooms 54			
with bath/shower 54			

Roebuck Inn   59%   £ D

This picturesque inn situated alongside the B197 has been providing hospitality since the 15th century, and it has managed to keep much of its original character. Open fires, beams and wall timbers bring charm to the public rooms, which include a reception-lounge and two bars. Bedrooms in modern extensions range from smart studio-style singles to standard rooms with fitted pine units. *Amenities* garden.

Room phone Yes	*Confirm by* 6	*Parking* Ample
Room TV Yes	*Last dinner* 9.45	*Banquets* 65/4

Steyning
Map 5 E4 West Sussex
High Street *BN4 3GG*
Steyning (0903) 81 2446

Credit Access, Amex,
Barclaycard, Diners

Rooms 10
with bath/shower 6

Springwells Hotel 56% Ⓜ £E

Built in 1772, this creeper-clad Georgian house with a secluded garden offers pleasant, homely accommodation. A restful atmosphere pervades the bar-lounge, which is tastefully decorated in Regency style and has a profusion of plants and prints. Bedrooms, two with four-posters, are attractively furnished and well maintained; second-floor ones have beams and sloping ceilings. *Amenities* garden, sauna, outdoor swimming pool.

Room phone Yes	*Confirm by* By arrang.	*Parking* Limited
Room TV Yes	*Last dinner* 9.30	

Steyning
Map 5 E4 West Sussex
High Street *BN4 3GG*
Steyning (0903) 81 2446

● **Set L** £5·95
About £32 for two

Springwells Hotel Restaurant ♕ Ⓢ

This restaurant makes a marvellously elegant setting for Andrew McGlennon's imaginative cooking. The well-balanced menu features dishes like our saddle of hare roasted with whole hazelnuts and paupiettes of veal in an orange-flavoured cream sauce. There's a tendency to overcook vegetables, but sweets such as chocolate marquise are delicious and beautifully presented.
🍷 *ABOVE AVERAGE. Credit* Access, Amex, Barclaycard, Diners ♿

Lunch 12.15–2 *Dinner* 7.15–9.30

Stoborough
Map 4 B4 Dorset
Grange Road
Near Wareham *BH20 5AL*
Wareham (092 95) 21 77
Proprietors Alford family
Credit Diners
Closed early Oct–late March

Rooms 36
with bath/shower 36

Springfield Country Hotel 58% Ⓜ £D

Once the Alfords' home, this extended 1930s house set amid peaceful meadows makes an attractive holiday hotel, and is also popular for conferences. Bedrooms are bright and inviting, with good darkwood furniture and smart bathrooms. Public areas include several comfortable lounges (one with TV). No children under two. *Amenities* garden, outdoor swimming pool, tennis, games room, riding, solarium, snooker, pool table, table tennis. ♿

Room phone No	*Confirm by* 5.30	*Parking* Ample
Room TV No	*Last dinner* 8	*Banquets* 100/40

Stockbridge
Map 4 C3 Hampshire
SO20 6EX
Stockbridge (026 481) 677
Proprietors
Ernest & Joan Fisher

● **Set L & Set D** £18·40
About £44 for two

Sheriff House Restaurant ★    

Booking is essential at this charming little *restaurant avec chambres*, where welcoming hosts Ernest and Joan Fisher are always happy to discuss guests' requirements in advance. The set dinners, a feast of fresh, natural flavours enhanced by garden herbs and judicious seasoning, offer simple joys like creamy chicken liver pâté, delicious ham and cheese pancakes, and succulent freshly caught lobster. The superbly rich yet exquisitely light chocolate roulade is not to be missed. Overnight guests have five pleasant bedrooms, each with bath or shower en suite.
Specialities sole à la Russe, farm goose in season, roast leg of spring lamb provençale, chocolate roulade. 🍷 *ABOVE AVERAGE.* ♿

Lunch by arrangement only *Dinner* at 8

Stockport
Map 10 B2 Greater Manchester
149 Buxton Road *SK2 6EL*
061–483 4431

Manager Mr Barry Stoyle
Credit Access, Amex,
Barclaycard, Diners

Rooms 74
with bath/shower 55

Alma Lodge Hotel 55% £D/E

The Victorian origins of this modernised businessman's hotel alongside the A6 are still visible in the panelled wainscotting and elaborate ceiling in the foyer. Public areas include meeting rooms, a large banqueting suite and a relaxing cocktail bar. The pleasant extension bedrooms, which have fitted units, good writing space and neat bathrooms, are larger and better equipped than the older rooms. *Amenities* dancing (Sat).

Room phone Yes	*Confirm by* 6	*Parking* Ample
Room TV Yes	*Last dinner* 9.30	*Banquets* 250/12

Stockton-on-Tees

Map 15 C5 Cleveland
10 John Walker Square *TS18 1AQ*
Stockton-on-Tees (0642) 69721
Telex 587895

Rooms 126
with bath/shower 126
Room phone Yes
Room TV Yes
Confirm by 6.30
Last dinner 10.30
Parking Ample
Banquets 300/4

Credit Access, Amex,
Barclaycard, Diners

Swallow Hotel   70%   £ E

Built over a modern shopping precinct, this five-storey brick and glass hotel is luxuriously appointed. An eye-catching spiral staircase in the marble-lined foyer leads to the spacious lounge and comfortable cocktail bar. Bedrooms have neat fitted furniture, radios and tea-makers plus excellent well-equipped bathrooms.
Amenities coffee shop (7am–10.30pm).

Stockton-on-Tees

Map 15 C5 Cleveland
10 John Walker Square
TS18 1AQ
Stockton-on-Tees (0642) 69721
Manager Mr A. Nossa

● **Set L** £6·95 **Set D** £7·95
About £31 for two

Swallow Hotel, Portcullis Restaurant

Cooking in this smartly appointed hotel restaurant shows enterprise and imagination, and the chef offers a wide choice of mainly French-inspired dishes ranging from escalope of veal in a cream sauce to fillet of salmon trout with dill and cucumber, as well as grills and a cold buffet. Vegetables are capably handled and there's an attractive sweet trolley.
Credit Access, Amex, Barclaycard, Diners

Lunch 12.30–2.30 *Dinner* 7.30–10.30
Closed L Sat, all Sun & 25 December

We welcome complaints and bona fide recommendations on the tear-out pages for readers' comments. They are followed up by our professional team. Please also complain to the management instantly.

Stoke Mandeville

Map 5 D2 Buckinghamshire
Risborough Road *HP22 5UT*
Stoke Mandeville (029 661) 2258
Proprietors Mr & Mrs Roy Bartman
Credit Access, Amex,
Barclaycard, Diners
Closed 3 days Christmas

Rooms 15
with bath/shower 15

Belmore Hotel   63%   Ⓜ   £ D

A modern extension houses most of the rooms at this converted farmhouse on the outskirts of town. The Bartmans run it very much on family lines, and the lounge, with its serve-yourself bar area, is a homely, relaxing room. Spacious, thoughtfully equipped bedrooms have carpeted bathrooms with smart up-to-date fittings. Breakfast is served in the bedrooms only.
Amenities garden, sauna, outdoor swimming pool, livery stable.

Room phone Yes	*Confirm by* By arrang.	*Parking* Ample
Room TV Yes	*Last dinner* 8.30	

Stoke-on-Trent

Map 10 B3 Staffordshire
Station Road *ST4 2AE*
Stoke-on-Trent (0782) 48501
Telex 36287

Credit Access, Amex,
Barclaycard, Diners

Rooms 70
with bath/shower 70

North Stafford Hotel   60%   £ D

Model kilns and pottery exhibits are especially apt in the Clayhanger's Bar of this red-brick Victorian hotel, while the Footlights Bar next door has a theatrical theme. Public areas also include a contemporary cocktail bar, a spacious lounge and various meeting rooms. Bedrooms have sleek modern units, coordinated colour schemes and simple, up-to-date bathrooms.

Room phone Yes	*Confirm by* 6	*Parking* Ample
Room TV Yes	*Last dinner* 9.45	*Banquets* 450/–

Ston Easton
Map 4 B3 Somerset
Near Bath, Avon *BA3 4DF*
Chewton Mendip (076 121) 631
Telex 444738

Rooms 12
with bath/shower 12
Room phone Yes
Room TV Yes
Confirm by By arrang.
Last dinner 9.30
Parking Ample
Banquets 24/8
Closed January

Credit Access, Amex, Diners

Ston Easton Park   89%   Ⓜ   £C

Eighteenth-century style and splendour have been expertly restored to this handsome Palladian mansion, which has been converted into a supremely comfortable and civilised hotel. The drawing room with its panelled murals and ornate plasterwork is the last word in elegance, and throughout the house there are fine antiques, tapestries and paintings (including one by Bellini in the library). Bedrooms are beautifully decorated and furnished, with replica Georgian travelling wardrobes, armchairs and sofas, and splendid bathrooms. Several rooms have magnificent four-posters and all have lovely views. Dogs in kennels only.
Amenities garden, game fishing, billiards, croquet.

Ston Easton
Map 4 B3 Somerset
Near Bath, Avon *BA3 4DF*
Chewton Mendip (076 121) 631

● **Set L** £8·50
About £40 for two

Ston Easton Park Restaurant   ★   ♕ Ⓢ

Jean-Luc Potier and his team have quickly made their mark at this friendly, coolly elegant restaurant. Sauces are deliciously smooth and light, and main courses like charcoal-grilled duck breast come with beautifully cooked vegetables. Fixed-price lunches, à la carte dinners. **Specialities** quenelles of pike Nantua sauce, lobster brioche, fillet of beef à la ficelle, tulip of sorbets.
🍷 *SUPERIOR. Credit* Access, Amex, Diners   ♿

Lunch 12.30–2 *Dinner* 7.30–9.30, Sat 7.30–10
Closed January

Stone
Map 10 B3 Staffordshire
High Street *ST15 8AS*
Stone (0785) 813535

Credit Access, Amex, Barclaycard

Rooms 29
with bath/shower 29

Crown Hotel   60%   £E

There's a marvellous solidity about this town-centre hostelry, which has been providing hospitality since Elizabethan times and now happily combines the best of past and present. The lounge and bar are pleasantly decorated, and a massive central staircase leads to the bedrooms, which have simple modern furniture and up-to-date bathrooms. The rooms in the new wing are especially smart and well equipped.

Room phone Yes	*Confirm by* By arrang.	*Parking* Ample
Room TV Yes	*Last dinner* 9	*Banquets* 150/25

Stoney Cross
Map 4 C4 Hampshire
Near Lyndhurst *SO47GN*
Cadnam (042 127) 2134

Credit Access, Amex, Barclaycard, Diners

Rooms 12
with bath/shower 12

Compton Arms Hotel   58%   £E

Ask for directions when you book for this modest hotel (it's on the A31, but access is tricky). Inside, it is all you would expect from a traditional country inn, with an oak-panelled lounge, two pleasant bars and a coffee lounge overlooking the garden. The welcoming atmosphere extends to the simple, well-maintained bedrooms, which have charming old-fashioned furniture and modern bathrooms. No dogs. *Amenities* garden.

Room phone Yes	*Confirm by* By arrang.	*Parking* Ample
Room TV Yes	*Last dinner* 9.45	*Banquets* 80/6

We do not necessarily recommend the cooking at hotels whose restaurants are not separately listed.

Storrington

Map 5 E3 West Sussex
Merrywood Lane *RH20 3HE*
Storrington (090 66) 4416

Rooms 7
with bath/shower 7
Room phone Yes
Room TV Yes
Confirm by By arrang.
Last dinner 9.30
Parking Ample

Closed Christmas & February

Credit Access, Amex,
Barclaycard, Diners

Little Thakeham   76%   Ⓜ   £ C/D

A tranquil setting on the South Downs, the house itself designed by Sir Edwin Lutyens and the gardens laid out by Gertrude Jekyll – it would be difficult to imagine a finer pedigree for a country house hotel. The public rooms are simple and dignified, with beautiful flower arrangements adding further to the picture of elegance; the main lounge (once the music room) is particularly impressive, with lovely antiques, log fire and plenty of comfortable chesterfields. Spacious, well-equipped bedrooms in pleasant pastel shades are furnished in a harmonious mixture of styles, and warm, carpeted bathrooms (two with bidets) have luxurious towels and bathrobes. *Amenities* garden, outdoor swimming pool, tennis, croquet.

Storrington

Map 5 E3 West Sussex
Merrywood Lane *RH20 3HE*
Storrington (090 66) 4416

● **Set L** Sun only £8·50
About £30 for two

Little Thakeham Restaurant

Attractive china, highly polished mahogany tables and a vast inglenook contribute to a traditional setting for a straightforward, well-cooked meal. Mushrooms aïoli or soup of the day (perhaps hearty leek and potato) might be among the simple starters, and main courses could include Dover sole (meunière or véronique), sautéed veal kidneys in Calvados, and tender roast lamb. 🍷 *ABOVE AVERAGE. Credit* Access, Amex, Barclaycard, Diners

Lunch 12.30–2.30 *Dinner* 7.30–9.30
Closed D Sun & all Mon to non-residents, Christmas & February

Storrington

Map 5 E3 West Sussex
Manley's Hill *RH20 4BT*
Storrington (090 66) 2331

● **Set L** Sun only £8·50
About £46 for two
Banquets 10/–

Manley's   ★   ⚘ Ⓢ

The elegant atmosphere of this stylish restaurant with its gleaming silverware and impeccably dressed waiters complements perfectly the refinement and originality of Karl Löderer's cooking. His vast menu features many French and German specialities like tender chicken Marengo faultlessly married with a light lobster sauce and the ever-popular sole ambassadeur (combined with avocado, tomatoes and scampi). Vegetables are excellent and there's a wide choice of wonderfully executed sweets such as rich chocolate parfait and meringues with raspberries in a Kirsch sauce. **Specialities** petite cocotte en feuilleté, entrecôte hôtelière, canard sauvage au porto, sorbet exotique.
Credit Access, Amex

Lunch 12–2 *Dinner* 7–9, Sat 7–9.30
Closed D Sun, all Mon & 1 week after Christmas

Stourbridge

Map 10 B4 West Midlands
High Street *DY8 1DW*
Stourbridge (038 43) 4350

Credit Access, Barclaycard
Closed 25 December

Rooms 20
with bath/shower 8

Talbot Hotel *(Inn)*   £ F

This brick-faced 15th-century coaching inn is full of charm and character, with an abundance of antiques, oak beams and carved panelling. There's a small, tiled reception area, and four cheerful bars ranging from traditional to modern, plus a residents' lounge with colour TV. A programme of refurbishment is updating bedrooms and bathrooms with modern decor and neat fitted units. *Amenities* dancing (Sat alternate months).

Room phone No	*Confirm by* 6	*Parking* Ample
Room TV No	*Last dinner* 9.15	*Banquets* 120/–

Stow-on-the-Wold

Map 4 C1 Gloucestershire
Fosse Way *GL54 1JX*
Stow-on-the-Wold
(0451) 30354
Proprietors Mr & Mrs R. Johnston
Credit Access, Amex,
Barclaycard, Diners

Fosse Manor Hotel   58%   Ⓜ   £ E

Set in five acres of grounds just outside Stow on the A429, this former vicarage is well maintained by the Johnstons. A plush foyer leads to the comfortable residents' lounge overlooking the lawns, and there's a pleasant bar. Bedrooms are mostly very large, with traditional furniture, attractive matching fabrics and tea-makers. Carpeted modern bathrooms. *Amenities* garden, croquet. **Closed** Christmas.

Continued

Rooms 23	*Room phone* No	*Confirm by* 6	*Parking* Ample
with bath/shower 14	*Room TV* No	*Last dinner* 9.30	*Banquets* 75/2

Stow-on-the-Wold
Map 4 C1 Gloucestershire
Park Street *GL54 1AG*
Stow-on-the-Wold
(0451) 30200

● **Set L** from £4·95 incl. service
Set D £7·95 incl. service
About £32 for two

Rafters 

Wonderfully imaginative starters, ranging from pumpkin soup to terrine of carp, almost steal the show in Keith Maby's simply decorated rustic restaurant. Carefully selected raw materials are skilfully handled in main courses like noisettes of venison and sautéed veal with a tasty vegetable garnish including celeriac purée. Home-made ice cream and chocolate mousse are typical delicious sweets. *Credit* Access, Amex, Barclaycard, Diners

Lunch 12.30–2.15, Sun 12.15–2.30 *Dinner* 7.15–10
Closed D Sun, all Mon & 4 days Christmas

Stow-on-the-Wold
Map 4 C1 Gloucestershire
Digbeth Street *GL54 1BN*
Stow-on-the-Wold
(0451) 30670

Credit Access, Amex,
Barclaycard, Diners

Royalist Hotel 53% Ⓜ £E/F

This quaint little hostelry is reputed to be the oldest building in Stow, the timber frame behind its Cotswold-stone facade being more than 1,000 years old. Charm and character abound in public rooms like the modest residents' lounge and cosy beamed bar, and heavy, ancient beams are also a feature of most of the simply furnished, unpretentious bedrooms. *Amenities* garden.

Rooms 15	*Room phone* No	*Confirm by* 6	*Parking* Limited
with bath/shower 7	*Room TV* Some	*Last dinner* 9.30	*Banquets* 50/–

Stow-on-the-Wold
Map 4 C1 Gloucestershire
Sheep Street *GL54 1HQ*
Stow-on-the-Wold
(0451) 30257

Credit Access, Amex,
Barclaycard, Diners

Unicorn Hotel 57% £D/E

Period charm is imaginatively combined with modern comforts at this quaint Cotswold-stone hotel. The public rooms are rich in oak beams, open hearths and inviting armchairs, while upstairs the bedrooms with their bright decor and freestanding furniture offer good contemporary comfort. Useful extras include colour TVs, trouser presses and tea/coffee-makers, and spotless bathrooms have coloured suites.

Rooms 20	*Room phone* Yes	*Confirm by* 6	*Parking* Ample
with bath/shower 20	*Room TV* Yes	*Last dinner* 9	*Banquets* 50/6

Stratford-upon-Avon
Town plan E2 Warwickshire
Clopton Bridge *CV37 7HP*
Stratford-upon-Avon
(0789) 204581
Telex 31324
Credit Access, Amex,
Barclaycard, Diners

Alveston Manor Hotel 67% £D

This handsome building – a mixture of period styles – stands in seven acres of grounds. The comfortable lounge has fine 16th-century oak panelling and the cocktail bar features a beautiful Moorish tapestry. Apart from some bedrooms with splendid old-fashioned furnishings, most are well-fitted rooms in the modern extensions; all have up-to-date bathrooms. *Amenities* garden, dancing (twice monthly January–end March).

Rooms 116	*Room phone* Yes	*Confirm by* 6	*Parking* Ample
with bath/shower 116	*Room TV* Yes	*Last dinner* 9.15	*Banquets* 130/2

Stratford-upon-Avon
Town plan D3 Warwickshire
44 Waterside *CV37 6BA*
Stratford-upon-Avon
(0789) 294949
Proprietor Mr J. N. Anker
Credit Access, Amex,
Barclaycard, Diners

Arden Hotel 60% Ⓜ £D/E

Right opposite the Royal Shakespeare Theatre, this pleasant hotel is an ideal spot for tourists and fans of the Bard. Guests and locals mingle in the smart bar, and there's a comfortable residents' lounge with views of the garden. Bedrooms in the original building are traditional and most attractive, while those in the extension are more modern. Most have simple bath or shower rooms. *Amenities* garden.

Rooms 64	*Room phone* Yes	*Confirm by* 6	*Parking* Ample
with bath/shower 54	*Room TV* Yes	*Last dinner* 9	*Banquets* 45/20

Map 4 C1
Town plan opposite

Population 22,000

A prosperous market-town on a lovely river site, with good Tudor and Jacobean architecture would be a fair description of Stratford-upon-Avon—if it wasn't for the Bard. It took 200 years after Shakespeare's birth for proper tribute to be paid to him in a festival staged by David Garrick. The first Theatre was not built until 1879; it was burnt down in 1926 and succeeded by the present theatre in 1932, with large overseas subscriptions, particularly from the U.S.A.

Annual Events
Mop Fair *12th October*
Shakespeare's Birthday *23rd April*
Shakespeare Theatre Season *from April*

Sights Outside Town
Coughton Court
Ragley Hall
Charlecote
Coventry Cathedral
Packwood House
Upton House
Warwick Castle

Information Centre
Judith Shakespeare's House
1 High Street
Telephone Stratford-upon-Avon
293127

Stratford-upon-Avon

1	Anne Hathaway's cottage *at Shottery*	A3
2	Guild Chapel, Guildhall, Grammar School and Almshouses *exceptional medieval buildings*	C3
3	Hall's Croft *fine Tudor house and walled garden, also houses Festival Club*	C3
4	Harvard House *1596 home of grandfather of Harvard's founder*	C2
5	Holy Trinity Church *contains Shakespeare's tomb*	C3
6	Information Centre	C2
7	Mary Arden's house *at Wilmcote, 3 miles. Tudor farmhouse, home of Shakespeare's mother, farming museum*	B1
8	New Place *Elizabethan garden on site of Shakespeare's last home*	C3
9	Picture Gallery and Museum *pictures and relics of famous actors*	D3
10	Railway Station	A1
11	Royal Shakespeare Theatre	D3
12	Shakespeare's birthplace *architectural interest and museum of rare Shakespeariana*	C1
13	Town Hall	C2

Fiat Dealers

Foster Motors, Western Road
Stratford-upon-Avon CV37 0AH
Tel: Stratford-upon-Avon 293532/
68913

Stratford-upon-Avon

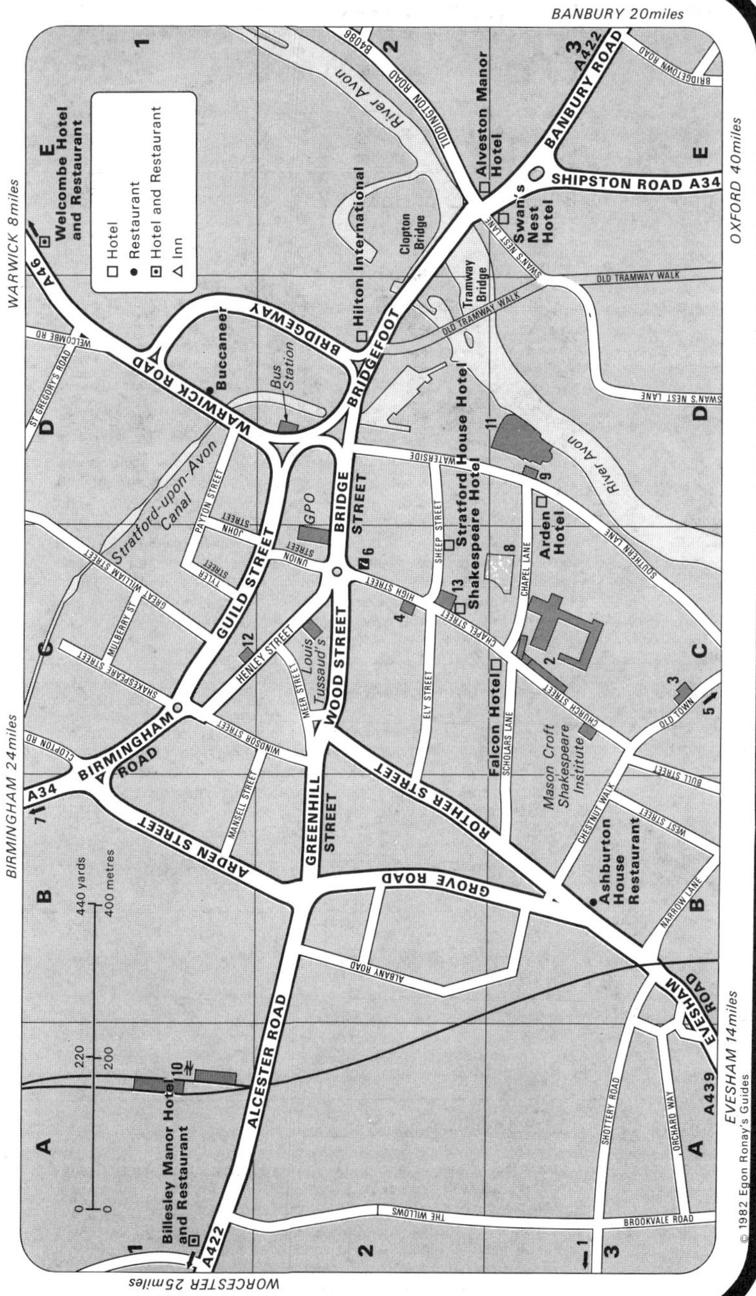

Stratford-upon-Avon   Ashburton House Restaurant

Town plan B3 Warwickshire
27 Evesham Place *CV37 6HT*
Stratford-upon-Avon
(0789) 292444
Proprietors Mr & Mrs A. R. Fraser

Booking is essential at this little guest house on the A439, whether for the four-course pre-theatre dinner or the later six-course meal (no choice). Mrs Fraser is a very competent cook, and her dishes originate from far and wide: typical treats are Chinese ramekins, groundnut soup, and tasty lamb à la Grecque. End with apple crumble or a deliciously refreshing peach sorbet.

● **Set D** £8 & £12 incl. service
About £23 for two

Dinner only 6–8 by arrangement only
Closed Sun & 3 days Christmas

Stratford-upon-Avon   Billesley Manor Hotel   73%   £ D/E

Town plan A1 Warwickshire
Billesley
Near Alcester *B49 6NF*
Alcester (0789) 763737

Rooms 12
with bath/shower 12
Room phone Yes
Room TV Yes
Confirm by By arrang.
Last dinner 9.30
Parking Ample
Banquets 40/6

Credit Access, Amex,
Barclaycard

Surrounded by lovely gardens, this fine stone 16th-century manor house stands four miles west of Stratford. The reception area is very elegant with Louis XIV furniture and Chinese rugs on a polished wood floor, and beyond is a splendid oak-panelled bar with a residents' lounge and writing room in the gallery above. First-floor bedrooms have oak panelling and solid antique furniture, including several four-poster beds; the Shakespeare Room also has a priests' hiding hole and an opulent bathroom with gold-plated fittings. Top-floor bedrooms are modern, with pretty fabrics and whitewood furniture. No dogs. *Amenities* garden, sauna, outdoor swimming pool, tennis, solarium, 24-hour laundry service.

Stratford-upon-Avon   Billesley Manor Restaurant

Town plan A1 Warwickshire
Billesley
Near Alcester *B49 6NF*
Alcester (0789) 763737

In a handsome oak-panelled dining room young Nigel Lambert presents his imaginative and well-balanced menus featuring both English country cooking and French nouvelle cuisine. Our smooth quenelles de brochet led happily to pork tenderloin with Cotswold dumplings, while smoked mackerel hotpot was followed by delicious aiguillettes de canard with kiwi-fruit sauce. Lovely ice creams. *Credit* Access, Amex, Barclaycard

● **Set L** £8·50 **Set D** £12
About £33 for two

Lunch 12.15–1.30, Sun 12.15–2 *Dinner* 7.30–9.30, Sat 7.30–10

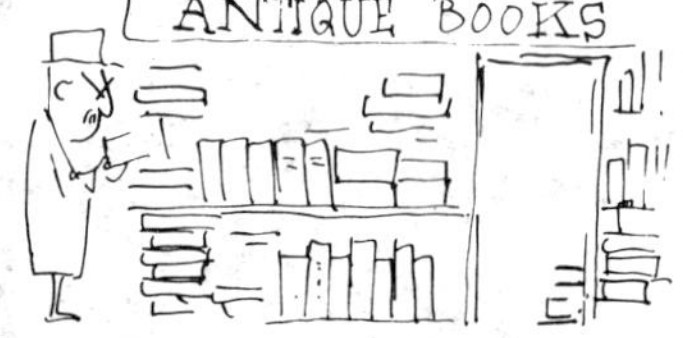

We publish annually, so make sure you use the current edition. It's worth it!

Stratford-upon-Avon   Buccaneer

Town plan D1 Warwickshire
11 Warwick Road *CV37 7YW*
Stratford-upon-Avon
(0789) 292550

Joanna Thor-Straten greets guests at this cosy restaurant decorated rather like a grotto, while husband Paul is at work in the kitchen. His fixed-price menus offer a good selection of well-prepared dishes ranging from onion soup or tasty terrine maison to scampi provençale or paupiettes de veau au saumon fumé. Carefully handled vegetables, and some simple, delicious desserts. *Credit* Access, Amex, Barclaycard, Diners

● **Set L & Set D** £8·75
About £26 for two

Lunch 12–2 *Dinner* 7–11.30
Closed L Sat & Sun, all Mon & February

Stratford-upon-Avon

Town plan C3 Warwickshire
Chapel Street *CV37 6HA*
Stratford-upon-Avon
(0789) 5777
Telex 312522
Credit Access, Amex,
Barclaycard, Diners

Falcon Hotel 60%   £ C/D

This charming timbered building in the centre of town has been a hotel since 1650, and its public rooms still retain their flagstoned floors, heavy beams and open fireplaces. Older bedrooms have a traditional appeal, too, while those in the modern rear extension, which also houses the reception area, have built-in units and wall-length windows. Bathrooms throughout have up-to-date fittings. *Amenities* garden.

Rooms 73
with bath/shower 73

Room phone Yes   *Confirm by* 6   *Parking* Ample
Room TV Yes   *Last dinner* 9   *Banquets* 160/6

Stratford-upon-Avon

Town plan D2 Warwickshire
Bridgefoot *CV37 6YR*
Stratford-upon-Avon
(0789) 67511   Telex 311127
Manager Mr Thomas W. Letham
Rooms 249
with bath/shower 249
Room phone Yes
Room TV Yes
Confirm by 6
Last dinner 11.30
Parking Ample
Banquets 450/10

Credit Access, Amex,
Barclaycard, Diners

Hilton International 75% *E*   £ C

Located on the north bank of the river Avon, this low, modern red-brick hotel is conveniently close to the Royal Shakespeare Theatre and the town centre. An enormous, comfortble foyer-lounge with an attractive flagstone floor has armchairs set around a fire, and there's a small Tavern Bar and a striking octagonal Actors' Bar, with riverside views and a handsome bronze ceiling. Bedrooms are large and well designed, many with convertible sofas; all have mini-bars, individually controlled air conditioning and beautifully kept, fully tiled bathrooms. Several acres of grounds contain a swan reserve. *Amenities* garden, dancing (Mon–Sat), hotel launch, shopping arcade, hairdressing.

Stratford-upon-Avon

Town plan C2 Warwickshire
Chapel Street *CV37 6ER*
Stratford-upon-Avon
(0789) 294771
Telex 311181
Credit Access, Amex,
Barclaycard, Diners

Shakespeare Hotel 64%   £ C/D

Dating from the 16th century, this appealing gabled and half-timbered building is a distinctive Stratford landmark. Public rooms skilfully blend comfortable traditional furniture and fitted carpets with heavy beams, pillars and panelling. Sturdily furnished bedrooms are full of character, with sloping floors and leaded windows; there are more modern rooms in the wing. Bathrooms are well equipped.

Rooms 66
with bath/shower 66

Room phone Yes   *Confirm by* 6   *Parking* Limited
Room TV Yes   *Last dinner* 9.30   *Banquets* 90/–

Stratford-upon-Avon

Town plan C2 Warwickshire
Sheep Street *CV37 6EF*
Stratford-upon-Avon
(0789) 68288
Credit Access, Amex,
Barclaycard, Diners
Closed 1 week Christmas

Stratford House Hotel 59% Ⓜ   £ D

Peter and Pamela Wade make this thoughtfully converted Georgian town house a most agreeable and charming place to stay. Guests can enjoy a drink in the cosy lounge, which also serves as the breakfast room. Bedrooms in the wing have pretty soft furnishings, tea/coffee-makers and spotlessly clean, well-equipped bathrooms; three beamed rooms in the original building are more traditional in style.

Rooms 9
with bath/shower 7

Room phone No   *Confirm by* By arrang.   *Parking* Difficult
Room TV Yes   *Last dinner* By arrang.

Stratford-upon-Avon

Town plan E3 Warwickshire
Bridgefoot *CV37 7LT*
Stratford-upon-Avon
(0789) 66761
Telex 31419
Credit Access, Amex,
Barclaycard, Diners

Swan's Nest Hotel 58%   £ D

On the banks of the Avon opposite the Royal Shakespeare Theatre, this pleasant red-brick hotel is no more than a stroll away from the town centre. It has a comfortable open-plan foyer-lounge and a popular bar. Large bedrooms (most in an extension at the rear) have attractive fitted units, matching fabrics and plenty of writing space. Spotlessly clean modern bathrooms. *Amenities* garden, dinner dance (Sat November–April).

Rooms 70
with bath/shower 52

Room phone Yes   *Confirm by* 6   *Parking* Ample
Room TV Yes   *Last dinner* 9.15   *Banquets* 120/2

Stratford-upon-Avon
Town plan E1 Warwickshire
Warwick Road *CV37 0NR*
Stratford-upon-Avon
(0789) 295252
Telex 31347
Rooms 84
with bath/shower 84
Room phone Yes
Room TV Yes
Confirm by By arrang.
Last dinner 9.15
Parking Ample
Banquets 160/–
Credit Access, Amex,
Barclaycard, Diners

Welcombe Hotel 73% £ C/D

A private road off the A46 leads to this impressive 19th-century mansion, which stands in 120 acres of beautiful lawns and parkland. You can relax in the restful American Bar or in the panelled lounge with a splendid marble fireplace. Bedrooms in the main house are positively enormous, with handsome traditional furnishings, and there's also a wing of smaller modern rooms enjoying fine garden views; old and new bathrooms are equally well equipped. Function facilities are lavish, and standards of service are delightfully old-fashioned.
Amenities garden, golf course, helipad, 24-hour laundry service, putting, garage, baby sitting.

Stratford-upon-Avon
Town plan E1 Warwickshire
Warwick Road *CV37 0NR*
Stratford-upon-Avon
(0789) 295252
French cooking

● **Set L** £8·80 **Set D** £9·75
incl. service
About £34 for two

Welcombe Hotel Restaurant

Service is most attentive in this elegant, formal dining room, where simple hors d'œuvre, delicious soups, grills such as halibut with parsley butter, and classical French dishes like gourmandise Brillat-Savarin and entrecôte Café de Paris are prepared to a consistently high standard. Home-made sorbets and superb crème caramel are among the sweets. *ABOVE AVERAGE.*
Credit Access, Amex, Barclaycard, Diners

Lunch 12.30–2.15 *Dinner* 7–9.15

Streatley-on-Thames
Map 5 D2 Berkshire
Near Reading *RG8 9HR*
Goring-on-Thames
(0491) 873737

Credit Access, Amex,
Barclaycard

Swan Hotel 66% Ⓜ £ D

This long, low hotel makes the most of its superb Thames-side setting, with many rooms overlooking the river. A colour scheme of brown, cream and pink creates a pleasingly unified interior. The foyer-lounge and the bar are attractively decorated and the bedrooms have good-quality furniture, pretty floral wallpapers and excellent, fully tiled bathrooms.
Amenities garden, coarse fishing, mooring.

Rooms 26	*Room phone* Yes	*Confirm by* 6	*Parking* Ample
with bath/shower 26	*Room TV* Yes	*Last dinner* 9.30	*Banquets* 100/6

Street
Map 4 A3 Somerset
High Street *BA16 0EF*
Street (0458) 43383
Proprietor Mr P. Boutin

Credit Access, Amex,
Barclaycard, Diners

Wessex Hotel 57% Ⓜ £ E

Purpose-built in the early '70s, this friendly high street hotel offers straightforward, comfortable accommodation. Modest twin-bedded bedrooms have large wardrobes, TV, radios and tea/coffee-makers, and their tiled modern bathrooms are very well fitted. The reception-cum-lounge has attractive low leather seating, and there is a small bar and useful function suite. *Amenities* dancing (Sat).

Rooms 50	*Room phone* Yes	*Confirm by* By arrang.	*Parking* Ample
with bath/shower 50	*Room TV* Yes	*Last dinner* 9.45	*Banquets* 250/–

Stroud
Map 4 B2 Gloucestershire
Rodborough Common *GL5 5DE*
Amberley (045 387) 3522

Credit Access, Amex,
Barclaycard, Diners

Bear of Rodborough 66% £ D

Situated high up in the Cotswolds a mile south of Stroud, this gabled hotel combines the best of old and new. Two stuffed bears stand guard in the smart entrance hall which leads to the bars and a comfortable residents' lounge. Bedrooms (especially those in the new wing) are extremely well fitted and have modernised, carpeted bathrooms. *Amenities* garden, dancing (Sat Oct–March), table tennis, 24-hour laundry service

Continued

| Rooms 48 | Room phone Yes | Confirm by 6 | Parking Ample |
| with bath/shower 48 | Room TV Yes | Last dinner 9.30 | Banquets 50/10 |

Stubbington
Map 5 D4 Hampshire
Titchfield Road *PO143NA*
Stubbington (032 95) 2014

Proprietor Mrs A. Bailey
Credit Access, Amex,
Barclaycard, Diners

Crofton Manor Hotel   55%   Ⓜ   £E

Peaceful grounds surround this mellow, ivy-clad stone house owned and run by the friendly Mrs Bailey. It has two pleasantly countrified lounges to relax in and a smart little bar. Bedrooms of different sizes and styles provide simple old-fashioned comfort, and bathrooms are well kept. No children under 11.
Amenities garden, outdoor swimming pool, croquet, pétanque.

| Rooms 7 | Room phone No | Confirm by By arrang. | Parking Ample |
| with bath/shower 3 | Room TV No | Last dinner 9.30 | |

Studland Bay
Map 4 C4 Dorset
Near Swanage *BH193AH*
Studland (092 944) 251

Proprietors Ferguson family

Closed late October–late March

Knoll House Hotel   63%   Ⓜ   £D

The Fergusons' rambling hotel near the sea is ideal for a family holiday (parents can even escape to the adults-only bar!). Well-furnished bedrooms are bright and roomy, tiled bathrooms neat and spotless. Inclusive weekly terms in high season. *Amenities* garden, outdoor swimming pool, tennis, 9-hole golf course, dancing (Wed in season, also Sat in high season), games room, children's dining room, nursery, playground, laundry room.

| Rooms 112 | Room phone Yes | Confirm by By arrang. | Parking Ample |
| with bath/shower 85 | Room TV No | Last dinner 8.15 | Banquets 150/– |

Sturminster Newton
Map 4 B4 Dorset
DT102AF
Sturminster Newton
(0258) 72507
Proprietor
Richard Prideaux-Brune
Rooms 12
with bath/shower 12
Room phone No
Room TV Yes
Confirm by By arrang.
Last dinner 9.30
Parking Ample
Banquets 60/20
Closed January & February

Plumber Manor   70%   Ⓜ   £E

This fine Jacobean mansion has been the Prideaux-Brune family home since the 17th century, and the book-lined sitting room and cosy bar still retain the warm, friendly feeling of a private house. Luxurious, elegant bedrooms have fine antiques and well-fitted, spacious bathrooms. There are six new rooms in a converted barn. No children under 12; no dogs.
Amenities garden, tennis, game fishing.

Sturminster Newton
Map 4 B4 Dorset
DT102AF
Sturminster Newton
(0258) 72507
Proprietor
Richard Prideaux-Brune

● **Set D** £10·50
About £29 for two

Plumber Manor Restaurant   ♟ ♛ Ⓢ

Dinner in these beautifully appointed rooms consists of a three-course set menu, with several choices supplemented by daily-changing specials. Brian Prideaux-Brune is the capable chef, and dishes like his salmon and walnut pâté with a tomato coulis or veal escalope with cream cheese, grapes and fresh mint are enjoyable for their forthright flavours, skilful saucing and attractive presentation. Smart, friendly service.

Dinner only 7.30–9.30, Sun 7.30–9
Closed Mon, also Sun Nov–March to non-residents & all Jan & Feb

Sudbury
Map 6 C3 Suffolk
Walnut Tree Lane *CC100BD*
Sudbury (0787) 75544

Manager Mr N. Fisher
Credit Access, Amex,
Barclaycard, Diners

Mill Hotel   65%   £E

Converted from a 300-year-old mill set on the river Stour, this hotel has been modernised in smart functional style, but still retains original features like the water wheel, which is visible behind glass in the large, comfortable bar. Simply furnished bedrooms in the main building and in the extension are equipped with radios and tea/coffee-makers. Well-fitted bathrooms.
Amenities coarse fishing.

Continued

Continued
Rooms 51
with bath/shower 51 | *Room phone* Yes
Room TV Yes | *Confirm by* 6
Last dinner 9.15 | *Parking* Ample
Banquets 70/20

Sunbury-on-Thames
Map 5 E2 Surrey
21 Thames Street *TW16 5QF*
Sunbury-on-Thames
(093 27) 83647
Proprietor Mr D. F. Newman

● **Set L & Set D** £9·20
incl. service
About £25 for two
Banquets 50/–

Castle Ⓢ

More like a private dining club than a restaurant, with its antiques and oil paintings, this elegant place offers tasty, reliable cooking and helpful service. Chicken Maryland, braised pheasant and delicious wild duck with morello cherries are typical items on the menu, and there are seafood dishes, too, like fish pâté, moules marinière and halibut hollandaise.
Credit Access, Amex, Barclaycard, Diners

Lunch 12.30–2.30 *Dinner* 6.30–9.30, Sat 6.30–10.30
Closed Sun & 26 December

Sunderland
Map 15 C4 Tyne & Wear
Borough Road *SR1 1PR*
Sunderland (0783) 78221
Telex 538231

Credit Access, Amex,
Barclaycard, Diners

Mowbray Park Hotel 55% £ E

This converted 19th-century house with a modern extension has a plush reception area and a choice of four bars including the Victorian-style Topper's Bar, a public bar and a cosy cocktail bar. Bedrooms have simple fitted units, tea/coffee-makers, radios and matching fabrics. Plain, adequate bathrooms have showers.

Rooms 58
with bath/shower 34 | *Room phone* Yes
Room TV Yes | *Confirm by* 6
Last dinner 9.45 | *Parking* Difficult
Banquets 84/2

Sunderland
Map 15 C4 Tyne & Wear
Queen's Parade
Seaburn *SR6 8DB*
Sunderland (0783) 292041

Credit Access, Amex,
Barclaycard, Diners

Seaburn Hotel 62% £ E

This 1930s seafront hotel has recently undergone some modernisation. There's a choice of three bars, including the smart, plush bar-lounge overlooking the sea. The best bedrooms are in the extension, with restful colour schemes and good fitted furniture; all rooms have TV, tea/coffee-makers and radios. Adequate bathrooms.
Amenities sea fishing, dancing (Sat). ♿

Rooms 82
with bath/shower 82 | *Room phone* Yes
Room TV Yes | *Confirm by* 6
Last dinner 9.30 | *Parking* Ample
Banquets 250/–

Sutton Benger
Map 4 B2 Wiltshire
Near Chippenham *SN15 4RH*
Seagry (0249) 720401

Credit Access, Amex,
Barclaycard, Diners

Bell House Hotel 67% £ D/E

Standing opposite the ancient village church, this is a charming little hotel in a lovely setting. A pleasant reception leads to the plush bar-lounge with its massive mahogany counter and comfortable seating. Bedrooms, individually fitted out in mock-Regency style, are provided with modern comforts like tea-makers and radios. Carpeted, up-to-date bathrooms. Immaculate housekeeping. *Amenities* garden.

Rooms 14
with bath/shower 14 | *Room phone* Yes
Room TV Yes | *Confirm by* By arrang.
Last dinner 10.30 | *Parking* Ample
Banquets 100/–

Sutton Coldfield
Map 10 C4 West Midlands
Four Oaks *B75 6LW*
021–308 3751

Proprietor M. J. Webb
Credit Access, Amex,
Barclaycard, Diners

Moor Hall Hotel 57% Ⓜ £ E

Standing in its own grounds next to a golf course, this secluded mansion is a popular place for conferences. It also offers comfortable overnight accommodation, bedrooms (mainly studio-style in an extension) being cheerful, roomy and well equipped. Almost all have excellent tiled bathrooms. There's a bright, modern reception-lounge area and four bars, two for residents only.
Amenities garden, dinner dance (Sat), discothèque (Wed).

Rooms 57
with bath/shower 52 | *Room phone* Yes
Room TV Yes | *Confirm by* 6
Last dinner 10.15 | *Parking* Ample
Banquets 120/–

Sutton Coldfield
Map 10 C4 West Midlands
Penns Lane, Walmley *B768LH*
021–351 3111
Telex 335789
Manager Mr C. D. Campbell
Credit Access, Amex,
Barclaycard, Diners

Rooms 116
with bath/shower 114

Penns Hall Hotel   66%   **£ D**

This 300-year-old lakeside hotel has been considerably extended over the years, and it now offers useful facilities for visiting businessmen. It has a traditionally furnished lounge and two bars, the '30s-style Richmond Room and a cosy cocktail bar. Bedrooms vary from smart studio rooms and lavish executive suites to modest compact ones.
Amenities garden, coarse fishing, dinner dance (Sat September–May).

Room phone Yes	*Confirm by* 6	*Parking* Ample
Room TV Yes	*Last dinner* 10	*Banquets* 600/4

Swallowfield
Map 5 D3 Berkshire
Basingstoke Road *RG7 1PY*
Reading (0734) 883124

● **Set L** £7·50 **Set D** £9·50
incl. service
About £27 for two
Banquets 50/–

Mill House Restaurant   ♔ ⓢ

Elegant decor, smartly laid tables and formal service set the style at this restaurant in a red-brick Georgian house. Menus offer enjoyable, attractively presented dishes such as roast beef, casseroled pheasant and venison pie. Starters might be hot smoked mackerel with gooseberry sauce or a smooth pâté with home-made herb bread. Rich chocolate mousse makes a tempting sweet. 🍷 *OUTSTANDING. Credit* Access, Amex, Barclaycard, Diners

Lunch 12.15–2 *Dinner* 7–9.30
Closed L Sat, D Sun, all Mon, 26 & 27 Dec, 1st wk Jan & last 2 wks Aug

Our inspectors never book in the name of the Egon Ronay Organisation; they disclose their identity only after paying their bills.

Sway
Map 4 C4 Hampshire
Mead End Road
Near Lymington *SO4 0EE*
Lymington (0590) 682288
Proprietors Betty & John David
Credit Amex, Barclaycard
Closed 25 & 26 December

Rooms 6
with bath/shower 4

Pine Trees Hotel   55%   Ⓜ   **£ E**

Visitors to Betty and John David's charming Victorian house are given the warmest of welcomes and treated very much like friends of the family. Old-fashioned comfort is the order of the day, with relaxing armchairs and sofas in the large TV lounge and lots of magazines to read. Homely bedrooms, which vary in style, provide simple accommodation. Adequate bathrooms. No children under 12. No dogs. *Amenities* garden.

Room phone No	*Confirm by* By arrang.	*Parking* Ample
Room TV No	*Last dinner* 9	

Swindon
Map 4 C2 Wiltshire
Blunsdon *SN2 4AD*
Swindon (0793) 721701

Proprietors Clifford family
Credit Access, Amex,
Barclaycard, Diners

Rooms 72
with bath/shower 72

Blunsdon House Hotel   68%   Ⓜ   **£ D/E**

The Clifford family continue to improve and expand their attractive converted country house, just north of the town off the A419. The entrance hall and roomy foyer-lounge are bright and modern, and there are three lively bars and extensive conference/banqueting facilities. Stylishly decorated bedrooms have mini-bars, tea-makers and well-appointed bathrooms. *Amenities* garden, children's playground, helipad, putting.   &

Room phone Yes	*Confirm by* 6	*Parking* Ample
Room TV Yes	*Last dinner* 10	*Banquets* 300/2

Swindon
Map 4 C2 Wiltshire
Oxford Road
Stratton St Margaret *SN3 4TL*
Swindon (0793) 822921
Telex 444456
Credit Access, Amex,
Barclaycard, Diners

Rooms 98
with bath/shower 98

Crest Hotel   58%   **£ D**

This low, modern hotel stands in its own grounds about four miles from junction 15 of the M4. There's a spacious air in the open-plan foyer and lounge, and the bar is a pleasant spot to relax in. Attractively decorated bedrooms in two wings are nicely furnished and well equipped; all have warm, tiled bathrooms.
Amenities garden, coffee shop (9.30am–6.30pm).   &

Room phone Yes	*Confirm by* 6	*Parking* Ample
Room TV Yes	*Last dinner* 9.45	*Banquets* 80/20

Swindon

Map 4 C2 Wiltshire
Marlborough Road *SN3 6AQ*
Swindon (0793) 24601
Telex 444464

Credit Access, Amex,
Barclaycard, Diners

Rooms 103
with bath/shower 103

Post House Hotel   59%   **£D**

Comfortable, no-nonsense accommodation and easy access to the M4 (junction 15) make this modern Cotswold-stone hotel a popular place with businessmen. Public areas (reception doubles as foyer-lounge and there are two bars) are bright and contemporary, with plenty of easy chairs. Bedrooms, too, are cheerful and functional, spotlessly clean and well equipped. Small bathrooms are simply fitted. *Amenities* outdoor swimming pool.

Room phone Yes	*Confirm by* 6	*Parking* Ample
Room TV Yes	*Last dinner* 10	*Banquets* 90/–

Swindon

Map 4 C2 Wiltshire
Fleming Way *SN1 1TN*
Swindon (0793) 28282
Telex 444250

Credit Access, Amex,
Barclaycard, Diners

Rooms 85
with bath/shower 85

Wiltshire Hotel   59%   **£D**

In the centre of town, this modern concrete hotel is particularly popular with business people. Bedrooms are neat and practical, with thoughtful extras such as fresh fruit and sewing kits, and all have compact, up-to-date bathrooms. There are two bars, including the Old Vic Bar in appealing Edwardian style, and a comfortable reception lounge.
Amenities dancing (Fri, Sat).

Room phone Yes	*Confirm by* 6	*Parking* Limited
Room TV Yes	*Last dinner* 10.30	*Banquets* 220/–

Stars in this Guide stand for the quality of the cooking only– our overriding criterion, irrespective of price, luxury or service.

Talkin Tarn

Map 13 D4 Cumbria
Brampton *CA8 1LS*
Brampton (069 77) 2340
Proprietor Mrs Claire Hoefkens

Set L £7·50 **Set D** £11·50
both incl. service
About £35 for two

Tarn End Hotel Restaurant

This charming *restaurant avec chambres* overlooking a lake is a pleasant setting in which to enjoy Martin Hoefkens' skilful cooking. An ambitious selection of often elaborate French dishes ranges from stuffed breast of chicken with Calvados and timbale of calf's sweetbreads périgourdine to lobster Thermidor and interesting specialities like preserved goose and home-smoked stuffed neck of duckling. Vegetables are capably prepared, and there's an impressive choice of sweets on the trolley. Diners wishing to stay overnight can make use of the five well-maintained bedrooms.
Credit Access

Lunch 12.30–1.45 *Dinner* 7.30–9, Sun 7.30–8.45
Closed 25 December

Taunton

Map 3 E2 Somerset
Castle Green *TA1 1NF*
Taunton (0823) 72671
Telex 46488
Proprietors Chapman family
Rooms 40
with bath/shower 40
Room phone Yes
Room TV Yes
Confirm by 6
Last dinner 9.30
Parking Ample
Banquets 125/–

Credit Access, Amex,
Barclaycard, Diners

Castle Hotel   78% Ⓜ   **£C**

With a dramatic and sometimes turbulent history stretching back hundreds of years, this magnificent creeper-clad building still retains echoes of its past, although some tasteful modernisation has taken place. The public rooms, which tend towards traditional in style, include a lofty reception hall with a heavy Jacobean table and a grandfather clock, a spacious lounge and an oak-panelled bar. There is also a functional modern cocktail bar. Most bedrooms have been thoughtfully and luxuriously improved, with good-quality furniture, smart floral fabrics and pastel colour schemes. Large, modern bathrooms.
Amenities garden, valeting, coffee shop (10am–2.30pm).

Taunton

Map 3 E2 Somerset
Castle Green *TA1 1NF*
Taunton (0823) 72674
Proprietors Chapman family
French cooking

● **Set L** from £6·50
Set D from £10·90 incl. service
About £38 for two

Castle Hotel Restaurant ★  

A revamped menu based on new French trends offers some very tempting choices in this dignified oak-panelled restaurant. Truly delicious dishes like marinated salmon with a delicate egg and dill sauce and grilled sliced breast of duck with fresh mango and lime sauce are ample proof of John Hornsby's abundant skills, and his vegetables and sweets are also outstanding.
Specialities steamed fresh seafood in a light chive, vermouth and cream sauce, fillet of lamb with garden thyme, chocolate marquise with coffee bean sauce.
🍷 *OUTSTANDING.*
Credit Access, Amex, Barclaycard, Diners

Lunch 12.30–2.15 *Dinner* 7.30–9.30

Taunton

Map 3 E2 Somerset
East Street *TA1 4LT*
Taunton (0823) 87651
Telex 46484

Credit Access, Amex,
Barclaycard, Diners

County Hotel   61%   £ D

This handsome Georgian building, formerly a coaching inn, is conveniently located right in the centre of town. The bright modern reception area is reached through the courtyard, and other public rooms, redesigned in open-plan style, include a lounge and a plush bar adorned with cricketing prints. Good-sized bedrooms have practical contemporary fitted or freestanding furniture. Compact, adequately equipped bathrooms.

Rooms 68	*Room phone* Yes	*Confirm by* 6	*Parking* Ample
with bath/shower 59	*Room TV* Yes	*Last dinner* 9.30	*Banquets* 300/–

Teignmouth

Map 3 E3 Devon
Little Haldon
Higher Easter Road *TQ14 9PB*
Teignmouth (062 67) 2196
Proprietors Mr & Mrs W. Russell
Credit Access, Amex,
Barclaycard, Diners

Venn Farm Country House Hotel   58%   Ⓜ   £ D/E

This comfortable converted farmhouse overlooking the town is nicely maintained by the Russell family. It has a lovely sunny lounge with paintings and fine old furniture and a simple bar. Bedrooms are individually decorated and have good-quality fitted units plus TV and tea/coffee-making facilities. Spotlessly clean, carpeted bathrooms. No children under seven. No dogs.
Amenities garden. **Closed** Christmas & New Year

Rooms 10	*Room phone* No	*Confirm by* By arrang.	*Parking* Ample
with bath/shower 9	*Room TV* Yes	*Last dinner* 8.30	*Banquets* 80/20

Teignmouth

Map 3 E3 Devon
Little Haldon
Higher Easter Road *TQ14 9PB*
Teignmouth (062 67) 2196
Proprietors Mr & Mrs W. Russell
About £24 for two

Venn Farm Restaurant   Ⓢ

Home-cooking is the great attraction of this friendly restaurant; where the freshest of ingredients are used – try the baked trout with herb butter. Book for Sunday lunch. *Credit* Access, Amex, Barclaycard, Diners *Lunch* 12–1.30, Sun 12–2 *Dinner* 6.30–8.30 **Closed** D Sun, L Mon & Sat, Bank Holidays to non-residents, Christmas & New Year ● **Set L** Sun only £4·50 **Set D** £6·50   ♿

Changes in data may occur in establishments after the Guide goes to press. Prices should be taken as indications rather than firm quotes.

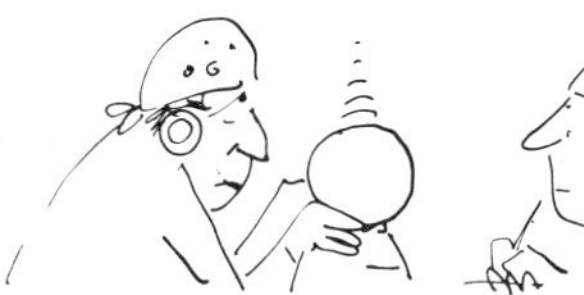

Tern Hill

Map 10 B3 Shropshire
Near Market Drayton *TF9 3PU*
Tern Hill (063 083) 310
Tenant Mr R. F. Caton
Credit Access, Amex,
Barclaycard, Diners
Closed 25 December

Tern Hill Hall Hotel   56%   Ⓜ   £ E/F

Built as a private house in 1911, this smart red-brick hotel stands in attractive grounds near the A41/A53 junction. Public rooms include a comfortable, freshly decorated residents' lounge, a large bar with striking mauve decor, and recently extended function facilities. All the practically furnished bedrooms have their own full bathroom or shower cubicle.
Amenities garden.

Rooms 10	*Room phone* No	*Confirm by* 6	*Parking* Ample
with bath/shower 6	*Room TV* Yes	*Last dinner* 9.30	*Banquets* 110/–

Tetbury

Map 4 B2 Gloucestershire
8 Long Street *GL8 8AQ*
Tetbury (0666) 52272
Telex 43232

Rooms 12
with bath/shower 12
Room phone Yes
Room TV Yes
Confirm by By arrang.
Last dinner 9.45
Parking Ample
Banquets 30/10

Credit Access, Amex,
Barclaycard, Diners

Close at Tetbury   71%   £D

In the 16th century, this impressive stone mansion was the home of a prosperous Cotswold wool merchant, and it still bears all the hallmarks of an elegant, dignified past. A massive stone fireplace lends character to the entrance hall, and there's a small bar as well as a delightful square lounge—once an open courtyard, but enclosed by an impressive dome in Georgian times. Bedrooms are mostly spacious with fine traditional furnishings (two have antique four-posters) and carefully chosen colour schemes. Tea-making facilities and trouser presses are up-to-date touches, and carpeted bathrooms are well equipped. No dogs.
Amenities garden, croquet.

Tetbury

Map 4 B2 Gloucestershire
8 Long Street *GL8 8AQ*
Tetbury (0666) 52272

● **Set L & D** £10
incl. wine & service
About £28 for two

Close at Tetbury Restaurant

Delicately moulded plaster ceilings and tall windows give this lofty hotel dining room a distinguished air. The daily-changing dinner menu is based on French-inspired dishes like escalope of veal normande and pork roasted with garlic, supplemented by seasonal fish and game; there's also an interesting cheeseboard and a nice choice of sweets. Set meals only at lunchtime.
Credit Access, Amex, Barclaycard, Diners

Lunch 12.30–1.45 *Dinner* 7.30–9.45
Closed 1 January

Tetbury

Map 4 B2 Gloucestershire
Market Place *GL8 8ES*
Tetbury (0666) 52436

Credit Access, Amex,
Barclaycard, Diners

Rooms 12
with bath/shower 12

White Hart Hotel   68%   £E

One of the oldest buildings in the town, this charming Cotswold-stone inn has lost none of its original character although it has benefited from modernisation. A neat reception-lounge leads to the lofty cocktail bar with exposed stone walls and a separate lounge with elegant brocade-covered seating. Expensively furnished bedrooms are especially impressive; all have tea-makers, trouser presses and spotless bathrooms.

| *Room phone* Yes | *Confirm by* By arrang. | *Parking* Limited |
| *Room TV* Yes | *Last dinner* 9.15 | *Banquets* 50/15 |

Tewkesbury

Map 4 B1 Gloucestershire
Lincoln Green Lane *GL20 7DN*
Tewkesbury (0684) 295405
Telex 43563

Credit Access, Amex,
Barclaycard, Diners

Rooms 52
with bath/shower 52

Tewkesbury Park Hotel   65%   £D

There are marvellous panoramic views from this much-extended 18th-century mansion, which now boasts extensive conference and sports facilities. Public rooms include four bars, while bedrooms in a modern block have pleasing decor, good fittings and smart bathrooms. *Amenities* garden, sauna, indoor swimming pool, squash, golf course, dancing (alternate Sats), discothèque (Thurs), helipad, table tennis, snooker, children's playground.

| *Room phone* Yes | *Confirm by* 7 | *Parking* Ample |
| *Room TV* Yes | *Last dinner* 9.30 | *Banquets* 150/8 |

Thame

Map 5 D2 Oxfordshire
Cornmarket *OX9 2BW*
Thame (084 421) 3661
Proprietors Mr P. I. Finestone &
Mr D. M. L. Barrington
Credit Access, Amex,
Barclaycard, Diners

Rooms 29
with bath/shower 16

Spread Eagle Hotel   59%   Ⓜ   £C/D

The facade of this pleasant town-centre hotel dates from its days as a coaching inn, but the inside has been extensively modernised. Hessian-covered walls and cane furniture are features of public rooms like the foyer, lounge and bar, and there are cane chairs, too, in the modest, cheerful bedrooms. No dogs. *Amenities* dancing (Sat monthly in winter).
Closed 2 days late December

| *Room phone* Yes | *Confirm by* By arrang. | *Parking* Ample |
| *Room TV* Yes | *Last dinner* 9.30 | *Banquets* 200/10 |

Thame

Map 5 D2 Oxfordshire
29 Lower High Street
OX9 2AA
Thame (084 421) 2146
Proprietor Terry Connor

● **Set L & Set D** £7·50 Mon–Fri
About £30 for two

Thatchers ⓢ

Fresh fish and seasonal game are among the attractions at this delightfully picturesque thatched cottage with a cosy, beamed dining room. There's also a wide choice of starters such as snails or avocado, as well as grills and sauced dishes like chicken suprême. Good ingredients are carefully handled, and service, supervised by the flamboyant Terry Connor, is very friendly.
Credit Barclaycard

Lunch 12–2, Sun 12–2.30 *Dinner* 7–10, Sat 7–10.30
Closed D Sun

Thetford

Map 6 C2 Norfolk
King Street *IP24 2AZ*
Thetford (0842) 4455

Credit Access, Amex,
Barclaycard, Diners

Rooms 42
with bath/shower 42

Bell Hotel   60%   £ D

Modern extensions blend well with the original Tudor inn at this pleasant hotel close to the river. A handsome leather-topped desk acts as a reception counter in the foyer, and there are beams and antiques throughout the public areas, which include two bars. Some bedrooms are quaint and cosy; most are modern, with pretty wallpapers and good carpets. Bathrooms are adequately fitted. *Amenities* buttery (10am–10pm).

Room phone Yes	*Confirm by* 6	*Parking* Ample
Room TV Yes	*Last dinner* 9.15	

Thornaby-on-Tees

Map 15 C5 Cleveland
Trenchard Avenue *TS17 6BR*
Stockton-on-Tees
(0642) 766511

Credit Access, Amex,
Barclaycard, Diners

Rooms 57
with bath/shower 57

Golden Eagle Hotel   60%   £ D/E

Several function rooms with their own bars make this well-run modern hotel next to Cleveland Leisure Centre (guests can use its facilities) a popular place for business and conference purposes. There are three other bars, one of them with a railways theme. Compact, functional bedrooms have geometric patterned wallpaper, simple fitted furniture and bright, tiled bathrooms. *Amenities* dancing (Mon–Sat), solarium.

Room phone Yes	*Confirm by* 6	*Parking* Ample
Room TV Yes	*Last dinner* 9.30	*Banquets* 300/–

Thornaby-on-Tees

Map 15 C5 Cleveland
Low Lane
Stainton Village *TS17 9LW*
Middlesbrough (0642) 591213
Telex 58426
Credit Access, Amex,
Barclaycard, Diners

Rooms 140
with bath/shower 140

Post House Hotel   61%   £ D

Turn off the A19 on the A174 towards Thornaby to locate this smart modern hotel. The tiled foyer-lounge has colourful orange upholstery and there is a relaxing bar and cheerful buttery. Bedrooms are simple and functional, with fitted units, tea/coffee-makers and mini-bars. Small bathrooms are adequate.
Amenities garden, coffee shop (7.30am–10.30pm). &

Room phone Yes	*Confirm by* 6	*Parking* Ample
Room TV Yes	*Last dinner* 10.15	*Banquets* 90/2

Thornbury

Map 4 B2 Avon
Near Bristol *BS12 1HH*
Thornbury (0454) 412647
Telex 449986
Proprietor Mr Kenneth Bell
Rooms 10
with bath/shower 10
Room phone Yes
Room TV Yes
Confirm by By arrang.
Last dinner 9.30
Parking Ample
Banquets 45/–
Closed 2 weeks Christmas

Credit Access, Amex,
Barclaycard

Thornbury Castle Hotel   80%   Ⓜ   £ C/D

For many years Kenneth Bell has been known for the restaurant he runs in a wing of his impresive 16th-century castle, and he has now expanded his interests by opening ten splendid bedrooms. The majority feature handsome antique furnishings, and all have pretty coordinated fabrics, dozens of useful accessories and luxuriously equipped bathrooms. Panelled public rooms, filled with antiques, oil paintings and comfortable armchairs, retain a lofty

Continued

Continued

dignity entirely in keeping with the history of the castle, which stands in beautifully laid-out formal gardens. No dogs, but kennels are available. No children under 12.
Amenities garden, helipad, croquet.

Thornbury
Map 4 B2 Avon
Near Bristol *BS12 1HH*
Thornbury (0454) 412647
Proprietor Mr Kenneth Bell

About £40 for two

Thornbury Castle Hotel Restaurant

The baronial setting, the friendly, professional service and the talents of chef-proprietor Kenneth Bell make a meal here a special occasion. Old favourites dominate the menu, and our pâté de foie de volaille was smooth and tasty. Main courses include sirloin steak with ratatouille and roast duck garnished with kumquats. Refreshing sorbets have lovely natural flavours.
♟ *OUTSTANDING. Credit* Access, Amex, Barclaycard

Lunch 12.30–2.30 *Dinner* 7–9.30
Closed some Bank Holidays & 2 weeks Christmas

Thornton-le-Dale
Map 15 D6 North Yorkshire
Near Pickering *YO18 7RR*
Pickering (0751) 74789

Credit Access, Amex,
Barclaycard, Diners

Hall Hotel 57% £E

An imposing stone-built mansion set in its own gardens and paddocks. The attractive lounge has a fine fireplace and handsome chesterfields, and two comfortable bars are popular local meeting places. Bedrooms vary from small singles and twins with balconies in the extension (which also has a splendid function room) to roomy, modernised ones in the main building. Adequate bathrooms. *Amenities* garden, squash, riding.

| *Rooms* 25 | *Room phone* Yes | *Confirm by* By arrang. | *Parking* Ample |
| *with bath/shower* 25 | *Room TV* Yes | *Last dinner* 8.30 | *Banquets* 120/– |

Thornton-le-Fylde
Map 10 A1 Lancashire
Skippool Creek
Near Blackpool *FY5 5LF*
Poulton-le-Fylde
(0253) 883497
Proprietors Scott family
Credit Amex

River House 61% Ⓜ £E

Mature gardens overlooking the river Wyre make a peaceful setting for the Scotts' charming hotel (ask for directions when booking). Antiques and flowers adorn public rooms like the chintzy lounge and cosy beamed bar, and the comfortable bedrooms are also traditional in style. The public bathroom features a splendid hooded Victorian bath, whereas the private one has modern fittings. *Amenities* garden, sea fishing, sailing, croquet.

| *Rooms* 4 | *Room phone* Yes | *Confirm by* By arrang. | *Parking* Ample |
| *with bath/shower* 1 | *Room TV* Yes | *Last dinner* 9.30 | *Banquets* 45/– |

Thornton-le-Fylde
Map 10 A1 Lancashire
Skippool Creek
Near Blackpool *FY5 5LF*
Poulton-le-Fylde
(0253) 883497
Proprietors Scott family

● **Set L** Sun only £4·75
Set D £6·75
About £28 for two

River House Restaurant

It's essential to book at this charming restaurant overlooking the lovely garden. Bill Scott does the cooking, making the very best of fresh local produce on a menu which could include lobster and salmon, guinea fowl with apricots and almonds, rare beef Wellington and moist, tasty roast suckling pig. Home-made puddings such as coffee gâteau make an appealing finish. *Credit* Amex

Lunch 12.30–2, Sun at 1 *Dinner* 7.30–9.30
Closed Mon (occasionally)

Thurlestone
Map 3 D3 Devon
Near Kingsbridge *TQ7 3NN*
Thurlestone (054 857) 382
Proprietors Grose family

Credit Access, Amex,
Barclaycard, Diners
Closed 2 weeks January

Thurlestone Hotel 63% Ⓜ £C/D

Set in 14 acres of picturesque gardens and parkland overlooking the sea, this imposing whitewashed building is a popular holiday hotel with a superb range of recreational facilities. Spacious, comfortably appointed public rooms include a bright, airy lounge and a cocktail bar. Bedrooms (some with balconies) are quite large, with modern furniture and matching soft furnishings. Spotlessly clean, carpeted bathrooms have contemporary suites. *Amenities* garden, sauna, indoor & outdoor swimming pools, tennis, squash, 9-hole golf course, dancing (Sat in winter), discothèque (twice weekly in summer), solarium, keep-fit equipment, billiards, badminton, petrol pumps, games room, ladies' hairdressing.

Continued

Rooms 74 *with bath/shower* 62	*Room phone* Yes *Room TV* Yes	*Confirm by* By arrang. *Last dinner* 9	*Parking* Ample *Banquets* 120/–

Tiverton

Map 3 D2 Devon
18 Newport Street *EX16 6NL*
Tiverton (0884) 254256

● **Set D** £8·50 incl. wine
About £27 for two
Banquets 50/25

Hendersons

A fresh, simply decorated restaurant, where Elizabeth Ambler keeps the customers happy with her excellent cooking. Beignets au fromage is a delicious starter, and main courses, served with a selection of imaginative vegetables, could include chicken in a delicate cream sauce, sole meunière and beef Stroganoff. An eye-catching sweet trolley is full of goodies like crème brûlée and coffee meringue. *Credit* Access, Barclaycard

Lunch 12.15–2 *Dinner* 7.15–10
Closed Sun & 2 days Christmas

Tonbridge

Map 7 B5 Kent
High Street *TN9 1DD*
Tonbridge (0732) 357966

Manager Mr S. Demutti
Credit Access, Amex,
Barclaycard, Diners

Rose & Crown Hotel   57%   £ D

Bedrooms in this old coaching inn provide good modern comforts in the beamed original part as well as the purpose-built extension, and neat bathrooms are also up to date. Downstairs are a pleasant residents' lounge and a cosy little bar with blackened beams.
Amenities garden, 24-hour laundry service.

Rooms 52 *with bath/shower* 52	*Room phone* Yes *Room TV* Yes	*Confirm by* 6 *Last dinner* 9	*Parking* Ample *Banquets* 75/–

Torquay

Map 3 D3 Devon
Asheldon Road
Wellswood *TQ1 2QS*
Torquay (0803) 23637
Proprietors
Mr & Mrs P. J. Phillips
Closed November–April

Gleneagles Hotel   61% Ⓜ   £ E

There are lovely views from the comfortable bar-lounge of this modern, family-run hotel, which has an attractive, welcoming entrance hall and a cosy TV lounge. Cheerful bedrooms, some with balconies, have fitted furnishings and compact, nicely appointed bathrooms. Family rooms have TVs. *Amenities* garden, outdoor swimming pool, dancing (Mon–Fri Whitsun–end September).

Rooms 42 *with bath/shower* 42	*Room phone* Some *Room TV* Some	*Confirm by* 6 *Last dinner* 8	*Parking* Ample

Torquay

Map 3 D3 Devon
Seafront *TQ2 6NT*
Torquay (0803) 25234
Telex 42891

Credit Access, Amex,
Barclaycard, Diners

Grand Hotel   69%   £ C

A Victorian seafront hotel, with lofty, comfortably modernised lounges (the sun lounge overlooks the bay), a relaxing cocktail bar in black and chrome and up-to-date conference facilities. Spacious bedrooms–many also with fine sea views–have smart darkwood furnishings and gleaming bathrooms.
Amenities garden, sauna, outdoor swimming pool, tennis, dinner dance (Sat), discothèque (Fri in summer), hairdressing, games room.

Rooms 110 *with bath/shower* 110	*Room phone* Yes *Room TV* Yes	*Confirm by* 7 *Last dinner* 9.15	*Parking* Ample *Banquets* 300/6

Torquay

Map 3 D3 Devon
Park Hill Road *TQ1 2DG*
Torquay (0803) 24301
Telex 42849
Manager Harry Murray
Rooms 180
with bath/shower 180
Room phone Yes
Room TV Yes
Confirm by By arrang.
Last dinner 9.30
Parking Ample
Banquets 450/2

Imperial Hotel   82% *E*   £ B

The facade is modern, but inside this luxury hotel overlooking Tor Bay everything is splendidly traditional. The spacious entrance hall has handsome panelling, and other public rooms are stylishly decorated and sumptuously furnished, with chandeliers, ornate ceilings, fine antiques and plenty of comfortable armchairs. Attractive flower displays add a fresh, bright look, and picture windows make the most of the sea views. The same high standards of

Continued

England

Continued
Credit Access, Amex,
Barclaycard, Diners

decor and furnishings extend to the large bedrooms, which all have comprehensively equipped tiled bathrooms. *Amenities* garden, sauna, indoor & outdoor swimming pools, tennis, squash, dancing (Mon–Sat), gymnasium, health centre, putting, hairdressing, croquet, curling, films (Sun). &

Torquay — John Dory 

Map 3 D3 Devon
7 Lisburne Square *TQ1 2PT*
Torquay (0803) 25217

Colin Brown's cosy little restaurant makes a pleasant setting for an enjoyable dinner. The menu, which changes every six months, is dominated by beautifully fresh seafood ranging from scallops and lobster in various guises to poached salmon and John Dory itself, grilled with fennel. There are also a few meat dishes such as steak and breast of pheasant in pâté sauce.
Credit Access

About £28 for two
Banquets 16/8

Dinner only 7–9.30
Closed Sun & Mon October–Whitsun & mid December–2nd week January

---

Torquay — Kistor Hotel 60% Ⓜ £D/E

Map 3 D3 Devon
Belgrave Road *TQ2 5HF*
Torquay (0803) 23219
Proprietors
Mr & Mrs Jonathan Hassell
Credit Access, Amex,
Barclaycard

Well-designed extensions have made this Victorian building near the seafront into a comfortable holiday hotel. A smart cocktail bar and several lounges offer plenty of attractive modern seating, and cheerful bedrooms have fitted units and up-to-date bathrooms. Staff are friendly and housekeeping is excellent. *Amenities* garden, sauna, indoor swimming pool, dancing (Fri, Sat also Mon Easter–October), croquet, putting, crazy golf.

Rooms 46
with bath/shower 46

Room phone No	*Confirm by* By arrang.	*Parking* Ample
Room TV Yes	*Last dinner* 8.30	*Banquets* 100/–

Torquay — Livermead Cliff Hotel 61% Ⓜ £D

Map 3 D3 Devon
Sea Front, Torbay Road *TQ2 6RQ*
Torquay (0803) 22110
Proprietors
Perry & Heather families
Credit Access, Barclaycard

A firm favourite with families on holiday, this friendly hotel enjoys a splendid position right on the seafront. The cheerful, sunny lounge has fine sea views, and there's a comfortable cocktail bar. Bedrooms and bathrooms are neat, bright and practical. Guests can use the extensive facilities of the Livermead House Hotel. *Amenities* garden, outdoor swimming pool, sea fishing, films, music (Wed in season).

Rooms 63
with bath/shower 51

Room phone No	*Confirm by* 6	*Parking* Ample
Room TV Most	*Last dinner* 8.30	*Banquets* 80/2

Torquay — Livermead House Hotel 63% Ⓜ £E

Map 3 D3 Devon
Sea Front, Torbay Road *TQ2 6QJ*
Torquay (0803) 24361
Telex 42918
Proprietors
Perry & Heather families
Credit Access, Barclaycard

A pleasant seafront hotel offering comfortable accommodation and extensive leisure facilities. Public rooms are bright and airy, with splendid views across Torbay, and cheerful bedrooms have smart built-in teak units and tea/coffee-makers. *Amenities* garden, sauna, outdoor swimming pool, tennis, squash, sea fishing, dancing (Mon, Wed), billiards, table tennis, hairdressing, solarium, laundry room, keep-fit equipment. &

Rooms 76
with bath/shower 56

Room phone No	*Confirm by* 6	*Parking* Ample
Room TV Most	*Last dinner* 8.30	*Banquets* 120/10

Torquay — Osborne Hotel 61% £C/D

Map 3 D3 Devon
Meadfoot Beach *TQ1 2LL*
Torquay (0803) 213311

Credit Access, Amex,
Barclaycard, Diners

This secluded hotel has lovely views of Torbay and offers modest, up-to-date comfort. Public areas include a smart reception lounge and a pleasant cocktail bar. Most bedrooms are simply fitted in modern style; a few have been attractively refurbished. Adequate tiled bathrooms. No dogs.
Amenities garden, sauna, outdoor swimming pool, tennis, children's games room, billiards, gymnasium, solarium, baby listening.

Rooms 40
with bath/shower 40

Room phone Yes	*Confirm by* 6	*Parking* Limited
Room TV Yes	*Last dinner* 10	*Banquets* 80/15

Torquay
Map 3 D3 Devon
Babbacombe Road *TQ13TG*
Torquay (0803) 22271
Telex 42606
Manager Paul Uphill

Credit Access, Amex,
Barclaycard, Diners

Palace Hotel 68% £C

Active holiday-makers are in their element at this vast, green-painted Victorian hotel, whose extensive sports facilities include professional coaching. Wooded grounds offer more leisurely exercise, and still less energy is required to enjoy the comfortable public rooms–an elegant bar, numerous lounges, two TV rooms and even a sun lounge overlooking the Italian garden. Cheerful bedrooms are equipped with armchairs and have good-quality fitted furniture; adequate bathrooms are carpeted.
Amenities garden, sauna, indoor & outdoor swimming pools, tennis, squash, 9-hole golf course, sea fishing, dancing (Mon–Sat), buttery (10.30am–6pm), nanny, hairdressing, petrol pumps, billiards, table tennis, putting.

Rooms 138
with bath/shower 114

Room phone Yes
Room TV Yes

Confirm by By arrang.
Last dinner 9

Parking Ample
Banquets 600/20

Torquay
Map 3 D3 Devon
Belgrave Road *TQ25HP*
Torquay (0803) 213232

Proprietor Mr A. F. Marshall
Credit Access, Amex,
Barclaycard, Diners

Rainbow House Hotel 55% Ⓜ £D

The emphasis at this cheerful, rambling hotel is on an impressive range of leisure activities. There's a wide choice of lounges and bars, and functionally fitted bedrooms offer adequate comforts. Compact tiled bathrooms. *Amenities* garden, sauna, indoor & outdoor swimming pools, squash, dancing (Mon–Sat), gymnasium, cabaret (in season), table tennis, buttery (10.30am–10.30pm), games room, solarium, in-house movies, baby listening. &

Rooms 97
with bath/shower 84

Room phone Some
Room TV Yes

Confirm by By arrang.
Last dinner 11.30

Parking Ample
Banquets 250/-

Torquay
Map 3 D3 Devon
Chestnut Avenue *TQ25JS*
Torquay (0803) 27135
Proprietors Mrs M. Edmonds &
Mr & Mrs J. Cowie

Toorak Hotel 64% Ⓜ £D

Several houses joined together make up this pleasant holiday hotel, which has numerous lounges (two with TV) and a large bar. Comfortable bedrooms of varying sizes are simply decorated and bathrooms are adequate.
Amenities garden, outdoor swimming pool, tennis, dinner dance (Wed, Sat in season), snooker, games room, bowling green, crazy golf, ladies' hairdressing, laundry room, croquet, coffee shop (10am–6 pm in summer).

Rooms 75
with bath/shower 62

Room phone No
Room TV No

Confirm by By arrang.
Last dinner 8.15

Parking Ample
Banquets 150/30

Totnes
Map 3 D3 Devon
6 North Street *TQ95NZ*
Totnes (0803) 863480
Proprietors Mr & Mrs B. J. Sellick

Elbow Room 

The talented Mrs Sellick prepares classic dishes from all over the world at this charming stone-walled restaurant. Flavour-packed crab chowder makes a rich, hearty starter, while main courses could include roast duckling, turbot Marguéry and tender bœuf smitane. Vegetables get the same careful treatment, and our hazelnut meringue gâteau was just one of the delicious desserts. Lighter lunches. *Credit* Amex, Barclaycard

Lunch 12–2 *Dinner* 7.30–9.30, Sat 7.30–10
Closed L Sat, all Sun, Mon, Bank Holidays & 2 weeks mid November

About £32 for two

Tresco
Map 2 A2 Isles of Scilly
(Cornwall) *TR240PU*
Scillonia (0720) 22883
Managers Mr & Mrs J. Pyatt

Credit Access, Amex,
Barclaycard, Diners

Island Hotel 65% £C

All is peace and tranquillity at this friendly modern hotel in a luxuriant garden setting by the sea. The lounge and bar (with sun terrace) are bright and airy, and cheerful bedrooms have fitted units and neat bathrooms. No dogs. Inclusive terms only. *Amenities* garden, outdoor swimming pool, sea fishing, croquet, bowls, sailing, rowing boats, table tennis, games room, private beach, golf driving range. **Closed** mid October–end March

Rooms 36
with bath/shower 29

Room phone Yes
Room TV Some

Confirm by By arrang.
Last dinner 8.15

Parking No cars
Banquets 25/-

Tresco

Map 2 A2 Isles of Scilly
(Cornwall) *TR24 0PU*
Scillonia (0720) 22883
Managers Mr & Mrs J. Pyatt

● **Set L** Sun only £7
Set D £12·50
About £33 for two

Island Hotel Restaurant ⓢ

Well-spaced tables, smart modern furnishings and fine sea views make for an attractive setting in which to enjoy a good choice of straightforward dishes ranging from chicken liver pâté and rich, creamy vegetable soup to braised oxtail, roast pork and chicken Bercy served with excellent vegetables. Well-stocked cheeseboard and delicious sweets. Cold buffet Sunday evenings.
 *ABOVE AVERAGE. Credit* Access, Amex, Barclaycard, Diners

Lunch 12.30–1.30, Sun 1–1.45 *Dinner* 7.15–8.15
Closed mid October–end March

Troutbeck

Map 13 D5 Cumbria
Near Windermere *LA23 1PL*
Ambleside (096 63) 3193

Proprietor Mr C. J. Poulsom
Closed mid November–mid
February

Mortal Man Hotel *(Inn)* Ⓜ £ E

Dating back to 1689, this charming inn was once a favourite haunt of the Lakeland poets. It's still a friendly, welcoming place, and its public rooms include a little TV lounge for residents and a popular beamed bar. Traditionally furnished bedrooms are well supplied with little extras to make one's stay a comfortable one. No children under five. Inclusive terms only.
Amenities garden.

Rooms 15	*Room phone* No	*Confirm by* 6	*Parking* Ample
with bath/shower 10	*Room TV* No	*Last dinner* 8	*Banquets* 50/10

Troutbeck

Map 13 D5 Cumbria
Near Windermere *LA23 1PL*
Ambleside (096 63) 3193
Proprietor Mr C. J. Poulsom

● **Set L** £6 **Set D** £9
incl. service
About £25 for two

Mortal Man Hotel Restaurant ⓢ

Honest traditional fare is Albert Miller's speciality in this charming Lakeland inn. His five-course fixed-price menus feature nourishing soups, light quiches and main courses ranging from excellent roasts and grills to local pigeon braised with red wine or baked trout. Vegetables are carefully cooked, and the sweet trolley has some delightful home-made creations like tangy lemon meringue tart.

Lunch Sun only 1–2 *Dinner* 7.30–8
Closed mid November–mid February

Truro

Map 2 B3 Cornwall
Tregolls Road *TR1 1JZ*
Truro (0872) 3513
Manager Mr J. C. McBride
Credit Access, Amex,
Barclaycard, Diners
Closed 25 & 26 December

Brookdale Hotel 60% Ⓜ £ E

Trim gardens surround this friendly hotel, which stands above the A39 St Austell road. Beautiful flower displays add splashes of colour to the crisply decorated public rooms, which include a relaxing lounge with smart white panelling and a stylish cocktail bar. Bright, cheerful bedrooms (larger in the annexes) have modern fitted units and colourful wallpaper. Bathrooms, public and private, are excellent. *Amenities* garden.

Rooms 55	*Room phone* Yes	*Confirm by* By arrang.	*Parking* Ample
with bath/shower 16	*Room TV* Yes	*Last dinner* 8.45	*Banquets* 100/4

Tunbridge Wells

Map 7 B5 Kent
Mount Ephraim *TN4 8XJ*
Tunbridge Wells (0892) 20331
Telex 957188
Manager Peter N. Hall
Credit Access, Amex,
Barclaycard, Diners

Spa Hotel 64% £ D

Dating from 1766, this impressive building stands in six acres of mature gardens. The huge reception-lounge area is luxuriously comfortable, and there's a TV room as well as a bar with equestrian decor. Good-sized bedrooms, traditional or modern, are nicely furnished, and bathrooms are well fitted. Caring staff provide excellent personal service.
Amenities garden, mini-golf, games room, croquet, 24-hour laundry service.

Rooms 71	*Room phone* Yes	*Confirm by* By arrang.	*Parking* Ample
with bath/shower 69	*Room TV* Yes	*Last dinner* 9.30	*Banquets* 250/–

Tunbridge Wells

Map 7 B5 Kent
Mount Ephraim *TN4 8XJ*
Tunbridge Wells (0892) 20331

Manager Mr Luigi

Spa Hotel Restaurant

Eat in style in this lofty, elegant room, whose windows look out over the hotel's attractive grounds. The menu ranges from simple favourites like onion soup or pâté maison to the more unusual snails with Pernod and almond butter or tender filet mignon Messina. Cooking is generally reliable and there's a tempting cheeseboard. Set meals only on Sunday.
Credit Access, Amex, Barclaycard, Diners

Continued

● **Set L** £6·25 **Set D** £7
About £30 for two
Banquets 250/–

Lunch 12.30–2 *Dinner* 7–9.30, Sun 7–8.30

Turvey
Map 5 E1 Bedfordshire
MK43 8DB
Turvey (023 064) 213
Proprietors
Mr & Mrs P. D. Galvani
About £26 for two

Laws at Turvey Restaurant　　　🍸 Ⓢ

A charming little hotel restaurant which proclaims the virtues of inventive home cooking. Tempting dishes range from chicken tarragon to poached Scotch salmon with yoghurt and cucumber sauce. Delicious sweets, too. *Credit* Access, Barclaycard *Lunch* 12.30–1.30 *Dinner* 7.30–9, Fri & Sat 7.30–10 **Closed** Sun, Easter & 25 December *Banquets* 36/–

Tutbury
Map 10 C3 Staffordshire
Nr Burton upon Trent *DE13 9LS*
Burton upon Trent
(0283) 813030
Props. Mr & Mrs D. J. Martindale
Credit Access, Amex,
Barclaycard, Diners

Ye Olde Dog & Partridge Hotel *(Inn)* Ⓜ　　£ E

Dating back to the 15th century, this charming town-centre inn has been attractively modernised. Bedrooms (most of them in an adjacent building) are spacious and colourful, and all have mini-bars; bathrooms are streamlined and spotless. There are also several popular, traditional bars, a patio and a peaceful first-floor residents' lounge. No children under ten. *Amenities* garden.

Rooms 18	*Room phone* Yes	*Confirm by* By arrang.	*Parking* Ample
with bath/shower 15	*Room TV* Yes	*Last dinner* 9.45	

Ullswater
Map 13 D5 Cumbria
Watermillock *CA11 0JJ*
Pooley Bridge (085 36) 444

Rooms 24
with bath/shower 24
Room phone Yes
Room TV No
Confirm by 6
Last dinner 9
Parking Ample
Banquets 85/–
Closed January–mid March

Credit Access, Amex,
Barclaycard, Diners

Leeming on Ullswater　75%　Ⓜ　　£ B/C

Comfort, luxury and service reach high levels at this immaculately kept Georgian manor house, which stands in beautiful mature gardens stretching down to the lake. Public rooms like the sumptuously furnished lounges and cosy bar are models of traditional elegance, and bedrooms, too, are most appealing, with pleasantly coordinated fabrics, attractive whitewood furniture and spotless, well-fitted bathrooms. Seven smart modern rooms are in a nearby converted stone cottage. In addition to its own amenities, the hotel can arrange deer stalking and driven pheasant shooting on an adjacent estate. No children under eight. No dogs. *Amenities* garden, coarse & game fishing, 24-hour laundry service, slipway, croquet, hotel boats. ♿

Ullswater
Map 13 D5 Cumbria
Watermillock *CA11 0JJ*
Pooley Bridge (085 36) 444

Leeming on Ullswater Restaurant　　👑 Ⓢ

Superb views across the gardens are a feature of this graceful dining room, where at lunch time an extensive buffet is served. Four-course dinners include excellent soups like our carrot and watercress, a seafood second course and meat dishes like lamb cutlets with Madeira sauce and roast venison. Linzer torte is one of many delicious desserts.
🍷 *OUTSTANDING. Credit* Access, Amex, Barclaycard, Diners ♿

● **Set L** £5 **Set D** £13
About £37 for two

Lunch 12.30–1.45 *Dinner* 7.45–8.45
Closed some Bank Holidays & January–mid March

Ullswater
Map 13 D5 Cumbria
Watermillock
Near Penrith *CA11 0JN*
Pooley Bridge (085 36) 204

Closed January–mid March

Old Church Hotel　57%　Ⓜ　　£ D/E

A serene lakeside setting, with smooth lawns running down to the water's edge, is a delightful feature of this immaculate Georgian house, most of whose individually furnished bedrooms have splendid lake views. Public rooms are warm and relaxing and include a charming pink lounge, a TV room and an attractive cocktail bar.
Amenities garden, coarse & game fishing, hotel boats, board sailing.

Rooms 12	*Room phone* No	*Confirm by* By arrang.	*Parking* Ample
with bath/shower 7	*Room TV* No	*Last dinner* 8.30	

Ullswater
Map 13 D5 Cumbria
Howtown, near Penrith *CA10 2LZ*
Pooley Bridge (085 36) 301
Proprietors
Francis Coulson & Brian Sack
Rooms 29
with bath/shower 21
Room phone Yes
Room TV Yes
Confirm by By arrang.
Last dinner 8.45
Parking Ample

Closed 5 December–5 March

Sharrow Bay Country House Hotel 78% Ⓜ £D/E

Brian Sack's and Francis Coulson's handsome greystone hotel stands in peaceful and stunningly beautiful countryside overlooking Ullswater and the surrounding hills. Comfortable sofas, pieces of period furniture and collections of glass and porcelain fill the two delightful lounges, where you can relax with a book or a drink. Sherry, iced water and biscuits are among the extras provided in the tastefully appointed bedrooms, all of which have lovely lake views; some rooms are in the even more tranquil Bank House, a delightful building 1½ miles away on the lake shore. Discreet, friendly service is of the highest standard. Inclusive terms only. No children under 13. No dogs. *Amenities* garden.

Ullswater
Map 13 D5 Cumbria
Howtown, near Penrith *CA10 2LZ*
Pooley Bridge (085 36) 301
Proprietors
Francis Coulson & Brian Sack

● **Set L** £15·50 **Set D** £19·50
incl. service
About £46 for two

Sharrow Bay Hotel Restaurant ★ ★ ♤ ♔ Ⓢ

Francis Coulson's consummate skills shine as brightly as the silverware in this elegant restaurant, where visitors continue to be delighted by his superb six-course meals. Starters ranging from curried apple soup to pâté in puff pastry are followed by a fish dish, a tangy sorbet and a main course which could be a simple omelette or an elaborate masterpiece like roast breast of duckling served with a mousseline of duckling and two sauces–redcurrant and Madeira, and juniper berry. Sweets are sensational too, and there's an excellent English cheeseboard. **Specialities** hot fish terrine with herb and cream sauce, game in season, marquise fondante au chocolat with coffee bean sauce. ♟ *OUTSTANDING.* ♿

Lunch 1–1.45 *Dinner* 8–8.45
Closed 5 December–5 March

Any person using our name to obtain free hospitality is a fraud. Proprietors, please inform the police and us.

Underbarrow
Map 13 D5 Cumbria
Near Kendal *LA8 8HF*
Crosthwaite (044 88) 387
Proprietors
Frank & Christine Jackson
Closed 27 Dec–mid Feb &
Mon–Thurs mid Feb–end Mar

Greenriggs Country House Hotel 62% Ⓜ £E

Set in lovely countryside three miles west of Kendal, this carefully converted 18th-century house is a pleasant and peaceful place to stay. A small entrance hall leads on to the garden. Cheerful bedrooms have pretty wallpaper and darkwood furniture; those in the annexe are more modern. Inclusive terms only except Sundays.
Amenities garden, croquet.

Rooms 14	*Room phone* No	*Confirm by* By arrang.	*Parking* Ample
with bath/shower 10	*Room TV* No	*Last dinner* 8	*Banquets* 45/10

Underbarrow
Map 13 D5 Cumbria
Near Kendal *LA8 8HF*
Crosthwaite (044 88) 387
Proprietors
Frank & Christine Jackson

● **Set D** £10
About £28 for two

Greenriggs Country House Hotel Restaurant ♤ Ⓢ

Frank Jackson has a passionate love of cooking and offers an enterprising choice of dishes on his four-course, fixed-price menu. Game livers in marjoram and cream might be followed by spiced apple soup, and then a main course like poached salmon with cucumber sauce and excellent vegetables. To finish there are tempting sweets such as raspberry brûlée or a choice of English cheeses. ♟ *ABOVE AVERAGE.*

Dinner only at 8
Closed Sun, 27 Dec–mid Feb & Mon–Thurs mid Feb–end Mar

Underbarrow

Map 13 D5 Cumbria
Near Kendal *LA8 8BB*
Crosthwaite (044 88) 397
Proprietors Johnson family
English cooking

● **Set D** £11
About £25 for two

Tullythwaite House ★  

Hospitality comes naturally to Mrs Johnson, who greets visitors to her delightful farmhouse restaurant as if they were dear friends invited for dinner (the gong sounds at 7 o'clock sharp). Daughter-in-law Barbara presides in the kitchen, maintaining some of the finest features of traditional English cooking: the centrepiece of her delicious set meal is a marvellous roast with excellent home-grown vegetables, preceded by starters like subtle cream of Stilton soup and finishing with *two* puddings for each guest. Unlicensed, so bring your own wine.
Specialities prawn cheesecake, tongue roll stuffed with chicken liver, roast duck with orange sauce, fresh fruit syllabub.

Dinner only at 7
Closed Sun, Mon & December–March

Upper Slaughter

Map 4 C1 Gloucestershire
Bourton-on-the-Water
Near Cheltenham *GL54 2JD*
Bourton-on-the-Water
(0451) 20243
Credit Access, Amex,
Barclaycard, Diners

Rooms 15
with bath/shower 14

Lords of the Manor Hotel   67%   Ⓜ   £D

A beautiful walled garden with mature trees and an attractive stream enhances the charm of this fine Cotswold manor house. The handsome, comfortably appointed public rooms retain much of their original elegance, and the bedrooms have traditional and antique furniture and well-fitted, carpeted bathrooms. Charming, caring hosts belong to the family that has owned the manor for over 200 years. *Amenities* garden, game fishing, croquet.

Room phone Yes	*Confirm by* 6	*Parking* Ample
Room TV No	*Last dinner* 9.30	

Upper Slaughter

Map 4 C1 Gloucestershire
Bourton-on-the-Water
Near Cheltenham *GL54 2JD*
Bourton-on-the-Water
(0451) 20243
About £25 for two

Lords of the Manor Hotel Restaurant   ♛ ⑤

Local produce features prominently on the daily-changing menu at this traditional hotel restaurant. Dishes range from grilled Cotswold trout to roast loin of veal, and puddings are particularly delicious.
Credit Access, Amex, Barclaycard, Diners
Lunch 12.30–1.45 *Dinner* 7.30–9.30 ● **Set L** £5, Sun £6

Uppingham

Map 11 E4 Leicestershire
High Street *LE15 9PY*
Uppingham (057 282) 3535

Credit Access, Amex,
Barclaycard, Diners

Rooms 26
with bath/shower 15

Falcon Hotel   56%   £E/F

Dating back to the 16th century, this stone coaching inn still prides itself on its hospitality. Windsor chairs and polished tables fill the charming lounge, and there are two bars with plenty of atmosphere. Bedrooms in the main building are cheerful and traditionally furnished (one has an Elizabethan four-poster), while those in the converted stable block are smaller, modern and functional. *Amenities* garden.

Room phone Yes	*Confirm by* By arrang.	*Parking* Ample
Room TV Yes	*Last dinner* 9.45	*Banquets* 80/10

Our inspectors are our full-time employees; they are professionally trained by us.

Uppingham

Map 11 E4 Leicestershire
High Street East *LE15 9PZ*
Uppingham (0572) 822951

French cooking

● **Set D** £10·50 incl. service
Sat £11
About £27 for two

Lake Isle   

Roy Richards does all the cooking in this rustic, simply furnished restaurant, offering an intriguing five-course set dinner menu that features carefully prepared French dishes. After a soup like spiced tomato there's perhaps terrine of whiting, followed by a main course such as chicken fricassee. Good cheeses, too, and sweets like lemon soufflé. Booking advisable.
🍷 *OUTSTANDING.*

Dinner only 7.30–9.30
Closed Sun & Mon

Uttoxeter
Map 10 C3 Staffordshire
Carter Street *ST14 8EU*
Uttoxeter (088 93) 2437

Credit Access, Barclaycard

White Hart Hotel *(Inn)*   **£E**

Market days are especially busy at this friendly, well-run inn, whose large and cheerful bar-lounge is a very popular meeting place. Residents have their own comfortable little lounge, too, and there's a splendid banqueting room with some fine panelling brought from Hampton Court. Homely bedrooms are furnished in styles ranging from antique to modern. Adequate bathrooms. *Amenities* patio.

Rooms 16	*Room phone* Yes	*Confirm by* By arrang.	*Parking* Ample
with bath/shower 12	*Room TV* No	*Last dinner* 10	*Banquets* 55/–

Ventnor
Map 5 D4 Isle of Wight
Belgrave Road *PO38 1JJ*
Ventnor (0983) 852186

Manager Mr D. Joyce
Credit Access, Amex,
Barclaycard, Diners

Royal Hotel   57%   **£D**

A relaxed atmosphere prevails at this solid sandstone hotel, where families are especially welcome. The comfortable entrance lounge overlooks the gardens, where there are extensive play areas, and the cosy little bar is a cheerful place. Bedrooms (many of family size) have practical furnishings and smart bathrooms. *Amenities* garden, outdoor swimming pool, discothèque (2 nights weekly in winter, 6 in summer), games room, laundry room.

Rooms 55	*Room phone* Yes	*Confirm by* 6	*Parking* Ample
with bath/shower 55	*Room TV* Yes	*Last dinner* 9	*Banquets* 110/–

Veryan
Map 2 B3 Cornwall
Carne Beach
Near Truro *TR2 5PF*
Veryan (087 250) 279
Credit Access, Amex,
Barclaycard, Diners
Closed early January–end March

Nare Hotel   62% Ⓜ   **£D**

A superb clifftop setting above a sandy beach is one of the delights of this well-run holiday hotel, which also has attractive gardens and a spacious terrace. Well-kept public rooms include two relaxing lounges and a smart bar with bamboo seating. Bedrooms and bathrooms are simply fitted in contemporary style. No dogs. *Amenities* garden, sauna, outdoor swimming pool, tennis, sea fishing, games room, table tennis.

Rooms 40	*Room phone* No	*Confirm by* By arrang.	*Parking* Ample
with bath/shower 33	*Room TV* No	*Last dinner* 9.15	*Banquets* 150/–

Virginia Water
Map 5 E3 Surrey
London Road *GU25 4QE*
Wentworth (099 04) 4424

● **Set L** £5·25 **Set D** £8·25
About £32 for two
Banquets 160/8

Sancho Panza   ♔ Ⓢ

Spanish classics and market-fresh fish are the mainstay of the menu at this comfortable, stylish restaurant. Crab basquaise and gazpacho Andaluz are among the tasty starters, while main courses include grills, roasts and specialities such as paella, superb fish stew and meltingly tender, crisp-skinned roast suckling pig served with apple sauce and very good vegetables. ♟ *ABOVE AVERAGE. Credit* Access, Amex, Barclaycard, Diners &

Lunch 12–2.30 *Dinner* 7.30–10.30, Fri & Sat 7.30–11
Closed D Sun, all 1 January & 26 December

Wadhurst
Map 7 B6 East Sussex
Wallcrouch *TN5 7JG*
Ticehurst (0580) 200430

● **Set D** from £9·50
About £30 for two

Spindlewood Hotel Restaurant   ♧ Ⓢ

Enjoy home-made canapés and an aperitif while perusing the menu of this delightful restaurant. Whatever your taste, you'll find something pleasing, whether it's a favourite like herby lamb fillet or an imaginative speciality such as wild duck with a pleasantly sharp citrus sauce. Vegetables are particularly good and presentation is most attractive.
♟ *ABOVE AVERAGE. Credit* Access, Barclaycard, Diners

Dinner only 7.15–9.30
Closed Sun & Mon to non-residents & 4 days Christmas

Wakefield
Map 10 C1 West Yorkshire
Queen's Drive
Ossett *WK5 9BE*
Wakefield (0924) 276388
Telex 55407
Credit Access, Amex,
Barclaycard, Diners

Post House Hotel   64%   **£D**

A low-rise modern building near junction 40 of the M1, this well-designed hotel has a spacious, comfortable lounge, a bright coffee shop and several conference rooms. There's also the attractive, intimate Turnpike Bar. Good-sized bedrooms have pleasant contemporary decor and fitted furnishings, with ample writing space, tea-makers, mini-bars and modern bathrooms. *Amenities* garden, dinner dance (Sat), coffee shop (7am–11pm). &

Continued

| Rooms 96 | Room phone Yes | Confirm by 6 | Parking Ample |
| with bath/shower 96 | Room TV Yes | Last dinner 10.30 | Banquets 160/– |

Wakefield

Map 10 C1 West Yorkshire
Queen Street *WF1 1JU*
Wakefield (0924) 72111

Credit Access, Amex,
Barclaycard, Diners

Swallow Hotel 59% £E

Designed with business people in mind, this functional modern hotel close to the city centre has numerous conference rooms and offers straightforward accommodation. Public rooms, which are situated on the first floor, include a small lounge, a striking contemporary cocktail bar and a wine bar. Centrally heated bedrooms (including four for families) have practical fitted furniture and tea-makers. Bathrooms are adequate.

| Rooms 68 | Room phone Yes | Confirm by 6 | Parking Ample |
| with bath/shower 52 | Room TV Yes | Last dinner 9.30 | Banquets 120/10 |

Walberton

Map 5 E4 West Sussex
Near Arundel *BN18 0LS*
Yapton (0243) 551215
Proprietor Mr Anthony Flynn

Credit Access, Amex,
Barclaycard

Avisford Park Hotel 60% Ⓜ £D

Originally a manor house and later a school, this fine Georgian building is very popular for conferences and functions. Public areas include a two-tier bar and lounge plus an ornate, lofty ballroom. Bedrooms (including many new studio singles) have fitted units, matching colour schemes and modern bathrooms. *Amenities* garden, outdoor swimming pool, tennis, squash, dinner dance (Sat), putting, croquet.

| Rooms 76 | Room phone Yes | Confirm by By arrang. | Parking Ample |
| with bath/shower 76 | Room TV Yes | Last dinner 9.30 | Banquets 150/– |

Wall

Map 15 B4 Northumberland
Near Hexham *NE46 4EE*
Humshaugh (043 481) 232

Tenant Mr A. H. White

Hadrian Inn *(Inn)* Ⓜ £E/F

Like much of the village, this sturdy roadside inn was built largely of stones from the nearby Roman landmark, and it makes an ideal base for tourists and sightseers. The rustic public bar is hung with agricultural implements, while a fine collection of firearms decorates the intimate cocktail bar; there are also two cosy lounges. Warm bedrooms have solid old-fashioned furniture, and bathrooms are spotless. *Amenities* garden.

| Rooms 8 | Room phone No | Confirm by By arrang. | Parking Ample |
| with bath/shower None | Room TV No | Last dinner 9.30 | Banquets 12/– |

Wallingford

Map 5 D2 Oxfordshire
High Street *OX10 0BS*
Wallingford (0491) 36665

Credit Access, Amex,
Barclaycard, Diners

George Hotel 58% £D

There's an attractive courtyard to the rear of this old whitewashed hostelry in the centre of town. The modernised interior holds a comfortable, well-carpeted lounge area and two bars, including the popular Tavern Bar with its inglenook fireplace. Bedrooms in the original building and the extension are all simply furnished and equipped with tea/coffee-makers. Bathrooms are adequate. *Amenities* discothèque (Fri).

| Rooms 18 | Room phone Yes | Confirm by 6 | Parking Ample |
| with bath/shower 9 | Room TV Yes | Last dinner 11 | Banquets 120/– |

Wallingford

Map 5 D2 Oxfordshire
OX10 8LZ
Warborough (086 732) 8567

Credit Access, Amex,
Barclaycard, Diners

Shillingford Bridge Hotel 52% Ⓜ £E

Situated on the A329 south of Shillingford, overlooking a quiet reach of the Thames, this low, white-painted hotel offers unfussy accommodation and varied entertainment. The large beamed bar has fine views, while bedrooms are simply furnished and equipped with tea/coffee-makers. Functional bathrooms. *Amenities* garden, outdoor swimming pool, squash, coarse fishing, dancing (Sat), cabaret (Sat monthly), mooring.

| Rooms 28 | Room phone Yes | Confirm by By arrang. | Parking Ample |
| with bath/shower 28 | Room TV Yes | Last dinner 9.45 | Banquets 150/80 |

Walsall

Map 10 C4 West Midlands
Walsall Wood *WS9 9AH*
Brownhills (0543) 376543
Telex 338212
Proprietor Mr B. T. Garrett
Credit Access, Amex,
Barclaycard, Diners

Rooms 76	
with bath/shower 76	

Baron's Court Hotel   68%   Ⓜ   £E

Situated three miles out of Walsall, this mock-Tudor hotel aims to re-create the past, with period portraits, suits of armour and coats of arms filling the public rooms. Bedrooms (including 17 bridal suites with four-posters) are nicely fitted out with Queen Anne-style furniture, and modern bathrooms are well-equipped.
Amenities dinner dance (Sat), folk music (Sun), night club (Fri, Sat).   &

Room phone Yes	*Confirm by* 7	*Parking* Ample
Room TV Yes	*Last dinner* 10	*Banquets* 150/5

Walsall

Map 10 C4 West Midlands
Birmingham Road *WS5 3AB*
Walsall (0922) 33555
Telex 335479
Credit Access, Amex,
Barclaycard, Diners
Closed Christmas

Rooms 106	
with bath/shower 106	

Crest Hotel   61%   £D

Refurbishment continues at this large modern businessman's hotel on the A34. There's an open-plan reception and a choice of three bars ranging from the intimate cocktail bar to the unusual Wharf Bar with tea chests and trap doors incorporated in its decor. Bedrooms have simple freestanding furniture except for a few studio-style rooms, and bathrooms are compact.
Amenities tennis, jazz (Tues).   &

Room phone Yes	*Confirm by* 6	*Parking* Ample
Room TV Yes	*Last dinner* 9.45	*Banquets* 120/10

Walshford

Map 15 C6 North Yorkshire
Wetherby *LS22 5HS*
Wetherby (0937) 62345
Proprietor Mr Donald Smiley

● **Set L** from £5·95
Set D from £7·95
About £32 for two

Bridge Inn, Byron Room   ♎ ♛♛ Ⓢ

Exquisite 18th-century plasterwork is a feature of this sumptuous restaurant, where William Bennett's set menus of three courses provide tantalising choice. Dishes like quenelles of sole with lobster sauce are well-judged, and to follow there are robust main courses like lamb noisettes with flageolet beans. Nice sweets such as raspberry brûlée and fluffy pear soufflé.
🍷 *OUTSTANDING. Credit* Access, Amex, Barclaycard, Diners   &

Lunch 12.30–2 *Dinner* 7.30–10
Closed D Sun, all Mon, Bank Holidays (except 26 Dec) & 1st week Jan

---

Waltham Abbey

Map 7 B4 Essex
20 The Market Square *EN9 1DU*
Lea Valley (0992) 712352
Proprietors
Jacob & Margaret Blunk

● **Set L & Set D** £15 incl. service
About £46 for two

Blunk's   Ⓢ

Fish looms large on Jacob Blunk's tempting menu at this gleaming restaurant with cane chairs and a polished tiled floor. Start with plump Spanish mussels in a pungent wine sauce, or lobster if you're feeling extravagant, and follow with halibut, chicken, duck or steak. Dishes are beautifully presented, and vegetables are delicious, as are the home-made ice creams. *Credit* Access, Amex, Barclaycard, Diners

Lunch 12.30–3 *Dinner* 7.30–11.30

Walton

Map 4 C1 Warwickshire
Near Wellesbourne *CV35 9HU*
Stratford-upon-Avon
(0789) 840011

Credit Access, Amex,
Barclaycard, Diners

Rooms 60	
with bath/shower 55	

Walton Hall Hotel   62%   £C/D

This grandiose Victorian mansion, designed on palatial lines, stands in impressive parkland complete with lake. Inside there's an ornate, marble-pillared reception hall, a plush Victorian Bar and a modern Clown's Bar. Bedrooms in the main building are vast, those in the annexe more modern and compact. *Amenities* garden, tennis, coarse fishing, dancing (Sat in winter), helipad, croquet, games room.

Room phone Yes	*Confirm by* 6	*Parking* Ample
Room TV Yes	*Last dinner* 9.30	*Banquets* 250/8

Walton-on-Thames
Map 5 E3 Surrey
32a High Street *KT12 1BZ*
Walton-on-Thames
(093 22) 44889

Italian cooking

● **Set L** £3·85
About £29 for two

La Bussola   Ⓢ

Nets, ropes and a ship's clock on the whitewashed walls give this restaurant a distinctly nautical flavour that's further manifest in the impressive display of hors d'œuvre and seafood. The menu also offers a wide choice of Italian dishes from lasagne to chicken breast stuffed with mortadella and cheese and served with a creamy sherry and paprika sauce. Generally careful cooking. *Credit* Access, Barclaycard

Lunch 12–2.15 *Dinner* 7–10.45
Closed L Sat & D Sun

Wansford
Map 6 A2 Cambridgeshire
Near Peterborough *PE8 6JA*
Stamford (0780) 782223

Credit Access, Amex,
Barclaycard, Diners

Rooms 28
with bath/shower 16

Haycock Hotel   62%   £ D/E

More than 200 years old when visited by Princess Victoria in 1835, this old coaching inn still has many delightful period features, including a huge inglenook fireplace in the comfortable smoke room. Bedrooms in the main building are large, those in the annexe smaller; all have colourful fabrics and attractive darkwood furniture. Bathrooms are well fitted.
Amenities garden, coarse fishing, pétanque.

Room phone Yes	*Confirm by* 6	*Parking* Ample
Room TV Yes	*Last dinner* 10	*Banquets* 100/–

Wansford
Map 6 A2 Cambridgeshire
Near Peterborough *PE8 6JA*
Stamford (0780) 782223

About £26 for two

Haycock Hotel Restaurant   Ⓢ

Fresh flowers adorn polished tables in this relaxing dining room. Basic fare is mainly traditional English, with succulent rare beef on the trolley and dishes like smoked trout with horseradish sauce and a rich, generously filled venison pie. Vegetables are imaginative, and there are delicious sweets like lemon mousse and real fruit salad to finish.
Credit Access, Amex, Barclaycard, Diners

Lunch 12.30–2.30 *Dinner* 7–10

Wantage
Map 5 D2 Oxfordshire
Market Place *OX7 1SZ*
Wantage (023 57) 66366

Credit Access, Amex,
Barclaycard
Closed 26–29 December

Rooms 15
with bath/shower 7

Bear Hotel   61%   Ⓜ   £ D

This charming 17th-century building in the centre of town is adorned with colourful window boxes. There's a cosy sitting room and cottage bar, as well as a coffee shop/wine bar across the flagstoned courtyard. Refurbished bedrooms have lovely old pine furniture and excellent private bathrooms; other bedrooms are adequate but more modest in style. No dogs.
Amenities wine bar/coffee shop (9.30am–5pm Tues–Sat).

Room phone Yes	*Confirm by* By arrang.	*Parking* Limited
Room TV Yes	*Last dinner* 9.30	*Banquets* 60/10

Wareham
Map 4 B4 Dorset
Church Green *BH20 4ND*
Wareham (092 95) 2772

Proprietor Mr John Turner
Rooms 15
with bath/shower 15
Room phone Yes
Room TV Yes
Confirm by By arrang.
Last dinner 9.45
Parking Ample
Banquets 40/20

Credit Access, Amex,
Barclaycard, Diners

Priory Hotel   72%   Ⓜ   £ D

Delightfully situated between the parish church and the river Frome, this fine old former priory, parts of which date back to the 16th century, has been carefully modernised and converted into an inviting and comfortable hotel. Arched doorways, flagstones and open stone hearths are charming reminders of the past, and the drawing room, with its antiques, deep sofas and rug-strewn polished floor, is a model of traditional elegance. There's also a cosy panelled bar and a residents' TV lounge upstairs. Bedrooms, including three new ones, are decorated and furnished to a very high standard and bathrooms are spacious and well equipped. No dogs.
Amenities garden, coarse fishing, sailing, mooring.   ♿

Warminster

Map 4 B3 Wiltshire
BA12 9HH
Warminster (0985) 21 2312

Rooms 14
with bath/shower 14
Room phone Yes
Room TV Yes
Confirm by By arrang.
Last dinner 9.30
Parking Ample

Closed January

Credit Access, Amex,
Barclaycard

Bishopstrow House   82%   Ⓜ   £ D

Elegance, comfort and service combine at a very high level in this immaculate late-Georgian mansion, which stands on the A36 in 25 acres of peaceful grounds reaching down to the river Wylye. Antiques, oil paintings and objets d'art abound in public rooms like the classically styled lounge and the blue and white morning room, and the whole place is beautifully carpeted and sumptuously furnished. Spacious bedrooms are models of tasteful luxury, with highly individual colour schemes and enormous beds, including some four-posters. The five new rooms have refreshing modern decor. Large bathrooms with Italian tile floors are superbly equipped. No children under seven. *Amenities* garden, tennis, game fishing.

Warminster

Map 4 B3 Wiltshire
BA12 9HH
Warminster (0985) 21 2312

● **Set D** £16, Sun £14
incl. service
About £42 for two

Bishopstrow House Restaurant   ♀ ♕ Ⓢ

A conservatory has added a new dimension to this elegant restaurant, which features excellent five-course dinners (no choice except desserts, and booking essential). After a light mousse or cool green vegetable salad comes a fish course, and main dishes like our juicy rack of lamb are served with a superb medley of crisp vegetables. Prime cheeses and delicate desserts end the meal in style. 🍷 *SUPERIOR. Credit* Access, Amex, Barclaycard

Lunch by arrangement only *Dinner* 8–9.30
Closed January

Warrington

Map 10 B2 Cheshire
Daresbury *WA4 4BB*
Warrington (0925) 67331
Telex 629330
Manager Mr Peter Friscuolo
Credit Access, Amex,
Barclaycard, Diners

Lord Daresbury Hotel   67%   £ D/E

This low, modern hotel stands amid smooth lawns three miles out of Warrington near the junction of the A56 and M56. The open-plan reception area has a smart bar-lounge, and there are several conference and function rooms. Uniform bedrooms are bright and practical, with smart modern decor, neat fitted furniture, colour TV and tea/coffee-makers. Fully tiled bathrooms are well kept. *Amenities* garden. **Closed** for accommodation 24–30 Dec

Rooms 141	*Room phone* Yes	*Confirm by* By arrang.	*Parking* Ample
with bath/shower 141	*Room TV* Yes	*Last dinner* 10	*Banquets* 300/–

Warwick

Map 10 C4 Warwickshire
1 High Street *CV34 4AP*
Warwick (0926) 492799
Proprietors
Signori Pancaldi & Bigliardi
About £30 for two

Aylesford   ♀ Ⓢ

A simple cellar-like restaurant offering a pleasant choice of standard Italian and French dishes, from stracciatella to entrecôte bordelaise. Seasonal specialities like mussels and pheasant. *Credit* Access, Amex, Barclaycard, Diners *Lunch* 12.30–2 *Dinner* 7.30–10 **Closed** D Mon, all Sun & Bank Holidays ● **Set L** £5 incl. service *Banquets* 50/–

Warwick

Map 10 C4 Warwickshire
Stratford Road *CV34 6RE*
Warwick (0926) 499555
Telex 31 2468

Rooms 131
with bath/shower 131
Room phone Yes
Room TV Yes
Confirm by 6
Last dinner 10.30
Parking Ample
Banquets 300/2

Ladbroke Mercury Hotel   70%   £ C

This attractive modern hotel on the A46 offers guests all the facilities of a motel combined with full and efficient hotel service. Open-plan public areas

                    Continued

Credit Access, Amex, Barclaycard, Diners	are spacious and stylish, with plenty of comfortable settees and Japanese-style bamboo screens. Good-sized bedrooms have smart pine furniture, tea/coffee-makers and well-equipped bathrooms. *Amenities* garden, indoor swimming pool, dancing (Fri, Sat), table tennis, helipad. ♿

Warwick   Westgate Arms   Ⓢ

Map 10 C4 Warwickshire
Bowling Green Street *CV34 4DD*
Warwick (0926) 42362
Proprietors
Mr J. W. Spencer & son

Fresh fish tops the bill at the Spencers' excellent pub restaurant, where the dining room features attractive lime-green decor and gleaming silverware. Sole, scampi, plaice and halibut appear alongside seasonal lobster, and enjoyable meat dishes are served with good vegetables. Prawn-garnished egg mayonnaise makes a simple, delicious starter, and desserts are equally appealing. Attentive service. *Credit* Access, Amex, Barclaycard, Diners

● **Set L** £7·50
About £31 for two

Lunch 12.30–2.30 *Dinner* 7.30–10
Closed Sun & Bank Holiday Mons

Washington   George Washington Hotel   67%   **£E**

Map 15 C4 Tyne and Wear
Stone Cellar Road
District 12 *HE37 1PH*
Washington (0632) 472626

Credit Access, Amex,
Barclaycard, Diners

Golfers and businessmen alike appreciate this purpose-built modern hotel, which has useful sporting and function facilities. There's a choice of three bars (one fitted out like a '30s speakeasy), and exposed brickwork is a pleasing feature throughout the public areas. Well-equipped bedrooms have attractive bamboo and cane furniture and up-to-date bathrooms.
Amenities squash, golf, pitch & putt, golf driving range, in-house movies.

Rooms 42	*Room phone* Yes	*Confirm by* By arrang.	*Parking* Ample
with bath/shower 42	*Room TV* Yes	*Last dinner* 9.30	*Banquets* 200/–

Washington   George Washington Hotel, Lincolns Restaurant   Ⓢ

Map 15 C4 Tyne & Wear
Stone Cellar Road
District 12 *NE37 1PH*
Washington (0632) 472626

The dinner menu caters for all tastes in this smart modern restaurant. There are charcoal grills, soups, fish, hot and cold starters, and a good range of imaginative specialities. We particularly enjoyed a piping hot, subtly flavoured onion soufflé and marvellous salmon gingembre (wrapped in pastry and glazed with hollandaise sauce). Smörgåsbord only at lunch time. *Credit* Access, Amex, Barclaycard, Diners   ♿

● **Set L** from £2·50 **Set D** £7
About £32 for two

Lunch 12–3, Sun 12–2 *Dinner* 7.30–9.30, Fri & Sat 7.30–10, Sun 7.30–9

We welcome complaints and bona fide recommendations on the tear-out pages for readers' comments. They are followed up by our professional team. Please also complain to the management instantly.

Washington   Post House Hotel   58%   **£D**

Map 15 C4 Tyne & Wear
Emerson District 5 *NE37 1LB*
Washington (0632) 462264
Telex 537574

Credit Access, Amex,
Barclaycard, Diners

Alongside the A1(M) and reached via the A1231, this neatly designed modern hotel with excellent conference facilities caters mainly for business people. A pleasant reception leads directly into the comfortably furnished lounge and bar area. Bedrooms in a seven-storey block are mostly studios and have fitted furniture, tea-makers and mini-bars. Compact bathrooms.
Amenities dancing (most Fris & Sats), coffee shop (7.30am–10.30pm). ♿

Rooms 145	*Room phone* Yes	*Confirm by* 6	*Parking* Ample
with bath/shower 145	*Room TV* Yes	*Last dinner* 10.30	*Banquets* 200/–

Washington   Post House Hotel, Presidents Restaurant   ♔ Ⓢ

Map 15 C4 Tyne & Wear
Emerson District 5 *NE37 1LB*
Washington (0632) 462264

About £29 for two

Chef's specials like juicy chicken stuffed with crab and delicately sauced supplement the carte in this elegantly refurbished dining room. Vegetables are interesting, and there's always a roast on the trolley. 🍷 *ABOVE AVERAGE.*
Credit Access, Amex, Barclaycard, Diners *Lunch* 12.30–2.30 *Dinner* 7–10
Closed L Sat & D Sun ● **Set L** £5·25 **Set D** £9·75 incl. service   ♿

Watford

Map 5 E2 Hertfordshire
Elton Way *WD2 8HA*
Watford (0923) 35881
Telex 923442

Credit Access, Amex,
Barclaycard, Diners

Rooms 182
with bath/shower 182

Ladbroke Mercury Hotel 65% £ C/D

Situated close to junction 5 of the M1, this is very much a businessman's hotel, with a separate block of function rooms. The spacious open-plan foyer-lounge has luxurious low seating and a profusion of greenery, and there's a handsome, really comfortable bar. Charming bedrooms have individual colour schemes, neat fitted units and well-equipped bathrooms. *Amenities* garden, dinner dance & cabaret (Sat).

Room phone Yes	*Confirm by* 6	*Parking* Ample
Room TV Yes	*Last dinner* 10.30	*Banquets* 400/–

Wellington

Map 10 B3 Shropshire
Ercall Lane, Telford *TF6 5AL*
Telford (0952) 51821

Manager Mr D. A. Bowen
Credit Access, Amex,
Barclaycard

Rooms 27
with bath/shower 27

Buckatree Hall Hotel 56% £ E/F

This former manor house stands in wooded grounds at the foot of the Wrekin within easy access of the M54. Modern extension bedrooms with balconies have simple fitted furniture, bedside controls and, like those in the original building, compact tiled bathrooms. An attractively arched bar-lounge features colourful carpets and glass-topped tables. *Amenities* garden, dancing (Sat).

Room phone Yes	*Confirm by* By arrang.	*Parking* Ample
Room TV Yes	*Last dinner* 10	*Banquets* 120/–

Welwyn

Map 7 A4 Hertfordshire
Danesbury Park Road *AL6 9SL*
Welwyn (043 871) 7064

Credit Access, Amex,
Barclaycard, Diners

Rooms 30
with bath/shower 26

Heath Lodge Hotel 58% Ⓜ £ E

Situated near the A1 in 19 acres of grounds (approach via the B197), this hotel features motel-style accommodation in modern chalets overlooking a large rockery. Bedrooms (including nine very luxurious ones) have good-quality fittings and attractive bathrooms. The original half-timbered building containing the traditionally furnished public rooms also has a few simple bedrooms. No dogs. *Amenities* garden.

Room phone Yes	*Confirm by* By arrang.	*Parking* Ample
Room TV Yes	*Last dinner* 9.30	*Banquets* 140/–

Welwyn Garden City

Map 7 B4 Hertfordshire
Homestead Lane *AL7 4LX*
Welwyn Gdn City (070 73) 24336
Telex 261523
Credit Access, Amex,
Barclaycard, Diners
Closed 3 days Christmas

Rooms 58
with bath/shower 58

Crest Hotel 59% £ D

Ask for directions when booking at this modern red-brick hotel, which stands south of the town centre on the edge of a residential area. Public rooms are bright and fresh looking, with attractive patterned carpets and bamboo-style furnishings. Good-sized bedrooms, all with tea-makers and trouser presses, have fitted units and functional tiled bathrooms. Extensive conference facilities. *Amenities* garden.

Room phone Yes	*Confirm by* 6	*Parking* Ample
Room TV Yes	*Last dinner* 9.45	*Banquets* 90/–

Wembley

Map 5 E2 Middlesex
Empire Way *HA9 8DS*
01–902 8839
Telex 24837

Credit Access, Amex,
Barclaycard, Diners

Rooms 325
with bath/shower 325

Crest Hotel 58% £ C

Built next to the Wembley Conference Centre and within shouting distance of the stadium, this modern hotel is naturally very popular. Public areas include a smart cocktail bar and a lounge. The best bedrooms have attractive matching fabrics and good fitted units; furnishings elsewhere are older. Compact, well-maintained bathrooms. Refurbishment would be welcome. *Amenities* coffee shop (10am–6.30pm).

Room phone Yes	*Confirm by* 6	*Parking* Ample
Room TV Yes	*Last dinner* 10	*Banquets* 300/2

Wembley

Map 5 E2 Middlesex
279 High Road *HA9 7DT*
01–902 3605
Proprietor Mr Hsu
Chinese cooking
About £16 for two

Peking Castle

Mr Hsu's delicious crispy duck is a great favourite among the Pekinese specialities available at this neat and tidy little Chinese restaurant. Dishes are mostly familiar, and cooking is reliable. *Credit* Access, Amex, Barclaycard
Lunch 12–2.30 *Dinner* 6–11.30, Fri & Sat 6–12
Closed 25 & 26 December ● **Set L & Set D** £5 *Banquets* 50/4

Wentbridge
Map 11 D1 West Yorkshire
Near Pontefract *WF8 3JJ*
Pontefract (0977) 620444
Proprietors
Mr & Mrs K. C. Dupuy
Credit Access, Amex,
Barclaycard, Diners

Rooms 20
with bath/shower 17

Wentbridge House Hotel   65%   (M)   **£D/E**

The Dupuys have created a hotel of great charm and character from their fine 18th-century house, which stands in peaceful parkland two miles from the M62/A1 interchange. Antiques and lovely pieces of porcelain grace the lounge and bar, and there are period pieces, too, in the cheerfully decorated bedrooms (three in an annexe). Smart carpeted bathrooms. Guide dogs only. *Amenities* garden. **Closed** 25 December evening   &

Room phone Yes	*Confirm by* By arrang.	*Parking* Ample
Room TV Yes	*Last dinner* 9.30	*Banquets* 150/4

Wentbridge
Map 11 D1 West Yorkshire
Near Pontefract *WF8 3JJ*
Pontefract (0977) 620444
Proprietors
Mr & Mrs K. C. Dupuy

● **Set** L £7·05
About £32 for two

Wentbridge House Hotel Restaurant

Two formal dining rooms, one with a splendid Adam fireplace, make an attractive setting for enjoying Charles Carter's capable cooking. The lengthy menu offers French-style dishes which may include cream of cauliflower soup, tournedos Rossini and delicious stuffed chicken breast. There's seasonal seafood as well—perhaps scallops, sole or lobster—and fresh, crisp vegetables. ♇ *OUTSTANDING. Credit* Access, Amex, Barclaycard, Diners

Lunch 12.30–2 *Dinner* 7.30–9.30, Sun 7.30–8.45
Closed D 25 December

Weobley
Map 4 A1 Hereford & Worcester
Broad Street *HR4 8SA*
Weobley (054 45) 220

Credit Access, Amex,
Diners

Rooms 7
with bath/shower 7

Red Lion Hotel   60%   **£E**

In a village full of delightful half-timbered buildings, this charming 14th-century inn is a particularly lovely one. Inside, all is cosy and welcoming: the cocktail bar has beams, natural stone walls and copper ornaments, and there's a peaceful little sitting room upstairs. Compact, homely bedrooms have spotless white decor, functional fitted units and neat modern bathrooms. *Amenities* garden.

Room phone Yes	*Confirm by* By arrang.	*Parking* Ample
Room TV Yes	*Last dinner* 9.30	*Banquets* 20/–

West Bromwich
Map 10 C4 West Midlands
Birmingham Road *B70 6RS*
021–553 6111
Telex 336232

Credit Access, Amex,
Barclaycard, Diners

Rooms 133
with bath/shower 133

West Bromwich Moat House   59%   **£D**

Formerly the Europa Lodge, this smart modern hotel is conveniently situated by junction 1 of the M5. The bright, spacious foyer and lounge both have plenty of comfortable seats, and there are two attractive bars. Cheerful bedrooms have fitted units, ample writing space and neat, well-equipped bathrooms. Extra accommodation and conference rooms are being added. *Amenities* garden, dinner dance (Sat November–April).   &

Room phone Yes	*Confirm by* By arrang.	*Parking* Ample
Room TV Yes	*Last dinner* 9.45	*Banquets* 120/–

West Chiltington
Map 5 E3 West Sussex
Monkmead Lane
Near Pulborough *RH20 2PF*
West Chiltington (079 83) 3123
Proprietor Mr R. Begley
Credit Access, Amex,
Barclaycard, Diners

Rooms 19
with bath/shower 19

Roundabout Hotel   59%   (M)   **£E**

Standing in peaceful countryside nowhere near a roundabout, this well-run hotel converted from a 1930s house offers all that is necessary for a quiet stay. Public areas include a simple lounge and a cheerful cocktail bar, and the comfortable bedrooms have attractive curtains, sturdy oak furniture and neat little bathrooms. No children under three.
Amenities garden. **Closed** 28 December–31 January

Room phone No	*Confirm by* 6	*Parking* Ample
Room TV Yes	*Last dinner* 8.45	*Banquets* 20/10

West Clandon
Map 5 E3 Surrey
Near Guildford *GU4 7TE*
Guildford (0483) 222447
Proprietor Mr A. J. Peck

About £36 for two

Onslow Arms   

A wealth of beams and rafters distinguish this pleasant restaurant in a picturesque pub. Cooking is capable, and the French-style menu varied. Excellent presentation; courteous, efficient service. *Credit* Access, Amex, Barclaycard, Diners *Lunch* 12.30–2 *Dinner* 7.30–10.15 **Closed** D Sun & all Mon ● **Set** L £5·85 *Banquets* 30/4   &

West Runton
Map 6 C1 Norfolk
Near Cromer *NR27 9QH*
West Runton (026 375) 691

Manager Mr R. M. Edwards
Credit Access, Amex,
Barclaycard, Diners

Links Country Park Hotel 66% £E

This attractive turreted Victorian building set in its own golf course offers splendid views across rolling countryside to the North Sea. Public rooms include a handsome panelled lounge with cocktail bar and a popular bar by the last green. Individually decorated bedrooms are bright and cheerful, with neat modern fittings and cosy little bathrooms.
Amenities garden, 9-hole golf course, table tennis, valeting, pool table.

Rooms 35	*Room phone* Yes	*Confirm by* By arrang.	*Parking* Ample
with bath/shower 35	*Room TV* Yes	*Last dinner* 9.30	*Banquets* 120/20

West Runton
Map 6 C1 Norfolk
Station Road *NR27 9QD*
West Runton (026 375) 396
Proprietor Mr Manfred Hollwoger

● **Set L** £5·60 **Set D** £8·50
About £28 for two
Banquets 80/6

Mirabelle

Daily table d'hôte menus and an à la carte provide plenty of choice at this cosy Austrian-style restaurant–try the hors d'œuvre variés for a bounteous sampling of tasty starters. To follow, there's Holstein schnitzel or entrecôte tyrolienne, as well as a range of grills, fresh fish and popular favourites like beef Wellington. Cooking is honest and enjoyable.
Credit Access, Amex, Barclaycard, Diners

Lunch 12.30–2 *Dinner* 7–9.30
Closed D Sun, all Mon, 25 December & 1st 3 weeks November

Westerham
Map 7 B5 Kent
Quebec Square *TN16 1TD*
Westerham (0959) 62139

● **Set L** £5·75 **Set D** £6·95
About £34 for two
Banquets 80/6

Montmorency

Originally a country house, this lavishly appointed restaurant overlooks formal gardens. Prime-quality produce is used skilfully in the preparation of a range of classic French and Italian dishes from moules marinière and cannelloni to duckling with Kirsch and black cherries. Vegetables are excellent, and a five-tier sweet trolley provides some tempting delights.
Credit Access, Amex, Barclaycard, Diners

Lunch 12–2.30 *Dinner* 7–11
Closed D Sun

Weston-super-Mare
Map 4 A3 Avon
Beach Road *BS23 1BA*
Weston-super-Mare
(0934) 26543
Manager Mr J. Hayward-Browne
Credit Access, Amex,
Barclaycard, Diners

Grand Atlantic Hotel 63% £D

This imposing hotel stands in attractive gardens on the esplanade overlooking the beach and the Bristol Channel. Large, comfortable sofas and armchairs abound in the roomy reception-lounge area, and there are also two bars and extensive banqueting and conference facilities. Bedrooms have modern fitted unit furniture and compact, well-kept bathrooms. *Amenities* garden, outdoor swimming pool, tennis, children's playground & playroom.

Rooms 79	*Room phone* Yes	*Confirm by* 6	*Parking* Ample
with bath/shower 79	*Room TV* Yes	*Last dinner* 9	*Banquets* 270/6

Weston-under-Penyard
Map 4 B1 Hereford & Worcester
Near Ross-on-Wye *HR9 7NT*
Ross-on-Wye (0989) 63541
Proprietor
Mr D. F. J. Walker

Credit Access, Barclaycard

Wye Hotel 57% Ⓜ £E

This fine Georgian house with a modern extension stands in secluded grounds on the A40 two miles east of Ross. The two lounges have comfortable contemporary furniture, and other public areas include function rooms and a smart cocktail bar. Bedrooms range from spacious and traditionally furnished in the main house to cheerful, modern and compact in the extension. Neat, adequately equipped bathrooms. *Amenities* garden, squash.

Rooms 46	*Room phone* Yes	*Confirm by* By arrang.	*Parking* Ample
with bath/shower 41	*Room TV* Yes	*Last dinner* 9.15	*Banquets* 150/–

Westonbirt
Map 4 B2 Gloucestershire
Near Tetbury *GL8 8QL*
Westonbirt (066 66) 233
Proprietors
Jeremy & Martin Price
Credit Access, Amex,
Barclaycard

Hare & Hounds Hotel 57% Ⓜ £E

There's a real old-fashioned charm about the Price brothers' welcoming hotel, a sturdy Cotswold-stone building standing in well-kept gardens back from the A433. Paintings and prints abound in the public rooms, which include two delightfully traditional lounges and a choice of bars. Bedrooms have solid furnishings and tea/coffee-makers; bathrooms are adequate.
Amenities garden, tennis, squash, table tennis, croquet, putting.

Continued

| Rooms 24 | Room phone Yes | Confirm by 5 | Parking Ample |
| with bath/shower 19 | Room TV Yes | Last dinner 9 | Banquets 150/20 |

Wetherby — Cardinal   ♀ ♕ Ⓢ
Map 11 D1 West Yorkshire

Bank Street *LS22 4NQ*
Wetherby (0937) 62751
Proprietors Mr & Mrs G. Dilasser

With the welcoming Dilassers as hosts and the talented Michel Mingam in the kitchen, it's a pleasure to eat at this comfortable, well-appointed restaurant. The menu, changed fortnightly, offers a good choice of soups and hors d'œuvre, while for main courses you could find loin of lamb and turkey fillet alongside French-inspired dishes such as seafood coquille or delicate darne de saumon. *Credit* Access, Amex, Barclaycard, Diners

About £24 for two
Banquets 70/25

Dinner only 7.30–10.30
Closed Mon

Wetherby — Ladbroke Mercury Hotel   59%   £C/D
Map 11 D1 West Yorkshire

Leeds Road *LS22 5HE*
Wetherby (0937) 63881
Manager Mr K. R. Radcliffe
Credit Access, Amex,
Barclaycard, Diners
Closed 4 days Christmas

Businessmen and tourists alike on the London to Edinburgh route find this modern hotel at the junction of the A58 and A1 a convenient stopping place. The flagstone-floored lounge-foyer has leather chesterfields, and leads to the intimate Macadam Bar with its alcove seating. Bedrooms have a restful caramel and beige decor and white melamine units. Compact bathrooms with shower units. *Amenities* garden.   ဦ

| Rooms 70 | Room phone Yes | Confirm by 6 | Parking Ample |
| with bath/shower 70 | Room TV Yes | Last dinner 10 | Banquets 110/– |

Weybourne — Gasché's Swiss Restaurant   Ⓢ
Map 6 C1 Norfolk

Near Holt *NR25 7SY*
Weybourne (026 370) 220
Proprietor
Mr Edgar Robert Steiner-Gasché

● **Set L** £4·95 & £5·95
Set D from £7·50
About £30 for two
Banquets 36/12

Inside this thatched stone cottage, scrubbed wooden tables and gingham napkins provide a cheerful Alpine note. The set menus combine Continental specialities like wiener schnitzel with local ones such as fresh Glaven trout. There are home-made ice creams to finish, as well as Swiss gâteaux, and the expert cooking of long-serving Nigel Massingham produces most enjoyable results. Book. *Credit* Amex, Diners   ဦ

Lunch 12.30–2 *Dinner* 7–9
Closed D Sun, all Mon & Bank Holidays

Changes in data may occur in establishments after the Guide goes to press. Prices should be taken as indications rather than firm quotes.

Weybourne — Maltings Hotel   62% Ⓜ   £E
Map 6 C1 Norfolk

Near Holt *NR25 7HJ*
Weybourne (026 370) 275

Credit Amex, Barclaycard,
Diners

Charm and character abound in this friendly, well-run hotel in a little village half a mile from the sea. Highly polished antiques mingle with comfortable armchairs and settees in the relaxing public rooms, and there's a delightfully rustic beamed bar in the old mash house. Compact, cheerfully decorated bedrooms, some in converted outbuildings, offer solid traditional comforts. One has a four-poster. *Amenities* garden.

| Rooms 23 | Room phone No | Confirm by By arrang. | Parking Ample |
| with bath/shower 18 | Room TV Yes | Last dinner 9 | Banquets 100/– |

We do not necessarily recommend the cooking at hotels whose restaurants are not separately listed.

Weybridge

Map 5 E3 Surrey
2 Temple Hall
Monument Hill *KT13 8RH*
Weybridge (0932) 43470
Proprietors Mr R. Ballerini
& Mr C. Di Michele
Italian cooking

● Set L £4·75, Sun £5·55
About £33 for two

Casa Romana

Fresh fish is a speciality of this stylish Italian restaurant, where excellent, robust cooking and swift, assured service make for very enjoyable meals. Deep-fried crab claws with Parmesan is a delicious starter, and main courses include variations on veal and chicken like an unusual cheese and herb-stuffed breast of chicken in a puff pastry case. Good sweets, super coffee. *Credit* Access, Amex, Barclaycard

Lunch 12.15–2.15 *Dinner* 7–10.45, Sun 7–10
Closed L Sat, all Mon & 25 & 26 December

Weybridge

Map 5 E3 Surrey
146 Oatlands Drive *KT13 9HB*
Weybridge (0932) 47242
Telex 262180

Credit Access, Amex,
Barclaycard, Diners

Oatlands Park Hotel   60%   £D

This sedate hotel in grounds of 40 acres offers good comfort and a wide range of amenities. There's an attractive panelled foyer, and the spacious lounge now has a bar. Bedrooms are pleasantly decorated in traditional style and bathrooms are well fitted.
Amenities garden, outdoor swimming pool, tennis, squash, 9-hole golf course, croquet, games room, putting, children's playground.

Rooms 145	*Room phone* Yes	*Confirm by* 6	*Parking* Ample
with bath/shower 92	*Room TV* Yes	*Last dinner* 8.30	*Banquets* 200/10

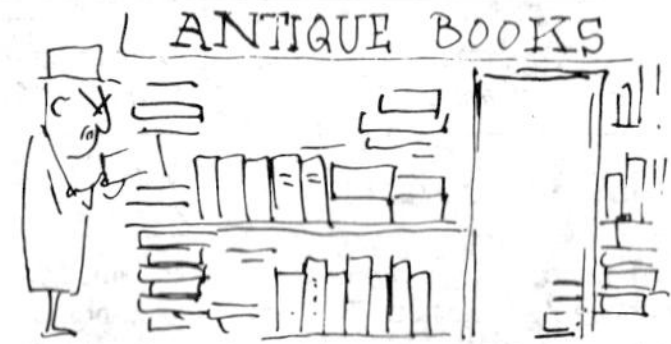

We publish annually, so make sure you use the current edition. It's worth it!

Weybridge

Map 5 E3 Surrey
Monument Green, High Street
KT13 8BQ
Weybridge (0932) 48364
Telex 894271
Credit Access, Amex,
Barclaycard, Diners

Ship Hotel   60%   £D

Pleasantly situated overlooking the green at the end of the High Street, this modest 16th-century hostelry retains much of its character in the traditional beamed foyer-lounge and the large rustic Nelson Bar, which is festooned with nautical bric-à-brac. Bedrooms are all in the modern extensions and most have fresh, attractive decor and darkwood fitted units. Bathrooms are spacious and well equipped. *Amenities* garden.

Rooms 39	*Room phone* Yes	*Confirm by* 6	*Parking* Ample
with bath/shower 39	*Room TV* Yes	*Last dinner* 10	*Banquets* 150/–

Whalley

Map 10 B1 Lancashire
Milton Road
Near Blackburn *BB6 9RH*
Whalley (025 482) 3446
Proprietors Mr & Mrs J. M. Camm

● Set D £7·25
About £22 for two
Banquets 38/12

Abbots Court

Simple, careful cooking is the hallmark of this welcoming restaurant in a former private house beside the B6246. Maurice Camm's four-course set dinner menu has enjoyable dishes like full-flavoured game soup and roast duckling with orange sauce. Vegetables are crisp and fresh, and there are some nice sweets like lemon soufflé served with home-made brandy snaps. Charming service. *Credit* Access

Dinner only 7–9.30
Closed Sun, Mon, Bank Holidays & last 2 weeks July

Whalley

Map 10 B1 Lancashire
Billington
Near Blackburn *BB6 9HY*
Whalley (025 482) 2556

● Set L £6·25
About £30 for two
Banquets *140/15*

Foxfields

Frequent trips to Manchester's markets ensure the freshness and quality of the produce used at this spacious restaurant just off the A59. There's a good choice of well-prepared, enjoyably different dishes ranging from lentil and bacon soup or salmon mousse with tangy lime mayonnaise to roast baby guinea fowl and nicely sauced veal fillet. Tempting sweet trolley. The Parkinsons are charming hosts. ▼ *ABOVE AVERAGE*. *Credit* Access

Lunch 12.30–1.30, Sun 12–1.30 *Dinner* 7–9.30, Sun 7–9
Closed L Sat & Mon & all Bank Holidays except Good Friday

Whimple

Map 3 E2 Devon
Near Exeter *EX5 2TD*
Whimple (0404) 822237

Rooms 6
with bath/shower 6
Room phone Yes
Room TV Yes
Confirm by By arrang.
Last dinner 8
Parking Ample
Banquets 10/–
Closed January

Credit Access, Barclaycard

Woodhayes 74%  £F

Set in three acres of nicely tended grounds not far from the A30, this is a delightful little country house hotel, maintained with impeccable taste by John Allan, who is the perfect host with a single-minded devotion to the well-being of his guests. Drinks can be enjoyed in two comfortable and delightfully traditional drawing rooms. Bedrooms are very pretty and, like the rest of the house, are fitted out in exemplary style, with freestanding period furniture, matching fabrics and thoughtful extras like flowers and mineral water. Excellent, well-equipped modern bathrooms. No children under 12. No dogs.
Amenities garden, croquet, 24-hour laundry service.

Whimple

Map 3 E2 Devon
Near Exeter *EX5 2TD*
Whimple (0404) 822237

● **Set D** £8·50
About £24 for two

Woodhayes Restaurant ♔ ⓢ

Graham Hartley is the chef at this elegant little country house restaurant. His skill is evident in deceptively simple dishes like pork rillettes with a superb clove-flavoured orange compote, a delicate tarragon and lettuce soup or pork tenderloin with a subtly spiced cream and cider sauce. Vegetables are enlivened with herbs like mint or caraway seeds, and sweets are enjoyable.
🍷*ABOVE AVERAGE. Credit* Access, Barclaycard   ♿

Dinner at 7.30 for 8
Closed January also all L & D Sun & Mon to non-residents

Whitehaven

Map 13 C5 Cumbria
Low Moresby *CA28 6RX*
Whitehaven (0946) 61572
Proprietors Grayson family
Credit Access, Barclaycard, Diners
Closed 25 December

Roseneath Country House Hotel 62%  £F

A homely, family-run hotel set in attractive grounds just off the A595. The oval entrance hall, with its antiques and polished wooden floor, sets the tone for public rooms like the comfortable lounge and cosy bar, and bedrooms in the main house are also solidly traditional. Three rooms in the coach house are more modern. No dogs. No children under 12.
Amenities garden, croquet.

Rooms 9	*Room phone* Yes	*Confirm by* By arrang.	*Parking* Ample
with bath/shower 7	*Room TV* Yes	*Last dinner* 8.45	*Banquets* 35/–

Whitehaven

Map 13 C5 Cumbria
Low Moresby *CA28 6RX*
Whitehaven (0946) 61572
Proprietors Grayson family

About £27 for two

Roseneath Country House Hotel Restaurant ♕ ⓢ

While Robert Grayson is looking after guests in the charming dining room, his mother Rachel is using her talents in the kitchen. Standards of cooking are high throughout the menu, which could include cream of pimento soup, pheasant casserole and fillet of beef with a mushroom sauce. Excellent vegetables, too, and well-laden hors d'œuvre, cheese and dessert trolleys.
🍷*ABOVE AVERAGE. Credit* Access, Barclaycard, Diners   ♿

Lunch by arrangement only *Dinner* 7.30–8.45
Closed D Sun to non-residents, 1 January & 25 & 26 December

Whitewell

Map 10 B1 Lancashire
Forest of Bowland
Near Clitheroe *BB7 3AT*
Dunsop Bridge (020 08) 222
Proprietor Mr R. Bowman
Credit Amex, Barclaycard, Diners

Whitewell Hotel 55%  £E/F

Private shooting and fishing are major attractions of this stone-built hotel set against a backdrop of rolling hills. The foyer, bar and TV lounge are all comfortable and welcoming, with fine old furniture and attractive prints. Double-glazed bedrooms, most with private baths, are traditionally furnished.
Amenities garden, game fishing, shooting, pool table.

Rooms 10	*Room phone* No	*Confirm by* 6	*Parking* Ample
with bath/shower 7	*Room TV* No	*Last dinner* 9.30	*Banquets* 80/4

CALOR TRANSPORT
60323
ERF
DDP 418 V

Engineering for World Transport

Putting a safe stop to all kinds of powered transport is the demanding job of Lucas Girling, a world leader in brakes and braking technology.

In the automotive field, Lucas Girling has responded to the massive challenge presented by trucks and buses by developing a highly advanced range of hydraulic and air operated drum and disc brakes, together with specialised air actuation equipment and an electronic anti-lock system of proven efficiency.

Lucas Girling

Whittlesey

Map 6 B2 Cambridgeshire
London Street *PE7 1BH*
Peterborough (0733) 203247

Falcon Hotel Restaurant   Ⓢ

A Georgian-style dining room with polished tables and gleaming silverware makes an appropriate setting for some well-prepared English fare including prime roast sirloin and game pie. There are also dishes like chicken in a tastily garnished white wine and cream sauce, and crisp fresh vegetables and an unusually attractive sweet trolley are sure to please.
Credit Access, Amex, Barclaycard, Diners

About £26 for two
Banquets 100/–

Lunch 12.30–2.30 *Dinner* 7–11, Sun 7.30–10.30
Closed D 25 & 26 December

Whitstable

Map 7 C5 Kent
101 Tankerton Road
Tankerton *CT52AJ*
Whitstable (0227) 272056
Proprietor
Mr James d'Alton-Bellas
French cooking

● **Set L** £4 **Set D** £7·85
About £23 for two

Le Pousse Bedaine   Ⓢ

It's a real pleasure to come upon this friendly, unassuming bistro. The menu offers a good choice of carefully prepared, largely uncomplicated French dishes ranging from onion soup and moules au gratin to veal escalopes with an outstanding Madeira sauce that's typical of the chef's first-class saucing. To finish, there are sweets like delicious tarte maison.
Credit Access, Amex, Barclaycard, Diners   ♿

Lunch 12–2 *Dinner* 6.30–11
Closed Sun & Bank Holidays except August Bank Holiday

Our inspectors never book in the name of the Egon Ronay Organisation; they disclose their identity only after paying their bills.

Whitwell-on-the-Hill

Map 15 C6 North Yorkshire
YO67JJ
Whitwell-on-the-Hill
(065 381) 551
Proprietor Lt Cdr Milner
Credit Access, Amex,
Barclaycard, Diners

Whitwell Hall Country House Hotel   68%   Ⓜ   £E

There's a cordial welcome at this beautifully situated 19th-century Gothic mansion. Part of the galleried entrance hall serves as a bar, and guests can take their drinks into the chintzy drawing room. Main-building bedrooms are warm, spacious and solidly furnished; those in the stables annexe are smaller. Some attention needed to housekeeping. Dogs in annexe only. No children under 12. *Amenities* garden, tennis, croquet, putting.   ♿

Rooms 20
with bath/shower 20

Room phone Yes   *Confirm by* By arrang.   *Parking* Ample
Room TV No   *Last dinner* 8.30

Wickham

Map 5 D4 Hampshire
The Square *PO175JG*
Wickham (0329) 833049
Proprietors
Mr & Mrs R. Skipwith
Credit Access, Barclaycard

Old House Hotel   66%   Ⓜ   £D

The Skipwiths are just as unstinting in their care of guests as of this picturesque Georgian building itself, which is a model of dedicated housekeeping. The two pleasant lounges and the simple bar are immaculate, as are the bedrooms, which are comfortably furnished and have compact modern bathrooms. Accommodation available Monday to Friday only. No dogs. *Amenities* garden. **Closed** 10 days Easter, 3 weeks July/August & Christmas

Rooms 10
with bath/shower 10

Room phone No   *Confirm by* By arrang.   *Parking* Ample
Room TV No   *Last dinner* 9.30   *Banquets* 12/–

Wickham

Map 5 D4 Hampshire
The Square *PO175JG*
Wickham (0329) 833049
Proprietors Mr & Mrs R. Skipwith
French cooking

Old House Hotel Restaurant   ♧ Ⓢ

Mrs Skipwith supervises the kitchen in this attractive hotel restaurant where cooking is a labour of love. The weekly-changing menu offers a small but varied choice of skilfully prepared French provincial dishes, like chicken with a creamy cider and Calvados sauce. Top-quality ingredients are carefully handled, vegetables are excellent, and sweets taste delicious.
Credit Access, Barclaycard

About £31 for two

Lunch 12–1.45 *Dinner* 7–9.30 **Closed** L Sat & Mon, all Sun, Bank Holidays, 10 days Easter, 3 weeks July/August & Christmas

Willerby
Map 11 E1 Humberside
Main Street *HU10 6EA*
Hull (0482) 655841

Credit Access, Amex,
Barclaycard, Diners

Rooms 14
with bath/shower 3

Grange Park Hotel   56%   Ⓜ   £E/F

This friendly red-brick Victorian hotel with modern extensions stands in peaceful grounds close to the A164. Good-sized bedrooms have cheerful decor, simple white fitted furniture and welcoming little extras like fresh fruit. An improvement programme planned by the new owner, which will begin with the expansion of conference facilities, will be welcome.
Amenities garden, dinner dance (Sat).

Room phone Yes	*Confirm by* 6	*Parking* Ample
Room TV Yes	*Last dinner* 9.15	*Banquets* 300/10

Willerby
Map 11 E1 Humberside
Well Lane *HU10 6ER*
Hull (0482) 652616
Manager Mr D. C. Baugh
Credit Access, Amex,
Barclaycard, Diners
Closed 25 December

Rooms 41
with bath/shower 41

Willerby Manor Hotel   57%   Ⓜ   £E

A Victorian building with a modern extension, this welcoming hotel stands in three acres of gardens about four miles west of Hull. The cocktail bar, which doubles as a lounge, retains much of its period charm, and bedrooms range from compact and fairly plain to larger and more attractively fitted. Good private bathrooms throughout, some being quite luxurious.
Amenities garden.

Room phone Yes	*Confirm by* 10	*Parking* Ample
Room TV Yes	*Last dinner* 9.45	*Banquets* 350/100

Wilmslow
Map 10 B2 Cheshire
Stanneylands Road *SK9 4EY*
Wilmslow (0625) 525225

Credit Access, Amex,
Barclaycard, Diners

Rooms 35
with bath/shower 35

Stanneylands Hotel   63%   Ⓜ   £D

Recent improvements to this attractive red-brick hotel include a smart new reception hall and a self-contained function complex; the comfortable bar has been refurnished and a new bedroom extension added. All rooms are pleasantly decorated and tastefully furnished, with their own neat bathrooms. The hotel stands just off the A34 in lovely gardens with specimen trees. No dogs. *Amenities* garden, 24-hour laundry service.   &

Room phone Yes	*Confirm by* 6	*Parking* Ample
Room TV Yes	*Last dinner* 10	*Banquets* 120/10

Wimbledon

San Lorenzo Fuoriporta & Worcester House

See under London and London Economy Hotels

Wimborne Minster
Map 4 C4 Dorset
The Square *BH21 1JA*
Wimborne (0202) 880101

Credit Access, Amex,
Barclaycard, Diners

Rooms 28
with bath/shower 12

King's Head Hotel   56%   £D

Dominating the town square, this handsome inn exudes serenity and offers pleasant facilities and accommodation. There's a convivial bar and a charming foyer-lounge with little alcoves, as well as two small meeting rooms. Simple, attractively decorated bedrooms with modern fitted units are equipped with tea-makers and radios. Bathrooms are adequate.

Room phone Yes	*Confirm by* 6	*Parking* Limited
Room TV Yes	*Last dinner* 9.30	*Banquets* 50/–

Wincanton
Map 4 B3 Somerset
Holbrook *BA9 8BS*
Wincanton (0963) 32377

Proprietors Mr & Mrs G. Taylor
Credit Access, Amex,
Barclaycard

Rooms 20
with bath/shower 10

Holbrook House Hotel   55%   Ⓜ   £E

Enlargement and modernisation over the years have not altered the gracious character of this well-ordered, family-run hotel, which has a history dating back to the 16th century. Public rooms, including a comfortable entrance-lounge, a charming drawing room and a simple bar, all have garden views, while spacious bedrooms are traditionally furnished. Adequate bathrooms.
Amenities garden, outdoor swimming pool, tennis, squash, games room.

Room phone No	*Confirm by* By arrang.	*Parking* Ample
Room TV No	*Last dinner* 8.30	*Banquets* 40/2

Winchester

Map 5 D3 Hampshire
Sparsholt, *SO21 2LT*
Winchester (0962) 63588
Telex 477375

Rooms 28
with bath/shower 28
Room phone Yes
Room TV Yes
Confirm by By arrang.
Last dinner 10.30
Parking Ample
Banquets 35/–

Credit Access, Amex,
Barclaycard

Lainston House 85% Ⓜ   £ C

A winding drive leads to this magnificent hotel, lovingly created from a listed
17th-century house. It has lost none of its homely qualities, and behind the
red-brick facade is a wealth of fine craftsmanship: the Delft-tiled fireplace in
the entrance hall, the gleaming oak and mahogany staircase, the lovely cedar
panelling in the bar. There's a bright and relaxing lounge, and the spacious
bedrooms are models of good taste, with beautifully coordinated decor and
furnishings and an impressive array of thoughtful extras; all have sparkling
tiled bathrooms. Friendly, concerned service perfectly complements the
elegant surroundings. No dogs.
Amenities garden.

Winchester

Map 5 D3 Hampshire
Sparsholt *SO21 2LT*
Winchester (0962) 63588

About £33 for two
Banquets 35/–

Lainston House Restaurant   ♔ Ⓢ

Light green decor gives a fresh, relaxing air to this tastefully appointed
restaurant, where the Swiss-trained chef offers a menu of skilfully prepared
classic European dishes. Our pâté en croûte with Cumberland sauce was a
superb starter, and main courses range from sautéed prawns provençale to
piccata Milanese, bœuf à la mode and Swiss-style veal with rösti potatoes.
🍷 *ABOVE AVERAGE. Credit* Access, Amex, Barclaycard

Lunch 12.30–3 *Dinner* 7–10.30

Winchester

Map 5 D3 Hampshire
1 Chesil Street *SO23 8HU*
Winchester (0962) 3177
Proprietor Mauro Bregoli
Italian cooking
About £26 for two

Old Chesil Rectory

This fine half-timbered building is a surprising setting for reliable Italian
cooking. The short menu includes home-made pasta, standard veal and
chicken dishes and some unusual items like charcoal-grilled venison. *Credit*
Access, Amex, Barclaycard, Diners *Lunch* 12–2.30 *Dinner* 7–10.30, Sun 7–
9.30 **Closed** Mon, Easter Sun & 25 & 26 Dec ● **Set L** £4·95 *Banquets* 65/–

Winchester

Map 5 D3 Hampshire
Paternoster Row *SO23 9LO*
Winchester (0962) 61611
Telex 47419

Credit Access, Amex,
Barclaycard, Diners

Rooms 94
with bath/shower 94

Wessex Hotel 66%   £ D

Major refurbishment is under way at this well-run 1960s hotel, which stands
close to the cathedral in the middle of the city. There's an Edwardian air
about the relaxing bar and lounge, while bedrooms are comfortably modern,
with practical fitted furniture and ample writing space. The majority are
double-glazed, and all have well-equipped, fully tiled bathrooms.
Amenities coffee shop (10am–10pm).

| *Room phone* Yes | *Confirm by* 6 | *Parking* Ample |
| *Room TV* Yes | *Last dinner* 10 | *Banquets* 110/4 |

Windermere

Map 13 D5 Cumbria
LA23 1LW
Ambleside (096 63) 2201

Credit Access, Amex,
Barclaycard, Diners

Rooms 35
with bath/shower 31

Langdale Chase Hotel 63% Ⓜ   £ D

Set in beautiful gardens, this Victorian mansion with a delightful boathouse
enjoys outstanding views over the lake. Both hall and lounge are panelled,
with antique furniture and fine carved fireplaces, and there's a bar opening
on to a terrace. Bedrooms, including six in a bungalow, are large and
comfortably furnished. *Amenities* garden, tennis, coarse fishing, putting,
croquet, rowing boats, mooring, baby listening, table tennis.

| *Room phone* Yes | *Confirm by* By arrang. | *Parking* Ample |
| *Room TV* Yes | *Last dinner* 8.30 | *Banquets* 100/10 |

Think of the number of dishes you can serve with Uncle Ben's.

Now treble it.

Announcing two new varieties of Uncle Ben's rice for you to serve.

Our Natural Wholegrain rice is left almost as nature intended. All we've done is remove the outer husk.

So all the bran, with its fibre and nutrients, is there for you to enjoy. And yet it still only takes 20 minutes to cook.

But perhaps our most exciting rice is Uncle Ben's Long Grain and Wild.

It comes with its own sachet of 18 herbs and seasonings, making it the perfect accompaniment for those really special dishes.

Uncle Ben's, now in three superb varieties, for perfect results every time.

FOR YOUR FREE, FULL-COLOUR UNCLE BEN'S RECIPE LEAFLET, JUST WRITE TO US ENCLOSING A SAE (A4 SIZE), DORNAY FOODS, ANSA ROAD, KING'S LYNN, NORFOLK. TEL: (0553) 61200.

Windermere

Map 13 D5 Cumbria
Rayrigg Road *LA23 1EY*
Windermere (096 62) 2536

Proprietor Mr John Tovey
Rooms 13
with bath/shower 13
Room phone No
Room TV No
Confirm by 4
Last dinner 8.30
Parking Ample
Banquets 30/20
Closed 9 December–3 March

Credit Amex, Diners

Miller Howe Hotel   72%   Ⓜ   £D

John Tovey generates a special warmth and charm at his splendid pebble-dash hotel on a hillside above Lake Windermere. There's no bar, but drinks are served in the three lounges, which have plenty of comfortable armchairs and fine lake views. Bedrooms (the best have their own balconies) are elegantly furnished and thoughtfully equipped; bathrooms are exceptionally luxurious. Demi-pension only. No children under 12. *Amenities* garden.

Windermere

Map 13 D5 Cumbria
Rayrigg Road *LA23 1EY*
Windermere (096 62) 2536
Proprietor Mr John Tovey

● **Set D** £14·50
About £40 for two

Miller Howe Hotel Restaurant   ♔ Ⓢ

John Tovey's five-course dinners (no choice except for the sweet) continue to delight guests in this smart split-level restaurant overlooking the lake. Tender, juicy calf's liver and superb cauliflower cheese soup started our meal in great style, and nicely poached salmon was served with a good hollandaise sauce and an assortment of seven vegetables. Details can sometimes disappoint. ♟ *SUPERIOR. Credit* Amex, Diners

Dinner only at 8.30, Sat at 7 & 9.30
Closed 9 December–3 March

Windermere

Map 13 D5 Cumbria
Crook *LA23 3NF*
Windermere (096 62) 5225

Credit Access, Amex,
Barclaycard, Diners

Wild Boar Hotel   60%   £D

Situated just outside a peaceful village in beautiful rolling countryside, this attractive whitewashed building has a history going back to the 17th century. Its homely residents' lounge has an open fire and plenty of comfortable sofas and armchairs, and there's also a welcoming little bar. Bedrooms are cheerfully furnished, and compact bathrooms are well fitted. *Amenities* garden, dinner dance (Sat mid October–Easter).

Rooms 38	*Room phone* Yes	*Confirm by* 6	*Parking* Ample
with bath/shower 38	*Room TV* Yes	*Last dinner* 8.45	*Banquets* 40/12

Windermere

Map 13 D5 Cumbria
Crook *LA23 3NF*
Windermere (096 62) 5225

● **Set L** £5·80 **Set D** £9·85
incl. service
About £29 for two

Wild Boar Hotel Restaurant   Ⓢ

Water from the hills above flows down a rock wall in this welcoming beamed restaurant, which actually offers wild boar among its seasonal specialities. Cooking maintains reliable standards throughout a long menu which includes game and seafood, omelettes, grills, casseroles and roast leg of lamb for two. A good selection of fresh vegetables and enjoyable desserts. ♟ *SUPERIOR. Credit* Access, Amex, Barclaycard, Diners

Lunch 12.30–2 *Dinner* 7–8.45

Windsor

Map 5 E2 Berkshire
High Street *SL4 1LJ*
Windsor (075 35) 51011
Telex 849220

Credit Access, Amex,
Barclaycard, Diners

Castle Hotel   58%   £D

Right in the centre of town, this is a Georgian building with a modern bedroom wing. Separated from the foyer by a glass partition is a large, elegant lounge-cum-bar, which contrasts with the cheerful modern buttery. Bedrooms are a fair size and all have solid built-in furniture. Bathrooms are tiled and neatly fitted.
Amenities buttery (7.30am–10pm).

Rooms 85	*Room phone* Yes	*Confirm by* 6	*Parking* Ample
with bath/shower 85	*Room TV* Yes	*Last dinner* 9.45	*Banquets* 300/–

Windsor

Map 5 E2 Berkshire
30 Thames Street *SL41PR*
Windsor (075 35) 60081
Proprietor Mr Peppino Battocchi
Italian cooking
About £30 for two

Don Peppino

Standard Italian dishes, including pasta, fish and veal are skilfully prepared and professionally served in this pleasant restaurant opposite the Castle walls. There are excellent fresh vegetables, too, and enjoyable desserts. *Credit* Access, Amex, Barclaycard, Diners *Lunch* 12.30–2.30 *Dinner* 6.30–11 **Closed** Sun & Christmas *Banquets* 20/7

Windsor

Map 5 E2 Berkshire
Windsor Road
Water Oakley *SL45UK*
Maidenhead (0628) 74141
Telex 849958
Rooms 92
with bath/shower 92
Room phone Yes
Room TV Yes
Confirm by 7
Last dinner 10
Parking Ample
Banquets 250/–

Credit Access, Amex,
Barclaycard

Oakley Court Hotel   82%   £ D

Superbly combining traditional elegance with modern facilities and high standards of service, this Victorian Gothic mansion with recent additions stands between Windsor and Maidenhead in landscaped gardens complete with a frontage along the Thames. Lovingly restored public rooms are resplendent with their decorative plasterwork and handsome oak panelling, and bedrooms, most of them in the modern blocks, have high-quality matching fabrics, excellent reproduction furniture and acres of fitted cupboards. Carpeted bathrooms are luxuriously equipped. The hotel has extensive self-contained conference facilities. No dogs. *Amenities* garden, coarse fishing, 12-hour laundry service (Mon–Sat), pitch & putt, billiards.

Windsor

Map 5 E2 Berkshire
Windsor Road
Water Oakley *SL45UK*
Maidenhead (0628) 74141

● **Set L** £7·50 **Set D** £12·50
incl. service
About £37 for two

Oakley Court Hotel Restaurant

An à la carte menu featuring nouvelle cuisine dishes and a traditional English table d'hôte with roast joints are the alternatives in this roomy, elegant restaurant. Cooking and presentation are excellent and the young English chef has a particularly sure touch with sauces like the smooth lobster one accompanying delicate sole quenelles. Mouthwatering desserts.
*ABOVE AVERAGE. Credit* Access, Amex, Barclaycard

Lunch 12.30–2 *Dinner* 7.30–10

Windsor

Map 5 E2 Berkshire
Thames Street *SL41PX*
Windsor (075 35) 61354
Proprietor Mr James Miers

Credit Amex, Diners

Old House Hotel   63% Ⓜ   £ D

Sir Christopher Wren built and lived in this fine house right on the banks of the Thames. The superb entrance hall with a gleaming floor of marble and black slate sets the tone of formal elegance, enhanced by a splendidly ornate drawing room. There's also a modest TV lounge and a cocktail bar. Bedrooms are tastefully furnished and have some attractive antiques. *Amenities* garden, coarse fishing, mooring.

| *Rooms* 39 | *Room phone* Yes | *Confirm by* 6 | *Parking* Limited |
| *with bath/shower* 36 | *Room TV* No | *Last dinner* 9.30 | *Banquets* 180/4 |

Winkleigh

Map 3 D2 Devon
EX198HQ
Winkleigh (083 783) 384
Proprietors Messrs D. C. Hawkes
& R. Falkner

● **Set D** £12·50
About £33 for two

King's Arms

Book early and arrive promptly for dinner at this cosy pub restaurant, where the six-course set menu (plus a refreshing sorbet) is marvellously varied. Dishes range from delicious cucumber and yoghurt soup and mousseline of salmon with delicate sorrel sauce to fine roast pork with imaginative vegetables. Glorious sweets and perfect Stilton complete a delightful experience. Smoking discouraged. *Credit* Access, Amex, Barclaycard, Diners

Dinner only at 8.15 **Closed** Sun, Mon, Bank Holidays, 2 weeks mid February & 2 weeks mid November

Winsford

Map 3 D2 Somerset
Near Minehead *TA24 7JE*
Winsford (064 385) 232
Proprietors
Sheila & Charles Steven
Credit Access, Amex,
Barclaycard, Diners

| *Rooms* 14 | *Room phone* No | *Confirm by* 6 | *Parking* Ample |
| *with bath/shower* 10 | *Room TV* No | *Last dinner* 9 | |

Royal Oak Inn *(Inn)* Ⓜ   £ E

This delightful old thatched inn in a picturesque village is an ideal base for touring the lovely Exmoor countryside. Three comfortable lounges include one with TV, and another that serves as a writing room, and there are two cosy beamed bars. Bedrooms – some in a converted stable block – have pretty wallpaper and practical modern furnishings, and there are modernised bathrooms throughout. *Amenities* garden, coarse fishing.

Wishaw

Map 10 C4 Warwickshire
Lichfield Road
Near Sutton Coldfield
West Midlands *B76 8BR*
Curdworth (0675) 70301
Telex 358848
Rooms 59
with bath/shower 59
Room phone Yes
Room TV Yes
Confirm by By arrang.
Last dinner 10.30
Parking Ample
Banquets 250/–

Credit Access, Amex,
Barclaycard, Diners

Belfry Hotel   73%   £ D/E

Golfing enthusiasts flock to this Victorian hotel, which boasts two championship courses. An attractive conservatory leads to the reception, and there are three bars, one with a golfing theme, and a cosy panelled lounge. Bedrooms vary from large traditional rooms to compact modern ones in the extension. Well-equipped bathrooms. No dogs. *Amenities* garden, two golf courses, discothèque (3 nights weekly), putting, buttery (7am–10.30pm).   ♿

Woburn

Map 5 E1 Bedfordshire
George Street
Near Milton Keynes *MK17 9PX*
Woburn (052 525) 441
Telex 825205
Credit Access, Amex,
Barclaycard, Diners

| *Rooms* 55 | *Room phone* Yes | *Confirm by* 6 | *Parking* Ample |
| *with bath/shower* 55 | *Room TV* Yes | *Last dinner* 10.30 | *Banquets* 60/20 |

Bedford Arms Hotel   66%   £ D/E

Substantially modernised, this Georgian coaching inn offers high standards of comfort and accommodation. Besides a comfortable foyer-lounge, there's a delightfully elegant cocktail bar and a beamed public bar. Bedrooms (including 20 new executive-style ones) are furnished in simple modern style and provided with bowls of fruit and drinks dispensers. All have well-equipped bathrooms. *Amenities* dancing (Fri).   ♿

Woking

Map 5 E3 Surrey
Chobham Road *GU21 4AL*
Woking (048 62) 73047

Credit Access, Amex, Barclaycard
Closed 2 weeks after Christmas

| *Rooms* 28 | *Room phone* Some | *Confirm by* 9 | *Parking* Ample |
| *with bath/shower* None | *Room TV* Yes | *Last dinner* 10 | *Banquets* 30/5 |

Wheatsheaf Hotel *(Inn)*   £ F

Standing near the town centre on the Chobham Road, this well-kept red-brick inn is a popular stopping place for businessmen. Bedrooms in the main building are the roomiest; those in the annexe are compact, bright and practical, and each pair share an up-to-date bathroom. There's a small foyer-lounge and a choice of three bars. No dogs.
Amenities garden.

Wolverhampton

Map 10 B4 West Midlands
Mount Road
Tettenhall Wood *WV6 8HL*
Wolverhampton (0902) 752055
Manager Mr T. M. Marshall
Credit Access, Amex,
Barclaycard, Diners

| *Rooms* 63 | *Room phone* Yes | *Confirm by* By arrang. | *Parking* Ample |
| *with bath/shower* 47 | *Room TV* Most | *Last dinner* 9.30 | *Banquets* 204/6 |

Mount Hotel   56%   £ E

A 19th-century, mock-Tudor hotel standing in landscaped gardens in a quiet suburb. The foyer-lounge area and a popular bar have handsome wood panelling, and function facilities include a splendid ballroom with a gallery. Bedrooms in the main building are furnished in traditional style, while those in the extension are modern, with neat, compact bathrooms. *Amenities* garden, dinner dance (Sat). **Closed** for accommodation 24–27 Dec.

Wolverhampton

Map 10 B4 West Midlands
Ednam Road
Goldthorn Park *WV45AJ*
Wolverhampton (0902) 331121
Credit Access, Amex,
Barclaycard, Diners
Closed 25 & 26 December

Rooms 57	
with bath/shower 49	

Park Hall Hotel   55%   £E

Ask for directions when booking at this converted Georgian mansion on the southern fringes of the city. Public areas include a modern cocktail bar, a simple public bar and a first-floor lounge-cum-conference room. Most bedrooms are in the extension and have practical fitted furniture and adequately equipped bathrooms. The hotel would benefit from refurbishment. *Amenities* garden, dancing (Sat in winter).

Room phone Yes	*Confirm by* 6	*Parking* Ample
Room TV Yes	*Last dinner* 9.45	*Banquets* 350/–

Stars in this Guide stand for the quality of the cooking only – our overriding criterion, irrespective of price, luxury or service.

Woodbridge

Map 6 D3 Suffolk
IP13 6NU
Woodbridge (039 43) 5678

Proprietor Mr M. S. Bunn
Rooms 24
with bath/shower 22
Room phone Yes
Room TV Yes
Confirm by By arrang.
Last dinner 9
Parking Ample
Banquets 85/10
Closed 25 December

Credit Access, Amex,
Barclaycard, Diners

Seckford Hall   71%   Ⓜ   £D/E

Mr Bunn, the long-time owner, keeps a loving eye on this impressive ivy-clad mansion, which was built in 1530 and is surrounded by 34 acres of beautiful parkland. The interior has been handsomely converted, with carved beams and oak panelling carefully preserved. Antiques abound, and there are deep, comfortable chairs to relax in. Some of the bedrooms have four-poster beds, others are more modern, but carefully chosen furniture blends well with the style of the house. All rooms are large and enjoy fine views over the grounds, and bathrooms, too, are bright and spacious. Staff are helpful and courteous.
Amenities garden, coarse fishing.

Woodhall Spa

Map 11 E2 Lincolnshire
Manor Estate *LN10 6QF*
Woodhall Spa (0526) 52588
Proprietors Mr & Mrs H. Plumb

Credit Barclaycard

Rooms 7	
with bath/shower 3	

Dower House Hotel   62%   Ⓜ   £E/F

The charming Plumbs have turned this secluded Edwardian house into a peaceful, well-run hotel. Homely comfort is the keynote of the reception hall, the relaxing lounge and the spacious bar with its delightful views of the grounds. Bedrooms vary in size but all are furnished in traditional style, with some very fine pieces here and there. Simple modern bathrooms.
Amenities garden.

Room phone No	*Confirm by* By arrang.	*Parking* Ample
Room TV Some	*Last dinner* 9.30	

Woodhall Spa

Map 11 E2 Lincolnshire
The Broadway *LN10 6SG*
Woodhall Spa (0526) 52434

Manager Mr A. Fothergill
Credit Access, Amex,
Barclaycard, Diners

Rooms 58	
with bath/shower 25	

Golf Hotel   61%   £E

Attractive soft furnishings and pleasant colour schemes give the public rooms of this half-timbered mock-Tudor hotel a warm, homely atmosphere. Bedrooms are cheerful and equipped with radios and trouser presses; a number also have modern private bathrooms. Adequate public bathrooms. The hotel has direct access to a championship golf course.
Amenities garden, croquet, table tennis, putting.

Room phone Yes	*Confirm by* By arrang.	*Parking* Ample
Room TV Yes	*Last dinner* 9	*Banquets* 200/–

Woodstock

Map 5 D1 Oxfordshire
Park Street *OX7 1SZ*
Woodstock (0993) 811511
Telex 837921 Bertel
Proprietor M. C. Porter
Rooms 44
with bath/shower 37
Room phone Yes
Room TV Yes
Confirm by By arrang.
Last dinner 10.30
Parking Ample
Banquets 100/–

Credit Access, Amex,
Barclaycard, Diners

Bear Hotel   75%   Ⓜ   £C

Splendidly laid out around the courtyard (now the hotel car park), this Cotswold-stone coaching inn can trace its origins back to the 16th century. Various periods and styles are reflected in the public rooms, which range from the rustic lounge bar with its blackened beams, wheelback chairs and huge open fireplaces to the residents' lounge, which has the exquisite style of an 18th-century drawing room with ornate gilt mirrors, elegant drapes and antique furniture. Traditional bedrooms have been furnished and decorated with impeccable taste and care. Excellent carpeted bathrooms– also marvellously fitted–have everything from bath caps to telephones.

Woody Bay

Map 3 D1 Devon
Near Parracombe *EX31 4QX*
Parracombe (059 83) 264

Credit Access, Amex,
Barclaycard, Diners

Woody Bay Hotel   57%   Ⓜ   £E

The Bennetts and the Johnses continue to make improvements to this white-painted hotel, which occupies a spectacular position on a wooded hillside overlooking the bay. The cheerful bar has splendid views, and there's a homely lounge with comfortable chairs and TV. Bedrooms are neat and tidy, with pretty floral wallpaper and fitted furniture; two rooms have four-posters. Adequate bathrooms. *Amenities* garden.

Rooms 14	*Room phone* No	*Confirm by* By arrang.	*Parking* Ample
with bath/shower 11	*Room TV* No	*Last dinner* 9	*Banquets* 40/12

Woolacombe

Map 2 C1 Devon *EX34 7BN*
Woolacombe (0271) 870388

Credit Access, Barclaycard

Closed January

Woolacombe Bay Hotel   58%   £D

There are fine views of the bay from this rambling Victorian building. Numerous public rooms have sleek contemporary furniture, while most of the attractive bedrooms have smart fitted units and modern tiled bathrooms. *Amenities* garden, sauna, outdoor and indoor swimming pool, tennis, squash, dancing (3 nights a week), children's playroom, laundry room, table tennis, solarium, billiards, hairdressing, pitch & putt.

Rooms 48	*Room phone* Yes	*Confirm by* 6	*Parking* Ample
with bath/shower 48	*Room TV* Yes	*Last dinner* 9	*Banquets* 160/–

Wooler

Map 14 B2 Northumberland
Cottage Road *NE71 6AD*
Wooler (066 82) 581

Proprietors Mr & Mrs B. Morton
& Mr & Mrs F. Park

Tankerville Arms Hotel *(Inn)*   Ⓜ   £E/F

The hospitable Parks and Mortons ensure a friendly, informal atmosphere at their attractive old creeper-covered inn. Besides a simple public bar, there's a cosy lounge bar with warm red decor and a residents' lounge with colour TV, contemporary fittings and views of the gardens. Bedrooms provide adequate comforts for short stays: bright, cheerful and quite roomy, they have radios and practical modern furniture. *Amenities* garden.

Rooms 17	*Room phone* No	*Confirm by* By arrang.	*Parking* Ample
with bath/shower 5	*Room TV* No	*Last dinner* 9.30	*Banquets* 80/6

Worcester

Map 4 B1 Hereford & Worcester
High Street *WR1 2QR*
Worcester (0905) 27155
Telex 338869

Credit Access, Amex,
Barclaycard, Diners

Giffard Hotel   62%   £D

This modern city-centre hotel in a shopping complex has superb views of the cathedral from some rooms. The public areas range from a smart foyer with smoked glass and suede-covered walls to an attractive lounge and gleaming coffee shop. The neat, comfortable bedrooms have space-saving units and cheerful decor, and the compact bathrooms are well equipped.
Amenities coffee shop (10am–10.15pm, Sun 10am–9.15pm).

Rooms 104	*Room phone* Yes	*Confirm by* 6	*Parking* Ample
with bath/shower 104	*Room TV* Yes	*Last dinner* 9.45	*Banquets* 80/6

The tastiest stars in our variety show

Munch a big crunch
FINDUS ®
25 YEARS
OF SUCCESS

2 French Bread
Pizzas
with Cheese and Tomatoes
FINDUS
WITH
CHEESE
French Bread Pizza
with Cheese and Tomatoes
FINDUS
WITH
CHEE

Worthing

Map 5 E4 West Sussex
Marine Parade *BN11 3QJ*
Worthing (0903) 34001

Manager Mr P. Nash
Credit Access, Amex,
Barclaycard

Rooms 94
with bath/shower 89

Beach Hotel   64%   £E

Since the 1930s this cream-painted seafront hotel has provided substantial comfort in traditional style. There are fine views of the sea from the picture windows in the spacious foyer-lounge, while the wood-panelled bar has a stylish, intimate atmosphere. Bedrooms (mostly double-glazed) are furnished with freestanding wooden units and armchairs. Bathrooms are adequate. No children under eight. No dogs. *Amenities* table tennis.

Room phone Yes   *Confirm by* By arrang.   *Parking* Ample
Room TV Yes   *Last dinner* 8.45   *Banquets* 250/–

Worthing

Map 5 E4 West Sussex
Steyne *BN11 3DU*
Worthing (0903) 36103
Telex 877046
Manager Mr John Walpole
Credit Access, Amex,
Barclaycard, Diners

Rooms 90
with bath/shower 76

Chatsworth Hotel   58%   £E

Standing right on the seafront overlooking an attractive lawned square, this four-storey Georgian building has been generally improved over the years. The entrance hall leads to a simple cocktail bar and several traditionally furnished lounge areas. Bedrooms vary in size from modest to large. All have functional built-in units and tea-makers, and most have modern, fully tiled bathrooms. *Amenities* 24-hour laundry service, games room.

Room phone Yes   *Confirm by* By arrang.   *Parking* Limited
Room TV Yes   *Last dinner* 9.15   *Banquets* 160/–

Worthing

Map 5 E4 West Sussex
Marine Parade *BN11 3PW*
Worthing (0903) 34444
Telex 877046
Manager Mr J. G. F. Stoy
Credit Access, Amex,
Barclaycard, Diners

Rooms 83
with bath/shower 56

Eardley Hotel   59%   £D

Ornamental gardens separate this imposing Victorian hotel from the seafront. The two traditionally furnished lounges and the attractive clubby bar are smart and comfortable. Bedrooms range from large sea-facing rooms boasting seating areas and spacious private bathrooms with bidets and showers, to smaller, neatly fitted singles. Extensive function facilities. *Amenities* garden, sea fishing, board sailing.

Room phone Yes   *Confirm by* By arrang.   *Parking* Limited
Room TV Yes   *Last dinner* 9.30   *Banquets* 150/2

Wotton

Map 5 E3 Surrey
Near Dorking *RH5 6QQ*
Dorking (0306) 5665

● **Set L** from £5·50
Set D from £7·90
About £25 for two
Banquets 60/30

Wotton Hatch

A pleasantly luxurious atmosphere pervades this attractive pub restaurant, where the young French chef offers a varied choice of capably prepared food. Starters like kedgeree or home-made Scotch broth are followed by a roast from the trolley or dishes such as sautéed chicken with cream and tarragon, while to finish there are simple sweets like apple pie.
Credit Access, Amex, Barclaycard, Diners

Lunch 12.30–2 *Dinner* 7.30–9.30, Fri & Sat 7.30–9.45
Closed D Sun, all Mon, 1 January & D 25 December

Wotton-under-Edge

Map 4 B2 Gloucestershire
Market Street *GL12 7AE*
Wotton-under-Edge
(045 385) 2329
Proprietor Mr M. T. Ramsland
Credit Access, Amex,
Barclaycard, Diners

Rooms 26
with bath/shower 19

Swan Hotel   57%   Ⓜ   £E

Past and present happily co-exist behind the distinctive blue Georgian-style facade of this town-centre hotel. Handsome beams and attractive panelling combine with plush seating in the reception and bar-lounge. Bedrooms vary in style and decor, most having modern freestanding furniture and fully tiled, up-to-date bathrooms (some with bidets). *Amenities* dinner dance (Sat).

Room phone Yes   *Confirm by* 6   *Parking* Difficult
Room TV Yes   *Last dinner* 10

Wrafton

Map 2 C2 Devon
Near Braunton *EX33 2DN*
Braunton (0271) 812149
Proprietor Mr B. Christmas

Poyer's

The setting – a thatched cottage in a country lane – is typical of rural England, but the menu is largely French-inspired, ranging from hearty vegetable soup and house pâté to roast quail in champagne and tender fillets of beef, pork and veal, each with its own sauce. To round off an enjoyable, well-cooked meal there's a trolleyful of tempting desserts. The little beamed dining rooms

Continued

Continued
● **Set L** £4·85 **Set D** £7
About £28 for two
Banquets 30/–

are cosy and homely. A modernised courtyard complex houses some ten attractive bedrooms, all with neat, up-to-date fittings and excellent bathrooms. There's also a comfortable lounge.
Credit Amex, Barclaycard

Lunch 12.30–2 *Dinner* 7.30–9.30, Sat 7.30–10
Closed L Sat, D Sun & 25 & 26 December

Wroxton

Map 5 D1 Oxfordshire
Near Banbury *OX15 6PZ*
Wroxton St Mary (029 573) 482
Manager Mr L. De Felice
Credit Access, Amex,
Barclaycard, Diners
Closed Christmas night

Wroxton House Hotel   69%   £ D

An attractive thatched Cotswold-stone hotel set in pleasant gardens. Beams, panelling and an open stone hearth add charm to the comfortable bar, and the residents' lounge is appealing, too. Compact bedrooms in the main house are prettily decorated and furnished, those in the annexe are quite luxurious. All have numerous little extras, like fruit and hairdryers, as do the good modern bathrooms. *Amenities* garden.

Rooms 15
with bath/shower 11

Room phone Yes
Room TV Yes

Confirm by By arrang.
Last dinner 10.30

Parking Ample
Banquets 70/–

Wroxton

Map 5 D1 Oxfordshire
Near Banbury *OX15 6PZ*
Wroxton St Mary (029 573) 482

Wroxton House Hotel Restaurant   ⑤

An elegant restaurant made up of three distinctively decorated rooms. The menu offers a varied choice of competently prepared dishes ranging from prawns Thermidor to veal escalope milanese, supplemented by seasonal specialities like Scotch salmon and roast pheasant. Simple, well-cooked vegetables and delicious sweets such as creamy chocolate mousse and crêpes suzette. *Credit* Access, Amex, Barclaycard, Diners

● **Set L** £5·70 **Set D** £6·85
incl. service
About £32 for two

Lunch 12–2.30 *Dinner* 7–10.30

Wye

Map 7 C5 Kent
4 Upper Bridge Street *TN25 5EB*
Wye (0233) 812540
Proprietors Mr R. Johnson &
Mr B. Boots

Wife of Bath   ♀ ⑤

Originally a private house, this attractive bow-windowed restaurant provides an elegant but homely setting in which to enjoy skilful, imaginative cooking. Bob Johnson is an experienced chef who changes his short, varied menu each week to make the best use of top-quality raw materials in dishes like fennel provençale and fillets of sole with prawns, brandy and cream. Sweets may include sorbets and chocolate mousse.

● **Set L & Set D** £9·50
About £28 for two
Banquets 50/35

Lunch 12.15–2 *Dinner* 7–10
Closed Sun, Mon & 25 December–1 January

Wymondham

Map 6 C2 Norfolk
16 Damgate Street *NR18 0BQ*
Wymondham (0953) 603533

Bullen's   ♀ ⑤

Edward and Stella Bullen share the duties in this endearing little restaurant. He does the cooking and offers a brief set menu each day featuring main courses like fillet of lamb en croûte or sautéed chicken with peppers, served with an abundance of excellent fresh vegetables. She looks after the guests and provides friendly deft service. Booking essential.
Credit Access, Barclaycard

● **Set D** £9·65
About £27 for two
Banquets 24/–

Dinner only at 8
Closed Sun, Mon & Bank Holidays

Changes in data may occur in establishments after the Guide goes to press. Prices should be taken as indications rather than firm quotes.

Yarm

Map 15 C5 Cleveland
Crathorne *TS15 0AR*
Stokesley (0642) 700398

Rooms 25
with bath/shower 25
Room phone Yes
Room TV Yes
Confirm by By arrang.
Last dinner 10
Parking Ample
Banquets 150/–

Credit Access, Amex,
Barclaycard, Diners

Crathorne Hall Hotel   74%　　　£ D

Built from local sandstone in the reign of Edward VII, this imposing country house stands in wooded grounds with lovely views of the river Leven and the Cleveland Hills beyond. A beautifully panelled entrance hall, with oil paintings and fine antiques, sets the tone for the impressive public rooms, which include a dignified drawing room with an ornately carved coat of arms above the fireplace, an elegant ballroom and a cocktail bar that's smartly contemporary. Spacious bedrooms, all with marvellous views, have pretty fabrics and high-quality mahogany furniture. Most bathrooms are modern, but three retain their splendid original huge tubs.
Amenities garden, croquet, games room, snooker.

Our inspectors are our full-time employees; they are professionally trained by us.

Yarm

Map 15 C5 Cleveland
Worsall Road *TS15 9PE*
Eaglescliffe (0642) 781050

Credit Amex, Barclaycard

Tall Trees Hotel   58%　　　£ E/F

Situated alongside the B1264, this low red-brick hotel overlooking the river Tees is noted for its superb sports and function facilities. There are two cheerful modern bars and a comfortable lounge for residents. Compact modern bedrooms are neatly furnished, and bathrooms are beautifully warm.
Amenities garden, sauna, squash, game fishing, dancing (Sat), golf driving range, solarium, clay-pigeon shooting, gymnasium.

Rooms 34	*Room phone* Yes	*Confirm by* By arrang.	*Parking* Ample
with bath/shower 34	*Room TV* Yes	*Last dinner* 9.30	*Banquets* 300/15

Yattendon

Map 5 D2 Berkshire
The Square *RG16 0UF*
Hermitage (0635) 201325
Proprietors Mr & Mrs John Behr
Credit Amex, Barclaycard,
Diners
Closed 24 & 25 December

Royal Oak Hotel *(Inn)* Ⓜ　　　£ D

Overlooking the square with its charming cottages and a blacksmith's shop, this 16th-century red-brick inn completes a beguiling picture of English village life. Mrs Behr's colourful floral displays create a sunny effect, while log fires in the traditional lounge and bar provide solace in winter. Bedrooms are pleasantly furnished in homely old-fashioned style, and each has its own compact bathroom. *Amenities* garden.

Rooms 5	*Room phone* Yes	*Confirm by* By arrang.	*Parking* Ample
with bath/shower 5	*Room TV* Yes	*Last dinner* 9.30	*Banquets* 30/20

Yattendon

Map 5 D2 Berkshire
The Square *RG16 0UF*
Hermitage (0635) 201325
Proprietors Mr & Mrs John Behr
English cooking

Set L & Set D from £7·75
About £26 for two

Royal Oak Hotel Restaurant　　　Ⓢ

Ingredients obtained fresh from local farms and shops form the basis of the satisfying fare offered in this cosy, civilised restaurant. Dishes range from hearty steak and kidney pudding or full-flavoured roast pheasant to more refined specialities like fillet of sole in a creamed lobster sauce; vegetables are tasty and sweets have a lovely home-made flavour.
Credit Amex, Barclaycard, Diners　　　

Lunch 12.30–1.30, Sun 12–1.30 *Dinner* 7.30–9.30, Sun 7.30–9
Closed D 24 & all 25 December

Yelverton

Map 2 C3 Devon
Plymouth *PL20 6DA*
Yelverton (082 285) 2245

Manager Mr Michael Jenkin
Credit Access, Amex,
Barclaycard, Diners

Rooms 23	*with bath/shower* 23

Moorland Links Hotel   61%   £ D

Nine acres of grounds provide a pleasant setting for this well-modernised hotel on the A386, just outside Plymouth. The foyer-lounge is a tastefully decorated room, and there is a panelled bar hung with firearms. Pleasant bedrooms–some with balconies–have smart fitted units or freestanding furniture; all are now equipped with good private bathrooms.
Amenities garden, outdoor swimming pool, tennis, putting.

Room phone Yes	*Confirm by* By arrang.	*Parking* Ample
Room TV Yes	*Last dinner* 10	*Banquets* 160/10

Yeovil

Map 4 B3 Somerset
Barwick *BA22 9TD*
Yeovil (0935) 23902

About £24 for two
Banquets 30/–

Little Barwick House   ⚘ ⓢ

Since the Colleys took over this charming Georgian dower house, the emphasis has changed from accommodation to food, though for overnight guests there are three warm, comfortable bedrooms. The simple, airy dining room is an apt setting for Veronica's fresh, wholesome cooking: the menu is straightforward, but everything is prepared and presented with great care, from the smoked mackerel pâté, garnished with tasty cucumber relish and served with brown and white bread as well as hot rolls, to the juicy pork fillet with lovely crisp vegetables and the mouthwatering strawberry Pavlova. Husband Christopher provides excellent cheerful service.
Credit Access, Amex, Barclaycard, Diners

Dinner only 7–9.30
Closed Sun, also Mon October–April, 1 January & 25 & 26 December

---

Yeovil

Map 4 B3 Somerset
Hendford *BA20 1TG*
Yeovil (0935) 23116
Telex 46580
Manager Mr K. C. Berry
Credit Access, Amex,
Barclaycard, Diners

Rooms 42	*with bath/shower* 42

Manor Hotel   68%   £ D/E

Situated near the town centre, this sturdy 18th-century house offers plush, up-to-date accommodation. Open-plan public rooms include a spacious reception-lounge leading into a comfortable bar. Smart, well-appointed bedrooms (half in an annexe) have good-quality fitted or freestanding furniture, pretty matching fabrics, tea-makers and trouser presses. Compact modern bathrooms. *Amenities* garden.

Room phone Yes	*Confirm by* 6	*Parking* Ample
Room TV Yes	*Last dinner* 10	*Banquets* 60/10

York

Town plan B1 North Yorkshire
Marygate Lane, Bootham *YO3 7DE*
York (0904) 34866
Proprietors
Mr & Mrs N. F. Dearnley
Credit Access, Amex,
Barclaycard, Diners

Rooms 27	*with bath/shower* 27

Abbots Mews Hotel   60%   Ⓜ   £ D/E

The Dearnleys and their staff take good care of visitors to this attractive hotel, handily placed for the station and the Minster, but away from the bustle and the traffic. Public rooms include a friendly bar and a sunny lounge with cane furniture and plenty of greenery; prettily decorated bedrooms have elegant white furniture and smart modern bathrooms (mostly showers only).
Amenities garden, solarium.

Room phone Yes	*Confirm by* By arrang.	*Parking* Ample
Room TV Yes	*Last dinner* 9.30	*Banquets* 80/–

York

Town plan A3 North Yorkshire
Tadcaster Road *YO2 2QQ*
York (0904) 707171
Proprietor Major P. B. Morris
Credit Access, Amex,
Barclaycard, Diners
Closed 2 days Christmas

Rooms 80	*with bath/shower* 78

Chase Hotel   62%   Ⓜ   £ D

This fine early Victorian hotel, which is within sight of York racecourse, has been run by the same family for over 25 years. Public rooms like the lounge and semicircular bar are comfortable and relaxing, and there are good conference facilities. Spacious, well-lit bedrooms are neatly furnished with fitted units; bathrooms spotlessly maintained. Guide dogs only.
Amenities garden, dancing (Sat November–Easter), putting.   ♿

Room phone Yes	*Confirm by* 6	*Parking* Ample
Room TV Yes	*Last dinner* 9	*Banquets* 134/12

A microwave cooker is the practical and perfect complement to the family freezer. And as the freezer experts, we at Bejam have naturally made microwave cookers very much our business, too. For years we've tried and tested models from every manufacturer; and we're better able than most to give a fair and balanced assessment.

All the microwave cookers in our selected range are well-designed, well-built and offer outstanding value for money.

So when you're making *your* choice, don't be bewildered – come straight to Bejam! As with our freezers, we offer easy credit terms, cash 'n' carry facilities, free delivery (within our service area), and free advice from our resident home economists.

All microwave cookers carry the full manufacturer's guarantee.

Make the most of your freezer with a microwave cooker from Bejam!

Bejam
The Freezer People

Map 15 C6
Town plan opposite

Population 97,240

A northern bastion and trading town from Roman times, in the 8th century York became a religious and learning centre, although the present university is fifteen years old. The great Minster spans 1,356 years. York's medieval wealth came from wool and monasteries, its modern prosperity from the advent of the railway, chocolate factories and tourists. Architectural gems blend the Middle Ages, pre-Reformation churches and the 18th century.

Sights Outside City
Castle Howard, Fountains Abbey, Ripley Castle, Harewood House, Knaresborough, Newby Hall (Boroughbridge), Kirkham Priory

Information Centre
De Grey Rooms, Exhibition Square, York YO1 2BH
Telephone York 21756/7

Lancia Dealers

Piccadilly Auto Centre
84 Piccadilly
York
Tel: 0904 34321

York

1	Art Gallery *English and European*	B1
2	Castle Folk Museum *unique reconstruction of period street and interiors*	C3
3	Clifford's Tower *13th-c keep*	C2/3
4	Guildhall and Mansion House	B2
5	Impressions Gallery of Photography	C2
6	Tourist Information Centre	C1
7	King's Manor *home of monks and kings*	B1
8	Merchant's Adventurers' Hall *medieval Chapel and Great Hall*	C2
9	Merchant Taylor's Hall *14th c*	C1
10	Minster *chief glory of York*	C1
11	Model Railway Exhibition	D3
12	Race-course	A3
13	Railway Museum *Britain's chief collection*	A1/2
14	St Mary's Abbey *ruins*	B1
15	St Mary's Heritage Centre (York Story)	C2
16	Shambles *meaning slaughterhouses; outstanding medieval street*	C2
17	Station	A/B2
18	Theatre Royal	B1
19	Treasurer's House *mainly 17th c valuable furniture and pictures*	C1
20	University *modern architectural interest*	E3
21	Yorkshire Museum *archaeology, natural history*	B1

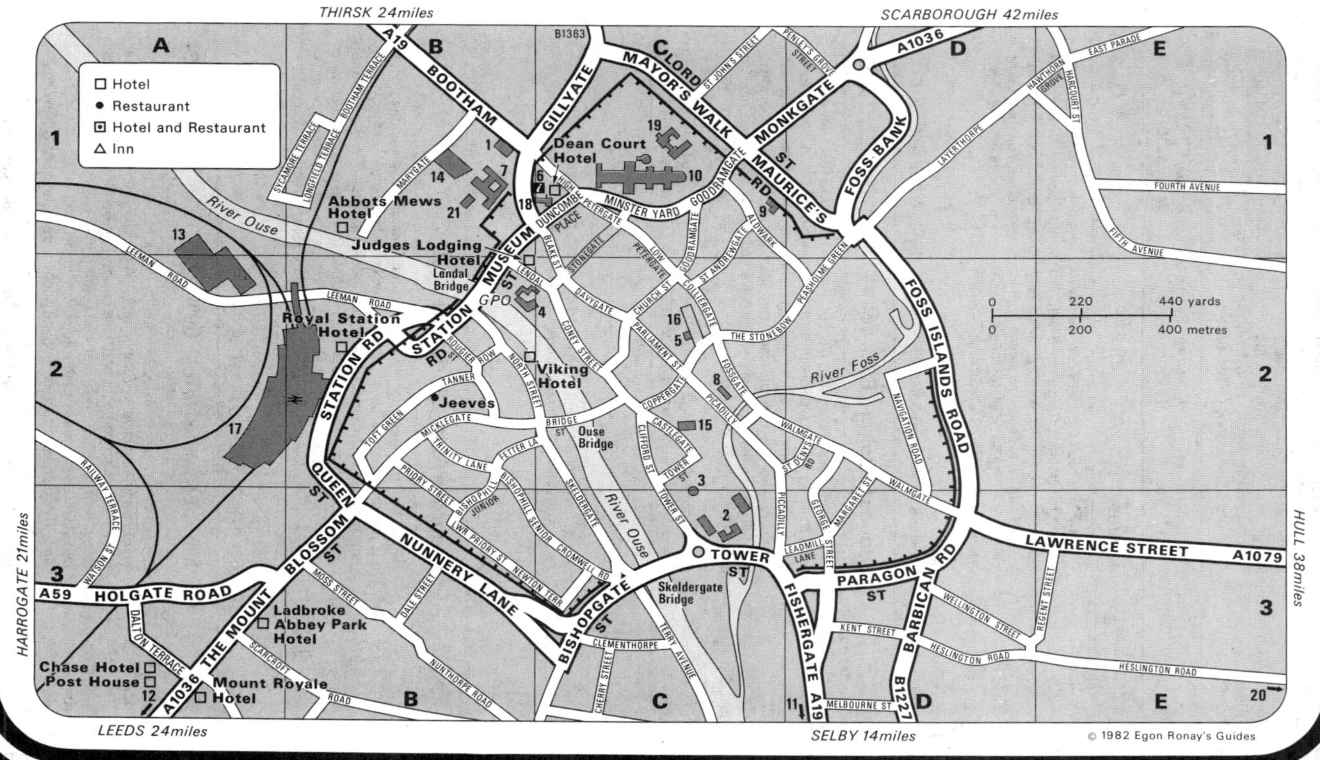

York LANCIA
LANCIA
THIRSK 24miles
SCARBOROUGH 42miles
HARROGATE 21miles
LEEDS 24miles
SELBY 14miles
HULL 38miles
© 1982 Egon Ronay's Guides
Hotel
Restaurant
Hotel and Restaurant
Inn
A
B
C
D
E
1
2
3
B1363
CLORD'S
GILLYGATE
MAYOR'S WALK
MONKGATE
MAURICE'S ST RD
FOSS BANK
ST JOHN'S STREET
PENLEY'S GROVE STREET
A1036
HAWTHORN GROVE
HARCOURT ST
EAST PARADE
LAYERTHORPE
FOURTH AVENUE
FIFTH AVENUE
BOOTHAM
BOOTHAM TERRACE
SYCAMORE TERRACE
LONGFIELD TERRACE
MARYGATE
Dean Court Hotel
19
10
Abbots Mews Hotel
14
7
6
18
MINSTER YARD
GOODRAMGATE
9
ALDWARK
PEASHOLME GREEN
FOSS ISLANDS ROAD
River Ouse
13
Judges Lodging Hotel
Lendal Bridge
LEEMAN ROAD
HIGH PETERGATE
DUNCOMBE PLACE
BLAKE ST
STONEGATE
LOW PETERGATE
CHURCH ST
ST ANDREWGATE
COLLIERGATE
THE STONEBOW
River Foss
NAVIGATION ROAD
MUSEUM ST
LENDAL
DAVYGATE
GPO
4
Royal Station Hotel
STATION RD
STATION RD
ROUGIER ST
ROW
NORTH STREET
CONEY STREET
PARLIAMENT ST
GOODRAMGATE
16
5
8
FOSSGATE
PICCADILLY
WALMGATE
ST DENYS RD
WALMGATE
0 220 440 yards
0 200 400 metres
Viking Hotel
TANNER
Jeeves
17
MICKLEGATE
TOFT GREEN
TRINITY LANE
FETTER LA
BRIDGE ST
Ouse Bridge
COPPERGATE
CASTLEGATE
CLIFFORD ST
TOWER ST
15
PICCADILLY
MARGARET ST
LEADMILL LANE
GEORGE STREET
RAILWAY TERRACE
WATSON ST
QUEEN ST
BLOSSOM ST
PRIORY STREET
BISHOPHILL JUNIOR
BISHOPHILL SENIOR
SKELDERGATE
LWR PRIORY ST
CROMWELL RD
NEWTON TERR
River Ouse
3
2
TOWER ST
Skeldergate Bridge
PARAGON ST
FISHERGATE A19
LAWRENCE STREET
A1079
HARROGATE 21miles
A59
HOLGATE ROAD
THE MOUNT
DALTON TERRACE
SCARCROFT ROAD
NUNNERY LANE
MOSS STREET
DALE STREET
NUNTHORPE ROAD
Ladbroke Abbey Park Hotel
Chase Hotel
Post House
12
A1036
Mount Royale Hotel
BISHOPGATE ST
CLEMENTHORPE
CHERRY STREET
TERRY AVENUE
11
MELBOURNE ST
B1227
BARBICAN RD
KENT STREET
WELLINGTON STREET
HESLINGTON ROAD
REGENT STREET
HESLINGTON ROAD
20

York — Dean Court Hotel 58% Ⓜ £C/D

Town plan C1 North Yorkshire
Duncombe Place *YO1 2EF*
York (0904) 25082
Telex 57450
Props. Mr & Mrs I. R. Washington
Credit Access, Amex,
Barclaycard, Diners

Its position close to York Minster makes this conversion of five Victorian houses a convenient base for tourists. The reception area and residents' lounges are comfortably and traditionally furnished, and there's also a coffee lounge and two bars. Good-sized bedrooms have tasteful decor and fittings. The best equipped are those in the modern wing. No dogs.
Amenities coffee lounge (10am–8pm).

Rooms 35	*Room phone* Yes	*Confirm by* By arrang.	*Parking* Difficult
with bath/shower 35	*Room TV* Yes	*Last dinner* 8.45	*Banquets* 15/–

York — Jeeves 🍷 Ⓢ

Town plan B2 North Yorkshire
39 Tanner Row *YO1 1JP*
York (0904) 59622

Timothy Mallinson produces consistently excellent dinners at this pleasant, family-run restaurant. Sauces are a feature of the main courses, which could include chicken breast with apricots, brandy and cream of pork fillet with mustard and wine sauce–all served with lovely vegetables. You might start with quiche or grilled scallops, and to finish there's cheese or a home-made dessert. 🍷 *SUPERIOR. Credit* Amex, Diners

● **Set D** £8·50
About £24 for two
Banquets 40/–

Dinner only 7–10
Closed Sun, also Mon Oct–April, Bank Hols, 25 Aug–3 Sept & 25–28 Oct

York — Judges Lodging 67% Ⓜ £D

Town plan B2 North Yorkshire
9 Lendal *YO1 2AQ*
York (0904) 38733

The Masons have imparted an elegant, French flavour to this 18th-century listed building, which was originally the residence of the local Assize Court judges. The entrance is full of lovely antiques, ornaments and plush armchairs, and a remarkable cantilever staircase leads to the traditional, tastefully furnished bedrooms, which have luxuriously appointed modern bathrooms. There's also a cellar bar.

Credit Barclaycard, Diners

Rooms 13	*Room phone* Yes	*Confirm by* By arrang.	*Parking* Limited
with bath/shower 13	*Room TV* No	*Last dinner* 10.30	*Banquets* 40/–

Any person using our name to obtain free hospitality is a fraud. Proprietors, please inform the police and us.

York — Ladbroke Abbey Park Hotel 60% £D

Town plan B3 North Yorkshire
The Mount *YO2 2BN*
York (0904) 58301
Telex 57993
Credit Access, Amex,
Barclaycard, Diners
Closed 2 weeks after Christmas

Helpful staff provide a friendly welcome at this modernised Georgian hotel not far from the city centre. Newly decorated bedrooms have colourful furnishings and laminated units with good writing space; extras in these 'gold star' rooms (book in advance) include fruit and sherry. Older-style rooms are gradually being refurbished. There's a cheerful cocktail bar and a cosy residents' lounge. *Amenities* dinner dance (Sat November–March)

Rooms 84	*Room phone* Yes	*Confirm by* 6	*Parking* Limited
with bath/shower 75	*Room TV* Yes	*Last dinner* 9.30	*Banquets* 150/20

York — Mount Royale Hotel 69% Ⓜ £E

Town plan A3 North Yorkshire
The Mount *YO2 2DA*
York (0904) 28856
Proprietors
Richard & Christine Oxtoby
Credit Access, Amex,
Barclaycard, Diners

Richard and Christine Oxtoby have turned two houses on the outskirts of town into an attractive, welcoming hotel. A panelled lounge overlooks the garden and swimming pool, and there's a cosy little bar. A fine staircase leads to the light, airy bedrooms, complete with potted plants and comfortable armchairs. Useful dressing areas adjoin the bright bathrooms.
Amenities garden, outdoor swimming pool. **Closed** Christmas & New Year

Rooms 18	*Room phone* Yes	*Confirm by* 6.30	*Parking* Limited
with bath/shower 18	*Room TV* Yes	*Last dinner* 9.30	*Banquets* 25/–

York
Town plan A3 North Yorkshire
Tadcaster Road *YO2 2QF*
York (0904) 707921
Telex 57798

Credit Access, Amex,
Barclaycard, Diners

Rooms 147	*Room phone* Yes	*Confirm by* 6	*Parking* Ample
with bath/shower 147	*Room TV* Yes	*Last dinner* 10	*Banquets* 64/–

Post House Hotel   62%   £ C/D

This large modern hotel south-west of the town on the A1036 was designed to make the most of views of the huge cedar of Lebanon in the grounds. The flagstoned foyer leads into a spacious lounge-bar with panoramic windows. Redecorated bedrooms are particularly attractive, and all are well equipped with colour TV, mini-bars, tea-makers and compact bathrooms.
Amenities garden, sauna, coffee shop (10.30am–6.30pm), putting.

York
Town plan B2 North Yorkshire
Station Road *YO2 2AA*
York (0904) 53681
Telex 57912
Credit Access, Amex,
Barclaycard, Diners
Closed Christmas

Rooms 129	*Room phone* Yes	*Confirm by* 6	*Parking* Limited
with bath/shower 110	*Room TV* Yes	*Last dinner* 9.15	*Banquets* 245/10

Royal Station Hotel   66%   £ E

Built in the grand Victorian manner, this well-run hotel, standing in attractive gardens near the old city wall, offers traditional service and modern comforts. The splendid panelled Oak Room is popular for functions and bars include the cosy cellar bar with an apt railway theme. Spacious bedrooms have solid freestanding furniture; bathrooms are adequate. *Amenities* garden, men's hairdressing, putting.

York
Town plan C2 North Yorkshire
North Street *YO1 1JF*
York (0904) 59822
Telex 57937

Rooms 187
with bath/shower 187
Room phone Yes
Room TV Yes
Confirm by By arrang.
Last dinner 10
Parking Ample
Banquets 350/4

Credit Access, Amex,
Barclaycard, Diners

Viking Hotel   70%   *E*   £ C/D

This large, modern, red-brick hotel occupies a pleasant site close to the historic city centre and right on the banks of the river Ouse. Overlooking the river is the pleasant Regatta Bar, whose walls are adorned with oars and boat club crests, and among the other smart public rooms is Plumes Coffee Shop, decorated in pink and home to a number of caged birds. Tastefully furnished bedrooms (newest ones are best) have plenty of writing space, direct-dial telephones, TVs and well-designed, fully tiled bathrooms. Up-to-the-minute conference and meeting facilities make this hotel a popular choice with businessmen.
Amenities coffee shop (10.30am–10.30pm).

WHERE TO GET LUCAS SERVICE.

ENGLAND

Ashford, Kent
Caffyns Ltd. — 0233 20334

Ashton-under-Lyne, Greater Manchester
Bowden Electrical & Diesel Services Ltd., — 061-339 6505

Avonmouth, Avon
Lucas Service UK Ltd. — 02752 4914/6987

Aylesbury, Buckinghamshire
Lucas Service UK Ltd. — 0296 83641

Banbury, Oxfordshire
Lucas Service Ltd. — 0295 50241

Barnsley, South Yorkshire
Lucas Service UK Ltd. — 0226 5151

Barnstaple, Devon
Diesel Electric (North Devon) — 0271 72181

Basingstoke, Hampshire
Lucas Service UK Ltd. — 0256 25655 & 3628

Bath, Avon
Lucas Service UK Ltd. — 0225 25341

Batley, West Yorkshire
Lucas Service UK Ltd. — 0924 472415

Bedford
Lucas Service UK Ltd.
18 Cauldwell Street — 0234 50331
Lucas Service UK Ltd.
7 Dallas Road — 0234 51581

Berkhamsted, Hertfordshire
T.W. Barford — 04427 4520

Berwick, Northumberland
Lucas Service UK Ltd. — 0289 6773

Birmingham, West Midlands
Lucas Service UK Ltd. — 021-327 1525
Car Lighting Services — 021-440 3663
Electric Services Co. (Birmingham) Ltd. — 021-622 2321
A.T. Gittins & Son Ltd.
15 Sutton Street — 021-692 1201
Ignition (Birmingham) Ltd. — 021-772 4911

Bishop's Stortford, Hertfordshire
Express Ignition — 0279 57827

Blackburn, Lancashire
Lucas Service UK Ltd. — 0254 60762 & 57551

Blackpool, Lancashire
Lucas Service UK Ltd. — 0253 61251

Boston, Lincolnshire
C.F. Parkinson Ltd. — 0205 63008

Bournemouth, Dorset
Lucas Service UK Ltd. — 02016 70507/79714
Express Ignition Co. Ltd. — 0202 36284

Bovey Tracey, Devon
Mid-Devon Auto Electrical Ltd. — Bovey Tracey 832595

Bradford, West Yorkshire
Lucas Service UK Ltd. — 0274 491495

Bridgnorth, Shropshire
Shropshire Diesel Service Ltd. — 07463 4245

Bridgwater, Somerset
H. N. Hickley & Co. Ltd. — 0278 3570

Brighton, East Sussex
Lucas Service UK Ltd. — 0273 772341

Bristol, Avon
Lucas Service UK Ltd.
345 Bath Road — 0272 773701
R. T. Crabbe Ltd. — 0272 555331/2/3
D. G. Whittle (Auto Electrical Fuel Injection
Services) — 0272 676959

Burnley, Lancashire
Injection Maintenance Ltd. — 0282 21957

Burton-on-Trent, Staffordshire
Dents (Burton-on-Trent) Ltd. — 0283 67578

Bury St. Edmunds, Suffolk
Specialist Electro Diesel Services Ltd. — 0284 2591

Cambridge
Lucas Service UK Ltd. — 0223 315931
Burchnells (Cambridge) Ltd. — 0223 59754

Canterbury, Kent
Lucas Service UK Ltd. — 0227 65241 & 66300

Carlisle, Cumbria
Lucas Service UK Ltd. — 0228 31138 & 25809

Chelmsford, Essex
Lucas Service UK Ltd. — 0245 466166

Chertsey, Surrey
Power Diesels & Electrical Ltd. — 09328 66031

Chester, Cheshire
Carlux Electrical Services Ltd. — 0244 378551
Miltons Battery Service (1974) Ltd. — 0244 371855

Chesterfield, Derbyshire
Automotive Electrical Engineers Ltd. — 0246 79181
Kirby & Son — 0246 70131

Chichester, West Sussex
Lucas Service UK Ltd. — 0243 781451/2

Christchurch, Dorset
Lucas Service UK Ltd. — 0202 484121

Cirencester, Gloucestershire
Severn Electrodiesel Ltd. — 0285 4725

Cleveleys, Lancashire
R. Bebbington Ltd. — 0253 853229

Colchester, Essex
Colchester Fuel Injection   0206 862049
Corby, Northamptonshire
C. A. Dieselectrics Ltd. 05 366 66983/67438
Coventry, West Midlands
Lucas Service UK Ltd.   0203 85735
R. J. Taberer Ltd.   0203 29382/23079
Crawley, West Sussex
Lucas Service UK Ltd.   0293 35372
Croydon, see Greater London

Dartford, Kent
Lucas Service UK Ltd.   0322 72538
Derby
Lucas Service UK Ltd.   0332 380454
Distington, Cumbria
Electrical & Diesel Services   0946 830247
Doncaster, South Yorkshire
Lucas Services UK Ltd. 0302 67952 & 62194

Dorchester, Dorset
Lucas Service UK Ltd.   0305 2987
Dover, Kent
Lucas Service UK Ltd. 0304 202653 & 208108
Dudley, West Midlands
F. H. Jennings   0384 55001
Durham,
Lucas Service UK Ltd.   0385 61223

Edgware, see Greater London
Ellesmere Port, Cheshire
Carlux Electrical Services Ltd.
                051-355 2101/3
Eltham, Kent
J. Kent Motor Factors Ltd.   01-850 2164/5/6
Eston
Carlec Batteries (Cleveland) Ltd.
                Eston Grange 60131/2/3
Exeter, Devon
Lucas Service UK Ltd.   0392 70235/6
EIC (Automotive) Ltd.   0392 54931

Falmouth, Cornwall
Lucas Service UK Ltd.
                0326 312754 & 312318
Folkestone, Kent
Ray Electricals (Folkestone) Ltd.
                0303 53194
Farnham, Surrey
Power Diesels & Electrical Ltd.
                0252 725918
Frome, Somerset
Lucas Service UK Ltd.   0373 64597 & 62866

Gerrards Cross, Buckinghamshire
Alpha Garages & Tool
                Gerrards Cross 82261
Gloucester
Lucas Service UK Ltd.   0452 26545 & 24951
Grantham, Lincolnshire
Burchnells Ltd.   0476 5191
Greenwich, see Greater London
Grimsby, Humberside
Lucas Service UK Ltd.   0472 59068
C. F. Parkinson (Lindsey) Ltd.   0472 58758

Guildford, Surrey
Bowden & Higlett Ltd.   0483 77411

Halifax, West Yorkshire
Elcar Ltd.   0422 65371
Hanley, Staffordshire
Lucas Service UK Ltd.   0782 22313
Harrow, see Greater London
Hartlepool, Cleveland
Lucas Service UK Ltd.   0429 74537
Hayes, see Greater London
Hereford
Lucas Service UK Ltd.   0432 267678
Autocar Electrical Services   0432 65771/2
High Wycombe, Buckinghamshire
Lucas Service UK Ltd.   0494 25793
Huddersfield, West Yorkshire
Elcar Ltd.   0484 21814/5
Hull, Humberside
Lucas Service UK Ltd.
    124 Anlaby Road   0482 29906
Kenning Specialised Services Ltd.
                0482 506911

Ipswich, Suffolk
Lucas Service UK Ltd.
    10 Bluestem Road   0473 710033
Lucas Service UK Ltd.
    Hadleigh Road Ind. Estate
                0473 52860/56189
Fuel Injection & Electrical (Ipswich) Ltd.
                0473 73161

ISLE OF MAN
Douglas
E. B. Christian & Co. Ltd.   0624 3211
ISLE OF WIGHT
Newport
Lucas Service UK Ltd.
                0983 524819 & 525297

Keighley, West Yorkshire
Highfield Auto Electrical Co. (Keighley) Ltd.
                0535 606231
Kendal, Cumbria
Andrew Brown   0539 24455
Kettering, Northamptonshire
Automatic Balance Complete Diesel Electric
    Services Ltd.   0536 85516
Kings Lynn, Norfolk
Lucas Service UK Ltd.   0553 3451
Kingston, see Greater London

Leatherhead, Surrey
W. T. Poole Engineering Ltd.
                03723 72122/72994
Leeds, West Yorkshire
Lucas Service UK Ltd.
    64 Roseville Road   0532 458591
Sewell of Leeds Ltd.   0532 435101
Leicester
A. B. Butt Ltd.   0533 23811
Wathes Electrodiesel Co. Ltd.   0533 64101

Lichfield, Staffordshire
The Battery Service Co. (Lichfield) Ltd.
54 23143/4
Lincoln
Lucas Service UK Ltd.   0522 24306
C. F. Parkinson (Lindsey) Ltd.   0522 30176
Liverpool, Merseyside
Lucas Service UK Ltd.
Vandries Street   051-236 7063 & 1886
Diesel & Battery Services (Liverpool) Ltd.
051-207 2362
Greater London
A.C.R. Ltd.   0784 55255
Atkinson (Kensington) Ltd.
82-84 New Kings Road   01-731 2333/4
Atkinson (Kensington) Ltd.
7 Pembridge Villas   01-727 0691/4
Auto Electrical Service (Harrow) Ltd.
01-952 4372
Autocar Marine & Diesel Ltd.   01-274 4041
Automobile Electric Service   01-790 8371
First Diesel Injection Ltd.   01-689 1806
Harrow Automobile Ignition Service Ltd.
55-57 Lowlands Road   01-422 1243
Harrow Automobile Ignition Services Ltd.
81A Wembley Hill Road   01-902 2281
J. Higgs (Electrical) Ltd.   01-534 3592
Injection Pump Repairs   01-960 0266
J. Kent Motor Factors Ltd.
01-850 2164/5/6
Lucas Service UK Ltd.
Park Royal NW10   01-961 1188
Lucas Service UK Ltd.
Croydon CR2   01-686 6151
Lucas Service UK Ltd.
Charlton SE7   01-858 6226
Lucas Service UK Ltd.
Kingston KT2   01-546 1244
Lucas Service UK Ltd.
New Southgate N11   01-361 1267
Lucas Service UK Ltd.
Woodford Green IG8   01-550 6711
Magenerator Ltd.   01-247 1098/9
Ranburn Ltd.
243 Tunnel Avenue   01-858 2293/3197
University Electrics Ltd.   01-573 8311
F. N. Wild   01-539 3151
Lowestoft, Suffolk
Lucas Service UK Ltd.   0502 66331
Luton, Bedfordshire
Lucas Service UK Ltd.   0582 507001/2/3

Maidstone, Kent
Lucas Service UK Ltd.   0622 55201
South Eastern Auto Electrical Services Ltd.
0622 55181
Malvern, Worcestershire
Malvern Diesel Services Ltd.
06845 4358-4126

Manchester
Lucas Service UK Ltd.   061-872 5271
Kingsway Auto Electrical Services Ltd.
061-432 0024
N.A.E.S. Ltd.   061-792 2213
G. E. Middleton & Co.   061-872 0923
Mansfield, Nottingham
F. Simpson Engineering (Jersey) Ltd.
0623 25682

Medway, Kent
Lucas Service UK Ltd.   0634 51161

Middlesbrough, Cleveland
T.H. Flory   0642 244451
Milton Keynes
Dieseltune Services   0908 640705 & 70727
Morecambe, Lancashire
Lucas Service UK Ltd.
0524 67455, 2799

Newark, Nottinghamshire
C. F. Parkinson (Notts) Ltd.   0636 72631
Newbury, Berkshire
Newbury Fuel Inj Services Ltd.
Newbury 200236
Newcastle-upon-Tyne, Tyne and Wear
Lucas Service UK Ltd.
Saltsmeadows Road   0632 773851
British Engines Ltd.   0632 659091
Tyneside Auto Electrical   0632 654426
Northallerton, North Yorkshire
Lucas Service UK Ltd.   0609 71609
Northampton
Northampton Diesel & Electrical Services Ltd.
0604 55321
Northwich, Cheshire
Irons & Dean   0606 3353/4
Norwich, Norfolk
Lucas Service UK Ltd. 0603 44979 & 410301
Kenning Specialised Services Ltd.
0603 29845
Panks Auto Electrical   0603 29967
Nottingham
Lucas Service UK Ltd.
Castle Boulevard   0602 46623
Frank Caldwell Ltd.   0602 782235
C. F. Parkinson (Notts) Ltd.
Derby Road NG7   0602 701176
C. F. Parkinson (Notts) Ltd.
Manvers Street NG2   0602 54468

Oswestry, Shropshire
Autoelectrix (Oswestry) Ltd.   0691 4771
Oxford
Borehams Car Electrical Service Ltd.
0865 44582/3
A. E. Malins   0865 40301

Pensnett, West Midlands
Kingswinford Fuel Injection Services Ltd.
0384 287608
Peterborough, Cambridgeshire
Auto Electrical Services (Peterborough) Ltd.
0733 62645
Burchnells (Peterborough) Ltd.   0733 43455
C. F. Parkinson (Peterborough) Ltd.
0733 311222
Plymouth, Devon
Lucas Service UK Ltd.
85 Cattedown Road   0752 660223
Brown & Williams Ltd.   0752 21811
Pontefract, West Yorkshire
Lucas Service UK Ltd.   0977 73537
Poole, Dorset
Hunts (Auto & Marine) Ltd.   0202 670505
Portsmouth, Hampshire
Lucas Service UK Ltd.   0705 661504
Preston, Lancashire
Lucas Service UK Ltd.   0772 58326
Smith & Davis (Auto & Elec) Ltd. 0772 57938

Reading, Berkshire
Lucas Service UK Ltd.   0734 861202/3/4

Redditch, Worcestershire
Auto Ignition Services (Redditch) Ltd.
    Redditch 64610/21

Retford, Nottinghamshire
Clarke's Auto Electrical   0777 703823

Ripon, North Yorkshire
Ripon Auto Electrics   0765 2253

Rochester, Kent
Squires & Knight Ltd.   0634 41651

St. Albans, Hertfordshire
Russell's Auto-Electric Co.   St. Albans 50517

St. Austell, Cornwall
Lucas Service UK Ltd.   0726 3249 & 3066
M.C.E.S. Electrodiesel Ltd.   0726 3271/2/3

St. Helens, Merseyside
Southport Electrical Services Ltd.
    0744 23228

St. Leonards-on-Sea, East Sussex
Lucas Service UK Ltd.   0424 430907/8

Salisbury, Wiltshire
Taplins Auto Electric Ltd.   0722 20233

Scarborough, North Yorkshire
Scarborough Ignition Co.   0723 65321

Scunthorpe, Humberside
Auto Electric Services Scunthorpe
    0724 68441 & 65831

Sheffield, South Yorkshire
Lucas Service UK Ltd.   0742 752522
Automotive Diesel Electric Service Ltd.
    0742 755177

Shrewsbury, Shropshire
Lucas Service UK Ltd.   0743 55061/2

Skipton, North Yorkshire
Highfield Auto Electrical Co. (Keighley) Ltd.
    0756 2247

Slough, Berkshire
Car Elec Repairs (Slough) Ltd.
    Slough 23401 & 24359

Southampton, Hampshire
Lucas Service UK Ltd.   0703 23276
Taplins Auto Electric Ltd.   0703 331331
P. B. Asher   0703 22139/27324

Southgate
Lucas Service UK Ltd.   01-361 1267/8/9

Stafford
Lucas Service UK Ltd.   0785 51476 & 52939

Staines, see Greater London

Stockton, Cleveland
Lucas Service UK Ltd.   0642 605050

Stoke Newington, see Greater London

Stoke-on-Trent, Staffordshire
Potteries Diesel Services   0782 45556

Sunderland, Tyne and Wear
Chloride Gaedor Ltd.   0783 58128

Swindon, Wiltshire
Gardiners Auto Electrical Service Ltd.
    0793 29254

Taunton, Somerset
H. N. Hickley & Co. Ltd.   0823 76041

Telford, Shropshire
The Battery Service Co. (Lichfield) Ltd.
    Telford 613707

Thornaby-on-Tees, Cleveland
Auto Electrics (Teesside) Ltd.   0642 607901

Tipton, West Midlands
Lucas Service UK Ltd.   021-557 9601/2

Torquay, Devon
Auto Maintenance Ltd.   0803 23268/9

Truro, Cornwall
Lucas Service UK Ltd.   0872 3054 & 2645

Tunbridge Wells, Kent
Lucas Service UK Ltd.   0892 23426 & 22094

Wakefield, West Yorkshire
J. E. Fowler Auto Electric Ltd. 0924 73948
F. Nettleton Ltd.   0924 376233/5

Walsall, West Midlands
Electro-Diesel Company   0922 33111

Warrington, Cheshire
Irons & Dean   0925 55251

Warwick
Lucas Service UK Ltd.   0926 45211

Watford, Hertfordshire
Russell's Auto-Electric Co.   Watford 28383

Wellingborough, Northamptonshire
Keith Legge Auto Electrical   0933 224296

Wembley, see Greater London

West Bromwich, West Midlands
Electromobile Engineering Co.
    (West Bromwich) Ltd.   021-558 3101/4

Westcliff-on-Sea, Essex
Kenning Specialised Services Ltd.
    0702 353096

Widnes, Cheshire
Irons & Dean   051-424 5416/7/8

Wigan
Irons & Dean   0942 495643

Winchester, Hampshire
Tapins Auto Electric Ltd.   0962 65071

Woodford Green, see Greater London

Worcester
Automobile Electrical Services
    (Worcester) Ltd.   0905 29391

Yeovil, Somerset
Lucas Service UK Ltd.   0935 23536

York, North Yorkshire
York Autoelectrics Ltd.   0904 54513

CHANNEL ISLANDS

Guernsey
Guernsey Auto & Electrical Supply
    Co. Ltd.   0481 26644

Jersey
Express Electrix Limited
    (Jersey)   0534 22524/5
A. E. A. Tostevin & Co.   0534 23035

SCOTLAND

Aberdeen
Lucas Service UK Ltd.   0224 895050
Ayr
Lucas Service UK Ltd.   0292 267132

Dumfries
Lucas Service UK Ltd.   Dumfries 4418
Dunoon, Argyllshire
Wilson Garage   Dunoon 3094
Dundee, Angus
Lucas Service UK Ltd.   0382 814929
Brayshay & Paterson Ltd.   0382 22393

Edinburgh, Midlothian
Lucas Service UK Ltd.   031-337 2311
Lothian Diesel Electrics Ltd.   031-346 0101
Elgin, Morayshire
Pentland Auto Elec Repairs Ltd.   Elgin 7462

Falkirk, Stirlingshire
Lucas Service UK Ltd.   0324 21189
Turners Auto Services Ltd.   0324 21222

Glasgow
Lucas Service UK Ltd.
4/24 Grant Street   041-332 6591
Argyll Diesel Electrical Ltd.   041-554 2504
T.W. Auto Electrics Ltd.   041-423 8891
Turner Diesels Ltd.   041-440 0666

Hawick, Roxburghshire
Lucas Service UK Ltd.   0450 6113

Inverness
Lucas Service UK Ltd.   0463 224855
Auto & General Electric Services
   (Inverness) Ltd.   0463 32211/3

Kilmarnock, Ayrshire
Lucas Service UK Ltd.   0563 22255
Templeton Brothers (Kilmarnock) Ltd.
                                          0563 24362
Kirkcaldy, Fifeshire
Lucas Service UK Ltd.   0592 263445
Kirkwall, Orkney & Shetland
Pentland Auto Electrical Repairs Ltd.
                                          Kirkwall 3094

Motherwell, Lanarkshire
Taggart & Wilson Ltd.   0698 64542

Paisley, Renfrewshire
Lucas Service UK Ltd.
                       041-889 6264 & 887 4197
Perth
Lucas Service UK Ltd.   0738 24183
J. Calderwood   0738 22416

Stranraer, Wigtownshire
Auto Services (Stranraer) Ltd.   0776 2677

Turriff, Aberdeenshire
Lucas Service UK Ltd.   Turriff 2251

Wick, Caithness-shire
Pentland Auto Electrical Repairs   0955 2181

WALES

Aberystwyth, Dyfed
Lucas Service UK Ltd.   09 7061 7013

Bridgend
A. L. Killick (Electrodiesel) Ltd.   0656 56612

Caernarvon, Gwynedd
Lucas Service UK Ltd.   0286 2888/2759
Cardiff, South Glamorgan
Lucas Service UK Ltd.   0222 28361
Fuel Injection Service (Wales) Ltd.
                                  0222 33717/25909
H. Regan & Co. Ltd.   0222 498503
Carmarthen, Dyfed
Lucas Service UK Ltd.   0267 5902/7504
Colwyn Bay, Clwyd
Lucas Service UK Ltd.   0492 49778/47373

Newport, Gwent
Lucas Service UK Ltd.   0633 56371/59479
Newtown, Powys
Grooms Industries   0686 26731

Swansea, West Glamorgan
Lucas Service UK Ltd.   0792 797824
Shorts Auto Electrical Services
                                          0792 469595

Wrexham, Clwyd
Lucas Service UK Ltd.   0978 263123

NORTHERN IRELAND

Ballymena, Antrim
Lucas Service UK Ltd.   0266 44708
Edgar Lowe Ltd.   0266 45231

Belfast, Antrim
Lucas Service UK Ltd.
   69/73 Glenmachan Street   0232 244731
Edgar Lowe Ltd.   0232 20005 & 28525
John Robertson (Belfast) Ltd.   0232 32066
Shields & McMurray   0232 58643

Dungannon, Tyrone
W. R. Hamilton Ltd.   086872 3941/2

Enniskillin, Fermanagh
T. P. Topping Ltd.   0365 3475

Lurgan, Armagh
Edgar Lowe (Ballymena) Ltd.   0762 82 3497

Newry, Down
Autoelectrics Ltd.   0693 2335/6

Omagh, Tyrone
T.E.S. Ltd.   0662 2686 & 44221 & 3680

Portadown, Armagh
W. R. Hamilton Ltd.   0762 35478 & 35398

REPUBLIC OF IRELAND

Arklow, Wicklow
Noble & Stevens Ltd.   0402 2638

Ballina, Co. Mayo
P.M.P.A. Diesel & Electrical Company Ltd.
                                       096 21155

Cork
Lucas Service Ireland Ltd.
                             021-20292/3/4/5/6

Dublin
Lucas Service Ireland Ltd.   01 746195
Diesel Services Ltd.   01 747718
Powderly's Car Electrical Services Ltd.
                                       01 749791
Robert Kemp Ltd.   01 778157

Galway
Lucas Service Ireland Ltd.   091 64729

Kilkenny
XL Battery & Electrical Services Ltd.
                                       056 21247

Limerick
Auto Diesel Services Ltd.   061 29222
Longford
W. & C. Pearse   043 6430 & 6116

Monaghan
Dieselec   047 81192

Portlaoighise, Leix
J. L. Bradshaw Ltd.   0502 21311 & 21206
Sligo
Car Electric Auto Electrical Service
                                       071 3852

Tralee, Kerry
Electrical & Diesel Engineers Ltd.   066 21530
Tullamore, Offaly
Tullamore Electrical Diesel Ltd.
                                       0506 41234
Waterford
A.B.E. Services Ltd.   051 73551

SCOTLAND

Aberdeen
Map 17 D4 Grampian
South Deeside Road *ABY 2YP*
Aberdeen (0224) 867355
Proprietor
Mr McKenzie-Smith
Credit Access, Amex,
Barclaycard, Diners

Ardoe House Hotel   67%   Ⓜ   £ D

Well-kept grounds, fine panoramic views and beautifully crafted woodwork contribute to the charm of this 19th-century stone mansion. Public rooms include an impressive foyer and a plush cocktail bar. A splendid staircase leads to the bedrooms which range from large, traditional ones to more modern rooms in the extension; compact singles have shower cubicles. *Amenities* garden, game fishing.

Rooms 21	*Room phone* Yes	*Confirm by* 6	*Parking* Ample
with bath/shower 13	*Room TV* Yes	*Last dinner* 9.30	*Banquets* 120/50

Aberdeen
Map 17 D4 Grampian
145 Crown Street *AB1 2HR*
Aberdeen (0224) 51403

Seafood
About £38 for two

Atlantis   Ⓢ

Seafood's the thing at this busy little basement restaurant, where the choice ranges from king prawns and Loch Sween oysters to salmon, sole and lobster in various guises. Booking is essential. *Credit* Access, Amex, Barclaycard, Diners *Lunch* 12–2 *Dinner* 7–10
Closed Sun & 1 week Christmas–New Year ● **Set L** £4

Aberdeen
Map 17 D4 Grampian
347 Union Street *AB1 2PT*
Aberdeen (0224) 20318
Proprietor David Fong
Chinese cooking

● **Set L** £3·50
About £26 for two

Dickens   ♕ Ⓢ

The name may be English, but the cooking is essentially Chinese in this very pleasant, tastefully furnished restaurant. Dishes like Peking diced pork with spiced chutney sauce or soo chow duck with pork and shrimps are delicious with perfectly cooked rice. There are also steaks and Western dishes like pâté and beef Stroganoff. Friendly young staff create a convivial atmosphere. *Credit* Access, Amex, Barclaycard, Diners

Meals 11.45am–11pm
Closed 1 & 2 January

Aberdeen
Map 17 D4 Grampian
Old Meldrum Road
Bucksburn *AB2 9LN*
Aberdeen (0224) 713911
Telex 73108
Rooms 99
with bath/shower 99
Room phone Yes
Room TV Yes
Confirm by 6
Last dinner 10.30
Parking Ample
Banquets 180/–

Credit Access, Amex,
Barclaycard, Diners

Holiday Inn   75%   *E*   £ C/D

Conveniently situated on the A96 between the city and the airport, this hotel is immediately recognisable by its startling futuristic facade. Public areas are all grouped around the indoor swimming pool, and they include a streamlined open-plan reception-lounge and two distinctive bars (one decorated with models of sailing clippers, the other more baronial in style). There are also extensive, fully equipped conference and function facilities. Bedrooms have well-designed fitted furniture, attractively patterned curtains and matching bedspreads, plus mini-bars and trouser presses. Bathrooms are smart. *Amenities* indoor swimming pool, in-house movies, hairdressing, transport for airport.   ♿

Aberdeen
Map 17 D4 Grampian
122 Huntly Street *AB1 1SU*
Aberdeen (0224) 630404
Telex 739707

Credit Access, Amex,
Barclaycard, Diners

Huntly Hotel   76%   £ B

Converted from a large old warehouse in the centre of the city, this luxurious three-storey hotel offers high standards of decor and service. Comfortable settees and chairs fill the plush reception-lounge area, and there's a fashionable cocktail bar with deep leather chairs, Victorian prints and potted plants as well as a disco platform. Bedrooms, all with double beds, are tastefully designed with matching colour schemes, upholstered easy chairs and smart built-in units. Brown and cream bathrooms are fully tiled and well equipped, with lovely big towels, shower caps and shampoo. The hotel is very efficiently staffed.
Amenities dinner dance (Sat).

Rooms 67	*Room phone* Yes	*Confirm by* 6	*Parking* Ample
with bath/shower 67	*Room TV* Yes	*Last dinner* 10.30	*Banquets* 200/2

Aberdeen

Map 17 D4 Grampian
349 Great Western Road *AB1 6NW*
Aberdeen (0224) 28901
Proprietors
Mrs P. Gray & Mr W. Gray
Credit Access, Amex,
Barclaycard, Diners

Malacca Hotel   60%   Ⓜ   £E

Skilfully converted from a bay-windowed stone town house, this comfortable small hotel has a bustling, popular streamlined bar with striking black
and green decor, gleaming brass rails and banquette seating (there is no
lounge). Modern, uncluttered bedrooms have duvets, melamine units with
useful shelf space, and compact bathrooms.

Rooms 10	*Room phone* Yes	*Confirm by* By arrang.	*Parking* Ample
with bath/shower 9	*Room TV* Yes	*Last dinner* 11	*Banquets* 30/–

Our inspectors are our full-time
employees; they are professionally trained by us.

Aberdeen

Map 17 D4 Grampian
78 Guild Street *AB9 2DN*
Aberdeen (0224) 27214
Telex 73161
Manager Mr T. L. Conboy
Credit Access, Amex,
Barclaycard, Diners

Station Hotel   65%   £C

Improvements continue at this impressive railway hotel, where standards of
service and housekeeping are commendably high. Plants and flowers adorn
the comfortable, spacious public areas, which have attractive pink seating
and art deco carpets. Spacious bedrooms have pretty wallpaper, good
solid furnishings, tea-makers and bedside controls. Well-equipped
bathrooms.   &

Rooms 60	*Room phone* Yes	*Confirm by* 6	*Parking* Limited
with bath/shower 50	*Room TV* Yes	*Last dinner* 9.30	*Banquets* 250/2

Aberdeen

Map 17 D4 Grampian
161 Springfield Road *AB9 2QH*
Aberdeen (0224) 33377
Telex 73794

Credit Access, Amex,
Barclaycard, Diners

Tree Tops Hotel   59%   £D

A beech-lined driveway leads to this 1960s hotel with a pleasantly
traditional appearance on the outskirts of town. Inside, there's a spacious
reception/lounge filled with chesterfield-style seating as well as a choice of
three bars to relax in. Cheerful, compact bedrooms are fitted with practical
modern furniture; most also have adequately equipped private bathrooms.
Amenities garden.

Rooms 108	*Room phone* Yes	*Confirm by* 6	*Parking* Ample
with bath/shower 83	*Room TV* Yes	*Last dinner* 10	*Banquets* 280/–

Aberdeen Airport

Map 17 D4 Grampian
Argyll Road, Dyce *AB2 0AF*
Aberdeen (0224) 725252
Telex 739239

Credit Access, Amex,
Barclaycard, Diners

Aberdeen Airport Hotel   68%   £D

This sleek, well-maintained hotel stands right alongside the airport. A
spacious reception hall doubles as a lounge, and there's a large modern bar.
Smart bedrooms range from studio-style with two single beds to de luxe
with two doubles; there are also two luxury suites. *Amenities* garden,
outdoor swimming pool, transport for airport, coffee shop (6am–11pm, Sun
8am–11pm), 24-hour laundry service.   &

Rooms 148	*Room phone* Yes	*Confirm by* 6	*Parking* Ample
with bath/shower 148	*Room TV* Yes	*Last dinner* 9.45	*Banquets* 300/–

We welcome complaints and bona fide recommendations on
the tear-out pages for readers' comments. They are followed up
by our professional team. Please also complain to the
management instantly.

In this guide you'll find the best restaurants in the UK, not far from them you'll find us.

The reason we're never far from the best restaurants is because we have more offices than anyone else. We also have more offices at UK airports and we're the only car hire company with offices on Inter-City stations.

Godfrey Davis Europcar is part of the Europcar International Car Rental network with over 2,500 offices, including over 500 airports in 101 countries and territories worldwide. For reservations anywhere in the UK or worldwide call 01-950 4080, or your local Godfrey Davis Europcar office.

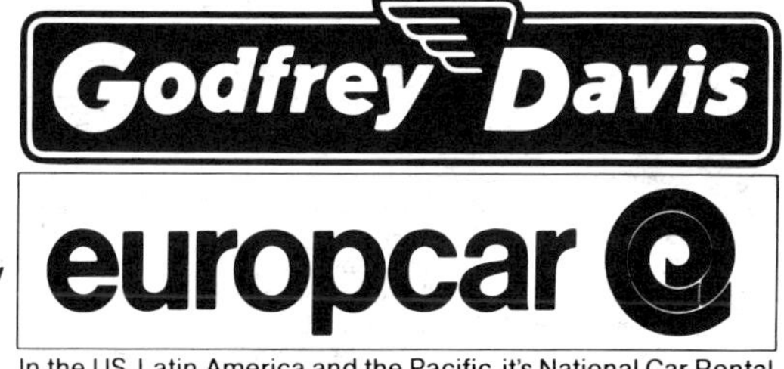

In the US, Latin America and the Pacific, it's National Car Rental.

Aberdeen Airport

Map 17 D4 Grampian
Riverview Drive, Farburn
Dyce *AB2 0AZ*
Aberdeen (0224) 770011
Telex 739651
Rooms 154
with bath/shower 154
Room phone Yes
Room TV Yes
Confirm by 6
Last dinner 11
Parking Ample
Banquets 300/–

Credit Access, Amex,
Barclaycard, Diners

Holiday Inn   77%   *E*   £C

Standing near the airport on the A947, this efficiently run, ultra-modern hotel caters well for the needs of the businessman. Luxurious and comfortable public rooms include a lounge with a blue tartan carpet and matching sofas, an inviting poolside bar and a number of comprehensively equipped banqueting and conference rooms. Spacious, double-glazed bedrooms have shag-pile carpets, colourful curtains and bedspreads, sensibly designed furniture units and good writing surfaces. Well-fitted bathrooms, with radio speakers and plenty of towels, have attractive mosaic-tiled floors and walls. *Amenities* sauna, indoor swimming pool, discothèque (Mon–Sat), in-house movies, gymnasium, coffee shop (7am–11pm).

Aberdeen Airport

Map 17 D4 Grampian
Farburn Terrace, Dyce *AB2 0DU*
Aberdeen (0224) 723101
Telex 73473
Manager Mr S. Gudd
Credit Access, Amex,
Barclaycard, Diners

Skean Dhu Hotel   66%   £D

A low, modern hotel built in a series of blocks, the main one housing a spacious reception/lounge area, a pleasant coffee shop and a cocktail bar in plush red velvet; there are also extensive function facilities. Smartly furnished, well-carpeted bedrooms are either studio-style or de luxe with two double beds. All rooms have parking outside. *Amenities* sauna, squash, coffee shop (6am–11pm, Sat & Sun 8am–11pm), solarium.

| *Rooms* 222 | *Room phone* Yes | *Confirm by* 6 | *Parking* Ample |
| *with bath/shower* 222 | *Room TV* Yes | *Last dinner* 10 | *Banquets* 350/– |

Achiltibuie

Map 16 B2 Highland
By Ullapool *IV26 2YG*
Achiltibuie (085 482) 282

Proprietors Mr & Mrs R. Irvine
Closed 2nd week October–
1 April

Summer Isles Hotel   60%   Ⓜ   £D

Guests return year after year to enjoy the scenic surroundings, the fishing and the wonderful walks at the Irvines' delightfully relaxing hotel. The lounge and bars are homely and inviting, and accommodation varies from the bright, simple rooms in the main building to the attractive pine-log chalet rooms, with their smart, modern bathrooms. No children under eight.
Amenities garden, game & sea fishing.

| *Rooms* 17 | *Room phone* No | *Confirm by* By arrang. | *Parking* Ample |
| *with bath/shower* 9 | *Room TV* No | *Last dinner* 7 | *Banquets* 25/4 |

Achiltibuie

Map 16 B2 Highland
by Ullapool *IV26 2YG*
Achiltibuie (085 482) 282
Proprietors Mr & Mrs R. Irvine

Summer Isles Hotel Restaurant    Ⓢ

Dinner starts bang on 7.30 in this simply appointed room, whose picture windows afford dramatic views across to the islands. There's no choice, but you can be sure that Mrs Irvine will use only the freshest ingredients, many of them home-produced, in her excellent four-course meals. Highlights of our visit were a velvet-smooth Stilton soup and a daintily delicious chocolate roulade. Book.

● **Set D** £13·50
About £33 for two

Dinner only 7 for 7.30
Closed 2nd week October–1 April

Airth

Map 17 C5 Central
By Falkirk *FK2 8JF*
Airth (032 483) 411
Telex 777975
Manager Mr R. Mitchell
Credit Access, Amex,
Barclaycard, Diners

Airth Castle Hotel   68%   £D/E

Standing on a hill south of Airth, this impressive greystone castle (part 15th century) has a spacious entrance hall and a lofty, Regency-style residents' lounge overlooking the extensive grounds. There's a cosy cocktail bar, and the modernised bedrooms have attractive reproduction furniture, co-ordinated fabrics and carpeted bathrooms with coloured fittings. No dogs.
Amenities garden, tennis, dancing (Sat), putting, badminton.

                                            Continued

Rooms 23	*Room phone* Yes	*Confirm by* By arrang.	*Parking* Ample
with bath/shower 23	*Room TV* Yes	*Last dinner* 9.45	*Banquets* 60/–

Alyth
Map 17 C4 Tayside
PH11 8JQ
Alyth (082 83) 2481
Proprietors
Mr & Mrs G. Billinghurst
Credit Amex, Barclaycard,
Diners

Lands of Loyal Hotel   63%   Ⓜ   £ D/E

Entering the hall, with its panelled walls, vast hearth and magnificent carved staircase, guests are reminded of the Victorian origins of this friendly, well-run hotel. Other public rooms like the comfortable lounge and bar retain much of their character, too, and the spacious bedrooms, all with lovely parkland views, boast some fine antiques, including a four-poster. Excellent housekeeping. *Amenities* garden, putting.

Rooms 14	*Room phone* No	*Confirm by* By arrang.	*Parking* Ample
with bath/shower 7	*Room TV* No	*Last dinner* 8.30	*Banquets* 30/2

Alyth
Map 17 C4 Tayside
PH11 8JQ
Alyth (082 83) 2481
Proprietors
Mr & Mrs G. Billinghurst

Lands of Loyal Hotel Restaurant   🍴 Ⓢ

Straightforward, unpretentious cooking is the hallmark of this hotel dining room with a lovely Victorian ceiling. Short daily menus feature dishes like leek and potato soup, poached salmon and roast shoulder of pork, plus grills, omelettes and salads. Vegetables might include delicious white cabbage with ham and raisins, while enjoyable sweets range from lemon sorbet to rhubarb pie. *Credit* Amex, Barclaycard, Diners

● **Set D** £10·50
About £27 for two

Lunch 12.45–2 *Dinner* 7–8.30

Anstruther
Map 17 D5 Fife
Bankwell Road *KY10 3DA*
Anstruther (0333) 310691
Proprietors Clarke family

Credit Access, Amex,
Barclaycard, Diners

Craw's Nest Hotel   60%   Ⓜ   £ E

Over the years, this old Scottish manse has been transformed into a pleasant, up-to-date hotel. It has a tiny cocktail bar and a smart panelled lounge bar, as well as a comfortable residents' lounge. Neat bedrooms (including some in the extension) are uniform in style with contemporary fitted furniture, tea-makers and radios, plus modern carpeted bathrooms. No dogs. *Amenities* garden, sauna, dancing (Sat), games room.

Rooms 31	*Room phone* Yes	*Confirm by* By arrang.	*Parking* Ample
with bath/shower 31	*Room TV* Yes	*Last dinner* 9	*Banquets* 300/–

Ardentinny
Map 17 B5 Strathclyde
PA23 8TR
Ardentinny (036 981) 209
Telex 8951994
Proprietors John & Sylvia Harris
Credit Amex
Closed Mon–Wed Nov–Mar

Ardentinny Hotel   60%   Ⓜ   £ E/F

Marvellously situated with large expanses of forest on one side and a loch on the other, this pleasant little hotel is a peaceful retreat and an ideal base for exploring the surrounding countryside. Old and new blend well in the two cosy bars, while bedrooms range from simple and old-fashioned to compact and up to date in the extension. Bathrooms are adequate. *Amenities* garden, sea fishing.

Rooms 10	*Room phone* No	*Confirm by* 6	*Parking* Ample
with bath/shower 6	*Room TV* No	*Last dinner* 8.30	*Banquets* 40/10

Ardnadam
Map 17 B5 Strathclyde
Sandbank
By Dunoon *PA23 8QG*
Sandbank (036 985) 210

Credit Barclaycard

Firpark Hotel   69%   Ⓜ   £ D/E

Known under its former owners as Ardnadam House, this handsome Victorian building by Holy Loch offers an appealing mixture of styles. The residents' lounge is all traditional elegance, with its fine wood panelling and charming minstrels' gallery, while the turquoise cocktail bar is strikingly modern. Simply decorated and individually furnished, the spacious bedrooms have TVs, radios, tea-makers and duvets. *Amenities* garden.

Rooms 6	*Room phone* No	*Confirm by* 5	*Parking* Ample
with bath/shower 2	*Room TV* Yes	*Last dinner* 9	*Banquets* 40/2

Arduaine
Map 17 B5 Strathclyde
Near Oban *PA34 4XG*
Kilmelford (085 22) 233
Proprietors
Mr & Mrs Colin Tindal
Credit Access, Amex
Closed late October–Easter

Rooms 26
with bath/shower 23

Loch Melfort Hotel   60%   Ⓜ   £ D/E

There are captivating views from this peaceful hotel beside Loch Melfort. Comfortable public rooms include a cocktail bar and the attractive Chart Bar with its Scandinavian pine decor; there are also two small lounges (one with TV). Bedrooms in the main house are pleasantly traditional; those in the wing are more modern, with doors opening on to patios or balconies. Well-equipped bathrooms. *Amenities* garden, mooring. &

| *Room phone* No | *Confirm by* 6 | *Parking* Ample |
| *Room TV* No | *Last dinner* 8.30 | |

Arduaine
Map 17 B5 Strathclyde
Near Oban *PA34 4XG*
Kilmelford (085 22) 233
Proprietors Mr & Mrs Colin Tindal

● **Set D** £10
About £26 for two

Loch Melfort Hotel Restaurant   Ⓢ

This friendly candlelit restaurant has an enchanting atmosphere, and the three-course set dinner is most enjoyable. Dishes like tasty crab quiche and mousseline of sole garnished with tiny prawns show a bias towards seafood. Pride of place, however, must go to the wonderful selection of sweets such as orange cake, featherlight gooseberry snow and gorgeous raspberry Pavlova. *Credit* Access, Amex &

Dinner only 7.15–8.30
Closed late October–Easter

We do not necessarily recommend the cooking at hotels whose restaurants are not separately listed.

Ardvasar
Map 17 A4 Highland
Isle of Skye *IV45 8RS*
Ardvasar (047 14) 223

Closed end October–beginning April

Rooms 12
with bath/shower 4

Ardvasar Hotel   57%   £ F

Excellent housekeeping is a feature of this cheerful little whitewashed hotel, which stands right by the harbour wall. Neat and tidy public rooms include a simple, homely lounge, a popular games room and two bars, one of them hung with clan prints. Nicely carpeted bedrooms are furnished with practical freestanding pieces; bathrooms have good modern fittings.
Amenities game fishing, games room, stalking.

| *Room phone* No | *Confirm by* By arrang. | *Parking* Ample |
| *Room TV* No | *Last dinner* 8 | *Banquets* 45/2 |

Auchterarder
Map 17 C5 Tayside
PH3 1NF
Auchterarder (076 46) 2231
Telex 76105

Rooms 207
with bath/shower 207
Room phone Yes
Room TV Yes
Confirm by 6
Last dinner 10
Parking Ample
Banquets 400/2

Credit Access, Amex,
Barclaycard, Diners

Gleneagles Hotel   88%   £ C

Renowned for its four championship golf courses and its atmosphere of grandeur and elegance, Gleneagles also offers an array of amenities. An impressive marble-pillared foyer sets the tone, and the opulent theme continues in the vast lounge with its elegant furniture. Bedrooms (undergoing refurbishment) are spacious, comfortable and luxuriously furnished. It is to be hoped that new owners will continue to provide the standards of service and maintenance for which the hotel is famous. *Amenities* garden, sauna, indoor swimming pool, tennis, squash, golf courses, coarse & game fishing, dancing (nightly), post office, bank, shops, bowling green, croquet, putting, pitch & putt, helipad, cinema, petrol pumps, hairdressing. &

Auchterarder

Map 17 C5 Tayside
PH3 1NF
Auchterarder (076 46) 2231

About £46 for two

Gleneagles Hotel, Eagles Nest ♛ ⑤

There's a warm, inviting atmosphere in this elegant new restaurant, where waiters in long white aprons provide discreet, efficient service. The extensive menu of French-inspired dishes has some delicious and subtle combinations like scallops with creamy saffron sauce and veal cutlet with mirabelle plums and wine sauce. Vegetables are perfectly prepared. 🍷*SUPERIOR.*
Credit Access, Amex, Barclaycard, Diners   ♿

Dinner only 7.30–10

Auchterhouse

Map 17 C5 Tayside
By Dundee *DD3 0QN*
Auchterhouse (082 626) 366

Credit Access, Amex, Diners
Closed 1–8 January

Old Mansion House Hotel   69%   Ⓜ   **£E**

This delightful hotel–a converted manor house–stands in ten acres of lovely grounds. The flagstoned entrance hall has a fine vaulted ceiling, and upstairs is a relaxing bar-lounge lined with books. Large, bright bedrooms are attractively decorated in traditional style, and modern bathrooms have coloured suites. *Amenities* garden, sauna, outdoor swimming pool, tennis, squash, croquet.

Rooms 6	*Room phone* Yes	*Confirm by* By arrang.	*Parking* Ample
with bath/shower 6	*Room TV* Yes	*Last dinner* 9.30	*Banquets* 20/10

Auchterhouse

Map 17 C5 Tayside
By Dundee *DD3 0QN*
Auchterhouse (082 626) 366

● Set L £5·95
About £34 for two

Old Mansion House Hotel Restaurant ♛ ♛

Tall windows overlook the garden in this elegant dining room with a huge Jacobean fireplace. There are Scottish dishes on the menu as well as tempting specialities like lobster Côte d'Azur and chicken suprême tastily sauced with cèpes. Everything is most enjoyably prepared and there's an imaginative choice of vegetables.
Credit Access, Amex, Diners

Lunch 12.30–2 *Dinner* 7.30–9.30, Sun 7.30–8.30
Closed 1–8 January

Aviemore

Map 17 C4 Highland
Aviemore Centre *PH22 1PH*
Aviemore (0479) 810261

Manager Mr I. Price
Credit Access, Amex, Barclaycard, Diners

Badenoch Hotel   58%   **£E**

This popular, well-run hotel offers a choice of accommodation: most bedrooms have modern built-in units, colour TV and compact, functional bathrooms, and there are also 20 bunk-bed rooms without these facilities. The basement Viking Bar is a boisterous centre for entertainment, while another bar and two lounges provide quieter, more relaxing surroundings. *Amenities* discothèque (Mon, Wed, Fri), folk music (Thurs). ♿

Rooms 81	*Room phone* Most	*Confirm by* 7	*Parking* Ample
with bath/shower 61	*Room TV* Most	*Last dinner* 9.30	*Banquets* 150/4

Aviemore

Map 17 C4 Highland
PH22 1QU
Aviemore (0479) 810661
Telex 75272

Credit Access, Amex, Barclaycard, Diners

Coylumbridge Hotel   60%   **£D/E**

A holiday-maker's paradise, this modern hotel complex offers an impressive range of recreational facilities. Public areas are stylishly open-plan and well-fitted contemporary bedrooms have excellent bathrooms. *Amenities* garden, sauna, indoor swimming pool, dinner dance (daily), discothèque (5 nights weekly), hairdressing, coffee shop (10am–6pm), clay pigeon shooting, archery, ice skating (winter), roller skating (summer).

Rooms 133	*Room phone* Yes	*Confirm by* 6	*Parking* Ample
with bath/shower 133	*Room TV* Yes	*Last dinner* 9.45	*Banquets* 550/–

Aviemore

Map 17 C4 Highland
Aviemore Centre *PH22 1PJ*
Aviemore (0479) 810771
Telex 75597

Credit Access, Amex, Barclaycard, Diners

Post House Hotel   58%   **£D**

This well-run early '70s hotel is being refurbished to bring it up to date. The bars and lounge feature Scandinavian-style wood decor, and there's a comfortable reception area and a sun terrace looking across to the Cairngorms. Standardised bedrooms have modern built-in units, bedside controls and neat, well-fitted bathrooms. *Amenities* garden, entertainment (Thurs–Sat), solarium, nursery, ski school (in winter), laundry room.

Continued

Continued
Rooms 103
with bath/shower 103   *Room phone* Yes   *Confirm by* By arrang.   *Parking* Ample
     Room TV Yes   *Last dinner* 10

Aviemore
Map 17 C4 Highland
Aviemore Centre *PH22 1PJ*
Aviemore (0479) 810771
Manager Mr Imperiali

Post House Hotel, Ben Macdui Restaurant   ♔ Ⓢ

There's a distinctly Scottish flavour to most of the dishes at this stylish restaurant. The Laird's Pot is a rich game soup, and baked trout, entrecôte steak stuffed with haggis, and tender escalope of venison are tempting main courses, with excellent vegetables. Prime ingredients, capable cooking and friendly, polished service all add up to a most enjoyable dinner.
Credit Access, Amex, Barclaycard, Diners

● **Set D** £7·50
About £27 for two   *Dinner only* 7–9.30

Aviemore
Map 17 C4 Highland
Aviemore Centre *PH22 1PF*
Aviemore (0479) 810681
Telex 75213

Credit Access, Amex,
Barclaycard, Diners

Strathspey Hotel   64%   £ D

Situated in the Aviemore leisure centre, this towering modern hotel has facilities for all the family. Smart public rooms include two lounges with mountain views, a plush cocktail bar and a basement disco-bar. Neat, well-fitted bedrooms have compact bathrooms.
Amenities garden, sauna, dancing (5 nights weekly in summer), solarium, nursery, pool table, ski school.

Rooms 90
with bath/shower 90   *Room phone* Yes   *Confirm by* By arrang.   *Parking* Ample
     Room TV Yes   *Last dinner* 9   *Banquets* 240/–

Ayr
Map 12 B2 Strathclyde
Belleisle Park
Alloway *KA7 4DU*
Ayr (0292) 42331

Credit Access, Amex

Belleisle House Hotel   64%   £ D/E

This imposing Scottish Baronial house standing in open parkland has some splendid public rooms, especially the oak-panelled entrance hall with its stone-carved illustrations of the works of Robert Burns and a magnificent dining room based on a room at Versailles. Solidly furnished bedrooms are bright and spacious; tiled bathrooms have modern fittings. Smart, friendly staff. *Amenities* dinner dance (most Sats).

Rooms 16
with bath/shower 14   *Room phone* Yes   *Confirm by* By arrang.   *Parking* Ample
     Room TV Yes   *Last dinner* 8.45   *Banquets* 400/6

Ayr
Map 12 B2 Strathclyde
Dalblair Road *KA7 1UG*
Ayr (0292) 69331

Credit Access, Amex,
Barclaycard, Diners

Caledonian Hotel   60%   £ D

There's a friendly air about this modern town-centre hotel, a popular place with businessmen and travellers. A spiral staircase leads up from the spacious foyer to an attractive lounge and bar area, and there's also a convivial public bar. Bright, cheerful bedrooms have contemporary free-standing furniture and adequately fitted bathrooms. No dogs.
Amenities sauna, dinner dance (Sat), dancing (4 nights weekly).   ♿

Rooms 127
with bath/shower 127   *Room phone* Yes   *Confirm by* By arang.   *Parking* Ample
     Room TV Yes   *Last dinner* 9.30   *Banquets* 150/2

Ayr
Map 12 B2 Strathclyde
19 Racecourse Road *KA7 2TD*
Ayr (0292) 60111

Credit Barclaycard, Diners

Pickwick Hotel   64%   £ E

Lofty spaciousness is a pleasing feature of this well-modernised Victorian house. The attractive lounge and bar are warmly welcoming with their patterned wallpaper and velvet seating, and there's also a useful function room with its own bar. Traditionally furnished bedrooms are well equipped with tea-makers, trouser presses and mini-bars, plus tiled shower or bathrooms. *Amenities* garden.

Rooms 15
with bath/shower 15   *Room phone* Yes   *Confirm by* By arrang.   *Parking* Ample
     Room TV Yes   *Last dinner* 9.30   *Banquets* 40/10

Ayr

Map 12 B2 Strathclyde
2a Academy Street *KA7 1HS*
Ayr (0292) 61391
Proprietors
Fran & Laurie Black

About £28 for two

Fouter's Bistro   Ⓢ

This little basement bistro with its check cloths, candles and Gallic posters has an enjoyably authentic atmosphere. Laurie and Fran Black's well-prepared menu of French and Italian favourites, such as sole meunière, bœuf bourguignonne, and saltimbocca, changes with the seasons and may include local venison. The smoked chicken with horseradish sauce makes an unusual starter. *Credit* Access, Amex, Barclaycard, Diners

Lunch 12–2 *Dinner* 6.30–10.30, Sun 7–10.30
Closed L Sun, all Mon, 1–3 Jan, 2 weeks Sept/Oct & 24–27 Dec

Ballachulish

Map 17 B4 Highland
Argyll *PA39 4JY*
Ballachulish (085 52) 239

Credit Access, Amex,
Barclaycard, Diners

Rooms 34
with bath/shower 16

Ballachulish Hotel   58%   £E

Bright, welcoming public rooms are an attraction of this turreted hotel, which enjoys a scenic setting overlooking Loch Leven and the mountains beyond. The spacious lounge is furnished with comfortable chintzy armchairs and, like the bar, has large windows which make the most of the views. Modestly equipped bedrooms have modern furniture and tea-makers. Bathrooms are up to date. *Amenities* garden, games room.

Room phone Yes	*Confirm by* 6	*Parking* Ample
Room TV No	*Last dinner* 8.45	*Banquets* 70/–

Ballachulish

Map 17 B4 Highland
Near Appin *PA38 4BW*
Duror (063 174) 268
Telex 778866

Credit Access, Amex,
Barclaycard, Diners

Rooms 29
with bath/shower 29

Stewart Hotel   58%   Ⓜ   £E

Standing in 15 acres of well-tended grounds with distant views of Loch Linnhe, this pleasant hotel is furnished in tasteful contemporary style throughout. A log fire burns in the comfortable bar, and there's an attractive lounge as well as a TV room. Cheerfully decorated bedrooms in the extension are fitted with practical modern furniture. Bathrooms are compact. *Amenities* garden. **Closed** Nov–Jan & weekdays Feb–Mar

Room phone No	*Confirm by* By arrang.	*Parking* Ample
Room TV No	*Last dinner* 8.30	*Banquets* 32/6

Ballater

Map 17 C4 Grampian
AB3 5SB
Ballater (0338) 55406
Proprietors Hector Macdonald &
Neil Bannister
Rooms 10
with bath/shower 10
Room phone Some
Room TV No
Confirm by 5
Last dinner 8.30
Parking Ample

Closed 1 December–
1st Sun in April
Credit Amex

Tullich Lodge   71%   Ⓜ   £C/D

Perched on a little hill with panoramic views of surrounding forests, this is a gem of a Victorian Gothic country house hotel where attentive personal service is a priority. A relaxed atmosphere pervades the public rooms, which include two lovely drawing rooms with tastefully arranged antiques and attractive panelling, as well as a simple bar. Bedrooms are stylishly appointed with antique furniture, good-quality curtains and comfortable beds all combining to create a pleasant effect. Bathrooms are modern and well equipped. Superb traditional Scottish breakfast with black pudding and home-made marmalade.
Amenities garden .

Ballater

Map 17 C4 Grampian
AB3 5SB
Ballater (0338) 55406
Proprietors Mr Hector Macdonald
& Mr Neil Bannister

● **Set D** £9
About £26 for two

Tullich Lodge Dining Room   Ⓢ

Neil Bannister transforms simple traditional food into a new experience in this lovely panelled dining room. There's no choice on the three-course set menu, but the quality of the cooking makes every dish a pleasure. Our home-made tomato soup deliciously flavoured with fresh basil was followed by tender roast leg of lamb with a nicely dressed green salad, and a liqueur-soaked hazelnut gâteau to finish. *Credit* Amex

Dinner only 7.30–8.30
Closed 1 December–1st Sun in April

Balquhidder
Map 17 B5 Central
Near Lochearnhead *FK19 8PQ*
Strathyre (087 74) 230

Credit Access, Amex,
Barclaycard, Diners

Rooms 4
with bath/shower 2

Ledcreich Hotel   63%   Ⓜ   £E

The friendly Hilditch family run this charming, whitewashed hotel, which enjoys a position of great tranquillity and beauty overlooking Loch Voil and the hills beyond. The relaxing residents' lounge has deep, comfortable chairs and lovely views, and there's a tiny bar, too. Cheerful bedrooms have smart whitewood furniture and excellent, fully modernised bathrooms. No dogs.
Amenities garden, game fishing, sailing boat.

Room phone No	*Confirm by* By arrang.	*Parking* Ample
Room TV No	*Last dinner* 9.30	*Banquets* 40/–

Balquhidder
Map 17 B5 Central
Near Lochearnhead *FK19 8PQ*
Strathyre (087 74) 230

●**Set L** £7·50 **Set D** £11·25
About £30 for two

Ledcreich Hotel Restaurant   🍴 Ⓢ

Book to be sure of a table at this attractive beamed restaurant. Duncan Hilditch offers set menus of delightfully tasty fare, and typical dishes could include cock-a-leekie soup or pâté maison to start, followed by roast venison, grilled trout or tender veal escalopes. Excellent vegetables, and sweets like sorbets or pear meringue glacé. Friendly, unhurried service.
🍷*ABOVE AVERAGE. Credit* Access, Amex, Barclaycard, Diners

Lunch Mon–Sat by arrangement only, Sun 12.30–2 *Dinner* 7.30–9.30
Closed Tues in winter

Banchory
Map 17 D4 Grampian
AB3 4ED
Banchory (033 02) 2622
Proprietors Mrs Peggy Jordan &
Mrs Kit Sabin
Rooms 23
with bath/shower 19
Room phone No
Room TV Most
Confirm by By arrang.
Last dinner 9.30
Parking Ample
Banquets 120/2

Credit Access, Amex,
Diners

Raemoir House Hotel   70%   Ⓜ   £C/D

Lovely grounds and really friendly personal service are among the many attributes of this handsome mansion (with a historic Ha' Hoose attached), which has been converted into a country house hotel. Fine antiques, beautiful tapestries and chandeliers provide interest in public rooms like the foyer, the spacious drawing room and the plushly furnished bar. Bedrooms are attractive, the Spanish and French rooms with their superb period furniture being especially delightful. Some of the bathrooms have marvellous old-fashioned baths.
Amenities garden, game fishing, helipad.   ♿

Banchory
Map 17 D4 Grampian
AB3 4ED
Banchory (033 02) 2622
Proprietors Mrs Peggy Jordan &
Mrs Kit Sabin
About £28 for two

Raemoir House Hotel Restaurant   ♛ Ⓢ

An elegant dining room offering fixed-price dinner menus. Sweets like chocolate gâteau and lemon mousse are especially successful. Light lunches except for Sunday. 🍷*ABOVE AVERAGE.*
Credit Access, Amex, Diners
Lunch 1–2 *Dinner* 8–9.30, Sat at 8 & 9.30 ● **Set D** £10   ♿

Banchory
Map 17 D4 Grampian
Inchmarlo Road *AB3 4AB*
Banchory (033 02) 2242

Credit Access, Amex,
Barclaycard, Diners

Rooms 25
with bath/shower 25

Tor-na-Coille Hotel   64%   £E

Six acres of delightful gardens surround this granite Victorian house, and there are fine views from the graceful, comfortable lounge and the spacious bar. Bedrooms at the front of the hotel are large and traditionally furnished, while others are more compact and modern with big shower rooms. All are prettily decorated.
Amenities garden, squash, game fishing, putting, pool table.

Room phone Yes	*Confirm by* By arrang.	*Parking* Ample
Room TV Yes	*Last dinner* 9.45	*Banquets* 80/–

Banchory

Map 17 D4 Grampian
AB3 4AB
Banchory (033 02) 2242

About £24 for two

Tor-na-Coille Hotel Restaurant   Ⓢ

This elegant dining room makes a pleasant setting for an enjoyable and competently prepared dinner. Good raw materials are used for dishes like tender beef medallions, and sweets are attractive. Light lunches except on Sunday when there's a traditional meal. *Credit* Access, Amex, Barclaycard, Diners *Lunch* 12.30–2 *Dinner* 7.30–10 ● **Set D** £8   ♿

Banff

Map 16 D3 Grampian
High Street *AB4 1AE*
Banff (026 12) 5353

Credit Access, Amex, Barclaycard, Diners
Closed 3 weeks January

County Hotel   64%   Ⓜ   £ D/E

Hard-working owners provide a warm welcome at this pleasant Georgian house which stands in attractive, well-kept gardens. There's no bar, but residents can relax with a drink in the lounge, an elegant room with antiques and chintzy armchairs. Bright bedrooms are individually decorated and furnished; one, with a four-poster, opens on to the garden. Sparkling modern bathrooms. *Amenities* garden.

Rooms 6	*Room phone* Yes	*Confirm by* By arrang.	*Parking* Ample
with bath/shower 6	*Room TV* Yes	*Last dinner* 9.15	*Banquets* 40/–

Banff

Map 16 D3 Grampian
High Street *AB4 1AE*
Banff (026 12) 5353

● **Set D** £10·95
About £29 for two

County Hotel Restaurant

A simply furnished restaurant, with neatly laid tables and views over the river Deveron. Reliably prepared four-course dinners start with crudités and a spicy dip followed perhaps by pâté maison or seafood cocktail. Main-course choice might be between scampi provençale, grilled lamb cutlets and veal Marsala, and to finish there are a few simple home-made puddings. Lighter lunches. 🍷 *ABOVE AVERAGE. Credit* Access, Amex, Barclaycard, Diners

Lunch 12.15–1.45, Sun 12.45–1.45 *Dinner* 7.30–9.30, Sun 7.30–9
Closed 3 weeks January

Barrhead

Map 12 B2 Strathclyde
Lochlibo Road *G78 1LG*
041–881 9211

Credit Access, Amex, Barclaycard, Diners

Dalmeny Park Hotel   59%   £ E/F

This handsome late-Victorian house stands in well-kept gardens on the A736 Glasgow–Irvine road. The comfortable lounge and bar have tall windows overlooking the lawn, and there's also a convivial public bar. Smart, freshly decorated bedrooms with matching curtains and bedspreads are furnished with traditional-style darkwood pieces. The hotel has a popular function suite. *Amenities* garden, dancing (Sat).

Rooms 19	*Room phone* Yes	*Confirm by* 7	*Parking* Ample
with bath/shower 10	*Room TV* Yes	*Last dinner* 9.30	*Banquets* 150/10

Beattock

Map 12 C3 Dumfries & Galloway
By Moffat *DG10 9SH*
Beattock (068 33) 407
Telex 777205
Props. Mr & Mrs Robert Beckh
Credit Access, Amex, Barclaycard, Diners

Auchen Castle Hotel   60%   Ⓜ   £ E

A mile north of the village, this fine Victorian mansion is set in spacious wooded grounds that include an attractive trout loch. The comfortable lounges retain their original lofty grandeur, while the cocktail bar is modern. Bedrooms range from spacious and traditional in the main building to smaller (with shower rooms) in an extension. *Amenities* garden, game fishing, dancing (Sat), rough shooting. **Closed** December–January

Rooms 28	*Room phone* No	*Confirm by* By arrang.	*Parking* Ample
with bath/shower 28	*Room TV* Yes	*Last dinner* 9	*Banquets* 100/–

Bellshill

Map 12 B2 Strathclyde
Hattonrigg Road *ML4 1RW*
Bellshill (0698) 748488

Credit Access, Amex, Barclaycard, Diners

Hattonrigg Hotel   53%   £ D/E

This modern two-storey hotel, a popular overnight stop for businessmen, is located just off the M74 a few miles south-east of Glasgow. It has a smart little residents' lounge with TV, a cosy cocktail bar and extensive conference and banqueting facilities. Cheerfully decorated bedrooms have central heating and tea/coffee-makers; bathrooms are neat and tidy. *Amenities* dancing (Sat, Sun).

Rooms 8	*Room phone* Yes	*Confirm by* By arrang.	*Parking* Ample
with bath/shower 4	*Room TV* No	*Last dinner* 9	*Banquets* 250/–

Biggar
Map 12 C2 Borders
Hartree *ML12 6JJ*
Biggar (0899) 20215

Credit Access
Closed 1 January

Rooms 39
with bath/shower 14

Hartree Country House Hotel   58%   £ E/F

Dating back more than 600 years, this impressive mansion set in rolling parkland still retains a sense of history. Massive oak doors open into the splendid public rooms, which are distinguished by antiques, fine paintings and chandeliers. Bedrooms vary considerably from spacious ones in the main house (some redecoration of rooms would be welcome) to compact modern ones in the extension. *Amenities* garden, putting, croquet.

Room phone No	*Confirm by* 8	*Parking* Ample
Room TV No	*Last dinner* 9.45	*Banquets* 24/5

Bonnyrigg
Map 12 C1 Lothian
Near Edinburgh *EH19 3JB*
Gorebridge (0875) 20153
Telex 72380

Rooms 24
with bath/shower 24
Room phone Yes
Room TV Yes
Confirm by By arrang.
Last dinner 10
Parking Ample
Banquets 100/–

Credit Access, Amex,
Barclaycard, Diners

Dalhousie Castle   78%   Ⓜ   £ C

A combination of comfort, style and traditional hospitality makes it a real delight to stay at this magnificent old castle, built of local sandstone and standing in wooded grounds by the winding river Esk. Moulded ceilings, polished floors, elegant antiques and comfortable leather chairs grace the public rooms, which include a splendid entrance hall and an attractive panelled drawing room. There's also a cosy bar down in the dungeons. Bedrooms of various sizes are decorated in restful shades and furnished with solid, Spanish-style pieces. Spacious, up-to-date bathrooms are fully tiled and luxuriously equipped.
Amenities garden, coarse fishing, croquet.

Bonnyrigg
Map 12 C1 Lothian
Near Edinburgh *EH19 3JB*
Gorebridge (0875) 20153

● **Set L** Sun only £8·50
About £34 for two

Dalhousie Castle Restaurant   ♛ Ⓢ

The castle dungeons, with their curved ceilings and armour-hung walls, make an intriguing setting for this friendly, comfortable restaurant, whose menu enjoyably combines Scottish and French cooking styles. Seasonal produce is used to good effect in dishes like scallops in cream and mushroom sauce or tasty venison and oyster pie, and home-made black bread is an appealing touch. *Credit* Access, Amex, Barclaycard, Diners

Lunch 12–2 *Dinner* 7–10

Borgue
Map 13 B4 Dumfries & Galloway
Near Kirkcudbright *DG6 4TP*
Borgue (055 77) 236
Proprietors
Mr & Mrs P. A. Baines

Rooms 9
with bath/shower 4

Senwick House Hotel   60%   Ⓜ   £ E

Situated between Borgue and Brighouse Bay, this pleasant family-run hotel is surrounded by 12 acres of lawned gardens and woodland. Inside there's a small entrance hall leading to the cosy residents' lounge with armchairs around the TV; the modern bar is bright and spacious. Cheerful bedrooms have sensible furniture and pretty wallpapers. Carpeted bathrooms are adequate. *Amenities* garden, tennis.

Room phone No	*Confirm by* By arrang.	*Parking* Ample
Room TV Some	*Last dinner* 9.30	*Banquets* 30/–

Bridge of Allan
Map 17 C5 Central
57 Henderson Street *FK9 4HL*
Bridge of Allan (0786) 832284

Credit Access, Amex,
Barclaycard, Diners

Royal Hotel   57%   £ D/E

Conveniently situated not far from the M9, this sturdy 19th-century hotel is popular with tourists and businessmen. Public rooms still retain their moulded ceilings, although there are now functional modern furnishings in the lounge and bar. Compact, well-maintained bedrooms have spacious wardrobes, trouser presses and radios. Functional half-tiled bath or shower rooms. *Amenities* table tennis.

Continued

Continued
Rooms 34
with bath/shower 14   *Room phone* Yes   *Confirm by* By arrang.   *Parking* Ample
                     Room TV Some   *Last dinner* 9.30   *Banquets* 110/8

Bridge of Cally

Map 17 C4 Tayside
By Blairgowrie *PH10 7JJ*
Bridge of Cally (025 086) 231

● Set D £6·95
About £20 for two
Banquets 25/2

Bridge of Cally Hotel Restaurant

A pleasant and unpretentious dining room with fresh flowers and attractive green decor. The short dinner menu features a varied choice of homely dishes ranging from full-flavoured leek soup to roast sirloin of beef with Madeira sauce and baked Ayrshire gammon; there's also an attractive sweet trolley. Lighter lunches feature salads and a daily hot dish.
Credit Access, Barclaycard

Lunch 12–1.45, Sun 12.30–2 *Dinner* 7.30–8.30
Closed Mon in winter & all November

Buckie

Map 16 C3 Grampian
Drybridge *AB5 2JB*
Buckie (0542) 32660

About £22 for two
Banquets 30/20

Old Monastery

Owner-chef Douglas Craig achieves consistently high standards at this pleasantly simple restaurant, once a chapel for monks in retreat. The menu features some Scottish specialities such as leek and potato soup, Spey salmon and tasty oatmeal-stuffed chicken breast, and there's also seasonal game. Anthea Craig makes some mouthwatering sweets, including grape and port trifle or a delicate fresh lime mousse. *ABOVE AVERAGE.*

Lunch 12.30–2 *Dinner* 7–9, Sat 7–9.30
Closed Sun, Mon, 25 & 26 Dec, 1st 3 weeks Jan & 2 weeks mid Oct

---

Cairnbaan

Map 17 B5 Strathclyde
By Lochgilphead
Argyll
PA31 8SH
Lochgilphead (0546) 2488
Credit Access, Amex,
Barclaycard, Diners

Cairnbaan Motor Inn   55%   Ⓜ   £E

Friendly staff greet visitors to this agreeable inn standing in wooded country right by the peaceful Crinan Canal. The original 18th-century building, which contains a simple modern bar-lounge and a sun lounge, has three annexes with comfortable fitted bedrooms; those in the most recent chalet block have verandahs overlooking the canal.
Amenities garden, pool table, games room, mooring, petrol pumps.

Rooms 24
with bath/shower 14   *Room phone* No   *Confirm by* By arrang.   *Parking* Ample
                     Room TV No   *Last dinner* 9.30   *Banquets* 120/6

Callander

Map 17 C5 Central
FK17 8BG
Callander (0877) 30003

Rooms 15
with bath/shower 11
Room phone Yes
Room TV Yes
Confirm by 6.30
Last dinner 8.55
Parking Ample

Roman Camp Hotel   70%   Ⓜ   £D

Built in 1625 on the site of a Roman camp beside the river Teith, this enchanting hotel stands in 20 acres of lovingly created formal gardens. Public areas are full of interest: there's a comfortable lounge with tapestry-covered walls and a ticking grandfather clock, a bright airy conservatory, and a marvellously peaceful oak-panelled library. Antiques and flowers line the corridors, and bedrooms are individually decorated, with fine period pieces and equipped with thoughtful extras like tea/coffee-makers and electric blankets, as well as biscuits and baskets of fruit. Bathrooms are spacious and well fitted.
Amenities garden, game fishing.

Callander

Map 17 C5 Central
FK17 8BG
Callander (0877) 30003

About £25 for two

Roman Camp Hotel Restaurant

An eye-catchingly simple modern dining room overlooking the garden. Samuel Denzler's short menu ranges from gazpacho to chicken breast with béarnaise and his dishes are well prepared and nicely presented. Friendly, informal service. *SUPERIOR.*
Lunch 12.30–1.55 *Dinner* 7–8.55

Canonbie
Map 12 D3 Dumfries & Galloway

DG14 0UX
Canonbie (054 15) 295
Proprietors
Robert & Susan Phillips

● **Set L** £5·95 **Set D** £8·75
About £24 for two
Banquets 30/12

Riverside Inn

Robert and Susan Phillips share the cooking in this delightful pub restaurant, and their daily-changing, fixed-price menu features reliably prepared, fresh-tasting dishes ranging from pan-fried trout and sirloin steak to medallions of veal with cream and vermouth. Vegetables are admirable and there's a nice choice of tempting puddings such as brandy and cream meringue. Booking essential.

Lunch by arrangement only *Dinner* 7.30–8.30
Closed D Sun & 2 weeks December/January

Castle Douglas
Map 13 B4 Dumfries & Galloway

DG7 1EL
Castle Douglas (0556) 2097

Credit Amex, Barclaycard, Diners
Closed 1 January

Rooms 15
with bath/shower 6

King's Arms Hotel *(Inn)* Ⓜ £D/E

This agreeable family-run hostelry, a coaching inn in former days, offers today's visitors a friendly welcome and simple comforts for short stays. The three bars are popular meeting places for the local farming community, and residents have a small lounge and a separate TV room. Cheerful bedrooms are adequately furnished; bathrooms are modern.

Room phone No	*Confirm by* By arrang.	*Parking* Ample
Room TV No	*Last dinner* 8	

Clachanseil
Map 17 B5 Strathclyde
By Oban
Balvickar (085 23) 276
Proprietors Pauline Jones & Maggie Symonds

About £22 for two

Willowburn Hotel Restaurant

Pauline Jones turns simple fresh ingredients into tasty, enjoyable dishes at this welcoming restaurant, which looks over Seil Sound to the mountains beyond. There's a good cold buffet at lunchtime, while in the evening the choice includes omelettes, home-baked ham, a flavour-packed bœuf bourguignonne and, with 24-hours' notice, lobster and crayfish.
Credit Access, Amex, Barclaycard, Diners

Lunch 12.30–2 *Dinner* 7–8.30
Closed November

Cleish
Map 17 C5 Tayside
Near Kinross *KY13 7LS*
Cleish Hills (057 75) 216

● **Set L** Sun only £5, winter £8
About £28 for two

Nivingston House Restaurant

You can have lunch in the simply furnished dining room or dinner in the more formal, elaborate main restaurant. The regularly changing à la carte menu features seasonal fare ranging from moules marinière to local venison in a black cherry cream sauce laced with Drambuie. On Sunday there's a set lunchtime buffet in summer, a traditional roast in winter.
Credit Access, Amex, Barclaycard, Diners

Lunch 12–2 *Dinner* 7–10
Closed 1st 2 weeks January

Coatbridge
Map 12 B1 Strathclyde
Glasgow Road *ML5 1EL*
Coatbridge (0236) 24392

Credit Access, Amex, Barclaycard, Diners

Rooms 24
with bath/shower 20

Coatbridge Hotel 55% £E

Catering mainly for business people, this modern hotel on the A89 offers modest short-stay accommodation and a range of conference and banqueting facilities. Public rooms include a simple lounge and three contrasting bars, one of them with a coach and horses theme. Compact bedrooms have functional fittings, TVs, radios and tea-makers. Their planned refurbishment will be welcome. *Amenities* discothèque (Fri–Sun).

Room phone Yes	*Confirm by* 6	*Parking* Ample
Room TV Yes	*Last dinner* 9.30	*Banquets* 150/40

We publish annually, so make sure you use the current edition. It's worth it!

Colbost

Map 16 A3 Highland
Dunvegan
Isle of Skye *IV55 8ZT*
Glendale (047 081) 258

About £23 for two
Banquets 30/2

Three Chimneys

Ask for directions when booking for this charming restaurant in a remote crofter's cottage. Mr Poyntz's cooking reaches great heights, and there are some memorable dishes on his varied menu: smoked haddock soup and seafood ragout are full of flavour, the salad (with 15 different ingredients) is outstanding, and sweets range from a delicious traditional cloutie dumpling to gorgeous caramel flan.

Lunch 12–2 *Dinner* 6.30–8.30
Closed Sun (except July–August) & mid October–beginning April

Connel

Map 17 B5 Strathclyde
North Connel *PA37 1RB*
Connel (063 171) 322
Proprietors
Mr & Mrs J. D. M. Stewart
Credit Barclaycard
Closed 10 October–Easter

Rooms 14
with bath/shower 4

Ossian's Hotel   56%   Ⓜ   £E

This immaculately kept modern hotel overlooking Loch Etive has been run for 12 years with great enthusiasm by Mr and Mrs Stewart. Public rooms, including a lounge, bar and TV room, have modest contemporary furnishings that combine with pine panelling and picture windows in pleasant Scandinavian style. Bedrooms, too, are simple and functional, gleaming bathrooms modern and well fitted. *Amenities* garden, game & sea fishing.

Room phone No	*Confirm by* 6	*Parking* Ample
Room TV No	*Last dinner* 8.15	*Banquets* 36/2

Connel

Map 17 B5 Strathclyde
North Connel *PA37 1RB*
Connel (063 171) 322
Proprietors
Mr & Mrs J. D. M. Stewart
About £21 for two

Ossian's Hotel Restaurant

Mrs Stewart's cooking is homely and straightforward at this hospitable restaurant, where set dinner menus range from soups and pâté to fresh fish, grills and sweets like an excellent light trifle. *Credit* Barclaycard
Dinner only 7–8.15
Closed 10 October–Easter ● **Set D** £6·50

Contin

Map 16 B3 Highland
By Strathpeffer *IV14 9EH*
Strathpeffer (099 72) 265

Rooms 19
with bath/shower 11

Craigdarroch Lodge Hotel   54%   Ⓜ   £E/F

Twelve acres of wooded grounds make a secluded setting for this friendly, family-run hotel, which is popular with sports-minded holiday-makers as well as those just wanting to relax. Unpretentious public rooms like the lounge and bar have attractive garden views, and bright bedrooms, simply and practically furnished, offer adequate comforts. Neat, modern bathrooms. *Amenities* garden, tennis, game fishing, snooker, clay-pigeon shooting.

Room phone No	*Confirm by* By arrang.	*Parking* Ample
Room TV No	*Last dinner* 9	*Banquets* 45/2

Craignure

Map 17 A5 Strathclyde
Isle of Mull *PA65 6BB*
Craignure (068 02) 351
Manager Mr John Patrick
Credit Access, Amex,
Barclaycard, Diners
Closed October–April

Rooms 60
with bath/shower 60

Isle of Mull Hotel   60%   £D

Not far from the Oban–Craignure ferry, this modern two-storey hotel has breathtaking views of the bay and the mountains beyond. Public areas include a cosy little bar and a comfortable lounge opening on to a paved terrace. Simply decorated bedrooms (including some for families) have good storage space, duvets, tea/coffee-makers and up-to-date bathrooms. Helpful staff. *Amenities* garden.

Room phone No	*Confirm by* By arrang.	*Parking* Ample
Room TV No	*Last dinner* 8.15	*Banquets* 18/6

Crinan

Map 17 B5 Strathclyde
Near Lochgilphead *PA31 8SR*
Crinan (054 683) 235
Proprietors Mr & Mrs N. Ryan
Credit Access, Amex,
Diners
Closed mid October–19 March

Rooms 22
with bath/shower 22

Crinan Hotel   67%   Ⓜ   £D

Situated on the lochside at the north end of the Crinan Canal, this delightful white-painted hotel is a popular holiday centre. Mrs Ryan has created highly artistic decor in the three relaxing bars and the very comfortable lounges. Bedrooms, too, are most attractive, with red pine furniture and colourful wallpapers; all have sea views. Excellent well-designed bathrooms. *Amenities* garden, hotel boat.

Room phone Yes	*Confirm by* 6	*Parking* Ample
Room TV No	*Last dinner* 9	*Banquets* 20/2

Crinan

Map 17 B5 Strathclyde
Near Lochgilphead *PA31 8SR*
Crinan (054 683) 235
Proprietors Mr & Mrs N. Ryan

● **Set D** £10
About £26 for two

Crinan Hotel Restaurant 

Charming hospitality and excellent local produce combine to make this a most pleasant restaurant. The set dinner menu features superb seafood ranging from locally smoked salmon to wonderfully fresh scallops, as well as meat dishes such as charcoal-grilled steak and roast lamb with fennel sauce. Vegetables are carefully handled and there are well-made sweets like Austrian grape torte. *Credit* Access, Amex, Diners

Dinner only 7–9
Closed mid October–19 March

Crinan

Map 17 B5 Strathclyde
Near Lochgilphead *PA31 8SR*
Crinan (054 683) 235
Proprietors Mr & Mrs N. Ryan
Seafood

● **Set D** £16·50
About £42 for two

Crinan Hotel, Lock 16 Seafood Rest. ★ 

Fresh seafood takes on a new meaning in this fascinating little restaurant. Each morning, Mr Ryan radios the local fleet to find out how they are faring, and then sets off to collect the very best from the day's haul. By lunchtime it is all in his kitchen ready for cooking. Every dish is an outstanding treat, and the range is astonishing: incomparably succulent jumbo prawns, lobsters, scallops, salmon and herring, all prepared in the simplest fashion to highlight their exquisite natural flavour. If the boats don't go out because of bad weather, the restaurant is closed, so it's wise to ring.
Credit Access, Amex, Diners

Lunch 12.30–2.30 *Dinner* 7–11
Closed mid October–19 March

Cullen

Map 16 D3 Grampian
Seafield Street
Near Buckie *AB5 2SE*
Cullen (0542) 40791

Credit Access, Amex,
Barclaycard, Diners

Rooms 25
with bath/shower 17

Seafield Arms Hotel 66% Ⓜ   £ D/E

Originally a coaching inn, this three-storey pebbledash building in the town centre is now a pleasantly modernised hotel. It has two lounges with comfortable chintz furnishings and a smart cocktail bar. Individually designed bedrooms have attractive coordinated fabrics, modern brass bedsteads and practical fitted units, as well as tea-makers and radios. Public and private bathrooms are well equipped. *Amenities* patio.

Room phone Yes	*Confirm by* 7	*Parking* Ample
Room TV Yes	*Last dinner* 9.30	

Cupar

Map 17 C5 Fife
25 Bonnygate *KY15 4BU*
Cupar (0334) 55574

About £24 for two

Ostlers Close

A pleasant, simply appointed restaurant, whose short menu includes a particularly good chicken liver pâté and nicely garnished fillets of beef, pork and veal served with rice and a light curry sauce.
Lunch 12.15–2 *Dinner* 7–9.30 **Closed** Sun & 1 January
Banquets 24/18

Dirleton

Map 12 D1 Lothian
EH39 5EG
Dirleton (062 085) 241
Telex 727887
Proprietor Mr Arthur Neil
Credit Access, Amex,
Barclaycard, Diners

Rooms 7
with bath/shower 7

Open Arms Hotel 66% Ⓜ   £ D

For more than 25 years Arthur Neil has been welcoming visitors to his delightful hotel overlooking Dirleton Castle and the village green. Chintzy lounges in soothing pastel shades are cosy and comfortable, and the cocktail bar is a popular meeting place. Bedrooms are tastefully decorated, and each one is furnished in individual style; bathrooms are well equipped and sparklingly clean. *Amenities* garden.

Room phone Yes	*Confirm by* By arrang.	*Parking* Ample
Room TV Yes	*Last dinner* 10	*Banquets* 30/5

Dirleton

Map 12 D1 Lothian
EH39 5EG
Dirleton (062 085) 241
Proprietor Mr Arthur Neil

Open Arms Hotel Restaurant 

Fixed-price menus offer an interesting selection of well-prepared dishes at this spacious restaurant, which has a glassed-in verandah for summer eating. Cock-a-leekie, mussel and onion stew and cranachan with blackcurrants are among the Scottish specialities, and other choices could include sautéed frogs' legs, smoked haddock mousse, game pies and roast beef.

Continued

● **Set L** £4·75, Sun £5·25
Set D £9·75
About £27 for two

🍷 *ABOVE AVERAGE. Credit* Access, Amex, Barclaycard, Diners

Lunch 12.30–2 *Dinner* 7–10

Dornoch
Map 16 C3 Highland
IV25 3HN
Dornoch (086 281) 212
Proprietors
Mr & Mrs N. W. G. Currie
Credit Amex, Barclaycard, Diners
Closed mid October–early April

Burghfield House Hotel 55% Ⓜ £E

Situated minutes from the Royal Dornoch course, this converted Victorian residence is popular with golfers. Public rooms include a spacious lounge and two modern bars. Bedrooms in the house are furnished in traditional style, and some have bathrooms to match; rooms in the annexe are more compact and modern. Some refurbishment is planned. *Amenities* garden, game fishing, discothèque (Fri, Sat), games room, putting.

Rooms 14
with bath/shower 7

Room phone No
Room TV No

Confirm by By arrang.
Last dinner 9

Parking Ample
Banquets 180/2

Dornoch
Map 16 C3 Highland
IV25 3HN
Dornoch (086 281) 212
Proprietors
Mr & Mrs N. W. G. Currie

● **Set L** £4·50 **Set D** £7·50
About £23 for two
Banquets 180/2

Burghfield House Hotel Restaurant Ⓢ

The fixed-price dinner menu in this large, well-proportioned hotel restaurant offers a nicely varied choice of dishes prepared from first-class ingredients. Starters like peppery haggis with whisky sauce or creamy turkey soup can be followed by main courses such as fresh haddock with scallop sauce or roast rib of beef. Sweets include an excellent Austrian pineapple cake. Buffet lunches. *Credit* Amex, Barclaycard, Diners

Lunch 12.30–2.30 *Dinner* 7.30–9
Closed mid October–beginning April

Dryburgh
Map 12 D2 Borders
St Boswells *TD6 0RQ*
St Boswells (0835) 22261
Telex 727396
Manager Mr D. A. Hogg
Credit Access, Amex,
Barclaycard, Diners

Dryburgh Abbey Hotel 62% £D

This fine Victorian mansion has gardens and lawns stretching down to the river Tweed. The comfortable foyer features an ancient vaulted alcove from the nearby abbey, and there are two relaxing lounges (one with TV) and a panelled bar. Bright, spacious bedrooms (three with four-posters) have central heating, tea-makers and trouser presses. Bathrooms are adequate. *Amenities* garden, game fishing, games room, croquet, putting. ♿

Rooms 29
with bath/shower 16

Room phone No
Room TV No

Confirm by 5
Last dinner 8.30

Parking Ample
Banquets 180/–

Drymen
Map 17 B5 Central
Near Glasgow *G63 0BQ*
Drymen (0360) 60588

Credit Access, Amex,
Barclaycard, Diners

Buchanan Arms Hotel 60% £D/E

There are fine views from the glass-covered sun terrace of this friendly, well-run hotel not far from Loch Lomond. The bar with its scrubbed wooden floor, stone arch and studded leather chairs has a cosy, welcoming atmosphere. Bedrooms, cheerfully decorated in pastel colours, have a pleasing mixture of modern furniture and reproduction pieces. Well-equipped bathrooms. *Amenities* garden.

Rooms 23
with bath/shower 21

Room phone Yes
Room TV Yes

Confirm by 6
Last dinner 9.15

Parking Ample
Banquets 100/6

Dulnain Bridge
Map 16 C3 Highland
Near Grantown-on-Spey
PH26 3LY
Dulnain Bridge (047 985) 257
Proprietors
Fone & Ogilvie families

Muckrach Lodge Hotel 56% Ⓜ £E/F

A friendly welcome and charming personal service are among the attractions of this delightful family-run hotel, a stone shooting lodge standing in peaceful countryside back from the A938. A log fire warms the homely panelled bar, and there's a comfortable, roomy residents' lounge. Simply furnished bedrooms and adequate public bathrooms are very well maintained. Guide dogs only. *Amenities* garden.

Rooms 9
with bath/shower None

Room phone No
Room TV No

Confirm by By arrang.
Last dinner 8

Parking Ample
Banquets 50/–

Dulnain Bridge — Muckrach Lodge Hotel Restaurant

Dulnain Bridge
Map 16 C3 Highland
Near Grantown-on-Spey *PH26 3LY*
Dulnain Bridge (047 985) 257
Proprietors Fone & Ogilvie families

About £25 for two

Set dinner menus at this simple, friendly restaurant range from pickled herrings and poached salmon to mushroom vol-au-vents and delicious chocolate pot. Generally capable cooking. Sunday buffet dinner during season.

Lunch by arrangement only *Dinner* 7.30–8.30 ● **Set D** £8·95

Dulnain Bridge — Skye of Curr Hotel 56% Ⓜ £ F

Dulnain Bridge
Map 16 C3 Highland
Near Grantown-on-Spey *PH26 3PA*
Dulnain Bridge (047 985) 345

Credit Amex, Barclaycard

Situated up a narrow lane from Dulnain Bridge, this converted 1920s stone mansion is now a charming little hotel. There's a warm welcome in the panelled entrance hall which leads to a simply furnished modern cocktail bar and the comfortable lounge. Cheerful bedrooms have practical modern furniture, and the three public bathrooms plus one shower room are old-fashioned but adequate. *Amenities* garden.

Rooms 8	*Room phone* No	*Confirm by* By arrang.	*Parking* Ample
with bath/shower None	*Room TV* No	*Last dinner* 8.30	*Banquets* 30/–

We do not necessarily recommend the cooking at hotels whose restaurants are not separately listed.

Dumfries — Cairndale Hotel 58% £ E

Dumfries
Map 13 C4 Dumfries & Galloway
English Street *DG1 2DF*
Dumfries (0387) 4111
Telex 777170
Manager Mr W. Jackson
Credit Access, Amex, Barclaycard, Diners

This cheerful red-brick hotel, originally three Victorian houses, is not far from the city centre. It has a charming residents' lounge and three modern bars, but the star of the public rooms is the old writing room, with its bureau tops folded into the wall. Bedrooms range from comfortably traditional to bright and modern in the rear wing; colourful tiled bathrooms.
Closed 1 & 2 January

Rooms 44	*Room phone* Yes	*Confirm by* 6	*Parking* Ample
with bath/shower 29	*Room TV* Yes	*Last dinner* 9	*Banquets* 150/2

Dunblane — Cromlix House 87% £ C

Dunblane
Map 17 C5 Central
FK15 9JT
Dunblane (0786) 822125

Rooms 11
with bath/shower 11
Room phone Yes
Room TV Most
Confirm by By arrang.
Last dinner 9.30
Parking Ample
Banquets 40/2

Credit Access, Amex, Barclaycard, Diners

A few minutes from the Stirling–Perth road, this late-Victorian mansion stands in 5,000 acres of grounds and gardens. The interior retains its full period flavour, with family portraits lining the staircase and fine antiques in the comfortable, bay-windowed morning room. The house also boasts a chapel, a gun room and an elegant, peaceful library. Large bedrooms are prettily furnished, with brass bedsteads and pastel colour schemes, and all have luxuriously equipped bathrooms. Six also have beautifully furnished sitting rooms. Bottled Malvern water and information folders are typically thoughtful touches in this most welcoming hotel. *Amenities* garden, tennis, game fishing, shooting, croquet.

Dunblane — Cromlix House Restaurant ♕ Ⓢ

Dunblane
Map 17 C5 Central
FK15 9JT
Dunblane (0786) 822125

About £36 for two

Discuss your preferences when booking at this elegant panelled restaurant, where you'll enjoy beautifully presented dishes ranging from fresh asparagus to poached sea trout, beef en croûte and lovely orange soufflé. ♟ *SUPERIOR*. *Credit* Access, Amex, Barclaycard, Diners *Lunch* by arrangement only *Dinner* 7–9.30 ● **Set L** from £8·50 **Set D** £15 incl. service

Dundee

Map 17 C5 Tayside
101 Marketgait *DD1 1QU*
Dundee (0382) 26874
Telex 76456

Credit Access, Amex,
Barclaycard, Diners

Rooms 57
with bath/shower 42

Angus Hotel   60%   **£ D**

There are fine views of the city and the Tay Bridges from the upper rooms of this business hotel. Stylish first-floor public areas include a modern lounge with hessian-hung walls and a boldly contemporary bar. Plain, neatly furnished bedrooms are bright with cheerful fabrics, and bathrooms are adequate. Executive suites and functional conference facilities are available. *Amenities* dinner dance (Sat).

Room phone Yes	*Confirm by* 6	*Parking* Limited
Room TV Yes	*Last dinner* 10.30	*Banquets* 500/4

Dundee

Map 17 C5 Tayside
Perth Road *DD1 9XJ*
Dundee (0382) 69231
Telex 76608

Credit Access, Amex,
Barclaycard, Diners

Rooms 27
with bath/shower 27

Invercarse Hotel   59%   **£ D/E**

This early Victorian house has been extended and modernised to form a comfortable, up-to-date hotel. Public rooms include three popular bars (one of which has pleasant views of the grounds), and there are extensive function facilities. Attractive modern bedrooms (mostly singles with compact shower rooms) have fitted furniture, radios and tea/coffee-makers. *Amenities* garden.

Room phone Yes	*Confirm by* 6	*Parking* Ample
Room TV Yes	*Last dinner* 10	*Banquets* 220/10

Dundee

Map 17 C5 Tayside
160 Nethergate *DD1 4DU*
Dundee (0382) 22515

Credit Access, Amex,
Barclaycard, Diners

Rooms 56
with bath/shower 12

Queen's Hotel   54%   **£ D/E**

Lofty, ornate ceilings and a splendid carved staircase stand as reminders of the grand Victorian origins of this pleasant, welcoming hotel. A simple lounge offers extensive views, and there's a little bar and a good choice of meeting and conference rooms. Bedrooms have attractive coordinated fabrics and smart natural-wood furniture. Adequate bathrooms, including many public ones. *Amenities* folk evenings (Wed in summer).

Room phone Yes	*Confirm by* 6	*Parking* Limited
Room TV Yes	*Last dinner* 9.30	*Banquets* 100/–

Dunfermline

Map 17 C5 Fife
West Pitcorthie Road *KY11 5DS*
Dunfermline (0383) 22611
Telex 727721

Credit Access, Amex,
Barclaycard, Diners

Rooms 48
with bath/shower 48

King Malcolm Hotel   60%   **£ D**

A most pleasing hotel in functional modern style popular with both businessmen and tourists. Public areas include a comfortable reception and a small bar, as well as several function rooms. Neat, compact bedrooms with fitted units have bedside controls and tea-making facilities, and bathrooms are simply equipped.
Amenities garden, dinner dance (Sat October–March).

Room phone Yes	*Confirm by* 6	*Parking* Ample
Room TV Yes	*Last dinner* 9.30	*Banquets* 130/20

Our inspectors never book in the name of the Egon Ronay Organisation; they disclose their identity only after paying their bills.

Dunkeld

Map 17 C5 Tayside
PH8 0HX
Dunkeld (035 02) 243

Proprietor Mrs G. B. Miller

Rooms 31
with bath/shower 26

Dunkeld House Hotel   68% Ⓜ   **£ D**

A tree-lined drive leads to this handsome turn-of-the-century house, which offers traditional comfort and friendly service in beautiful, tranquil surroundings. The panelled lounges and cocktail bar command lovely views across the lawns to the river Tay. Spacious bedrooms are attractively furnished; bathrooms are well equipped. *Amenities* garden, tennis, game fishing, dancing (Sat in summer), pitch & putt, croquet, bowls.

Room phone No	*Confirm by* By arrang.	*Parking* Ample
Room TV Yes	*Last dinner* 9	*Banquets* 35/2

Dunkeld

Map 17 C5 Tayside
PH8 0HX
Dunkeld (035 02) 243
Proprietor Mrs G. B. Miller

● **Set L** £5·75, Sun £6
Set D £8·75, Sat & Sun £10
About £26 for two

Dunkeld House Hotel Restaurant ♛ Ⓢ

Fabulous views of the river Tay are part of the attraction of this pleasant, spacious dining room. The à la carte and set menus offer a good choice of dishes from chicken Kiev and beef Stroganoff to roast duckling with Calvados sauce and Pernod-flavoured lamb vol-au-vent. Sweets include a delicious lemon torte. Cooking is generally acceptable although lapses can occur. ♿

Lunch 12.30–2 *Dinner* 7–9, Sun 7–8.30

Dysart

Map 17 C5 Fife
By Kirkcaldy *KY1 2TP*
Kirkcaldy (0592) 51211

About £26 for two
Banquets 18/–

Old Rectory Inn Ⓢ

A charming little dining room in a pub that was once a rectory. The young chef shows flair and considerable expertise in preparing an interesting selection of French-inspired dishes, ranging from devilled crab croquettes and smoked ham mousse with figs to entrecôte au poivre and roast duck with grapefruit sauce. Excellent vegetables and a tempting sweet trolley. Sunday lunch features a cold table and a roast. ♿

Lunch Sun only 12.30–2 *Dinner* 7–9.15
Closed D Sun & Mon, 25 December & 1st week January

East Kilbride

Map 12 B2 Strathclyde
Cornwall Street *G74 1AF*
East Kilbride (035 52) 29771
Telex 778428
Credit Access, Amex, Barclaycard, Diners
Closed 1 Jan & 25 Dec

Bruce Hotel 66% £ D/E

Next to a town-centre shopping precinct, this popular hotel sports an ultra-modern split-level reception area leading to a colourful cocktail bar-cum-lounge. There are also useful conference facilities. Warm, comfortable bedrooms (some studio-type) have fitted units, tea-makers, radios and fully tiled bath or shower rooms.
Amenities dinner dance (Sat), discothèque (Sun), hairdressing.

Rooms 84	*Room phone* Yes	*Confirm by* 6	*Parking* Ample
with bath/shower 84	*Room TV* Yes	*Last dinner* 9.45	*Banquets* 250/10

Stars in this Guide stand for the quality of the cooking only— our overriding criterion, irrespective of price, luxury or service.

East Kilbride

Map 12 B2 Strathclyde
2 Cornwall Way *G74 1JR*
East Kilbride (035 52) 21161
Telex 778504
Manager Mr W. J. Tennyson
Credit Access, Amex, Barclaycard, Diners

Stuart Hotel 63% £ D/E

Refurbishment has improved standards and facilities at this modern businessman's hotel in the centre of East Kilbride. Public areas include several meeting rooms, a tastefully decorated bar and a functional lounge. Compact, sensibly laid out bedrooms have good writing and storage space plus tea-makers. Adequate, half-tiled bathrooms.
Amenities dinner dance (Sat). ♿

Rooms 30	*Room phone* Yes	*Confirm by* Noon	*Parking* Limited
with bath/shower 30	*Room TV* Yes	*Last dinner* 9.30	*Banquets* 160/2

East Linton

Map 12 D1 Lothian
Station Road *EH40 3DP*
East Linton (062 086) 395

Credit Access, Amex, Barclaycard, Diners

Harvester's Hotel 57% Ⓜ £ D

This fine Georgian house, standing in the middle of a village just off the A1, has two comfortable, chintzy lounges and an appealing bar. Cheerfully decorated bedrooms have modern built-in units, duvets and tea-makers. Like the bathrooms, they are tidy and well maintained. Seven rooms are in a converted coach house across the garden.
Amenities garden, game fishing.

Rooms 10	*Room phone* No	*Confirm by* 6	*Parking* Ample
with bath/shower 7	*Room TV* No	*Last dinner* 8.30	

East Linton

Map 12 D1 Lothian
Station Road *EH40 3DP*
East Linton (062 086) 395

Harvester's Hotel Restaurant

This comfortable dining room with its green trelliswork is an agreeable setting in which to enjoy uncomplicated, well-prepared food. There's a choice of dishes on the menu to suit all tastes, from moules marinière and trout with almonds to crisp, tender duckling bigarade or quail with rosemary, as well as steaks and grills. Attractive sweets.
Credit Access, Amex, Barclaycard, Diners

Dinner only 7–8.30

About £22 for two

Changes in data may occur in establishments after the Guide goes to press. Prices should be taken as indications rather than firm quotes.

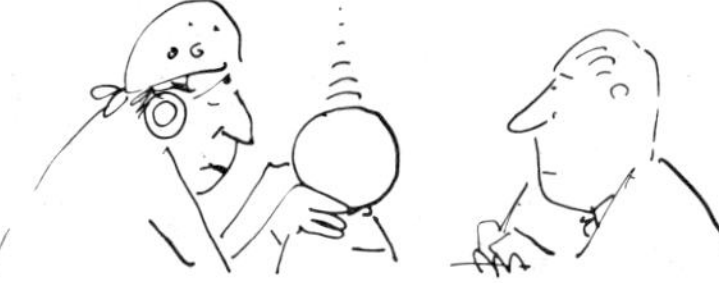

Edinburgh

Town plan C2 Lothian
167 Rose Street *EH2 4LS*
031–225 4787

Swiss cooking

About £22 for two
Banquets 20/–

Alp Horn

An enormous Alp horn catches the eye on the wall of this cosy restaurant, where the food is authentically Swiss in style. Dishes like pork chop cooked with a piquant sweet pepper sauce and venison in a savoury sauce served with noodles are well prepared and full of flavour. Air-dried meats, fondues and rösti potatoes help to complete the picture. Polite, helpful service.
Credit Access

Lunch 12–2 *Dinner* 6.30–10
Closed Sun, Mon & last 3 weeks September

Edinburgh

Town plan E3 Lothian
56 St Mary's Street *EH1 1SX*
031–556 5888

French cooking

● **Set L** £3·75, Sun £5·65
About £28 for two
Banquets 45/–

L'Auberge

Everything about this friendly restaurant is unmistakably French, from the decor to the cooking of Daniel Martelat, who hails from Lyons. Dishes like terrine maison, monkfish fillets with green peppercorns and meaty duckling à l'orange are competently prepared and most enjoyable. There's a nice choice of vegetables, and sweets range from sorbets to crêpes suzette.
*ABOVE AVERAGE. Credit* Access, Amex, Barclaycard

Lunch 12.30–2.30 *Dinner* 6.30–10, Fri & Sat 6.30–11.30
Closed L Sat

Edinburgh

Town plan A2 Lothian
Queensferry Road *EH4 6AS*
031–339 1144
Telex 727928

Credit Access, Amex,
Barclaycard, Diners

Barnton Hotel   57%   £ D/E

A few miles out of the city on the A90, this Victorian building with modern extensions is popular both with businessmen and tourists. Public areas with contemporary furnishings include a small foyer and three pleasant bars. Up-to-date bedrooms (some reserved for non-smokers) have built-in furniture, tea/coffee-makers and tiled bath or shower rooms.
Amenities dinner dance (Sat), jazz (Sun lunchtime).

Rooms 50	*Room phone* Yes	*Confirm by* 6	*Parking* Ample
with bath/shower 50	*Room TV* Yes	*Last dinner* 10	*Banquets* 100/2

Edinburgh

Town plan B5 Lothian
134 Braid Road *EH10 6JD*
031–447 8888

Credit Access, Amex,
Barclaycard, Diners

Braid Hills Hotel   57% Ⓜ   £ D

There's a homely, old-fashioned air about this friendly Victorian hotel, which stands high on a bank beside the A702 near the Braid Hills golf course. Public rooms include a spacious foyer-lounge, a separate TV lounge and two bars (one of them, the public Buckstone Bar, stands in the grounds). Bedrooms have freestanding furniture of various styles; private bathrooms are well equipped. *Amenities* garden.

Rooms 51	*Room phone* Yes	*Confirm by* By arrang.	*Parking* Ample
with bath/shower 24	*Room TV* Some	*Last dinner* 9	*Banquets* 70/–

FIAT Edinburgh

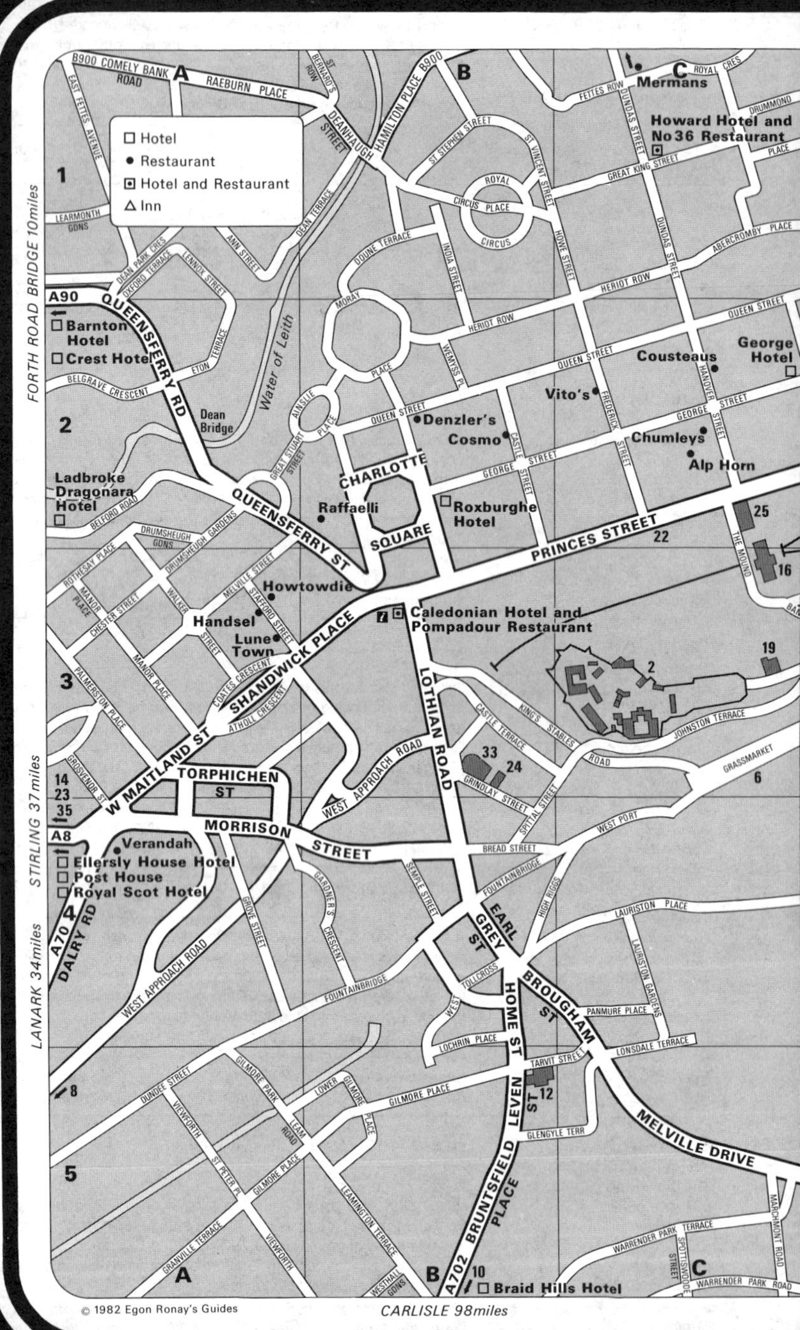

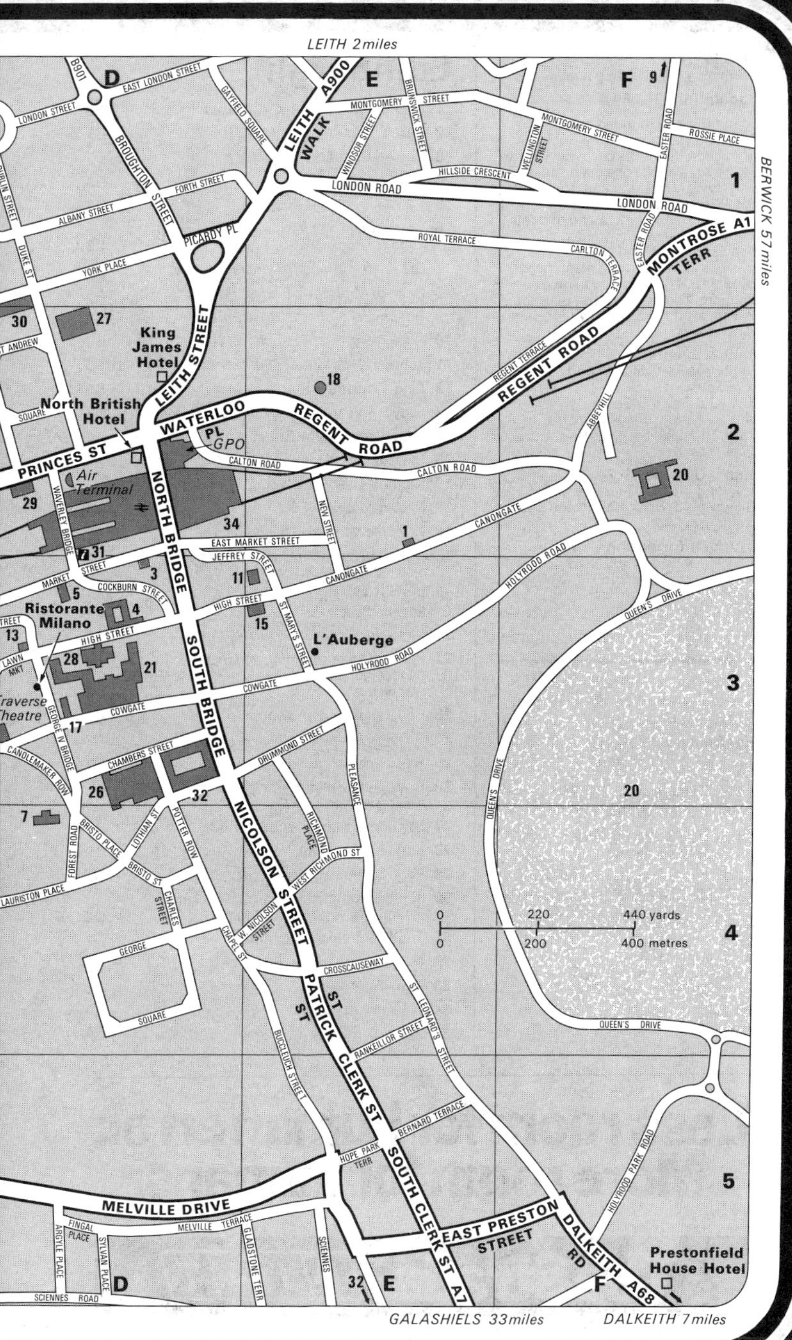

F I A T
LEITH 2 miles
BERWICK 57 miles
B901
D
EAST LONDON STREET
E
LEITH A900
WALK
F
9
LONDON STREET
GAYFIELD SQUARE
MONTGOMERY STREET
BRUNSWICK STREET
MONTGOMERY STREET
EASTER ROAD
ROSSIE PLACE
BROUGHTON STREET
FORTH STREET
WINDSOR STREET
WELLINGTON STREET
HILLSIDE CRESCENT
1
DUBLIN STREET
ALBANY STREET
LONDON ROAD
LONDON ROAD
DUKE ST
PICARDY PL
ROYAL TERRACE
CARLTON TERRACE
EASTER ROAD
MONTROSE A1
TERR
YORK PLACE
30
27
LEITH STREET
King
James
Hotel
REGENT TERRACE
REGENT ROAD
MONTROSE A1
TERR
ST ANDREW
18
North British
Hotel
WATERLOO
REGENT ROAD
2
PL
GPO
ABBEYHILL
PRINCES ST
SQUARE
NORTH BRIDGE
CALTON ROAD
CALTON ROAD
20
Air
Terminal
NEW STREET
CANONGATE
29
WAVERLEY BRIDGE
34
EAST MARKET STREET
1
HOLYROOD ROAD
QUEEN'S DRIVE
7 31
STREET
JEFFREY STREET
CANONGATE
MARKET
3
5
COCKBURN STREET
11
HIGH STREET
15
ST MARY'S STREET
Ristorante
Milano
4
L'Auberge
HOLYROOD ROAD
13
HIGH STREET
28
21
HOLYROOD ROAD
LAWN
MKT
3
Traverse
Theatre
COWGATE
20
17
COWGATE
SOUTH BRIDGE
CANDLEMAKER ROW
CHAMBERS STREET
DRUMMOND STREET
26
PLEASANCE
32
QUEEN'S DRIVE
7
NICOLSON STREET
BRISTO PLACE
POTTER ROW
RICHMOND
PLACE
FOREST ROAD
LOTHIAN ST
WEST RICHMOND ST
BRISTO ST
CHARLES
STREET
LAURISTON PLACE
CHAPEL ST
W. NICOLSON
STREET
440 yards
4
GEORGE
CROSSCAUSEWAY
ST
PATRICK CLERK ST
ST LEONARD'S
STREET
220
400 metres
SQUARE
RANKEILLOR STREET
QUEEN'S DRIVE
5
BUCCLEUCH STREET
BERNARD TERRACE
HOLYROOD PARK ROAD
HOPE PARK
TERR
MELVILLE DRIVE
FINGAL
PLACE
MELVILLE TERRACE
GLADSTONE TERR
SOUTH CLERK ST
EAST PRESTON
DALKEITH
Prestonfield
House Hotel
ARGYLE PLACE
SYLVAN PLACE
STREET
RD
A68
D
SCIENNES
SCIENNES ROAD
GLADSTONE TERR
32
E
CLERK ST A7
F A68
GALASHIELS 33 miles
DALKEITH 7 miles

Map 12 C1
Town plan on preceding page

Population 470,085

Edinburgh was founded about a thousand years ago on the Rock which dominates the city. The narrow Old Town, with its one main street (the Royal Mile stretching from the Castle to Holyroodhouse) is the city of John Knox and Mary Queen of Scots. Its Royal Charter was granted by Robert the Bruce in 1329. The gracious New Town is a magnificent example of 18th-century town planning. Today Edinburgh is a centre of festival and pageantry, culture and conferences.

Annual Events
Edinburgh Festival *21st Aug–10th Sept*
Highland Games *August*
Military Tattoo *19th Aug–10th Sept*
Royal Highland Show *20th–23rd June*

Sights Outside City
Cramond Village, Duddingston Village, Forth Bridge, Lauriston Castle, Craigmillar Castle

Tourist Information Centre
5 Waverley Bridge EH1 1BQ
Telephone 031–226 6591

Fiat Dealers

Croall & Croall
Glenogle Road
Edinburgh EH3 5HW
Tel: Edinburgh 556 6404/9

John Croall & Sons (Motors) Ltd
162 St Johns Road
Corstorphine
Edinburgh EH12 8AZ
Tel: Edinburgh 334 6248

William Swanson
300 Colinton Road
Edinburgh, EH13 0LE
Tel: Edinburgh 441 4567/8

Edinburgh

1	Canongate Tolbooth *City Museum*	E2
2	Castle	C3
3	City Art Centre	D3
4	City Chambers	D3
5	Festival Booking Office	D3
6	Grassmarket *picturesque old buildings and antique shops*	C3
7	Greyfriars Kirk *and Greyfriars Bobby statue*	D4
8	Heart of Midlothian F.C.	A5
9	Hibernian F.C. *Easter Road Park*	F1
10	Hillend *dry ski centre open all year*	B5
11	John Knox's House *1490, timber galleries*	D/E3
12	King's Theatre	B5
13	Lady Stair's House *1692, literary museum*	D3
14	Murrayfield Rugby Ground	A4
15	Museum of Childhood	E3
16	National Gallery *try 'Sound Guide'*	C3
17	National Library	D3
18	Nelson's Monument *viewpoint*	E2
19	Outlook Tower *Camera obscura and Scottish life exhibition*	C3
20	Palace of Holyroodhouse and Arthur's Seat and the Park	F2
21	Parliament House and Law Courts	D3
22	Princes Street *shopping and gardens, bandstand, floral clock, war memorials*	B3/C2/D2
23	Royal Highland Showground	A3
24	Royal Lyceum Theatre	B3
25	Royal Scottish Academy	C2
26	Royal Scottish Museum *largest museum of science and art in U.K.*	D3
27	St Andrew Square Bus Station	D2
28	St Giles' Cathedral	D3
29	Scott Monument *viewpoint*	D2
30	Scottish National Portrait Gallery and National Museum of Antiquities	D2
31	Tourist Information Centre	D2
32	University of Edinburgh	D3
33	Usher Hall	B3
34	Waverley Station	D2
35	Zoo	A3

Edinburgh
Town plan B3 Lothian
Princes Street *EH1 2AB*
031–225 2433
Telex 72179

Credit Access, Amex,
Barclaycard, Diners

Caledonian Hotel   69% **£C**

This imposing, turn-of-the-century railway hotel is undergoing a complete transformation. Public areas are stylishly furnished and relaxing, and some original features like the splendid old staircase have been retained. Bedrooms range from standard ones with pleasant fabrics and bedside controls to luxury suites with sitting areas. Tiled bathrooms are well fitted.
Amenities garden, dinner dance (Fri, Sat), hairdressing

Rooms 212	Room phone Yes	Confirm by 6	Parking Ample
with bath/shower 212	Room TV Yes	Last dinner 10.30	Banquets 220/2

Edinburgh
Town plan B3 Lothian
Princes Street *EH1 2AB*
031–225 2433

Caledonian Hotel, Pompadour Restaurant

This grand restaurant has been refurbished in luxurious style, and there's an air of refinement about much of the cooking. The menu is in two parts, one featuring haute cuisine specialities like sautéed veal and kidney with brandy and wild mushrooms, the other has a Scottish flavour with dishes such as smoked haddock soup and venison in a pickled walnut sauce.
ABOVE AVERAGE. Credit Access, Amex, Barclaycard, Diners

● **Set L** from £12 incl. service
About £40 for two

Lunch 12.30–2.15 *Dinner* 7.30–11, Sat 7.30–12
Closed L Sat & all Sun

Edinburgh
Town plan B2 Lothian
70 Rose Street
North Lane *EH2 3DX*
031–225 3106

Chumleys

Faultless service and light airy decor make eating here a real pleasure. You can compose your meal from a combination of starters like fish mousseline with spinach and smoked venison with Cumberland sauce, or there are more substantial dishes such as tender loin of veal Magyar and roast wild duck with black cherries. Sweets include an unusual banana and avocado terrine.
Credit Access, Amex, Barclaycard, Diners

● **Set L** £5
About £35 for two

Lunch 12.30–2.30 *Dinner* 7–10.30
Closed Sun

Edinburgh
Town plan B2 Lothian
58a North Castle Street *EH2 3LU*
031–226 6743
Proprietor Cosmo Tamburro
Italian cooking
About £28 for two

Cosmo

Flavoursome minestrone makes a tasty start to an acceptably prepared meal of Italian favourites, including home-made pasta. The spacious, quietly elegant setting is a real attraction. *Credit* Access, Barclaycard
Lunch 12.30–2.15 *Dinner* 6.30–10.15
Closed L Sat, all Sun, Mon, 1 January & 25 December

Edinburgh
Town plan C2 Lothian
109 Hanover Street *EH2 1DR*
031–226 3355

Seafood
About £30 for two

Cousteaus

Seafood is well prepared in this coolly decorated basement restaurant. Mussels in various guises are a speciality, and the menu could also offer salmon (smoked or fresh), sole, trout and turbot. Enjoyable desserts, too.
Credit Access, Amex, Barclaycard, Diners
Dinner only 6–12

Edinburgh
Town plan A2 Lothian
Queensferry Road *EH4 3HL*
031–332 2442
Telex 72541

Credit Access, Amex,
Barclaycard, Diners

Crest Hotel   62% **£D**

Wide windows give a pleasant feeling of airiness to this modern hotel above the A90 Queensferry Road. The open-plan foyer/lounge has deep, comfortable sofas and low glass tables, and the relaxing bar looks down grassy slopes to the road. Exposed brickwork features in the bedrooms, which all have built-in furniture, tea/coffee-makers and compact tiled bathrooms.

Rooms 120	Room phone Yes	Confirm by 6	Parking Ample
with bath/shower 120	Room TV Yes	Last dinner 9.45	Banquets 140/2

Edinburgh
Town plan B2 Lothian
80 Queen Street *EH2 4NF*
031–226 5467

About £24 for two
Banquets 40/2

Denzler's   ⑤

A change of ownership has not affected the reliability of the cooking in this bustling restaurant. Swiss specialities like fondues, air-dried meats and veal sausages feature prominently on the regularly changing menu along with dishes such as trout meunière and tender venison in a piquant sauce served with authentic spätzle. Delicious sweets, too. One dining area is reserved for non-smokers. *Credit* Access, Barclaycard   &

Lunch 12–2 *Dinner* 7–10
Closed Sun & Bank Holidays

Edinburgh
Town plan A4 Lothian
Ellersly Road *EH12 6HZ*
031–337 6888
Manager Mr W. F. Wright

Credit Access, Amex,
Barclaycard, Diners

Rooms 58
with bath/shower 58

Ellersly House Hotel   60%   £ D

Set in two acres of grounds in a quiet residential part of the city, this Edwardian building is a pleasant, comfortably appointed hotel. There's a spacious lounge-bar as well as a second bar with a dance floor. Bedrooms range from large and traditionally furnished in the original building to more compact modern ones in the two extensions. Bathrooms are adequately fitted. *Amenities* garden, dancing (Fri–Sun), croquet.   &

Room phone Yes	*Confirm by* 7	*Parking* Ample
Room TV Yes	*Last dinner* 8.45	*Banquets* 100/4

Edinburgh
Town plan C2 Lothian
19 George Street *EH2 2PB*
031–225 1251
Telex 72570

Rooms 198
with bath/shower 198
Room phone Yes
Room TV Yes
Confirm by 6
Last dinner 10
Parking Difficult
Banquets 200/6

Credit Access, Amex,
Barclaycard, Diners

George Hotel   76%   *E*   £ C

Extensive refurbishment has greatly improved this handsome city-centre hotel. The most eye-catching of the splendid public areas is the Carver's Table, a magnificent lofty room with marble-effect pillars, arched windows and pleasant furnishings. There are also two bars (a plush little cocktail bar for residents and the relaxing Clans Bar) as well as superb banqueting facilities. Bedrooms in two wings of the building are spacious, comfortable and attractively furnished, and some have fine views of Edinburgh. Bathrooms are compact, modern and well fitted. Smart, uniformed staff provide polite and helpful service.   &

Edinburgh
Town plan A3 Lothian
22 Stafford Street *EH3 7BD*
031–225 5521

●**Set L** £4·25
About £30 for two
Banquets 60/40

Handsel   ♛ ⑤

On the first floor of a refurbished terrace house, this elegant Georgian dining room is impeccably laid out. The extensive menu features popular dishes like beef Stroganoff and chicken cacciatore along with grills, fresh seafood and flambéed specialities. Vegetables are nicely seasoned and there are familiar sweets like pineapple gâteau on the trolley.
Credit Access, Amex, Barclaycard, Diners

Lunch 12.30–2.30 *Dinner* 6.30–10
Closed L Sat, all Sun & Bank Holidays

Edinburgh
Town plan C1 Lothian
36 Great King Street *EH3 6QH*
031–556 1393
Telex 727887

Credit Access, Amex,
Barclaycard, Diners

Rooms 26
with bath/shower 26

Howard Hotel   59%   £ D

Set in an elegant Georgian terrace, this hotel has smartly refurbished public rooms, including a cosy lounge and an attractive cocktail bar; there's also the popular Claret Jug Bar with a separate entrance. Sizeable bedrooms have either functional modern furniture or solid Edwardian pieces. Planned refurbishment of the bedrooms will improve the overall standard of the hotel. *Amenities* garden.   &

Room phone Yes	*Confirm by* 6	*Parking* Limited
Room TV Yes	*Last dinner* 9.30	*Banquets* 50/–

Edinburgh

Town plan C1 Lothian
36 Great King Street *EH3 6QH*
031–556 1393

About £25 for two

Howard Hotel, No. 36 Restaurant ♕

Flowers, candles and portraits give this dining room an elegant atmosphere. The menu features a wide choice of reliably prepared, uncomplicated dishes based on good-quality raw materials. *Credit* Access, Amex, Barclaycard, Diners *Lunch* 12–2 *Dinner* 7–9.30 **Closed** L Sat & Sun, D 25 Dec & all 31 Dec & 1 Jan ● **Set L** from £4·90 **Set D** from £7·50 *Banquets* 50/– &

Edinburgh

Town plan A3 Lothian
27a Stafford Street *EH3 7BJ*
031–225 6291

● **Set L & Set D** from £8·75
About £48 for two
Banquets 40/–

Howtowdie ♕ Ⓢ

A really civilised atmosphere pervades this intimate basement restaurant, where local produce is used to good effect. Dishes range from traditional cullen skink (Finnan haddock soup) to poached salmon and roast pheasant in apricot sauce, while colourful petits fours and excellent coffee round off a meal with a flourish. Cooking is generally acceptable, although there may be occasional lapses. *Credit* Access, Amex, Barclaycard, Diners

Lunch 12–2.30 *Dinner* 7–11
Closed Sun, 1 & 2 January & 25 & 26 December

Edinburgh

Town plan D2 Lothian
St James Centre
Leith Street *EH1 3SW*
031–556 0111
Telex 727200
Credit Access, Amex,
Barclaycard, Diners

Rooms 161
with bath/shower 161

King James Hotel   62%   £ C/D

A modern concrete and glass building in the heart of the city. Public rooms on the third floor include two plush bars which also serve as lounges. Double-glazed bedrooms have modern built-in units, good writing space and tea-makers, as well as fully tiled bath or shower roor..s Very friendly, helpful staff. Extensive refurbishment is planned.
Amenities dancing (Tues–Sat), discothèque (nightly).

Room phone Yes	*Confirm by* 6	*Parking* Ample
Room TV Yes	*Last dinner* 10	*Banquets* 230/6

Edinburgh

Town plan A2 Lothian
69 Belford Road *EH4 3DG*
031–332 2545
Telex 727979

Rooms 146
with bath/shower 146
Room phone Yes
Room TV Yes
Confirm by 6
Last dinner 10.30
Parking Ample
Banquets 250/2

Credit Access, Amex,
Barclaycard, Diners

Ladbroke Dragonara Hotel   75%   *E*   £ B

Flanked by the Water of Leith and conveniently close to Princes Street, this modern hotel in prime condition is a useful base for businessmen and visitors to the city. Apart from the comfortable foyer-lounge, public areas are open-plan, and decor is quite stylish, with plush upholstery, good lighting and large picture windows; there's also a rustic public bar in an adjoining 17th-century building. Bedrooms (including 32 superior Gold Star rooms) are well equipped, with good-quality furniture, plenty of writing space, bedside controls and tea-making facilities. Compact bathrooms are nicely planned. Staff are very pleasant.
Amenities garden. &

Edinburgh

Town plan A3 Lothian
38 William Street *EH3 7LJ*
031–225 9388

Chinese cooking

● **Set L & Set D** from £5·20
About £20 for two
Banquets 12/–

Lune Town ♧

The presence of chef-proprietor Mr Liu ensures that high standards are maintained at this unassuming Chinese restaurant. A good range of authentic Cantonese dishes, expertly prepared from first-class ingredients, includes various dim sum, exceptionally delectable crispy beef, and duck in a tasty sauce with lightly cooked vegetables and pineapple. Jasmin tea makes a refreshing accompaniment. *Credit* Access, Amex, Barclaycard, Diners

Meals noon–2.30pm & 6pm–12.30am, Sat 2pm–1.30am, Sun 4pm–midnight. **Closed** Chinese New Year

Edinburgh
Town plan C1 Lothian
8 Eyre Place *EH3 5EP*
031–556 1177

About £24 for two

Mermans   ♧ ⑤

A tiny little restaurant with colourful modern decor. The set dinner menu includes a fish and a meat course (with interesting vegetables), plus starters and sweets. Skilful, enthusiastic cooking.
Credit Access, Amex, Barclaycard, Diners
Dinner only 7–10.30 **Closed** Sun & Bank Holidays ● **Set D** £7·50

Edinburgh
Town plan D2 Lothian
Princes Street *EH2 2EQ*
031–556 2414
Telex 72332

Credit Access, Amex,
Barclaycard, Diners

Rooms 193
with bath/shower 171

North British Hotel   67%   £ D

This massive railway hotel with a prominent clock tower stands next to Waverley Station overlooking Princes Street. The reception area and lofty central lounge have modern furnishings, and there are some handsome banqueting rooms and a choice of three bars. Bedrooms with built-in units are bright and roomy, and private bathrooms are up to date. Courteous helpful staff. *Amenities* hairdressing, beauty salon.

Room phone Yes	*Confirm by* 6	*Parking* Difficult
Room TV Yes	*Last dinner* 10.30	*Banquets* 430/–

Edinburgh
Town plan A4 Lothian
Corstorphine Road *EH12 6UA*
031–334 8221
Telex 727103

Credit Access, Amex,
Barclaycard, Diners

Rooms 208
with bath/shower 208

Post House Hotel   59%   £ C/D

There are uninterrupted views of the city from this well-maintained modern hotel situated next to the zoo. Public rooms, which are pleasantly decorated in contemporary style, include a comfortable lounge and two popular bars. Refurbished bedrooms have soft colour schemes, attractive built-in units, tea-makers and mini-bars. Up-to-date bathrooms are functionally equipped. *Amenities* coffee shop (noon–10pm).   &

Room phone Yes	*Confirm by* 6	*Parking* Ample
Room TV Yes	*Last dinner* 10	*Banquets* 100/10

Edinburgh
Town plan F5 Lothian
Priestfield Road *EH16 5UT*
031–667 8000
Telex 727396
Manager Mr G. Fabbroni
Credit Access, Amex,
Barclaycard, Diners

Rooms 5
with bath/shower None

Prestonfield House Hotel   60%   £ C/D

Designed by the architect of Holyroodhouse, this historic 17th-century building set in 23 acres of grounds retains many original features including marble floors, enormous tapestries, ornate ceilings and antique furniture, especially in its public rooms. Bedrooms (two with shower cubicles) are comfortably furnished in keeping with the rest of the hotel, and public bathrooms are well equipped. *Amenities* garden.

Room phone Yes	*Confirm by* By arrang.	*Parking* Ample
Room TV No	*Last dinner* 10	*Banquets* 500/2

Edinburgh
Town plan B2 Lothian
10 Randolph Place *EH3 7TA*
031–225 6060

Italian cooking

About £26 for two
Banquets 60/35

Raffaelli   ♔ ⑤

This stylishly decorated restaurant makes a pleasing setting for some very capable Italian cooking. The menu has a good choice of dishes including enjoyable al dente pasta and an outstanding osso bucho. Interesting vegetables are well prepared and sweets such as creamy chocolate mousse and home-made lemon cheesecake are truly delicious. Service is alert and helpful. *Credit* Access, Amex, Barclaycard, Diners   &

Meals noon–9pm, Sat 6pm–11pm
Closed L Sat, all Sun & Bank Holidays

Edinburgh
Town plan D3 Lothian
7 Victoria Street *EH1 2HE*
031–226 5260
Proprietor Mr Giuseppe Ferrari
Italian cooking

About £28 for two

Ristorante Milano   ⑤

Reliable cooking is the hallmark of this large, nicely appointed restaurant. The menu offers a wide choice of Italian dishes: fresh soups, well-cooked pasta, tender veal (ours was served with a tasty Marsala sauce) and vegetables such as excellent, crispy fried zucchini. Home-made sweets include a deliciously light chocolate roll. Friendly attentive service.
Credit Amex, Barclaycard, Diners   &

Lunch 12–3 *Dinners* 6.30–11
Closed Sun & Bank Holidays

Edinburgh

Town plan B2 Lothian
38 Charlotte Square *EH2 4HG*
031–225 3921
Telex 727054
Manager Mr Donald A. Addison
Credit Access, Amex,
Barclaycard, Diners

Roxburghe Hotel   66%   £C

Improvements continue at this handsome hotel in an Adam-designed square just off Princes Street. The foyer and lounge are elegant and spacious, and there's a bright, comfortable buttery and a plush bar. Some bedrooms, including two suites, boast fine traditional furnishings, while others, more modern in style, have practical fitted units. Up-to-date bathrooms are well equipped. *Amenities* buttery (10am–6pm Mon–Sat). &

Rooms 72	*Room phone* Yes	*Confirm by* 4	*Parking* Difficult
with bath/shower 61	*Room TV* Yes	*Last dinner* 10.30	*Banquets* 200/4

Edinburgh

Town plan A4 Lothian
111 Glasgow Road *EH12 8NF*
031–334 9191
Telex 727197

Credit Access, Amex,
Barclaycard, Diners

Royal Scot Hotel   65%   £D

Improvements continue at this well-maintained modern hotel five miles out of the city centre on the Glasgow Road. Public areas include a spacious foyer and two bars, as well as extensive banqueting facilities. Bedrooms vary in size, all being comfortably equipped, and bathrooms are spotlessly clean. *Amenities* garden, sauna, dinner dance (Fri, Sat), hairdressing, coffee shop (7.30am–10pm) &

Rooms 254	*Room phone* Yes	*Confirm by* 6	*Parking* Ample
with bath/shower 254	*Room TV* Yes	*Last dinner* 10.30	*Banquets* 220/2

Edinburgh

Town plan A4 Lothian
17 Dalry Road *EH11 2BQ*
031–337 5828
Bangladeshi cooking

About £23 for two

Verandah   Ⓢ

Waiters in richly embroidered waistcoats serve well-prepared spicy Bangladeshi and North Indian dishes, such as tandoori chicken and lamb pasanda, in this pleasantly furnished restaurant. Try the home-made almond ice cream to finish. *Credit* Access, Amex, Barclaycard, Diners *Lunch* 12–2.15 *Dinner* 5–11.45 ● **Set L & Set D** from £7·10 &

Edinburgh

Town plan C2 Lothian
55 Frederick Street *EH2 1LH*
031–225 5052
Proprietor Mr Vito Crolla
Italian cooking
About £28 for two

Vito's   Ⓢ

A lively, colourful basement restaurant where you'll enjoy well-cooked Italian favourites like home-made pizza and fettuccine, ravioli in a smooth cream sauce and tender, tasty saltimbocca. Cheerful service.
Credit Amex, Barclaycard
Lunch 12–2.30 *Dinner* 6.30–11 **Closed** Sun, 1 & 2 Jan & 25 & 26 Dec

Ellon

Map 16 D3 Grampian
AB4 9NP
Ellon (0358) 20666
Telex 739200

Credit Access, Amex,
Barclaycard, Diners

Ladbroke Mercury Motor Inn   57%   £C/D

Popular with businessmen, this low, modern hotel overlooking the river Ythan offers a good range of comfortable, up-to-date accommodation. Simply decorated bedrooms have practical furniture providing plenty of storage and writing space, colour TVs, radios and well-equipped tiled bathrooms. Discreetly contemporary public areas include an open-plan reception-lounge, and three bars. *Amenities* games room. &

Rooms 40	*Room phone* Yes	*Confirm by* 6	*Parking* Ample
with bath/shower 40	*Room TV* Yes	*Last dinner* 9.30	*Banquets* 180/10

Erskine

Map 12 B1 Strathclyde
Near Glasgow *PA8 6AN*
041–812 0123
Telex 777713

Credit Access, Amex,
Barclaycard, Diners

Crest Hotel   65%   £D

Combining a peaceful setting overlooking the Clyde with easy access to the airport, this well-run modern hotel is popular with business people and tourists alike. A feeling of pleasant spaciousness extends from the foyer, bars and conference rooms to the practically furnished, well-equipped bedrooms, all with smart tiled bathrooms. *Amenities* garden, dinner dance (Sat), coffee shop (noon–9pm), games room. &

Rooms 200	*Room phone* Yes	*Confirm by* By arrang.	*Parking* Ample
with bath/shower 200	*Room TV* Yes	*Last dinner* 10	*Banquets* 150/10

Falkirk

Map 12 C1 Central
Kemper Avenue *FK1 1UF*
Falkirk (0324) 27421

Proprietor Mr W. L. Reid
Credit Access, Amex,
Barclaycard, Diners

| *Rooms* 33 | | | |
| *with bath/shower* 33 | | | |

Hotel Cladhan 55% Ⓜ £ E

This low modern hotel lies within easy reach of the town centre. Open-plan public areas, which include a pleasant bar-lounge, are cheerful and well kept, and there is a large function suite. Good-sized bedrooms have sensibly planned fitted units, trouser presses and well-equipped, carpeted private bathrooms. All rooms are double-glazed.
Amenities dinner dance (Sat), discothèque (Sun).

Room phone Yes	*Confirm by* By arrang.	*Parking* Ample
Room TV Yes	*Last dinner* 9.15	*Banquets* 200/50

Fochabers

Map 16 C3 Grampian
High Street *IV32 7DH*
Fochabers (0343) 820508
Proprietor Mr C. Pearn

Credit Access, Amex,
Barclaycard, Diners

Rooms 13
with bath/shower 8

Gordon Arms Hotel 56% Ⓜ £ D/E

A popular base for sporting holidays, this well-maintained, whitewashed hotel stands on the edge of town on the A96 Aberdeen–Inverness road. Comfortable, relaxing public rooms include a bar-lounge with plenty of settees and wheelback chairs. Bedrooms have simple built-in units, colour TVs, and tea/coffee-makers. Plain but adequate bathrooms.
Amenities garden. &

Room phone Yes	*Confirm by* 6	*Parking* Ample
Room TV Yes	*Last dinner* 9	*Banquets* 100/10

Fochabers

Map 16 C3 Grampian
High Street *IV32 7DH*
Fochabers (0343) 820508
Proprietor Mr C. Pearn

About £28 for two

Gordon Arms Hotel Restaurant

Trout, salmon, lobster and steaks are popular choices at this simply furnished restaurant, along with home-made soups, pâtés and tasty sweets. Capable, reliable cooking. Restricted winter menu. *Credit* Access, Amex, Barclaycard, Diners *Lunch* 12.30–2.15 *Dinner* 7.30–9.15 **Closed** 1 January
● **Set L** £3·50 **Set D** winter only £7·50 &

Forfar

Map 17 C4 Tayside
Castle Street *DD8 3AE*
Forfar (0307) 62691

Credit Diners

Rooms 15
with bath/shower 7

Royal Hotel 59% Ⓜ £ E

Recent improvements have turned this former coaching inn into a smart, comfortable little hotel. The panelled reception and cosy residents' lounge bar are on the first floor, while two more bars at street level include the stylish new Royal, with green baize walls and plush red seating. Bright, compact bedrooms have well-designed fitted units; bathrooms are neat and modern.
Amenities discothèque (Fri, Sat).

Room phone Some	*Confirm by* 7	*Parking* Ample
Room TV Some	*Last dinner* 9	*Banquets* 170/2

Fort William

Map 17 B4 Highland
Torlundy *PH33 6SN*
Fort William (0397) 2177

Proprietors Mr & Mrs Hobbs
Rooms 13
with bath/shower 13
Room phone Yes
Room TV Yes
Confirm by 4
Last dinner 8
Parking Ample
Closed November–March

Credit Access, Barclaycard

Inverlochy Castle 92% Ⓜ £ A

It is no wonder that this splendid 19th-century castle has gained an enviable international reputation, with its glorious grounds beneath Ben Nevis, its superb furnishings and its faultless service. The stately public rooms are most beautifully decorated especially the entrance hall graced by a lovely Italian painted ceiling and crystal chandeliers. Bedrooms are large and exquisitely fitted with tastefully chosen colour schemes and fabrics. Fully carpeted bathrooms have excellent modern fittings, and there are also two lavishly appointed suites. Mrs Hobbs and her marvellous staff ensure a delightful atmosphere of family intimacy. No dogs. *Amenities* garden, tennis, game fishing, billiards.

Fort William
Map 17 B4 Highland
Torlundy *PH33 6SN*
Fort William (0397) 2177
Proprietors Mr & Mrs Hobbs

● **Set D** £21
About £56 for two

Inverlochy Castle Restaurant ★  

Book early and discuss your meal in advance, as this beautifully appointed restaurant with only a few tables has no menu, and specialities vary with the seasons. The new young chef is experienced, has finesse and also a capacity to gain still-higher gradings. Our meal had some really outstanding features, like sole mousse wrapped with thin slices of salmon and garnished with lobster coral, as well as the most tender fillet steak au poivre and lamb cutlets. There were highlights, too, among the sweets, such as delicately flavoured orange soufflé and wonderful crème brûlée with raspberries. Light lunches. Service is formal but friendly.
♟ *OUTSTANDING. Credit* Access, Barclaycard

Lunch 12–2 *Dinner* 8–9
Closed November–March

Fort William
Map 17 B4 Highland
Achintore Road *PH33 6RW*
Fort William (0397) 3117

Credit Access, Amex,
Barclaycard, Diners
Closed 2 weeks Christmas

Ladbroke Mercury Motor Inn   56%   £ C/D

Separated from Loch Linnhe by the busy main road, this modern hotel offers a cheerful welcome, fine views and adequate accommodation. The open-plan public area, pleasantly decorated in browns and creams, has comfortable tweedy chairs and picture windows that overlook the loch and mountains. Simply decorated bedrooms, some of them quite small, are equipped with tea-makers. Functional bathrooms. *Amenities* garden, sauna.

Rooms 61	*Room phone* Most	*Confirm by* 6	*Parking* Ample
with bath/shower 61	*Room TV* Yes	*Last dinner* 9.30	*Banquets* 150/10

Fortingall
Map 17 C5 Tayside
By Aberfeldy *PH15 2NQ*
Kenmore (088 73) 367
Proprietors
Michael & Maureen Turner

● **Set L** £4·95 **Set D** £10·95
incl. service
About £27 for two

Fortingall Hotel Restaurant   ♟ ♕ Ⓢ

Maureen Turner does the cooking in this welcoming hotel restaurant, and offers a five-course set dinner menu (no choice except last course). Appetisers like mushroom vol-au-vent are followed by soup, fish, a main course such as sautéed chicken provençale and delicious sweets. There's also a Victorian gastronomic extravaganza on Saturday evenings. Lighter lunches. Booking advisable. *Credit* Access, Amex, Barclaycard

Lunch 12.30–1.45 *Dinner* at 7.30
Closed end October–early April

Gairloch
Map 16 B3 Highland
IV21 2BL
Gairloch (0445) 2001
Manager Mr G. Lagermans
Credit Access, Amex,
Barclaycard, Diners
Closed 1 October–1 May

Gairloch Hotel   58%   £ D

With its location overlooking Gair Loch and its sporting facilities, this rugged greystone hotel is a popular holiday base. The lounge areas have a traditional, comfortable elegance, and there's a cosy little cocktail bar. Prettily decorated, practically furnished bedrooms include large front ones with fine sea views; bathrooms are adequate. *Amenities* garden, sauna, tennis, game & sea fishing, solarium, board sailing.   ♿

Rooms 50	*Room phone* No	*Confirm by* 6	*Parking* Ample
with bath/shower 46	*Room TV* No	*Last dinner* 9	*Banquets* 120/–

Gairloch
Map 16 B3 Highland
IV21 2AW
Badachro (044 583) 250

Credit Access, Barclaycard
Closed end October–Easter

Shieldaig Lodge Hotel   55%   £ D/E

Peace and tranquillity reign at this former shooting lodge, which enjoys a lovely secluded position on the shores of Loch Shieldaig. Public rooms are spacious and comfortable, the lounges being equipped with attractive traditional pieces. Bedrooms vary from large with sturdy antiques, to smaller and more modestly furnished. Modern bathrooms are well maintained. *Amenities* garden, tennis, game fishing, stalking, hotel boat.

Rooms 15	*Room phone* No	*Confirm by* By arrang.	*Parking* Ample
with bath/shower 3	*Room TV* No	*Last dinner* 8	*Banquets* 40/2

Garve
Map 16 B3 Highland
IV23 2PH
Aultguish (099 75) 269

Inchbae Lodge   58%   Ⓜ   £F

Built as a shooting lodge about 100 years ago, this pleasant hotel on the road to Ullapool is surrounded by craggy hills and forests, with the rushing river Black Water at the bottom of the garden. There are plenty of deep sofas and armchairs in the cosy bar and lounge, and bedrooms, furnished in a simple, modern style, offer homely comforts. Some are in a chalet-type annexe. *Amenities* garden, game fishing.

Rooms 12	*Room phone* No	*Confirm by* By arrang.	*Parking* Ample
with bath/shower 9	*Room TV* No	*Last dinner* 7.30	*Banquets* 50/10

Garve
Map 16 B3 Highland
IV23 2PU
Garve (099 74) 204

Proprietors Mr & Mrs Parke

Closed 1 October–1 May

Strathgarve Lodge   62%   Ⓜ   £D

Mr and Mrs Parke take great pride in their splendid Highland lodge, which stands in 100 acres of its own delightful grounds, with sporting rights over thousands more. There's a feeling of warmth and homeliness about the spotless public rooms, which include an elegant drawing room and a handsome panelled bar. Bedrooms, too, offer solid, traditional comforts. *Amenities* garden, game fishing, putting, sailing, fishing boats.

Rooms 17	*Room phone* No	*Confirm by* By arrang.	*Parking* Ample
with bath/shower 11	*Room TV* No	*Last dinner* 8.30	

Gatehouse of Fleet
Map 13 B4 Dumfries & Galloway
DG7 2DL
Gatehouse of Fleet
(055 74) 341

Cally Palace Hotel   65%   £E

New owners have made substantial improvements to this splendid Regency house set in 100 acres of parkland. Magnificent public rooms all have newly restored plaster ceilings, while bedrooms are spacious, comfortably furnished and provided with tea-makers. Well-fitted bathrooms. *Amenities* garden, sauna, outdoor swimming pool, game fishing, tennis, dancing (Sat), putting, croquet, rowing boats, nursery, children's playground, games room.

Rooms 60	*Room phone* Yes	*Confirm by* By arrang.	*Parking* Ample
with bath/shower 60	*Room TV* Yes	*Last dinner* 9.30	*Banquets* 120/–

Gatehouse of Fleet
Map 13 B4 Dumfries & Galloway
DG7 2HY
Gatehouse of Fleet
(055 74) 207
Manager Mr R. Raphael
Credit Access, Amex,
Barclaycard, Diners

Murray Arms Hotel   58%   £E

This friendly white-painted posting house is a pleasing blend of old and new. Public rooms include two cosy bars and four cottage lounges (one with TV). Bedrooms (including some family rooms in the annexe across the road) have either traditional or fitted furniture. Neat, compact bathrooms. *Amenities* garden, tennis, rough shooting, 9-hole golf course, clock golf, game & sea fishing, croquet, coffee shop (10am–5pm Easter–Oct).

Rooms 20	*Room phone* Yes	*Confirm by* By arrang.	*Parking* Ample
with bath/shower 16	*Room TV* Most	*Last dinner* 8.45	

Giffnock
Map 12 B2 Strathclyde
Eastwood Toll *G46 6RA*
041–638 2225
Telex 779138
Manager Mr J. Magennis
Credit Access, Amex,
Barclaycard, Diners

Macdonald Hotel   60%   £D

Thanks to dedicated, long-serving staff, this busy hotel with popular function facilities has a well-managed air. Public areas have attractive warm decor, and this extends to the comfortable bedrooms, which are provided with plenty of wardrobe space and tea/coffee-makers; there's also a luxurious suite with handsome yew furniture. Good bathrooms are tiled. *Amenities* dancing (Sat).

Rooms 59	*Room phone* Yes	*Confirm by* 6.30	*Parking* Ample
with bath/shower 59	*Room TV* Yes	*Last dinner* 10	*Banquets* 220/–

Glamis
Map 17 C5 Tayside
DD8 1RS
Glamis (0307 84) 248
Managers
Mr & Mrs R. B. McMillen
About £18 for two

Strathmore Arms   Ⓢ

A pleasant, efficiently run pub dining room where the lunch menu features a tempting cold buffet and acceptably cooked dishes like country casserole and veal escalope. More elaborate dinner menu. *Credit* Amex, Diners
Lunch 12.30–2 *Dinner* 7.30–9
Closed Sun ● **Set L** £4·50 *Banquets* 80/10

Tasty inside, Toasty outside

Make anyday a Findus Crispy Pancake Day

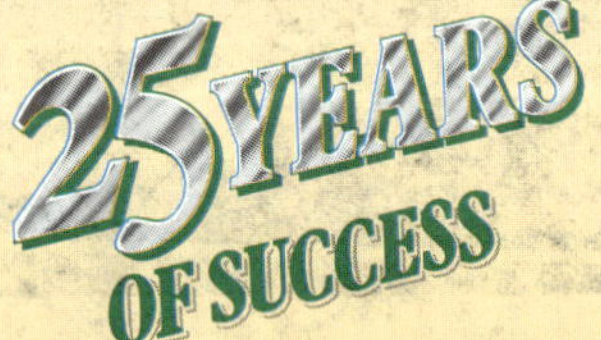

Glasgow

Town plan B3 Strathclyde
Bothwell Street *G2 7EN*
041–248 2656
Telex 77440

Rooms 248
with bath/shower 248
Room phone Yes
Room TV Yes
Confirm by 6
Last dinner 11
Parking Ample
Banquets 750/7

Credit Access, Amex,
Barclaycard, Diners

Albany Hotel   72%   *E*   £ B/C

Definitely designed with the executive in mind, this tall modern hotel boasts a comprehensively equipped new business centre. A spacious, marble-floored foyer leads to the intimate lounge and bar area, where smart furnishings and spotlights create a sophisticated atmosphere. The Norwegian-style Cabin Bar, in contrast, is much more informal in style, and there's also a small TV lounge with tweedy sofas. Really comfortable bedrooms have restful colour schemes and practical built-in furniture, as well as tea-makers and adjustable air conditioning. Fully tiled bathrooms are well fitted. No dogs. *Amenities* dancing (Sat).

Glasgow

Town plan B3 Strathclyde
Bothwell Street *G2 7EN*
041–248 2656

● **Set L** £9·95 **Set D** £11·75
About £40 for two

Albany Hotel, Four Seasons Restaurant   Ⓢ

Vibrant colour schemes and velvet seating give this modern restaurant a warm, elegant atmosphere. The set menus offer well-known favourites and French-inspired dishes like medallions of beef in a cream and brandy sauce, plus seasonal Scottish specialities such as Arbroath smokies, roast saddle of hare and gamekeeper's pie. Sweets are carefully prepared.
Credit Access, Amex, Barclaycard, Diners   ♿

Lunch 12.30–2.30 *Dinner* 7–11
Closed L Sat, all Sun & Bank Holidays except 25 December

Glasgow

Town plan A5 Strathclyde
517 Paisley Road West *G51 1RW*
041–427 3146
Telex 778795
Manager Mr J. N. Griffin
Credit Access, Amex,
Barclaycard, Diners

Bellahouston Hotel   60%   £ D/E

Friendly, helpful reception staff create an excellent first impression at this well-run modern hotel, which stands near the M8 to the south-west of the city. Apart from the pleasant foyer, which has a small seating area, there's also a lounge, a cocktail bar and several conference and banqueting rooms. Neat, tidy bedrooms have smart fitted units, TVs, radios, tea-makers and adequate bathrooms.   ♿

Rooms 122	*Room phone* Yes	*Confirm by* 6	*Parking* Ample
with bath/shower 122	*Room TV* Yes	*Last dinner* 9.30	*Banquets* 275/10

Glasgow

Town plan C3 Strathclyde
Gordon Street *G1 3SP*
041–221 9680
Telex 777771

Credit Access, Amex,
Barclaycard, Diners

Central Hotel   66%   £ D

This massive 19th-century hotel by Central Station has retained much of its Victorian appeal, with its lofty ceilings and marble colonnades. There's a splendid staircase in the foyer and the comfortable cocktail bar smartly combines old and new. Spacious bedrooms have traditional furniture, many with bright contemporary colour schemes. Adequate bathrooms.
Amenities hairdressing.   ♿

Rooms 211	*Room phone* Yes	*Confirm by* 6	*Parking* Difficult
with bath/shower 173	*Room TV* Yes	*Last dinner* 10.30	*Banquets* 700/–

Glasgow

Town plan B4 Strathclyde
377 Argyle Street *G2 8LL*
041–248 2355
Telex 779652
Credit Access, Amex,
Barclaycard, Diners
Closed 1 week Christmas

Centre Hotel   56%   £ D

Admirably fulfilling its chief role as an overnight stop for businessmen, this cheerful, well-maintained hotel stands in an office-block development near Central Station. A public bar leads off the welcoming foyer, while upstairs there's another bar and restful lounge. Neat, tidy bedrooms have practical built-in units, tea/coffee-making facilities, trouser presses and smart tiled bathrooms.

Rooms 123	*Room phone* Yes	*Confirm by* 6	*Parking* Difficult
with bath/shower 123	*Room TV* Yes	*Last dinner* 9.30	*Banquets* 100/20

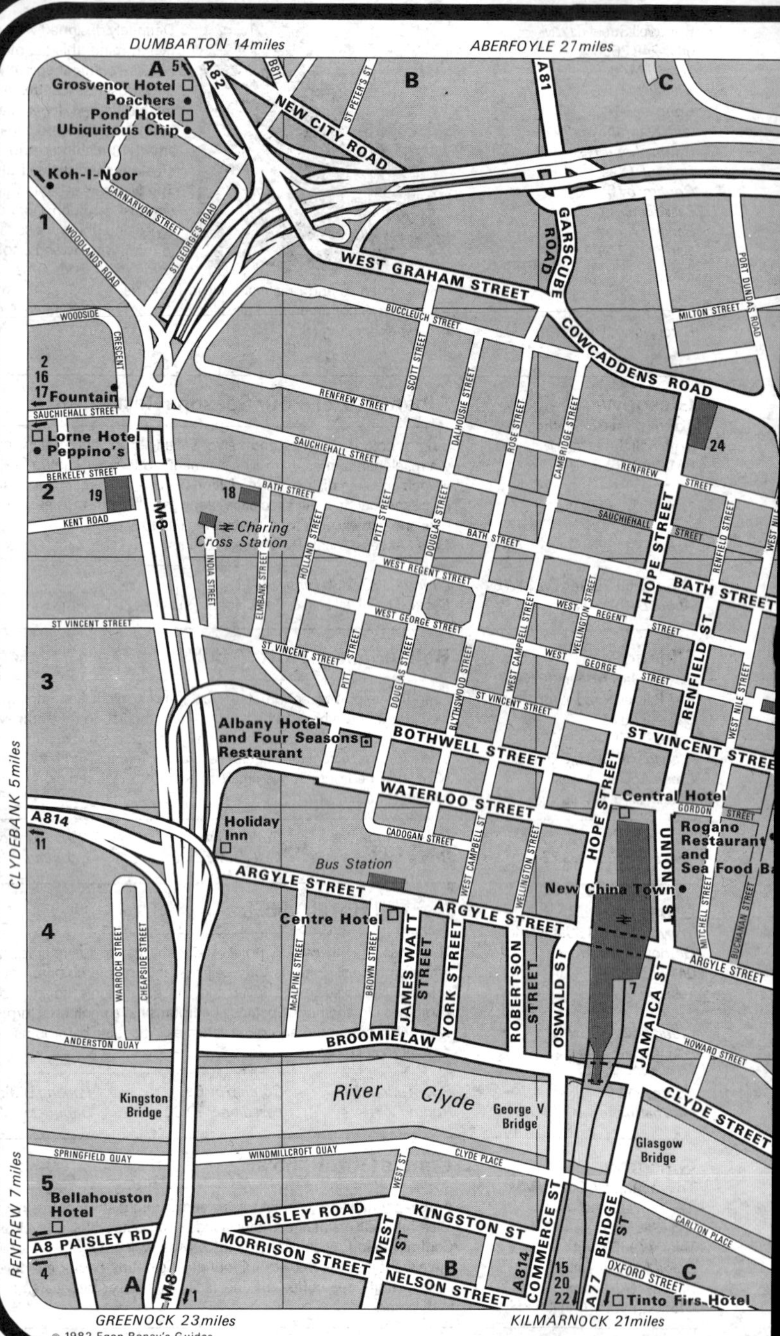
LANCIA
Glasgow
DUMBARTON 14 miles
ABERFOYLE 27 miles
A
B
C
Grosvenor Hotel
Poachers
Pond Hotel
Ubiquitous Chip
Koh-I-Noor
NEW CITY ROAD
ST PETERS ST
A82
A81
GARSCUBE ROAD
PORT DUNDAS ROAD
WEST GRAHAM STREET
COWCADDENS ROAD
WOODLANDS ROAD
CARNARVON STREET
ST GEORGES ROAD
WOODSIDE
CRESCENT
BUCCLEUCH STREET
MILTON STREET
Fountain
RENFREW STREET
SCOTT STREET
DALHOUSIE STREET
ROSE STREET
CAMBRIDGE STREET
RENFREW STREET
SAUCHIEHALL STREET
SAUCHIEHALL STREET
SAUCHIEHALL STREET
24
Lorne Hotel
Peppino's
BERKELEY STREET
BATH STREET
BATH STREET
HOPE STREET
BATH STREET
RENFIELD STREET
WEST NILE
19
18
KENT ROAD
HOLLAND STREET
PITT STREET
DOUGLAS STREET
Charing
Cross Station
WEST REGENT STREET
M8
ELMBANK STREET
WEST GEORGE STREET
WEST
WELLINGTON
REGENT
STREET
ST VINCENT STREET
INDIA STREET
WEST
GEORGE
STREET
ST VINCENT STREET
ST VINCENT STREET
PITT STREET
DOUGLAS STREET
BLYTHSWOOD STREET
WEST CAMPBELL STREET
ST VINCENT STREET
RENFIELD ST
WEST NILE ST
Albany Hotel
and Four Seasons
Restaurant
BOTHWELL STREET
ST VINCENT STREET
CLYDEBANK 5 miles
WATERLOO STREET
Central Hotel
GORDON
STREET
A814
Holiday
Inn
CADOGAN STREET
WEST CAMPBELL ST
WELLINGTON STREET
HOPE STREET
Rogano
Restaurant
and
Sea Food Bar
11
Bus Station
ARGYLE STREET
New China Town
MITCHELL STREET
BUCHANAN STREET
ARGYLE STREET
Centre Hotel
McALPINE STREET
BROWN STREET
JAMES WATT STREET
YORK STREET
ROBERTSON STREET
OSWALD STREET
JAMAICA ST
ARGYLE STREET
WARROCH STREET
CHEAPSIDE STREET
BROOMIELAW
HOWARD STREET
ANDERSTON QUAY
River   Clyde
George V
Bridge
CLYDE STREET
Kingston
Bridge
Glasgow
Bridge
RENFREW 7 miles
SPRINGFIELD QUAY
WINDMILLCROFT QUAY
CLYDE PLACE
Bellahouston
Hotel
WEST ST
KINGSTON ST
BRIDGE ST
CARLTON PLACE
A8 PAISLEY RD
PAISLEY ROAD
COMMERCE ST
OXFORD STREET
MORRISON STREET
WEST ST
A814
A77
15
20
22
M8
NELSON STREET
B
Tinto Firs Hotel
A
C
GREENOCK 23 miles
KILMARNOCK 21 miles
© 1982 Egon Ronay's Guides

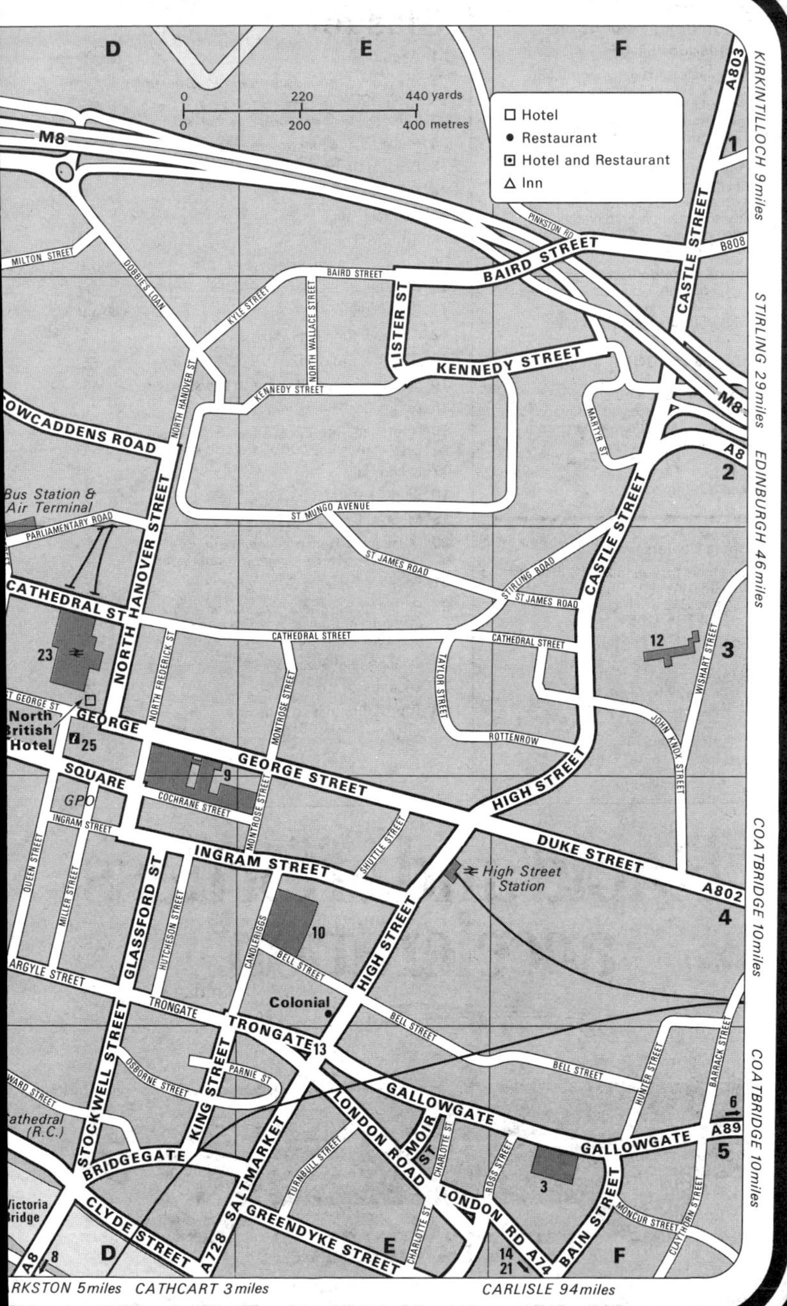

LANCIA
KIRKINTILLOCH 9miles
STIRLING 29miles
EDINBURGH 46miles
COATBRIDGE 10miles
COATBRIDGE 10miles
RKSTON 5miles   CATHCART 3miles
CARLISLE 94miles
Hotel
Restaurant
Hotel and Restaurant
Inn
0   220   440 yards
0   200   400 metres
D
E
F
1
2
3
4
5
6
M8
A803
B808
A8
M8
A8
A802
A89
A728
A74
MILTON STREET
DOBBIE'S LOAN
OWCADDENS ROAD
Bus Station & Air Terminal
PARLIAMENTARY ROAD
NORTH HANOVER STREET
NORTH HANOVER ST
KYLE STREET
NORTH WALLACE STREET
BAIRD STREET
LISTER ST
KENNEDY STREET
KENNEDY STREET
BAIRD STREET
PINKSTON RD
MARTYR ST
CASTLE STREET
CASTLE STREET
ST MUNGO AVENUE
ST JAMES ROAD
ST JAMES ROAD
STIRLING ROAD
WISHART STREET
CATHEDRAL ST
CATHEDRAL STREET
CATHEDRAL STREET
CATHEDRAL STREET
23
12
3
NORTH FREDERICK ST
MONTROSE STREET
TAYLOR STREET
ROTTENROW
JOHN KNOX STREET
ST GEORGE ST
North British Hotel
GEORGE
25
SQUARE
GPO
INGRAM STREET
COCHRANE STREET
GEORGE STREET
HIGH STREET
DUKE STREET
9
QUEEN STREET
MILLER STREET
INGRAM STREET
GLASSFORD ST
HUTCHESON STREET
MONTROSE STREET
SHUTTLE STREET
HIGH STREET
High Street Station
ARGYLE STREET
CANDLERIGGS
BELL STREET
10
BELL STREET
HUNTER STREET
BELL STREET
BARRACK STREET
Colonial
TRONGATE
TRONGATE
13
WARD STREET
STOCKWELL STREET
OSBORNE STREET
KING STREET
PARNIE ST
BRIDGEGATE
SALTMARKET
GREENDYKE STREET
LONDON ROAD
MOIR ST
CHARLOTTE ST
CHARLOTTE ST
LONDON RD
TURNBULL STREET
GALLOWGATE
GALLOWGATE
ROSS STREET
BAIN STREET
MONCUR STREET
CLAYTHORN STREET
athedral (R.C.)
Victoria Bridge
CLYDE STREET
8
14
21
3

Map 12 B1
Town plan on preceding page

Population 755,429

Prime factors in Glasgow's history were the River Clyde and the Industrial Revolution (helped by the Lowland genius for shipbuilding and engineering). In the Clyde, Glasgow possesses the loveliest waterway approach of any British city. Famous for learning (two universities), sport (soccer capital of Britain), the port, shops, museums, art galleries and fifty-one parks, it also leads Britain in Turkish baths (six).

Sights Outside City
Loch Lomond, Rouken Glen, Firth of Clyde, Isle of Arran, Kyles of Bute, Bothwell Castle, Provan Hall, Trossachs

Information Office
George Square G2 1ES
Open June–September Mon–Sat 9am–9pm Sun 2pm–9pm Open October–May Mon–Sat 9am–5pm Sun Closed
Telephone 041–221 7371 and 041–221 6136
Telex 779504

Lancia Dealers

Callanders (Jordanhill) Motors Ltd
595 Great Western Road
Glasgow G12 8XH
Tel: 041–334 8155

Ritchies
393 Shields Road
Glasgow
Tel: 041–429 5611

Glasgow

1	Airport	A5
2	Art Gallery and Museum *paintings, ceramics, silver, costumes, etc.*	A2
3	The Barrows *weekend street market*	F5
4	Bellahouston Park *sports centre*	A5
5	Botanic Gardens	A1
6	Calderpark Zoo	F5
7	Central Station	C4
8	Citizens' Theatre	D5
9	City Chambers *fine loggia*	D3/4
10	City Hall	E4
11	Clyde Tunnel	A4
12	Glasgow Cathedral *impressive Gothic*	F3
13	Glasgow Cross *1626 Tolbooth Steeple*	E5
14	Glasgow Green *city's oldest riverside park*	F5
15	Haggs Castle–children	C5
16	Hunterian Museum & Art Gallery (Glasgow University) *early books, archaeology*	A2
17	Kelvin Hall	A2
18	King's Theatre	A2
19	Mitchell Library and Theatre	A2
20	Museum of Transport *comprehensive collection. Also enginering, shipbuilding*	C5
21	People's Palace *local history*	F5
22	Pollok House *Spanish paintings, English furniture, rare silver, in Adam building amid parkland*	C5
23	Queen Street Station	D3
24	Theatre Royal	C2
25	Tourist Information Bureau	D3

Glasgow
Town plan E4 Strathclyde
25 High Street *G1 1LX*
041–552 1923
Proprietor Mr Romano Salvi

● **Set L** from £2·50
About £24·50 for two

Colonial

There's a solid, old-fashioned atmosphere about this restaurant with its beams, wrought iron and high curved ceiling. The lengthy menu has a wide choice of mainly French-inspired dishes ranging from duck à la orange and tournedos Rossini to sole véronique and scampi provençale, as well as various grills. Vegetables are crisp and simply cooked, and sweets include crêpes suzette. *Credit* Access, Amex, Barclaycard, Diners

Lunch 12–2.30 *Dinner* 6–10.30
Closed L Sun & L & D Bank Holidays

Glasgow
Town plan A2 Strathclyde
2 Woodside Crescent *G3 7UL*
041–332 6396
Manager Ronnie Mitchell

● **Set L** £7 **Set D** £10 incl. wine
About £35 for two
Banquets 20/3

Fountain

Elegant decor and attentive service add to the enjoyment of a meal in this comfortable restaurant. The short menu offers a nice balance of familiar and unusual dishes, from mussel and onion stew or poached chicken breast with leek sauce to simple grills. Vegetables are well prepared, and tempting sweets include sorbets and items like hazelnut and chocolate gâteau.
♍ *SUPERIOR. Credit* Access, Amex, Barclaycard, Diners

Lunch 12–2.15 *Dinner* 6–9.30
Closed Bank Holidays & last 2 weeks July

Glasgow
Town plan A1 Strathclyde
10 Grosvenor Terrace *G12 0TA*
041–339 8811
Telex 776247

Rooms 96
with bath/shower 96
Room phone Yes
Room TV Yes
Confirm by 6
Last dinner 10.30
Parking Ample
Banquets 300/10

Credit Access, Amex,
Barclaycard, Diners

Grosvenor Hotel   75%   *E*   £D

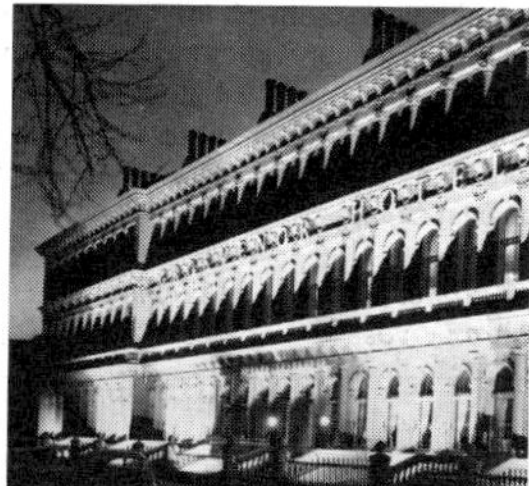

Ten minutes' drive from the city centre and almost as close to the airport, this impressive new hotel is a luxurious and convenient base for tourists as well as businessmen. Attractive flower arrangements enhance the spacious foyer, which has a seating area with comfortable chesterfields. There's also a roomy lounge whose picture windows look out on to the terrace, a welcoming bar and excellent function facilities. Bedrooms (those at the front overlook the Botanical Gardens) range from singles to twins, double doubles and a bridal suite complete with four-poster. All are elegantly furnished and comprehensively equipped, with beautifully fitted bathrooms. *Amenities* dancing (Sat October–March), in-house movies, hairdressing.

Glasgow
Town plan B4 Strathclyde
Argyle Street *G3 8RR*
041–226 5577
Telex 776355

Credit Access, Amex,
Barclaycard, Diners

Holiday Inn   80%   *E*   £C

Standing near the city centre just by the Anderston exit of the M8, this smart 13-storey hotel is a comfortable and convenient base for business people and tourists alike. Attractive public rooms like the foyer, lounge and bars are roomy and relaxing, and there are a number of superbly equipped conference rooms and a leisure centre. Spacious, well-furnished bedrooms have such modern facilities as air conditioning, double glazing, direct-dial telephones, mini-bars, trouser presses and hairdryers. Bathrooms feature smart marble-effect fitments and pulsating showers. Friendly and efficient staff.
Amenities sauna, indoor swimming pool, squash, solarium, keep-fit equipment, hairdressing, coffee shop (11am–11pm).

| *Rooms* 297 | *Room phone* Yes | *Confirm by* 6 | *Parking* Ample |
| *with bath/shower* 297 | *Room TV* Yes | *Last dinner* 11.30 | *Banquets* 800/8 |

Glasgow
Town plan A1 Strathclyde
2 Gibson Street *G12 8NX*
041–339 4275
Proprietor Mr Ghulam Rasul Tahir
Indian cooking
About £13 for two

Koh-I-Noor

This long-standing, family-run Indian restaurant specialises in authentic Punjabi dishes like chicken biryani and bhuna lamb with lots of delicious sundries and side dishes. Unlicensed, but bring your own.
Credit Access, Amex, Barclaycard, Diners *Meals* noon–midnight
● **Set L** £2·10

Glasgow

Town plan A2 Strathclyde
923 Sauchiehall Street
G3 8NY
041–334 4891

Credit Access, Amex,
Barclaycard, Diners

Rooms 83
with bath/shower 40

Lorne Hotel   54%   £E

New owners are planning a welcome refurbishment programme at this
modern hotel, whose position makes it a useful base for tourist or businessman. Ground-floor rooms include a neat foyer and cheerful public bar, while
upstairs there's a residents' bar and two function rooms. Simply decorated
bedrooms with built-in units are compact and functional; adequate bathrooms. *Amenities* entertainment (6 nights weekly).

Room phone Yes	*Confirm by* 6	*Parking* Limited
Room TV Yes	*Last dinner* 10	*Banquets* 80/1

Glasgow

Town plan C4 Strathclyde
54 Union Street *G66 1DH*
041–248 5996
Manager Steve Yip
Chinese cooking

● **Set L** £1·85 **Set D** £4·50
About £20 for two
Banquets 120/2

New China Town   Ⓢ

Chinese lanterns and a dragon suspended from the ceiling create a colourful
atmosphere in this popular second-floor restaurant. There's a vast menu of
Cantonese dishes ranging from tender king prawns with ginger and spring
onions to roast duck with a sweet orange sauce or thick noodles with beef
and vegetables, as well as a selection of dim sum. Cooking is competent and
reliable

Meals noon–midnight

Glasgow

Town plan D3 Strathclyde
40 George Square *G2 1DS*
041–332 6711
Telex 778147

Credit Access, Amex,
Barclaycard, Diners

Rooms 124
with bath/shower 98

North British Hotel   59%   £E

Situated in the heart of the city, next to the railway station, this handsome
building is benefiting from refurbishment. A cosy foyer opens into the
elegant cocktail bar, while the vividly decorated Devil's Elbow Bar is a
popular local haunt. Bedrooms range from traditional in the original building
(some with enormous private bathrooms) to more compact modern ones in
the extension. *Amenities* restaurant (12.30pm–10.30pm).   &

Room phone Yes	*Confirm by* 6	*Parking* Difficult
Room TV Yes	*Last dinner* 10	*Banquets* 120/2

Glasgow

Town plan A2 Strathclyde
11 Hyndland Street *G11 5QE*
041–339 6523
Italian cooking

About £25 for two

Peppino's

This brightly decorated basement restaurant offers a balanced menu of nicely
sauced Italian dishes, as well as steaks and grills. Vegetables are carefully
prepared, and there are tasty sweets like zabaglione. *Credit* Access, Amex,
Barclaycard, Diners *Lunch* 12–2.15 *Dinner* 6–10.30 **Closed** Sun, Mon, 1st
week January & 3 weeks July/August ● **Set L** £2·50 *Banquets* 50/35

Glasgow

Town plan A1 Strathclyde
Ruthven Lane *G12 9BG*
041–339 0932

About £36 for two
Banquets 15/2

Poachers   Ⓢ

Pretty Japanese parasols give this simple restaurant a pleasant atmosphere,
and the menu shows variety and imagination. Starters like chilled melon and
ginger soup can be followed by daily fish specialities such as halibut in
lobster sauce or a meat dish like lamb's sweetbreads Madeira. Good
selection of fresh vegetables, plus delicious sweets to finish.
Credit Access, Amex, Barclaycard, Diners

Lunch 12–2.30 *Dinner* 6.30–11
Closed Sun, 1 January, Easter Monday & 25 December

Glasgow

Town plan A1 Strathclyde
2 Shelley Road
Great Western Road *G12 0XP*
041–334 8161
Telex 777804
Credit Access, Amex,
Barclaycard, Diners

Rooms 137
with bath/shower 137

Pond Hotel   58%   £D/E

Overlooking a pond about two miles from the city centre, this modern hotel
provides practical, comfortable accommodation. Bedrooms are uniform in
style with large windows, functional built-in units, radios and tea-makers
and all have compact bathrooms with showers. Open-plan public areas,
including two bars, are pleasantly furnished in contemporary style.
Amenities dancing (Sat in winter).

Room phone Yes	*Confirm by* 6	*Parking* Ample
Room TV Yes	*Last dinner* 10.30	*Banquets* 130/30

Glasgow

Town plan C4 Strathclyde
11 Exchange Place *G1 3AN*
041–221 5677
Proprietor
Mr Donald Grant

About £32 for two
Banquets 22/10

Rogano Restaurant & Seafood Bar   Ⓢ

Service with a smile adds to the pleasure of a meal at this popular restaurant and oyster bar, whose decor includes painted panels from an old ocean liner. Fresh seasonal seafood, including Helford oysters and sole, is the mainstay of the lengthy menu, supplemented by veal, chicken, steaks and grills for meat-eaters. Everything is capably and straightforwardly prepared.
Credit Access, Amex, Barclaycard, Diners

Lunch 12–2.30 *Dinner* 6–10
Closed Sun & Bank Holidays

Any person using our name to obtain free hospitality is a fraud. Proprietors, please inform the police and us.

Glasgow

Town plan C5 Strathclyde
470 Kilmarnock Road *G43 2BB*
041–637 2353
Telex 778329

Credit Access, Amex,
Barclaycard, Diners

Rooms 30
with bath/shower 27

Tinto Firs Hotel   58%   £D

Standing by the A77 Ayr road in Glasgow's south-western suburbs, this modern two-storey hotel is used mainly by short-stay business visitors. The bright, pleasant reception area is open-plan with a lounge and cocktail bar, and there's another comfortable bar. Bedrooms are compact and functional, with simple fitted units, tea/coffee-makers and bowls of fruit. Bathrooms have adequate modern fittings.

Room phone Yes	*Confirm by* 6	*Parking* Limited
Room TV Yes	*Last dinner* 9.30	*Banquets* 120/4

Glasgow

Town plan A1 Strathclyde
12 Ashton Lane
Hillhead *G12 8SJ*
041–334 5007
Proprietors
Mr Clydesdale & Mr Bryden

About £27 for two
Banquets 50/20

Ubiquitous Chip

Eat in the dining room or in the covered courtyard of this charmingly informal, friendly restaurant. The short menu changes daily to make the best use of fresh local produce and some dishes, such as venison with rowan jelly, have a distinctly Scottish flavour. There are imaginative ideas, too, like plaice with Stilton sauce and lamb stuffed with mussels, and interesting vegetables. 🍷 *SUPERIOR. Credit* Access, Amex, Barclaycard   ♿

Lunch 12–2.30 *Dinner* 5.30–11
Closed Sun, 1 January & 25 December

Glasgow Airport

Map 12 B1 Strathclyde
91 Glasgow Road
Renfrew *PA4 8YB*
041–886 3771   Telex 779032
Manager Richard Castelow
Credit Access, Amex,
Barclaycard, Diners

Rooms 120
with bath/shower 120

Dean Park Hotel   53%   £E

Five minutes' drive from the airport, this low concrete hotel provides unfussy facilities for business travellers. Public areas include a plain lounge and brightly furnished cocktail bar, as well as a variety of function rooms. Bedrooms are adequately equipped with unit furniture, plenty of writing and wardrobe space, and tea-makers. Some refurbishment is planned.
Amenities garden, dancing (alternate Weds).

Room phone Yes	*Confirm by* 7.30	*Parking* Ample
Room TV Yes	*Last dinner* 10	*Banquets* 230/2

Glasgow Airport

Map 12 B1 Strathclyde
Abbotsinch
Near Paisley *PA3 2TR*
041–887 1212
Telex 777733
Credit Access, Amex,
Barclaycard, Diners

Rooms 316
with bath/shower 316

Excelsior Hotel   68%   £C

Catering well for the traveller and businessman, this tall modern hotel right next to the airport terminal has a bustling marble-floored foyer and lounge-bar, and a quieter panelled cocktail bar. Studio-style bedrooms are double-glazed and have soothing pale decor, neat fitted units, tea-makers and well-equipped bathrooms. Good conference facilities.
Amenities discothèque (Sun), hairdressing, transport for airport.

Room phone Yes	*Confirm by* 6	*Parking* Ample
Room TV Yes	*Last dinner* 10.30	*Banquets* 350/-

Engineering for World Transport

Bringing a fast, modern passenger or freight train to a safe stop calls for something rather special in the way of braking equipment, bearing in mind that the total weight of the train is likely to be several hundred tons.

Lucas Girling is deeply involved in railway braking technology and is a world leader in the design, manufacture and supply of specialised braking equipment for railway locomotives and rolling stock.

Glasgow Airport
Map 12 B1 Strathclyde
Inchinnan Road
Renfrew *PA4 9AJ*
041–886 4100
Telex 778897
Credit Access, Amex,
Barclaycard, Diners

Normandy Hotel 62% **£ D**

An eye-catching reproduction of the Bayeux Tapestry graces the walls of the spacious reception area at this cheerful modern hotel, which has three popular bars. Double-glazed bedrooms are bright, comfortable and well equipped, with good tiled bathrooms.
Amenities garden, dinner dance (Sat in winter), coffee shop (10am–11pm), discothèque, transport for airport, golf driving range, in-house movies.

Rooms 142	*Room phone* Yes	*Confirm by* 6	*Parking* Ample
with bath/shower 142	*Room TV* Yes	*Last dinner* 10	*Banquets* 1,000/–

Glenborrodale
Map 17 A4 Highland
Ardnamurchan *PH36 4JP*
Glenborrodale (097 24) 266
Manager Mr Brian Rahilly
Credit Access, Amex,
Barclaycard, Diners
Closed early Nov–mid March

Glenborrodale Castle Hotel 64% **£ D**

Towers and turrets give a dream-like appearance to this welcoming red-stone hotel, which stands in lovely gardens amid the rugged splendour of lochs and glens. Public rooms, including a panelled bar and a roomy modern lounge, command fabulous views, as do most of the bedrooms, which have attractive patterned wallpaper and comfortable furnishings. Helpful staff.
Amenities garden, sea fishing, putting, croquet.

Rooms 23	*Room phone* Yes	*Confirm by* By arrang.	*Parking* Ample
with bath/shower 2	*Room TV* Yes	*Last dinner* 9.30	

Glencoe
Map 17 B4 Highland
PA39 4HZ
Kingshouse (085 56) 259

Credit Access, Amex,
Closed November & December

King's House Hotel 52% (M) **£ E**

Set in remote, rugged countryside some ten miles along the A82 from Glencoe, this smart pebbledash building makes a good base for lovers of the open air. The small entrance hall leads to a large rustic bar and two lounges—one with picture windows to take advantage of the splendid views. Well-maintained bedrooms and bathrooms provide simple, adequate comforts.
Amenities garden, game fishing.

Rooms 22	*Room phone* No	*Confirm by* By arrang.	*Parking* Ample
with bath/shower 10	*Room TV* No	*Last dinner* 8.15	*Banquets* 50/–

Glenlivet
Map 16 C3 Grampian
AB3 9DJ
Glenlivet (080 73) 376

Credit Access, Barclaycard,
Diners
Closed 3 days Christmas

Blairfindy Lodge Hotel 60% (M) **£ E**

New owners Michael and Miranda Blunt make their guests feel very much at home at this pleasant, secluded country lodge, a popular centre for outdoor holidays. The lounges are spacious and comfortable, with traditional chintzy armchairs, and there's a cheerfully relaxed bar. Redecorated bedrooms have good carpets and practical modern furnishings; simple bathrooms are up to date. *Amenities* garden, game fishing.

Rooms 13	*Room phone* Yes	*Confirm by* By arrang.	*Parking* Ample
with bath/shower 8	*Room TV* No	*Last dinner* 9.30	*Banquets* 20/2

Glenlivet
Map 16 C3 Grampian
AB3 9DJ
Glenlivet (080 73) 376

About £24 for two

Blairfindy Lodge Hotel Restaurant

Dinner at this well-furnished restaurant offers enjoyable dishes ranging from smoked mackerel pâté and colourful orange and carrot soup to nicely sauced entrées served with fresh, crisp vegetables. *Credit* Access, Barclaycard, Diners *Lunch* by arrangement only *Dinner* 7.30–9.30 **Closed** 3 days Christmas ● **Set D** £8

Glenrothes
Map 17 C5 Fife
Leslie Road *KY6 3ET*
Glenrothes (0592) 742511
Proprietors Mr & Mrs Crombie
Credit Access, Amex,
Barclaycard
Closed 1 & 2 January

Balgeddie House Hotel 63% (M) **£ E**

Standing among attractive lawns high above Glenrothes, this family-run hotel combines the charm of its 1930s origins with modern comforts. There's a bright residents' lounge, a contemporary cocktail bar and the spotlit Paddock Bar with a horsy theme. Bedrooms vary from spacious and traditionally furnished to neat attic conversions with modern units. Well-equipped bathrooms. Excellent housekeeping. *Amenities* garden, croquet.

Rooms 18	*Room phone* Yes	*Confirm by* By arrang.	*Parking* Ample
with bath/shower 18	*Room TV* Yes	*Last dinner* 9	*Banquets* 60/20

Glenrothes
Map 17 C5 Fife
Leslie Road *KY6 3ET*
Glenrothes (0592) 742511
Proprietors Mr & Mrs Crombie

About £25 for two

Balgeddie House Hotel Restaurant

A well-furnished, traditional dining room is the comfortable setting for an extensive choice of capably prepared dishes. The menu features seafood, grills, flambées and mainly French-inspired specialities. 🍷 *ABOVE AVERAGE. Credit* Access, Amex, Barclaycard *Lunch* 12.30–2 *Dinner* 7–9, Sat 7–9.30 **Closed** 1 & 2 January ● **Set L** Sun only £4·50   ♿

Grantown-on-Spey
Map 16 C3 Highland
Woodlands Terrace *PH26 3JX*
Grantown-on-Spey (0479) 2597

Manager Mr D. L. Small
Credit Access, Barclaycard
Closed end October–end March

Rooms 81
with bath/shower 58

Craiglynne Hotel   55%   £E

Homely comforts are provided at this turreted greystone hotel near the town centre. It has a spacious reception-lounge, a smaller lounge with colour TV and an attractive pine-panelled bar. Compact bedrooms, most of which have simple contemporary furnishings, are neat and tidy, as are the well-fitted shower and bathrooms. *Amenities* garden, dancing (once weekly, also Sat May–September).   ♿

Room phone No	*Confirm by* 6	*Parking* Ample
Room TV No	*Last dinner* 8	

Gullane
Map 12 D1 Lothian
Muirfield *EH31 2EG*
Gullane (0620) 842144
Telex 727396
Proprietors Mr & Mrs G. Weaver
Rooms 24
with bath/shower 21
Room phone Yes
Room TV No
Confirm by By arrang.
Last dinner 9
Parking Ample
Banquets 30/2
Closed 1 January–mid March

Credit Access, Amex,
Barclaycard, Diners

Greywalls Hotel   72%   Ⓜ   £B

This delightful Lutyens-designed country house, built in 1901 and since tastefully extended, is a haven of peace and civilised comfort. Standing next to Muirfield and within easy reach of several championship courses, it's also a paradise for golfers, and there are lovely views down to the Firth of Forth. Four charming lounges include a traditional panelled library and an airy bamboo-furnished sun room overlooking the pretty walled garden. Comfortable, spacious bedrooms are furnished with antiques and fine mahogany pieces; well-equipped bathrooms are sparklingly clean. Standards of service and housekeeping are commendably high. *Amenities* garden, tennis, croquet.

Gullane
Map 12 D1 Lothian
Muirfield *EH31 2EG*
Gullane (0620) 842144
Proprietors
Mr & Mrs G. Weaver

● **Set L** £5·90 **Set D** £11·50
About £29 for two

Greywalls Hotel Restaurant   ★   ♛ⓢ

Julian Waterer has taken over at this elegant restaurant, producing superb set meals which include both traditional dishes and examples of modern French cuisine. Starters like carrot and orange soup or subtle Stilton, port and celery pâté precede a choice of, say, Dover sole, lamb cutlets with tarragon butter or roast duck with kiwi fruit and ginger sauce. Vegetables are excellent, too, and delicious desserts include refreshing ice creams and sorbets.
Specialities turbot mousse with puréed scallops and watercress sauce, chicken, veal and asparagus terrine, pastry case filled with strawberries and hazelnut ice cream, baked with soft meringue.
🍷 *ABOVE AVERAGE. Credit* Access, Amex, Barclaycard, Diners   ♿

Lunch 12.30–2 *Dinner* 7.30–9
Closed January–mid March

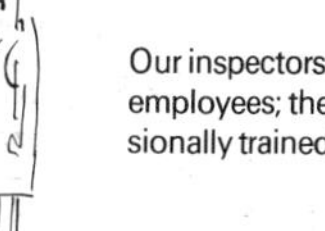

Our inspectors are our full-time employees; they are professionally trained by us.

Gullane

Map 12 D1 Lothian
EH31 2AA
Gullane (0620) 843214
Proprietors
David & Hilary Brown

● **Set L** £6·50 **Set D** £9·75
About £22 for two
Banquets 24/16

La Potinière

It's essential to book at this cosy little restaurant, where a meal is a leisurely social occasion. The well-balanced set menu (no choice) offers delicate soups, featherlight soufflés and maybe plump, beautifully roasted chicken or a pork speciality. Creamy sweets are followed by excellent coffee. David Brown's unflappable service complements his wife's culinary skills. No smoking. *OUTSTANDING.*

Lunch at 1 *Dinner* Sat only at 8
Closed L Sat, all Wed, 1 January, 25 December & October

Hawick

Map 12 D3 Borders
West Stewart Place *TD9 8BH*
Hawick (0450) 72263
Proprietors
Joan & Barrie Newland

Closed 1 week Christmas

Rooms 6
with bath/shower 3

Kirklands Hotel 57% Ⓜ £E

The Newlands make constant improvements to their converted Victorian house on the outskirts of town. The residents' lounge has relaxing tapestry-covered settees, and bedrooms are attractively papered; all have solid traditional furniture, as well as tea-making sets and thoughtful extras like tissues and fresh fruit. The bar features an impressive collection of Toby jugs. *Amenities* garden.

Room phone Yes	*Confirm by* By arrang.	*Parking* Ample
Room TV Yes	*Last dinner* 8.30	

Hawick

Map 12 D3 Borders
West Stewart Place *TD9 8BH*
Hawick (0450) 72263
Proprietors
Joan & Barrie Newland

● **Set D** £7·95
About £25 for two

Kirklands Hotel Restaurant

A finely moulded plasterwork ceiling and lace tablecloths contribute to the elegant decor of this spacious restaurant. For dinner there's a good choice of popular dishes like sautéed chicken provençale, beef Stroganoff and trout with tomatoes and almonds, as well as a familiar selection of sweets (home-made trifle, fruit salad) on the trolley. The lunchtime menu features simpler items such as omelettes, grills and salads.

Lunch 12–2 *Dinner* 7–8.30, Fri & Sat 7–9.30
Closed L Sat & all Sun to non-residents & 1 week Christmas

We welcome complaints and bona fide recommendations on the tear-out pages for readers' comments. They are followed up by our professional team. Please also complain to the management instantly.

Hollybush

Map 12 B3 Strathclyde
By Ayr *KA6 7EA*
Dalrymple (029 256) 214
Telex 779358
Proprietor R. L. White
Credit Access, Amex, Barclaycard
Closed 25–28 December

Rooms 12
with bath/shower 7

Hollybush House Hotel 67% Ⓜ £E

Salmon and trout fishing on the river Doon are among the attractions of this friendly, well-kept country house, which stands in extensive wooded grounds five miles from Ayr. Public areas include a comfortable oak-panelled entrance lounge, a ballroom and a delightful library doubling as a sitting room. Best bedrooms (with private bathrooms) have handsome Victorian furnishings. *Amenities* garden, game fishing, clay-pigeon shooting.

Room phone No	*Confirm by* 6.30	*Parking* Ample
Room TV No	*Last dinner* 9.30	*Banquets* 70/8

Hollybush

Map 12 B3 Strathclyde
By Ayr *KA6 7EA*
Dalrymple (029 256) 214
Proprietor Mr R. L. White

● **Set L** Sun only £4·75
About £23 for two

Hollybush House Hotel Restaurant

An elegant, spacious dining room, with an ornate marble fireplace, comfortable leather chairs and fresh flowers on the tables. The menu of capably prepared dishes includes hearty soups and smooth pâté maison (served with delicious home-made soda bread), and main courses like entrecôte maison or devilled chicken in curry sauce are based on excellent-quality ingredients. *Credit* Access, Amex, Barclaycard

Lunch Sun 12.30–2, Mon–Sat by arrangement only *Dinner* 7–9.30, Sun 7–8
Closed 25–28 December

Humbie

Map 12 D2 Lothian
Near Edinburgh *EH36 5PL*
Humbie (087 533) 696
Telex 727897

Rooms 11
with bath/shower 11
Room phone Yes
Room TV Yes
Confirm by 6
Last dinner 8.30
Parking Ample
Banquets 60/–

Credit Access, Amex,
Barclaycard, Diners

Johnstounburn House   70%   Ⓜ   £C

Beautiful grounds, complete with a formal walled garden, a little lake and an 18th-century dovecote, surround this splendid house, which dates back to 1625. Mr and Mrs Vere-Nicholl have taken great care to preserve its grand country-house atmosphere, and there are period features, oil paintings and fine antiques throughout the public rooms–the comfortable morning room and bar, a small drawing room and the lovely panelled Cedar Room lounge. Traditionally furnished bedrooms include some charming ones in the attic; all have carefully matched fabrics and wallpapers and bright, well-fitted modern bathrooms. *Amenities* garden, coarse fishing, croquet, clay-pigeon shooting.

Humbie

Map 12 D2 Lothian
Near Edinburgh *EH36 5PL*
Humbie (087 533) 696

● **Set D** £11
About £36 for two

Johnstounburn House Restaurant   ♔ Ⓢ

A formal dining room with panelling and long drapes is a fine setting for Raymond Baudon's skilful cooking. Excellent materials, including fresh seafood and local game, are used for a Franco–Scottish menu ranging from mussel soup and coquilles St Jacques to a superb whisky-flavoured pâté or filet mignon Robert Burns (with haggis). Finish with home-made ice cream and good coffee. *Credit* Access, Amex, Barclaycard, Diners

Lunch by arrangement only *Dinner* 7–8.30, Sun 7–9

Invergarry

Map 17 B4 Highland
PH35 4HJ
Invergarry (080 93) 206

Closed beginning November–end March

Rooms 11
with bath/shower 5

Inn on the Garry *(Inn)*   Ⓜ   £E

Ian and Fiona MacLean take a keen interest in the running of their pleasant roadside inn, whose little ground-floor rooms include a lounge with comfortable modern sofas and a smart pine-furnished public bar. Good-sized bedrooms, reached by a fine old wooden staircase, are decorated in a variety of styles and colours; bathrooms are adequate. Housekeeping could be improved.

Room phone No	*Confirm by* 6		*Parking* Ample
Room TV No	*Last dinner* 9		*Banquets* 15/2

Invergarry

Map 17 B4 Highland
PH35 4HJ
Invergarry (080 93) 206

About £24 for two

Inn on the Garry Restaurant   ♧

Haggis and neeps is a tasty, spicy favourite at this unpretentious family-run roadside inn, which also provides delicious trout, local kippers and tender rump steak. A few simple sweets, some ice-cream based.
Lunch 12–2 *Dinner* 7.30–9 **Closed** beginning November–end March
● **Set D** £8   &

Inverness

Map 16 C3 Highland
Church Street *IV1 1DX*
Inverness (0463) 35181

Credit Access, Amex,
Barclaycard, Diners

Rooms 118
with bath/shower 118

Caledonian Hotel   56%   £D

Popular with tourists in the summer and business people in the winter, this modern city-centre hotel offers reasonable accommodation. Functional public rooms include the busy Tenerife Lounge and the Victorian-style lounge bar. Uniform bedrooms have practical modern furniture and tea-making facilities. Compact, adequately fitted bathrooms.
Amenities dancing (Fri, Sat), cabaret (nightly).

Room phone Yes	*Confirm by* 6		*Parking* Ample
Room TV Yes	*Last dinner* 9.15		*Banquets* 400/2

COMPLETE CO-ORDINATION TO MATCH YOUR LIFESTYLE.

Perfect Harmony is arguably
the most important development
in room decor of the last decade.

Offered by one of the world's
leading manufacturers of prestigious carpets,
this fine collection introduces the
completely co-ordinated room where carpet,
rug, wallcarpet and curtains are all in perfect harmony.

The Perfect Harmony range offers
literally hundreds of combinations
of glorious colours, textures and materials.

To find out more about Perfect Harmony
simply write to us for our full colour brochure.

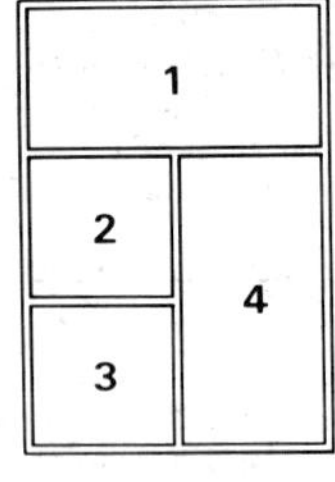

Shown opposite:

1. **CORAL** *Carpet* Reprise
   Wallcarpet Collage
   Curtain Fabric Masque

2. **JADE** *Carpet* Intermezzo
   Wallcarpet Figurine
   Curtain Fabric Ballet

3. **FLAX** *Carpet* Ensemble
   Rug Andante
   Wallcarpet Figurine
   Curtain Fabric Masque

4. **ICE** *Carpet* Finale
   Wallcarpet Pastiche
   Curtain Fabric Gavotte

Gaskell Broadloom Ltd.,
Wheatfield Mill, Rishton,
Blackburn, Lancashire BB1 4NV.

PERFECT HARMONY

Inverness

Culloden House Hotel   **77%**   Ⓜ   **£C**

Map 16 C3 Highland
Culloden *IV1 2NZ*
Inverness (0463) 790461
Telex 75402

Rooms 20
with bath/shower 20
Room phone Yes
Room TV Yes
Confirm by By arrang.
Last dinner 9.30
Parking Ample
Banquets 45/2

Credit Access, Amex,
Barclaycard, Diners

A sweeping drive leads to this handsome mansion, steeped in history and standing near the site of the Battle of Culloden. Interesting antiques and a portrait of Bonnie Prince Charlie grace the entrance hall, and the lofty drawing room features ornate blue and white plasterwork. A handsome staircase leads up past a wall tapestry to the bedrooms, many of which have lovely views across the rolling hills. Impressively roomy, comfortably furnished and thoughtfully equipped, they all have spotless, well-appointed bathrooms. Three rooms have four-posters.
Amenities garden, sauna, tennis, solarium.

Inverness

Dunain Park Hotel   **68%**   Ⓜ   **£C**

Map 16 C3 Highland
Dunain Park *IV3 6JN*
Inverness (0463) 30512
Telex 75446
Proprietors
Judith & Michael Bulger
Closed beginning Nov–mid Mar

This well-maintained Georgian house, set in six acres of gardens and woodland just off the A82, offers good standards of comfort and service in tranquil surroundings. Antiques, paintings and prints adorn the lounges, which have plenty of armchairs and a good supply of magazines. There are antiques, too, in the attractive bedrooms, four of which have their own well-equipped bathrooms. *Amenities* garden, croquet, badminton.

Rooms 6
with bath/shower 4

| *Room phone* No | *Confirm by* By arrang. | *Parking* Ample |
| *Room TV* No | *Last dinner* 9 | *Banquets* 22/4 |

Inverness

Dunain Park Hotel Restaurant   ♀ ⑤

Map 16 C3 Highland
Dunain Park *IV3 6JN*
Inverness (0463) 30512
Proprietors
Judith & Michael Bulger

Gleaming silverware, flowers and candles make an attractive setting for Judith Bulger's delightful four-course dinners, with each dish notable for the quality of the ingredients and the honest, natural flavours. Potted shrimps or delicate egg and cucumber mousse could precede creamy mushroom soup, with a main course choice of trout, roast leg of lamb or a really excellent chicken, mushroom and cranberry pie. *ABOVE AVERAGE.*

● **Set D** £13
About £34 for two

Dinner only 7.30–9
Closed beginning November–mid March

Inverness

Kingsmills Hotel   **67%**   Ⓜ   **£D**

Map 16 C3 Highland
Damfield Road *IV2 3LP*
Inverness (0463) 37166
Telex 75566

Credit Access, Amex,
Barclaycard, Diners

A tasteful blending of old and new has made this much-extended 18th-century country house a pleasant and comfortable hotel. One of the elegant lounges features an indoor garden, the other has antiques and a magnificent ornate ceiling; there are also two bars. Well-kept bedrooms have attractive floral decor, practical fitted furniture and colourful well-equipped bathrooms. *Amenities* garden, squash.

Rooms 54
with bath/shower 54

| *Room phone* Yes | *Confirm by* By arrang. | *Parking* Ample |
| *Room TV* Yes | *Last dinner* 9.45 | *Banquets* 60/– |

Inverness

Ladbroke Mercury Hotel   **60%**   **£C**

Map 16 C3 Highland
Nairn Road *IV2 3TR*
Inverness (0463) 39666
Telex 75377

Credit Access, Amex,
Barclaycard, Diners

This pleasant modern hotel stands on the A9 on the southern edge of town. Automatic doors lead into the bright reception-lounge-bar area, which is roomy and attractively furnished. There's also a smart public bar, and conference facilities are ample. Colour-coordinated bedrooms have TVs, radios, tea-makers and neat little bathrooms. Good maintenance and housekeeping. *Amenities* discothèque (3 nights weekly).   ♿

Continued

Rooms 108	*Room phone* Yes	*Confirm by* By arrang.	*Parking* Ample
with bath/shower 108	*Room TV* Yes	*Last dinner* 10	*Banquets* 160/2

Inverness
Map 16 C3 Highland
Academy Street *IV1 1LG*
Inverness (0463) 31926
Telex 75275

Credit Access, Amex,
Barclaycard, Diners

Station Hotel   63%   £ C/D

Extensive refurbishment is breathing new life into this elegant Victorian hotel next to the station. The pillared foyer-lounge is dominated by a grand central staircase; other public rooms include the pleasant, cane-furnished Robbie's Bar and a cheerful public bar. Fair-sized bedrooms have comfortable chairs, pretty floral curtains and toning pastel paintwork. Adequate bathrooms.

Rooms 65	*Room phone* Yes	*Confirm by* 6	*Parking* Limited
with bath/shower 52	*Room TV* Yes	*Last dinner* 9	*Banquets* 150/2

Inverness
Map 16 C3 Highland
Academy Street *IV1 1LG*
Inverness (0463) 31926

● **Set D** £8·75 incl. service
About £35 for two

Station Hotel Restaurant   ★   Ⓢ

Skilled, imaginative cooking, artistic presentation and courteous, efficient service make a meal in this lofty Victorian dining room a rare pleasure. Embracing the best of English, Scottish and French cuisine, chef Bland and his diligent team keep the customers happy with a good choice of dishes ranging from hearty beef and chicken broth to grilled salmon with truffle-flavoured hollandaise, or superb medallions of venison with a delicious plum sauce.
Specialities seafood avocado with red wine and raspberry dressing, veal with wild mushrooms on a bed of creamed spinach, fresh strawberries with pear sorbet and Kirsch sauce. 🍷 *ABOVE AVERAGE.*
Credit Access, Amex, Barclaycard, Diners

Lunch 12.30–2.30 *Dinner* 7–9
Closed L Sat & Sun

Invershin
Map 16 B2 Highland
IV27 4ET
Invershin (054 982) 202
Proprietors Hedley family
Credit Access, Amex,
Barclaycard, Diners
Closed 1–4 January

Invershin Hotel   54%   Ⓜ   £ F

This pleasant hotel is run on friendly lines by the Hedley family, who are adding to the comforts of the place with substantial refurbishment. Compact, up-to-date bedrooms, plainly furnished with freestanding pieces, have excellent beds; all are equipped with colour TVs and tea-makers. Modern bathrooms are well maintained. Superb Scandinavian-style breakfasts.
Amenities garden, game fishing.   &

Rooms 27	*Room phone* Yes	*Confirm by* By arrang.	*Parking* Ample
with bath/shower 14	*Room TV* Yes	*Last dinner* 9	*Banquets* 120/2

Invershin
Map 16 B2 Highland
IV27 4ET
Invershin (054 982) 202
Proprietors Hedley family

Invershin Hotel Restaurant   

Thoroughly enjoyable, uncomplicated cooking is the hallmark of this popular restaurant, where fresh local produce is skilfully handled to preserve all its natural flavour. Herring salad or really meaty beef and vegetable soup can be followed by a main course such as excellent poached turbot with nicely prepared vegetables. Simple sweets like strawberry sponge.
Credit Access, Amex, Barclaycard, Diners   &

● **Set L** £3 **Set D** £5
About £18 for two

Lunch 12.30–3 *Dinner* 6.45–9, Fri, Sat & Sun 6.45–10
Closed 1–4 January

Isle of Gigha
Map 17 A6 Strathclyde
PA41 7AD
Gigha (058 35) 254
Managers
Mr & Mrs K. L. Roebuck

Gigha Hotel   60%   £ D/E

The friendly Roebucks treat you as one of the family at this delightful hotel on a peaceful island. Pine decor gives a bright, fresh look to the rustic public bar, and the bar lounge and a little sitting room with TV are very cosy. There's pine, too, in the bedrooms, which have attractive cottage fabrics and simple, practical furnishings. Good modern bathrooms.
Amenities garden, transport for ferry.

Rooms 9	*Room phone* No	*Confirm by* By arrang.	*Parking* Limited
with bath/shower 3	*Room TV* No	*Last dinner* 9	

Isle Ornsay
Map 17 A4 Highland
Isle of Skye *IV43 8QY*
Isle Ornsay (047 13) 214
Telex 75442
Proprietors
The Lord & Lady Macdonald

Kinloch Lodge Hotel   60%      £E

A long winding driveway leads to this remote and beautifully situated hotel which is run by the Lord and Lady Macdonald. Fine old paintings add character to the cosy bar and the comfortable, modestly furnished lounge, while most of the neat bedrooms with white fitted units and pretty floral wallpapers enjoy marvellous views. Bathrooms are adequately equipped. *Amenities* garden, game fishing, stalking.

Rooms 12	*Room phone* No	*Confirm by* By arrang.	*Parking* Ample
with bath/shower 6	*Room TV* No	*Last dinner* 8	*Banquets* 40/–

Isle Ornsay
Map 17 A4 Highland
Isle of Skye *IV43 8QY*
Isle Ornsay (047 13) 214
Proprietors
The Lord & Lady Macdonald
About £28 for two

Kinloch Lodge Hotel Restaurant   

There's a real home-made flavour about the three-course dinners at this charming hotel restaurant: soups are delicate, bread is freshly baked, roasts are perfectly cooked and fudge is lovely with coffee.
Dinner only at 8
● **Set D** £10·50

Kelso
Map 12 D2 Borders
TD5 7HT
Kelso (0573) 24168
Proprietor Mr R. A. Brooks

Closed for accommodation
12 days Christmas/New Year

Ednam House Hotel   60%      £D/E

This popular fishing hotel, a handsome Georgian building standing beside the river Tweed, offers friendly, caring service and old-fashioned comforts. The two large, relaxing lounges have lovely plasterwork ceilings and chintzy furnishings, and there are two bars. Bedrooms—large first-floor ones have river views—are solidly and traditionally furnished, and bathrooms are acceptably equipped. *Amenities* garden.

Rooms 32	*Room phone* Yes	*Confirm by* 6	*Parking* Ample
with bath/shower 22	*Room TV* No	*Last dinner* 9	*Banquets* 200/10

Kelso
Map 12 D2 Borders
Sprouston Road *TD5 8ES*
Kelso (0573) 24594

Closed 2 weeks January

House O'Hill Hotel   56%   Ⓜ   £E/F

There are fine views over the town, river and castle from this friendly hotel, built as a private house in 1962. You can relax in the simple modern cocktail bar or round the fireplace in the pleasantly traditional lounge. Compact, plainly furnished bedrooms provide adequate comforts. Rooms without private baths have washbasins. *Amenities* garden, tennis, putting.

Rooms 7	*Room phone* No	*Confirm by* 6	*Parking* Ample
with bath/shower 3	*Room TV* Most	*Last dinner* 8.30	*Banquets* 100/30

Kenmore
Map 17 C5 Tayside
PH15 2NA
Kenmore (088 73) 205

Credit Access, Amex,
Barclaycard

Kenmore Hotel   53%   £D/E

Built in 1572, not far from the arched gateway of Taymouth Castle, this hotel provides acceptable accommodation for tourists and Tay fishermen. An open fire warms the pleasantly comfortable lounge, and there are two bars. Bedrooms are simply appointed with plain colour schemes; bathrooms are functional. Some refurbishment would be very welcome. *Amenities* garden, golf course, game fishing.

Rooms 48	*Room phone* Yes	*Confirm by* By arrang.	*Parking* Ample
with bath/shower 36	*Room TV* No	*Last dinner* 8.45	*Banquets* 90/2

Kentallen of Appin
Map 17 B4 Highland
PA38 4BX
Duror (063 174) 227
Proprietors
Mr & Mrs Robert Taylor

Closed mid-October–Easter

Ardsheal House   63%   Ⓜ   £E

Jane & Robert Taylor extend a delightfully friendly welcome to guests at this charming manor house set in an attractive garden overlooking Loch Linnhe. The three homely lounges (one with TV) are wonderfully relaxing and warm. Tastefully appointed bedrooms have lovely old-fashioned furniture and pretty wallpapers, and modern bathrooms are carpeted and well equipped. *Amenities* garden, tennis, billiards.

Rooms 13	*Room phone* No	*Confirm by* 6	*Parking* Ample
with bath/shower 8	*Room TV* No	*Last dinner* 8.30	*Banquets* 24/2

Kentallen of Appin
Map 17 B4 Highland
PA38 4BX
Duror (063 174) 227
Proprietors
Mr & Mrs Robert Taylor

● **Set D** from £10·50
About £28 for two

Ardsheal House Restaurant

Dinner is served in the charming candlelit conservatory of this hotel, and reveals a very talented young chef. The four-course set menu offers no choice, although there are dishes to suit all tastes: starters like tasty haggis or home-made pasta are followed by soups such as authentic borsch and main courses like delicious trout with fried parsley or roast duckling. Vegetables are superb and sweets are beautifully light.

Lunch by arrangement only *Dinner* 8–8.30
Closed mid October–Easter

Kilchrenan
Map 17 B5 Strathclyde
By Taynuilt *PA35 1HE*
Kilchrenan (086 63) 333

Rooms 15
with bath/shower 15
Room phone Yes
Room TV No
Confirm by 6.30
Last dinner 9
Parking Ample

Closed 1 November–Easter

Credit Access, Amex,
Barclaycard

Ardanaiseig Hotel   74%   £ D

Occupying a magnificent position on the shores of Loch Awe, this secluded mansion set in beautiful grounds is a glorious retreat for holiday-makers, tourists and sports enthusiasts. The entrance hall leads directly into the public areas, which include a comfortably furnished lounge (with a grand piano for visitors to play) and a cosy library with a little bar. Tastefully decorated, individually furnished bedrooms all have their own bathrooms. Michael and Frieda Yeo are perfect hosts, and the hotel is maintained in immaculate condition. Inclusive terms only.
Amenities garden, tennis, game fishing, croquet, clay-pigeon shooting, billiards.

Kilchrenan
Map 17 B5 Strathclyde
By Taynuilt *PA35 1HE*
Kilchrenan (086 63) 333

● **Set L** Sun only £7·15
Set D £12·95
About £32 for two

Ardanaiseig Hotel Restaurant

A meal in this beautifully proportioned dining room is a highly enjoyable, leisurely experience enhanced by skilful, friendly service. The dinner menu makes use of the finest ingredients, with dishes ranging from tasty smoked haddock mousse to veal in cream and mushroom sauce and roast duckling with cranberries and port. Outstanding sweets. Lighter lunches except on Sundays.  *ABOVE AVERAGE. Credit* Access, Amex, Barclaycard

Lunch 12.30–2 *Dinner* 7.30–9.30
Closed end October–Easter

Kilchrenan
Map 17 B5 Strathclyde
Near Taynuilt *PA35 1HQ*
Kilchrenan (086 63) 211
Proprietors
Mr & Mrs J. D. Taylor
Credit Access, Amex,
Barclaycard, Diners

Rooms 22
with bath/shower 11

Taychreggan Hotel   62%   Ⓜ   £ D/E

The Taylors continue to improve this peaceful country house on the shores of Loch Awe. Public rooms include two modern lounges and a TV room, and there's an inviting bar. Some bedrooms have antique furniture, others modern built-in units, but all are neat and well appointed, with lovely views. Very friendly service. *Amenities* garden, coarse & game fishing, hotel boats.
Closed mid-October–week before Easter

Room phone No	*Confirm by* By arrang.	*Parking* Ample
Room TV No	*Last dinner* 8.45	*Banquets* 40/4

We do not necessarily recommend the cooking at hotels whose restaurants are not separately listed.

Kilchrenan

Map 17 B5 Strathclyde
Near Taynuilt *PA35 1HQ*
Kilchrenan (086 63) 211
Proprietors Mr & Mrs J. D. Taylor

● **Set L** £4·95 **Set D** £9·50
About £26 for two

Taychreggan Hotel Restaurant

A charming modern restaurant, where the daily-changing set dinner menu (three courses plus cheese) is skilfully prepared from first-rate materials. Dishes range from baked mushrooms to nicely flavoured chicken Kiev and Danish smoked pork with parsley sauce; vegetables are carefully cooked and sweets are delicious. At lunch time there's a Danish cold table.
ABOVE AVERAGE. Credit Access, Amex, Barclaycard, Diners

Lunch 12–2.15 *Dinner* 7.30–8.45
Closed mid October–week before Easter

Kildary

Map 16 C3 Highland
IV18 0NP
Kildary (086 284) 2330
Proprietor Mrs H. Attwood

About £24 for two

Delny House Hotel Restaurant

Mrs Attwood produces an enjoyable help-yourself buffet in this spacious dining room. The choice ranges from vegetable soup and soused herrings to cold meats, salads and in the evening tasty hot roasts with all the trimmings.
Lunch 1–3 *Dinner* at 8 **Closed** Sun ● **Set L** £6·50 **Set D** £9
Banquets 25/20

Kildrummy

Map 17 C4 Grampian
By Alford *AB3 8RA*
Kildrummy (033 65) 288
Proprietor Mr T. Hanna
Credit Access, Amex,
Barclaycard
Closed 4 January–4 March

Kildrummy Castle Hotel   69% Ⓜ   £ D

Built in 1900, this handsome greystone mansion stands in attractive gardens close to the ruins of the 14th-century castle. Carved woodwork is a feature of the public rooms, which include an impressive entrance hall, a relaxing drawing room and a cosy library. Spacious bedrooms are attractively furnished with solid period pieces. Modern bathrooms.
Amenities garden, game fishing, billiards, children's playground.

Rooms 13	*Room phone* Yes	*Confirm by* By arrang.	*Parking* Ample
with bath/shower 10	*Room TV* Yes	*Last dinner* 9	*Banquets* 50/4

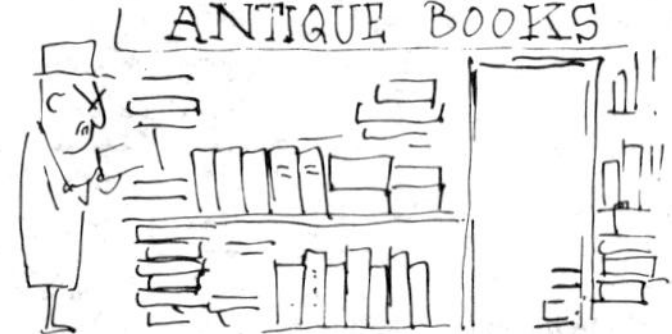

We publish annually, so make sure you use the current edition. It's worth it!

Killiecrankie

Map 17 C4 Tayside
By Pitlochry *PH16 5LG*
Pitlochry (0796) 3220
Proprietors
Mr & Mrs D. Hattersley Smith

Closed mid October–Easter

Killiecrankie Hotel   54% Ⓜ   £ E/F

A smart white-painted building under a slate roof, the Hattersley Smiths' welcoming little hotel stands in delightful countryside just off the A9. The cosy bar makes the most of the fine views, and upstairs is a large comfortable residents' lounge with colour TV. Cheerful, compact bedrooms are adequately furnished in modern style; bathrooms are well equipped and very tidy. *Amenities* garden, putting.

Rooms 12	*Room phone* No	*Confirm by* By arrang.	*Parking* Ample
with bath/shower 10	*Room TV* No	*Last dinner* 8.30	*Banquets* 30/10

Kilwinning

Map 12 A2 Strathclyde
KA13 6PG
Kilwinning (0294) 53689
Proprietor Mr Alastair Hood

● **Set D** £9
About £25 for two

High Smithstown Farm Restaurant

Ask for directions when booking dinner at this isolated farmhouse restaurant two miles outside Kilwinning. The fixed-price menu, which changes daily, offers tasty dishes like pâté and soup flavoured with home-grown herbs, followed by main courses such as coq au vin or poached trout béarnaise, with particularly good vegetables. Simple sweets like cherry and raisin pie.
ABOVE AVERAGE. Credit Amex

Dinner only 7.30–9
Closed Sun, Mon, 1 January & last 3 weeks October

The best of the catch

3·WAY COOK
OVEN, GRILL OR FRY
FINDUS®

Broccoli À La Polanaise with Cod in Parsley Sauce

1 x Findus 225g/8oz Broccoli
45ml/3 tbsp breadcrumbs
25g/1oz butter
½ small packet ready salted crisps
50g/2oz Mature Cheddar
Cheese, grated

Cook broccoli according to directions,
drain. Fry breadcrumbs in butter until
light brown. Add seasoning and leave to
cool. Break up crisps slightly. Mix with
breadcrumbs and grated cheese. Place
broccoli in serving dish, sprinkle with
cheese mix and grill until cheese bubbles.

Whole Plaice with Egg and Caper Dressing

3 hard-boiled eggs
Pinch of garlic salt
10ml/2 tsp French mustard
2.5ml/½ tsp salt   Pepper
Pinch of dill   30ml/2 tbsp olive oil
10ml/2 tsp white wine vinegar
30ml/2 tbsp lemon juice
15ml/1 tbsp finely chopped capers

Rub eggs through sieve into bowl.
Add garlic salt, mustard, salt, pepper and
dill. Beat briskly until mixture forms a
smooth paste. Stir in oil a little at a time.
Add vinegar and lemon juice. Mix well
and stir in capers. Chill before serving.

Fish Cake Extravaganza

4-6 Findus Fish Cakes
1 finely chopped clove garlic
1 small, finely chopped onion
15ml/1 tbsp oil 12.5g/½ oz cornflour
400g/14oz tin tomatoes
15ml/1 tbsp tomato purée
2.5ml/½ tsp sugar 1.25ml/¼ tsp sage
Seasoning 50g/2oz grated cheese

Fry garlic and onions in oil until transparent.
Mix cornflour with 30ml/2 tablespoons of
the tomato juice. Add to pan with tomatoes,
remaining juice from can, tomato purée, sugar,
sage and seasoning. Bring to the boil and
simmer for 5 minutes. Cook fish cakes as directed.
Pour sauce onto a serving dish and arrange fish
cakes overlapping each other. Top with grated
cheese and grill until cheese melts.

Traditional Fish and Chips

With Batter Crisp Findus Cod
you get traditional fish and
chips with a new crispier batter
and the modern choice of
cooking-oven, grill or fry.

AND HERE'S TO ANOTHER
25 YEARS
OF SUCCESS
FINDUS ®

Kinclaven by Stanley

Map 17 C5 Tayside
PH1 4QN
Meikleour (025 083) 268
Telex 727396
Proprietor Mrs P. E. Brassey
Rooms 23
with bath/shower 23
Room phone Yes
Room TV Yes
Confirm by By arrang.
Last dinner 9.45
Parking Ample
Banquets 25/–
Closed 1 December–13 January

Credit Access, Amex,
Diners

Ballathie House   70%   Ⓜ   £ C/D

Built in 1850 on the west bank of the river Tay, this impressive turreted mansion is a friendly, well-maintained hotel. Comfortable sofas and armchairs fill the spacious entrance hall and the cosy residents' lounge, and in the bar, a stuffed salmon in a glass case serves as a reminder of angling pleasures. Bedrooms range from large and traditional to more modern ones with practical darkwood furniture, with bathrooms to match. A Scandinavian-style lodge nearby offers more modest accommodation for sportsmen and families.
Amenities garden, tennis, coarse & game fishing, putting, croquet, helipad.

Kinclaven by Stanley

Map 17 C5 Tayside
PH! 4QN
Meikleour (025 083) 268

Proprietor Mrs P. E. Brassey

● **Set L** £5 **Set D** £9
About £30 for two

Ballathie House Restaurant   ♕ Ⓢ

A friendly atmosphere pervades this lofty, formal dining room overlooking the hotel's lawned gardens. Local produce features on the daily set menus with main courses like roast rib of Angus beef and pan-fried trout after soup or perhaps pâté. Specialities such as baked Tay salmon with cream and champagne sauce provide further choice on the short à la carte dinner menu.
Credit Access, Amex, Diners   &

Lunch 12–2, Sun 12–2.30 *Dinner* 7–9.45, Sun 7–8.30
Closed 1 December–13 January

Kinloch Rannoch

Map 17 C4 Tayside
By Pitlochry *PH16 5PS*
Kinloch Rannoch (088 22) 201

Credit Access, Amex,
Barclaycard, Diners

Rooms 20
with bath/shower 20

Loch Rannoch Hotel   61%   £ D

Set in 250 acres of wooded grounds by Loch Rannoch, this modernised hotel has extensive amenities, catering for all tastes. Attractive bedrooms have whitewood furniture and up-to-date bathrooms. There's also a spacious bar and a residents' lounge. *Amenities* garden, sauna, indoor swimming pool, coarse & game fishing, in-house movies, dry ski slope, solarium, gymnasium, nature trails, hotel boats, bicycles, pool table.

Room phone Yes	*Confirm by* By arrang.	*Parking* Ample
Room TV Yes	*Last dinner* 8.45	*Banquets* 50/–

Our inspectors never book in the name of the Egon Ronay Organisation; they disclose their identity only after paying their bills.

Kinlochbervie

Map 16 B2 Highland
By Lairg *IV27 4RP*
Kinlochbervie (097 182) 275
Proprietors
Mr & Mrs B. Davidson
Closed 3 days New Year &
Christmas

Rooms 10
with bath/shower 10

Kinlochbervie Hotel   68%   Ⓜ   £ D

The Davidsons are charming, friendly hosts at this appealing modern hotel perched above a fishing harbour. The large bar has splendid views from its picture windows and there's a cosy little lounge. Bedrooms are very attractively appointed, with good fitted units, nice Scottish fabrics, tea-makers and plenty of writing space. All have fully carpeted, up-to-date bathrooms.

Room phone Yes	*Confirm by* By arrang.	*Parking* Ample
Room TV Yes	*Last dinner* 8.30	*Banquets* 50/2

Kinlochbervie

Map 16 B2 Highland
By Lairg *IV27 4RP*
Kinlochbervie (097 182) 275
Proprietors
Mr & Mrs B. Davidson

About £26 for two

Kinlochbervie Hotel Restaurant ★  

Mr Davidson's excellent food comes as a delightful surprise in such a remote restaurant, with its spectacular mountain and sea views. He is an experienced chef who knows the value of using the best raw materials; seafood straight from the local fishing fleet is handled with great subtlety to preserve its fine flavour, the smoked salmon is cured with oak chips, juniper berries and wild myrtle, vegetables are simple and fresh, and sweets like a delicate chocolate gâteau show a very skilful touch.
Specialities tranche of salmon with king prawns and champagne sauce, brioche of sole with prawn sauce, turbot with saffron and Pernod sauce.

Dinner only 7.30–8.30
Closed 3 days New Year & Christmas

Knipoch

Map 17 B5 Strathclyde
Near Oban *PA34 4QT*
Kilninver (085 26) 208

Rooms 22
with bath/shower 22
Room phone Yes
Room TV Yes
Confirm by By arrang.
Last dinner 9.30
Parking Ample
Banquets 50/8

Credit Access, Amex,
Barclaycard, Diners

Knipoch Hotel 75% Ⓜ £C/D

Situated six miles south of Oban on the A816, this modernised and extended country house is a most friendly establishment. The elegant reception hall with its oak panelling and leather armchairs gives way to a relaxing lounge and a small bar. A wide staircase leads to the charming bedrooms, which are tastefully fitted with lovely furniture and fabrics; all have fine views of Loch Feochan. Well equipped bathrooms. No dogs. *Amenities* garden.

Knipoch

Map 17 B5 Strathclyde
Near Oban *PA34 4QT*
Kilninver (085 26) 208

● **Set D** £10
About £30 for two

Knipoch Hotel Restaurant ★  

A Scottish-Danish team runs the kitchen of this pleasant hotel restaurant with painstaking care and single-minded devotion. Standards of cooking never falter and the choice of local raw materials is excellent: salmon is smoked on the premises, venison is beautifully tender while items like ham broth have a robust, traditional flavour. Vegetables are cooked to perfection and sweets such as raspberry fool and chocolate gâteau show a professional touch. Thoughtful, friendly service.
Specialities Loch Feochan home-cured salmon, West Coast crawfish with mousseline, local game.
Credit Access, Amex, Barclaycard, Diners

Dinner only 7.30–9.30

Kyle of Lochalsh

Map 16 A3 Highland
Ferry Road *IV40 8AF*
Kyle (0599) 4202

Credit Access, Amex,
Barclaycard, Diners

Lochalsh Hotel 61% £D

There are fine views across to the rugged mountains of Skye from this large white building near the ferry. Afternoon tea is a speciality of the comfortable lounge and there are two bars, one popular with locals. Bright, spacious bedrooms have many comforts including colour TV and a lovely peaceful atmosphere, and smart bathrooms are well kept.
Amenities garden, sea fishing, dancing (Fri in winter), hairdressing. &

Rooms 45	*Room phone* Yes	*Confirm by* 6	*Parking* Limited
with bath/shower 28	*Room TV* Yes	*Last dinner* 8.30	*Banquets* 120/–

Lanark
Map 12 C2 Strathclyde
ML11 9UF
Lanark (0555) 4426
Proprietors
D. I. Laird & M. Russell
Credit Access, Amex,
Diners

Rooms 15
with bath/shower None

Cartland Bridge Hotel 53% Ⓜ £E

Spires and turrets set the tone of this 19th-century country retreat in 18 acres of wooded grounds, and the interior is dominated by marvellous pine panelling. There are two bars with modern chrome and vinyl fittings. Spacious, comfortable bedrooms vary in style, some boasting fine antiques, others having simple traditional furniture.
Amenities garden, game fishing, dancing (Sat).

Room phone Yes	*Confirm by* By arrang.	*Parking* Ample
Room TV No	*Last dinner* 9.15	*Banquets* 250/–

Langbank
Map 12 B1 Strathclyde
PA14 6YE
Langbank (047 554) 711
Telex 779801

Rooms 18
with bath/shower 18
Room phone Yes
Room TV Yes
Confirm by By arrang.
Last dinner 9.30
Parking Ample
Banquets 110/2

Credit Access, Amex,
Barclaycard, Diners

Gleddoch House Hotel 72% £C/D

Part of a 250-acre estate overlooking the river Clyde, this fine hotel is favoured by foreign visitors who appreciate its pleasant accommodation and numerous leisure facilities. Public areas include a foyer with a bold red colour scheme, a cosy lounge and a spacious bar. Large comfortable bedrooms in the original house have excellent beds and good-quality fabrics; those in the new wing are slightly smaller, but attractively furnished. There are also two luxurious executive rooms and three suites with lovely views. Bathrooms are modern. Management and staff are exceptionally welcoming. *Amenities* garden, sauna, indoor swimming pool, squash, golf course, game fishing, snooker, riding.

Langbank
Map 12 B1 Strathclyde
PA14 6YE
Langbank (047 554) 711

French cooking

● **Set L** £5·50
Set D £12, Sat £12·50
About £30 for two

Gleddoch House Hotel Restaurant Ⓢ

The young French chef is establishing a reputation for very capable cooking in this hotel restaurant. His short menu begins with appetisers like smoked quail and soups such as delicate pheasant consommé; main courses range from beef fillet with well-made green peppercorn sauce to turbot coated in hazelnut cream sauce, and there are some delicious sweets.
🍷 *ABOVE AVERAGE. Credit* Access, Amex, Barclaycard, Diners

Lunch 12.15–2.15 *Dinner* 7.30–9.30
Closed 1 January & 26 December

Stars in this Guide stand for the quality of the cooking only—
our overriding criterion, irrespective of price, luxury or service.

Largs
Map 12 A2 Strathclyde
South Promenade *KA30 8DZ*
Largs (0475) 674551

Credit Access, Amex,
Diners

Rooms 50
with bath/shower 36

Marine & Curlinghall Hotel 59% Ⓜ £D/E

A wealth of magnificent 19th-century carved wood and panelling distinguishes this peaceful hotel, which has lovely gardens overlooking the sea. The spacious bars and lounges have mostly modern furnishings, as do the simple, practical bedrooms; sea-facing rooms are larger, and all have radios and tea/coffee-makers. *Amenities* garden, table tennis, dancing (Sat), putting, billiards, pool table.

Room phone No	*Confirm by* 6.30	*Parking* Ample
Room TV Most	*Last dinner* 8.30	*Banquets* 120/12

Lucas
Service
A F Glaze Ltd
Luc
Lucas Service

Engineering for World Transport

Lucas Service, in the UK, is a nationwide network of over 300 company-owned and independent agents, supplying motorists and the automotive trade with the right auto-electrical, braking and fuel injection parts for British, European and Japanese vehicles.

Every Lucas Service agent also offers specialised product knowledge and service facilities, stemming from Lucas manufacturing experience and from the global activities of Lucas World Service, who offer similar facilities to the automotive aftermarket throughout Europe and beyond.

Lucas Service

Ledaig

Map 17 B5 Strathclyde
Connel *PA37 1SD*
Ledaig (063 172) 371
Telex 727897
Proprietors
Mr & Mrs Robin Buchanan-Smith
Rooms 22
with bath/shower 22
Room phone Yes
Room TV No
Confirm by By arrang.
Last dinner 8.30
Parking Ample
Banquets 20/–
Closed December–March

Credit Amex

Isle of Eriska 73% Ⓜ £B/C

Cross the bridge from the mainland and you're in a different world on this idyllic, tranquil island, where the friendly Buchanan-Smiths run this splendid Victorian hotel. Decor and furnishings throughout are tasteful and homely, with plenty of chintzy easy chairs in the panelled hall, bright, airy lounge and restful bar-lounge. Individually decorated bedrooms (singles are compact) have a combination of traditional and more modern furnishings and a vast list of extras including clothes brushes, trouser presses, sewing kits, books, information folders and fresh fruit. Spotless bathrooms have modern suites. Inclusive terms only. *Amenities* garden, tennis, sea fishing, croquet, riding, yacht for hire, rowing boat. &

Ledaig

Map 17 B5 Strathclyde
Connel *PA37 1SD*
Ledaig (063 172) 371
Proprietors
Mr & Mrs Robin Buchanan-Smith

● **Set L** from £6·50
Set D £13·50
About £35 for two

Isle of Eriska Restaurant ★

Beautifully fresh local ingredients are used whenever possible in this dignified panelled dining room. The six-course dinner could start with hot sherried grapefruit or smoked salmon wrapped around prawn mousse, to be followed by an excellent soup, perhaps lettuce or onion and parsley. The main course is usually a beautifully cooked roast served with vegetables from the garden, and the sweet trolley is loaded with goodies like strawberry mousse or peach, hazelnut and meringue cake. Light lunches, except for Sunday roast. Buffet Sunday evenings. **Specialities** lemon-stuffed chicken with tarragon and wine sauce, lettuce soup, raspberry brûlée, Uppingham pâté. ▼ *ABOVE AVERAGE. Credit* Amex

Lunch 1–2 *Dinner* 7.30–8.30
Closed December–March

Letham

Map 17 C5 Fife
KY7 7RU
Letham (033 781) 209
Telex 727369
Manager Mr D. V. Wellings
Credit Access, Amex

Rooms 11
with bath/shower 10

Fernie Castle Hotel 58% £E

Suits of armour and medieval weapons in the hall and bar are reminders that this stone-built hotel was once a castle. Best of the public rooms is the elegant lounge, with its gold-painted plasterwork and relaxing armchairs. Good-sized bedrooms, with plenty of storage and writing space, have TVs, tea-makers and a welcoming glass of sherry. Planned redecoration will be welcome. *Amenities* garden, dinner dance (Sat).

Room phone Yes	*Confirm by* 6	*Parking* Ample
Room TV Yes	*Last dinner* 9	*Banquets* 120/30

Lewiston

Map 16 B3 Highland
Near Drumnadrochit *IV3 6UN*
Drumnadrochit (045 62) 225
Proprietors
Mr & Mrs N. J. Quinn

Credit Barclaycard

Rooms 8
with bath/shower None

Lewiston Arms Hotel *(Inn)* Ⓜ £F

This bustling 200-year-old hostelry close to Loch Ness provides pleasant accommodation for tourists and monster hunters alike. The charmingly decorated new lounge bar opens on to the garden, and there's a cosy residents' lounge with an open fire, also a small TV room. Simple bedrooms (including four in a nearby cottage) have traditional furniture and pretty floral wallpapers. Public bathrooms are adequate. *Amenities* garden, tennis.

Room phone No	*Confirm by* 6	*Parking* Ample
Room TV No	*Last dinner* 9.30	*Banquets* 20/2

Linlithgow

Map 12 C1 Lothian
Champany Farm *EH49 7LW*
Philipstoun (050 683) 532
Proprietor Malcolm King

About £32 for two

Champany

This charming stone-walled restaurant offers starters and a seasonal choice of well-prepared main courses ranging from baked salmon with hollandaise to tasty veal in orange and ginger. *Credit* Access, Amex, Diners
Lunch 12–2.30 *Dinner* 7–9.30 **Closed** Sun & 1 & 2 January
● **Set L** £4·50 *Banquets* 25/6 &

Lochgair

Map 17 B5 Strathclyde
By Lochgilphead *PA31 8SA*
Lochgair (054 682) 233

Credit Amex, Barclaycard
Diners

Lochgair Hotel 54% £E

This unassuming little hotel with a garden running down to the shores of Loch Fyne makes a pleasant setting for a short stay. Guests can choose between the panelled public bar and the cosy lounge bar, or relax before TV in one of the old-fashioned lounges. Bedrooms (including balconied ones in the wing) have modern freestanding furniture and tea-makers. Bathrooms are adequate. *Amenities* garden, coarse & game fishing.

| *Rooms* 20 | *Room phone* No | *Confirm by* 6.30 | *Parking* Ample |
| *with bath/shower* 10 | *Room TV* No | *Last dinner* 8.30 | |

Lockerbie

Map 12 C3 Dumfries & Galloway
DG11 2SF
Lockerbie (057 62) 2427

Credit Amex, Barclaycard,
Diners

Dryfesdale Hotel 55% Ⓜ £F

A pleasant avenue of beech trees leads from the A74 to this cream-painted converted 18th-century manse, which stands in its own grounds just north of town. Well-used public rooms include a comfortable bar and a relaxing lounge with a bow-fronted glass sun lounge. Plainly furnished bedrooms are bright and cheerful; bathrooms well fitted.
Amenities garden, stabling.   &

| *Rooms* 12 | *Room phone* Yes | *Confirm by* By arrang. | *Parking* Ample |
| *with bath/shower* 5 | *Room TV* Yes | *Last dinner* 9 | *Banquets* 80/– |

Lybster

Map 16 C2 Highland
KW3 6BS
Lybster (059 32) 208
Proprietors
Mr & Mrs R. I. Mowat

Closed 1–4 January

Portland Arms Hotel 57% Ⓜ £E

Owned and run by Mr and Mrs Mowat for nearly 30 years, this pleasantly old-fashioned hotel is popular with shooting parties. Antiques mingle with modern pieces in the foyer and lounge, and bedrooms, too, vary greatly in furnishings as well as size: one room has a splendid half-tester, and many have attractive old bedsteads. Well-equipped modern bathrooms. There are two simple bars. *Amenities* garden, shooting.

| *Rooms* 22 | *Room phone* No | *Confirm by* By arrang. | *Parking* Ample |
| *with bath/shower* 7 | *Room TV* No | *Last dinner* 8.15 | *Banquets* 125/2 |

Lybster

Map 16 C2 Highland
KW3 6BS
Lybster (059 32) 208
Proprietors
Mr & Mrs R. I. Mowat

Portland Arms Hotel Restaurant Ⓢ

Exceptionally tender and tasty roast beef, served with nicely cooked vegetables, was the highlight of a meal at this roomy, traditionally furnished restaurant, where two long-serving lady cooks produce their excellent set meals. Scottish vegetable soup made a simple, nourishing starter, and the cold salmon was deliciously fresh and moist. Brisk, helpful waitresses put the seal on a really enjoyable dinner.   &

● **Set L** £3·50 **Set D** £5·75
About £18 for two

Lunch 12.45–2 *Dinner* 7.30–8.15
Closed 1–4 January

Melrose

Map 12 D2 Borders
TD6 9PD
Melrose (089 682) 2308

Credit Access, Amex,
Barclaycard, Diners

George & Abbotsford Hotel 55% £E

Sir Walter Scott was a frequent visitor to this pleasant town-centre hotel, whose smart new cocktail bar is a favourite local meeting place. There's also a comfortable little TV lounge and a function room. Compact bedrooms, which overlook the pretty rose garden, have decent modern furniture and are equipped with tea/coffee-making facilities. Bathrooms are adequate. *Amenities* garden.

| *Rooms* 22 | *Room phone* No | *Confirm by* By arrang. | *Parking* Ample |
| *with bath/shower* 13 | *Room TV* No | *Last dinner* 8.30 | *Banquets* 70/20 |

Milngavie

Map 12 B1 Strathclyde
Main Street *G62 6BY*
041–956 2291
Telex 778323

Credit Access, Amex,
Barclaycard, Diners

Black Bull Hotel 61% £E

This town-centre hotel, built some 250 years ago, has been extensively modernised throughout. There's a small lounge on the first floor as well as a choice of four different bars (one with a Glasgow tram motif). Bedrooms in the main building and the extension are functional in style, with fitted units, tea-makers and radios, and spacious bathrooms are well equipped.
Amenities jazz (Sun September–June).

Continued

Continued
Rooms 28
with bath/shower 27

Room phone Yes	*Confirm by* 7	*Parking* Ample
Room TV Yes	*Last dinner* 9.30	*Banquets* 120/10

Moffat   Annandale Hotel   51%   Ⓜ   £ F

Map 12 C3 Dumfries & Galloway
High Street *DG10 9HF*
Moffat (0683) 20013
Proprietor Mr Peter Toni
Credit Access, Amex,
Barclaycard, Diners
Closed mid Dec–mid Mar

Behind the Georgian facade of this four-storey building is a friendly, well-kept hotel. It has a spacious entrance hall, a residents' lounge with colour TV and a smart, contemporary lounge bar. Bedrooms in the main building are simply and solidly furnished, while the five in the converted stable block have modern fitted units, a useful luggage area and carpeted private bathrooms.

Rooms 30
with bath/shower 5

Room phone No	*Confirm by* By arrang.	*Parking* Ample
Room TV Some	*Last dinner* 8.30	*Banquets* 120/10

Moffat   Beechwood Country House Hotel   56%   Ⓜ   £ E

Map 12 C3 Dumfries & Galloway
Off Harthope Place *DG10 9RS*
Moffat (0683) 20210

Credit Access, Amex,
Barclaycard, Diners
Closed January

Keith & Sheila McIlwrick extend a warm welcome at their Victorian grey-stone mansion, which stands high above the town against a background of lovely beech trees. An assortment of objets d'art adorns the tall, attractively furnished lounge and bar. Well-kept bedrooms of varying size and style are bright and homely, all with radios, tea-makers and duvets. Compact carpeted bedrooms. No dogs. *Amenities* garden.

Rooms 8
with bath/shower 6

Room phone Most	*Confirm by* 6	*Parking* Ample
Room TV No	*Last dinner* 9.30	

Moffat   Ladbroke Mercury Motor Inn   56%   £ D

Map 12 C3 Dumfries & Galloway
Ladyknowe *DG10 9DY*
Moffat (0683) 20464

Credit Access, Amex,
Barclaycard, Diners

This two-storey town-centre hotel offers unfussy accommodation. A simple modern reception hall leads to the straightforward bar and nicely decorated residents' lounge with comfortable armchairs and glass-topped tables. Bedrooms, equipped with tea/coffee-making facilities and radios, have practical fitted units and pastel colour schemes. Adequately equipped bathrooms. *Amenities* pool table.

Rooms 51
with bath/shower 48

Room phone Some	*Confirm by* 6	*Parking* Ample
Room TV Yes	*Last dinner* 9.30	*Banquets* 30/–

Moniaive   Woodlea Hotel   60%   Ⓜ   £ E/F

Map 12 B3 Dumfries & Galloway
Near Thornhill *DG3 4EN*
Moniaive (084 82) 209
Proprietors Mr & Mrs. R. McIver

Closed occasionally
November–March

A wide range of leisure activities is a feature of the McIvers' hotel, which has a large, modern lounge, an attractive cellar bar and a games room with separate TV area. Spacious bedrooms have pine furnishings and pretty duvet covers. *Amenities* garden, sauna, outdoor swimming pool, tennis, dancing (some Fris July–August), keep-fit equipment, croquet, bicycles, putting, solarium, games room, badminton, children's play area.

Rooms 15
with bath/shower 2

Room phone No	*Confirm by* By arrang.	*Parking* Ample
Room TV No	*Last dinner* 8.30	*Banquets* 76/–

Moniaive   Woodlea Hotel Restaurant   ♧ Ⓢ

Map 12 B3 Dumfries & Galloway
Near Thornhill *DG3 4EN*
Moniaive (084 82) 209
Proprietors Mr & Mrs R. McIver

Local game and fish and home-grown vegetables feature on the menu of this informal, pine-furnished restaurant with lovely mountain views. The McIvers share the cooking, producing wholesome, tasty dishes ranging from grilled trout and steaks to duckling in cherry sauce and venison in red wine. Finish with delicious apple crumble or fruit salad. Cold buffet for lunch.   ♿

● **Set L** £3·80, incl. service
Set D £6·80, incl. service
About £24 for two

Lunch 12.30–2 (summer only) *Dinner* 7.30–8.30
Closed D 25 December & occasionally November–March

Muir of Ord   Ord Arms Hotel *(Inn)*   Ⓜ   £ F

Map 16 B3 Highland
North Road *IV6 7XR*

This homely stone-built inn stands on the A9 on the northern outskirts of the

Continued

Inverness (0463) 870286

Credit Access
Closed 1–6 January

Rooms 14
with bath/shower 7

Nairn
Map 16 C3 Highland
IV12 4HU
Nairn (0667) 53119
Proprietor
Mr J. Gordon Macintyre
Rooms 17
with bath/shower 12
Room phone No
Room TV No
Confirm by By arrang.
Last dinner 9.30
Parking Ample
Banquets 70/2
Closed beginning December–
end February
Credit Amex, Barclaycard
Diners

Clifton Hotel 70%    £ E

With an amazing collection of paintings, prints, antiques and mirrors filling its sumptuous public rooms, this splendid Victorian house is like a miniature museum. Charming bedrooms also feature some good antique pieces, and rooms at the top command fine sea views. Bathrooms have excellent up-to-date fittings. The beauty of the decor is matched by immaculate housekeeping and excellent service. *Amenities* garden.

Muir of Ord. It has a pleasantly modernised reception/lounge area and two cheerful bars. Three simply appointed bedrooms are on the ground floor but the best are upstairs, individually styled, with prettily patterned wallpaper and white unit furniture. Compact, well-fitted bathrooms and shower rooms. *Amenities* garden.

Room phone No	*Confirm by* 7	*Parking* Ample
Room TV Yes	*Last dinner* 9	*Banquets* 120/20

Nairn
Map 16 C3 Highland
IV12 4HU
Nairn (0667) 53119
Proprietor
Mr J. Gordon Macintyre

About £28 for two

Clifton Hotel Restaurant & Green Room

Dinner in the restaurant–an elegant room with fresh flowers and lace tablecloths–brings a selection of well-prepared dishes ranging from excellent thick oxtail soup to omelettes, roast chicken and beef Stroganoff. Tangy cold lemon soufflé is just one of the splendid desserts. Seafood lunches are served in the delightful little Green Room. *ABOVE AVERAGE.*
Credit Amex, Barclaycard, Diners

Lunch 12.30–2.30 *Dinner* 7–9.30
Closed beginning December–end February

Nairn
Map 16 C3 Highland
Seabank Road *IV12 4HD*
Nairn (0667) 52301

Credit Access, Amex,
Barclaycard, Diners

Rooms 55
with bath/shower 55

Golf View Hotel 60%   £ D

With its numerous leisure activities, this solid Victorian hotel by the Moray Firth is popular for family holidays. The two lounges and the cocktail bar are comfortably up to date, and bedrooms have modern furnishings and compact bathrooms. *Amenities* garden, sauna, outdoor swimming pool, tennis, dancing (Mon, Wed, Sat in season), cabaret (Fri in season), putting, films, hairdressing, games room, trampoline, paddling pool.

Room phone Yes	*Confirm by* 6	*Parking* Ample
Room TV Yes	*Last dinner* 9.30	*Banquets* 140/–

Nairn
Map 16 C3 Highland
Inverness Road *IV12 4RX*
Nairn (0667) 53144

Rooms 44
with bath/shower 44
Room phone Yes
Room TV Yes
Confirm by By arrang.
Last dinner 9.30
Parking Ample
Banquets 60/–

Newton Hotel 70%   £ C/D

There are marvellous views of the Moray Firth from this impressive stone hotel set in 27 acres of mature gardens. The grand panelled entrance hall immediately creates an impression of gracious elegance, which extends to the peaceful library and the comfortable lounge with its velvet-covered armchairs and sofas; there's also a more up-to-date cocktail bar. Attractively decorated bedrooms (including some very modern ones in the court-

Continued

Continued	yard block) have good-quality furniture and well-fitted bathrooms. Guests
Credit Access, Amex,	can use the facilities of the nearby Golf View Hotel.
Barclaycard, Diners	*Amenities* garden, sauna, tennis, hotel coach, solarium, table tennis, putting, croquet.

Newburgh   Udny Arms Hotel   60%   £E

Map 16 D3 Grampian
Main Street *AB4 0BL*
Newburgh (035 86) 444
Telex 739187

Credit Access, Amex,
Barclaycard

A homely atmosphere prevails at this grand little hotel, a popular base for outdoor holidays. Two delightful lounges, two bars and a newly converted bistro/wine bar are among the welcoming public rooms, and there's also a self-contained function suite with its own leafy bar. Cosy, compact bedrooms, furnished in contemporary or traditional style, have TVs, radios and neat little bathrooms. *Amenities* garden.

Rooms 20	*Room phone* Yes	*Confirm by* 7	*Parking* Ample
with bath/shower 20	*Room TV* Yes	*Last dinner* 10	*Banquets* 100/–

Newburgh   Udny Arms Hotel Restaurant   Ⓢ

Map 16 D3 Grampian
Main Street *AB4 0BL*
Newburgh (035 86) 444

Local game and seafood find their seasonal place on the menus of this charmingly traditional restaurant. Cooking is consistently capable throughout the menu which could include Scotch broth or spicily sauced cheese aigrettes, followed by game pie, roast rib of beef or chicken with ginger and walnuts. To finish, there's an enjoyable selection of sweets and a few well-kept cheeses. *Credit* Access, Amex, Barclaycard

● **Set D** £11·50
About £30 for two

Dinner only 6.30–10, Sun 7–10

Newton Stewart   Bruce Hotel   60%   Ⓜ   £E

Map 13 B4 Dumfries & Galloway
Queen Street *DG8 6JL*
Newton Stewart (0671) 2294
Proprietor
Mrs John M. Wyllie
Credit Access, Amex,
Barclaycard, Diners

This grey-stone hotel has a smart modern interior. Striking contemporary decor is a feature of the public rooms, which include a stylish cocktail bar, a simple public bar and a luxurious first-floor residents' lounge with TV. Prettily decorated bedrooms (mainly in the extension) are equipped to a high standard and have plenty of storage space. Colourful bathrooms are well fitted. *Amenities* solarium.

Rooms 17	*Room phone* Yes	*Confirm by* By arrang.	*Parking* Ample
with bath/shower 15	*Room TV* Yes	*Last dinner* 8.30	*Banquets* 60/20

North Berwick   Marine Hotel   68%   £D

Map 12 D1 Lothian
Cromwell Road *EH39 4LZ*
North Berwick (0620) 2406
Telex 727363

Credit Access, Amex,
Barclaycard, Diners

A large, turreted building overlooking a golf course and the sea. Restful decor and deep windows give a special appeal to public rooms like the roomy, comfortable lounge and bar. Attractive bedrooms range from large ones in the tower to smaller ones in a modern wing. Good bathrooms.
Amenities garden, sauna, outdoor swimming pool, tennis, squash, dancing (Sat), games room, billiards, table tennis, putting.

Rooms 85	*Room phone* Yes	*Confirm by* By arrang.	*Parking* Ample
with bath/shower 85	*Room TV* Yes	*Last dinner* 9	*Banquets* 240/2

Oban   Alexander Hotel   58%   £D

Map 17 B5 Strathclyde
Esplanade *PA34 5AA*
Oban (0631) 62381

Credit Access, Amex,
Barclaycard, Diners
Closed mid October–1 May

Overlooking the harbour, this modernised Victorian building offers reasonable standards of comfort and simple accommodation. There are three pleasantly furnished lounges (one with TV) as well as an attractive new bar. Bedrooms of varying size are well maintained and provided with tea-makers. Most have neat little bathrooms, and public bathrooms are adequate. *Amenities* entertainment (2 nights weekly), games room.

Rooms 56	*Room phone* No	*Confirm by* By arrang.	*Parking* Limited
with bath/shower 43	*Room TV* No	*Last dinner* 8.30	

Old Meldrum
Map 16 D3 Grampian
AB5 0AE
Old Meldrum (065 12) 2294
Proprietor Robin Duff of Meldrum
Credit Amex, Diners
Closed mid December–mid March

Rooms 9
with bath/shower 7

Meldrum House Hotel   67%   £ D

Traces of the 13th-century castle still remain in the Lairds of Meldrum's ancestral house, a fine turreted mansion set in 300 acres of beautiful wooded grounds. Antiques and modern furniture mingle in the public rooms, which include an imposing hall, an airy lounge and an interesting vaulted bar. Large bedrooms have solid period furnishings and attractive views. Spacious modern bathrooms. *Amenities* garden.

Room phone Most	*Confirm by* By arrang.	*Parking* Ample
Room TV Yes	*Last dinner* 9	*Banquets* 60/10

Peat Inn
Map 17 D5 Fife
Near Cupar *KY15 5LH*
Peat Inn (033 484) 206
Proprietors
David & Patricia Wilson

● **Set L** £6·50 incl. service
About £26 for two

The Peat Inn   ★

This plushly furnished inn makes an elegant setting for David Wilson's excellent cooking, which is very much a labour of love. He uses superb local ingredients and herbs from his own garden to create marvellous dishes like venison liver in a light Madeira sauce with a garnish of root vegetables and poached fillet of sole filled with subtle lobster mousse and served with a creamy crayfish sauce. Presentation is in the true nouvelle cuisine style. Set lunch menu (no choice).
Specialities lobster and prawn cake in a crayfish sauce, escalope of salmon in pastry with Vermouth and dill, saddle of venison in a port sauce, pineapple and grenadine sorbet with fresh fruits. *OUTSTANDING. Credit* Amex

Lunch at 12.30 for 1 *Dinner* 7.30–9.30
Closed Sun, Mon, 25 Dec, 1st week Jan, 1 week April & 1 week Oct

Peebles
Map 12 C2 Borders
Eddleston *EH45 8PL*
Eddleston (072 13) 233
Proprietors
Mr & Mrs S. L. Maguire
Closed late December–mid March

Rooms 16
with bath/shower 11

Cringletie House Hotel   63%   Ⓜ   £ D/E

There's a delightfully homely air to this turreted Victorian mansion set in 28 acres of gardens and woods. A splendid carved oak staircase leads to the first-floor public rooms, which include a bar in the former library and a superb panelled lounge with a beautiful painted ceiling. Bedrooms are furnished in traditional style, and bathrooms are up to date.
Amenities garden, tennis, croquet, putting.

Room phone No	*Confirm by* 5	*Parking* Ample
Room TV No	*Last dinner* 8.30	*Banquets* 28/15

Peebles
Map 12 C2 Borders
Eddleston *EH45 8PL*
Eddleston (072 13) 233
Proprietors Mr & Mrs S. Maguire

● **Set L** Sun only £6 **Set D** £10
About £26 for two

Cringletie House Hotel Restaurant

Mrs Maguire gives visitors to this elegantly formal restaurant a real taste of home cooking, with good use made of garden-fresh fruit and vegetables. The four-course set dinner menu features dishes like roast loin of pork with orange and Madeira sauce or beef kebabs, plus some delicious puddings such as rhubarb charlotte. There are simpler weekday lunch menus and a traditional roast on Sundays. *ABOVE AVERAGE.*

Lunch 1–1.45 *Dinner* 7.30–8.30
Closed late December–mid March

Peebles
Map 12 C2 Borders
Innerleithen Road *EH45 8BA*
Peebles (0721) 20451

Credit Access, Amex, Barclaycard, Diners

Rooms 32
with bath/shower 24

Park Hotel   63%   £ E

Picture windows in the spacious bar-lounge give fine views of the grounds and far-distant hills at this comfortable turn-of-the-century hotel. There's also a relaxing residents' lounge with traditional furniture. Bedrooms range from large and luxurious in the main building to simpler, modern ones in the extension. Bathrooms are spick and span.
Amenities garden, dancing (Sat, October–March), putting.

Room phone Yes	*Confirm by* 6	*Parking* Ample
Room TV Yes	*Last dinner* 9	*Banquets* 80/6

Peebles

Map 12 C2 Borders
Innerleithen Road *EH45 8LX*
Peebles (0721) 20602
Telex 72568
Manager Mr Pieter J. Van Dijk
Rooms 134
with bath/shower 134
Room phone Yes
Room TV Yes
Confirm by By arrang.
Last dinner 9
Parking Ample
Banquets 352/2

Credit Access, Amex,
Barclaycard

Peebles Hotel Hydro   70%   £ C

Helpful and smartly uniformed staff create an immediately favourable impression at this superbly run Edwardian hotel, beautifully situated high above the valley of the Tweed. The elegantly furnished lounges are lofty and dignified, and there's a relaxing bar, as well as a terrace and a number of splendid conference rooms. Cheerfully decorated bedrooms, including some family-size, are comfortable and well equipped, bathrooms neat and sparkling. No dogs. *Amenities* garden, sauna, indoor swimming pool, tennis, squash, dancing (Fri, Sat, also 3 extra nights weekly in season), badminton, pitch & putt, putting, games room, riding, billiards, cinema, solarium, laundry room, children's playground.

Peebles

Map 12 C2 Borders
High Street *EH45 8AJ*
Peebles (0721) 20892

Credit Access, Amex,
Barclaycard, Diners

Rooms 37
with bath/shower 37

Tontine Hotel   60%   £ D

Built by public subscription in 1808, this well-maintained stone building occupies a prominent position in the main street. Public rooms like the large, comfortable lounge and the panelled bar lead off a little entrance hall with a fine staircase. Simply decorated bedrooms, some in the original building, the rest in a modern extension, have central heating, tea-makers (with Scottish shortbread) and well-fitted bathrooms.

Room phone Yes	*Confirm by* 6	*Parking* Ample
Room TV Yes	*Last dinner* 9.30	

Perth

Map 17 C5 Tayside
West Mill Street *PH1 5QP*
Perth (0738) 28281
Telex 778704

Credit Access, Amex,
Barclaycard, Diners

Rooms 78
with bath/shower 78

City Mills Hotel   57%   £ D/E

The cottagy public areas of this town-centre hotel are full of heavy timbers, and the sight of the millstream flowing beneath the floor leaves you in no doubt as to the building's past. Bedrooms in the main building have fitted units and autumnal colour schemes, while those in the extension are decorated in soft colours and have reproduction antique furniture. Bathrooms are adequate. *Amenities* garden.

Room phone Yes	*Confirm by* 6	*Parking* Ample
Room TV Yes	*Last dinner* 10.30	*Banquets* 200/–

Perth

Map 17 C5 Tayside
Crieff Road *PH1 3JT*
Almondbank (073 088) 241
Manager Tony Heath

About £25 for two

Huntingtower

A peaceful house in lovely gardens two miles outside Perth. First-class meat is used for dishes like tournedos with Madeira sauce and lamb's liver with onions. Sweets can disappoint. *SUPERIOR. Credit* Access, Amex, Barclaycard, Diners *Lunch* 12.30–2 *Dinner* 7.15–9.30 **Closed** D Sun, all Mon, 25 December & 2–9 January ● **Set L** £5·25 **Set D** £8·50 *Banquets* 46/2

Perth

Map 17 C5 Tayside
Tay Street *PH1 5LD*
Perth (0738) 24455

Credit Access, Amex,
Barclaycard, Diners

Rooms 43
with bath/shower 43

Royal George Hotel   62%   £ D

A pleasant tree-lined road by the river Tay leads to this sturdy city-centre hotel, whose large reception area has plenty of comfortable seating. There are other places for guests to relax, too, including a spacious panelled bar with a terrace overlooking the river. Bedrooms, some attractively refurbished, have good solid furnishings and well-equipped bathrooms. *Amenities* garden.

Room phone Yes	*Confirm by* 6	*Parking* Limited
Room TV Yes	*Last dinner* 9	*Banquets* 80/2

Perth

Map 17 C5 Tayside
Leonard Street *PH2 8HE*
Perth (0738) 24141
Telex 76481

Credit Access, Amex,
Barclaycard, Diners

Rooms 55			
with bath/shower 42			

Station Hotel   64%   £E

This imposing Victorian hotel with turrets and crenellated gables still has a feeling of solidity. Lofty public rooms, which include a convivial cocktail bar and an elegant lounge, bear the marks of a more gracious age, with pillars and thick carpeting complementing modern furniture. Spacious bedrooms are boldly decorated in various styles and have tastefully chosen furniture. Bathrooms are compact. *Amenities* garden.

Room phone Yes	*Confirm by* 6	*Parking* Ample
Room TV Yes	*Last dinner* 9	*Banquets* 260/–

Perth

Map 17 C5 Tayside
24 St John Street *PH1 5SP*
Perth (0738) 26641
Smørrebrød

About £17 for two

Timothy's

Friendliness and informality are the hallmarks of this enterprising, cosy little restaurant. The mainstay of the menu is a wide selection of appetising smørrebrød (Danish open sandwiches), but there are also soups, jacket potatoes and puddings. *Lunch* 12–2.30 *Dinner* 7–10.15
Closed Sun, Mon, 1 & 2 January & Christmas

Pitcaple

Map 16 D3 Grampian
By Inverurie *AB5 9HS*
Pitcaple (046 76) 202
Telex 739935
Proprietors Theo & Maggie Smith
Rooms 11
with bath/shower 7
Room phone Yes
Room TV Yes
Confirm by By arrang.
Last dinner 9
Parking Ample
Banquets 40/2
Closed 25 & 26 December

Credit Access, Amex,
Barclaycard, Diners

Pittodrie House Hotel   70%   Ⓜ   £E/F

A peaceful country house atmosphere prevails at this splendid little castle, which stands in a lovely garden on a 3,000-acre estate. The spacious drawing room is a model of traditional elegance and comfort, with antiques, family portraits, a large open fireplace and plenty of chintzy chairs. There's also a handsome chandeliered entrance hall, a panelled bar, a billiards room and a library which doubles as a function room. Spacious bedrooms also have some fine antiques, and one has a magnificent old half-tester. Good modern bathrooms. The building itself is in a mixture of styles, the oldest part dating back to 1480.
Amenities garden, tennis, squash, billiards, croquet.

Pitcaple

Map 16 D3 Grampian
By Inverurie *AB5 9HS*
Pitcaple (046 76) 202
Proprietors
Theo & Maggie Smith

● **Set L** £7 **Set D** £14
About £35 for two

Pittodrie House Hotel Restaurant

A lofty dining room in the grand style, with narrow arched windows and elegant Regency-style furniture. Set dinners offer a good choice of simple, enjoyably cooked dishes ranging from delicate smoked mackerel pâté and tender deep-fried clams to flavoursome rare roast beef and an excellent lemon and brandy syllabub. Booking essential for lunch.
Credit Access, Amex, Barclaycard, Diners

Lunch 12–1.30 *Dinner* 7.30–9
Closed 25 & 26 December

Pitlochry

Map 17 C4 Tayside
PH16 5LY
Pitlochry (0796) 2400
Telex 76406

Credit Access, Amex,
Barclaycard, Diners

Rooms 92			
with bath/shower 92			

Atholl Palace Hotel   61%   £D

This imposing Victorian hotel stands in 48 acres of private parkland and offers many leisure facilities. Public rooms are on a grand scale and have traditional furnishings, while the bedrooms have quiet, modern decor and practical fitted units. Spotless bathrooms. *Amenities* garden, sauna, outdoor swimming pool, tennis, helipad, cinema, nature trails, putting, pitch & putt, games room, children's playroom, badminton.

Room phone Yes	*Confirm by* 6	*Parking* Ample
Room TV Yes	*Last dinner* 9	*Banquets* 200/–

Pitlochry

Map 17 C4 Tayside
Clunie Bridge Road *PH16 5JY*
Pitlochry (0796) 2537

Proprietors
Mr & Mrs Graham Brown
Closed 2 November–26 March

Green Park Hotel 56% Ⓜ £ D/E

Occupying a superb position on the banks of Loch Faskally, this Victorian building is a well-maintained hotel. The panelled reception hall is a welcoming sight, and there's a delightful sun lounge, a TV lounge and a modern cocktail bar. Bedrooms in the main house are traditional, whereas extension rooms are in simple modern style, with good bathrooms. *Amenities* garden, coarse & game fishing, putting, table tennis, children's play area.

Rooms 38	*Room phone* No	*Confirm by* By arrang.	*Parking* Ample
with bath/shower 28	*Room TV* No	*Last dinner* 8	

Pitlochry

Map 17 C4 Tayside
Knockard Road *PH16 5JH*
Pitlochry (0796) 2666

Credit Access, Amex,
Barclaycard, Diners
Closed 15 October–end March

Pitlochry Hydro Hotel 59% £ E

Lovely gardens and lawns surround this handsome Victorian hotel, which commands fine views from its position high above the town. There's a spacious reception hall, two traditional lounges and a roomy, comfortable bar-lounge. Simply furnished bedrooms have tea/coffee-making facilities. Some bedrooms and bathrooms are in need of refurbishment. *Amenities* garden, tennis, 9-hole golf course, dancing (Sat), solarium, putting, croquet. &

Rooms 64	*Room phone* No	*Confirm by* 6	*Parking* Ample
with bath/shower 56	*Room TV* No	*Last dinner* 8.30	*Banquets* 60/2

Any person using our name to obtain free hospitality is a fraud. Proprietors, please inform the police and us.

Port Appin

Map 17 B5 Strathclyde
PA38 4DF
Appin (063 173) 236

Closed end October–week before Easter

Airds Hotel 63% Ⓜ £ D/E

Mr and Mrs Allen offer real Scottish hospitality at their splendid old ferry inn, which overlooks lovely Loch Linnhe and the mountains of Morvern. The warm, homely feeling that makes the lounge and bar so cosy extends to the traditionally styled bedrooms, which have thoughtful extras. Bathrooms, private and public, have functional modern fittings. Housekeeping is excellent. *Amenities* garden.

Rooms 16	*Room phone* No	*Confirm by* By arrang.	*Parking* Ample
with bath/shower 5	*Room TV* No	*Last dinner* 7.30	*Banquets* 40/2

Port Appin

Map 17 B5 Strathclyde
PA38 4DF
Appin (063 173) 236

Airds Hotel Restaurant 🍷 Ⓢ

Dinner is at 7.30 in this neat, simply decorated restaurant, where Betty Allen turns excellent local produce into some very enjoyable dishes on her four-course menus. Smoked mackerel pâté, rich cream of spinach soup and trout with cream and chives were carefully prepared and attractively presented; other choices might include haggis and rib of beef. Delicious puddings, too. Lighter lunches.  *OUTSTANDING.* &

● **Set D** £10	*Lunch* 12.30–1.30 *Dinner* at 7.30
About £27·50 for two	**Closed** end October–week before Easter

Port William

Map 13 B4 Dumfries & Galloway
Near Newton Stewart *DG8 9RL*
Mochrum (098 886) 254

Closed mid January–end February

Corzemalzie House Hotel 65% Ⓜ £ E

The McDougalls have boldly converted this 19th-century mansion into a smart modern hotel. A central Swedish fireplace dominates the bar, and there's a large lounge with bamboo furniture and contemporary sofas and chairs. Bedrooms are also up to date and comfortable, with freestanding units and tea-making facilities. Compact, fully tiled bathrooms. Breakfasts are outstanding. *Amenities* garden, game fishing, shooting, croquet, putting.

Rooms 15	*Room phone* No	*Confirm by* By arrang.	*Parking* Ample
with bath/shower 15	*Room TV* No	*Last dinner* 9.15	*Banquets* 80/–

Port William
Map 13 B4 Dumfries & Galloway
Near Newton Stewart *DG8 9RL*
Mochrum (098 886) 254

Corsemalzie House Hotel Restaurant   ⓢ

Local specialities, including salmon, beef and game, dominate the menu at this lofty restaurant, where prime ingredients and careful preparation produce some excellent dishes. Our mussel salad with a tangy lemon dressing made a splendid starter, and we also enjoyed hearty lentil soup and richly sauced carbonnade of beef. Help yourself from a sideboard of delicious desserts. Service is charming and efficient.   ♿

● **Set L** Sun only £5 **Set D** £7·50   *Lunch* Sun 1–2, Mon–Sat by arrangement only *Dinner* 7.30–9.15
About £27 for two   **Closed** mid January–end February

Our inspectors are our full-time employees; they are professionally trained by us.

Portpatrick
Map 13 A4 Dumfries & Galloway
Near Stranraer *DG9 9AD*
Portpatrick (077 681) 471

Credit Amex, Barclaycard
Closed January–March

Knockinaam Lodge Hotel   66%   £ D/E

Check for directions when booking at this secluded Victorian house with 30 acres of wooded grounds and its own private bay. A charming entrance hall leads to the cosy panelled bar and a spacious lounge designed for relaxation. Cheerfully decorated bedrooms vary in size, but all have luxurious curtains and attractive freestanding and antique furniture. Large, carpeted bathrooms. *Amenities* garden, sea fishing, croquet, slipway, putting.

Rooms 10	*Room phone* No	*Confirm by* By arrang.	*Parking* Ample
with bath/shower 8	*Room TV* No	*Last dinner* 9	*Banquets* 40/–

Portpatrick
Map 13 A4 Dumfries & Galloway
Near Stranraer *DG9 9AD*
Portpatrick (077 681) 471

Knockinaam Lodge Hotel Restaurant   ⓢ

Chef John Henry's menus have a French flavour at this comfortable dining room. The choice ranges from quite simple dishes like ham and green pea soup and delicious chicken pancakes to inventive specialities such as smoked salmon pâté with green peppercorns and pork fillet with asparagus sauce. Vegetables are fresh and enjoyable, and sweets include a beautifully light strawberry Pavlova. *Credit* Amex, Barclaycard   ♿

● **Set D** £11   *Lunch* by arrangement only *Dinner* 7.15–9
About £30 for two   **Closed** January–March

Portree
Map 16 A3 Highland
Isle of Skye *IV51 9DB*
Portree (0478) 2531
Proprietors
H. M. & M. B. Andrew

Closed October–May

Rosedale Hotel *(Inn)* Ⓜ   £ E

A row of cheerful white-painted harbourside dwellings makes up this friendly, peaceful hotel, run by the Andrew family since 1950. There are two lounges with simple modern furnishings (one has TV) and two smart and cosy little bars. Neat bedrooms are furnished mainly in traditional style, and bathrooms are well kept and adequate.
Amenities sea fishing.

Rooms 21	*Room phone* No	*Confirm by* By arrang.	*Parking* Ample
with bath/shower 10	*Room TV* No	*Last dinner* 8	

Prestwick
Map 12 B2 Strathclyde
Ayr Road *KA9 1TP*
Prestwick (0292) 76811

Manager Mr N. Smith
Credit Access, Amex,
Barclaycard, Diners

Carlton Hotel   55%   £ E

Within easy reach of the town centre and the airport, this modern hotel is useful for business visitors. Decor throughout is functional, from the lounge bar and comfortable TV lounge to the simple bedrooms, which have practical furniture, tea/coffee-makers and fully tiled bathrooms. Some redecoration would be welcome.
Amenities dinner dance (Fri, Sat), pool table.

Rooms 39	*Room phone* Yes	*Confirm by* 6	*Parking* Ample
with bath/shower 39	*Room TV* Yes	*Last dinner* 9.30	

Renfrew

Map 12 B1 Strathclyde
63 Hairst Street *PA48QY*
041–886 3055
Proprietors
Mr A. Pierotti & Mr S. Izzi
Italian cooking
● **Set L** from £3·50
Set D from £6·75
About £32 for two
Banquets 180/70

Piccolo Mondo

Dancing to a live band every evening is an added attraction in this comfortable modern restaurant, where the menu features a varied selection of authentic Italian fare–from home-made cannelloni to tender, tasty saltimbocca alla romana. There are also grills, seasonal game and good fresh fish. Vegetables are nicely prepared and the sweet trolley has many popular favourites. *Credit* Access, Amex, Barclaycard, Diners

Lunch 12–2.15 *Dinner* 6.30–11
Closed Sun

Renfrew

See also under Glasgow Airport

Rockcliffe

Map 13 C4 Dumfries & Galloway
Near Dalbeattie *DG54QF*
Rockcliffe (055 663) 225

Closed mid October–April

Baron's Craig Hotel   65%   £D

Standing in fine mature gardens and woodland, with views of the Solway Firth through the trees, this impressive 19th-century building is a haven of peace and seclusion. Antiques fill the entrance hall, and there's also a beautifully furnished lounge and a bright, airy cocktail bar. Bedrooms range from attractive and traditional in the main house to more modern ones in the extension. Well-fitted bathrooms. *Amenities* garden.

| *Rooms* 28 | *Room phone* No | *Confirm by* By arrang. | *Parking* Ample |
| *with bath/shower* 20 | *Room TV* No | *Last dinner* 9 | |

Rothes-on-Spey

Map 16 C3 Grampian
IV33 7AH
Rothes (034 03) 254
Proprietors
Mr & Mrs D. C. Carmichael

Closed mid November–14 March

Rothes Glen Hotel   65%      £C/D

Turreted like a small castle, this delightful mansion (designed by the architect of Balmoral) is set in 40 acres of grounds in the tranquil Spey valley. Fine antiques and a galleried staircase give the entrance hall an air of gracious elegance, which extends to the serene drawing room and cocktail bar. Some bedrooms are traditional, others more compact and modern. Bathrooms are adequate. *Amenities* garden, putting.

| *Rooms* 19 | *Room phone* Yes | *Confirm by* By arrang. | *Parking* Ample |
| *with bath/shower* 8 | *Room TV* No | *Last dinner* 8.30 | *Banquets* 30/– |

Rothes-on-Spey

Map 16 C3 Grampian
IV33 7AH
Rothes (034 03) 254
Proprietors
Mr & Mrs D. C. Carmichael

● **Set L** £5 **Set D** £9·75
About £30 for two

Rothes Glen Hotel Restaurant

An attractive, airy restaurant with pleasant views from its large windows. The table d'hôte menus (three courses for lunch, four for dinner) offer honest, capably prepared dishes ranging from grilled herrings in oatmeal with mustard sauce to roast loin of lamb, and there are some creamy sweets such as chocolate mousse. A more extensive à la carte is also available in summer.

Lunch 12.30–2 *Dinner* 7–8.30
Closed mid November–14 March

Rothesay

Map 12 A1 Strathclyde
Isle of Bute *PA20 9JD*
Rothesay (0700) 2500
Telex 778982
Credit Access, Amex,
Barclaycard, Diners
Closed 5 January–end February

Glenburn Hotel   61%   £E

A beautiful hillside position affords fine sea views from this sturdy Victorian mansion. Spacious smartly refurbished public rooms like the lounges and bar are decorated in contemporary style, and bedrooms of various sizes offer simple, practical comforts. Adequate bathrooms. *Amenities* garden, tennis, dinner dance (Sat), cabaret, putting, badminton, table tennis, billiards, laundry room, hairdressing, jetty, hotel boats, hotel coach.

| *Rooms* 103 | *Room phone* Yes | *Confirm by* 6 | *Parking* Ample |
| *with bath/shower* 44 | *Room TV* No | *Last dinner* 8.30 | *Banquets* 200/2 |

St Andrews
Map 17 D5 Fife
Old Station Road *KY16 9SP*
St Andrews (0334) 74371
Telex 76280
Credit Access, Amex,
Barclaycard, Diners
Closed end Nov–mid March

Old Course Hotel 63%   £C

New owners have just taken over this large stone-built hotel alongside the 17th fairway of the Old Course at St Andrews and plan to make substantial improvements. At present, public areas include a spacious reception-lounge and two simply furnished bars. Well-designed bedrooms have fitted units, tea-makers and radios. Bathrooms are fully tiled.

Rooms 82
with bath/shower 82

Room phone Yes	*Confirm by* 6	*Parking* Ample
Room TV Yes	*Last dinner* 9.30	*Banquets* 175/4

St Andrews
Map 17 D5 Fife
Strathkinness Low Road *KY16 9TX*
St Andrews (0334) 72594
Proprietors Mr & Mrs Cook
& Mrs Russell
Credit Access, Amex,
Barclaycard, Diners

Rufflets Hotel 68% Ⓜ   £D

Run by the same family for the last 30 years, this extended private house offers excellent comforts and friendly hospitality. There's a pleasant lounge with views of the garden from its huge bay window, a cosy TV room and an attractive bar. Tastefully decorated bedrooms are in modern or traditional style and tiled bathrooms are spotless. No dogs. *Amenities* garden, putting.
Closed mid January–mid February   &

Rooms 21
with bath/shower 21

Room phone Yes	*Confirm by* 6	*Parking* Ample
Room TV Some	*Last dinner* 9	*Banquets* 60/–

St Fillans
Map 17 C5 Tayside
Near Crieff *PH6 2NF*
St Fillans (076 485) 333

Credit Access, Barclaycard
Closed end October–beginning April

Four Seasons Hotel 60% Ⓜ   £D

Close to the shores of Loch Earn, this attractive modern hotel offers pleasant accommodation and hospitality. Public rooms, including the long Tarken Bar, have a Scandinavian air with their extensive panelling. Bedrooms are simply furnished in modern style, and have adequate bathrooms; there are also six family chalets in the grounds. Some redecoration will be welcome.
Amenities garden.   &

Rooms 18
with bath/shower 18

Room phone Yes	*Confirm by* By arrang.	*Parking* Ample
Room TV Yes	*Last dinner* 9.45	*Banquets* 120/6

St Fillans
Map 17 C5 Tayside
Near Crieff *PH6 2NF*
St Fillans (076 485) 333

Four Seasons Hotel Restaurant   

There are lovely views from the windows of this long modern dining room with its Scandinavian-style panelled ceiling. The menu offers a good choice of straightforward dishes like pâté maison, chicken basquaise, braised silverside and grills, as well as seasonal salmon and game, while sweets on the trolley include a rich chocolate mousse.
🍷 *SUPERIOR. Credit* Access, Barclaycard

● **Set L** £5·50 **Set D** £7·90
About £27 for two

Lunch 12.15–2 *Dinner* 7.15–9.45
Closed end October–beginning April

We welcome complaints and bona fide recommendations on the tear-out pages for readers' comments. They are followed up by our professional team. Please also complain to the management instantly.

Scourie
Map 16 B2 Highland
IV27 4TH
Scourie (0971) 2080

Eddrachilles Hotel 59% Ⓜ   £E

Mr and Mrs Wood's charming white-painted hotel enjoys a setting of great beauty and tranquillity at the head of Badcall Bay, a fascinating sight with its dozens of little islands. Housekeeping is immaculate throughout, from the homely public rooms to the comfortable bedrooms, which have practical modern furnishings and sparkling, up-to-date bathrooms.
Amenities garden, game & sea fishing, hotel boats.

Rooms 11
with bath/shower 11

Room phone No	*Confirm by* By arrang.	*Parking* Ample
Room TV No	*Last dinner* 8.30	*Banquets* 40/2

Scourie
Map 16 B2 Highland
IV27 4TH
Scourie (0971) 2080

Eddrachilles Hotel Restaurant

Triumphantly overcoming the supply problems caused by the isolated position, Mrs Wood has turned this delightful restaurant into an outpost of civilised eating. Seafood features when local supplies are available, and other choices could include smooth chicken liver pâté, tasty farmhouse broth and a nicely sauced tournedos served with lovely crisp vegetables. Simple sweets are enjoyable too. Light lunches in high season.

● **Set D** £4·65
About £24 for two

Lunch (high season only) 12–2 *Dinner* 6.30–8.30
Closed 1 January & 25 December

Scourie
Map 16 B2 Highland
IV27 4SX
Scourie (0971) 2396

Proprietors Mr & Mrs Hay
Credit Barclaycard
Closed end October–mid March

Scourie Hotel 60% Ⓜ £E

Anglers return year after year to this peaceful, relaxing hotel, parts of which date back to the 15th century. The two spacious lounges feature grandfather clocks and deep, comfortable armchairs, and fishermen's tales are told in the cosy modern bar. Bedrooms have functional contemporary furniture, and bathrooms are up to date. Owners are friendly and welcoming and the whole place sparkles. *Amenities* garden, game fishing, hotel boats.

Rooms 22
with bath/shower 11

Room phone No	*Confirm by* 7	*Parking* Ample
Room TV No	*Last dinner* 8.30	*Banquets* 60/2

Selkirk
Map 12 D2 Borders
TD7 5LS
Selkirk (0750) 20747
Proprietors
Mr & Mrs J. C. M. Hill

Closed 2 weeks January

Philipburn House Hotel 59% Ⓜ £D/E

This Georgian house has been imaginatively converted to suit the needs of families on holiday. The lounge has relaxing chairs and there's a smart cocktail bar. Well-equipped bedrooms vary from those with four-posters to family suites and a pine lodge. Bathrooms are modern. Demi-pension only. *Amenities* garden, outdoor swimming pool, discothèque (Sat), laundry room, children's playground & playroom, baby listening.

Rooms 17
with bath/shower 10

Room phone No	*Confirm by* 6	*Parking* Ample
Room TV Yes	*Last dinner* 9	

Selkirk
Map 12 D2 Borders
TD7 5LS
Selkirk (0750) 20747
Proprietors
Mr & Mrs J. C. M. Hill

Philipburn House Hotel Restaurant

There's a fresh, attractive look about this cosy restaurant, with its pine tables and chairs and picture windows overlooking the swimming pool. Mr Hill does most of the cooking, and good fresh ingredients allied to careful preparation ensure the success of dishes ranging from hearty soups to lasagne, omelettes, nicely garnished main courses and some splendid traditional puddings. No smoking. 🍷 *SUPERIOR*.

● **Set L** £5·50 **Set D** £9
(residents only)
About £20 for two

Luinch 12.30–2 *Dinner* 7.30–9.30
Closed 2 weeks January

Skeabost Bridge
Map 16 A3 Highland
Isle of Skye *IV51 9NP*
Skeabost Bridge (047 032) 202
Proprietors Mr & Mrs I. Stuart,
Mr & Mrs I. McNab,
Mr & Mrs J. R. Stuart
Closed mid October–mid April

Skeabost House Hotel 58% Ⓜ £E

Many original features remain in this turreted Victorian building, once a hunting lodge, that stands in 12 acres of grounds. There's beautiful panelling in the hall, and two comfortable lounges feature fine antiques and roaring log fires. Bedrooms range from attractive old-fashioned rooms in the main house to neat modern ones in the extension. Bathrooms are adequate. *Amenities* garden, game & sea fishing, putting, billiards.

Rooms 27
with bath/shower 13

Room phone No	*Confirm by* 6	*Parking* Ample
Room TV No	*Last dinner* 8.30	

We do not necessarily recommend the cooking at hotels whose restaurants are not separately listed.

Skelmorlie
Map 12 A1 Strathclyde
PA17 5HE
Wemyss Bay (0475) 520832

Proprietor Mr C. Sebire
Closed early January–mid February

Rooms 18
with bath/shower 18

Manor Park Hotel 64% Ⓜ £ D

Guests at this hotel overlooking the Firth of Clyde profit doubly from the proprietor's green fingers. Not only are the gardens a delight, but beautiful flower displays adorn smart public rooms like the Adam-style foyer and spacious lounge. And the bar has its own attraction, too–a notable collection of whiskies. Comfortable bedrooms are simply furnished, and bathrooms have good modern fittings. No dogs. *Amenities* garden.

Room phone Yes	*Confirm by* By arrang.	*Parking* Ample
Room TV Yes	*Last dinner* 8.45	*Banquets* 120/2

Skelmorlie
Map 12 A1 Strathclyde
PA17 5HE
Wemyss Bay (0475) 520832
Proprietor Mr C. Sebire

About £22 for two

Manor Park Hotel Restaurant Ⓢ

A neat, simply furnished dining room whose short menu offers well-prepared, straightforward choices ranging from nourishing soup and meaty pâté to beef, veal, lobster and seasonal specialities like our succulent salmon with a fine hollandaise sauce. *Lunch* 1–2.30 *Dinner* 7–8.45
Closed early January–mid February ● **Set L** Sun only £4·75 **Set D** £7·50

South Queensferry
Map 12 C1 Lothian
EH30 9SF
031–331 1199
Telex 727430

Credit Access, Amex, Barclaycard, Diners

Rooms 107
with bath/shower 107

Forth Bridges Moat House 55% £ D

Spectacular views are a feature of this modern hotel within a service area on the A90 south of the Forth Bridge. The spacious bar-lounge area has comfortable contemporary seating, and there's a lively bar as well as a coffee shop. Usefully equipped bedrooms have neat built-in units and smart tiled bathrooms. *Amenities* garden, dancing (Fri in winter), coffee shop (8.30am–7pm, 9am–5pm in winter).

Room phone Yes	*Confirm by* 6	*Parking* Ample
Room TV Yes	*Last dinner* 9.45	*Banquets* 200/–

Spean Bridge
Map 17 B4 Highland
PH34 4DZ
Invergloy (039 784) 222

Proprietors Forsyth family

Closed November–March

Rooms 15
with bath/shower 5

Letterfinlay Lodge Hotel 56% Ⓜ £ E/F

North-east of Spean Bridge on the shores of Loch Lochy, this extended shooting lodge enjoys magnificent views over the loch. It's a friendly, welcoming place, with a cosy TV lounge and comfortable, traditionally furnished bedrooms. The extension features four compact modern rooms with tiled bathrooms, as well as a bar with plush velvet seating and picture windows. *Amenities* garden, game fishing, stalking, mooring.

Room phone No	*Confirm by* 6	*Parking* Ample
Room TV No	*Last dinner* 8.30	*Banquets* 60/12

Stepps
Map 12 B1 Strathclyde
Cumbernauld Road *G33 6DR*
041–779 2111

Manager Mr T. N. G. Willet
Credit Access, Amex, Barclaycard, Diners

Rooms 19
with bath/shower 19

Garfield Hotel 59% £ E

Situated some five miles from Glasgow, this converted house is popular for its conference and function facilities, as well as its comfortable accommodation. Bedrooms are neatly fitted with built-in furniture; those in the extension, which include a luxurious suite, are more modern. All have tiled bathrooms with showers. There's also a pleasant lounge and cocktail bar. *Amenities* garden, dinner dance (Sat).

Room phone Yes	*Confirm by* 6	*Parking* Ample
Room TV Yes	*Last dinner* 8	*Banquets* 150/–

Stonehaven
Map 17 D4 Grampian
2 Bath Street *AB32 DE*
Stonehaven (0569) 62044
Proprietor Mr I. V. Mackenzie

Credit Barclaycard, Diners

Rooms 14
with bath/shower 3

St Leonard's Hotel 53% Ⓜ £ E

Simple comforts for short stays are offered at this unpretentious greystone hotel, many of whose rooms overlook the sea. Plainly furnished public areas include a residents' lounge and bar, and there's a ballroom in the extension. Cheerful, well-maintained bedrooms have practical modern built-in or freestanding furniture, television sets and tea-makers. Adequate bathrooms. No dogs. *Amenities* garden, dinner dance (some Sats).

Room phone Yes	*Confirm by* 7	*Parking* Ample
Room TV Yes	*Last dinner* 9	*Banquets* 130/2

Stonehaven

Map 17 D4 Grampian
Cowie Park *AB3 2PZ*
Stonehaven (0569) 62936
Telex 739111

Credit Access, Amex,
Barclaycard, Diners

Rooms 40
with bath/shower 40

Stonehaven Commodore Hotel   64%   £E

Attractive public rooms in this modern glass and concrete hotel near the seafront include a comfortable lounge, two function rooms, a stylish cocktail bar and a locally favoured public bar with four pool tables. Well-kept bedrooms have flowery decor, practical built-in units and well-fitted carpeted bathrooms. Helpful staff.
Amenities discothèque (Sat), pool table.

Room phone Yes   *Confirm by* By arrang.   *Parking* Ample
Room TV Yes   *Last dinner* 10   *Banquets* 400/2

Stornoway

Map 16 A2 Highland
Perceval Road South
Isle of Lewis *PA87 2EU*
Stornoway (0851) 2604

Credit Access, Amex,
Barclaycard, Diners

Rooms 40
with bath/shower 40

Caberfeidh Hotel   52%   £E

Oilmen and tourists make good use of the simple facilities at this modern, purpose-built hotel not far from the car ferry terminal and the airport. The spacious reception hall features stags' heads on the walls and a MacKenzie tartan carpet, and the huge Viking Bar has Nordic echoes; there's also a quiet cocktail bar. Bedrooms are large and functional in style, and bathrooms are adequate. *Amenities* garden.

Room phone Some   *Confirm by* By arrang.   *Parking* Ample
Room TV No   *Last dinner* 9.30   *Banquets* 250/–

Strachur

Map 17 B5 Strathclyde
PA27 8BX
Strachur (036 986) 279
Telex 727396
Manager Mrs L. Huggins
Credit Access, Amex,
Barclaycard

Rooms 22
with bath/shower 17

Creggans Inn   60%   £D/E

A comfortable, friendly atmosphere and breathtaking views of Loch Fyne combine to make this hotel very popular with overseas visitors. Public rooms are tastefully fitted with fine oak furniture and original prints, while bedrooms have great individuality, with pretty colour schemes, frilly curtains and whitewood furniture. Bathrooms are compact and well equipped.
Amenities garden, sea fishing.

Room phone Yes   *Confirm by* By arrang.   *Parking* Ample
Room TV No   *Last dinner* 9.30   *Banquets* 100/20

Strachur

Map 17 B5 Strathclyde
PA27 8BX
Strachur (036 986) 279
Manager Mrs L. Huggins

About £23 for two

Creggans Inn Restaurant

A cheerful, cosy restaurant where kilted staff serve enjoyable dishes based on local produce. Native oysters, sea trout and smoked salmon feature with a small selection of meat dishes like stuffed loin of pork.
Credit Access, Amex, Barclaycard
Lunch 12.30–2.30 *Dinner* 7.30–9.30

Stranraer

Map 13 A4 Dumfries & Galloway
Royal Crescent *DG9 8HB*
Stranraer (0776) 4413
Telex 777088
Proprietor Mr H. C. McMillan

Rooms 83
with bath/shower 83

North West Castle Hotel   65%   Ⓜ   £E/F

Originally the home of Sir John Ross, the Arctic explorer, this extended Regency house is now a pleasant and absolutely spotless hotel with a fine leisure complex. There are two superb lounges for relaxation, as well as three bars. Thoughtfully designed bedrooms have built-in units and well-fitted bathrooms. No dogs. *Amenities* garden, sauna, indoor swimming pool, dancing (Sat), solarium, games room, in-house movies, curling (Oct–May).

Room phone Yes   *Confirm by* 6   *Parking* Ample
Room TV Yes   *Last dinner* 9.30   *Banquets* 175/–

Strathblane

Map 12 B1 Strathclyde
G63 9AA
Blanefield (0360) 70621

Credit Access, Amex,
Barclaycard, Diners

Rooms 19
with bath/shower 11

Kirkhouse Inn   55%   £F

This neat little stone and plaster inn has been dispensing hospitality since 1601 and still provides a popular stopping place just north of Glasgow. There are two bars, including one bedecked with horse tack, and a separate lounge-cum-meeting room. Well-kept bedrooms have modern freestanding furniture, central heating and radios; private bathrooms are tiled and spotless. *Amenities* garden.

Room phone Yes   *Confirm by* 8   *Parking* Ample
Room TV Yes   *Last dinner* 10

Strathmiglo
Map 17 C5 Fife
KY14 7PR
Strathmiglo (033 76) 252

● **Set L** £4·50
About £28 for two

Strathmiglo Inn   🍴 Ⓢ

A cottagy pub restaurant on two levels, charmingly run by friendly Allan and Jan Corbett. The short menu has a choice of well-known favourites ranging from fried mussels in a creamy wine sauce and scampi provençale to veal saltimbocca and fillet steak. Vegetables, like red cabbage with caraway seeds, show touches of imagination, and sweets include creamy strawberry mousse. *Credit* Access, Amex, Barclaycard

Lunch 12–2, Sun 12.30–2 *Dinner* 7–9.30
Closed D Sun, all Thurs, 1–10 January & last 2 weeks July

Strathtummel
Map 17 C4 Tayside
Near Pitlochry *PH16 5RU*
Tummel Bridge (088 24) 233
Proprietors
Mr & Mrs Gordon C. Hallewell

Closed mid October–mid April

Port-an-Eilean Hotel   67%   Ⓜ   £E/F

This handsome former shooting lodge enjoys a position of great beauty and tranquillity on the shores of Loch Tummel. The reception hall sports some fine antiques, and the comfortable bar and residents' lounge, with its sun lounge, have magnificent loch views. Traditionally decorated bedrooms are enormous and bathrooms old-fashioned. *Amenities* garden, coarse & game fishing, loch bathing, sailing, grouse shooting.

Rooms 12	*Room phone* No	*Confirm by* By arrang.	*Parking* Ample
with bath/shower 6	*Room TV* No	*Last dinner* 9	

Symington
Map 12 C2 Strathclyde
Near Biggar *ML12 6PQ*
Tinto (089 93) 454

Credit Access, Amex,
Barclaycard, Diners

Tinto Hotel   54%   Ⓜ   £E

This solid pebbledash hotel set in peaceful rolling countryside is popular for business courses and small conferences. The unassuming public bar is a favourite local meeting place, and there's also a plush cocktail bar and a foyer-lounge with comfortable tweedy armchairs. Simply decorated bedrooms have tea-making facilities and writing tables. Adequate bathrooms. *Amenities* garden, dancing (Sat), putting, games room.

Rooms 34	*Room phone* No	*Confirm by* By arrang.	*Parking* Ample
with bath/shower 3	*Room TV* No	*Last dinner* 8.30	*Banquets* 170/6

Talladale
Map 16 B3 Highland
By Achnasheen *IV22 2HN*
Loch Maree (044 589) 200
Proprietor
Miss Kathleen Moodie

Closed November–end March

Loch Maree Hotel *(Inn)*   Ⓜ   £D

Stuffed salmon on the walls of the airy lounge testify to the real concern of this modest hotel, which has sole fishing rights on the loch it overlooks. There's also another lounge and a cosy cocktail bar. Bright, homely bedrooms provide good comfort and have superb views, and public bathrooms are immaculate.
Amenities garden, game fishing.

Rooms 15	*Room phone* No	*Confirm by* 7	*Parking* Ample
with bath/shower None	*Room TV* No	*Last dinner* 8	

Tarbert
Map 12 A1 Strathclyde
Loch Fyne, Argyll *PA29 6YJ*
Tarbert (088 02) 207
Managers Mr & Mrs G. H. Scott
Credit Access, Amex,
Barclaycard, Diners
Closed October–Easter

Stonefield Castle Hotel   67%   Ⓜ   £C/D

Lovely gardens, marvellous views and a friendly atmosphere add to the charm of this splendid 19th-century castle. Public rooms are filled with oil paintings, marble fireplaces and gilt-framed mirrors, and there's a delightful library. Comfortable bedrooms range from traditional to modern, with bathrooms to match. *Amenities* garden, tennis, sauna, outdoor swimming pool, sea fishing, solarium, putting, mooring, games room, children's play area.

Rooms 34	*Room phone* No	*Confirm by* By arrang.	*Parking* Ample
with bath/shower 32	*Room TV* No	*Last dinner* 9	*Banquets* 120/20

Tarbert
Map 12 A1 Strathclyde
Loch Fyne, Argyll *PA29 6YJ*
Tarbert (088 02) 207
Managers Mr & Mrs G. H. Scott

Stonefield Castle Restaurant   ★   Ⓢ

This simple modern dining room is a showcase for some of the finest traditional cooking in Scotland. Materials are selected with the utmost care from local sources and there's a convincing authenticity about the results. The cock-a-leekie soup is an outstanding blend of chicken, prunes and leeks, delicious mussels are baked with breadcrumbs and garlic butter, and

Continued

Continued ● **Set D** £10·50 *About £29 for two*	full-flavoured giant prawns come with a beautifully sweet Drambuie sauce. It is to be hoped that the new young Scottish chef will remain in residence. **Specialities** cock-a-leekie soup, lobster with melted butter, peppered fillet steak. *Credit* Access, Amex, Barclaycard, Diners

Dinner only 7–9
Closed October–Easter

Tiroran   Tiroran House   64%   Ⓜ   £D

Map 17 A5 Strathclyde
Isle of Mull *PA69 6EF*
Tiroran (068 15) 232

Robin and Sue Blockey take good care of guests at their beautifully situated hotel, reached by the A849 from Craignure. There's no bar, but drinks are served in the sitting rooms, which are filled with curios like antique swords and a Chinese screen. Individually furnished bedrooms are decorated to a high standard; bathrooms are well equipped. No children under ten.
Amenities garden, games room, croquet, hotel boats.

Credit Barclaycard
Closed mid October–May

Rooms 7 *with bath/shower* 4	*Room phone* No *Room TV* No	*Confirm by* By arrang. *Last dinner* 8	*Parking* Ample

Tiroran   Tiroran House Restaurant

Map 17 A5 Strathclyde
Isle of Mull *PA69 6EF*
Tiroran (068 15) 232

Excellent fresh produce and capable home cooking result in very enjoyable dinners at this traditionally furnished restaurant. After avgolemono soup or tasty ratatouille and anchovy flan, the main course (no choice) could be gigot served with a good selection of nicely prepared vegetables. Our meringue balls with orange sauce made a delicious dessert, and to finish there are some Scottish cheeses. *Credit* Barclaycard

● **Set L** £4 **Set D** £9
About £25 for two

Lunch 12.30–2 *Dinner at* 8
Closed mid October–1 May

Troon   Marine Hotel   67%   £D

Map 12 B2 Strathclyde
Crosbie Road *KA10 6HE*
Troon (0292) 314444

Overlooking the Royal Troon championship golf course by the Firth of Clyde, this handsome sandstone hotel is popular with sporting enthusiasts and tourists. There's much wood panelling in the public rooms, which enjoy fine views out to sea. Comfortable bedrooms, with a mixture of traditional and modern furnishings, have tea-makers and well-maintained bathrooms.
Amenities garden, dancing (Sat), ladies' hairdressing.

Credit Access, Amex,
Barclaycard, Diners

Rooms 70 *with bath/shower* 70	*Room phone* Yes *Room TV* Yes	*Confirm by* By arrang. *Last dinner* 10.30	*Parking* Ample *Banquets* 150/2

Troon   Marine Hotel, L'Auberge de Provence   Ⓢ

Map 12 B2 Strathclyde
Crosbie Road *KA10 6HE*
Troon (0292) 314444

This smart and warmly inviting little restaurant makes a pleasant setting for a short menu of capably cooked French dishes like steak with green pepper-corn sauce. Seasonal specialities, too, plus tasty fresh vegetables and light sweets. *Credit* Access, Amex, Barclaycard, Diners *Dinner only* 7.30–10.30
Closed Sun & Mon ● **Set D** from £10·75

French cooking
About £33 for two

Troon   Sun Court Hotel   60%   Ⓜ   £E

Map 12 B2 Strathclyde
19 Crosbie Road *KA10 6HF*
Troon (0292) 312727
Proprietors
Mr & Mrs A. Breckenridge
Credit Access, Amex

Very much a sportsman's hotel, with, unusually, a Real tennis court and resident coaches for tennis and squash, this converted Edwardian house is also popular with business visitors. There's an oak-panelled hall and staircase plus a simple lounge and a functional bar. Large bedrooms have spacious wardrobes, and bathrooms are simply fitted. General maintenance could be improved. *Amenities* garden, tennis, squash, Real tennis.

Rooms 21 *with bath/shower* 19	*Room phone* Some *Room TV* Yes	*Confirm by* By arrang. *Last dinner* 9.30	*Parking* Ample *Banquets* 40/2

Turnberry

Map 12 A3 Strathclyde
KA26 9LT
Turnberry (065 53) 202
Telex 777779

Rooms 125
with bath/shower 125
Room phone Yes
Room TV Yes
Confirm by By arrang.
Last dinner 9.30
Parking Ample
Banquets 400/10

Credit Access, Amex,
Barclaycard, Diners

Turnberry Hotel   77%   £ C

Two championship golf courses are among the attractions of this magnificent Edwardian hotel with views across the sea to Arran and Ailsa Craig. Superb plaster friezes blend with the pastel colour schemes in the spacious, relaxing public areas, and the emphasis on tasteful design is also evident in the smart, individually styled bedrooms which have good freestanding furniture and most acceptable bathrooms (many with bidets).
Amenities garden, sauna, indoor swimming pool, tennis, 2 golf courses, dancing (Sat, also Thurs, Fri Easter–October), putting, pitch & putt, gymnasium, solarium, cinema (weekly), helipad, billiards, table tennis, croquet, valeting, coffee shop (8am–8pm April–October).

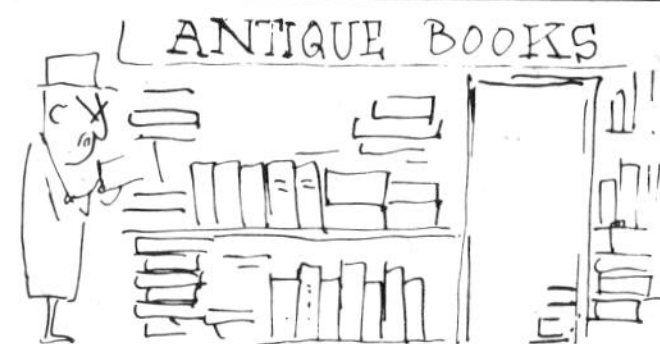

We publish annually, so make
sure you use the current
edition. It's worth it!

Uig

Map 16 A3 Highland
Isle of Skye *IV51 9YE*
Uig (047 042) 205
Proprietors
Graham & Taylor family
Credit Access, Amex,
Barclaycard, Diners

Rooms 25
with bath/shower 25

Uig Hotel   61% Ⓜ   £ E

A whitewashed building with arched windows and a striking slate roof, this welcoming, family-run hotel overlooks picturesque Uig Bay. Two tweedy lounges are relaxing, and there's a pleasant, leafy sun lounge. Bright, spacious bedrooms (eight in a separate modern block in the garden) are individually decorated and very well appointed, with excellent bathrooms.
Amenities garden, sailing dinghies. **Closed** 30 September–Easter

Room phone No	*Confirm by* By arrang.	*Parking* Ample
Room TV No	*Last dinner* 8	

Ullapool

Map 16 B2 Highland
North Road *IV26 2UD*
Ullapool (0854) 2314

Credit Access, Amex,
Barclaycard, Diners
Closed 24 October–Easter

Rooms 60
with bath/shower 60

Ladbroke Mercury Motor Inn   57%   £ D

This well-maintained modern hotel makes a pleasant base for foreign tourists and families on holiday. Open-plan public areas include a smartly decorated foyer-lounge and bar. Compact bedrooms have fitted pine units, good carpeting and spotlessly clean, nicely equipped bathrooms.
Amenities garden, sauna, Scottish music (4 nights weekly in summer), putting, games room.

Room phone Yes	*Confirm by* 6	*Parking* Ample
Room TV Yes	*Last dinner* 9	*Banquets* 50/–

Ullapool

Map 16 B2 Highland
North Road *IV26 2UD*
Ullapool (0854) 2314

● **Set D** £7·50
About £30 for two

Ladbroke Mercury Motor Inn Restaurant   Ⓢ

This attractive candlelit restaurant makes a charming setting for an enjoyable dinner. On the Laird's Table there's a fine selection of starters, local seafood, roast joints and salads to supplement the short à la carte, which includes skilfully prepared dishes like poached salmon with light hollandaise sauce and venison casserole. A traditional lunch is served on Sundays.
Credit Access, Amex, Barclaycard, Diners

Lunch Sun only 12–2 *Dinner* 6–9.30
Closed 24 October–Easter

Ullapool
Map 16 B2 Highland
Garve Road *IV26 2SY*
Ullapool (0854) 2181

Credit Access, Amex,
Diners

Royal Hotel 62%   £E

There's a feeling of spaciousness about this sleek modern hotel, whose enormous curved windows povide sweeping views over lovely Loch Broom. An efficiently manned reception area leads to the comfortable lounge, and there's a TV lounge as well as two bars. Cheerfully decorated bedrooms have good modern fittings; some have sun terraces overlooking the loch. *Amenities* garden, game & sea fishing, cabaret (nightly June–September), games room.

Rooms 61	*Room phone* Yes	*Confirm by* By arrang.	*Parking* Ample
with bath/shower 46	*Room TV* No	*Last dinner* 9.30	*Banquets* 180/-

Uphall
Map 12 C1 Lothian
EH52 6JS
Broxburn (0506) 853831
Telex 727148
Proprietors Mr & Mrs K. Knight
Credit Amex

Houston House 69% Ⓜ   £D

This well-maintained 16th-century house stands off the A89 in extensive gardens and parkland. Flagstone floors, beautiful rugs and fine furnishings grace the public rooms, while bedrooms vary from modern and neatly fitted in the newer wing to larger and traditionally furnished (ten of them have four-posters) in the main building. Spacious bathrooms are attractively tiled, and shower rooms are compact. *Amenities* garden, croquet.

Rooms 29	*Room phone* Yes	*Confirm by* By arrang.	*Parking* Ample
with bath/shower 29	*Room TV* Yes	*Last dinner* 9.30	*Banquets* 42/12

Uphall
Map 12 C1 Lothian
EH52 6JS
Broxburn (0506) 853831
Proprietors
Mr & Mrs K. Knight
About £29 for two

Houston House Restaurant   ♛ Ⓢ

Two elegant dining rooms provide an attractive setting for enjoyable dishes like carrot and orange soup, seafood pie and julienne of veal with a creamy paprika sauce. Set meals only, no choice for dinner. 🍷 *OUTSTANDING.*
Credit *Amex* Lunch *12.30–2* Dinner *7.30–9.30*
● **Set L** £7·50 **Set D** £11.50 incl. service

Weem
Map 17 C4 Tayside
By Aberfeldy *PH15 2LD*
Aberfeldy (0887) 20346
Proprietor Mr A. Gillespie

Ailean Chraggan Hotel Restaurant    Ⓢ

Chef-proprietor Mr Gillespie has built up a strong local following in this friendly, well-run restaurant, where the menu offers straightforward, carefully prepared dishes. Simple starters like pâté maison or tasty chicken broth might precede main courses ranging from omelettes and grills to casseroled chicken and a well-flavoured carbonnade de bœuf. We particularly enjoyed beautifully fresh, moist Tay salmon.

About £21 for two

Lunch 12.30–2 *Dinner* 7.30–9
Closed 3 days New Year & 25 & 26 December

Wester Howgate
Map 12 C2 Lothian
Near Penicuik *EH26 8QB*
Penicuik (0968) 74244
Proprietors Mr & Mrs I. di Rollo
Smørrebrød

Old Howgate Inn    Ⓢ

Danish open sandwiches are the speciality of this pub restaurant, and they come in an endless variety of appetising guises. You'll find that two or three will make a delicious meal–perhaps smoked trout with horseradish sauce, salami with potato salad, and tongue with creamed mushrooms, all served on excellent bread. There's soup to start with, and cheese or simple sweets to finish. *Credit* Access, Amex, Barclaycard

About £20 for two

Lunch 12–2, Sun 12.30–2 *Dinner* 6.30–10, Sun 6.30–9.30
Closed 1 & 2 January & 25 December

Wick
Map 16 C2 Highland
Riverside *KW1 5AT*
Wick (0955) 3344
Credit Access, Amex,
Barclaycard, Diners
Closed 25 December–
1st week January

Ladbroke Mercury Motor Inn 55%   £C/D

This modern, three-storey hotel offers modest but convenient accommodation for travellers. Public areas include a simple bar and a comfortably furnished lounge. Bedrooms are equipped with bedside controls, radios and tea-makers; the best are those on the top floor, which have contemporary built-in units. Bathrooms are well planned and spotlessly clean. *Amenities* garden, dinner dance (Sat in winter), games room. ♿

Rooms 45	*Room phone* Yes	*Confirm by* 6	*Parking* Ample
with bath/shower 45	*Room TV* Yes	*Last dinner* 8.30	*Banquets* 200/10

WALES

Aberdyfi
Map 8 B3 Gwynedd
LL35 0SB
Aberdovey (065 472) 213

Credit Access
Closed 18 October–end March

Rooms 48			
with bath/shower 33			

Trefeddian Hotel 55% Ⓜ £E

This family-run hotel, popular with holiday-makers, overlooks the dunes and the beach. There are three lounges with contemporary furnishings and pleasant sea views, plus a simple bar. Functional modern bedrooms are equipped with radio/baby listening facilities, and most have well-fitted, tiled bathrooms. *Amenities* garden, solarium, indoor swimming pool, tennis, table tennis, badminton, putting.

Room phone No	*Confirm by* 6	*Parking* Ample
Room TV No	*Last dinner* 8.30	

Abergwesyn
Map 9 C4 Powys
Near Llanwrtyd Wells *LD5 4TW*
Llanwrtyd Wells (059 13) 238

Proprietor Mr J. M. L. Yates

Closed end October–Easter

Rooms 10		
with bath/shower 10		

Llwynderw Hotel 68% Ⓜ £D

No TV or radio disturbs the peace at this Georgian house in a beautiful setting among hills and forests. Guests can browse in the well-stocked library, enjoy a board game in the Palm Court room, or sink back into a deep settee in the elegant lounge. Attractive, traditionally furnished bedrooms with pretty lace bedspreads have modern bathrooms. No children under 10. Inclusive terms only. *Amenities* garden.

Room phone No	*Confirm by* By arrang.	*Parking* Ample
Room TV No	*Last dinner* 7.45	

Abergwesyn
Map 9 C4 Powys
Near Llanwrtyd Wells *LD5 4TW*
Llanwrtyd Wells (059 13) 238
Proprietor Mr J. M. L. Yates
English cooking

● **Set D** £12
About £30 for two

Llwynderw Hotel Restaurant ♧ Ⓢ

Sturdy oak tables and a huge stone fireplace give a pleasantly rustic air to this friendly, informal restaurant, where set meals (no choice except for sweets) offer uncomplicated, flavoursome dishes capably prepared by Mr Yates from the best of local produce. Typical treats could include delicately flavoured cauliflower soup, Welsh mutton or oxtail in cider, crème caramel and poached pears. Booking is essential.

Lunch by arrangement only *Dinner* at 7.45
Closed end October–Easter

Abersoch
Map 8 B2 Gwynedd
Bwlch Tocyn *LL53 7BU*
Abersoch (075 881) 2966
Proprietors Fletcher-Brewer family
Credit Access, Amex, Diners
Closed November–Easter
(except Christmas period)

Rooms 18		
with bath/shower 15		

Porth Tocyn Hotel 64% Ⓜ £D

Splendid views across Cardigan Bay are a major asset of this friendly, family-run hotel which stands on a headland in well-tended grounds. Behind the white facade are several delightfully relaxing lounges, including a sun lounge and TV room. Bedrooms are bright and homely, with occasional antique pieces, and bathrooms are up to date.
Amenities garden, outdoor swimming pool, tennis.

Room phone No	*Confirm by* By arrang.	*Parking* Ample
Room TV No	*Last dinner* 9.30	*Banquets* 60/4

Abersoch
Map 8 B2 Gwynedd
Bwlch Tocyn *LL53 7BU*
Abersoch (075 881) 2966
Proprietors
Fletcher-Brewer family

● **Set L** £4·60
Set D from £7·95
About £32 for two

Porth Tocyn Hotel Restaurant ♧ Ⓢ

Mrs Fletcher-Brewer presides over this charming restaurant, while her daughter-in-law supervises the kitchen, with most satisfactory results. Table d'hôte menus (simpler at lunch) include imaginative choices like guinea fowl with peach ginger stuffing, as well as more familiar dishes such as salmon with hollandaise, and delicious puddings. Home-made petits fours too.
♟ *ABOVE AVERAGE. Credit* Access, Amex, Diners

Lunch 1–2 *Dinner* 7.30–9.30
Closed November–Easter (except Christmas period)

Aberystwyth
Map 9 B4 Dyfed
Chancery *SY23 4DE*
Aberystwyth (0970) 617941

Credit Access, Amex,
Barclaycard, Diners

Conrah Country Hotel 62% Ⓜ £E/F

Oak pillars and panels grace the entrance hall of this pleasant country mansion, which stands on the A487 three miles south of Aberystwyth. There are also two comfortable lounges and a roomy bar. Bright bedrooms are simply decorated and furnished, most with neatly fitted bathrooms; nine in the motel annexe (without TV) have shower rooms. No dogs. *Amenities* garden, sauna, indoor swimming pool.

Continued

Rooms 22	*Room phone* Yes	*Confirm by* 6	*Parking* Ample
with bath/shower 19	*Room TV* Most	*Last dinner* 9	*Banquets* 80/20

Barry
Map 9 C6 South Glamorgan
Porthkerry Road *CF6 8XY*
Barry (0446) 740069
Proprietors
Wyn & Linda Pryce-Jones
Credit Access, Amex,
Barclaycard, Diners

Mount Sorrel Hotel   60%      £E

An elegant modern interior hides behind the Victorian facade of this friendly, well-run hotel, which clings to a steep hill with views of the town and the sea. Attractive dark cane and bamboo furniture and potted plants give a crisp, fresh look to the public rooms, and compact bedrooms, decorated in soothing shades, have smart fitted furniture and carpeted, well-equipped bathrooms. *Amenities* dancing (Sat).

Rooms 37	*Room phone* Yes	*Confirm by* 6	*Parking* Limited
with bath/shower 37	*Room TV* Yes	*Last dinner* 10	*Banquets* 85/–

Beaumaris
Map 8 C1 Gwynedd
Castle Street *LL58 8AW*
Beaumaris (0248) 810415
Manager Mr Peter F. Wood

Bulkeley Arms   56%   £E

Built in 1832 overlooking the Menai Strait, this greystone hotel has a solidly traditional atmosphere. There's some fine mahogany furniture in the spacious public rooms, which include three comfortable lounges (one with TV) and two simple bars. Well-maintained bedrooms with '30s-style furniture are pleasantly decorated. Adequate bathrooms. Very friendly, helpful staff. No dogs. *Amenities* garden, clock golf.

Rooms 42	*Room phone* No	*Confirm by* By arrang.	*Parking* Ample
with bath/shower 18	*Room TV* Some	*Last dinner* 8.15	*Banquets* 130/–

Beaumaris
Map 8 C1 Gwynedd
Castle Street, Anglesey
LL58 8AP
Beaumaris (0248) 810329
Proprietors Mr & Mrs Barnett
Credit Access
Closed Sun (November–March)

Ye Olde Bull's Head Hotel *(Inn)*    £F

Close to the historic castle in the town's main street, this former posting house has great warmth and character. The little beamed bar is full of polished brass and other interesting ornaments, and the lounge and TV room are as comfortable as they are charming. Cheerful bedrooms, many of them with exposed beams, provide modest but pleasant accommodation; bathrooms are adequate. No dogs.

Rooms 17	*Room phone* No	*Confirm by* By arrang.	*Parking* Limited
with bath/shower 7	*Room TV* No	*Last dinner* 8.30	

Beddgelert
Map 8 C2 Gwynedd
LL55 4YE
Beddgelert (076 686) 224

Manager Mrs A. Pierce
Credit Access, Amex,
Barclaycard, Diners

Royal Goat Hotel   55%   £E/F

Superb mountain views are an attraction of this much-extended Georgian house in the heart of Snowdonia. Modernised public rooms include a stylish cocktail bar, inviting lounge bar and small TV lounge. Welsh tapestry bedspreads add a touch of colour to the simply furnished bedrooms, and the small, tiled bathrooms are adequate.
Amenities coarse fishing, dancing (Fri or Sat).

Rooms 29	*Room phone* Yes	*Confirm by* 6	*Parking* Ample
with bath/shower 15	*Room TV* No	*Last dinner* 8.30	*Banquets* 100/25

Betws-y-Coed
Map 8 C2 Gwynedd
LL24 0BT
Betws-y-Coed (069 02) 217
Proprietor
Miss Violet Connell-Smith

Gwydyr Hotel   55% (M)   £F

Very popular with salmon and trout fishermen, this traditional Victorian hotel is a most welcoming place thanks to Miss Connell-Smith and her staff. Public rooms include a comfortable old-fashioned lounge with upholstered settees and some fine mahogany and walnut pieces, and there are two simple bars. Pleasant, homely bedrooms have functional fittings, and bathrooms are adequate. *Amenities* garden, coarse & game fishing.

Rooms 24	*Room phone* No	*Confirm by* 6	*Parking* Ample
with bath/shower 13	*Room TV* Yes	*Last dinner* 8	

Map 9 D6
Town plan opposite

Population 284,400

Though it enshrines Welsh culture and history, Cardiff is both modern and cosmopolitan. Its population was less than 2,000 at the beginning of the 19th century, when its port developed with export of coal from the near-by mines
No British city is more compact in its many offerings to visitors, everything dominated by the comprehensive City Centre and the lovingly restored Castle.
It is a matter of choice whether Welsh tradition, commerce or sport matter most to the visitor, though certainly the last attracts the most visitors *en masse*, especially to Cardiff Arms Park.
Though Cardiff is an ideal base for touring South Wales, a short visit offers more than enough to remain within the city limits.

Annual Events
Cardiff Festival *July/August*
Festival of 20th-century Music *March*
Horticultural Show *June*
International Horse Show *June*
International Welsh Rally
Llandaff Festival *June*

Information Office
Public Relations Officer
City Hall
Cardiff
Telephone Cardiff (0222) 31033
Ext 578

Wales Tourist Board
Brunel House
2 Fitzalan Road
Cardiff

Cardiff

1	Bute Park	C1/2
2	Cardiff Castle *fairy-tale magnificence bequeathed by the Bute family*	C2
3	Civic Centre	C1/2
4	General Station	C/D3
5	Llandaff Cathedral	A1
6	National Museum of Wales	D1
7	National Sports Centre for Wales	B1
8	New Theatre, Park Place	D2
9	Queen Street Station	E2
10	Sherman Theatre	D1
11	St John's Church, St John Square (City Centre)	D2
12	Welsh Industrial and Maritime Museum, Bute Street	D3
13	Wood Street Bus Station	C3

Fiat Dealers

T. S. Grimshaw Ltd
329 Cowbridge Road East
Cardiff CF5 1JD
Tel: Cardiff 395322

Yapp's Garages Ltd
Fidlas Road, Llanishen
Cardiff CF4 5YW
Tel: Cardiff 751323

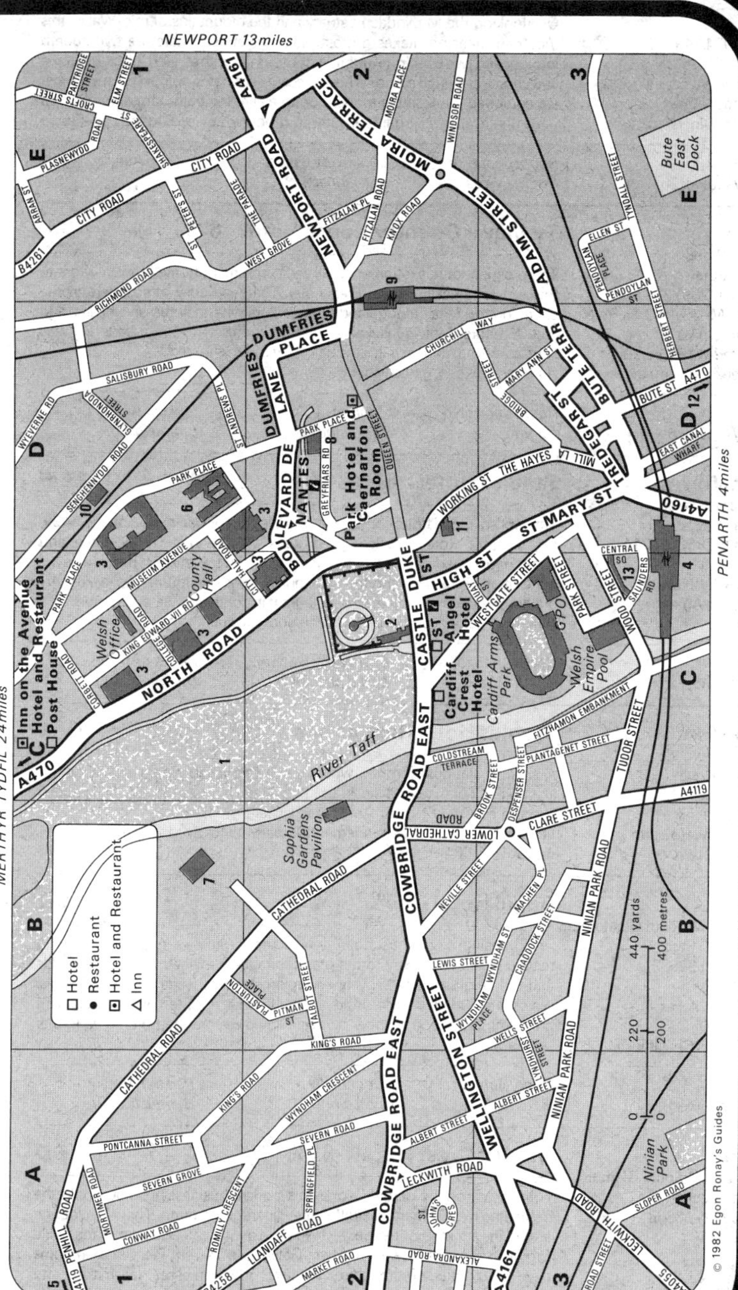

NEWPORT 13 miles
MERTHYR TYDFIL 24 miles
PENARTH 4 miles
PORT TALBOT 34 miles
Bute East Dock
CROFTS STREET
ELM STREET
PARTRIDGE STREET
SHAKESPEARE ST
PLASNEWYDD ROAD
ARRAN ST
B4261
CITY ROAD
CITY ROAD
THE PARADE
ST PETER'S ST
WEST GROVE
RICHMOND ROAD
SALISBURY ROAD
WEVERNE RD
GLYNRHONDDA STREET
SENGHENNYDD ROAD
PARK PLACE
PARK PLACE
MUSEUM AVENUE
CORBETT ROAD
COLLEGE ROAD
KING EDWARD VII RD
CATHAYS PLACE
ST ANDREWS PL
PARK PLACE
Welsh Office
County Hall
NORTH ROAD
NEWPORT ROAD
MOIRA TERRACE
MOIRA PLACE
WINDSOR ROAD
FITZALAN PL
FITZALAN ROAD
KNOX ROAD
ADAM STREET
DUMFRIES PLACE
DUMFRIES LANE
BOULEVARD DE NANTES
GREYFRIARS RD
QUEEN STREET
Park Hotel and Caernarfon Room
CHURCHILL WAY
MARY ANN STREET
BRIDGE STREET
WINDSOR ROAD
ELLEN ST
PENDOYLAN PLACE
PENDOYLAN ST
TYNDALL STREET
HERBERT STREET
EAST CANAL WHARF
BUTE ST A470
MILL LA
TREDEGAR ST
BUTE TERR
WORKING ST
THE HAYES
ST MARY ST
HIGH ST
CASTLE ST
DUKE ST
Angel Hotel
Cardiff Crest Hotel
Cardiff Arms Park
WESTGATE STREET
QUAY ST
PARK STREET
GPO
CENTRAL SQ
WOOD STREET
SAUNDERS RD
Welsh Empire Pool
River Taff
Sophia Gardens Pavilion
CATHEDRAL ROAD
COWBRIDGE ROAD EAST
LOWER CATHEDRAL ROAD
CLARE STREET
COLDSTREAM TERRACE
FITZHAMON EMBANKMENT
BROOK STREET
DESPENSER STREET
PLANTAGENET STREET
MACHEN PL
TUDOR STREET
NINIAN PARK ROAD
NEVILLE STREET
LEWIS STREET
WYNDHAM ST
CRADDOCK STREET
WYNDHAM PLACE
WELLINGTON STREET
LYNDHURST STREET
WELLS STREET
ALBERT STREET
PONTCANNA STREET
MORTIMER ROAD
CONWAY ROAD
SEVERN GROVE
SEVERN ROAD
SPRINGFIELD PL
ROMILLY CRESCENT
WYNHAM CRESCENT
KING'S ROAD
KING'S ROAD
TALBOT STREET
PITMAN ST
PLASTURION PLACE
PENHILL ROAD
A4119
CATHEDRAL ROAD
LLANDAFF ROAD
B4258
MARKET ROAD
ALEXANDRA ROAD
ST JOHN'S CRES
LECKWITH ROAD
LECKWITH ROAD
BROAD STREET
SLOPER ROAD
A4055
Ninian Park
COWBRIDGE ROAD EAST
A4161
A470
A4160
A4119
□ Hotel
● Restaurant
◉ Hotel and Restaurant
△ Inn
◉ Inn on the Avenue Hotel and Restaurant
□ Post House
440 yards
400 metres
220
200
0

Bontddu

Map 8 C3 Gwynedd
LL40 2SU
Bontddu (034 149) 661
Telex 35142
Proprietor Mr W. S. Hall
Credit Access, Amex,
Barclaycard, Diners

Bontddu Hall Hotel 69%  £E

Overlooking the Mawddach Estuary and the mountains of mid-Wales, this Victorian mansion makes a most pleasing retreat. There are two superb lounges and two bars (one intriguingly designed with stained-glass windows and church pews). Bedrooms have nicely coordinated colour schemes. Most are equipped with simple modern units, as are the bathrooms. No children under three. *Amenities* garden, putting, in-house movies. **Closed** Jan–Feb

Rooms 25	*Room phone* Yes	*Confirm by* By arrang.	*Parking* Ample
with bath/shower 25	*Room TV* Yes	*Last dinner* 9	

Brechfa

Map 9 B5 Dyfed
Near Carmarthen *SA32 7RA*
Brechfa (026 789) 332
Proprietors Mr & Mrs C. D. Ross
Credit Barclaycard
Closed 1st 2 weeks February
& 1st 2 weeks November

Ty Mawr Country House Hotel 62%  £E

The prospect of relaxation amid all the comforts of home draws visitors to this sympathetically modernised hotel. There's a cosy atmosphere in the charming residents' lounge and the two bars with their massive beams and pine furniture. Individually decorated bedrooms with brass beds are well kept, as are the modern carpeted bathrooms with showers.
Amenities garden, game fishing.

Rooms 5	*Room phone* No	*Confirm by* 7	*Parking* Ample
with bath/shower 5	*Room TV* No	*Last dinner* 9	*Banquets* 60/–

Caernarfon

Map 8 B2 Gwynedd
Llanwnda *LL54 5SD*
Llanwnda (0286) 830711
Proprietors
Mr & Mrs R. W. Howarth
Credit Access, Amex,
Barclaycard

Stables Hotel 64% £E/F

This well-planned hotel complex, three miles out of Caernarfon on the A499, has a single-storey block of bedrooms. All are prettily decorated and comfortably fitted with modern units, radios and tea-makers; bathrooms are quite smart. Reception and the traditionally furnished lounge are in a nearby building, and the bar adjoins the restaurant in converted Victorian stables. *Amenities* garden, outdoor swimming pool, croquet.

Rooms 12	*Room phone* Yes	*Confirm by* By arrang.	*Parking* Ample
with bath/shower 12	*Room TV* Yes	*Last dinner* 9.45	*Banquets* 90/–

Caernarfon

Map 8 B2 Gwynedd
Llanwnda *LL54 5SD*
Llanwnda (0286) 830711
Proprietors
Mr & Mrs R. W. Howarth
About £28 *for two*

Stables Hotel Restaurant

A smart rustic dining room, where you'll find reliably prepared favourites like duck à l'orange and steak and kidney pie, supplemented by flambéed specialities. *Credit* Access, Amex, Barclaycard
Lunch 12–1.45, Sat by arrangement *Dinner* 7–9.45, Sun by arrangement
● **Set L** £5·50 **Set D** £7

Cardiff

Town plan C2 South Glamorgan
Castle Street *CF1 2QZ*
Cardiff (0222) 32633
Telex 498132
Credit Access, Amex,
Barclaycard, Diners
Closed 2 days Christmas

Angel Hotel 65% £D

An imposing city-centre hotel, where the impressive entrance hall with marble pillars gives way to the grand lounges furnished with chesterfields and ornate gilt tables. A lovely sweeping staircase leads to the bedrooms, which are modern in style, as are the bathrooms. A three-year refurbishment programme planned by new owners should restore the hotel to its former splendour.

Rooms 97	*Room phone* Yes	*Confirm by* 6	*Parking* Ample
with bath/shower 82	*Room TV* Yes	*Last dinner* 10	*Banquets* 320/–

Cardiff

Town plan C2 South Glamorgan
Westgate Street *CF1 1JB*
Cardiff (0222) 388681
Telex 497258

Credit Access, Amex,
Barclaycard, Diners

Cardiff Crest Hotel 61% £D

Formerly called the Cardiff Centre, this modern business hotel overlooks the castle, the river Taff and Cardiff Arms Park rugby ground. There is a lounge area in the smartly contemporary foyer, and guests can also relax in the Triple Crown Bar or the Edwardian-style Gatehouse Tavern. Pleasant bedrooms have fitted units, comfortable armchairs, trouser presses, tea-makers and neat, compact bathrooms. Extensive conference facilities.

Rooms 160	*Room phone* Yes	*Confirm by* 6	*Parking* Ample
with bath/shower 160	*Room TV* Yes	*Last dinner* 10	*Banquets* 250/25

Cardiff — Inn on the Avenue   67%   Ⓜ   £ D

Town plan C1 South Glamorgan
Circle Way East
Llanedeyrn *CF3 7XF*
Cardiff (0222) 732520
Telex 497582
Credit Access, Amex,
Barclaycard, Diners

Opened in 1980, this strikingly designed modern hotel stands in neatly landscaped grounds on the eastbound A48. Handsome chandeliers are a feature of the open-plan foyer and bar and the large, relaxing residents' lounge. Spacious bedrooms on four floors are thoughtfully planned, with attractive colour schemes, good fitted units and comfortable armchairs. Excellent bathrooms. *Amenities* garden, dancing (Sat).

Rooms 150	*Room phone* Yes	*Confirm by* 6	*Parking* Ample
with bath/shower 150	*Room TV* Yes	*Last dinner* 11	*Banquets* 100/–

Cardiff — Inn on the Avenue Restaurant   ♔ Ⓢ

Town plan C1 South Glamorgan
Circle Way East
Llanedeyrn *CF3 7XF*
Cardiff (0222) 732520

This restful modern dining room makes a stylish setting for an enjoyable meal. There's always a succulent roast on the trolley, and the interesting menu features Welsh favourites like local trout and salmon, in addition to chef's specials such as chicken suprême or a delicious avocado and fruit salad. The beautifully presented sweet trolley makes choice difficult.
Credit Access, Amex, Barclaycard, Diners

● **Set L** £6·50 **Set D** £7·50
About £33 for two

Lunch 12.30–2.30 *Dinner* 7–10.45

Cardiff — Park Hotel   70%   £ D

Town plan D2 South Glamorgan
Park Place *CF1 3UD*
Cardiff (0222) 23471
Telex 497195

Rooms 108
with bath/shower 108
Room phone Yes
Room TV Yes
Confirm by 6
Last dinner 11
Parking Ample
Banquets 250/10
Closed 25 & 26 December

Credit Access, Amex,
Barclaycard, Diners

Overlooking a shopping precinct in the heart of the city, this imposing late-Victorian hotel offers a pleasing combination of traditional style and up-to-the-minute comfort. Well-furnished public rooms like the entrance hall with its glittering chandeliers and the spacious cocktail bar-cum-lounge retain much of their elegance and grandeur, though some improvements in maintenance would be welcome. Good-sized bedrooms (those overlooking Park Place or Queen Street are the brightest) have high-quality mahogany units giving plenty of storage and writing space, relaxing armchairs and excellent tiled bathrooms. The hotel offers an extensive range of conference and banqueting facilities. *Amenities* in-house movies.

Cardiff — Park Hotel, Caernarfon Room   ♔ Ⓢ

Town plan D2 South Glamorgan
Park Place *CF1 3UD*
Cardiff (0222) 23471

An elegant dining room with gleaming silverware, crisp linen and comfortable chairs. Laver bread and cawl cennin (leek and vegetable soup) are two Welsh specialities on the menu, which might also include stuffed mushrooms, grills, roast lamb with rosemary, and an excellent chicken suprême stuffed with crabmeat. Capable cooking, with due care given to sauces and vegetables. *Credit* Access, Amex, Barclaycard, Diners

● **Set L** £5·50 **Set D** £6·50
About £33 for two

Lunch 12.30–2 *Dinner* 7–9.45, Sun 7–9.15
Closed 25 & 26 December

Cardiff — Post House Hotel   59%   £ D

Town plan C1 South Glamorgan
Pentwyn Road
Pentwyn *CF2 7XA*
Cardiff (0222) 731212
Telex 497633
Credit Access, Amex,
Barclaycard, Diners

Occupying a six-acre site about four miles from the city centre, this modern hotel near the M4 is popular with businessmen. Smart public rooms include a comfortable lounge area and two relaxing bars, and there's also a well-equipped conference suite. Good-sized bedrooms have mini-bars, tea/coffee-makers and compact tiled bathrooms.
Amenities garden, coffee shop (7.30am–10.30pm).   ♿

Rooms 150	*Room phone* Yes	*Confirm by* 6	*Parking* Ample
with bath/shower 150	*Room TV* Yes	*Last dinner* 11	*Banquets* 120/10

Carmarthen
Map 9 B5 Dyfed
Spilman Street *SA31 1LG*
Carmarthen (0267) 5111
Telex 48520

Credit Access, Amex,
Barclaycard, Diners

Rooms 88
with bath/shower 82

Ivy Bush Royal Hotel   60%   £ D/E

Uniformed staff provide a courteous reception at this much-extended hotel close to the centre of town. A colourful stained-glass window provides a striking note in the lounge, which, like other public areas, is decorated in restful modern style. Bedrooms, though not large, are comfortably furnished with solid wooden units, and bathrooms are adequately fitted.
Amenities garden, sauna, dinner dance (Sat).

| *Room phone* Yes | *Confirm by* 6 | *Parking* Ample |
| *Room TV* Yes | *Last dinner* 8.45 | *Banquets* 200/– |

Castleton
Map 9 D6 Gwent
Near Cardiff *CF3 8UQ*
Castleton (0633) 680591

Credit Access, Amex,
Barclaycard, Diners

Rooms 55
with bath/shower 55

Ladbroke Wentloog Castle Hotel   59%   £ D

Standing alongside the A48, not far from junction 28 of the M4, this gabled Victorian house has a two-storey wing of well-equipped modern bedrooms with simple fitted furniture and fully tiled bathrooms (some with showers only). In the original building there's a panelled bar decorated with hunting prints and, upstairs, a range of meeting rooms.
Amenities garden, sauna, dinner dance (Sat).

| *Room phone* Yes | *Confirm by* 6 | *Parking* Ample |
| *Room TV* Yes | *Last dinner* 10.30 | *Banquets* 95/– |

Chepstow
Map 9 D6 Gwent
St Pierre Park *NP6 6YA*
Chepstow (029 12) 5261
Telex 497562

Credit Access, Amex,
Barclaycard, Diners

Rooms 76
with bath/shower 76

St Pierre Golf & Country Club   62%   £ D

A veritable sportsman's paradise, this greatly extended old building is popular with businessmen and holiday-makers alike. Public areas still retain links with the past, while modern bedrooms have fitted pine furniture and streamlined bathrooms. No dogs. *Amenities* garden, sauna, indoor swimming pool, tennis, squash, two golf courses, coarse fishing, coffee shop (11am–10pm), badminton, snooker, table tennis, gymnasium.

| *Room phone* Yes | *Confirm by* 6 | *Parking* Ample |
| *Room TV* Yes | *Last dinner* 9.30 | *Banquets* 180/– |

Colwyn Bay
Map 8 C1 Clwyd
Penmaenhead *LL29 9LD*
Colwyn Bay (0492) 56555
Telex 61362
Proprietor Mr M. L. Sexton
Credit Access, Amex,
Barclaycard, Diners

Rooms 44
with bath/shower 44

Hotel Seventy Degrees   66%   Ⓜ   £ D

An unusual modular construction gives every room at this modern clifftop hotel a splendid sea view. The warmly decorated foyer-lounge is very relaxing and there's also an attractive bar with elegant modern decor. Well-maintained bedrooms have simple built-in units, coordinated fabrics and compact, fully tiled bathrooms.
Amenities dancing (Sat), in-house movies. **Closed** 10 days Christmas

| *Room phone* Yes | *Confirm by* By arrang. | *Parking* Ample |
| *Room TV* Yes | *Last dinner* 9.30 | *Banquets* 120/12 |

Cowbridge
Map 9 C6 South Glamorgan
High Street *CF7 7AF*
Cowbridge (044 63) 4814

Credit Access, Barclaycard

Rooms 31
with bath/shower 28

Bear Hotel   59%   £ E

This stone-fronted hotel in the middle of a busy little town retains much of the charm of its days as a coaching inn. Original oak beams and exposed stone walls are attractive features of the public rooms, which include three popular bars. Older bedrooms are furnished in a variety of styles, while the ten bright, cheerful rooms in the modern wing have contemporary fitted furniture.

| *Room phone* Yes | *Confirm by* 7 | *Parking* Ample |
| *Room TV* Yes | *Last dinner* 9.45 | |

Coychurch
Map 9 C6 Mid Glamorgan
Near Bridgend *CF35 6AF*
Pencoed (0656) 860621
Proprietors Mr & Mrs Taylor
Credit Access, Amex,
Barclaycard, Diners
Closed 3 days Christmas

Coed-y-Mwstwr Hotel   67%   Ⓜ   £ D

The Taylors' handsome Victorian house on a wooded hillside offers visitors very comfortable accommodation in peaceful surroundings. There are plenty of relaxing armchairs and settees in the open-plan lounge bar, and the attractively decorated bedrooms, reached by a fine staircase, have smart freestanding furniture and good modern bathrooms. No children under seven. Guide dogs only. *Amenities* garden, outdoor swimming pool, tennis.

Continued

Rooms 16	*Room phone* Yes	*Confirm by* 6	*Parking* Ample
with bath/shower 16	*Room TV* Yes	*Last dinner* 10	*Banquets* 80/–

Coychurch
Map 9 C6 Mid Glamorgan
Near Bridgend *CF35 6AF*
Pencoed (0656) 860621
Proprietors Mr & Mrs V. Taylor

● **Set L** from £7·95 incl. wine
Set D £10·75
About £36 for two

Coed-y-Mwstwr Hotel, Eliot Room

Two beautiful chandeliers adorn this elegant panelled room, where classically prepared dishes are served with style. Starters could include smoked salmon pâté and veal kidneys with sherry, while main courses like pepper steak or our superbly fresh poached sewin are served with excellent vegetables. A light chocolate and Grand Marnier soufflé makes a lovely finale. ▼ *ABOVE AVERAGE. Credit* Access, Amex, Barclaycard, Diners

Lunch 12.30–2 *Dinner* 7.30–10
Closed D Sun, Bank Holidays & 3 days Christmas

Crickhowell
Map 9 D5 Powys
Brecon Road *NP8 1BW*
Crickhowell (0873) 810408

Bear Hotel *(Inn)* Ⓜ   £F

In the heart of the town, this charming and welcoming old inn is full of character. Exposed stone walls, vast fireplaces and interesting antique furniture are features of the public rooms, which include a roomy lounge and two congenial, cottage bars. Cheerful bedrooms have colourful decor, duvets and double glazing. Adequate modern bathrooms.
Amenities garden.

Rooms 12	*Room phone* No	*Confirm by* 6	*Parking* Ample
with bath/shower 9	*Room TV* No	*Last dinner* 8.45	*Banquets* 65/10

Crickhowell
Map 9 D5 Powys
Brecon Road *NP8 1SG*
Crickhowell (0873) 810775
Proprietor Barbara Ambrose

About £30 for two

Nantyffin Cider Mill Inn

A cosy little dining room with a log fire makes this old country pub attractive to the passing motorist. Lunchtime food revolves mainly round grills, sturdy home-made pies and salads, while in the evening there are such delights as devilled kidneys, delicious mussels in white wine, jugged hare, steaks and venison. Vegetables are fresh and crisp, and afters include tipsy trifle and lovely light pancakes.

Lunch 12–2.30, Sun 12–1.30 *Dinner* 7–10, Sun 7–9.30

Cross Inn
Map 9 B4 Dyfed
Llanon *SY23 5PB*
Nebo (097 46) 644
Proprietors
Chris & Sue Riley

● **Set D** £8
About £22 for two
Banquets 30/–

Rhos-yr-Hafod Inn Restaurant

Chris and Sue Riley's lively country inn is situated a few miles down a lane off the A487. It's the perfect setting in which to enjoy Sue's robust cooking and imaginative set menus, which offer really good value. You might begin with kidneys Turbigo and go on to seafood soup, followed perhaps by pork chops and spiced plum sauce and a delicious home-made pudding to finish. Booking essential.

Dinner only 7.30–9.30
Closed Sun, Mon (except Bank Holidays) & 25 & 26 December

Deganwy
Map 8 C1 Gwynedd
Conwy Road *LL31 9DA*
Deganwy (0492) 83358

Credit Access, Amex,
Barclaycard

Deganwy Castle Hotel   63%   £E

Overlooking the Conwy estuary with views of Snowdonia in the distance, this turn-of-the-century hotel is a delightful place to stay. Tastefully designed public rooms include two comfortable lounges (one with TV) and two bars, one with inglenook fireplace and rough stone walls. Best bedrooms, on the first floor, have coordinated colour schemes and trouser presses; other bedrooms are adequate. *Amenities* garden, hairdressing.

Rooms 36	*Room phone* Most	*Confirm by* 6	*Parking* Ample
with bath/shower 12	*Room TV* Yes	*Last dinner* 9	*Banquets* 120/10

Dolgellau

Map 8 C3 Gwynedd
Lion Street *LL40 1DG*
Dolgellau (0341) 422579

Proprietor Mr G. G. Hall
Credit Amex, Barclaycard
Closed 18 Dec–1 Jan

Golden Lion Royal Hotel 59% Ⓜ £E

Bedrooms are comfortably furnished in this charming, creeper-clad hotel. Some have four-posters and sturdy antiques, while others (including all of those in the stable wing) are neat and modern. Welcoming log fires burn in the three lounges, and a striking military theme animates the plush cocktail bar. There's also a popular coffee shop and public bar.
Amenities garden, coffee shop (10.30am–5pm).

| *Rooms* 23 | *Room phone* No | *Confirm by* 6 | *Parking* Limited |
| *with bath/shower* 14 | *Room TV* Most | *Last dinner* 9 | *Banquets* 100/– |

Dolgellau

Map 8 C3 Gwynedd
LL40 1TL
Dolgellau (0341) 422488
Proprietors
Mr & Mrs Peter Hall

Closed 14 October–Easter

Gwernan Lake Hotel *(Inn)* Ⓜ £F

Nestling by the side of a lake some two miles outside Dolgellau, this little whitewashed stone inn makes a most tranquil retreat. Immaculate public rooms include a comfortable panelled residents' lounge and a cosy bar popular with locals. Bedrooms are unpretentious and simply furnished, and there are two well-kept public bathrooms. No children under four. No dogs.
Amenities garden, coarse & game fishing.

| *Rooms* 11 | *Room phone* No | *Confirm by* By arrang. | *Parking* Ample |
| *with bath/shower* None | *Room TV* No | *Last dinner* 8.30 | |

Dolgellau

Map 8 C3 Gwynedd
Queen's Square *LL40 1AR*
Dolgellau (0341) 422209

Credit Access

Royal Ship Hotel 53% £E

Charming Brenda Parry is the life and soul of this simple town-centre hostelry, where unfussy accommodation is the order of the day. Public rooms offer plenty of variety: there are four little bars, including the smart, contemporary-style St John's Bar, and three simply furnished lounges (one with TV). Comfortable bedrooms have functional modern units, radios and tea-makers. Simple bathrooms are spotlessly clean. ♿

| *Rooms* 26 | *Room phone* No | *Confirm by* 6 | *Parking* Limited |
| *with bath/shower* 7 | *Room TV* No | *Last dinner* 8.30 | *Banquets* 90/– |

Eglwysfach

Map 8 C3 Dyfed
Near Machynlleth, Powys
SY20 8TA
Glandyfi (065 474) 209
Credit Access, Amex,
Barclaycard, Diners
Closed 4 January–3 February

Ynyshir Hall Country House Hotel 68% Ⓜ £D

Close to the Snowdonia National Park, this modernised 16th-century house in lovely gardens is a good base from which to explore the Welsh countryside. The entrance hall with its flowers and ornaments is most welcoming and there are two relaxing drawing rooms as well as an intimate bar. Attractive bedrooms have nice extras like fresh fruit, and bathrooms are well fitted. Inclusive terms only. *Amenities* garden. ♿

| *Rooms* 11 | *Room phone* No | *Confirm by* By arrang. | *Parking* Ample |
| *with bath/shower* 7 | *Room TV* No | *Last dinner* 9 | |

Eglwysfach

Map 8 C3 Dyfed
Near Machynlleth, Powys
SY20 8TA
Glandyfi (065 474) 209

Ynyshir Hall Restaurant ⚘ Ⓢ

Prime ingredients are competently prepared in this discreetly elegant dining room. The short fixed-price menu features tempting dishes like grilled red mullet and noisettes of lamb with mint and lemon sauce, which are served with nicely cooked vegetables. The sweet trolley is a great attraction and there's also a vegetarian menu. No smoking in the dining room.
🍷 *ABOVE AVERAGE. Credit* Access, Amex, Barclaycard, Diners

● **Set L** £6·95 **Set D** £10·25
About £28 for two

Lunch Sun 12–1.45, Mon–Sat by arrangement *Dinner* 7–9.30
Closed 4 January–1 February

Erbistock

Map 8 D2 Clwyd
Near Wrexham *LL13 0DL*
Overton-on-Dee (097 873) 243
Manager Miss E. Grundy

Boat Inn Ⓢ

Right on the banks of the Dee at the end of a long narrow road, this 16th-century stone house is absolutely delightful. In the beamed dining room you can enjoy a regularly changing menu which includes classical French dishes like poached sole with prawn sauce and guinea fowl provençale, grills and skilfully prepared vegetables. Finish with a pleasant

Continued

sweet and excellent coffee. *Credit* Access, Amex, Barclaycard, Diners

● **Set L & Set D** £7·50
About £27 for two
Banquets 25/2

Lunch 12.30–2.15, Sun 12.30–2
Dinner 7.30–9.15, Sat 7.30–9.30, Sun 7.30–9

Fishguard
Map 9 A5 Dyfed
Goodwick *SA64 0BT*
Fishguard (0348) 873571
Proprietor Mr G. J. Schell

Credit Access, Amex,
Barclaycard, Diners

Fishguard Bay Hotel   60%   Ⓜ   £ E

This rambling Victorian building stands in pleasant wooded grounds overlooking Fishguard Bay. Spacious public rooms, furnished with a mixture of fine old mahogany and simpler modern pieces, include two lounges and three bars. Comfortable bedrooms (some with balconies) have practical fittings and plenty of space. There's a sumptuous honeymoon suite. Helpful, friendly staff. *Amenities* garden, outdoor swimming pool, snooker.   &

Rooms 62
with bath/shower 27

Room phone Some	*Confirm by* 7	*Parking* Ample
Room TV Some	*Last dinner* 9.30	*Banquets* 300/–

Glyn Ceiriog
Map 8 D2 Clwyd
Llwynmawr
Near Llangollen *LL20 7BB*
Glyn Ceiriog (069 172) 281
Proprietor Miss Jenny Turner
Credit Access, Amex

Golden Pheasant Hotel   58%   Ⓜ   £ E

Modern comforts blend happily with the old-fashioned charm of a country inn at this attractive 18th-century hotel in a delightful wooded valley. There are fine views from the two comfortable lounges, and there's a friendly public bar as well as a plush lounge bar. Cheerful bedrooms (best in the wing) have traditional furnishings and well-equipped bathrooms.
Amenities garden, coarse & game fishing, riding, shooting.

Rooms 19
with bath/shower 19

Room phone No	*Confirm by* By arrang.	*Parking* Ample
Room TV No	*Last dinner* 8.30	*Banquets* 70/10

Gwbert-on-Sea
Map 9 B4 Dyfed
Near Cardigan *SA43 1PP*
Cardigan (0239) 613241
Telex 48440

Credit Access, Amex,
Barclaycard, Diners

Cliff Hotel   60%   £ E

Panoramic views of Cardigan Bay and a good range of leisure amenities make this an ideal holiday hotel. Public rooms include two spacious lounges, a continental-style sun lounge and a chintzy bar. Bedrooms, in a mixture of styles, have good modern bathrooms. *Amenities* garden, outdoor swimming pool, squash, sea fishing, dancing (Sat in summer), 9-hole golf course, games room, helipad, laundry room, surfing, putting.   &

Rooms 70
with bath/shower 70

Room phone Yes	*Confirm by* 6	*Parking* Ample
Room TV Most	*Last dinner* 9	*Banquets* 220/16

Lake Vyrnwy
Map 8 C3 Powys
Via Oswestry, Shropshire *SY10 0LY*
Llanwddyn (069 173) 244
Proprietors Mrs J. F. Moir &
Lt Col Sir John Baynes Bt
Closed 14 January–1 March
except by arrangement

Lake Vyrnwy Hotel   56%   Ⓜ   £ D/E

Renowned for its fishing and shooting, this sturdy Victorian hotel also has spectacular views of Lake Vyrnwy. Public rooms have a charming, old-fashioned atmosphere enhanced by period furniture. Bedrooms of various sizes are also traditional in style, and bathrooms are adequate. No dogs, but kennels available.
Amenities garden, tennis, game fishing, shooting, table tennis, games room.

Rooms 31
with bath/shower 11

Room phone No	*Confirm by* By arrang.	*Parking* Ample
Room TV No	*Last dinner* 7.30	*Banquets* 25/–

Stars in this Guide stand for the quality of the cooking only—
our overriding criterion, irrespective of price, luxury or service.

Llandewi Skirrid
Map 9 D5 Gwent
Near Abergavenny *NP7 8AW*
Abergavenny (0873) 2797
Proprietors
Mr & Mrs Taruschio

About £33 for two

Walnut Tree Inn ★ 

A profusion of potted plants greets guests at this well-loved restaurant, where Franco Taruschio produces a long, daily-changing choice of dishes featuring seafood as well as classics like steak tartare and chilli con carne. Beautifully fresh ingredients are handled with great skill and care throughout a menu which ranges from simple lasagne and gravad lax to crispy crab pancakes, roast quails with sage and mignon de veau with orange and peppercorns. An amazing sweet selection includes ice creams, sorbets, Toulouse chestnut pudding and splendidly rich dolce torinese.
Specialities tenerelli deliziosa, plateau de fruits de mer, salmon with rhubarb, torte with three liqueurs.  *OUTSTANDING.*

Lunch 12–2.30 *Dinner* 7–10
Closed Sun & 25 & 26 December

Llandudno
Map 8 C1 Gwynedd
LL30 1RS
Deganwy (0492) 84466

Rooms 20
with bath/shower 20
Room phone Yes
Room TV Yes
Confirm by By arrang.
Last dinner 9
Parking Ample

Credit Access, Amex,
Barclaycard, Diners

Bodysgallen Hall   74%   Ⓜ   £ D

In former times, part of this beautiful stone building was a watch tower for Conwy Castle, and inside and out it has been wonderfully preserved; the formal 18th-century gardens are enchanting, and the interior of the house is a model of good taste. The entrance hall, drawing room and library are traditionally appointed, with much panelling and a profusion of oil paintings; there's also a new bar. Superb, individually decorated bedrooms have excellent oak and mahogany furniture, coordinated colour schemes and extras ranging from trouser presses to bottled water. Bathrooms have good-quality fittings. No children under six.
Amenities garden, tennis, croquet.

Llandudno
Map 8 C1 Gwynedd
Church Walk *LL30 2HE*
Llandudno (0492) 79955
Telex 617161
Proprietors L. & E. Maddocks
Credit Access, Amex,
Barclaycard, Diners

Rooms 56
with bath/shower 56

Empire Hotel   62%   Ⓜ   £ E/F

Situated a short walk from the promenade, this friendly, family-run hotel boasts excellent recreational facilities. Smart public rooms, which include a fine lounge and two bars, have a Victorian theme, while compact bedrooms have neat built-in units, colourful decor and thoughtfully equipped bathrooms. *Amenities* sauna, indoor swimming pool, dancing (Sat), games room, roof garden, solarium, children's pool. **Closed** 2 weeks Christmas

Room phone Yes	*Confirm by* By arrang.	*Parking* Ample
Room TV Yes	*Last dinner* 8.30	

Llandudno
Map 8 C1 Gwynedd
The Promenade *LL30 1AP*
Llandudno (0492) 77466

Credit Access, Amex,
Barclaycard

Rooms 150
with bath/shower 75

Imperial Hotel   58%   £ E

A recent facelift has brightened this large Victorian hotel on the seafront. Public rooms include spacious open-plan lounge areas, a colourful cocktail bar and the lively Speakeasy Bar in the basement. Simply decorated bedrooms are fitted in an unfussy modern style. Well-equipped bathrooms. *Amenities* dancing (3 nights weekly May–Sept), discothèque (6 nights weekly), sauna, keep-fit equipment, snooker, pool table, table tennis, solarium.

Room phone Yes	*Confirm by* 6	*Parking* Limited
Room TV Yes	*Last dinner* 8.30	*Banquets* 350/–

Llandudno
Map 8 C1 Gwynedd
St George's Place *LL30 2LG*
Llandudno (0492) 77544
Telex 61520

Credit Access, Amex,
Barclaycard, Diners

St George's Hotel   67%   £ D

This hotel built in 1853 dominates the promenade, and its traditionally furnished lounge overlooks the sea. Other well-maintained public areas include two smart bars. Most of the spacious bedrooms have fitted units and pretty floral bedspreads. Front rooms on the first floor have balconies, and the Grecian and Roman rooms have especially luxurious bathrooms. *Amenities* dancing (Mon–Sat), buttery (10am–3pm).

                    Continued

| Rooms 82 | Room phone Yes | Confirm by 6 | Parking Ample |
| with bath/shower 82 | Room TV Yes | Last dinner 8.30 | Banquets 245/10 |

Llanelli
Map 9 B6 Dyfed
Furnace *SA15 4HA*
Llanelli (055 42) 58171
Telex 48521

Credit Access, Amex,
Barclaycard, Diners

Stradey Park Hotel 60% £E

A crenellated mansion with a modern bedroom extension, this pleasant hotel stands high on a hill overlooking the town. There's a comfortable reception-lounge area and a spacious bar as well as versatile conference facilities. Good-sized bedrooms have simple, contemporary decor and furnishings and tea/coffee-makers. Bathrooms are neatly fitted and well maintained. *Amenities* dancing (most Sats).　&

| Rooms 77 | Room phone Yes | Confirm by 6 | Parking Ample |
| with bath/shower 77 | Room TV Yes | Last dinner 9.30 | Banquets 400/– |

Llangollen
Map 8 D2 Clwyd
Bridge Street *LL20 8PL*
Llangollen (0978) 860303
Telex 61160
Manager Mr David Morris
Credit Access, Amex,
Barclaycard, Diners

Hand Hotel 57% £E

The public rooms of this rambling old coaching inn with steeply terraced gardens overlooking the river Dee provide good modern comfort. The best of the bedrooms are prettily decorated and equipped with simple fitted units and compact carpeted bathrooms.
Amenities garden, game fishing, dancing (Sat), entertainment (nightly in summer, 3 nights weekly in winter).

| Rooms 60 | Room phone Yes | Confirm by By arrang. | Parking Ample |
| with bath/shower 60 | Room TV Yes | Last dinner 10 | Banquets 100/– |

Llangollen
Map 8 D2 Clwyd
Bridge Street *LL20 8PG*
Llangollen (0978) 860202

Credit Access, Amex,
Barclaycard, Diners

Royal Hotel 58% £D

Strategically placed in the centre of town, this fine old black and white building beside an ancient stone bridge enjoys splendid views of the bubbling river Dee. Inside are two bars and a large, peaceful residents' lounge. Modernised bedrooms, which provide practical comforts, have colour TVs, radios, tea/coffee-makers and tiled, adequately fitted bathrooms.

| Rooms 33 | Room phone Yes | Confirm by 6 | Parking Ample |
| with bath/shower 33 | Room TV Yes | Last dinner 9 | Banquets 80/6 |

Machynlleth
Map 8 C3 Powys
Maengwyn Street *SY20 8AE*
Machynlleth (0654) 2289

Credit Access, Amex,
Barclaycard, Diners
Closed 1 week Christmas

Wynnstay Hotel 57% £D

Gradual improvements are enhancing the traditional appeal of this former coaching inn in the town centre. Fresh flowers, potted plants and a grandfather clock create a homely atmosphere in the public rooms, among which are two lounges and two cosy little bars. Good-sized bedrooms, uniformly furnished with light oak fitted units, have tea/coffee-making facilities. Bathrooms are adequate.

| Rooms 31 | Room phone Yes | Confirm by 6 | Parking Ample |
| with bath/shower 10 | Room TV Yes | Last dinner 8.30 | |

Merthyr Tydfil
Map 9 C5 Mid Glamorgan
Head of the Valley Road
Aberdare *CF44 0LX*
Merthyr Tydfil (0685) 6221
Proprietors Baverstock family
Credit Access, Amex,
Barclaycard, Diners

Baverstock's Hotel 62% Ⓜ £E

This modern hotel on the A465 just outside Merthyr is run with care by the Baverstock family, who keep it in tip-top condition. Public rooms like the lounge and bars are decorated and furnished in attractive contemporary style, and the bedrooms (the newest being especially handsome) have smart fitted units and prettily patterned duvets. Immaculate tiled bathrooms. Guide dogs only. **Closed** 25 December. *Amenities* garden, dinner dance (Sat).　&

| Rooms 43 | Room phone Yes | Confirm by By arrang. | Parking Ample |
| with bath/shower 43 | Room TV Yes | Last dinner 10.15 | Banquets 400/– |

Monmouth
Map 9 D5 Gwent
Agincourt Square *NP5 3DY*
Monmouth (0600) 2177

Proprietor Mr K. L. Gough
Credit Access, Amex,
Barclaycard, Diners

Rooms 28
with bath/shower 26

King's Head Hotel 68% Ⓜ **£E**

This half-timbered 17th-century building retains much original style and character. There's a feeling of recaptured elegance in the grand ballroom, while guests wanting a drink can choose between the plush cocktail bar and the more rustic public bar. Bedrooms tastefully decorated with bold floral prints have mainly darkwood built-in units and compact, well-fitted bathrooms.

Room phone Yes	*Confirm by* 6	*Parking* Limited
Room TV Yes	*Last dinner* 9	*Banquets* 200/–

Mumbles
Map 9 C6 West Glamorgan
Norton Road *SA3 5TQ*
Swansea (0792) 66174
Props. Mr & Mrs Claude Rossi
Credit Access, Barclaycard
Closed Christmas &
Bank Holidays

Rooms 13
with bath/shower 12

Norton House Hotel 69% Ⓜ **£E**

The Rossis are welcoming hosts at this large Georgian house near the seafront. A fine walnut staircase with a minstrels' gallery leads to the bedrooms, which are spacious and traditionally furnished (three have four-posters); rooms in the new wing are smaller and have Regency-style furniture. Simple modern bathrooms. There's also a comfortable bar-lounge. No dogs. *Amenities* garden, sauna, solarium.

Room phone Yes	*Confirm by* By arrang.	*Parking* Ample
Room TV Some	*Last dinner* 9.45	*Banquets* 40/–

Newport
Map 9 D6 Gwent
The Coldra *NP6 2YA*
Newport (0633) 413000

Rooms 17
with bath/shower 17
Room phone Yes
Room TV Yes
Confirm by By arrang.
Last dinner 10.30
Parking Ample
Banquets 100/6

Credit Access, Amex,
Barclaycard, Diners

Celtic Manor 79% **£D**

There's an air of restful luxury about this Victorian mansion, which stands on a hill above junction 24 of the M4. The elegant, spacious foyer sets the right note of comfort, continued in the superb residents' lounge with its deep, chintzy chairs and lovely old fireplace. The lounge bar has a pleasing combination of leather chesterfields and pink velour-clad armchairs, and among the other public rooms are an arched cellar bar and a leafy, bamboo-furnished conservatory. Spacious bedrooms, decorated to a very high standard, have attractive darkwood furniture which contrasts beautifully with the light blue carpets. Well-equipped bathrooms. Guide dogs only. *Amenities* garden, Patio coffee shop (7am–11pm).

Newport
Map 9 A5 Dyfed
Market Street *SA42 0PH*
Newport (0239) 820420
Proprietors
Joan & Robin Evans

About £30 for two

Pantry ★

A warm welcome and the rustic decor enhance the excellence of the food in the Evans' charming little restaurant. The short menu shows how memorable essentially simple dishes can be when good raw materials are handled with skill and enthusiasm. Rich onion soup and delicate salmon trout mousse with cucumber mayonnaise have distinct, well-defined flavours, local lamb is cooked to perfection, and delicious vegetables include outstanding cream and garlic potatoes. Lovely sweets like hazelnut meringue gâteau with raspberries round off a marvellous meal.
Specialities roast carré of lamb with a mushroom, tomato and caper sauce, salmon in crust with fennel sauce, meringue glacé with hot chocolate sauce.

Dinner only 7.30–9.30
Closed Sun, Mon & 1 week Christmas

Newtown
Map 8 D3 Powys
Broad Street *SY16 2LU*
Newtown (0686) 26964

Credit Access, Amex,
Barclaycard, Diners

Bear Hotel 57% **£F**

This attractive half-timbered hotel is popular with holiday-makers and businessmen alike. The modern wing contains a pleasant lounge with cane furniture and a lounge-bar. Bedrooms (the best are in the wing) have simple colour schemes and functional contemporary furniture. Compact bathrooms are adequately equipped. *Amenities* dinner dance (Sat).

Continued

Rooms 37	*Room phone* Yes	*Confirm by* 6	*Parking* Ample
with bath/shower 31	*Room TV* Yes	*Last dinner* 9.15	

Northophall
Map 8 D2 Clwyd
Near Mold *CH7 6JH*
Deeside (0244) 816181
Telex 617112
Proprietor Mr John Hayter
Credit Access, Amex,
Barclaycard, Diners

Chequers Hotel   55%   Ⓜ   £ E

Set off the A56 in grounds of 40 acres, this extended Victorian house is a pleasant combination of old and new. There's a cocktail bar with a large mullioned bay window on the ground floor, while a fine Canadian pine staircase with a gallery leads to the peaceful lounge and the original, simply furnished bedrooms. Best rooms, however, are those in the new wing. Compact, well-equipped bathrooms. *Amenities* garden.   &

Rooms 30	*Room phone* Yes	*Confirm by* 6	*Parking* Ample
with bath/shower 30	*Room TV* Yes	*Last dinner* 9.45	*Banquets* 110/–

Pant Mawr
Map 9 C4 Powys
Near Llangurig *SY18 6SY*
Llangurig (055 15) 240
Proprietors
Mr & Mrs W. T. Edwards

Closed 20–30 December

Glansevern Arms *(Inn)*   Ⓜ   £ F

There are superb views from this charming little inn which stands in a beautiful valley four miles outside Llangurig on the A44. It's easy to unwind in the old-fashioned lounge with its comfortable seating or in the two delightful beamed bars. Bedrooms are sturdily furnished and–like the bathrooms–spotless. The friendly Edwardses serve marvellous breakfasts. *Amenities* garden, game fishing, rough shooting.

Rooms 6	*Room phone* No	*Confirm by* By arrang.	*Parking* Ample
with bath/shower None	*Room TV* No	*Last dinner* 8	

Pembroke
Map 9 A5 Dyfed
Main Street *SA71 4JS*
Pembroke (0646) 683611
Telex 48598
Proprietors Mr & Mrs G. Wheeler
Credit Access, Barclaycard
Closed 1 week Christmas

Wheeler's Old King's Arms Hotel   58%   Ⓜ   £ E/F

The plain exterior gives no hint of the unspoilt charm of this friendly, family-run hotel. The cheerful public bar offers a roaring fire and rustic antiques, while the cocktail bar near the comfortable residents' lounge is elegant in shades of brown. Pine furniture contrasts with dark soft furnishings in the Nordic-style bedrooms, with the newer rooms being largest and best. All have well-fitted modern bathrooms.

Rooms 21	*Room phone* Yes	*Confirm by* By arrang.	*Parking* Limited
with bath/shower 21	*Room TV* Yes	*Last dinner* 10	

Penarth
Map 9 D6 South Glamorgan
Esplanade *CF6 2AS*
Penarth (0222) 702424
Proprietor Mr E. Rabaiotti

Caprice   ♔ Ⓢ

A wide selection from the international repertoire is offered at this smart restaurant overlooking the sea. French onion soup and lasagne verdi are among the simple starters, while main courses include fish and game in season, grills and flambéed dishes. Capable, reliable cooking, with very good sauces, nice crisp vegetables and a trolleyload of tempting desserts.
 *SUPERIOR. Credit* Access, Amex, Barclaycard, Diners

● **Set L** £6·95 **Set D** £9·75
About £34 for two
Banquets 100/–

Lunch 12–2.30 *Dinner* 7–11
Closed Sun & Bank Holidays

Penmaenpool
Map 8 C3 Gwynedd
Near Dolgellau *LL40 1YD*
Dolgellau (0341) 422525

Proprietor Mr John Hall
Credit Access, Amex,
Barclaycard, Diners

George III Hotel *(Inn)*   Ⓜ   £ D/E

Dating back some 300 years, this pleasant hostelry overlooking the Mawddach estuary is full of character. One bar has a balcony and a bar front made from a converted Welsh dresser; there's another rustic bar in the cellar. Bedrooms are compact, simply furnished and equipped with tea-makers; those in the nearby lodge are slightly larger and more luxurious. Well-fitted bathrooms. *Amenities* garden, sea fishing.   &

Rooms 12	*Room phone* No	*Confirm by* 6	*Parking* Ample
with bath/shower 7	*Room TV* Yes	*Last dinner* 9	

Penrhyndeudraeth
Map 8 C2 Gwynedd
LL48 6ER

HOTEL PORTMEIRION   Ⓜ   £ E

It will take at least three years to restore this Victorian mansion to its former

Continued

Continued
Penrhyn (0766) 770228
Manager Mr T. McDermott
Credit Access, Amex,
Barclaycard, Diners
Closed October–Easter

state after a disastrous fire. A simple bar and modest reception are in operation, but accommodation at present is in a number of cottages dotted throughout the village; these are comfortably furnished in traditional style and most have fine views of the estuary and hills beyond.
Amenities garden, outdoor swimming pool, sea fishing, tennis.

Rooms 18 — *Room phone* No — *Confirm by* By arrang. — *Parking* Ample
with bath/shower 18 — *Room TV* Yes — *Last dinner* 9.30

Port Dinorwic
Map 8 B2 Gwynedd
20 Snowdon Street *LL56 4HQ*
Port Dinorwic (0248) 670546
Proprietors Keith Rothwell &
David Robertson

Seahorse

Check cloths, candles and a blazing fire in the old-fashioned grate give a bistro air to this refined restaurant where they welcome you with plates of smoked salmon canapés. First-class ingredients including local fish are the basis for an appetising menu of simple, carefully prepared dishes like roast quails or scampi with Pernod, served with crisp salads and good vegetables.
Credit Access, Barclaycard

About £25 for two

Dinner only 7.30–9.30
Closed Sun, 1 January & 25 & 26 December

Presteigne
Map 9 D4 Powys
High Street *LD8 2BE*
Presteigne (0544) 267406

Managers Mr & Mrs Hodgetts
Credit Access, Amex,
Barclaycard, Diners

Radnorshire Arms Hotel   55%   £ D

Parts of this classic half-timbered building date back to the early 1600s and there are still echoes of the past in the charming lounge and bar, both of which have an abundance of oak panelling. Two bedrooms upstairs continue this theme, although most (including eight in the garden wing) have simple fitted units. All are equipped with tea-makers and well-maintained modern bathrooms. *Amenities* garden.

Rooms 16 — *Room phone* Yes — *Confirm by* 6 — *Parking* Ample
with bath/shower 16 — *Room TV* Yes — *Last dinner* 8.30

Robeston Wathen
Map 9 A5 Dyfed
Near Narberth *SA67 8EU*
Narberth (0834) 860392
Proprietors
Grahame & Pamela Barrett
Credit Access
Closed 4 days Christmas

Robeston House   66%      £ E

There's an air of quiet elegance about the Barretts' welcoming hotel, which stands on the A40. Antiques, pictures and objets d'art grace the comfortable public rooms, while bright, cheerful bedrooms, some with attractive views, are furnished in a pleasing mixture of traditional and contemporary styles. Modern bathrooms. No children under 14. Dogs in kennels only.
Amenities garden, outdoor swimming pool, game fishing.

Rooms 6 — *Room phone* No — *Confirm by* 6 — *Parking* Ample
with bath/shower 3 — *Room TV* Yes — *Last dinner* 9.30 — *Banquets* 50/12

Robeston Wathen
Map 9 A5 Dyfed
Near Narberth *SA67 8EU*
Narberth (0834) 860392
Proprietors Barrett family

Robeston House Restaurant

There's a touch of elegance about this charming restaurant with its polished oak tables and lovely glassware. Dishes on the fixed-price menu are robust and full of flavour, with local produce used to good effect. We enjoyed a tasty carrot and orange soup, smoked baby chicken with thick Stilton sauce and delicious vegetables (including superb garlic potatoes), and, to finish, rich walnut charlotte. *Credit* Access

● **Set L & Set D** £9
About £24 for two

Lunch by arrangement only *Dinner* 7.30–9.30
Closed 4 days Christmas

Ruthin
Map 8 C2 Clwyd
St Peter's Square *LL15 1AA*
Ruthin (082 42) 2479
Telex 617074

Credit Access, Amex,
Barclaycard, Diners

Castle Hotel   55%   £ E/F

A tall Georgian building and its smaller Tudor neighbour make up this pleasant family-run hotel, which new owners are in the process of redecorating. The bright little entrance hall leads to an attractive bar-lounge area, and there's another bar with a delightfully rustic air. Bedrooms in a variety of styles are simple, cheerful and comfortable. Good modern bathrooms.
Amenities garden.

Rooms 25 — *Room phone* Yes — *Confirm by* 7 — *Parking* Ample
with bath/shower 13 — *Room TV* Yes — *Last dinner* 11 — *Banquets* 130/–

Ruthin

Map 8 C2 Clwyd
Castle Street
Corwen Road *LL15 2NU*
Ruthin (082 42) 2664
Telex 61169
Credit Access, Amex,
Barclaycard, Diners

Ruthin Castle   65%

£ D/E

Peacocks strut through the impressive landscaped grounds of this much enlarged and altered medieval castle high above the river Clwyd. Magnificent public rooms, decorated in the grand manner, include two beautiful lounges and an octagonal cocktail bar, once the library. Spacious bedrooms are simply furnished; best ones are in the main building. Adequate bathrooms. *Amenities* garden, coarse fishing, helipad.

Rooms 60	*Room phone* Yes	*Confirm by* 6	*Parking* Ample
with bath/shower 60	*Room TV* No	*Last dinner* 9	*Banquets* 150/2

St David's

Map 9 A5 Dyfed
Catherine Street *SA62 6RJ*
St David's (0437) 720239

Proprietor Mr A. W. Falconer
Credit Access, Barclaycard,
Diners

St Non's Hotel   57%   Ⓜ

£ F

Lovers of the open air will find this unpretentious little hotel an ideal base for exploring the beauty of the Welsh countryside. Enjoy a drink on the patio when the weather's fine, or choose between the relaxing TV lounge and the attractive bars, where log fires burn. Bedrooms with built-in units are brightened up by a floral-patterned feature wall. Simple modern bathrooms. *Amenities* garden, dinner dance (Sat).

Rooms 20	*Room phone* No	*Confirm by* 6	*Parking* Ample
with bath/shower 20	*Room TV* No	*Last dinner* 9.30	*Banquets* 120/2

St David's

Map 9 A5 Dyfed
SA62 6BN
St David's (0437) 720300
Proprietors
Grahame & David Lloyd
Credit Access, Amex
Closed January

Warpool Court Hotel   64%   Ⓜ

£ D/E

The traditional comforts and amenities of this peaceful manor house are appreciated by families and businessmen alike. Decor is dominated by a collection of 3,000 hand-painted tiles, and there are many antiques, too. Bedrooms are comfortably furnished, and have well-fitted bath or shower rooms.
Amenities garden, indoor swimming pool, sea fishing, dancing (3 Sats monthly October–May), chamber music (1 Sat monthly October–May).

Rooms 25	*Room phone* No	*Confirm by* 8	*Parking* Ample
with bath/shower 25	*Room TV* Yes	*Last dinner* 9.30	*Banquets* 40/–

St David's

Map 9 A5 Dyfed
SA62 6BN
St David's (0437) 720300
Proprietors
Grahame & David Lloyd

Warpool Court Hotel Restaurant   ♧ Ⓢ

A pleasantly traditional dining room—candlelit in the evening—where the cooking is based on fine local produce like salmon trout and hare. Dishes ranging from veal kidney with Madeira sauce to plain grills come with al dente vegetables, and there's an excellent choice on the sweet trolley. Lighter lunches offer things like nourishing Welsh cawl, lasagne and filled pancakes. *Credit* Access, Amex

● **Set D** from £9·25
About £27 for two

Lunch 11–3 *Dinner* 7–9.30
Closed January

St Mellons

Map 9 D6 South Glamorgan
Near Cardiff *CF3 8XR*
Castleton (Gwent)
(0633) 680355
Proprietors M. S. & E. Arino
Credit Access, Amex,
Barclaycard, Diners

St Mellons Hotel   54%   Ⓜ

£ E

A well-equipped leisure centre is the main attraction of this modernised Victorian hotel, which stands just off the A48 in the middle of the St Mellons golf course. Public rooms like the lounge and bar are plainly furnished in contemporary style, as are the bedrooms (the best are those in the motel-style blocks). No dogs. *Amenities* garden, sauna, indoor swimming pool, tennis, squash, gymnasium, snooker, table tennis.

Rooms 27	*Room phone* Yes	*Confirm by* 6	*Parking* Ample
with bath/shower 27	*Room TV* Yes	*Last dinner* 10	*Banquets* 200/18

Saundersfoot

Map 9 B5 Dyfed
Cambrian Terrace *SA69 9ER*
Saundersfoot (0834) 812448

Credit Access, Amex,
Barclaycard

Cambrian Hotel   59%   Ⓜ

£ D

This welcoming harbourside hotel, a comfortable holiday base, is also popular for conferences. Red and gold decor adds warmth to the public rooms, which include four bars and a residents' lounge. You can also relax on a cheerful patio. Simply decorated bedrooms have trouser presses, tea-makers and modern tiled bathrooms.
Amenities dancing (Sat October–April, Wed April–October).

Continued

Continued			
Rooms 28	*Room phone* Yes	*Confirm by* 7	*Parking* Ample
with bath/shower 28	*Room TV* Yes	*Last dinner* 9.30	

Swanbridge

Map 9 D6 South Glamorgan
Near Penarth *CF6 2XR*
Cardiff (0222) 530448
Proprietor Mr Eduardo Ferrandez

About £35 for two
Banquets 50/10

Sully House Hotel Restaurant

Turn off the B4267 towards St Mary Well Bay to find this charming *restaurant avec chambres* overlooking Sully Island. Paul Westmacott's classically based à la carte menu is supplemented by seasonal specialities, ingredients are wonderfully fresh and dishes like fresh asparagus spears with hollandaise sauce and lobster cardinal are cooked to perfection. Vegetables are nicely garnished, and sweets from the trolley include a truly delicious Black Forest gâteau. Upstairs there are five spacious, attractively decorated bedrooms with colour TVs and their own bathrooms. Staff are extremely pleasant and attentive.
Credit Access, Barclaycard, Diners

Lunch 12.30–2.30 *Dinner* 7–10
Closed Sun (except Mothering Sun) & Bank Holidays except Good Friday

---

Swansea

Map 9 C6 West Glamorgan
Whitewalls *SA1 3AB*
Swansea (0792) 50011
Telex 48128

Credit Access, Amex,
Barclaycard, Diners

Dolphin Hotel   55%   £E/F

A popular place with the business community, this unpretentious hotel in a shopping centre retains the style and decor of its '60s origins. Public areas on the first floor include two spacious lounges, a comfortable cocktail bar and several conference rooms. Simple bedrooms with functional fitted furniture and neat tiled bathrooms offer adequate comforts for short stays.

Rooms 65	*Room phone* Yes	*Confirm by* By arrang.	*Parking* Difficult
with bath/shower 65	*Room TV* Yes	*Last dinner* 9.30	*Banquets* 300/5

Swansea

Map 9 C6 West Glamorgan
The Kingsway *SA1 5LS*
Swansea (0792) 51074
Telex 48309

Credit Access, Amex,
Barclaycard, Diners

Dragon Hotel   65%   £D

Right in the centre of town, this purpose-built modern hotel is popular with overnight business visitors and provides a wide range of function and conference suites. Italian marble and smart light fittings feature in the foyer, and there are two comfortable bars, as well as a busy public bar. Practical bedrooms with attractive colour schemes have colour TVs, radios, tea/coffee-makers and well-kept bathrooms.

Rooms 118	*Room phone* Yes	*Confirm by* 6	*Parking* Ample
with bath/shower 118	*Room TV* Yes	*Last dinner* 9.30	*Banquets* 260/6

Swansea

Map 9 C6 West Glamorgan
66 Wind Street *SA1 1EQ*
Swansea (0792) 461397
Proprietor Colin Pressdee

● Set L £4·85
Set D £7·95 & £12·50
About £30 for two
Banquets 35/10

Drangway

A friendly, informal restaurant with bottle-green walls, modern prints and pine tables. The menus are an interesting combination of local specialities– oysters, sewin, laverbread–French classics and imaginative creations such as duck liver mousse with truffles and redcurrant sauce. Vegetables are excellent, and desserts include a very good apple and almond tart.
SUPERIOR. Credit Access, Amex, Barclaycard, Diners

Lunch 12.15–2.15 *Dinner* 7–10.15
Closed Sun & Bank Holidays

Tal-y-Llyn

Map 8 C3 Gwynedd
Near Tywyn *LL36 9AJ*
Abergynolwyn (065 477) 282
Proprietors
Mr & Mrs Thompson
Credit Access, Barclaycard

Tyn-y-Cornel Hotel   55%   Ⓜ   £D

This 500-year-old farmhouse in a secluded rugged valley overlooks a trout-filled lake. Simple public rooms include a pleasant reception-cum-bar and comfortable lounge with a cosy log fire. Bedrooms are furnished in simple modern style, the best being those in converted outbuildings, which have splendid views. Adequate carpeted bathrooms. *Amenities* garden, game fishing, rowing boats, water sports tuition (July & August).

Rooms 15	*Room phone* Some	*Confirm by* 6	*Parking* Ample
with bath/shower 13	*Room TV* No	*Last dinner* 8.45	

Talsarnau

Map 8 C2 Gwynedd
LL47 6YA
Harlech (0766) 780200

Credit Access, Amex,
Barclaycard

Rooms 14
with bath/shower 11

Maes-y-Neuadd Hotel   61%   Ⓜ   £ D/E

Parts of this traditional Welsh granite and slate house date back to the 14th century, and it succeeds in combining period charm with modern amenities. There's a comfortable lounge with upholstered chesterfields and an informal bar. Good-sized bedrooms have melamine units and Welsh tweed bedspreads, and bathrooms are carpeted. New owners maintain the hotel in spotless condition. No children under seven. *Amenities* garden, game fishing.

Room phone No
Room TV Yes
Confirm by By arrang.
Last dinner 9
Parking Ample

Three Cocks

Map 9 D5 Powys
Near Brecon *LD3 0SL*
Glasbury (049 74) 215

Credit Access, Amex,
Barclaycard, Diners
Closed January

Rooms 7
with bath/shower None

Three Cocks Hotel *(Inn)*   Ⓜ   £ F

This delightful 15th-century roadside inn between Brecon and Hereford is run with great enthusiasm by Barry and Jill Cole. It has a comfortable openplan lounge area with heavy beams and traditional decor and furnishings, a relaxing TV room and a cheerful bar. Some of the prettily decorated bedrooms have fine old carved oak furniture. Simple, well-maintained bathrooms. *Amenities* garden.

Room phone No
Room TV No
Confirm by 6
Last dinner 9.30
Parking Ample

Three Cocks

Map 9 D5 Powys
Near Brecon *LD3 0SL*
Glasbury (049 74) 215

● **Set D** £8·95 incl. service
About £32 for two

Three Cocks Hotel Restaurant   Ⓢ

Imagination and flair combine with cooking skills of a high order to produce some excellent dishes at this smart, comfortable restaurant. On a monthly-changing menu you might find a superb starter of chicken terrine with kumquat sauce, and main courses such as venison pie or veal escalope with mango and sage sauce. Sorbets make a colourful, refreshing sweet.
Credit Access, Amex, Barclaycard, Diners

Dinner only 7.30–9.30, Sat 7–10

Tintern Parva

Map 9 D6 Gwent
Near Chepstow *NP6 6SF*
Tintern (029 18) 202

Credit Access, Amex,
Barclaycard, Diners

Rooms 26
with bath/shower 26

Beaufort Hotel   59%   £ E

A stone's throw from the ruins of Tintern Abbey, this pleasant hotel still retains original arched doorways and lattice windows, although it has been soberly modernised. Pretty floral designs and pastel colours characterise the lounge, while attractive prints enhance the beamed bar. Neat, cheerful bedrooms have simple freestanding furniture and fully tiled bathrooms (some with showers only). *Amenities* garden.

Room phone Yes
Room TV Yes
Confirm by 6
Last dinner 9
Parking Ample
Banquets 200/–

Tintern Parva

Map 9 D6 Gwent
Near Chepstow *NP6 6SF*
Tintern (029 18) 205

Credit Access, Amex,
Barclaycard, Diners

Rooms 19
with bath/shower 15

Royal George Hotel   56%   £ D

Set in a peaceful village ringed by hills, this stone-built house offers a delightful mixture of old-world charm and modern comforts. Relax in the welcoming lounge bar with its open fire and parquet floor, or join the locals in the flagstoned public bar. Cheerful bedrooms, mostly in chalet wings round the garden, have neat fitted units, and bathrooms are up to date. *Amenities* garden.

Room phone Yes
Room TV Yes
Confirm by 6
Last dinner 9.30
Parking Ample

We welcome complaints and bona fide recommendations on the tear-out pages for readers' comments. They are followed up by our professional team. Please also complain to the management instantly.

Tintern Parva
Map 9 D6 Gwent
Near Chepstow *NP6 6SP*
Tintern (029 18) 441

Credit Access, Barclaycard
Closed January

Rooms 9			
with bath/shower 4			

Wye Valley Hotel *(Inn)* (M)   £ F

Keen fishermen and walkers will revel in the superb Wye Valley setting of this unpretentious little country inn, enthusiastically run by the friendly young Cowburns. There are two bars (one mock Tudor) and a residents' TV lounge. Attractive duvets add a touch of colour to the simple bedrooms, which have tea/coffee-making facilities. Private bathrooms also have shower units.

Room phone No	*Confirm by* By arrang.	*Parking* Ample
Room TV No	*Last dinner* 9.30	*Banquets* 80/30

Usk
Map 9 D5 Gwent
Bridge Street *NP5 1BQ*
Usk (029 13) 2133

Manager Mr K. Close
Credit Access, Barclaycard

Rooms 30			
with bath/shower 27			

Three Salmons Hotel   54%   £ E

Once a coaching inn, this black-and-white town-centre hostelry still provides a warm welcome and comfortable accommodation for short stays. Light oak panelling is a feature of the public rooms, which include a little reception with leather chesterfields and a splendid lounge bar. Bedrooms, in the main hotel and two nearby annexes, have radios, tea-makers and mainly modern furniture; adequate bathrooms. *Amenities* garden.

Room phone Yes	*Confirm by* By arrang.	*Parking* Ample
Room TV Yes	*Last dinner* 9.30	*Banquets* 150/10

Our inspectors are our full-time employees; they are professionally trained by us.

Wolf's Castle
Map 9 A5 Dyfed
Near Haverfordwest *SA62 5LZ*
Treffgarne (043 787) 225
Proprietor
Andrew M. Stirling
Credit Access, Barclaycard
Closed 4 days Christmas

Rooms 12		
with bath/shower 6		

Wolfscastle Country Hotel   57% (M)   £ F

There's always a warm welcome at this extended Georgian building standing just off the A40 between Haverfordwest and Fishguard. The entrance hall is full of notices about local events, and there's also a sociable bar with oak tables and an amusing collection of toy clowns; upstairs is a quiet residents' lounge. Cheerfully decorated bedrooms offer ample comfort. Simple modern bathrooms. *Amenities* garden, tennis, squash.

Room phone No	*Confirm by* By arrang.	*Parking* Ample
Room TV Yes	*Last dinner* 9	

Wolf's Castle
Map 9 A5 Dyfed
Near Haverfordwest *SA62 5LZ*
Treffgarne (043 787) 225
Proprietor Andrew M. Stirling

About £25 for two

Wolfscastle Country Hotel Restaurant   (S)

There's a fresh, homely appeal about this friendly restaurant, where dishes ranging from seafood mousse and stuffed peppers to coq au vin and coulibiac are capably prepared and charmingly served. Booking is essential. *Credit* Access, Barclaycard *Lunch* Sun 12–2, Mon–Sat by arrangement only *Dinner* 7–9.30 **Closed** 4 days Christmas

Wrexham
Map 8 D2 Clwyd
Yorke Street *LL13 8LP*
Wrexham (0978) 53431
Telex 61674

Credit Access, Amex,
Barclaycard, Diners

Rooms 80			
with bath/shower 80			

Crest Hotel   54%   £ D

Everything today behind the red-brick Georgian facade of this town-centre hotel is thoroughly modern, from the spacious multi-level reception-cum-lounge-cum-bar area, with its banquette seating and subdued lighting, to the practical bedrooms (popular with businessmen) with their ample writing space, fitted units, bedside controls for TV and tea-making facilities. Good, fully tiled bathrooms.

Room phone Yes	*Confirm by* 6	*Parking* Ample
Room TV Yes	*Last dinner* 9.45	*Banquets* 70/10

CHANNEL ISLANDS

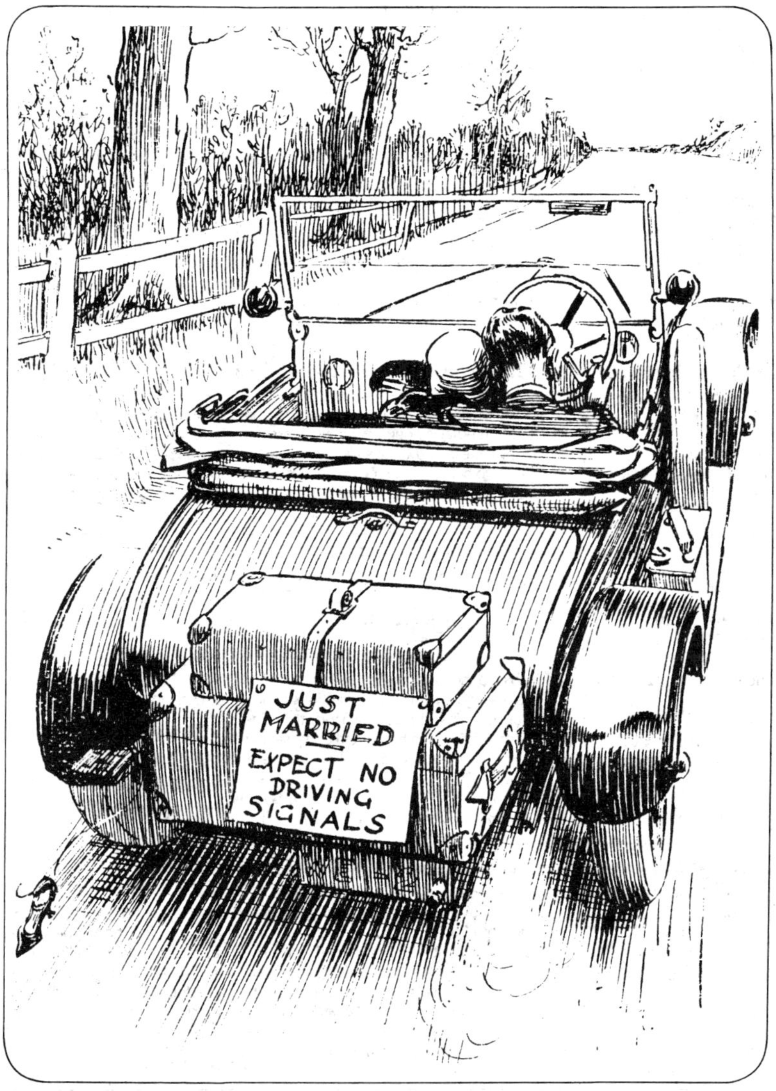

Guernsey

Pleinmont

Map 3 E4 Guernsey
Torteval
Guernsey (0481) 64044
Proprietor Mr J. H. Henke

Credit Access, Barclaycard

Rooms 12
with bath/shower 10

Imperial Hotel *(Inn)*  £ E/F

This pleasant, white-painted hotel is tucked away in a remote part of the island, overlooking a little bay. There's a choice of three bars to relax in, from the lively public bar to the delightfully intimate Beau Rivage Bar and the Continental Bar. Spacious, immaculately maintained bedrooms have simple melamine units and tea/coffee-makers. Nicely equipped modern bathrooms are also large and spotlessly clean. *Amenities* garden.

Room phone No *Confirm by* By arrang. *Parking* Ample
Room TV Yes *Last dinner* 9.45

St Martin's

Map 3 E4 Guernsey
Forest Road
Guernsey (0481) 35757
Telex 4191144
Manager Nino Campelli
Credit Access, Amex,
Barclaycard, Diners

Rooms 43
with bath/shower 43

St Margaret's Lodge Hotel 55% £ F

Attractive gardens surround this modern hotel set close to the airport. Bedrooms of varying sizes are neatly decorated, with practical whitewood units and colourful, well-fitted bathrooms; some have balconies overlooking the swimming pool. Three comfortably furnished lounges include one with a bar opening on to the garden. *Amenities* garden, outdoor swimming pool, dancing (Fri, Sat), pool table. &

Room phone Yes *Confirm by* By arrang. *Parking* Ample
Room TV Yes *Last dinner* 10 *Banquets* 100/–

St Peter Port

Map 3 E4 Guernsey
Cambridge Park
Guernsey (0481) 26221
Telex 4191462
Manager Mr N. J. Adams
Credit Access, Amex,
Barclaycard, Diners

Rooms 75
with bath/shower 75

Duke of Richmond Hotel 61% £ E/F

Just across the park from the town's conference and leisure complex, this modern hotel is popular with businessmen. The plush reception area boasts a royal crest, and there's also an elegant lounge, flower-decked sun terrace and two bars (one rigged out as a man-of-war). Bedrooms have fitted units, bold fabrics and well-equipped bathrooms. *Amenities* outdoor swimming pool, dancing (5 nights weekly in summer, 3 in winter).

Room phone Yes *Confirm by* 6 *Parking* Ample
Room TV Yes *Last dinner* 9.30 *Banquets* 300/–

St Peter Port

Map 3 E4 Guernsey
Les Cotils
Guernsey (0481) 24624

Manager G. Toffanello
Credit Access, Amex,
Barclaycard, Diners

Rooms 13
with bath/shower 13

La Frégate Hotel 64% £ D

A secluded haven with fine views of the harbour, this hilltop hotel is also close to the town centre. Dating from the 18th century it still retains much of its elegance, with polished antiques and curios enhancing the charm of the public rooms. No radio or TV disturbs the calm atmosphere in the spacious bedrooms, which have fitted units, easy chairs and well-kept bathrooms. No children under 14 or dogs. *Amenities* garden.

Room phone Yes *Confirm by* By arrang. *Parking* Ample
Room TV No *Last dinner* 9.30 *Banquets* 14/8

St Peter Port

Map 3 E4 Guernsey
Les Cotils
Guernsey (0481) 24624
Manager Mr G. Toffanello
French cooking

● **Set L** £5·75
About £30 for two

La Frégate Hotel Restaurant Ⓢ

The choice of raw materials and preparation are both excellent at this delightful hillside restaurant. Dishes like the eye-catching 'noir et blanc' (a veal steak with asparagus and hollandaise sauce paired with a fillet steak with mushrooms and Madeira sauce) are typical of the imaginative style of the menu; there's also a fine selection of local seafood, delicious vegetables and well-made sweets. *Credit* Access, Amex, Barclaycard, Diners

Lunch 12.30–1.30 *Dinner* 7–9.30, Sun 7–9

St Peter Port
Map 3 E4 Guernsey
Quay Steps
Guernsey (0481) 21714
Proprietors
Carlo Graziani & Olivier Diverio
French cooking

About £28 for two
Banquets 30/6

Le Nautique

The classical French menu in this attractive quayside restaurant has a distinctly marine flavour, with fresh seafood much in evidence. The choice of skilfully prepared dishes ranges from lightly poached oysters and tender grilled lobster to brill with green peppercorns and orange, while meat items such as rump steak with chanterelles add further variety.
ABOVE AVERAGE. Credit Access, Amex, Barclaycard, Diners

Lunch 12–2 *Dinner* 7–10
Closed Sun & 1st 3 weeks January

St Peter Port
Map 3 E4 Guernsey
Ann's Place
Guernsey (0481) 24921
Telex 4191144

Rooms 74
with bath/shower 72
Room phone Yes
Room TV Yes
Confirm by By arrang.
Last dinner 9.15
Parking Limited
Banquets 220/25

Credit Access, Amex,
Barclaycard, Diners

Old Government House Hotel   70%   £C/D

Before 1858 this white-painted hotel overlooking the harbour was the governor's residence, but it now offers superb accommodation for visitors to the island. Comfortable bedrooms have undergone extensive refurbishment and are attractively appointed with ornate classical fittings or military-style furniture. Bathrooms are fully tiled and well equipped. Public areas reflect the elegance of the building's past and include a lovely bar with bamboo furniture and even a grand piano; there's also a plush cocktail bar and a tranquil lounge with relaxing Queen Anne-style fireside chairs. *Amenities* garden, outdoor swimming pool, dancing (Mon–Sat in summer, weekends in winter), discothèque, hairdressing.

Jersey

Bouley Bay
Map 3 F4 Jersey
Trinity
Jersey (0534) 62777
Telex 4191462
Manager Mr B. Oliver
Rooms 56
with bath/shower 56
Room phone Yes
Room TV Yes
Confirm by By arrang.
Last dinner 10
Parking Ample
Banquets 70/–
Closed end October–1 April

Credit Access, Amex,
Barclaycard, Diners

Water's Edge Hotel   74%   £D

Award-winning gardens stretch up the hill behind this secluded hotel on the edge of a small bay, and the location is a marvellous one for a peaceful holiday. An atmosphere of classical elegance pervades the reception hall with its reproduction Louis XV furniture and crystal chandeliers; there are also three bars ranging from the stylish cocktail and residents' bars to the lively public bar that's popular with locals. Spacious bedrooms are sumptuously appointed with onyx tables and ornately moulded units, and colour schemes are attractively coordinated. Bathrooms are spotlessly clean. Inclusive terms only in high season. *Amenities* garden, sauna, outdoor swimming pool, dancing (Mon–Sat), diving school, solarium.

La Corbière
Map 3 F4 Jersey
Petit Port
Jersey (0534) 42687
Proprietor Mr Victor Comaglia

About £25 for two
Banquets 50/–

Sea Crest Hotel Restaurant Ⓢ

A friendly bustling atmosphere adds to the popularity of this comfortable little restaurant with picture windows overlooking the sea. Cooking styles range from traditional Italian pasta and classic French meat and seafood dishes to a straightforward English roast on Sundays. The chef is an expert at smooth, delicate sauces and his sweets are very tempting.
Credit Access, Barclaycard

Lunch 12.30–2 *Dinner* 7.30–10
Closed 2 months winter

Gorey
Map 3 F4 Jersey
Gorey Pier
Jersey (0534) 53633
Telex 4192085
Manager Mr Pedro Martinez
Credit Access, Barclaycard

Rooms 16
with bath/shower 16

Moorings Hotel   64%   £ D/E

Mont Orgeuil towers impressively above this friendly little hotel down by the picturesque fishing harbour. Well-kept public rooms include two smart bars, one with cosy red plush seating, and a spacious first-floor lounge. They are outshone, however, by the delightful bedrooms with their tasteful contemporary decor, thick carpets and large, comfortable beds. Bathrooms are equally luxurious. *Amenities* sea fishing.

Room phone Yes	*Confirm by* By arrang.	*Parking* Limited
Room TV Yes	*Last dinner* 10.30	*Banquets* 50/–

Gorey
Map 3 F4 Jersey
Gorey Pier
Jersey (0534) 53633
Manager Mr Pedro Martinez

● **Set L** £4 **Set D** £4·75
About £28 for two
Banquets 70/20

Moorings Hotel Restaurant Ⓢ

Although it includes a selection of grills and classic meat dishes, the menu – and a tank of live lobsters – make it clear that top-quality local seafood is the speciality of this intimate little restaurant. Choose from skate, turbot, sole, scallops, oysters and scampi, all of them beautifully fresh and appetising. The flamboyant service is a star turn.
Credit Access, Barclaycard

Lunch 12.30–2.15 *Dinner* 7–10.30

Our inspectors never book in the name of the Egon Ronay Organisation; they disclose their identity only after paying their bills.

Gorey
Map 3 F4 Jersey
Jersey (0534) 54444
Telex 4192032

Credit Access, Amex,
Barclaycard, Diners
Closed November–April

Rooms 28
with bath/shower 28

Old Court House Hotel   64%   £ E/F

There are fine views out to sea from the large balconies of this white-fronted hotel, which also boasts a spacious, welcoming bar and a relaxing function room that is used for breakfasts. Well-carpeted hallways lead to the comfortable bedrooms, which are attractively furnished and have plenty of cupboard space. Carpeted bathrooms are fully tiled. No dogs.
Amenities garden, sauna, outdoor swimming pool, solarium.

Room phone Yes	*Confirm by* 6	*Parking* Ample
Room TV Yes	*Last dinner* 10	*Banquets* 100/–

Gorey
Map 3 F4 Jersey
Gorey Village
Jersey (0534) 54395
Proprietor Bryan Mollet

● **Set L** from £3·50
Set D £5·95
About £21 for two

Seascale Hotel Restaurant

Seafood's the speciality of Bryan Mollet's homely little restaurant, and the day's local catch could range from prawns and plaice to sand eels, sea bass, lemon sole and lobster. It's all excellent, and the best way to enjoy a selection is the spectacular plateau de fruits de mer. Other choices on the long international menu could include wild duck, escalope de veau and beef vindaloo.

Lunch 12.30–2 *Dinner* 7.30–10
Closed L Mon, D Sun to non-residents & January–February

Havre des Pas

Map 3 F4 Jersey
St Helier
Jersey (0534) 23493
Telex 4192225
Manager Mr Marcus Troy
Credit Amex, Barclaycard,
Diners

Rooms 84
with bath/shower 73

Ommaroo Hotel   56%   £ D

Originally four private houses, this gabled and balconied hotel offers modest comforts. Two lounges (one with TV) and a sun lounge all have a homely atmosphere, and there's a club-like cocktail bar. Bedrooms are quite large and have functional melamine units; bathrooms are simple and modern. The hotel could do with some redecoration. *Amenities* garden, dancing (4 nights weekly May–October), 24-hour laundry service, table tennis.

Room phone Yes	*Confirm by* By arrang.	*Parking* Ample
Room TV Most	*Last dinner* 8.30	*Banquets* 180/25

Havre des Pas

Map 3 F4 Jersey
St Helier
Jersey (0534) 23474
Telex 4192328
Credit Access, Amex,
Barclaycard, Diners
Closed 1 November–4 March

Rooms 96
with bath/shower 96

Hotel de la Plage   65%   £ D

Situated on the seafront, this is a very popular holiday hotel with modern facilities. The comfortable open-plan lounge leads to a sun terrace, while the lively Caribbean Bar has a colourful tropical theme. Bedrooms (including six with extra-large balconies) are fitted with light oak units and armchairs. Compact, up-to-date bathrooms. No dogs. *Amenities* dancing (6 nights weekly in summer), dinner dance (Sat in winter).

Room phone Yes	*Confirm by* By arrang.	*Parking* Ample
Room TV Yes	*Last dinner* 9	

Stars in this Guide stand for the quality of the cooking only–
our overriding criterion, irrespective of price, luxury or service.

Portelet Bay

Map 3 F4 Jersey
Near St Brelade
Jersey (0534) 41204
Telex 4192039
Manager Mr J. M. Heslop
Credit Access, Amex,
Barclaycard, Diners

Rooms 86
with bath/shower 86

Portelet Hotel   64%   £ E

Tucked away in a secluded spot, this hotel has fine views of St Brelade's Bay from its public areas, which include a delightful sun terrace, two cosy lounges and a split-level bar. Most of the comfortable bedrooms have contemporary furnishings, and compact bathrooms are well equipped. No dogs. *Amenities* garden, outdoor swimming pool, tennis, dancing (nightly), cabaret (Tues in season), games room, snooker. **Closed** 9 October–Easter

Room phone Yes	*Confirm by* By arrang.	*Parking* Ample
Room TV Yes	*Last dinner* 8.45	*Banquets* 150/–

St Aubin

Map 3 F4 Jersey
La Haule
Jersey (0534) 41426

Credit Amex, Barclaycard,
Diners
Closed November–April

Rooms 20
with bath/shower 14

La Haule Manor   62%   £ D/E

Set in extensive grounds by the sea, this skilfully converted 18th-century house retains much of its original homely character. There are three comfortable modern lounges (one with TV), as well as a simply decorated cocktail bar. Sizeable bedrooms have attractive melamine units and colourful prints on the walls. Bathrooms are fitted with good modern suites. *Amenities* garden, croquet, 24-hour laundry service.

Room phone No	*Confirm by* By arrang.	*Parking* Ample
Room TV No	*Last dinner* 8.30	

St Aubin's Harbour

Map 3 F4 Jersey
Jersey (0534) 41156

Proprietors Jonty, Vicky &
Caroline Sharp

Closed 25 & 26 December

Rooms 9
with bath/shower 2

Old Court House Inn *(Inn)* Ⓜ   £ E

Situated right on the quay overlooking St Aubin's Bay, this historic inn is charmingly run by the Sharp family. The choice of bars ranges from the beamed Westward, with a bar counter formed from the gig of a schooner, to the Mizzen Mast, where you sit inside the stern of an old galleon; there's also a smart lounge with TV. Bedrooms are simply furnished and there's a well-appointed penthouse suite. No children or dogs.

Room phone Yes	*Confirm by* By arrang.	*Parking* Limited
Room TV Yes	*Last dinner* 10.15	*Banquets* 18/–

St Brelade

Map 3 F4 Jersey
La Pulente, La Moye
Jersey (0534) 44101
Telex 4192341
Manager Mr M. Dugini
Rooms 46
with bath/shower 46
Room phone Yes
Room TV Yes
Confirm by By arrang.
Last dinner 9.15
Parking Ample
Banquets 130/–
Closed 3 January–3 March

Credit Access, Amex,
Barclaycard, Diners

Atlantic Hotel   72%   £ D

Sitting on a sunny balcony overlooking the swimming pool and exotic gardens, it's easy to forget the cares of the world at this smoothly run modern hotel. The bright, spacious lounge has colourful contemporary decor and high-quality, ultra-modern furniture, and there's a similarly luxurious little bar. Comfortable bedrooms are extremely well equipped; the four de luxe rooms in a wing (reached by a bridge over the goldfish pond) are outstanding, with tasteful military-style furnishings and gold-plated fittings in the sumptuous bathrooms. No babies.
Amenities garden, outdoor swimming pool, tennis, dancing (twice weekly in summer).

St Brelade

Map 3 F4 Jersey
Route du Coin, La Haule
Jersey (0534) 44261

Credit Access, Amex,
Barclaycard, Diners

La Place Hotel   69%   £ D/E

Originally a granite farmhouse, this peaceful hotel has been considerably extended and offers stylish comfort in its two lounges–one traditional, the other more modern–and Caribbean-style bar overlooking the attractive courtyard and swimming pool. Bedrooms vary from luxurious ones facing the pool to simpler upstairs rooms. Excellent, spacious bathrooms. Only inclusive terms in high season. *Amenities* garden, sauna, outdoor swimming pool. &

Rooms 41	*Room phone* Yes	*Confirm by* By arrang.	*Parking* Ample
with bath/shower 41	*Room TV* Yes	*Last dinner* 9.30	*Banquets* 90/–

St Brelade

Map 3 F4 Jersey
Route du Coin, La Haule
Jersey (0534) 44261

● **Set L** £5·50
Set D £7·50
About £30 for two

La Place Hotel, Cartwheel Restaurant

Cartwheels are an ornamental feature of this charming restaurant, which also boasts blackened oak beams, gleaming copperware and pretty floral displays. The chef copes very well with a long menu of dishes ranging from classics like sole meunière and veal Cordon Bleu to mildly curried scampi with mango and coconut or excellent tournedos Maxim with a spicy herb sauce. *Credit* Access, Amex, Barclaycard, Diners

Lunch 12.30–2 *Dinner* 7–9.45

Changes in data may occur in establishments after the Guide goes to press. Prices should be taken as indications rather than firm quotes.

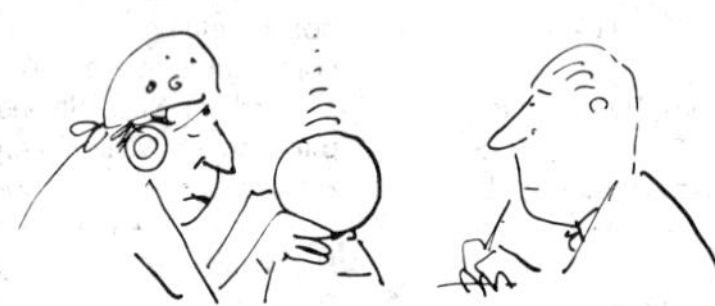

St Brelade's Bay

Map 3 F4 Jersey
Jersey (0534) 43476

Managers Mr & Mrs C. Magris
Credit Access, Barclaycard
Closed January & February

Hotel Château Valeuse   63%   £ E/F

Sea-facing balconies make the most of the view from this cheerful, chalet-like hotel on a hillside above the bay. A large, airy lounge is very relaxing and there are two comfortable bars, including the Hapsburg Bar recalling old Vienna. Bedrooms are bright and neatly fitted, nearly all having excellent bathrooms. No children under five. No dogs.
Amenities garden, outdoor swimming pool.

Rooms 26	*Room phone* No	*Confirm by* By arrang.	*Parking* Ample
with bath/shower 23	*Room TV* No	*Last dinner* 10	*Banquets* 80/–

St Brelade's Bay

Map 3 F4 Jersey
Jersey (0534) 43101
Telex 4192281
Manager John Wileman

Rooms 103
with bath/shower 103
Room phone Yes
Room TV Yes
Confirm by By arrang.
Last dinner 9.45
Parking Ample
Banquets 230/–

Credit Access, Amex,
Barclaycard, Diners

Hotel l'Horizon   75% *E*   £C/D

There's plenty of room to relax at this luxurious holiday hotel, which enjoys an unrivalled position right on the sandy beach of beautiful St Brelade's Bay. The lounges are roomy and comfortable, and there are three attractive bars and a delightful sun terrace. Recent improvements include an attractive new foyer and reception area. Bright, spacious bedrooms (front ones with balconies are especially desirable) have good-quality freestanding furniture and well-equipped tiled bathrooms. No dogs.
Amenities sauna, indoor swimming pool, dancing (Easter–November Mon–Sat, November–Easter Thurs, Sat), beauty salon, hairdressing, solarium, massage.

St Brelade's Bay

Map 3 F4 Jersey
Jersey (0534) 43101
Manager John Wileman

About £30 for two

Hotel l'Horizon, Star Grill   ♔♔ Ⓢ

A smartly furnished modern restaurant, with gleaming silverware, fresh flowers and picture windows looking out over the bay. The international menu offers a wide range of capably prepared dishes including soups and a varied hors d'œuvre selection, a number of grills and classic specialities, from succulent salmon and lobster to sautéed kidneys and duckling à l'orange.
♟ *SUPERIOR. Credit* Access, Amex, Barclaycard, Diners

Lunch 12.45–2.45 *Dinner* 7.45–10.45
Closed Mon

St Brelade's Bay

Map 3 F4 Jersey
Jersey (0534) 43281
Proprietor
Mr Digby Brecknell
Credit Access, Amex,
Barclaycard, Diners
Closed October–May

Rooms 80
with bath/shower 80

St Brelade's Bay Hotel   68%   Ⓜ   £C

A spacious terraced garden with palm trees is one of the attractions of this white-painted hotel on the seafront. Public areas include two comfortable lounges and a lively cocktail bar. Well-maintained bedrooms (some with balconies) have modern fitted units and fully carpeted bathrooms. Guide dogs only. *Amenities* garden, sauna, outdoor swimming pool, tennis, dancing (nightly), solarium, games room, table tennis, children's play room.

Room phone Yes	*Confirm by* By arrang.	*Parking* Ample
Room TV Some	*Last dinner* 9	

St Clement's Bay

Map 3 F4 Jersey
Jersey (0534) 24455
Telex 4192296
Manager R. Corral

Credit Access, Amex,
Barclaycard, Diners

Rooms 41
with bath/shower 41

Hotel Ambassadeur   66%   £E

Smart Scandinavian-style decor is a feature of this attractive hotel overlooking St Clement's Bay. Bedrooms (including several for families) have good-quality modern furniture and excellent fully tiled bathrooms. Public areas include a spacious lounge and two smart bars. *Amenities* garden, outdoor swimming pool, sea fishing, cabaret (Sat), discothèque (Tues), children's playroom, pool bar café (11am–6pm).

Room phone Yes	*Confirm by* By arrang.	*Parking* Ample
Room TV Yes	*Last dinner* 9.30	*Banquets* 50/–

St Helier

Map 3 F4 Jersey
St Saviour's Road
Jersey (0534) 25441
Telex 4192086

Credit Access, Amex,
Barclaycard, Diners

Apollo Hotel   64%   £D

This well-designed modern hotel, built round a courtyard, has a bright, spacious reception area which doubles as a comfortable, relaxing lounge. There are also two bars, one of them reserved for residents. Attractively decorated bedrooms have white fitted furniture, giving ample storage and writing space, and neat, well-equipped bathrooms. Excellent housekeeping. No dogs. *Amenities* dancing (Wed, Sat in Summer).

Continued

Continued
Rooms 53
with bath/shower 53   *Room phone* Yes   *Confirm by* By arrang.   *Parking* Ample
Room TV Yes   *Last dinner* 8.30   *Banquets* 120/–

St Helier

Map 3 F4 Jersey
Green Street
Jersey (0534) 32471
Telex 4192160
Manager Mr F. Pietrogiovanna
Credit Access, Amex,
Barclaycard, Diners

Beaufort Hotel   64%   £E

Within easy reach of the town centre and the beach, this modern three-storey hotel is popular with businessmen and families on holiday. The large lounge with picture windows and comfortable modern seating leads to the sun terrace, and there's also a bar downstairs. Well-maintained bedrooms have white fitted furniture, subtle colour schemes and neat, compact bathrooms with showers. No dogs.

Rooms 50
with bath/shower 50   *Room phone* Yes   *Confirm by* By arrang.   *Parking* Limited
Room TV Yes   *Last dinner* 9   *Banquets* 120/–

St Helier

Map 3 F4 Jersey
65 Halkett Place
Jersey (0534) 34602
Proprietor Mr V. Rossi
Italian cooking

La Capannina   Ⓢ

Set in a small street by the market, this congenial, welcoming restaurant makes a feature of expertly prepared, fresh-tasting Italian fare ranging from mixed seafood risotto to veal chop cooked in butter and sage. There are also some French dishes like entrecôte bordelaise, as well as a host of seasonal specialities including wild duck and oysters.
Credit Access, Amex, Barclaycard, Diners

About £25 for two
Banquets 40/–

Lunch 12–2 *Dinner* 7–10
Closed Sun & Bank Holidays

St Helier

Map 3 F4 Jersey
Esplanade
Jersey (0534) 22301
Telex 4192104
Manager Mr David Lapidus
Rooms 116
with bath/shower 116
Room phone Yes
Room TV Yes
Confirm by By arrang.
Last dinner 10.30
Parking Limited
Banquets 300/–

Credit Access, Amex,
Barclaycard, Diners

Grand Hotel   70%   £C/D

Fully living up to its name, this marvellous seafront hotel combines all the gracious style of the past with up-to-date comfort and facilities like the comprehensively equipped health centre. The elegant reception is flanked by sun terraces which are reached through the smart, traditionally furnished bar, and there's also a tranquil residents' lounge overlooking St Brelade's Bay. Accommodation varies from studio-style rooms to excellent, immaculately designed suites with attractive contemporary furniture, perfectly coordinated fabrics and plush carpeting. Bathrooms are equipped to a very high standard. No dogs. *Amenities* sauna, indoor swimming pool, dancing (6 nights weekly), snooker, health centre.

St Helier

Map 3 F4 Jersey
Esplanade
Jersey (0534) 72255
Manager Mr A. Travaglini

Grand Hotel, Victoria's Restaurant   ♛♛

An attractive hotel restaurant designed in plush Victorian style. The main menu has familiar dishes like charcoal-grilled lamb cutlets and roast duckling with black cherry sauce, plus nouvelle cuisine specialities such as baked sea bass with béarnaise sauce. Raw materials are excellent and preparation generally quite acceptable.
Credit Access, Amex, Barclaycard, Diners   ♿

● **Set L** £5 **Set D** £6
About £28 for two

Lunch 12.30–2 *Dinner* 7–10.30
Closed Sun

St Helier

Map 3 F4 Jersey
37 La Motte Street
Jersey (0534) 20147
Proprietors
Mauro & Irene Mori

Mauro's   Ⓢ

Hospitable Mauro Mori presides cheerfully over this smart town-centre restaurant, which has built up a strong following with its extensive à la carte selection of ably cooked French and Italian dishes. The choice ranges from deliciously fresh and tasty mussels alla marinara and minestrone to tender veal chops with sage, duck à l'orange and steak pizzaiola. Vegetables and desserts are very good, too. *Credit* Barclaycard

Continued

About £27 for two

Lunch 12.30–2 *Dinner* 7.30–10
Closed Sun, Bank Holidays & 21 December–31 January

St Helier

Map 3 F4 Jersey
The Esplanade
Jersey (0534) 78644
Telex 4192309
Manager Mr Richard Heron
Credit Access, Amex,
Barclaycard, Diners

Rooms 151
with bath/shower 151

Pomme d'Or Hotel   61%   £ D/E

Extensively refurbished throughout, this hotel overlooks the busy marina and ferry terminal. The spacious lobby also serves as a lounge area, and there's a separate lounge on the first floor, plus a choice of three attractively decorated bars. Immaculate bedrooms have functional freestanding units, tea-makers and simple modern bathrooms. *Amenities* dancing (nightly May–October, Sat & Sun October–May), coffee shop (7am–11pm). &

Room phone Yes	*Confirm by* 6	*Parking* Difficult
Room TV Yes	*Last dinner* 9	*Banquets* 180/8

St Peter

Map 3 F4 Jersey
Jersey (0534) 41255
Telex 4192249

Credit Access, Amex,
Barclaycard

Rooms 68
with bath/shower 68

Mermaid Hotel   66%   £ D

Set in 18 acres of attractive grounds opposite the airport, this is a well-maintained hotel. Guests can choose between the intimate cocktail bar and the lively atmosphere of the Tavern Bar; there's also a stylish, comfortably furnished lounge. Bedrooms (most with balconies) have fitted units and compact modern bathrooms. Guide dogs only. *Amenities* garden, outdoor swimming pool, dancing (3 nights weekly May–October). &

Room phone Yes	*Confirm by* By arrang.	*Parking* Ample
Room TV Yes	*Last dinner* 9	*Banquets* 120/20

St Saviour

Map 3 F4 Jersey
Jersey (0534) 25501
Telex 4192306
Proprietors Lewis family &
Mr & Mrs Duffy
Rooms 36
with bath/shower 36
Room phone Yes
Room TV Yes
Confirm by By arrang.
Last dinner 9
Parking Ample
Banquets 50/–

Credit Access, Amex,
Barclaycard, Diners

Longueville Manor Hotel   76%      £ C

Surrounded by 15 acres of beautiful landscaped gardens, this large, creeper-clad manor house has been carefully extended over the years by caring hosts Mr and Mrs Lewis. Elegant public areas, which include a comfortable lounge and a panelled bar, show the owners' impeccable taste, with lots of antiques and interesting curios that help to give the place its highly individual character. Bedrooms are also most attractive, with good-quality furniture and coordinated colour schemes. There are four very luxurious rooms with ultra-smart bathrooms. No children under seven.
Amenities garden, outdoor swimming pool. riding, putting. &

St Saviour

Map 3 F4 Jersey
Jersey (0534) 25501
Proprietors Lewis family &
Mr & Mrs Duffy
French cooking

● **Set L** £6·75
Set D from £11·50
About £36 for two

Longueville Manor Restaurant   ★

Stone walls, dark oak panelling and colourful wallhangings give this excellent restaurant the feel of a medieval hall. Items on the inventive menus are described over cocktails in the bar and fully live up to expectations, superb preparation being matched by beautiful presentation. Lamb's sweetbreads with mushroom chausson is a lovely starter, and main courses could include rosettes of veal Curaçao or succulent poached baby salmon served with perfectly prepared vegetables. Sweets are irresistible, too. **Specialities** three terrines of Longueville Manor, romance of the sea, breast of duck with pink grapefruit, raspberry parfait and hot glazed pears. 🍷 *ABOVE AVERAGE.*
Credit Access, Amex, Barclaycard, Diners &

Lunch 12.30–2 *Dinner* 7.30–9.30

Sark

Sark

Map 3 E4 Sark
Sark (048 183) 2036

Proprietors
Peter & Nita Hauser
Credit Barclaycard
Closed October–April

Rooms 7
with bath/shower 5

Aval du Creux Hotel   59%      £ E/F

A short tractor drive takes guests from the harbour up to this converted granite farmhouse, which offers simple, pleasant accommodation under the charming care of Peter and Nita Hauser. The bar and lounges (one with TV) are homely and relaxing, and bedrooms, all with pretty duvets and showers, are maintained in spotless condition. Book well in advance. Inclusive terms only. No dogs. *Amenities* garden.

Room phone No	*Confirm by* By arrang.	*Parking* No cars
Room TV No	*Last dinner* 9	*Banquets* 20/-

Sark

Map 3 E4 Sark
Sark (048 183) 2036
Proprietors
Peter & Nita Hauser

● **Set D** £6
About £22 for two

Aval du Creux Hotel Restaurant   ★   

Enthusiastic Peter Hauser uses only the finest and freshest ingredients to produce a tempting range of dishes in this simple, homely restaurant. Seafood takes pride of place, with choices like the cold mixed platter, deep-fried scallops, grilled sole or our excellent lobster américaine. Simple starters include well-made soups and pâtés, and main courses such as wiener schnitzel and grilled steak are served with delicious vegetables. Charming service is provided by Nita Hauser and her friendly young team.
Specialities cocktail de crevettes 'Super Maison', brochette fruits de mer hongroise, filet de sole au lard fumé à l'aneth, omelette Stéphanie.
Credit Barclaycard

Lunch 12–2 *Dinner* 7–9
Closed October–April

Sark

Map 3 E4 Sark
Sark (048 183) 2046

Proprietors Mr & Mrs T. Scott
Credit Access, Barclaycard,
Diners
Closed October–Easter

Rooms 16
with bath/shower 11

Hotel Petit Champ   59%   M   £ E/F

It's essential to book well in advance at this peaceful, welcoming hotel, whose comfortable public areas include a traditionally furnished lounge, a sun lounge, TV room and bar. Brightly decorated bedrooms (four with balconies) are homely and attractive; like the rest of the hotel, they are kept sparklingly clean. Inclusive terms only. No children under seven. Guide dogs only. *Amenities* garden, outdoor swimming pool, horse & carriage hire.

Room phone No	*Confirm by* By arrang.	*Parking* No cars
Room TV No	*Last dinner* 8	*Banquets* 20/-

Our inspectors are our full-time employees; they are professionally trained by us.

Sark

Map 3 E4 Sark
Sark (048 183) 2046

Proprietors Mr & Mrs T. Scott

About £20 for two

Hotel Petit Champ Restaurant

Non-residents must book at this attractive pine-furnished restaurant, where lunch time brings a simple three-course meal—perhaps creamy spinach soup, omelette with salad, and fresh fruit and cheese. The evening choice is greater, and could include chicken liver pâté, trout meunière, entrecôte au poivre and delicious Sark lobster. Our whisky parfait made an enjoyable dessert. *Credit* Access, Barclaycard, Diners

Lunch at 1 *Dinner* at 8
Closed October–Easter

ISLE OF MAN

Ballasalla

Map 13 B5 Isle of Man
Main Road
Ballasalla (0624) 822940

About £21 for two

La Rosette 

Bob and Rosa Phillips have quickly gained a reputation for serving good food in this tiny rustic restaurant. We enjoyed herby pâté and perfectly cooked brill with Calvados, accompanied by a nice selection of fresh vegetables. Lighter lunches. Unlicensed, but bring your own. Book. *Credit* Access *Lunch* 12–3 *Dinner* 7.30–10.30 **Closed** Sun & Mon

Castletown

Map 13 A6 Isle of Man
Fort Island
Castletown (062 482) 2201
Telex 627636
Proprietors Mr P. W. Makinson
& Mr W. Forster
Credit Access, Amex, Barclaycard

Rooms 82
with bath/shower 82

Castletown Golf Links Hotel 62%  £ D

Golfers especially appreciate this comfortable hotel built on a peninsula overlooking its own championship course. A lovely panelled hall leads to the relaxing bar, and there's also a sun lounge with fine views. Many of the traditionally furnished bedrooms open on to the grounds, and all have adequate bathrooms. *Amenities* garden, outdoor swimming pool, tennis, golf course, sea fishing, putting, billiards, table tennis. **Closed** 7 Oct–29 Mar

Room phone Yes	*Confirm by* By arrang.	*Parking* Ample
Room TV Some	*Last dinner* 9	*Banquets* 150/–

Douglas

Map 13 B6 Isle of Man
Summerhill
Douglas (0624) 23103

French cooking

● **Set D** from £7
About £25 for two

L'Expérience

Colourful decor matches the French style of cooking in this friendly, popular restaurant. Three fixed-price dinner menus offer tasty dishes made with good-quality local ingredients, including 'queenies' (small scallops) in a creamy curry sauce and rich beef bourguignonne. The locally baked French bread is excellent, vegetables are well prepared and sweets include a delicious apple flan. Simpler à la carte menu at lunch time.

Lunch 12–2 *Dinner* 7–11
Closed Sun, 25 & 26 December & January

Douglas

Map 13 B6 Isle of Man
Central Promenade
Douglas (0624) 4521
Manager Mr Tony Woodrow

Credit Access, Amex,
Barclaycard, Diners

Rooms 138
with bath/shower 138

Palace Hotel 58% £ D

Built on the promenade as a casino, this large modern hotel is still noted for its range of evening entertainment. There's an attractive, plant-filled bar and a comfortable TV lounge, as well as a number of small function rooms. Bedrooms are practical with fitted units, coordinated soft furnishings and tea/coffee-makers. Compact bathrooms are fully tiled. *Amenities* outdoor swimming pool, dinner dance (Sat), discothèque (nightly), casino, nightclub.

Room phone Yes	*Confirm by* 7	*Parking* Ample
Room TV Yes	*Last dinner* 12	*Banquets* 900/–

Douglas
Map 13 B6 Isle of Man
Harris Promenade
Douglas (0624) 26011
Manager Mr C. R. Robertshaw

Credit Access, Amex,
Barclaycard, Diners

Rooms 85
with bath/shower 70

Sefton Hotel   59%   £ E

This friendly Victorian hotel standing on the promenade commands fine views over the sweep of Douglas Bay. There's a smartly decorated foyer, a lounge and a popular bar with a dance floor. Spacious bedrooms have fitted furniture, pretty matching curtains and wallpapers and tea/coffee-makers. Tiled bathrooms are well equipped. No dogs. *Amenities* sauna, laundry room, children's play room, table tennis, solarium, film shows.

| *Room phone* Yes | *Confirm by* By arrang. | *Parking* Limited |
| *Room TV* Yes | *Last dinner* 8.45 | *Banquets* 75/– |

Ramsey
Map 13 B5 Isle of Man
East Street
Ramsey (0624) 814182
Proprietor Karl Meier

About £26 for two

Harbour Bistro

There's a distinctly marine flavour to this busy quayside bistro, where the dinner menu ranges from fresh seafood to casseroles and dishes like roast guinea fowl with interesting vegetables. Less choice at lunchtime.
Lunch 12.15–2.30 *Dinner* 6.30–10.30 **Closed** Sun, Bank Holidays & January ● **Set** L £3·25

NORTHERN IRELAND

Map 18 D2
Town plan opposite

Population 360,000

Belfast, capital of Northern Ireland, gained city status as recently as 1888. The magnificent domed City Hall, lavish Opera House and decorated facades of many banks and shops as well as the ornamented interiors of Belfast's public houses typify its Victorian character. The area stretching from the pedestrianised shopping centre (plenty of car parking) to Queen's University is theatre and cinema land, popular for eating and drinking. There are few tall buildings and wherever you are you can see the green hills which ring the city. Riverside paths follow the Lagan's course for nine miles through rose gardens and parkland.

Sights Outside City
Belfast Zoo, Belmont
Carrickfergus Castle
Holywood
Strangford Lough
Ulster Folk and Transport Museum

Annual Events
Belfast Civic Festival & Lord Mayor's Show *May*
International Arts Festival *November*
International Rose Trials *July–Sept*
Ireland International motor rally *Easter weekend*
Royal Ulster Academy Art Exhibition *Autumn*
Royal Ulster Agricultural Show, Balmoral *May*
Twelfth Processions *12th July*

Belfast

1	Arts Theatre	A4
2	Belfast Cathedral	B2
3	Belfast Central Library	A2
4	Belfast Central rail station	C3
5	Bord Failte information office	A3
6	Botanic rail station	A4
7	Bus station, Great Victoria Street	A3
8	Bus station, Oxford Street	B3
9	City Hall *Victorian splendour*	A/B3
10	Grand Opera House	A3
11	Law Courts	B3
12	Linenhall Library *established 1788*	B5
13	Lyric Theatre	B5
14	Northern Ireland Tourist Board information centre	B2
15	Ormeau Park	C4/5
16	Queen's University	A5
17	Transport Museum	C2
18	Ulster Museum *treasures from Spanish Armada*	A5
19	Windsor Park/Celtic Park football ground	A4

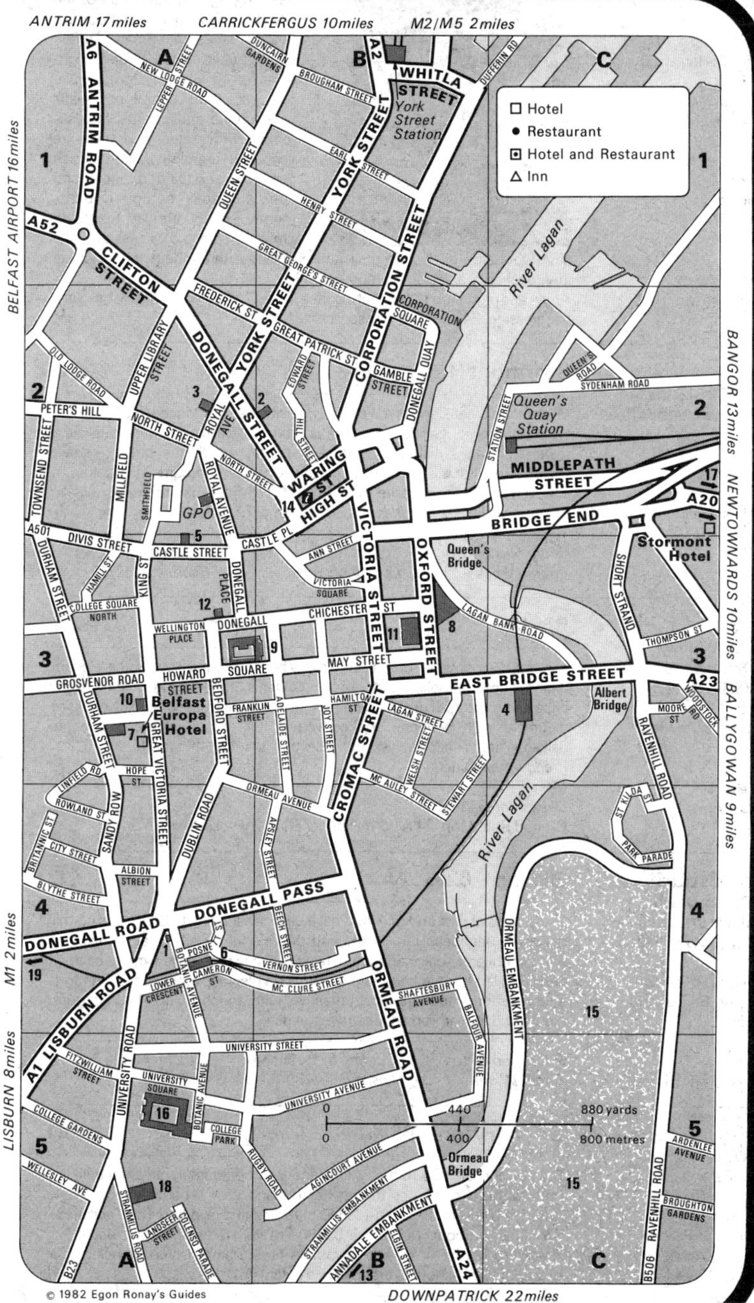

Belfast LANCIA
ANTRIM 17 miles
CARRICKFERGUS 10 miles
M2/M5 2 miles
Hotel
Restaurant
Hotel and Restaurant
Inn
BELFAST AIRPORT 16 miles
ANTRIM ROAD
A6
A52
A501
CLIFTON STREET
DONEGALL STREET
YORK STREET
CORPORATION STREET
WHITLA STREET
A2
York Street Station
DUFFERIN RD
River Lagan
NEW LODGE ROAD
LEPPER STREET
DUNCAIRN GARDENS
BROUGHAM STREET
EARL STREET
HENRY STREET
QUEEN STREET
GREAT GEORGE'S STREET
FREDERICK ST
GREAT PATRICK ST
EDWARD STREET
HILL STREET
GAMBLE STREET
DONEGALL QUAY
CORPORATION SQUARE
Queen's Road
SYDENHAM ROAD
Queen's Quay Station
BANGOR 13 miles
OLD LODGE ROAD
PETER'S HILL
UPPER LIBRARY STREET
NORTH STREET
ROYAL AVE
WARING ST
HIGH ST
MIDDLEPATH STREET
A20
17
NEWTOWNARDS 10 miles
TOWNSEND STREET
MILLFIELD
SMITHFIELD
NORTH STREET
GPO
ROYAL AVENUE
CASTLE PL
CASTLE STREET
VICTORIA STREET
OXFORD STREET
Queen's Bridge
BRIDGE END
Stormont Hotel
DURHAM STREET
DIVIS STREET
HAMIL ST
KING ST
DONEGALL PLACE
ANN STREET
VICTORIA SQUARE
CHICHESTER ST
Lagan Bank Road
SHORT STRAND
THOMPSON ST
A23
COLLEGE SQUARE NORTH
WELLINGTON PLACE
DONEGALL SQUARE
MAY STREET
EAST BRIDGE STREET
Albert Bridge
MOORE ST
WOODSTOCK RD
BALLYGOWAN 9 miles
GROSVENOR ROAD
HOWARD STREET
BEDFORD STREET
Belfast Europa Hotel
FRANKLIN STREET
ADELAIDE STREET
JOY STREET
HAMILTON ST
LAGAN STREET
WELSH STREET
STEWART STREET
CROMAC STREET
RAVENHILL ROAD
ST KILDA ST
DURHAM STREET
LINFIELD RD
HOPE ST
GREAT VICTORIA STREET
DUBLIN ROAD
ORMEAU AVENUE
MC AULEY STREET
River Lagan
PARK PARADE
M1 2 miles
ROWLAND ST
SANDY ROW
BRITANNIC ST
CITY STREET
ALBION STREET
BLYTHE STREET
APSLEY STREET
DONEGALL PASS
BEECH STREET
ORMEAU EMBANKMENT
DONEGALL ROAD
LISBURN 8 miles
A1 LISBURN ROAD
BOTANIC AVENUE
LOWER CRESCENT
POSNE
CAMERON ST
VERNON STREET
MC CLURE STREET
ORMEAU ROAD
SHAFTESBURY AVENUE
BALFOUR AVENUE
15
FITZWILLIAM STREET
UNIVERSITY ROAD
UNIVERSITY SQUARE
UNIVERSITY STREET
UNIVERSITY AVENUE
BOTANIC AVENUE
COLLEGE GARDENS
COLLEGE PARK
RUGBY ROAD
AGINCOURT AVENUE
440
400
880 yards
800 metres
Ormeau Bridge
A24
5
ARDENLEE AVENUE
WELLESLEY AVE
STRANMILLS ROAD
LANDSEER STREET
COLENSO PARADE
STRANMILLIS EMBANKMENT
ANNADALE EMBANKMENT
ELGIN STREET
13
15
RAVENHILL ROAD
BROUGHTON GARDENS
B23
B2
B506
C
DOWNPATRICK 22 miles
© 1982 Egon Ronay's Guides

Belfast
Town plan A3 Co. Antrim
Great Victoria Street *BT2 7AP*
Belfast (0232) 45161
Telex 74491
Manager Mr R. Harper Brown
Rooms 200
with bath/shower 200
Room phone Yes
Room TV Yes
Confirm by By arrang.
Last dinner 10.30
Parking Limited
Banquets 500/–

Credit Access, Amex,
Barclaycard, Diners

Belfast Europa Hotel   71%   *E*   £ D

Standing right in the centre of the city, this towering modern hotel is a notable landmark. Smartly refurbished public areas include a bright coffee shop and a popular public bar; upstairs are a sumptuous open-plan lounge and cocktail bar festooned with plants. Bedrooms are very well appointed, with stylish contemporary fitted furniture and compact, fully equipped bathrooms. The Penthouse nightclub provides splendid views over the city. Standards of decor, repair and cleanliness throughout the hotel are irreproachable, and staff are most helpful.
Amenities nightclub (Mon–Sat), coffee shop (7.30am–11.30pm Mon–Sat), hairdressing, 24-hour laundry service.

Belfast
Town plan C2 Co. Antrim
587 Upper Newtownards Road
BT4 3LP
Belfast (0232) 658621

Credit Access, Amex,
Barclaycard, Diners

Stormont Hotel   66%   £ D

Progressive extensions to a Victorian mansion have produced this fine hotel, which stands opposite the grounds of Stormont Castle. Bright colours are a feature of the stylish public rooms, among which the brilliant green Grasshopper Bar is particularly appealing. Cheerful bedrooms have colourful soft furnishings, neat white furniture and well-fitted bathrooms. Extensive function facilities. *Amenities* garden, dancing (Tues, Sat).

Rooms 51	*Room phone* Yes	*Confirm by* 6	*Parking* Ample
with bath/shower 51	*Room TV* Yes	*Last dinner* 9.45	*Banquets* 250/10

Comber
Map 18 D2 Co. Down
41a High Street *BT23 5HJ*
Comber (0247) 872229
Proprietors
Mr & Mrs Denis Crawford

● **Set D** £10·50
About £29 for two
Banquets 25/10

Blades

In a charming private house tucked away behind the main street, this elegant dining room overlooks beautiful gardens. Denis Crawford's interesting fixed-price menu includes dishes like pheasant in red wine sauce or fillets of plaice meunière with perfectly cooked vegetables, and there are also some delicious home-made sweets plus a savoury to round things off.
Credit Amex, Diners

Dinner only 7–10.30
Closed Sun, Mon, 24 & 25 December & last 2 weeks July

Crawfordsburn
Map 18 D2 Co. Down
15 Main Street *BT19 1JH*
Helen's Bay (0247) 853255

Proprietor Mrs H. E. Avis
Credit Access, Barclaycard,
Diners

Old Inn   62%   Ⓜ   £ D

Thirty years of care and affection have been lavished by Heather Avis on this delightful Jacobean inn. Inside and out, it's full of charm and character: thatch above the black and white facade, a minstrels' gallery in the beamed and panelled lounge and magnificent floral displays everywhere. Comfortable bedrooms, too, are most attractive, with armchairs and fine antiques. Good modern bathrooms. *Amenities* garden.

Rooms 26	*Room phone* Yes	*Confirm by* By arrang.	*Parking* Ample
with bath/shower 15	*Room TV* Yes	*Last dinner* 9.30	*Banquets* 70/–

Dunadry
Map 18 D2 Co. Antrim
Muckamore *BT41 2HA*
Templepatrick (084 94) 32474
Telex 747245
Proprietor Mr N. Falloon
Credit Access, Amex,
Barclaycard, Diners

Dunadry Inn   66%   Ⓜ   £ D

Built on the site of a former village and incorporating an old linen mill, this unusual hotel combines the best of old and new. Antiques and modern furniture blend in the open-plan lounge area and two bars (one galleried). Spacious bedrooms vary in size; bathrooms are well equipped. No dogs.
Amenities garden, outdoor swimming pool, game fishing, dancing (Sat except July), 24-hour laundry service (Mon–Fri).

Rooms 77	*Room phone* Yes	*Confirm by* By arrang.	*Parking* Ample
with bath/shower 77	*Room TV* Yes	*Last dinner* 9.30	*Banquets* 300/4

Dunmurry
Map 18 D2 Co. Antrim
Near Belfast *BT17 9ES*
Belfast (0232) 612101
Telex 74281
Manager Mr M. K. Kraft
Rooms 77
with bath/shower 77
Room phone Yes
Room TV Yes
Confirm by 7
Last dinner 10.45
Parking Ample
Banquets 350/10

Credit Access, Amex,
Barclaycard, Diners

Conway Hotel   70%   £ C/D

This friendly modern hotel stands in 12 acres of neat gardens and woodland less than five miles from the centre of Belfast. Public areas are a fine example of good contemporary design: the open-plan reception area incorporates a striking cocktail bar and a handsome lounge whose picture windows overlook the gardens. There are also extensive facilities for conferences and functions, including an enormous ballroom. Bedrooms are mainly studio style, with attractive pastel pink decor, modern built-in units, plenty of well-lit writing space and compact tiled bathrooms. Efficient, helpful staff.
Amenities garden, outdoor swimming pool, squash, entertainment (Sat), restaurant (noon–10.45pm).

Helen's Bay
Map 18 D2 Co. Down
Near Bangor *BT19 1TN*
Helen's Bay (0247) 852841

● **Set L** £5·75
About £33 for two
Banquets 22/15

Carriage

Domenico Traversari transformed a station waiting room to make this cosy restaurant, where he offers an imaginative choice of well-prepared dishes with some unusual touches. Seafood is a feature of the daily-changing menu which could also include game in season or richly sauced fillet of beef, enterprising vegetables and tempting sweets like lemon soufflé. Best to book. Unlicensed. *Credit* Access, Amex, Barclaycard, Diners

---

Lunch Sun only 12–3 *Dinner* 7.30–11
Closed Mon, 1 January & 24–26 December

Any person using our name to obtain free hospitality is a fraud.
Proprietors, please inform the police and us.

Holywood
Map 18 D2 Co. Down
Craigavad *BT18 0EX*
Holywood (023 17) 5223
Telex 74617
Manager Mr P. J. Weston
Rooms 74
with bath/shower 74
Room phone Yes
Room TV Yes
Confirm by 6
Last dinner 9.30
Parking Ample
Banquets 350/2
Closed 25 December

Credit Access, Amex,
Barclaycard, Diners

Culloden Hotel   77%   £ C

Built in Scottish Baronial style with stone specially imported from Scotland, this splendid piece of Victorian architecture is set amid acres of meticulously maintained grounds. Guests can enjoy the view from the sumptuously furnished lounge or admire the original oil paintings on the walls; there's also a large bar with a panelled ceiling. Bedrooms in the original house are large and traditional in style, whereas those in the new wing are carefully designed and tastefully decorated to a very high modern standard, with particularly luxurious, fully tiled bathrooms.
Amenities garden, tennis, squash, dancing (Thurs), table tennis, putting, grill room (11am–11pm Mon–Sat), croquet, 24-hour laundry service.

Holywood
Map 18 D2 Co. Down
30 High Street *BT18 9AD*
Holywood (023 17) 5880

About £35 for two

Schooner

A nautical theme runs through this smart, modern restaurant, where the menu offers a choice of tempting, soundly prepared dishes. Fresh local seafood is a feature, and there are some delicious desserts. *Credit* Access, Amex, Barclaycard, Diners *Lunch* 12.30–2 *Dinner* 7–10 **Closed** L Sat, all Sun, 1 week Easter, 2 weeks July & 1 week Christmas

Londonderry
Map 18 C1 Co. Londonderry
Prehen Road *BT47 2PA*
Londonderry (0504) 46722
Telex 748005
Credit Access, Amex,
Barclaycard, Diners
Closed 25 & 26 December

Everglades Hotel   69%   £E

Just outside the town, this well-run modern hotel is stylishly designed, with relaxing lounge areas and an attractive cane-furnished bar. Bedrooms have good-quality fitted units, colour TV and gleaming, fully tiled bathrooms. Helpful staff. No dogs. *Amenities* garden, sauna, indoor swimming pool, dancing (Sat), buttery (Mon–Fri 11.30am–10pm, Sat 11.30am–7pm), in-house video, 24-hour laundry service.

Rooms 38
with bath/shower 38

Room phone Yes   *Confirm by* 5   *Parking* Ample
Room TV Yes   *Last dinner* 10   *Banquets* 250/4

Newtownards
Map 18 D2 Co. Down
92 Church Street *BT23 4AL*
Newtownards (0247) 814141
Manager Mrs Elizabeth Miller
Credit Access, Amex,
Barclaycard, Diners
Closed 2 days Easter & 12/13 July

Strangford Arms Hotel   57%   £D

With easy access to Belfast, this extended Victorian hotel makes a useful base for visiting businessmen. A carpeted entrance hall leads to the large contemporary-style Horseshoe Bar, and there's a cosy lounge on the first floor. The best bedrooms are in the recent extension; all have functional fitted furniture and stylish lighting. Bathrooms are modern and well equipped. No dogs. *Amenities* dancing (Sat), in-house movies.

Rooms 36
with bath/shower 32

Room phone Yes   *Confirm by* By arrang.   *Parking* Ample
Room TV Yes   *Last dinner* 9.45   *Banquets* 160/10

Portaferry
Map 18 D2 Co. Down
Shore Road *BT22 1PE*
Portaferry (024 772) 231

Credit Access, Amex,
Barclaycard, Diners

Portaferry Hotel *(Inn)* Ⓜ   £F 

Standing opposite the ferry terminus at the southern end of Lough Strangford, this pretty, cream-painted inn is professionally run by the Herlihy family. The rustic bar is spotlessly clean, and there's a modern lounge. Brightly decorated bedrooms (some with views of the lough) have white laminate furniture. Public bathrooms are adequate, private ones being more modern. No dogs. *Amenities* sea fishing, folk music (Tues), mooring.

Rooms 5
with bath/shower 2

Room phone No   *Confirm by* 6   *Parking* Ample
Room TV No   *Last dinner* 9

Saintfield
Map 18 D2 Co. Down
120 Monlough Road *BT24 7EU*
Saintfield (0238) 510396
Proprietors
Misses M. McDonald &
B. Jackson

● **Set D** £11·50
About £31 for two

Barn ★

This peaceful, cosy farmhouse restaurant is a delightful setting for the lovely dinners which the talented Miss McDonald prepares from tip-top ingredients. Simple starters could include mushroom soup with cream or avocado vinaigrette, while main courses range from grilled salmon and stuffed sole to bœuf bourguignonne and our marvellously tender roast lamb stuffed with lemon, sage and breadcrumbs. Accompanying vegetables like ratatouille and waxy new potatoes are outstanding, too, and desserts from the trolley are absolutely irresistible. Charming service by local ladies. Booking essential. **Specialities** lobster mousseline, roast venison in port and wine with cherry sauce, plum and Kirsch mousse.

Dinner Wed (by arrangement), Fri & Sat only 7.30–9.30
Closed 26 December, 1st 2 weeks May & last 2 weeks September

EIRE

Adare

Map 19 B5 Co. Limerick
Limerick 94209
Telex 70202

Manager Mr Brian Murphy
Credit Access, Amex,
Barclaycard, Diners

Rooms 25
with bath/shower 25

Dunraven Arms Hotel   59%   Ⓜ   £ D

Improvements continue at this welcoming hotel, converted from a row of Georgian cottages and standing in its own attractive gardens. Antiques, paintings and prints are dotted around the public rooms, which include a chintzy residents' lounge and a pleasant bar. Refurbished bedrooms have pretty matching fabrics and modern bathrooms; other rooms are larger and more traditionally furnished. *Amenities* garden, 24-hour laundry service. &

Room phone Yes	*Confirm by* 6	*Parking* Ample
Room TV No	*Last dinner* 9.15	*Banquets* 150/10

Annamoe

Map 19 D4 Co. Wicklow
Near Glendalough
Wicklow 5194
Proprietor Mr Paul Tullio

● **Set D** £15·50
About £40 for two
Banquets 60/10

Armstrong's Barn   ♧ Ⓢ

Paul Tullio is the hardworking chef-patron of this delightful restaurant in an old farmhouse. His set dinners offer a selection of carefully prepared dishes ranging from nettle soup and chicken liver pâté to delicately poached sea bass, Chinese beef and chicken casserole. Vegetables are well handled, too, and lemon and orange syllabub makes a lovely refreshing dessert.
🍷 *ABOVE AVERAGE. Credit* Amex, Barclaycard &

Dinner only 7.30–10
Closed Mon, Bank Holidays & end December–17 March

Annestown

Map 19 C5 Co. Waterford
Waterford 96160
Proprietors
John & Pippa Galloway

● **Set D** £9
About £33 for two
Banquets 20/6

Annestown House   ♧ Ⓢ

A charming family atmosphere pervades this 150-year-old house on the edge of the town. Pippa Galloway makes good use of local produce, and her short menu ranges from chicken Chinese-style and roast duck with apple and cinnamon stuffing to lasagne and grills. Nicely cooked seasonal vegetables and delicious sweets such as Grand Marnier pancakes complete the picture. *Credit* Amex, Barclaycard, Diners

Dinner only 7–10.30
Closed Sun & October–April

Prices quoted for Eire are in Irish punts

Ballina

Map 18 B3 Co. Mayo
Ballina 21033
Telex 33796
Proprietors Mr & Mrs B. Moylett
Credit Access, Amex,
Barclaycard, Diners
Closed 14–28 December

Rooms 56
with bath/shower 49

Downhill Hotel   64%   Ⓜ   £ C/D

The landscaped grounds of this well-maintained hotel overlook the sparkling Brusna Falls. Welcoming public rooms include three chintzy lounges (one with TV) and a large modern bar. Bedrooms are comfortably equipped with fitted units; most have attractive tiled bathrooms. *Amenities* garden, sauna, indoor swimming pool, tennis, squash, coarse & game fishing, 24-hour laundry service, in-house video, billiards, table tennis, pool table.

Room phone Yes	*Confirm by* 6.30	*Parking* Ample
Room TV Yes	*Last dinner* 9.15	*Banquets* 350/2

Ballinahinch

Map 18 B3 Co. Galway
Clifden 135
Telex 28809

Credit Access, Amex,
Barclaycard
Closed February & March

Rooms 20
with bath/shower 20

Ballinahinch Castle   59%   £ F

Surrounded by woodland, this ornate 200-year-old hotel has a spectacular setting overlooking a river. Drinks are served in the two comfortable lounges (one with TV), and guests can chat with locals in the friendly Fisherman's Bar. Simply furnished bedrooms have good-quality carpets, and pleasant modern bathrooms. No dogs.
Amenities garden, tennis, game fishing.

Room phone No	*Confirm by* 6	*Parking* Ample
Room TV No	*Last dinner* 9	*Banquets* 60/2

Ballylickey

Map 19 B6 Co. Cork
Near Bantry
Bantry 50071

Proprietors Mr & Mrs Graves
Rooms 25
with bath/shower 25
Room phone Yes
Room TV No
Confirm by 5.30
Last dinner 8.30
Parking Ample

Closed mid October–
end March
Credit Amex, Diners

Ballylickey House Hotel   71%   Ⓜ   £E

With lovely gardens stretching down to the shores of Bantry Bay, this is a most beguiling and beautifully situated hotel. Inside, the decor is a tribute to the impeccable taste of Mrs Graves, especially in the two cosy, delightfully furnished drawing rooms and the charming little bar. Bedrooms (including some which can be made into suites for families) show the same care and thoughtful design, and all have attractive bathrooms with modern fittings. There are also three comfortable Scandinavian-style chalets built round the pool.
Amenities garden, outdoor swimming pool, game fishing.

Ballylickey

Map 19 B6 Co. Cork
Bantry 50071
Proprietors Mr & Mrs Graves
French cooking

● **Set D** £13·25 incl. service
About £36 for two

Ballylickey House Hotel Restaurant   ♔ Ⓢ

Antique furniture and soft comfortable seating make this a most pleasant and welcoming dining room. The four-course set dinner menu, plus daily specialities, is based on classical French cuisine, with dishes like creamy mushroom soup, lightly battered goujonettes of sole and tender veal tongue with sauce ravigote and delicious fresh vegetables. Cooking is accurate and presentation thoughtful. *Credit* Amex, Diners

Lunch by arrangement only *Dinner* 7.30–9
Closed mid October–end March

Ballylickey

Map 19 B6 Co. Cork
Near Bantry
Bantry 50073
Proprietor
Miss Kathleen O'Sullivan

Closed 31 October–31 March

Sea View Hotel   57%   Ⓜ   £F

Run on personal lines, rather like a guest house, Kathleen O'Sullivan's attractive little white-painted hotel is spotlessly maintained. Public rooms like the pretty bar and the three traditional-style lounges are neat and homely. Bedrooms are simply furnished with freestanding pieces, and many of them enjoy fine views of Bantry Bay. Bathrooms are adequate.
Amenities garden.

Rooms 12	*Room phone* No	*Confirm by* 5	*Parking* Ample
with bath/shower 6	*Room TV* No	*Last dinner* 9	*Banquets* 48/6

Ballyvaughan

Map 19 B4 Co. Clare
Ballyvaughan 5
Telex 28110
Proprietors Peter & Moira Haden
Credit Access, Amex,
Barclaycard
Closed November–February

Gregan's Castle Hotel   62%   Ⓜ   £E

At the foot of Corkscrew Hill, with spectacular views across the rugged Burren, this hotel with the air of a private residence provides a friendly welcome. Stylish public rooms include a homely lounge looking out to Galway Bay, a TV lounge with a huge open fireplace and a delightful beamed bar. Bedrooms have pretty fabrics and wallpapers; tiled bathrooms are well fitted. No dogs. *Amenities* garden.

Rooms 16	*Room phone* No	*Confirm by* 5.30	*Parking* Ample
with bath/shower 12	*Room TV* No	*Last dinner* 8	

Ballyvaughan

Map 19 B4 Co. Clare
Ballyvaughan 5

Proprietors
Peter & Moira Haden

Gregan's Castle Hotel Restaurant   ♧ Ⓢ

The day's local catch–oysters, sole, cod and lobsters–is a feature of Peter Haden's excellent five-course dinners at this pleasant, traditional hotel restaurant. Alternatives might include local lamb or Limerick ham. A choice of soups follows the starter, and to finish there's Burren goat's milk cheese followed by some mouthwatering desserts. Friendly, attentive service.

Continued

Continued

ABOVE AVERAGE. *Credit* Access, Amex, Barclaycard

● **Set D** from £11
About £31 for two

Dinner only 7–8
Closed November–February

Baltimore
Map 19 B6 Co. Cork
The Pier
Baltimore 36

Seafood

● **Set L & Set D** £5–£16
About £30 for two
Banquets 45/6

Chez Youen

Friendly collaboration with local fishermen ensures that Youen Jacob gets the best of the catch, and his interest in seafood is matched by real culinary skills. This enchanting quayside restaurant has all the atmosphere of Youen's native Brittany, and his short menus highlight the superb freshness of succulent lobster, clams, oysters, John Dory, skate and brill while the magnificent mixed seafood platter is a feast in itself. There are also some meat dishes, such as wild duck with orange sauce or fillet steak, and tarte Tatin makes an excellent finish.
Credit Access, Amex, Barclaycard, Diners

Meals summer 12.30–midnight; winter dinner only 7–11.30
Closed 24 & 25 December & 3 weeks October

Blessington
Map 19 D4 Co. Wicklow
Naas 65199
Proprietors
Mr & Mrs L. M. Byrne

Closed mid Dec–mid Jan

Downshire House Hotel 57% Ⓜ £E

Very popular with fishermen, this pleasant modern hotel is run by Mr and Mrs Byrne, who make guests feel most welcome. There are functional modern furnishings in the friendly bar and the two comfortable lounges, one of which has TV. Bedrooms (including ten in the annexe) are all similar in style with simple contemporary furniture and adequate bathrooms.
Amenities garden, tennis, coarse & game fishing.

Rooms 25	*Room phone* Yes	*Confirm by* By arrang.	*Parking* Ample
with bath/shower 25	*Room TV* No	*Last dinner* 9.30	*Banquets* 250/12

Bunratty
Map 19 B4 Co. Clare
Limerick 61177
Telex 26214

Manager Mr Michael Rice
Credit Access, Amex,
Barclaycard, Diners

Fitzpatrick's Shannon Shamrock Hotel 60% £C

Efficient, friendly staff enhance the appeal of this low modern hotel between Limerick and Shannon Airport. Bedrooms (a few smartly redecorated) have good-quality fitted units, and bathrooms are well equipped. There's a large bar and a relaxing lounge area with glass-topped cane tables.
Amenities garden, sauna, indoor swimming pool, transport for airport & Limerick, beauty salon, in-house movies, 24-hour laundry service.

Rooms 110	*Room phone* Yes	*Confirm by* 6	*Parking* Ample
with bath/shower 110	*Room TV* Yes	*Last dinner* 9.30	*Banquets* 50/4

Cahir
Map 19 C5 Co. Tipperary
The Square
Cahir 205

● **Set D** £11·50
About £35 for two
Banquets 35/10

Earl of Glengall

New owners have quickly made their mark at this smart first-floor restaurant, and their young Belgian chef sets high standards in the kitchen. Shellfish bisque and chicken liver terrine are full-flavoured starters, while main courses range from rich navarin of lamb to poached trout with creamed leeks. Vegetables are tasty and sweets include a delicious apple pie.
ABOVE AVERAGE. *Credit* Access, Amex, Barclaycard, Diners

Dinner only 7–9.30
Closed Sun, Good Friday & 25 & 26 December

Cahir
Map 19 C5 Co. Tipperary
Ballylooby
Cahir 261

Credit Access, Amex,
Barclaycard, Diners

Kilcoran Lodge Hotel 60% Ⓜ £E

Patricia Haines and her staff provide a warm, cheerful welcome at this pleasant hotel that was once the Earl of Glengall's hunting lodge. There are deep, chintzy armchairs in the two peaceful lounges, and bedrooms, furnished in varying styles, are comfortable and carefully kept; many have superb views across lovely countryside to the mountains. No dogs.
Amenities garden, game fishing, shooting.

Rooms 22	*Room phone* Yes	*Confirm by* 7	*Parking* Ample
with bath/shower 12	*Room TV* No	*Last dinner* 9.15	*Banquets* 200/10

Cahir

Map 19 C5 Co. Tipperary
Ballylooby
Cahir 261

Kilcoran Lodge Hotel Restaurant   ♧ ⓢ

George Haines' superb-quality ingredients and expert cooking make a meal at this quiet country restaurant a most worthwhile experience. Smooth pâté with an excellent Cumberland sauce, and fresh salmon with mayonnaise are typical starters, and stuffed lamb or perfect roast beef with Yorkshire pudding is a delicious main course. Even the bread is home-made, as are the simple sweets. *Credit* Access, Amex, Barclaycard, Diners

● **Set L** £5·50 **Set D** £9·50
About £25 for two

Lunch 12.30–2.45 *Dinner* 7–9.15

Caragh Lake

Map 19 A5 Co. Kerry
Caragh Lake 5

Rooms 20
with bath/shower 12
Room phone No
Room TV No
Confirm by By arrang.
Last dinner 9
Parking Ample

Closed end September–April

Credit Access, Amex,
Barclaycard, Diners

Ard-na-Sidhe   70%   £E

Everything is in tip-top condition at this delightful old lakeside hotel in the peaceful setting of a large secluded garden. The attractive public rooms contain some fine furniture; drinks are served in the pleasant lounge. Bright bedrooms with fitted wardrobes and freestanding quality furniture are very comfortable. Bathrooms are well equipped. No dogs. *Amenities* garden, game fishing, entertainment (Wed, Sat).

Caragh Lake

Map 19 A5 Co. Kerry
Caragh Lake 15

Proprietors
Dr Rolf & Christine Schaper

Closed 20 September–1 April

Caragh Lodge   66%   Ⓜ   £E/F

Cordial Dr Schaper devotes much loving care to his splendid garden full of rare plants, shrubs and trees at this peaceful lakeside hotel. Public rooms are furnished with fine antique pieces, and simply decorated bedrooms–mostly in the annexes–are thoroughly relaxing. All have comfortable beds with duvets, and bright modern bathrooms. No children under ten. No dogs. *Amenities* garden, sauna, tennis, game fishing, games room, hotel boats.

Rooms 10	*Room phone* No	*Confirm by* 6	*Parking* Ample
with bath/shower 10	*Room TV* No	*Last dinner* 8	

We welcome complaints and bona fide recommendations on the tear-out pages for readers' comments. They are followed up by our professional team. Please also complain to the management instantly.

Carrickmacross

Map 18 C3 Co. Monaghan
Carrickmacross 61438

Proprietors
Mr & Mrs G. Gilhooly
Credit Access, Amex,
Barclaycard, Diners

Nuremore Hotel   59%   Ⓜ   £D/E

A hundred acres of grounds surround this leisure-orientated hotel. Public rooms like the lounges and bar of the extended Victorian mansion are spacious and modern; bedrooms have neat fitted units and well-kept bathrooms. *Amenities* garden, sauna, indoor swimming pool, squash, 9-hole golf course, coarse & game fishing, folk music (Sun), discothèque (most Sats), helipad, in-house video, putting, hotel boat, snooker, pool table.   ♿

Rooms 40	*Room phone* Yes	*Confirm by* 6	*Parking* Ample
with bath/shower 40	*Room TV* Yes	*Last dinner* 9.45	*Banquets* 350/4

Prices quoted for Eire are in Irish punts

Cashel

Map 18 A3 Co. Galway
Clifden 252
Telex 28812
Proprietors
Dermot & Kay McEvilly
Rooms 30
with bath/shower 30
Room phone No
Room TV No
Confirm by 6
Last dinner 9
Parking Ample

Credit Access, Amex,
Barclaycard
Closed 1 November–1 March

Cashel House Hotel 70%  £E

Overlooking Cashel Bay and sur-rounded by 50 acres of lovely gardens and woodland walks, this 19th-century building has a delight-ful country-house atmosphere. Good-quality modern furniture and handsome antique pieces blend happily in the public rooms, which include a clubby bar. Bedrooms with pretty pastel colour schemes have tasteful furnishings. Nine attractive, well-equipped mini-suites in the wing have lounge areas with large windows that make the most of the views. Staff are very friendly and helpful. No children under eight.
Amenities garden, tennis, sailing & rowing boats.

Cashel

Map 18 A3 Co. Galway
Clifden 252
Proprietors
Dermot & Kay McEvilly

● **Set D** from £11
About £31 for two

Cashel House Hotel Restaurant

Charming service by young girls brings a smile to this tall-windowed traditional dining room. Locally caught fish is a feature of the interesting menu, and the tasty mussels from the hotel's own bed are well worth sampling. Dishes like beef Wellington, lobster Newburg and salmon hollan-daise are skilfully prepared from first-class ingredients, and the home-made sweets are delicious. *Credit* Access, Amex, Barclaycard

Dinner only 7.30–9
Closed 1 November–1 March

Cashel

Map 19 C5 Co. Tipperary
Tipperary 61411
Telex 26938

Credit Access, Amex,
Barclaycard, Diners
Closed 24 & 25 December

Rooms 20
with bath/shower 20

Cashel Palace Hotel 69% £C

New owners have recently taken over this fine 18th-century red-brick mansion standing in 22 acres of grounds. High ceilings, moulded pillars and crystal chandeliers are features of the elegant public rooms. Bedrooms range from large and traditional to simpler, more up-to-date ones. Neat, modern-ised bathrooms. No dogs. *Amenities* garden, game fishing, folk music (Sun), buttery (11am–11pm), 24-hour laundry service.

Room phone Yes	*Confirm by* 6	*Parking* Ample
Room TV No	*Last dinner* 9.30	*Banquets* 50/10

Castlebar

Map 18 B3 Co. Mayo
Castlebar 22033
Telex 33790
Proprietors Mrs Una Lee
Credit Access, Amex,
Barclaycard, Diners
Closed 8–10 days Christmas

Rooms 41
with bath/shower 41

Breaffy House Hotel 58%  £E/F

Two miles out of town, this sturdy 18th-century mansion set in 60 acres of parkland provides a pleasant holiday base. Simply furnished public rooms include several comfortable lounges with fine garden views. Bedrooms in the main house and extension are cheerfully decorated, all with neat modern units and small, well-fitted bathrooms.
Amenities garden, children's playground, pitch & putt.

Room phone Yes	*Confirm by* 6	*Parking* Ample
Room TV No	*Last dinner* 9	*Banquets* 220/10

Castledermot

Map 19 C4 Co. Kildare
Carlow 45156
Telex 25388
Manager Mr Oliver Deane

Credit Access, Amex,
Barclaycard, Diners

Rooms 46
with bath/shower 46

Kilkea Castle 62% £C/D

This quiet retreat–a 12th-century castle–provides up-to-date comforts. Rough stone arches contrast with comfortable banquettes in the Cavalier Bar, and there's a lofty beamed lounge. Bedrooms (most in converted outbuildings) have modern units and well-fitted bathrooms. *Amenities* garden, sauna, outdoor swimming pool, tennis, game fishing, discothèque (Sun), dinner dance (Fri, Sat), gymnasium, beauty salon, solarium.

Room phone Yes	*Confirm by* By arrang.	*Parking* Ample
Room TV No	*Last dinner* 9.15	*Banquets* 300/8

Claremorris
Map 18 B3 Co. Mayo
Brize
Balla 118
Managers Gay and Carmel Nevin

● **Set L** £3·80 **Set D** £6·80
About £36 for two
Banquets 600/–

Beaten Path, Regency Room 

This charming Regency-style restaurant is part of a modern catering complex on the Balla road. Local meat, game and seafood are featured on the extensive à la carte and set menus, with dishes ranging from lobster Thermidor to venison with oyster stuffing and black cherry sauce, in addition to grills and flambéed specialities. Vegetables are tasty and sweets are well made. *Credit* Access, Amex, Barclaycard, Diners

Lunch Sun only 12.30–3 *Dinner* 7–10.30
Closed Mon–Fri week before Easter & 25 & 26 December

Clarinbridge
Map 19 B4 Co. Galway
Galway 86107
Manager Mr Bob D'Silva

About £26 for two
Banquets 70/5

Paddy Burke's

Clarinbridge is the scene of an annual oyster festival, and oysters appear on the menu of this simple pub with three little dining rooms. Here you can choose from the bar menu (perhaps seafood chowder and smoked cod casserole) or the more elaborate à la carte, which offers yet more delicious seafood plus meat dishes like fillet steak or roast duck. Homely desserts to finish. *Credit* Access

Lunch 12.30–3, Sun 12.30–2 *Dinner* 7.30–10
Closed D Sun, all Mon in winter, Good Friday & 25 December

Clifden
Map 18 A3 Co. Galway
Sky Road
Clifden 33   Telex 28366
Proprietor Mr Paul Hughes
Credit Access, Barclaycard
Closed 10 Nov–10 Dec
& 10 Jan–10 Mar

Rooms 40
with bath/shower 40

Abbeyglen Hotel   63%   Ⓜ   £E

This efficiently run hotel enjoys a position of great beauty in extensive grounds overlooking the sea. The welcoming foyer leads to an equally pleasant, well-furnished lounge, and there's a plush bar. Bedrooms range from the newest, with excellent furnishings and lovely views, to simpler, more modestly fitted rooms. Good modern bathrooms.
Amenities garden, outdoor swimming pool, tennis, dancing (Fri, Sat).

Room phone Yes	*Confirm by* 7	*Parking* Ample
Room TV No	*Last dinner* 9	

Clifden
Map 18 A3 Co. Galway
Sky Road
Clifden 33
Proprietor Mr Paul Hughes

● **Set D** £9·90
About £25 for two

Abbeyglen Hotel Restaurant 

A spacious first-floor dining room, with flowers and candles on the smart, yellow-clothed tables. Set menus make the most of excellent ingredients like fresh local fish and prime beef, cooked straightforwardly and served with good sauces and carefully prepared vegetables. Soups and pâtés, too, are tasty, and there are some delicious desserts such as apple pie and strawberry gâteau. *Credit* Access, Barclaycard

Dinner only 7.30–9
Closed 10 November–10 December & 10 January–10 March

Clifden
Map 18 A3 Co. Galway
The Square
Clifden 134
Proprietors McEvaddy family
Credit Amex, Barclaycard,
Diners
Closed October–May

Rooms 20
with bath/shower 20

Hotel Alcock & Brown   59%   Ⓜ   £F

The upper floors of this pleasant, family-run hotel have fine views across the rooftops to the surrounding hills. The bright entrance lounge is furnished in modern style and cheerful colours adorn the functional bar. Bedrooms offer clean, simple accommodation, with comfortable beds, new chintz curtains, and small tweedy sofas. Compact, carpeted bathrooms are well kept. No children.

Room phone Yes	*Confirm by* 6	*Parking* Ample
Room TV No	*Last dinner* 9.15	

We do not necessarily recommend the cooking at hotels whose restaurants are not separately listed.

FIAT GUIDE TO SIGHTS

Cork

Map 19 B6
Town plan opposite

Population 130,000

Despite its 7th-century foundation as a place of scholarship by St Fin Barre, sustained today by University College, Cork's present tranquillity belies a turbulent history from 819 (the coming of the Danes) to 1921 (the end of the Troubles).
It is a place of water—the River Lee that divides into channels to give the city centre four fascinating quays—and the sea, with all its harbours and resorts. It is also a hill-surrounded valley; and despite its intense Irishness, has the physical aspect of an 18th-century town in France.

Annual Events
Cork Choral Festival *Late April*
Cork Summer Show *June*
Grand Opera Week *May*
International Film Festival *Oct*
St Patrick's Week *14th–20th March*

Sights Outside City
Airport, Blackrock, Blarney, Cobh Harbour and Yacht Clubs, Crosshaven, Fermoy, Kinsale

Tourist Office
Grand Parade
Telephone 23251

1	Bus Office	D2
2	Christchurch	C3
3	Church of St Francis *Byzantine with Italian mosaics*	B/C2
4	Crawford School of Art and Gallery	C2
5	Fitzgerald Park and Public Museum	A2
6	G.A.A. Athletic Grounds	E2
7	Mardyke Walk	A2
8	Marina	E2
9	Opera House	C2
10	Railway Station	E1
11	Red Abbey *oldest ruin*	C3
12	St Ann's Church, Shandon	C1
13	St Fin Barre's Cathedral *Church of Ireland*	B3
14	The Lough	B3
15	Tourist Office	C2
16	University College	A3
17	University Sports Ground, Mardyke	A2

Handbuilt by robots.

The Strada. FIAT

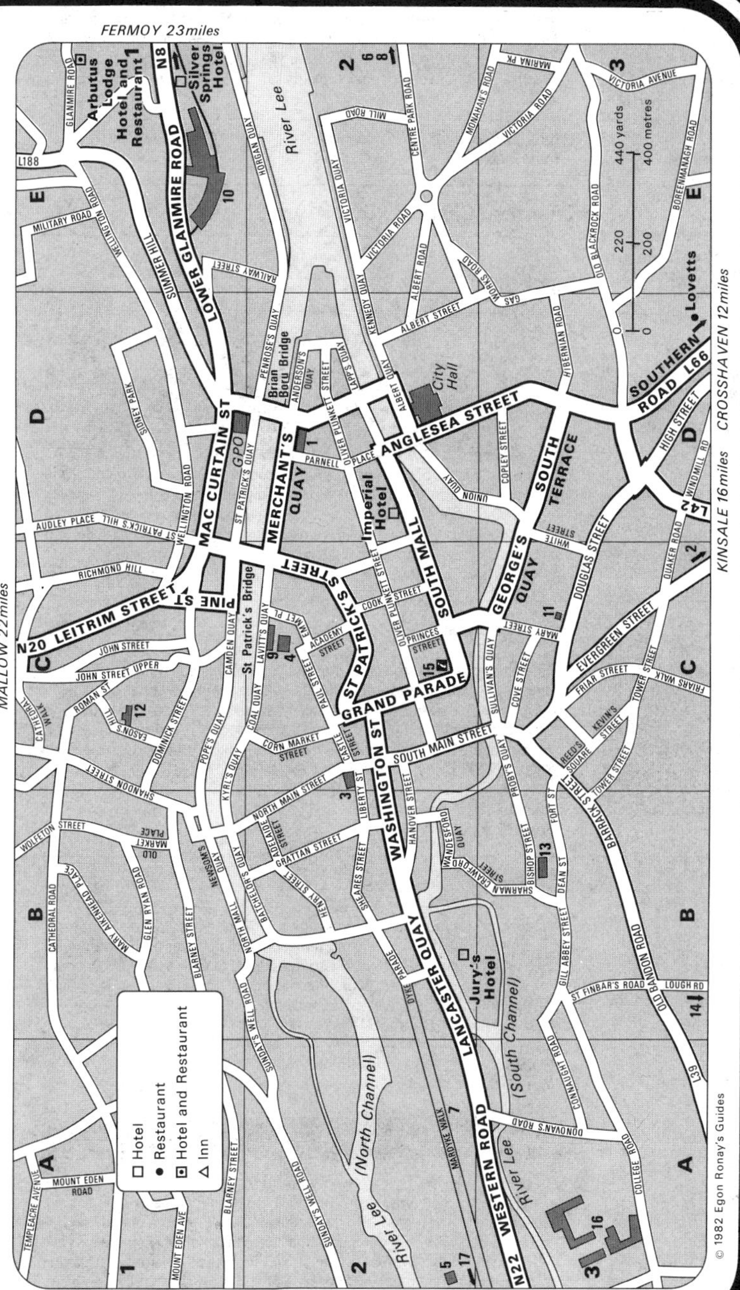

Cork
FIAT
FERMOY 23miles
Arbutus Lodge Hotel and Restaurant 1
N8
Silver Springs Hotel
GLANMIRE ROAD
River Lee
2
6
8
MARINA PK
MONAHAN'S ROAD
VICTORIA ROAD
VICTORIA AVENUE
3
BORENMANAGH ROAD
440 yards
400 metres
220
200
L188
MILITARY ROAD
WELLINGTON ROAD
SIDNEY PARK
SUMMER HILL
LOWER GLANMIRE ROAD
RAILWAY STREET
HORGAN QUAY
PENROSE'S QUAY
MILL ROAD
VICTORIA QUAY
KENNEDY QUAY
CENTRE PARK ROAD
ALBERT ROAD
WORKS ROAD
GAS WORKS ROAD
ALBERT STREET
HIBERNIAN ROAD
OLD BLACKROCK ROAD
10
E
D
C
B
A
E
D
C
B
A
SOUTHERN ROAD L66
Lovetts
CROSSHAVEN 12miles
KINSALE 16miles
HIGH STREET
WINDMILL RD
QUAKER ROAD
L42
2
MALLOW 22miles
MILITARY ROAD
GLANMIRE ROAD
N20 LEITRIM STREET
MAC CURTAIN ST
GPO
ST PATRICK'S QUAY
ST PATRICK'S HILL
WELLINGTON ROAD
AUDLEY PLACE
RICHMOND HILL
PINE ST
PINE STREET
MERCHANT'S QUAY
ANDERSON'S QUAY
LAPP'S QUAY
ALBERT QUAY
Brian Boru Bridge
PARNELL
O PLACE
OLIVER PLUNKETT STREET
Imperial Hotel
ANGLESEA STREET
City Hall
ALBERT QUAY
COPLEY STREET
UNION QUAY
SOUTH TERRACE
WHITE STREET
DOUGLAS STREET
1
ST PATRICK'S STREET
SOUTH MALL
GEORGE'S QUAY
MARY STREET
11
EVERGREEN STREET
FRIAR STREET
TOWER STREET
St Patrick's Bridge
LAVITT'S QUAY
EMMET PL
ACADEMY STREET
PRINCES STREET
COOK STREET
OLIVER PLUNKETT STREET
SULLIVAN'S QUAY
COVE STREET
KEVIN'S STREET
9
4
15
7
GRAND PARADE
CAMDEN QUAY
COAL QUAY
PAUL STREET
CASTLE STREET
LIBERTY ST
PROBY'S QUAY
REED'S SQUARE
FORT ST
FRIARS WALK
C
JOHN STREET
JOHN STREET UPPER
ROMAN ST
EASON'S HILL
S.NON'S
DOMINICK STREET
SHANDON STREET
POPES QUAY
KYR'S QUAY
CORN MARKET STREET
NORTH MAIN STREET
SOUTH MAIN STREET
WASHINGTON ST
HANOVER STREET
WANDESFORD QUAY
BISHOP STREET
DEAN ST
BARRACK STREET
12
3
13
WOLFETON STREET
OLD MARKET PLACE
NEWSOM'S QUAY
ADELAIDE STREET
GRATTAN STREET
SHEARES STREET
MARY STREET
SHARMAN CRAWFORD STREET
GILL ABBEY STREET
ST FINBAR'S ROAD
OLD BANDON ROAD
LOUGH RD
14
L39
CATHEDRAL ROAD
MARY AHERN
GLEN RYAN ROAD
BLARNEY STREET
BATCHELOR'S QUAY
DYKE PARADE
Jury's Hotel
CONNAUGHT ROAD
COLLEGE ROAD
A
B
MOUNT EDEN ROAD
TEMPLEACRE AVENUE
MOUNT EDEN AVE
CATHEDRAL WALK
SUNDAY'S WELL ROAD
MARDYKE WALK
River Lee (North Channel)
LANCASTER QUAY
WESTERN ROAD
N22
River Lee (South Channel)
DONOVAN'S ROAD
DONOVAN'S ROAD
5
17
16
7
1
2
3
Hotel
Restaurant
Hotel and Restaurant
Inn
MACROOM 25miles
© 1982 Egon Ronay's Guides

Clifden

Map 18 A3 Co. Galway
Clifden 16
Telex 28936
Proprietors
John & Evangeline Roche
Credit Access, Barclaycard
Closed end October–mid March

Rooms 31
with bath/shower 31

Rock Glen 60% Ⓜ   £E

This converted 18th-century shooting lodge with a modern extension stands in its own peaceful grounds overlooking Mannin Bay. There are fine views from the chintzy lounge and bar, which have deep, relaxing armchairs and sofas, and there's also a TV room. Well-proportioned bedrooms with attractive soft furnishings have plenty of storage space, and carpeted bathrooms are up to date. *Amenities* garden.

Room phone No   *Confirm by* 6   *Parking* Ample
Room TV No   *Last dinner* 8.30

Cong

Map 18 B3 Co. Mayo
Castlebar 22644
Telex 4749
Manager Mr Rory Murphy

Rooms 77
with bath/shower 77
Room phone Yes
Room TV No
Confirm by 6
Last dinner 9.15
Parking Ample
Banquets 140
Closed January–early April

Credit Access, Amex,
Barclaycard, Diners

Ashford Castle 90%   £C

Five hundred acres of glorious grounds surround this majestic turreted castle overlooking Lough Corrib. A marvellously dignified atmosphere permeates its stately public rooms, which are filled with antiques, fine oil paintings and crystal chandeliers. Spacious bedrooms are furnished in traditional style, and bathrooms have good modern fittings. No dogs.
Amenities garden, tennis, 9-hole golf course, game fishing, shooting.

Cong

Map 18 B3 Co. Mayo
Castlebar 22644
Manager Mr Rory Murphy

● **Set L** £7 **Set D** £14·50
About £40 for two

Ashford Castle Restaurant   👑👑👑 Ⓢ

Skilled formal service matches the opulence of this splendid dining room hung with crystal chandeliers. Dennis Lenehan, the new chef, provides a well-prepared meal based on excellent materials. You might start with vichyssoise before going on to trout, beef Stroganoff or pepper steak with Cognac sauce. Salads, sandwiches or a simple table d'hôte at lunch time.
🍷 *SUPERIOR. Credit* Access, Amex, Barclaycard, Diners

Lunch 1–2.30 *Dinner* 7–9.15
Closed 3 January–Easter

Cork

Town plan E1 Co. Cork
Montenotte
Cork 501237
Telex 75079
Proprietors Ryan family
Credit Access, Amex,
Barclaycard, Diners

Rooms 20
with bath/shower 20

Arbutus Lodge Hotel 66% Ⓜ   £C/D

Amiably run for more than 20 years by the Ryan family, this pleasant hotel has a most peaceful and relaxing atmosphere. The foyer and corridors are hung with portraits, and there's also a plush little lounge and a large modern bar. Attractively decorated bedrooms have floral wallpapers and reproduction furniture. Compact, well-equipped bathrooms. No dogs.
Amenities garden. **Closed** 24–30 December

Room phone Yes   *Confirm by* 6   *Parking* Ample
Room TV Yes   *Last dinner* 9   *Banquets* 80/10

Cork

Town plan E1 Co. Cork
Montenotte
Cork 501237
Proprietors Ryan family

● **Set L** £10 **Set D** £12·95
incl. service
About £48 for two

Arbutus Lodge Hotel Restaurant ★    Ⓢ

For a while Declan Ryan was absent from the kitchen of this graceful, spacious restaurant. Now that he says he has taken charge once again, the cooking is likely to regain its high reputation. The French-inspired menu is supplemented by an intriguing, carefully chosen list of daily specialities like thinly sliced salmon with sorrel sauce and roast rack of lamb with garden herbs, which are prepared with great skill and most beautifully presented. Vegetables are cooked to perfection, and the choice of sweets is a delight to both eye and palate. **Specialities** mosaïque de légumes, grilled scallops with fennel, loin of venison with prune and port sauce. 🍷 *OUTSTANDING.*

Continued

Credit Access, Amex, Barclaycard, Diners

Lunch 1–2 *Dinner* 7–9.15
Closed L Sun, D Sun to non-residents & 24–30 December

Cork

Town plan D2 Co. Cork
South Mall
Cork 23304

Rooms 80
with bath/shower 80
Room phone Yes
Room TV Yes
Confirm by 7
Last dinner 10.15
Parking Difficult
Banquets 350/2

Credit Access, Amex,
Barclaycard, Diners
Closed Christmas week

Imperial Hotel   71%   £ D

An atmosphere of spaciousness and luxury pervades this hotel in the heart of the city. The splendid foyer with its impressive marble floors, mirrors and crystal chandeliers leads to the Orangery, a light, airy room, with modern glass tables and chromium chairs, which serves as a lounge; there are also two bars, one plush and roomy, the other more functional and up to date in style. Compact bedrooms are furnished to a very high standard, with practical built-in units, cane chairs and bedside controls, as well as thoughtful touches like welcoming baskets of fresh fruit. Bathrooms are fully equipped. No dogs.
Amenities discothèque (Thurs).

Cork

Town plan B2 Co. Cork
Western Road
Cork 966377
Telex 26073

Rooms 140
with bath/shower 140
Room phone Yes
Room TV Yes
Confirm by 6
Last dinner 11
Parking Ample
Banquets 350/10

Credit Access, Amex,
Barclaycard, Diners

Jurys Hotel   70%   *E*   £ B/C

Serving the needs of travelling businessmen, this smart modern hotel has a whole range of recreational and conference facilities. The public area is one vast open space on several levels, with large windows, green plants and plenty of comfortable seating for guests to relax in; there are also two stylish bars with plush contemporary furniture. Bedrooms (including many excellent new ones) are very well equipped with good-quality built-in units, bedside controls and attractive tiled bathrooms provided with telephone extensions. *Amenities* garden, sauna, indoor/outdoor swimming pool, squash, discothèque (weekends), games room, health centre, gymnasium, children's playground.   &

Cork

Town plan D3 Co. Cork
Churchyard Lane, Well Road
Douglas
Cork 294909

About £32 for two

Lovetts   Ⓢ

Excellent fresh seafood–from grilled turbot to prawns and scallops provençale–is skilfully cooked at this attractive restaurant in a town house. There are a few meat dishes, too. ♀ *SUPERIOR*. *Credit* Access, Amex, Barclaycard, Diners *Lunch* 12.45–2.45 *Dinner* 7.30–9.45 **Closed** L Sat, all Sun & Bank Holidays ● **Set L** £8·50 **Set D** £10 *Banquets* 28/4

Cork

Town plan B2 Co. Cork
Tivoli
Cork 507533
Telex 26111
Credit Access, Amex,
Barclaycard, Diners
Closed 1 week Christmas

Rooms 72
with bath/shower 72

Silver Springs Hotel   60%   £ D

This angular, concrete and glass hotel stands in its own grounds on the A25 Dublin–Waterford road. Comfortable, freshly decorated public rooms include a large lounge with smart cane chairs and a lounge bar in similar style with a wood-lined ceiling. White-painted bedrooms have practical built-in furniture and well-equipped tiled bathrooms.
Amenities garden, discothèque (Wed, Fri).

Room phone Yes	*Confirm by* 6	*Parking* Ample
Room TV Yes	*Last dinner* 9.45	*Banquets* 140/–

Map 19 D4
Town plan opposite

Population 983,683

Dublin (from the Erse for 'dark pool'), came into historic prominence when the Norman conquerors in England were invited to help the King of Leinster campaign against the High King of Ireland. The chapter of 'troubles' began. In 1800 the Irish Parliament was absorbed by Westminster, but in 1922 that chapter ended and Dublin is the bustling capital of the Irish Republic, remaining home from home for the Irish everywhere.

Annual Events
Dublin Horse Show *3rd–7th August*
Dublin Spring Show *4th–8th May*
Gaelic Football Finals *18th September*
Hurling Finals *4th September*
St Patrick's Day Parade *17th March*

Sights Outside City
Malahide Castle,
Hill Abbey of Howth,
The Curragh, Bray,
Enniskerry Village,
Powerscourt House, Vale of Avoca

Information Office
14 Upper O'Connell Street
Telephone Dublin 747733

Dublin

1	Abbey Theatre	D1
2	Airport	C1
3	Bank of Ireland *in old Parliament building*	C1
4	Botanic Gardens	B1
5	Castle	C2
6	Christ Church Cathedral *11th-c Strongbow's tomb*	C2
7	City Hall *18th-c*	C2
8	Civic Museum *record of Dublin's history*	C2
9	Connolly Station	D1
10	Croke Park *hurling and Gaelic football*	C1
11	Eblana Theatre	D1
12	Four Courts *Law Courts*	B1
13	Gaiety Theatre	C2
14	Gate Theatre	C1
15	Government Buildings	D2
16	Heuston Station	A1
17	Hugh Lane Municipal Gallery of Modern Art	C1
18	Lansdowne Road Rugby Ground	E3
19	Leinster House *Dail; National Library; Museum*	D2
20	Mansion House *Queen Anne period*	D2
21	Olympia Theatre	C2
22	Pearse Station	D2
23	Phoenix Park and Zoo	A1
24	Pro-Cathedral	C1
25	Royal Dublin Society Showgrounds	E3
26	St Audoen's Church *oldest parish church*	B2
27	St Michan's Church *remarkable vaults*	B1
28	St Patrick's Cathedral *impressive interior, Swift's tomb*	C2
29	St Stephen's Green *oasis in city's heart*	C/D2
30	Tourist Information Centre	C1
31	Trinity College and Library *Book of Kells*	D2

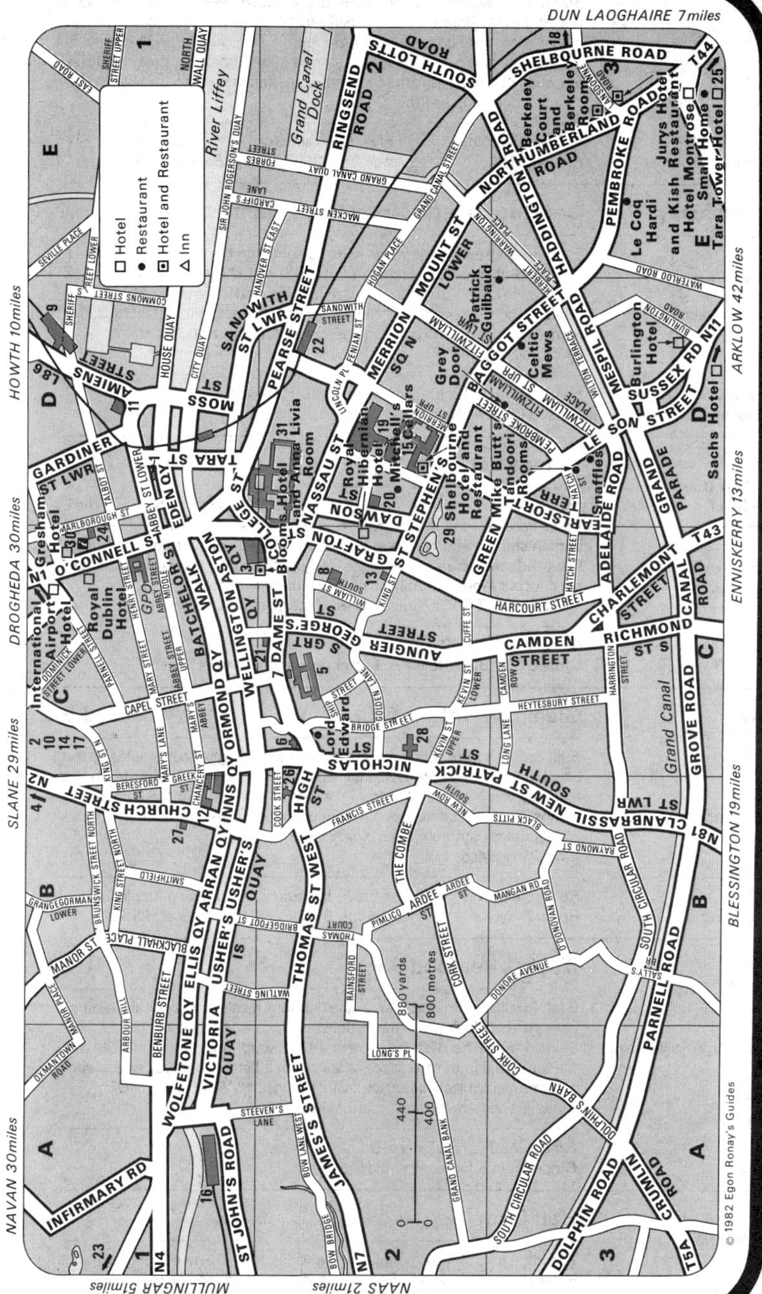

DUN LAOGHAIRE 7 miles
ARKLOW 42 miles
ENNISKERRY 13 miles
BLESSINGTON 19 miles
NAAS 21 miles
MULLINGAR 51 miles
NAVAN 30 miles
SLANE 29 miles
DROGHEDA 30 miles
HOWTH 10 miles
Hotel
Restaurant
Hotel and Restaurant
Inn
River Liffey
Grand Canal Dock
SOUTH LOTTS ROAD
SHELBOURNE ROAD
NORTHUMBERLAND ROAD
HADDINGTON ROAD
PEMBROKE ROAD
Berkeley Court and Berkeley Room
Jurys Hotel and Kish Restaurant
Hotel Montrose
Tara Tower Hotel
Small Home
Le Coq Hardi
Burlington Hotel
SUSSEX RD N11
Sachs Hotel
MESPIL ROAD
BAGGOT STREET
Patrick Guilbaud
Celtic Mews
FITZWILLIAM ST LWR
FITZWILLIAM ST UPR
MOUNT ST LOWER
MERRION SQ N
Grey Door
Mitchell's Cellars
Royal Hibernian Hotel
SANDWITH ST LWR
PEARSE STREET
SANDWITH STREET
GRAND CANAL QUAY
SIR JOHN ROGERSON'S QUAY
RINGSEND ROAD
WALL QUAY
NORTH WALL QUAY
EAST ROAD
SHERIFF STREET UPPER
SEVILLE PLACE
COMMONS STREET
HOUSE QUAY
CITY QUAY
MOSS ST
TARA ST
EDEN QY
AMIENS STREET
GARDINER ST LWR
Gresham Hotel
International Airport Hotel
Royal Dublin Hotel
GPO
O'CONNELL ST
TALBOT ST
ABBEY ST LOWER
MARLBOROUGH ST
HENRY STREET
MARY STREET
CAPEL STREET
PARNELL STREET
DOMINICK STREET LOWER
BATCHELOR WALK
ASTON QY
WELLINGTON QY
ORMOND QY
INNS QY
ARRAN QY
ELLIS QY
WOLFE TONE QY
USHER'S QUAY
USHER'S ISLAND
VICTORIA QUAY
ST JOHN'S ROAD
INFIRMARY RD
JAMES'S STREET
THOMAS ST WEST
Blooms Hotel
Livia Room and Anna Livia
NASSAU ST
DAWSON ST
GRAFTON ST
COLLEGE ST
DAME ST
S GRT GEORGE'S STREET
AUNGIER STREET
NICHOLAS ST
NEW ST
ST PATRICK ST LWR
HIGH ST
FRANCIS STREET
THE COMBE
Shelbourne Hotel and Restaurant
ST STEPHEN'S GREEN
Mike Butt's Tandoori Rooms
Snaffles
HARCOURT STREET
CAMDEN STREET
CAMDEN ROW
KEVIN ST LOWER
KEVIN ST UPPER
CUFFE ST
HEYTESBURY STREET
LONG LANE
NEW ROW SOUTH
BLACK PITTS
RAYMOND ST
DONORE AVENUE
ADELAIDE ROAD
HATCH STREET
CHARLEMONT STREET
RICHMOND ST S
GRAND PARADE
GROVE ROAD
Grand Canal
CHARLESFORT ROAD
RANELAGH
RATHMINES
CLANBRASSIL ST LWR
SOUTH CIRCULAR ROAD
DOLPHIN ROAD
CRUMLIN ROAD
PARNELL ROAD
CORK STREET
ARDEE ST
PIMLICO
THOMAS COURT
BRIDGEFOOT ST
WATLING STREET
BENBURB STREET
MANOR ST
BLACKHALL PLACE
CHURCH STREET
SMITHFIELD
KING STREET NORTH
BRUNSWICK STREET NORTH
GRANGEGORMAN LOWER
OXMANTOWN ROAD
ARBOUR HILL
MANOR PLACE
BOW BRIDGE
STEEVEN'S LANE
800 metres
880 yards
440
400
© 1982 Egon Ronay's Guides
A B C D E
1 2 3

Courtmacsherry

Map 19 B6 Co. Cork
Near Bandon
Bandon 46198
Proprietors
Mr & Mrs Terry Adams

Closed October–March

Courtmacsherry Hotel 61% Ⓜ £ E/F

Surrounded by ten acres of gardens, this secluded, seaside hotel – converted from a private house – makes a peaceful place to stay. Simple, well-kept public rooms include a popular bar and a cosy lounge with plenty of comfortable chairs. There are lovely sea views from the neat, modestly furnished bedrooms, and modern bathrooms are adequate.
Amenities garden, sea fishing, riding.

Rooms 16	*Room phone* No	*Confirm by* By arrang.	*Parking* Ample
with bath/shower 5	*Room TV* No	*Last dinner* 9.30	*Banquets* 70/2

Courtmacsherry

Map 19 B6 Co. Cork
Near Bandon
Bandon 46198
Proprietors
Mr & Mrs Terry Adams

Courtmacsherry Hotel Restaurant

This attractive restaurant features fish straight from the sea: Terry Adams is a dab hand at preparing salmon, plaice, brill and shellfish, as well as meat dishes such has shish kebabs or roast duckling, and his family provide willing service. The good-value set dinner, which changes every night, includes home-made soups and pâtés and delicious homely sweets.
♟ *ABOVE AVERAGE.*

● **Set L** from £5 **Set D** from £8
About £22 for two

Lunch Sun only 12.30–2.30 *Dinner* 7.30–9.30
Closed October–March

Dalkey

Map 19 D4 Co. Dublin
17 Railway Road
Dublin 859055
Proprietors
Mr & Mrs Mervyn Stewart

Guinea Pig

The Stewarts are friendly hosts at this popular, informal restaurant, where super-fresh seafood is the mainstay of the interesting menus. Our poached salmon stuffed with crabmeat was excellent, and sole, lobster, roast duck, steak and seasonal game also appear regularly. Vegetables are first class, and our chocolate meringue gâteau made a triumphant finale.
♟ *ABOVE AVERAGE. Credit* Access, Amex, Barclaycard, Diners

● **Set D** Mon–Fri £11·95
About £40 for two
Banquets 40/30

Dinner only 7–11.30
Closed Sun, Bank Holidays, 1 week January & 2 weeks Easter

Delgany

Map 19 D4 Co. Wicklow
Glen o' the Downs
Dublin 862896

Manager Mr Vincent O'Donoghue
Credit Amex

Glenview Hotel 60% £E

Built on the top of a hill in the shadow of the Sugar Loaf mountain, this beautifully situated hotel is maintained in very good condition, and there are fabulous views of the glen from the picture windows of the comfortable lounge. Spacious bedrooms have simple modern furniture, floral wallpapers and fully tiled bathrooms with bidets. No dogs.
Amenities garden.

Rooms 23	*Room phone* Yes	*Confirm by* By arrang.	*Parking* Ample
with bath/shower 23	*Room TV* No	*Last dinner* 9.45	*Banquets* 95/20

Dingle

Map 19 A5 Co. Kerry
John Street
Dingle 144
Proprietors John & Stella Doyle
Seafood

Doyle's Seafood Bar

Fresh local fish form the basis of the delicious meals at this popular seafood bar where Stella Doyle is the skilful cook and John Doyle the helpful host. Starters might be oysters or creamy crab soup, and the main dish sole, salmon, squid in tomato sauce or succulent lobster. Gorgeous sweets such as home-made blackcurrant ice cream to finish. ♟ *ABOVE AVERAGE.*
Credit Access, Amex, Barclaycard, Diners

Lunch 12.30–2.15 *Dinner* 6–9
Closed Sun & December–mid March

About £26 for two

Dingle

Map 19 A5 Co. Kerry
John Street
Dingle 300
Seafood

Half Door

Friendly John Slye's hospitality pervades this charming unpretentious restaurant, where lovely fresh seafood is cooked simply to highlight its natural flavour. Steaks and delicious sweets, too. *Credit* Access, Amex, Barclaycard, Diners *Lunch* 12.30–2.15, Sun 12.30–1.45 *Dinner* 6–9, Sun 6–8 **Closed** Tues & November–March ● **Set L** £3·50 *Banquets* 12/2

About £25 for two

Dingle

Map 19 A5 Co. Kerry
Dingle 104
Telex 26900
Manager Mr Peter Coyle
Credit Access, Amex,
Barclaycard, Diners
Closed November–February

Rooms 80
with bath/shower 80

Sceilig Hotel   59%   **£ E**

Overlooking Dingle Bay, this modern two-storey building has a rustic bar and a cheerfully furnished lounge, as well as a pleasant patio. Sizeable bedrooms have practical built-in units and well-fitted, up-to-date bathrooms.
Amenities garden, outdoor swimming pool, tennis, sea fishing, children's play area, games room, entertainment (2–3 nights weekly), pony trekking.

Room phone Yes	*Confirm by* 6	*Parking* Ample
Room TV No	*Last dinner* 9	*Banquets* 160/–

Dublin

Town plan E3 Co. Dublin
Lansdowne Road
Dublin 601711
Telex 30554

Rooms 200
with bath/shower 200
Room phone Yes
Room TV Yes
Confirm by 6
Last dinner 10.15
Parking Ample
Banquets 200/10

Credit Access, Amex,
Barclaycard, Diners

Berkeley Court   85%   *E*   **£ B**

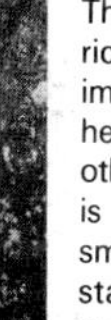

The entrance hall with its striking, richly patterned carpet gives an immediate impression of opulence heightened by fine antiques and other quality furnishings. Reception is friendly and efficient, and the smart porters very helpful. Outstandingly comfortable public rooms include a large bar with luxurious settees and a popular split-level coffee shop. There are splendid conference rooms and four luxury suites. Bedrooms have attractive traditional decor and handsome canopied beds, and large mirrors and pretty tiling are features of the well-planned bathrooms. No dogs.
Amenities sauna, indoor swimming pool, solarium, hairdressing, coffee shop (7.30am–11.30pm).

Dublin

Town plan E3 Co. Dublin
Lansdowne Road
Dublin 601711

About £45 for two

Berkeley Court, Berkeley Room   ♔ Ⓢ

Formal, attentive service and an elegant, Regency-style ambience back up an impressive menu of international dishes competently prepared from quality ingredients. 🍷 *SUPERIOR*.
Credit Access, Amex, Barclaycard, Diners
Lunch 12.30–2.30 *Dinner* 6.30–10.15, Sun 6.30–9.30 ● Set L £9·95   &

Dublin

Town plan C2 Co. Dublin
Anglesea Street
Dublin 715622
Telex 31688

Rooms 84
with bath/shower 84
Room phone Yes
Room TV Yes
Confirm by 6
Last dinner 10.30
Parking Limited
Banquets 60/10

Credit Access, Amex,
Barclaycard, Diners

Blooms Hotel   76%   *E*   **£ B**

This stylish hotel–named after the hero of James Joyce's *Ulysses*–has an eye-catching circular lounge where glass and glittering mirrors provide a spectacular setting for velvet settees, cane chairs and potted plants. Glass features, too, in the smart basement cocktail bar, while the coffee shop and main bar are luxuriously traditional. Bedrooms, attractively decorated in green or beige, are equipped with trouser presses, bedside controls and a supply of soft drinks. The tiled bathrooms, with telephone extensions, are models of good design. Polite, helpful staff. No dogs.
Amenities coffee house (7.30am–11.30pm).

Dublin

Town plan C2 Co. Dublin
Anglesea Street
Dublin 715622

Blooms Hotel, Anna Livia Room   ♔ Ⓢ

Silk-hung walls and red plush settees give a luxurious air to this very civilised restaurant with impeccable formal service. The menu of traditional favourites features fish dishes and a few Irish specialities, and Sunday lunch brings roast beef carved on the trolley. Quality ingredients are competently handled and sauces are well made.

                                                    Continued

---

Continued

● **Set L** £10·50 **Set D** £14
About £40 for two

📍 *SUPERIOR. Credit* Access, Amex, Barclaycard, Diners

Lunch 12.30–2.30 *Dinner* 6.30–10.30, Sun 6.30–9

Dublin

Town plan D3 Co. Dublin
Upper Leeson Street
Dublin 605222
Telex 25517

Rooms 420
with bath/shower 420
Room phone Yes
Room TV Yes
Confirm by 6
Last dinner 11
Parking Ample
Banquets 1,300/10

Credit Access, Amex,
Barclaycard, Diners

Burlington Hotel 71% *E*   £C

Marble, handsome carpeting and deep armchairs and settees set the tone in the spacious foyer of this very large modern hotel in a quiet part of the city. There are three comfortable bars, including a delightfully plush and mellow room with much wood panelling. Bedrooms, smartly fitted with lightwood units, have colour TV and thoroughly up-to-date, well-equipped bathrooms. Reception and room service are efficient and helpful. No dogs.
Amenities sauna, indoor swimming pool, dancing (Mon–Sat), hairdressing, grill room (12.30pm–11pm), in-house movies.　　♿

Dublin

Town plan D3 Co. Dublin
109a Lower Baggot Street
Dublin 760796
Proprietors Gray family

About £50 for two
Banquets 20/6

Celtic Mews   ♛ Ⓢ

Maura and Joe Gray make guests very welcome at this smart little mews restaurant, where uncomplicated dishes are prepared to a consistently high standard. Fresh seafood, like our delicious poached salmon with hollandaise sauce, is a speciality, along with steaks, seasonal game, beef Stroganoff and traditional Irish stew. There's an attractive sweet trolley. Booking essential.
Credit Access, Amex, Barclaycard

Dinner only 6.30–11.45
Closed Sun, Bank Holidays & last 2 weeks July

Dublin

Town plan E3 Co. Dublin
35 Pembroke Road
Dublin 684130
Proprietor John Howard

● **Set L** £9
About £45 for two
Banquets 20/8

Le Coq Hardi   ♢ ♛ Ⓢ

This smart, intimate restaurant with a bar in the basement makes a luxurious setting for John Howard's reliable cooking. Dishes like rich French onion soup and calf's liver with fresh apricots are supplemented by daily seafood specialities such as salmon with hollandaise sauce. Sauces are well made, vegetables are excellent and sweets include a subtly flavoured lemon cheesecake. 📍 *OUTSTANDING. Credit* Access, Amex, Diners

Lunch 12.30–3 *Dinner* 7–11
Closed L Sat, all Sun, Bank Holidays & 23 December–15 January

---

Prices quoted for Eire are in Irish punts

Dublin

Town plan C1 Co. Dublin
O'Connell Street
Dublin 746881
Telex 25308
Credit Access, Amex,
Barclaycard, Diners
Closed 3 days Christmas

Rooms 179
with bath/shower 179

Gresham Hotel 69%   £D

A well-known city-centre landmark, this imposing Victorian hotel has a spacious marble-floored foyer and a smartly furnished bar-lounge. There are also several function rooms. Comfortable bedrooms, including some luxurious suites, vary in style from '30s to very modern, and some bathrooms retain their splendid original fittings. *Amenities* coffee shop (7.15am–11.30pm), discothèque, 24-hour laundry service (Mon–Fri).　　♿

Room phone Yes	*Confirm by* 6	*Parking* Limited
Room TV Yes	*Last dinner* 11.30	*Banquets* 350/4

Dublin
Town plan D2 Co. Dublin
23 Upper Pembroke Street
Dublin 763286

● **Set L** £7·95
About £40 for two
Banquets 50/–

Grey Door   Ⓢ

Russian and Scandinavian specialities dominate the menu in this appealing little restaurant. Dishes range from authentic borsch, blinis, forschmak (an interesting blend of minced lamb and salt herring) and honey-basted duck served on a bed of kasha, to steaks, sauced veal and Swedish cured salmon. Enterprising, competent cooking.
Credit Access, Amex, Barclaycard

Lunch 12–2.30 *Dinner* 7–11
Closed L Sat, all Sun & Christmas

Dublin
Town plan E3 Co. Dublin
Pembroke Road, Ballsbridge
Dublin 605000
Telex 25304
Manager Mr Lee Kidney
Rooms 314
with bath/shower 314
Room phone Yes
Room TV Yes
Confirm by 6
Last dinner 10.30
Parking Ample
Banquets 1,000/5

Credit Access, Amex,
Barclaycard, Diners

Jurys Hotel   74%   *E*   **£B**

From coach parties to conferences, there's accommodation for all at this impressive modern hotel where the range of amenities includes an ultra-modern complex with a sunken bar and swimming pool, and nine luxurious private suites. There is ample lounge space in the vast foyer, and no less than four bars, including the smart, sober Dubliner. Bedrooms (including three specially designed for the disabled) are attractively decorated and comfortable, with space for armchairs and settees; the newer bathrooms are particularly well equipped. Friendly staff provide 24-hour room service.
Amenities garden, indoor/outdoor swimming pool, cabaret (May–October), hairdressing, coffee shop (23 hours).   &

Dublin
Town plan E3 Co. Dublin
Pembroke Road, Ballsbridge
Dublin 605000

Seafood

About £44 for two

Jurys Hotel, Kish Restaurant

A four-piece palm-court orchestra brings a note of nostalgia to this modern dining room luxuriant with greenery. The menu offers exclusively seafood, with a more elaborate choice at night. Fresh local salmon, sole and lobsters are well cooked and served in a variety of ways, and starters include tasty scallops and smokies. Finish with fruit salad or home-made ice cream.
Credit Access, Amex, Barclaycard, Diners   &

Lunch 12.30–2 *Dinner* 6.30–10
Closed L Sat & all Sun

Dublin
Town plan C2 Co. Dublin
23 Christchurch Place
Dublin 752557

Proprietor Mr Tom Cunniam
Seafood

About £42 for two

Lord Edward   Ⓢ

This popular Edwardian-style restaurant above an old tavern specialises in seafood, and the long meatless menu offers mussels, crab, gorgeous scallops and Dublin Bay prawns as well as classics like sole Walewska, grilled turbot and lobster Thermidor. Everything's splendidly fresh, vegetables are good, and there's a small range of simple desserts. Service is courteous and efficient. *Credit* Access, Amex, Barclaycard, Diners

Lunch 12.30–2.30 *Dinner* 6–10.45
Closed L Sat, all Sun & Bank Holidays

Dublin
Town plan D3 Co. Dublin
27 Lower Leeson Street
Dublin 762286
Proprietor Mr Mike Butt

About £36 for two
Banquets 65/–

Mike Butt's Tandoori Rooms   ♁ Ⓢ

Drawing inspiration from all parts of the globe, Mike Butt offers a large range of exotic and highly enjoyable creations, with the emphasis on spicy tandooris, tikkas, kebabs and curries. Special thali menus are popular, too, and other international choices include sea trout belle meunière, paella à la valenciana and rib of beef rickshawboy. Mango sorbet makes a refreshing sweet. *Credit* Access, Amex, Barclaycard, Diners

Dinner only 7–12
Closed Sun & Bank Holidays

Dublin

Town plan D2 Co. Dublin
21 Kildare Street
Dublin 680367

About £19 for two

Mitchell's Cellars

A friendly, bustling little basement restaurant, where two young women prepare a small choice of tasty, homely fare such as pâté, soups, quiches and casseroles, along with delicious desserts. *Credit* Access, Barclaycard *Lunch only* 12.15–2.30 **Closed** Sun, also Mon & Sat of Bank Holiday weekends, Good Friday & 24 December–2 January

Dublin

Town plan E3 Co. Dublin
Stillorgan Road, Donnybrook
Dublin 693311
Telex 91207
Manager Mr W. Kingston
Credit Access, Amex,
Barclaycard, Diners

Rooms 190
with bath/shower 190

Hotel Montrose 58% £ D/E

A modern balconied hotel to the south-east of the city, with palm trees in the car park. The streamlined reception hall is open-plan with a lounge area, and there's a large bar with plush burgundy seating. Bright bedrooms have colourful bedspreads and curtains, attractive freestanding furniture and half-tiled bathrooms. No dogs. *Amenities* sauna, grill (noon–midnight), hairdressing, massage, 24-hour laundry service (Mon–Fri).

Room phone Yes	*Confirm by* 7.30	*Parking* Ample
Room TV Yes	*Last dinner* 10	*Banquets* 160/30

Dublin

Town plan D3 Co. Dublin
46 James's Place
Off Lower Baggot Street
Dublin 764192
French cooking

● **Set L** £7·50
About £45 for two
Banquets 65/40

Patrick Guilbaud ★

Patrick Guilbaud spent three years creating this stylish city-centre restaurant, whose well-spaced tables are set with lovely glassware and china. Outstanding materials, delicate sauces and beautiful presentation are features of the skilfully prepared French dishes, including some nouvelle cuisine items. Our hot fish terrine with a basil-flavoured sauce was quite superb, and the pink-cooked duck with green peppercorn sauce was fittingly accompanied by excellent dauphinoise potatoes and delicious ratatouille. Finish with home-made sorbets or the pâtissier's magnificent Pithiviers and mille-feuilles.

♟ *SUPERIOR*. *Credit* Access, Amex, Barclaycard, Diners

Lunch 12.30–2 *Dinner* 7.30–10
Closed L Sat, all Sun & Bank Holidays

Dublin

Town plan C1 Co. Dublin
O'Connell Street
Dublin 749351
Telex 24288

Credit Access, Amex,
Barclaycard, Diners

Rooms 110
with bath/shower 110

Royal Dublin Hotel 57% £ C

This functional modern hotel stands in the heart of the city. The spacious, stone-floored foyer has a seating area, and there's a large panelled bar/lounge, a small contemporary cocktail bar and some meeting rooms. Identical bedrooms in pastel shades have simple fitted units and compact tiled bathrooms. Standards of maintenance and housekeeping could be improved. No dogs. *Amenities* 24-hour laundry service (Mon–Fri).

Room phone Yes	*Confirm by* 6	*Parking* Limited
Room TV No	*Last dinner* 9.15	*Banquets* 150/4

Dublin

Town plan D3 Co. Dublin
19 Morehampton Road
Dublin 680995   Telex 31667
Manager Mr Jack Donnelly
Credit Access, Amex,
Barclaycard, Diners
Closed 25 & 26 December

Rooms 21
with bath/shower 21

Sachs Hotel 64% £ B

A well-maintained, efficiently run hotel converted from a row of sturdy Georgian houses. The small, sumptuous lounge is an inviting room with an open fireplace, a lovely chandelier and relaxing period furniture; there's also a bright cocktail bar and a popular Victorian-style bar. Imaginatively decorated bedrooms have deep carpeting, excellent reproduction or modern furniture and colourful tiled bathrooms. No dogs. *Amenities* night club.

Room phone Yes	*Confirm by* By arrang.	*Parking* Ample
Room TV Yes	*Last dinner* 10.30	*Banquets* 100/4

Dublin

Town plan D2 Co. Dublin
St Stephen's Green
Dublin 766471
Telex 25184
Manager Mr P. M. C. Browne
Credit Access, Amex,
Barclaycard, Diners

Shelbourne Hotel 69% £ B

Work continues at this comfortable city-centre hotel, whose foyer and lounge retain many elegant Victorian features. Other stylish public areas include two bars and several function rooms. Bedrooms are gradually being refurbished to a very high standard, with quality furnishings and luxuriously fitted bathrooms. *Amenities* cabaret & dancing (in summer), barber, coffee shop (10.30am–11.30pm), 24-hour laundry service.

Continued

Rooms 176	*Room phone* Yes	*Confirm by* 6	*Parking* Limited
with bath/shower 176	*Room TV* Yes	*Last dinner* 10.30	*Banquets* 500/–

Dublin   Shelbourne Hotel Restaurant   ♕♕ Ⓢ

Town plan D2 Co. Dublin
St Stephen's Green
Dublin 766471

A splendidly traditional restaurant, whose menus provide an enjoyable choice of seafood, including lobster, sole and salmon, plus grills, sauced meat and chicken dishes, and some tempting sweets. 🍷 *ABOVE AVERAGE. Credit* Access, Amex, Barclaycard, Diners *Lunch* 12.30–2.30 *Dinner* 6.30–10.30

About £52 for two

Closed Sun & Bank Holidays ● **Set L** from £13·50 **Set D** from £17·50

Dublin   Small Home   Ⓢ

Town plan E3 Co. Dublin
41 Shelbourne Road
Dublin 608087

Familiar dishes from the international repertoire are skilfully prepared and cheerfully served in the two panelled rooms of this homely restaurant. Starters like lasagne or seafood cocktail precede main courses ranging from stuffed sole to kidneys Turbigo and our hearty, flavour-packed navarin of lamb. Desserts include home-made ice cream. Simpler lunchtime choice. *Credit* Access, Amex, Barclaycard, Diners

● **Set D** £9·95 (Sun–Thurs)
About £36 for two
Banquets 32/6

Lunch 12.30–2 *Dinner* 7–10.30, Sat 7–11.30
Closed L Sat, all Sun, Bank Holidays & 1 week before Easter

Dublin   Snaffles   Ⓢ

Town plan D3 Co. Dublin
47 Lower Leeson Street
Dublin 760790
Proprietor Mr N. Tinne

Prime fresh ingredients and reliable cooking produce very enjoyable results in this elegant and friendly basement restaurant. You could start with bacon and potato soup, perhaps, or a deliciously light mousse flavoured with cheese and garlic, and go on to grilled steak, coq au vin or pink-roasted rack of lamb served with redcurrant jelly. Oysters, salmon and game in season. *Credit* Access, Amex, Barclaycard, Diners

About £44 for two
Banquets 8/4

Lunch 12.30–2.30 *Dinner* 7–11
Closed L Sat, D Mon, all Sun, Bank Holidays & 1 week Christmas

Dublin   Tara Tower Hotel   55%   £ D

Town plan E3 Co. Dublin
Merrion Road
Dublin 694666

Standing halfway between the city and Dun Laoghaire ferry terminal, this functional modern hotel is useful for business people and tourists alike. The open-plan reception-lounge area is bright and cheerful, and there's a large, comfortable bar as well as useful conference facilities. Uniformly decorated bedrooms have simple fitted units and compact, well-equipped bathrooms. No dogs. *Amenities* coffee shop (7.15am–11.15pm).   ♿

Credit Access, Amex,
Barclaycard, Diners

Rooms 83	*Room phone* Yes	*Confirm by* By arrang.	*Parking* Ample
with bath/shower 83	*Room TV* Yes	*Last dinner* 11.15	*Banquets* 250/–

Dublin Airport   International Airport Hotel   58%   £ B/C

Town plan C1 Co. Dublin
Collinstown
Dublin 379211
Telex 24612

A marble-floored sunken lounge is an unusual feature of this modern low-rise hotel near the airport. There's also a lofty entrance hall, a large, comfortable bar and a bright coffee shop. Spacious bedrooms (including 45 smart new ones) have practical fitted furniture, tea/coffee-makers and compact bathrooms. No dogs. *Amenities* coffee shop (6.30am–10.30pm), 24-hour laundry service, transport for airport.   ♿

Credit Access, Amex,
Barclaycard, Diners

Rooms 195	*Room phone* Yes	*Confirm by* 6	*Parking* Ample
with bath/shower 195	*Room TV* Yes	*Last dinner* 10.30	*Banquets* 100/4

Dun Laoghaire   Digby's   ♟ Ⓢ

Map 19 D4 Co. Dublin
5 Windsor Terrace
Dublin 804600

Lunch is served downstairs, dinner upstairs in this pretty seafront restaurant, owned and run by the capable, enthusiastic Cathcarts. Paul's seasonal menu shows great versatility, with imaginative ideas like mushroom and walnut soup and local plaice stuffed with crab alongside more familiar dishes such as spring lamb and spaghetti bolognese. The home-made ice creams are delicious, too. *Credit* Access, Amex, Barclaycard, Diners

Continued

Continued
About £27 for two
Banquets 50/12

Lunch 12–3 *Dinner* 7.15–11
Closed L Sat, all Sun, Good Friday & 24–26 December

Dun Laoghaire   Restaurant na Mara

Map 19 D4 Co. Dublin
1 Harbour Road
Dublin 806767
Manager Mr Bernard Nicholson
Seafood

This elegant salmon-pink restaurant, converted from the booking hall of a Victorian railway terminus, specialises in super-fresh seafood. Starters include Galway oysters, smoked eel and prawn chowder, while for main courses there's a wide range of shellfish, a number of classic sole recipes and specialities like seafood brochette with sauce américaine. Lovely homely desserts. *Credit* Access, Amex, Barclaycard, Diners

● **Set L** £6 & £8
Set D (Tues–Thurs) £12·95
About £40 for two

Lunch 1–2.30 *Dinner* 7–10.30 **Closed** Sun, Mon, Bank Holidays except 17 March 10 days Easter & 10 days Christmas

---

Dun Laoghaire   Oliver's

Map 19 D4 Co. Dublin
62 Upper Georges Street
Dublin 802204

Georgina Foley's excellent cooking and a friendly atmosphere make a meal here a most pleasant experience. After some Dublin Bay prawns or an interesting watercress and cucumber soup, you could enjoy a main course of plaice, lamb or steak, carefully prepared and served with excellent vegetables. Delicious sweets include a spirited chocolate mousse and home-made ice creams. *Credit* Access, Amex, Barclaycard, Diners

About £32 for two

Dinner only 7–10.45, Sun 7–10
Closed Good Friday, Easter Sunday & 24 & 25 December

Dundalk   Ballymascanlon Hotel   57%   Ⓜ   £E

Map 18 D3 Co. Louth
Dundalk 71124
Telex 33860
Proprietors Quinn family
Credit Access, Amex,
Barclaycard, Diners
Closed 25 December

The Quinn family are always on hand to look after the guests at their fine hotel set in attractive parkland. The well-proportioned lounge, handsome marble fireplaces and a grand oak staircase are reminders of its Victorian origins, while the compact bedrooms are comfortably contemporary.
Amenities garden, sauna, indoor swimming pool, tennis, squash, dancing (Sat, Sun), children's playground, solarium, gymnasium, billiards.

Rooms 40	*Room phone* Yes	*Confirm by* 6	*Parking* Ample
with bath/shower 37	*Room TV* No	*Last dinner* 9.30	*Banquets* 340/20

Prices quoted for Eire are in Irish punts

Dunderry   Dunderry Lodge Restaurant ★

Map 18 C3 Co. Meath
Robinstown, near Navan
Navan 31671
Proprietors Nicholas &
Catherine Healy

Booking is essential at this peaceful farmhouse restaurant, where you'll enjoy a truly delightful dinner prepared with skill and flair by Catherine Healy. Superbly fresh fish and seasonal game are offered as available, and our salmon with a spinach and sorrel sauce was unbeatable. Cervelle provençale and mushrooms in tarragon cream are popular starters, and main courses could include Dover sole with mussels, suprême of chicken and entrecôte béarnaise. Desserts are just as delicious, and service is charming and helpful. No pipes or cigars. **Specialities** terrine of crab, roast wild duck sauce groseille, cassolette of lamb's sweetbreads, summer pudding.
🍷*OUTSTANDING. Credit* Access, Amex, Barclaycard, Diners

● **Set D** £7·50
About £34 for two

Dinner only 7.30–9.30
Closed Sun, Mon, 1 week Easter, mid Aug–mid Sept & 22 Dec–2 Jan

---

Dungarvan   Seanachie

Map 19 C5 Co. Waterford
Ballymacart 35

Five miles west of Dungarvan on the N25, this delightful thatched pub provides simple, carefully prepared fare ranging from soup and pâté to seafood pancake, chicken mornay and traditional Irish stew.
Lunch 12–3 *Dinner* 6.30–9.30 **Closed** Sun & 1 November–Easter

About £26 for two
Banquets 60/20

Dunmore East
Map 19 C5 Co. Waterford
Near Waterford
Waterford 83215
Proprietors Charlie &
Antoinette Boland

● **Set L** Sun only £5·70
Set D £10·50
About £25 for two

Candlelight Inn

Seafood dishes, simply and deliciously prepared from the pick of the day's catch, are the stars of this cosy restaurant overlooking the harbour. Sprats, prawns, scallops, sole, turbot, lobster and salmon all appear on the menu, along with a few meat dishes, tasty starters like deep-fried mushrooms and homely desserts. Set menu only Sunday lunchtime.
Credit Access, Amex, Barclaycard

Lunch 12.30–2.30 *Dinner* 6–10, Sun 6–9.30
Closed 1 November–28 February

Ennis
Map 19 B4 Co. Clare
Station Road
Ennis 21127
Telex 28103

Credit Access, Amex,
Barclaycard, Diners

Rooms 63
with bath/shower 63

Old Ground Hotel   65%   £ C

Opposite the cathedral, this attractive ivy-clad hotel dates back in parts to the 17th century. There's a quiet elegance about the entrance foyer and the two lounges, with their antique furniture and paintings, and the function suite (once the town hall) is positively baronial. The cocktail bar is newly refurbished, and the comfortable, well-furnished bedrooms have up-to-date bathrooms. *Amenities* garden, 24-hour laundry service.

Room phone Yes	*Confirm by* 6	*Parking* Ample
Room TV Yes	*Last dinner* 9	*Banquets* 180/4

Ennis
Map 19 B4 Co. Clare
Clare Road
Ennis 21421
Telex 28294
Manager Mr John Madden
Credit Access, Amex,
Barclaycard, Diners

Rooms 120
with bath/shower 120

West County Inn   60%   £ E

An efficiently run modern hotel on the southern outskirts of the town. Public rooms include conference suites, a comfortable foyer-lounge and two bars, and for summer sipping there's a pleasant sunken garden. Cheerfully decorated bedrooms (original ones are smaller than the newer rooms) have smart fitted furniture and compact tiled bathrooms.
Amenities garden, dancing (Sat), Irish cabaret (Tues, Fri).

Room phone Yes	*Confirm by* 6	*Parking* Ample
Room TV Yes	*Last dinner* 9.15	*Banquets* 600/20

Galway
Map 19 B4 Co. Galway
Taylor's Hill
Galway 21433   Telex 28873
Manager Mr MacCarthy-O'Hea
Credit Access, Amex,
Barclaycard, Diners
Closed 1 week Christmas

Rooms 72
with bath/shower 72

Ardilaun House Hotel   62%   £ D/E

Modernisation has not detracted from the appeal of this comfortable, friendly hotel, which stands on the outskirts of the city in its own peaceful grounds. The foyer is attractive and welcoming, as are the chintzy lounge and the popular Blazers Bar. Cheerfully decorated bedrooms, many recently refurbished, have freestanding, mainly reproduction furniture and modern tiled bathrooms. *Amenities* garden, dancing (Sat).

Room phone Yes	*Confirm by* 5	*Parking* Ample
Room TV No	*Last dinner* 9	*Banquets* 100/10

Galway
Map 19 B4 Co. Galway
Dublin Road
Galway 65281   Telex 28844
Manager Mr Paul O'Connor
Credit Access, Amex,
Barclaycard, Diners
Closed 1 week Christmas

Rooms 113
with bath/shower 113

Corrib Great Southern Hotel   57%   £ D

A popular concrete-and-glass hotel, located just outside Galway on the Dublin road. Public rooms include streamlined reception-lounge, a TV lounge and a spacious bar with picture windows and fine views. Bright bedrooms with simple fitted units have compact, well-equipped bathrooms. *Amenities* garden, sauna, indoor swimming pool, bar entertainment (weekends), 24-hour laundry service (Mon–Sat), snooker, table tennis.

Room phone Yes	*Confirm by* 6	*Parking* Ample
Room TV No	*Last dinner* 9	*Banquets* 120/10

Galway
Map 19 B4 Co. Galway
Dublin Road
Galway 63181
Telex 28349

Credit Access, Amex,
Barclaycard, Diners

Galway Ryan Hotel   58%   £ D

On the outskirts of town, this low modern hotel is attractively designed, with a sunken lounge, full of potted plants, an eye-catching feature round which the public areas are arranged. There are also two smart bars and a cheerful coffee shop. Bright bedrooms all feature extra beds for families and have roomy modern bathrooms. *Amenities* garden, bar entertainment (nightly), children's playroom, coffee shop (noon–9.30pm).

Continued

Continued
Rooms 96
with bath/shower 96

Room phone Yes
Room TV No

Confirm by 6
Last dinner 9.30

Parking Ample
Banquets 150/10

Galway
Map 19 B4 Co. Galway
Eyre Square
Galway 64041
Telex 28364

Credit Access, Amex,
Barclaycard, Diners

Great Southern Hotel   66%   £ C

This elegant Victorian hotel in the city centre has been carefully modernised over the years. Its reception hall and lounge are spacious and comfortable, and there are two stylish bars. Freshly decorated bedrooms have smart reproduction furniture and luxuriously equipped bathrooms. *Amenities* sauna, indoor swimming pool, discothèque & night club (Tues–Sun), cabaret (Wed, Thurs in summer), in-house video, coffee shop (7.30am–11pm).

Rooms 120
with bath/shower 120

Room phone Yes
Room TV Yes

Confirm by 6
Last dinner 10.30

Parking Limited
Banquets 480/10

Gap of Dunloe
Map 19 A5 Co. Kerry
Beaufort
Killarney 44111
Telex 28233

Rooms 143
with bath/shower 143
Room phone Yes
Room TV No
Confirm by By arrang.
Last dinner 9.15
Parking Ample
Banquets 190/4
Closed end October–Easter

Credit Access, Amex,
Barclaycard, Diners

Dunloe Castle   82%   £ E

Luxurious modern comfort and a wide range of indoor and outdoor facilities are the attractions of this smart hotel by the spectacular Gap of Dunloe. A spacious entrance hall with a polished tiled floor leads to the cool airy bar attractively fitted with good reproduction furniture; there are also several comfortable lounges (one with TV). Bedrooms are maintained in excellent condition and have simple contemporary furniture. Large, well-equipped bathrooms. *Amenities* garden, sauna, indoor swimming pool, tennis, game fishing, entertainment (Thurs), 24-hour laundry service, coffee shop (noon–7pm), pitch & putt, golf driving range, croquet, table tennis, badminton, riding.

Glen of Aherlow
Map 19 B5 Co. Tipperary
Tipperary 56153

Credit Access, Amex,
Barclaycard, Diners
Closed 25 December

Aherlow House Hotel   64%   £ E

Streams flow through the wooded grounds of this converted private house in the shadow of the Gatty Mountains. The entrance hall leads to the large bar-lounge with antique furniture and hunting mementoes, and there's a TV lounge as well as a vast sun terrace. Individually decorated bedrooms have a mixture of modern and period furniture, and bathrooms are fully carpeted. *Amenities* garden, coarse fishing, discothèque (Fri).

Rooms 10
with bath/shower 10

Room phone Yes
Room TV No

Confirm by 7
Last dinner 9.15

Parking Ample
Banquets 500/10

Glengarriff
Map 19 A6 Co. Cork
Glengarriff 10

Proprietor Miss M. Deasy

Closed 30 September–Easter

Casey's Hotel   50% Ⓜ   £ E

This immaculate family-run hotel in a sleepy fishing village is ideal for a quiet holiday. The Deasys have been here for three generations, and May Deasy provides a warm welcome. There's a lofty old-fashioned lounge where guests can relax in the inviting armchairs, and gleaming corridors lead to homely bedrooms with solid traditional furnishings. Simple bathrooms are nicely tiled and papered. No dogs. *Amenities* garden.

Rooms 20
with bath/shower 4

Room phone No
Room TV No

Confirm by By arrang.
Last dinner 8.30

Parking Ample

Glounthaune
Map 19 B6 Co. Cork
Cork 953319

Credit Access, Amex,
Barclaycard, Diners

Rooms 27
with bath/shower 25

Ashbourne House Hotel   60%   Ⓜ   £ E

This rambling 19th-century country house stands back from the main road in extensive botanical gardens of rare beauty. There's an attractive panelled foyer, and the residents' lounge and bar have plush, comfortable seating. Good-sized bedrooms have built-in units, and some have duvets; bathrooms are modern. *Amenities* garden, sauna, outdoor swimming pool, tennis, croquet, putting, folk music (Fri June–September).

Room phone Yes	*Confirm by* By arrang.	*Parking* Ample
Room TV Most	*Last dinner* 9.30	*Banquets* 120/2

Prices quoted for Eire are in Irish punts

Gorey
Map 19 D5 Co. Wexford
Gorey 21124

Rooms 11
with bath/shower 11
Room phone Yes
Room TV No
Confirm by 6
Last dinner 9.30
Parking Ample
Banquets 35/2
Closed mid December–mid February

Marlfield House Hotel   74%   Ⓜ   £ D/E

Mrs Bowe and her staff have a really warm welcome for guests at this fine Regency country house, where high standards of decor, comfort and service are maintained. Antiques, paintings and crystal chandeliers grace the spacious public rooms (most of them overlooking the pretty gardens) and the bar, with its warming log fire and comfortable armchairs, is a particularly pleasant spot. A handsome wide staircase leads up to the superb bedrooms, which feature colourful wallpaper, lovely coordinated fabrics and a wealth of antique furniture. Bathrooms have attractive tiles and excellent modern fittings (most have bidets). No children under five. No dogs. *Amenities* garden, tennis.

Gorey
Map 19 D5 Co. Wexford
Gorey 21124

About £31 for two

Marlfield House Hotel Restaurant   ♣ ♕ ⓢ

Seafood takes pride of place at Mary Bowe's friendly restaurant, with appealing items like goujons of monkfish and beautifully fresh salmon. There are also pâtés, soups, a few meat and chicken dishes, and some tempting desserts. 🍷 *ABOVE AVERAGE. Dinner only* 7.30–9.30
Closed 15 December–15 February ● **Set D** £13   &♿

Howth
Map 19 D4 Co. Dublin
East Pier, Harbour Road
Dublin 325235
Proprietor Mr Aidan MacManus
Seafood

About £32 for two
Banquets 18/10

King Sitric   ♣ ⓢ

There's always a warm welcome at this simple, well-loved seafood restaurant, where many of the beautifully fresh ingredients are landed on the quay right opposite. Preparation is excellent, and the menu ranges from oysters, mussels, squid and fish soup to brill à l'orange and monkfish Wellington. Some meat dishes, too, and excellent ice cream and meringues to finish.  *SUPERIOR. Credit* Access, Amex, Diners

Dinner only 6.30–11.15
Closed Sun, Bank Holidays & 12 days Christmas

Kanturk
Map 19 B5 Co. Cork
Assolas
Kanturk 15
Proprietors
Hugh & Eleanore Bourke

Closed October–Easter

Rooms 7
with bath/shower 6

Assolas Country House   64%   Ⓜ   £ E

A lovely garden complete with a lake and a river surrounds this peaceful old house, where the Bourkes are the most congenial hosts. There's a flagstoned entrance-lounge, and guests can relax and enjoy a drink in the exquisitely furnished drawing room. Neat, homely bedrooms in traditional style have a few antiques here and there. Adequate bathrooms. No dogs. *Amenities* garden, tennis, coarse & game fishing, croquet, games room, hotel boats.

Room phone No	*Confirm by* 6	*Parking* Ample
Room TV No	*Last dinner* 8	

Kenmare
Map 19 A6 Co. Kerry
Kenmare 41300
Telex 28180

Credit Access, Amex,
Barclaycard, Diners

Rooms 100
with bath/shower 100

Kenmare Bay Hotel 58% £E

Popular with Continental coach parties, this smoothly run glass and concrete hotel stands just outside the town centre. The flagstoned entrance features a tropical fish tank, and there is an attractive Scandinavian-style bar-lounge, as well as a small TV lounge. Best bedrooms are large and smartly furnished, with good units and matching fabrics; bathrooms are bright and well kept. *Amenities* garden.

Room phone Yes	*Confirm by* 6	*Parking* Ample
Room TV No	*Last dinner* 9	*Banquets* 200/–

Kenmare
Map 19 A6 Co. Kerry
Killarney 41200
Telex 70005

Rooms 50
with bath/shower 50
Room phone Yes
Room TV Some
Confirm by 6
Last dinner 9.30
Parking Ample
Banquets 30/12

Credit Access, Amex,
Barclaycard, Diners

Park Hotel 88% £C/D

The many attractions of this splendid Victorian hotel include a position of great beauty overlooking sea and mountains and friendly, efficient service from a likeable young team. Public rooms are a model of sumptuous elegance, with beautiful paintings, marble fireplaces, rich curtains and a stylish combination of fine antiques and excellent reproduction furniture. Comfortable bedrooms range from graceful and traditional to more modern with built-in units; there are also eight luxurious suites, some with four-posters. Bright, modern bathrooms with Italian marble tiling are comprehensively equipped.
Amenities garden, tennis, dancing (Fri & Mon in season), games room.

Kenmare
Map 19 A6 Co. Kerry
Killarney 41200

● **Set L** £8·25 **Set D** £15
incl. service
About £45 for two
Banquets 30/4

Park Hotel Restaurant ★ ♛♛ ⑤

Colin O'Daly is making his mark at this elegant, spacious restaurant, matching his high cooking skills with a brilliant eye for presentation. The long French menu includes many unusual and imaginative dishes: our Irish smoked salmon with delicate sea-urchin quenelles was a superb starter, and main courses range from perfectly poached sole with lobster sauce to sirloin of beef with stuffed vine leaves or breast of chicken with pine-kernel sauce. Desserts are delicious, too, and you can sample several in a special chef's selection. **Specialities** feuilleté de gras-double à la sauge, escalope de saumon au pouliot, palet de nos desserts.
🍷 *SUPERIOR. Credit* Access, Amex, Barclaycard, Diners

Lunch 1–2 *Dinner* 7–9

Kenmare
Map 19 A6 Co. Kerry
Henry Street
Kenmare 41016
Proprietor Grainne O'Connel
Seafood
About £27 for two

Purple Heather ♧

Skilfully prepared seafood is served at tables in the bar of this modest pub. Dishes ranging from cod mornay to scallops in wine sauce are full of natural flavour, and there's a choice of simple sweets.
Lunch 12.30–2.30 *Dinner* 6–8.30
Closed Sun & mid October–Easter

Kilkenny
Map 19 C5 Co. Kilkenny
Castlecomer Road
Kilkenny 22122   Telex 80080
Proprietors Bobby Kerr,
John Walsh & Aidan Prior
Credit Access, Amex,
Barclaycard, Diners

Newpark Hotel 60% Ⓜ £C/D

The Scandinavian-style reception and large, intimately lit bar area designed by one of the owners of this hotel are especially attractive, and the setting in 50 acres of parkland is a pleasant one. Colourful bedrooms in the wing have modern units and compact private bathrooms, while those in the main building are more simply furnished. *Amenities* garden, tennis, discothèque (Tues, Sun), children's playground, grill room (12.30pm–11pm).

Continued

| Rooms 46 | Room phone Yes | Confirm by 6 | Parking Ample |
| with bath/shower 38 | Room TV Most | Last dinner 11 | Banquets 500/10 |

Killarney

Map 19 A5 Co. Kerry
Killarney 31766
Telex 26942
Managers Mr Louis O'Hara &
Miss Sandra Williamson
Credit Access, Amex, Barclaycard
Closed 19 December–20 January

Aghadoe Heights Hotel 66% Ⓜ £C/D

Picture windows make the most of the superb lake and mountain views from this well-kept hilltop hotel. Clean modern design characterises the public areas, which include a comfortable entrance lounge and a large bar. Spacious, neatly fitted bedrooms are also up to date, with good bathrooms. *Amenities* garden, tennis, coarse & game fishing, dancing (6 nights weekly in summer, Fri, Sat in winter), 24-hour laundry service. ♿

| Rooms 55 | Room phone Yes | Confirm by 6 | Parking Ample |
| with bath/shower 55 | Room TV Yes | Last dinner 9.30 | Banquets 80/– |

Killarney

Map 19 A5 Co. Kerry
Mucross Road
Killarney 31895
Telex 28123
Manager Mr Denis Tucker
Credit Access, Amex,
Barclaycard, Diners

Cahernane Hotel 69% £D/E

An elegant foyer with a panelled ceiling, a carved staircase and an ornate fireplace preserves the Victorian character of this fine greystone mansion. There are also two gracious lounges and a striking cellar bar. Bedrooms vary from solidly traditional rooms–some smartly refurbished–in the main building to simple modern ones in the extension. *Amenities* garden, tennis, game fishing, pitch & putt, croquet. **Closed** 1 October–1 April ♿

| Rooms 37 | Room phone Yes | Confirm by By arrang. | Parking Ample |
| with bath/shower 37 | Room TV No | Last dinner 9.30 | Banquets 95/10 |

Killarney

Map 19 A5 Co. Kerry
Mucross Road
Killarney 31895
Manager Mr Denis Tucker

Cahernane Hotel, Pembroke Room ♛ Ⓢ

Skilful cooking produces consistently enjoyable results at this intimate little restaurant with friendly, attentive service. The menu ranges near and far to include dishes like pâté with Cumberland sauce, local salmon, Irish stew, richly sauced seafood pancakes, steak Diane and Hungarian goulash. Vegetables are carefully handled, and there are some tempting desserts. Shorter lunch menu. *Credit* Access, Amex, Barclaycard, Diners

● **Set L** from £5 **Set D** from £8
About £32 for two

Lunch 1–2.30 *Dinner* 7–9.30
Closed 1 October–1 April

Killarney

Map 19 A5 Co. Kerry
Killarney 31144
Telex 70010

Credit Access, Amex,
Barclaycard, Diners
Closed January & February

Castlerosse Hotel 57% £D

Right beside a championship golf course, this low whitewashed motel enjoys splendid views across Lough Leane to the mountains beyond. There's a reception hall with TV and an airy lounge with a Scandinavian-style timbered ceiling. Well-kept bedrooms have lightwood panelling, fitted units and partly tiled bathrooms. *Amenities* garden, outdoor swimming pool, tennis, bar entertainment (most nights in season), petrol pumps, games room. ♿

| Rooms 42 | Room phone Yes | Confirm by 6 | Parking Ample |
| with bath/shower 42 | Room TV No | Last dinner 9.30 | Banquets 200/10 |

Killarney

Map 19 A5 Co. Kerry
Fossa
Killarney 31900
Telex 28213

Rooms 175
with bath/shower 175
Room phone Yes
Room TV No
Confirm by 8
Last dinner 9.30
Parking Ample
Banquets 500/12
Closed December–February

Hotel Europe 73% £E

A beautiful lakeside setting with lovely views of the mountains is just one of the attractions of this comfortable modern hotel. Picture windows enhance

Continued

Continued *Credit* Access, Amex, Barclaycard, Diners	the spacious, traditionally furnished public rooms, many of which boast Persian carpets, French prints and fine antiques. There are several airy lounges, two bars and extensive conference facilities. Bedrooms are simply but pleasantly decorated, with attractive modern furniture and luxuriously appointed bathrooms, many with bidets. Front rooms have balconies overlooking the lake. *Amenities* garden, sauna, indoor swimming pool, game fishing, discothèque (twice weekly), entertainment (nightly June–September), health centre, billiards, riding, hairdressing, boating.

Killarney — Hotel Europe, Panorama Restaurant 

Map 19 A5 Co. Kerry
Fossa
Killarney 31900

A large, bright restaurant, whose enormous picture windows offer spectacular vistas of the lake and mountains beyond. The capable German chef Willi Steinbeck offers an interesting selection of international dishes ranging from Irish cabbage soup and finely textured liver pâté to fresh local seafood – including scallops, lobster and sole – and succulent veal steak.
Credit Access, Amex, Barclaycard, Diners

● **Set L** £7·50 **Set D** £11
incl. service
About £35 for two

Lunch 12.30–2 *Dinner* 7–9.30
Closed December–February

Killarney — Gaby's 

Map 19 A5 Co. Kerry
17 High Street
Killarney 32519
Proprietor Ireen Maes
Seafood
About £33 for two

A friendly family-run seafood restaurant, where you can choose your lobster from a tank or enjoy a speciality such as scallops maison or black sole meunière. Fillet steak for meat-eaters. ♥ *SUPERIOR*.
Lunch 12.30–3 *Dinner* 6–10 **Closed** L Sun & Mon, June & August Bank Holiday Suns & 15 December–15 March

Killarney — Great Southern Hotel   67%   £ D

Map 19 A5 Co. Kerry
Killarney 31262
Telex 26998
Manager Dennis A. Hurley

Credit Access, Amex,
Barclaycard, Diners

Pillars and chandeliers are features of the lounge of this grand Victorian hotel, and the cocktail bar has a marble fireplace. Bedrooms in the original part are comfortably appointed in traditional style; those in the extension have modern units. *Amenities* garden, sauna, indoor swimming pool, tennis, cabaret (6 nights weekly in summer), putting, 24-hour lounge service, massage, table tennis, valeting, 24-hour laundry service.

Rooms 180 *with bath/shower* 180	*Room phone* Yes *Room TV* Most	*Confirm by* 6 *Last dinner* 10.30	*Parking* Ample *Banquets* 550/–

Killarney — Torc Great Southern Hotel   61%   £ D

Map 19 A5 Co. Kerry
Park Road
Killarney 31611
Telex 28207
Credit Access, Amex,
Barclaycard, Diners
Closed October–March

Light, airy and functional, this popular, well-run glass and metal hotel dates from the late '60s. Modern paintings and potted plants adorn the public areas, which include an open-plan foyer-lounge and a bar with comfortable cane furniture. Good-sized bedrooms have simple white units and well-equipped bathrooms with bidets. No dogs. *Amenities* garden, sauna, indoor swimming pool, tennis, entertainment (Mon, Wed, Sat).

Rooms 96 *with bath/shower* 96	*Room phone* Yes *Room TV* Some	*Confirm by* 6 *Last dinner* 9	*Parking* Ample

Prices quoted for Eire are in Irish punts

Killiney — Court Hotel   69%      £ D

Map 19 D4 Co. Dublin
Killiney Bay
Dublin 851622
Telex 33244
Manager Mr N. Kenny
Credit Amex

This friendly, well-run hotel is an impressive Victorian building standing in pleasant gardens overlooking Killiney Bay. A comfortable cocktail bar leads off the little reception area, while upstairs there's a spacious, traditionally furnished bar-lounge. The 25 bedrooms in a modern wing are the best, with attractive built-in wooden units and luxuriously appointed bathrooms. *Amenities* garden, squash, discothèque (Sun).

Rooms 34 *with bath/shower* 34	*Room phone* Yes *Room TV* Yes	*Confirm by* 7.30 *Last dinner* 10.30	*Parking* Ample *Banquets* 250/–

Killiney
Map 19 D4 Co. Dublin
Dublin 851533
Telex 230353
Proprietor Mr P. Fitzpatrick

Rooms 48
with bath/shower 48
Room phone Yes
Room TV Yes
Confirm by By arrang.
Last dinner 10.45
Parking Ample
Banquets 290/10

Credit Access, Amex,
Barclaycard, Diners

Fitzpatrick Castle Hotel   71%      £ C

A well-run hotel, whose public rooms like the long lounge and smart cocktail bar have a Victorian opulence, with lots of velvet, leather and mahogany. Spacious bedrooms vary considerably, from functional and modern to luxurious four-poster rooms with fully equipped bathrooms. *Amenities* garden, sauna, indoor swimming pool, tennis, squash, dancing (Sat Sept–Feb), pitch & putt, grill room (noon–midnight), hairdressing, beauty salon.

Killiney
Map 19 D4 Co. Dublin
Dublin 851329
Proprietors Mr & Mrs Rolland
French cooking

● **Set D** £10·50 & £12·50
About £35 for two
Banquets 45/20

Rolland   

Henri Rolland cooks and his wife Helena takes good care of guests in this cheerful, cosy restaurant. The two fixed-price menus offer enjoyable French dishes like tasty monkfish Américaine or sautéed kidneys with mustard sauce, as well as steaks and seasonal game. There's also a small selection of tempting sweets such as poached pears and tangy lemon cheesecake.
Credit Amex, Barclaycard, Diners

Dinner only 7–10
Closed Sun, Mon, Bank Holidays, 1st week July & 1 week August

---

Kinsale
Map 19 B6 Co. Cork
Cork 72135
Telex 32443

Credit Access, Amex,
Barclaycard, Diners

Rooms 59
with bath/shower 48

Actons Hotel   60%   £ D

Separated from the quayside by its trim lawns and swimming pool, this popular holiday hotel, converted from a row of handsome town houses, commands fine views over the estuary towards the sea. Public rooms like the lounge and bars have an unfussy appeal, and bedrooms are neat and comfortable, with modern built-in units; bathrooms are adequate. *Amenities* garden, outdoor swimming pool, games room, children's play area.

Room phone Yes | *Confirm by* 6 | *Parking* Ample
Room TV Yes | *Last dinner* 8.30 | *Banquets* 40/2

Kinsale
Map 19 B6 Co. Cork
Guardwell
Cork 72470
Proprietor Mrs Heide Roche

About £32 for two
Banquets 50/20

Bistro   

This smart, attractive restaurant is noted for the very capable cooking of its German chef, whose extensive menu gives equal billing to seafood and meat. Specialities range from Kinsale oysters, superb scallop soup and poached salmon with hollandaise sauce to carpetbag steak, roast quail with juniper sauce and duckling à l'orange. Vegetables are carefully cooked, and sweets are based mainly on ice cream. *Credit* Access, Barclaycard

Dinner only 7.30–10.30
Closed Mon & end January–end February

Kinsale
Map 19 B6 Co. Cork
Long Quay
Cork 72209
Proprietors Anne & Brian Cronin
Credit Access, Amex,
Barclaycard, Diners
Closed 24 & 25 December

Rooms 12
with bath/shower 1

Blue Haven Hotel *(Inn)*      £ E

Anne and Brian Cronin make visitors feel most welcome at their pretty blue and white hostelry in the centre of town. The cosy little TV lounge is furnished in modern style and there's an attractive L-shaped bar bedecked with nautical mementoes. Bedrooms, all with washbasins, are cheerful, neat and tidy, and the compact public bathrooms are adequately equipped. No dogs.

Room phone No | *Confirm by* By arrang. | *Parking* Limited
Room TV No | *Last dinner* 10 | *Banquets* 55/6

Kinsale
Map 19 B6 Co. Cork
Long Quay
Cork 72209
Proprietors
Anne & Brian Cronin
Seafood

About £36 for two

Blue Haven Hotel Restaurant

Fresh seafood is the mainstay of the menu in this cosy, stone-walled restaurant. Attractive, carefully prepared dishes range from brill with shrimps and capers to monkfish with Irish Mist; meat lovers might choose escalopes of beef with green noodles and mead sauce. Starters include a delightful courgette and celery soup, and strawberry gâteau makes a good finish.
Credit Access, Amex, Barclaycard, Diners

Dinner only 7–10, Sat 7–10.30
Closed 31 October–28 February

Kinsale
Map 19 B6 Co. Cork
Scilly
Cork 72260

About £32 for two

Man Friday

Feel transported to the tropics in this relaxing restaurant decked out like a Caribbean log cabin. The cooking is equally colourful and exotic, with a choice of dishes from all over the world: rich, sweet Chinese beef and Polynesian pork kebabs exist happily alongside steak au poivre, sole Colbert and veal zurichoise. There are firm, fresh vegetables, too, and home-made ice creams. *ABOVE AVERAGE. Credit* Access, Barclaycard

Dinner only 7.30–10 **Closed** Sun, also Mon in winter, Good Friday, 2 weeks February & 1 week Christmas

Kinsale
Map 19 B6 Co. Cork
Lower O'Connell Street
Cork 72664
Proprietors
Tony & Kieran Greenway

● **Set L** Sun only £5·50 **Set D** £8
About £29 for two
Banquets 45/6

Skipper's

An informal and friendly bistro-style restaurant attached to a wine bar. The Greenway brothers produce carefully prepared dishes ranging from superb monkfish with a seafood sauce to poached salmon with cucumber sauce and shredded beef with green peppers. Sweets might include a delicious orange cheesecake. Weekday lunches (summer only) offer a selection of cold seafood. *Credit* (dinner only) Access, Amex, Barclaycard, Diners

Lunch Sun 1–3, Mon–Sat in summer only *Dinner* 7.30–10.30
Closed D Sun & Mon, last 2 weeks February & last 2 weeks November

Kinsale
Map 19 B6 Co. Cork
Main Street
Cork 72502
Proprietors
Gerry & Marie Galvin

About £35 for two
Banquets 25/10

Vintage

Gerry and Marie Galvin have devised an imaginative and varied menu at their pretty beamed restaurant. Fresh seafood features in dishes like mussel soup and baked crab cakes, and there are plenty of other choices, ranging from oxtail pâté to Japanese-style chicken and beautifully tender loin of lamb with onion stuffing. Desserts include home-made ice creams and sorbets.
*SUPERIOR. Credit* Access, Barclaycard

Dinner only 7–10.30
Closed Tues, Wed & beginning November–end February

Letterfrack
Map 18 A3 Co. Galway
Moyard 7

Proprietors Foyle family

Closed November–Easter

Rosleague Manor Hotel 61%  £ E

Beautifully situated overlooking Ballynakill Bay, the Foyles' secluded country house is a peaceful, tranquil retreat. The lounge has solid Victorian furnishings and an elegant marble fireplace, whereas the bar is plainer and more modern. Bedrooms, too, vary in style, but all are pleasantly decorated and well furnished. Bathrooms have up-to-date equipment. Friendly owners and staff. *Amenities* garden, sauna.

Rooms 17	*Room phone* No	*Confirm by* By arrang.	*Parking* Ample
with bath/shower 15	*Room TV* No	*Last dinner* 9.30	*Banquets* 80/10

Letterfrack
Map 18 A3 Co. Galway
Moyard 7

Proprietors Foyle family

Rosleague Manor Hotel Restaurant

Four-course set menus offer first-class simple fare in this light, well-proportioned restaurant. Sea-fresh fish tops the bill—perhaps grilled black sole or turbot hollandaise—and other choices could include quiche lorraine or turkey and sorrel soup, and main courses like baked gammon or roast duckling. Delicious desserts and excellent coffee. Cold buffet only on Sunday. *ABOVE AVERAGE.*

Continued

● **Set D** from £9·50
About £26 for two

Dinner only 8–9.30, Sun at 7.30
Closed November–Easter

Limerick
Map 19 B5 Co. Limerick
Ennis Road
Limerick 53033
Manager Mr T. Murphy
Credit Access, Amex,
Barclaycard, Diners
Closed 25 December

Greenhills Hotel   60%   £ D/E

An extensive refurbishment programme is greatly improving this neat modern hotel fronted by palm trees. Relax in the comfortable entrance lounge or in the bright, split-level bar. Stylish bedrooms, which include 30 in a new wing, have deep green carpeting and smart fitted units, and compact bathrooms are well equipped. No dogs.
Amenities garden, discothèque (Thurs–Sun), in-house video.   &

Rooms 55
with bath/shower 55

Room phone Yes
Room TV Yes

Confirm by 6
Last dinner 12

Parking Ample
Banquets 520/10

Limerick
Map 19 B5 Co. Limerick
Ennis Road
Limerick 55266
Telex 28266
Manager Mr Brendan Gallagher
Credit Access, Amex,
Barclaycard, Diners

Jurys Hotel   65%   £ C

Close to the centre of town, this comfortable modern hotel is especially popular with business people. The lounge with its glass-topped tables and potted plants is very relaxing, and there's a smart bar. Large bedrooms feature good lighting and writing space, and bathrooms with shower attachments are well equipped. Guide dogs only. *Amenities* garden, in-house video, valeting, 24-hour laundry service (Mon–Fri), coffee shop (7am–11pm).   &

Rooms 96
with bath/shower 96

Room phone Yes
Room TV Yes

Confirm by 6
Last dinner 11.30

Parking Ample

Limerick
Map 19 B5 Co. Limerick
Ennis Road
Limerick 51544
Telex 28121
Manager Mr Matt Sherlock
Credit Access, Amex,
Barclaycard, Diners

Limerick Inn   69%   £ C

Near Shannon Airport, this well-kept modern hotel in smart Mediterranean style provides excellent comfort. The chintzy lounge and warmly decorated bar are very relaxing, and large bedrooms are attractively furnished, with first-rate bathrooms. *Amenities* garden, tennis, dancing (Wed, Fri, Sat June–September), transport to airport & Limerick, children's playground, putting, grill room (7.30am–11pm), 24-hour laundry service, in-house video.   &

Rooms 133
with bath/shower 133

Room phone Yes
Room TV Yes

Confirm by 6
Last dinner 10

Parking Ample
Banquets 600/6

Malahide
Map 18 D3 Co. Dublin
9 St James's Terrace
Dublin 452206
Proprietors
Mr & Mrs Johnny Oppermann

Johnny's   ♚ ⓢ

Johnny Oppermann can be seen at work in the kitchen of this smart cellar restaurant producing the tempting dishes on his seasonal menu. Choices range from subtle crabmeat with Pernod and garlicky hot mushrooms to tender breast of duck with a bittersweet orange, lemon and port sauce. Excellent vegetables, too. Gentlemen should wear jackets and ties.
🍷*ABOVE AVERAGE. Credit* Access, Amex, Barclaycard, Diners   &

About £37 for two

Dinner only 7.30–10.30
Closed Sun, Mon, 4 days Christmas, 1 week Easter & 1 Sept–mid Oct

---

Mallow
Map 19 B5 Co. Cork
Mallow 27156
Proprietors
Michael & Jane O'Callaghan

Rooms 18
with bath/shower 18
Room phone No
Room TV No
Confirm by 6
Last dinner 8.30
Parking Ample
Banquets 30/10
Closed mid October–Easter

Longueville House   74% Ⓜ   £ D/E

It's a real pleasure to stay at Michael and Jane O'Callaghan's lovely hotel, an impressive mansion set in secluded woodland and offering peace, comfort,

Continued

Continued

country-house elegance and polite, friendly service. The lofty entrance hall with its flagstoned floor and sweeping staircase is splendidly baronial, and its dignity is matched by the imposing library and a relaxing drawing room with fine antiques, oil paintings, beautiful mirrors and an elaborate plastered ceiling. Attractively decorated bedrooms are bright and spacious, with antique beds and wardrobes and well-designed, fully modernised bathrooms. No children under 12 or dogs.
Amenities garden, coarse & game fishing, games room.

Mallow
Map 19 B5 Co. Cork
Mallow 27156
Proprietors
Michael & Jane O'Callaghan

Longueville House, President's Rest.

Full of bounce and charm, Mrs O'Callaghan not only cooks with flair but finds time to chat to customers in her elegant restaurant. The four-course set-price dinner menu offers a good choice of dishes based on first-class ingredients—local salmon is particularly good—and prepared with skill and imagination. Vegetables are fresh and crisp, and desserts light and refreshing.
SUPERIOR.

● **Set D** £13·50
About £35 for two

Dinner only 7–8.30, Sun 7–8
Closed Sun, Mon & mid October–Easter

Monkstown
Map 19 D4 Co. Dublin
Monkstown Crescent
Dublin 805174

Abbot of Monkstown

A cool atmosphere pervades this light modern restaurant, where the seasonal menu offers a varied choice of well-prepared dishes. Some, like brill with white wine and herbs, are French-inspired while others, such as velvety home-smoked mackerel and apple mousse or a stuffed chicken breast crêpe with creamy tarragon sauce, show real touches of inventiveness. Helpful service. *Credit* Access, Amex, Barclaycard

● **Set L** from £6
About £43 for two

Lunch 12.30–2.30 *Dinner* 6.30–10.30
Closed Sun, Bank Holidays & 24 December–2 January

Moyard
Map 18 A3 Co. Galway
Connemara
Moyard 9

Proprietor Joanne Fretwell
Credit Amex, Barclaycard
Closed end October–1 April

Crocnaraw 61% Ⓜ £E

Twenty acres of lovely gardens are an appropriate setting for Joanne Fretwell's delightful Georgian house. Open fires and deep, comfortable chairs give a warm, homely air to the lounges, where guests can relax with a book or a drink. Charming bedrooms vary in size and decor, and furnishings range from antiques to modern. Bathrooms are adequate. Excellent housekeeping. *Amenities* garden, game fishing, croquet, riding.

Rooms 10	*Room phone* No	*Confirm by* 6	*Parking* Ample
with bath/shower 6	*Room TV* No	*Last dinner* 9.45	

Moyard
Map 18 A3 Co. Galway
Moyard 21
Proprietors
Moira & Fraser Stephenson
Seafood
About £18 for two

Doon

Freshly caught seafood is simply prepared with delicious results in Moira and Fraser Stephenson's welcoming little cottage restaurant. Daily lunch menus might also offer excellent home-made vegetable soup and sweets like rich chocolate mousse. *Lunch only* 12–3 **Closed** Wed (except July & August) & 2nd week October–Easter

---

Moycullen
Map 19 B4 Co. Galway
Galway 85109
Proprietors
Mr B. Casey & Mr S. Deviney

About £31 for two

Silver Teal

Delicious fried crab claws and tasty pork in a cream and mushroom sauce are typical examples of this homely restaurant's careful handling of good local produce. Vegetables and simple sweets are equally appetising. *Credit* Amex
Lunch 12.30–2.30, Sun 12.30–2 *Dinner* 6.30–10.30, Sun 6.30–9.30 **Closed** Good Friday & 4 days Christmas ● **Set L** £5·50 **Set D** Mon–Fri £8·90

Navan
Map 18 C3 Co. Meath
Dublin Road
Navan 23119

Credit Access, Amex,
Barclaycard

Ardboyne Hotel 57% £E/F

The small-paned windows give a mock-Dickensian atmosphere to the bar at one end of the spacious foyer-lounge of this modern hotel perched high above the river Boyne. The good conference and banqueting facilities attract businessmen, who also appreciate the neat, functional bedrooms with ample writing space and well-equipped tiled bathrooms. No dogs. *Amenities* garden, discothèque (Wed, Fri, Sun), grill room (7.30am–10.15pm).

Continued

Rooms 26	*Room phone* Yes	*Confirm by* 6	*Parking* Ample
with bath/shower 26	*Room TV* Yes	*Last dinner* 10.15	*Banquets* 400/10

New Ross
Map 19 C5 Wexford
The Quay
New Ross 21723
Proprietor Mr R. Fletcher

● **Set L** £10 **Set D** £17·50,
incl. service
About £38 for two
Banquets 88/By arrang.

Galley Cruising Restaurant ⑤

The wooded scenery along the banks of the river Barrow is part of the pleasure of eating aboard this cruising restaurant. The set menus (three-course lunch and four-course dinner plus fruit and coffee) include simple, enjoyable food such as a tasty pâté or creamy home-made soup, and much use is made of local produce like fresh salmon and Irish cheeses. Booking is essential. Polite, friendly service.

Lunch 12.30–2.30 *Dinner* 7–10
Closed D Sun, all Mon & November–March

Newbridge
Map 19 C4 Co. Kildare
Newbridge 31666
Telex 24326
Proprietors Mr & Mrs O'Loughlin
Credit Access, Amex,
Barclaycard, Diners
Closed 25 & 26 December

Hotel Keadeen 64% Ⓜ £E

This converted private house not far from the Curragh racecourse has benefited from recent refurbishment. A spacious reception hall leads to the smart lounge and cocktail bar, and there's another bar with an Edwardian theme. Large bedrooms (in single-storey wings built round a courtyard) have matching floral fabrics and wallpaper and reproduction furniture. Compact bathrooms. *Amenities* garden, dancing (Sun, also some Sats).   &

Rooms 35	*Room phone* Yes	*Confirm by* 6	*Parking* Ample
with bath/shower 35	*Room TV* Yes	*Last dinner* 10	*Banquets* 500/10

Newmarket-on-Fergus Clare Inn 76% £D
Map 19 B4 Co. Clare
Shannon 71161
Telex 24025
Manager Miss Mary Vaughan

Rooms 121
with bath/shower 121
Room phone Yes
Room TV No
Confirm by 6
Last dinner 9
Parking Ample
Banquets 300/10

Credit Access, Amex,
Barclaycard, Diners

There are sweeping views across the Shannon estuary from the tall arched windows of this long, low hotel. Cheerfully decorated public rooms include two traditionally furnished lounges, one a regular suntrap, and a large bar. Bedrooms are spacious, with fresh, attractive decor, comfortable beds and cosy armchairs. Bathrooms are well equipped. No dogs. *Amenities* garden, 9-hole golf course, entertainment (nightly), cabaret (Thurs, Sat).   &

Newmarket-on-Fergus Dromoland Castle 83% £B
Map 19 B4 Co. Clare
Shannon 71144
Telex 26854

Manager Miss P. Barry
Rooms 67
with bath/shower 67
Room phone Yes
Room TV No
Confirm by 5
Last dinner 9
Parking Ample
Banquets 160/8
Closed 2 November–late March

Credit Access, Amex,
Barclaycard, Diners

Like something out of a fairy tale, this splendid turreted castle stands in lovely parkland complete with its own lake. Oil portraits, crystal chandeliers, rich carpets and fine furnishings grace the magnificent entrance hall and sumptuous lounges, and there's a stately bar with a huge gilded mirror and ornate plasterwork. Cheerfully decorated bedrooms have smart contemporary furniture and well-equipped tiled bathrooms. The largest rooms are in

Continued

Continued

the turrets, while some overlook a pretty courtyard. Housekeeping is immaculate. No dogs, but kennels are available.
Amenities garden, sauna, tennis, 9-hole golf course, coarse & game fishing, croquet, cycling, boating, ladies' hairdressing, 24-hour laundry service.

Newport
Map 18 A3 Co. Mayo
Newport 41222   Telex 33740
Proprietors Mr & Mrs Francis Mumford-Smith
Credit Amex, Barclaycard, Diners
Closed 1 October–31 March

Newport House Hotel   59%   Ⓜ   £E

The Mumford-Smiths have created a feeling of tranquillity at their graceful manor house, set in rambling gardens by the old town bridge. Time has stood still in the elegant, antique-filled public rooms, and bedrooms, too, are comfortably traditional, with homely touches everywhere and neat bathrooms. *Amenities* garden, 9-hole golf course, game & sea fishing, games room, billiards, shooting, croquet, water-skiing, riding.   &

Rooms 20
with bath/shower 20

Room phone No
Room TV No

Confirm by By arrang.
Last dinner 9.30

Parking Ample

Newport
Map 18 A3 Co. Mayo
Newport 41222
Proprietors
Mr & Mrs Francis Mumford-Smith

Newport House Hotel Restaurant   Ⓢ

An elegant Regency dining room, overlooking the gardens, is a delightful setting for some simple, enjoyable dishes making the most of local fish and home-grown vegetables. After tasty vegetable soup or terrine de canard, you might choose a grill, an omelette or superb salmon with hollandaise sauce. Lovely desserts include light, crisp apple tart and smooth chocolate mousse. ♉*ABOVE AVERAGE. Credit* Amex, Barclaycard, Diners   &

● **Set L** from £6 **Set D** from £10
incl. service
About £28 for two

Lunch 12–2.30 *Dinner* 7.30–9.30
Closed 1 October–31 March

Oughterard
Map 18 B3 Co. Galway
Galway 82328
Telex 28905
Credit Access, Amex, Barclaycard
Closed 1st week December–1st week February

Connemara Gateway Hotel   58%   Ⓜ   £D/E

Major improvements are adding to the appeal of this friendly modern hotel. There's a pleasant rustic bar, as well as a comfortable lounge with colour TV. Spacious bedrooms, with practical built-in furniture and tea/coffee-makers, have large windows to take advantage of the fine views. Compact, well-fitted bathrooms. *Amenities* garden, outdoor swimming pool, tennis, folk music (Sat), putting, children's playground, croquet.   &

Rooms 48
with bath/shower 48

Room phone Yes
Room TV No

Confirm by 6
Last dinner 9.30

Parking Ample
Banquets 200/2

Oughterard
Map 18 B3 Co. Galway
Galway 82313
Proprietors
Harry & June Hodgson

Closed early October–Easter

Currarevagh House   61%   Ⓜ   £D/E

The friendly Hodgsons' handsome Victorian house, standing near the shores of Lough Corrib, is an ideal base for fishing or for touring the Connemara countryside. Public rooms are tall and elegant, with marble fireplaces, fine antiques and wide windows overlooking the gardens, and bedrooms are attractively decorated and solidly furnished. Tiled bathrooms have modern fittings. *Amenities* garden, game fishing, croquet, hotel boats.

Rooms 15
with bath/shower 10

Room phone No
Room TV No

Confirm by 6
Last dinner 8

Parking Ample

Prices quoted for Eire are in Irish punts

Oughterard
Map 18 B3 Co. Galway
Galway 82207
Telex 28902
Proprietors
Patric & Moira Higgins
Credit Access, Barclaycard, Diners

Sweeney's Oughterard House   61%   Ⓜ   £C

Set in colourful grounds by a fast-flowing river, this creeper-clad building is a pleasant, family-run hotel. Public areas include a spacious modern bar and a TV lounge as well as a reading room. Some bedrooms have modern fitted units, whereas others are furnished with solid antique pieces. Simple bathrooms are well equipped. Some redecoration would be welcome. *Amenities* garden.   &

Rooms 21
with bath/shower 21

Room phone Yes
Room TV No

Confirm by 6
Last dinner 7.45

Parking Ample

Rathmullan

Map 18 C1 Co. Donegal
Near Letterkenny
Rathmullan 4
Proprietors
Mr & Mrs R. Wheeler
Credit Access, Amex, Diners
Closed mid October–Easter

Rathmullan House   63%   Ⓜ   £E

Peace and tranquillity reign at the Wheelers' lovely Georgian mansion, which stands in prizewinning gardens by the shores of Lough Swilly. The drawing room and library are restful and elegant, and there's an appealing cellar bar. Bedrooms of varying sizes are comfortably and traditionally furnished; bathrooms are spotless. No dogs. *Amenities* garden, tennis, game & sea fishing, putting, croquet, hotel boat, pool table, table tennis.

| *Rooms* 21 | *Room phone* No | *Confirm by* 6 | *Parking* Ample |
| *with bath/shower* 16 | *Room TV* No | *Last dinner* 8.15 | *Banquets* 30/– |

Redcastle

Map 18 C1 Co. Donegal
Near Moville
Moville 243

Credit Access, Amex,
Barclaycard, Diners

Red Castle Hotel   63%   £E

Part of a loughside leisure centre, this modernised mansion retains a traditional air in its public rooms, which include a panelled lounge and bar. Pleasantly decorated bedrooms have solid built-in units made by a local craftsman and roomy, well-fitted bathroom. No dogs.
Amenities sauna, tennis, squash, 9-hole golf course, game & sea fishing, entertainment (Sat & Sun), solarium, games room.

| *Rooms* 14 | *Room phone* Yes | *Confirm by* By arrang. | *Parking* Ample |
| *with bath/shower* 14 | *Room TV* Yes | *Last dinner* 10 | *Banquets* 200/– |

Redcastle

Map 18 C1 Co. Donegal
Near Moville
Moville 243

Red Castle Hotel Restaurant   ♛

In this stylish restaurant right on the edge of Loch Foyle you can choose from a wide-ranging menu offering grills and roasts alongside familiar French dishes like caneton à l'orange or coquilles St Jacques mornay. Start with a simple hors d'œuvre or hearty home-made soup, and round off a pleasant meal with a delicious dessert from the colourful trolley.
🍷*ABOVE AVERAGE. Credit* Access, Amex, Barclaycard, Diners   &

● **Set L** £6 **Set D** £10
About £36 for two

Lunch 12.30–2.45 *Dinner* 7–10

Renvyle

Map 18 A3 Co. Galway
Connemara
Renvyle 3
Telex 28896
Proprietor Mr Hugh Coyle
Credit Access, Barclaycard
Closed 6 January–mid March

Renvyle House Hotel   59%   Ⓜ   £D/E

This friendly hotel by the sea caters well for the active holiday-maker. Rustic-style public rooms include a TV lounge, a sun lounge and a panelled bar. Best bedrooms are bright and practical, with well-fitted bathrooms.
Amenities garden, sauna, tennis, golf course, game & sea fishing, entertainment (weekends in summer), croquet, games room, diving school, rowing boats, riding, snooker, children's playground, bowls, badminton.   &

| *Rooms* 76 | *Room phone* Yes | *Confirm by* 6 | *Parking* Ample |
| *with bath/shower* 76 | *Room TV* No | *Last dinner* 9 | *Banquets* 180/2 |

Rosses Point

Map 18 B2 Co. Sligo
Sligo 77112
Proprietor Mr Tim Corcoran
Seafood

About £30 for two

Moorings   ♧ Ⓢ

Tim Corcoran's menu varies with the success of his day's fishing, but whatever the choice, it's all very carefully prepared, from tasty chowder to succulent grilled turbot. A few meat dishes, too, and simple sweets.
Credit Access, Barclaycard, Diners *Dinner only* 6.30–10 **Closed** Sun, 20 December–8 January, 1 week June & 1st 2 weeks November   &

Rosslare

Map 19 D5 Co. Wexford
Wexford 32124
Telex 8586
Proprietors
Mr & Mrs Seamus Casey

Casey's Cedars Hotel   68%   Ⓜ   £E

Vera and Seamus Casey are the dedicated owners of this smart, purpose-built hotel a short walk from the beach. Spacious public rooms are plushly furnished in contemporary style, while bedrooms have well-designed fitted furniture and matching fabrics. Large, modern tiled bathrooms. No dogs.
Amenities garden, dancing (Fri, Sat, plus 3 nights weekly in summer), children's play area & playroom, table tennis, pool table.   &

| *Rooms* 35 | *Room phone* Yes | *Confirm by* 7 | *Parking* Ample |
| *with bath/shower* 35 | *Room TV* No | *Last dinner* 9.30 | *Banquets* 700/10 |

Rosslare
Map 19 D5 Co. Wexford
Wexford 32114

Manager Mr Austin Cody

Closed mid Dec–mid Feb

Kelly's Strand Hotel 66% Ⓜ £E

This modernised Victorian building is a popular hotel for family holidays. Public areas include a relaxing residents' lounge, a sun lounge and two bars. Bedrooms and bathrooms of varying size and style offer adequate comforts; some rooms overlook the sea. No dogs. *Amenities* garden, sauna, indoor & outdoor swimming pools, tennis, squash, dancing (Mon–Sat), films (Sun), hairdressing, health centre, games room, children's playroom.

Rooms 99	Room phone Yes	Confirm by 6	Parking Ample
with bath/shower 93	Room TV No	Last dinner 9	Banquets 40/4

Rosslare
Map 19 D5 Co. Wexford
Wexford 32114

Manager Mr Austin Cody

About £25 for two

Kelly's Strand Hotel Restaurant Ⓢ

Superb roast beef is a highlight of the menu in this spacious, formal dining room. There are plenty of other delights, too, including lovely fresh seafood and mouthwatering desserts. Service is a model of smart, friendly efficiency. *Lunch* 1–2.30 *Dinner* 7.30–9.30 **Closed** mid December–mid February
● **Set L** £5·95 **Set D** £9·25

Rossnowlagh
Map 18 B2 Co. Donegal
Bundoran 65343
Telex 33460

Proprietors
Vincent & Mary Britton
Credit Amex, Diners

Closed October–Easter

Sand House Hotel 63% Ⓜ £E

Situated by the 'heavenly cove' of Rossnowlagh, this fine modern hotel is perfect for family holidays and offers a range of amenities to suit all tastes. The pleasant reception-lounge is warmed in cold weather by a turf fire, and there are several other lounges to relax in, as well as a superb cocktail bar. Bedrooms (many looking out to sea) are delightfully furnished with antiques and locally made modern units, while bathrooms are thoughtfully designed and well equipped.
Amenities garden, tennis, 9-hole golf course, sea fishing, dancing (Sat), surfing, board-sailing, miniature golf, putting, pony trekking, canoeing, games room.

Rooms 40	Room phone Yes	Confirm by By arrang.	Parking Ample
with bath/shower 40	Room TV No	Last dinner 9	

Sandycove
Map 19 D4 Co. Dublin
Marine Parade
Dublin 809873
Proprietors
Sean & Audrey Kinsella

About £55 for two
Banquets 30/10

Mirabeau ♧ Ⓢ

Fine views across Dublin Bay are among the attractions of this welcoming restaurant. Superb seafood and meat are presented for your inspection before being skilfully cooked by owner Sean Kinsella, and the choice ranges from lobster, prawns, scallops and sole to delicious crispy duckling and a variety of steaks. Excellent vegetables and simple sweets.  *ABOVE AVERAGE. Credit* Access, Amex, Barclaycard, Diners ♿

Dinner only 7.30–11
Closed Sun, Bank Holidays & last 3 weeks September

Schull
Map 19 A6 Co. Cork
Skibbereen 28181

Credit Amex, Barclaycard, Diners
Closed 1 October–Easter

Ard na Greine 55% Ⓜ £D/E

Frank and Rhona O'Sullivan are charming hosts at this peaceful converted farmhouse within walking distance of the sea. There's a simple rustic bar, as well as a first-floor lounge with a view of the Fastnet Rock on fine days. Most bedrooms are in an extension, and have been carefully designed in modern style. Smart, black-tiled bathrooms are spotlessly clean. No dogs.
Amenities garden. ♿

Rooms 8	Room phone No	Confirm by 7	Parking Ample
with bath/shower 6	Room TV No	Last dinner 9	

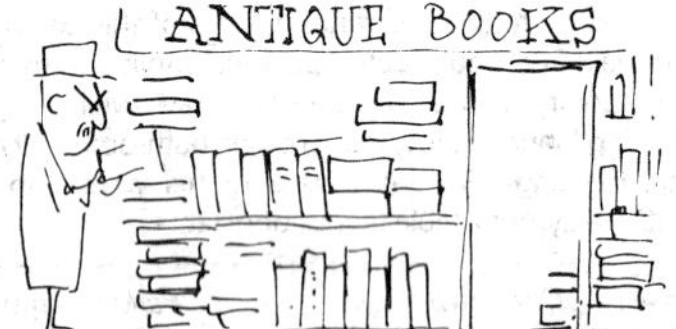

We publish annually, so make sure you use the current edition. It's worth it!

Shanagarry

Map 19 C6 Co. Cork
Near Midleton
Midleton 652531
Telex 75208
Proprietors Mr & Mrs Allen

Closed 24–26 December

Rooms 24
with bath/shower 22

Ballymaloe House   58%   Ⓜ   £ D

Including part of a Geraldine castle, this beguiling old house is full of simple charm and character. Guests can enjoy a drink in the large lounge or relax in the TV room. Individually decorated bedrooms vary in style from traditional in the main building to more modern in the coachyard. Compact bathrooms, some with showers only. *Amenities* garden, outdoor swimming pool, tennis, 9-hole golf course, games room, riding, croquet.   ♿

Room phone Yes	*Confirm by* By arrang.	*Parking* Ample
Room TV No	*Last dinner* 9.30	*Banquets* 45/6

Shanagarry

Map 19 C6 Co. Cork
Near Midleton
Midleton 652531
Proprietors Mr & Mrs Allen

● **Set L** £5·50 **Set D** £11·50
About £33 for two
Banquets 45/6

Ballymaloe House Restaurant   ★   ♿ Ⓢ

Irish country cooking is closest to Mrs Allen's heart, and her five-course daily menus transform farm-fresh produce into a memorable experience. Accuracy and flair mark everything she does, from full-flavoured mushroom soup to succulent salmon topped with a sprig of fennel and a perfect béarnaise sauce. Delicious combinations of vegetables might include cucumber with tomato and mint or cauliflower with spinach; and sweets such as a gorgeous meringue gâteau end the meal in fitting style. Buffet lunches; cold buffet Sunday evenings. Smoking discouraged.
Specialities sauté of calf's liver with whiskey and tarragon, home-made breads and ice creams, fresh Ballycotton fish. ♟ *OUTSTANDING.*   ♿

Lunch 1–1.30 *Dinner* 7–9.30, Sun 7.30–8
Closed 24–26 December

Prices quoted for Eire are in Irish punts

Shannon

Map 19 B5 Co. Clare
Shannon Airport
Shannon 61122
Telex 24018
Manager Miss Frances Ringrose
Credit Access, Amex,
Barclaycard, Diners

Rooms 126
with bath/shower 126

Shannon International Hotel   67%   £ D

Well insulated from noise, this smart modern hotel lies within easy walking distance of the airport terminal. The foyer and several lounge areas are very stylish, and there's a distinctive circular bar with fine views over the estuary. Spacious bedrooms are prettily furnished and have neat, well-equipped bathrooms. Restaurant closed for dinner October–June. No dogs. *Amenities* 24-hour laundry service. **Closed** 24 & 25 December   ♿

Room phone Yes	*Confirm by* 6	*Parking* Ample
Room TV No	*Last dinner* 8.30	

Skibbereen

Map 19 B6 Co. Cork
Skibbereen 21109
Telex 32137

Credit Access, Amex,
Barclaycard, Diners

Rooms 10
with bath/shower 5

Liss Ard House Hotel   68%   £ C/D

Set in grounds of 60 acres, this beautifully kept Georgian house makes a very elegant hotel. Two sitting rooms have deep armchairs and crystal chandeliers, and there's a marble fireplace in the cosy bar. Individually styled bedrooms feature pretty matching fabrics and antiques or built-in units; modernised bathrooms are well equipped. *Amenities* garden, tennis, game fishing, riding, carriage driving, pony trekking, hotel boat, croquet.

Room phone Yes	*Confirm by* By arrang.	*Parking* Ample
Room TV No	*Last dinner* 9	*Banquets* 120/–

Sligo

Map 18 B2 Co. Sligo
Pearse Road
Sligo 3291
Telex 24397
Manager Mr J. Feeney
Credit Access, Amex,
Barclaycard, Diners

Rooms 60
with bath/shower 60

Sligo Park Hotel   56%   £ D

This modern hotel on the main Dublin road is popular with businessmen who make good use of its extensive function facilities. Showcases of Irish crystal glassware decorate the reception-cum-lounge, and there's an ultra-modern TV lounge and cheerful canopied bar. Well-proportioned bedrooms are fitted with built-in units. Compact bathrooms. *Amenities* garden, 24-hour laundry service, children's playground, in-house video.   ♿

Room phone Yes	*Confirm by* 6	*Parking* Ample
Room TV Yes	*Last dinner* 9	*Banquets* 300/–

Sneem

Map 19 A6 Co. Kerry
Sneem 45122
Telex 26899

Manager Mr Brendan Maher
Rooms 59
with bath/shower 59
Room phone Yes
Room TV Yes
Confirm by 4
Last dinner 8.30
Parking Ample
Banquets 120/15
Closed 31 October–Easter except
23 December–3 January
Credit Access, Amex,
Barclaycard, Diners

Parknasilla Hotel   77%   £D

In its own grounds on the banks of the Kenmare River, this substantial Victorian mansion has lovely views of the Atlantic. There are three distinctive lounges comfortably furnished in different styles (one with TV), as well as a plush bar with green silk-covered walls and velvet upholstered armchairs; many of the public rooms retain their Victorian marble or carved wooden fire surrounds. Bedrooms vary from vast luxuriously equipped suites to more modest standard rooms. Bathrooms have excellent modern fittings. *Amenities* garden, sauna, indoor swimming pool, tennis, 9-hole golf course, dancing (Wed, Sat, Sun in season), billiards, hairdressing, games room, riding, sailing, hotel launch, shooting.

Sneem

Map 19 A6 Co. Kerry
Sneem 45122
Manager Mr Brendan Maher

Parknasilla Hotel, Pygmalion Restaurant   ♛♛ Ⓢ

Luxurious decor in tobacco brown and white enhances the civilised atmosphere in this fine restaurant. The table d'hôte and gastronomic menus feature a selection of skilfully prepared dishes ranging from veal escalope and loin of lamb to lobster Thermidor and poached salmon with hollandaise sauce; vegetables are nicely judged, and Kirsch gâteau makes a delightful sweet.  *ABOVE AVERAGE. Credit* Access, Amex, Barclaycard, Diners

● **Set L** £6 **Set D** £10
About £35 for two

Lunch 1–2 *Dinner* 7–8.30
Closed 31 October–Easter except 23 December–3 January

Strandhill

Map 18 B2 Co. Sligo
Sligo 78122

Knockmuldowney   ♧ Ⓢ

The Coopers maintain a high standard of cooking in this delightful country restaurant overlooking Ballisodare Bay. The short, daily-changing menus make good use of fresh local produce, and we thoroughly enjoyed our blue cheese mille-feuille with fresh herbs followed by chicken in tarragon sauce. Vegetables showed an imaginative touch, and our sweet was a creamy orange soufflé.  *SUPERIOR. Credit* Access, Amex, Barclaycard, Diners

● **Set D** £9
About £28 for two
Banquets 35/–

Dinner only 7.30–10
Closed Sun, Mon except Bank Holidays, Good Friday, 25 Dec & Feb

---

Virginia

Map 18 C3 Co. Cavan
Cavan 32096

Credit Access, Amex,
Barclaycard, Diners
Closed possibly January

Park Hotel   57%   Ⓜ   £D

New owners now run this charming converted farmhouse set in 100 acres of grounds by Lough Ramor. Public rooms include a comfortable lounge with TV and a large modern bar. Most of the pretty, simply furnished bedrooms have compact bathrooms with showers. *Amenities* garden, tennis, 9-hole golf course, coarse & game fishing, children's playroom, hotel boats, table tennis, putting, croquet, nature trails, grill room (10am–10pm).   ♿

Rooms 30	*Room phone* Yes	*Confirm by* By arrang.	*Parking* Ample
with bath/shower 26	*Room TV* Some	*Last dinner* 9	*Banquets* 110/–

Waterford

Map 19 C5 Co. Waterford
Ferrybank
Waterford 32111   Telex 80684
Proprietors Joan & Tony Breen
Credit Access, Amex,
Barclaycard, Diners
Closed 24 & 25 December

Ardree Hotel   62%   Ⓜ   £D

Magnificent views over the city and estuary are a feature of this sleek, modern hotel. Public areas like the reception-lounge and the bar are comfortable, roomy and cheerfully contemporary. Bedrooms have practical fitted furniture and colourful bathrooms equipped with bidets. No dogs. *Amenities* garden, tennis, discothèque (4 nights weekly), bar entertainment (in summer), in-house movies, 24-hour laundry service.   ♿

Rooms 100	*Room phone* Yes	*Confirm by* 6	*Parking* Ample
with bath/shower 100	*Room TV* Yes	*Last dinner* 10.45	*Banquets* 600/–

Waterford

Map 19 C5 Co. Waterford
Dunmore East Road
Waterford 74138

● **Set L & Set D** (Tues–Fri)
£11 incl. service
About £34 for two

Ballinakill House Restaurant   

A civilised atmosphere pervades this stylish restaurant, where Martin Dwyer's regularly changing menu features enterprising creations like sweetbreads in puff pastry with caper sauce and brill with Seville orange sauce, as well as more familiar classical French dishes such as steak au poivre. Vegetables are carefully handled, and there are some outstanding sweets. ▼ *SUPERIOR. Credit* Access, Amex, Barclaycard

Lunch by arrangement only *Dinner* 7.30–10
Closed Sun, Mon, Bank Holidays & following Tues & 10 days Christmas

---

Waterford

Map 19 C5 Co. Waterford
The Quay
Waterford 55111
Telex 80188

Credit Access, Amex,
Barclaycard, Diners

Rooms 50
with bath/shower 50

Granville Hotel   68%   Ⓜ   **£ E/F**

Friendly staff and caring owners make it a real pleasure to stay at this smoothly run, thoroughly modernised hotel. A feature of the foyer is the lovely old mahogany panelling, while deep red velvet seating adds a touch of luxury to the spacious bar. Bedrooms have coordinated fabrics, practical modern units and up-to-date bathrooms with pretty tiles. No dogs. *Amenities* dinner dance (Sat), grill room (12.30pm–10.30pm).

Room phone Yes	*Confirm by* 7	*Parking* Ample
Room TV Yes	*Last dinner* 9.30	*Banquets* 150/–

Waterford

Map 19 C5 Co. Waterford
The Quay
Waterford 55111

About £27 for two

Granville Hotel, Sword Restaurant   ♛ Ⓢ

An elegant, comfortable restaurant where lunch and dinner menus offer a choice of straightforward well-prepared dishes ranging from pâté to plaice, grills and roast beef. Homely sweets and good service. *Credit* Access, Amex, Barclaycard, Diners *Lunch* 12.30–2.30 *Dinners* 7–9.30
Closed 25 & 26 December ● **Set L** from £3·60 **Set D** from £8·50

Waterville

Map 19 A6 Co. Kerry
Waterville 5
Proprietor Mr Peter Huggard

● **Set D** from £9·85
About £27 for two
Banquets 24/10

Butler Arms Restaurant   ♧ Ⓢ

Prime raw materials, careful cooking and attractive presentation characterise Peter Huggard's four-course menus in this friendly restaurant overlooking a little garden. Start with pâté or a tasty seafood terrine before going on to home-made soup, followed by delicious salmon or perhaps pork steak Wellington. Enjoyable sweets might include gâteau or lemon meringue pie, and coffee is excellent. *Credit* Access, Barclaycard   ♿

Dinner only 7.30–9
Closed 12 October–Easter

Waterville

Map 19 A6 Co. Kerry
Waterville 11

Proprietor Mr Raymond Hunt

● **Set L** £5 **Set D** £10·50
About £28 for two
Banquets 60/35

Huntsman   ♧ Ⓢ

This smart, friendly restaurant stands right on the seashore (with fine views over the bay), so it's quite appropriate that sea-fresh fish and shellfish should dominate the menu. Raymond Hunt puts his considerable talents to good use in producing a wide selection of delicious dishes, ranging from rich prawn bisque to grilled turbot béarnaise and monkfish tails with a cheese and mustard sauce. *Credit* Access, Barclaycard

Lunch 12–3.30 *Dinner* 6–9.45
Closed November–March

Waterville

Map 19 A6 Co. Kerry
Tralee 23100
Telex 28246

Credit Access, Amex,
Barclaycard, Diners
Closed mid October–mid April

Rooms 100
with bath/shower 100

Waterville Lake Hotel   69%   **£ C**

Spectacular lake and mountain views are a feature of this modern hotel, whose spacious public rooms include three lounges and two bars. Bedrooms have smart darkwood furniture and well-equipped bathrooms. Maintenance could be improved. No dogs. *Amenities* garden, sauna, indoor swimming pool, tennis, golf, game & sea fishing, dancing (Tues–Sat), table tennis, snooker, grill bar (noon–10pm), children's playroom and playground.   ♿

Room phone Yes	*Confirm by* 6	*Parking* Ample
Room TV No	*Last dinner* 10	*Banquets* 70/4

Wexford

Map 19 D5 Co. Wexford
North Main Street
Wexford 23591

Seafood

● **Set L** £6·95
About £34 for two
Banquets 40/8

Captain White's Seafood Restaurant   Ⓢ

Beautifully fresh local seafood cooked to order is well worth waiting for at this friendly, comfortable restaurant. Start with some famous Wexford mussels (in winter months) or perhaps a delicious chowder, and go on to baked sea bass, poached salmon or skewered scallops. Cooking does justice to the quality of the ingredients, and there's a choice of steaks for meat-lovers. *Credit* Access, Amex, Barclaycard, Diners

Lunch 12.30–2.30 *Dinner* 7–10.15
Closed Sun & 25 December

Wexford

Map 19 D5 Co. Wexford
Trinity Street
Wexford 22566
Telex 80658
Manager Mr Liam B. Lynch
Credit Access, Amex,
Barclaycard, Diners

Rooms 116
with bath/shower 94

Talbot Hotel   60%   Ⓜ   £ D

Three bars and several lounges (one with TV) provide ample scope for relaxation at this friendly modern hotel. Compact bedrooms have well-designed fitted furniture; bathrooms are adequate. No dogs. *Amenities* sauna, indoor swimming pool, squash, dancing (Sat), discothèque (Sun), solarium, 24-hour laundry service, children's playroom, hairdressing, beauty parlour, games room, grill room (12.30pm–11pm), cabaret (Wed–Sat in summer). ♻

Room phone Yes	*Confirm by* 6	*Parking* Ample
Room TV No	*Last dinner* 8.45	*Banquets* 600/–

Wexford

Map 19 D5 Co. Wexford
Abbey Street
Wexford 22311
Telex 80630
Manager Peter Hussey
Credit Access, Amex,
Barclaycard, Diners

Rooms 100
with bath/shower 60

White's Hotel   61%   Ⓜ   £ C/D

This smart modern hotel, built in 1970, has a car park in front. The simple foyer extends into a plush open-plan lounge and bar with red velvet seating. There are also spacious banqueting facilities. Bedrooms (all twins or doubles) are fitted with functional built-in furniture. More than half have compact tiled bathrooms.
Amenities dancing (Thurs, Sat, Sun in high season).

Room phone Yes	*Confirm by* 6	*Parking* Ample
Room TV Yes	*Last dinner* 10.45	*Banquets* 700/20

Youghal

Map 19 C6 Co. Cork
163 North Main Street
Youghal 2424
Proprietors Fitzgibbon family
Seafood
About £33 for two

Aherne's Pub & Seafood Bar   ♧ Ⓢ

Superbly fresh seafood is the attraction of this family-run restaurant, where lobsters, oysters, mussels and salmon are simply prepared and full of flavour. A few meat dishes, too. 🍷 *ABOVE AVERAGE. Credit* Access, Amex, Barclaycard, Diners *Lunch* 12.30–2.30 *Dinner* 6.30–10, Sun 6.30–9 **Closed** L Sun, D Mon, Good Friday & 5 days Christmas ● **Set L** £6 *Banquets* 50/6   ♻

Readers' comments

Please use this sheet for complaints on establishments included in the Guide or for recommending new establishments which you would like our inspectors to visit.

Please post to Egon Ronay Organisation Greencoat House, Francis Street, London SW1P 1DH.

Please use an up-to-date Guide. We publish annually

N.B. We regret that owing to the enormous volume of readers' communications received each year, we will be unable to acknowledge these forms, but they will certainly be seriously considered.

Name and address of establishment	Your recommendation or complaint

Name of sender (in block letters) _______________________

Address of sender (in block letters) _______________________

(1983)

Readers' comments

Please use this sheet for complaints on establishments included in the Guide or for recommending new establishments which you would like our inspectors to visit.

Please post to Egon Ronay Organisation
Greencoat House, Francis Street, London SW1P 1DH.
Please use an up-to-date Guide. We publish annually.

N.B. We regret that owing to the enormous volume of readers' communications received each year, we will be unable to acknowledge these forms, but they will certainly be seriously considered.

Name and address of establishment	Your recommendation or complaint

Name of sender (in block letters) ___________________________

Address of sender (in block letters) ___________________________

(1983)

Readers' comments

Please use this sheet for complaints on establishments included in the Guide or for recommending new establishments which you would like our inspectors to visit.

Please post to Egon Ronay Organisation Greencoat House, Francis Street, London SW1P 1DH.

Please use an up-to-date Guide. We publish annually

N.B. We regret that owing to the enormous volume of readers' communications received each year, we will be unable to acknowledge these forms, but they will certainly be seriously considered.

Name and address of establishment	Your recommendation or complaint

Name of sender (in block letters) ___________________________

Address of sender (in block letters) ___________________________

(1983)

Readers' comments

Please use this sheet for complaints on establishments included in the Guide or for recommending new establishments which you would like our inspectors to visit.

Please post to Egon Ronay Organisation Greencoat House, Francis Street, London SW1P 1DH.

Please use an up-to-date Guide. We publish annually.

N.B. We regret that owing to the enormous volume of readers' communications received each year, we will be unable to acknowledge these forms, but they will certainly be seriously considered.

Name and address of establishment	Your recommendation or complaint

Name of sender (in block letters) ____________________

Address of sender (in block letters) ____________________

(1983)

ADVERTISERS' INDEX

Engineering for World Transport

Used by the Navy and offshore oil rigs for rescues and patrols, the Avon Searider inflatable dramatically illustrates the need for marinisation in marine electrical equipment.

Fully marinised products, as chosen for the Searider, are the speciality of Lucas Marine, a company which has studied the effects of maritime pollution on materials, finishes and components. By applying its own rigorous protective standards to every product, Lucas Marine has brought new confidence and safety to thousands of boat owners.

‘The House red, sir.’

WINE MERCHANTS
GEO. G. SANDEMAN
SONS & CO. LIMITED
NDEMAN
CLARET
BORDEAUX
ATION BORDEAUX CONTRÔLÉE
1978
PRODUCE OF FRANCE
ED IN BLANQUEFORT, GIRONDE
FRANCE FOR
G. Sandeman
ons & Co. Ltd.
LONDON, ENGLAND
70
63 mm

Sandeman Claret. From The House of Sandeman.

MAPS

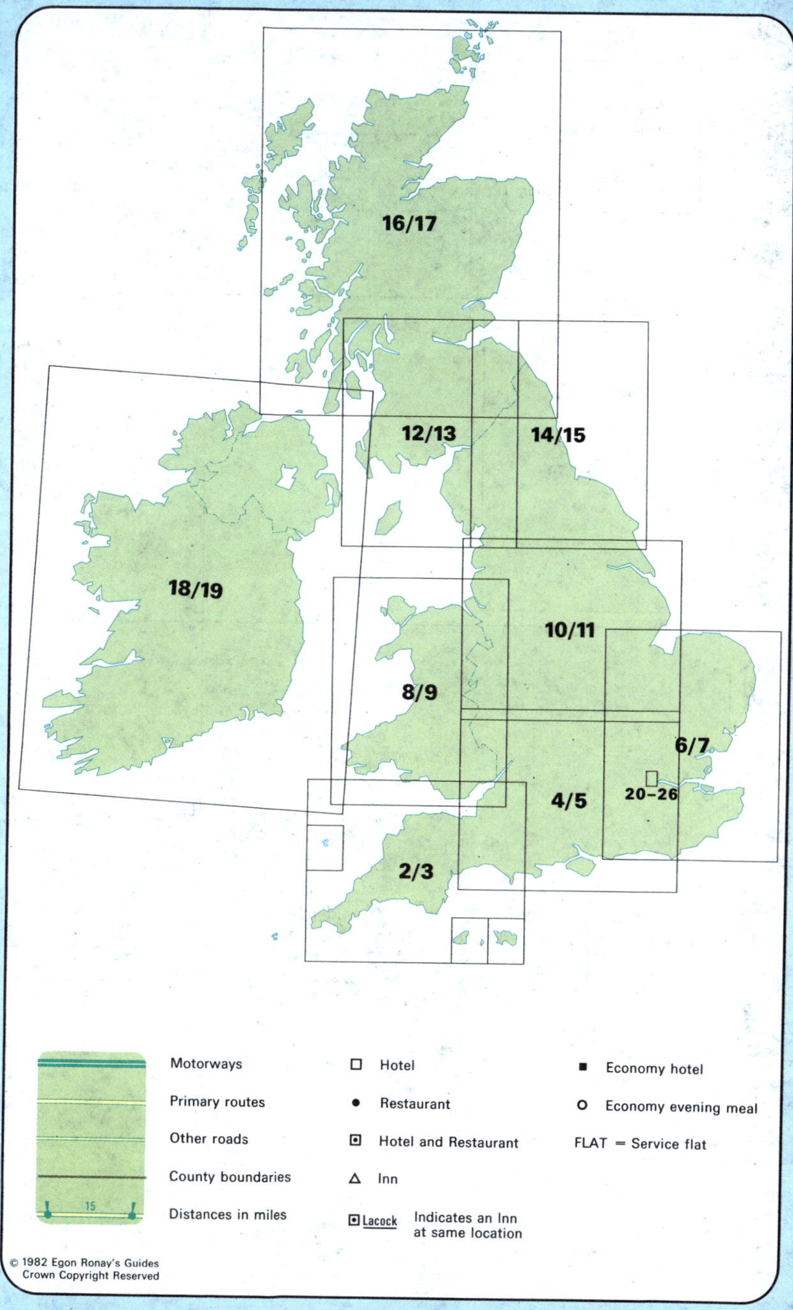

16/17
12/13
14/15
18/19
10/11
8/9
6/7
20–26
4/5
2/3
Motorways
Primary routes
Other roads
County boundaries
Distances in miles
15
Hotel
Restaurant
Hotel and Restaurant
Inn
Lacock   Indicates an Inn at same location
Economy hotel
Economy evening meal
FLAT = Service flat

Simply the best there is.

Simply the best there is.

Britvic is a Registered Trade Mark

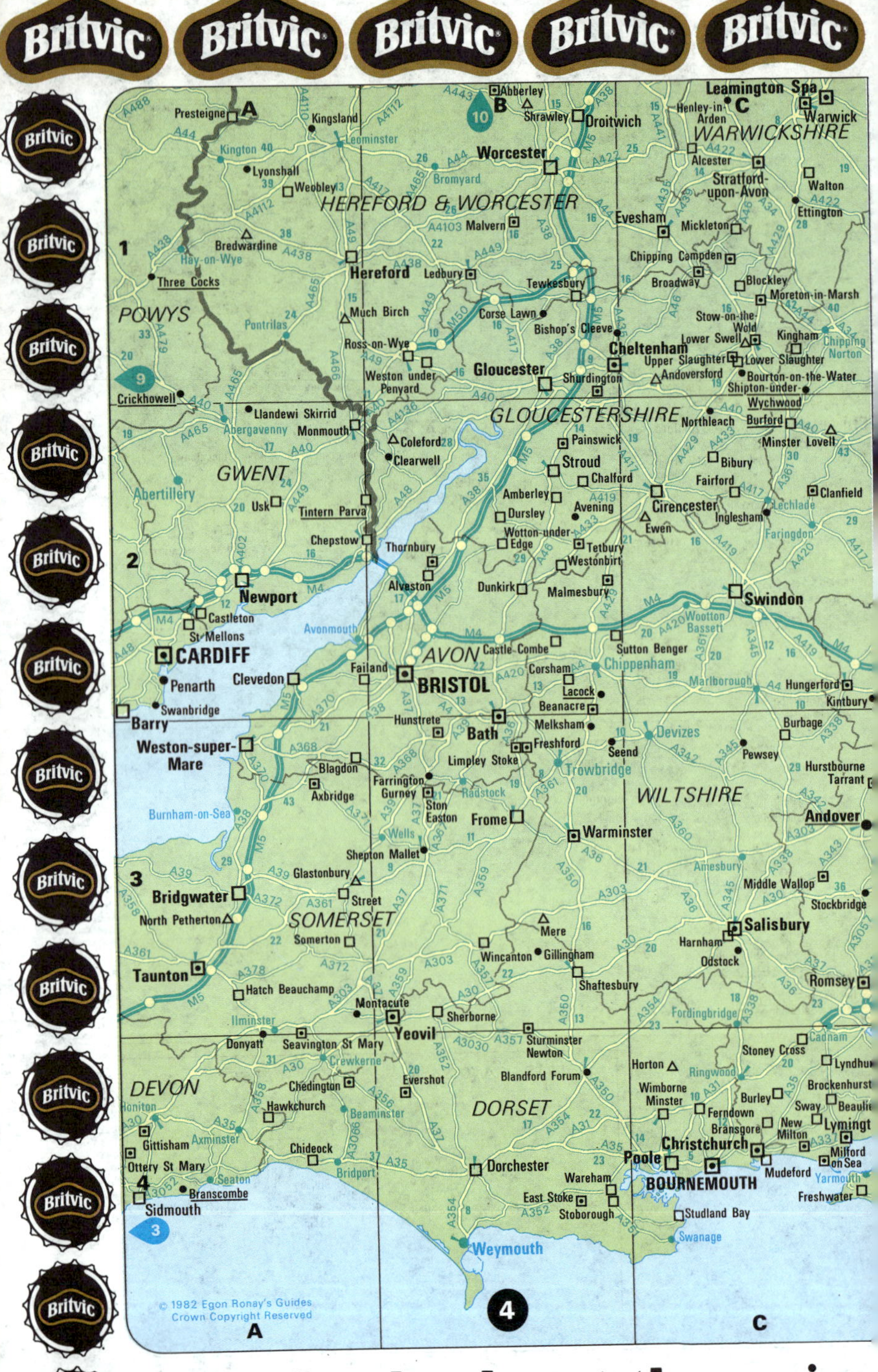

Simply the best there is.

Britvic Britvic Britvic Britvic Britvic

NORTHAMPTONSHIRE
Daventry NORTHAMPTON Wellingborough St Neots Newmarket
Southam Horton Turvey Bedford CAMBRIDGESHIRE Cambridge Six Mile Bottom
Wroxton Towcester Newport Pagnell Sandy Haverhill
Banbury Brackley BEDFORDSHIRE Ampthill Shefford Royston Saffron Walden
Milton Keynes Woburn Flitton Letchworth Bishop's Stortford Great Dunmow Felsted
Steeple Aston Buckingham Leighton Buzzard Hitchin Little Wymondley High-Easter
Bicester Middleton Stoney Chesterton BUCKINGHAMSHIRE Dunstable LUTON Stevenage HERTFORDSHIRE Old Harlow Harlow
Woodstock Aylesbury Ivinghoe Harpenden Welwyn Garden City Hertford Hertingfordbury ESSEX
OXFORD Stoke Mandeville Aston Clinton Redbourn St Albans Hatfield Waltham Abbey Epping
OXFORDSHIRE Thame Berkhamsted Hemel Hempstead South Mimms Newgate Street Brentwood
Abingdon Chenies Watford Elstree Hadley Wood Borehamwood
Amersham Beaconsfield Hatch End Harrow Weald Mill Hill
Wallingford Marlow Gerrards Cross Wembley GREATER LONDON North Stifford
Wantage North Stoke Henley-on-Thames Hurley Cookham Farnham Common Hillingdon Ealing LONDON Stepney Limehouse
Streatley-on-Thames Burnham Slough West Drayton Kew Greenwich Blackheath
Pangbourne Maidenhead London Airport Richmond LONDON Catford Gravesend
Yattendon Bray-on-Thames Sonning-on-Thames Windsor Heathrow Ashford Dulwich
READING BERKSHIRE Ascot Egham Sunbury-on-Thames Kingston Bromley KENT
Newbury Burghfield Sindlesham Shepperton East Molesey
Shinfield Bagshot Virginia Water Walton-on-Thames Cheam Keston Sevenoaks
Silchester Swallowfield Weybridge Claygate Cobham Sanderstead Westerham Tonbridge
Basingstoke Camberley Woking Leatherhead Chipstead Bletchingley Limpsfield
Fleet Aldershot East Horsley West Clandon SURREY South Godstone Chiddingstone
Crondall Guildford Dorking Reigate Penshurst Speldhurst
HAMPSHIRE Godalming Wotton Bramley London Airport Gatwick Blindley Heath
Alton Farnham Milford Hascombe Ockley Lowfield Heath Tunbridge Wells
Crawley New Alresford Churt Chiddingfold Cranleigh Rusper East Grinstead Frant
Grayshott Alfold Crossways Crawley Wadhurst
Winchester Haslemere Horsham Lower Beeding Mayfield
Petersfield Billingshurst Haywards Heath
Eastleigh Midhurst Petworth WEST SUSSEX West Chiltington Uckfield Rushlake Green
Botley Shedfield Chilgrove Pulborough Storrington EAST SUSSEX
SOUTHAMPTON Wickham Havant Goodwood Steyning Herstmonceux
Stubbington Fareham Chichester Walberton Arundel Poynings Lewes Boreham Street
Gosport Bosham Climping A27 BRIGHTON Alfriston Selmeston Jevington
PORTSMOUTH Southsea South Hayling Littlehampton Worthing Newhaven
Cowes Ryde Selsey Bognor Regis Seaford Eastbourne
Newport St Helens Bembridge
ISLE OF WIGHT Sandown Shanklin
Bonchurch Ventnor

□ Hotel
● Restaurant
◉ Hotel and Restaurant
△ Inn
▣ Lacock Indicates an Inn at same location
■ Economy hotel
○ Economy evening meal

0 5 10 15 Miles
0 5 10 15 20 25 Kilometres

Simply the best there is.

Britvic is a Registered Trade Mark

Britvic
Simply the best there is.
LINCOLNSHIRE
Grantham
Grimsthorpe
Melton Mowbray
Langham
Oakham
LEICESTER-SHIRE
Uppingham
Wansford
Stamford
Market Deeping
Boston
Spalding
Long Sutton
King's Lynn
Wisbech
Downham Market
PETERBOROUGH
Whittlesey
March
Market Harborough
Corby
Oundle
Thrapston
Kettering
NORTHAMPTON-SHIRE
Wellingborough
Rushden
Huntingdon
St Ives
Needingworth
NORTHAMPTON
Horton
Turvey
Bedford
Newport Pagnell
Ampthill
Milton Keynes
Shefford
Flitton
Woburn
Leighton Buzzard
Little Wymondley
Letchworth
Stevenage
Bishop's Stortford
St Neots
Cambridge
CAMBRIDGESHIRE
Chatteris
Ely
Littleport
Mildenhall
Newmarket
Six Mile Bottom
Royston
Saffron Walden
Haverhill
Great Dunmow
Braintree
Coggeshall
Hunstanton
Burnham Market
Wells-next-the-Sea
Blakeney
Weybourne
West Runton
Cromer
Holt
Aldborough
Fakenham
Guist
Aylsham
Hoveton
Horning
Ormesby St Margaret
South Walsham
East Dereham
Swaffham
NORFOLK
NORWICH
Shipdham
Barnham Broom
Hethersett
Wymondham
Great Yarmouth
Thetford
Brockdish
Diss
Scole
Harleston
Eye
Bungay
Beccles
Carlton Colville
Lowestoft
Fressingfield
Halesworth
Southwold
Yoxford
Framlingham
Aldeburgh
Orford
Woodbridge
Bury St Edmunds
Stowmarket
Earl Stonham
Bradfield Combust
Cockfield
SUFFOLK
Lavenham
Long Melford
Hintlesham
Clare
Sudbury
Hadleigh
Copdock
IPSWICH
Nayland
Dedham
Felixstowe
Harwich
Halstead
Colchester
BEDFORDSHIRE
Sleaford

Simply the best there is.
Britvic is a Registered Trade Mark
Hotel
Restaurant
Hotel and Restaurant
Inn
Lacock Indicates an Inn at same location
Economy hotel
Economy evening meal
© 1982 Egon Ronay's Guides
Crown Copyright Reserved
Miles
Kilometres
continued
HERTFORDSHIRE
ESSEX
Aylesbury
Ivinghoe
Aston-Clinton
Harpenden
Welwyn
Welwyn Garden City
Felsted
Frinton-on-Sea
Stoke Mandeville
Redbourn
Hertford
Hertingfordbury
Old Harlow
High Easter
Clacton-on-Sea
Berkhamsted
St Albans
Hatfield
Harlow
Chelmsford
Maldon
Hemel Hempstead
South Mimms
Newgate Street
Epping
Chenies
Hadley Wood
Waltham Abbey
Burnham-on-Crouch
Amersham
Elstree
Watford
Borehamwood
Brentwood
Rochford
Beaconsfield
Hatch End
Harrow
Mill Hill
BASILDON
Great Wakering
Henley-on-Thames
Marlow
Gerrards Cross
Weald
Wembley
GREATER LONDON
North Stifford
SOUTHEND-ON-SEA
Cookham
Farnham Common
Burnham
Slough
Hillingdon
Ealing
Stepney
Limehouse
Hurley
West Drayton
Maidenhead
Bray
London Airport
Kew
LONDON
Greenwich
Tilbury
Gravesend
Rochester
Sheerness
Sonning-on-Thames
Windsor
Heathrow
Ashford
Richmond
Blackheath
BERKSHIRE
Egham
Wimbledon
Catford
Sindlesham
Shepperton
Sunbury-on-Thames
Dulwich
Shorne
Herne Bay
Margate
Shinfield
Ascot
Kingston
Bromley
Whitstable
Broadstairs
Bagshot
Virginia Water
Walton-on-Thames
East Molesey
Keston
Sittingbourne
Herne
Woking
Weybridge
Cheam
Ramsgate
Camberley
Claygate
Chipstead
Sanderstead
Chartham Hatch
Fordwich
Canterbury
SURREY
Cobham
Sevenoaks
Maidstone
Aldershot
East Horsley
Leatherhead
Limpsfield
Hollingbourne
Deal
Guildford
West Clandon
Dorking
Westerham
KENT
Pett Bottom
Barham
Crondall
Reigate
Bletchingley
Wye
Godalming
Wotton
South Godstone
Ashford
Farnham
Bramley
London Airport
Chiddingstone
Milford
Hascombe
Ockley
Gatwick
Blindley Heath
Penshurst
Speldhurst
Goudhurst
Biddenden
Dover
Churt
Chiddingfold
Lowfield Heath
Tonbridge
High Halden
Grayshott
Alfold
Cranleigh
Rusper
Crawley
East Grinstead
Tunbridge Wells
Frant
Folkestone
Haslemere
Crossways
Wadhurst
New Romney
Hythe
Horsham
Lower Beeding
Mayfield
Bodiam
Billingshurst
Haywards Heath
EAST
Northiam
Petersfield
Petworth
WEST
West Chiltington
Uckfield
Rushlake Green
Sedlescombe
Rye
Midhurst
Battle
Lydd
Chilgrove
Pulborough
Storrington
SUSSEX
Herstmonceux
Hastings
Goodwood
SUSSEX
Steyning
Poynings
Lewes
Boreham Street
Chichester
Walberton
Arundel
Worthing
Alfriston
Selmeston
Jevington
Cooden Beach
Bosham
Climping
BRIGHTON
Newhaven
Seaford
Eastbourne
Bognor Regis
Littlehampton
Selsey
4
5
7
6
A
B
C
D
Britvic

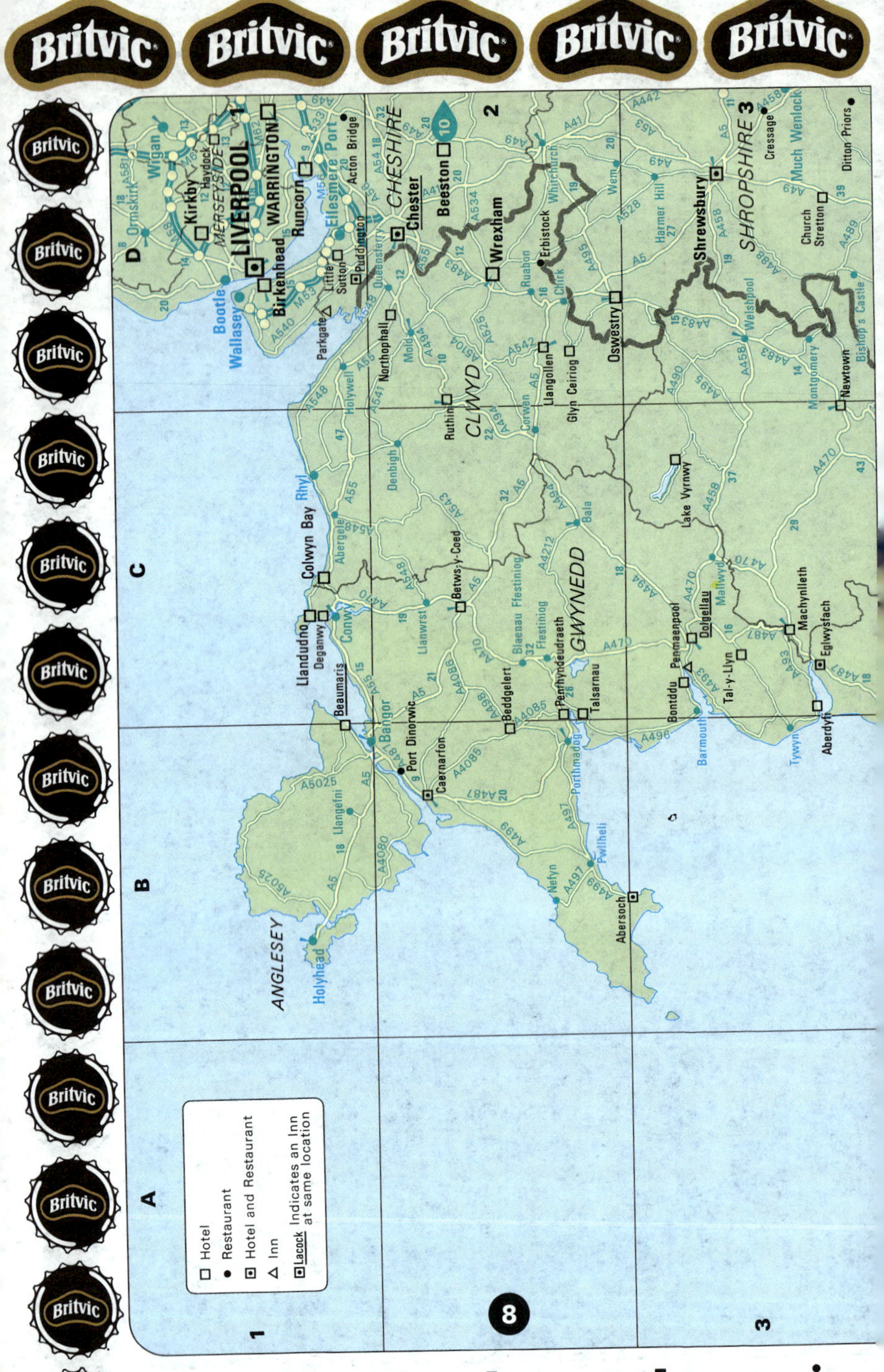

Britvic
Britvic
Britvic
Britvic
Britvic
CHESHIRE
CLWYD
GWYNEDD
SHROPSHIRE
ANGLESEY
MERSEYSIDE
Liverpool
Warrington
Birkenhead
Bootle
Wallasey
Wigan
Kirkby
Ormskirk
Haydock
Runcorn
Ellesmere Port
Acton Bridge
Chester
Beeston
Wrexham
Oswestry
Whitchurch
Wem
Shrewsbury
Much Wenlock
Cressage
Church Stretton
Ditton Priors
Bishop's Castle
Newtown
Montgomery
Welshpool
Lake Vyrnwy
Harmer Hill
Erbistock
Ruabon
Chirk
Llangollen
Glyn Ceiriog
Corwen
Denbigh
Ruthin
Mold
Northophall
Holywell
Rhyl
Colwyn Bay
Abergele
Llandudno
Deganwy
Conwy
Beaumaris
Bangor
Port Dinorwic
Caernarfon
Betws-y-Coed
Llanrwst
Blaenau Ffestiniog
Ffestiniog
Beddgelert
Penrhyndeudraeth
Porthmadog
Talsarnau
Bala
Dolgellau
Mallwyd
Machynlleth
Eglwysfach
Aberdyfi
Tywyn
Barmouth
Bontddu
Pennaenpool
Tal-y-Llyn
Pwllheli
Nefyn
Abersoch
Holyhead
Llangefni
Parkgate
Puddington
Queensferry
Little Sutton
Simply the best there is.
Hotel
Restaurant
Hotel and Restaurant
Inn
Lacock Indicates an Inn at same location
8

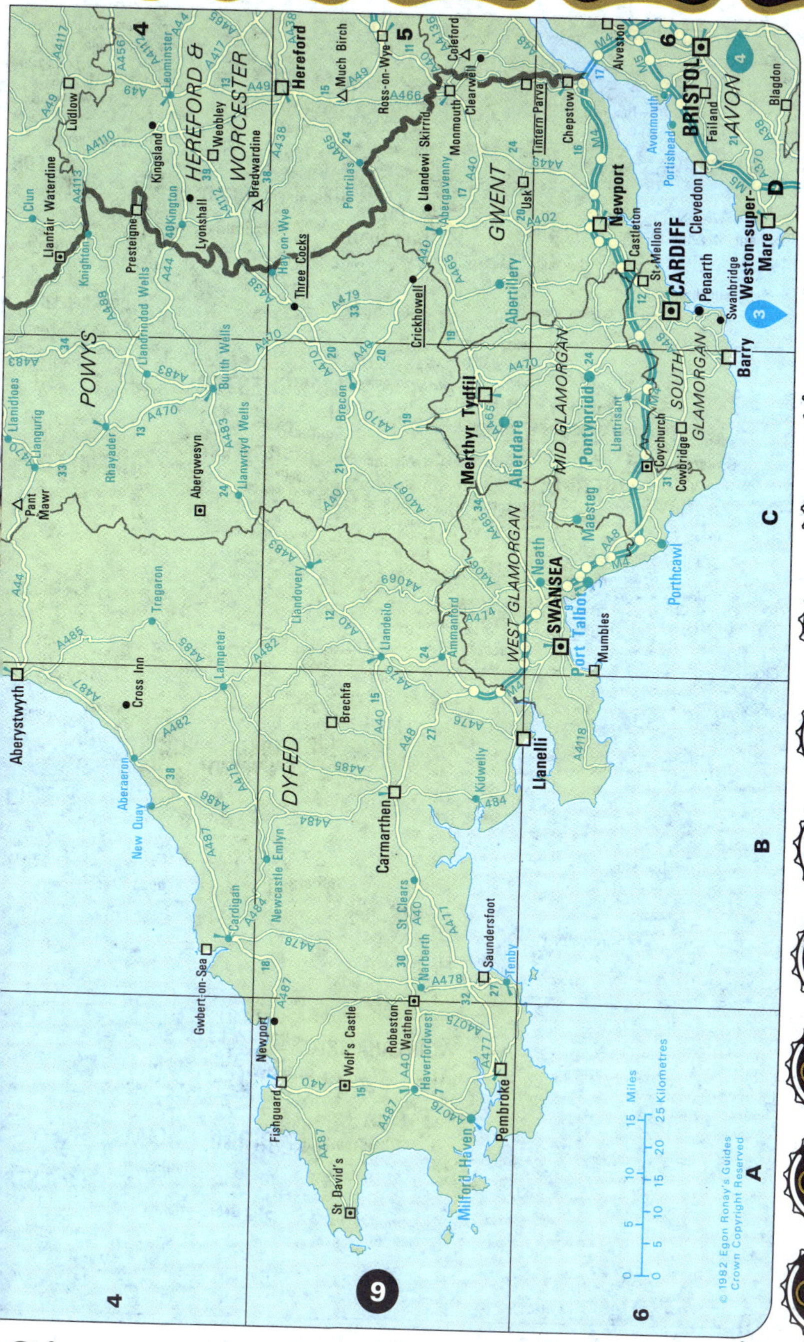

Britvic   **Britvic**   **Britvic**   **Britvic**   **Britvic**

Simply the best there is.

Britvic is a Registered Trade Mark

Simply the best there is.

Britvic
Britvic
Britvic
Britvic
Britvic
Hotel
Restaurant
Hotel and Restaurant
Inn
Lacock Indicates an Inn at same location
Simply the best there is.
Britvic is a Registered Trade Mark
1982 Egon Ronay's Guides
Crown Copyright Reserved

Simply the best there is.

Britvic

Hotel
Restaurant
Hotel and Restaurant
Inn
Lacock Indicates an Inn at same location

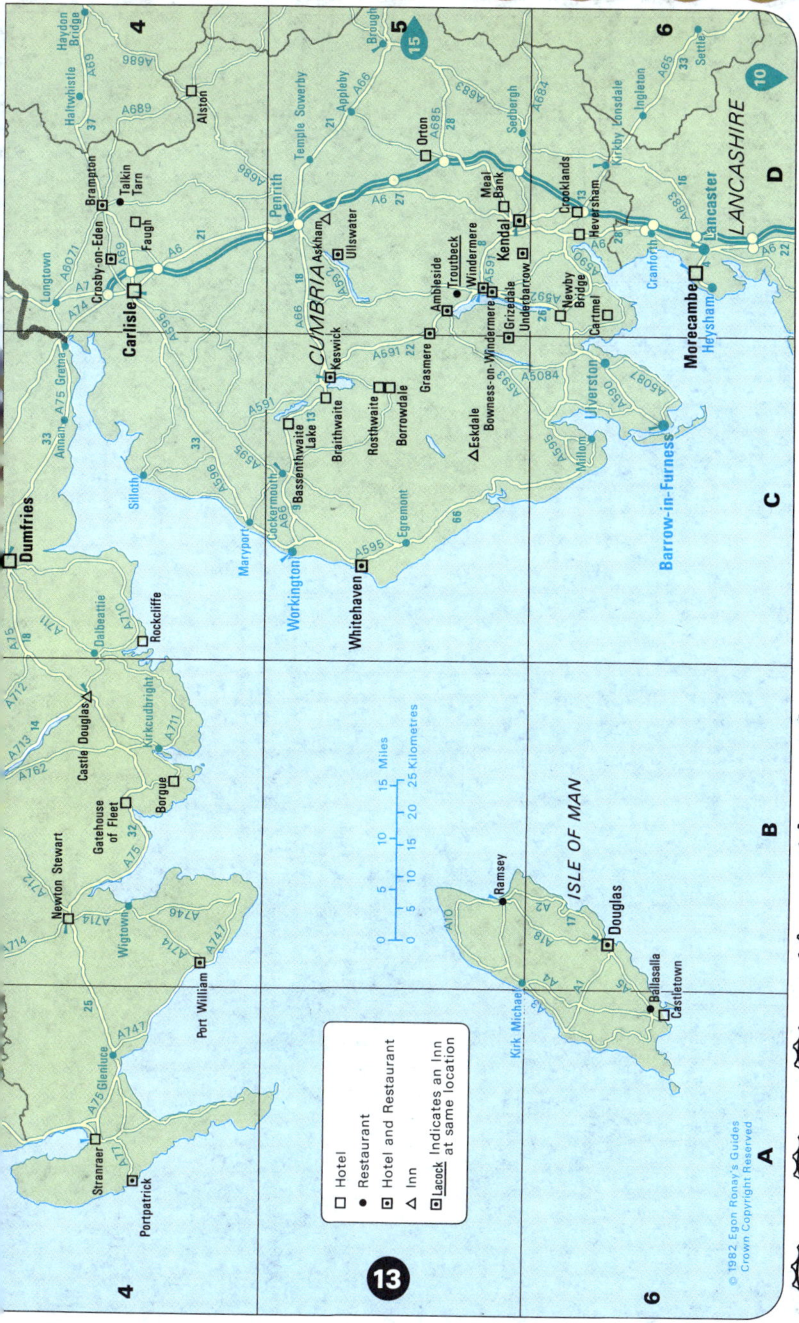

Simply the best there is.

Britvic is a Registered Trade Mark

Simply the best there is.
Britvic
A
B
C
D
Hotel
Restaurant
Hotel and Restaurant
Inn
Lacock Indicates an Inn at same location
0 5 10 15 Miles
0 5 10 15 20 25 Kilometres
Anstruther
Methil
Dysart
North Berwick
Gullane
Dirleton
Dunbar
East Linton
Haddington
Dalkeith
Bonnyrigg
Humbie
Eyemouth
Berwick-upon-Tweed
Duns
Lauder
Cornhill-on-Tweed
Bamburgh
Belford
Galashiels
Melrose
Dryburgh
Kelso
Wooler
Selkirk
BORDERS
Jedburgh
Hawick
Alnwick
Carter Bar
Amble
Longframlington
Otterburn
Longhorsley
NORTHUMBERLAND
Morpeth
Ashington
Langholm
Blyth
1
2
3
12
14

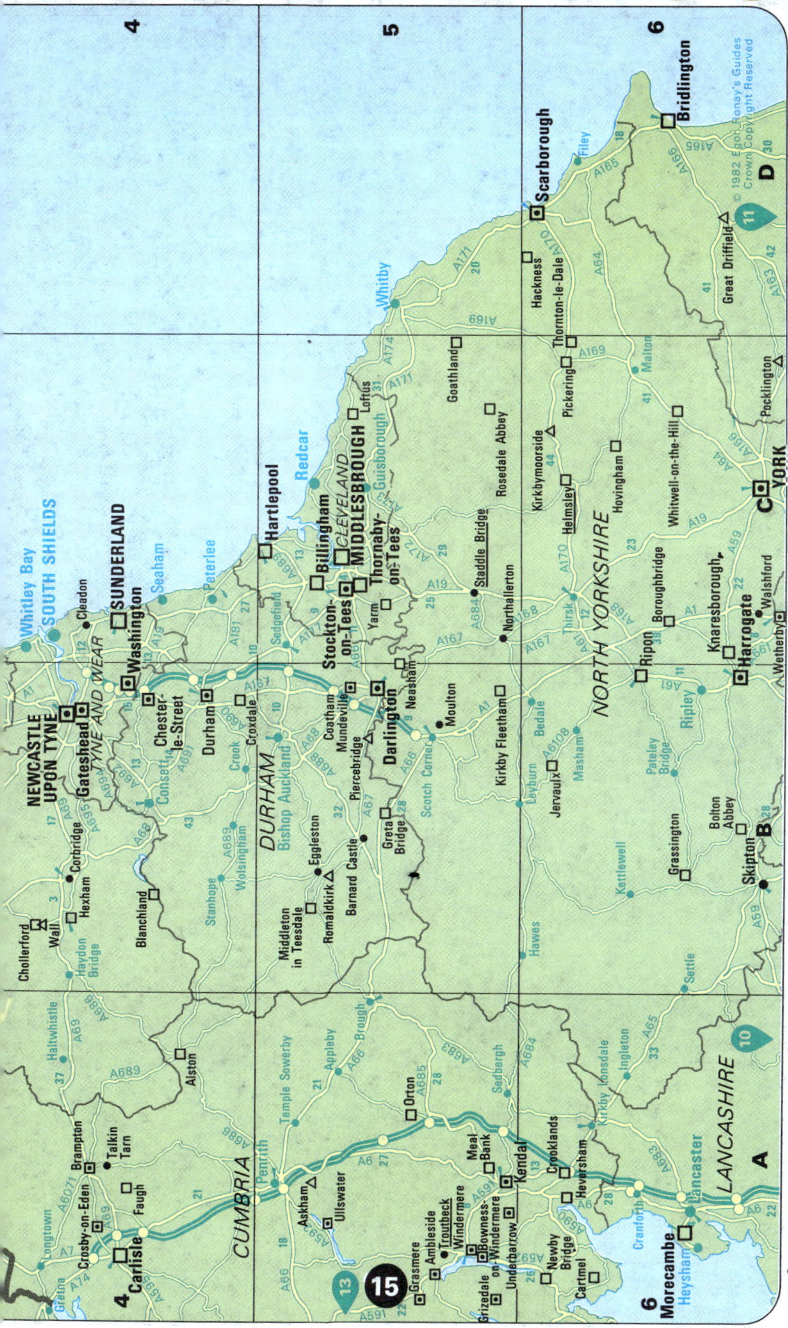

Simply the best there is.

Britvic is a Registered Trade Mark

Simply the best there is.
Britvic
Britvic
Britvic
Britvic
Britvic
A   B   C   D
1   2   3
16
Hotel
Restaurant
Hotel and Restaurant
Inn
Lacock Indicates an Inn at same location
0   10   20   30 Miles
0   10   20   30   40   50 Kilometres
ORKNEY
WESTERN ISLES
LEWIS
SKYE
HIGHLAND
John o' Groats
Durness
Port of Ness
Kinlochbervie
Tongue
Thurso
Wick
Scourie
Lybster
Stornoway
Helmsdale
Achiltibuie
Lairg
Brora
Ullapool
Invershin
Bonar Bridge
Dornoch
Tain
Kildary
Gairloch
Invergordon
Lossiemouth
Cullen
Banff
Fraserburgh
Talladale
Cromarty
Elgin
Buckie
Kinlochewe
Garve
Dingwall
Fortrose
Forres
Fochabers
Uig
Contin
Nairn
Rothes-on-Spey
Keith
Turriff
Peterhead
Calbost
Muir of Ord
Beauly
Charlestown of Aberlour
Dufftown
Huntly
Dunvegan
Skeabost Bridge
Portree
Inverness
Grantown-on-Spey
Glenlivet
Old Meldrum
Ellon
Kyle of Lochalsh
Lewiston
Dulnain Bridge
Pitcaple
Inverurie
Newburgh
A857
A858
A859
A855
A856
A863
A850
A838
A836
A897
A895
A882
A894
A835
A839
A9
A837
A838
A832
A896
A890
A832
A836
A82
A96
A939
A947
A98
A95
A97
A96
A920
A92
A952
A947
A836
21
43
37
37
61
59
38
35
28
26
18
42
32
1

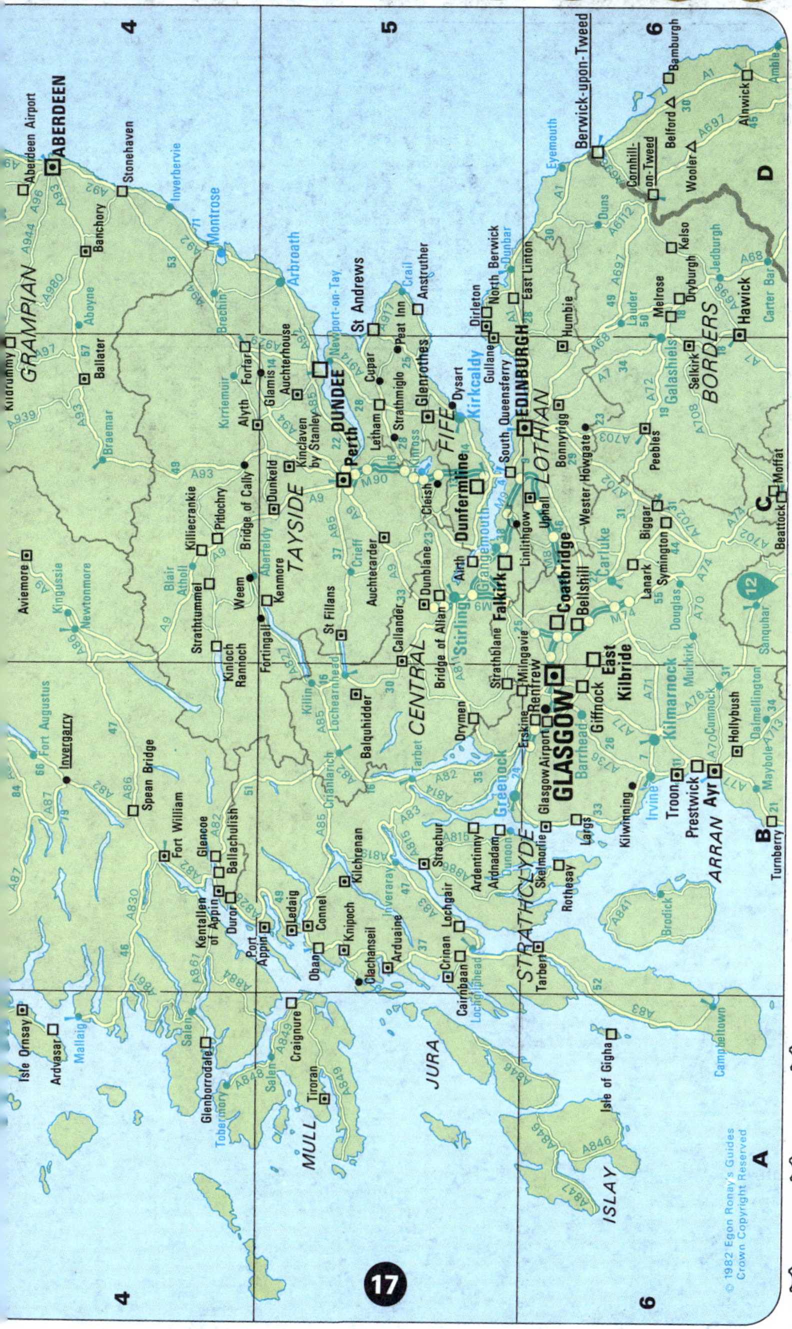

Simply the best there is.

Britvic is a Registered Trade Mark

Simply the best there is.
Britvic
A   B   C   D
1   2   3
18
0   10   20   30 Miles
0   10   20   30   40   50 Kilometres
DONEGAL
LONDONDERRY
ANTRIM
TYRONE
FERMANAGH
DOWN
ARMAGH
MONAGHAN
SLIGO
LEITRIM
CAVAN
MAYO
ROSCOMMON
LONGFORD
MEATH
WESTMEATH
LOUTH
DUBLIN
Londonderry
BELFAST
Redcastle
Rathmullan
Rosapenna
Coleraine
Limavady
Ballymena
Larne
Carrickfergus
Helen's Bay
Bangor
Crawfordsburn
Newtownards
Comber
Pontaferry
Holywood
Dunadry
Antrim
Dunmurry
Lisburn
Saintfield
Portadown
Downpatrick
Newcastle
Strabane
Donegal
Omagh
Cookstown
Dungannon
Armagh
Newry
Rossnowlagh
Ballyshannon
Enniskillen
Monaghan
Clones
Carrickmacross
Dundalk
Rosses Point
Strandhill
Sligo
Collooney
Ballina
Cavan
Virginia
Ceannanas Mor
Dunderry
Navan
Drogheda
Newport
Castlebar
Charlestown
Claremorris
Longford
Roscommon
Renvyle
Moyard
Letterfrack
Clifden
Ballynahinch
Cong
Tuam
Oughterard
Mullingar
Kinnegad
Malahide

Simply the best there is.

Britvic is a Registered Trade Mark

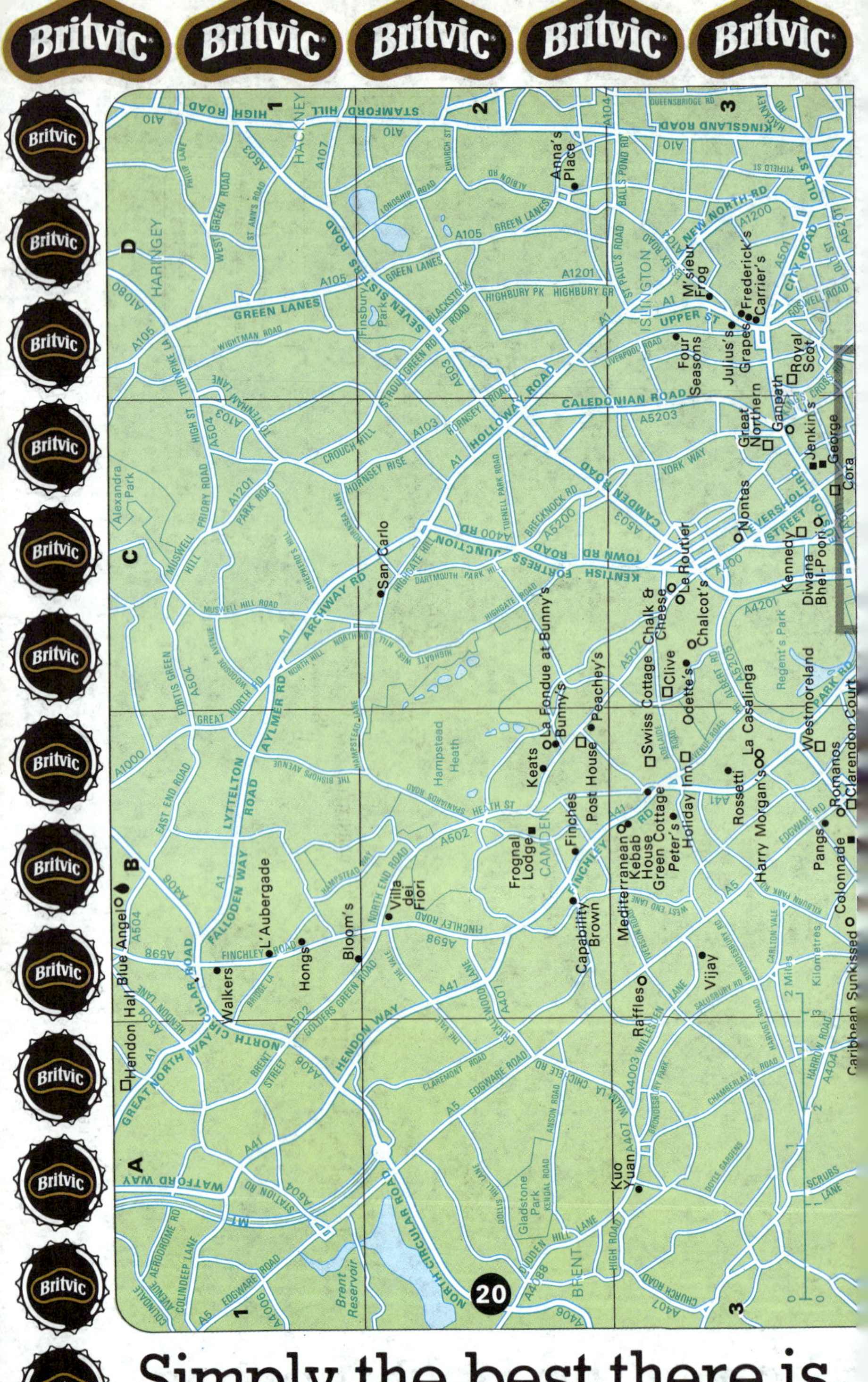

Britvic
Britvic
Britvic
Britvic
Britvic
Simply the best there is.
20
HACKNEY
HARINGEY
ISLINGTON
CAMDEN
HENDON WAY
HAMPSTEAD
FINCHLEY
BRENT
GREEN LANES
HOLLOWAY ROAD
CALEDONIAN ROAD
ARCHWAY RD
SEVEN SISTERS ROAD
HIGH ROAD
STAMFORD HILL
KINGSLAND ROAD
NEW NORTH RD
CITY ROAD
UPPER ST
YORK WAY
CAMDEN ROAD
KENTISH TOWN RD
FORTRESS ROAD
WATFORD WAY
NORTH CIRCULAR ROAD
GREAT NORTH WAY
FALLODEN WAY
LYTTELTON ROAD
AYLMER RD
EAST END ROAD
FINCHLEY ROAD
NORTH END ROAD
EDGWARE ROAD
PARK RD
REGENT'S PARK
ALEXANDRA PARK
MUSWELL HILL
Anna's Place
Frederick's
Carrier's
M'sieur Frog
Grapes
Julius's
Four Seasons
Royal Scot
Great Northern
Ganpath
Jenkin's
George
Cora
Nontas
Kennedy
Le Routier
Diwana Bhel-Poori
Chalk & Cheese
Clive
Chalcot's
Odette's
La Casalinga
Westmoreland
Rossetti
Romanos
Clarendon Court
Swiss Cottage
Holiday Inn
Harry Morgan's
Pangs
Colonnade
San Carlo
Keats
Bunny's
La Fondue at Bunny's
Peachey's
Post House
Finches
Green Cottage
Mediterranean Kebab House
Peter's
Vijay
Frognal Lodge
Capability Brown
Villa dei Fiori
Bloom's
Hongs
L'Aubergade
Walkers
Hendon Hall
Blue Angel
Raffles
Kuo Yuan
Caribbean Sunkissed
Gladstone Park
Brent Reservoir
Hampstead Heath
2 Miles
3 Kilometres

Britvic Britvic Britvic Britvic Britvic

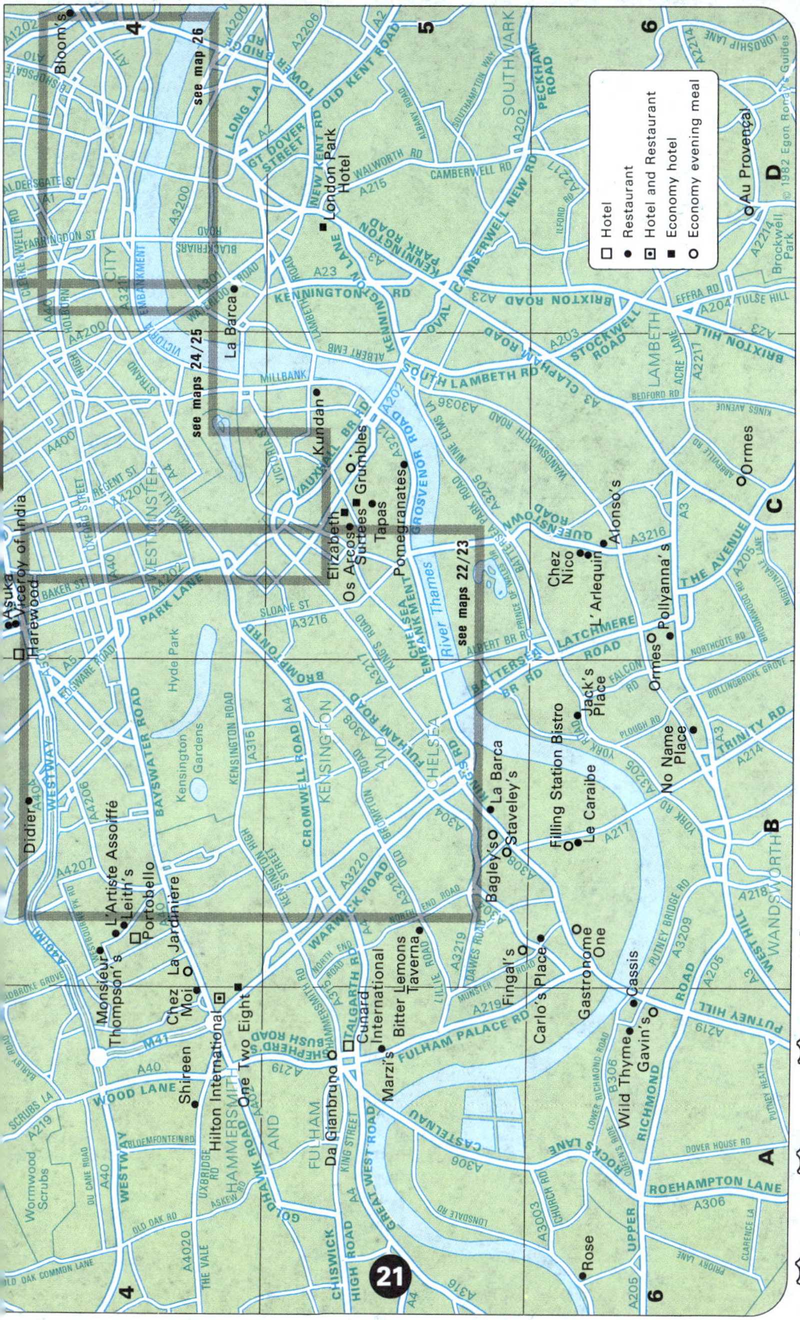

21

Simply the best there is.

Britvic is a Registered Trade Mark

24
25
1
2
3
22
D
C
B
A
HARLEY STREET
WEYMOUTH STREET
WIMPOLE STREET
NEW CAVENDISH STREET
A5204
HENRIETTA PL
WIGMORE STREET
DAVIES STREET
DUKE STREET
GROSVENOR STREET
BROOK STREET
SOUTH AUDLEY STREET
UPPER GROSVENOR STREET
DEANERY
HAMILTON PLACE
DOWN ST
CURZON
CONSTITUTION HILL
GROSVENOR
GROSVENOR CRES
GROSVENOR
HARLEY STREET
ANNE STREET
HARLEY STREET
BEAUMONT STREET
WEYMOUTH STREET
MARYLEBONE HIGH STREET
THAYER STREET
JAMES ST
ORCHARD STREET
PORTMAN
MOXTON STREET
PADDINGTON STREET
CHILTERN STREET
BAKER STREET
GLOUCESTER PLACE
MONTAGU STREET
MONTAGU SQUARE
MONTAGU PLACE
GREAT CUMBERLAND PLACE
OLD QUEBEC ST
CUMBERLAND
PARK LANE
PARK LANE
PARK STREET
GREEN STREET
UPPER BROOK STREET
PARK STREET
Grosvenor House
GROSVENOR
Clifton Ford
Londoner
Woodlands
La Pavona
Masako
Yakitori
Ikeda
Chaopraya
Strafford Court
Claridge's
Europa
Shogun
Britannia
Scott's
Connaught
Greenhouse
Chesterfield
Relais des Amis
Tibério
Athenaeum
Hard Rock Café
Hilton
Londonderry
Inn on the Park
Inter-Continental
Trader Vic's
Dorchester
Sheraton Park Tower
Upper Crust
Berkeley
Salloos
Newports
Basil Street
Hyde Park
Nanteu
Serai
Caravan
Verbanella
Durrants
New
Mandeville
Le Ptit Montmartre
Selfridge
Churchill
Le Gavroche
Le Chef
La Lupa
O Le Dodo
Gourmand
Sidi Bou Said
Parkwood
Stanhope
Great Mughal
Merryfield House
Milford House
Der Monica's
Holiday Inn
Salino
London Metropole
Great Western Royal
Grosvenor Court
Lancaster Court
Royal Lancaster
Royal Park
Park Plaza
Columbia
White's
Century
Mornington
Lancaster
Henry VIII
Craven Gardens
Leinster Towers
Leinster Terr
Apollo
Kalamaras
Central Park
Coburg
London Embassy
Texas Lone Star West
Eden Park
Hung Toa
Mandarin Kitchen
Diwana Bhel-Poori
Chez Franco
Baba
Topo D'Oro
Geale's
Costas Grill
Mildred's
La Paesana
Verbanella
Pembridge Court
Hyde Park
Kensington Gardens
The Serpentine
The Long Water
Round Pond
Kensington Palace
Royal Garden
Holy Cow
Wheeler's
Ark
Kensington Palace
Maggie Jones
John Howard
MARYLEBONE ROAD
EDGWARE ROAD
CHAPEL ST
SALE PL
SUSSEX GARDENS
BAYSWATER ROAD
WESTWAY
A40(M)
NOTTING HILL GATE
Paddington Station
Paddington Basin
WEST CARRIAGE DRIVE
NORTH CARRIAGE DRIVE
KNIGHTSBRIDGE
KENSINGTON ROAD
KENSINGTON CHURCH STREET
KENSINGTON HIGH STREET
PALACE GARDENS TERRACE
BRUNSWICK GARDENS
PEMBRIDGE ROAD
PEMBRIDGE GARDENS
PEMBRIDGE VILLAS
CHEPSTOW ROAD
CHEPSTOW PLACE
QUEENSWAY
PORCHESTER ROAD
INVERNESS TERRACE
LEINSTER TERRACE
GLOUCESTER TERRACE
EASTBOURNE TERRACE
WESTBOURNE TERRACE
PRAED STREET
SUSSEX PLACE
LANCASTER GATE
WESTBOURNE TERRACE
Royal Albert Hall

Hotel
Restaurant
Hotel and Restaurant
Economy hotel
Economy evening meal

RIVER THAMES
Chelsea Reach
Chelsea Bridge
Albert Bridge
Battersea Bridge
Battersea Park
CHELSEA EMBANKMENT
CHEYNE WALK
QUEENSTOWN RD A321
A3212
© 1982 Egon Ronay's Guides

Science Museum
Victoria and Albert Museum
Natural History Museum
Royal Hospital
Air Terminal
Earl's Court Exhibition Building

PRINCE CONSORT ROAD
BROMPTON ROAD
CROMWELL ROAD
WEST CROMWELL ROAD
PEMBROKE ROAD
EARL'S COURT ROAD
WARWICK ROAD
FINBOROUGH ROAD
REDCLIFFE GARDENS
GUNTER GROVE
EDITH GROVE
A304 FULHAM ROAD
FULHAM ROAD
SLOANE STREET
ECCLESTON ST
EBURY BRIDGE ROAD
A302
A321
A3220
A308
A3031
A3220
B314

Yangtze
Byblos
Phoenicia
Kensington Close
London Tara
Casa Porrelli
Siam
Gondoliere
Embassy House
Le Quai St Pierre
Lexham
Oliver
Atlas
Apollo
Elizabetta
Concord
Hogarth
London International
Crystal Palace
Ladbroke Kensington Court
Terstan
Barkston
Leicester Court
Tudor Court
Stanhope Court
London Penta
Manor Court
Eden Plaza
Gloucester
Onslow Court
Il Falconiere
Chanterelle
Cranley Gardens
Blake's
Pontevecchio
Tiger Lee
Adam's Rib
L'Artiste Affame
Philbeach
Lily
West Centre
La Croisette
Foxtrot Quango
Brinkley's
Hungry Horse
Golden Duck
September
La Famiglia
Bagatelle
Barbarella
William F.
Eden House
Parsons
Busabong
Eleven Park Walk
La Corse
Ho Lee Fook
Dan's
Good Earth
Eden House
Daquise
Paper Tiger
Rembrandt
Brasserie St Quentin
Park House
Tai-Pan
Luba's Bistro
Executive
Cadogan
Montpeliano
Shezan
Parkes
Ménage à Trois
Rascals
Brasserie des Amis
Mes Amis
Wolfe's
Verbanella
Capital
Campden Court
San Ruffillo
Holiday Inn
Lowndes
Scats
Motcombs
Hyatt
Carlton Tower
London Belgravia
Chesham House
Ebury Court
Ken Lo's
Alison House
Colin House
Mimmo d'Ischia
Eatons
Ebury Wine Bar
Miljanou
Pulcinella
Shu
Shan II
Prince
Sumner
Alexander
Astor House
Tandoori
Drakes
Meridiana
Ma Cuisine
Walton's
Daphne's
Le Suquet
English House
Nineteen
Wilbraham
English Garden
Culford House
Willett House
Standard
Gavvers
Como Lario
Hunan
Pimlico Ristorante Italiano
La Tante Claire
Foxtrot Oscar

23

ROSEBERY AVENUE
MOUNT PLEASANT
PHOENIX PLACE
GOUGH STREET
CHANCERY LANE
BELL YARD
MILFORD LANE
ARUNDEL STREET
SURREY STREET
TEMPLE PLACE
Howard
Somerset House
VICTORIA EMBANKMENT
Royal Courts of Justice
SERLE STREET
CAREY STREET
LINCOLN'S INN FIELDS
PORTUGAL STREET
KINGSWAY
ALDWYCH
STRAND
LANCASTER PLACE
Waldorf
Flounders
Thomas de Quincey's
Paulos'
Joe Allen
Strand Palace
Simpson's
Savoy
GRAY'S INN ROAD
DOUGHTY STREET
JOHN STREET
GT. JAMES'S ROAD
BEDFORD ROW
JOCKEY'S FIELDS
Brasserie du Coin
Les Halles
PROCTER ST
LAMB'S CONDUIT STREET
ORDE HALL STREET
HARPUR STREET
THEOBALD'S ROAD
RED LION STREET
EAGLE STREET
HIGH HOLBORN
NEWTON STREET
PARKER STREET
GREAT QUEEN STREET
WILD STREET
DRURY LANE
WELLINGTON STREET
BOW STREET
Covent Garden
see inset below
BRUNSWICK SQUARE
Bloomsbury Crest
B504
MARCHMONT STREET
HERBRAND STREET
CORAM STREET
BERNARD STREET
GUILFORD STREET
Tagore
Russell
President
Il Fornello
QUEEN SQUARE
GREAT ORMOND STREET
OLD GLOUCESTER STREET
Imperial
Bonnington
Lonsdale
Montague
Ruskin
SOUTHAMPTON ROW
BOSWELL STREET
BEDFORD PLACE
MONTAGUE PLACE
Kingsley
BLOOMSBURY WAY
BURY PLACE
BLOOMSBURY STREET
COPTIC ST
NEW OXFORD STREET
HIGH ST
ST GILES HIGH ST
Drury Lane
Last Days of the Raj
LONG ACRE
Floral Street
NEW ROW
BEDFORDBURY
GARRICK STREET
ST MARTIN'S LANE
ENDELL STREET
MONMOUTH STREET
Seven Dials
SHELTON STREET
SHORTS GARDENS
NEAL STREET
La Corée
Gay Hussar
CHARING CROSS ROAD
Cambridge Circus
WEST ST
LEICESTER SQUARE
WHITCOMB
Tavistock
Kites
WOBURN PLACE
BEDFORD WAY
Royal National
MONTAGUE PLACE
RUSSELL SQUARE
British Museum
University of London
MALET STREET
BEDFORD SQUARE
GOWER STREET
University College
GORDON SQUARE
TAVISTOCK SQUARE
TAVISTOCK PLACE
GORDON STREET
A4200
Anemos
Chez Gerard
White Tower
Bertorelli Bros
Cyriana
Kebab House
New Berners
Mahagopal
Efes Kebab House
Gaylord
St Moritz
Kaya
Lev-On's
Melati
Topo Gigio
Melati
Fuji
Yamaju
Estoril da Luigi e Roberto
Café Royal
Legends
Apicella 81
Cecconi's
Westbury
St Moritz
Vasco & Piero's Pavilion
Arirang
New Berners
TOTTENHAM COURT ROAD
GOODGE STREET
CHARLOTTE STREET
CLEVELAND STREET
WHITFIELD STREET
GREAT RUSSELL STREET
HANWAY STREET
RATHBONE PLACE
NEWMAN STREET
BERNERS STREET
WELLS STREET
EASTCASTLE STREET
OXFORD STREET
MORTIMER STREET
GREAT TITCHFIELD STREET
GREAT PORTLAND STREET
MARGARET STREET
REGENT STREET
HANOVER STREET
CONDUIT STREET
NEW BOND STREET
OLD BOND STREET
SAVILE ROW
BURLINGTON STREET
CLIFFORD STREET
CORK STREET
SACKVILLE STREET
GLASSHOUSE STREET
BEAK STREET
CARNABY STREET
BROADWICK STREET
POLAND STREET
BERWICK STREET
WARDOUR STREET
DEAN STREET
FRITH STREET
GREEK STREET
SOHO SQUARE
SUTTON ROW
FALCONBERG COURT
MANETTE STREET
The White House
Gurkha Tandoori
Regent Crest
EUSTON ROAD
A501
A400
A4201
PARK SQ EAST
B522
WARREN STREET
CONWAY STREET
FITZROY STREET
FITZROY SQUARE
GRAFTON WAY
MAPLE STREET
BOLSOVER STREET
CLIPSTONE STREET
GREAT PORTLAND STREET
BOLSOVER STREET
CARBURTON STREET
DEVONSHIRE STREET
WEYMOUTH STREET
PORTLAND PLACE
GOSFIELD ST
St George's
LANGHAM STREET
CHANDOS ST
CAVENDISH SQUARE
Chicago Pizza Pie Factory
HOLLES ST
DERING ST
PRINCES STREET
HANOVER SQUARE
ST GEORGE STREET
MADDOX STREET
Guinea Grill
Ikeda
Café Jardin
Claridge's
Westbury
NEW CAVENDISH STREET
HARLEY STREET
WIMPOLE STREET
WELBECK STREET
WIGMORE STREET
QUEEN ANNE STREET
HENRIETTA PLACE
MANSFIELD STREET
DUKE STREET
BROOK STREET
GROSVENOR STREET
DAVIES STREET
SOUTH MOLTON STREET
BOND STREET
BROOK'S MEWS
GILBERT STREET
BINNEY STREET
GROSVENOR SQUARE
Europa
Shogun
Scott's
Britannia
Connaught
CARLOS PLACE
MOUNT STREET
Odin's
Langan's Bistro
La Napten Yakitori
Pavona
Woodlands
Clifton Ford
Londoner
New Mandeville
Le P'tit Montmartre
Masako
Chaopraya
Stratford Court
DEVONSHIRE PLACE
BEAUMONT STREET
MARYLEBONE HIGH STREET
MARYLEBONE LANE
JAMES STREET
WIGMORE STREET
WESTMORELAND STREET
BENTINCK STREET
THAYER STREET
MARYLEBONE HIGH ST
DUKE STREET
BALDERTON ST
PARK STREET
GROSVENOR STREET
26
24
22
440 yards
400 metres
A B C D
1 2 3

Hotel
Restaurant
Hotel and Restaurant
Economy hotel
Economy evening meal

Brown's
Bentley's Oyster Bar
Piccadilly
National Gallery
Royal Trafalgar
TRAFALGAR
Charing Cross
Charing Cross Station
RIVER THAMES
Waterloo Bridge
Reach
May Fair
A l'Ecu de France
STRAND
National Theatre
Greenhouse
Chesterfield
Tiberio Mirabelle
Bristol
Colombina
Cavendish
CHARLES II ST
COCKSPUR ST
TRAFALGAR SQUARE
VILLIERS ST
King's
4
Relais des Amis
Washington
Ritz
Wilton's
Lafayette
PALL MALL
CRAVEN STREET
NORTHUMBERLAND AVENUE
VICTORIA EMBANKMENT
Royal Festival Hall
4
Dorchester
L'Artiste Musclé
Langan's Brasserie
SCOTLAND YARD
WHITEHALL PLACE
Royal Horseguards
WHITEHALL
BELVEDERE ROAD
CONCERT HALL APPROACH
Trader Vic's
Curzon
Suntory
Stafford
Duke's
CARLTON GARDENS
Horse Guards
HORSEGUARDS AVENUE
Hilton Londonderry
Park Lane
THE MALL
HORSE GUARDS ROAD
Inn on the Park
Inter-Continental
Athenæum
Green Park
St James's Palace
St James's Park
Au Jardin des Gourmets
Ajimura
Neal Street
ENDELL STREET
B401
SHELTON STREET
LONG ACRE
B402
DRURY LANE
Hard Rock Café
CONSTITUTION HILL
St James's Park Lake
CHARING CROSS ROAD
SHAFTESBURY AVENUE
Seven Dials
MERCER STREET
EARLHAM STREET
SHORTS GARDENS
NEAL STREET
Interlude de Tabaillau
BOW STREET
25
Buckingham Palace Gardens
Buckingham Palace
L'Escargot
FRITH STREET
OLD COMPTON ST
MOOR ST
Cambridge Circus
TOWER STREET
MONMOUTH STREET
LANGLEY STREET
Covent Garden
5
GROSVENOR PLACE
BIRDCAGE WALK
ANNE'S GATE
Equatorial
ROMILLY STREET
WEST STREET
LITCHFIELD ST
ST MARTIN'S STREET
SLINGSBY PLACE
The Royal Mews
BUCKINGHAM GATE
PETTY FRANCE
St Ermin's
CATHERINE PLACE
WILFRED ST
PALACE PLACE
CASTLE LANE
CAXTON STREET
BROADWAY
A302
Gallant
Tai Ka Lok
Happy Garden
GREAT NEWPORT STREET
Inigo Jones
ROSE STREET
Grange
Poons of Covent Garden
LWR GROSVENOR PL
Goring
Royal Westminster
STAG PLACE
Poons & Co
Loon Fung
LITTLE NEWPORT ST
CRANBOURN STREET
GARRICK STREET
HOBART PL
BEESTON
Chesham House
GROSVENOR GDNS
BUCKINGHAM PALACE ROAD
VICTORIA STREET
ARTILLERY ROW
STRUTTON GROUND
Diamond
New Rasa Sayang
Shu Shan
Chez Solange
Boulestin
6
HOWICK PLACE
GREYCOAT PLACE
HORSEFERRY RD
Poon's
LISLE ST
BEAR STREET
NEW ROW
Porters
Ebury Court
Grosvenor
Ken Lo's
Victoria Station
WILTON ROAD
ROCHESTER ROW
Manzi's
Sheekeys
HOP GARDENS
BEDFORDBURY
BEDFORD CT
MAIDEN LANE
L.S. Grunts
6
Alison House
ECCLESTON STREET
B310
VAUXHALL BR RD
A202
Yasmine
Gran Paradiso
A
Swiss Centre, Chesa
Swiss Centre, Rendezvous
Royal Angus
Pastoria
Trattoria Imperia
B404
© 1982 Egon Ronay's Guides
C
D

COMMERCIAL STREET
A1202
A11
A13
MANSELL STREET
TWR BR APP
ST KATHARINE'S WAY
Tower
Tower Bridge
A100
Hotel
Restaurant
Hotel and Restaurant
Economy hotel
Economy evening meal
© 1982 Egon Ronay's Guides
D
MINORIES
Fenchurch Street Station
TOWER HILL
SHAD THAMES
VINE LANE
ABBOTS LANE
MORGAN'S LANE
LITTLE LANE
TOOLEY STREET
A2205
A200
Tower of London
Great Eastern
Bill Bentley's
Liverpool Street Station
BISHOPSGATE
HOUNDSDITCH
ST MARY AXE
LEADENHALL STREET
BILLITER ST
FENCHURCH STREET
FENCHURCH AVE
MARK LANE
HART
SEETHING LA
TRINITY SQ
PEPYS STREET
COOPERS ROW
CRUTCHED FRIARS
ROYAL MINT ST
CROSSWALL
LOWER THAMES STREET
BYWARD STREET
Shares
Broad Street Station
OLD BROAD STREET
WORMWOOD STREET
THREADNEEDLE
Bank of England
CORNHILL
LOMBARD STREET
GRACECHURCH STREET
BIRCHIN LANE
FINCH LANE
KING WILLIAM STREET
PHILPOT LANE
EASTCHEAP
MINCING LANE
GT TOWER ST
BOTOLPH
ST MARY AT HILL
LOWER THAMES STREET
Upper Pool
ARTHUR STREET
MONUMENT STREET
Southwark Cathedral
Ashley's
MOORGATE
COLEMAN STREET
PRINCE'S STREET
LOTHBURY
POULTRY
QUEEN VICTORIA ST
WALBROOK
Cotillion Room
Cannon Street Station
CANNON STREET
SWAN LA
ALLHALLOWS LANE
London Bridge
BOROUGH HIGH STREET
BEDALE ST
CATHEDRAL STREET
STONEY STREET
CLINK STREET
London Bridge Station
ST THOMAS STREET
JOINER ST
MAZE
BASINGHALL STREET
KING STREET
QUEEN ST
CHEAPSIDE
BREAD STREET
CLOAK LANE
COLLEGE ST
DOWGATE HILL
SKINNERS LANE
UPPER THAMES STREET
PLACE
COUSIN LANE
BANK END
BANKSIDE
PARK STREET
SOUTHWARK BRIDGE ROAD
A300
Le Poulbot
GRESHAM STREET
MILK ST
WOOD STREET
WATLING STREET
QUEEN ST
QUEEN ST
Southwark Bridge
PARK STREET
EMERSON STREET
SUMNER STREET
SOUTHWARK STREET
GREAT GUILDFORD STREET
Baron of Beef
GUTTER LANE
FOSTER LANE
NOBLE STREET
ST MARTIN'S LE GRAND
NEW CHANGE
CANNON STREET
RIVER THAMES
BANKSIDE
HOPTON STREET
LAVINGTON ST
EWER STREET
ALDERSGATE STREET
LITTLE BRITAIN
ANGEL STREET
NEWGATE STREET
Ginnan
St Paul's Cathedral
ST PAUL'S CHURCHYARD
GODLIMAN ST
CARTER LANE
WHITE LION HILL
QUEEN VICTORIA STREET
HOPTON STREET
BEAR LANE
SUFFOLK ST
GREAT SUFFOLK STREET
GAMBIA STREET
Le Gamin
Holborn Viaduct Station
ARWICK LANE
OLD BAILEY
LUDGATE HILL
PILGRIM ST
ST ANDREW'S HILL
CREED LA
BLACKFRIARS LANE
Blackfriars Station
BURRELL STREET
TREVERIS STREET
DOLBEN STREET
Central Markets
West Smithfield
Bubb's
SNOW HILL
HOSIER LANE
GILTSPUR STREET
SEACOAL LANE
FLEET LANE
BEAR ALLEY
NEW BRIDGE STREET
Blackfriars Bridge
BLACKFRIARS ROAD
A201
UPPER GROUND
PARIS GARDEN
COLOMBO ST
MEYMOTT ST
JOAN STREET
HOLBORN VIADUCT
FARRINGDON STREET
ST BRIDE ST
SHOE LANE
SALISBURY COURT
DORSET RISE
JOHN CARPENTER STREET
UPPER GROUND
HATFIELDS
A201
HATTON GARDEN
A521
ST ANDREW ST
SHOE LANE
WHITEFRIARS ST
CARMELITE ST
National Theatre
DUCHY STREET
STAMFORD ST
COIN STREET
CORNWALL RD
LEATHER LANE
GREVILLE STREET
NORWICH ST
FETTER LANE
NEW FETTER LANE
HARDING STREET
FLEET STREET
BOUVERIE STREET
TEMPLE AVENUE
UPPER GROUND
RSJ
STAMFORD ST
THEED STREET
ROUPELL STREET
EXTON ST
GRAY'S INN RD
A5200
HOLBORN
CURSITOR ST
FURNIVAL STREET
BREAM'S BUILDINGS
CHANCERY LANE
CAREY STREET
Royal Courts of Justice
STRAND
BELL YARD
VICTORIA EMBANKMENT
MIDDLE TEMPLE LANE
TEMPLE PLACE
Howard
A40
SOUTHAMPTON
A4
A3211
24
26
25